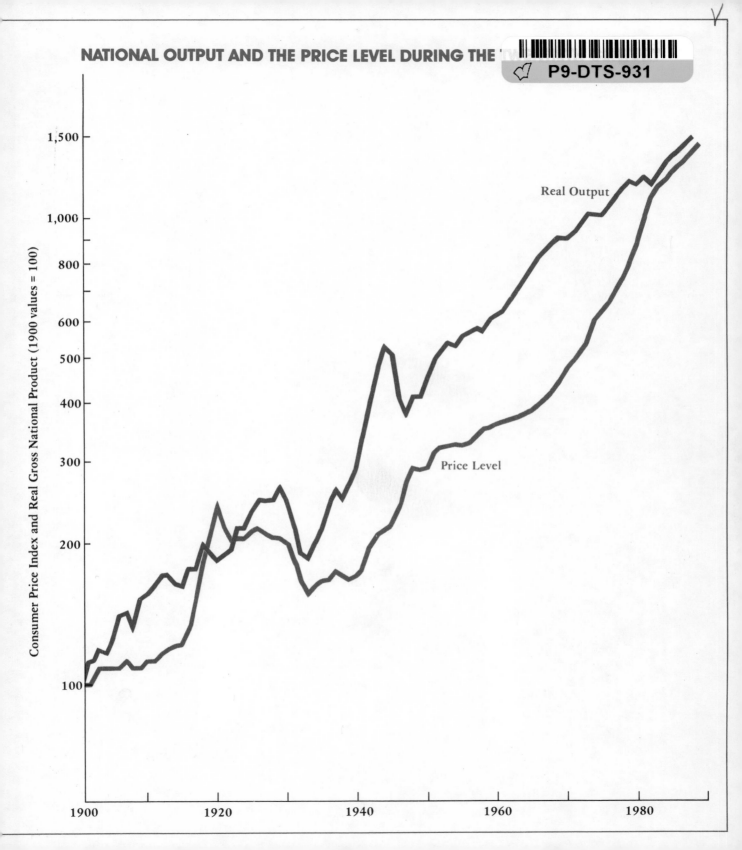

NATIONAL OUTPUT AND THE PRICE LEVEL DURING THE TW

P9-DTS-931

Real Output

Price Level

Consumer Price Index and Real Gross National Product (1900 values = 100)

1,500
1,000
800
600
500
400
300
200
100

1900   1920   1940   1960   1980

ECONOMICS

ECONOMICS

PAUL A. SAMUELSON

Institute Professor Emeritus
Massachusetts Institute of Technology

WILLIAM D. NORDHAUS

John Musser Professor of Economics
Yale University Cowles Foundation

THIRTEENTH EDITION

McGRAW-HILL BOOK COMPANY

New York	St. Louis	San Francisco	Auckland	Bogotá	Caracas
Colorado Springs	Hamburg	Lisbon	London	Madrid	Mexico
Milan	Montreal	New Delhi	Oklahoma City	Panama	Paris
San Juan	São Paulo	Singapore	Sydney	Tokyo	Toronto

ECONOMICS

1 2 3 4 5 6 7 8 9 0 D O C D O C 8 9 4 3 2 1 0 9

ISBN 0-07-054786-6

This book was set in Times Roman by York Graphic Services, Inc.
The editors were Elisa Adams, Scott D. Stratford, and
Peggy C. Rehberger; the designer was Joan E. O'Connor;
the production supervisor was Diane Renda.
Cover illustration by Roy Wiemann.
New drawings were done by Fine Line Illustrations, Inc.
R. R. Donnelley & Sons Company was printer and binder.

Library of Congress Cataloging-in-Publication Data

Samuelson, Paul Anthony, (date).
  Economics / Paul A. Samuelson, William D. Nordhaus.–13th ed.
  p.   cm.
  Includes bibliographical references and index.
  ISBN 0-07-054786-6
  1. Economics. I. Nordhaus, William D. II. Title.
HB171.5.S25 1989
330—dc19   88-28134

ABOUT THE AUTHORS

Thomas Moon

Paul A. Samuelson *(left)* founder of the renowned MIT graduate department of economics, was trained at the University of Chicago and Harvard. His many scientific writings brought him world fame at a young age, and he was the first American to receive a Nobel Prize in economics (1970). One of those rare scientists who can communicate with the lay public, Professor Samuelson long wrote an economics column for *Newsweek*. He testifies often before Congress and serves as academic consultant to the Federal Reserve, the U.S. Treasury, and various private, nonprofit organizations. He was economic adviser to President John F. Kennedy. Professor Samuelson plays tennis daily, and his family's size doubled when triplets arrived.

William D. Nordhaus *(right)* is one of America's eminent economists. Born in New Mexico, he was an undergraduate at Yale, received his Ph.D. in economics at MIT, and is now the John Musser Professor of Economics at Yale University and a member of the Cowles Foundation for Research in Economics. His economic research has spanned a wide variety of topics—including inflation, energy, technological change, regulation, resource and environmental economics, and trends in profits and productivity. In addition, Professor Nordhaus takes a keen interest in economic policy. He served as a Member of President Carter's Council of Economic Advisors from 1977 to 1979 and writes occasionally for *The New York Times* and other periodicals. From 1986 to 1988, he served as Provost of Yale University; in this capacity he negotiated a labor contract, helped invest a large endowment, oversaw a major investment program, and managed a large organization. He regularly teaches the Principles of Economics course at Yale. Professor Nordhaus and his family live in New Haven, Connecticut and share an enthusiasm for music, hiking, and skiing.

To Our Children and Students

PREFACE

Books are the carriers of civilization. Without books, history is silent, literature dumb, science crippled, thought and speculation at a standstill. They are engines of change, windows on the world, lighthouses erected in a sea of time.

Barbara Tuchman

THIS book has served as the standard bearer for the teaching of elementary economics since the landmark 1948 edition. Each new edition has distilled the deepest thinking of economists about how the economy works and about what society can do to improve people's living standards.

But economics is an evolving science; it must solve emerging puzzles and grapple with current dilemmas of public policy. The 1980s saw the emergence of a new approach to economic policy called "supply-side economics"; the United States began to incur huge federal budget deficits and trade deficits; East Asian countries challenged American preeminence in world economic affairs; the rich in America became richer as the poor became poorer.

All these and a host of other issues test the ingenuity of modern economics. The need to keep *Economics* at the forefront of modern economic analysis in the rapidly evolving world economy motivated the fruitful collaboration of the twelfth edition—a collaboration between two scholarly generations. This thirteenth edition continues that new tradition, affording the authors an exciting opportunity to forge a synthesis of modern mainstream economics and to present the doctrines of the warring factions of Keynesian and classical macroeconomics along with supply-side, libertarian, and Marxist principles.

Our task in these pages is straightforward: to present a clear, accurate, and interesting introduction to the principles of modern economics and to the institutions of the American and world economy. Our primary goal is to survey economics. But in doing this we would rather be right than exciting; our experience shows that modern economics no longer deserves its old title as "the dismal science," and besides it is anything but dull.

THE THIRTEENTH EDITION

The thirteenth edition continues the last edition's sweeping reorganization and rewriting. The book has been through a searching review for superfluous elements: every paragraph, every figure, and every table has been scrutinized to ensure that it is both necessary and clearly expressed. Many a sentence and appendix has fallen before the merciless scissors. While we have ruthlessly trimmed unnecessary details or outmoded theories, nothing essential has been sacrificed.

We are sometimes asked our philosophy in writing an introductory textbook. Above all, we want this book to be authoritative, comprehensive, and clear:

▪ The thirteenth edition contains an *authoritative* statement of modern economic science. The road to economic knowledge has been an arduous one traveled by many generations of economists. The outcome of this journey, surveyed in these pages, is an improved understanding of comparative advantage and international trade, the pricing of products and inputs, the quasi-random movements of the stock market, and the principles underlying the determination of national output. This text will explain how modern economics views each of these pivotal topics.

▪ A *comprehensive* survey of modern economics needs 950 pages. Reports of teachers advised us that no major topic has been omitted. Between these covers you will find all the major themes and topics of our subject, from absolute advantage to zero-pollution emissions, from mercantilism to supply-side economics. There is freedom to choose.

▪ Most of all, we try to be *clear*. What good are deep theorems that no student can understand? Every page has been studied by reviewers and students to weed out inessential digressions or inapt phrasing. Nietzsche once complained about "the offensive simplicity of the style" of the nineteenth century economist John Stuart Mill. We would love to be indicted for that offense.

Revisions in this Edition

Economics is a dynamic science—changing to reflect the shifting trends in economic affairs, in finance, in the world economy, and in society at large. This book evolves along with the science it surveys. Every chapter has moved forward in time to keep pace with economic analysis and policy. What are the major changes?

1. Increased Emphasis on International Economics
Americans are learning that no nation is an island. Our living standards are affected by technological developments in Japan and Germany; our companies must contend with

competitors from Korea and Brazil. Similarly, no complete understanding of modern economics is possible without a thorough grounding in the world economy. The thirteenth edition therefore contains a new emphasis on the essential elements of international economics.

The major new theme in this edition is a completely revised treatment of open-economy macroeconomics, for which the primary discussion occurs in Chapter 9. This exposition demonstrates the linkage between international trade and domestic output and employment and explains how events abroad can cause business cycles at home.

Other new material on the world economy includes: an application of open-economy macroeconomics to cities and regions in Chapter 9; analysis of the relation of protectionism to game theory in Chapters 25 and 39; an up-to-date analysis of the debt crisis in Chapter 37; a new presentation of the theory of comparative advantage in Chapter 38; an analysis of the reasons behind economists' realistic disillusionment with floating exchange rates in Chapter 40; and a survey of the problem of the stubborn U.S. trade deficit and growing foreign indebtedness in Chapter 40.

2. Microeconomic Foundations of Macroeconomics

Some may feel that an analysis of the microeconomic foundations of macroeconomics is too advanced for introductory textbooks. We disagree. Our thirteenth edition presents a straightforward survey of the economic underpinnings of modern mainstream macroeconomics. This includes an analysis of the reason for the non-vertical aggregate supply curve and of the role of contracts in the inflexibility of wages. Our exposition provides an analysis of the foundations of aggregate supply theory in Chapter 8; a survey of the microeconomic foundations of the theory of involuntary unemployment in Chapter 13; and a concise description of the theory and evidence on rational-expectations macroeconomics in Chapter 16.

3. Balanced Treatment of Modern Macroeconomics

This new edition features all major schools of modern macroeconomics: Keynesian, classical, monetarist, and supply-side. Each is clearly presented and compared with its competitors in a balanced and evenhanded way. For each, the empirical evidence is presented and evaluated.

Among the major revisions are Chapter 8's alternative approaches to macroeconomics with a special emphasis on the contrast of Keynesian and classical viewpoints, Chapter 10's appraisal of the theory and experience of supply-side economics, and Chapter 16's analysis of new trends in monetary thinking.

4. Earlier Coverage of Money and the Banking System

In response to requests from many users of this book, the coverage of money and of the banking system has been placed earlier in the text. It has also been substantially revised. Chapter 11 now brings together such topics as the history of money and banks, the demand for money, and the money supply. Chapter 12, on the Federal Reserve System, also placed earlier than in previous editions, is fully updated. It contains a new section on interest rates, as well as an explanation of the changing views on the effectiveness of targeting the money supply. Instructors can now explore the policy issues of unemployment and inflation, and input-output determination, with a firm foundation on the monetary system.

5. Comprehensive Modern Treatment of Factor Markets

In a modern economy, factor markets are just as important as product markets. Our approach is to present a thorough analysis of the general principles of price and output determination in factor markets, a lucid treatment of marginal productivity theories, and thoughtful studies of labor, resource, and capital markets.

This analysis of factor markets contains a number of special topics that are indispensable for understanding today's complex world: the theory of rent and unique factors of production; the tragedy of the commons related to global environmental problems; the theory of capital and interest along with an application to the determination of business profits; two chapters on labor markets, including the modern theory of discrimination and the doctrine of comparable worth; and a discussion of the economic roots of poverty, including an audit of neoconservative fears that the mixed economy is losing ground on economic betterment of poorer groups.

6. Unified Treatment of Production and Cost

Earlier editions treated production and cost theory separately. The thirteenth edition has unified these two topics into a pair of chapters, Chapters 21 and 22, so that the essential duality of these two topics can be exploited. The exposition is buttressed by a real-world example of oil pipelines, based on engineering data, that allows students to appreciate how cost and production data are grounded in technological data and shows diminishing returns at work.

7. Clear Exposition of Major Ideas

We have pored over every chapter to improve the clarity of the exposition. The comments of over 1000 students as well as suggestions of teachers, practitioners, and experts have been incorporated in the thirteenth edition.

The introductory chapter now spells out the essence of economics with intriguing and important illustrations; more than 100 new end-of-chapter examples have been added to focus student attention on key concepts or policy issues; Chapter 18's elementary analysis of supply and demand now includes additional examples and has been redrafted for ease of comprehension; the treatment of comparative advantage in Chapter 38 has been revised for greater coherence; new tables help summarize essential points of analysis, and new sections on interest rates, expectations, price and income elasticities, and comparative advantage help deepen students' understanding.

The glossary, which was first introduced in the twelfth edition, has been carefully tuned to meet the needs of this edition; all major terms now have a capsule definition that students can easily turn to. As a new study aid, the most important terms are printed in boldface when first defined in the text; they all then appear again in the glossary to reinforce the indispensable vocabulary of economics in the student's mind.

One of the distinguishing features of *Economics* has been the presentation of central but sometimes advanced theories in understandable ways. For the thirteenth edition we have redrafted the chapters on general equilibrium, public choice, and decisions of the firm to make these topics understandable to beginning students.

8. Increased Emphasis on History and Policy

Economics is at its core an empirical science. It first aims to explain the world around us and then helps us craft economic policies, based on sound economic principles, that can improve society's real-world functioning.

Drawing upon history, economic chronicles, and the authors' experience, the thir-teenth edition places a renewed emphasis on empirical evidence to illustrate economic theories. Understanding of macroeconomic analysis is aided by an understanding of the trends in federal budget deficits and a description of the Gramm-Rudman legislation; the dilemmas of monetary policy become clearer when the political business cycle and the 1979–1982 monetarist experiment are surveyed; international economics comes to life when the surging U.S. trade deficit and the successes of outward-oriented countries are analyzed.

The microeconomic chapters draw upon case studies, economic history, business decisions, and real-world experience to illustrate the fundamental principles. Examples such as OPEC pricing, airline deregulation, the comparable worth controversy, anti-trust policy and practice, collective bargaining by labor unions, the history of stock markets, production theory, and an analysis of tax reform help bring the theorems of microeconomics to life.

This "hands-on" approach to economics allows students to understand better the relevance of economic analysis to real-world problems.

Optional Matter

Economics courses range from one-quarter surveys to year-long intensive honors courses. This textbook has been carefully designed to meet all situations. The more advanced materials have been placed in appendixes or specially designated sections. These will appeal to curious students and to demanding courses that want to survey the entire discipline thoroughly. As is traditional with this book, we have included ad-vanced problems to test the mettle of the most dedicated student.

If yours is a fast-paced course, you will appreciate the careful layering of the more advanced material. Hard-pressed students can skip the advanced sections, encounter-ing the core of economic analysis without losing the thread of economic reasoning. And for those who teach the bright honors students, this book will challenge the most advanced young scholar. Indeed, many of today's leading economists have written to say they have used parts of *Economics* all along their pilgrimage to the Ph.D.

Format

The thirteenth edition has adapted the successful new format introduced in the last edition. There are more headings to remind the student of the thrust of the argument. Special footnotes (in gray boxes) are reserved for important and useful illustrations of the core material in the chapter.

New features in this edition include scores of fresh end-of-chapter questions, with a special emphasis upon short problems that reinforce the major concepts surveyed in the chapter. Terms printed in bold type mark the first occurrence and definition of the most important words that constitute the language of economics. And many tables and figures have been added or redrawn to crystallize essential parts of the analysis.

But these many changes have not altered one bit the central stylistic beacon that has guided *Economics* since its first days: to use simple sentences, clear explanations, and concise tables and graphs.

Microeconomics or Macroeconomics First?

Should you teach microeconomics or macroeconomics first? Some say that teaching macroeconomics first is preferable because the first-time student finds macro more approachable and will more quickly develop a keen interest in economics. Others believe that the principles of macroeconomics can be more thoroughly appreciated after the rigorous reasoning of microeconomics has been mastered. We have taught economics in both sequences and find both work well. Our colleagues across the country are split virtually evenly on the best approach.

Whatever your philosophy, this text has been carefully designed for it. Instructors who deal with macroeconomics first can move straight through the chapters. Those who wish to tackle microeconomics first should skip from Part One directly to Part Four, knowing that the exposition and cross-references have been tailored with their needs in mind.

An important innovation in this new edition is the availability of two paperback volumes, *Macroeconomics* (Chapters 1–17 and 36–40 of the text) and *Microeconomics* (Chapters 1–4 and 18–40).

Auxiliary Teaching and Study Aids

Students of this edition will benefit greatly from the *Study Guide*. This carefully designed aid has been prepared by Professor Gary Yohe of Wesleyan University, who worked in close collaboration with us in our revision. Both when used alongside classroom discussions and when employed independently for self-study, the *Study Guide* has proved to be an impressive success.

In addition, instructors will find the *Instructor's Manual and Test Bank* useful for planning their courses and preparing multiple sets of test questions in both print and computerized format. Moreover, McGraw-Hill has designed a beautiful set of two-color overhead transparencies for presenting the tabular and graphical material in the classroom. Additional figures from the text are available on transparency masters. These items can all be obtained by contacting your local McGraw-Hill sales representative.

Economics in the Computer Age

This edition is accompanied by the *Interactive Economic Graphic Tutorial to accompany Samuelson/Nordhaus* which combines text, graphics, page references to the book, and key concepts on the same screen. Shifts in curves are shown by arrows that guide the student through economic processes step by step. The program is available for the IBM PC and compatibles; it will reinforce the text and provide personal instruction for the central concepts of *Economics*.

Acknowledgments

This book has two authors but a multitude of collaborators. We are profoundly grateful to colleagues, reviewers, students, and McGraw-Hill's staff for contributing to the timely completion of the thirteenth edition of *Economics*.

Colleagues at MIT, Yale, and elsewhere who graciously contributed their comments and suggestions include E. Cary Brown, Robert J. Gordon, Lyle Gramley, Paul Joskow, Alfred Kahn, Richard Levin, Robert Litan, Joseph Pechman, Merton J. Peck, Gustav Ranis, Paul Craig Roberts, Herbert Scarf, Robert M. Solow, James Tobin, Janet Yellen, and Gary Yohe.

In addition, we have benefitted from the tireless devotion of those whose experience in teaching elementary economics is embodied in this edition. We are particularly grateful to John E. Anderson, Eastern Michigan University; Jeff A. Ankrom, Wittenberg University; Mark Bagnoli, University of Michigan; James H. Barrow, Wilkes Community College; Gerald E. Breger, University of South Carolina; Thomas P. Breslin, Trenton State College; Kristyn C. Brown, Baylor University; Dennis M. Byrne, University of Akron; Sue Cain, Pittsburgh State University; K. Laurence Chang, Case Western Reserve University; Charles R. Chittle, Bowling Green State University; Raymond L. Cohn, Illinois State University; Christopher M. Cornwell, West Virginia University; Michael J. Cravatta, Richland Community College; Ross P. Daniel, Louisiana State University; William Dawes, SUNY an Stony Brook; Loraine Donaldson, Georgia State University; Joseph Earley, Loyola Marymount University; Paul G. Farnham, Georgia State University; Raymond P. H. Fishe, University of Miami; Eric Fisher, Cornell University; Kevin F. Forbes, Catholic University; Ralph G. Fowler, Diablo Valley College; George C. Georgiou, Towson State University; Frank W. Gery, St. Olaf College; Ron D. Gilbert, Texas Tech University; Amihai Glazer, University of California–Irvine; Michael J. Gootzeit, Memphis State University; Mitchell Harwitz SUNY—University at Buffalo; Roger S. Hewett, Drake University; Ann Helwege, Tufts University; John Hillard, University of Leeds, England; Harold Hotelling, Oakland University; John Huttman, San Francisco State University; Eric Jensen, College of William and Mary; Nasrin Jewell, College of St. Catherine; Warren L. Jones, Western Illinois University; M. Barbara Killen, University of Minnesota; Philip A. Klein, Pennsylvania State University; Soyon Lee, Illinois Benedictine College; Dennis Patrick Leyden, University of North Carolina at Greensboro; David Loschky, University of Missouri—Columbia; Steven J. Matusz, Michigan State University; Richard A. Miller, Wesleyan University; Robert M. Mulligan, Providence College; Alannah Orrison, New York University; John E. Page, Dominican College of Blauvelt; Hong Y. Park, Saginaw Valley State University; Barbara B. Reagan, Southern Methodist University; Paul D. Roman, Saint Louis University; Howard N. Ross, Baruch College; Marc Rubin, Loyola College; Jean Hart Sandver, Capital University; John L. Solow, University of Iowa; Allen D. Stone, Southwest Missouri State University; Gilbert S. Suzawa, University of Rhode Island; William O. Thweatt, Vanderbilt University; Darwin Wassink, University of Wisconsin at Eau Claire; Arthur Welsh, Pennsylvania State University; James N. Wetzel, Virginia Commonwealth University; Jack C. Wimberly, University of Southern Mississippi; Larry A. Wohl, Gustavus Adolphus College; William C. Wood, Bridgewater College; and Gavin Wright, Stanford University.

Students at MIT, Yale, and other colleges and universities have served as an "invisible college." They constantly challenge and test us, helping to make this edition less imperfect than its predecessor. Although they are too numerous to enumerate, their influence is woven through every chapter.

A small group of student coworkers devoted their time and energy to this edition, especially Larry Burtschy, Howard Chang, Akiva Dickstein, Elizabeth Gregory, Keith

Hwang, Martin Lariviere, John Garen, and Don Smythe. The statistical and historical material was prepared and double-checked by Tan Yong Hui. Clerical assistance was provided by Glena Ames. Judith Hickey provided invaluable editorial, logistical, and stylistic assistance.

McGraw-Hill's New York team included Designer Joan O'Connor, Senior Editing Supervisor Peggy Rehberger, Assistant Production Manager Diane Renda, and Economics Editor Scott Stratford, along with Senior Editor Elisa Adams who provided unerring advice from the inception of this edition to its completion. This group of skilled professionals turned a mountain of paper into a finely polished work of art.

TO THE SOVEREIGN READER

The thirteenth edition marks the fortieth birthday of *Economics*. The first twelve editions of this book have opened the world of economics to millions of students around the world, and this edition can also serve you well.

One book studied in a single course cannot make you an expert in the subject. But then, most students are not pursuing careers in economics. Rather, you are likely to be concerned with gaining a basic understanding of how our complex economy works. We have therefore laid out a survey of the essential concepts and policy problems of modern economics as simply as we can, omitting no important topics, using no misleading oversimplifications, but burdening you with no unnecessary complications.

Who has been uppermost in our minds as we rewrote this thirteenth edition? You, the beginning student. On every page we have asked: What are the crucial forces that will influence our economy in the 1990s and the early twenty-first century? What tools will be most helpful for men and women entering careers in business, law, government, and the 1001 other paths that young people follow?

At every point in the writing of this edition we have worked to clarify and sharpen the analysis, to make sure the tables and charts are well labeled, and to check for the relevance of each historical illustration.

The Intellectual Marketplace

Markets will hold center stage in the pages that follow: markets for corn and wheat, stocks and bonds, French francs and Japanese yen, unskilled labor and highly trained neurosurgeons. There is also a marketplace of ideas, where contending schools of economists develop their theories and attempt to persuade their colleagues. You will find a fair and impartial review of the thinking of the intellectual giants of our profession in the chapters that follow—from the early economists like Adam Smith, David Ricardo, and Karl Marx to modern-day titans like John Maynard Keynes, Milton Friedman, and Robert Solow.

You have probably read in the newspaper about the gross national product, the consumer price index, the stock market, and the unemployment rate. After you have completed a thorough study of the chapters in this textbook, you will not only know precisely what these words mean; you will also understand the economic forces that influence and determine them.

How to Study Economics

We have designed this book so that it can be fruitfully used by the beginning freshman as well as by advanced students in the severest honors course. It is carefully layered so that each reader can pursue topics quickly or in depth.

Divide and Conquer

No one can tell you the best way to read a textbook, for individual styles differ greatly among students. But educators and psychologists offer counsel about certain tried-and-true methods that will help you learn the subject more quickly and retain the material longer.

To begin with, this is obviously not a novel or a detective story. Economics is best learned by daily study in small chunks. Don't wait until 2 or 3 days before a test to begin your studies; make steady progress through the material by keeping up with the assigned reading.

For each chapter, begin by searching for the basic ideas for perspective. You may first want to skim through the material, look at the summary, and study the major concepts and definitions. Next, read the material carefully, underlining the important sentences and taking notes on focal ideas. Then refresh your memory by reading the final summary, reviewing the major concepts, and going back through the chapter to doublecheck the highlights.

Read Actively

Above all, be an active participant in your study. Always ask yourself, ''Why is this important?'' or ''What is a current example of this theory?'' Think of new examples as you study the text. Read the newspaper to witness economic history unfolding daily. Argue about the analysis or examples with your teachers and classmates. Do the end-of-chapter questions and work through Professor Gary Yohe's *Study Guide* to help cement the important concepts in your mind and test the limits of your understanding.

Skoal!

Our envy goes with you, the beginning student, as you set out to explore the exciting world of economics for the first time. This is a thrill that, alas, you can experience only once in a lifetime. So, as you begin, we wish you bon voyage!

Paul A. Samuelson
William D. Nordhaus

CONTENTS IN BRIEF_____

CONTENTS_____

PART FOUR   MICROECONOMICS: SUPPLY, DEMAND, AND PRODUCT MARKETS   419

18   SUPPLY AND DEMAND IN INDIVIDUAL MARKETS   421

PART FIVE   WAGES, RENT, AND PROFITS: THE DISTRIBUTION OF INCOME   637

ECONOMICS

PART ONE

BASIC CONCEPTS

CHAPTER 1
INTRODUCTION

The Age of Chivalry is gone; that of sophisters, economists, and calculators has succeeded.

Edmund Burke

As YOU begin your reading, you are probably wondering, why study economics? In fact, people do it for countless reasons.

Some study economics because they hope to make money.

Others worry that they will be illiterate if they cannot understand the laws of supply and demand.

People are also concerned to learn how budget deficits and inflation will affect their future.

For Whom the Bell Tolls

All these reasons, and many more, make good sense. Still, we have come to realize, there is one overriding reason to learn the basic lessons of economics.

All your life—from cradle to grave—you will run up against the brutal truths of economics. As a voter, you will have to make decisions on issues—the budget deficit, taxes, and foreign trade—that cannot be understood until you have mastered the rudiments of this subject.

Choosing your life's occupation is the most important economic decision you will make. Once you have earned your income, economics will help you decide how much to spend or save. Of course, studying eco-

3

nomics is not guaranteed to make you a genius. But without economics the dice of life are simply loaded against you.

No need to belabor the point. We hope you will find that, in addition to being useful, economics is a fascinating field in its own right. Generations of students, often to their surprise, have discovered how stimulating economics can be.

WHAT IS ECONOMICS?

Economics covers all kinds of topics. But at the core it is devoted to understanding the way businesses, households, and governments behave; it attempts to figure out the 1001 puzzles of everyday life.

Have You Ever Wondered . . .

You have undoubtedly asked a multitude of economic questions even before you picked up your first textbook on economics. You might come into your first class with questions like these:

Why is it sometimes hard to find a summer job? Sometimes easy? Why do people worry about the government budget deficit? What are the effects of the deficit on inflation? For that matter, why do people worry about inflation? What is the money supply and why is it important? Why are women so often paid less than men? Why are some people rich and others poor? How can foreign countries like Japan or Korea produce goods so much more cheaply than America? What would happen if we kept foreign cars out of the United States to ''protect'' domestic workers and firms? How much is it really costing me to go to college?

The list could go on for pages, and the answers will fill this book, for trying to answer these questions forms the very essence of economic science.

A Historical Perspective

As a scholarly discipline, economics is two centuries old. Adam Smith published his pathbreaking book *The Wealth of Nations* in 1776, a year also notable for the Declaration of Independence. It is no coincidence that both documents appeared in the same year. The movement for political freedom from the tyranny of European monarchies appeared almost simultaneously with attempts to emancipate prices and wages from heavy-handed government regulation.

Adam Smith, of course, represented only a beginning. Almost a century later, as vibrant capitalist enterprises in railroads, textiles, and other sectors began to spread their influence into every region of the world, there appeared the massive critique of capitalism: Karl Marx's *Capital* (1867, 1885, 1894). Marx proclaimed that capitalism was doomed and would soon be followed by business depressions, revolutionary upheavals, and government-run socialism. More than a century later, one-third of the world's population live in countries where Marxian doctrines are economic gospel.

In the decades that followed, Marx's predictions seemed borne out. Economic panics and deep depressions in the 1890s and 1930s led intellectuals of the twentieth century to question the viability of private-enterprise capitalism. In the trough of the Great Depression, however, appeared John Maynard Keynes' *The General Theory of Employment, Interest and Money* (1936). This landmark work described a new approach to economics, one that would help government monetary and fiscal management tame the worst ravages of business cycles.

Smith, Marx, and Keynes are but three of the many thinkers who have shaped economics and made it the vital science it is today.

Definitions of Economics

On first encountering economics, you may want a definition. Here are a few that are commonly heard:

▪ Economics is the study of those activities that involve the production and exchange of goods.

▪ Economics analyzes movements in the overall economy—trends in prices, output, and unemployment. Once such phenomena are understood, economics helps develop the policies by which governments can improve the performance of the economy.

▪ Economics is the science of choice. It studies how people choose to use scarce or limited productive resources (land, labor, equipment, technical knowledge), to produce various commodities (such as wheat, beef, overcoats, concerts, roads, and missiles), and to distribute these goods to various members of society for their consumption.

- Economics is the study of commerce among nations. It helps explain why nations export some goods and import others, and analyzes the effects of putting economic barriers at national frontiers.

- Economics is the study of money, banking, capital, and wealth.

The list is a good one, yet you could extend it many times over. But if we boil down all these definitions, we would find a common theme like the following:

Economics is the study of how societies use scarce resources to produce valuable commodities and distribute them among different groups.

Macroeconomics and Microeconomics A major distinction is made between **macroeconomics,** which studies the functioning of the economy as a whole, and **microeconomics,** which analyzes the behavior of individual components like industries, firms, and households.

Parts Two and Three of this book cover macroeconomics—asking about the determination of national income and output, studying the overall inflation and unemployment rates, asking about the total money supply, and investigating why some nations thrive while others stagnate.

Parts Four and Five, which cover microeconomics, in a sense look at the economy through a microscope—studying, among other things, how individual prices are set, asking about the behavior of labor unions, and inquiring into the effect of higher taxes on people's work effort or saving.

THE SCIENTIFIC APPROACH

The list of economic questions is so long that you might naturally ask how we could even hope to answer them. How could anyone hope to know in a rigorous, scientific way why teenagers have such high unemployment rates? Can economists really understand the reasons why some people are fabulously rich while others can hardly scratch out one square meal a day?

Of course, economists have no monopoly on the truth about the important issues of the day. Indeed, many puzzling phenomena are poorly understood and highly controversial. But economists and other scientists have developed techniques—sometimes called the *scientific approach*—that give them a head start in understanding the forces that underlie issues like unemployment, prices and wages, income distribution, or foreign trade.

Observation One of the major sources of economic knowledge is observation of economic affairs, especially drawing upon the historical record. As an example, consider inflation, which occurs when there is a rise in the general level of prices.[1] Citizens, bankers, and political leaders often fret about high inflation rates when prices are rising 10 or 20 or even 100 percent per year.

How can we understand the damage done by inflation? One way is to study historical inflations. For example, we will later investigate the German inflation of the 1920s, during which prices rose 1,000,000,000,000 percent in 2 years. This destroyed much of the wealth of the middle class, led to social unrest, and, many people believe, abetted Hitler's rise to power. By examining the impacts of these virulent forms of inflation, we can gain insight into the more moderate inflations of the 1970s and 1980s.

The philosopher Santayana said that those who forget history are condemned to repeat it. Economics too has much to learn from the history books, and the lessons are found on virtually every page of this textbook.

Analysis History and facts are central to an empirical science like economics, but facts cannot tell their own story. To recorded history we must add economic analysis, for only by developing and testing economic theories can we shape the jumble of data and facts into a coherent view of reality.

What do we mean by *economic analysis*? This is an approach which deduces or predicts certain kinds of

---

[1]Developing an understanding of economic issues requires a specialized vocabulary. If you find yourself confused about a particular word or phrase, you should consult the Glossary at the back of this book. The Glossary contains most of the major technical economic terms used in this book. All terms printed in boldface are also defined in the Glossary.

economic behavior on the basis of prior assumptions about how people or firms are motivated or will act. As an example of analysis, consider the drive to protect domestic workers and firms from foreign competition. In recent years, the United States has bought much more from abroad than it has sold to foreigners. As a result employment in heavy manufacturing industries has declined. Workers in industries such as automobile, steel, machinery, and textiles have complained that "cheap foreign labor" is stealing their jobs. What might be done? Some people suggest putting barriers on trade, say by taxing imports or by setting quotas limiting their quantity. In recent years, for example, imports of Japanese autos have been limited to 2.2 million per year.

People could argue endlessly about the impacts of such import restraints. Or they could study the predictions of economic supply-and-demand analysis. Such an analysis shows that, under certain assumptions, import restraints on cars increase the number of jobs in the domestic car industry, raise car prices, but lower the total national income. And case study piled on case study confirms the validity of these kinds of predictions.

In the pages that follow, you will find an array of analytical tools: supply and demand, cost schedules, and the like. Mastery of the use of these tools will help you answer myriad economic questions that arise every day.

Statistical Analyses As we move into advanced topics, the use of statistics grows in importance. Governments and businesses issue volumes of data that can be analyzed to help us understand economic behavior quantitatively. While the actual use of these tools requires mathematical methods in probability and econometrics, understanding the results requires primarily careful reading and common sense.

Where might we use statistics? Let's say that you are wondering why, on average, women earn only 60 percent of the wages of men. With millions of workers, you can hardly hope to compile a history of each one to explain the disparity. Instead, you collect representative data on wages of men and women, along with their personal characteristics (education, years of experience, occupation, and so forth). Using these data, you might then employ statistical techniques to estimate what fraction of the difference in earnings of men and women is due to differences in characteristics. For example, studies have found that a significant part of the difference in earnings is associated with the fact that men have tended to spend more time in the work force and have generally entered higher-paying occupations. But after all the statistical dust has settled, studies generally leave a significant part of the wage differential unexplained, and some believe this remaining differential is due to discrimination.

Experiments Sometimes history, analysis, and statistics still are unable to provide a clear answer to important questions. The economic world is enormously complicated, with thousands of prices and millions of households. In an exciting new development, economists are turning to laboratory and other controlled experiments to understand complex economic processes.

What are *controlled experiments*? A scientist sets up a controlled experiment by dividing a population into two or more groups, each of which is treated exactly the same except for a single factor. In a test to determine whether saccharin causes cancer in rats, a "control" group would get no saccharin, while the "experimental" group might get different amounts of saccharin in its diet each day. The key ingredient in such a controlled experiment is to vary saccharin and hold all other things (water, light, diet, genetics) equal, thereby allowing the scientist to determine whether saccharin has any measurable impact on the rats.

Experiments in economics are more difficult than in most sciences. To begin with, economists cannot measure economic variables with the precision that physical scientists can measure mass, velocity, or distance. Moreover, it is difficult to replicate the real economy in a laboratory, and people often behave peculiarly in experimental situations. Nevertheless, in one group of controlled experiments over the last 15 years, economists and others have measured people's reactions to different kinds of government programs to raise the incomes of the poor. These experiments were extremely helpful in showing how changes in government programs might affect people's work habits and saving behavior.

In the last decade, economists have turned increasingly to laboratory experiments. In these, groups of people are set up as firms and consumers to determine how prices would behave in different markets. Already we have seen some surprising differences that no one had imagined before the experiments were run.[2]

These four techniques—observation, analysis, statistics, and experiments—form the approach by which economic science progresses. Every day, a new puzzle arises. In response, economists test new ideas and reject old ones, and economics evolves and changes. Textbooks embody both the established wisdom and the hot controversies of today. But in a decade or two, new facts will have toppled old theories, and the subject will evolve anew.

PITFALLS IN ECONOMIC REASONING

No matter what the problem or what the approach, certain pitfalls lie in the path of the serious economist. This section reviews a few of them.

Failing to Keep "Other Things Equal"

In most economic problems, many variables are at work. For example, the number of cars bought in a given year is determined by the price of cars, by consumer incomes, by gasoline prices, and so forth. How can we isolate the impact on car sales of a single variable, such as the price of cars?

As we noted in our discussion of controlled experiments, the key step in isolating the impact of a single variable is to hold **other things equal.** This phrase means that the factor under consideration is varied while all other factors are held constant. If we want to measure the impact of car prices on the number of cars purchased, we must examine the effect of changing car prices while ensuring that consumer incomes, gasoline prices, and other such variables are unchanged, that these "other things are held equal."

Say that you are interested in determining the impact on car sales of the big drop in gasoline prices in 1986. You will be vexed by the facts that consumer incomes rose sharply in 1986 and that fear of terrorist attacks abroad led many people to vacation in America in their automobiles. Nevertheless, you must try to isolate the effects of the lower gasoline prices by attempting to determine what would happen if other things were equal. Unless you exclude the effects of other variables changing, you cannot accurately understand the impact of changing gasoline prices.

The *Post Hoc* Fallacy

A common fallacy which often arises in interpreting cause-and-effect relationships is the "*post hoc* fallacy." This occurred in ancient times when the medicine man believed that both witchcraft and a little arsenic were necessary to kill his enemy. Another example is a reporter's claim that, because Florida has the highest death rate of any state, it must have a terribly unhealthful climate.

In each case we see the **post hoc fallacy.**[3]

The fact that event A is observed before event B does not prove that event A caused event B. To conclude that "after the event" implies "because of the event" is to commit the *post hoc* fallacy.

The medicine man committed the *post hoc* fallacy because he concluded that witchcraft caused death because it preceded death. The reporter committed the same fallacy when assuming that Florida's climate must be responsible for the high death rate, forgetting to take into account that Florida's residents are older than those of any other state. Only after we have corrected the mortality figures for the age of the population and other important variables can we judge whether Florida is a healthful or dangerous place to live.

The Whole Is Not Always the Sum of the Parts

Have you ever seen people jump up at a football game to gain a better view? They usually find that, once everybody is standing up, the view has not improved at all. Such behavior, where what is true for an indi-

---

[2]A nontechnical survey of such experiments is provided in Charles R. Plott, "Laboratory Experiments in Economics: The Implications of Posted-Price Institutions," *Science,* vol. 232, May 9, 1986, pp. 732–738.

[3]In logic, this is known as the *post hoc, ergo propter hoc* fallacy (translated from the Latin as "after this, therefore necessarily because of this").

vidual is not necessarily true for everyone, illustrates the "fallacy of composition," which is defined as follows:

The **fallacy of composition** occurs when what is true of a part is therefore believed to be true for the whole.

The following examples are true statements that might surprise people who had fallen into the fallacy of composition.

- If all farmers produce a big crop, total farm income will probably fall.

- Attempts of individuals to save more in a depression may lessen the community's total savings.

- If a single individual receives more money, that person will be better off; if everybody receives more money, no one will be better off.

- It may benefit the United States to reduce tariffs charged on imported goods, even if other countries refuse to lower their tariffs.

In the course of this book, these apparent paradoxes will be related to the fallacy of composition. There are no magic formulas or hidden tricks. Rather, these are examples in which what seems to be true for individuals is not always true for society as a whole. You might, at the end of your studies, check over the above examples to see how they involve the fallacy of composition.

Subjectivity

Perhaps the deepest pitfall in studying economics arises from the *subjectivity* we bring to studying the world around us. People sometimes believe that there is an objective reality outside themselves and that the task of science is to discover the facts and laws of nature or society.

Alas, learning is not so simple. When we are young, our minds are open to new ideas. Newborn babies see light but do not yet perceive that the light forms objects. As they grow up, they begin to organize light, touch, and sound into parents, food, and dogs. But no sooner do we begin to understand the world around us, than we become captives of our own knowledge. Growing up on planet Earth, it was natural for our ancestors to believe that the rest of the

universe revolved around them. Growing up in a capitalist economy, we may find it hard to sympathize with or even understand socialist systems. In the end, the way we perceive the observed facts depends on the theoretical spectacles we wear.

The same is true of scientists. Like other people, they are prisoners of their theoretical preconceptions. If physicists learned Newtonian physics well, this might actually hinder their grasp of Einsteinian relativity theories.

That is why science belongs to the young. The old "know" too many things that they cannot forget. A striking illustration of this is given by Nobel laureate Max Planck, the physicist renowned for his discovery of the revolutionary quantum theory. In his *Scientific Autobiography,* Planck reports what he observed in the development of physics:

> This experience gave me also an opportunity to learn a fact—a remarkable one in my opinion: A new scientific truth does not triumph by convincing its opponents and making them see the light, but rather because its opponents eventually die, and a new generation grows up that is familiar with it.

Just as Newton, Einstein, and Planck revolutionized perceptions in physics, so did the giants of economics like Smith, Marx, and Keynes—indeed, all whose names appear on the family tree of economics shown on the back endpaper of this book—transform economic understanding by converting the young and open-minded.

Is It a Bird? A simple picture can illustrate the subjectivity that exists in every science. Does picture *(b)* in Figure 1-1 show a bird looking to the left? Or is it an antelope looking to the right?

There is no right answer. Either may be correct depending upon the context. In the presence of Figure 1-1*(a)*'s field of birds, most people think it is a bird. But next to *(c)*'s field of antelopes, people see it as an antelope.

So it is with scientific facts and theories. *After you have studied and learned a body of economic principles, you comprehend reality in a new and different way.* This important insight helps us understand why people who live on the same planet can have funda-

BIRD OR ANTELOPE?

(a)   (b)   (c)

Figure 1-1   The same facts may tell different stories to scientific observers who wear different theoretical spectacles

Is **(b)** a bird or an antelope? When **(c)** is covered up, most people think it is a bird. But when **(a)** is covered, most will see it as an antelope. [Source: N. R. Hanson, *Patterns of Discovery* (Cambridge University Press, London, 1961).] Thus do differences in perception affect people's views on economic policy.

mentally different economic perceptions—why some believe capitalism is the best system while others hold communism to be optimal, or why some believe government spending is wasteful and others believe it useful.

So let us be forewarned to question the inevitable subjectivity of our own beliefs and philosophies and to be open-minded about views that differ from our own.

Uncertainty in Economic Life

More than a century ago, the French mathematician Laplace thought that, with sufficient data and time for computation, we could see the future as clearly as the present. In today's age of uncertainty, we know this is not so; there is an inherent unpredictability in even the most precise physical sciences. The social sciences are even less precise than the physical sciences, for they involve more complex relationships and must attempt to predict human behavior. More and more today, economists must cope with the fact that uncertainty pervades economic life.

In the last 40 years, economics has been in the forefront of developing tools that explain how uncertainty affects human behavior. As a result of this work, we now understand more about chess strategies, about how to invest in the stock market, and even about the arms race.

One of the first principles to understand is that economic laws hold on average and not in every particular case. For example, economics would hold that, other things equal, lower gasoline prices raise the amount of gasoline used. A skeptic would retort, "But my cousin Jane hasn't changed her driving habits at all." Or, "You say that lower unemployment tends to raise inflation. What about 1983? It didn't happen then!"

The critics have apt observations; economics is not an exact science. Rather:

Economic laws hold true only on the average, not as exact relationships.

Figure 1-2 gives a preview of a vital statistical relationship whereby consumption (spending by households on goods like food, clothing, and housing) can be related to income. Note that the dots do not fall exactly on the line, as they might in chemistry or astronomy. This consumption-income relationship illustrates that even very accurate-looking economic laws are still only approximate, not exact.

What lies behind the consumption-income relation in Figure 1-2 is a country of 90 million households, each spending a certain amount in light of its income, wealth, tastes, and idiosyncratic elements. The consumption of individual households may be highly unpredictable in a given year, depending on whether they bought a new car or went on a long vacation or were unemployed. But individual differences largely

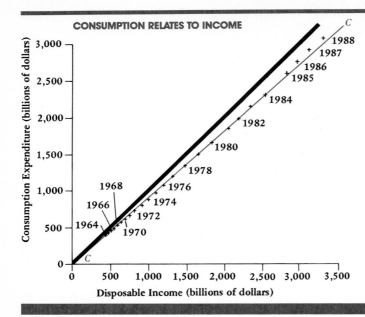

CONSUMPTION RELATES TO INCOME

Figure 1-2   Economic laws hold on average, but are not exact relationships

Observed points of consumption spending fall near the red line, which displays average behavior. Thus, the black point for 1986 is so near the *CC* line that it could have been quite accurately predicted from that line even before the year was over. This regularity between dollar income and spending is typical of economic relationships. (Source: Figure 7-6.)

disappear when overall behavior is examined. *The law of averages states that the average behavior of groups will be much more predictable than the behavior of individuals.*

Thus, even when there are enormous differences in individual behavior (such as consumption or saving or buying gasoline) we can often see great regularities of overall community behavior.

THE USES OF ECONOMICS

After seeing the way economics advances and the pitfalls that lie on the road to progress, we might wonder, What is the ultimate destination? Why do we study economics? What are its uses?

As we suggested earlier, our economic knowledge serves us in managing our personal lives, understanding society, and designing better economic policies.

The role of better economic understanding in guiding our individual lives will be as varied as are our personalities or physiognomies. Learning about the stock market or about interest rates may help people manage their own finances better; knowledge about price theory and antitrust policy may improve the skills of a lawyer; better awareness of the determinants of cost and revenue will produce better business decisions. The doctor, the investor, and the farmer all

need to understand about accounting and regulation to make the highest profit from their businesses.

Economic Description and Policy

In addition to helping people in their personal lives, economics is required for understanding key national issues and for making progress in dealing with them. People who have never made a systematic study of economics are handicapped in even thinking about national issues; they are like the illiterate trying to read.

Economics plays two distinct roles in promoting the understanding of national economic issues. It first helps to describe, explain, and predict economic behavior—as for example when it helps us understand the causes of poverty. But for many people, the payoff from such economic knowledge comes when it is applied to a second task, that of improving economic performance. This distinction between description and prescription is central to modern economics.

Normative vs. Positive Economics When using economics, we must be careful to distinguish between normative statements (or value judgments) and positive (or factual) statements.

Positive economics describes the facts and behavior in the economy. What percent of teenagers are unemployed? How many people earn less than $12,000 a year? What will be the effect of higher cigarette taxes on the number of smokers? These are questions that can be resolved only by reference to facts—they may be easy or tough questions, but they are all in the realm of positive economics.

Normative economics involves ethics and value judgments. Should the government give money to poor people? Should the public sector (government) or the private sector (business) provide extra jobs for unemployed teenagers? Should the budget deficit be reduced by higher taxes or lower spending? These are questions involving deeply held values or moral judgments. They can be argued about, but they can never be settled by science or by appeal to facts. There simply is no right or wrong answer to how high inflation should be, whether society should help poor people, or how much the nation should spend on defense. These questions are resolved by political decision, not by economic science.

Economics in Government

Economists have in recent years become the counselors of presidents and prime ministers. The political agenda is full of economic issues: Should we raise taxes to curb the budget deficit? Should the nation protect the automobile industry from Japanese competition? What should we do to curb acid rain? Political leaders need economic advisers to provide counsel on such complicated questions.

Increasingly, the international side of economic activity concerns policymakers. As the nation's trade deficit climbed in the 1980s, Congress labored to rewrite the rules of international commerce. And, as we note in the last chapter of this book, historian Paul Kennedy has shown the close link of relative economic strength with military and political power, forecasting a future decline of the United States as a Great Power in the years ahead.

The heads of government must constantly make vital decisions that involve economics. But of course national leaders need not themselves be professional experts in economics. Rather, they need to be literate "consumers" of the conflicting economic advice given them.*

Similarly, few students will become professional economists. Many will study economics for only a term or two. This book is intended to give a thorough introductory overview of the whole subject. Your view of the world will never be the same after a single semester of economics.

Why Economists Disagree

In recent years, economists have developed a reputation for being a querulous lot who can't agree on anything. One writer complained, "If you laid all economists end to end, they still wouldn't reach a conclusion." A randomly selected radio or television show will often find two economists disputing about almost anything. Why?

The media are partly to blame. Heated arguments make exciting theater and, seeing a row of nodding economists, you would probably nod off yourself.

But surveys reveal that economists have fewer disagreements than is popularly supposed. A broad consensus exists on many questions of positive economics: economists agree on many issues in microeconomics, such as the effects of rent control, minimum wages, and tariffs upon the economy. Many areas of macroeconomics, by contrast, stir up controversy, especially the role of money and the sources of unemployment in today's society. Many economists are desperately seeking solutions to these puzzles.

The major disagreements among economists, however, lie in the normative arena. Economists differ as much as the rest of the population on issues such as the appropriate size of government, the power of unions, the relative importance of inflation and unem-

---

*As an example of how leaders require economic advice, consider the distinguished British statesman Winston Churchill. He was a great orator, gifted writer, and shrewd judge of the Hitlerian threat while most around him slept. Yet, all his life, Churchill felt himself to be a babe in the woods when it came to the subject of economics. Critics noted that he was "without a deep appreciation of decimal points."

Thus, in 1925, as chancellor of the exchequer, Churchill was persuaded by his advisers to put England back on the gold standard at the wrong price level. Outside experts warned at the time against such folly, and history has recorded that England never quite recovered from the stagnation of the 1920s that this mistake produced.

ployment, and the fair distribution of income. They are as divided as their parents or cousins on the broad political and ethical issues of the day.

■　■　■

We have come to the end of our overture. Return briefly to our opening theme, Why study economics? Perhaps the best answer to the question is a famous one given by Lord Keynes in the final lines of his 1936 classic, *The General Theory of Employment, Interest and Money:*

> The ideas of economists and political philosophers, both when they are right and when they are wrong, are more powerful than is commonly understood. Indeed the world is ruled by little else. Practical men, who believe themselves to be quite exempt from any intellectual influences, are usually the slaves of some defunct economist. Madmen in authority, who hear voices in the air, are distilling their frenzy from some academic scribbler of a few years back. I am sure that the power of vested interests is vastly exaggerated compared with the gradual encroachment of ideas. Not, indeed, immediately, but after a certain interval; for in the field of economic and political philosophy there are not many who are influenced by new theories after they are twenty-five or thirty years of age, so that the ideas which civil servants and politicians and even agitators apply to current events are not likely to be the newest. But, soon or late, it is ideas, not vested interests, which are dangerous for good or evil.

After a careful study of economics you will begin to recognize the ideas that lie behind the arguments in the popular press or political platform. To understand the ideas of generations of economists and how they apply to the problems of personal life and national issues—ultimately, this is why we study economics.

Preview

Before we begin our journey into the realm of economics, let's preview the major themes of this book.

Part One deals with the fundamental tools needed to analyze the basic facts and institutions of modern economic life.

Part Two turns to microeconomics, beginning with the forces of competition and monopoly. These forces act through supply and demand to help determine—efficiently or inefficiently—the composition of the national output, in terms of both goods and services produced and their prices.

Part Three treats the distribution of income: determination of wages, rent, interest, and profits and the pricing of the factors of production.

Part Four then ties several strands of the microeconomics chapters together, weighing the role of the private versus the public sector, reviewing capitalism versus socialism, and asking how society can change the distribution of income.

Part Five deals with issues of trade, growth, and development: How do nations grow over a period of decades, and why do some nations prosper while others stagnate in underdevelopment? The last chapters turn an eye to the country's economic relations with the rest of the world, delving into determinants of exchange rates, examining the gains from trade, and weighing the arguments about protectionism.

SUMMARY

1. Economics, both a science and an art, is studied for a variety of reasons: to understand problems facing the citizen and family, to help governments promote growth and improve the quality of life while avoiding depression and inflation, and to analyze fascinating patterns of social behavior. Because economic questions enter into both daily life and national issues, a basic understanding of economics is vital for sound decision making by individuals and nations.

2. Among many definitions, the most comprehensive is: *Economics is the study of how societies choose to use scarce productive resources that have alternative uses, to produce commodities of various kinds, and to distribute them among different groups.*

3. Economists and other scientists have a variety of weapons that can be deployed to attack economic questions. Observation of economic history provides countless episodes from which to find patterns of behavior. Economic analysis allows the facts to be arrayed into general propositions. Often statistical studies permit understanding of complex situations. And experiments are a recent way to test for economic relationships. In approaching economic questions, we confront basic methodological problems that must be solved: holding other things equal; trying to keep descriptions distinct from value judgments; avoiding the *post hoc* and composition fallacies; realizing the inevitable subjectivity in observation and theory.

CONCEPTS FOR REVIEW

economics	fallacy of composition
normative vs. positive economics	*post hoc* fallacy
macroeconomics vs. microeconomics	other things equal
the scientific approach	uncertainty, law of averages
controlled experiment	

QUESTIONS FOR DISCUSSION

1. Give some definitions of economics. Which is the most comprehensive one?

2. Define each term in your own words: *post hoc* fallacy; other things equal; normative and positive economics.

3. Identify which of the following are normative and which are positive statements:

(a) Lower gasoline prices lead to higher consumption of gasoline.

(b) Bread prices should be lower.

(c) The poor should pay no taxes.

(d) Restricting the imports of Japanese cars will raise GM's profits and is therefore desirable.

(e) Rising food prices contributed to the French Revolution.

4. Is it possible to be "objective" in a social science like economics? On what can conservatives and liberals agree? Give examples of the fallacy of composition and of the *post hoc, ergo propter hoc* fallacy. Is the former involved in the debate over cigarette smoking and longevity? (Why not?) Might the latter be involved in this debate? (Why so?)

5. In commenting on the role of economics in government, one economic adviser to presidents said, "Economists should be on tap, not on top." What did he mean? Do you agree?

6. The gravestone of Karl Marx contains the following words he wrote at the age of 26:

> Up 'til now the philosophers have only
> interpreted the world in various ways. The
> point, though, is to change it!

Could a scientist believe in "changing the world," but not necessarily agree with a Marxian program for thoroughgoing violent revolution? How would different people draw the line? How would you, before beginning your first course in economics?

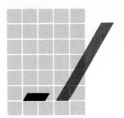

APPENDIX: 1 _____
How to Read Graphs

A picture is worth a thousand words.
　　　　　　　Chinese proverb

Before you can master economics, you must have a working knowledge of graphs. They are as indispensable to the economist as a hammer is to a carpenter. So if you are not familiar with the use of diagrams, invest some time in learning how to read them— it will be time well spent.

What is a *graph*? It is an illustration showing how two or more sets of data or variables are related to one another. And its power arises from the fact that so much data can be packed into a small space and can be easily comprehended.

You will encounter a wide variety of graphs in this book: graphs showing how variables move over time (as you see inside the front cover), relationships between variables (as in Figure 1-2, page 10), as well as diagrams dealing with supply and demand. We begin with a simple example that will arise in the next chapter.

THE PRODUCTION-POSSIBILITY FRONTIER

One of the first graphical diagrams you will encounter in this text is the production-possibility frontier. At any point in time, a country can produce only a certain amount of goods and services with its limited resources. The United States can produce only so much gasoline, so much heating oil, so many aircraft, and so forth. Moreover, the country cannot increase its production of one good without giving up at least some of another good: for example, the more gasoline produced, the less heating oil can be produced.

In economics, we represent this limitation on a country's productive potential by the **production-possibility frontier *(PPF)*.** The *PPF* represents the maximum amounts of a pair of goods or services that can both be produced with an economy's given resources.

Let's look at a basic example using food and machines. The essential data for the *PPF* are shown in Table 1A-1. Of the two sets of data, one set gives possible outputs of food; the other set gives possible outputs of machines. Each level of output of food is paired with the number of machines that could be produced at the same time. Thus if the economy produced 10 units of food, it could produce a maximum of 140 machines.

Production-Possibility Graph

The data shown in Table 1A-1 can also be presented as a graph. To construct the graph, we represent each of the pairs of data of Table 1A-1 by a single point on a two-dimensional plane:

ALTERNATIVE PRODUCTION POSSIBILITIES

POSSIBILITIES	FOOD	MACHINES
A	0	150
B	10	140
C	20	120
D	30	90
E	40	50
F	50	0

Table 1A-1   The pairs of possible outputs of food and machines

The table shows six potential pairs of outputs that can be produced with the given resources of a country. The country can choose one of the six output couples.

A graph is an illustration showing how two or more sets of data are related to one another.

Figure 1A-1 displays in a graph the relationship between food and machines shown in Table 1A-1. It is constructed by representing each pair of numbers by a single point in the graph. Thus the row labelled A in Table 1A-1 is graphed as point *A* in Figure 1A-1, and similarly for points *B*, *C*, and so on.

In Figure 1A-1, the vertical line at left and the horizontal line at bottom correspond to the two *variables*—machines and food. A *variable* is an item of interest that can be defined and measured. Important variables studied in economics are prices, quantities, hours of work, acres of land, dollars of income, and so forth. Each line is marked off to show the range of numbers that the goods might take.

The horizontal line is referred to as the *horizontal axis* (or sometimes the *X axis*). The horizontal axis is simply a convenient line for measuring the quantity of one of the variables. In Figure 1A-1, food is on the red horizontal axis, which has been divided into numbers from 0 to 50.

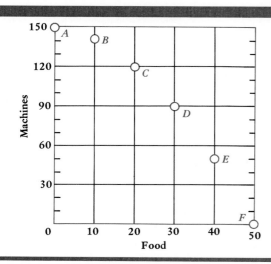

Figure 1A-1   Six possible pairs of food-machines production levels

This figure shows the data of Table 1A-1 in graphical form. The data are *exactly* the same, but note how a visual display strikes the eye more vividly.

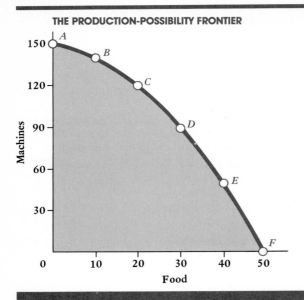

THE PRODUCTION-POSSIBILITY FRONTIER

Figure 1A-2

A smooth curve fills in between the plotted points of the numerical production possibilities, creating the production-possibility frontier.

Similarly, the vertical line at the left is known as the *vertical axis* or *Y axis*. In this example, it measures the number of machines produced. Thus, any point on the horizontal line running through point *C* on the red vertical axis stands for 120 machines.

The lower left-hand corner at which the two axis lines meet is the *origin*. It signifies 0 food and 0 machines.

A Smooth Curve   When drawing graphs, we go beyond simply putting a few dots on a page. *A graph is usually a continuous curve, filling in the space between the points expressed in a table*. Figure 1A-2 fills in the space between each pair of points with a smooth curve from *A* to *F*.

Why do economists often use graphs rather than tables? The food versus machine diagram in Figure 1A-2 can illustrate a number of interesting points. The smooth curve *ABCDEF* reflects the menu of choice for the economy. It is a visual device for showing what types of goods are available in what quantities. By using graphs like the production-possibility frontier, we can more easily understand economic principles.

Slopes and Lines

The essential elements of graphs have been introduced. Let's move on to further aspects of their use.

Most graphs have lines on them. In Figure 1A-2, for example, we see a line depicting the relationship (or ''function'') between output of food and machines. An important way to describe the relationship between the two variables is by the slope of the line. Let's first define slope and then see why it is an important concept.

The **slope** of a line represents the change in one variable that occurs when another variable changes. More precisely, it is the change in the variable on the vertical axis per unit change in the variable on the horizontal axis. For example, in Figure 1A-2, say that food production rose from 25 to 26 units. The slope of the curve in Figure 1A-2 tells us the exact change in machine production that would take place. To repeat, slope is an exact measure of the relationship between the change in Y and the change in X.

Consider the case of straight lines, shown in Figure 1A-3. We want to measure the relationship between the quantities on the X and Y axes as given by the slope of the line AE. Let's calculate the slope of the line between points B and D. Think of the movement from B to D as coming in two stages. First comes a horizontal movement from B to C indicating a 1-unit increase in the X value (with no change in Y). Second comes a compensating vertical movement up or down, shown as s in Figure 1A-3. (The movement of 1 horizontal unit is purely for convenience. The formula holds for movements of any length.) The two-step movement assures us that at the end we are still on the straight line.

Assuming the BC movement is a 1-unit increase in X, then the length of CD (marked as s in Figure 1A-3) indicates the change in Y per unit change in X. On a graph, this change is called the *slope* of the line $ABDE$.

Some important points to remember are:

1. Slope is always expressed as a number. It measures the change in Y per unit change in X.

2. If the line is straight, its slope is constant everywhere.

3. The slope of the line indicates whether the relationship between X and Y is *direct* or *inverse*. Direct relationships occur when variables move in the same direction (that is, they increase or decrease together); inverse relationships occur when the variables move in opposite directions (that is, one increases as the other decreases). Thus a negative slope indicates the X-Y relation is inverse, as in Figure 1A-3(*a*). Why? Because an increase in X calls for a decrease in Y.

Often slope is defined as ''the rise over the run.'' The rise is the vertical distance involved; in Figure 1A-3, the rise is the distance from C to D. The run is the horizontal distance; it is BC in Figure 1A-3. The rise over the run in this instance would be CD over BC. Thus the slope is CD/BC.

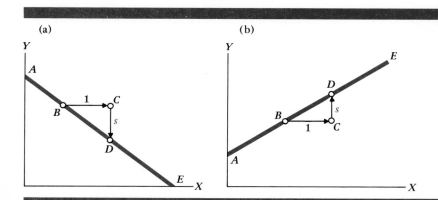

(a)   (b)

Figure 1A-3   Calculation of slope for straight lines

It is easy to calculate slopes for straight lines as "rise over run." Thus in both **(a)** and **(b)**, the numerical value of the slope is rise/run = $CD/BC = s/1 = s$. Note that in **(a)**, CD is negative, indicating a negative slope, or an inverse relationship between X and Y.

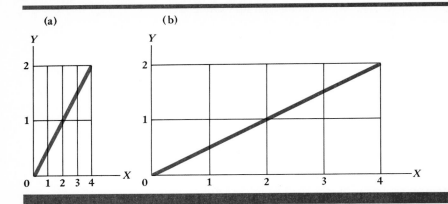

Figure 1A-4 Steepness is not the same as slope

Note that even though **(a)** looks steeper than **(b),** they display the same relationship. Both have slope of $\frac{1}{2}$, but the X axis has been stretched out in **(b).**

People sometimes confuse slope with the appearance of steepness. This conclusion is often valid—but not always. The steepness depends on the scale of the graph. Diagrams *(a)* and *(b)* in Figure 1A-4 both portray exactly the same relationship, and both are accurate. But in *(b)*, the horizontal scale has been stretched out compared to *(a)*. If you calculate carefully, you will see that the algebraic slopes are exactly the same (and equal to $\frac{1}{2}$).

Slope for Curved Lines   A curved line is one whose slope is different at different points. Consider the curved line *ABCDEF* in Figure 1A-5. Suppose we are at point *B*. We can easily calculate the slope from *B* to other points on the curve. To calculate the slope from *B* to *E*, we would draw a right-angled triangle underneath, with corners at *B* and *E*, just as in Figure 1A-3. The slope of the curve between *B* and *E* is then calculated using the right-angle measuring technique shown in Figure 1A-3; the slope

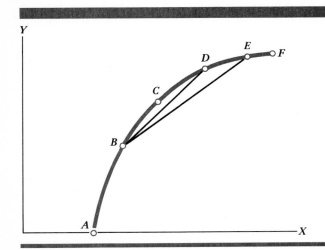

Figure 1A-5 Slopes of curved lines

The lines *BE* and *BD* can be used to calculate the average slope between two points. These are called *arc slopes.*

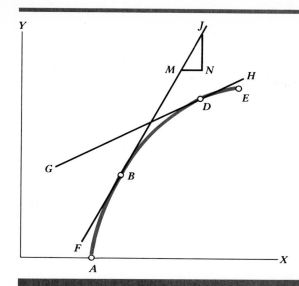

Figure 1A-6   The slope at a point

By constructing a tangent line we can calculate the slope at a point. Thus the line *FBMJ* is tangent to smooth curve *ABD* at point *B*. The slope at *B* is calculated as the slope of the tangent line, i.e., as *NJ/MN*.

is called the *arc slope* between two points. Note that, because the line is curved, the arc slope between *B* and *E* is different from that between *B* and *D*.

Sometimes arc slopes are sufficient for the problem at hand. On other occasions it is useful to ask what the slope of the curved line is *at a point,* such as *B*.

The easiest way to calculate the slope at a point is to draw a *tangent* to the curved line at the point. The tangent to a curved line is itself by definition a straight line; it does not cross the curved line but only touches it, and it touches it at one point only. The slope of this tangent line measures the slope of the curve at that point, where we can use the usual right-angle measuring technique to calculate the slope. By inspection of Figure 1A-6, we see how the slope of the tangent line *FJ* measures the slope of the curved line at point *B*. Similarly, the tangent line *GH* gives the slope of the curved line at point *D*.

Shifts of and Movement along Curves

One of the key distinctions in economics is between shifts of curves and movements along curves. We can examine the distinction in Figure 1A-7. The inner production-possibility frontier reproduces the *PPF* in Figure 1A-2. At point *D* society chooses to produce 30 units of food and 90 units of machines. If society decides to consume more food *with a given PPF*, then it could *move along* the *PPF* to point *E*. This movement along the curve represents choosing more food and fewer machines.

The inner *PPF* might represent society's production possibilities for 1990. If we return to the same country in 2000, the *PPF* has *shifted* from the inner 1990 curve to the outer 2000 curve. (This shift would occur as the economy grew and became more efficient, as we will see in the next chapter.) In the later year, society might choose to be at point *G*, with more food and machines than at either *D* or *E*.

The key point to remember as similar examples occur later in this text is that in one

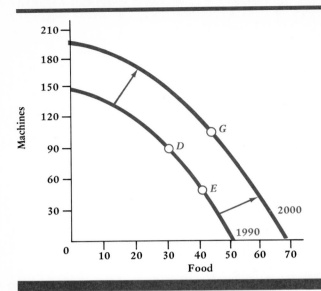

Figure 1A-7   Shift of curves versus movement along curves

In using graphs, it is essential to distinguish *movement along* a curve (such as from high-investment *D* to low-investment *E*) from a *shift of* a curve (as from *D* in an early year to *G* in a later year).

case (moving from *D* to *E*) we witnessed movement along a curve, while in the second case (from *D* to *G*) we witnessed a shift of the curve.

Some Special Graphs

We have encountered one of economics' most important graphs in Figure 1A-2: that which shows the relationship between two economic variables (such as food and machines, or guns and butter). You will encounter other types of graphs in the pages that follow.

Time Series   Some graphs show how a particular variable has changed over time. Some examples appear on the inside front cover of this book, where output, capital, population, and the real interest rate are plotted against time. Generally, in time-series graphs such as these, the horizontal axis is time while the vertical axis shows an economic variable under consideration.

Scatter Diagrams   Sometimes individual pairs of points will be plotted, like the points of the food-or-machines diagram in Figure 1A-1; more often, combinations of variables for different years will be plotted. An important example is the consumption function, shown in Figure 1-2, page 10. By showing whether the points lie tightly or loosely around the line, scatter diagrams allow us to see whether a relationship (say, between consumption and income) is reliable or unreliable.

Diagrams with More Than One Curve   Often it will be extremely useful to put two curves in the same graph, thus obtaining a "multicurve diagram." The most important example is the supply-and-demand diagram, shown in Chapter 4 (see page 64). These graphs can show two different relationships simultaneously, such as how consumers' purchases respond to price (demand) and how businesses' production responds to price (supply). By graphing the two relationships together, we can determine the price and quantity that will hold in a market.

■ ■ ■

This concludes our brief excursion into graphs. With these basic principles mastered, the graphs in this book, and in other areas, can be both fun and instructive.

SUMMARY TO APPENDIX

1. Graphs are an extremely important tool of modern economics. They allow a quick visual presentation of data or of the relationship between two variables.
2. The important points to understand about a graph are: What is on each of two axes (horizontal and vertical)? What are the units on each axis? What kind of relationship is depicted in the curve or curves shown in the graph?
3. The relationship between the two variables in a curve is given by its slope. The slope is defined as "the rise over the run," or the increase in Y per unit increase in X. If it is upward (or positively) sloping, the two variables are directly related and move upward or downward together. If it has a downward (or negative) slope, then the two variables are inversely related.
4. In addition, we sometimes see special examples of graphs: time series, which show how a particular variable moves over time; scatter diagrams, which show the observations on a pair of variables; and multicurve diagrams, which show two or more relationships on a single figure.

CONCEPTS FOR REVIEW

horizontal, or X, axis
vertical, or Y, axis
origin
slope (negative, positive, zero)
slope as "rise over run"

direct, inverse relationship
slope of curved line: arc slope, tangent
  at a point
special graphs: time series, scatter,
  multicurve

QUESTIONS FOR DISCUSSION

1. Consider the following problem for a student. You have 16 hours a day to divide between leisure and study. Let leisure be the X variable and study hours be the Y variable. Plot the straight-line relationship between all combinations of X and Y on a blank piece of graph paper. Be careful to label the axes and mark the origin.
2. In question 1, what is the slope of the line showing the relationship between study and leisure hours? Is it a straight line?

3. Let us say that you absolutely need 6 hours of leisure per day, no more, no less. Mark the point on the graph that you will choose. Now consider a *movement along the curve:* Assume that you decide that you need only 4 hours of leisure a day. Plot the new point.

4. Next show a *shift of the curve:* You find that you need less sleep, so that you have 18 hours a day to devote to leisure and study. Draw the new (shifted) curve.

5. Keep a record of your own leisure and study for a week. Plot the hours of leisure and study each day as a point on a graph. This is a scatter diagram. Do you see any relationship between the hours of study and leisure?

6. Consider the following data. Plot the relationship on a scatter diagram. Why can't you be sure which of the variables "causes" movement in the other variable (remember the *post hoc* fallacy)?

YEAR	MONEY SUPPLY (billions)	GNP (billions)
1965	$170	$ 705
1970	217	1,016
1975	291	1,598
1980	414	2,732
1985	627	3,998

Source: *Economic Report of the President,* 1987.

CHAPTER 2

BASIC PROBLEMS
OF ECONOMIC
ORGANIZATION

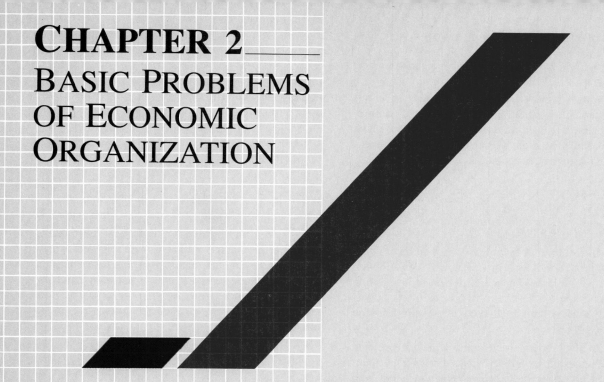

Every gun that is made, every warship launched,
every rocket fired signifies, in the final sense, a theft
from those who hunger and are not fed.

President Dwight D. Eisenhower

WHENEVER PEOPLE gather into a community, they must necessarily confront a few universal economic problems. These fundamental questions are as crucial today as they were in the days of the Romans or the Greeks. And they will just as surely be faced by the brave new world of the future.

Section A of this chapter describes the three central problems of economic organization. There we see that every society must determine *what* commodities shall be produced, *how* these goods should be made, and *for whom* they will be produced. In addition, in this first section we will begin to understand that scarcity is a key fact of economic life.

Section B then illustrates the problem of scarcity in terms of the limited levels of production available to an economy. It shows that society's choices between different goods and services are limited by the amount of resources available and by the technological knowledge of the society. Given the production possibilities, society must choose between necessities and luxuries, between public and private goods, or between consumption and investment.

A. PROBLEMS OF ECONOMIC ORGANIZATION

Every human society—whether it consists of an advanced industrial nation, a centrally planned communist society, a Taos commune, or an isolated island society—must confront and answer three fundamental and interdependent economic problems.

- *What* commodities are to be produced and in what quantities? How much of each of the many possible goods and services should the economy make? And when will they be produced? Should we produce pizzas or shirts today? A few high-quality shirts or many cheap shirts? Should we produce many consumption goods (like pizzas and concerts), or few consumption goods and many investment goods (like pizza factories and concert halls), allowing more consumption tomorrow?

- *How* shall goods be produced? By whom and with what resources and in what technological manner are they to be produced? Who hunts, and who fishes? Is electricity to be generated from oil and coal, or waterfalls and atoms, or sun and wind? Handicrafts or mass production? In large privately owned corporations or in state-owned companies? If from all these sources, in what quantities from each?

- *For whom* shall goods be produced? Who is to enjoy and get the benefit of the nation's goods and services? Or, to put it another way, how is the national product to be divided among different individuals and families? Are we to have a society in which a few are rich and many poor? Or in which all share the nation's output equally? Shall high earnings go to muscles or to IQ? Shall selfish go-getters inherit the earth? Shall the lazy eat well?

These three problems are fundamental and common to all economies. But, as we will see later, different societies try to solve them using different institutions.

Inputs and Outputs

Now that we have outlined the three major economic tasks of every society, we can translate these into economic language. On close reading, we see that the three problems are really about the limitations and choices among an economy's *inputs* and *outputs*.

Inputs are commodities or services used by firms in their production processes. Inputs are combined to produce outputs, while **outputs** consist of the varied array of useful goods or services that are either consumed or used for further production.

For example, when a cook makes an omelette, the eggs, salt, heat, frying pan, and the chef's skilled labor are the inputs. A fluffy omelette is the output.

We classify inputs, also called *factors of production,* into three broad classes: natural resources, labor, and capital.

Natural resources represent the gifts of nature to our productive processes. They consist of the land used for farming or for supporting houses, factories, and roads; energy resources to fuel our cars or heat our homes; nonenergy resources like copper and yttrium and sand. We might view our physical environment—the air we breathe and the water we drink—as part of the natural resources of an economy.

Labor consists of the human time spent in production—working in automobile factories, tilling the land, teaching in schools, or cooking omelettes. Thousands of occupations and tasks, at all skill levels, are performed by labor. It is at once the most familiar input and the most crucial to an advanced industrial economy.

Capital resources form the durable goods of an economy, produced by the economy in order to produce yet other goods. Capital goods include the countless machines, roads, computers, hammers, trucks, steel mills, and buildings that dot the landscape of any modern economy. As we will later see, the accumulation of numerous specialized capital goods is essential to the task of economic development.

Restating the three economic problems, a society must decide: (1) *what* outputs to produce, and in what quantity; (2) *how* to produce them—that is, by what techniques should inputs be combined to produce the desired outputs; and (3) *for whom* should the outputs be produced and distributed.

Alternative Economic Systems: Custom, Command, and Market

The three economic problems faced by societies are universal, but the solutions vary from place to place. The study of *alternative economic systems* is concerned with the different mechanisms that a society can use to allocate its scarce resources.

Custom rules every facet of behavior in many primitive civilizations. *What, how,* and *for whom* may be decided by traditions passed on from elders to youths. In ancient Egypt and even sometimes today in India, a son unswervingly adopts the trade of his father. Sometimes the customs appear bizarre to outsiders; the Kwakiutl Indians consider it desirable not to accumulate wealth but to give it away in the potlatch—a roisterous celebration.

However strange many customs look to outsiders, they often are efficient at performing the three functions of organizing the economy. In some cases, though, customs may be so unyielding that societies become extinct defending their traditions.

Another system is a **command economy**—one in which the government makes all decisions about production and distribution. Such a government might be dictatorial or it might be democratic; in the extreme it would tell people what to eat and drink, how food and steel should be made, and who should live well or poorly.

A final approach, developed at length in Chapter 3, is the **market economy.** Here, a system of prices, of markets, of profits and losses, of incentives and rewards determines *what, how,* and *for whom.* Firms produce those commodities that yield the highest profits (the *what*) by the techniques of production that are least costly (the *how*), and people's consumption arises from their decisions about how to spend the wages and property incomes generated by their labor and property ownership (the *for whom*).

No economy today is one of these pure forms. Rather, societies are **mixed economies,** with elements of market, command, and custom. There has never been a 100 percent market economy (although nineteenth-century England came close). In American capitalism today, the government has an important role in setting the legal framework for economic life, producing education and police services, and regulating pollution and business. But most decisions in the United States today are made when markets determine prices and quantities.

The Law of Scarcity

Why are we concerned with the fundamental questions of *what, how,* and *for whom*? These problems arise because people want to consume far more than an economy can produce. If infinite quantities of every good could be produced, or if human desires were fully satisfied, people would not worry about the efficient use of scarce resources. Nor would business managers lose sleep over wasteful use of labor or energy. Moreover, since all of us could have as much as we pleased, no one would care about the distribution of incomes among different people or classes.

In such an Eden of prosperity, there would be no **economic goods**—that is, no goods that are scarce or limited in supply. There would be no need to economize on consumption, and indeed economics would no longer be a vital science. All goods would be free, like sand in the desert or water at the beach.

Limited Goods But no society has reached a utopia of limitless possibilities. Goods are limited while wants seem unbounded. Even in the United States, the most productive society yet known, annual production in the mid-1980s has averaged around 80 million tons of steel, 8 million cars, and 3.2 billion barrels of oil. The country has but a few hundred miles of sandy beaches. Ski areas and concert halls have limited capacity, and our rock idols can hardly sing more than 300 live concerts a year. Our national output would have to be many times larger before the average American could live at the level of the average doctor or lawyer. And outside the United States, particularly in Africa and Asia, hundreds of millions of people suffer from undeniable hunger and material deprivation.

Unlimited Wants By comparison with the poor nations or early civilizations, advanced industrial economies seem very wealthy indeed. But higher incomes bring in their train higher consumption standards and ever higher "needs." An investigation of consumption patterns would find that people want and need central heating and cooling, movies and compact disks, autos and personal computers, concerts and recreation, leisure time and privacy, clean air and pure water, safe factories and clean streets, and innumerable other goods and services. If you add up all the wants, you quickly find that there are simply not enough goods and services to satisfy a small fraction of everyone's consumption desires.

It is little comfort that the biologist tells us that we can be adequately nourished for a few cents a day.[1] Anyone who has kept a budget knows that the social necessities of life in America—the absolute musts—far surpass the minimum physiological needs for food, clothing, and shelter. Thirty years ago, in *The Affluent Society,* John Kenneth Galbraith analyzed how consumers often flit from one purchase to an-

other in response to the pressures of fashion and advertising.[2]

But economics must reckon with consumer wants and needs whether they are genuine or contrived. Shakespeare's King Lear said, "Reason not the need"—and economists do not; rather they analyze how limited goods get rationed among whatever wants a society generates.

The **law of scarcity** states that goods are scarce because there are not enough resources to produce all the goods that people want to consume.

Faced with this undeniable truth—that goods are scarce relative to wants—economics describes and analyzes how different societies cope with limited resources—choosing different bundles of goods (the *what*), selecting among different techniques of production (the *how*), and deciding in the end who should consume the goods (the *for whom*).

B. SOCIETY'S TECHNOLOGICAL POSSIBILITIES

We have seen how limitations of resources force people and society to choose among alternative uses of the scarce resources. We now illustrate the law of scarcity with the help of examples.

THE PRODUCTION-POSSIBILITY FRONTIER

Consider an economy with only so many people, so much technical knowledge, so many factories and tools, and so much land, water power, and natural resources. In deciding *what* shall be produced and *how,* the economy must really be deciding just how these resources are to be allocated among the thousands of different possible commodities. How much land should go into wheat growing? Or into pasturage? How many factories are to produce knives? How much skilled labor for shoelaces?

These problems are complicated even to discuss, much less solve. Therefore, we must simplify. So let us assume that only two economic goods (or classes of economic goods) are to be produced. For dramatic purposes we can choose the pair—guns and butter—used to illustrate the problem of choosing between military spending and civilian goods. This example applies equally to the tradeoffs involved in President Reagan's defense buildup of the 1980s, to America's massive mobilization during World War II, and to the choices of military versus civilian spending faced by any nation. Moreover, the choice could apply to any pair of goods. The appendix to Chapter 1 examined food and machines, but we could also consider food versus clothing, consumption today versus consumption tomorrow, or public goods versus private goods.

Numerical Example We can begin our study of guns and butter with the numerical example of Table 2-1. Suppose that our economy threw all its energy into producing the civilian good, butter. There will still be

---

[1] A study suggests that standard requirements of adult nutrition could be bought in 1988 for about $360 per year, or a little less than a dollar a day. But what a diet this implies: cabbage, spinach, pork liver, and flour!

[2] John Kenneth Galbraith, *The Affluent Society* (Houghton Mifflin, Boston, 1958).

ALTERNATIVE PRODUCTION POSSIBILITIES

POSSIBILITIES	BUTTER (millions of pounds)	GUNS (thousands)
A	0	15
B	1	14
C	2	12
D	3	9
E	4	5
F	5	0

Table 2-1   Limitations of scarce resources implies the guns-butter tradeoff

As we go from A to B . . . to F, we are transferring labor, materials, and other resources from the gun industry to the butter industry.

a maximum amount of butter that can be produced per year. (The exact amount depends upon the quantity and quality of resources of the economy in question and the technological efficiency with which they are used.) Suppose 5 million pounds of butter is the maximum amount that can be produced with the existing technology and resources.

At the other extreme, imagine that 100 percent of society's resources had instead been devoted to the production of guns. Only some maximum number of guns could then be produced: 15 thousand guns of a certain description can perhaps be produced if we are willing to produce no butter.

These are two extreme possibilities. In between there are many others. If we are willing to give up some butter, we can have some guns. If we are willing to give up still more butter, we can have still more guns.

A schedule of possibilities is given in Table 2-1. Combination F shows the extreme where all butter and no guns are produced, while A depicts the opposite extreme where all resources go into guns. In between—at E, D, C, and B—increasing amounts of butter are being given up in return for more guns.

Butter is transformed into guns, not physically, but by the alchemy of diverting resources from one use to the other.

We can represent an economy's production possi-

bilities more vividly in the diagram shown in Figure 2-1. This diagram measures butter along the horizontal axis and guns along the vertical one.

Recalling the principles on using graphs outlined in Chapter 1's appendix, you should be able to go directly from the numerical table to the diagram: to F, by counting over 5 butter units to the right and going up 0 gun units; to E, by going 4 butter units to the right and going up 5 gun units; and finally, to A, by going over 0 butter units and up 15 gun units.

We may fill in all intermediate positions with new red dots, even those involving fractions of a million pounds or fractions of a thousand guns. When we have filled in all the points, we have the continuous red curve shown as the production-possibility frontier in Figure 2-2.

Efficiency

We have up to now implicitly assumed that the economy was on, rather than inside, the production-possibility frontier. Operating on the frontier implies that the economy was producing *efficiently*.

Efficiency is one of the central concepts of economics. **Efficiency** means absence of waste, or using the economy's resources as effectively as possible to

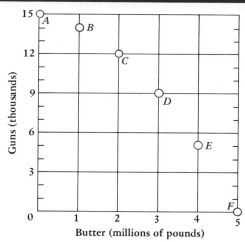

Figure 2-1   Graphical depiction of alternative production possibilities

This figure displays the data from Table 2-1.

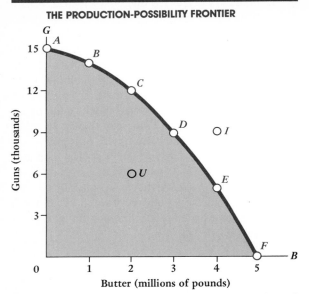

THE PRODUCTION-POSSIBILITY FRONTIER

Figure 2-2 A smooth curve connects the plotted points of the numerical production possibilities

This frontier shows the menu of choice along which society can choose to substitute guns for butter, assuming a given state of technology and a given total of resources. Points outside the frontier (such as point *I*) are impossible or unattainable. Any point inside the curve, such as *U*, indicates that resources are unemployed, or not used in the best possible way.

satisfy people's needs and desires. More specifically, *the economy is producing efficiently when it cannot produce more of one good without producing less of another*—when it is on the production-possibility frontier.

How do we know that any point on that frontier is efficient? Let us start in the situation shown by point *D* in Figure 2-2. Decree that we want another million pounds of butter. If we ignored the constraint shown by the *PPF*, we might think it possible to produce more butter without reducing gun production, as in moving to point *I*, due east of point *D*. But point *I* is in the "impossible" region, outside the frontier. Starting from *D*, we cannot get more butter without

giving up some guns. Hence point *D* is efficient, and point *I* is infeasible.

Productive efficiency occurs when society cannot increase the output of one good without cutting back on another good. An efficient economy is on its production-possibility frontier.

One further point about an efficient economy can be illustrated using the *PPF*: Being on the *PPF* means that producing more of one good inevitably implies sacrificing other goods. When we produce more guns, we are substituting guns for butter. Substitution is the law of life in a full-employment economy, and the production-possibility frontier depicts the menu of society's choices.

Unemployed Resources and Inefficiency Even casual observers of modern life know that we often witness unemployed resources in the form of idle workers, idle factories, and idle land. Chapter 1 hinted that economic laws might be different when resources are less than fully employed. Being inside the *PPF* is one such instance.

With unemployment of resources we are not on the production-possibility frontier at all, but rather somewhere *inside* it. Thus, *U* in Figure 2-2 represents a point inside the *PPF*; at *U* society is producing only 2 units of butter and 6 units of guns. Some resources are idle, and by putting them to work we can have more butter and more guns. We can move from *U* to *D*, thereby producing more butter and more guns and improving the economy's efficiency.

Taking into account the possibility of unemployed resources throws important light on the historical experience in World War II of two countries: the United States and the Soviet Union. After 1940, how was the United States able to become the "arsenal of democracy" and to enjoy civilian living standards higher than ever before? Largely by taking up the slack of unemployment and moving toward the *PPF*.

The case of wartime U.S.S.R. was different. The Soviets had little unemployment before the war and were already on their rather low production-possibility frontier. To move northwest along their *PPF* the Soviets had no choice but to substitute war goods for civilian goods—with consequent privation.

Having unemployed resources is not the only reason why an economy might be inside its *PPF*. If an economy is inefficiently organized, it may also fall well short of the frontier. Such a case occurred during an outbreak of general strikes in Poland in 1981 and 1982. There, output fell dramatically as the price system broke down. Political turmoil pushed Poland inside its *PPF*.

Less dramatic, but no less important, are cases where an economy is inside its *PPF* because it is riddled with monopoly or inefficient regulation, or because a command economy is subject to arbitrary decrees by inept bureaucrats. Deregulation or removing government rules on business operations, such as occurred for airlines in the United States in the last decade, can improve efficiency and move the economy toward its frontier.

No Free Lunches? You may have heard the saying, "There is no such thing as a free lunch." This adage expresses the notion that you can't get something for nothing. Someone who treats you to a lunch often wants something in return—perhaps a favor, a job, or some free help. We can illustrate the no-free-lunch principle with the *PPF,* for this shows that an efficient economy cannot produce more guns without sacrificing butter; that is, it cannot get more of one good (lunch) without sacrificing another (money to buy other things).

But the no-free-lunch principle might break down if you were inside the frontier: If your luncheon host simply has free time and wants company, then you both might move toward the happiness-possibility frontier. More generally, a genuine improvement in economic conditions can take place by getting rid of waste and inefficiency. When waste is rooted out or when people exchange goods, everyone may end up better off, in a sense getting something for nothing.

PUTTING THE *PPF* TO WORK

In addition to illustrating efficiency, the production-possibility curve can help introduce many of the most basic concepts of economics.

1. Figure 2-2 illustrates the basic definition of eco-

nomics given in Chapter 1; there we defined economics as the science of choosing what goods to produce. Should we live in a fortress economy bristling with guns but with austere living habits, as at point *B* in Figure 2-2? Or should we reduce the military to a pittance and instead enjoy an economy with much bread and butter, as at point *E*?

Such debates are heard in peacetime as well as in wartime. During the 1980s, President Reagan lobbied successfully for a larger share of national output going to defense, and real defense spending rose almost 50 percent from 1980 to 1988.

2. The production-possibility frontier provides a rigorous definition of scarcity.

Economic scarcity refers to the basic fact of life that there exists only a finite amount of human and nonhuman resources, which the best technical knowledge is capable of using to produce only limited maximum amounts of each economic good. The *PPF* shows the outer limit of the combination of producible goods.

And thus far, nowhere on the globe is the supply of goods so plentiful or are tastes so limited that the average family can have more than enough of everything it might fancy. Scarcity is a reflection of the fact that the *PPF* constrains our living standards.

3. The production-possibility schedule can also illustrate the three basic problems of economic life: *what, how,* and *for whom.*

What goods are produced and consumed can be depicted by the point that ends up getting chosen on the *PPF*.

How goods are to be produced involves an efficient choice of methods and a proper assignment of different amounts and kinds of limited resources to the various industries.

For whom goods are to be produced cannot be discerned from the *PPF* alone. Sometimes, though, you can make a guess from it. If you find a society on its *PPF* with many yachts and furs, but few potatoes and compact cars, you might suspect that it experiences considerable inequality of income and wealth among its people.

4. The production-possibility frontier can also illustrate the inherent need to choose among limited op-

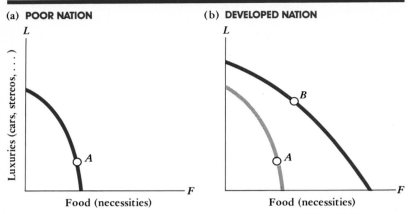

Figure 2-3 Economic development and progress shifts PPF outward

(a) Before development, the nation is poor. It must devote almost all its resources to food, enjoying few comforts.
(b) Economic development and invention shift out the PPF. After development, a nation goes from A to B, expanding its food consumption little compared with its increased consumption of luxuries. Note that it can increase its consumption of both goods if it wishes.

portunities of many kinds. People have limited time available to pursue different activities. For example, as a student, you might have 10 hours to study for upcoming tests in economics and math. If you study only math you will get a high grade there and do poorly in economics, and vice versa. Treating the grades on the two tests as the "output" of your studying, sketch out the PPF for grades, given your limited time resources.

Alternatively, if the two student commodities are "grades" and "fun," how would you draw this PPF? Where are you on this frontier? Where are your lazier friends?

Pictures at an Exhibition

The same analysis that applies to choosing between the pair of goods—guns and butter—applies to any choice of goods. Thus the more resources the government uses to build public goods (like roads), the less will be left to produce private goods (like houses); the more we choose to consume of food, the less we can consume of clothing; the more society decides to con-

sume today, the less can be its production of capital goods (durable productive goods like equipment or factories) to turn out more consumption goods for the next year or decade.

The graphs of Figures 2-3 to 2-6 are self-explanatory. They show that the production-possibility frontier can illustrate many familiar and basic economic processes. Later chapters will deal with each of these in depth, and it is necessary here only to comprehend the common-sense ideas involved.

Figure 2-3 shows the effect of economic growth and development. As a result of an increase in both inputs and an improvement in a nation's technology, the PPF shifts out. A nation can have more of all goods as its economy grows. The figure illustrates as well how a society devotes most of its effort to food production when it is poor but shifts toward comforts and luxuries as it develops.

Figure 2-4 illustrates how the electorate must choose between private goods (bought at a price) and public goods (paid for by taxes).

Figure 2-5 illustrates how an economy chooses between (a) current consumption goods and (b) invest-

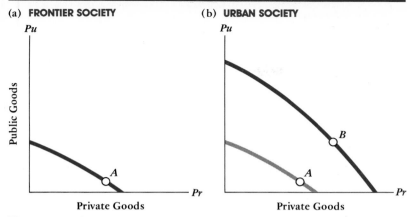

Figure 2-4   With prosperity comes greater emphasis on public rather than private goods

(a) The first economy is poor and dispersed, as in Thomas Jefferson's frontier days. The proportion of resources going to public goods (defense, roads, public health) is low.

(b) The second economy is more prosperous and chooses to spend more of its higher income on public goods or governmental services (roads, defense, sewage systems, education).

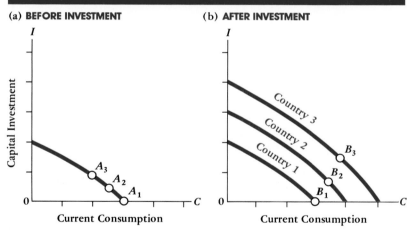

Figure 2-5   Investment for future consumption requires sacrifice of current consumption

A nation can produce either current consumption goods (bread, concerts) or investment goods (trucks and trains, houses and factories, computers and steel mills).

(a) Three countries start out even: They have the same *PPF* shown in the panel on the left. They have different investment rates, however. Country 1 does no investment for the future and remains at A_1 (merely replacing machines). Country 2 abstains modestly from consumption and invests a bit at A_2. Country 3 invests much and sacrifices much of current consumption.

(b) In the following years, countries that invest more forge ahead. Thus thrifty country 3 has shifted its *PPF* far out, while country 1's *PPF* has moved not at all. After thrift, country 3 is still investing but has more current consumption as well.

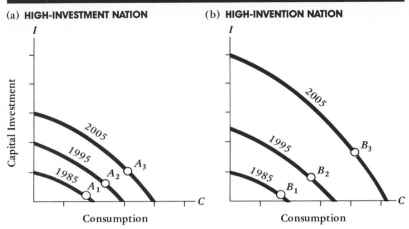

Figure 2-6   Innovative country can outpace country that only invests

(a) Country A plods ahead, advancing by accumulating capital goods.
(b) Country B stresses ingenuity and innovation, investing in science, education, and research. From 1985 to 1995, growth is by invention alone; after 1995, country B grows even faster by combining innovation and investment.

ment or capital goods (machines, factories, etc.). By sacrificing current consumption and producing more capital goods, a nation's economy can grow more rapidly, making possible more of *both* goods (consumption and capital) in the future.

Figure 2-6 shows how the economy of country B, blessed by scientific and engineering discoveries and providing generous incentives for innovators, might surpass thriftier A, which was investing more for the future but with less rapidly advancing technology.

These four diagrams illustrate key themes of later chapters—how societies choose among different patterns of output, how they pay for their choice, how they benefit or lose in the future. A careful study of these diagrams is a good investment—just as a nation sometimes benefits from investing in capital goods for future enjoyment, so a few extra minutes spent here will bring rewards in later chapters.

OPPORTUNITY COST

Life is full of choices. Because resources are scarce, we are constantly deciding which good we want to buy or which activity we will pursue. Should we go to a movie or read a book? Should we take a vacation or get some extra work done? Should we take a year off from college to travel or try out a job? In each of these cases, making a choice in a world of scarcity requires us to give up alternative activities, in effect costing us the opportunity to do something else. That alternative forgone is called the *opportunity cost*.

To take a simple example, say that, after necessary expenses, your income is $100. With that sum you can either take a trip to Chicago or buy a radio. If you decide to go to Chicago, economists would say that the opportunity cost of your trip was the pleasure of enjoying the new radio.

The concept of opportunity cost can also be illustrated using the production-possibility frontier. Look back at the frontier in Figure 2-2 on page 28. Suppose the country has decided to step up its purchases of guns from 9000 guns at D to 12,000 guns at C. What is the opportunity cost of this decision? You might calculate it in dollar terms, but on the most fundamental level, the cost is the alternative butter that must be given up to produce the extra guns. In this example the opportunity cost of the 3000 guns is easily seen to be 1 million pounds of butter.

The **opportunity cost** of a decision arises because choosing one thing in a world of scarcity means giving up something else. The opportunity cost is the value of the good or service forgone.

The concept of opportunity cost is a useful reminder that the actual dollar outlays are not always an accurate index of true costs. For example, if the government decides to run a highway through a national park, the needed land might look cheap in out-of-pocket or budget costs, but the opportunity cost of paving over the park would be paid when people enjoyed fewer picnics or hikes or camping trips.

Another important example of opportunity cost is the cost of going to college. If you went to a public university, you might calculate the total costs of tuition, room, board, books, and travel to be about $9000 in 1989. Does this mean that $9000 is the opportunity cost of going to school? Definitely not! You must include as well the opportunity cost of the *time* spent studying and going to classes. A full-time job for a 20-year-old high school graduate would on average pay around $15,000 in 1989. If we add up both the actual expenses and the earnings forgone, we find the opportunity cost of college was $24,000 (equal to $9000 + $15,000) rather than $9000 per year.

In the end, the opportunity cost concept reinforces the point made by the no-free-lunch doctrine. Often, the real costs of our actions—whether going to college or building roads or increasing military outlays—are subtle and go far beyond the actual dollar outlays. This central lesson of economics—to look to the genuine costs of our decisions—will reappear again and again in the chapters that follow.

THE LAW OF DIMINISHING RETURNS

We can also use the production-possibility frontier to illustrate one of the most famous economic relationships: the law of diminishing returns. This law concerns the relationship between inputs and outputs in the productive process. More specifically, *the law of diminishing returns holds that we will get less and less extra output when we add successive doses of inputs while holding other inputs fixed.*

As an example of diminishing returns, consider the following controlled experiment: Given a fixed amount of land, say 100 acres, we shall first have no

LAW OF DIMINISHING RETURNS

UNITS OF LABOR (person-years)	TOTAL OUTPUT (bushels)	EXTRA OUTPUT ADDED BY ADDITIONAL UNIT OF LABOR (bushels per person-year)
0	0	
		2,000
1	2,000	
		1,000
2	3,000	
		500
3	3,500	
		___
4	3,800	
		100
5	3,900	

Table 2-2   Diminishing returns is a fundamental law of economics and technology

According to the law of diminishing returns, as additional units of labor are added, with land held fixed, the extra output tends to decline.

labor at all. We note that with zero labor input there is no corn output. So, in Table 2-2, we record zero product when labor is zero.

Now we make a second related experiment. We add 1 unit of labor to the same fixed amount of land. How much output do we now get? Say we observe that we now have produced 2000 bushels of corn.

Now make a third controlled experiment. We still hold land fixed. Once more we vary the labor input, adding exactly the same extra unit of labor as before. That is, we now go from 1 unit of labor to 2 units of labor to match our earlier increase from 0 labor to 1 labor. We await the outcome of the experiment in terms of extra corn produced.

We can now observe whether diminishing returns has set in—that is, we can now see whether the quantity of extra output declines as equal-sized doses of additional inputs are added. Do we have proportional returns, with an extra output of 2000 bushels added to the original output of 2000 bushels? Or do we find diminishing returns, with the additional inputs adding less than the original 2000 bushels of output?

Table 2-2 demonstrates that diminishing returns has indeed set in. The second extra unit of labor added only 1000 bushels of additional output, which is less than what the first unit of labor added. A third extra unit of labor adds even less additional output than does the second, and the fourth unit adds yet a bit less. The hypothetical experiment reported in Table 2-2 thus shows numerically what happens when the law of diminishing returns holds.

The law of diminishing returns is an important and often-observed economic relationship. But it is not valid for all technologies. Often the law holds only after a number of units of inputs have been added. Put differently, the first few units of inputs might actually yield increasing extra returns, since we may need a minimum amount of labor just to walk to the field and pick up a shovel. But, ultimately, decreasing returns will prevail at high levels of inputs for most technologies.

Some Examples

In fact, the law of diminishing returns makes good sense. Consider what happens as more and more labor cultivates the same 100-acre farm. For a while, output will increase smartly as we add labor—the fields will be more thoroughly seeded and weeded, irrigation ditches well-tended, scarecrows well-oiled. After a while, however, the additional labor becomes less and less productive. The third hoeing of the day, the fourth oiling of the machinery—these add little. Eventually, so many people crowd onto the farm that the crop gets trampled, as too many tillers spoil the crop. Ultimately, output may even turn down.

We can again use the example of studying to illustrate the law of diminishing returns. You might find that the first hour of studying economics on a given day was productive—learning new laws and facts, insights and history. The second hour might find your attention wandering a bit, with less learned. The third hour might show that diminishing returns had set in with a vengeance—that by the next day you could remember nothing of what you had read during the third hour. Does the law of diminishing returns suggest why the hours devoted to studying in an economics course should be evenly spaced rather than crammed into the day before exams?

We shall see in Part Five that the wage paid to workers depends upon the extra output added by the last worker. Diminishing returns reveals that living standards in crowded China or India are low because there are many workers per acre of land in these regions and not because land happens to be owned by the state or by absentee landlords. In conclusion, we may summarize as follows:

An increase in some inputs, with other inputs held constant, will increase total output. But after some point, the extra output resulting from additional doses of inputs will tend to become smaller and smaller.

■ ■ ■

With the fundamental concepts of economic organization and key concepts like the *PPF* behind us, the next chapter turns to an analysis of the way our own economy determines prices, quantities, and incomes.

SUMMARY

A. Problems of Economic Organization

1. Every economy must solve the three fundamental economic problems: *What* kinds and quantities shall be produced of all possible goods and services? *How* shall resources be used in producing these goods? And *for whom* shall the goods be produced (that is, what shall be the distribution of consumption among different individuals and classes)?

2. Societies meet these problems in different ways—by custom, by command and centralized control, and, in our mixed economy, largely by a system of prices and markets.

3. The basic problems matter because of the fundamental fact of economic life: Wants far outstrip the economy's capacity to produce goods and services. Economic goods are *scarce,* not free. Society must choose among them because not all needs and desires can be satisfied.

B. Society's Technological Possibilities

4. With given resources and technology, the production choices open to a nation between two such goods as butter and guns can be summarized in the *production-possibility frontier (PPF).* This indicates the way that one good can be transformed into another by transferring resources from its production to that of the other.

5. Productive *efficiency* occurs when production of one good cannot be increased without curtailing production of another good. This is illustrated by the *PPF*. When an economy is operating efficiently on its frontier, it can only produce more of one good by producing less of others. In our example, an economy increases its production of guns by sacrificing some butter.

Societies are not always on the frontier—for example, when unemployment is excessive, when there are monopolistic abuses, or when government regulation hampers firms' activities, the economy is inefficient and operates inside the frontier.

6. Production-possibility frontiers can illustrate many basic economic processes: how economic growth pushes out the frontier, how a nation uses relatively less resources for food and other necessities as it develops, how a country chooses between private market goods and public governmental goods, and how societies choose between current consumption goods and capital goods that enhance future capacity to produce. The *PPF* also shows technological change as a *PPF* that shifts out over time.

7. Dollar costs are not the same as true economic costs. When we measure the total cost of making choices in a world of scarcity, we calculate the *opportunity cost,* which measures the value of the things given up, or opportunities forgone.

8. The *law of diminishing returns* asserts that, after a point, as we add equal extra doses of a variable input (such as labor) to a fixed input (such as land), the amount of extra output will decline.

CONCEPTS FOR REVIEW

what, how, and *for whom*
organization by custom, command, market
economic goods and free goods
the law of scarcity
production-possibility frontier *(PPF)*

opportunity cost
alternative economic systems
efficiency
law of diminishing returns
inputs, outputs

QUESTIONS FOR DISCUSSION _____

1. Explain what economists mean by *scarcity, free goods,* and *efficiency*.

2. What does it mean for an economy to be on its production-possibility frontier? How can an economy be inside its frontier? Why can it not be outside (or to the northeast) of the frontier?

3. Assume Econoland produces haircuts and shirts with inputs of labor. Econoland has 1000 hours of labor available. A haircut requires $\frac{1}{2}$ hour of labor, while a shirt requires 5 hours of labor. Construct Econoland's production-possibility frontier.

4. Redraw society's production-possibility frontier in Figure 2-2 after scientific inventions have doubled the productivity of its resources in butter production only, and not in guns.

5. "Compulsory military service allows the government to fool itself and the people about the true cost of a big army." Compare the budget cost and the opportunity cost of a voluntary army (where army pay is high) and compulsory service (where pay is low). What does the concept of opportunity cost contribute to analyzing the quotation?

6. Many scientists believe that we are depleting our natural resources. Assume that there are only two inputs (labor and natural resources) producing two goods, haircuts and gasoline, and there is no improvement in society's technology over time. Show what would happen to the *PPF* over time as natural resources are exhausted. How would invention and technological improvement modify your answer? Can you see from this example why economic growth is a contest between depletion and invention?

7. Would the production-possibility frontier look different in a command economy, a market economy, and an economy based on custom?

8. The *how, what,* and *for whom* are solved differently in different systems. Consider each of the following and explain how the three big questions of economic organization are solved: within your family, within your college or university, in the food industry, and in the army.

9. From 1982 to 1984, the American economy grew rapidly as unemployment fell and capital equipment was utilized more intensively. Draw a *PPF* for 1982 and 1984 and put in two points to illustrate where the economy might have been in both those years.

CHAPTER 3

MARKETS AND COMMAND IN A MODERN ECONOMY

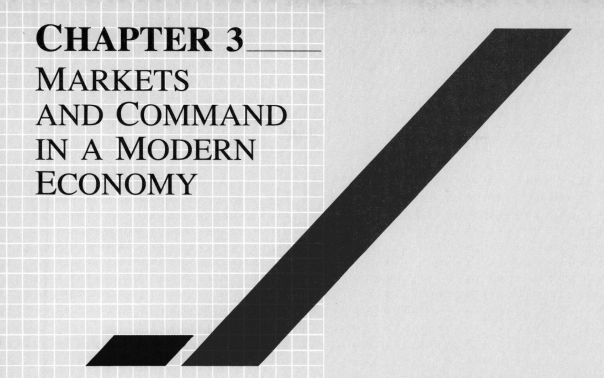

Every individual endeavors to employ his capital so that its produce may be of greatest value. He generally neither intends to promote the public interest, nor knows how much he is promoting it. He intends only his own security, only his own gain. And he is in this led by an invisible hand to promote an end which was no part of his intention. By pursuing his own interest he frequently promotes that of society more effectually than when he really intends to promote it.

Adam Smith
The Wealth of Nations (1776)

BEFORE WE begin to study the economic life of an advanced industrial economy like the United States, we should turn our eyes back to the history and evolution of the modern mixed economy. Centuries ago, government councils or town guilds directed much economic activity in regions of Europe and Asia. However, around the time of the American Revolution, governments began to exercise less and less direct control over prices and economic conditions. Feudal relationships were gradually replaced by what is called the market mechanism, sometimes also labelled "free enterprise" or "competitive capitalism."

The nineteenth century became the age of **laissez-faire.** This doctrine, which translates as "leave us alone," holds that government should interfere as little as possible in economic affairs. Many governments followed this approach in the middle and late nineteenth century. But before this trend had attained a condition of full laissez-faire, the tide turned the other way. Beginning a century ago, in almost all countries of North America and Europe, the economic functions of government expanded steadily.

Then, around 1980, the tide shifted yet again, as conservative economic policies produced a decline from the high-water mark of intervention in owner-ship, taxation, and control of the economy.

What are the principles that lie behind the market economy and government's command of economic affairs? In this chapter we will study in detail both these forms of economic organization.

Market, Command, and Mixed Economies

Recall our earlier definitions of market and command economies:

The *market mechanism* is a form of economic organization in which individual consumers and businesses interact through markets to solve the three central problems of economic organization. A *command economy* is one in which the resource allocation is determined by governments, commanding individuals and firms to follow the state's economic plans.

Today, neither of these polar extremes represents the reality of the American economic system. Rather, ours is a *mixed economy,* in which both private and public institutions exercise economic control: the private system through the invisible direction of the market mechanism, the public or government institutions through regulatory commands and fiscal incentives.

Section A of this chapter shows how a market mechanism tackles the three problems of economic organization that must be met by any society. Section B briefly reviews the role of the command economy as government directs a modern mixed economy. Section C describes some fundamental characteristics of the present economic order: its use of capital, division of labor, and use of money.

A. HOW MARKETS SOLVE THE BASIC ECONOMIC PROBLEMS

In a country like the United States, most economic questions are resolved through the market, so we begin our systematic study there. Who solves the three basic questions—*how, what,* and *for whom*—in a market economy? You may be surprised to learn that no individual or organization is consciously concerned with the triad of economic problems. Rather, millions of businesses and consumers interact through markets to set prices and outputs.

To see how remarkable this fact is, consider the city of New York. Without a constant flow of goods in and out of the city, it would be on the verge of starvation within a week. A wide variety of the right kinds and amounts of food is required. From the surrounding counties, from 50 states, and from the far corners of the world, goods have been traveling for days and months with New York as their destination.

How is it that 10 million people are able to sleep easily at night, without living in mortal terror of a breakdown in the elaborate economic processes upon which the city's existence depends? The surprise is that all these economic activities are undertaken without coercion or centralized direction by anybody.

Everyone in the United States notices how much the government does to control economic activity: it legislates police protection, speed limits, antipollution laws, minimum wages, taxation, national defense, drug prohibitions, highway construction, and so forth. But we often overlook how much of our ordinary economic life proceeds without government intervention.

Thousands of commodities are produced by millions of people, willingly, without central direction or master plan.

Not Chaos but Economic Order

Before they have studied the way the market works, most people see only a jumble of different firms and products. People seldom stop to wonder how it is that food is produced in the right amounts, gets transported to the right place, and arrives in a palatable form at the dinner table. But a close look at the example of New York is convincing proof that a market system is not a system of chaos and anarchy. A market system contains an internal logic. It works.

A market economy is an elaborate mechanism for unconscious coordination of people, activities, and businesses through a system of prices and markets. It is a communication device for pooling the knowledge and actions of millions of diverse individuals. Without a central intelligence, it solves a problem that today's largest computer could not solve, involving millions of unknown variables and relations.

Nobody designed it, and like human society, it is changing. But it does meet the first test of any social organization—it can survive.

History's most dramatic example of the importance of the market economy came in West Germany after World War II. In 1947, production and consumption had dropped to a low level. Neither bombing damage nor postwar reparation payments could account for this breakdown. Paralysis of the market mechanism was clearly to blame. Price controls and overarching government regulation hobbled markets. Money was worthless; factories closed down for lack of materials; trains could not run for lack of coal; coal could not be mined because miners were hungry; miners were hungry because peasants would not sell food for money and no industrial goods were available for them to purchase in return. Markets were not functioning properly. People could not buy what they needed or sell what they produced at free-market prices.

Then in 1948, the government freed prices from controls and introduced a new currency, quickly putting the market mechanism back into effective operation. Very quickly production and consumption soared; once again *what, how,* and *for whom* were being resolved by markets and prices. People called it "an economic miracle," but in fact the recovery was largely the result of a smoothly running market mechanism.

The fact to emphasize is that markets are performing similar miracles around us all the time—if only we look around and alert ourselves to the everyday functioning of the market mechanism. So central are markets to the high levels of output of a capitalist economy that history often witnesses political crises when the market mechanism breaks down. Indeed, a revolutionary out to destroy Western democracies could ask for nothing better than a galloping inflation or depression to paralyze markets and produce political chaos.

THE MARKET MECHANISM

Just how does the market mechanism go about determining wages, prices, outputs, and other economic variables? We can describe its workings easily.

Originally, a market meant a place where goods were bought and sold. Economic histories of the Middle Ages record that market stalls—filled with slabs of butter, pyramids of cheese, wet fish, and heaps of vegetables—would form the commercial centers of villages and towns.[1] Today, important markets include the Chicago Board of Trade, where oil, wheat, and other commodities are traded, and the New York Stock Exchange, where titles to ownership of the largest American firms are bought and sold.

Market transactions are often made over the telephone or electronically (as for many financial transactions), and sometimes markets are not centrally organized but operate through individuals buying and selling a house or a car.

A **market** is an arrangement by which buyers and sellers of a commodity interact to determine its price and quantity.

In a market system, everything has a price—each commodity and each service. Even the different kinds of human labor have prices, namely, wage rates. We receive income for what we sell, and we use this income to buy what we want.

Moreover, prices provide important signals to market participants. If consumers want more of any good—say, wheat—a flood of new orders will be placed for it. As buyers scramble around to buy more wheat, the sellers will raise the price of wheat to ration out a limited supply. And the higher price will encourage greater wheat production.

On the other hand, what if a commodity such as cars becomes overstocked at the going market price? Sellers will lower car prices in their rush to unload

---

[1] For a detailed account of how markets grew and flourished in Western Europe, see Fernand Braudel, *The Wheels of Commerce* (Perennial Library, Harper & Row, New York, 1986).

unwanted models. At the lower price, more consumers will want cars, and producers will want to produce fewer cars. As a result, a balance (or equilibrium) between buyers and sellers (or what the next chapter and Part Four will call an "equilibrium of supply and demand") will be restored.

What is true of the markets for consumer goods is also true of markets for factors of production. Recall that a factor of production is an input into the productive process—one of the classical triad of land, labor, and capital. If computer programmers rather than typists are needed, job opportunities will be more favorable in the computing field. The price of computer programmers (their hourly wage) will tend to rise, and that of typists will tend to fall. The shift in relative wages will cause a shift of workers into the growing occupation.

Solution to the Three Problems

What happens when we put all the different markets together—wheat, cars, land, labor, capital, and everything else? These form a market mechanism that grinds out an equilibrium of prices and production.

By matching sellers and buyers (supply and demand) in each of these markets, a market economy solves our three problems simultaneously. Here are the bare outlines of such a market equilibrium.

1. *What* things will be produced is determined by the dollar votes of consumers—not every 2 or 4 years at the polls, but every day in their decisions to purchase this item instead of that one. The money that they pay into business cash registers ultimately provides the payrolls, rents, and dividends that consumers, as employees, receive as income.

Firms in turn are driven by the desire for profits—**profits** being net revenues or the difference between total sales and total costs. Firms are lured into production of goods in high demand by the high profits there, leaving behind areas of low profits.

2. *How* things are produced is determined by the competition among different producers. The best way for producers to meet price competition and maximize profits is to keep costs at a minimum by adopting the most efficient methods of production. Producers are spurred on by the lure of profit—the production method that is cheapest at any one time will displace a more costly method.

History is filled with examples of how more efficient and lower-cost technologies replaced more expensive ones. Steam engines displaced horses because steam was cheaper per unit of useful work. Diesel and electric locomotives replaced coal-driven ones because of the higher efficiency of the new technologies. In the 1990s, glass fibers and lightwave communications will displace Alexander Graham Bell's traditional copper telephone lines.

We can see the same phenomenon across nations. Bob Smith farms extensively, with much American land relative to each hour of labor. Pierre Reny farms intensively, using much labor to each hectare of French land.

Who makes sure that these *how* decisions reflect the fact that land is scarcer in France than in America? Is it Congress? The National Assembly? The United Nations? Of course not.

The price system is society's signaling device. It tells farmer Smith that he should farm extensively by presenting him with a high ratio of wage rates to land rents. Peasant Reny, on the other hand, faces a low wage/rent ratio and uses more labor per unit of land than does Smith. By looking at price signals, farmers, firms, and other producers can choose the most appropriate technique of production.

3. *For whom* things are produced is determined by supply and demand in the markets for factors of production. Factor markets determine the wage rates, land rents, interest rates, and profits—such prices being termed *factor prices*. By adding up all the revenues from factors we can calculate people's incomes. The distribution of income among the population is thus determined by the *amounts* of factors (person-hours, acres, etc.) owned and the *prices* of the factors (wage rates, land rents, etc.).

Be warned, however, that there are also important extra-market influences that affect the resulting distribution of income. This distribution is highly dependent upon the ownership of property, upon acquired or inherited abilities, upon luck, and upon the presence or absence of racial and gender discrimination.

Who Rules?

Who is in charge of a market economy? If we look beyond the details, we see that the economy is ultimately ruled by two monarchs: consumers and technology. Consumers direct by their innate or learned tastes, as expressed in their dollar votes, the ultimate uses to which society's resources are channeled. They pick the point on the production-possibility frontier.

But the available resources place a fundamental constraint on consumers. The economy cannot go outside its *PPF*. You can fly to London, but there are no flights to Mars. An economy's resources, along with the available science and technology, limit the places where consumers can put their dollar votes.

In other words, consumers are not the dictators in deciding *what* goods should be produced. Consumer demand has to dovetail with business supply of goods. Businesses set their prices based on production costs—moving into areas with high profits and leaving unprofitable sectors. So business cost and supply decisions, along with consumer demand, do help to determine *what*. Just as a broker may help arrange a match between buyer and seller, markets act as the go-betweens who reconcile the consumer's tastes with technology's limitations.

It is important to see the role of profits in guiding the market mechanism. Profits provide the rewards and penalties for businesses. Profits lead firms to enter areas where consumers want more goods, to leave areas where consumers want fewer goods, and to use the most efficient (or least costly) techniques of production.

Like a master using carrots and kicks to coax a donkey forward, the market system deals out profits and losses to get *how, what,* and *for whom* decided.

A Picture of Prices and Markets

We can picture the circular flow of economic life as shown in Figure 3-1. This provides an overview of how market prices reconcile household transactions with business needs. Note two different kinds of markets: one set for outputs like tea and shoes and the second for inputs like land and labor. Further see how decisions are made by two different entities, households and businesses.

Households buy goods and sell factors of production; businesses sell goods and buy factors of production. Households use their income from sale of inputs such as labor and property to buy goods; businesses base their prices of goods on the costs of labor and property. Prices in goods markets are set to balance consumer demand with business supply; prices in factor markets are set to balance household supply with business demands.

All this sounds complicated. But it is just this intricate web of interdependent supplies and demands through which the prices in a market mechanism solve the *how, what,* and *for whom*. A few minutes spent studying Figure 3-1 now will pay many dividends later in furthering your understanding of the workings of a market economy.

The Invisible Hand and "Perfect Competition"

Adam Smith, whose *The Wealth of Nations* (1776) is the germinal book of modern economics, was thrilled by his recognition of an order in the economic system. Smith proclaimed the principle of the "invisible hand." This principle holds that every individual, in selfishly pursuing only his or her personal good, is led, as if by an invisible hand, to achieve the best good for all. Smith held that, in this best of all possible worlds, any government interference with free competition is almost certain to be injurious. (Reread carefully this chapter's introductory quotation.)

The *invisible-hand* doctrine is a concept for explaining why the outcome of a market mechanism looks so orderly. Smith's insight about the guiding function of the market mechanism has inspired modern economists—both the admirers and the critics of capitalism. After two centuries of experience and thought, however, we now recognize the scope and realistic limitations of this doctrine. We know that the market sometimes lets us down, that there are "market failures," and that markets do not always lead to the most efficient outcome. One of the major market failures, whose consequences will run as a theme through this book, is imperfect competition.

Perfect Competition Smith himself recognized that the virtues of the market mechanism are fully realized

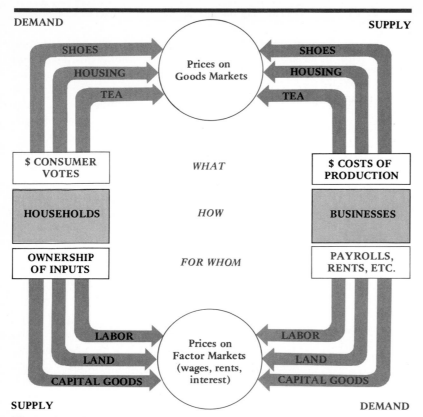

Figure 3-1   The market system relies on supply and demand to solve the trio of economic problems

We see here the circular flow of a market economy. Note how dollar votes of households interact with business supply in goods market at top, helping to determine *what* is produced. Further, business demand for inputs or productive factors meets the public's supply of labor and other inputs in the lower factor markets to help determine wage, rent, and interest payments. Business competition to buy factor inputs and sell goods most cheaply determines *how* goods are to be produced. (But all parts of the diagram interact together. *What* depends on the lower part, just as *for whom* depends on the upper part—carpenter wages depend on housing demand, and demand for yachts depends on oil-land royalties.)

only when the checks and balances of perfect competition are present. What is meant by **perfect competition**? It is a technical economic term that refers to a market in which no firm or consumer is large enough to affect the market price. For example, the wheat market is perfectly competitive because the largest wheat farm, producing only a minuscule fraction of

the world's wheat, can have no appreciable effect upon the price of wheat.

On the other hand, when a computer company, a steelworkers' labor union, or an airline is large enough to exert an influence on the price of computers, of steelworkers' labor, or of air transportation, some degree of ''imperfect competition'' has set in.

The invisible-hand doctrine is about economies in which all the markets are perfectly competitive. In such a circumstance, the economy will generate an efficient allocation of resources—where an efficient economy is on its production-possibility frontier. When all industries are subject to the checks and balances of perfect competition, as we will see later in this book, markets will produce the efficient bundle of outputs with the most efficient techniques and using the minimum quantity of inputs.

By contrast, when imperfect competition arises, society may move inside its *PPF*. This would occur, for example, because a single seller (or monopolist) raised the price of a good sky-high in order to earn extra profits. The output of that good would be re-duced below the most efficient level, and the efficiency of the economy would thereby suffer. When sellers are few, inadequate checks exist to ensure that prices are determined by the costs of production. And in such a situation, the invisible-hand property of markets may vanish.

In summary, Adam Smith discovered a remarkable property of a competitive market economy: under perfect competition without market failures, markets will squeeze as many useful goods and services out of the available resources as is possible. But where monopolies or pollution or similar market failures become pervasive, the remarkable efficiency properties of the invisible hand may be destroyed.

B. THE ECONOMIC ROLE OF GOVERNMENT

The last section described the remarkable efficiency properties of the market mechanism. We saw how an ideal, perfectly competitive economy—where resource-allocation decisions are made through prices and markets—could squeeze the maximum amount of useful goods and services out of the available resources.

But the market does not always behave in an ideal fashion. Indeed, there has probably never been an absolutely pure and perfect competitive market. Rather, market economies suffer from monopoly and pollution, along with unemployment and inflation, and the income distribution in market economies is sometimes found unacceptable by voters.

In response to these flaws in the market mechanism, democracies have chosen to introduce the visible hand of government into the mixed economy. Governments displace markets by owning and operating certain enterprises (like the military); governments regulate businesses (like telephone companies); governments spend money on space exploration and scientific research; governments tax their citizens and redistribute the proceeds to poor people. In this section we provide a first survey of the rationale and techniques of government intervention in a modern economy.

THE THREE FUNCTIONS OF GOVERNMENT

In discussing government's role, we generally take for granted that government sets the rules of the road, writing laws and enforcing contracts. But what are government's economic functions? They are to promote efficiency, equity, and stability. Government actions concerning *efficiency* are attempts to correct market failures like monopoly. Government programs to promote *equity* use taxes and spending to redistribute income when society shows its concerns for the poor or for particular groups. *Stabilization policy* attempts to shave the peaks and troughs of the business cycle, reducing unemployment and inflation, and promoting economic growth. We will examine briefly each function.

Efficiency

As we saw earlier, economies sometimes suffer from market failures. In actual markets, a firm may profit as much by keeping prices high as by keeping production high. In some markets, firms emit pollution into the air or water or dump toxic wastes into the soil. In each of these cases market failure leads to inefficient production or consumption, and there may be a role for government to cure the disease. But, while evaluating the role of government in curing economic ailments, we must also be alert to ''government failures''—situations in which governmental attempts to solve problems may make them worse or cause other problems.

Imperfect Competition One serious deviation from perfect competition comes from *imperfect competition* or *monopoly elements*.

Recall how strict is the economist's definition of a ''perfect competitor.'' The mere presence of a few rivals is not enough for perfect competition. Rather, perfect competition in a market arises when there is a *sufficient number of firms or degree of rivalry such that no one firm can affect the price of that good.* An *imperfect competitor* is one whose actions *can* affect a good's price. In reality, then, almost all business owners, except possibly the millions of farmers who individually produce a negligible fraction of the total crop, are imperfect competitors. At the extreme of imperfect competition is the *monopolist*—a single supplier who determines the price of a particular good by himself.

All economic life is a blend of competitive and monopolistic elements. Imperfect competition, not perfect competition, is the prevailing mode. But to say that a firm can affect the price of its output does not mean it is a dictator. As we shall later see, a business cannot set its prices completely as it pleases and still be profitable. It must take into account the prices of goods that are substitutes for its own. Even if it produces a trademarked heating oil with unique properties, it must reckon with prices charged for other heating oils, as well as for wood, gas, and insulation. Hence, there are always some checks on the economic power of imperfect competitors.

When monopoly power—the ability of a large firm to affect the price in a given market—does become economically significant, we see prices that rise above cost and that depress the amount of output that consumers will buy. The pattern of too high price and too low output is the hallmark of the inefficiencies associated with monopoly power. High prices also mean high profits, which may be turned to misleading

advertising, or even to buying influence from legislatures.

The government does not accept as inevitable all exercise of monopoly power. Since the 1890s, the federal government has imposed both antitrust laws and economic regulation in the name of improving the workings of our imperfectly competitive market system—as Chapters 24 and 25 will discuss.

Externalities A second way in which an unregulated market mechanism may lead to an inefficient outcome arises when there are spillovers or externalities. Look back for a moment to the circular-flow diagram in Figure 3-1. Note that all the transactions between households and businesses take place in voluntary exchange *through markets*. When a firm uses a scarce resource like land, it buys this from the owner in the land market; when a firm produces valuable goods like oil, it receives full value from the buyer in the oil market.

But many interactions in fact take place outside markets. Firm A uses scarce resources like clean air or water without paying those whose air or water is fouled. Firm B, by contrast, decides to provide its employees free vaccinations against a communicable disease; once immunity is achieved, people outside the firm benefit from the reduced dangers of contracting the disease as well. In these cases, an economic bad and an economic good have been transferred outside of market transactions.

Externalities (or spillover effects) occur when firms or people impose costs or benefits on others without those others receiving the proper payment or paying the proper costs.

(You can illustrate a spillover in Figure 3-1 by drawing a direct line from a business to a household. This is an externality because the transaction takes place involuntarily, outside markets.)

As our society has become more densely populated, as production is increasingly based on processes involving harmful substances, negative spillover effects have grown from little nuisances to major threats. Government *regulations* operate with varying degrees of effectiveness to control externalities like air and water pollution, strip mining, hazardous wastes, unsafe drugs and foods, and radioactive materials.

Critics of regulation complain that government economic activity is unnecessarily coercive. Governments are like parents, always saying no: Thou shalt not employ child labor. Thou shalt not pour out smoke from thy factory chimney. Thou shalt not sell dangerous drugs. And so forth.

Many government edicts are in fact controversial: Do we really need to tell firms about how clean they should keep the air inside factories? Do people need to be forced to wear seatbelts?

While the optimal scope of government intervention will never be resolved, most people will agree that government is needed to prevent some of the worst spillovers created by the market mechanism.

Public Goods It is possible to prevent firms from dumping wastes by imposing regulations; it is much more difficult for governments to encourage the production of **public goods.** These are the economic activities—conveying large or small benefits to the community—that cannot efficiently be left to private enterprise. Important examples of production of public goods are the maintenance of national defense and of internal law and order, the building of a highway network, and the support of pure science and public health. Private provision of these public goods will not occur because the benefits of the goods are so widely dispersed across the population that no single firm or consumer has an economic incentive to provide them.*

Because private provision of public goods will generally be insufficient, government must step in to provide public goods. In buying public goods like national defense or lighthouses, government is behaving exactly like any other large spender. By casting sufficient dollar votes in certain directions, it causes resources to flow there. The price system then takes over and ensures that the government-purchased lighthouses or fighter aircraft get produced.

Taxes Government must find the revenues to pay for its public goods and for income-redistribution programs. Such revenues come from taxes levied on incomes, wages, consumer sales, and similar items. Moreover, taxes are raised at all levels of government—city, state, and federal.

Taxes differ from other uses of our incomes in one important respect: Everyone is subject to the tax laws; we are all forced to contribute our share of payments to the government. It is true that the citizenry as a whole imposes that tax burden on itself, and surely we would agree that each citizen has the right to his or her share of the public goods produced by government. However, the close connection between spending and consumption that we see for private goods does not hold for taxes and public goods. I buy a hamburger or a wool sweater only if I want one, but I must pay my share of the taxes used to finance defense, space research, and public education even if I don't care a bit for these activities.

■   ■   ■

This brief discussion of how government intervenes in markets to improve their efficiency indicates that such actions are firmly grounded in economic logic. Government sets the rules of the road, levies taxes and tolls to pay for collective activities, and buys public goods such as highways, thereby facilitating the smooth driving of private enterprise, preventing abuses when firms become monopolistic road hogs, and curbing firms' activities when their exhaust fumes threaten lives and property.

Equity

Up to now we have focused on defects in the guiding role of the invisible hand—imperfections that perhaps could be corrected by judicious intervention. But as-

*Here is a typical example of a public good provided by government: lighthouses. These save lives and cargos. But lighthouse keepers cannot reach out to collect fees from ships; nor, if they could, would it serve an efficient social purpose for them to exact an economic penalty on ships who use their services. The light can be most efficiently provided free of charge, for it costs no more to warn 100 ships than to warn a single ship of the nearby rocks. We have here a positive externality, a divergence between *private* and *social* advantage. Philosophers and political leaders have always recognized the necessary role of government as provider of such public goods.

sume for the moment that the economy functioned with complete efficiency—always on the production-possibility frontier and never inside it, always choosing the right amount of public versus private goods, and so forth. Even if the market system worked as perfectly as just described, many would not consider it ideal. Why not?

In the first place, goods follow dollar votes and not the greatest need. A rich person's cat may receive the milk that a poor child needs to remain healthy. Does this happen because the market is failing? Not at all, for the market mechanism is doing its job—putting goods in the hands of those who can pay the most, of those who have the most money votes. Simply put, even the most efficient market system may generate great inequality.[2] If a country spends more on pet food than on paying for college education for the poor, that is a defect of income distribution, not of the market.

Income inequalities may be politically or ethically unacceptable. A nation does not need to accept the outcome of competitive markets as predetermined and immutable; people may examine the distribution of income and decide it is unfair. If a democratic society does not like the distribution of dollar votes under a laissez-faire market system, it can take steps to change the distribution of income.

Often the income distribution in a market system appears to be the result of accidents of technology or birth. Suppose the invention of robots should cause the competitive price of labor to fall greatly, thereby reducing incomes of the poor and turning 95 percent of national income over to robots and their owners. Would everyone regard that as necessarily right or ideal? Probably not. Yet that could be the way the cookie crumbles under the market system. Does someone who inherited 500 square miles of rangeland, for which oil companies offer $50 million per year, necessarily deserve so large an income? People are deeply divided on whether such high incomes should be heavily taxed.

Let's say that voters decide to reduce income in-

equality. What tools could Congress use? First, it could engage in *progressive taxation,* taxing a larger fraction of incomes of rich than of poor. The federal income and inheritance taxes are examples of such redistributive progressive taxation.

Second, because low tax rates cannot help those who have no incomes at all, governments have in recent decades built up a system of **transfer payments,** or payments to people for which no services are received. Such transfers include aid for the elderly, blind, disabled, and for those with dependent children, as well as unemployment insurance for the jobless. This system of transfer payments provides a "safety net" to protect the unfortunate from economic destruction. And, finally, governments sometimes subsidize consumption of low-income groups by providing food stamps, subsidized medical care, and low-cost housing.

Through the process of economic growth and welfare programs that established minimum standards of living, much of the great and visible destitution of nineteenth-century capitalism has been erased in the twentieth century. But relative poverty and deprivation have proven difficult to eradicate.

What can economics contribute to debates about equality? Economics as a science cannot answer such normative questions as how much of the competitively determined incomes—if any—should be transferred to poor families. But it can analyze the economic costs or benefits of different redistributive systems. Economists have devoted much time to analyzing whether different income-redistribution devices (such as taxes and food stamps) lead to social waste (such as people working less or buying less nutritious food). They have studied whether giving poor people cash rather than goods is likely to be a more or less efficient use of society's resources. Economics is like a good travel agent. You, the traveler, must decide whether you want sun or snow. But once you choose, the agent can help you get to your destination quickly and cheaply.

Stability

In addition to its role as promoter of efficiency and equity, government also engages in the macroeconomic function of promoting economic stability.

---

[2]One of the most dramatic instances of how markets can produce inequality occurred in 1848–1849, when Queen Victoria's laissez-faire government let millions of Irish children, women, and men starve in the great famine when a fungus suddenly destroyed the potato crop.

Since its origins, capitalism has been plagued by periodic bouts of inflation (rising prices) and depression (very high unemployment). Sometimes these episodes were so violent, as in the German hyperinflation during the 1920s, that social turmoil, revolution, and war followed in their wake.

At times, as during the Great Depression in America in the 1930s, hardship persisted for a decade because political leaders had insufficient economic understanding to take steps for economic revival. More recently, in the early 1980s, governments here and abroad took steps to reduce high rates of inflation; these measures led to high unemployment and declining inflation.

Today, thanks to the intellectual contribution of John Maynard Keynes, his followers, and also his critics, we have a better understanding of how to control the ups and downs of the business cycle. We now understand that, by careful use of the government's monetary and fiscal powers, the levels of output, employment, and inflation can be influenced. The *fiscal powers* of government are those just discussed—the power to tax and to spend. The *monetary powers* involve regulating banks and the financial system with an eye toward determining the supply of money, interest rates, and credit conditions. Through these two central tools of macroeconomic policy, governments can influence the rate of growth and level of output, the level of employment, and the price level of an economy.

Governments in advanced industrial countries successfully applied the lessons of the Keynesian revolution over the last half-century. Spurred on by expansionary monetary and fiscal policies, the market economies of the world witnessed a period of unprecedented economic growth from World War II until the early 1970s. In the 1970s, however, the advanced economies encountered foul economic weather: two major oil-price increases, harvest failures, commodity shortages, a breakdown in the international financial system, and an increasingly heavy burden of government regulatory and redistributive programs. As

FAILURE OF INVISIBLE HAND	GOVERNMENT INTERVENTION	CURRENT EXAMPLES OF GOVERNMENT POLICY
Inefficiency		
Monopoly	Intervene in markets	Antitrust laws
Externalities	Intervene in markets	Antipollution regulations, speed limits
Public goods	Subsidize worthwhile activities	National defense, lighthouses
Inequality		
Unacceptable inequalities of income and wealth	Redistribute incomes	Progressive taxation of income and wealth
		Income-support programs (e.g., food stamps)
Instability		
Inflation, unemployment, low growth	Stabilize through macroeconomic policies	Monetary policies (e.g., changes in money supply and interest rates)
		Fiscal policies (e.g., taxes and spending programs)

Table 3-1 Government can sometimes remedy shortcomings of the market

economic growth slackened and inflation soared, people became skeptical about the ability of monetary and fiscal policies to attain the goals of macroeconomic stabilization.

Today, policymakers are realizing that a modern economy faces a fundamental macroeconomic dilemma: *No country has for long periods of time succeeded in having free enterprise, low inflation, and full employment.* Just as today's market economy cannot have both guns *and* butter, so a market economy cannot simultaneously attain full employment *and* stable prices.

Table 3-1 (see page 47) presents a succinct summary of the economic role played by government today, showing why, as government actively promotes efficiency, equity, and stability, the United States in the 1980s is called a "mixed economy." Indeed, in all advanced industrial economies, the market determines most individual prices and quantities while government steers the overall economy with programs of taxation, spending, and regulation. Both halves—market and government—are essential for a soundly functioning economy. To operate a modern economy without both is like trying to clap with one hand.

C. SPECIALIZATION, MONEY, AND CAPITAL

The first two sections of this chapter described the two major systems of economic organization—by market direction and by government command. But no matter what mechanism is used to organize economic activity, we will always find three distinguishing features in an advanced industrial economy: specialization, money, and capital.

▪ The present-day economy is characterized by an elaborate degree of *specialization* and an intricate *division of labor*.

▪ The economy today makes extensive use of *money*. The flow of money is the lifeblood of our system. Money provides the yardstick for measuring the economic value of things. But improper management of money by the central bank can cause inflation or depression.

▪ Modern industrial technologies rest upon the use of vast amounts of *capital:* precision machinery, large-scale factories, and stocks of inventories. The ability to rely on such capital goods leverages human labor power into a much more productive factor of production and allows productivity many times greater than in an earlier age.

We will now turn to describe each of these three features of a modern economy. But in analyzing them, we will also see that they are all closely interrelated. Specialization makes possible great efficiencies and increased production. Use of money allows trade to take place quickly and with minimal time and energy. Without the great facility for trade and exchange that money provides, an elaborate division of labor would not be possible. Money and capital are related because the funds for buying capital goods are funnelled through money markets, where people's savings can be transformed into other people's capital. And the relationship between the price mechanism and trade is intrinsic: the complex, many-sided exchange that takes place in markets could not occur without money to function as a unit of account and a medium of exchange.

SPECIALIZATION AND DIVISION OF LABOR

One of the major differences between a modern economy and that of frontier days is found in the extensive division of labor and specialization of the modern work force. Our standards of living today are vastly higher than those of an earlier age because of the economies of mass production, which is in turn made possible by specialization.

Specialization occurs when people concentrate their efforts on a particular, sometimes narrow, set of tasks—it permits each person and region to use to best advantage any peculiar differences in skill and resources. Even in a primitive economy people learn that, rather than have everyone do everything in a mediocre way, it is better to establish a *division of labor*—a breaking up of production into a number of small specialized steps or tasks. A division of labor permits slow people to fish and swift people to hunt, all exchanging what they make for what they need.

To illustrate the increased productivity of specialization, Adam Smith provided the classical example of pinmaking. One worker could at best make a few dozen imperfect pins per day. But when a small group of workers is subdivided with respect to function so that each performs simple repetitive operations, they can turn out hundreds of thousands of perfect pins per day.

Perhaps the epitome of specialization is the modern automobile assembly line, where cars move down a conveyor belt and workers, or even robots, perform highly specialized functions. A worker might spend years just putting left tires on Chevrolets. The result of such specialization is the enormous increase in labor productivity in many manufacturing industries.[3]

The Perils of Overspecialization

Like too much sun or wine, too much specialization can be unhealthy. Despite its efficiency, specialization may also have the effect of making work tedious and without purpose. Extreme specialization means that a worker does but one single thing. Charlie Chaplin's classic movie *Modern Times,* in which the worker spends his whole lifetime accomplishing nothing more than the turning of bolt 999 on the remorseless assembly line, highlights the hazards of overspecialization.

Specialization may stunt personal development. Someone who spends all day mopping floors or digging holes or cutting buttonholes finds little stimulation on the job and earns little job satisfaction. Who can wonder that, as people's incomes rise, men and women complain that their specialized occupations are "alienating." As a result, many enlightened companies today encourage greater flexibility, job rotation, and worker participation in production.

Specialization and division of labor produce a further serious problem—interdependence. In medieval times, the artisan made one type of article and exchanged it for many others. Today, very few of us produce a single final good; we make but the tiniest fraction of what we consume. We might teach a small part of a college curriculum, or produce part of an article of clothing, or assemble part of an automobile or computer. In exchange for this specialized labor, we will receive an income adequate to buy goods from all over the world.

But note how our specialization makes us dependent on everyone else. If we produce only one of a thousand different items, we depend on other people to produce the other 999 items. When the great chain of production and distribution is broken, problems follow. For example, when a transformer failed in upper New York in 1965, the entire northeast of the United States plunged into darkness. The fall of the Shah of Iran in 1979 triggered rising oil prices, global recession, and a debt crisis for Mexico. A disruption of transportation systems and the economic fabric of trade reveals how dangerously modern economic life depends upon specialized exchange.

Is our affluence worth the perils of alienation and fragility? Should we turn back the clock to a simpler and poorer life? Should we sacrifice the last few percent of our income to attain a more secure but still specialized existence? These are valid questions asked today by thoughtful people. However we answer these questions, we should recognize one crucial fact: Our present high standard of living rests in good measure on an economic order that promotes a great specialization and division of labor. Turning back the clock to an earlier, less specialized way of life would inevitably reduce our real incomes.

MONEY: THE LUBRICANT OF EXCHANGE

If specialization permits people to concentrate on particular tasks, money then allows people to trade their

---

[3] One of the most controversial areas of specialization arises in international trade. Should the United States specialize in computers, buying cars from the Japanese and oil from OPEC? Such might be the efficient pattern of production in which each region produced according to its comparative advantage.

But Michigan autoworkers might protest the use of "cheap foreign labor" and persuade Congress that "protectionist" legislation, limiting the number of imported automobiles, would better serve the country (as it clearly serves the autoworkers). Part Seven shows how total U.S. national income is improved by international specialization—each country producing goods in which it has comparative advantage.

specialized outputs for the vast array of goods produced by others.

To be sure, we could imagine a state of *barter,* where one kind of merchandise is traded directly for another. In less advanced cultures, it is not uncommon for food to be traded for weapons, or for aid in the building of a house to be exchanged for help in clearing a field.

But exchange today in all economies—capitalist or communist—takes place through the medium of money. What is *money*? **Money** is the means of payment or the medium of exchange; in our economy, money consists of currency and checking accounts with which households and businesses pay for things. When you buy gum with a quarter, lunch with a $10 bill, or a stereo set with a check, in each case you are employing money.

Money is a lubricant that facilitates exchange. But like other lubricants, it can get gummed up. Under barter, if I am hungry and you are naked, I can always sew your clothes while you bake my bread. But after 1929, in the richest capitalistic country in all history, the banks failed, money was hoarded, some people went hungry and other people went in rags. Poverty can prevail amid plenty when money is not properly managed by the central bank.

The whole of Parts Two and Three of this book will deal with the problems of macroeconomics, problems rooted in society's dependence on a money economy.

CAPITAL

The economy rests on three major factors of production: labor, capital, and land. Land and labor are often called *primary factors of production.* A primary factor of production is one that is produced or given outside the economy (by sociological forces in the case of labor or geological history in the case of land) rather than produced by the economic system.

Capital is a different kind of productive factor. *Capital is a produced factor of production, a long-lived input which is itself an output of the economy.* For example, we build a textile factory, then use the factory to produce shirts; we assemble a computer, then employ the computer in educating students; and so forth.

Capital goods are durable goods, produced by the economy for further use in the production process. By contrast, labor and land are primary factors, given from outside the economy and not produced by the economy.[4]

Capital, Time, and Interest

Capital has a special relationship to time. Why so? We will see that capital inherently involves time-consuming, indirect, roundabout methods of production. Indeed, one of the paradoxes of capital is that by using indirect or roundabout methods the economy becomes enormously more productive.

If farmers had to work with their hands, without any capital such as tractors or shovels, productivity and consumption would be very low indeed. This fact is reflected in a strange tale. When an anthropologist asked of mourning tribe members, "Who died?" they replied, "Death, what is that? We have lost the needle that helped us sew our clothing."

People learned long ago that direct methods of production are less efficient than indirect or roundabout techniques. A direct method for catching fish would be to wade into the stream and catch fish with your hands, but this direct technique will produce few fish. Instead, people learned to build nets or fishing rods or fishing boats (all these being capital equipment). After we make the effort to construct the fishing capital, fishing time becomes vastly more productive in terms of fish caught per day.

Other examples of indirect or roundabout techniques that lead to greater efficiency are the following: A farmer spends time in clearing fields or digging ditches, so that the wheat yield will improve. A steelworker makes sheet steel, which will be used to manufacture a tractor, which will clear a field. A biologist injects DNA into a cell to produce a new and hardy seed. All these are roundabout ways of increasing the amount of wheat our economy can produce.

While we who toil inside the economy hardly stop

---

[4] Some qualifications are evident. Land can sometimes be made by drainage of swamps or filling in lakes, as can be seen on Chicago's lakefront or in almost one-third of the Netherlands. And labor supply does respond to economic incentives, as higher wages may increase the number of teenagers in the labor force.

to wonder about its roundaboutness, a moment's reflection will present us with the fact that almost no one in our system seems to be producing final consumer goods. Everyone is doing work of a preparatory nature, with the final consumption a distant future goal.

Growth from the Sacrifice of Current Consumption
The fact that it takes time and resources to get things started and synchronized is important. It explains why society does not automatically replace all direct processes by more productive, roundabout ones, and all roundabout processes by still more roundabout processes.

The advantage in using roundabout processes is offset by the initial disadvantage of having *to forgo present consumption goods* by diverting resources from current consumption to uses that will bear fruit only after some time. We could invest time and resources in making our highways even wider and our railroad beds even flatter than they are, thereby reducing fuel and repair costs and driving time. Why don't we engage in even more roundabout production than we do? Because that would cause too great a reduction in today's consumption.

To the extent that people are willing to save—to abstain from present consumption and wait for future consumption—to that extent, society can devote resources to new capital formation. New capital formation helps the economy to grow by pushing out the *PPF;* the higher is investment, the more rapid is the outward shift in the *PPF.* (Turn back to Figure 2-5 to see how forgoing current consumption in favor of capital formation adds to future production possibilities.)

We summarize as follows:

Much of economic activity is forward-looking. Every time we build a new factory or road, add to the stock of trucks or computers, increase the years or quality of education, increase the intensity of our research and development—we are enhancing the future productivity of our economy. By the same token, much of our current high living standard is the consequence of past investments.

In short, growing economies devote a significant share of their current output to net capital formation to bolster future economic output.

Interest Rates
Factors of production, like other commodities, have prices—wages are the price of labor while rents are the prices of land.[5] What is the price of capital? Its price is called the **interest rate.** Because capital involves increasing future consumption at the expense of current consumption, the interest rate is measured as a gain in dollars per dollar per unit of time.

Let's say that by forgoing $100 worth of consumption today—building a factory or computer or satellite—we gain $10 of consumption for every year in the future. This return of 10 percent per year is capital's yield. The market interest rate will be determined as firms, desiring funds for the factory or other projects, bid for funds in money markets. Firms will borrow funds as long as the cost of funds is less than the return on capital; the ruling interest rate then stands as the price that rations society's scarce supply of capital goods.

Capital and Private Property
Physical capital goods are important in any economy because they help to increase productivity. This is as true of socialism as it is of capitalism. But there is one important difference. By and large, it is private firms and individuals who own the tools of production in our market economy.

What is the exception in our system—government ownership of the means of production—is the rule in a communist state, where productive property is collectively owned. The return on capital goods accrues to the state, not to individuals, in a communist state; the government then decides how capital income should be distributed.

In a market economy, capital is generally privately owned, and capital income goes to individuals. Every patch of land has a deed, or title of ownership; almost every machine and building belongs to an individual or corporation. *Property rights* bestow on their owners the ability to use, exchange, paint, dig, drill, or exploit their capital goods. These capital goods also

---

[5] We must carefully distinguish *physical* capital from *financial* capital. Physical capital takes the form of factories, equipment, houses, and inventories; physical capital is an input or factor of production. Financial capital is ''paper'' assets or claims, like bonds, common stocks, checking and savings accounts, or home mortgages; financial capital is often the claims to physical capital, but they are never inputs into the productive process.

have market values, and people can buy and sell the capital goods for whatever price they will fetch. *The ability of individuals to own and profit from capital is what gives capitalism its name.*

But while our society is one built on private property, property rights are limited. Society determines how much of "your" property you may bequeath to your heirs and how much must go in inheritance and estate taxes to the government. Society determines how much the owners of public-utility companies—such as electric and gas firms—can earn and how much pollution your car can emit. Even your home is not your castle. You must obey zoning laws and, if necessary, make way for a road.

Interestingly enough, the most valuable economic resource, labor, cannot be turned into a commodity that is bought and sold as private property. Since the abolition of slavery, it is against the law to treat human earning power like other capital assets. You are not free to sell yourself; you must rent yourself at a wage.

■   ■   ■

We have now completed our overview of the functioning of a market economy. In the next chapter we describe in detail how supply and demand interact to determine the prices and quantities of goods and see how this basic analytical approach can be used to analyze a wide variety of economic problems.

SUMMARY

A. How Markets Solve the Basic Economic Problems

1. In an economy like the United States, most economic decisions flow through markets, which are arrangements by which buyers and sellers set quantities and prices for commodities. Adam Smith proclaimed that the *invisible hand* of markets would lead to the optimal economic outcome as individuals pursue their own self-interest. And while markets are far from perfect, they have the virtue of solving the problems of *how, what,* and *for whom.*

2. The market mechanism works as follows: The dollar votes of people affect prices of goods; these prices serve as guides for the amounts of the different goods to be produced. When people demand more of a good, a competitive business can make a profit by expanding production of that good. Under perfect competition, a business must find the cheapest method of production, efficiently using labor, land, and other factors; otherwise, it will incur losses and be eliminated from the market.

At the same time that the *what* and *how* problems are being resolved by prices, so is the problem of *for whom.* The distribution of income is determined by the ownership of factors of production (land, labor, and capital) and by their prices—wages of each kind of labor, rents of land, royalties of books, and various returns to capital. People possessing fertile land or the ability to hit home runs will earn many dollar votes to buy consumer goods. Those without property or education and with skills, color, and sex that the market does not value will receive low incomes.

B. The Economic Role of Government

3. Although the market mechanism is an admirable way of producing and allocating goods, sometimes market failures lead to deficiencies in the economic outcomes. To correct these failures, the government may step in to ensure *efficiency, equity,* and *stability*.

4. The market fails to provide an efficient allocation of goods when there are imperfections of competition or externalities. Imperfect competition, such as monopoly, often leads to regulation or even government ownership of production. Externalities arise when firms impose costs or bestow benefits on others outside of markets—such as when a steel mill pumps out smoke and soils the neighborhood without paying for the damages. When externalities occur, government may decide to step in and regulate these spillovers (as it does with air pollution), or engage in *public-good* provision itself (as in the case of national defense).

5. A second governmental function arises when citizens choose to alter the pattern of incomes (the *for whom*) generated by market wages, rents, interest, and dividends. Modern governments use progressive taxation to raise revenues for transfers or income-support programs that place a financial safety net under the poor.

6. Since the development of macroeconomic theory and policy in the 1930s, government has undertaken a third role: using fiscal powers (of taxing and spending) and monetary policy (affecting the supply of money, credit conditions, and interest rates) to curb inflation and unemployment and to increase economic growth.

C. Specialization, Money, and Capital

7. As economies develop, they become more specialized. Division of labor allows a task to be broken into smaller pieces that can be mastered and performed more quickly by a single worker. Specialization arises in part from innate or acquired skills of workers, but even more from the increasing tendency to use roundabout methods of production that require many specialized skills.

8. Elaborate systems of exchange of specialized goods and services today rely on money to lubricate the wheels of trade. Money is the universally acceptable medium of exchange—currency and checks—used to pay for everything from apples to zebra skins. By accepting money, people and nations can specialize in producing a few goods and exchange them for others; without money, we would waste much time constantly bartering one good for another.

9. Capital goods—produced inputs such as machinery, housing, and inventories of goods in process—permit roundabout methods of production that add much to a nation's output. These roundabout, time-consuming methods take time and resources to get started; hence, adding to the stock of capital goods requires a temporary sacrifice of present consumption. In a well-functioning market system, the interest rate serves to ration out capital to the most worthwhile investments.

10. Under a mixed economy, capital goods are largely owned as private property; the incomes they produce go to their owners and to the government as taxes. Under communism, the state owns capital goods. In no system are private-property rights unlimited.

CONCEPTS FOR REVIEW

market mechanism

markets for goods and for factors of production

perfect and imperfect competition

roundabout or indirect production

efficiency, equity, stability

specialization, division of labor, interdependence

money

factors of production (labor, land, capital)

market

invisible-hand doctrine

interest rate

public goods, externalities

QUESTIONS FOR DISCUSSION

1. Consider an economy where the only activity is farming and where land and labor produce a single output, corn. Briefly describe the solution to *what, how,* and *for whom* in this rural country. Draw a circular flow like Figure 3-1 for this economy.

2. Consider the following cases of government intervention in the economy: pollution limitations; ''Star Wars'' defense purchase; the food-stamp program; price regulation of AT&T; a monetary-policy step to curb inflation. What role of government is being pursued in each case?

3. Give some examples you know of specialization and division of labor. Can you think of cases where overspecialization has occurred?

4. If it cannot borrow abroad, what must a poor country do if it wishes to become an efficient, industrialized nation in the next few generations?

5. ''Lincoln freed the slaves. With one pen stroke he destroyed much of the capital the South had been able to accumulate over the years.'' Comment.

6. In what sense does a market mechanism ''ration'' scarce goods and services?

7. The circular flow of goods and inputs in Figure 3-1 has a corresponding flow of money. Draw a circular flow for the monetary side of the economy, and compare it with the circular flow of goods and inputs.

8. In addition to writing the opening quotation of this chapter, Adam Smith wrote, ''I have never known much good done by those who affected to trade for the public good.'' Explain the logic behind this statement and relate it to the invisible-hand doctrine.

9. This chapter discusses many ''market failures,'' areas in which the invisible hand guides poorly, and describes the role of government. Is it possible that there are, as well, ''government failures,'' government attempts to curb market failures that are worse than the original market failures? Think of some examples of government failures. Can you imagine a case where government failures are so bad that it is better to live with the market failures than to try to correct them?

CHAPTER 4

THE ELEMENTS OF SUPPLY AND DEMAND

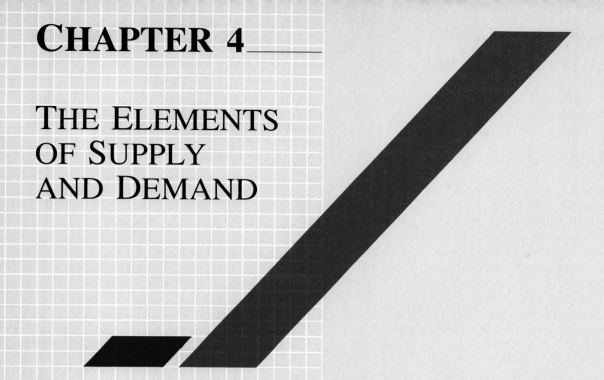

*You can make even a parrot into a learned economist—
all it must learn are the two words "supply" and
"demand."*

Anonymous

UP TO NOW we have seen that every economy must somehow solve three fundamental problems, *how, what,* and *for whom.* These are solved sometimes by custom and sometimes by government command. However, the American economy, along with most other advanced industrial countries, relies on a system of markets and prices to guide most economic decisions. In a market system, you will recall, consumers are like voters, using their money votes to buy what they want most. Your votes compete with my votes, and the people with the most dollar votes exercise the most influence over what gets produced and to whom goods flow.

Our task is now to understand exactly how this spending of dollar votes operates in a market system. Why are diamonds useless but expensive, while water is vital but cheap? Why does land in Manhattan command astronomical prices, while desert land in Arizona goes for a song? Why did few people own personal computers yesterday, while many own them today?

The answers to these and a thousand other questions can be found in the *theory of supply and demand.* This theory shows how consumer preferences determine consumer demand for commodities, while business costs underpin the supply of commodities. And finally we will see how supply and demand are brought into balance by the movement of prices, by the price mechanism.

THE MARKET MECHANISM

Suppose you wake up one morning with an urge for a new stereo set. How could you get one? Surely you wouldn't say, "I'll head down to the voting booth and vote for the president or senator most likely to give me a new stereo. Of course, I mean one with twin 100-watt channels, Dolby, and a built-in compact disk player."

Or to take an actual historical case, suppose that people decide that they want to travel in automobiles rather than on horseback. How does this desire get translated into action? Do politicians tell workers and firms to move to Detroit to make cars? Would the Senate tell horse breeders to slow down horse production? How would government get producers to make cotton for car seats rather than hay for horses?

Of course, the transition did not occur under government direction. Rather, consumers bought more cars and fewer horses. With higher profits in car production, automobile production geared up, new firms like Cadillac and Ford sprouted all over Detroit, and workers hungry for good jobs moved there. As horses languished in the pastures, horse prices fell and horse breeders turned to other fields. As less hay was needed for horses, the price of hay fell and other crops were planted instead. At the same time, the demand for automotive components, such as steel, cotton, and rubber, increased, and the prices of these goods rose, attracting manufacturers into the production of automotive-based commodities.

Through just such forces, we have witnessed a veritable revolution in American transportation during this century, with the horse population falling by 90 percent while the car population grew from nothing to 140 million vehicles.

What brought about this revolution? It occurred as changes in taste and technology operated through the forces of supply and demand.

Similar revolutions are taking place in the economic marketplace all the time. As people's tastes change, as the stocks of factors of production change, or as methods of production evolve, the marketplace registers these changes in the prices and quantities of inputs and outputs. By using prices, sales, and profits as signals to producers and consumers, the price mechanism acts to *ration out* the available resources among the competing uses.

ANALYSIS OF SUPPLY AND DEMAND

The purpose of this chapter is to show how supply and demand work themselves out in the competitive market for *individual commodities*. We shall define a demand curve and then a supply curve. Using these basic tools, we shall see how the market price is determined (or reaches its competitive equilibrium) where these two curves intersect—where the forces of demand and supply are just in balance.

The Demand Schedule

Let us start with demand. It is commonly observed that the quantity of a good that people will buy at any one time depends on its price. The higher the price charged for an article, the less of it people will be willing to buy. And, other things being equal, the lower its market price, the more units of it will be demanded.

Thus there exists at any one time a definite relationship between the market price of a good and the quantity demanded of that good. This relationship between price and quantity bought is called the **demand schedule,** or the **demand curve.**

Table 4-1 presents a hypothetical demand schedule. At any price *(P)*, such as $5 per bushel, a definite quantity of corn will be demanded by all the consumers in the market—in this case 9 million bushels per year.

At a lower price, such as $4, the quantity bought is even greater, 10 million units. At lower *P* of $3, the quantity demanded *(Q)* is greater still—namely, 12 million. By lowering *P* enough, we could coax out sales of more than 20 million units. From Table 4-1 we can determine the quantity demanded at any price by comparing column (2) with column (1).

DEMAND SCHEDULE FOR CORN

	(1) PRICE ($ per bu) *P*	(2) QUANTITY DEMANDED (million bu per year) *Q*
A	5	9
B	4	10
C	3	12
D	2	15
E	1	20

Table 4-1   **The demand schedule relates quantity demanded to price**

At each market price, consumers will want to buy a definite quantity of corn. At each lower price of corn, the quantity of corn demanded will rise.

The Demand Curve

The numerical data can also be given a graphic interpretation in Figure 4-1, showing the quantity of corn demanded at each level of the price of corn. This graphical depiction of the demand schedule is called the *demand curve*. Note that quantity and price are inversely related, *Q* going up when *P* goes down. The curve slopes downward, going from northwest to southeast. This important property is given a name: the *law of downward-sloping demand*. This law has strong intuitive appeal and has been known in a general way since the time of the Greeks; it has been empirically tested and verified for practically all commodities—corn, gasoline, cars, and theater tickets being a few examples.

The **law of downward-sloping demand:** When the price of a commodity is raised (and other things are held constant), buyers tend to buy less of the commodity. Similarly, when the price is lowered, other things equal, quantity demanded increases.

What is the rationale for the law of downward-sloping demand? Quantity demanded for a good tends to rise as price falls because consumers will generally substitute the now less expensive good for other goods.

The reasons behind the law are easily illustrated for the case of personal computers (PCs). When the price of PCs was sky-high, only the richest people could afford them. Everybody did calculations by hand and used typewriters or pens to write papers. Even today, in poor countries like India, only the richest businesses and banks own PCs.

As the price of PCs began to fall, more and more people found them worthwhile—for work, for school, or for fun. Hence one reason for the law of downward-sloping demand comes from the fact that lower prices coax in new buyers.

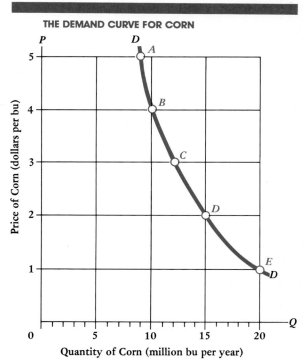

Figure 4-1   **A downward-sloping demand curve relates quantity demanded to price**

In the demand curve for corn, prices are measured on the vertical axis while quantity demanded is measured on the horizontal axis. Each pair of (*P*,*Q*) numbers from Table 4-1 is plotted as a point and then a smooth curve is passed through the points to give us a demand curve. The negative slope of the demand curve illustrates the law of downward-sloping demand.

In addition, a price reduction will induce some extra purchases by a good's existing consumers. For example, when water is very dear, we demand only enough of it to drink. Then when its price drops, we buy some to wash with. At still lower prices, we resort to still other uses. Finally, when it is really very cheap, we water flowers and use it lavishly for any possible purpose. Conversely, a rise in the price of a good will cause some of us to buy less.

Why does quantity demanded tend to fall as price rises? For two main reasons. First is the **substitution effect.** When the price of a good rises, I naturally try to substitute other similar goods for it (for example, chicken for beef or synthetic shirts for cotton shirts). A second factor, known as the **income effect,** comes into play because when a price goes up, I find myself somewhat poorer than I was before. If gasoline prices double, I have in effect less income, so I will naturally curb my consumption of gasoline and other goods.

Our discussion of demand has referred to ''the'' demand curve. But whose demand is it? Mine? Yours? Everybody's? In general, we can determine each person's demand for corn or other products. When we analyze the price and quantity for a market, however, we will refer to the *market demand,* which represents the sum total of all individual demands. As we will see in Chapter 19, the market demand curve is found by adding together the amounts demanded by all individuals at each price. In this chapter, we will always be speaking of the market demand.

Behind the Demand Curve

What determines the market demand for corn or cars or computers? We have up to now mentioned only a commodity's own price as a factor. But other factors weigh importantly: average levels of income, the size of the population, the prices and availability of related goods, individual tastes, and other special factors.

The average *income* of consumers is a key determinant of demand. As people's incomes rise, they tend to buy more of almost everything—apples, boats, cars, etc.

Second, the size of the market—measured say by the population—clearly affects the amount demanded at each price. California's 30 million people tend to buy 30 times more apples and cars than do Rhode Island's 1 million people.

Third, the price and availability of *related goods* will influence the demand for a commodity. A particularly important relationship exists among substitute goods—ones that tend to perform the same function, such as pens and pencils, cotton and wool, or oil and natural gas. Demand for good A tends to be low if the price of substitute product B is low. (For example, if the price of natural gas is high in Boston, will the demand for oil tend to be low or high?)

Fourth, in addition to these objective factors we must add a set of subjective factors called *tastes* or *preferences.* Tastes represent a variety of social and historical factors. They may reflect genuine psychological or physiological needs (for liquids, salt, warmth, or love). They may include artificially contrived cravings (for cigarettes, drugs, or fancy sports cars). They may contain a large element of tradition or religion (so that eating beef is popular in America but taboo in India, while curried jellyfish is a delicacy in Japan).

Finally, individual goods will generally have *particular factors* behind their demand—rainfall for umbrellas, snow depth for skis, and ocean temperature for surfboards.

Much of our analysis will focus on price as a factor tending to balance supply and demand, but we must never lose sight of these other factors that ultimately determine the strength of demand. The different factors behind the demand for a typical good like automobiles are sketched in Table 4-2.

A Change in Demand Demand for different goods changes over time. Demand curves won't sit still except in a textbook.

Why does the demand curve shift? Because factors other than the price of the commodity change. As an example, what were some possible reasons for the increase in the American demand for cars from 1950 to 1988? First, the average real income of Americans almost doubled, so higher incomes induced higher demand for cars. Second, the number of adults rose by more than half, increasing the number of potential drivers. Third, there was a general decline in the

FACTORS AFFECTING DEMAND	EXAMPLE FOR AUTOMOBILES
1. Own price	Higher own price reduces quantity demanded
2. Average income	As incomes rise, people increase car purchases
3. Population	Higher population increases car purchases
4. Prices of related goods	Lower gasoline prices raise the demand for cars
5. Tastes	Americans buy more cars than Europeans, other things equal
6. Particular factors	Special factors include availability of subways, TV viewing, dating patterns, etc.

Table 4-2   Many factors, price and non-price, affect demand

availability of alternative forms of transportation (bus, trolley, and rail). As for tastes, who can say?

The final result of all these changes in factors other than own price was to shift the demand curve for cars far to the right.

A shift in the demand for automobiles is illustrated in Figure 4-2. As a result of the change in the non-own-price factors just discussed, we say there is an *increase in demand*. This leads to the rightward shift in the demand curve as shown in Figure 4-2. Note that the shift means that more cars will be bought at every price.

You can test yourself by answering the following: Will a warm winter shift the demand curve for heating oil leftward or rightward? Why? What would happen to the demand for ski-lift tickets if snowfall were especially light? What about the effect of a large oil-price increase on the demand for coal?

Supply Schedule and Supply Curve

Let us now turn from demand to supply. By supply we mean the quantity of a good that businesses willingly produce and sell. More precisely, we relate the quantity supplied of a good to its market price, hold-

ing equal other things, such as costs of production, the prices of substitute goods, and the organization of the market.

The **supply schedule** (and **supply curve**) of a commodity means the relationship between its market price and the amount of that commodity that producers are willing to produce and sell.

Table 4-3 shows a hypothetical supply schedule for corn. Figure 4-3 plots the same data as the supply curve for corn. What do these data show? At low corn prices, farmers will shut down the farm or devote cornland to the production of substitute products like wheat or soybeans. According to the table, at a corn price of $1 per bushel, no corn at all will be produced. As the corn price rises (holding constant things like the price of wheat), land will be shifted from wheat production to corn production. At ever-higher corn prices, each farmer will find it profitable to add even

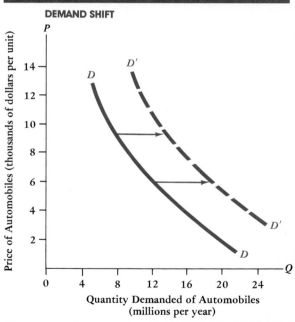

Figure 4-2   Increase in demand for automobiles

As factors other than own price change, the demand for automobiles is affected. Here we see the effect of factors like rising average income, increased population, lower gasoline prices, and a shift of tastes toward cars.

SUPPLY SCHEDULE FOR CORN

	(1) PRICE ($ per bu) P	(2) QUANTITY SELLERS WILL SUPPLY (million bu per year) Q
A	5	18
B	4	16
C	3	12
D	2	7
E	1	0

Table 4-3 Supply relates quantity supplied to price

The table shows, for each price, the quantity of corn that the country's farmers want to produce and sell. Note the direct or positive relation between price and quantity supplied.

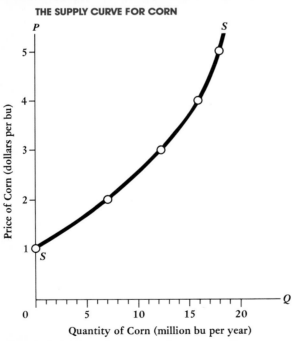

THE SUPPLY CURVE FOR CORN

Figure 4-3 Supply curve relates quantity supplied to price

The supply curve plots the price and quantity pairs from Table 4-3. A smooth curve is passed through these points to give the upward-sloping supply curve, *SS*.

more land, labor, tractors, irrigation, and fertilizer. All these tend to increase the output of corn at the higher market prices.

Note that the supply curve slopes upward and to the right, rising from southwest to northeast. By contrast, the demand curve sloped downward. What explains the upward slope of the supply curve for the output of an individual commodity? One important reason is found in the law of diminishing returns. If society wants more wine, then more and more labor will have to be added to the same limited hill sites suitable for producing wine grapes. Each new worker will—according to the law of diminishing returns—be adding less and less extra product; hence, the price needed to coax out additional product will have to rise. By raising the price of wine, society can persuade grape farmers and wine merchants to produce and sell more wine, and the supply curve for wine therefore is upward-sloping.

Behind the Supply Curve Just as we looked behind demand to uncover its fundamental determinants, we now examine the forces operating on supply. A detailed study of the conditions of cost and supply will occupy much of Part Four of this text, so we will treat the subject briefly at this point.

The fundamental point to grasp about businesses' supply behavior is that firms supply commodities for profit, not for fun or charity. As a result, a competitive farmer will supply more corn when prices are higher because it is more profitable to do so; conversely, when the corn price falls below the cost of production, as it did in the mid-1980s, farmers plant other crops, let the fields go to seed, or even sell the farm or go into bankruptcy.

We see then that a key dominant factor lying behind supply decisions is the *costs of production*. When the costs of production of a particular good are low relative to the market price, then it will be profitable for producers to produce a great deal. When production costs are very high relative to price, producers will produce little or may quit producing.

Among the forces affecting production costs are technology and input costs. *Technological advance* will certainly affect costs. A better computer program for crop rotation, genetically engineered seeds,

FACTORS DETERMINING SUPPLY	EXAMPLE FOR AUTOMOBILES
1. Own price	Higher own price increases most profitable production level
2. Production costs	
a. Technology	Robots lower production cost and increase supply
b. Input prices	Autoworkers' wage cuts lower costs and increase supply
3. Prices of production substitute	If bus and truck prices fall, supply of cars increases
4. Market organization	Removal of quota on Japanese car imports increases supply
5. Particular factors	If government lowers standards on auto-safety equipment, supply may increase

Table 4-4 Supply is affected by price, production costs, and other factors

and new drip irrigation systems—all these would lower a farmer's production costs and increase his supply.

Similarly, if technology did not change, but the *prices of inputs* changed, this would change the costs of production and thereby affect supply. For example, when fuel prices fell in 1986, this lowered production costs and increased supply of all foodstuffs.

A second major factor affecting supply stems from the *prices of production substitutes;* these goods are ones that can be readily substituted for one another in the production process. If the price of one production substitute rises, this will decrease the supply of the other substitute. Farmers can produce wheat as well as corn; McDonald's can sell McChickens as well as McHamburgers; an oil refinery can produce diesel fuel as well as gasoline. For each pair, as the price of one (e.g., diesel fuel) rises, this will tend to decrease the supply of the other (e.g., gasoline).

A third factor affecting supply is the *market organization*. If a market becomes monopolized, this would tend to raise the price at each level of output.

When some producers are excluded—as was the case in recent years for foreign sugar producers or Japanese cars—then prices of the remaining goods tend to rise at each output level. Generally, for given input prices and technology, a perfectly competitive market will produce the highest possible level of output at each price level.

Finally, *idiosyncratic factors* enter supply. The weather exerts an important influence on farming and on the ski industry. The computer industry has been marked by a keen spirit of innovation as well as by imitation, which has led to rapid change in the availability of new products. In some industries, like telecommunications and airlines, government regulation has shunted supply decisions off their competitive track.

Table 4-4 highlights the important determinants of supply using the case of automobiles as an illustration.

Shifts in Supply Supply behavior is constantly changing. What then leads to such changes? Recall that our supply schedule in Table 4-3 or supply curve in Figure 4-3 relates quantity supplied to the market price. These schedules shift, and supply is said to change, when any factors other than the commodity's own price change. In terms of a supply curve, supply is said to increase when the amount supplied increases at each market price.

To consider a shift in supply, take the automobile market. Supply might increase because introduction of cost-saving robots cut down the labor required to produce cars, or because autoworkers took a pay cut, or because bus and truck prices fell, or because the Japanese were allowed to export more cars to the United States, or because government removed some of the regulatory burden on the industry. *Each of these factors would tend to increase the supply of automobiles in the United States.* Figure 4-4 illustrates an increase in supply for automobiles.

To test your understanding of supply shifts, think about the following: What would happen to the supply of oil if a new invention made oil exploration easier? What happens to the supply curve for corn in Figure 4-3 after a disastrous drought? What does a Florida freeze do to the supply of orange juice?

SUPPLY SHIFT

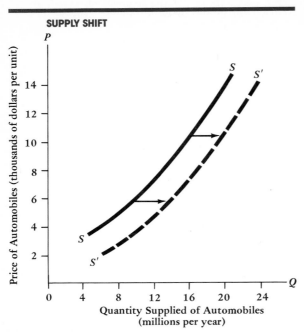

Figure 4-4   Increased supply of automobiles

As production costs fall or foreign competition increases, the supply of automobiles increases. At each price, therefore, producers will supply more automobiles and the supply curve shifts to the right.

EQUILIBRIUM OF SUPPLY AND DEMAND

We have seen how consumers demand different amounts of corn, cars, and computers as a function of these goods' prices. Similarly, producers willingly supply different amounts of these and other goods depending on their prices. What happens when suppliers and demanders meet?

The answer is that the supply and demand forces in the marketplace will produce an equilibrium price and equilibrium quantity, or a market equilibrium. The **market equilibrium** comes at that price and quantity where the supply and demand forces are in balance. At such a price and quantity, the amount that buyers wish to buy is just equal to the amount that sellers wish to sell. At that equilibrium, price and quantity

tend to stay the same, as long as other things remain equal, until something operates to change supply and demand.

Let us work through the corn example in Table 4-5 to see how supply and demand determine a market equilibrium; the numbers from this table come from the data shown in Tables 4-1 and 4-3. Recall that up to now we have been considering in the demand schedule what people would buy at different prices, while the supply schedule shows what firms want to sell at different prices. We have said, "If price is A, quantity demanded will be X; if price is B, quantity sold will be Y; and so forth." But now we want to know the exact level that price and quantity will settle on. Neither the supply schedule nor the demand schedule alone can tell us the answer. Rather the answer will depend on the interaction of supply and demand.

To find the right level of price and quantity, proceed the way a middleman or broker might—by trying to find a price at which the desired amounts to be bought and sold just match. Could a price of $5 per bushel prevail for long? Clearly not, as row A in Table 4-5 shows: at $5 producers will be supplying 18 units (million bushels per year) while demanders will be buying only 9 units per year. The amount supplied at $5 will exceed the amount demanded, and stocks of corn will pile up in the granary. Because too much corn is chasing too few consumers, the price of corn will tend to fall, as shown in column (5) of Table 4-5.

Say our broker tries $2 instead. Does that price clear the market? A quick look at row D shows that at $2, consumption exceeds production. The storehouses of corn begin to empty at that price. Indeed, as people scramble around to find their desired quantity of corn, they will tend to bid up the price of corn, as is shown in column (5) of Table 4-5.

We could try other prices, but by now the answer is clearly $3, or row C in Table 4-5. Only at $3 will the amount demanded by consumers exactly equal the amount willingly supplied by producers—in each case 12 units. At $3, price is at equilibrium because there is no tendency for price to rise or fall, and no stocks of corn are piling up or dwindling down. We also say that $3 is the *market-clearing price,* by which we mean that we have cleared the books of the supply and demand orders; there are no extra supply

COMBINING DEMAND AND SUPPLY FOR CORN

	(1) POSSIBLE PRICES ($ per bu)	(2) QUANTITY DEMANDED (million bu per year)	(3) QUANTITY SUPPLIED (million bu per year)	(4) STATE OF MARKET	(5) PRESSURE ON PRICE
A	5	9	18	Surplus	Downward
B	4	10	16	Surplus	Downward
C	3	12	12	Equilibrium	Neutral
D	2	15	7	Shortage	Upward
E	1	20	0	Shortage	Upward

Table 4-5 Equilibrium price comes where quantity demanded equals quantity supplied

Only at the equilibrium price of $3 per bushel does amount supplied equal amount demanded. At too low a price there is a shortage and price tends to rise. Too high a price produces a surplus which will depress price.

or demand orders left over after we have found the market-clearing or equilibrium price. Everybody is satisfied—demanders, suppliers, and our broker.

Equilibrium with Supply and Demand Curves The same story is told in Figure 4-5. Here we have placed the supply curve from Figure 4-3 right on top of the demand curve from Figure 4-1. This was possible because they were drawn with exactly the same units on each axis. The supply and demand curves cross or intersect at only one point, C. We will see that the equilibrium price and quantity come at just this intersection point.

We can now repeat our earlier experiment that attempted to find the equilibrium price. Start with the initial high price of $5 per bushel, shown at the top part of Figure 4-5. At that price, suppliers want to sell more than demanders want to buy; the result is a *surplus* or excess of quantity supplied over quantity demanded, shown by the labelled black line in the figure. The arrows show the direction that price tends to move when a market is in surplus.

When we examine a price of $2 per bushel, the market shows a *shortage* or excess of quantity demanded over quantity supplied, again shown by a la-

belled black line. Under conditions of shortage, the competition among buyers for limited goods causes price to rise, as shown by rising arrows in the figure.

We now see that the balance of forces or equilibrium comes at point C, *where the supply and demand curves intersect*. At point C, with a price of $3 per bushel and a quantity of 12 units, the quantities demanded and supplied are equal; there are no shortages or surpluses; there is no tendency for price to rise or fall. At point C and only at point C, the forces of supply and demand are in balance and the price has settled at a sustainable level.

The equilibrium price and quantity come at that level where the amount willingly supplied equals the amount willingly demanded. In a competitive market, this equilibrium is found at the intersection of the supply and demand curves. No shortages or surpluses are found at the equilibrium price.

Effect of a Shift in Supply or Demand Curves

Our supply-and-demand apparatus can do much more than tell us about the equilibrium price and quantity—

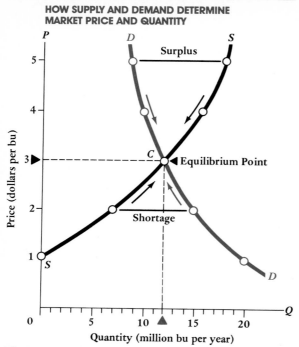

HOW SUPPLY AND DEMAND DETERMINE MARKET PRICE AND QUANTITY

Figure 4-5   Market equilibrium comes graphically at the intersection of supply and demand curves

To determine equilibrium price and quantity in supply-and-demand diagrams, look for the intersection of two curves. At a price of $3 at point *C*, quantity willingly supplied just equals quantity willingly demanded. When price is too low (say at $2), quantity demanded exceeds quantity supplied; shortages occur, driving price back up to equilibrium. What occurs at a price of $4?

it can tell us about the effect of changes in economic conditions on prices and quantities.

The key to understanding the impact of changes is the concept of a shift in supply or demand schedules or curves. Recall that we explored the non-own-price elements lying behind supply and demand. We can now see how, when one of these non-own-price elements changes, supply or demand shifts and the equilibrium price and quantity adjust.

A Shift in Supply Gregory King, an English writer of the seventeenth century, noticed that when the harvest was bad, food prices rose. When food was plentiful, farmers got a lower price. Why was this so?

A spell of bad growing weather reduces the amount that farmers will supply at each and every market price; it thereby shifts the supply curve to the left. This is illustrated in Figure 4-6*(a)*, where the supply curve has shifted from *SS* to *S'S'*. But the demand curve has not shifted; I am as hungry when it rains in Iowa as when it is dry.

What happens in the corn market? The new supply curve *S'S'* intersects the original demand curve at *E'*, to the left of the old equilibrium at *E*. At the old price there was too little corn to satisfy consumer demand. So price rose, raising quantity supplied and lowering quantity demanded; finally, at the new equilibrium price, the amounts demanded and supplied are once again equal.

Thus a bad harvest (or any leftward shift of the *SS* curve) raises prices and, by the law of downward-sloping demand, lowers quantity demanded.

Suppose, instead, that because of good weather or cheap fertilizers or a new miracle seed, the supply increased. Draw in a new *S"S"* curve, along with the new equilibrium *E"* and the lower price and higher quantity of corn.

A Shift in Demand We can also use our apparatus to examine the effect of forces that change demand. Suppose that there is a sharp increase in family incomes, so that everyone wants more corn. This is represented in Figure 4-6*(b)* as a "demand shift." In this case, at every price, consumers demand a higher quantity of corn. The demand curve thus shifts *rightward* from *DD* to *D'D'*.

The demand shift produces a shortage of corn at the old price. The equilibrium price and quantity thus move upward from *E* to *E"* in panel *(b)*. Why? Because, after the demand curve shifts, at the old price consumers demand more than suppliers produce. Shortages arise. A scramble for corn ensues. Prices are bid upward until at *E"* supply and demand come back into balance.

So forces that affect consumer demand—incomes, population, the prices of substitute goods, tastes—

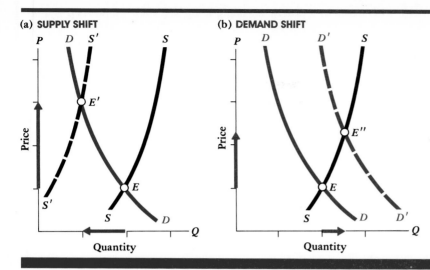

Figure 4-6 When either the supply or the demand curve shifts, equilibrium price changes

(a) If supply shifts leftward, a shortage will develop at the prior price. Price will be bid up until quantities supplied and demanded equilibrate at new equilibrium, *E'*. **(b)** A shift in the demand curve leads to excess demand. Price will be bid up as equilibrium price and quantity move upward to *E"*.

will shift the demand curve and affect the equilibrium price and quantity.

Three Hurdles

We pause to consider three hurdles that must be overcome before the tools of supply and demand can be usefully employed. The first point deals with our insistence, when we draw up a demand or supply schedule, that other things remain equal. The second concerns the difference between shifts of curves and movements along curves. The third deals with the exact meaning of an equilibrium of supply and demand.

"Other Things Equal" In drawing up a demand schedule for corn, we vary its price and observe what would happen to the quantity bought, always assuming that *no other factors change to cloud our experiment.*

Specifically, this means that, as we change the price of corn, we must not at the same time change family income, or the price of wheat, or do anything else that would shift the demand schedule for corn. Like any scientist who wants to isolate the effects of one causal factor, we must vary only that one factor.

What happens when we fail to hold other things

equal as we define a demand curve? As Figure 4-7 will illustrate, failure to hold other things equal can lead us into erroneous reasoning.

Let's say you are interested in the market for pizzas. You observe that the demand curve is *DD* in Figure 4-7 when jobs are plentiful and people have the incomes to go out to pizza parlors. However, when business activity is depressed and many people are out of work, incomes are low and the demand for pizzas is also low.

In boom times, you would record the equilibrium point shown at point *E* in Figure 4-7, while in bad times you would observe the equilibrium point *E'*. Suppose you take a ruler and join points *E* and *E'*. You pronounce, ''I have disproved the law of downward-sloping demand, for note that when *P* was high, so too was *Q*—as shown by *E*. And when *P* was lowered, instead of that change increasing *Q*, it actually lowered *Q*—as shown by *E'*. My straight line joining *E* and *E'* represents an upward-sloping, not a downward-sloping, demand curve. So I have refuted a basic economic law.''

Alas, you would be crestfallen to discover that you had broken one of the cardinal rules of economics: You did not hold other things equal. Like the person who pronounces the retirement paradise of Florida an

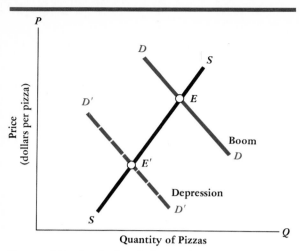

Figure 4-7   Analysis of demand curve must hold other things equal

Lower demand occurs when the economy is depressed, while a boom produces higher demand. Does the curve drawn through *E* and *E'* yield a demand curve? Why not?

unhealthful state because its death rate is so high, you omitted an important variable. At the same time that *P* dropped, other things were *not* held constant; rather, income was also lowered. The tendency for a drop in *P* to raise purchases was more than masked by the countertendency of lowered income to decrease purchases.

Not only is this a poor application of economic reasoning, but you might well be suspicious of the argument because it leads to nonsensical conclusions. It would predict such things as that in years of large harvests corn will sell for a higher rather than for a lower price, because the demand curve is upward-sloping. Not only does such reasoning lead to absurd predictions, but it would also lose the fortunes of a corn farmer or a speculator. Make sure, then, to hold other things equal when analyzing the impact of a change in supply or demand.

Movement along Curves vs. Shift of Curves
Closely related to the problem of other things equal is the common confusion of shifts of curves with movement along curves. Great care must be taken when a

problem is being discussed not to confuse an *increase in demand* (by which is meant a shift of the whole demand curve to the right) with an *increase in the quantity demanded* (as a result of moving to a lower price on the same demand curve). Recall that a demand or supply curve represents the pairs of possible prices and quantities that satisfy either buyers or sellers. A single point on a demand curve represents the "quantity bought" or the "quantity demanded" at a particular price.

Hence an increase in supply (or, equivalently, a rightward shift in the supply curve) will lead to an increase in the quantity demanded, not to an increase in demand, as a result of the price decrease. This represents a movement down the demand curve, not a shift in the demand curve. A similar distinction applies to shifts in supply vs. changes in quantity supplied.

Figure 4-8 illustrates this key distinction. A demand increase denotes a shift of the demand curve or schedule. Such a shift occurs when factors behind demand change (say income increases). As a result of the demand shift illustrated in Figure 4-8(*a*), the equilibrium quantity increases from 10 to 15 units.

The case of a movement along the demand curve is shown in Figure 4-8(*b*). In this case, the quantity demanded changes because of a shift in *supply,* rather than a shift in demand. A supply shift changed the market equilibrium from point *E* to point *E''*, and the quantity demanded changed from 10 to 15 units. But demand did not change in this case; rather quantity demanded changed and there was a movement along the demand curve from *E* to *E''*.

Let's put this distinction to work by analyzing the following incorrect argument: "A bad harvest does not always raise price. The price might rise at first. But a higher price will diminish the demand. And a reduced demand will send the price down again. Therefore, it is not certain, after all, that the bad harvest will really raise the price of corn!"

What is wrong with this statement? It errs because "demand" is used incorrectly in the third sentence; it uses the word "demand" in the sense of "quantity demanded," thus confusing a movement along a curve with a shift of the demand curve. The correct statement would run as follows:

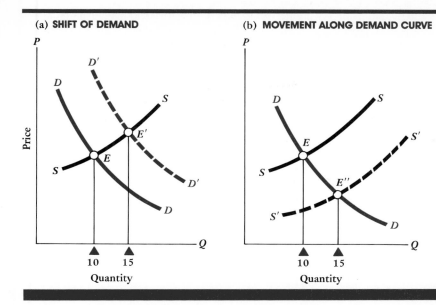

(a) SHIFT OF DEMAND

(b) MOVEMENT ALONG DEMAND CURVE

Figure 4-8 Shifts of and movements along curves

Start out with initial equilibrium at *E* with a quantity of 10 units. Case **(a)** produces an increase in demand (i.e., a shift of the demand curve) leading to new equilibrium of 15 units at *E'*. In case **(b)**, a shift of supply produces a movement along the demand curve from *E* to *E"*.

"A bad harvest will raise price as the leftward shift in the supply curve raises the equilibrium price of corn. The higher equilibrium price will reduce the quantity demanded, as consumers move up the downward-sloping demand curve. But since no shift in the demand curve occurred, there is no reason to expect that price will fall as a result of a decrease in the quantity demanded."

Meaning of Equilibrium The last hurdle is a more subtle one, less likely to arise but more difficult to surmount. It is seen in the following statement by a skeptic: "How can you say that supply and demand determine a particular equilibrium quantity? After all, the amount one person sells is precisely what another person buys. The quantity bought must always equal the quantity sold, no matter what the price, whether or not the market is in equilibrium."

The economist might reply as follows: You are quite right that measured quantity bought and measured quantity sold must be identical. But the important question is this: At which price is the amount that consumers willingly buy just matched by the amount that producers willingly sell? Only at such a price—where there is equality between the amounts that demanders and suppliers willingly plan to go on buying and selling—will there be no tendency for price to rise or for price to fall.

At any other price, such as where price is above the intersection of supply and demand, obviously the measured amounts bought and sold are equal. But at too high a price there is a surplus of goods, with producers eagerly trying to sell more goods than demanders will buy. Moreover, this excess of desired supply over desired demand will put downward pressure on price until price has finally reached that equilibrium level where the two curves intersect. And where price is below its equilibrium, many buyers will be unhappy as the too low price produces a shortage of the good.

At the equilibrium intersection of supply and demand, and there alone, will everybody be happy: the suppliers, the demanders, and the economist who is seeking the price at which there is neither surplus nor shortage.

Rationing by Prices

Having seen how supply and demand operate, let us take stock of what the market mechanism accomplished. Once the equilibrium prices and quantities of all inputs and outputs have been determined, the market has allocated or rationed out the scarce goods of the society among the possible uses. Who did the rationing, a planning board or a legislature or some central authority? No. The marketplace, through the interaction of supply and demand, did the rationing. It was rationing by the purse.

What goods were being produced? This was answered by the signals of the market prices. High coal prices coaxed out more coal as low corn prices drove resources out of agriculture. Those who had more dollar votes had the greatest influence on what goods were produced.

For whom were goods delivered? The power of the purse dictated who got the largest quantity of goods. If you have a high income, you will end up with a larger house, more clothing, and longer vacations. When backed up by cash, the most urgently felt needs got fulfilled through the operation of the demand curve.

Even the *how* question was being decided by supply and demand. With corn prices low, farmers could no longer afford expensive tractors and fertilizers, and only the best land was cultivated. With high coal prices, coal companies bought fancy new machines that could mine many tons an hour.

A market economy solves the basic economic problems through the operation of supply and demand.

The Role of Perfect Competition

Strictly speaking, our supply-and-demand analysis applies only to perfectly competitive markets—ones in which neither sellers nor buyers are large enough to affect the market price. In fact such markets are rare and can be found mainly in organized commodity markets, like Chicago's Board of Trade, which sells corn, wheat, and metals. Securities markets like the New York Stock Exchange, which trades ownership rights to America's largest companies, are also perfectly competitive. Such institutions are also called ''auction markets''; prices clear the auction markets virtually every minute of the working day.

Most other markets, however, show some traces of imperfect competition, for there are usually a few buyers or sellers who have at least a tiny effect on the market price. Hence for near-competitive markets, the assumptions of the competitive market do not literally apply.

Nonetheless, the tools of supply and demand do summarize in an idealized way the behavior of many markets. For this analysis to apply, several elements must be present: There must be numerous buyers and sellers; they must be well informed about quality and about prices; and the actions of individual buyers and sellers must not have an appreciable effect on the prevailing market price. So long as all this is true, price and quantity will behave much as is predicted by our supply-and-demand analysis.

Three Markets

We will rely on the supply-and-demand analysis throughout this textbook. Before we conclude this introduction, however, we examine in Figure 4-9 three cases where such analysis gives a good approximation of how prices and quantities are determined. Panel *(a)* pictures a competitive market for used cars. What would happen to used-car prices in an economic boom when family incomes are high? Panel *(b)* shows how a high oil price was produced when OPEC (the Organization of Petroleum Exporting Countries) organized a price-fixing group (called a cartel). What happened to the quantity of oil demanded after OPEC collapsed and oil prices fell sharply? The third case shows the supply and demand for land in Manhattan. Note how little the supply of land responds to higher prices. Can you see why increased demand for land raises prices a great deal and affects land quantity only a little?

Having concluded our introductory discussion of supply-and-demand analysis, we will explore in later chapters the forces lying behind supply and demand and show how this analysis can be applied to yet further examples. In addition, we will incorporate monopoly elements, or imperfect competition, into the analysis. After all these further refinements are included, we will see that competitive supply-and-demand analysis is an indispensable tool for interpreting the economic world in which we live.

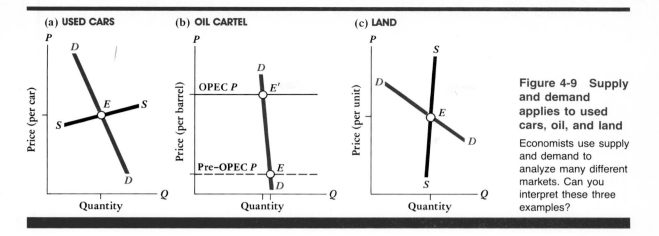

Figure 4-9   Supply and demand applies to used cars, oil, and land

Economists use supply and demand to analyze many different markets. Can you interpret these three examples?

SUMMARY

1. Supply-and-demand analysis shows how a market mechanism grapples with the triad of economic problems, *what, how,* and *for whom.* It shows how dollar votes decide the prices and quantities of different goods.

2. A demand schedule represents the relationship between the quantity of a good that people want to buy and the price of that good. Such a demand schedule, represented graphically as a demand curve, always holds equal other things like family incomes, tastes, etc. Almost all commodities obey the "law of downward-sloping demand," which holds that quantity demanded falls as a good's price rises. This law is represented as a downward-sloping demand curve.

3. Many factors lie behind the demand relationship for an entire market: average family incomes, population, the prices of related goods, tastes, and peculiar factors. When these factors change, the demand curve will shift.

4. The supply schedule (or supply curve) gives the relationship between the quantity that producers will be willing to sell—other things equal—and that good's price. Generally quantity supplied responds positively to price, so that the supply curve rises upward and to the right.

5. Factors other than the good's price affect its supply, the most important being the cost of production of the good, determined by the state of technology and by input prices. Other factors in supply include the prices of substitute goods, the market organization, and particular factors.

6. The equilibrium of supply and demand in a competitive market takes place at a price where forces of supply and demand are in balance. This occurs at the price where the quantity demanded just equals the quantity supplied, or graphically at the intersection of the supply and demand curves. At a price above the equilibrium, the amount that producers want to supply will exceed the amount that consumers want to buy, producing a surplus of goods and exerting downward pressure on prices. Similarly, a price lower than the equilibrium price will generate shortages, and buyers will therefore tend to bid prices upward to the equilibrium.

7. Competitively determined prices ration out the limited supply of goods to those with the desires and the necessary dollar votes.

8. To avoid pitfalls in the use of supply-and-demand analysis, we must observe certain strictures: *(a)* Hold other things equal, which requires distinguishing the effect of changing a commodity's own price from the effect of changes in other factors; *(b)* distinguish a change in demand or supply (which produces a shift in a curve) from a change in the quantity demanded or supplied (which represents a movement along a curve); *(c)* recognize a supply-and-demand equilibrium, which is where buyers and sellers willingly engage in trades.

CONCEPTS FOR REVIEW_____

demand schedule or curve, *DD*
law of downward-sloping demand
supply schedule or curve, *SS*
forces behind supply curves and
  demand curves
shifts of curve versus movements along
  curve

other things equal
competitive equilibrium
auction market
surplus, shortage
rationing by prices
equilibrium

QUESTIONS FOR DISCUSSION_____

1. Explain why each of the following is false:
  (a) Failure of Brazil's coffee crop will lower the *P* of coffee.
  (b) Fad for short skirts will raise wool *P*.
  (c) A new yen for meat will lower the *P* of grains and raise the *P* of hide and horn.
  (d) Development of the sugar beet raised rents on tropical sugar cane lands.
2. Define carefully what is meant by a demand schedule or curve. State the law of downward-sloping demand. Illustrate the law of downward-sloping demand with two cases from your own experience.
3. Define the concept of a supply schedule or curve. Show that an increase in supply means a rightward and downward shift of the supply curve. Contrast this with the rightward and upward shift in the demand curve implied by an increase in demand. Why the difference?
4. What factors might increase the demand for corn? The supply? What would cheap oil do to the supply of gasoline? To coal miners' wages?
5. Spell out arguments to show that competitive price settles down at the equilibrium intersection of supply and demand. Trace through what happens if the market price started out too high or too low.

6. "An increase (or decrease) in supply will lower (or raise) price." Verify. Now interpret: "An increase (decrease) in demand will generally raise (lower) price."

7. Identify whether each of the following involves a shift in the demand curve or a change in the quantity demanded: (1) Auto sales rise as consumer incomes rise; (2) fish prices fall after the Pope allows Catholics to eat meat on Friday; (3) a gasoline tax lowers the consumption of gasoline; (4) after a disastrous wheat blight, bread sales go down; (5) after a disastrous wheat blight, peanut butter and jelly sales go down; (6) after the Black Death struck Europe in the fourteenth century, wages rose.

8. "A simultaneous increase of demand and decrease of supply is statistically and logically impossible. Demand and supply are the same thing." Comment in terms of the section "Three Hurdles."

9. From the following data, plot the supply and demand curves and determine the equilibrium price and quantity.

SUPPLY AND DEMAND FOR PIZZAS

PRICE ($ per pizza)	QUANTITY DEMANDED (pizzas per semester)	QUANTITY SUPPLIED (pizzas per semester)
10	0	40
8	10	30
6	20	20
4	30	10
2	40	0
0	125	0

What would happen if the demand for pizzas tripled at each price? What would occur if the price were initially set at $4 per pizza?

10. Under political pressure from the steel industry, the federal government has undertaken the following measures to bolster the sagging production and employment of that industry. For each, discuss the impact upon supply, demand, output, and price of steel in the United States.

  (a) On three occasions in the last two decades, the government has put limitations on foreign supply of steel into the United States.

  (b) In the 1970s, the government reduced the tax burden on the steel industry by lowering the effective amount of taxes paid by steel companies on their profits.

  (c) In the 1970s, the government undertook to increase the purchases of steel by the Department of Defense.

  (d) In the 1970s and 1980s, the government reduced the regulatory burden on steel companies by relieving them of the need to comply with certain air-pollution rules.

  (e) During periods of wage and price guidelines, the government put pressure on the coal industry to settle for lower wage increases.

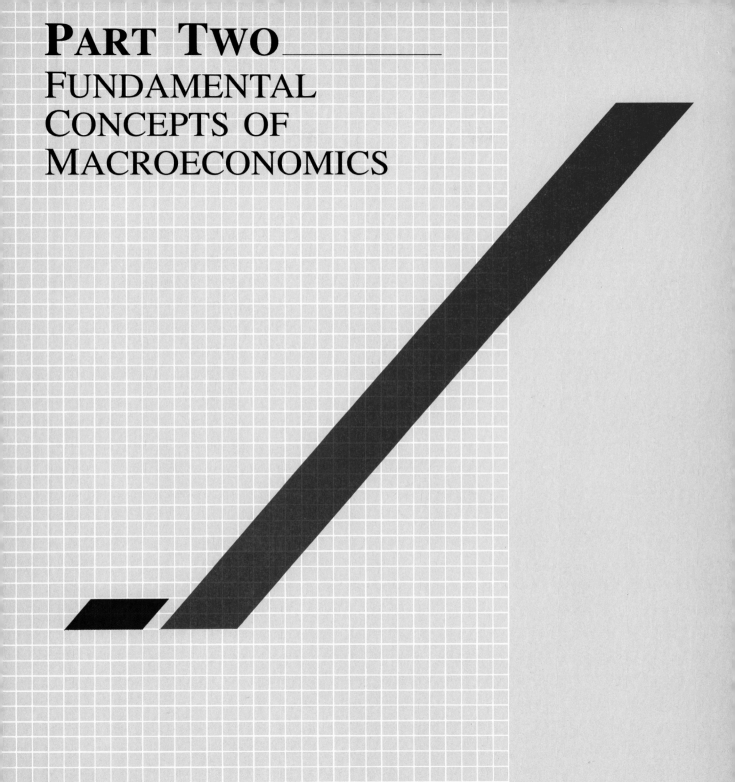

PART TWO
FUNDAMENTAL
CONCEPTS OF
MACROECONOMICS

CHAPTER 5

OVERVIEW OF MACROECONOMICS

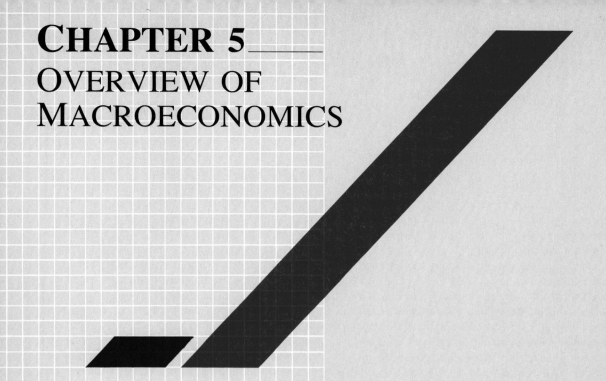

The whole purpose of the economy is production of goods or services for consumption now or in the future. I think the burden of proof should always be on those who would produce less rather than more, on those who would leave idle men or machines or land that could be used. It is amazing how many reasons can be found to justify such waste: fear of inflation, balance-of-payments deficits, unbalanced budgets, excessive national debt, loss of confidence in the dollar.

James Tobin
National Economic Policy (1966)

PART ONE served to introduce the major themes of economics. We turn in the following 13 chapters to an analysis of the ebb and flow of the economy as a whole—to the study of macroeconomics.

Macroeconomics studies the major trends of the entire economy. It examines such historical issues as the following: Why did production and prices in America and the rest of the industrial world collapse during the Great Depression of the 1930s? What forces propelled America into a sustained boom during World War II? Why did unemployment rise to almost 11 percent of the labor force in 1982, only to decline gradually over the next 6 years? Why did the rate of price increase, or the rate of inflation, rise from almost zero in 1961 to above 10 percent per year in 1980–1981? What forces led to slow productivity growth during the last two decades? And why did the United States in the late 1980s spend almost twice as much on imports as it earned from exports?

Macroeconomics does not settle for a mere study of history. Most macroeconomists want to understand the sources of the business cycle so that they can tame it. Economists study the institutions affecting taxes, spending, and money not only for the satisfaction of

75

better understanding how the world operates but also to help them devise more effective policies to stabilize the economy. Some economists advocate that government take an active role toward stabilizing the economy, while others lean toward a laissez-faire, or "hands off," attitude by government.

This chapter provides a general introduction to the subject of macroeconomics. Section A surveys the major concepts and issues that come up time and time again in any discussion of macroeconomic issues; it examines major definitions and important goals of macroeconomic policy. Then section B introduces the major tool of macroeconomic analysis—aggregate supply and demand—and applies this tool to three historical periods.

As we launch into a detailed study of macroeconomics, let us recall the definitions that we first encountered in Chapter 1: **Macroeconomics** is the study of the behavior of the economy as a whole. It examines the overall level of a nation's output, employment, prices, and foreign trade.

By contrast, **microeconomics** comprises the study of individual prices and quantities and markets. It analyzes perfectly and imperfectly competitive markets, the markets for inputs and outputs, the impact of

unions or discrimination on labor markets, the efficiency of competitive markets, and many similar questions.

A few examples will clarify this distinction. Microeconomics considers the behavior of steel prices versus energy prices, while macroeconomics studies the behavior of all producer and consumer prices. Microeconomics studies whether going to college is a good use of your time when young, while macroeconomics examines what determines the unemployment rate of young adults. Microeconomics examines the individual items of foreign trade—why we import Hondas and export heavy trucks. Macroeconomics examines the overall trends in our imports and exports, and asks why the exchange value of the dollar rose in the early 1980s and then fell in the late 1980s.

We must add one final point before plunging into our subject. This chapter is an overview of the entire subject of macroeconomics. It therefore packs a great deal of new material into a few pages as we provide a broad outline of macroeconomic issues. The new concepts and ideas sketched here will be filled in during the next 12 chapters, which are devoted to developing, clarifying, and extending the introductory analysis of this overview chapter.

A. Macroeconomic Concepts and Goals

The political, social, and military fate of nations depends greatly upon their economic success, and no area of economics is today more vital or more controversial than macroeconomics. Countries like Japan, which have grown rapidly while winning export markets for their products, experience great prestige as their citizens enjoy high and rising living standards. At the opposite extreme are countries that stagnate and suffer from rapid inflation, large trade deficits, and large foreign indebtedness. Countries tend to emulate the policies of the successful countries while avoiding the mistakes of the poor performers.

Macroeconomics is an important subject because a nation can affect its economic performance. By a judicious choice of macroeconomic policies—such as the level and structure of taxation or expenditure—a

nation can speed or slow its economic growth, ignite a rapid inflation or slow price increases, produce a trade deficit or a trade surplus. We cannot do anything about the weather, but whether economic policies are wise or foolish will have a major impact on our future living standards.

OBJECTIVES AND INSTRUMENTS IN MACROECONOMICS

As we weigh the claims of competing political figures, or puzzle over the rise and decline of nations, it quickly becomes clear that a few key variables stand out in importance. In judging a nation's performance, time and again we encounter gross national product

OBJECTIVES	INSTRUMENTS
Output: High level Rapid growth rate	**Fiscal policy:** Government expenditure Taxation
Employment: High level of employment Low involuntary unemployment	**Monetary policy:** Control of money supply affecting interest rates
Price-level stability with free markets	**Foreign economics:** Trade policies Exchange-rate intervention
Foreign balance: Export and import equilibrium Exchange-rate stability	**Incomes policies:** From voluntary wage-price guidelines to mandatory controls

Table 5-1   Objectives and instruments of macroeconomics

The left-hand column displays the major objectives of macroeconomic policy. These goals can be found in national laws and in the statements of political leaders. The right-hand column contains the major instruments or policy measures available to modern economies. These are the ways that policymakers can affect the pace and direction of economic activity. These objectives and instruments will be discussed in the first part of this chapter.

(GNP), employment, inflation, and net exports. These are the central measures by which we judge macroeconomic performance.

For much of history, nations did little to affect their overall economic performance. But with the development of modern macroeconomics, knowledge has grown about how public policies affect the economy. We now understand better the instruments or tools of macroeconomic policy. We know why changes in the money supply or taxes and expenditures affect our economies. And having tasted the fruit of macroeconomic knowledge, few governments abstain from attempting to affect output, employment, inflation, and foreign trade.

Table 5-1 is a list of the major objectives and instruments of macroeconomic policy. We will now turn to a detailed discussion of each—thereby illustrating some key questions that confront modern macroeconomics.

Objectives

Four objectives are central to evaluating macroeconomic performance—those concerning output, employment, prices, and the foreign sector.

Output   The ultimate yardstick of a country's economic success is its ability to generate a high level of production of economic goods and services for its population. What could be more important for an economy than to produce and consume large quantities of housing, shelter, food, education, and recreation? The most comprehensive measure of the total quantity of production in an economy is the **gross national product.** GNP is the measure of the market value of all goods and services, from apples to zippers, produced in a country during a year.

GNP can be measured in current or actual market prices, which is called *nominal GNP.* Or we can measure GNP in a set of constant or invariant prices (say for the year 1982), which is called *real GNP.* (A more complete discussion of the concepts underpinning GNP is presented in the next chapter.) Movements in real GNP are the best widely available measure of the level and growth of output; they serve as the carefully monitored pulse of the nation's economy.

Figure 5-1 shows the history of real GNP in the United States since 1929. A careful examination of the figure will reveal the economic decline during the Great Depression, the recovery and boom during the wartime economy of World War II, rapid and stable growth during the 1960s, recessions in 1975 and 1982, and steady recovery from 1982 to 1988.

A study of the past patterns of output growth in major countries reveals that capitalist economies have been subject to **business cycles,** periods of expansion and contraction in real GNP. During business downturns, millions of people are thrown out of work, and billions of dollars of production of goods and services are lost. Business cycles tended to be less violent after 1945 than they had been before, in part because the

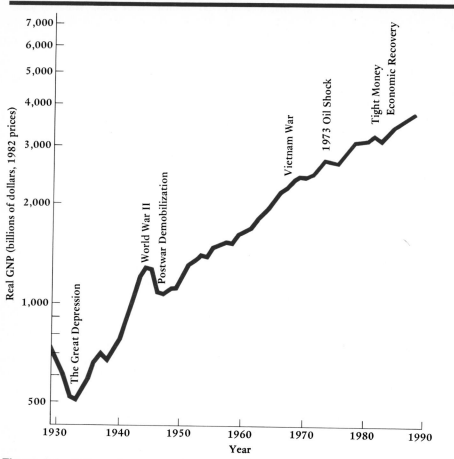

Figure 5-1   U.S. real gross national product, 1929–1988

This figure shows the growth of real GNP over the period since 1929. Note that, in the Depression, output actually fell sharply. In the period since World War II, growth in output was very steady until the economy was hit by numerous shocks in the 1970s and 1980s. (Source: U.S. Department of Commerce.)

knowledge and practice of macroeconomic policy became widespread after World War II. However, even considering the major progress made in macroeconomics over the last half-century, business cycles continue to haunt developed countries.

But the ripples or waves which represent business cycles cannot mask the central historical fact of mixed capitalist economies—their slow but steady growth in real GNP and the improvement in living standards of their populations. The American economy has proven itself a powerful engine of progress over a period of more than a century, as shown by the growth in trend GNP or **potential output.**

Although we postpone a complete discussion of potential output to later chapters, we can sketch the basic points here. An economy has a certain amount of labor, capital, and land available to it at a given time. Combining these inputs with the available technology will allow a maximum sustainable level of output to be produced. (We described this maximum sustainable level of output in Chapter 2 using the production-possibility frontier.) If the economy attempts to produce more than its potential output, prices will begin to rise more and more rapidly as resources are utilized too intensively. If the economy produces less than its potential, then unnecessarily high levels of unemployment of labor and excess capacity of factories will prevail. Between the extremes of too high utilization of capacity and too high unemployment

of inputs is a threshold level of output that we designate potential output. We will present a complete analysis of the determinants of potential output in later chapters.

When potential GNP exceeds actual GNP, the difference between them is the **GNP gap.** A large GNP gap means that the economy is not operating up to its potential, or that the economy is inside its *PPF*. When a GNP gap exists, goods are lost just as much as if they were dumped into the sea.

Figure 5-2 shows an estimate of potential output

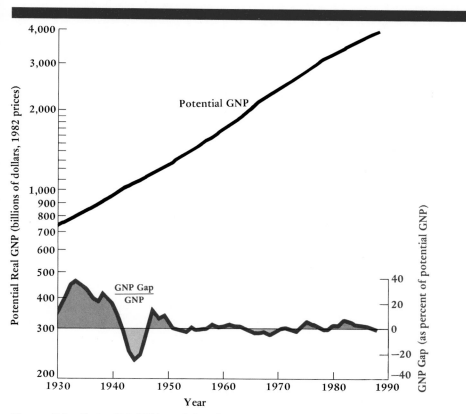

Figure 5-2   Potential GNP and the GNP gap

This figure shows the trend of potential GNP along with the contours of the business cycle.

The top smooth line, with a scale at the left, shows potential output over the period 1930–1988. Potential output is defined as the maximum sustainable GNP. Potential output has grown about 3 percent annually over the last half-century.

The lower curve, with its scale on the right-hand side, shows the GNP gap. This shows the extent to which actual output fell below its potential, as a percent of potential GNP. Note the large GNP gaps in the 1930s and 1980s. (Source: U.S. Department of Commerce and authors' estimates.)

and the GNP gap for the period 1930–1988. Note the periods in which much output was lost—particularly the 1930s and the early 1980s.

Why do large GNP gaps sometimes open up? Why might an economy move well inside its *PPF*? These are among the most important questions addressed by macroeconomic analysis, and some tentative answers are the following. A large GNP gap may occur be-cause economic policy was unable to counteract forces tending to depress the economy or because policymakers decided that a downturn was sound economic medicine. The Great Depression of the 1930s persisted for a decade because President Roosevelt, the Congress, and the Federal Reserve possessed insufficient macroeconomic knowledge to attempt expansionary economic policies. In other periods, such

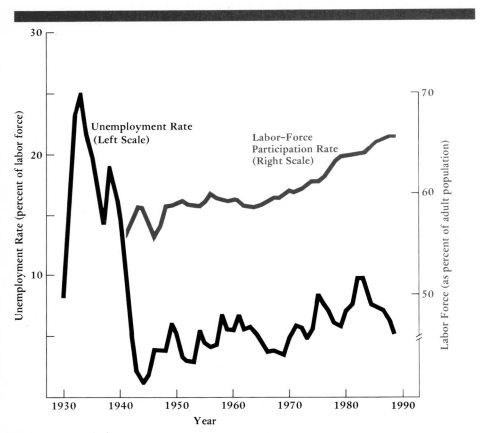

Figure 5-3   Trends in the labor force and unemployment

The red line and the right-hand scale show trends in the labor-force participation rate (the fraction of the population 16 years of age and over that is in the labor force). Note the gradual upward trend, particularly after 1965, as a larger fraction of adult women moved from work in the home to work in the marketplace.

The black line and the left-hand scale show the unemployment rate, or the fraction of the labor force that was looking for but could not find work. Unemployment reached tragic proportions during the 1930s, peaking at 25 percent of the labor force in 1933. Also note the upward creep of the unemployment rate since 1969, reaching a postwar high of 9.7 percent in 1982. (Source: U.S. Department of Labor.)

as from 1980 to 1983, policymakers intentionally raised unemployment and GNP gaps in order to reduce the rate of inflation (or price increase)—such periods were "investments in disinflation."

High Employment, Low Unemployment The next major objective of macroeconomic policy is *high employment,* which also requires *low unemployment.* People want to be able to find good, high-paying jobs and to find them easily.

Figure 5-3 shows trends in labor-force participation and in unemployment over the last six decades. As Chapter 13 discusses in greater detail, the labor force includes all persons either employed or unemployed, but excludes those without work who are not looking for jobs. Over the period since 1929, there has been a gentle increase in the fraction of the adult population that is in the labor force (from around 53 percent in 1929 to 66 percent in 1988). Unemployment reached epidemic proportions in the Great Depression of the 1930s, with a quarter of the work force idled. Over the last four decades, the nation has been more fortunate in its employment experience, with the unemployment rate averaging $5\frac{1}{2}$ percent of the labor force.

Unfortunately, as we see in the bottom part of Figure 5-3, there has been a marked upward drift in the fraction of the labor force that has been unemployed over the last two decades. The goal of ensuring good jobs for all who want them has proven increasingly elusive.

Stable Prices The third macroeconomic objective is to ensure *stable prices with free markets.* This objective contains two parts. Price stability denotes that the overall price level does not rise or fall rapidly. Why do societies prefer stable prices? The reason is that prices are a yardstick whereby economic values are measured. When the economic yardstick changes quickly during periods of rapidly changing prices, contracts and other economic agreements become distorted, and the price system tends to become less valuable. The second half of the objective of stable prices, maintenance of free markets, means that prices and quantities should be determined by market forces, by supply and demand, to the maximum possible extent. The objective of stable prices with free

markets is pursued in the United States today because many people believe that stable prices determined by free markets allow the economy to allocate resources efficiently and in a way that is responsive to individual tastes.

The most common way to measure the overall price level is the **consumer price index,** popularly known as the CPI. The CPI measures the cost of a fixed basket of goods (items like food, shelter, clothing, and medical care) bought by the typical urban consumer. The overall price level is often denoted by the letter *P*. The rate of **inflation** is the rate of growth or decline of the price level, say, from one year to the next.[1]

Figure 5-4 on the next page illustrates the rate of inflation for the CPI from 1929 to 1988. Over this entire period, inflation averaged 3.4 percent per year. Note that inflation fluctuated greatly over the years, varying from *minus* 10 percent in 1932 to a high of *plus* 14 percent in 1947. When prices decline, or the rate of inflation is negative, we have **deflation.**

The objective of price stability with free markets is more subtle than those objectives concerning output and employment (a fuller treatment of the desirability of stable prices is contained in Chapter 14). It is clearly undesirable to impose an absolutely rigid set of prices, such as has sometimes been the case in communist countries or during times of wartime price controls in market economies. A frozen price structure would prevent the invisible hand from directing markets efficiently. Without changes in relative prices, how would firms know to reallocate their production from horse-drawn buggies to automobiles or from records to compact disks?

At the other extreme, we must avoid *hyperinflation,* where the price level rises a thousand or a million percent a year. In such situations, as in Weimar Germany of the 1920s or Bolivia in the 1980s, prices are useless. Those foolish or naive enough to hold on to currency become impoverished. An economy returns to barter.

Thus we seek a golden mean of price flexibility,

---

[1]More precisely the rate of inflation of the CPI is:

$$\text{Rate of inflation of consumer prices (in percent)} = \frac{\text{CPI (this year)} - \text{CPI (last year)}}{\text{CPI (last year)}} \times 100$$

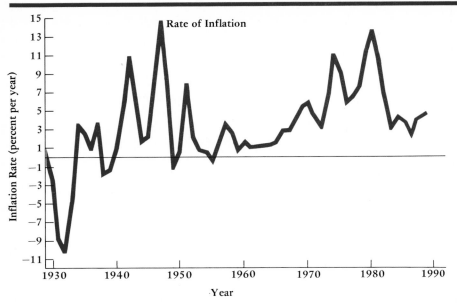

Figure 5-4   The rising trend of consumer price inflation, 1929–1988

This figure shows the year-over-year increase in consumer prices as measured by the consumer price index (CPI). During the Depression, prices actually fell. Since World War II, however, deflation (or falling prices) has been rare. Note the upward trend of inflation from 1960 to 1980. During the 1980s, high unemployment and declining oil prices brought the rate of inflation down to a more acceptable level. (Source: U.S. Department of Labor.)

perhaps tolerating a gentle inflation, as the best way to allow the price system to function efficiently.

Foreign Economic Policy The final goal of policy is to promote a proper *foreign economic policy*. This aim has become increasingly important as the nations of the globe have become more closely tied by international trade and finance.

All economies are open. They import and export goods and services; they borrow or lend money to foreigners; they imitate foreign technologies or sell their inventions abroad; their people travel to all parts of the world for business and pleasure. Declines in the costs of transportation and communication have made these international linkages even tighter than they were a generation ago. Some economies today trade over half their national output.

International economics involves trade between nations. The United States exports computers, grain,

aircraft, and a variety of other goods and services to other countries; it imports oil, VCRs, automobiles, cameras, and a host of other commodities. The difference between the dollar value of exports and the dollar value of imports is called **net exports.** In the 1980s, the United States moved from a net export balance (where exports and imports were approximately equal) to a tremendous negative net export position, with exports totaling only three-fourths of imports in 1987.

While foreign trade represents only a small fraction of our total GNP, the global economy exercises a disproportionate influence on our own living standards and economic life. Events abroad reverberate at home, and America's economic policies have profound impacts on Latin America, Japan, and Europe. Poor harvests in the Soviet Union caused an upturn in grain prices and triggered a major food-price inflation in the early 1970s in the United States. A rise in oil prices by oil-exporting countries twice raised inflation and unemployment in the United States. In the early 1980s, a sharp rise of interest rates in the United States sent shock waves through Latin American countries struggling to repay their foreign indebtedness.

Nations also keep a close eye on their **foreign exchange rates,** which represent the price of their own currency in terms of the currencies of other nations. The foreign exchange rate of the U.S. dollar rose from 1.7 German marks to the dollar in 1980 to 3.2 deutsche marks in 1985, and then fell sharply to 1.8 deutsche marks in 1988. When a nation's exchange rate rises, its exports become more expensive and therefore less competitive in world markets, causing exports to shrink relative to imports. By contrast, when a nation's exchange rate falls, import prices rise and the inflation rate therefore tends to increase. These and other impacts on the economy make the exchange rate increasingly important for all nations.

When net exports turn to deficit or surplus, or when the foreign exchange rate rises or falls sharply, countries move to correct the imbalance in their foreign economic relations. The most important recent case came for the United States in the 1980s. In the early part of the 1980s, the exchange rate on the dollar rose sharply and the U.S. economy grew more rapidly than did foreign economies. As a result, imports grew rapidly while exports stagnated, and the U.S. net exports moved from a balanced position in 1979 to a deficit of $110 billion in 1988. By the end of the 1980s, the foreign trade deficit had accumulated to the point where the United States had become the world's largest debtor nation.

■   ■   ■

We can summarize the objectives of macroeconomic policy as follows:

1. A high and rising level of real output

2. High employment and low unemployment, providing good jobs at high pay to those who want to work

3. A stable or gently rising price level, with prices and wages determined by free markets

4. Foreign economic relations marked by a stable foreign exchange rate and exports more or less balancing imports

Few nations succeed in meeting these objectives, but most advanced countries are continually searching for the means of attaining them more fully.

Instruments

Most advanced countries seek to attain some combination of the four sets of goals described above. But how can these goals be met? What policy measures are at hand for the nation wishing to improve its economic performance? We can find the answer to these questions in the instruments of macroeconomic policy.

Looking back to Table 5-1, we see on the right side the four major sets of instruments of macroeconomic policy. A *policy instrument* is an economic variable under the direct or indirect control of government; changes in policy instruments affect one or more of the macroeconomic objectives. That is to say, by changing monetary, fiscal, and other policies governments can steer the economy toward a better mix of output, price stability, employment, and foreign targets.

Fiscal Policy The first instrument of macroeconomic management is *fiscal policy,* which consists of setting the levels of taxation and expenditure to affect macroeconomic performance. Begin by considering *expenditures,* which means government spending on goods and services: purchases of tanks and pencils, building of dams and roads, salaries of judges and Army generals, and so forth. Federal expenditures are the instrument by which the government determines the relative size of the public and private sectors, that is, how much of our GNP is consumed collectively rather than privately. In addition, government expenditure affects the overall level of spending in the economy and can thereby affect the level of GNP.

The other half of fiscal policy is *taxation.* In macroeconomics, taxation plays two key roles. First, taxes reduce people's incomes. By leaving households with less spendable income, higher taxes tend to reduce their consumption spending, lowering aggregate demand and actual GNP.

In addition, taxes help determine the prices that businesses and individuals face in markets and thereby affect incentives and behavior. One important set of taxes are those affecting the cost of investing in capital goods. For example, the Tax Reform Act of 1986 contained a provision that made equipment relatively more expensive, thus discouraging businesses from investing in such goods. As a result, business investment, and real GNP itself, were relatively depressed in the period following removal of the investment tax credit. Many other provisions of the tax code have an important effect on economic activity.

A more complete analysis of how taxes and expenditures affect GNP will be given in the chapters that follow.

Monetary Policy The second major tool of macroeconomic policy is *monetary policy,* which comprises the management of a nation's money, credit, and banking system by the nation's central bank. You may have read how our central bank, the Federal Reserve, operates to affect the money supply. But what exactly is the money supply? **Money** consists of the means of exchange or method of payment in our economy: the currency and checking accounts that people use to pay their bills. By engaging in central-bank operations, the Federal Reserve can regulate the amount of money available to the economy.

Why does such a minor activity turn out to be of prime importance for macroeconomic activity? The point of supplying money is not to make profit for the Federal Reserve by turning trees into greenbacks. Rather, by speeding or slowing the growth of the money supply, the Federal Reserve makes interest rates lower or higher and induces or retards investment in houses, plant, equipment, and inventories. In periods of tight money, higher interest rates lead to falling GNP and to declining inflation.

The exact nature of monetary policy—the way that the central bank controls the money supply and the linkage between money, output, and inflation—is one of the most fascinating yet controversial areas of macroeconomics. A policy of tight money in the United States—lowering the rate of growth of the money supply—raised interest rates, slowed economic growth, and raised unemployment in the period 1979–1982. At the end of the period, the restrictive policy had succeeded in lowering the country's inflation rate. Exactly how did the Federal Reserve engineer the 1980–1982 recession? Was this policy well or ill-designed? These are issues to which we will turn in the chapters that follow on monetary policy.

The Foreign Connection As economies become more and more open, their policymakers devote increasing attention to managing their *foreign economic policies.* The major tools fall into two categories. First, nations can affect their trade by *trade policies.* These consist of tariffs, quotas, and other devices that restrict or encourage imports and exports. Most trade policies have little effect on macroeconomic performance, but from time to time, as was the case in the 1930s, the restrictions on trade are so severe as to cause major economic dislocations, inflations, or recessions.

A second set of policies specifically aimed toward the foreign sector is *exchange-market management.* There are a number of different systems whereby nations can regulate their foreign exchange markets. Some systems involve leaving exchange rates completely to the marketplace; others involve setting a fixed exchange rate vis à vis other currencies. The United States falls in between these extremes, allowing exchange rates to move with the market but occasionally intervening to nudge the dollar's exchange rate up or down.

In addition, central bankers and political leaders increasingly gather to *coordinate* their macroeconomic policies, for the monetary and fiscal policies of different countries spill over to affect their neighbors. It used to be said that "when America sneezes, Europe catches cold," suggesting the high degree of dependence of European economies on the United States. Since 1975, the heads of government of the major industrial countries have gathered each year at economic summit meetings to discuss joint economic issues and to take appropriate measures for attaining commonly agreed-upon goals. Such meetings, along with conferences of finance ministers and central bankers, led to attempts in 1986–1988 to stabilize the exchange rate of the dollar and to reduce trade imbalances among major countries.

Incomes Policies A final set of macroeconomic policies are **incomes policies,** more accurately denoted wage-price policies. When inflation threatens to get out of control, governments grope for ways to stabilize prices. The traditional route for slowing inflation has been for governments to take fiscal or monetary steps to slow economic activity and raise unemployment.

Macroeconomic studies over the last three decades indicate that this traditional strategy is very costly. It takes hundreds of billions of dollars in the GNP gap to reduce inflation by a few percentage points—a fact demonstrated as recently as the 1980–1986 period. Faced with the need to take such unpleasant medicine, governments have often searched for alternative methods of containing inflation. These alternatives ranged from wage and price controls (used particularly in wartime), to less drastic measures like voluntary wage and price guidelines, to public sermons by governments to persuade labor unions and large firms to moderate wage and price increases.

Incomes policies are the most controversial of all macroeconomic policies. A generation ago, many economists found them a worthwhile approach, and they were used in 1980 by the Carter administration. In the last decade, however, skepticism about their effectiveness along with a more conservative attitude toward government intervention has led to a general disenchantment with price-wage policies. Many economists believe they are simply ineffective. Others think they are worse than useless—that they interfere with free markets, gum up relative price movements, and fail to reduce inflation. In any case, with inflation having all but disappeared from the scene during the mid-1980s, the demand for incomes policies became virtually nonexistent.

Will price-wage policies reemerge if inflation reignites in the future? It is too early to tell, but it seems a good bet that they will. Some economists will argue that, like old age, incomes policies are better than the alternative—i.e., direct action on wages and prices is better than high unemployment. While this approach will remain controversial, we shall review its pros and cons in Chapter 15.

■   ■   ■

To summarize:

A nation has a wide variety of policy instruments that can be used to pursue its macroeconomic objectives. The major ones are these:

1. Fiscal policy consists of government expenditures and taxation. Government expenditures influence the relative size of collective as opposed to private consumption. Taxation subtracts from incomes and reduces private spending; in addition, it affects investment and potential output. Fiscal policy affects total spending and thereby influences actual real GNP and inflation, at least in the short run.

2. Monetary policy, operated by the central bank, sets the money supply. Changes in the money supply move interest rates up or down and affect spending on items like machinery or buildings. Monetary policy has an important effect on both actual GNP and potential GNP.

3. Foreign economic policies—trade policies, exchange-rate setting, or even monetary and fiscal policies—attempt to keep imports in line with exports and to stabilize foreign exchange rates. Governments increasingly meet to coordinate their macroeconomic objectives and policies.

4. Incomes policies are government actions that attempt to moderate inflation by direct steps, whether by verbal persuasion or by legislated wage and price controls. These policies have fallen out of favor in the low-inflation and conservative 1980s.

Macroeconomic Policies and Objectives in Practice

Earlier sections have surveyed the objectives and policies of macroeconomics. These issues must be faced by all governments in all countries. But exactly what policies have been chosen in the United States?

In the period before World War II, understanding of macroeconomics was primitive. Aside from familiar homilies like "balance the budget," there was nothing resembling a coherent theory for managing the economy.

The 1930s marked the first stirrings of the science of macroeconomics, initiated by the germinal contribution of John Maynard Keynes. After World War II, reflecting both the increasing influence of Keynesian views and fear of recurrence of a depression, the U.S. Congress formally proclaimed federal responsibility for macroeconomic performance. It enacted the landmark Employment Act of 1946, which stated:

> The Congress hereby declares that it is the continuing policy and responsibility of the federal government to use all practicable means consistent with its needs and obligations . . . to promote maximum employment, production, and purchasing power.

Note that three of the four objectives discussed above were formally included in the Employment Act.

At the same time that Congress set forth these lofty but somewhat vague goals, the Employment Act established a Council of Economic Advisers (or CEA) as a part of the presidential staff, to diagnose the health of the economy and prescribe appropriate remedies.[2]

In the middle 1970s, the poor performance of the American economy led Congress to reassess the 1946 act. As a result, Congress passed the 1978 Full Employment and Balanced Growth Act, more generally known after its two sponsors as the Humphrey-Hawkins Act. Not satisfied with the vague standards of the 1946 Employment Act, the new bill established quantitative goals—a 4 percent unemployment rate and an interim target of 3 percent inflation—as the nation's economic objectives.

By the mid-1980s, macroeconomic circumstances in the United States had shifted concern to gaping budget deficits. Because of large tax cuts and an extensive military buildup in the early 1980s, the federal budget deficit (equal to the difference between government expenditures and tax revenues) grew to over $200 billion. People became alarmed about the impact of large deficits on economic growth, and in re-

sponse Congress passed the Balanced Budget Act of 1985 (also known as the Gramm-Rudman Act after its chief sponsors).

According to the Act, the budget deficit was targeted to decline each year, aiming for a balanced budget by 1991 (this target was subsequently postponed). If the required decline in the deficit were not met, government expenditures would be cut automatically across-the-board. A balanced budget became the central objective of American macroeconomic policy during the late 1980s.

The goals of the Gramm-Rudman Act proved just as difficult to attain as those of the earlier Humphrey-Hawkins approach. Why has it proved so difficult to attain the goals of full employment with stable prices, or of a balanced budget with rapid economic growth?

The answer to these questions lies in the nature of the *constraints* and *tradeoffs* that face the macroeconomy. The production-possibility curve showed that we cannot have maximum guns and maximum butter, or high consumption today and high consumption tomorrow, or much private and collective consumption. You cannot eat your cake today and have it tomorrow.

There are, as well, tradeoffs in macroeconomics. Macroeconomics involves choice among alternative central objectives. A nation cannot simultaneously have high consumption and rapid growth. To lower a high inflation rate requires either a period of high unemployment and low output, or interfering with free markets through wage-price policies. These difficult choices are among those that must be faced by macroeconomic policymakers in every nation.

Of all the macroeconomic issues, the most agonizing is the difficulty of securing full employment of labor and other resources. Policymakers are constantly on the alert for an outbreak of inflation. As a result, they are generally unwilling to allow as much production and employment as many would desire. In effect, output and employment are restrained to prevent high or rising inflation. Such restraint can explain why unemployment stayed above 6 percent for most of the 1980s.

An example of how policymakers reacted to inflation by slowing economic growth came during the late 1970s and early 1980s. After the Iranian revolution in 1978, oil production fell and oil prices jumped

---

[2]In addition to advising the President, the major visible responsibility of the CEA is to prepare the *Economic Report of the President and the Council of Economic Advisers,* published annually along with the presidential budget. This document is required reading for macroeconomists for it contains a wealth of statistics and a diagnosis of current economic trends, along with analysis and defense of the administration's economic policies. Sometimes this dry document becomes controversial. In 1984, President Reagan's Secretary of the Treasury said that the report of President Reagan's CEA should be "thrown in the wastebasket."

from \$14 to \$34 per barrel. Inflation in the United States rose from 6 percent in 1977 to 14 percent in 1980.

Economic policymakers in the United States and abroad were frightened by the accelerating inflation. President Carter agonized: Should he slow the economy, allow unemployment to rise, stifle economic growth, and incur the wrath of labor unions and half the electorate? And all of this to slow inflation? Or should he introduce expansionary fiscal and monetary policies, risk igniting even greater inflation, and raise the hackles of the business community and the other half of the electorate? Carter opted for an economic slowdown and a rise in unemployment.

This same dilemma was faced by all industrial countries in the wake of the 1979 oil-price increase. Some, like Britain, opted for a deep recession. Others, like France, attempted to stimulate the economy.

But the lesson each country faced was identical:

Whether a leader is a Democrat or Republican in the United States, a conservative in Britain, or a socialist in France, a country cannot escape the short-run tradeoff between unemployment and inflation.

All have learned that in an economy where prices and wages are determined in free markets, a policy to reduce inflation must pay a high toll in high unemployment and large GNP gaps.

The converse of this dilemma is also true. If a nation wishes to enjoy the fruits of extremely low unemployment, with output far above its potential GNP, inflation will surely follow. As we will see in the second half of this chapter, when President Johnson pushed the economy far above its potential output in the 1960s, the nation reaped the whirlwind in a rising inflation rate.

Other macroeconomic dilemmas confront policymakers. A country can temporarily curb inflation by wage and price controls, but the result is distorted prices and economic inefficiency. To increase the rate of growth of potential GNP requires greater investment in knowledge and capital, but when a high-employment economy invests more, it enjoys less consumption, that is, less food, clothing, and recreation. These are the kinds of painful choices that macroeconomic policymakers in all industrial countries must face.

B. AGGREGATE SUPPLY AND DEMAND

The first part of this chapter provided an introduction to the major concepts and issues of macroeconomics. We now turn to an analysis of the forces determining aggregate output and the price level in a modern industrial economy. We begin with an overview of the macroeconomic mechanism, examining those variables which affect the macroeconomy. The next section introduces a simple analytical apparatus for understanding macroeconomic forces, the analysis of aggregate supply and demand. We then conclude with some applications of aggregate supply-and-demand analysis.

INSIDE THE MACROECONOMY: AGGREGATE SUPPLY AND DEMAND

We begin with a simple picture of the forces operating on the macroeconomy, shown in Figure 5-5. This fig-

ure shows on the left the major variables affecting the macroeconomic system. First are the instruments or policy variables discussed in the last section: taxes, monetary policy, and so forth. A second set of variables affecting the economy are *external* to the economy; that is, they influence economic activity but are for the most part unaffected by it. These variables include wars, the weather, population growth, and many other factors.

The policy and external variables interact in Figure 5-5 through the black box that we call the macroeconomy. These variables influence overall economic activity, including the goals or target variables that we discussed in the last section: output, employment and unemployment, prices, and net exports (recall especially Table 5-1). To state the matter in another way, policy and external variables are inputs to the macroeconomy, while targets are the outputs of the macroeconomy.

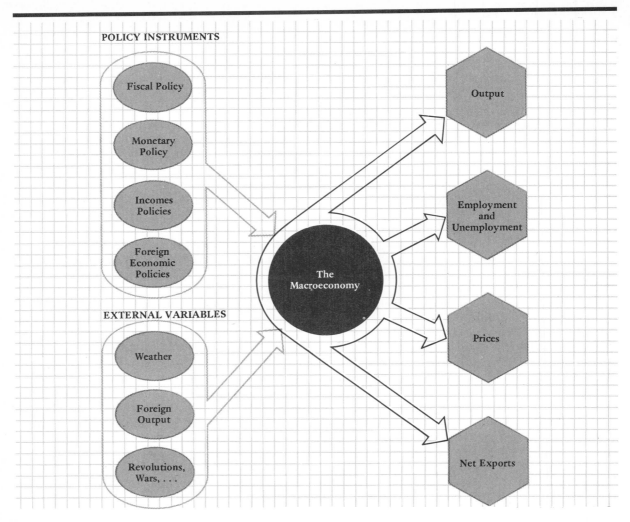

Figure 5-5 Major variables affecting the macroeconomy
Policy variables (such as monetary or fiscal policy) along with external variables (those outside the control of economic forces, like wars or the weather) interact in the macroeconomy to determine output, prices, employment, and net exports.

These distinctions apply equally well to the microeconomic supply-and-demand analysis of Chapter 4. If we were analyzing the supply and demand for wheat, the external variables would be the weather (affecting the supply curve) along with tastes (affecting the demand curve). We might also consider the impact of policies, such as to provide aid to drought-stricken farmers. The outcomes or targets are the price and quantity of wheat sold in a given period.

Definitions of Aggregate Supply and Demand

With this overview of the forces operating on the macroeconomy, we can now sketch in a preliminary way how they operate. Figure 5-6 is the key diagram for understanding the interaction of these forces. It expands Figure 5-5 by showing the relationship among the different variables inside the macroeconomy.

The new diagram in Figure 5-6 organizes the policy and external variables into two categories: those affecting aggregate supply and those affecting aggregate demand. The division of variables into these two categories will be essential to understanding what determines the level of output, prices, and unemployment in both the long and the short run. In the balance of this chapter, we will define and analyze the twin concepts of aggregate supply and demand.

Aggregate Supply Begin by examining the lower part of Figure 5-6, which shows the forces affecting aggregate supply. **Aggregate supply** refers to the amount of total national output that businesses willingly produce and sell in a given period. Aggregate supply (often written *AS*) depends upon the price level, upon businesses' productive capacity, and upon the level of costs.

In general, businesses would like to sell all they can produce at high prices. However, in certain circumstances, prices and spending levels may be depressed, so businesses might sell less than their capacity or potential output. In other circumstances, such as wartime booms, businesses might for a time produce above their sustainable potential output.

We see, then, that aggregate supply is closely linked to the nation's capacity or potential output. But what determines potential output and aggregate sup-

ply? As shown in the bottom left of Figure 5-6, aggregate supply is determined by the amount of productive inputs (labor and capital being the most important) and the efficiency with which those inputs are combined (that is, the technology of the society). We will inquire further into the determinants of potential output and aggregate supply in Chapter 10.

Aggregate Demand The other half of the mechanism determining overall output, employment, and prices is the set of forces affecting aggregate demand. **Aggregate demand** refers to the total or aggregate quantity of output that consumers, businesses, foreigners, and governments willingly spend in a given period. Aggregate demand (often written *AD*) depends upon the level of prices and incomes, as well as upon policy variables such as monetary and fiscal policy.

In other words, aggregate demand measures total spending by all the different entities in the economy—on cars, food, and other consumption goods bought by consumers; on plant and equipment bought by businesses; on tanks, weather forecasters, and computers bought by government; and on net exports bought by other countries. The total purchases are affected by the prices at which the goods are offered, by people's incomes, by financial conditions and expectations about the future, and by foreign economic conditions, as well as by government policies in the monetary and fiscal arenas.

Macroeconomic Equilibrium The overall outcome or equilibrium for the macroeconomy is determined by the interaction of aggregate supply and demand. That is, national output, the price level, and total employment will settle at levels that reflect the quantities that businesses willingly sell to willing buyers. We must remember, however, that important background forces of labor supply, capital stock, technology, and monetary and fiscal policies lie behind aggregate supply or demand. The interaction of *AS* (chiefly driven by potential GNP) and *AD* (driven by spending and its determinants) produces the outcomes we are analyzing: the level of actual GNP, the number of jobs and the unemployment rate, prices, and thus the rate of inflation.

Figure 5-6 may look complicated, but it has actu-

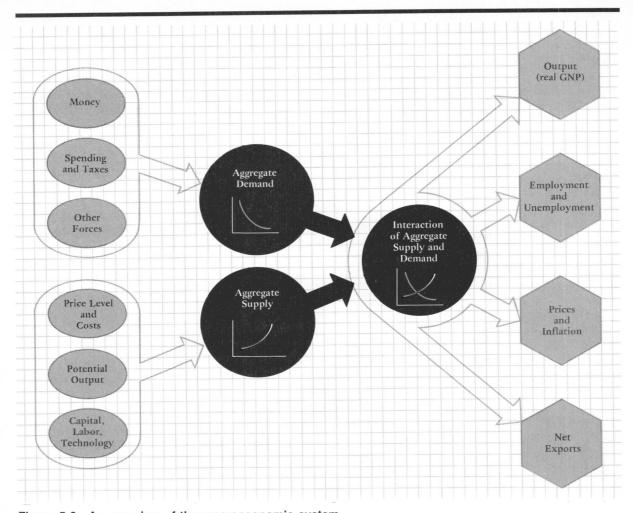

Figure 5-6   An overview of the macroeconomic system

This diagram shows the major elements affecting the macroeconomy. On the left are the major variables determining aggregate supply and demand: policy variables like monetary and fiscal policy along with stocks of capital and labor. As highlighted in color at the center of the figure, aggregate supply and demand interact as the level of demand beats upon the available resources. The chief outcomes are shown on the right in hexagons: output, employment, prices, and net exports.

The purpose of macroeconomic analysis is to understand the forces behind this diagram, which we will meet repeatedly in the next 12 chapters.

ally oversimplified reality somewhat. One of the outcomes on the right is the level of investment in plant and equipment (which is part of GNP). Investment adds to the capital stock. As the economy accumulates capital, workers have more and better tools to work with, and the level of potential output rises. Hence, we might draw a thin line from output (real GNP) back to capital.

Nor is this the only influence of output back to the forces affecting aggregate supply. Education, research and development, depletion of subsoil minerals and fuels—each of these leaves a smaller or larger stock of useful capital assets for the future. In such ways does the interaction of *AS* and *AD* feed back to influence the economy's aggregate supply.

Aggregate Supply and Demand Curves

We can deepen our understanding of macroeconomic equilibrium with the help of a familiar set of tools: supply and demand curves. Recall that in Chapter 4 we introduced the notion of market supply and demand curves and used that apparatus to analyze the prices and quantities of individual products. We applied this tool to the wheat market, the oil market, and the real estate market.

This graphical apparatus can also help us understand major macroeconomic issues of output determination, inflation, and stagflation. Using aggregate supply and demand, we can see how monetary expansion leads to rising prices and higher output. We can also see why increases in efficiency may lead to higher output and to a *lower* overall price level. Moreover, this analysis will show why a tax cut might lead to an expansion of output and employment in the short run, while higher spending may end up only raising prices and leaving output unaffected in the long run.

Figure 5-7 shows the aggregate supply and demand schedules for the output of an entire economy. On the horizontal, or quantity, axis is the total output (real GNP) of the economy. On the vertical axis is the overall price level (say, as measured by the CPI).

The downward-sloping black curve is the **aggregate demand schedule,** or *AD* curve. It represents

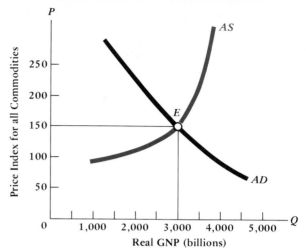

AGGREGATE SUPPLY AND DEMAND CURVES

Figure 5-7   Aggregate price and output are determined by the interaction of aggregate supply and demand

National output and the overall price level are determined at the intersection of the aggregate demand and supply curves.

The *AD* curve represents the quantity of total spending at different price levels. The *AS* curve shows what firms will produce and sell at different price levels.

At point *E* lies the macroeconomic equilibrium; this occurs at an overall price level where firms willingly produce and sell an output of *Q* = 3000, and spenders willingly buy just that amount.

what all the entities in the economy—consumers, businesses, foreigners, and governments—would buy at different aggregate price levels.

The upward-sloping red curve in Figure 5-7 is the **aggregate supply schedule,** or *AS* **curve.** This curve represents the relationship between the prices businesses will charge and the volume of output they produce and sell. Thus as the level of total output demanded rises, businesses as a whole will charge higher prices: along the *AS* curve, overall *P* rises as real output *Q* rises.

Combining *AS* and *AD,* we can also find the *equilibrium values of price and quantity;* that is, we find

AGGREGATE SUPPLY IN THE LONG AND SHORT RUN

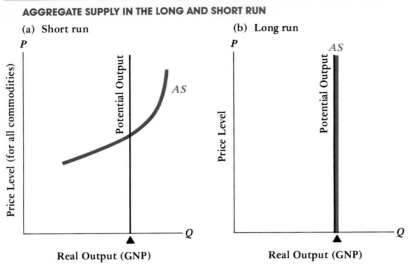

Figure 5-8 _AS_ may slope gently upward in the short run but tends to be vertical in the long run

The short-run _AS_ curve on the left slopes up gently for low levels of output. Why? Because in the short run many of a firm's costs are inflexible: wage rates, rents, and similar contractual commitments provide some fixity to firm's costs. An increase in _AD,_ therefore, leads firms to raise output but also to raise their prices somewhat.

The _AS_ curve on the right shows the shape of the curve in the very long run. Because all input and output prices are flexible in the long run, the aggregate supply curve is vertical. Firms will supply the same level of output, namely potential output, no matter what the price level and no matter what the level of aggregate demand.

the real GNP and the associated price level that would satisfy both buyers and sellers. Given the forces determining _AS_ and _AD_ in Figure 5-7, the overall economy is in equilibrium at point _E_. Only at that point, where the level of output is _Q_ = 3000 and _P_ = 150, are spenders and sellers content. Only at point _E_ is the overall price level such that buyers are willing to buy exactly what sellers are willing to produce and sell.

Slopes of _AS_ and _AD_ Curves Why do the curves have the pictured slopes in Figure 5-7? Start with the _AD_ curve. It slopes downward, indicating that the volume of spending increases as the overall price level falls. The reason for this lies in the consumption spending of households. As the dollar price of things I buy falls, my dollar income enables me to buy more

units of food, clothing, or books. For example, if the CPI falls 5 percent, my income and wealth are unlikely to fall 5 percent as well: my wage may be set for 1 to 3 years, and the dollar value of my money holdings won't fall at all. Since my real purchasing power increases, my real consumption spending is likely to rise. Even after the lower price level begins to undermine my income (through lower wages), I find the value of my dollar wealth (cash, bonds, bank accounts) does not shrink as much as the price level does. Thus a lower overall price level leads to higher real consumption and higher total demand—i.e., the _AD_ curve slopes down.

Must the _AS_ curve slope upward? Actually, as we will see in the coming chapters, the exact shape of the aggregate supply schedule is intensely debated among macroeconomists today. Most economists agree that in the very long run the *AS* curve is vertical. But in the short and medium runs, the *AS* curve slopes upward from southwest to northeast. Let's analyze more carefully, then, the way aggregate supply relates to prices.[3]

Long-Run vs. Short-Run Aggregate Supply

The major controversies about modern macroeconomics today swirl around the determination and shape of aggregate supply. Some economists, particularly those adhering to the Keynesian approach, believe that the *AS* curve is relatively flat; others, especially those who argue for the classical approach, hold that the *AS* curve is relatively steep or even vertical.

Figure 5-8 depicts two *AS* curves. On the left is one that is relatively flat, particularly at low levels of output. This relatively flat *AS* curve would pertain to the short run; that is, it would show the relationship between the price level and output for a period of a year or two. For the short run, firms are willing to increase their output levels in response to a higher price level. In other words, as the level of aggregate demand rises, firms are willing to supply more and more output if they can also increase their prices as output rises.

Why do firms raise both prices and output in the short run as aggregate demand increases? Because they have certain costs that are fixed in the short run, it is profitable to raise prices and sell extra output as aggregate demand increases. Let us see why.

Suppose that a burst of extra spending occurs. Firms know that in the short run many of their costs are fixed in dollar terms—workers are paid $15 per hour, rent is $1500 per month, and so forth. If firms can successfully raise their prices in response to the extra burst of spending, they will also find it profitable to increase their output. Hence, in the short run,

before wages and rents and other dollar-fixed costs have adjusted, firms will rationally react to aggregate demand increases by raising both prices and output. This positive association between prices and output is seen in the upward-sloping *AS* curve.

As an aside, we note that the most important of these temporarily fixed costs is wage rates. Many firms, covering almost one-half of manufacturing workers, have long-term agreements with labor unions. These agreements generally extend for 3 years and specify a dollar wage rate (with partial adjustment for price changes). Thus for the life of the labor contract, the wage rates facing firms are partially fixed in dollar terms. When consumers or businesses demand more cars or trucks or other goods in the short run, firms react by raising prices, earning higher profits, and producing more output.

Once we appreciate why the *AS* curve may slope gently upward in the short run, we can begin to understand why it is likely to be vertical or near-vertical in the long run. As the inflexible or "sticky" elements of cost—wage contracts or rent agreements, for example—expire and are renegotiated, wages, rents, and other costs begin to adjust to the higher prices. If the price *(P)* in Figure 5-8(a) moves up 10 percent because of the higher demand, then money wages will eventually move up 10 percent as well. As a result, the firm will in the long run be unable to profit from the higher level of aggregate demand. As costs move up to meet prices, the level of output will come back to its long-run equilibrium level at potential output. Therefore, output may increase in response to higher aggregate demand for a while, but in the long run, as costs rise proportionally with prices, output will come back to its long-run equilibrium level.

The right-hand panel of Figure 5-8 illustrates the long-run response of aggregate supply to different price levels. We see there that the long-run *AS* curve is drawn as a vertical line at a level of real output equal to potential output. The long-run *AS* curve is vertical because, given sufficient time, all costs adjust. Firms cannot take advantage of fixed money wage rates in their labor agreements forever: after a time, labor will recognize that prices have risen. Workers will insist on compensating increases in wages. Eventually, after all elements of cost have fully adjusted, firms will face the same ratio of price

---

[3]Care must be taken not to confuse the reasons behind the slopes of macro *AD* or *AS* curves with the reasons behind micro *DD* or *SS* curves. Chapters 4, 18, 19, and 23 show that the slopes of micro curves relate to diminishing marginal utility (for *DD*) or diminishing returns (for *SS*). The slope of macro curves rests on the fixity of costs or the presence of dollar-fixed assets.

to costs as in the initial state, and there will no longer be any incentive for the firms to increase their output. Thus, the long-run *AS* curve is vertical.

Output in the Short and Long Run

The shape of the *AS* curve has an implication that is absolutely critical to understanding certain important controversies in modern macroeconomics. Numerous empirical studies confirm that the *AS* curve is relatively flat for a year or two, as pictured in Figure 5-8(*a*). On the other hand, for periods of a decade or more, the *AS* curve tends to be nearly vertical, as shown in Figure 5-8(*b*). This difference in behavior is key to understanding the determinants of real output. It suggests that, as long as output is at or below potential, changes in spending can have a significant effect upon output; as demand changes sweep back and forth on a relatively flat *AS* curve, output tends to decrease and increase.

In the longer run, however, aggregate demand becomes less important for real output. If the *AS* curve is vertical, output is solely determined by the level of potential output; *AD* changes affect the price level but not the level of real output.

Aggregate demand has a significant impact upon movements of real output in the short run. In the long run, however, real output is determined chiefly by potential output, and aggregate demand affects mainly the level of prices.

This completes our introduction to the analysis of aggregate supply and demand. However, before we proceed to examine some applications of aggregate supply-and-demand analysis, one word of caution is in order. We must take care not to confuse this set of curves with the market supply and demand curves of microeconomics, such as those discussed in Chapter 4. Aggregate supply and demand refer to the determination of output and price for the entire economy; market supply and demand refer to the equilibrium for one small part of the economy. The difference can be seen on the axes of the diagrams. The wheat supply-and-demand diagram has bushels of wheat and the price of wheat on the axes; by contrast, the *AS* and *AD* diagrams have the national output and the overall price level on the axes. Keep these different approaches clearly distinct in your mind as you move

into the exciting world of macroeconomics in the pages that follow.

AGGREGATE SUPPLY AND DEMAND AT WORK

We can use the tools of aggregate supply and demand to understand some of the major events of post–World War II American history—the Vietnam war boom, the stagflation of the 1970s, and the deep recession of the early 1980s.

Vietnam War Boom The American economy experienced a period of unprecedented recovery and prosperity during the early 1960s. GNP grew 4 percent annually, unemployment declined, and inflation was virtually absent.

What forces lay behind this vigorous expansion? During this period, macroeconomic policymakers took fiscal measures to stimulate the economy by increasing aggregate demand. In 1964 and 1965, personal and corporate taxes were cut sharply. By 1965, the economy was at its potential output.

Unfortunately, the administration underestimated the size of the buildup for the Vietnam war; defense spending grew by 55 percent from 1965 to 1968. Even when it became clear that a major inflationary boom was underway, President Johnson refused to take painful fiscal steps to slow the economy—tax increases and civilian expenditure cuts came only in 1968, too late to prevent overheating. The Federal Reserve allowed rapid money growth and low interest rates to prevail. As a result, for much of the period 1966–1970, the economy operated far above its potential output.

Figure 5-9 illustrates the events of this period. The tax cut and defense expenditures increased aggregate demand, shifting the *AD* curve to the right from *AD* to *AD'*. The equilibrium moved from *E* to *E'*. Output and employment rose sharply, but prices began to creep upward as output bumped capacity limits.

The lesson of this episode is that increasing aggregate demand produces a harvest of higher output and employment, but if expansion takes the economy well beyond potential output, an overheated economy and price inflation will soon follow.

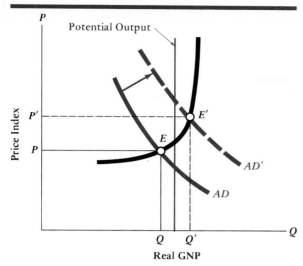

Figure 5-9 Vietnam war boom

This figure illustrates the overheating of the economy that occurred in the late 1960s. The economy was close to potential output in 1964. As a result of the 1964 tax cut and the Vietnam war buildup, aggregate demand moved from *AD* to *AD'*, with the equilibrium moving from *E* in 1964 to *E'* in 1969. Output moved far above potential output, and the price level moved up sharply from *P* to *P'*. Thus output increased and prices rose.

Supply-Side Inflation Another important macroeconomic phenomenon, known as a supply shock, was seen during the 1970s. A **supply shock** refers to a sudden change in conditions of cost or productivity that has a discontinuous impact upon aggregate supply. Supply shocks occurred with particular virulence in 1973, called the "year of the seven plagues," which included crop failures, shifting ocean currents, massive speculation on world commodity markets, turmoil in foreign exchange markets, and a quadrupling of the price of OPEC crude oil. An "end-of-the-world" mentality arose, with the cover of a popular magazine showing an empty cornucopia entitled "Running Out of Everything?".

This jolt to crude material and fuel supplies showed up dramatically in their prices. The prices of crude materials and fuels rose more from 1972 to 1973 than they had in the entire period from the end of World War II to 1972.

This sudden rise in the cost of raw materials constituted a supply shock. We can depict it as a sharp upward shift in the aggregate supply curve; to coax the same level of output from businesses would require them to charge substantially higher prices. This is illustrated in Figure 5-10, where the *AS* curve moves up from *AS* to *AS'*.

The results of a supply shock are striking:

A supply shock, seen as a sharp upward shift in the *AS* curve, results in higher prices along with a decline in output. Supply shocks thus lead to a deterioration of all the major goals of macroeconomic policy.

Tight Money, 1979–1982 By 1979 the economy had recovered from the 1973 supply shock. Output had returned to its potential. Just when inflation had slowed, however, another round of oil-price increases contributed to an accelerating two-digit inflation rate—

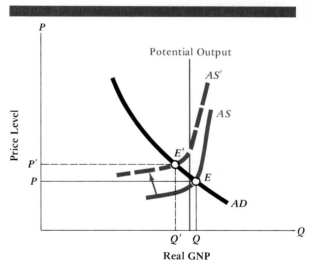

Figure 5-10 Effects of supply shocks

The effect of sharply higher oil, commodity, or labor costs was to increase the costs of doing business. This led to stagflation—stagnation combined with inflation.

As a result of the higher costs of oil and other inputs, businesses charged more for their products. The *AS* curve shifted up from *AS* to *AS'* and the equilibrium shifted from *E* in 1973 to *E'* in 1975. Output declined from *Q* to *Q'*, while prices rose. The economy thus suffered a double whammy—lower output *and* higher prices. A similar pattern followed the second oil-price increase of 1979.

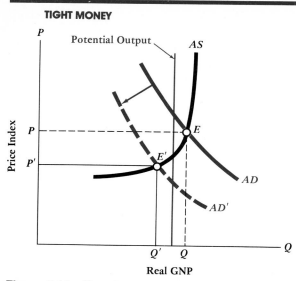

TIGHT MONEY

Figure 5-11 Monetary restraint reduces output and inflation

From 1979 to 1982, the Federal Reserve slowed growth in money and credit, reducing aggregate demand, and producing a sharp downturn in economic activity. As a result, wage and price inflation slowed to a crawl for the rest of the 1980s.

averaging 12 percent per year for 1979–1980. Such a rate was regarded as unacceptably high by political leaders of both the left and the right.

Faced by an unacceptable inflation rate, policy-makers took steps to slow economic growth and raise unemployment. The slowdown began when Paul Volcker, former chairman of the Federal Reserve Board, used monetary policy to raise interest rates in 1979 (these steps constitute "tight money"). After Ronald Reagan took office in 1981, his administration encouraged the tight-money policies.

What was the impact? The higher interest rates led to a slowdown in spending on interest-sensitive components of aggregate demand. After 1979, we saw declines in housing construction, automobile purchases, business investment, and so forth.

Figure 5-11 pictures the impact of monetary restraint on the economy. Tight money raised interest

rates and reduced aggregate demand. This can be seen as a downward shift of the aggregate demand curve—exactly the opposite of the impact of the defense buildup during the 1960s. The decrease in aggregate demand reduced output almost 10 percent below its potential by the end of 1982, and the unemployment rate rose from below 6 percent in 1979 to over 10 percent at the end of 1982. What was the reward for these austere measures? Inflation declined from an average of 12 percent per year in the 1979–1980 period to 4 percent during the period from 1983 to 1988. High unemployment succeeded in wringing inflation out of the economy.

Economic Policy

Our brief review of modern economic history highlights some of the crucial forces that impinge upon the macroeconomy. Some of the forces operate on the spending side, changing aggregate demand because of changes in consumer preferences or military expenditures. Other disturbances arise on the supply side, as when a revolution leads to a doubling of oil prices or when bad harvests lead to major food-price increases.

The major task of macroeconomic policy today is to diagnose the different ailments affecting aggregate supply and demand and to prescribe the appropriate policies. In some cases, policymakers face no dilemmas. If the economy is operating at potential output, and if the President signs an accord with the Soviet Union leading to deep cuts in military spending, then the diagnosis is straightforward. The military cuts would tend to decrease aggregate demand; most economists would agree that economic policy should respond by taking measures to offset the spending cut—using monetary or fiscal policy to increase aggregate demand.

Other kinds of shocks pose more difficult policy questions, and in some cases these seem to be irreconcilable dilemmas. What would be the appropriate response if global weather patterns in 1988 produced a terrible drought, sending food prices sky-high? As aggregate supply contracted (in a manner shown in Figure 5-10), should policymakers "accommodate" the price rise by increasing aggregate demand to pre-

THE ROAD AHEAD

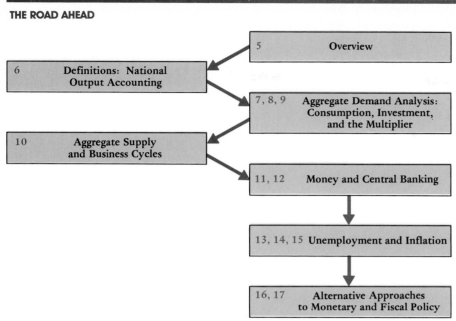

Figure 5-12   Road map to the macroeconomic chapters

This chart shows the road that we will follow in the survey of macroeconomics that follows. We begin with definitions of major concepts and an analysis of the determinants of aggregate demand; examine aggregate supply and business cycles; analyze monetary economics; move on to unemployment and inflation; and finish with a study of the major alternative approaches to macroeconomic policy.

vent any output loss? Or should economic policy be "nonaccommodative," contracting aggregate demand to prevent any increase in the overall price level? An accommodative policy will lead to high inflation and low unemployment; a nonaccommodative approach will produce an economic downturn and high unemployment while preventing rising prices.

Which approach is the correct one? Economics can provide no scientifically correct answer to such questions, for they are *normative* issues involving dilemmas of social and political values. But economics can strive to answer *positive* questions, providing quantitative estimates of the gains and losses from inflation and unemployment associated with different policy approaches. Then the political leaders must make the ultimate choices.

The Road Ahead

Having gained an overview of the policies and objectives of macroeconomics, along with a preview of the elements of aggregate supply and demand, we turn in the following chapters to a detailed discussion. Figure 5-12 provides a road map of the terrain in the pages ahead of us. Here is the plan.

We begin with a close look at the measurement of national output and income (Chapter 6). The next three chapters (7 through 9) introduce the basic elements which determine aggregate demand— including the demand for investment and consumption along with Keynesian and classical theories. Chapter 10 examines the determinants of aggregate supply, along with modern supply-side economics.

The next five chapters analyze money, unemployment, and inflation. We introduce money in Chapters 11 and 12, which show why households hold money and how the Federal Reserve controls the money supply. Once money is understood, we turn to an analysis of the policy issues of unemployment and inflation in Chapters 13 through 15.

The final two chapters on macroeconomics turn to the major policy issues of today: the way that money affects the economy, the use of fiscal policy to stabilize the economy, the stubborn fiscal deficits that have plagued the American economy in the 1980s, and alternative approaches to macroeconomics. The concluding chapters will help to explain why macroeconomics is both the most exciting and the most controversial area of economics today.

SUMMARY _____

A. Macroeconomic Concepts and Goals

1. This chapter begins the study of macroeconomics—the study of broad aggregates of economic life: total output, overall unemployment and inflation, the money supply and the budget deficit. This contrasts with microeconomics, which studies the behavior of individual markets, prices, and outputs.

2. The major objectives of a macroeconomy are:

(a) High level and rapid growth of output and consumption. Output is usually measured by the gross national product, which is the total value of all goods and services produced in a given year. Also, GNP should be high relative to potential GNP, the maximum sustainable or high-employment level of output.

(b) High employment and low involuntary unemployment.

(c) Price-level stability (or low inflation), through prices and wages set in free markets.

(d) Foreign balance, where exports roughly balance imports and the nation has a stable exchange rate against foreign currencies.

3. Before the science of macroeconomics was developed, countries tended to drift around in the shifting macroeconomic currents without a rudder. Today, there are numerous instruments that can be used by governments to steer the economy:

(a) Fiscal policy (government spending and taxation) helps determine the allocation of resources between private and collective goods, affects people's incomes and consumption, and provides incentives for investment and many important factor-supply decisions.

(b) Monetary policy (particularly influencing interest rates and credit conditions through setting the money supply) affects sectors in the economy that are interest-sensitive. The most important are housing and business investment—which move up and down as the nation's central bank moves interest rates down and up.

(c) Depending on external circumstances, nations may take steps to affect their foreign trade and commerce—they can restrict imports through tariffs and quotas, and they can affect their foreign exchange rate by a fixed rate system or by buying or selling currencies.

(d) Incomes policies (government programs that directly affect wage and price decisions) attempt to control inflation without incurring the high costs of recessions and unemployment. Their past successes in peacetime have been modest and they have fallen from favor in recent years.

4. The United States has developed legislative macroeconomic objectives only since World War II. The Employment Act of 1946 declared a federal policy "to promote maximum employment, production, and purchasing power." An attempt to make this more precise in 1978 has had little effect on economic policy. The 1985 Balanced Budget (or Gramm-Rudman) Act elevated deficit reduction to a paramount status, mandating a gradual reduction of deficits toward a balanced-budget goal in 1991.

5. The United States, along with other industrial countries, was dogged by stagflation (stagnation plus inflation) during most of the 1970s and 1980s. No major industrial country has achieved the twin goals of price stability and low unemployment since the 1960s. This poor performance reflects the existence of tradeoffs in macroeconomics, ones much like the tradeoff shown by the production-possibility frontier in Chapter 2. The central tradeoff in the short run is that no nation has for long experienced full employment, low inflation, and free markets.

B. Aggregate Supply and Demand

6. The central concepts for understanding macroeconomic forces are aggregate supply *(AS)* and aggregate demand *(AD)*. Aggregate demand is composed of the total spending in an economy by households, businesses, governments, and foreigners. It represents the total real output that would be bought at each price level. Aggregate supply describes how much real GNP businesses would produce and sell given prices, costs, and market conditions.

7. *AS* and *AD* curves have the same shapes as the familiar microeconomic supply and demand curves analyzed in Chapter 4—although the reasons behind the slopes are different here. Aggregate demand slopes down in part because consumers are able to stretch their dollar incomes and wealth further at a lower price level. Similarly, *AS* slopes up in the short run because businesses face some dollar-fixed costs (such as those in wage contracts); in such a circumstance, firms will both produce more goods and raise prices somewhat as demand increases. They can make a higher profit at higher goods prices and are thus willing to produce more.

8. The overall macroeconomic equilibrium, determining both aggregate price and output, comes where the *AS* and *AD* curves intersect. In the short run (for all but very high output levels), the *AS* curve slopes gently upward, so the level of real output is primarily determined by where the *AD* curve cuts the upward-sloping *AS* curve. In the long run, the *AS* curve turns vertical. This reflects the fact that in the long run all costs are variable, so wages and other costs will soon follow up output prices. Because long-run *AS* is vertical at potential output, the long-run level of potential output determines the level of output. This result arises from the intersection of a downward-sloping *AD* curve with a vertical *AS* curve.

9. Recent American experience provides important applications of the *AS-AD* apparatus:

   (a) In the mid-1960s, Vietnam war–bloated deficits plus easy money led to a rapid outward shift in the *AD* curve. The result was a sharp upturn in prices and inflation.

(b) In the early 1970s, a series of adverse supply shocks led to an upward movement in the *AS* curve. This led to a reduction of output along with an increase in prices and inflation.

(c) At the end of the 1970s, economic policymakers induced a sharp recession to reduce inflation. Tight money shifted the *AD* curve to the left—pursuing the opposite policies from those taken during the Vietnam war. The stagnation of the early 1980s led to a sharp reduction in inflation along with high unemployment.

CONCEPTS FOR REVIEW

macroeconomics vs. microeconomics
gross national product (GNP), actual
  and potential
employment, unemployment
consumer price index (CPI)
inflation, deflation
incomes policy
net exports

fiscal policy (expenditures, taxation)
money, monetary policy
aggregate supply, aggregate demand
AS curve, *AD* curve
why *AD* slopes down; why *AS* slopes
  up
long-run vs. short-run *AS* slope

QUESTIONS FOR DISCUSSION

1. What are the major objectives for macroeconomic performance? Write a brief definition of each of the major objectives. Describe why each of the major objectives is thought to be important.

2. If a nation desires to have stable prices (or low inflation), why might it be undesirable simply to decree that all prices should be immutably fixed by law? (HINT: Recall the importance of the price mechanism for economic efficiency.)

3. If the CPI were 300 in 1990 and 315 in 1991, what is the inflation rate for 1991?

4. What would be the effect of each of the following on aggregate demand or on aggregate supply, as indicated:

    (a) A large oil-price increase (on *AS*)?
    (b) An arms-reduction agreement reducing defense spending (on *AD*)?
    (c) A severe drought (on *AS*)?
    (d) A monetary loosening that lowers interest rates (on *AD*)?

5. For each of the events listed in question 4, use the *AS-AD* apparatus to show the effect on output and on the overall price level.

6. Using the *AS-AD* curves, explain the following statement: "In the short run, pumping up spending and demand will lead to higher output and employment, along with higher prices. But in the long run, it is not possible to keep output sustainably above potential output."

7. Why does the *AD* curve slope downward? Why is the *AS* curve not vertical in the short run in an economy like that of the United States? How might the short-run *AS* curve appear in an economy where all goods and services were sold on "auction markets"—i.e., where prices were set so that supply and demand were always in balance?

8. Put yourself in the shoes of an economic policymaker. The economy is in equilibrium with $P = 100$ and $Q = 3000 =$ potential GNP. You are absolutely "nonaccommodative" about inflation; i.e., you want to keep prices absolutely stable at $P = 100$, no matter what happens to output. Finally, you have instruments at your control to affect aggregate demand but you cannot affect aggregate supply.

   Given these tools and objectives, how would you respond to:
   (a) A surprise increase in investment spending?
   (b) A sharp food price increase following a major drought?
   (c) A productivity decline that decreases potential output?
   (d) An agreement to cut conventional military forces and associated expenditures by 20 percent?
   (e) A sharp increase in net exports that followed a fall in the dollar's foreign exchange rate?

9. In 1982–1983, the Reagan administration reduced taxes and increased government spending. Explain why this policy would tend to increase aggregate demand. What effect would this policy have upon output and prices in the short run? In the long run?

CHAPTER 6
MEASUREMENT OF NATIONAL OUTPUT AND INCOME

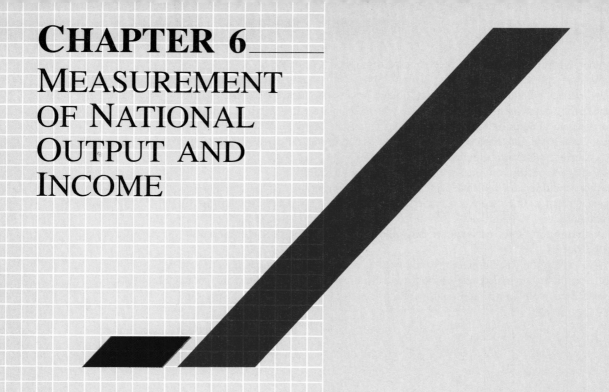

When you can measure what you are speaking about, and express it in numbers, you know something about it; when you cannot measure it, when you cannot express it in numbers, your knowledge is of a meager and unsatisfactory kind; it may be the beginning of knowledge, but you have scarcely, in your thoughts, advanced to the stage of science.

Lord Kelvin

MACROECONOMICS is the study of the behavior of the entire economy—of national output and income, the overall price level, unemployment, foreign trade, and so forth. But modern economics, like all empirical sciences, concerns not only abstract concepts. It involves items that can actually be measured by statisticians: prices of wheat, quantities of automobiles, number of unemployed people, national output, or the price level.

To begin our study of macroeconomics, we undertake a detailed investigation of exactly how the major macroeconomic variables are measured. This chapter focuses on one of the most important concepts in all economics, the gross national product (or GNP), which measures the total dollar value of the national output. With this measure we can calculate the overall economic performance of an entire economy.

Measuring national output is indispensable for macroeconomic theory and policy. It prepares us for tackling the central issues concerning the economic growth of nations, the business cycle, the relationship between economic activity and unemployment, along with the measurement and determinants of inflation.

Before the concept of GNP was invented, it was difficult to know whether the economy was healthy or sick, or whether its health was improving or deteriorating. Without the detailed GNP accounts that this chapter analyzes, Chapters 5 through 17 in this book would have far less to talk about. The world is indebted to people like Harvard's Simon Kuznets, recipient of the Nobel Prize for his pathbreaking work on GNP measurement. Although the discovery of the GNP has no patent and is not displayed in the Museum of Science and Technology, it is truly one of the great inventions of the twentieth century. Without measures of economic aggregates like GNP, macroeconomics would be adrift in a sea of unorganized data.

Today, there is much talk about the "underground economy," which denotes that part of economic activity that is unrecorded, informal, or illegal and which generally does not bear its share of society's taxes. Using national income accounts, economists can estimate the size of the underground economy so that Congress can take appropriate measures to tax or otherwise regulate the hidden economy.

Of course, we do not live by bread alone. Nor does society live on GNP alone. These days, we are increasingly concerned lest material growth be gained at the expense of the quality of life and the quality of the environment. People wonder whether, in producing more electricity and cars, we are also generating more acid rain and polluted air. To answer this question, we must devise ways of correcting and converting the GNP concept into a more adequate measure of economic activity—hence the concept of *net economic welfare,* or *NEW.*

In sum, the purpose of this chapter is to help us understand the exact meaning of central macroeconomic concepts, after which we will proceed to study how output, prices, and employment are determined.

GROSS NATIONAL PRODUCT: THE YARDSTICK OF AN ECONOMY'S PERFORMANCE

What is the **gross national product**? It is the name we give to the total dollar value of the goods and services produced by a nation during a given year. It is the figure you arrive at when you apply the measuring rod of money to the diverse goods and services—from apples to zithers, from battleships to machine tools—that a country produces with its land, labor, and capital resources. It equals the sum of the money values of all consumption and investment goods, government purchases, and net exports to other lands.

GNP is used for many purposes, but the most important one is that it measures the overall performance of an economy. If you ask an economic historian just what happened during the Great Depression, his best short answer would be:

> From a 1929 GNP of $104 billion, there was a drop to 1933 GNP of $56 billion. This near-halving of the money value of the flow of goods and services in the American economy caused hardship, bankruptcies, bank failures, riots, and political turmoil.

The gross national product (or GNP) is the most comprehensive measure of a nation's total output of goods and services. It is the sum of the dollar values of consumption, investment, government purchases of goods and services, and net exports.

With this preview, we now turn to a discussion of the elements of the national income and product accounts. We start by distinguishing between real and nominal GNP increases. Then, we turn to the different ways of measuring GNP, as well as the major components of GNP. Finally, we reflect on shortcomings of GNP as an index of economic welfare, suggest an alternative approach in net economic welfare (NEW), and consider the importance of the underground economy.

Real vs. Nominal GNP: "Deflating" GNP by a Price Index

In defining GNP, we measured the dollar value of goods and services using the measuring rod of *market prices* for oranges, apples, machines, and other commodities. But prices change over time, as inflation generally sends prices upward year after year. Who would want to measure things with a rubber yardstick—one that stretches in your hands from day to day—rather than a rigid yardstick?

SAMPLE CALCULATION OF REAL GNP

DATE	(1) NOMINAL GNP (billions of current dollars)	(2) INDEX NUMBER OF PRICES (GNP deflator)	(3) REAL GNP (billions of dollars, 1929 prices) $(3) = \frac{(1)}{(2)} \times 100$
1929	104	100	$\frac{104}{100} \times 100 = 104$
1933	56	77	$\frac{56}{77} \times 100 = 73$

Table 6-1   To convert nominal GNP into real GNP, we deflate, dividing by price index

Using price index of column (2), we deflate column (1) to get real GNP, column (3).

(Riddle: Can you show that 1929's real GNP was $80 billion in terms of 1933 prices? HINT: With 1933 as a base of 100, 1929's price index is 130.)

The problem of changing prices is one of the problems economists have to solve when they use money as their measuring rod. Clearly, we want a measure of the nation's output and income that uses an invariant yardstick.

How can this be done? Economists can repair most of the damage wrought by the elastic yardstick by using a *price index*.[1] (We first encountered price indexes in Chapter 5. A full discussion will follow in Chapter 14.)

A 1929–1933 comparison will illustrate the process by which we use a price index number to "deflate" a current or "*nominal GNP*," converting it into "*real GNP*." Real GNP measures the total quantity of output, while nominal GNP measures the current-dollar value of output. The ratio of nominal GNP to real GNP is the "price of GNP," which is called the **GNP deflator.**

---

[1] A price index is a weighted average of prices—here of the thousands of items that enter into GNP. The price index used to remove inflation (or "deflate" the GNP) is called the *GNP deflator*. It is defined as a weighted average of price changes of all commodities in the GNP, with each good given as a weight of its percentage importance in the total GNP.

Table 6-1 gives the actual 1929 and 1933 nominal GNP figures of $104 and $56 billion. It shows a 46 percent drop in nominal GNP from 1929 to 1933, but the government estimates that prices on average dropped about 23 percent in the Depression. Using 1929 as a base of 100, this means that the 1933 price index was about 77. So our $56 billion 1933 GNP was really worth much more than half the $104 billion GNP of 1929.

How much more? Table 6-1 divides nominal GNP by the GNP deflator to obtain real GNP, or GNP in 1929 prices. This calculation shows that real GNP fell to only seven-tenths of the 1929 level: in terms of 1929 prices, or dollars of 1929 purchasing power, real GNP fell to $73 billion. Hence, part of the near-halving shown by the nominal GNP was due to the optical illusion of the shrinking price yardstick.

Figure 6-1 shows in black the history of nominal GNP (expressed in the actual dollars and prices that were current in each historical year). Then, for comparison, the real GNP (expressed in 1982 dollars) is shown in red.

Note that part of the increase in nominal GNP over the last half-century is really illusory, being due merely to inflation of the price units of our money yardstick.

To summarize:

Nominal GNP represents the total money value of goods and services produced in a given year, where the values are in terms of the market prices of each year. **Real GNP** corrects nominal GNP by valuing output in terms of the prices of a base year, creating a constant-dollar measure of output. Because we define the GNP deflator as the price of GNP, we have:

$$\text{Real GNP} = \frac{\text{nominal GNP}}{\text{GNP deflator}}$$

Two Measures of National Product: Goods-Flow and Earnings-Flow

How do we actually go about measuring GNP? As we will see, and as is illustrated in Figure 6-2 on p. 106, GNP can be measured either as a flow of products or as a sum of earnings.

In this introductory discussion, we will consider

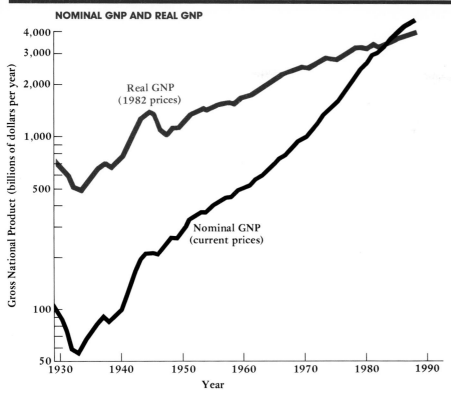

NOMINAL GNP AND REAL GNP

Figure 6-1   Nominal GNP grows faster than real GNP because of price inflation

The rise in nominal GNP exaggerates the rise in real GNP. Why? Because growth in nominal GNP includes price inflation as the overall price level moves up year after year. To obtain an accurate measure of real output, we must divide nominal GNP by the GNP deflator. (Source: U.S. Department of Commerce.)

GNP measurement in an economy with no government or foreign sector and with no investment taking place. For the moment, consider an economy that produces only *consumption goods,* which are items that are purchased by households to satisfy their wants.

Flow-of-Product Approach Each year the public consumes a wide variety of final goods and services: goods such as apples, oranges, and bread; services such as health care and haircuts. We include only *final goods*—goods ultimately bought and used by

consumers—for reasons to be discussed shortly. We spend our family incomes for these consumer goods, as in the upper loop of Figure 6-2. Add together all the consumption dollars spent on these final goods, and you will arrive at this simplified economy's total GNP.

Thus, in our simple economy, you can easily calculate national income or product as the sum of the annual flow of *final* goods and services: (price of oranges × number of oranges) plus (price of apples × number of apples) plus. . . . The gross national product is defined as the total money value of

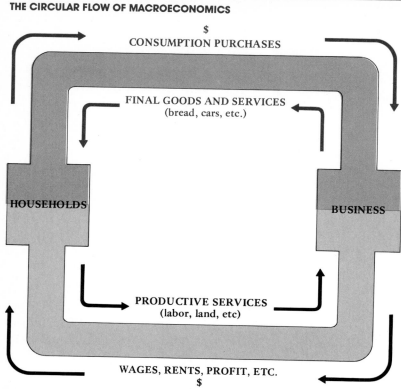

THE CIRCULAR FLOW OF MACROECONOMICS

$
CONSUMPTION PURCHASES

FINAL GOODS AND SERVICES
(bread, cars, etc.)

HOUSEHOLDS

BUSINESS

PRODUCTIVE SERVICES
(labor, land, etc)

WAGES, RENTS, PROFIT, ETC.
$

Figure 6-2   Gross national product can be measured as (a) flow of final products, or equally, as (b) flow of costs

In the upper loop, people spend their money on final goods. The total dollar flow of these each year is one measure of gross national product.

The lower loop measures the annual flow of costs of output: the earnings that business pays out in wages, rent, interest, dividends, and business profits. The two measures of GNP must always be identical. Note that this figure is the *macroeconomic* counterpart of Fig. 3-1, which presented the microeconomic circular flow of supply and demand.

the flow of final products produced by the nation.[2]

Why use market prices as weights in evaluating and summing diverse physical commodities and services? Because, as we shall see in Part Four, market prices reflect the relative economic value of diverse goods

[2]Our simple example considers only consumption expenditures. When we complete our analysis, GNP will include all final goods and services; that is, GNP is consumption, private investment, government spending on goods and services, and net exports to the rest of the world.

and services. That is, the relative prices of different goods reflect how much consumers value their last (or marginal) units of consumption of these goods. Thus the choice of market prices as weights for different goods is not arbitrary: in a smoothly functioning market economy these weights reflect the relative satisfactions that consumers receive from each good.

Earnings or Cost Approach There is a second and equivalent way to calculate GNP: the earnings or cost approach. Go to the lower loop in Figure 6-2. Through it flow all the costs of doing business, which are also the earnings that households receive from the firm. These costs include the wages paid to labor, the rents paid to land, the profits paid to capital, and so forth.

The lower-loop costs represent the factor earnings of land, labor, and capital and are the costs of production of the upper-loop flow of products. Statisticians can measure the annual flow of these earnings or income.[3] In this way they will again arrive at the GNP.

Hence, a second way to calculate GNP is as the total of factor earnings (wages, interest, rents, and profits) that are the costs of producing society's final products.

Equivalence of the Two Approaches Now we have calculated GNP by the upper-loop flow-of-product approach and by the lower-loop earnings-flow approach. Which of these two is greater? They are *exactly* the same.

We can understand the identity of the two approaches if we examine a simple economy with one barber producing only haircuts. Say the barber has no expenses other than labor. If he sells 10 haircuts at $6 each, then GNP is $60. But the barber's earnings (in wages and profits) are also exactly $60. Hence, the GNP here is identical whether measured as flow of products ($60 of haircuts) or as cost and income ($60 of wages and profits).

More generally, the two approaches are identical because we have included "profit" in the lower loop—along with wages, interest, and rents. What exactly is profit? Profit is what you have left over from the sale of product (your oranges, apples, bread, and haircuts) after you have paid the other factor costs—wages, interest, and rents.

So profit is the residual that automatically adjusts to make the lower loop's costs or earnings exactly match the upper loop's value of goods.

To sum up:

GNP, or gross national product, can be measured in two different ways: (1) as the flow of final products, or (2) as the total costs or earnings of inputs producing output. Because profit is defined as a residual cost, both approaches will yield exactly the same total GNP.

A Simple Example

It will be helpful to show how the national income and product accounts can be built up from businesses' income statements. An *account* for a firm or nation is a numerical record of all flows (outputs, costs, etc.) during a given period. The top half of Table 6-2 (see top of page 108) shows the results of a year's farming operations for a single, typical farm. (This account is similar to the income statements analyzed in detail in the appendix to Chapter 20.) We simply put sales of final products on the left-hand side and the various costs of production on the right. Once we include profit as an item of cost, total sales must by definition equal total costs.

The bottom half of Table 6-2 shows how we can easily construct a set of GNP accounts. In this example we analyze a simple agrarian economy with no government or investment, and in which all final products are produced on 10 million identical farms. The national output account simply adds together the outputs and costs of the 10 million identical farms to get the two different measures of GNP.

The Problem of "Double Counting"

Recall that GNP is the total production of final goods and services. A *final* product is one that is produced and sold for consumption or investment by consumers, governments, or foreigners. GNP excludes *intermediate* goods, i.e., ones that are used up to produce other goods. GNP hence includes bread but not wheat, and cars but not steel.

For the flow-of-product calculation of GNP, excluding intermediate products poses no major complications. We simply include the bread and cars in GNP but avoid including the wheat and dough that went into the bread or the steel and glass that went into the car. If you turn back to the upper loop in Figure 6-2, you will see that bread and cars appear in the flow of

---

[3] When we leave our simple world in which GNP is only consumption, we will have to introduce government transfer payments and taxes into the calculations.

(a) INCOME STATEMENT OF TYPICAL FARM

OUTPUT IN FARMING		EARNINGS	
Sales of goods (corn, apples, etc.)	$1,000	**Costs of production**	
		Wages	$ 800
		Rents	100
		Interest	25
		Profit (residual)	75
Total	**$1,000**	Total	**$1,000**

(b) NATIONAL PRODUCT ACCOUNT *(in millions)*

UPPER-LOOP FLOW OF PRODUCT		LOWER-LOOP FLOW OF EARNINGS	
Final output (10 × 1,000)	$10,000	**Costs or Earnings**	
		Wages (10 × 800)	$ 8,000
		Rents (10 × 100)	1,000
		Interest (10 × 25)	250
		Profit (10 × 75)	750
GNP total	**$10,000**	**GNP total**	**$10,000**

Table 6-2　**Construction of national product accounts from business accounts**

Part **(a)** shows the income statement of a typical farm. Part **(b)** then adds up (or aggregates) the 10 million identical farms into total GNP. Note that profit is included as an item of cost or earnings in national income accounting, so the product calculation of GNP exactly equals the earnings estimate of GNP.

products, but you will not find any wheat, flour, or steel.

Where are products like wheat and steel? They are so-called intermediate products and are simply cycling around inside the block marked "business." They are never bought by consumers, and they never show up as final products in GNP.

"Value Added" in the Lower Loop　A new statistician who is being trained to make GNP measurements might be puzzled, saying:

I can see that, if you are careful, your upper-loop product approach to GNP will avoid including intermediate products. But aren't you in some trouble when you use the lower-loop cost or earnings approach?

After all, we at the Commerce Department gather income statements from the accounts of firms. Won't we then be

picking up what grain merchants pay to wheat farmers, what bakers pay to grain merchants, and what grocers pay to bakers? Won't this result in double counting or even triple counting of items going through several productive stages?

These are good questions, but there is an answer that will resolve the problem. The statisticians making lower-loop earnings measurements are very careful to use what they call the "value-added" approach. **Value added** is the difference between a firm's sales and its purchases of materials and services from other firms.

In other words, in calculating the value added by a firm, the statistician includes all costs that go to factors other than businesses and excludes all payments made to other businesses. Hence business costs in the form of wages, salaries, interest payments, and dividends are included in value added, but purchases of wheat or steel or electricity are excluded from value added. Why are all those purchases from other firms excluded from value added to obtain GNP? Because those purchases will get properly counted in GNP from the reports of other firms.

Table 6-3 illustrates by means of the several stages of a loaf of bread how careful adherence to the value-added approach will enable you to subtract the intermediate expenses that show up in the income statements of farmers, millers, bakers, and grocers. We then end up with the desired equality between (*a*) final sales of bread and (*b*) total earnings, calculated as the sum of all values added in all the different stages of bread production.

All this can be summarized as follows:

Value-added approach: To avoid double counting, we take care to include in gross national product only final goods and not the intermediate goods that go to make the final goods. By measuring the value added at each stage, taking care to subtract expenditures on the intermediate goods bought from other firms, the

lower-loop earnings approach properly avoids all double counting and records wages, interest, rent, and profit exactly one time.

DETAILS OF THE NATIONAL ACCOUNTS

We have now seen the bare bones of the national income and product accounts. The rest of this chapter fleshes out how the various sectors fit together. We first describe the way that investment, government, and the foreign sector are treated. We then turn to the earnings or cost side.

Before we start on the journey to understanding the full national income and product accounts, look at Table 6-4 to get an idea of where we are going. This table shows a summary set of accounts for both the product and income sides. If you know the structure of the table and the definitions of the terms in it, you will be well on your way to understanding GNP and

---

BREAD RECEIPTS, COSTS, AND VALUE ADDED (*in cents per loaf*)

STAGE OF PRODUCTION	(1) SALES RECEIPTS	(2) COST OF INTERMEDIATE MATERIALS OR GOODS		(3) VALUE ADDED (wages, profit, etc.) (3) = (1) − (2)
Wheat	24	−0	=	24
Flour	33	−24	=	9
Baked dough	60	−33	=	27
Delivered bread	90	−60	=	30
	207	−117	=	90 (sum of value added)

Table 6-3 **GNP sums up value added at each production stage**

To avoid double counting of intermediate products, we carefully calculate value added at each stage, subtracting all the costs of materials and intermediate products not produced in that stage but bought from other business firms. Note that every black intermediate-product item both appears in column (1) and is subtracted, as a negative element, in the next stage of production in column (2). (How much would we overestimate GNP if we counted all receipts, not just value added? The overestimate would be 117 cents per loaf.)

NATIONAL ACCOUNTS OVERVIEW

PRODUCT APPROACH	EARNINGS APPROACH
Components of gross national product: Consumption *(C)* Gross investment, domestic *(I)* Government *(G)* Net exports *(X)*	**Earnings or costs as sources of gross national product:** Wages Interest, rent, and other property income Indirect taxes Depreciation Profits
Equals: Gross national product	**Equals: Gross national product**
Less: Depreciation	Less: Depreciation
Equals: Net national product	**Equals: Net national product**

Table 6-4   Overview of the national income and product accounts

This table shows the major components of the two sides of the national accounts. The left side shows the components of the product approach (or upper loop); the symbols *C, I, G,* and *X* are often used to represent these four items of GNP. The right side shows the components of the earnings or cost approach (or lower loop). Each approach will ultimately add up to exactly the same GNP and NNP.

The full national accounts are presented in Table 6-6 below, with the actual data for 1987.

its family of components. We will return to this table with data for 1987 in Table 6-6.

Investment and Capital Formation

So far, we have banished all capital goods from our discussion. We talked of people wanting to consume bread, apples, oranges, and haircuts. In real life, however, nations devote part of their output to production of new capital goods, to investment.

In Chapter 2, we saw that investment involves the sacrifice of current consumption to increase future consumption. Instead of eating more bread now, people choose to build new ovens to make it possible to produce bread for future consumption. People want to make provision for investment as well as for current consumption. *Investment* (or capital formation) consists of the additions to the nation's stock of buildings, equipment, and inventories. It is the new houses, factories, trucks, and inventories produced in a year.

A warning is in order here: To economists, invest-

ment always means real capital formation—adding goods to the stock of inventories, or production of new factories, houses, or tools. Often, in common usage, investment means using money to buy some General Motors stock, to buy a corner lot, or to open a savings account. Try not to confuse these two different uses of the word "investment."

If I take $1000 from my safe and put it in the bank or buy some common stock from a stockbroker, in economic terms, no investment has taken place. All that has happened is that the composition of my financial assets has changed. Only when production of a physical capital good takes place, through building a home or producing a truck or such activities, is there what the economist calls investment.

Turning to our national accounts, how does investment enter? If people are using part of society's production possibilities for capital formation rather than for consumption, economic statisticians recognize that such outputs must be included in the upper-loop flow of GNP. So we must modify our original definition to read:

GROSS AND NET INVESTMENT *(in billions of dollars, 1982 prices)*

INVESTMENT COMPONENTS	1929	1933	1965	1987
Residential fixed	35.4	7.7	114.2	195.2
Business fixed	93.0	25.7	227.6	445.1
Change in business inventories	10.8	−10.7	25.2	34.4
Gross private domestic investment	**139.2**	**22.7**	**367.0**	**674.7**
Allowances for depreciation or capital consumption (also = difference between GNP and NNP)	−86.8	−86.5	−183.6	−460.8
Net private domestic investment	**52.4**	**−63.8**	**183.4**	**213.9**

Table 6-5   To go from gross to net investment we subtract depreciation of capital

Gross births minus deaths equals any population's change. Similarly, net capital formation (or net investment) will equal gross capital formation (gross investment in all new capital goods) minus depreciation (or allowance for used-up capital goods). (Source: U.S. Department of Commerce.)

Gross national product is the sum of all final products. Along with consumption goods and services, we must also include gross investment.

Net vs. Gross Investment In our revised definition of GNP, note that we included "gross investment" along with consumption.

Why the word "gross"? This word indicates that investment is not adjusted for **depreciation,** which makes an allowance for the amount of capital that has been used up.[4] Thus gross investment includes all the machines, factories, and houses built during a year— even though some were bought simply to replace some old capital goods that were thrown on the scrap heap.

If you want to get a measure of the increase in society's capital, gross investment is not a sensible measure. It excludes a necessary allowance for depreciation and is thus too large—too gross.

An analogy to population will make clear the im-

portance of considering depreciation. If you want to measure the increase in the size of the population, you cannot simply count the number of births, for this would clearly exaggerate the net change in population. To get population growth, you must subtract the number of deaths.

The same point holds for capital. To find the net increase in capital, you must take the gross investment and subtract the deaths of capital in the form of depreciation, or the amount of capital used up.

Thus to estimate capital formation we measure net investment: net investment is always births of capital (gross investment) less deaths of capital (capital depreciation).

Net investment equals gross investment minus depreciation.

Table 6-5 gives typical figures relating net and gross investment. They differ only by depreciation. Typically net investment is substantial. In the Great Depression, however, net investment was *negative,* indicating we were not investing enough to replace our capital stock.

---

[4] The treatment of depreciation in the income statements of firms is presented in the appendix to Chapter 20.

From Gross National Product to Net National Product

Gross investment can be estimated fairly accurately, involving no difficult depreciation estimate. For this reason governments generally rely primarily on gross national product rather than net national product (NNP). How would we calculate NNP from GNP?

Gross national product (GNP) is defined as the sum of final products: this includes consumption goods plus gross investment (plus, as we will shortly see, government purchases and net exports). **Net national product** includes consumption, government purchases, and net exports, along with net investment. Hence

$$GNP = NNP + depreciation$$

A little thought suggests that NNP is a sounder measure of a nation's output than is GNP. Including depreciation is a little like including wheat as well as bread.

Why is it, then, that everyone from economists to journalists works with GNP? Because GNP is available more quickly and is more reliable, given the perils of estimating depreciation; in addition, GNP and NNP move closely together over periods of a year or so.[5]

Treatment of Government

Up to now we have talked about consumers but ignored the biggest consumer of all—federal, state, and local governments. Somehow GNP must take into account the billions of dollars of product a nation *collectively* consumes or invests; we must include public goods along with private goods. How do we do this?

After some debate, the income statisticians of the United States and United Nations decided on using the simplest method of all. To the flow of consumption, investment, and net exports, we simply add all government expenditures on goods and services.

These government expenditures include costs of roads and missiles, spending on the services of teach-

ers and judges, wages of marine colonels and weather forecasters. In short, all the government payroll expenditures on its employees plus the goods (typewriters, roads, and airplanes) it buys from private industry are included in this third great category of flow of products, called "government expenditure on goods and services."

Exclusion of Transfer Payments Does this mean that every dollar of government expenditure gets included in GNP? Definitely not. GNP includes only government spending on goods and services and excludes spending on transfer payments.

What are government **transfer payments**? These are government payments to individuals that are not made in exchange for goods or services supplied. Examples of government transfers include unemployment insurance, veterans benefits, old-age or disability payments, income support to the blind, and similar items. They are intended to meet some form of need. Because transfers are not for purchase of a current good or service, they are omitted from GNP.

Thus if you receive a payment from the government because you did some work for a government agency, that would be a factor payment and would be included in GNP. If you receive welfare payments because you are poor, that payment is not for a good or service but is a transfer payment excluded from GNP.

Many other government transfer items could be mentioned. But we can conclude with one large item: interest on the government debt. Years ago, it was decided to exclude this item from GNP. Why so? Because the interest on the debt is a return on debt borrowed to pay for past wars or government programs and is not a payment for current government goods or services.

Finally, do not confuse the way the national accounts measure government spending on goods and services *(G)* with the official government budget. When the Treasury measures its expenditures, these include expenditures on goods and services *(G) plus* transfers.

Treatment of Taxes In using the flow-of-product approach to compute the GNP, we need not worry about how the government finances its spending. It

---

[5] Table 6-6 will show how we can easily calculate NNP from GNP once we know depreciation. A rule of thumb for recent years is that NNP is about 90 percent of GNP.

does not matter whether the government pays for its goods and services by taxing, by printing money, or by borrowing. Wherever the dollars come from, the statistician computes the governmental component of GNP as the actual cost to the government of the goods and services.

It is fine to ignore taxes in the flow-of-product approach. But what about in the earnings or cost approach to GNP? We must indeed account for taxes here.

Consider wages, for example. Part of what my employer pays me in wages I have to give to the government in the form of personal income taxes. So these direct taxes definitely do get included in the wage component of business expenses and the same holds for direct taxes (personal or corporate) on interest, rent, and profit.

Or take the sales and other indirect taxes that manufacturers and retailers have to pay on a loaf of bread (or on the wheat, flour, and dough stages). Suppose these indirect taxes total 10 cents per loaf, and suppose wages, profit, and other value-added items add up to 90 cents in cost to the bread industry. What will the bread sell for in the product approach? For 90 cents? Surely not. The bread will sell for $1, equal to 90 cents of factor costs plus 10 cents of indirect taxes.

Thus the cost approach to GNP includes both indirect and direct taxes as elements of the cost of producing final output.

Net Exports

The United States is an open economy engaged in imports and exports of goods and services. A final component of GNP—increasingly important in recent years—is **net exports,** the difference between exports and imports of goods and services.

How do we draw the line between our GNP and other countries' GNPs? The U.S. GNP represents all goods and services produced by labor, capital, and other factors owned by U.S. residents. U.S. production differs from what is purchased by all sectors in the United States in two respects. First, some of our output (Iowa wheat and Boeing aircraft) is bought by foreigners and shipped abroad. Combining these sales abroad with earnings on American capital located abroad, we obtain *exports.*

Second, some of what we consume (French perfume and Japanese cars) is produced abroad and shipped to the United States. Adding these to the dividends and other factor payments paid to foreigners, we calculate our *imports.*

For most of the last half-century, net exports have been positive, as exports exceeded imports. Since 1983, however, U.S. imports have increased extremely rapidly while net exports have decreased sharply; as a result, the United States has incurred a large trade deficit. We study the sources and implications of the large trade deficit in the final three chapters of this text.

A Numerical Example We can use a simple farming economy to understand how the national accounts work. Suppose that Agrovia produces 100 bushels of wheat. Of these, 87 bushels are consumed (in C), 10 go for government purchases to feed the army (as G), 6 go into domestic investment as increases in inventories *(I)*. In addition, 4 bushels are exported while 7 bushels are imported, for net exports *(X)* of minus 3.

What then is the composition of the GNP of Agrovia? It is the following:

$$GNP = 87 \text{ of } C + 10 \text{ of } G + 6 \text{ of } I - 3 \text{ of } X$$
$$= 100 \text{ bushels}$$

A Simplification In our treatment of macroeconomics, we will sometimes simplify our discussion by combining domestic investment with net exports to get *total national gross investment,* which we will call I_n. Put differently, we can include net exports as part of total investment. Let us see why. When a nation exports more than it imports, it is investing the excess (the net exports) abroad, so this component is called *net foreign investment.* In subsequent chapters we will sometimes find it convenient to combine net foreign investment with domestic investment.

■   ■   ■

We can now give a final comprehensive definition of GNP and NNP.

GNP is the sum of four major components as listed below:

1. Personal consumption expenditure on goods and services *(C)*, plus

2. Gross private domestic investment *(I)*, plus

3. Government expenditures on goods and services *(G)*, plus

4. Net exports *(X)*, or exports minus imports.

NNP is calculated as follows:

$$\text{NNP} = \text{GNP} - \text{depreciation}$$

GNP is also definable as a total of costs:

1. Wages, interest, rents, and profit (always carefully excluding, by the value-added technique, double counting of intermediate goods bought from other firms) plus

2. Indirect business taxes that do show up as an expense of producing the flow of products, and

3. In the case of gross national product, there will also be included a depreciation allowance—whereas the net national product will be less than the gross national product by the amount of this estimated depreciation allowance.

The two measures of GNP yield identical amounts by definition (i.e., by adherence to the rules of double-entry bookkeeping and the definition of profit as a residual).

GROSS NATIONAL PRODUCT, 1987 *(in billions of current dollars)*

FLOW-OF-PRODUCT APPROACH			EARNINGS OR COST APPROACH		
1. Personal consumption expenditure		$3,012	1. Wages and other employee supplements		$2,684
Durable goods	$ 422		2. Net interest		354
Nondurable goods	998		3. Rent income of persons		18
Services	1,592		4. Indirect business taxes, adjustments, and statistical discrepancy		369
2. Gross private domestic investment		713	5. Depreciation		479
Residential fixed	227		6. Income of unincorporated enterprises (adjusted)		313
Business fixed	447		7. Corporate profits before taxes (adjusted)		310
Change in inventories	39		Dividends	95	
3. Government purchases of goods and services		925	Undistributed profits	47	
			Corporate profit taxes	134	
4. Net exports		−123			
Exports	428		Reported profits (unadj.)	276	
Imports	551		Valuation adjustments	34	
Gross national product		**$4,527**	**Gross national product**		**$4,527**
Less: Depreciation (or capital consumption allowance)		−480	*Less:* Depreciation (or capital consumption allowance)		−480
Net national product		**$4,047**	**Net national product**		**$4,047**

Table 6-6   Here are the two ways of looking at the GNP accounts in actual numbers
The left side measures flow of products (at market prices). The right side measures flow of costs (factor earnings and depreciation plus indirect taxes). To get NNP, we subtract depreciation from each side. (Source: U.S. Department of Commerce.)

GNP and NNP: A Look at Numbers

Armed with an understanding of the concepts, we can turn to a look at the actual data in the important Table 6-6.

Flow-of-Product Approach Look first at Table 6-6's left side. It gives the upper-loop *flow-of-product* approach to GNP. Each of the four major components appears there, along with the production in each component for 1987. Of these, *C* and *G* and their obvious subclassifications require little discussion.

Gross private domestic investment does require one comment. Its $713 billion total includes all new business fixed investment in plant and equipment, residential construction, and increase in inventory of goods. This gross total makes no subtraction for depreciation of capital. Thus, gross investment exceeds the $233 billion of net investment by $480 billion of depreciation.

Finally, note the large negative entry for *net exports*, −$123 billion. This negative entry represents the fact that the United States imported $123 billion more in goods and services than it exported in 1987.

Adding up the four components on the left gives the total GNP of $4527 billion. This is the harvest we have been working for: the money measure of the American economy's overall performance for 1987.

Lower-Loop Flow-of-Cost Approach Now turn to the right-hand side of the table. Here we have all *net costs of production* plus *taxes* and *depreciation*.

A few explanations are in order. *Wages* and other employee supplements include all take-home pay, fringe benefits, and taxes on wages.

Net interest is a similar item. Remember that interest on government debt is not included as part of *G* or of GNP but is treated as a transfer.

Rent income of persons includes rents received by landlords. In addition, if you own your own home, you are treated as *paying rent to yourself*. This is a so-called imputed item and makes sense if we really want to measure the housing services the American people are enjoying and do not want the estimate to change when people decide to own a home rather than

renting it. This imputed item has to be estimated, since people do not report rental receipts on their own homes.

Indirect business taxes, as we saw earlier, do have to be included as a separate item in the income approach if we are to match the product approach. Any direct taxes on wages, interests, or rents were already included in those items themselves, so they must not be included again. (As shown in Table 6-6, we have included with indirect business taxes some adjustments: business transfer payments and the inevitable "statistical discrepancy," which reflects the fact that the officials never have every bit of needed data.[6])

Depreciation on capital goods that were used up must appear as an expense in GNP, much like other expenses.

Next, turn to *profit*. This should come last because it is the residual, what is left over after all other costs have been subtracted from total sales. There are two kinds of profits: profit of corporations and net earnings of unincorporated enterprises (i.e., proprietorships and partnerships).

Income of unincorporated enterprises (adjusted) refers to earnings of partnerships and single-ownership businesses. This includes much farm and professional income.

Finally, *corporate profits before taxes (adjusted)* is shown. Its $310 billion includes corporate profit *taxes* of $134 billion. The remainder then goes to dividends or to undistributed corporate profits, the latter amount of $47 billion being what you leave or "plow back" into the business, called *net corporate saving*.

Note that profits are corrected for inflation. The costs of inventories and of plant and equipment—that you've used up and will have to replace at prices in-

---

[6] Statisticians must always work with incomplete reports and must fill in some gaps by estimation. Just as a measurement in a chemistry lab may differ from the ideal, so, in fact, do errors creep into both upper- and lower-loop GNP estimates. These are reconnected by an item called the "statistical discrepancy." Along with the civil servants who are heads of units called Wages, Interest, and so forth, there actually used to be someone with the title "Head of the Statistical Discrepancy." If data were perfect, that unit head would be out of a job; but as real life is never so ideal, this person's task of reconciliation was one of the hardest of all.

flated over what you originally bought them for—are "adjusted" upward to allow for inflation.[7]

Again, on the right side, the flow-of-cost approach gives us the same $4527 billion of GNP, and the same NNP figure of $4047 billion (after subtracting depreciation). The right and left sides do agree.

From GNP to Disposable Income

We have now constructed the basic GNP accounts. These topics are of interest not only for themselves, but also because of their importance for the consumption function in the next chapter. One further distinction will help illuminate the way the nation's books are kept. This shows how personal income can be derived from GNP. We now show how accountants move from GNP, to personal income, and finally to disposable income.

Personal Income To help us understand movements in personal consumption and saving, we often need to measure the total income received by households. For this, we have a monthly series of data on *personal income,* or *PI. PI* represents all income—whether as earnings on factors or as transfers—actually received by households. It is constructed principally by (1) starting with NNP; then (2) subtracting those profits withheld by businesses, indirect and social-insurance taxes paid to governments, and net interest payments to non-household sectors; then (3) adding in all transfer payments received by households. Note that *PI* includes personal income taxes.

Disposable Income How many dollars per year do private individuals and families have available to spend? The concept of disposable income tries to answer this question. To get disposable income, you simply subtract personal taxes from personal income. *Disposable income* is, so to speak, what actually gets into the public's hands, to dispose of as it pleases.

Disposable income *(DI)* is important because, as we will see in the next chapters, it is *DI* that people divide between *(a)* consumption spending including interest payments and *(b)* net personal saving. For most of the period since World War II, personal saving represented 6 percent of disposable income, with the balance going to consumption and interest payments. Since 1985, however, the personal savings rate dropped precipitously, reaching a postwar low of 3.2 percent in 1987. Movements in *DI,* consumption, and saving are crucial topics that will be analyzed in depth in the next chapter.

The Identity of Measured Saving and Investment

One of the most important relationships arising from national-income accounting is that between saving and investment. To pave the way for the discussion of income determination in Chapter 8, we show here that, under the accounting rules described above, *measured saving is exactly equal to measured investment.* This equality is an identity of national-income accounting and holds by definition.

What is the measure of investment? Assuming for the moment that there is no government or foreign sector, we know I is that part of upper-loop output that is not C. What is the measure of saving, S? Again ignoring government, foreign, and corporate saving, we know that S is that part of the lower-loop disposable income, or GNP, that is not spent on C. To summarize:

$$I = \text{product-approach GNP minus } C$$
$$S = \text{earnings-approach GNP minus } C$$

But the two loops do give the same measure of GNP. Hence, we have

$$I = S: \text{ the identity between measured}$$
$$\text{saving and investment}$$

[7]During periods of inflation, firms' accounts typically do not charge as costs of production the full amount that it would cost to replace their inventories or their depreciated plant and equipment. They are allowed by the Treasury to write off only the historical cost rather than the replacement cost of a truck or building. Reported profit is too high when true real costs are thus underestimated. So the Commerce Department subtracts from reported profits an adjustment to allow for price rise of inventory that has been sold and needs to be replaced ("inventory valuation adjustment"). And it also subtracts an adjustment for rise in reproduction cost of depreciated capital items ("capital consumption adjustment"). Thus in the inflationary year of 1980, the reported $175 billion of corporate profits contained $57 billion of these two items of "paper profits."

That is the simplest case. Our task will be done when we bring businesses, government, and net exports into the picture. For this discussion, total national gross investment (I_n) will include both domestic gross investment (I) and net foreign investment (X). But gross saving (S) must be divided into three different categories: (1) net personal savings, NPS, which comes out of people's disposable incomes; (2) gross business saving, GBS, which is depreciation plus any earnings retained in the firm; and finally, (3) net government surplus (or "saving"), NGS, which represents the algebraic excess of government's tax revenues over its expenditures on goods and services *and* on transfers. Our identity of measured national saving and investment, S and I_n, now has to be written in terms of the three components of total S.[8]

$$I_n = NPS + GBS + NGS = \text{total saving}$$

Again, remember this identity must hold whether the economy is in equilibrium, going into depression, or in a wartime boom.

BEYOND GNP TO NET ECONOMIC WELFARE (NEW)

Reliance on statistics like gross national product has led to a backlash. Critics complain that GNP represents the excessive consumerism of a society devoted to endless production of useless material goods. In the striking words of a young radical, "Don't speak to me of all your numbers and dollars, your gross national product. To me, GNP stands for gross national pollution."

What are we to think? Isn't it true that GNP includes government purchases of missiles in G and sulfur-emitting smoke along with the electricity in C? Must modern economics make a fetish of quantity at the expense of quality of life? Or can we correct the defects of the official GNP numbers so that they better reflect the true satisfaction-producing products of our economy?

Economists have attempted to adjust the national accounts to construct a more meaningful measure of national output, one called **net economic welfare,** or NEW. NEW is based upon GNP but makes two major changes.[9] First, GNP includes many components that make no obvious contribution to individual well-being, and second, some key satisfaction-producing consumption items are omitted from GNP.

Net economic welfare is an adjusted measure of total national output that includes only consumption and investment items that contribute directly to economic well-being.

We will describe the major elements of NEW.

Pluses: Value of Leisure Time Suppose you decide, as you become more affluent, to work fewer hours, to get your psychic satisfactions from leisure as well as from goods and services. Then the measured GNP goes down even though welfare goes up. So, to correct for the psychic satisfaction of leisure, a positive correction must be added to get NEW from GNP.

Consider also do-it-yourself work done in the

---

[8]This fundamental identity can be derived by recalling the definitions of GNP and of saving. The fundamental identity for GNP from the product side is

$$GNP = C + I + G + X$$

But gross national investment is defined as $I_n = I + X$, so the product side can be written as

$$GNP = C + I_n + G$$

Next turn to the breakdown of GNP from the earnings or cost side:

$$GNP = DI + GBS + Tx - Tr$$

where $Tx =$ taxes and $Tr =$ transfers. Recalling that $DI = C + NPS$, we have

$$GNP = C + (NPS + GBS) + (Tx - Tr - G) + G$$
$$= C + I_n + G$$

Because $NGS = Tx - Tr - G$, we can cancel C and G to obtain the saving-investment identity:

$$I_n = NPS + GBS + NGS$$

[9]The discussion here is drawn from William Nordhaus and James Tobin, "Is Growth Obsolete?" in *Fiftieth Anniversary Colloquium V* (National Bureau of Economic Research, Columbia University Press, New York, 1972). We have replaced the earlier concept, a measure of economic welfare (MEW), by the more informative label net economic welfare (NEW). The 1929–1965 estimates have been updated through 1988. Further refinements have been undertaken by Japanese economists (who have constructed a series known as net national welfare) and by Robert Eisner, who estimates broader income and output measures in a total incomes system of accounts, or TISA [see Robert Eisner, "The Total Incomes System of Accounts," *Survey of Current Business* (January 1985), pp. 24–48].

home—cooking meals or insulating walls. Because the values added are not bought or sold in markets, they never enter into the goods and services of the GNP—neither in the upper loop nor in the lower loop. An estimate of NEW will need to include the value of similar do-it-yourself activities.

Pluses: The Underground Economy

In recent years, many economists claim to have detected an explosive growth in the underground economy. Underground activities are of two kinds: activities that are illegal (such as the drug trade or murder-for-hire), and activities that are legal but unrecorded for tax purposes (such as a carpenter who builds your garage in the evenings in return for your personal advice about his finances).

In general, national accountants exclude illegal activities from a measure of national output—these are by social consensus "bads" and not "goods." A swelling cocaine trade will not enter into either GNP or NEW.

What about the second source of underground activity: the array of carpenters, doctors, babysitters, and farmers who produce valuable goods and services but might escape the net of national output statisticians?

Several economists, led by Edward Feige and Peter Gutmann, claim such a sector is booming. They examine financial data (particularly the use of cash, which is the major means of payment in the underground) and conclude that real GNP growth in the last two decades was significantly understated because of the omission of underground activity. Some point to high tax rates as an incentive to work in the underground economy.

Independent evidence confirms these views. Recent studies indicate that the overall level of compliance with the federal income-tax system has been falling in recent years. The result is that a larger fraction of national income escapes the tax collector's beady eye.[10]

Others are skeptical. While not denying that 5, 10, or 15 percent of economic output is unreported to the Internal Revenue Service, these skeptics doubt whether the amount is growing. They point out that the national accounts already make imputations for unreported activities.

Another bit of evidence comes from a review of the national accounts and employment data. After a careful analysis of the GNP data, Edward Denison concludes that the major source of error would arise from understatement of employment. But the reported employment data come from two completely independent sources (households and firms), and these two sources are highly consistent and both show that the ratio of employment to population rose sharply over the last two decades. Denison concludes that, given the upward surge in reported employment, "growth of national income and product is not being understated much as a result of growth of the underground economy."[11]

Minuses: Environmental Damage

The above understatements and inadequacies of the GNP are not hard to understand. More difficult are some overstatements contained in conventional GNP measures. Along with adding in "goods" (e.g., air conditioning), GNP should be adjusted so that it subtracts out the "bads" or disamenities of modern life (e.g., the pollution of air and water, property damage, and health risks that arise when coal is burned to generate electricity for the air conditioning). Clearly we should subtract the economic cost of such "bads" whenever they are not reflected in market outputs and prices.

For example, suppose the residents of Suburbia enjoy 10 million kilowatt-hours of power, paying Utility Co. 10 cents per kilowatt-hour. That $1 million covers the cost of labor, plant costs, and fuel costs. But suppose the company damages the neigh-

---

[10] How does the Internal Revenue Service estimate the extent of noncompliance? They have instituted a program called the Taxpayers' Compliance Measurement Program (TCMP). This takes a small sample of households and traces every scrap of paper and expenditure to reconstruct the household's true income. Some-

times, the IRS even asks how you got the money for your fancy car or Persian rug. Using estimates of underreporting from the TCMP sample, accountants increase the *reported* income statements to obtain the national accounts of income shown in Table 6-6 on p. 114.

[11] Edward F. Denison, "Is U.S. Growth Understated Because of the Underground Economy? Employment Ratios Suggest Not," *Review of Income and Wealth* (October 1982).

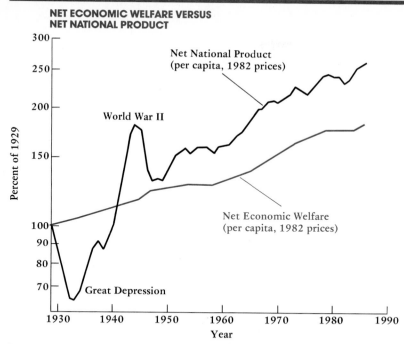

NET ECONOMIC WELFARE VERSUS NET NATIONAL PRODUCT

Figure 6-3   Net economic welfare (NEW) has grown more slowly than NNP

Adjustments for leisure would swell per capita NEW growth beyond per capita NNP. But disamenities of modern urbanization (growing pollution, etc.) slow down NEW growth. How much of NNP growth would you be willing to sacrifice to enhance the quality of life and NEW growth? [Source: W. Nordhaus and J. Tobin, "Is Growth Obsolete?" *Fiftieth Anniversary Colloquium V* (National Bureau of Economic Research, Columbia University Press, 1972); updated by the authors.]

borhood with sulfur from oil and coal, acid rain, or radiation exposure. It incurs no money costs for these externalities.

Why do we emphasize that the firm "incurs no *money* costs"? Because pollution damages do involve a cost to society—an externality—that is not paid for by the firm or the users of electricity (see Chapter 3 for a discussion of externalities). Suppose that in addition to the 10 cents of direct costs, the surrounding neighborhood suffers 1 cent per kilowatt-hour of environmental damage. This is the cost (to trees, trout, streams, and people of the sulfur, oil slicks, acid rain, etc.) not paid by Utility Co. Then the total "external" cost is $100,000. To correct for these hidden costs, we must subtract $100,000 of "pollution bads" from the $1,000,000 flow of "electricity goods" in constructing NEW.

We shall not describe here all the various adjustments to go from real NNP to NEW. The other major modifications are subtraction of government intermediate goods and adjustment for the congestion of urban life. Economists have made calculations of net economic welfare, and these are shown in Figure 6-3. For comparison, we show per capita NEW against per capita NNP, for NNP is the most appropriate measure from the national income accounts. We see that NEW grows more slowly than does NNP. This difference may be inevitable in a world that is becoming more congested and relies ever more heavily on large-scale power plants and sophisticated organic chemicals.

Having reviewed the measurement of national output and analyzed the shortcomings of the GNP, what should we conclude about the adequacy of our national accounts as measures of economic welfare? The answer has never been more aptly stated than in a summary by Arthur Okun:

It should be no surprise that national prosperity does not guarantee a happy society, any more than personal pros-

perity ensures a happy family. No growth of GNP can counter the tensions arising from an unpopular and unsuccessful war, a long overdue self-confrontation with conscience on racial injustice, a volcanic eruption of sexual mores, and an unprecedented assertion of independence by the young. Still, prosperity . . . is a precondition for success in achieving many of our aspirations.[12]

[12] *The Political Economy of Prosperity* (Norton, New York, 1970), p. 124.

SUMMARY

1. The gross national product (or GNP) is the most comprehensive measure of a nation's production of goods and services. It comprises the dollar value of consumption *(C)*, gross private domestic investment *(I)*, government purchases of goods and services *(G)*, and net exports *(X)*. Recall the formula:

$$GNP = C + I + G + X$$

This will sometimes be simplified by combining domestic investment and net exports into total national gross investment (I_n):

$$GNP = C + I_n + G$$

2. By use of a price index, we can "deflate" nominal GNP (GNP in current dollars) to arrive at a more accurate measure of real GNP (GNP expressed in dollars of some base year's purchasing power). Use of such a price index is an approximate way of correcting for the rubber yardstick implied by changing levels of prices.

3. Because of the way we define residual profit, we can match the upper-loop flow-of-product measurement of GNP with the lower-loop flow-of-cost measurement, as shown in Figure 6-2. The flow-of-cost approach uses factor earnings, carefully computing values added to eliminate double counting of intermediate products. And after summing up all (before-tax) wage, interest, rent, depreciation, and profit income, it adds to this total all indirect tax costs of business. GNP definitely does not include transfer items such as receipt of interest on government bonds or receipt of welfare payments.

4. Net investment is positive when the nation is producing more inventory and buildings and equipment than are currently being used up in the form of depreciation. Since depreciation is hard to estimate accurately, statisticians have more confidence in their measures of gross than of net investment.

5. Personal and disposable income are two additional official measurements. Disposable income *(DI)* is what people actually have left—after all tax payments, corporate saving of undistributed profits, and transfer adjustments have been made—to spend on consumption or to save. Personal income is *DI* plus personal taxes.

6. Using the rules of the national accounts, measured saving must exactly equal measured investment. This is easily seen in a hypothetical economy with nothing but households. In a complete economy, the identity is

$$I_n = NPS + GBS + NGS$$

where total national gross investment (I_n, which equals both domestic and foreign investment) equals net personal saving (NPS) plus gross business saving (GBS) plus net government saving (NGS).

The identity between saving and investment is just that: saving must equal investment no matter whether the economy is in boom or recession, war or peace. It is a consequence of the definitions of national-income accounting.

7. Gross national product is an imperfect measure of genuine economic welfare. An alternative approach is net economic welfare (NEW). The calculation of NEW adds to NNP certain items—such as value of leisure, homemakers' services, and do-it-yourself activities. It also subtracts from NNP unmet costs of pollution, other disamenities of modern urbanization, and still other adjustments. The result still shows a positive growth in NEW, but at a slower rate than in NNP.

CONCEPTS FOR REVIEW

GNP
GNP deflator
nominal and real GNP
GNP = $C + I + G + X$
    = $C + I_n + G$
GNP in two equivalent views: product
  (upper loop) and earnings (lower loop)
intermediate goods, value added
net investment = gross investment −
  depreciation

NNP = GNP − depreciation
government transfers
disposable income *(DI)*
$I_n = S$
    = $NPS + GBS + NGS$
NEW = GNP + leisure and
  underground activity − pollution and
  disamenities

QUESTIONS FOR DISCUSSION

1. Define carefully the following and give an example of each:
  (a) Consumption
  (b) Gross private domestic investment
  (c) Government purchase of a good (in GNP)
  (d) Government transfer payment (not in GNP)
  (e) Export

2. "You can't add apples and oranges." Show that by using prices we can do this.

3. Consider the following data: Nominal GNP for 1987 was $4527 billion, as compared to $4240 for 1986. The GNP deflator for 1987 was 117.7, as compared to 113.9 for 1986. The GNP deflator was 100 in 1982.

Calculate real GNP for 1986 and 1987, in 1982 prices. Calculate the rates of growth of nominal GNP and real GNP for 1987. What was the rate of inflation (as measured by the GNP deflator) for 1987?

4. R. Crusoe produces upper-loop product of $1000. He pays $750 in wages, $125 in interest, and $75 in rent. What *must* his profit be? If three-fourths of Crusoe's output is consumed and the rest invested, calculate Crusoeland's GNP in both the product and income approaches and show they must agree exactly.

5. "Political economy has finally, after too long a delay, begun to grapple with the quality of economic life. By examining NEW rather than GNP we can begin to weigh true economic costs and benefits rather than only those seen in markets." Evaluate.

6. Here are some brain teasers. Can you see why the following are *not* counted in GNP:

    (a) The home meals produced by a fine chef

    (b) Purchase of a plot of land

    (c) Purchase of an original Rembrandt painting

    (d) The value I get from playing a 1985 Rolling Stones compact disk

    (e) The increased value to consumers of costless improvements in the quality of weather forecasting

7. Consider the country of Agrovia, whose GNP is discussed in "A Numerical Example" on page 113. Construct a set of national accounts like that in Table 6-6 assuming that wheat costs $5 per bushel, there is no depreciation, wages are three-fourths of national output, indirect business taxes are used to finance government spending, and the balance of income goes as rent income to farmers.

CHAPTER 7
CONSUMPTION
AND INVESTMENT

There's many a slip 'twixt the cup and the lip.

Anonymous

MACROECONOMICS is the study of the behavior of the overall economy. Now that we have completed our overview, it is natural that we turn to an analysis of the largest components of GNP, consumption and investment. Recall that *consumption* consists of spending by households on final goods and services, including durable goods like furniture, nondurables like food, and services like education. *Investment,* on the other hand, is composed of produced goods that are used for further production, including equipment like power looms, structures like houses or factories, and inventories like cars on dealers' lots.

Patterns of consumption and investment play a crucial role in a nation's economy. Nations that consume a large fraction of their incomes—such as the United States—tend to invest relatively little and show modest rates of economic growth. By contrast, those nations that consume a small fraction of their incomes tend to invest heavily; these countries, as exemplified by Japan or South Korea, have rapidly growing output and productivity.

This chapter will probe the reasons lying behind trends in consumption and investment. We will at-

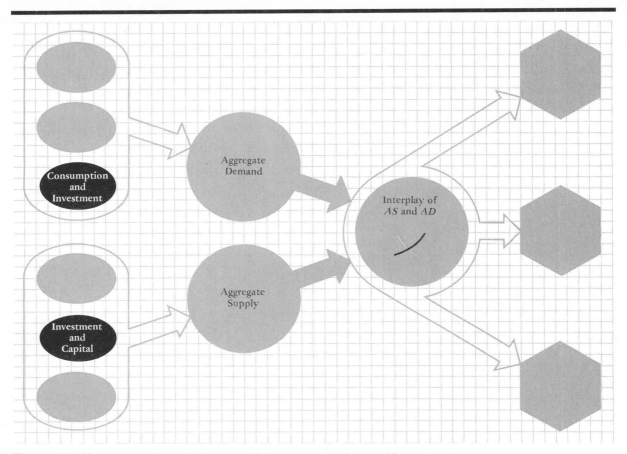

Figure 7-1   Here we analyze the forces driving consumption and investment

We begin our analysis of macroeconomics with a survey of two major components of GNP: consumption and investment. In later chapters, we will see that they affect both the supply and the demand sides of the macroeconomy.

tempt to understand how people choose between saving and consumption and will see that poor people tend to save less than well-to-do people. In addition, we will study the determinants of investment, including such factors as taxes, interest rates, and expectations.

We study these topics not only for their intrinsic interest but also because consumption and investment are important determinants of the overall level of out-

put and employment in the short run. When spending on investment and consumption grows rapidly, output as a whole tends to grow as well. Why is this? We will see in the next chapters that total output in the short run is significantly affected by the interplay of consumption and investment. When innovations or favorable tax treatment or growing markets give a spur to business investment—as was the case in the 1960s and the late 1980s—aggregate demand moves ahead and output and employment grow rapidly. When business confidence withers or when markets shrink—as happened during the 1930s and in the early 1980s—investment declines, aggregate demand contracts, and output and employment fall.

This chapter begins the thorough study of the determination of aggregate demand by focusing upon the behavior of consumption and investment. Figure 7-1 shows how this chapter's analysis fits into the overall structure of the macroeconomy. Once we have surveyed consumption and investment, we can in the next chapter put these two components together into the simplest model of income determination—the multiplier model.

The tools introduced in this and the next chapter form the intellectual core of what is called *Keynesian economics*. When introduced a half-century ago by the English economist, John Maynard Keynes,[1] these concepts were as foreign to the then practicing economists as "quarks" or "charm" are to freshmen in a modern college physics course. Today, many of the elements of Keynes' thinking—such as the ideas presented in the next two chapters—are part of the language of modern economics.

A. CONSUMPTION AND SAVING

We begin our discussion with an analysis of consumption and savings behavior, first examining individual spending patterns and then looking at aggregate consumption behavior. Recall from Chapter 6 that household consumption is spending on final goods and services bought for the satisfaction gained or needs met by their use. Household saving, on the other hand, is by definition that part of income not spent on consumption.

Consumption is the largest single component of GNP, constituting 65 percent of total spending over the last decade. What are the major elements of consumption? Among the most important categories are housing, motor vehicles, food, and medical care. Table 7-1 on the next page displays the major elements, broken down into the three categories of durable goods, nondurable goods, and services. The items themselves are familiar, but their relative importance, particularly the increasing importance of services, is worth a moment's study.

Budgetary Expenditure Patterns

How do the patterns of consumption spending differ across different households in the United States?

No two families spend their money in exactly the same way. Yet statistics show that there is a predictable regularity in the way people allocate their expenditures among food, clothing, and other major items. Thousands of budgetary investigations have been made of the spending patterns of people at different levels of income, and there is remarkable agreement on the general, qualitative patterns of behavior.[2]

What are they? Figure 7-2 tells the story. Poor families must spend their incomes largely on the necessities of life, food and shelter. As income increases, expenditure on many food items goes up. People eat more and eat better. They shift away from cheap, bulky carbohydrates to more expensive meats, fruits, and vegetables. There are, however, limits to the extra money people will spend on food when their incomes rise. Consequently, the proportion of total spending devoted to food declines as income increases.

---

[1]Keynes himself (1883–1946) was a many-sided genius who won eminence in the fields of mathematics, philosophy, and literature. In addition, he found time to run a large insurance company, advise the British Treasury, help govern the Bank of England, edit a world-famous economics journal, collect modern art and rare books, and sponsor ballet and drama. He was also an economist who knew how to make money by shrewd speculation, both for himself and for King's College, Cambridge. His 1936 book, *The General Theory of Employment, Interest and Money,* presented a challenge to current macroeconomic thinking and provides the groundwork for mainstream macroeconomics.

[2]Figure 7-2's behavior patterns are called "Engel's Laws," after the nineteenth-century Prussian statistician Ernst Engel. The average behavior of consumption expenditure does change fairly regularly with income. But averages do not tell the whole story. Within each income class, there is a considerable spread of consumption around the average.

CONSUMPTION, 1987

CATEGORY OF CONSUMPTION	VALUE OF CATEGORY (billions of dollars)	PERCENT OF TOTAL
Durable goods	**422**	14
Motor vehicles	196	
Household equipment	148	
Other	78	
Nondurable goods	**998**	33
Food	526	
Energy	77	
Clothing and apparel	178	
Other	216	
Services	**1,592**	53
Housing	468	
Medical care	360	
Personal business	216	
Education	51	
Other	497	
Total, personal consumption expenditures	**3,012**	**100**

Table 7-1   The major components of consumption
There are three major types of consumption: durables like cars, nondurables like food, and services like college education. The size of the service sector is becoming increasingly large as basic needs for food are met and as health, recreation, and education claim a larger part of family budgets. (Source: U.S. Department of Commerce.)

Above the very lowest income level, the proportion of income spent on shelter is largely constant. This constancy is expressed in a familiar rule of thumb: One week's salary should cover 1 month's expenditure on housing.

Expenditure on clothing, recreation, and automobiles increases more than proportionately to after-tax income, until high incomes are reached. Spending on luxury items, by definition, increases in greater proportion than income.

Finally, as we look across families, note that saving rises very rapidly as income increases. Saving is the greatest luxury good of all.

Consumption, Income, and Saving

We suggested above that there is a close tie between income, consumption, and saving. What is the exact relationship?

Actually, the idea is simple. **Saving** is that part of income that is not consumed. That is, saving equals income minus consumption. The relationship between income, consumption, and saving for 1987 is shown in Table 7-2. Begin with personal income (made up, as Chapter 6 showed, of wages, interest, rents, dividends, transfer payments, and so forth). In 1987, 15 percent of personal income went to personal tax and nontax payments. This left $3210 billion of personal disposable income. Household outlays for consumption (including interest) amounted to 96.8 percent of income, or $3106 billion, leaving $104 billion as personal saving.

Studies of savings behavior show that rich people save more than poor people, not only absolutely but also as a percent of their incomes. The very poor are unable to save at all. Instead, as long as they have any wealth to draw down or can borrow, they tend to *dissave*. That is, they tend to spend more than they earn,

EXPENDITURES FOR CONSUMPTION AT DIFFERENT INCOME LEVELS, 1989

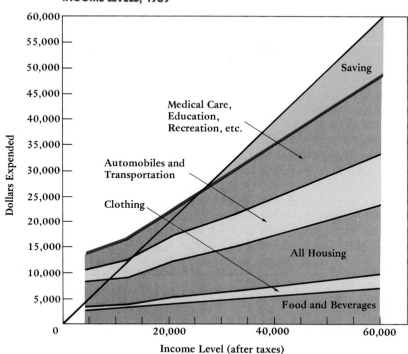

Figure 7-2   Family budget expenditures show regular patterns

Careful sampling of families and of individuals verifies the importance of income as a determinant of consumption expenditure. Notice the drop in food as a percentage of higher incomes. Note also the rise in saving, from below zero at low incomes to substantial amounts at high incomes. [Source: U.S. Department of Labor, *Consumer Expenditure Survey: Interview Survey 1984* (August 1986), updated to 1989 prices by authors.]

ITEM	AMOUNT (billions of dollars), 1987
Personal income	3,780
Less: Personal tax and nontax payments	570
Equals: Personal disposable income	3,210
Less: Personal consumption outlays (consumption and interest)	3,106
Equals: Personal saving	104

Source: U.S. Department of Commerce.

Table 7-2   Saving equals disposable income less consumption

thereby reducing their accumulated saving or going deeper into debt. In short, income is a prime determinant of saving, as shown in Figure 7-2.

Table 7-3 on the next page contains illustrative data on disposable income, saving, and consumption drawn from budget studies on American households. The first column shows seven different levels of disposable income. The second column indicates saving at each level of income, and the third column indicates consumption spending at each level of income.

The *breakeven point*—where the representative household neither saves nor dissaves but is consuming all its income—comes at around $16,000. Below this, say at $15,000, the household actually consumes more than its income; it dissaves (see the −$110 item). Above $16,000 it begins to show positive saving [see the +$150 and other positive items in column (2)].

Column (3) shows the consumption spending for

HOUSEHOLD SAVING AND CONSUMPTION

	(1) DISPOSABLE INCOME	(2) NET SAVING (+) OR DISSAVING (−)	(3) CONSUMPTION
A	$15,000	$ −110	$15,110
B	**16,000**	**0**	**16,000**
C	17,000	+150	16,850
D	18,000	+400	17,600
E	19,000	+760	18,240
F	20,000	+1,170	18,830
G	21,000	+1,640	19,360

Table 7-3   Consumption and saving are primarily determined by income

This table shows average levels of consumption and saving at different levels of disposable income. The breakeven point at which people cease to dissave and begin to do positive saving is shown here at $16,000. How much of each extra dollar do people devote to extra consumption at this income level? How much to extra saving? (Answer: About 85 cents and 15 cents, respectively, when we compare row B and row C.)

each income level. Since each dollar of income is divided between the part consumed and the remaining part saved, columns (3) and (2) are not independent; they must always exactly add up to column (1).

The relationship between income and consumption or saving is central to a number of economic issues. But at this stage we turn to the aspect of consumption that relates to aggregate output and employment. For this purpose we need to understand how many *extra* dollars of consumption and saving each *extra* dollar of income induces.

To understand how saving and investment determine the level of national output and employment, we must study in detail:

- The consumption function, relating consumption and income; and its twin,

- The savings function, relating saving and income.

The Consumption Function

A key tool for analyzing consumption is the consumption function. The **consumption function** shows the relationship between the level of consumption expenditures and the level of household disposable income. This concept, introduced by Keynes, is based on the hypothesis that there is a stable empirical relationship between consumption and income.

We can display the consumption function most vividly in the form of a graph. If we take the seven levels of income listed in Table 7-3, we can plot them in Figure 7-3. This figure plots household disposable income [column (1) of Table 7-3] on the horizontal axis, and household consumption [column (3)] on the vertical axis. Each of the income-consumption combinations is represented by a single point. We have then connected the points *A*, *B*, *C*, *D*, *E*, *F*, and *G* by a smooth curve.

The relation between consumption and income shown in Figure 7-3 is called the consumption function.

To understand the figure, it is helpful to look at the 45° line drawn northeast from the origin. Because the vertical and horizontal axes have exactly the same scale, the 45° line has a very special property: At any point on the 45° line, the distance up from the horizontal axis (which is consumption) exactly equals the distance across from the vertical axis (which is income). You can use your eyes or a ruler to verify this fact.

Thus at any point on the 45° line, consumption exactly equals income.

The "Breakeven" Point The 45° line tells us immediately, therefore, whether consumption spending is equal to, greater than, or less than the level of income. The point on the consumption schedule where it intersects the 45° line shows us the level of disposable income at which households just break even.

This breakeven point is at *B* in Figure 7-3. Here, consumption expenditure is exactly equal to disposable income: The household is borrowing nothing and on balance saving nothing.

Similarly, at any other point on the consumption function, the household cannot be just breaking even.

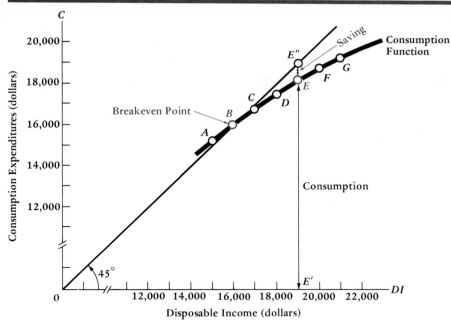

Figure 7-3   A plot of the consumption function

The curve through A, B, C, . . . G, is the consumption function. The horizontal axis depicts the level of disposable income (DI). For each level of DI, the consumption function shows the dollar level of consumption (C) for the household. Note that consumption rises with increases in DI. The 45° line helps locate the breakeven point and helps our eye measure net saving. Can you see how? (Source: Table 7-3.)

To the right of point B, the consumption function lies below the 45° line: We can see the relationship between income and consumption by examining the thin black line from E' to E in Figure 7-3. At an income of $19,000 the level of consumption is $18,240 (see Table 7-3). We can see that consumption is less than income by the fact that the consumption function lies below the 45° line at point E.

If the household is not spending all its income, it must be saving the remainder. The 45° line tells us more than that: It enables us to find how much the household is saving. Net saving is measured by the distance from the consumption function up to the 45° line, as shown by the EE'' savings arrow in red.

To the left of point B, our 45° line tells us that the household is spending more than its income. The ex-

cess of consumption over income is its "net dissaving" and is measured by the vertical distance between the consumption function and the 45° line.

To review:

When the consumption function lies above the 45° line, the household is dissaving. When the two curves meet at the breakeven point, the household is neither saving nor dissaving. When the consumption function lies below the 45° line, the household has positive saving. The amount of dissaving or saving is always measured by the vertical distance between the consumption function and the 45° line.

The Savings Function The fact that saving equals income minus consumption means that we can easily derive a new relationship: the **savings function.**

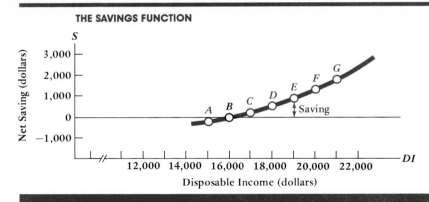

THE SAVINGS FUNCTION

Figure 7-4 The savings function is the mirror image of the consumption function

This savings schedule comes from subtracting consumption from income. Graphically, the savings function is obtained by subtracting vertically the consumption function from the 45° line in Figure 7-3. Note that the breakeven point *B* is at the same $16,000 income level as in Figure 7-3.

Graphically, this is shown in Figure 7-4. Again we show disposable income on the horizontal axis; vertically, we now show net saving, whether negative or positive in amount.

This savings function comes directly from Figure 7-3. It is simply the vertical distance there between the 45° line and the consumption function. At a point such as *A* in Figure 7-3, the fact that the household's saving was negative can be seen by the fact that the consumption function lies above the 45° line. Figure 7-4 shows the dissaving directly—the savings function is below the horizontal axis at point *A*. Similarly, positive saving occurs to the right of point *B* as is shown by the savings function lying above the horizontal axis at points *C, D,* and so forth.

The Marginal Propensity to Consume

Many modern macroeconomic theories attach much importance to the response of consumption to changes in income, which is called the marginal propensity to consume, or *MPC*. The **marginal propensity to consume** is the extra amount that people consume when they receive an extra dollar of income.

The word "marginal" is used throughout economics to mean extra or additional. For example, "marginal cost" means the additional cost of producing an extra unit of output. "Propensity to consume" in macroeconomics designates the desired level of consumption. *MPC*, then, is the additional or extra consumption that results from an extra dollar of income.

Table 7-4 rearranges Table 7-3's data in a more

convenient form. First, verify its similarity to Table 7-3. Then, look at columns (1) and (2) to see how consumption expenditure goes up with higher levels of income.

Column (3) in Table 7-4 shows how we compute the marginal propensity to consume. From *B* to *C,* income rises by $1000, going from $16,000 to $17,000. By how much does consumption rise? Consumption grows from $16,000 to $16,850, an increase of $850. The extra consumption is therefore 0.85 of the extra income. Out of each extra dollar of income, 85 cents goes to consumption and 15 cents goes to saving. We can see, then, that as we move from point *B* to point *C* the marginal propensity to consume, or *MPC*, is 0.85—as we show in column (3) of Table 7-4.

You can compute *MPC* between other income levels. In Table 7-4, *MPC* begins at 0.89 for the poor and finally falls to 0.53 at higher incomes.

Marginal Propensity to Consume as Geometrical Slope We now know how to calculate the *MPC* from data on income and consumption. What is the geometrical meaning of *MPC?* The *MPC* is a numerical measure of the slope of the consumption function.

Figure 7-5 on p. 132 shows how to calculate the *MPC* graphically. Near points *B* and *C* a little triangle is drawn. As income increases by $1000 from point *B* to point *C,* the amount of consumption rises by $850, according to the consumption function. This means that the *MPC* in this range is $850/$1000 = 0.85. But, as the appendix to Chapter 1 showed, the slope

CONSUMPTION AND SAVING

	(1) DISPOSABLE INCOME (after taxes)	(2) CONSUMPTION EXPENDITURE	(3) MARGINAL PROPENSITY TO CONSUME (MPC)	(4) NET SAVING (4) = (1) − (2)	(5) MARGINAL PROPENSITY TO SAVE (MPS)
A	$15,000	$15,110		$−110	
			$\frac{890}{1,000} = 0.89$		$\frac{110}{1,000} = 0.11$
B	16,000	16,000		0	
			$\frac{850}{1,000} = 0.85$		$\frac{150}{1,000} = 0.15$
C	17,000	16,850		+150	
			$\frac{750}{1,000} = 0.75$		$\frac{250}{1,000} = 0.25$
D	18,000	17,600		+400	
			$\frac{640}{1,000} = 0.64$		$\frac{360}{1,000} = 0.36$
E	19,000	18,240		+760	
			$\frac{590}{1,000} = 0.59$		$\frac{410}{1,000} = 0.41$
F	20,000	18,830		+1,170	
			$\frac{530}{1,000} = 0.53$		$\frac{470}{1,000} = 0.47$
G	21,000	19,360		+1,640	

Table 7-4 The marginal propensities to consume and to save

This table shows consumption and savings schedules and marginal propensities. Each dollar of income that is not consumed is saved. And each dollar of extra income goes into extra consumption or extra saving—giving important concepts we need: marginal propensity to consume and to save, MPC and MPS.

of a line is "the rise over the run." We can therefore see that the slope of the consumption function between points B and C is 0.85.*

The slope of the consumption function, which measures the change in consumption per dollar change in income, is the marginal propensity to consume.

*The slope of lines was discussed in Chapter 1's appendix, but a brief review may be helpful. The numerical slope of a line can be illustrated with the help of the accompanying triangle. By the numerical slope of the line XW, we always mean the numerical ratio of the length of ZW to the length XZ. The slope is "the rise over the run."

If the line XW were not straight, as is the case of many curves in economics, then we would calculate the slope as the tangent. That is, if you want to find the slope at point G in Figure 7-5, you (1) first place a ruler tangent to the curve at point G, then (2) calculate the slope as the rise over the run of the tangent line created by the ruler.

In the case of the consumption function, its slope is the MPC, or the marginal propensity to consume. Similarly, if the curve is the savings function, its slope is defined as the marginal propensity to save, or the MPS.

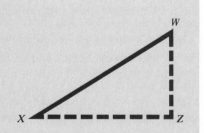

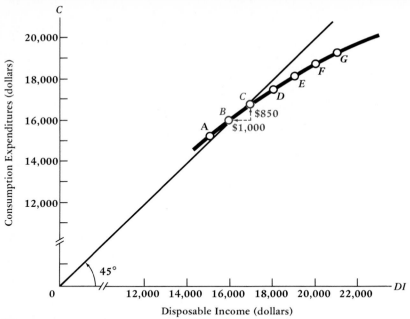

Figure 7-5   The slope of the consumption function is its *MPC*

To calculate the marginal propensity to consume *(MPC)*, we measure the slope of the consumption function by forming a little right triangle and relating height to base. From point *B* to point *C*, the increase in consumption is $850 while the change in disposable income is $1000. The slope, equal to the change in *C* divided by the change in *DI*, gives the *MPC*. If the consumption function is everywhere upward-sloping, what does this imply about the *MPC*?

The Marginal Propensity to Save

Along with the marginal propensity to consume goes its mirror image, the marginal propensity to save, or *MPS*. The **marginal propensity to save** is defined as the fraction of an extra dollar of income that goes to extra saving.

Why are *MPC* and *MPS* related like mirror twins? Recall that income equals consumption plus saving. This implies that each extra dollar of income must be divided between extra consumption and extra saving. Thus if *MPC* is 0.85, then *MPS* must be 0.15. (What would *MPS* be if *MPC* were 0.6? Or 0.99?) A comparison of columns (3) and (5) of Table 7-4 confirms

that at any income level, *MPC* and *MPS* must always add up to *exactly* 1, no more and no less.

Thus we know that, everywhere and always, $MPS \equiv 1 - MPC$.

Brief Review of Definitions

Let's review briefly the main definitions we have learned:

1. The consumption function relates the level of consumption to the level of disposable income.

2. The savings function relates saving to disposable income. Since what is saved is the same as what is not consumed, savings and consumption schedules are mirror images in the sense that

Saving + consumption = disposable income

3. The marginal propensity to consume *(MPC)* is the amount of extra consumption generated by an extra dollar of income. Graphically, it is given by the slope of the consumption function—a steep slope meaning a high *MPC* and a flat one meaning a low *MPC*.

4. The marginal propensity to save *(MPS)* is the extra saving generated by an extra dollar of income, or the slope of the savings schedule. Because the part of each dollar that is not consumed is necessarily saved, $MPS \equiv 1 - MPC$.

NATIONAL CONSUMPTION BEHAVIOR

Up to now we have examined the budget patterns and consumption behavior of typical families at different levels of income. We now turn to a discussion of consumption for the nation as a whole. This transition from household behavior to national trends exemplifies the way that macroeconomics proceeds—by first examining economic activity on the individual level and then aggregating individuals in order to understand the way the overall economy operates.

Why are we interested in national consumption trends? Consumption is important, first, because it is a major component of total or aggregate spending, and our task in these chapters is to understand the determination of aggregate demand. Second, we have seen that what is not consumed—what is saved—is available to the nation for investment, and investment serves as a driving force behind long-term economic growth. The behavior of consumption and saving is therefore among the most important issues of macroeconomics.

Determinants of Consumption

We begin by analyzing the major forces that affect consumer spending. What factors in a nation's life and livelihood set the pace of its consumption outlays?

Disposable Income Informal observation and statistical studies show that income is the central factor determining a nation's consumption. Look at Figure 7-6 on the next page to see how closely consumption followed yearly disposable income over the period 1929–1988. The only period when income and consumption were not moving in tandem was during World War II, when goods were scarce and rationed, and people were urged to save to help the war effort.

Permanent or Life-Cycle Income The simplest theory of consumption uses only the current year's income to predict consumption expenditures. A moment's thought indicates, however, that past and future incomes will also affect consumption. Careful studies have shown that people base their consumption expenditures not only on current income but also on long-run income trends.

What are some examples? If bad weather destroys a crop, farmers will draw upon their previous saving. If the stock market rises sharply in a given year, investors probably will not spend all of their higher wealth immediately. Because medical students can look forward to high professional earnings, they will dissave by borrowing for consumption purposes while young. In all these cases, consumers take the long view, asking, ''Is this year's income temporarily high or low? Given my current and future income, what level of consumption can I sustain for several years without saving too much or running up debts?''

Evidence indicates that consumers generally choose their consumption levels with an eye to their long-run income prospects. Analyses that have been developed to explain the reliance of consumption on long-term income trends include the *permanent-income theory* and the *life-cycle hypothesis. Permanent income* is the level of income that would be received by a household when temporary or transient influences—such as the weather, a short business cycle, or a windfall gain or loss—are removed.[3]

---

[3]The pathbreaking studies on longer-term influences were by Milton Friedman (on the permanent-income hypothesis) and Franco Modigliani (for the life-cycle model). Both received the Nobel Prize in economics for their accomplishments in these and other areas.

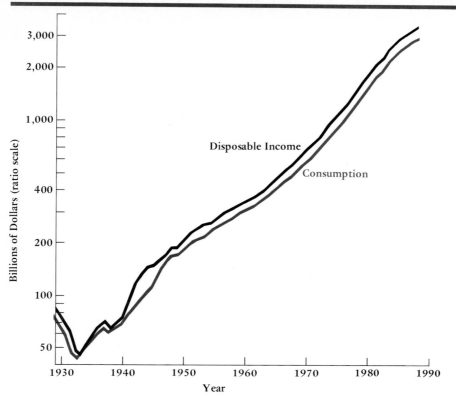

Figure 7-6 Consumption and disposable income, 1929–1988
U.S. consumption spending has closely tracked the level of personal disposable income over the last six decades. Macroeconomists can make good consumption forecasts based on the historical consumption function. (Source: U.S. Department of Commerce.)

The notion of permanent income is of great importance because it suggests that consumers do not respond equally to all income shocks. If a change in income appears permanent (such as being promoted to a secure and high-paying job), then consumers are likely to raise consumption proportionally to the increased income. On the other hand, if the change is clearly transitory (like a spell of bad weather or a temporary salary bonus), then the marginal propensity to consume might be quite low. Thus consumer *expectations* about the nature of income shocks—such as whether they are likely to be permanent or transitory—may have a major impact on the marginal propensity to consume.

Wealth A further important determinant of the amount of consumption is wealth. Consider two consumers, both earning $25,000 per year. One has $100,000 in the bank while the other has no saving at all. The first consumer can consume more without acting imprudently or going bankrupt, and studies indicate such a *wealth effect* does occur.

Normally, wealth does not change rapidly from year to year. Therefore, the wealth effect seldom causes sharp movements in consumption. From time to time, however, exceptions occur. When the stock market tumbled after 1929, fortunes collapsed and paper-rich capitalists became paupers overnight. Many wealthy people were forced to curtail their consumption. Similarly, as stock prices soared in the mid-1980s, adding more than a trillion dollars to people's wealth after 1982, consumption was probably bolstered by the flush of wealth people felt.

Other Influences   From time to time, economists have pointed to other variables as important determinants of saving or consumption. Over the last decade, in response to a declining national savings rate, some pointed to high tax rates and low real (or inflation-corrected) yields on saving. Martin Feldstein, Harvard professor and the chairman of the Council of Economic Advisers under President Reagan, has argued that a generous Social Security system reduces personal saving. Because we expect to get a large government pension when we retire, we save less for retirement today. Other economists have found that consumers tend to save more when inflation is heating up.

How important are influences other than income in determining consumption? Few doubt the importance of wealth, social factors, and expectations in affecting savings levels. But from year to year, the major determinant of changes in consumption appears to be changes in consumer incomes.

The National Consumption Function

Having reviewed the determinants of consumption, we may conclude that the level of disposable income is the primary determinant of the level of national consumption. Armed with this result, we can plot recent annual data on consumption and disposable income in Figure 7-7. The *scatter diagram* shows data for the period 1964–1988, with each point representing the level of consumption and income for a given year.

In addition, we have drawn a red line through the scatter points—labelled *CC* and marked "fitted consumption function." This fitted consumption function shows how closely consumption follows disposable income over the last quarter-century; indeed, economic historians have found that the close relationship between disposable income and consumption holds back to the nineteenth century. This relationship—that consumers always saved 6 percent of their disposable income—was thought to be among the most durable empirical regularities of macroeconomics. And you can see from Figure 7-7 that the fitted line tracks the actual data very closely.

But discrepancies arise from time to time. In the

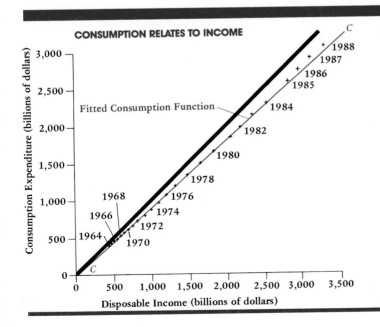

CONSUMPTION RELATES TO INCOME

Figure 7-7   A consumption function for the United States, 1964–1988

A straight line has been passed through the scatter of data points. Can you verify that the *MPC* slope of the fitted line is close to 0.94? How can you identify a falling personal savings rate for the 1986–1988 period? (Source: Figure 7-6.)

late 1980s, savings behavior in the United States departed from its long-term trend, with personal saving reaching a low of 3.2 percent in 1987. (We discusse the declining national savings rate later in this chapter.) This departure of behavior from the norm will remind us that economics is not a precise laboratory science where behavior is invariant from one year to the next. One of the great challenges of macroeconomics is to remain alert to changes in the structure of the economy—in this case, to try to understand the dramatic decline in the personal savings rate of the United States in the late 1980s.

B. THE DETERMINANTS OF INVESTMENT

The second major component of private spending is investment.[4] Investment plays two roles in macroeconomics. First, because it is a large and volatile component of spending, sharp changes in investment can have a major impact on aggregate demand and thence on output and employment.

In addition, investment leads to capital accumulation. Adding to the stock of useful buildings and equipment increases the nation's potential output and promotes economic growth in the long run. Thus investment plays a dual role, affecting short-run output through its impact on aggregate demand and influencing long-run output growth through the impact of capital formation on potential output.

We will return in later chapters to more specific theories of investment (the "accelerator mechanism" is derived in Chapter 10, while Chapter 30 provides the microeconomic theory of capital). It will be useful to foreshadow those later chapters at this point.

Recall from Table 6-5 that investment is broken down into three categories—purchases of residential structures, investment in business fixed plant and equipment, and additions to inventory. Of the total, about a quarter is residential housing, a twentieth normally is change in inventories, and the rest—averaging 70 percent of total investment over the last 5 years—is investment in business plant and equipment.

Ultimately, businesses invest when they expect that building a new factory or buying a new machine will earn them a profit—that is, will bring them revenues greater than the costs of the investment. This simple statement contains the three elements essential to understanding investment: revenues, costs, and expectations.

Revenues An investment will bring the firm additional revenues only if investing allows the firm to sell more. This suggests that a very important determinant of investment will be the overall level of output (or GNP). When factories are sitting idle, firms have relatively little need for *new* factories, so investment is low. More generally, investment depends upon the revenues that will be generated by the state of overall economic activity. For example, in the last major business downturn, output fell sharply from 1979 to 1982, and investment as a result declined by 22 percent.

Some studies suggest that the impact of output dominates the movement of investment over the business cycle. It is so important that we will return to a fuller discussion in Chapter 10's treatment of the accelerator.

Costs A second important determinant of the level of investment is the costs of investing. When we examine costs of investment, however, we find that they are somewhat more complicated than the costs for other commodities like haircuts or movies. This added complexity arises because investment goods last many years. Moreover, when a purchased good lasts many years, businesses and home buyers often tend to pay for such investments by borrowing funds (say through a mortgage).

---

[4]Remember that the term "investment" is used in a special way in macroeconomics. We define investment as the addition to the community's stock of tangible capital goods—capital goods being equipment, structures, or inventories. When IBM builds a new factory or when the Smiths build a new house, these activities are investment. Many people speak of "investing" when buying a piece of land, an old security, or any title to property. For economists these purchases clearly involve financial transaction or portfolio changes, for what one person is buying, someone else is selling. There is *investment* only when real capital is created.

What is the cost of borrowing? It is the *interest rate* on borrowed funds. Recall that the interest rate is the price paid for borrowing money for a period of time; you might have to pay 13 percent to borrow $1000 for a year. In the case of a family buying a house, the interest rate is the mortgage interest rate.

In addition, government *taxes* can affect the cost of investment. The federal government has a large array of fiscal weapons that either encourage or discourage investment in particular sectors. The federal corporation income tax takes up to 34 cents of every dollar of corporate profits, thereby discouraging investment in the corporate sector. Until 1986, the government gave a 10 percent credit on investment in equipment, partially offsetting the drag from other taxes. The overall level of taxation and the relative tax rates in different sectors, or even in different countries, will have a profound effect upon the investment behavior of profit-seeking companies.[5]

Expectations   The third element in the determination of investment is the state of expectations and business confidence. Investment is above all a gamble on the future, a bet that present and future revenues will be greater than present and future costs. If businesses are concerned that future economic conditions in Mexico will be depressed, or that a revolution in South Africa may lead to nationalization of their investments, or that the prices at which they can sell their oil will fall in the future—they will be reluctant to invest in Mexico, South Africa, or oil production.

Conversely, when businesses see the likelihood of a sharp business recovery in the near future, they begin to plan for plant expansion.

Thus investment decisions hang by a thread on expectations about future events—even worse, they ultimately hang on future events that are very hard to predict. It is not surprising that governments and central bankers spend many hours worrying about how to improve the state of business confidence.

We can sum up our review of the forces lying behind the investment decisions as follows:

Businesses invest to earn profits. Because capital goods last many years, investment decisions depend on (a) the demand for the output produced by the new investment, (b) the interest rates and taxes that influence the costs of the investment, and (c) the businessperson's expectation about the state of the economy.

Policy Channels on Investment

Because of the importance of investment in both short-run economic activity and long-run economic growth, policymakers often desire to increase the level of private investment. What channels exist for policy to affect investment?

The most powerful effect is through monetary policy, which affects interest rates and the cost of capital. Although this channel will be examined in depth in later chapters, we can summarize the mechanism at this point. The major point to understand is that the central bank, the Federal Reserve System, can operate monetary policy to raise or lower interest rates and thereby affect investment.

Suppose that the Federal Reserve wishes to take steps to increase investment spending. How would it go about this? As we explain in depth in Part Three, the Federal Reserve would use monetary policy to lower interest rates, which would make loans cheaper for businesses and households. With lower interest rates, businesses would tend to borrow more for their investments, and households would borrow more for new or larger homes. The pace of housing construction would quicken, and businesses would buy more equipment and structures. In short, investment spending would increase. Similarly, if the Federal Reserve desired to slow investment, it could raise interest rates and choke off borrowing for houses, factories, and equipment.

A second major route for affecting investment is through tax policy. As we explained above, the government takes some of the profits of enterprise by taxing business profits. Studies have shown that when taxes on profits, or tax provisions directly affecting

---

[5]In assessing the impact of taxation upon investment, economists want to know the overall "marginal tax rate" on the return on investment. The marginal tax rate is the additional tax paid on an additional dollar of income. For 1988, the marginal tax rate on income from corporate investments, including taxes levied by all levels of government (federal, state, and local), is about 38 percent (see *Economic Report of the President, 1987* for a discussion). This means that if an investment earns $100 of profit, the corporate investor keeps $62 and governments get $38. The high tax rate on corporate profits has led some to say that government is the largest single shareholder in American capitalism.

investment, are changed, business investment is affected. Changes in personal taxation can also affect investment in certain sectors of the economy, as was the case after the 1986 Tax Reform Act made many "tax shelters," such as those covering real estate, less attractive.

In addition, a country's microeconomic policies can influence the business climate and thereby affect the pace of investment. When France threatened to nationalize many of its industries in 1981, businesses cut back on their investment programs. When American regulatory programs became more stringent in the 1970s, imposing costly and complicated pollution-control requirements on new investment, businesses sometimes decided to patch up their outdated plants for a while longer rather than build brand-new factories. These and many other microeconomic programs affect the "tone" of the business climate and spill over to affect the overall state of investment.

Governments affect investment through active monetary policies, through tax programs, and through the general tone of microeconomic policies.

The Investment Demand Curve

Although a wide range of economic policies and events influence investment, the link between monetary policy, interest rates, and investment is all-impor-

INTEREST RATES AND INVESTMENT

(1) PROJECT	(2) TOTAL DOLLAR INVESTMENT IN PROJECT (millions)	(3) ANNUAL REVENUES PER $1,000 INVESTED	(4) (5) COST PER $1,000 OF PROJECT AT ANNUAL INTEREST RATE OF		(6) (7) ANNUAL NET PROFIT PER $1,000 INVESTED AT ANNUAL INTEREST RATE OF	
			10%	5%	10%	5%
A	$ 1	$1,500	$100	$50	$1,400	$1,450
B	4	220	100	50	120	170
C	10	160	100	50	60	110
D	10	130	100	50	30	80
E	5	110	100	50	10	60
F	15	90	100	50	−10	40
G	10	60	100	50	−40	10
H	20	40	100	50	−60	−10

Table 7-5   The net profit on investment depends on the interest rate

The economy has eight investment projects, ranked in order of return. Column (2) shows the total size of the projects. Column (3) calculates the perpetual return each year per $1000 invested.

Columns (4) and (5) then show the cost of the project, assuming all funds are borrowed, at interest rates of 10 and 5 percent; this is shown per $1000 of the project.

The last two columns calculate the annual net profit per $1000 invested in the project. If net profit is positive, then profit-maximizing firms will undertake the investment; if negative, the investment project will be rejected.

Note how the cutoff between profitable and unprofitable investments moves as the interest rate rises. (Where would the cutoff be if the interest rate rose to 15 percent per year?)

tant. Monetary policy is made each month; interest rates and other asset yields fluctuate daily. We should dwell a minute, then, on the relationship between interest rates and investment—what we will call the *investment demand curve.*

Consider a simplified economy where firms have numerous investment projects: project A, B, C, and so forth up to H. For simplicity, assume that they are so long-lived (like power plants or buildings) that we can ignore the need for replacement. In addition, assume that they yield a constant stream of net income each year. There is no inflation. Table 7-5 shows the financial data on each of the investment projects.

Consider project A. This project costs $1 million. It has a very high return—$1500 per year of revenues per $1000 invested (this is a return of 150 percent per year). Columns (4) and (5) show the cost of investment. For simplicity, assume that the investment is financed purely by borrowing at the market interest rate, here taken alternatively as 10 percent per year in column (4) and 5 percent in column (5).

Thus at a 10 percent annual interest rate, the cost of borrowing $1000 is $100 a year, as is shown in all entries of column (4); at a 5 percent interest rate, the borrowing cost is $50 per $1000 borrowed per year.

Finally, the last two columns show the *annual net profit* from the investment. For lucrative project A, the net annual profit is $1400 a year per $1000 invested at 10 percent interest rate. Project H loses money.

To review what we have found up to now: Firms can compare the annual revenues from an investment with the annual cost of capital, where the cost of capital depends upon the interest rate. The difference between annual revenue and annual cost is the annual net profit. When annual net profit is positive, the investment makes money, while a negative net profit denotes that the investment loses money.[6]

The annual net profit on an investment is shown in the last two columns of Table 7-5. Examine the last column, corresponding to a 5 percent interest rate. Note that at this interest rate, investment projects A through G would be profitable. We would thus expect profit-maximizing firms to invest in all seven projects, which [from column (2)] total up to $55 million in investment. Thus at a 5 percent interest rate, the demand for investment would be $55 million.

Say, however, that because of a tightening of monetary policy the interest rate rose to 10 percent. Then the cost of financing these investments would double. We see from column (6) that investment projects F and G become unprofitable at an interest rate of 10 percent; the demand for investment would fall to $30 million.

We can show the results of this analysis in Figure 7-8. This figure shows the *demand-for-investment schedule,* which is here a downward-sloping step function of the interest rate. Each step reflects the amount of investment that would be undertaken at the breakeven interest rate for projects A, B, and so forth.

What level of investment will come forth? If the market interest rate is 5 percent, the desired level of investment will occur at point *M,* which shows investment of $55 million. At this interest rate, projects A through G are undertaken.

If, because of the Federal Reserve's tightening of money or other conditions, interest rates were to rise to 10 percent, projects F and G would be squeezed out; the total demand for investment would lie at point *M'* in Figure 7-8, with a total investment demand of $30 million.

Shifts in the Investment Demand Curve

We have seen how interest rates affect the level of investment. Our earlier review suggests that investment is affected by other forces as well. For example, an increase in the total level of output in the economy will shift the investment demand curve out.

An increase in business taxation would have a depressing effect upon investment. Say that the government taxes away half the net yield in column (3) of Table 7-5, with interest costs in column (4) or (5) not being deductible. The net profits in column (6) or (7) would therefore decline. [Verify that at a 10 percent interest rate, a 50 percent tax on column (3) would

---

[6]This example is greatly simplified relative to most actual investment calculations. More often, they involve an uneven stream of returns, depreciation of capital, taxes, and multiple interest rates on borrowed funds. Chapter 30 and its appendix discuss the issue in greater detail, with stress on the need to "discount" future dollars because the interest rate is positive. A more complete discussion can be found in an advanced book on finance.

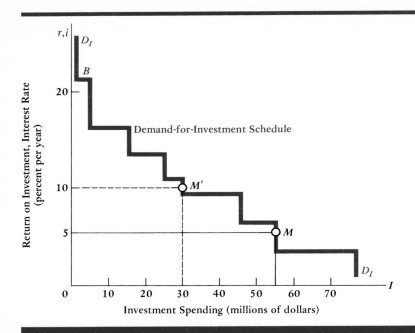

Figure 7-8 Demand for investment relates investment to the interest rate

The downward-stepping demand-for-investment schedule plots the level of investment that would occur at each interest rate, as calculated from the data in Table 7-5. Each sideward step represents a lump of investment: Project A has such a high rate that it is off the figure; the highest visible step is project B, shown at the upper left.

At each interest rate, all investments that have positive net profit will be undertaken. Thus at an interest rate of 5 percent, $55 million of investment will take place, as shown by the intersection at point M of the red demand-for-investment curve and the solid black interest-rate line. If interest rates were to rise to 10 percent, the new equilibrium would be at M', with $30 million of investment.

raise the cutoff to between projects B and C, and the demand for investment would decline to $5 million.]

Finally, note the importance of expectations. The yield shown in column (3) involves events in the distant future. What if investors become pessimistic and think that yields will soon halve? Or double? By working through these cases you can see how powerful an effect expectations can have on investment.

Figure 7-9 displays how each of these events—an increase in GNP, an increase in capital taxation, and a bout of business pessimism—would tend to shift the investment demand schedule, D_I.

Real vs. Nominal Interest Rates

If you look at a newspaper for the late 1970s or early 1980s, you will see *nominal* (or money) *interest rates* of 8, 15, or even 18 percent per year. These compare with rates of 3 or 4 or 5 percent in the early 1960s. Does this comparison suggest that investment should have collapsed in recent years? Or take Brazil, where interest rates have been more than 100 percent per year. Wouldn't this dampen even the most robust entrepreneurial spirits?

Surprisingly, the answer is no. Investment in the late 1970s and early 1980s in the United States was actually high by historical standards. And Brazil showed extremely high levels of real investment even though nominal interest rates were astronomical.

The answer to this puzzle lies in the concept of the *real rate of interest*. In the United States or Brazil, the high money interest rates were matched by extremely high inflation rates. True, you had to pay a great deal to borrow, but when you repaid, it was in depreciated dollars or cruzados. The interest rate in terms of real goods was actually low or even negative.

An example will clarify the point. Say that the interest rate and the inflation rate are both 20 percent. If you borrow $1000 today, you have to pay back $1200 next year. But because of inflation the real value of the $1200 next year is exactly the same as the $1000 this year. So, in effect, you are repaying the exact same amount of real goods. In this case, the interest rate in terms of real goods (the *real interest rate*) is zero, not 20 percent.

More generally, we have the following:

The real interest rate is the interest that borrowers pay in terms of real goods and services. It is equal to the nominal (or money) interest rate less the rate of inflation.

Chapter 12 contains a more detailed discussion of different kinds of interest rates, while Figure 12-3 shows the behavior of real and nominal interest rates in recent years.

How does this concept relate to investment? Recall that our analysis shown in Table 7-5 assumed no inflation, so the real and nominal rates of interest were the same. If there is inflation, then the yield shown in column (3) is no longer constant; it would be growing at the rate of inflation. Future returns would actually be higher than the first-period return, so the dollar value of the investment would be higher with inflation. In terms of our investment demand schedule in Figure 7-8, if the interest rate shown there is a nominal interest rate, then inflation will shift the curve up vertically.

Often, to remove the distortionary effects of inflation both on revenues and on nominal interest rates, economists find it easier to analyze investment in inflation-corrected terms. That is, the demand for investment can be analyzed by examining the effect of real output and real interest rates on real investment outlays (where "real" output and investment refer to the values of these variables in constant prices).

The concept of the real interest rate then resolves the paradox of high investment accompanying high interest rates, seen in Brazil and the United States in the 1970s. While nominal interest rates were high, *real* interest rates were low. The low real interest rates led to robust investment in the late 1970s.

Volatile Investment

After learning of the factors affecting investment, you will not be surprised to discover that investment is extremely volatile. Investment behaves unpredictably because it depends on such volatile factors as the success or failure of new and untried products, changes in tax rates and interest rates, political attitudes and approaches to stabilizing the economy, and similar changeable events of economic life.

Because it depends on jittery expectations about highly unpredictable future events, investment is extremely volatile.

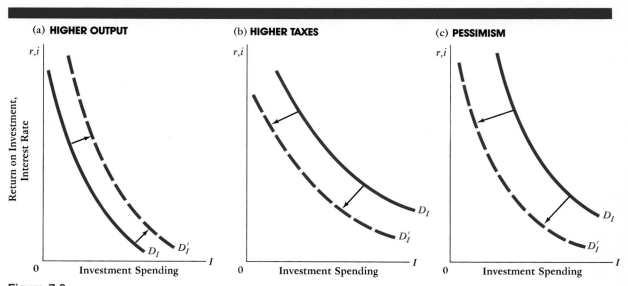

Figure 7-9

In the demand-for-investment (D_I) schedule, the arrows show the impact of **(a)** a higher level of GNP; **(b)** higher taxes on capital income; and **(c)** a burst of business pessimism such as might follow the election of a socialist government advocating nationalization of all major businesses.

INVESTMENT: A VOLATILE COMPONENT OF GNP

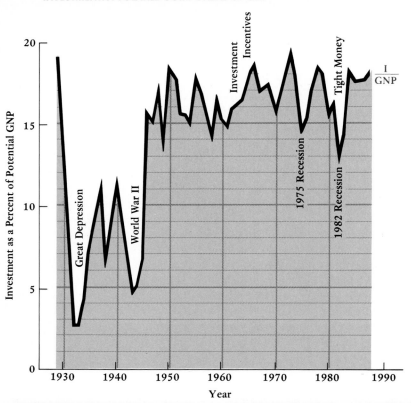

Figure 7-10   The volatility of investment, 1929–1988

This figure shows gross private domestic investment as a share of potential GNP. Note the extreme drop in investment during the 1930s and during World War II (when the economy was investing in the future of democracy rather than in factories). Note as well the sharp drop in the recessions of 1975 and 1982. (Source: U.S. Department of Commerce.)

We can get a picture of the instability of investment from Figure 7-10. This shows investment as a percentage of potential GNP. Note the low levels of investment during the Great Depression of the 1930s and during World War II; see how the investment incentives of the 1960s increased the share of investment in GNP; and note that business recessions, such as in 1975 and 1982, tend to produce a sharp decline in the investment-GNP ratio.

THE DECLINING U.S. SAVINGS RATE

In the last chapter we saw that saving always equals investment. This relationship holds in peace and war, in recession and boom, as a consequence of the defi-

nitions of the national income accounts. Because of the identity, and since capital formation is so important to long-run economic growth, people pay a great deal of attention to trends in national savings rates. Table 7-6 lists the gross savings rates of major countries in a recent year. It shows that Japan leads the list in saving as a percent of national income while the United States lags behind other major countries.

Moreover, the already low U.S. savings rate has declined even further over the last decade. Figure 7-11 shows trends in net private saving (equal to the sum of net foreign investment and net private domestic saving) over recent decades. This measure of the national savings rate has declined from over 10 percent after World War II to around 2 percent in the mid-1980s.

NATIONAL SAVINGS RATES

COUNTRY	NATIONAL SAVINGS RATE, 1984 (gross private saving as percent of GNP)
Japan	26
West Germany	19
Canada	17
France	16
United Kingdom	15
United States	14

Source: United Nations, *National Accounts Statistics,* 1986, and U.S. Department of Commerce.

Table 7-6   U.S. savings rate trails that of other major industrial countries

The table shows gross national private saving (equal to gross saving of households and businesses at home and abroad) divided by GNP.

What are the reasons for the precipitous decline in the national savings rate? This is a highly controversial question today, but economists point to the following potential causes:

• *Federal budget deficits*   Beginning in the early 1980s, the federal government began to incur large budget deficits. The budget deficit grew from a few billion annually in the late 1970s to an average of around $200 billion annually by the mid-1980s. Most economists believe that high budget deficits stimulate consumption and thereby lower national saving. Some have calculated that most of the recent decline in the national savings rate is due to the high budget deficits of the 1980s.[7]

• *Social Security system*   Many economists have argued that the introduction of the Social Security system has removed some of the need for private saving. In earlier times, a family would save during working years to build up a nest egg for retirement. Today, the government collects social security taxes

[7]One school of thought, originating in studies of Rochester's Robert Barro and adopted by the Treasury Department under the Reagan presidency, holds that government deficits will not stimulate consumption. The logic of the Barro theory is that, when the government incurs deficits, people know that the government will eventually have to raise taxes to pay the interest and principal on the debt. Rational and farsighted consumers will accordingly save just enough to offset the stimulative effect of government deficits. This theory has been found defective in a number of empirical studies.

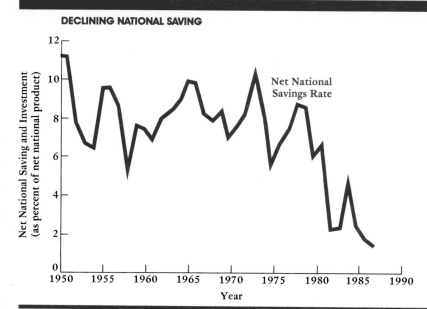

DECLINING NATIONAL SAVING

Net National Savings Rate

Figure 7-11   U.S. national saving has evaporated

The net national savings rate equals total private savings (domestic and foreign) minus depreciation, all divided by NNP; by identity, net national saving equals net private domestic and foreign investment. The savings rate has declined sharply since 1980. (Source: Congressional Budget Office, *Trends in Public Investment,* December 1987, updated by authors.)

and pays out social security benefits, displacing some of the need for private saving for retirement. In recent years, 9 percent of personal disposable income has come in the form of government pensions, health care, and disability pay for older persons.

Other income-support systems have a similar effect, reducing the need to save for a rainy day: crop insurance for farmers, unemployment insurance for workers, and medical care for the indigent all alleviate the precautionary motive for people to save.

▪ *Capital markets and attitudes about debt* Before the modern era, capital markets had numerous imperfections. People found it hard to borrow funds for worthwhile purposes, whether for buying a house, financing an education, or starting a business. As capital markets developed, often with the help of government, new loan instruments developed, allowing people to borrow more easily. One good example of this is student loans. Decades ago, college educations were financed either by parents paying or by students working. Today, because the federal government guarantees many student loans, students can borrow to pay for their education and repay their educational loans from their own earnings later in life.

In addition, some people believe that Americans have adopted a psychology of debt quite different from that of an earlier age. Whereas Shakespeare's Polonius warned his son, ''neither a borrower nor a lender be,'' the widespread availability of credit-card debt, installment credit, and home-equity loans tells people today, ''buy now, pay later.''

▪ *Other sources* Many other suspects have been indicted in an attempt to find the culprit in the case of the declining national savings rate. Some pointed to high inflation in the late 1970s and early 1980s, although this cause would seem to be acquitted given the continued decline of saving as inflation disappeared in the mid-1980s. Others pointed to attenuated incentives to save in recent years in the form of high

tax rates and low post-tax returns as an important cause of the low savings rate; here again, the argument appears wanting because saving did not recover even after tax rates fell and real interest rates rose in the 1980s. Further suggestions include the rapid increase in the value of household wealth (which might lead people to save less of their income) and sociological hypotheses such as a perceived decline in the Protestant ethic (an ethic that Tawney and other historians thought was a major contributor to the rise of capitalism in earlier centuries).

The declining national savings rate remains a puzzling phenomenon testing the ingenuity of macroeconomists. While no one has demonstrated conclusively why the U.S. national savings rate has dropped so sharply in recent years, virtually all believe that the savings rate is too low to guarantee a vital and healthy rate of investment in the 1990s.

ON TO OUTPUT DETERMINATION

We have now completed our survey, in the last chapter, of the major components of income and output and, in this chapter, of the determinants of investment and consumption. We have seen that consumption and investment can fluctuate from year to year, and in the case of investment the fluctuations can be quite sharp. This suggests that the total flow of dollar spending, of aggregate demand, is not guaranteed to grow smoothly from year to year.

The next two chapters investigate how the forces of spending and production interact to give an equilibrium level of national output. We will see that actual GNP can diverge from its potential. And when GNP gaps occur, we will see high or low levels of unemployment while inflation gathers steam or abates. At the heart of the theories we will investigate, however, are the movements of consumption and investment analyzed in this chapter.

SUMMARY

A. Consumption and Saving

1. Income is an important determinant of consumption (food, clothing, and other items of household spending) and of saving. The *consumption function* is the schedule relating total consumption to total income. Because any dollar of income is either saved or consumed, the *savings schedule* is the other side or mirror image of the consumption function. The characteristics of the consumption and savings schedules are summarized on pages 132–133 and should be reviewed.

2. We can add together individual consumption functions to obtain a national consumption function. In simplest form, this shows total consumption expenditures as a function of disposable income. Other variables also affect consumption: Wealth and expectations about future income have a significant impact on consumption patterns.

B. The Determinants of Investment

3. The second large component of spending is investment in housing, plant, and equipment. The major motivation behind investment is to earn a net profit, that is, to invest where present and future expected revenues exceed present and future expected costs. The major economic forces that determine investment are therefore the revenues produced by investment (primarily influenced by the state of the business cycle), the cost of investment (determined by interest rates and tax policy), and the state of expectations about the future. Because the determinants of investment depend on highly unpredictable future events, investment is the most volatile component of aggregate spending.

4. An important relationship is the investment demand schedule, connecting the level of investment spending and the interest rate. When firms' choices of investment projects are driven by profits, this will lead to a downward-sloping investment demand curve. A higher interest rate will lead firms to cancel some investment projects.

5. In making investment decisions, the real interest rate is particularly relevant. The real rate of interest corrects the nominal interest rate for the rate of inflation. Thus, real interest rate = nominal interest rate − rate of inflation.

6. The national savings rate has declined sharply in the last decade. Studies point to the growing fiscal deficit of the federal government, to social security pension programs, to changes in capital markets, and to changed attitudes about debt as possible reasons. Most economists believe that a lower federal deficit is the best single way to increase the national savings rate today.

CONCEPTS FOR REVIEW

consumption and savings functions
marginal propensity to consume *(MPC)*
  and marginal propensity to save *(MPS)*

determinants of consumption: permanent
  income, wealth
role of interest rates in *I*

$MPC + MPS \equiv 1$
breakeven point, 45° line
disposable income
national consumption function vs.
  household consumption function

determinants of investment: revenues,
  costs, expectations
investment demand function
real vs. nominal interest rate
trends in savings rate

QUESTIONS FOR DISCUSSION

1. Summarize the budget patterns for food, clothing, luxuries, saving.

2. What are some of the reasons why people save? Why has the U.S. savings rate declined in recent years?

3. Exactly how were the *MPC* and *MPS* in Table 7-4 computed? Illustrate by calculating *MPC* and *MPS* between points *A* and *B*. Explain why it must always be true that $MPC + MPS \equiv 1$.

4. I consume *all* my income at every level of income. Draw my consumption and savings schedules. What are my *MPC* and *MPS?*

5. A noted economist has written: "The 1986 Tax Reform Act raises the tax rate on corporations by as much as 20 percentage points [e.g., from 18 percent of profits to 38 percent of profits]. In the long run, this may well reduce the stock of plant and equipment by 10 to 15 percent." Explain the reasoning behind this statement. Illustrate using the demand-for-investment schedule.

6. Estimate your income, consumption, and saving for last year. If you dissaved (consumed more than your income) how did you finance your dissaving? Estimate the composition of your consumption in terms of each of the major categories listed in Table 7-1.

7. "Along the consumption function, income changes more than consumption." What does this imply for the *MPC* and *MPS?*

8. What would be the effects of the following on the investment demand function illustrated in Table 7-5 and Figure 7-8:

    (a) A doubling of the annual revenues per $1000 invested shown in column (3)

    (b) A rise in interest rates to 15 percent per year

    (c) The addition of a ninth project with data in the first three columns of: (J, 10, 70)

    (d) A 50 percent tax on *net* profits shown in columns (6) and (7)

9. Using the augmented investment-demand schedules in Question 8, and assuming that the interest rate is 10 percent, calculate the level of investment for cases (a) through (d).

10. Advanced problem: Suppose the consumption function is $C = 450 + \frac{2}{3} DI$. Now calculate the *MPC* as $dC/d(DI) = \frac{2}{3}$. From the identity $S + C \equiv DI$, verify the formula for the *SS* schedule: $S = -450 + \frac{1}{3} DI$. From this, calculate *MPS* as $dS/d(DI)$ and verify that it does equal $1 - MPC = 1 - \frac{2}{3} = \frac{1}{3}$.

11. Advanced problem: According to the life-cycle model, people consume each year an amount related to their *lifetime* income, not simply to the income of the given year. Assume that you expect to receive future incomes (in constant dollars) according to the following schedule:

(1) YEAR	(2) INCOME	(3) CONSUMPTION	(4) SAVING	(5) CUMULATIVE SAVING (end of year)
1	$30,000			
2	30,000			
3	25,000			
4	15,000			
5	0 (retired)			0

Assume that there is no interest paid on saving. You have no initial saving. Further assume that you want to ''smooth'' your consumption (or have equal consumptions each year) because of diminishing extra satisfaction from extra consumption. Derive your best consumption trajectory, filling the figures into column (3). Then in column (4) calculate your saving and put your end-of-period wealth, or cumulative saving, for each year into column (5). What is your average savings rate in the first 4 years?

Next, assume that a government social security program taxes you $2000 in each of your working years and provides you an $8000 pension in year 5. If you still desire to smooth consumption, calculate your revised savings plan. How has the social security program affected your consumption? What is the effect on your average savings rate in the first 4 years?

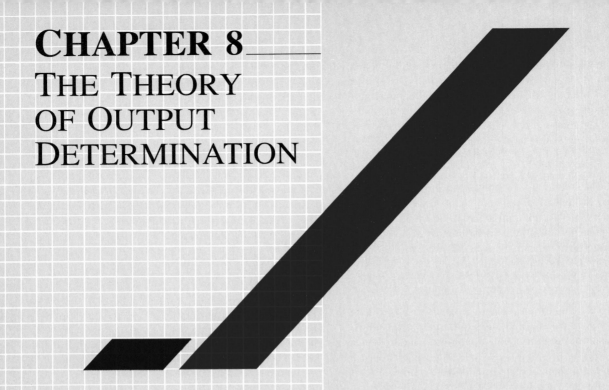

CHAPTER 8

THE THEORY
OF OUTPUT
DETERMINATION

*If the propensity to consume and the rate of new
investment result in a deficient effective demand, the
actual level of employment will fall short of the
supply of labour potentially available.*

J. M. Keynes
General Theory (1936)

WE HAVE MET the major personae—aggregate demand and supply, output and prices, the consumption function, saving, and investment. In the background is a history of inflation and unemployment, growth and stagnation. The stage is set for the central economic drama of our times: Can a capitalist economy achieve full employment with stable prices? Or is it doomed to repeated cycles of inflation and unemployment, boom and bust?

This chapter and the following one are addressed to these central issues. In the present chapter we start with a return to the tools of aggregate demand and supply. The first section presents the underpinnings of aggregate demand-and-supply analysis, examines the differences between the classical and the Keynesian approaches, and then shows how opposite are their views of both the functioning of the macroeconomy and the best policies to combat inflation and unemployment.

Section B then presents the Keynesian "multiplier" model. This approach shows how, when output is below the full-employment level, consumption

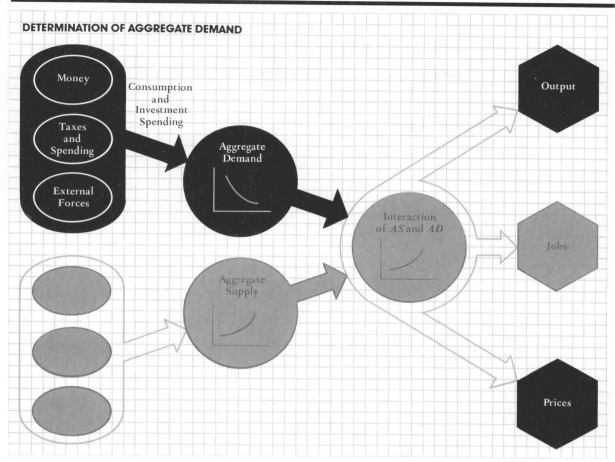

DETERMINATION OF AGGREGATE DEMAND

Figure 8-1   Chapter 8 analyzes the determination of output

We now concentrate on the role of aggregate demand in output determination. The first section examines the complete aggregate supply-and-demand interaction; it shows the crucial role of price flexibility.

  The second section examines an underemployed economy, where prices are inflexible in the short run. It shows that aggregate demand is then the primary determinant of output.

and investment spending interact to determine the equilibrium level of GNP. The multiplier model is important today as a way of providing a simple explanation of how shocks to investment, foreign trade, and government tax and spending policies can affect output and employment. Although the multiplier model is an oversimplified approach to output determination, it contains a valid and enduring insight into the behavior of an advanced industrial economy in the short run.

  Figure 8-1 provides a schematic overview of the major issues addressed in this chapter.

A. FOUNDATIONS OF AGGREGATE SUPPLY AND DEMAND ———

Earlier chapters have provided an overview of the major concepts of macroeconomics and have introduced the tools of aggregate supply and demand. In this section, our task is threefold. We will first examine in depth the foundations of aggregate demand analysis. Second, we will discuss the foundations of aggregate supply, focusing especially upon the way output supplied responds to changes in the price level. Finally, we will sketch the major differences between the Keynesian and the classical approaches to macroeconomics—with respect to both their analysis of the business cycle and their prescriptions for economic policy.

ANALYTICAL FOUNDATIONS OF AGGREGATE DEMAND

Chapter 5 explained that national output and the price level are determined by the interplay of aggregate demand and supply. This means that the actual level of production is determined in part by aggregate demand (the quantity of goods and services that people, businesses, and governments want to buy) and in part by aggregate supply (the quantity of goods and services that businesses want to sell). We begin by describing the important determinants of aggregate demand.

Aggregate demand (or *AD*) is the total or aggregate quantity of output that will be willingly bought at a given level of prices. *AD* is the total spending in all product sectors: on consumption, private domestic investment, government purchases of goods and services, and net exports. Its four components are the following.

1. As Chapter 7 indicated, *consumption (C)* is primarily determined by personal disposable income, which is personal income less taxes, and by consumer wealth. Aggregate demand analysis focuses on the reaction of *real* consumption (that is, consumption in constant prices) to the aggregate price level. Studies indicate that, when the price level rises, consumers tend to buy fewer goods and services because their real incomes and real wealth tend not to keep pace with the price level.[1]

2. The last chapter also examined the determinants of *investment (I)* spending, that is, of purchases of structures and equipment and accumulation of inventories. This analysis suggested that the major determinants of investment were the level of output, the cost of capital (as determined by tax policies along with interest rates and other financial conditions), and expectations about the future. The major channel by which economic policy can affect investment is through monetary policy, which tends to raise interest rates and reduce investment when the money supply grows more slowly, and to lower interest rates and stimulate investment when the money supply grows more rapidly.

3. A third component of aggregate demand is *government spending on goods and services (G)*. As Chapter 6 explained, such expenditures, on all levels of government, consist of purchases of goods like tanks or road-building equipment as well as of the services of judges and public-school teachers. Unlike the first two terms, this component of aggregate demand is determined directly by the spending decisions of governments; when the Pentagon buys a new fighter aircraft, this output immediately adds to the GNP.

4. A final component of aggregate demand is *net exports (X)*, which is equal to the value of exports minus the value of imports. A detailed discussion of the determinants of net exports is postponed until the second half of the next chapter, but we can mention the

---

[1] The tendency of real consumption to lag when prices rise relates to a famous law called the "real balance effect" or the "Pigou effect," after the classical economist A. C. Pigou. The rationale behind this effect is that part of people's wealth consists of holdings of money or money balances (currency and checking accounts), which are fixed in dollar terms. As the price level rises, the *real* value of the money balances declines. For example, say that you hold $500 in money, in cash and in your checking account, and the price level is 1. If the price level doubles to 2, then your money balances will buy only half the quantity of consumption goods.

As a result of the diminution of the real value of your wealth, your consumption spending will tend to decline. This inverse relation between the price level and real consumption spending is one of the major reasons for the downward-sloping *AD* curve.

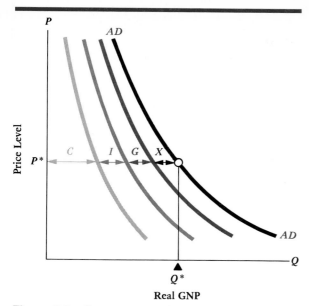

Figure 8-2   Components of aggregate demand

Aggregate demand *(AD)* consists of four spending streams—consumption *(C)*, domestic private investment *(I)*, government spending on goods and services *(G)*, and net exports *(X)*.

Aggregate demand shifts arise from changes in economic policies (such as monetary changes or changes in government expenditures or tax rates) or from shifts in external events affecting spending (as would be the case with changes in foreign output, affecting *X*, or business confidence, affecting *I*).

major factors at this point. Imports are significantly affected by domestic income and output, by the ratio of domestic to foreign prices, and by the foreign exchange rate of the dollar. Exports are heavily affected by foreign incomes and outputs, by relative prices, and by foreign exchange rates. Net exports, then, will be determined by domestic and foreign incomes, by relative prices, and by exchange rates.

We show the *AD* curve in Figure 8-2, where aggregate demand is built up from its four major components. For example, at price level P^*, we can read the level of consumption, investment, government spending, and net exports. The sum of the four spending streams at the reference price level is then aggre-

gate spending, or aggregate demand, at that price level.

Behind the Aggregate Demand Curve

Figure 8-2 is a highly simplified depiction of the determinants of aggregate demand. As we use the *AD* curve in the chapters that follow, we should remember what variables or forces lie behind the *AD* curve, and that this is a *macro*economic demand function, not a *micro*economic curve.

Behind Aggregate Demand   What forces lie behind the aggregate demand curve in Figure 8-2? Table 8-1 on the next page outlines some of the major ones. Most discussion in the popular press and in technical economic literature focuses on the policy variables—monetary and fiscal actions—because those are ones that governments can use to affect economic performance. The second part of the table includes variables that either are outside the scope of macroeconomic analysis proper (such as demographic changes) or have significant independent movement (such as movements of the stock market).

What would be the effect of changes in the variables lying behind the *AD* curve? Let us suppose, for example, that the government decided to increase defense spending on missiles or tanks. The effect of this step would be to increase the spending on *G*. Unless some other component of spending declined to offset the increase in *G*, the total *AD* curve would shift out and to the right as *G* increased. Similarly, an increase in the money supply, an improvement in business confidence, an increase in the value of consumer wealth (say because of a stock-price increase), or a population increase would lead to an increase in aggregate demand.

A Warning about Aggregate Demand Curves   Having introduced the *AD* curve, we should pause for a warning that the aggregate demand curve is quite distinct from a microeconomic demand curve. What are the major differences? Recall from Chapter 4 that the microeconomic demand curve, say for corn, has the price of corn on the vertical axis and the quantity of corn on the horizontal axis. In constructing the

VARIABLE	IMPACT ON AGGREGATE DEMAND
Policy variables	
Monetary policy	Increase in money supply lowers interest rates and improves credit conditions, producing higher levels of investment and consumption of durable goods.
Fiscal policy	Increases in expenditures on goods and services directly increase spending; tax reductions raise income and thereby spur spending increases.
External variables	
Expectations and business confidence	Greater confidence leads businesses to expect greater profits and thereby increases investment.
Foreign output	Foreign boom leads to an increase in net exports.
Asset values	Stock-price or housing-price rise produces greater level of wealth of consumers and thereby increases consumption; may also lead to lower cost of capital and thereby increase investment.
Demographic changes	Higher population levels increase consumption; growth in number of family units increases demand for housing investment.

Table 8-1   Many factors lie behind aggregate demand

The simplest aggregate demand curve relates total spending to the price level. This table displays other important factors that affect aggregate demand—some of these factors represent policy variables while others are external factors. Changes in any of these would produce a shift in the *AD* curve.

microeconomic demand curve, we keep all other prices and total consumer incomes constant.

In the aggregate demand curve, by contrast, the general price level is allowed to vary on the vertical axis. Moreover, total output and incomes vary along the *AD* curve, rather than being fixed as in the case of the microeconomic demand curve.

Finally, the negative slope of the microeconomic demand curve comes from the ability of consumers to substitute other goods for the good in question. If the corn price rises, demand falls because consumers substitute wheat and meat for corn, using more of the relatively inexpensive commodities and less of the relatively expensive one. The reasons underlying the slope of the aggregate demand curve are different. Total spending falls when the overall price level rises, among other reasons, because the real purchasing power of consumer wealth (or real money balances) declines as higher prices eat away at its dollar value.

To summarize, recall that macroeconomic *AD* curves differ from their microeconomic cousins because they refer to changes in the prices and output for the economy as a whole and because the negative relation between aggregate price and quantity depends upon the impact of price upon the real wealth of consumers.

Alternative Views of Aggregate Demand

Most macroeconomists find the theory of aggregate demand essential to understanding both the process of economic growth and the division of GNP into different components. Economists differ in the emphasis they place on different forces affecting aggregate demand. We will mention some of these differences briefly here.

In analyzing movements in aggregate demand, some economists concentrate on the importance of monetary forces, especially on the role of the supply of money. (Recall that money has a precise meaning in economics: It refers to those things—dollar bills, nickels, checks—that serve as a medium of exchange and a standard of value.) According to these economists, the supply of money is the primary determinant of the total *dollar* value of spending. More precisely, this group holds that there is a strict relationship between the dollar value of all purchases and the amount of money available. If we identify total dollar spending with nominal GNP (nominal GNP being the current-price value of total purchases), then nominal GNP will be proportional to the money supply. (The importance of monetary forces will be extensively analyzed in later chapters.)

Other economists have a different emphasis. Some believe that autonomous spending flows play a major role in aggregate demand. Such spending streams include government spending, investment, and exports. In analyzing the ups and downs of the business cycle, this approach focuses on changes in spending decisions of governments, along with changes in investment and foreign economic conditions, particularly in the short run.

The majority of macroeconomists today adhere to an eclectic approach, believing that a wide variety of forces operate to affect aggregate demand. Table 8-1 lists many of the most important policy and external variables that would be examined by this group. These macroeconomists point to different forces moving the economy during different periods. During World War II, with military spending absorbing almost half of GNP, fiscal policy would be seen as the leading determinant of demand; a similar analysis might have applied during the Korean and Vietnam wars. In recent years, particularly during the period of tight money from 1979 to 1982, monetary policy exercised a dominant influence over the macroeconomy.

Macroeconomists generally look to yet other forces in different times. From 1855 to 1875, due to increased investment opportunities, railroads were built all over the world, and the industrial economies enjoyed a sustained economic expansion. In the next two decades, nothing took the place of the railroads, and the United States suffered from a business depression. The early 1980s witnessed a massive decline in U.S. net exports, which had the effect of contracting greatly the X portion of the AD curve in Figure 8-2, and thereby shifting the AD curve sharply to the left.

This concludes our survey of the major elements of aggregate demand. These form one blade of the scissors that determine national output and the overall price level. We turn next to the other blade, aggregate supply, after which we will put aggregate supply and demand together and analyze today's schism between classical and Keynesian macroeconomics.

DETERMINANTS OF AGGREGATE SUPPLY

Turn now to the supply side of the macroeconomy. While aggregate demand tells how much people will want to spend on GNP given prices, taxes, the money supply, and so forth, aggregate supply tells how much output businesses will want to supply given prices, productive capacity, costs, and other conditions.

Aggregate supply is central to both the long-run and the short-run evolution of the economy. In the short run, the interaction between aggregate demand and aggregate supply determines the level of output, unemployment, and capacity utilization as well as the impetus to inflation. Over periods of a decade or more, aggregate supply is the major factor behind economic growth. Why does North America have so much higher a living standard than does South America? Why is national output in the United States so much higher in 1990 than it was in 1890? The answers lie in the fact that aggregate supply is so much

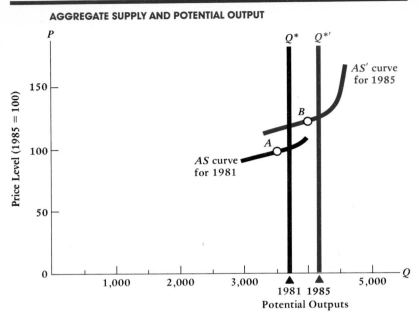

AGGREGATE SUPPLY AND POTENTIAL OUTPUT

Figure 8-3   Potential-output increase shifts out aggregate supply

For two selected years, we plot potential output as the vertical lines marked Q^* and $Q^{*'}$.

From 1981 to 1985, potential output increased, which shifted aggregate supply (AS) to the right. In addition, the AS curve shifted up somewhat from 1981 to 1985, reflecting the rise in wages and other costs of production. As we show above, the upward-sloping AS curves for each year are relatively flat until they reach the potential-output line, and then they turn sharply vertical when output exceeds potential output.

higher in the United States in 1990 than it was a century earlier or than it is today in South America.

Our detailed study of aggregate supply is contained in the economic-growth survey in Chapters 36 and 37. At this stage we will present only a skeletal analysis, one that will help to explain the key issues in aggregate supply theory.

Aggregate Supply and Potential Output

Aggregate supply (or *AS*) refers to the total national output that businesses willingly produce and sell during a given year. We can construct the aggregate supply curve as the graph that shows the level of real output that will be produced at each possible price level. But just as we asked what lay behind the aggregate demand curve, here we are interested in knowing the forces that determine aggregate supply.

Aggregate supply depends fundamentally upon two distinct sets of forces: potential output and wage-price behavior. Let us examine each of these influences.

Potential Output In the long run, aggregate supply is derived from the capacity of the economy to produce; that is, over time, aggregate supply depends primarily upon potential output.

Recall that potential GNP represents the sustainable capacity or high-employment output of the economy. More precisely, potential GNP equals the level of output that the economy could produce if only 6 percent of the labor force were unemployed.

What is the relation between potential output and aggregate supply? Figure 8-3 shows potential output and the aggregate supply curve for two different years, 1981 and 1985. The vertical lines, marked $Q*$ and $Q*'$, show the levels of potential output in the two years. According to studies, real potential output grew 2.3 percent per year over this 4-year period.

In addition, Figure 8-3 shows an illustrative short-run aggregate supply curve for each of the two years, with the 1981 AS curve in solid black and the 1985 curve drawn as a solid red curve. Note two points in Figure 8-3. First, an increase in potential output tends to shift the entire AS curve to the right. Second, an increase in the cost of production, with no change in potential output, shifts the AS curve straight up. The overall change in the AS curve from 1981 to 1985 can be found by combining these two factors: The rightward shift from the increase in potential output along with the upward shift from higher production costs yields the upward and rightward shift in AS from 1981 to 1985.

Wage-Price Behavior The second major influence on aggregate supply is the behavior of wages and prices. We can see in Figure 8-3 that potential output serves as a kind of hinge to which the AS curve is attached. Below potential output, the AS curve is fairly flat because prices and wages are sticky when GNP is below its potential. As real output begins to exceed potential output, prices come unstuck and start to move up rapidly, so that to the right of potential output, the AS curve turns up sharply.

What forces lie behind the slope of the AS curve? Put in terms of real-world behavior, why do prices respond relatively little to output changes when unemployment is high, whereas output increases tend to drive prices up sharply when capacity utilization is high? For that matter, why is there any relationship at all between the level of aggregate output and the overall price level?

The answers to these questions lie in the way that wages and prices are determined in a modern industrial economy. The key point is that, because some

elements of cost are sticky or inflexible in the short run, businesses will respond to higher levels of total spending by producing and selling higher levels of output. The emphasis here is upon the *stickiness* of costs in the *short run*.

Example for a Firm Figure 8-4 will illustrate the point. Let us say that a typical firm is producing 800 units of output at a price of $100 per unit in a factory that has a capacity of 1100 units. We can represent the initial situation as point A in Figure 8-4. Now suppose a burst of spending occurs. The firm knows that many of its costs are set in dollar terms in the short run: Workers are paid $14.50 per hour, rent for the building is $1400 per month, managers are paid a total of $11,000 per month, and so forth. How will the typical

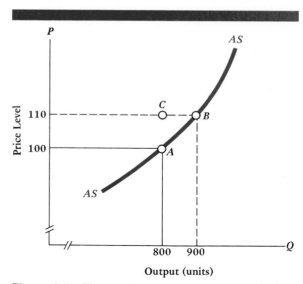

Figure 8-4   Firms will produce more output at a higher price level in short run

In the short run, because of some sticky costs, a typical firm at point A will respond to higher demand by producing more output at a higher price level at point B. Because of this output response, the short-run aggregate supply curve slopes upward.

In the long run, after all costs have adjusted and have risen by the same 10 percent as output price, the firm will desire to produce the original level of output at point C.

firm react? Faced with this situation, the firm could rationally decide that its best response is to raise the price to $110 per unit and increase production to 900 units, shown in Figure 8-4 as point *B*.

This reaction—raising prices and output in response to higher demand—can carry over to the economy as a whole. As aggregate demand increases, say because the government buys more boots for the army or builds more roads, all firms together will react by increasing production and raising the prices of boots, cement, and other goods. In sum, when some elements of costs are sticky and where there is excess productive capacity, firms will respond to an increase in spending by increasing both output and prices.

Sources of Inflexibility   We should pause to consider the sources of the stickiness in prices and costs. The most important of these is wages. Almost half of all manufacturing workers are covered by long-term union contracts. In the United States, these contracts generally extend for 3 years and specify a dollar wage rate, e.g., $14.50 per hour for the hypothetical example discussed above. For the life of the labor agreement, the wage rate faced by the firm will be largely fixed in dollar terms. When spending on cement or boots or other goods increases, firms can raise their prices and outputs without having wages react; that is, if spending rises, firms can for a while increase output and prices and earn higher profits.

Many other prices and costs are similarly sticky in the short run. When a firm rents a building, the lease will often last for a year and sometimes will extend for a decade. The rental will generally be set in dollar terms. In addition, firms often sign contracts with their suppliers that specify the prices to be paid for materials or components, with the prices predetermined for a month or even a year. Some prices are fixed by government regulation, particularly those for utilities like electricity, gas, water, and telephones. Because these costs are rigid, firms can expand their output, raise their output prices, and make greater profits in the face of higher levels of aggregate demand.

Using this analysis, we can understand why, as aggregate demand rises higher and higher, firms respond with greater and greater price increases. As a

firm's output approaches its capacity, there is less and less room to increase production. Moreover, because competing firms are also close to capacity, all firms can raise prices to a greater extent without losing customers to rivals. Therefore, as production rises above potential output, a larger fraction of the response to demand increases comes as price increases and a smaller fraction comes as output increases. In terms of the aggregate supply curve, this implies that the short-run *AS* curve will be relatively flat to the left of the potential-output line, where output is less than potential output, but will become steeper and steeper as output increases, that is, further and further to the right of the potential-output line.

If the sticky wages, rents, and other costs allow firms in the short run to raise output when demand increases, the *AS* curve will be upward-sloping rather than vertical in the short run. By contrast, we can begin to understand why *AS* is likely to become vertical or near-vertical in the long run as the sticky prices come unstuck. A review of the list of dollar-fixed elements of cost—wages, rents, prices of materials and components, and regulated prices—will reveal that all these elements are unlikely to remain unchanged forever. As the sticky elements of cost, whether labor-union contracts or rent agreements, expire and are renegotiated, these costs will begin to adjust to the higher prices. After the general price level shown in Figure 8-4 has risen 10 percent because of the higher demand, money wages are eventually likely to respond by moving up 10 percent as well. Rents, purchased materials and components, regulated prices—all these will eventually also move up 10 percent.

What will be the net effect, in the long run, when both costs and prices have moved up 10 percent together? When this happens, firms will no longer be able to profit from the higher level of aggregate demand, so output will return to its original level. In terms of Figure 8-4, if both costs and prices rise by 10 percent, the desired level of production will move from point *A* to point *C*, with output remaining at its original level of 800 units.

We can summarize as follows: The aggregate supply for an economy will differ from potential output in the short run because of inflexible elements of cost. In the short run, firms will respond to higher demand

AGGREGATE SUPPLY IN THE LONG AND SHORT RUN

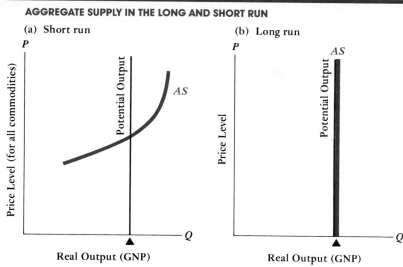

Figure 8-5   Mainstream macroeconomists hold that aggregate supply curve slopes upward in short run but turns vertical in long run

Because of the stickiness of wages and other costs, mainstream macroeconomists hold that the *AS* curve tends to slope upward gently in the short run, indicating that increases in aggregate demand will coax out higher output to be sold at higher prices. In the long run, as all wages and costs adjust to the higher price level, output tends to be unaffected by the level of aggregate demand, so the *AS* curve turns vertical.

The classical approach holds that the short run is vanishingly small, so the *AS* curve is vertical for all practical purposes.

by raising both production and prices. In the longer run, as costs respond to the higher level of prices, most or all of the response to higher demand comes in prices and little or none comes in higher output.

Alternative Views of Aggregate Supply

The discussion of aggregate supply has pointed to the reasons why in the short run output supplied may increase at higher levels of aggregate demand. It further suggested that in the long run the output response might well disappear as costs and prices all adjusted to demand changes. In terms of the *AS* curve, this distinction translates into a difference between a short-run upward-sloping *AS* curve and a long-run

vertical *AS* curve. Figure 8-5 shows how aggregate supply curves would look for both the short run and the long run.

One of the liveliest macroeconomic controversies surrounds the behavior of aggregate supply or the shape of the *AS* curve. As explained above, modern mainstream macroeconomists point to long-term contracts and slowly adjusting expectations, arguing that the short run may last years or even decades. Other economists believe that most markets are workably competitive and that prices and wages are sufficiently flexible, so that the short run is very short indeed. These two groups find markedly different answers to questions about aggregate supply behavior. Having analyzed the mainstream approach, we describe here the alternative view.

Classical Analysis Classical economists, including many distinguished economists from the time of Adam Smith up to today's new classical school, tend to hold that wages and prices are sufficiently flexible that markets will "clear," or come to equilibrium, very quickly. They might point to the stock market or the commodity markets, where supply and demand shocks get reflected in prices in a matter of minutes. If prices and wages adjust rapidly, then the short run will be so short that it can be neglected for practical purposes of macroeconomic analysis. In other words, for the purpose of understanding most macroeconomic phenomena, the long-run analysis with its vertical or near-vertical *AS* curve is the appropriate approach. The classical macroeconomists conclude that the economy always operates at full employment or at its potential output. In terms of the above discussion, the short run is so short that it disappears.

It follows from the classical analysis that output does not respond to changes in aggregate demand. To understand this argument, consider an economy in an initial full-employment equilibrium. An increase in aggregate demand might initially tempt producers to produce more. But the increased demand would, in a classical world of flexible wages and prices, quickly lead to rising output prices and higher costs for factors of production. The new equilibrium might be one in which output prices rose 10 percent, but this would be followed almost immediately by a 10 percent increase in wages, rents, oil prices, highway tolls, taxes, and all other costs. In the new equilibrium, then, the overall price level might have increased by 10 percent, but this would be quickly followed by a 10 percent cost increase, so that all relative prices (that is, the ratio of output price to production cost or the relative prices of different outputs) would remain unchanged.

But, the classical economist continues, why would a supplier change its output level if all prices and costs were increased by the same percentage? That is, why would a firm change its desired supply if all dollar magnitudes moved together while leaving all relative prices in the same relationship? The answer is that rational firms and workers in smoothly functioning markets would not change their output supply or labor supply. In sum, in a situation where prices and wages were completely flexible, supplies and demands in individual markets would lead to a situation where higher aggregate demand would simply raise all costs and prices and leave overall output unchanged.

Before concluding this section, we should reiterate the modern mainstream view on aggregate supply. A considerable body of evidence suggests that wages and prices adjust slowly to economic shocks. In the case of wages, often set by multiyear collective bargaining agreements, full adjustment to labor market changes can take a decade as opposed to the minutes or seconds required for prices to change in stock or commodity markets. Because of this slow response of wages and prices to changing economic conditions, output will for a substantial period of time respond to aggregate demand, and the aggregate supply curve is therefore upward-sloping.

Having analyzed the mainstream and the classical approaches, turn back to Figure 8-5 on the last page to review the two views.

The classical view holds that aggregate supply is independent of the overall price level and that the *AS* curve is therefore vertical; this behavior occurs when prices and wages are flexible, responding quickly to economic shocks.

The classical approach contrasts with modern mainstream macroeconomics, which holds that sticky wages and prices allow output to respond to changes in aggregate demand over an extended period; that is, the *AS* curve is gently upward-sloping rather than vertical for a considerable number of years. Virtually all major schools of macroeconomics hold that the *AS* curve is vertical over the long run.

KEYNESIAN AND CLASSICAL APPROACHES COMPARED

We can now consider the different approaches to examine their predictions for macroeconomic behavior and their implications for economic policy.

The Classical Model

The classical macroeconomic view is shown in Figure 8-6, which combines a conventional aggregate demand curve and a vertical or classical aggregate supply curve. Let us trace out the impact of a shift in aggregate demand upon the economy. Suppose that aggregate demand falls, say because slow growth in the money supply raises interest rates and lowers investment spending. As a result, the *AD* curve shifts leftward to *AD'* in Figure 8-6. Initially, at the original price of *P*, total spending falls to point *B* and there might be a very brief period in which output tends to fall. But the demand shift is followed by a rapid adjustment of wages and prices, with the overall price level falling from *P* to *P'* in Figure 8-6. As the price level falls, total output demanded moves to point *C*, reestablishing full employment.

What has been the impact of an aggregate demand shift in our classical world? *The price level has fallen, but the levels of output and employment have not changed at all.* Employment is maintained at the full-employment level, and output remains at potential output. Why has this happened? The reason is that the price mechanism has functioned properly: prices and wages have fallen sufficiently to maintain real spending at the original level. In the new equilibrium at point *C*, wages have declined enough to ensure that all workers willing to work at existing wage rates can find jobs, so that no involuntary unemployment exists.

Policy Consequences   The classical view has two conclusions that are vitally important for economic policy. First, there is never any waste from unutilized resources. Output is always at potential output, and workers who want to work at the going wage rate can find jobs.

Does this imply that there is no unemployment? Surely not, for there will always be *microeconomic* waste in any real-world economy. We will find high-paid ski instructors who sit idle during a rainstorm, or labor unions who have set such high wage rates that their workers cannot find jobs all the time. But a classical economy has no *macroeconomic* waste in the sense of underutilized resources due to insufficient aggregate demand.

The second element of the classical view is even more striking: Macroeconomic policy cannot affect the level of unemployment and output. Rather, monetary and fiscal policies can only affect the economy's price level (or its inflation rate), along with the composition of real GNP. This second classical proposi-

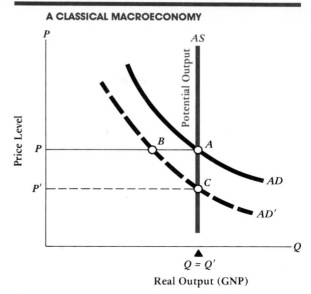

Figure 8-6   Aggregate demand shifts lead to price changes but leave output unaffected in a classical economy

A classical economy is one with a vertical *AS* curve, reflecting rapid adjustment in wages and prices. A decline in aggregate demand leads to a lower price level but to no decline in real GNP. The economy will produce its potential output no matter what the level of demand.

What is the effect if macroeconomic policymakers attempt to contract the economy by tightening monetary or fiscal policy? The *AD* curve shifts downward, but because the *AS* curve is vertical only the price level will decline; output will be unchanged and workers will continue to enjoy full employment.

tion is easily seen in Figure 8-6. Consider an economy in equilibrium at point *A*, given by the intersection of the initial *AD* and the vertical *AS* curves. What happens as a result of the monetary contraction? For a brief instant, at the initial price level *P*, there is excess supply. However, as prices and wages quickly begin to fall under the pressure of excess supply, the economy moves to the new equilibrium at point *C*. The net effect of the contractionary economic policy has been to leave output and employment unaffected, while lowering the overall price level sufficiently to cause the initial full-employment equilibrium to be restored.

The Great Divide This discussion reveals the heart of the classical view along with the deep intellectual divide between the classical and the modern mainstream view of macroeconomics. The difference resides in the assumption in classical macroeconomics that prices and wages are flexible—in the belief that, very quickly after an economic shock, price flexibility can restore full employment. As we will shortly see, most modern mainstream economists are profoundly skeptical about the ability of an economy to maintain full employment automatically from year to year.

Economists who held these classical views include John Stuart Mill, Alfred Marshall, and A. C. Pigou. But we discuss their ideas not in the way that a biologist analyzes dinosaurs, merely for their historical value. Rather, classical economics is alive and thriving in the new classical school, sometimes called the ''rational-expectations school.'' The new classicists—featuring prominently Robert Lucas, Thomas Sargent, and Robert Barro—have presented some of the greatest challenges to modern macroeconomic thinking.

The Keynesian Revolution

While the classical economists were preaching that persistent unemployment was impossible, economists of the 1930s could hardly ignore the vast army of unemployed workers—begging for work and selling pencils on street corners. How could classical economics explain such massive and persistent idleness?

Enter Keynes. The timing of his *General Theory* (1936) could hardly have been better. But more important is that this treatise offered for the first time a new way to understand the peaks and troughs of the business cycle and ushered in the era of modern macroeconomics.

In fact, the Keynesian revolution combined two different elements: First, Keynes presented the concept of aggregate demand, in which aggregate spending would be driven by the consumption function and by investment decisions. Second, Keynes argued that prices and wages were inflexible or sticky, so that the vertical classical *AS* curve would have to be replaced by the upward-sloping or horizontal *AS* curve.

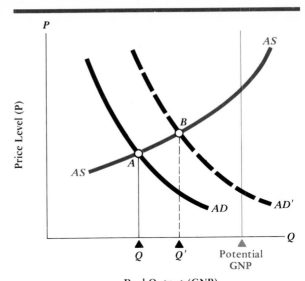

Figure 8-7   Aggregate demand determines output in the Keynesian approach

In the Keynesian model, aggregate supply slopes gently upward, implying that output will increase with higher aggregate demand as long as there are unused resources. When *AD* is depressed, output will be in equilibrium at point *A*, with high unemployment.

If aggregate demand increases from *AD* to *AD'*, the level of real output increases from *A* to *B*, with but a modest increase in prices. In this Keynesian paradigm, with *AS* upward-sloping in the short run, economic policies that increase aggregate demand succeed in increasing output and employment.

The Surprising Consequences By introducing the two new elements, Keynes brought a veritable revolution to macroeconomics. The result can be shown in Figure 8-7, which includes an aggregate demand curve along with an upward-sloping aggregate supply curve.

The first point is that a modern economy like the United States can easily settle into an equilibrium with unemployed resources, or even massive unemployment. For example, if the *AD* curve intersects the *AS* curve far to the left, as is illustrated at point *A* in Figure 8-7, equilibrium output may lie far below potential output. Moreover, because wages and prices are sticky, there is no economic force that will quickly return the economy to potential output. Using this approach, Keynes proclaimed that unemployment could be a persistent feature of an industrial economy. A nation could remain at the high-unemployment, high-misery condition at point *A* for many years because there is no equilibrating mechanism that will guarantee a quick return of GNP to its potential.

Keynes' second conclusion follows from the first. Through monetary or fiscal policies, government can stimulate the economy back toward high employment. For example, if the government were to increase its purchases, aggregate demand would be increased, say from *AD* to *AD'* in Figure 8-7. The impact would be to increase output from *Q* to *Q'*, reducing the gap between actual and potential GNP. In short, by appropriate use of economic policy, government can help to ensure that the economy will move toward a desirable level of output and employment.

What was the impact of Keynes' revolutionary analysis? The impact is described by an economist who was present at its creation in the 1930s:

> The *General Theory* caught most economists under the age of 35 with the unexpected virulence of a disease first attacking and decimating an isolated tribe of South Sea islanders. Economists beyond 50 turned out to be quite immune to the ailment. . . .
>
> Of course, the Great Depression of the Thirties was not the first to reveal the untenability of the classical synthesis. The classical philosophy always had its ups and downs along with the great swings of business activity. Each time it had come back. But for the first time, it was confronted by a competing system—a well-reasoned body of thought . . . a synthesis.[2]

Theories and Policy

In economics, people's views on policy are often determined by the theoretical spectacles they wear. Does a president or a senator or an economist lean toward a classical or a Keynesian view? The answer

to this question will often give an accurate prediction of how that person feels about many of the major economic-policy debates of the day.

Examples are legion. Economists who tend toward the classical view will often be skeptical about the need for government to take steps to stabilize business cycles. They argue that a government policy to increase aggregate demand will instead lead to higher prices or higher inflation. In addition, a classical-thinking economist would worry about government spending "crowding out" investment; that is, if the government spends more, then—because the economy is near its potential output—the increased government spending will merely displace spending on private goods.

A Keynesian, by contrast, will hold a different view. Because the macroeconomy is liable to remain in a depressed condition, with high levels of unemployed resources for long periods of time, a Keynesian economist might believe that government can stimulate the economy by taking steps to affect aggregate demand. These policies might increase aggregate demand in periods of slow economic activity or curb spending in periods of boom with threatening inflation. This economist might argue that government spending would crowd out nothing at all. Higher government spending increases output and allows private spending to continue; when the government takes a larger slice out of the pie, the pie actually becomes larger. Government spending, tax cuts, or more rapid money growth—all create more output and thus stimulate more investment rather than crowding out investment.

Which of these is the correct view—classical or Keynesian? As we shall see, neither has an unqualified claim to the truth, and both are oversimplified. In the chapters to come, we will see the strengths and weaknesses in both positions. For now, the key point to recognize is that many of the debates about economic policy arise because one participant has the classical model in mind while the other has the Keynesian view. The art of good macroeconomic judgment is to sense the strengths and weaknesses of each paradigm.

We now turn to a detailed analysis of the Keynesian multiplier model, which is a close relative of the

[2] Paul A. Samuelson, "Lord Keynes and the General Theory," *Econometrica* (1946), pp. 187–199.

Keynesian model just outlined. We start with this simple model as a first and highly useful approach to output determination. Many of the most important insights about modern macroeconomics, and particularly about the modern mainstream view, can be easily grasped once this rudimentary multiplier model is understood. But we must always remember that the multiplier model is a first and not the last word on macroeconomic theory, and that macroeconomics has evolved a long way since the multiplier model was first introduced a half-century ago.

B. OUTPUT DETERMINATION: THE MULTIPLIER MODEL

What forces determine the level of output and employment in a nation? Why did output fall by almost a third from 1929 to 1933? Why did output rise so dramatically during World War II? Why did output fall in 1982 as net exports and other components of investment slacked off? We can use our aggregate demand-and-supply apparatus to address these important questions. But in some circumstances, the impact of sharp changes in investment or government spending or exports can be seen more easily using the Keynesian multiplier model.

What is the **multiplier model**? This approach receives its name because it shows that each dollar change in investment spending leads to more than a dollar change in GNP—i.e., to a ''multiplied'' change. Once we have mastered the simple multiplier model in this chapter, we are prepared for the next chapter, which analyzes how government spending and taxes can alter equilibrium output and then examines the impact of changes in a nation's foreign trade on its income, output, and employment.

Using the Consumption and Savings Schedules

Chapter 7 gave a simplified picture of the consumption and savings functions for the nation. These *CC* and *SS* schedules are drawn up on the basis of our knowledge of the thriftiness of different families, their wealth, and so forth.

Initially we shall here make the further simplifying assumptions that there are no taxes, undistributed corporate profits, foreign trade, depreciation, or government expenditures or transfers of any kind to worry about. Hence, we do not have to concern ourselves yet with any distinction between gross national product and disposable income. In what follows, ''income'' is disposable income and equals GNP.

Figure 8-8 shows the national consumption and savings functions. Each point on the consumption function shows desired or planned consumption at that level of disposable income. Each point on the savings schedule shows desired or planned saving at that income level. Recall that the two schedules are closely related: Since $C + S$ always equals income, the *CC* and *SS* curves are mirror twins that will always add up to the 45° line.

HOW OUTPUT IS DETERMINED AT THE LEVEL WHERE SAVINGS AND INVESTMENT SCHEDULES INTERSECT

We have seen that saving and investment are dependent on quite different factors: Saving tends to depend in a passive way upon income, while investment depends on output as well as on various other factors (such as expected future output, interest rates, tax policy, and business confidence).

For simplicity, first suppose investment opportunities are such that investment would be exactly $200 billion per year regardless of the level of GNP. This means that, if we now draw a schedule of investment against GNP, it will have to be a horizontal line—always the same distance above the horizontal axis. This case is shown in Figure 8-9, where the investment schedule is labelled *II* to distinguish it from the *SS* savings schedule. (Note that *II* does not mean Roman numeral 2.)

By examining the interaction of saving and investment, we can find the equilibrium level of GNP. The

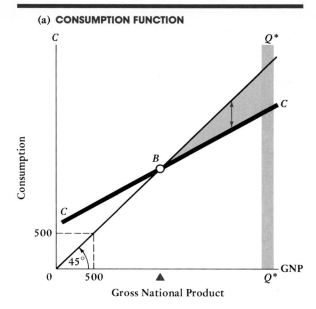

(a) CONSUMPTION FUNCTION

(b) SAVINGS FUNCTION

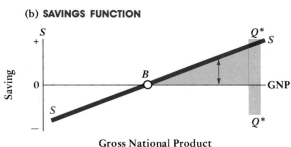

Figure 8-8   Society's national output determines its levels of consumption and saving

CC is the consumption function for the country, while SS is the savings function for the country.

Recall that these are closely related in a mirror-image fashion. The breakeven point is shown at point B—on the upper diagram where CC intersects the 45° line and on the lower diagram where SS intersects the horizontal axis. Can you explain why the vertically aligned arrows *must* be of equal length? The two points marked 500 emphasize the important property of the 45° line: Any point on it depicts a vertical distance exactly equal to the horizontal distance. The gray band marked Q*Q* shows the level of potential GNP.

savings and investment schedules intersect at point E in Figure 8-9. This point, which corresponds to a level of GNP equal to the distance from 0 to M as shown by the red pointer, represents the equilibrium level of output in the multiplier model.

This intersection of the savings and investment schedules is the equilibrium toward which national output will gravitate.

The remaining pages of this chapter are devoted to the single task of explaining and interpreting this important theory of the determination of GNP.

The Meaning of Equilibrium

Central to understanding the nature of output determination is to see why point E in Figure 8-9 is an equilibrium. The reason is that only at point E does the desired saving of households equal the desired investment of firms. And when desired saving and desired investment are not equal, output will tend to adjust up or down.

Let's begin by emphasizing that the savings and investment schedules shown in Figure 8-9 represent

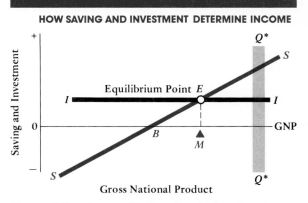

Figure 8-9   The equilibrium level of national output is determined by intersection of savings and investment schedules

E marks the spot where investment and savings curves intersect. Equilibrium GNP comes at intersection of SS and II curves because at no other level of GNP could the desired saving of households exactly match the desired investment of business.

desired or planned levels. Thus at output level *M*, businesses desire their investment to be equal to the vertical distance *ME*. Also households desire to save the amount *ME*. But there is no logical necessity for the actual saving (or investment) to be equal to the planned saving (or investment). People can make mistakes. Or they may forecast events incorrectly. In either case, actual *S* or *I* might deviate from planned levels of *S* or *I*.

To see how output adjusts until desired saving and desired investment are equal we consider three cases. The first case is that in which the system is at *E* itself, where the *II* schedule of what business firms want to invest just intersects the *SS* schedule of what families want to save. When everyone's plans are satisfied, all will be content to go on doing just what they have been doing.

At equilibrium, firms will not find inventories piling up on their shelves; nor will they find sales so brisk as to force them to produce more goods. So production, employment, income, and spending will remain the same. GNP in this first case does truly stay at point *E*, and we can rightly call it an *equilibrium*.

The second case is where the system is first at a GNP higher than at *E*; thus, GNP is to the right of *M*, at an income level where the *SS* schedule is higher than the *II* schedule. Why can't the system stay there indefinitely? Because at such an income level, families are saving—are refraining from spending on consumption—more than business firms will be willing to go on investing.

Firms will thus find that they have too few customers and that their inventories are piling up against their wishes. They will not want to maintain such undesired inventory investment. What can they do about it? They can cut back production and lay off workers. This moves GNP gradually downward, or leftward in Figure 8-9. When does the system stop being in disequilibrium? Only when it gets back to *E*, the equilibrium intersection point. There the tendency to change has disappeared.

You should master the third case. Show that if GNP were *below* its equilibrium level, strong forces would be set up to move it eastward back to *E*.

All three cases then lead to the same conclusion:

The only equilibrium of GNP is at *E*, where the savings and investment schedules intersect. At any

other point, the desired saving of households will not match the desired investment of business, and this discrepancy will cause businesses to change their production and employment levels to return the system to the equilibrium GNP.

Output Determination by Consumption and Investment

There is a second way of showing how output is determined, other than by the intersection of the savings and investment schedules. The final equilibrium is the same, but our understanding of output determination is deepened if we work through this second approach.

This second method is called the consumption-plus-investment (or *C + I*) rather than the saving-investment approach. How does the *C + I* approach work? Figure 8-10 shows a curve of total spending graphed against total output or income. The black *CC* line is simply our consumption function, showing the level of desired consumption at each level of income. We then add desired investment (at fixed level *I*) on top of the consumption function. Thus the level of total spending is *C + I*, and is shown by the red *C + I* curve in Figure 8-10.

We next put in a 45° line to help us identify the equilibrium. At any point on the 45° line, the total level of consumption plus investment spending (measured vertically) exactly equals the total level of output (measured horizontally).

We can now easily calculate the equilibrium level of output in Figure 8-10. Only where the desired amounts of spending, as represented by the *C + I* curve, equal total output is the economy in equilibrium. In summary:

The total spending or *C + I* curve shows the level of desired expenditure by consumers and businesses at each level of output. The economy is in equilibrium at the point where the *C + I* curve crosses the 45° line—at point *E* in Figure 8-10. Point *E* represents an equilibrium because at that level desired spending on consumption and investment exactly equals the level of total output.

The Adjustment Mechanism It is important to understand why point *E* is an equilibrium. Equilibrium occurs when planned spending (on *C* and *I*) equals planned output. If the system were to find itself away from equilibrium, say, at output level *D* in Figure 8-10, what would happen? At this level of output, the *C* + *I* spending line is above the 45° line, so planned *C* + *I* spending is greater than planned output. This means that consumers will be buying more cars and shoes than producers are producing. Auto dealers will find their lots emptying, and shoe stores will be running low on many sizes.

In this disequilibrium, auto dealers and shoe stores respond by increasing their orders. Automakers and shoe manufacturers recall workers from layoff and gear up their production lines. *Output increases*.

By following this chain of reasoning, we see that only when firms are producing what households and firms plan to spend on *C* and *I*, precisely at point *E*, will the economy be in equilibrium. (You should also work through what happens when output is above equilibrium.)

Planned vs. Actual Amounts A final word: This chapter repeatedly uses words such as ''planned'' and ''desired.'' These are to call attention to the difference between *(a)* the amount of planned or desired consumption given by the consumption function or by the investment demand schedule and *(b)* the actual amount of consumption or investment measured after the fact.

This distinction is necessary to emphasize that GNP is at equilibrium only where firms and consumers are on their schedules of desired spending and investment. Saving and investment will always be exactly equal, in recession or boom, as measured by a national accounts statistician. But, *actual* investment will often differ from *planned* investment when firms find their actual sales unequal to their planned production and they consequently face an involuntary buildup or reduction of inventories. Only when the level of output is such that planned spending on *C* + *I* equals planned output will there be no tendency for output, income, or spending to change.

An Arithmetic Analysis

An arithmetic example may help show why the equilibrium level of output occurs where planned spending and planned output are equal. Table 8-2 on the

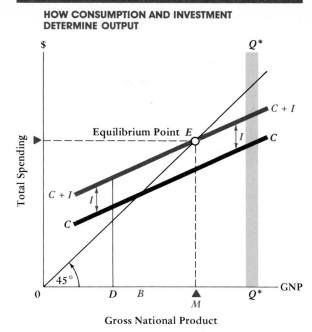

HOW CONSUMPTION AND INVESTMENT DETERMINE OUTPUT

Figure 8-10   Alternatively, equilibrium GNP level can be shown by intersection of *C* + *I* schedule with 45° line

Adding *II* to *CC* gives the *C* + *I* curve of total desired spending. At *E*, where this intersects the 45° line, we get the same equilibrium as in the saving-and-investment diagram. (Note the similarities between this figure and Fig. 8-9: the investment added to *CC* is the same as *II* of Fig. 8-9; breakeven point *B* and potential-output band *Q** each come at the same GNP levels on the two diagrams, and so must the *E* intersection.)

next page shows a simple example of consumption and savings functions.

The breakeven level of income, where the nation is too poor to do any net saving on balance, is assumed to be $3000 billion ($3 trillion). Each change of income of $300 billion is assumed to lead to a $100 billion change in saving and a $200 billion change in consumption; in other words, *MPC* is for simplicity here assumed to be constant and exactly equal to $\frac{2}{3}$, with $MPS = \frac{1}{3}$.

What shall we assume about investment? For simplicity, let us suppose again that the only level of investment that will be sustained indefinitely is ex-

GNP DETERMINATION WHERE OUTPUT EQUALS PLANNED SPENDING *(in billions of dollars)*

(1) LEVELS OF GNP AND *DI*	(2) PLANNED CON-SUMPTION	(3) PLANNED SAVING (3) = (1) − (2)	(4) PLANNED INVEST-MENT	(5) LEVEL OF GNP (5) = (1)		(6) TOTAL PLANNED SPENDING ON CONSUMPTION AND INVESTMENT (6) = (2) + (4)	(7) RESULTING TENDENCY OF OUTPUT
4,200	3,800	400	200	4,200	>	4,000	Contraction
3,900	3,600	300	200	3,900	>	3,800	Contraction
3,600	3,400	200	200	3,600	=	3,600	Equilibrium
3,300	3,200	100	200	3,300	<	3,400	Expansion
3,000	3,000	0	200	3,000	<	3,200	Expansion
2,700	2,800	−100	200	2,700	<	3,000	Expansion

Table 8-2   The tendency for output to go to its equilibrium level is shown by arithmetic table

The red row depicts the equilibrium GNP level, where the $3600 that is being produced is just matched by the $3600 that households plan to consume and that firms plan to invest. In upper rows, firms will be forced into unintended inventory investment and will respond by cutting production and GNP back to equilibrium. Interpret the lower rows' tendency toward expansion of GNP toward equilibrium.

actly $200 billion, as shown in column (4) of Table 8-2. That is, at each level of GNP businesses desire to purchase $200 billion of investment goods, no more and no less.

Columns (5) and (6) are the crucial ones. Column (5) shows the total GNP—this is simply column (1) copied once again into column (5).

Then column (6) shows what business firms would actually be selling year in and year out; this represents the planned consumption spending plus planned investment. It's really Figure 8-10's red *C + I* schedule in numbers.

When businesses as a whole are temporarily producing too high a level of total product (higher than the sum of what consumers and businesses want to purchase), businesses will find themselves involuntarily piling up inventories of unsalable goods.

Thus, reading the top row of Table 8-2, we see that if firms are temporarily producing $4200 billion of GNP, planned or desired spending [shown in column (6)] is only $4000 billion. Thus firms will find that they are piling up inventories of cars, shoes, and books. They will thus contract their operations, and GNP will fall. In the opposite case, represented by the bottom row of Table 8-2, total spending is $3000 billion compared to output of $2700 billion. Inventories

are being depleted and firms will expand operations, raising output.

We see, then, that when business firms as a whole are temporarily producing more than they can profitably sell, they will want to contract their operations, and GNP will tend to fall. When they are selling more than their current production, they increase their output and GNP rises.

Only when the level of output in column (5) exactly equals planned spending in column (6) will business firms be in equilibrium. Their sales will then be just enough to justify continuing their current level of aggregate output. GNP will neither expand nor contract.

■ ■ ■

Let us return for a moment to review what has been accomplished. In our overview of macroeconomics, we saw that one of the major indicators of economic success for a nation is the level and growth of its national output, or GNP. A country's standard of living—its ability to support education and the arts, or to defend itself—rests crucially on its ability to produce useful goods and services.

What then determines the level of GNP? In the very long run, potential output limits the amount a country can produce. But in the short run, particularly when wages and prices are inflexible, output is determined by aggregate demand, or total spending. The last few pages showed how investment and the consumption function interact in a simple economy to determine the level of national output. While this approach is drastically simplified, its essence will remain valid even when extended to more realistic situations involving government, monetary policy, and foreign trade.

THE MULTIPLIER

We are now prepared to discuss one of the central concepts of modern macroeconomics—the multiplier. To see where the idea of a multiplier arises, recall that we have just discussed how the interaction of consumption and investment spending determines the level of national output. Clearly, an increase in investment will increase the level of output and employment. Thus, an investment boom may bring a nation out of a depression—by having a higher $C + I$ schedule cut the 45° line at a higher level of equilibrium GNP. In the Keynesian multiplier model described here, an increase in private investment will cause output and employment to expand; a decrease in investment will cause them to contract.

This is not a very surprising result. After all, we have learned that investment is one part of GNP, so when one of the parts increases in value, we should naturally expect the whole to increase in value. But that is only part of the story. Our Keynesian theory of output determination will give us a still more striking result, that an increase in investment will increase GNP by an amplified or multiplied amount—by an amount greater than itself. Investment spending is high-powered spending.

This amplified effect of investment on output is called the *multiplier*. The word ''multiplier'' itself is used for the numerical coefficient showing the size of the increase in output resulting from each unit increase in investment.

Some examples will make this terminology clear. Let there be an increase of investment of $100 billion. If this causes an increase in output of $300 billion, then the multiplier is 3. If, instead, the resulting increase in output were $400 billion, then the multiplier would be 4.

The **multiplier** is the number by which the change in investment must be multiplied in order to determine the resulting change in total output.

Woodsheds and Carpenters No proof has yet been presented to show that the multiplier will be greater than 1. But the discussion up to now indicates how, when I hire unemployed resources to build a $1000 woodshed, there will be a *secondary* expansion of national income and production, over and above my *primary* investment. Here is why.

My carpenters and lumber producers will get an extra $1000 of income. But that is not the end of the story. If they all have a marginal propensity to consume of $\frac{2}{3}$, they will now spend $666.67 on new consumption goods. The producers of these goods will now have an extra income of $666.67. If their *MPC* is also $\frac{2}{3}$, they in turn will spend $444.44, or $\frac{2}{3}$ of $666.67 (or $\frac{2}{3}$ of $\frac{2}{3}$ of $1000). So the process will go on, with each new round of spending being $\frac{2}{3}$ of the previous round.

The Chain of Respending Thus an endless chain of *secondary consumption respending* is set in motion by my primary $1000 of investment spending. But, although an endless chain, it is a dwindling chain. And it eventually adds up to a finite amount.

Using straightforward arithmetic, we can find the total increase in spending:

$$
\begin{array}{rcl}
\$1000.00 & & 1 \times \$1000 \\
+ & & + \\
666.67 & & \frac{2}{3} \times \$1000 \\
+ & & + \\
444.44 & & \left(\frac{2}{3}\right)^2 \times \$1000 \\
+ & = & + \\
296.30 & & \left(\frac{2}{3}\right)^3 \times \$1000 \\
+ & & + \\
197.53 & & \left(\frac{2}{3}\right)^4 \times \$1000 \\
+ & & + \\
\vdots & & \vdots \\
\hline
\$3000 & & \dfrac{1}{1 - \frac{2}{3}} \times \$1000, \text{ or } 3 \times \$1000
\end{array}
$$

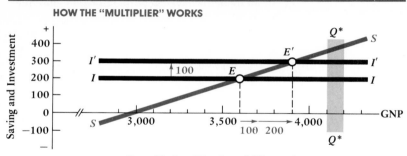

Figure 8-11   Each dollar of investment here is "multiplied" into 3 dollars of output

New investment shifts *II* up to *I'I'*. *E'* gives the new equilibrium output, with output increasing by 3 for each 1 increase in investment. (Note: The broken horizontal red arrow is 3 times the length of the vertical red arrow of investment shift, and is broken to show 2 units of secondary consumption responding for each 1 unit of primary investment.)

This shows that, with an *MPC* of $\frac{2}{3}$, the multiplier is 3, consisting of the 1 of primary investment plus 2 extra of secondary consumption responding.

The same arithmetic would give a multiplier of 4 if the *MPC* were $\frac{3}{4}$, for the reason that $1 + \frac{3}{4} + (\frac{3}{4})^2 + (\frac{3}{4})^3 + \cdots$ finally adds up to 4. If the *MPC* were $\frac{1}{2}$, the multiplier would be 2.

The size of the multiplier thus depends upon how large the *MPC* is; or it can be expressed in terms of the twin concept, the *MPS*. If the *MPS* were $\frac{1}{4}$, the *MPC* would be $\frac{3}{4}$, and the multiplier would be 4. If the *MPS* were $\frac{1}{3}$, the multiplier would be 3. If the *MPS* were $1/X$, the multiplier would be X.

By this time it should be clear that the simple multiplier is always the inverse, or "reciprocal," of the marginal propensity to save.[3] Equivalently, it is equal to

$$\frac{1}{1 - MPC}$$

[3]The formula for an infinite geometric progression is

$$1 + r + r^2 + r^3 + \cdots + r^n + \cdots = \frac{1}{1 - r}$$

as long as the *MPC*, *r*, is less than 1 in absolute value.

Our simple multiplier formula is

$$\begin{aligned}\text{Change in output} &= \frac{1}{MPS} \times \text{change in investment} \\ &= \frac{1}{1 - MPC} \times \text{change in investment}\end{aligned}$$

In other words, the greater the extra consumption respending, the greater the multiplier. The greater the *MPS* "leakage" into extra saving at each round of spending, the smaller the final multiplier.

Graphical Picture of the Multiplier

Up to this point, we have discussed the multiplier in terms of common sense and arithmetic. Will our saving-investment analysis of income give us the same result? The answer is yes.

Suppose, as back in Table 8-2, the *MPS* is $\frac{1}{3}$ and a new series of inventions comes along and gives rise to an extra $100 billion of continuing investment opportunities, over and above our previous $200 billion. Then the increase in investment should raise equilibrium GNP from $3600 billion to what? To $3900 billion if the multiplier is indeed correctly given as 3 by our previous analysis.

A look at Figure 8-11 can confirm this. Our old

investment schedule *II* is shifted upward by $100 billion to the new level *I'I'*. The new intersection point is *E'*; the increase in income is exactly 3 times as much as the increase in investment. This is true because an *MPS* of only $\frac{1}{3}$ means a relatively flat *SS* savings schedule. As the red arrows show, the horizontal output distance is 3 times as great as the upward shift in the investment schedule, the excess being the secondary "consumption responding."

What is happening? We know that desired saving must rise to equal the new and higher level of investment. The only way that saving can rise is for national income to rise. With an *MPS* of $\frac{1}{3}$, and an increase in investment of $100, income must rise by exactly $300 to bring forth $100 of additional saving to match exactly the new investment. Hence, in equilibrium $100 of additional investment induces $300 of additional income, verifying our multiplier arithmetic.[4]

THE MULTIPLIER IN MACROECONOMICS TODAY

The multiplier model just outlined—suitably elaborated—has been enormously influential in macroeconomic analysis over the last half-century. We turn now to see how it fits into the broader macroeconomic conception of the *AS* and *AD* analysis of the first half of this chapter.

The relationship between the multiplier analysis and the *AS-AD* approach is shown in Figure 8-12. Begin at the bottom. This shows a gently sloping *AS* curve that becomes quite steep as output exceeds potential output. In the region where there are unused resources, to the left of potential output *(Q*)*, output is determined primarily by the strength of aggregate demand. As investment increases, this increases *AD*, and equilibrium output rises.

The same economy can be described in a slightly

---

[4] Alter Table 8-2, on page 166, to verify this answer. In column (4), we now put in $300 billion instead of $200 billion of investment. The new equilibrium level of output now shifts one row up from the red equilibrium row. The multiplier can also work downward; a decline of $100 billion in investment spending will induce an endless chain of negative items, leading ultimately to a $300 billion reduction in equilibrium output. (Check this by cutting *I* from 200 to 100 in Table 8-2.)

OUTPUT DETERMINATION IN TWO APPROACHES

(a) Multiplier Model

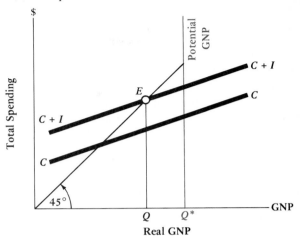

(b) *AS-AD* Approach

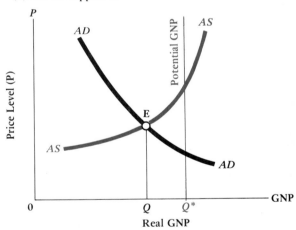

Figure 8-12 Two approaches to the short-run macroeconomic equilibrium

The multiplier model of section B of this chapter is simply a different way of examining the *AS-AD* equilibrium.

(a) The top panel shows the output-expenditure equilibrium. At point *E,* the spending line just cuts the 45° line, leading to equilibrium output of *Q*.

(b) This can also be seen in the bottom panel, where the *AD* curve cuts the *AS* curve at point *E*. Both approaches lead to exactly the same equilibrium output, *Q*.

different way by the multiplier diagram in the top panel of Figure 8-12. The multiplier equilibrium is at the same level of output as the *AS-AD* equilibrium— both lead to a real GNP of *Q*. They simply stress different features of output determination.

It will be useful to put all this in clear language. In real life, when the multiplier operates on a system with considerable excess capacity and unemployed workers, most of the increments to total spending will end up in extra real output, with only small increases in the price level. However, as the economy reaches and surpasses potential output, it is not possible to coax out more production at the going level of prices; thus higher spending (upward shifts in Figure 8-12's bottom *AD* curve) will simply end up in higher price levels, and little or none of the *AD* increase will end up in higher real output or employment.

A Key Limitation These points show a very important limitation on the multiplier model as a realistic tool. While it may be a highly useful approach in depressions or even recessions, it cannot apply to periods of full employment, when real GNP exceeds potential output. Once factories are operating at full capacity and when all the workers are employed, the economy simply cannot produce more output. This fact rein- forces the point that the multiplier model applies only in an economy with unemployed resources.

A Summing Up

Much ink has been spent in attempts to explain why a nation experiences business cycles, but it is only in the last few decades that economists have learned how to separate myth from reality. The ideas introduced in this chapter are indispensable for anyone attempting to understand business conditions or trying to cure unemployment or inflation. The multiplier model of section B allows us to see how consumption and investment interact to determine output, and this approach also shows why changes in the level of investment will produce multiplied effects upon output.

But this analysis remains oversimplified. The next chapter elaborates on the simple multiplier model by introducing government fiscal policy into the model. It also shows the impact of international trade on output. In later chapters, we shall consider the role of money, and then see the determinants of inflation and unemployment. But mastery of the basic elements of aggregate supply and demand will provide a glimpse into the way that different forces operate upon the overall economy.

SUMMARY _____

A. Foundations of Aggregate Supply and Demand

1. Aggregate demand represents the total quantity of output that is willingly bought at a given price level. It is comprised of *(a)* consumption spending, which depends upon personal disposable income, wealth, and other factors and which tends to decline as the overall price level rises; *(b)* investment, which depends upon output, the cost of capital (which in turn is affected by interest rates and taxes), and expectations; *(c)* government spending on goods and services; and *(d)* net exports, which is exports (depending upon foreign output and foreign exchange rates) minus imports (which depend upon domestic income and output and exchange rates). Aggregate demand hence depends upon all the elements that might affect any of its major components.

2. Macroeconomic or aggregate demand curves differ from the microeconomic varieties in that the former relate overall spending on all components of output to the overall price level.

3. Aggregate supply describes the relationship between the output that businesses willingly produce and the overall price level, technology, and potential output. In the long run, aggregate supply is closely tied to an economy's potential output. In the short run, price and wage relations will affect how production responds to different levels of aggregate demand.

4. Two major approaches to aggregate supply theory are: *(a)* The modern mainstream view, which holds that prices and wages are sticky in the short run due to contractual rigidities such as labor-union agreements. In this kind of economy, output responds positively to higher levels of demand, that is, the *AS* curve slopes upward gently or is relatively flat, particularly at low levels of output. *(b)* The classical view, in which prices and wages are highly flexible, so that prices move quickly to erase any excess supply or demand in markets. This leads to a situation in which total output is insensitive to the overall price level, i.e., in which the *AS* curve is vertical.

5. The classical model holds that output will be unaffected by changes in aggregate demand, so that economic policy can play no role in stabilizing the business cycle or reducing unemployment in periods of depression. By contrast, the Keynesian model holds that output is significantly affected in the short run by fluctuations in aggregate demand. In a Keynesian world, the economy can experience long periods of persistent unemployment. Monetary and fiscal policy can therefore play a major role in alleviating business-cycle swings since well-designed policies can propel the economy toward a more desirable level of output and employment.

B. Output Determination: The Multiplier Model

6. The multiplier model is a rudimentary approach by which aggregate demand determines the level of output. In this approach, household consumption is a function of disposable income and investment is fixed. People's desires to consume and the willingness of businesses to invest are brought into line with each other by means of changes in output. The equilibrium level of national output must be at the intersection of savings and investment schedules *SS* and *II*. Or, to put it another way, equilibrium output comes at the intersection of the consumption-plus-investment schedule $C + I$ with the 45° line.

7. If output were temporarily above its equilibrium level, businesses would find output higher than sales, with inventories piling up involuntarily and profits plummeting. Firms would therefore cut production and employment back toward the equilibrium level. The only equilibrium path of output that can be maintained is at the output level where households will voluntarily continue to save exactly as much as businesses will voluntarily continue to invest.

8. Thus for the simplified Keynesian model of this chapter: Investment calls the tune, and consumption dances to the music. Investment determines output, while saving responds passively to income changes. Output rises or falls until planned saving has adjusted itself to the level of planned investment.

9. Investment has a *multiplier effect* on output. When investment changes, there is an equal primary change in national output. But as the income receivers in the capital-goods industries get more income, they set into motion a whole chain of additional secondary consumption spending and employment.

   If people always spend about $\frac{2}{3}$ of each extra dollar of income on consumption, the total of the multiplier chain will be

$$1 + \tfrac{2}{3} + (\tfrac{2}{3})^2 + \cdots = \frac{1}{1 - \tfrac{2}{3}} = 3$$

The multiplier works upward or downward, amplifying either increases or decreases in investment. The simplest multiplier is numerically equal to the reciprocal of the *MPS* or, equivalently, to

$$\frac{1}{1 - MPC}$$

This result occurs because it always takes more than a dollar of increased income to bring forth a dollar of increased saving.

CONCEPTS FOR REVIEW

major components of aggregate demand
aggregate supply: role of potential
  output and price-wage behavior
aggregate supply: mainstream and
  classical approaches
flexible vs. sticky wages and prices
classical and Keynesian economics:
  impact of demand shifts, effectiveness
  of policy
classical vs. Keynesian models: vertical
  and upward-sloping *AS* curves
C + *I* schedule

two ways of viewing GNP
  determination:
    planned saving = planned investment
    planned *C* + planned *I* = GNP
investment equals saving: planned vs.
  actual levels
multiplier effect of investment
multiplier = $1 + (MPC) + (MPC)^2 + \cdots$

$$= \frac{1}{1 - MPC} = \frac{1}{MPS}$$

QUESTIONS FOR DISCUSSION

1. Can you recall from the last chapter how the *CC* and *SS* schedules are in a mirror-image relationship, with $MPC + MPS \equiv 1$ always? Why does the breakeven point in the consumption and savings functions come at the same level of income (or, why will breakeven point *B* be at the same output on the horizontal axis in the lower part of Figure 8-8 and on the 45° line in the upper part)?

2. In the multiplier model, assume that investment is always zero. Show that equilibrium output would in this special case come at the breakeven point of the consumption function. Why would equilibrium output *not* occur at the breakeven point when investment is not zero?

3. The saving-and-investment diagram and the 45° line *C* + *I* diagram are two different ways of showing how national output is determined. Describe each. Show their equivalence.

4. Reconstruct Table 8-2 assuming that net investment is equal to *(a)* $300 billion, *(b)* $400 billion. What is the resulting difference in GNP? Is this difference greater or smaller than the change in *I*? Why? When *I* drops from $200 billion to $100 billion, how much must GNP drop?

5. Give *(a)* the common sense, *(b)* the arithmetic, *(c)* the geometry of the multiplier. What are the multipliers for *MPC* = 0.9? 0.8? 0.5? For *MPS* = 0.1? 0.8?

6. Work out the explosive(!) chain of spending and respending when *MPC* = 2. Try to explain the economics of the arithmetic of the divergent infinite geometric series.

7. Compare the effects of the following changes in both the Keynesian and the classical models. You will find that the answers are best given in the framework of the *AS-AD* analysis of Figures 8-6 and 8-7.

(a) What will be the effect of an increase in potential output on the level of actual output in the two models for given aggregate demand curves?

(b) For a given level of potential output, what is the effect of a small outward shift in the *AD* curve in each case? Of a very, very large shift in the *AD* curve?

8. Assume that GNP is $1000, while *C* = $800 and *I* = $200 (all figures are in millions). The *MPC* is 0.50. Now assume that a computer firm decides to build a new warehouse, with investment rising from $200 to $210. Using the multiplier model, describe in words the transition from the old equilibrium to the new equilibrium, and explain with hypothetical examples who ends up with the higher levels of income and spending.

9. Assume that consumption is equal to 100 plus 0.80 of each dollar of disposable income; that there are no taxes, foreign savings, or business savings; and that there is no government or foreign sector. Further assume that businesses invest 50 plus 0.10 for each dollar of GNP. Determine the equilibrium level of GNP. How much would GNP change if investment were to increase by an additional 10? Can you restate the multiplier when both consumption and investment respond to output? (HINT: Substitute "marginal propensity to spend" for "marginal propensity to consume.")

CHAPTER 9

THE MULTIPLIER EXTENDED: FISCAL POLICY AND INTERNATIONAL TRADE

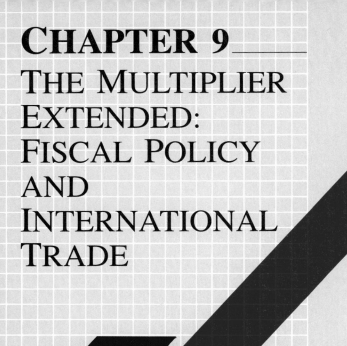

The only good budget is a balanced budget.

Adam Smith of Glasgow (1776)

THE LAST CHAPTER set forth the essentials of modern macroeconomic theory of output determination. It introduced both the classical and the Keynesian approaches, and then began to explore the Keynesian multiplier model.

This chapter presses on to develop the Keynesian multiplier model, with a number of important applications and extensions. We ask, What are the effects on output and employment of government fiscal policies like public expenditures and government taxation? Do these outlays have ''multiplier'' effects as does investment? We shall see that fiscal policy can help tame the business cycle.

In section B of this chapter we analyze the impact of international trade on the macroeconomy. We see that a large decrease in net exports, such as occurred in the United States in the early 1980s, can slow the pace of economic activity. This section shows that the increasing integration of the world economy, with greater volumes of world trade, has profound effects on economic activity at home.

While this chapter focuses on the income flows associated with fiscal policy and international trade, be

CHAPTER OVERVIEW

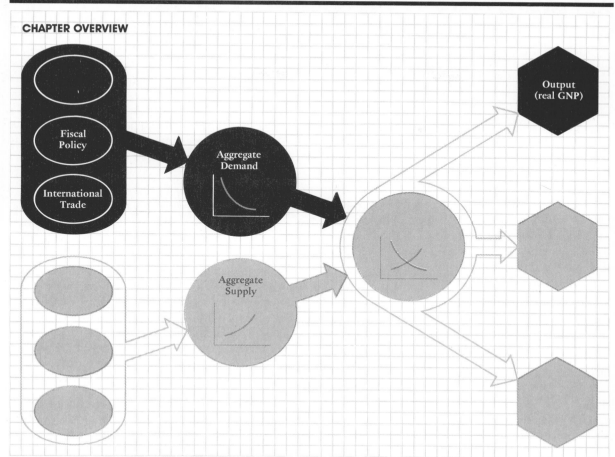

Figure 9-1   Fiscal policy and international trade affect output through the multiplier model

This chapter further develops the Keynesian multiplier model. Section A shows how government fiscal policy—changes in expenditures or taxation—can affect output. The second section analyzes the impact of foreign economies on economic activity.

warned that one of the major forces in macroeconomic activity, money and monetary policy, has so far been ignored. This is so, we emphasize, not because money is less important than fiscal policy; indeed, money today plays a leading role in the macroeconomic drama. Rather, the treatment of money has been postponed because of its greater complexity. Moreover, understanding the way that fiscal policy works is a useful prelude to the later task of understanding the way that money affects economic activity.

Figure 9-1 shows the subject matter of this chapter. We begin where the last chapter ended, with the multiplier model, and then extend this approach to two important aspects of the modern economy, fiscal policy and international trade.

A. FISCAL POLICY IN THE MULTIPLIER MODEL _____

In the last chapter, we saw how fluctuations in aggregate demand could lead to changes in national output. Depending on the relationship between the level of actual GNP and the economy's potential GNP, we might be suffering from a period of acute unemployment (as we were during the 1930s and again in the early 1980s), or from overemployment and rapid inflation (as during World War II and the Vietnam war period).

In order to show how the nation has alternated between boom and recession, Figure 9-2 plots the history of actual and potential GNP over the last 35 years.[1] Those parts of the figure that are shaded represent periods when output was below potential, and when inflation tended to subside. Those that are unshaded were periods when output was above potential GNP and inflation tended to rise.

Figure 9-2 is a reminder of the eternal trials of a macroeconomic policymaker. The economy just won't sit still. Like a small child, it is constantly getting into trouble of one kind or another. In early 1980, the country was near hysteria with fears of inflation and speculation—these concerns led policymakers to institute credit controls along with the most restrictive monetary policy in recent history. There soon ensued a steep recession—so steep, indeed, that by 1982 concerns about inflation had evaporated to be replaced by fears of unemployment as the prime economic danger. A sustained recovery from 1982 to 1988 reduced unemployment to full-employment levels in many parts of the country, but a mounting government budget deficit along with a huge trade deficit displaced earlier worries. The central macroeconomic problem at the end of the 1980s revolved around the best way to reduce the federal budget deficit and the impact on the United States of its mounting external debt. Each year, each decade, and each generation faces a different set of macroeconomic problems.

In the midst of debates about the large federal budget deficit, some people argued that reducing the deficit too quickly would lead to a recession and rising unemployment. It is likely that they were thinking

about the "multiplier" impact of fiscal policy on aggregate demand. In this section, then, we explore the impact of fiscal policy upon the economy. We begin by showing the way the multiplier model of the last chapter can be augmented to include both government expenditures and taxation. We then demonstrate that the fiscal-policy multipliers are closely related to the investment multipliers analyzed in the last chapter.

THE IMPACT OF FISCAL POLICY

The last chapter introduced the Keynesian multiplier model of output determination. In this approach, investment spending (given autonomously outside the model) interacted with induced consumption spending (set according to the consumption function) to determine the level of output. We now extend this by adding the impact of fiscal policy, which consists of government expenditures on goods and services *(G)* and taxes and transfers *(T)*. We will see in this section that, as long as there are unemployed resources, changes in *G* and *T* will affect the level of national output.

Before proceeding, we should reiterate the conditions under which the Keynesian multiplier model is most appropriate. We saw at the end of the last chapter that in this model aggregate supply is passive and output is determined by changes in aggregate demand (see especially Figure 8-12). Changes in spending lead to shifts in the aggregate demand curve, which then moves back and forth along a gently sloping *AS* curve to determine the equilibrium level of GNP. It would be useful to review that figure and the summary of the last chapter if these points are not firmly planted in your mind.

Enter Government

Let us now explicitly introduce government into our multiplier model to see how output determination is affected. As you might guess, we now consider a *C + I + G* spending schedule (instead of last chap-

---

[1] Chapter 10 contains a more detailed discussion of the history and determinants of potential GNP.

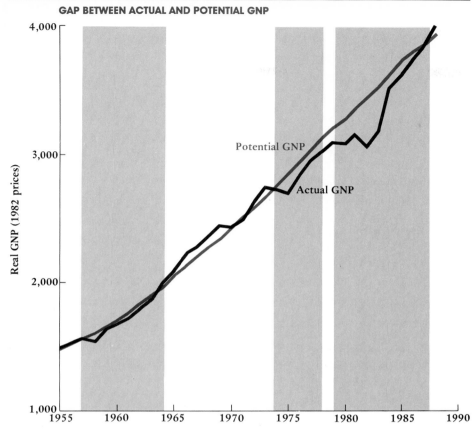

Figure 9-2   The economy alternates between periods of underproduction and overproduction

The figure shows the levels of actual and potential GNP since 1955. The shaded periods are those when the economy experienced underemployment. In those periods inflation often declined. The unshaded periods were ones of full employment; inflation tended to rise.

One of the important tasks of macroeconomic policy is to reduce the gap between actual and potential output, but the job is never finished. (Source: Fig. 5-2.)

ter's $C + I$ schedule) and use that to chart the equilibrium when government, with its spending and taxing, is in the picture.

It will simplify our task in the beginning if we analyze the effects of government expenditure with taxes held constant (these are called ''lump-sum taxes''). Even with a constant dollar value for taxes, we can no longer ignore the distinction between disposable income and gross national product. If we continue for now to rule out business saving and foreign trade, we know from Chapter 6 that GNP equals disposable income plus taxes. But with the tax revenue held constant, GNP and DI will always differ by the same amount; moreover, after taking account of such taxes, we can still plot the CC consumption schedule against GNP rather than against DI.

An example will clarify how we can depict our consumption function when taxes are present. In Figure 9-3, we have drawn our original consumption function with zero taxes as the black CC line. In this

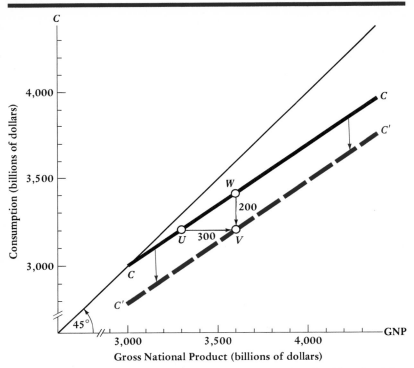

Figure 9-3   Taxes reduce disposable income and shift *CC* schedule to the right and down

Each dollar of tax shifts the *CC* schedule to the right by the amount of the tax. A rightward *CC* shift also means a downward *CC* shift, but the downward *CC* shift is less than the rightward shift. Why? Because the downward shift is equal to the rightward shift times the *MPC*. Thus, if the *MPC* is ⅔, the downward shift is ⅔ times $300 billion = $200 billion. Verify that *WV* = ⅔ *UV*.

case, GNP = *DI*. Here, consumption is 3000 at a *DI* of 3000; consumption is also 3400 at a GNP of 3600.

Now introduce taxes of 300. At a *DI* of 3600, GNP must be equal to 3600 + 300 = 3900. Consumption is thus 3400 at a *DI* of 3600 or at a GNP of 3900. So we can write consumption as a function of GNP by shifting the consumption function to the right to the red *C'C'* curve; the amount of the rightward shift is exactly equal to the amount of taxes, 300.

Alternatively, we can plot the new consumption function as a *downward* shift by 200. As Figure 9-3 shows, the 200 is calculated as a decrease of income of 300 times the *MPC* of ⅔.

Turning next to the different components of aggre-

gate demand, recall from Chapter 6 that GNP consists of four different parts:

GNP = consumption expenditure
+ gross private domestic investment
+ government expenditure on goods and services
+ net exports
= *C + I + G + X*

In the first section of this chapter, we assume that there is no foreign trade, so our GNP consists of the first three of the components, *C + I + G*. The second half of this chapter then adds the final component, net exports *(X)*, to the multiplier model.

We can show the effect of *G* in Figure 9-4, a diagram that—with one exception—is exactly the same as the one used in the last chapter to explain output determination. We have added one new variable (*G*, government spending on goods and services) on top of the consumption function and the fixed amount of investment. That is, the vertical distance between the *C + I* line and the *C + I + G* line is the amount of government spending on goods and services (on police, tanks, roads, etc.).

Why do we simply add *G* on the top? Because spending on government buildings *(G)* has the same macroeconomic impact as spending on private buildings *(I)*, and collective consumption expenditure involved in maintaining a public library *(G)* has the

same effect upon jobs as private consumption expenditure for newspapers or books *(C)*.

We end up with the three-layered *C + I + G* schedule showing the amount of total spending forthcoming at each level of GNP. We now must go to its intersection with the 45° line to read off the equilibrium level of national product. At this equilibrium GNP level, denoted by point *E* in Figure 9-4 below, total planned spending exactly equals total planned output. Point *E* is thus the equilibrium level of output.

Impact of Taxation on Aggregate Demand

Next turn to see how government taxation tends to reduce aggregate demand and the level of GNP. We

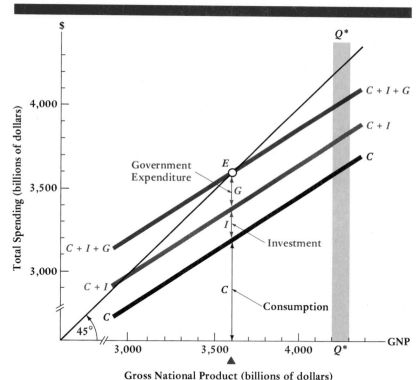

Figure 9-4   Government expenditure adds on just like investment to determine equilibrium GNP

On top of consumption spending and investment spending, we now add government spending on goods and services. This gives us the *C + I + G* schedule. At *E*, where this intersects the 45° line, we find the equilibrium level of GNP.

do not need graphs to tell us what happens when the government increases our taxes while at the same time holding its expenditures constant.

Extra taxes mean that we have lower disposable incomes, and lower disposable incomes tend to reduce our consumption spending. Clearly, if investment and government expenditure remain the same, a reduction in consumption spending will then reduce gross national product and employment. Thus, in our Keynesian model, when output is below its potential, higher taxes without increases in government spending will tend to reduce real GNP.

The earlier Figure 9-3 confirms this reasoning. In this figure, the upper CC curve represents the level of the consumption function with no taxes. The CC curve is unrealistic, of course, because consumers must pay taxes on their incomes. For simplicity, we assume that consumers pay $300 billion in taxes at every level of income; thus DI is exactly $300 billion less than GNP at every level of output. As is shown in Figure 9-3, this level of taxes can be represented by a rightward shift in the consumption function of $300 billion. This rightward shift will also appear as a downward shift; if the MPC is $\frac{2}{3}$, then the rightward shift of $300 billion will be a downward shift of $200 billion, as shown in Figure 9-3.

We thus easily see that taxes lower output in our multiplier model. A glance back at Figure 9-4 will show why. $I + G$ is unchanged when taxes increase, but the increase in taxes will lower disposable income, thereby shifting the CC consumption schedule downward. Hence, the $C + I + G$ schedule shifts downward. You can pencil in a new, lower $C' + I + G$ schedule in Figure 9-4. Confirm that its new intersection with the 45° line must be at a lower equilibrium level of GNP.

Before we leave our discussion of taxes, recall that G is government outlays on goods and services. It excludes spending on transfers such as unemployment insurance or social security payments. These transfers are treated as *negative taxes,* so that the taxes (T) considered here are actually best thought of as taxes less transfers. Therefore, if direct and indirect taxes total $400 billion, while all transfer payments are $100 billion, then we will say that net taxes, T, equal $400 - $100 = $300 billion.

A Numerical Example

The points made up to now can be illustrated by Table 9-1 below. This table is very similar to Table 8-2 in the last chapter, which illustrated output determina-

OUTPUT DETERMINATION WITH GOVERNMENT (*in billions of dollars*)

(1) INITIAL LEVEL OF GNP	(2) TAXES (T)	(3) DISPOS-ABLE INCOME (DI)	(4) PLANNED CONSUMP-TION (C)	(5) PLANNED INVEST-MENT (I)	(6) GOVERNMENT EXPEND-ITURE (G)	(7) TOTAL SPENDING (C + I + G)	(8) RESULTING TENDENCY OF ECONOMY
4,200	300	3,900	3,600	200	200	4,000	Contraction
3,900	300	3,600	3,400	200	200	3,800	Contraction
3,600	300	3,300	3,200	200	200	3,600	Equilibrium
3,300	300	3,000	3,000	200	200	3,400	Expansion
3,000	300	2,700	2,800	200	200	3,200	Expansion

Table 9-1 **Government spending, taxes, and investment determine equilibrium GNP**

This table shows how output is determined when government spending on goods and services is added to the multiplier model. In this example, taxes are "lump sum" or independent of the level of income. Disposable income is thus GNP minus $300 billion. Total spending is $I + G$ + (the consumption determined by the consumption function).

At levels of output less than $3600 billion, spending is greater than output, so output expands. Levels of output greater than $3600 are unsustainable and lead to contraction. Only at output of $3600 is output in equilibrium—that is, planned spending equals output.

tion in the multiplier model. The first column shows a reference level of GNP, while the second shows a fixed level of taxes, $300 billion. Disposable income in column (3) is then GNP less taxes. Consumption, taken as a function of *DI*, is shown in column (4). Column (5) shows the fixed level of investment, while column (6) exhibits the level of government spending.

To find total aggregate demand in column (7), we add together the *C + I + G* of columns (4) through (6).

Finally, we should compare total spending in column (7) with the initial level of GNP in column (1). If spending is above GNP, output rises; if spending is below GNP, output falls. This tendency, shown in the last column, assures us that output will tend toward its equilibrium at $3600 billion.

FISCAL-POLICY MULTIPLIERS

We have now seen that government fiscal policy affects equilibrium GNP in the multiplier model in a way quite similar to the impact of investment. Investment, taxes, and government spending represent autonomous spending streams that interact with induced consumption spending to determine the equilibrium level of national output. The parallel between investment and fiscal policy suggests that fiscal policy should also have multiplier effects upon output. And this is exactly right.

The *government expenditure multiplier* is the increase in GNP resulting from $1 increase in government expenditures on goods and services. An initial government purchase of a good or service will set in motion a chain of respending: If the government builds a road, the road-builders will spend some of their incomes on consumption goods, which in turn will generate incomes, some of which will be respent. In the simple model examined here, the ultimate effect on GNP of an extra dollar of *G* will be the same as an extra dollar of *I*: The multipliers are equal to $1/(1 - MPC)$. Figure 9-5 shows how a change in *G* will result in a higher level of GNP, with the increase being a multiple of the increase in government purchases.

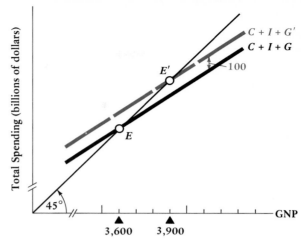

THE GOVERNMENT EXPENDITURE MULTIPLIER

Figure 9-5   The effect of higher G on output

Suppose that the government raises defense expenditures by $100 billion. This shifts upward the *C + I + G* line by $100 billion to *C + I + G'*.

The new equilibrium level of GNP is thus read off the 45° line at *E'* rather than at *E*. Because the *MPC* is $\frac{2}{3}$, the new level of output is $300 billion higher. That is, the government expenditure multiplier is

$$3 = \frac{1}{1 - \frac{2}{3}}$$

(What would the government expenditure multiplier be if the *MPC* were $\frac{3}{4}$? $\frac{9}{10}$?)

To show the effects of an extra $100 billion of *G*, the *C + I + G* curve in Figure 9-5 has been shifted up by $100 billion. The ultimate increase in GNP is equal to the $100 billion of primary spending times the expenditure multiplier. In this case, because the *MPC* is $\frac{2}{3}$, the multiplier is 3, so the equilibrium level of GNP rises by $300 billion.

Note, as well, that this horse can be ridden in both directions. If government expenditures were to fall, with taxes and other influences held constant, then GNP would decline by the change in *G* times the multiplier.

This example as well as common sense shows that the government expenditure multiplier is exactly the same number as the investment multiplier. Because they are equal, they are both called *expenditure multipliers.*

We can sum up:

Government expenditures on goods and services *(G)* are an important force in the determination of output and employment. In the multiplier model, if *G* increases, output will rise by the increase in *G* times the expenditure multiplier. Government spending therefore has the potential to stabilize, or destabilize, output over the business cycle.

The effect of *G* on output can be seen as well in the numerical example of Table 9-1. You can pencil in a different level of *G*—at $300 billion—and find the equilibrium level of GNP. It should give the same answer as Figure 9-5.

Impact of Taxes

Taxes will also have an impact upon equilibrium GNP, although the size of tax multipliers is smaller than that of expenditure multipliers.

To understand the impact of taxes on equilibrium GNP, consider the following example. Suppose the economy is at its potential GNP, and the nation gears up to meet foreign military threats by raising defense spending by $200 billion. Such sudden increases have occurred at many points in the history of the United States, such as in the early 1940s for World War II, in 1951 for the Korean war, in the mid-1960s for the Vietnam war, and in the early 1980s during the Reagan defense buildup. Say that economic planners wish to raise taxes just enough to offset the economic impact of the $200 billion increase in *G*. How much would taxes have to be raised?

We are in for a surprise. To offset the $200 billion increase in *G*, we need to increase tax collections by more than $200 billion. In our numerical example, we can find the exact size of the tax or *T* increase from Figure 9-3. That figure shows that a $300 billion increase in *T* reduces disposable income by just that amount and will lead to a consumption decline of just $200 billion when the *MPC* is $\frac{2}{3}$. Put differently, a tax increase of $300 billion will shift the *CC* curve

down by $200 billion. Hence, while a $1 billion increase in defense spending shifts up the *C + I + G* line by $1 billion, a $1 billion tax increase shifts down the *C + I + G* line by only $$\frac{2}{3}$ billion (when the *MPC* is $\frac{2}{3}$).

Thus offsetting an increase in defense spending, when non-defense outlays are constant, requires a larger increase in *T* than the increase in *G*.

The reason for this differential impact of *T* and *G* is that the tax multiplier is smaller than the expenditure multiplier. How much smaller?

Dollars of tax changes are almost as powerful a weapon against unemployment or inflation as are changes in dollars of government expenditures. The tax multiplier is smaller than the expenditure multiplier by a factor equal to the *MPC:*

Tax multiplier = *MPC* × expenditure multiplier

The reason the tax multiplier is smaller than the expenditure multiplier is straightforward. When government spends $1 on *G*, that $1 gets spent directly on GNP. On the other hand, when government cuts taxes by a dollar, only part of that dollar is spent on *C*, while a fraction of that $1 tax cut is saved. The difference in the response to a dollar of *G* and a dollar of *T* is enough to lower the tax multiplier below the expenditure multiplier.[2]

Fiscal Policy in Practice

Over the last quarter-century, fiscal policy was one of the nation's main tools in fighting off recession or

---

[2] The different multipliers can be seen using the device of the "expenditure rounds" shown on pp. 167–168 above. Let the *MPC* be *r*. Then if *G* goes up by 1 unit, the total increase in spending is the sum of secondary respending rounds:

$$1 + r + r^2 + r^3 + \cdots = \frac{1}{1 - r}$$

Now, if taxes are reduced by $1, consumers save $(1 - r)$ of the increased disposable income and spend *r* dollars on the first round. With the further rounds, the total spending is thus:

$$r + r^2 + r^3 + \cdots = \frac{r}{1 - r}$$

Thus the tax multiplier is *r* times the expenditure multiplier, where *r* is the *MPC*.

inflation. The Kennedy-Johnson tax cut of 1964 propelled the nation to, and then beyond, its potential output. It was followed by a tax increase in 1968 to offset the increased Vietnam war expenditures. President Ford lowered taxes in 1975 to fight a deep recession; President Carter was dissatisfied with the speed of the recovery and introduced further stimulative fiscal measures in 1977 and 1978. By 1979, however, inflation became the major concern, and further tax cuts were opposed by the Carter administration.

The 1980s provided a dramatic demonstration of the impact of fiscal policy. In 1981, President Reagan proposed a tax cut along with spending reductions,[3] but the Congress passed a fiscal program that was extremely expansionary. These steps propelled the American economy out of the deep recession of 1981–1982 into a rapid expansion in 1983–1985. From 1985 to 1988, however, the country became alarmed about the mounting budget deficit, and fiscal policy turned contractionary. Fortunately, as fiscal policy began to slow the economy, other forces (particularly net exports and investment) took up the slack and helped sustain the long economic expansion of the 1980s.

THE PARADOX OF THRIFT[4]

The growth of nations depends crucially on savings and investment. And from youth we are taught that thrift is an important virtue; *Poor Richard's Almanac* tells us that "A penny saved is a penny earned." Presidents and prime ministers are constantly urging their people to increase saving so that their nations can prosper.

But will higher saving necessarily benefit the economy? In a striking argument, Keynes pointed out that when people attempt to save more, this will not necessarily result in more saving for the nation as a whole. Let us analyze this "paradox of thrift."

Begin in a simple Keynesian world without any government spending or taxes. Suppose the President

successfully persuades the populace to save a larger part of their incomes, or more precisely, to save more at every level of income. Then, as is shown in Figure 9-6 on p. 184, the savings schedule (labelled *SS*) shifts up. Or equivalently, in our expenditure diagram of Figure 9-4, the consumption function shifts down.

What would be the impact of this increase of thrift in a Keynesian multiplier model? The answer is that the higher savings schedule will intersect the unchanged investment schedule (marked as *II* in Figure 9-6) at a lower equilibrium level of GNP. That is, the greater thrift represented by the upward shift in the savings schedule will tend to reduce the level of GNP.

We can use our intuition to understand the process. If people try to increase their saving and lower their consumption for a given level of business investment, sales (equal to $C + I$ spending) will fall. Businesses will cut back on production. How far will production fall? GNP will fall until people stop trying to save more than businesses are investing.

Perhaps this point seems obvious. But Figure 9-6 tells us something more surprising. It shows, for a Keynesian multiplier model in which the *MPC* is $\frac{2}{3}$, that a \$1 upward shift in the savings schedule will kill off \$3 of income. Contrariwise, a \$1 downward shift in the savings schedule, which means a \$1 upward shift in the consumption schedule, will produce a similar multiplied \$3 increase in income. (The horizontal red arrow in Figure 9-6 is 3 times the vertical red arrow.)

In short, just as investment spending is "high-powered spending" with multiplier effects on income, so too will consumption spending that represents a genuine shift in the consumption and savings functions be high-powered spending.

This surprising result leads to the **paradox of thrift:** In a multiplier model with unchanged investment, an upward shift in the savings function, reflecting an increase in thriftiness, will actually reduce income and output. How much? Output is reduced in a multiplied way until income falls low enough to bring people's new desired saving again into equality with investment. Thus an attempt to save more may lead, instead, to lower income and no more saving or investment.

Just when we have learned Poor Richard's wisdom,

---

[3] Problem 13 in the Questions for Discussion puts together taxes and spending to analyze a "balanced-budget multiplier."

[4] This section can be omitted in short courses.

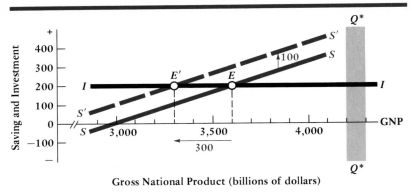

Figure 9-6 Saving-and-investment diagram shows how thriftiness can kill off income

In an underemployed economy, desire to consume less at every income level will shift the savings schedule upward. With the investment line *(II)* unchanged, equilibrium drops to the *E'* intersection. Why? Because when planned saving is higher than planned investment, income has to fall—and fall in a *multiplied* way—until people feel poor enough that they will want to save only the amount of planned investment.

along comes a new generation of financial wizards who show that in depressed times the old virtues may be modern sins.

Paradox Resolved

Let's try to untangle the paradox in a dispassionate manner. Two considerations help to clarify things.

The first is this: In economics, we must always be on guard against the fallacy of composition. That is to say, what is good for each person separately need not therefore always be good for all; under some circumstances, private prudence may be social folly.

Specifically, this means that the *attempt* of each and every person to increase saving may—under the conditions to be described—result in no more *actual* saving by all the people. The italicized words "attempt" and "actual" are keys to the paradox. They remind us that when people attempt to save more, the actual outcome may be only a lower level of output with no additional saving.

The second clue to the paradox of thrift lies in the question of whether or not the economy is at a depressed level. In a classical world, we would always

be at full employment; thus the more of our national product we devoted to current consumption, the less would be available for saving and capital formation. If output could be assumed to be always at its potential, then the old-fashioned doctrine of thrift would be absolutely correct—correct, be it noted, from both the individual and the social standpoints. In primitive agricultural communities, such as the American colonies of Ben Franklin's day, Franklin's prescription probably contained much truth. Similarly, if people saved more during full-employment periods such as World War I or II, more of the full-employment output would have been made available for investment.

To Save More in Recessions? The explanation of the paradox raises a question for today: Why would a modern economist or policymaker try to increase saving at a time when there are substantial unemployed resources? Should Congress and the Reagan administration have devoted so much effort in 1982 to patching up the Social Security system? In the depressed year of 1982, should not Congress and the president have tried to get people to save *less* and thereby raise consumption, output, and employment?

As in many other macroeconomic debates, the answer lies in one's view of whether the economy is classical or Keynesian. The two cases are illustrated by Figure 9-7, which shows two polar extremes of the aggregate supply curve. Let us say that you lean toward the classical view, believing that the *AS* curve is extremely steep. You would hold this view if you believe that prices and wages are flexible and that output is always near its potential. In this case, which is illustrated in the upper right of Figure 9-7, an increase in thrift would lower aggregate demand from *AD* to *AD'*, reducing prices but leaving output unaffected.

By contrast, say that you favor the Keynesian viewpoint. We here depict an extreme or depression Keynesian view, one in which wages and prices are absolutely rigid. In this example, the aggregate supply curve would be horizontal, as shown on the lower left of Figure 9-7. Consequently, an increase of thrift would reduce aggregate demand from *AD''* to *AD'''* and would produce a sharp decrease in output and employment.

We see, then, that economists might differ about the impact of thrift upon output not because one group cared much and the other little about unemployment or GNP gaps. Instead, the classical and Keynesian economists disagree because they have different pictures of the economy in mind. Classical economists wish to increase thrift because they believe that the higher saving will result in higher investment; they may care deeply about unemployment, but they believe that higher thrift will not produce higher joblessness. Similarly, Keynesian economists who wish to encourage consumption in deep recessions are not opposed to investment. Instead, they may believe that

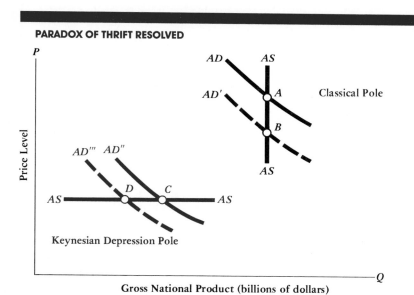

PARADOX OF THRIFT RESOLVED

Figure 9-7   Paradox of thrift in Keynesian and classical poles

As in many macroeconomic debates, different approaches produce different answers. In the classical pole shown at the upper right, an increase in thrift reduces *AD* to *AD'*. Classical aggregate supply implies that output will be unchanged while prices fall. The increased thrift and lower consumption make way for higher levels of investment.

In the depression Keynesian approach shown on the lower left, an increase in thrift lowers *AD''* to *AD'''*. This brings lower levels of output as lower income brings voluntary or desired saving in line with desired investment in a way displayed in Fig. 9-6.

the *AS* curve is relatively flat in the short run, that the major economic enemy is unemployment, and that they should postpone stimulating investment until the economy is closer to its potential.

■   ■   ■

This concludes our description of the elementary application of multiplier models to government fiscal policy. In later chapters, particularly Chapters 16 and 17, we return to provide a more detailed discussion of the institutions of American fiscal policy along with an analysis of the interaction of fiscal policy with monetary policy.

The next section of this chapter applies the multiplier model to international trade. We see there how exports have an effect very similar to that of investment and government spending, and the section concludes with a set of estimates of the size of real-world multipliers.

B. OUTPUT DETERMINATION IN OPEN ECONOMIES

No nation is an island unto itself. Every nation is an open economy, trading goods and services with others, exporting those commodities that are produced most inexpensively at home and importing products in which others have a cost advantage.

In an earlier era, foreign trade exerted only a modest impact upon the macroeconomic performance of the United States. Most citizens, students, and politicians could afford to ignore the economic linkages between nations, leaving that topic to specialists who toiled in universities or in the State Department.

But revolutionary developments in communications, transportation, and trade policy have increasingly linked together the economic fortunes of nations. Japan, Canada, and the United States are today more closely integrated than were New York and California a century ago; the international business cycle exerts a powerful effect on every nation of the globe; monetary-policy actions in Washington can lead to starvation, poverty, and revolution in South America; movements in trade balances can drive countries into boom or recession. To ignore international trade is to miss half the economic ball game.

The theories of international trade and development are analyzed in depth in Chapters 37 through 40. In this section, we highlight some of the major trends and then show how changes in net exports exert an impact on the macroeconomy analogous to that of investment spending.

IMPACTS OF FOREIGN TRADE ON ECONOMIC ACTIVITY

Net Exports: Concepts and Trends

Begin by recalling some basic definitions. In Chapter 6 we showed that GNP has four components: consumption, investment, government purchases, and net exports. Net exports are defined as exports of goods and services minus imports of goods and services.

What are the major components of international trade? For the United States during 1987, exports totalled $428 billion while imports were $551 billion, for net exports of minus $123 billion.

The major components of exports were merchandise exports of $258 billion, of which the principal items were $25 billion of foodstuffs, $67 billion of industrial products, $88 billion of capital goods, and $26 billion of automotive goods. Other exports totalled $170 billion, including $32 billion of travel and transportation and $96 billion of income on U.S. assets abroad.

Imports for 1987 totalled $551 billion. Of this, $413 billion was merchandise trade, including $25 billion of foodstuffs, $110 billion of industrial supplies, $85 billion of capital goods, $85 billion of automotive products, and $63 billion of other consumer goods. Non-merchandise trade of $138 billion in-

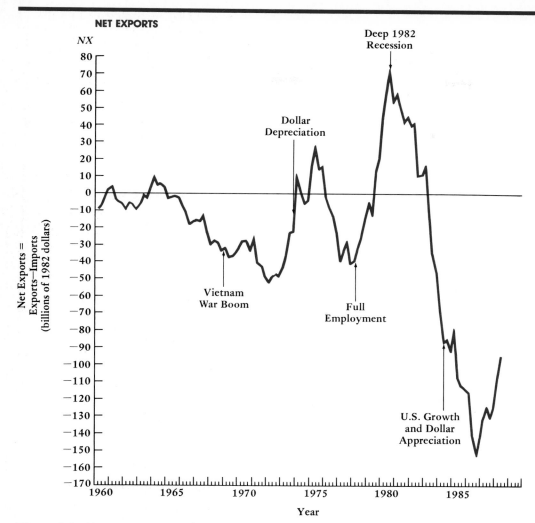

NET EXPORTS

Figure 9-8   Net exports turned sharply negative in the 1980s

The history of real net exports (exports minus imports, both measured in 1982 prices) showed ups and downs until 1980. The rise (or "appreciation") of the U.S. dollar in the early 1980s, along with relatively slow growth of U.S. trading partners, led to a massive external deficit after 1982. (Source: U.S. Department of Commerce.)

cluded $47 billion of travel and transportation and $67 billion of income from foreign assets in the United States.

Over most of the twentieth century, the United States has had a positive balance on its net exports.

Net exports turned negative during the Vietnam war boom, but then improved after the depreciation of the dollar in the early 1970s and again during the deep recession of the early 1980s. A dramatic deterioration in the U.S. trade position occurred in the mid-1980s, so that by 1987 imports exceeded exports by $129 billion (in 1982 prices). The huge trade deficit of the late 1980s has become one of the major political problems for the United States and its trading partners. Figure 9-8 displays U.S. net exports over the last three decades.

Once we take into account the possibility of exports and imports, we must also recognize that a nation's expenditure may differ from its production. Total *domestic expenditure* (sometimes called domestic demand) is equal to consumption plus domestic investment plus government purchases. It will differ from total *national product* (or GNP) for two reasons. First, some part of domestic expenditure will be on goods produced abroad, these items being imports (denoted by *m*) like Colombian coffee or Japanese automobiles. In addition, some part of America's production will be sold abroad as exports (denoted by *e*)—items like Iowa wheat or Boeing aircraft. The difference between national output and domestic expenditure is simply $e - m$ = net exports = X.

When we want to calculate the *total* demand for American goods and services, we need to include not only domestic demand but also foreign demand; that is, we need to know the total spending of American residents as well as the net purchases of foreigners. This total must include domestic expenditures (*C + I + G*) plus sales to foreigners *(e)* less domestic purchases from foreigners *(m)*. That is, expenditure on national output, or GNP, equals consumption plus domestic investment plus government purchases plus net exports:

$$\text{Total aggregate demand} = \text{GNP}$$
$$= C + I + G + X$$

Determinants of Net Exports What determines the movements of exports and imports and therefore net exports? It is best to think of the import and export components of net exports separately. Imports of goods and services consist of items like Japanese cars, Mexican tomatoes, and French wine. Purchases of such items by American residents are positively related to American income and output, to U.S. GNP. When U.S. GNP is rising rapidly, U.S. imports tend to rise even more quickly.

In addition, the choice between foreign and domes-

tic goods responds to the relative price of the two. If the price of domestic cars rises relative to the price of Korean cars, say because productivity growth is more rapid in Korea or because the exchange rate on the Korean won falls relative to the U.S. dollar, Americans will buy more Korean and fewer American cars. Hence the volume and value of imports will be affected by the relative prices of domestic and foreign goods, which in turn depend on both the domestic price levels and the foreign exchange rate of the dollar.[5]

Exports are the mirror image of imports: Our exports are the imports of the rest of the world. They depend, therefore, primarily upon the incomes and outputs of our trading partners, as well as upon the relative prices of our exports and the goods with which they compete. As foreign output rises, or as the foreign exchange rate of the dollar falls, the volume and value of our exports tend to grow.

What caused the major changes in net exports shown in Figure 9-8? From 1960 to 1969, the American economy grew rapidly and American prices rose relative to those of its trading partners; consequently, imports tended to grow faster than exports. From 1969 to 1975, the American economy slumped. In addition, as the world's monetary system broke down, the value of the dollar fell relative to other major currencies. Consequently, U.S. goods became relatively cheaper, the growth of imports slowed, exports boomed, and net exports became positive.

The period since 1982 can be seen as one in which all major elements became unfavorable to the U.S. trade position. The value of the dollar rose sharply from 1980 to 1985, so that in America, imports became relatively cheap while exports became uncompetitive. Foreign economies grew less rapidly than the

---

[5] Recall from Chapter 5 that the *foreign exchange rate* is the price of a nation's currency in terms of foreign currencies. Take wine as an example. The relative prices of U.S. wine and French wine will depend upon both countries' prices and upon the foreign exchange rate. Say that California chardonnay wines sell for $6 per bottle, while the equivalent French chardonnay sells for 40 French francs. Then at the 1984 exchange rate of 10 French francs to the dollar, French wine sells at $4 per bottle while California wine sells at $6, giving an advantage to the imported variety.

Say that the foreign exchange rate of the dollar fell to 5 francs to the dollar. Then the French wine would sell for $8 as compared to $6 for the California wine. The fall in the exchange rate on the dollar would therefore turn relative prices against imports and in favor of domestic products.

home economy, so again exports sagged while imports grew sharply. The effect was a massive turn toward deficit in real net exports.

Impact of Trade on GNP

How do changes in a nation's trade flows affect its GNP and employment? Surprisingly, the answer is that this small tail can wag the entire American economy. Let us see how.

Table 9-2 shows how introducing net exports affects output determination. This table begins with the same components shown for a closed economy in Table 9-1. Total domestic demand in column (2) is composed of the consumption, investment, and government purchases we analyzed earlier (although we have pushed taxes out of the picture in this table). Column (3) then adds the exports of goods and services. These depend *(a)* upon foreign incomes and outputs, which are assumed to be external, given or fixed from the outside, and *(b)* upon prices and exchange rates, which are also taken as given in this simple multiplier model of an open economy. Exports are therefore a constant level of $360 billion of foreign spending on domestic goods and services.

The interesting new element arises from imports, shown in column (4). Like exports, imports depend upon external variables like prices and exchange rates. But in addition, imports depend upon domestic incomes and output, which clearly change in the different rows of Table 9-2. For simplicity, we assume that people always import 10 percent of their total incomes, so imports in column (4) are 10 percent of column (1).

Subtracting column (4) from column (3) gives net exports in column (5). This is a negative number when imports exceed exports and a positive number when exports are greater than imports. Net exports in column (5) are the net addition to the spending stream contributed by foreigners. Equilibrium output in an open economy comes at the point where total spending in column (6) exactly equals total output. In this case, equilibrium comes with net exports of exactly zero, although generally the net export position would differ from zero. You can examine other rows to see why, when spending does not equal output, the economy is not in equilibrium.

Figure 9-9 on the next page shows the open-economy equilibrium graphically. The upward-sloping black line marked $C + I + G$ is the same curve as Figure 9-4 used to illustrate output determination with government spending. To this line we must add the level of net exports that is forthcoming at each level of GNP. Net exports from column (5) of Table 9-2 are added to get the red line of total aggregate demand or total spending. To the left in the figure, net exports are positive so the red line lies above the black curve; at the right, imports exceed exports and net exports are negative so the total spending line lies below the line for domestic demand.

OUTPUT DETERMINATION WITH FOREIGN TRADE *(in billions of dollars)*

(1) INITIAL LEVEL OF GNP	(2) DOMESTIC DEMAND ($C + I + G$)	(3) EXPORTS *(e)*	(4) IMPORTS *(m)*	(5) NET EXPORTS *(X)*	(6) TOTAL SPENDING ($C + I + G + X$)	(7) RESULTING TENDENCY OF ECONOMY
4,200	4,000	360	420	−60	3,940	↓ Contraction
3,900	3,800	360	390	−30	3,770	↓ Contraction
3,600	**3,600**	**360**	**360**	**0**	**3,600**	**Equilibrium**
3,300	3,400	360	330	30	3,430	↑ Expansion
3,000	3,200	360	300	60	3,260	↑ Expansion

Table 9-2 Net exports add to aggregate demand of economy

To the domestic demand of $C + I + G$, we must add net exports of $X = e - m$ to obtain total aggregate demand for the economy. Note that higher net exports have the same multiplier as do investment and government expenditure increases.

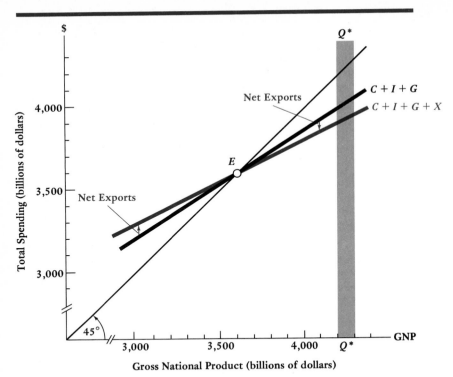

Figure 9-9 Adding net exports to domestic demand gives equilibrium GNP in open economy

The black line represents domestic demand, purchases by domestic consumers, businesses, and governments. To this must be added net foreign spending; net exports plus domestic demand produces the red line of total spending. Equilibrium comes at point E, where total GNP equals total spending on goods and services produced in the U.S. Note that the slope of the red total demand curve is less than that of domestic demand to reflect leakage from spending into imports.

Equilibrium GNP occurs where the red line of total spending intersects the 45° line. This intersection comes at exactly the same point, at $3600 billion, that is shown as equilibrium GNP in Table 9-2. Only at $3600 billion does GNP exactly equal what consumers, businesses, governments, and foreigners want to spend on goods and services produced in the United States.[6]

[6] Note that the two lines in Fig. 9-9 cross where net exports are zero, but the fact that equilibrium comes at zero net exports is purely coincidental. Redraw an equilibrium of Fig. 9-9 that has positive net exports.

The Marginal Propensity to Import and the Spending Line

Note that the aggregate demand curve, the red $C + I + G + X$ curve in Figure 9-9, has a slightly smaller slope than the black curve of domestic demand. This important fact arises because of the leakage from spending into imports. We assumed for this example that 10 cents of every dollar of income was spent on imports. It will be convenient to introduce a new term, the marginal propensity to import, to explain the implications of this assumption. The **marginal**

propensity to import, which we will denote *MPm,* is the increase in imports for each $1 increase in GNP. It will be recalled that we labelled the increase in consumption per unit increase of income the "marginal propensity to consume." The marginal propensity to import is closely related. It tells how much is imported for each dollar increase in total GNP. What marginal propensity to import is assumed to hold in Table 9-2? Clearly, the answer is $MPm = 0.10$, for every $300 billion of increased income leads to $30 billion of increased imports. (What is the marginal propensity to import in an economy with no foreign trade? Zero.)

Returning to Figure 9-9, let us examine the slope of the total spending line (that is, the line showing total spending on $C + I + G + X$). Note that the slope of the total spending line is less than the slope of the domestic demand line of $C + I + G$. As GNP and total incomes rise by $300, spending on consumption rises by the income change times the *MPC* (assumed to be two-thirds), or by $200. At the same time, spending on imports, or foreign goods, also rises by $30. Hence spending on domestic goods rises by only $200 − $30 = $170. Thus the slope of the total spending line falls from 0.667 in our closed economy to 0.567 in our open economy.[7]

The Open-Economy Multiplier

You might suspect that the leakage of spending outside the economy into imports would change the multiplier in an open economy, and your suspicion would be reinforced by your observation that the import leakage changes the slope of the spending line. You would be correct. Let us see why.

[7] Up to now we have considered only leakages from income into saving and into imports. In a complete account of the economy, two further important *leakages* should be included: (*a*) those into taxes, for some taxes (such as income or sales taxes) rise with higher levels of incomes and output, and (*b*) those into business savings when businesses earn higher profits but do not pay those profits out to individuals.

In addition, a complete model would include one further item of induced *spending:* As Chapter 7 hinted, private investment tends to respond positively as output rises, for businesses tend to spend more on investment to increase capacity at higher levels of output.

These further leakages and induced spending streams will change the slope of the aggregate spending curve and will also change the economy's multiplier.

One way of understanding the expenditure multiplier in an open economy is to calculate the rounds of spending and responding generated by an additional dollar of government spending, investment, or exports. To take the last example, say that the Germans decide to buy an extra dollar of U.S. computer software. This extra dollar will generate $1 of income, of which $\$\frac{2}{3} = \$0.667$ will be spent by Americans on consumption. However, because the marginal propensity to import is 0.10, of the $0.667 of extra consumption, one-tenth of the extra dollar of income or $0.10 will be spent on foreign goods and services, leaving only $0.567 of spending on domestically produced goods. That $0.567 of domestic spending will generate $0.567 of U.S. income, from which $0.567 \times (\$0.567) = \$0.321$ will be spent on consumption of domestic goods and services. Hence the total increase in output, or the **open-economy multiplier** will be

$$\text{Open-economy} \atop \text{multiplier} = 1 + 0.567 + (0.567)^2 + \cdots$$

$$= 1 + (\tfrac{2}{3} - \tfrac{1}{10}) + (\tfrac{2}{3} - \tfrac{1}{10})^2 + \cdots$$

$$= \frac{1}{1 - \tfrac{2}{3} + \tfrac{1}{10}} = \frac{1}{\tfrac{13}{30}} = 2.3$$

This compares with a closed-economy multiplier of $1/(1 - 0.667) = 3$.

Another way of calculating the multiplier is as follows: Recall from the last chapter that the multiplier in the simplest model was $1/MPS$, where $MPS =$ the marginal propensity to save. This result can be extended by noting that the analogy to the *MPS* in an open economy is the *total leakage* per dollar of extra income, that amount leaking into saving (the *MPS*) plus that amount leaking into imports (the *MPm*). Hence, the open-economy multiplier should be $1/(MPS + MPm) = 1/(0.333 + 0.1) = 1/0.433 = 2.3$. Note that both the leakage analysis and the rounds analysis provide exactly the same answer.

To summarize, because a fraction of any income increase leaks into imports in an open economy, the open-economy multiplier effect is somewhat smaller than that of a closed economy. The exact relationship is

$$\text{Open-economy multiplier} = \frac{1}{MPS + MPm}$$

where MPS = marginal propensity to save and MPm = marginal propensity to import.

Regional Multipliers A little reflection will suggest that we can apply the analysis of open economies to regions or cities as well. Say that you are the mayor of a medium-sized city called Urbana, asked to consider the relevance of the multiplier analysis to your city. A group of developers is meeting with you to propose the establishment of a science and industrial park. The group wants the city to put up $50 million in seed money and argues that the investment will yield a handsome return because it will be respent time and time again. Indeed, one enthusiast argues that, on the basis of elementary economics, expenditure multipliers are at least 3, and perhaps 5, so that the city's $50 million will generate at least $150 million, and perhaps $250 million, in additional business.

As you think about the argument, you are troubled because you think the enthusiast has a closed economy in mind. Your city, by contrast, is a very open economy, importing and exporting most of its business. After all, many of the workers, all of the construction materials, and most of the construction businesses and architects are likely to come from outside Urbana.

You consult your local economist, who provides estimates that indicate that the MPm of medium-sized cities like Urbana is as high as 0.80. If the MPS is around 0.25, this suggests that the total multiplier is only $1/(0.25 + 0.80) = 0.95$.

The ingenious argument of the developer is therefore far off the mark, for, after accounting for imports into the city, the increase of incomes and net output in the city would actually be somewhat less than the cost of the $50 million project.

POLICY IMPLICATIONS

In a world where nations are increasingly linked by trade and commerce, heads of government today concern themselves more and more with the state of the world economy, the prospects for international trade, and the economic linkages between them. We shall mention some of the major issues of international macroeconomics here, reserving a more detailed discussion for Chapters 38 through 40.

Impacts of Trade Flows and Exchange Rates

Turn back to Figure 9-8, which shows the recent history of net exports in the United States. This graph depicts one of the major economic events of the last decade—the deterioration of the U.S. net export position over the early 1980s. To get a rough measure of the size of the shift, we can compare 1980 and 1986, years in which the overall utilization of resources was approximately the same. From 1980 to 1986, real net exports in 1982 prices moved from a surplus of $57 billion to a deficit of $138 billion. This decline of $195 billion in real net exports is 6 percent of the average real GNP for this period.

What was the impact of this sharp deterioration upon the American economy? Unless other spending items offset this change, the sharp decline in net exports would exert a contractionary effect upon the economy. The change would be the approximate equivalent of a $195 billion decrease in government spending on goods and services. Fortunately for the economy, the decrease in net exports occurred at just the time when the federal government budget was shifting in an *expansionary* direction. From 1980 to 1986, the federal government deficit increased by $143 billion. Had the sharp expansionary shift in the government or some other sector not occurred, the economy would have suffered a prolonged and deep recession.

Using this analysis, we can also understand the impact of changes in foreign exchange rates. The exchange rate of the dollar is today largely market-determined, that is to say, determined by the interaction of supply and demand of private traders and investors. When the exchange rate of the dollar rises, so that the dollar will buy more of foreign currencies, this is called an **appreciation** of the currency. For example, from 1980 to 1985 the price of a British pound fell from $2.33 to $1.30. This falling price represented a rise in the dollar's value, or an appreciation of the dollar. By contrast, when the value of a currency falls, this is called a **depreciation.**

Let us explore the impact of an appreciation of the dollar, such as occurred from 1980 to 1985. Over this period, the value of the dollar rose 55 percent. As a result, in a way explained in footnote 5 above, American exports became less competitive abroad and foreign imports became more competitive in the United States. This sharp rise in the value of the dollar was in good measure responsible for the sharp deterioration of net exports shown in Figure 9-8, and provided a contractionary impetus to aggregate demand over the 1980–1985 period.

Hence, an appreciation of a country's currency will lead to a decline in real net exports and this tends to reduce aggregate demand and output. A currency depreciation will tend to increase a country's real net exports and to boost aggregate demand and output.

Impacts of Trade Policies

Most people do not personally experience macroeconomic disturbances. Rather, they feel the impact of global events on their individual towns, companies, or jobs or on the prices they pay. As the U.S. foreign-trade position swung sharply from surplus to deficit, people experienced losses of jobs and profits in agriculture and manufacturing, along with an invasion of foreign products, particularly from Japan and the Pacific Basin. Workers and companies in automobiles, steel, electronics, farming, and many other affected industries saw their livelihood threatened by relatively inexpensive foreign goods.

The age-old reaction to foreign-trade problems, dating back to Alexander Hamilton, is to lobby the government for "protection from cheap foreign goods." Such protection takes the form of tariffs or quotas on competitive products, such as Japanese cars, Brazilian steel, Italian footwear, Canadian wheat, and so forth.

A detailed analysis of the economics of protection will be provided in Chapters 38 and 39, but one important macroeconomic point should be made here: If the United States keeps out foreign goods, it lowers imports and thereby raises U.S. net exports. The impact on the United States is therefore to raise its GNP. Suppose that a protectionist policy succeeded in lowering imports by $130 billion. Pencil a new set of

numbers reflecting that policy into Table 9-2 and calculate how much this will increase U.S. GNP. (Alternatively, you can calculate the impact on the United States by multiplying the change in net exports by the open-economy multiplier.)

But the change in trade policies also affects the economies of other countries. A decrease in our imports by $130 billion will be reflected in a decrease in other countries' *exports* by $130 billion. Other countries will therefore experience an economic contraction when we protect our own industries. Such policies were followed by many nations during the 1930s and tended to worsen the Great Depression. Because protectionist policies tend to aid the domestic economy at the expense of foreign countries, they are sometimes called a "beggar-thy-neighbor" approach.

Improving International Cooperation

The discussion of this chapter suggests that economic interdependence now plays a major role in the economic health and material wealth of nations. Output, prices, employment, real incomes, as well as the fate of individual industries all depend upon the output and trade policies of other nations. This fact is captured in the old saying, "When America sneezes, Europe catches cold." An updated adage might read, "When the global economy is sick, the contagion spreads to everyone."

Over the period since World War II, international economic cooperation has become a major part of the economic policy of nations. These are the major issues today:

▪ *Trade agreements.* We showed above that protectionist measures like tariffs and quotas could curb trade deficits, and at the same time increase domestic output and employment. But this cure would be a "beggar-thy-neighbor" policy, in a sense exporting trade deficits and unemployment. Having learned the dangers of protectionism in the 1930s, nations banded together in multinational trade treaties and agreements to desist from imposing trade restrictions.

▪ *International monetary arrangements.* Foreign exchange rates necessarily affect many nations. In earlier years, nations would sometimes manipulate their exchange rates to attain domestic political objectives—forcing a depreciation of their currency to increase net exports, output, and employment. At other times, nations have allowed their domestic inflation to spill over to other regions. In an attempt to curtail undesirable manipulation of exchange rates, nations have agreed on certain international monetary arrangements, overseen by the multinational International Monetary Fund (IMF).

■ *Macroeconomic coordination.* The most recent and controversial of cooperative steps include attempts to coordinate macroeconomic policy. Suppose the world economy is in recession. No single nation is powerful enough to bring the world economy back to its potential output. Moreover, if one small nation takes fiscal or monetary steps to increase its output, much of the stimulus spills over to other countries and, because open-economy multipliers are small, the home economy enjoys relatively less economic expansion. (Recall how the benefits of the construction project tended to spill over to other regions for our hypothetical case of the town of Urbana above. This kind of spillover happened in real life when the French took expansionary fiscal steps by themselves in 1981 and found that the multiplier was disappointingly small.)

Even worse, if a small country expands on its own, it will find that not only does much of the stimulus spill over its borders, but also it is likely to witness a turn in its trade account toward deficit. This fact can be seen in Figure 9-9, where an increase in GNP with no increase in exports will produce a negative net export position.

To break out of this bind, economists and policymakers have sometimes proposed "coordinated expansion," wherein all countries would take expansionary steps simultaneously. A coordinated fiscal or monetary expansion would find each country both causing and enjoying expansionary spillovers. Moreover, because foreign countries would be expanding, a nation could hope that its exports (driven up by expansion abroad) would rise as much as its imports (driven up by expansion at home). Such coordinated macroeconomic policies could also be used to contract global economic activity if that were called for. Such coordination of macroeconomic policies was

proposed by President Carter at economic summits in 1977 and 1978, and was endorsed by European leaders at economic summits in the 1980s.

In summary, the macroeconomic fates of nations are closely linked through international trade and capital flows. Nations have agreed to manage their international trade policies, their macroeconomic policies, and their exchange rates so as to encourage a free and open trading system, to prevent imposing hardships on other nations, and to prevent undesired unemployment or inflation. Much has been accomplished in these areas, but much remains to be done.

HOW LARGE ARE MULTIPLIERS?

In order to understand the impact of fiscal policy or of investment decisions or of changes in foreign trade, economists must be able to estimate the size of fiscal, investment, or foreign-trade multipliers. Further, if policymakers are to construct effective countercyclical policies, their economic advisers must possess economic models that will project the effects of different doses of fiscal or monetary policies. Just as a physician prescribing a pain-killer must know the effect of different-sized doses, so must an economist know whether the expenditure and tax multipliers are 2 or 4 or 6.

In fact, the last decades have seen an outpouring of statistical studies of macroeconomic models of the kind we have analyzed. Early work in this area began with pioneers like Jan Tinbergen of the Netherlands and Lawrence Klein of the University of Pennsylvania—both winners of the Nobel Prize for work in macroeconomic modeling. Today, there is an entire industry of econometricians estimating macroeconomic models, determining multipliers, and forecasting the future of the economy.

Estimates of Multipliers   Simple textbook models give a highly simplified picture of the functioning of the macroeconomy, and for this reason textbook multipliers are too crude to use in real-world policymaking. In order to get a more realistic picture of the response of output to changes in government expenditures, economists estimate large-scale econometric

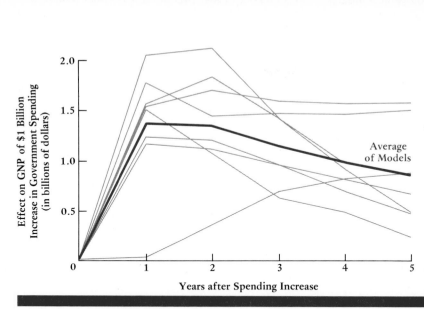

Figure 9-10 Expenditure multipliers in macroeconomic models

A recent study shows the estimated government expenditure multipliers in different macroeconomic models at different intervals following a fiscal policy change. These experiments show the estimated impact of a permanent $1 billion increase in the real value of government purchases of goods and services on real GNP. The heavy red line shows the average for the different models while the light gray lines represent the estimated multiplier in the individual models. [Source: Ralph C. Bryant, Gerald Holtham, and Peter Hooper, "Consensus and Diversity in Model Simulations," in *Empirical Macroeconomics for Interdependent Economies* (Brookings, Washington, D. C., 1988).]

models and then perform numerical experiments by calculating the impact of a change in government expenditures on the path of the economy.

A recent comprehensive survey of econometric models of the United States economy provides a representative sample of multiplier estimates. The models surveyed include equations that represent all major sectors of the economy (including both monetary and financial sectors, along with investment demand schedules and consumption functions) and they incorporate a full set of links with the rest of the world. In the experiments, the level of real government purchases of goods and services is permanently increased by $1 billion. The models then calculate the impact on real GNP. The change in real GNP resulting from the increase in government spending provides an estimate of the size of the government expenditure multiplier.

Figure 9-10 shows the results of this survey. The heavy red line shows the average government expenditure multiplier estimated by eight models, while the light lines show the range of estimates of the individual models. The average multiplier for the first and second years is around 1.4, but after the second year

the multiplier tends to decline slightly as monetary forces and international impacts come into play. (The monetary forces represent the impact of higher GNP on interest rates, which leads to a "crowding out" of investment, as we will explain in Chapters 16 and 17.)

One interesting feature of these estimates is that the different models (shown by the light lines in Figure 9-10) suggest a great deal of disagreement about the size of multipliers. Why cannot economists agree on as elementary a concept as the expenditure multiplier?

The disagreements arise for two reasons. First, there is an inherent uncertainty about the nature of economic relationships. Uncertainty is the stuff of all sciences, and even in an exact science like physics, estimates of the age of the universe recently changed from 8 to 16 billion years. Because of the difficulty of making controlled experiments, along with the fact that the economy itself evolves through time, economics contains even greater challenges for those who estimate its empirical structure.

In addition, economists have fundamental disagreements about the underlying nature of the macroeconomy. Some economists tend toward a classical approach while others stay with the conventional Keynesian model. Moreover, different statistical approaches may lead to divergent estimates.

Given all the alternative approaches to macroeconomics, it is not surprising that the size of multipliers is a subject of great controversy.

Qualifications

We have now completed our survey of the most important applications of the Keynesian multiplier model. This approach has been extremely useful in helping to explain business fluctuations and the linkage between international trade and national output. It shows how government fiscal policy can be used to fight unemployment and inflation.

But it would be a mistake to believe that an economist can be made out of a parrot by simply teaching it to say "$C + I + G + X$" or "multiplier." Behind such concepts are important assumptions and qualifications.

First, recall that the multiplier model assumes investment is fixed and that prices are sticky. A more realistic approach takes into account that investment responds to monetary conditions and to the level of output, while prices will rise more rapidly as output and employment increase. Only after we have mastered elements of monetary theory and policy, along with the essentials of inflation analysis, can the full impact of fiscal policy and trade flows be understood. When all these realistic aspects are included in the analysis, the multiplier on government purchases or taxes or foreign trade may be attenuated, or in some cases may even approach zero.

The key qualifications are ones that will concern us for the rest of the chapters on macroeconomics. Before we turn to analyze monetary policy as well as inflation and unemployment, however, the next chapter begins to examine the shape of business cycles that have plagued capitalism throughout its history.

SUMMARY

A. Fiscal Policy in the Multiplier Model

1. Ancient societies suffered famines due to harvest failures. The modern market economy can suffer from poverty amidst plenty. Here there may be large gaps between potential and actual output due to deficient aggregate demand. Or, excessive spending may lead to inflation. We now study how fiscal policy can do something to smooth the cycle of boom and bust.

2. The analysis of fiscal policy presented here continues the Keynesian multiplier model of Chapter 8. For clarity, it is best understood as a world in which prices and wages are inflexible, so that the aggregate supply curve is relatively flat for output levels below potential GNP.

3. An increase in government expenditure—taken by itself with taxes and investment unchanged—has expansionary effects on national product much like those of investment. The schedule of $C + I + G$ shifts upward to a higher equilibrium intersection with the 45° line.

4. A decrease in taxes—taken by itself with investment and government expenditure unchanged—raises the equilibrium level of national product. The CC schedule of consumption plotted against GNP is shifted upward and leftward by a tax cut, but since extra dollars of disposable income go partly into saving, the dollar increase in consumption will not be quite so great as the dollars of new disposable income. Therefore, the tax multiplier is smaller than the government expenditure multiplier.

5. The attempt to save more does not automatically produce increased saving for society as a whole. The "paradox of thrift" shows that an increase in thriftiness during depressed times may, in fact, reduce output with no increase in saving or investment. Only in the classical world, where employment remains full, are consumption and investment necessarily competing. Only then is the private virtue of saving always a social virtue.

The moral is not for each individual to squander money during a depression, trying to be patriotic. Instead, it is to note that policies can recreate a high-employment environment in which private virtues are no longer social follies.

B. Output Determination in Open Economies

6. An open economy is one that engages in foreign trade, exporting goods to other countries and importing goods produced abroad. The difference between exports and imports of goods and services is called net exports. For most of the twentieth century, the United States had net exports near zero, but in the 1980s net exports moved sharply into deficit.

7. When foreign trade is introduced, domestic demand can differ from national output. Domestic demand is comprised of consumption, investment, and government purchases $(C + I + G)$. To obtain GNP, exports (e) must be added and imports (m) subtracted, so that

$$GNP = C + I + G + X$$

where X = net exports = $e - m$. Imports are determined by domestic income and output along with the prices of domestic goods relative to those of foreign goods; exports are the mirror image, determined by foreign income and output along with relative prices. The dollar increase of imports for each dollar increase in GNP is called the marginal propensity to import (MPm).

8. Foreign trade has an effect on GNP similar to that of investment or government purchases. As net exports rise, this leads to an increase in aggregate demand for domestic output. Net exports hence have a multiplier effect on output. But the expenditure multiplier in an open economy will be smaller than that in a closed economy because of leakages from spending into imports—the multiplier being

$$\frac{\text{Open-economy}}{\text{multiplier}} = \frac{1}{MPS + MPm}$$

where MPS = marginal propensity to save and MPm = marginal propensity to import. Clearly, other things equal, the open-economy multiplier is smaller than the closed-economy multiplier, where $MPm = 0$.

9. Because of the increasing interdependence of national economies, national leaders can ignore international linkages only at their economic and political peril. Among the important policy issues are:

(a) Nations' trade policies will affect other countries' output and employment. A policy of protecting one's own industries by trade barriers is a "beggar-thy-neighbor" approach, in essence exporting unemployment and trade deficits.

(b) Foreign exchange rates—the price of one nation's currency in terms of other nations' currencies—can affect relative prices and net exports. A rise in a nation's foreign exchange rate (called an appreciation) will depress that nation's net exports and output, while a fall in a nation's foreign exchange rate (called a depreciation) will increase net exports and output. Because of the significant impact of exchange rates on national economies, countries have entered into agreements on international monetary arrangements.

(c) In recent years, countries have from time to time attempted to coordinate their macroeconomic policies, simultaneously trying to increase their national outputs or to lower their national inflation rates. By cooperating in fiscal or monetary policies, countries can take advantage of the expansionary or contractionary impacts that inevitably spill over the borders when output changes.

10. Numerous econometric studies have estimated real-world expenditure multipliers. For mainstream models, these tend to show multipliers of between 1 and $1\frac{1}{2}$ for periods of up to 4 years.

CONCEPTS FOR REVIEW

stabilization policy
fiscal policy:
   G effect on equilibrium GNP
   T effect on CC and on GNP
multiplier effects of government
  spending (G) and taxes (T)
paradox of thrift
$C + I + G$ curve for closed economy
$C + I + G + X$ curve for open
  economy
net exports $= X = e - m$
domestic demand vs. spending on GNP

foreign exchange rate
marginal propensity to import (MPm)

$$\text{multiplier in closed economy} = \frac{1}{MPS}$$

$$\text{and in open economy} = \frac{1}{(MPS + MPm)}$$

impact on GNP of trade flows,
  exchange rates
coordination of macroeconomic policy

QUESTIONS FOR DISCUSSION

1. Explain the following concepts: government expenditure multiplier, marginal propensity to consume, marginal propensity to import.

2. Explain in words and using the notion of expenditure rounds why the tax multiplier is smaller than the expenditure multiplier.

3. Give the pros and cons of attempting to increase saving when output is below potential output.

4. During most of the 1980s, many political leaders have argued for lowering government deficits. Analyze the impact of lowering government purchases of goods and services on the government deficit and on output.

5. Explain why governments might choose to employ fiscal policy to stabilize the economy. Why would fiscal policy be effective in raising output in a depression Keynesian economy but not in a classical economy?

6. Explain the impact upon net exports and GNP of the following, using Table 9-2 where possible:

(a) An increase in investment *(I)* of $100 billion

(b) A decrease in government purchases *(G)* of $50 billion

(c) An increase of foreign output which increased exports by $10 billion

(d) A depreciation of the exchange rate that raised exports by $30 billion and lowered imports by $20 billion at every level of GNP.

7. What would the expenditure multiplier be in an economy without government spending or taxes where the *MPC* is 0.80 and where the *MPm* is 0? Where the *MPm* is 0.1? Where the *MPm* is 0.9?

Can the multiplier ever be less than 1? Explain how this might be possible.

8. Suppose America is running a trade deficit with output at the desired level, while Europe has a trade surplus with excessively high unemployment. What combination of coordinated exchange-rate changes and fiscal policies could move trade positions toward balance and output toward the desired levels?

9. ''Even if the government spends billions on 'wasteful' Star-Wars armaments, this action can create jobs in a recession and will be socially worthwhile.'' Discuss.

10. Give arguments for and against thriftiness. Contrast *(a)* the individual and community viewpoints, *(b)* conditions of boom and depression, and *(c)* classical vs. depression Keynesian views.

11. Explain the impact of a protectionist tariff or quota on imports as it affects net exports, domestic GNP, and foreign GNP.

12. If an arms-control agreement were reached and defense spending were cut 20 percent, how might we preserve full employment? Explain your alternative programs in terms of shifts of the $C + I + G$ schedule.

13. Add $1 billion of government spending on goods and services to a system in output-spending equilibrium. Pay for it by legislating an extra $1 billion of taxes. Will such a balanced-budget fiscal expansion leave equilibrium income unchanged? No: The positive spending multiplier, we've seen, outweighs the negative tax-increase multiplier. By how much? By exactly enough to give us a new *balanced-budget multiplier* of exactly 1. Here's why:

We write down our spending and tax geometric progressions

New spending:	$1 + r + r^2 + r^3 + \cdots$
New taxing:	$- r - r^2 - r^3 - \cdots$
Balanced-budget multiplier:	$1 + 0 + 0 + 0 + \cdots = 1$

(Of course in real life many complications have to be taken into account when using this result—for example, the Federal Reserve's monetary policies as well as corporate savings and spending decisions have to be combined with individuals' savings behavior.)

In 1981, President Reagan proposed a $300 billion decrease in both taxes and *G* spending. Show the effect of this policy in the $C + I + G$ spending-output equilibrium diagram, like that of Figure 9-4. What will be the effect of such a balanced-budget decrease in the size of government on GNP in the Keynesian multiplier model?

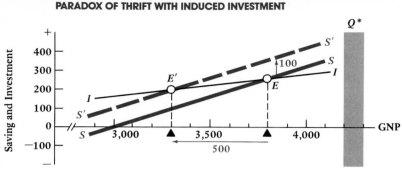

Gross National Product (billions of dollars)

Figure 9-11

14. In certain cases, we will find a stronger version of the paradox of thrift than that in the text. Assume that investment responds positively to higher levels of GNP, as is shown by the *II* line in Figure 9-11. This case is more realistic than the fixed-investment case because businesses tend to add to their plant and equipment if sales are high relative to plant capacity.

Using the analysis in Figure 9-11, explain what happens to GNP, saving, and investment when people try to save more (as represented by an upward shift in the savings function). Can you use this analysis to argue that an increase in the desire to save will actually lead to lower saving? Why does increased thrift in a depression actually make the depression worse?

CHAPTER 10

AGGREGATE SUPPLY AND BUSINESS CYCLES

The fault, dear Brutus, is not in our stars—but in ourselves.

William Shakespeare,
Julius Caesar

EARLIER CHAPTERS have examined the major forces operating to determine aggregate demand and national output. In this chapter we begin to apply these earlier concepts to important economic issues of the day. What are the major determinants of potential output and of long-term economic growth? What are the "supply-side policies" that dominated economic policymaking during the 1980s? And what is the important relationship between the GNP and the overall unemployment rate? These are among the topics treated in the first part of this chapter.

The second half of the chapter then turns to the empirical side of the same coin. What is the nature of the fluctuations in economic activity that we call business cycles? Are there regular historical patterns of movements in most business cycles? Can wise macroeconomic policies prevent business cycles?

Because economics is an empirical science, bold theoretical formulations must be tested against the empirical facts of life before they can be accepted. It is here, in the history of business cycles, that macroeconomists have found the laboratory for evaluating their most prized theories.

Figure 10-1 presents a chapter overview, using our familiar flowchart.

201

CHAPTER OVERVIEW

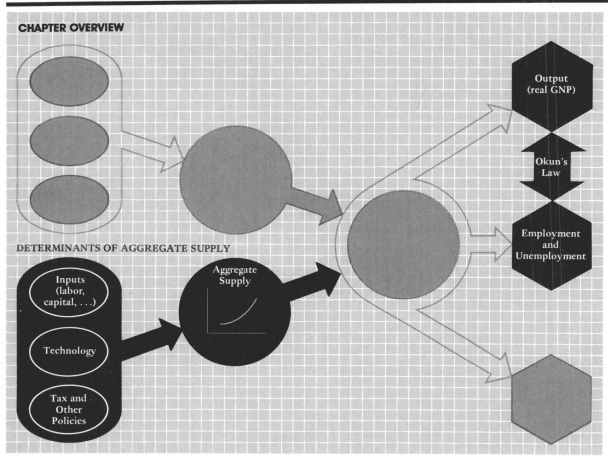

DETERMINANTS OF AGGREGATE SUPPLY

Inputs (labor, capital, ...)

Technology

Tax and Other Policies

Aggregate Supply

Output (real GNP)

Okun's Law

Employment and Unemployment

Figure 10-1   The supply side and business cycles are treated here

Section A of this chapter investigates two major topics. First, we review the determinants of aggregate supply, particularly the factors affecting potential output. We also examine the relationship between real output and unemployment, known as Okun's Law. Then in section B we examine theories and facts of the business cycle—which is, in essence, the entire macroeconomic system.

Incessant Fluctuations

Business conditions never stand still. Prosperity may be followed by a panic or a crash. Economic expansion then gives way to recession. GNP, employment, and real incomes fall. Inflation and profits decline, and people are thrown out of work.

Eventually the bottom is reached, and recovery begins. The recovery may be slow or fast. It may be incomplete, or it may be so strong as to lead to a new boom. The new prosperity may represent a long, sustained plateau of brisk demand, plentiful jobs, and increased living standards. Or it may represent a quick, inflationary flaring up of prices and speculation, to be followed by another slump.

Such upward and downward movements in output,

prices, interest rates, and employment form the **business cycle** that has characterized the industrialized nations of the world for the last two centuries—ever

since an elaborate, interdependent money economy began to replace the relatively self-sufficient precommercial society.

A. THE SUPPLY SIDE

How do business cycles fit into the economic analysis of aggregate supply and demand? Does output decline in a recession because of a shift of aggregate demand, because investment or government spending declines? Or does a decline in output reflect a contraction of the economy's ability to produce, following a decline in potential output? Before we can answer these questions, we must briefly describe the determinants of aggregate supply.

Determinants of Aggregate Supply

Our discussion of macroeconomics has up to now largely taken aggregate supply for granted, focusing instead on forces operating on aggregate demand. This focus is perhaps appropriate for the short run, but it cannot explain the major differences in the growth of nations over periods of a decade or a century. To understand why, for example, Japan has grown so much more rapidly than other major industrial countries and why Japan now challenges America and Europe in the contest for markets around the world, we must understand why Japan's potential output has grown so fast.

The determinants of potential output will be studied in depth in Chapters 36 and 37. Here we will sketch the major forces affecting long-run economic growth.

Review Recall that potential output is the economy's high-employment output, or its sustainable level of real GNP. It represents the maximum level of output that can be produced without straining the nation's productive capacity and igniting inflationary tendencies. In the late 1980s, economists estimate that output is at its potential when 94 percent of the labor force is employed—that is to say, when the unemployment rate is around 6 percent. When actual output exceeds potential output, prices begin to rise more

and more rapidly, and the level of output cannot be long sustained.

Chapter 8 discussed the relationship between potential output and aggregate supply. That chapter showed, in Figure 8-3, how aggregate supply was largely determined by the level of potential output. As potential output increases over time, the *AS* curve shifts to the right along with the increase in potential output. To the right of potential output, the *AS* curve becomes very steep as demand responses are increasingly met by price increases; to the left of potential output, *AS* is relatively flat, reflecting the empirical finding that increases in aggregate demand during periods of economic slack are largely met by output increases rather than by price increases.

Source of Potential-Output Growth

We have seen that aggregate supply tends to increase because of growth in potential output. What determines growth in potential output? We can preview here the major forces determining the long-run growth of potential output, although a complete analysis is provided in Chapter 36. That chapter also discusses the slowdown in the growth of labor productivity over the last 15 years.

It is customary to divide the sources of growth in potential output into two categories: growth in inputs (capital, labor, land), and improvements in technology or efficiency. Using statistical techniques we can even estimate the quantitative contribution of each of these.

Thus, take the period 1948–1986. During this period real potential output is estimated to have grown at 3.2 percent per year. Of this, 0.9 percent per year was accounted for by growth in labor inputs, 0.9 percent per year by a larger capital stock, 1.0 percent per year due to improved knowledge and technology, and the balance due to miscellaneous sources.

What Causes Business Cycles?

Business cycles occur when economic activity speeds up or slows down. What shifts in aggregate supply and demand underlie typical movements of the business cycle? The answer is illustrated in Figure 10-2, which shows how a typical recession is generated. A **recession** is an economic downturn; today, a recession is said to occur when real GNP has declined for two successive calendar quarters.

Say that the economy is originally in short-run equilibrium at point *B*. Then, as a result of lower *G* or *I*, or of consumers desiring to save more, there is a shift to the left in the *AD* curve of aggregate spending. If the shift in the *AD* curve is sudden, the *AS* curve is unlikely to have shifted much; assume it is unchanged. The net effect, after multipliers, is that the economy has a new equilibrium at point *C*. Note that output has declined from *Q* to *Q'* and that prices are lower (or in a more realistic model, the rate of inflation has declined).

The case of a boom is, naturally, just the opposite—with the *AD* curve shifting to the right, output rising closer to potential GNP or perhaps even overshooting it, and prices (and inflation) rising.

OKUN'S LAW

According to Figure 10-2, business cycles are generated because the gap between potential and actual GNP widens or shrinks. But the story does not end with output. Business cycles spill over to affect employment and unemployment.

What happens to unemployment in recessions? As orders and output fall, workers are laid off. The stickiness in wages prevents workers from finding new jobs quickly at lower wage rates. In sum, the unemployment rate rises in recessions.

Figure 10-3 shows how close is the relationship between output changes and unemployment: This relationship, discovered by Arthur Okun,* is called *Okun's Law*.

Okun's Law states that for every 2 percent that GNP falls relative to potential GNP, the unemployment rate rises 1 percentage point. For example, if GNP begins at 100 percent of its potential and falls to 98 percent of potential, the unemployment rate rises from 6 to 7 percent.

We can easily understand Okun's Law with some illustrative examples.[1]

Examples You sometimes hear the expression, ''You have to keep running just to stay in the same place.'' This is true of GNP growth and unemployment because GNP must grow as rapidly as potential GNP to keep the unemployment rate from rising. Say that potential GNP is growing at 3 percent per year. Then to keep the unemployment rate constant requires that real GNP also grow at 3 percent each year.

A second example involves the 3 years of economic stagnation from 1979 to 1982. From 1979 to 1982, actual GNP didn't grow at all. But potential GNP grew for 3 years at 3 percent per year. Hence, to illustrate Okun's Law, we start with a 9 percent increase in potential GNP from 1979 to 1982. What should have happened to the unemployment rate from 1979 to 1982? Recall from Okun's Law that each 2

[1]In early studies, Okun found that the relationship was about 3 to 1; that is, 1 point of *U* for every 3 points of the GNP gap. However, more recent data and more advanced econometric techniques suggest that the 2-to-1 figure is more representative for recent periods.

*Arthur Okun (1929–1979) was one of the most creative American economic policymakers of the postwar era. Educated at Columbia, he taught at Yale until he joined President Kennedy's Council of Economic Advisers as a staff member in 1961. He became a CEA member in 1964 and President Johnson's chairman in 1968. After he left the CEA, Okun stayed in Washington at the Brookings Institution.

In his last years, Okun waged a tireless battle to find ways of reducing inflation without throwing millions of people out of work; one of his ideas was the ''Tax-Based Incomes Policies'' (or ''TIPs'') discussed in Chapter 15.

In addition, Okun was renowned for his use of simple homilies to illustrate economic points. He compared arguments against the 1968 tax increase to his 7-year-old's arguments against taking medicine: ''He is perfectly well; he is so sick that nothing can possibly help him; he will take it later in the day if his throat doesn't get better; it isn't fair unless his brothers take it too.'' [Arthur M. Okun, *The Political Economy of Prosperity* (Norton, New York, 1970), p. 99.] Okun proved time and again that a well-told tale is often worth more than 1000 equations.

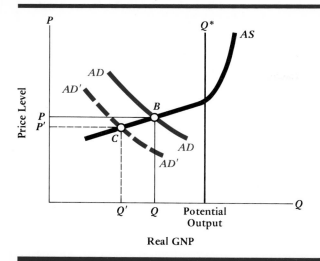

Figure 10-2 A decline in aggregate demand leads to an economic downturn

A shift in the *AD* curve along a relatively flat and unchanging *AS* curve leads to lower levels of output (declining from *Q* to *Q'*), also producing lower prices and lower inflation. Note that as a result of the downward shift in the *AD* curve, the gap between actual and potential GNP becomes greater during the recession.

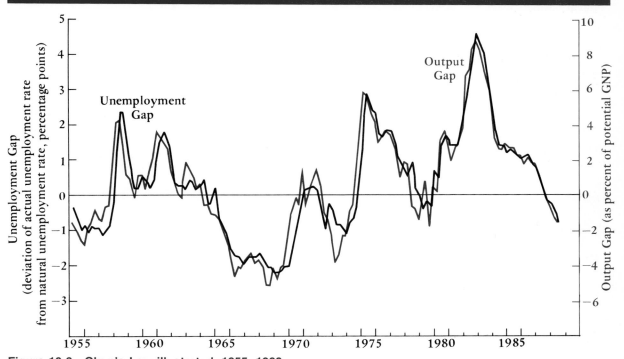

Figure 10-3 Okun's Law illustrated, 1955–1988

The two lines show the output gap and the unemployment gap over the last three decades. The output gap is the percentage deviation of GNP from its potential. The unemployment gap is the deviation of the unemployment rate from the natural rate, in percentage points.

According to Okun's Law, whenever output moves 2 percent below potential GNP, the unemployment rate rises 1 percentage point above the natural rate. Thus in 1983, output was 7 percent below potential GNP, and the unemployment rate was 9.5 percent (= 6 percent for the natural rate plus $\frac{1}{2}$ the output gap of 7 percent).

percent shortfall of GNP relative to potential adds 1 percentage point to the unemployment rate. A 9 percent shortfall in GNP should have led to a rise in the unemployment rate of 4.5 percentage points. Starting with an unemployment rate of 5.8 percent in 1979, then, Okun's Law would predict a 10.3 percent unemployment rate in 1982. The official statistics show the slightly lower number of 9.7 percent unemployed for 1982. This is surprisingly accurate for an inexact science like economics.

Here is still another example. Let us say you are the newly elected president, planning your macroeconomic policy at the end of 1988. The unemployment rate in late 1988 is 7 percent, and you would like to get the economy back to potential GNP by the time your program is judged by the voters in November 1992. (This kind of policy is sometimes called "a political business cycle.")

Question: How fast must the economy grow over the 4 years from 1988 to 1992? Answer: It must grow at the growth rate of potential GNP (about 3 percent annually), plus enough to reduce the unemployment rate about $\frac{1}{4}$ percentage point each year. The average annual growth rate for GNP must then be $3 + \frac{1}{2} = 3\frac{1}{2}$ percent annually over the 4-year period.

Thus Okun's Law provides the missing link between output markets and labor markets in recession and recovery.

Supply-Side Business Cycles

Until recently, most discussion has presumed that business cycles are caused by changes in aggregate demand—this approach is illustrated in Figure 10-2. Events of the last two decades cast significant doubt on that presumption. That period witnessed several shocks to productivity or to costs that shifted aggregate supply and affected overall business conditions.

Among the important examples were (1) those that affected the level of potential output, including droughts and crop failures in agriculture or, more generally, a slowdown in the growth of productivity, and (2) shocks that drove costs or prices up or down in an unanticipated fashion, such as two major oil-price increases, one oil-price decline, and major fluctuations in the foreign exchange rate of the dollar.

The impact of a supply shock on business condi-

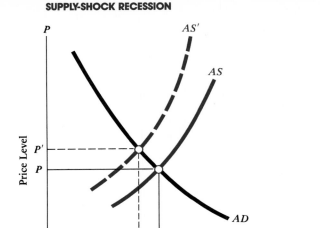

SUPPLY-SHOCK RECESSION

Figure 10-4   Productivity decrease or cost increase can cause business downturn

Sometimes business cycles are caused by changes in aggregate supply. Either a decrease in potential output (perhaps because of a productivity decline) or a rise in the cost of production (perhaps because of a crop failure) can lead to a leftward shift in the AS curve. This produces a recession, with output falling but prices and inflation rising. What are the observable differences between demand-side and supply-side business cycles?

tions is shown in Figure 10-4. Either of the two types of shocks—a productivity decrease that lowers potential output or a cost increase that raises the costs of production—will have the effect of shifting the AS curve to the left. That shift will tend to raise prices (or increase the rate of inflation) and decrease output. The impact on prices contrasts with the impact of a demand-induced business cycle, shown in Figure 10-2, where we find prices or inflation declining in a recession. This pattern of output and inflation moving in opposite directions has been found in business downturns in 1974 and 1980, suggesting that these periods, which followed major increases in oil prices, were in part supply-side business cycles.

Some economists, particularly those associated

with the rational-expectations or new classical school, have gone further to argue that economic fluctuations are indeed *real business cycles*. Real business cycle theory assumes that aggregate supply is classical—that is, the *AS* curve is vertical. By constructing an aggregate supply-and-demand diagram, it is easily verified that with a vertical *AS* curve *all* the month-to-month or year-to-year fluctuations in real GNP are due to shocks to aggregate supply, say through changes in productivity or labor supply, while none of the changes in real GNP are due to changes in aggregate demand.

Critics of real business cycle theory question whether changes in productivity are large enough to produce the major fluctuations in output seen in some business cycles. They point to the Great Depression, asking whether technological regress caused the economy's potential output to decline by 30 percent from 1929 to 1933, as would be suggested by real business cycle theories. Few economists accept this explanation.

SUPPLY-SIDE ECONOMICS[2]

During most of the period from World War II until 1980, economists and policymakers emphasized the role of aggregate demand in understanding the business cycle and in pursuing corrective countercyclical policies. Whenever unemployment rose, there would be a call for tax cuts or expenditure increases; whenever inflation threatened, some would call for a tightening of monetary or fiscal policies.

Toward the end of the 1970s, critics of the conventional approach to macroeconomics argued that economic policy had become too oriented toward the management of aggregate demand. They claimed that excessive concerns with short-run fiscal-policy actions tended to threaten the long-run vitality of the economy. Some critics, including orthodox economists of a more conservative persuasion, pressed for a return to more traditional policies of balancing the

budget and squeezing inflation out of the economy.

In addition, in reaction to the perceived excesses of demand-side economics, there arose a new phalanx of theorists espousing **supply-side economics.** As we will describe below, this school emphasized the importance of incentives for people to work and to save, downplayed the role of demand management, and proposed large tax cuts as a way of curing the diseases of slow economic growth and slumping productivity growth.

Supply-side economic theory arose in the political arena rather than in university classrooms. Its chief strategists were Arthur Laffer (professor of economics at Pepperdine College and business consultant), Jude Winniski (journalist), Paul Craig Roberts (assistant secretary of the Treasury in the Reagan administration and professor of economics at Georgetown University), and Norman Ture (undersecretary of the Treasury in the Reagan administration and business economist). Supply-side economics was espoused forcefully by President Reagan in the United States (1981–1989), by Prime Minister Thatcher in the United Kingdom (from 1979 on), and in less vocal forms by several other government leaders in countries of Western Europe.

Although these economists and political leaders have embraced a wide variety of positions, three central features of supply-side economics emerge: the retreat from Keynesian theories, the emphasis on incentives and supply effects, and the advocacy of large tax cuts.

Retreat from Keynes Keynesian economics holds that, in the short run, national output and employment are primarily determined by aggregate demand. Further, the Keynesian approach holds that monetary and fiscal changes should be undertaken to combat undesirable levels of unemployment or inflation.

Toward the end of the 1970s, a disenchantment with the Keynesian approach became widespread within the economics profession. An influential article by Harvard's Martin Feldstein laid out the case against demand-oriented policies.[3] Feldstein argued for a greater emphasis on factors that would increase

---

[2]An excellent set of readings on the political and social debate over supply-side economics is contained in Thomas R. Swartz, Frank J. Bonello, and Andrew F. Kozak, *The Supply Side: Debating Economic Issues* (Dushkin, Guilford, Conn., 1983).

[3]See Martin Feldstein, ''The Retreat from Keynesian Economics,'' *The Public Interest* (Summer 1981), pp. 92–105.

the growth in potential output—factors such as increased saving and investment, regulatory reform, and reduced taxation of capital income.

This retreat from Keynesian policies of active demand management was part of the economic program of the supply siders and was espoused by both the Reagan and the Thatcher governments. They set their macroeconomic policies with an eye to long-run economic growth rather than short-run economic stabilization. They vowed to determine the appropriate long-run policies and then to stick with them. Fine-tuning of the economy—with constant changes of policy as the economic winds shifted—would be avoided.

What was the basis of this abrupt about-face in economic philosophy? In part, the supply-side policies stemmed from a classical conception of the macroeconomy. Although supply siders failed to produce a coherent macroeconomic theory, their views appeared to arise from a belief that aggregate supply responded more to incentives, taxes, and post-tax factor returns than to changes in aggregate demand. In terms of the *AS-AD* framework, supply siders believed that the *AS* curve would be quite steep or vertical, so that any recession would be short-lived and most of the reaction to changes in aggregate demand would come through changes in the overall price level.

In addition, supply-side economists and political leaders believed that government had become too intrusive—that their economies had become like addicts dependent upon government stimulus packages and income-support programs. They thought that a "cold turkey" withdrawal of active government management of the economy would increase innovation and improve productivity.

At the end of the Reagan era, we can now ask whether the supply-side approach was successful in bringing better economic performance. While the final verdict is not in, there is no evidence of an economic sea change in the United States during the 1980s. Inflation was brought down sharply in the early 1980s, but the reduction in inflation was, as the Keynesians had predicted, bought at a high price in terms of unemployment during the deep and sharp recession and very high unemployment in 1981–1983.

Under Prime Minister Thatcher, Britain has pursued supply-side policies for a decade, with an emphasis on enlarging the role of the market and reducing high tax rates. Britain appears to have achieved a significant change in its economic performance, with major improvements in productivity growth during the 1980s. Some believe that the upturn in Britain's economic fortune resulted from reforms in a very rigid industrial structure and from supply-side policies that were more consistently applied than those in the United States.

A New Emphasis on Incentives A second theme of supply-side economics was the key role played by *incentives,* which are complete market returns to working, saving, and entrepreneurship. Supply siders emphasized the loss of incentives that occurs when tax rates are excessively high and argued that Keynesians, in their excessive concern with demand management, had ignored the impact of tax rates and incentives on aggregate supply. A paraphrase of the argument is as follows:

> Supply-side economics emphasizes the role of fiscal policy in the determination of economic growth and aggregate supply. Our analysis relies upon straight classical price theory. According to supply-side economics, tax changes affect the economy through their effect on post-tax factor rewards rather than on dollar flows of incomes and spending; tax rates affect the relative prices of goods and thereby affect supplies of labor and capital. We seek to raise the after-tax rewards to growth activities such as labor, saving, and investment relative to leisure and consumption.

> It is far more important to analyze the impact of a tax change on the rate of return to labor or saving or investment than to look at the dollar amount of the tax change on disposable income. By lowering tax rates on labor or interest or dividends, we can increase saving, investment, and economic growth.[4]

[4]This excerpt is a paraphrase of Stephen J. Entin, "Comments on the Critics" in a symposium, "Supply Side Economics: What Remains?" American Economic Association Annual Meeting, December 1985, *Treasury News*.

A favorable account is contained in Paul Craig Roberts, *The Supply-Side Revolution: An Insider's Account of Policymaking in Washington* (Harvard University Press, Cambridge, Mass., 1984). For a critical analysis, see the papers by Martin Feldstein, Lawrence Chimerene and Richard Young, and George von Furstenberg and F. Jeffrey Green in *American Economic Review* (May 1986).

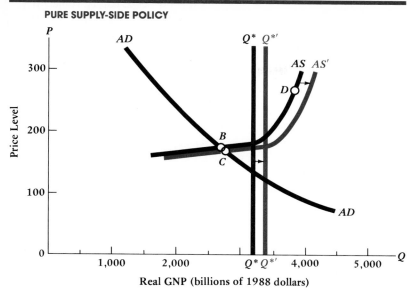

PURE SUPPLY-SIDE POLICY

Figure 10-5   Impact of a pure supply-side policy

Before a pure supply-side policy, potential output is $Q^* = 3200$; an impressive increase in aggregate supply might raise potential output to $Q^{*\prime} = 3400$.

   If the economy is on the flat portion of the *AS* curve, the impact on actual GNP will be relatively modest if *AD* does not change. In the illustrated case, actual GNP changes from *B* to *C*, with an increase of real GNP from 2700 to 2750.

   On the other hand, what would happen to actual GNP if *AD* cut the *AS* curve in its near-vertical classical section, such as at point *D*? Almost all the increase in potential output would show up in actual output.

What is the hypothesized relationship between tax policy and overall economic activity? In the context of aggregate supply-and-demand analysis, a lowering of tax rates would raise the post-tax return to capital and labor; higher post-tax returns would induce greater labor and capital supply, along with higher rates of innovation and productivity growth; and the increase of inputs and innovation would increase the growth of potential output and thereby shift aggregate supply to the right.

Figure 10-5 illustrates the impact of a hypothetical supply-oriented program. For analytical convenience, assume that the supply-side program has the net effect of increasing the total supply of inputs like labor and capital. For concreteness, say that the supply-side policy produces a very large increase in potential out-put. The example in Figure 10-5 increases potential GNP by about 6 percent, or $200 billion, from $3200 billion at Q^* to $3400 billion at $Q^{*\prime}$. This increase shifts the *AS* curve outward as shown in the figure.

What is the impact of this supply-side measure? The answer depends upon the shape of the aggregate supply curve. If the economy is Keynesian, or in a recession, with a relatively flat *AS* curve as shown at point *B* in Figure 10-5, the impact of the supply shift on actual output will be relatively modest. In the illustrated case, the equilibrium moves from point *B* to point *C*, with an increase of output of approximately $50 billion and a tiny decrease in the overall price level.

On the other hand, suppose the economy were in a more classical supply position, such as that shown at point *D* on the *AS* curve in Figure 10-5. In this case, the increase in potential output from Q^* to $Q^{*\prime}$ would translate into a substantial increase in actual output—with each 1 percent increase in potential output causing approximately a 1 percent increase in actual output.

The first conclusion is that supply-side policies are likely to be most effective when the economy behaves in a near-classical fashion. That is, when prices and wages are flexible, so that prices move rapidly in response to demand or supply shocks, then an increase in supply will be quickly transformed into an equivalent increase in actual output. The effectiveness of supply-oriented policies in a classical economy may explain the attraction of this approach to non-Keynesian economists.

How large an impact are supply-side policies likely to have in reality? In the heady, early days, supply siders forecasted extremely beneficial impacts of their policies. In the 1981 Economic Recovery Program of the Reagan administration, they predicted that the program would lead to rapid economic recovery, with an anticipated growth in real GNP of 4.8 percent per year over the next 4 years. In fact, the actual growth rate fell far short of the forecast, averaging only 2.5 percent per year.

One reason for the shortfall is the great difficulty of creating a major increase in the growth of potential output. Skeptics of the supply-side approach point to studies indicating that increasing the growth rate of potential output by more than a few tenths of a percentage point per year requires strenuous efforts. Take for example an ambitious program to increase saving; suppose that such policies succeed in raising the personal savings rate from 6 to 8 percent of disposable income (a prodigious increase by historical standards); further assume that this 2-percentage-point increase is channeled completely into business investment (a most unlikely occurrence); and say that we wait for 10 years to observe the outcome. Studies by Edward Denison and others indicate that such a policy would increase potential output at the end of a decade by only 1 percent (say from $4000 billion to $4040 billion). Put in terms of growth rates, this would increase the growth rate of potential GNP from 3.0 percent per year to 3.1 percent per year. The wheels of supply policies grind exceedingly slowly.

What do the data show about the net impact of the supply-side experiment after 8 years? Have the tax cuts and other policies succeeded in providing a significant boost to saving, investment, and productivity growth in the United States? A partial answer is provided by Table 33-6 (p. 792). This shows that in fact the personal savings rate has actually declined during the 1980s: All the supply-side encouragement, all the theorizing about the impacts of higher after-tax returns quoted above appear to have had no net positive effect on the national savings rate. Other indicators of real economic performance fared poorly in the 1980s as well: Productivity growth was relatively slow and unemployment remained on average high.

Tax Cuts The final strand of supply-side thinking emerged in its advocacy of large tax cuts. We saw in the last chapter how taxes could affect aggregate demand and output. Supply-side economists argue that the role of taxes in affecting aggregate demand has been overemphasized. They argue that government in the 1960s and 1970s used taxes to raise revenues or stimulate demand while ignoring the impacts of the rising tax burden on incentives. The high taxes, it was argued, led people to reduce their labor and capital supply. Indeed, some supply-side economists, particularly Arthur Laffer, suggested that high tax rates might actually lower tax revenues. This ''Laffer-curve'' proposition held that high tax rates shrink the tax base because of a lower level of economic activity. Many mainstream economists and even some supply-side economists scoffed at the Laffer proposition, and the evidence of the 1980s has not been kind to this heretical view.[5]

To counter earlier approaches to taxation, supply-side economists proposed a radical restructuring of the tax system, sometimes called the ''supply-side tax cuts.'' The philosophy underlying supply-side tax cuts was that the reforms should improve incentives by lowering tax rates on the last dollar of income (or marginal tax rates); that the tax system should be less

---

[5]Say that R = total tax revenues, t = tax rate, and B = the tax base. For capital, R would be the total taxes on capital income, t the tax rate on capital income, and B total capital income. The Laffer proposition holds that, after a point, as t rises toward 100 percent, B shrinks so rapidly that $R = tB$ actually declines. Further evidence and discussion is contained in Chapter 33.

progressive (that is, it should lower the tax burden on high-income individuals); and that the system should be designed toward encouraging productivity or supply rather than toward manipulating aggregate demand.

Figure 10-6 illustrates the impact of a supply-side tax cut in terms of the *AS-AD* analysis. We know from the analysis of the last chapter that tax cuts will increase consumption and increase aggregate demand (this analysis assumes that monetary policy does not offset the expansionary impact of the fiscal expansion). A large permanent tax cut—such as the 25 percent cut in personal taxes enacted in 1981—produces the large shift in *AD* shown in Figure 10-6. In addition, such a tax cut might increase potential output; however, as the last section indicated, the size of the potential-output increase would be extremely modest in the short run. We therefore show the tax cut as shifting the *AS* curve only slightly to the right.

The net effect of a massive supply-side tax cut is, just as the supply siders predict, to increase output significantly, as is shown by the movement from point *A* to point *B* in Figure 10-6. In the short run, for a period of up to 5 years, the major source of the economic expansion from supply-side tax cuts is the impact on aggregate demand, not the effect on potential output and aggregate supply.

The lessons learned from Figure 10-6 and its analysis are of great importance for understanding recent American history. It is no accident that the recovery from the deep recession of 1982 occurred just when the supply-side tax cuts were providing large increases in the disposable income of Americans and thereby stimulating the economy. Moreover, because the expansion was largely fueled by demand-side

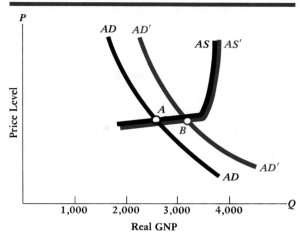

Figure 10-6   Macroeconomic impact of a supply-side tax cut

Many supply siders recommend massive tax cuts as a measure for combating the ills of today's economy. Tax cuts have two effects: They shift out the *AD* curve (from *AD* to *AD'*) as shown by the multiplier analysis of the last chapter. And they may increase potential output if lower taxes draw in larger supplies of labor or capital—thus shifting out the *AS* curve from *AS* to *AS'*. Such tax cuts do, as supply siders suggest, increase real GNP. But statistical studies suggest that for periods up to a decade, the major impact on actual output comes through the effect upon aggregate demand.

stimulus, when the economy had again attained its potential output in 1987, the overall rate of economic growth had not changed markedly as compared to the pre-supply-side era. The Reagan economic expansion of the mid-1980s was indeed a demand-side recovery dressed up in a supply-side cloak.

B. BUSINESS CYCLES

Recessions did not just happen; they reflected the vulnerability of an industrial economy to cumulative movements upward and downward. While they have diverse specific causes, cyclical fluctuations can usually be viewed as the result of imbalances between the growth of productive capacity and the growth of final demands for its output.

Arthur Okun
The Political Economy of Prosperity (1970)

The first half of this chapter showed how the interaction of aggregate supply and demand might lead to business cycles. We now turn to a more careful factual description: What are the patterns of the business cycle? We then inquire into the major economic theories of business cycles and describe the art of forecasting. What are the major business-cycle theories? And how well can economists forecast cycles?

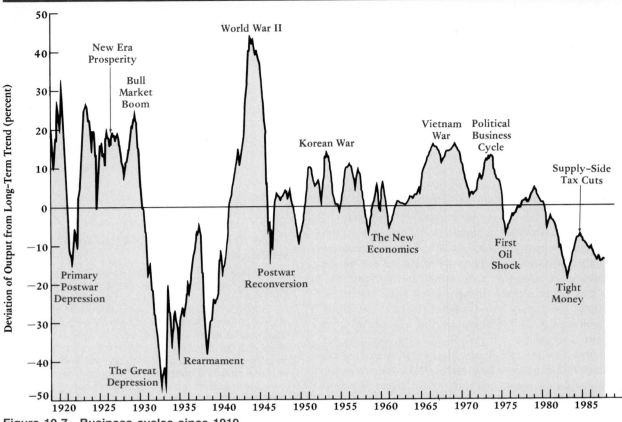

Figure 10-7   Business cycles since 1919

Industrial production has fluctuated incessantly around its long-run trend. Can a more stable economy be seen over the last 30 years? (Source: Federal Reserve Board, detrended by authors.)

BUSINESS-CYCLE HISTORY

No two business cycles are quite the same. Yet they have much in common. Though not identical twins, they are recognizable as belonging to the same family. No exact formula, such as might apply to the motions of the moon or of a pendulum, can be used to predict the timing of business cycles. Rather, in their irregularities, business cycles more closely resemble the fluctuations of the weather.

Figure 10-7 shows how the American economy has been buffeted by the business cycle throughout our recent history.[6]

Features of the Business Cycle

Early writers on the business cycle, possessing little quantitative information, tended to attach disproportionate attention to panics and crises. They wrote of the collapse of the South Sea Bubble in 1720, the Jay Cooke panic of 1873, the Grover Cleveland panic of

---

[6]How are the diagrams depicting business cycles derived? Statisticians first remove ''seasonal variation'' from the data; that is, systematic influences (like the effect of Christmas on toy sales) are taken out of the monthly or quarterly figures. Sometimes the data are ''detrended;'' that is, the data are recalculated as a deviation from the long-term trend. Both these procedures are explained in statistics textbooks.

1893, the "rich man's panic" of 1904, and, of course, the cataclysmic stock market crash of "black Tuesday," October 29, 1929. Memories of these distant events came alive after the dramatic stock market crash of October 19, 1987, when many people wondered whether a new depression was just over the horizon.

Phases Today, modern analysts divide the business cycle into phases. "Peaks" and "troughs" mark the turning points of the cycles, while "recession" and "expansion" are the major phases.

Figure 10-8 shows the successive phases of the business cycle. The economy enters a recession when real GNP has declined for two consecutive quarter-years. The recession ends at a "trough"—the most recent trough being in November 1982, according to the unofficial dater of business cycles, the National Bureau of Economic Research. Next follows recovery, peak, recession, trough, recovery, . . . and an endless succession of ups and downs.

Note, again, that the pattern of cycles is irregular. Figure 10-7 shows that cycles are like mountain ranges, with different levels of heights and valleys. Some valleys are very deep—as in the Great Depres-

sion; others are shallow, as was that of 1970. Moreover, the duration of cycles differs. Sometimes a major depression can last a decade; at other times, as in 1975, the downturn may be relatively brief.

Salient Characteristics While business cycles are not identical twins, they often have a familial similarity. If a trusted economic forecaster announces that a recession is about to arrive, are there any typical phenomena that you should expect to accompany the recession? The following are but a few of the customary cyclical relationships:

▪ Often, consumer purchases decline sharply while business inventories of automobiles and other durable goods increase unexpectedly. As businesses react by curbing production, real GNP falls. Shortly afterward, business investment in plant and equipment also falls sharply. As we showed in Chapter 7, investment is one of the most volatile components of GNP.

▪ The demand for labor falls—first seen in a drop in the average workweek, followed by layoffs and higher unemployment.

▪ As output falls, demand and supplies of crude materials decline, and the prices of many commodi-

FOUR PHASES OF THE CYCLE

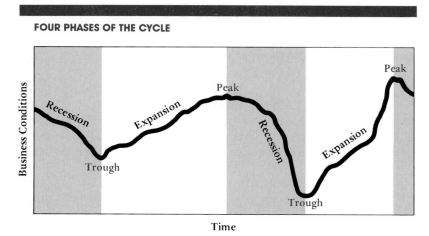

Figure 10-8   A cycle, like the year, has its seasons

Expansions follow recessions with turning points in between. The National Bureau of Economic Research has dated these phases for the history of the United States and of many other countries.

ties tumble. Wages and manufacturing prices are less likely to decline, but they tend to rise less rapidly in economic downturns.

▪ Business profits fall sharply in recessions. In anticipation of this, common-stock prices usually tumble as rational investors sniff the scent of a business downturn. However, because the demand for credit falls, interest rates generally also fall in recessions.

We have spoken in terms of recessions. Booms are the mirror image of recessions, with each of the above factors operating in the opposite direction.

BUSINESS-CYCLE THEORIES

The previous section pointed to shifts in aggregate demand as the source of cycles. Can we go further and find common patterns of initiators and propagators of cycles?

One place to start in understanding business cycles is to look for patterns of cyclical fluctuations. One important pattern, noted above, is that purchases of investment and other durable goods tend to move sharply up in expansions and down in recessions. This should not be surprising, for we know we can postpone the purchase of a new car or factory or machine, stretching out the life of the old one, whereas perishable necessities like food cannot be made to last until prices decline.

Most theories of business cycles today stress the importance, then, of durable consumption goods and investment. We could easily find dozens of cycle theories, but, after discarding those which are empty or obviously contradict the facts or the rules of logic, we are left with only a few really different explanations.[7] Most of these differ only in emphasis.

We may classify the different theories into two categories, primarily external and primarily internal. The *external* theories find the root of the business cycle in the fluctuations of something outside the economic system—in sunspots or the climate; in wars, revolutions, and elections; in gold discoveries, rates of growth of population, and migrations; in discoveries of new lands and resources; in scientific breakthroughs and technological innovations.

The *internal* theories look for mechanisms within the economic system itself that will give rise to self-generating business cycles, so that every expansion will breed recession and contraction, and every contraction will breed revival and expansion—in a quasi-regular, repeating chain.

Let's review some of the well-known business-cycle theories.

The Political Business Cycle

One of the major examples of an external business cycle is the "cycle of politics." This view rests on the observation that macroeconomic policy is determined by elected officials who may attempt to manipulate the economy to promote their electoral fortunes.[8] The theory is based on these three premises:

▪ Since the time of Keynes, policymakers have had the tools to stimulate the economy.

▪ Voters like periods of low unemployment, rapid economic growth, and low inflation.

▪ Politicians like to get reelected.

What follows from these three propositions? A *political business cycle*. Here is how a politician might attempt to manage the cycle: Right after elections, use a year or two to impose austerity on the econ-

---

[7]We may mention just a few of the better-known theories: (1) The *monetary* theory attributes the cycle to the expansion and contraction of money and credit (Hawtrey, Friedman, et al.); (2) the *innovation* theory attributes the cycle to the clustering of important inventions such as the railroad (Schumpeter, Hansen, et al.); (3) the *psychological* theory treats the cycle as a case of people infecting each other with pessimistic and optimistic expectations (Pigou, Bagehot, et al.); (4) the *underconsumption* theory claims too much income goes to wealthy or thrifty people compared with what can be invested (Hobson, Sweezy, et al.); (5) *political* theories of the

cycle (Kalecki, Nordhaus, Tufte); (6) the *equilibrium business cycle* claims that misperceptions lead people to work or search too much (Lucas, Barro, Sargent); and (7) *real business cycles*—in which productivity shocks are propagated through the economy (Prescott, Long, Plosser).

[8]This view is thus closely related to the theory of public choice of Chapter 32. The emphasis is not on the wickedness of politicians, but upon the incentives and rewards that influence political decision makers.

omy; raise unemployment and idle factories, thereby reducing inflationary pressures. Make sure the voters take their anti-inflationary medicine early, in the hopes that the bad taste will be forgotten by election day.

Then a year or so before election day, stimulate the economy. Reduce taxes, increase G, persuade the Federal Reserve to keep interest rates low. As citizens come into the voting booth, they may remember only the boom and not the recession.

Is this but cynical science fiction? No, according to the most careful study of the subject, by Edward Tufte:

> There is an electoral rhythm to the national economic performance of many capitalist democracies. . . . The timing of elections influences the rate of unemployment and growth in real disposable income, the short-term management of inflation and unemployment, the flow of transfer payments, the undertaking of expansionary or contractionary economic policies, and the time perspective of economic policymaking. . . . Economic life vibrates with the rhythms of politics.[9]

The best case study of this syndrome is Richard Nixon's 1972 reelection campaign—with pressure on the Federal Reserve to expand the money supply, with tax cuts, and with wage-price controls instituted 15 months before the election. On the other hand, Jimmy Carter preached and practiced austerity in his reelection year, 1980—and was trounced by Ronald Reagan. Some people detected a political cycle behind the unemployment movements in the 1981–1984 period, with high unemployment in the first 2 years and high economic growth in the second 2 years.

Combining External and Internal Factors

Many business-cycle theories integrate internal and external approaches. In a combined approach, shocks may originate outside the economy, but then the internal workings of the economy propagate and continue the shock. An analogous situation occurs if you bump

a rocking chair, setting in motion a cyclical rocking according to the internal design of the chair. Shocks external to the economy might come from wars or demobilization, from political cycles or oil-price shocks, from innovations or gold discoveries. These external shocks are then transmitted through the economy in a fashion that leads to the more or less regular fluctuations we call business cycles.

What might be the internal mechanism that would propagate the external shocks? When economists look at the economy, they usually see investment as an important factor. The reason was hinted at in Chapter 7, where we saw that the expectation of revenue or output changes would affect the demand for investment. If sales are increasing, businesses are likely to increase their investment; by contrast, when sales and output fall in recessions, businesses tend to cut back on their investment plans. Hence, years of rapid output growth like 1975–1978 witnessed a considerable volume of capital formation, while in recession years like 1981–1982 investment fared poorly.

What is occurring in these examples? We find here that investment is affected by the *growth* of sales and output. This relationship is known as the "accelerator principle," which enters almost all business-cycle theories. We turn in the next section to a description of the accelerator principle, after which we return to an important business-cycle theory that combines the accelerator principle with the multiplier model.

The Accelerator Principle[10]

The **accelerator principle** (or *accelerator*) is a theory of the determinants of investment. It states that society's needed stock of capital, whether inventory or equipment, depends primarily upon the level of production; additions to the stock of capital, net investment, will take place only when output is growing. As a result, a prosperous period may come to an end, not simply because sales have gone down, but merely because production and sales have stabilized at a high level.

A numerical example will make this clear. Imagine a typical textile firm whose stock of capital equipment

---

[9]E. R. Tufte, *Political Control of the Economy* (Princeton University Press, Princeton, N.J., 1978).

[10]This section may be omitted in short courses.

is always kept equal to 2 times the annual production (or constant-dollar value of sales) of cloth.[11]

Thus, when its sales have remained at $30 million per year for some time, its balance sheet will show $60 million of capital equipment, consisting perhaps of 20 machines of different ages, with 1 wearing out each year and being replaced. Because replacement just balances depreciation, there is no net investment or saving being done by the firm. Gross investment takes place at the rate of $3 million per year, representing the yearly replacement of 1 machine. The other $27 million of sales may be assumed to be wages and dividends. The first phase of Table 10-1 shows this.

Now let us suppose that, in the fourth year, sales rise 50 percent—from $30 to $45 million. To keep the ratio of capital to output at 2, the number of machines must also rise 50 percent, or from 20 to 30 machines. In that fourth year, instead of 1 machine, 11 machines must be bought—10 new ones in addition to the replacement of the worn-out one.

Sales rose 50 percent. How much has investment in machines gone up? From 1 machine to 11; or by 1000 percent! This *accelerated* response of investment to a change in output gives the accelerator principle its name.

If sales go on rising in both the fifth and sixth years by the same $15 million, we'll continue to need 11 new machines (10 + 1) every year.

So far, the accelerator principle has given us no trouble. On the contrary, it has given us a tremendous burst in investment spending as a result of a moderate increase in sales. But now we are riding a tiger. *According to the accelerator principle, sales must continue to keep increasing at the same speed in order for investment to stand still.*

If sales should stop growing at so rapid a rate—if they should level off in the seventh year even at the high level of $75 million per year—then net investment will fall away to zero, and gross investment will for many years fall back to only 1 machine (see Table 10-1). In other words, a drop to no growth in sales

will result in a 90 percent drop in gross investment and a 100 percent drop in net investment. (See the third phase of Table 10-1.)

The accelerator principle can work in both directions. Should sales now drop below $75 million, gross investment would drop away to nothing for a long time; in fact, the firm might want to disinvest by selling off some of its used machinery. (Fill in the fourth phase with the needed zeros—to signify that now nothing needs to be replaced.) Hence, investment can drop sharply, perhaps causing a recession, just because output has stopped growing.

The accelerator principle is a powerful factor producing economic instability: Changes in output may become magnified into larger changes in investment.

Interaction of Multiplier and Accelerator

An important theory of the business cycle comes from the combination of the accelerator and the multiplier models. To understand the *multiplier-accelerator model,* consider what happens when there is a drop in the production of machine-producing industries. This will curtail income and spending on food and clothing and will lead to multiplied changes in output. This itself might cause textile sales to stop growing, or even to decline, which will in turn cause a further accelerated drop in net investment.

At some point, investment will reach rock bottom. When output has fallen quickly, the accelerator principle will call for negative investment. But gross investment in plant and equipment can hardly be negative, and this fact puts a floor on how far investment can fall. So the slump contains the seeds of its own recovery. Once investment has hit the basement, it must stop falling. But then output must also stop falling. At this point, firms will need some replacement investment, so gross investment will pick up, and a business upturn has begun.

So the Mr. Hyde of depression can turn itself into the Dr. Jekyll of expansion. Once output begins to grow, the rising production induces new investment via the accelerator. The new investment induces yet further growth in output via the multiplier. At some point, however, output begins to strain against capacity. Output growth slows. But then the accelerator

---

[11]To keep the discussion simple, we use a capital-output ratio of 2 to 1 and ignore changes in interest rates, prices, or in the utilization of capacity. To be complete, inventory changes and plant changes should be included in the analysis along with equipment changes.

THE ACCELERATOR PRINCIPLE *(in millions of dollars)*

TIME	YEARLY SALES	STOCK OF CAPITAL	NET INVESTMENT (*NI*)	GROSS INVESTMENT (*NI* + REPLACEMENT)
First phase				
First year	$30	$ 60	$ 0	1 machine at $3 = $3
Second year	30	60	0	1 machine at $3 = $3
Third year	30	60	0	1 machine at $3 = $3
Second phase				
Fourth year	**$45**	$ 90	**$30**	(10 + 1) machines at $3 = $33
Fifth year	60	120	30	(10 + 1) machines at $3 = $33
Sixth year	75	150	30	(10 + 1) machines at $3 = $33
Third phase				
Seventh year	**$75**	$150	**$ 0**	1 machine at $3 = $3
Fourth phase (to be filled in)				
Eighth year	$73½	$147	–$ 3	_____ machines at $3 = $_____

Table 10-1   Accelerator principle links the level of investment to GNP's rate of growth

If the required capital stock is closely tied to production, investment will rise and fall with GNP *growth*. To keep investment from falling, the growth of sales cannot falter. Hence, investment will fluctuate more then sales? (Verify that gross investment is zero in the fourth phase, as no machines need be ordered.)

begins to operate against expansion. Like an airplane that falls once it slows and stalls, the economic system plummets downward.

We thus have constructed a simple model of the business cycle—one in which external forces set the cycle in motion and internal forces keep it going. When augmented by other realistic features of a modern economy—inventories, money and financial markets, and inflation—the multiplier-accelerator mechanism can explain many of the characteristic features of today's business cycles.

FORECASTING BUSINESS CYCLES

Given the wide swings in economic activity—and the drastic effects these fluctuations sometimes have on business profits and economic well-being—it is not surprising that economic forecasting is one of the most important tasks of economists. If businesses know that a downturn is ahead, they can trim inventories, production, and employment, just as sailors reef their sails in preparation for a squall. Similarly, if economic policymakers see that a speculative boom is gaining momentum, they may take monetary or fiscal steps to restrain the economy. Like bright headlights on a car, good forecasts cast light on the economic terrain ahead and help decision makers adapt their actions to economic conditions.

Before plunging into an examination of the different forecasting methods, let us emphasize that forecasting is as much an art as a science. Because business cycles are not mechanical repetitions of the past, judgment is a necessary ingredient in good forecasting. Forecasts often turn out to be far off the mark, as we will shortly see. But the strength of economic forecasting is that, year in and year out, professional forecasters outdo those who are untrained, or nonsystematic, or use unscientific techniques like basing their forecasts on the phases of the moon.

Econometric Modeling and Forecasting

In an earlier era, economists forecasted the business cycle by looking at a wide variety of data on things like money, boxcar loadings, and steel production. Sometimes the series were added together to form an "index of leading indicators" that, they hoped, would be a barometer of future economic conditions.

Just as weather forecasting has made major advances in reliability through the use of good physics, ample data, and supercomputers, economics has come into the age of computers and statistics with large-scale macroeconomic models. Thanks to the pioneering work of Holland's Nobel laureate Jan Tinbergen, today we have dozens of macroeconomic models. Lawrence Klein of the Wharton School, who won the 1980 Nobel Prize for his contribution to economic modeling, has built a number of forecasting systems over the last three decades. Commercial consulting firms, such as Data Resources Inc. (DRI), have developed models that are widely used by firms and policymakers.

How are these large computer models constructed?[12] Generally modelers start with an analytical framework, with equations representing both aggregate demand and aggregate supply. Using the techniques of modern econometrics, each equation is "fitted" to the data to obtain parameter estimates (such as the *MPC,* the accelerator coefficient, the growth of potential GNP, etc.). Of course, at each stage modelers use their own experience and judgment to assess whether the results are reasonable or unacceptable.[13]

Finally, the whole "model" is put together and run as a system of equations. In small models there were one or two dozen equations. Today's large systems forecast from a few hundred to 10,000 variables. Once the forecaster is willing to bet on the external and policy variables (population, government spending and taxing, monetary policy, etc.), then this system of equations can be used to project into the future—i.e., the economy is forecast.

How might a typical forecast look? Table 10-2 shows the forecast of one of the most influential forecasters (DRI) right after the Reagan economic policy was announced. In April 1981, DRI made a relatively rosy forecast for the last quarter of 1982—forecasting low unemployment, rapid GNP growth, and high inflation. In fact, the economy entered its steepest decline in the postwar period. Not until the end of 1981 (about a year before the trough of the deep recession) did DRI and other forecasters begin to sniff serious economic problems ahead.

The Accuracy of Economic Forecasts

Businesses and governments pay millions of dollars for economic forecasts. How well have the forecasters performed? Was the information provided more reliable than simple guesswork? The best single test of macroeconomics as an objective science comes in its success in forecasting the future.

Studies of the record of forecasts versus actual outcomes indicate that professional forecasters have generally made a significant improvement over naive extrapolations or uninformed guesses. For example, over the period from 1959 to 1984, naive extrapolation of trends for real GNP growth had an average forecast error of 2.5 times that of professional forecasters. More precisely, over that period, a simple extrapolation of past trends in real GNP growth had an average forecast error of 2.8 percentage points, while the consensus of forecasts had an average error of 1.1 percentage points. For the inflation rate, simple extrapolation had an average error over the 1962–1984 period of 1.3 percentage points, while the consensus of forecasts had an average forecast error of 1.0 percentage point.

Is the Business Cycle Avoidable?

Just as there are waves of prosperity and recession, there also follow swings in popular views about the necessity of business cycles. When recessions were frequent, they were often viewed as unavoidable. During the long period of prosperity of the 1960s—

---

[12]For the autobiography of a forecast, see Lawrence Klein and Richard Young, *An Introduction to Econometric Forecasting and Forecasting Models* (Heath, Lexington, Mass., 1980).

[13]The process by which forecasts are generated is somewhat mysterious to their users. The mixture of art and science has led one observer to ask: "What does an economic forecast have in common with a dog's breakfast? Simple: You never know what's in it."

FORECASTING TURBULENT TIMES—AND RESULTS

	(1) DRI FORECAST OF APRIL 1981 FOR 4th QUARTER OF 1982	(2) ACTUAL DATA FOR 4th QUARTER OF 1982	(3) PERCENTAGE ERROR
GNP (billions of $)			
Real	1,582	1,477	−7
Nominal	3,482	3,108	−11
Inflation rate (percent per year, GNP deflator)	10.1	3.7	−63
Unemployment rate (percent)	6.6	10.7	+62
Interest rates (percent per year)			
3-month Treasury bills	13.8	7.9	−43
Long-term bonds (Aaa)	13.1	11.1	−15
Federal deficit (billions of $)	24	203	+746
Stock prices (index)	146	137	−6

Table 10-2   A forecast of the economy 18 months in advance
This shows the macroeconomic forecast of the performance of the U.S. economy made in the euphoria of spring 1981 for economic conditions for late 1982. The recession was not foreseen, nor was the accompanying reduction in inflation. While DRI launched a poor forecast, most others (including the government) did even worse. According to DRI's Otto Eckstein, "[1982] has proved to be the most difficult for forecasting that has been experienced in modern memory." (Source: *The Data Resources Review of the U.S. Economy,* April 1981 and February 1983.)

the longest expansion in our history—great optimism set in. Indeed, in 1965 President Johnson stated, "I do not believe recessions are inevitable."

Such pronouncements were overly sanguine. A more balanced view was taken by Arthur Okun:

> Recessions are now generally considered to be fundamentally preventable, like airplane crashes and unlike hurricanes. But we have not banished air crashes from the land, and it is not clear that we have the wisdom or the ability to eliminate recessions. The danger has not disappeared. The forces that produce recurrent recessions are still in the wings, merely waiting for their cue.[14]

Over the last two decades, we have been reminded of the shocks that send a mixed economy into booms or

recessions: OPEC oil boycotts and price hikes in 1973 and 1979; monetary stringency in 1979–1982; investment collapses in 1975 and 1982; large federal tax cuts in 1981–1983; a massive swing toward trade deficits during the 1980–1986 period; a rapid decline in unemployment and a resurgence of inflation in 1988. These and other forces produced virulent worldwide business cycles in 1973–1975 and 1980–1982. Business cycles are very much alive today.

How likely are deep depressions? Although nothing can be ruled impossible in an inexact science like economics, the probability of a great depression—a prolonged, cumulative slump like that of the 1870s, 1890s, or 1930s—has been markedly reduced over the last half-century. Some worried that the market crash of October 1987 was the harbinger of a new great depression, and many parallels were drawn between the speculative excesses of the 1920s and the stock market euphoria of the 1980s. But most econo-

[14]Arthur M. Okun, *The Political Economy of Prosperity* (Norton, New York, 1970), pp. 33f.

mists are quoting long odds against a recurrence in the 1980s and 1990s of the steep GNP declines and unemployment increases that occurred from 1929 to 1933.

What has changed in the last 50 years? Two factors stand out. First, economics has shown that monetary and fiscal policies can keep the occasional recession that breaks out from snowballing into a persistent and profound slump. And second, the electorates of mixed economies insist that any political party in power take the expansionary actions necessary to cure lasting depressions.

If Marxists wait for capitalism to collapse in a final cataclysmic crisis, they wait in vain. The wild business cycle that savaged capitalism during its early years has been tamed.

SUMMARY

A. The Supply Side

1. Aggregate supply is derived from the capability of the economy to produce—that is, from its potential output. For the short run, we can best describe the AS curve as relatively flat up to the level of potential output, then turning sharply toward the vertical at higher levels of output. Increases in potential output, at unchanging costs, shift the AS curve to the right; increases in costs (such as wage costs) move the AS curve upward.

2. If potential output is a kind of hinge to which the AS curve is attached, what determines potential output? The major determinants of potential output growth are increases in inputs of capital and labor, and improvement in the state of knowledge and technology. Over long periods, the growth in potential output tends to be quite smooth, being in the range of $2\frac{1}{2}$ to 4 percent per year over the last five decades.

3. There is a clear connection between movements in output and the unemployment rate over the business cycle. According to Okun's Law, for every percent that actual GNP declines below potential GNP, the unemployment rate rises $\frac{1}{2}$ percentage point above the natural rate of unemployment. Such a rule is useful in translating cyclical movements of GNP into their effects on unemployment.

4. Until the 1980s, most economists focused on Keynesian remedies for stabilizing the economy; this approach emphasized changing monetary and fiscal policy in demand-management policies. By contrast, during the 1980s, supply-side economics had the ascendancy. This school emphasizes (*a*) a non-Keynesian approach to macroeconomic policy—focusing on the medium run, avoiding fine-tuning of the economy, and downplaying the importance of changes in aggregate demand; (*b*) a new emphasis on economic incentives—with particular attention to the impact of tax policy on after-tax returns to labor and capital as determining saving, investment, and labor supply; and (*c*) advocacy of large tax cuts—with some holding that these might actually pay for themselves by generating larger revenues and others simply holding that lower taxes would improve economic efficiency.

By the end of the 1980s, no major change in productivity growth, in the growth of potential GNP, or in overall economic performance could be detected as the result of the supply-side experiment.

B. Business Cycles

5. The business cycle is a pulse common to most sectors of the economy and to all advanced market economies. In business cycles we see movements in GNP, unemployment, prices, and profits—although the movements are not so regular and predictable as the orbits of the planets or the oscillations of a pendulum. Today, we distinguish the phases of expansion, peak, recession, and trough.

6. Most business-cycle theories today stress the role of shifts in aggregate demand in causing business fluctuations. In recent years, supply shocks (such as oil-price changes) have added to the list of factors affecting cycles.

7. A first clue to the source of business cycles is found in the large amplitude of fluctuations of investment or durable capital goods. Although most economists agree on this fact, they differ in their emphasis upon external or internal factors. Increasingly, however, they lean toward a synthesis of external and internal factors. On the one hand, importance is attached to fluctuations in such external factors as population growth, gold discoveries, and political events or wars. On the other hand, economists stress the way that these external factors interact with the economic system. Important interactions include the multiplier and the accelerator principle.

8. Forecasting is still inexact. Today, the most successful forecasters use medium- to large-scale computer models, based on statistical estimates, to forecast future changes in the economy. Postmortems show that the forecasters have been quite successful in forecasting movements in real GNP but only modestly successful in predicting inflation.

CONCEPTS FOR REVIEW

business cycle
relation of aggregate supply and
  potential output
tenets of supply-side economics
business-cycle phases:
  peak, trough
  expansion, recession

sources of growth of potential output
external and internal cycle theories:
  war, innovations, political cycles
Okun's Law
accelerator principle
accelerator and multiplier interactions
macroeconomic models

QUESTIONS FOR DISCUSSION

1. How do you expect to fare in the next recession?

2. Describe the different phases of the business cycle. In which phase is the economy now?

3. Assume that the unemployment rate is 8 percent and GNP is $4000. What is a rough estimate of potential GNP? Assume that potential GNP is growing at 3 percent annually. What will potential GNP be in 2 years? How fast will GNP have to grow to reach potential GNP in 2 years?

4. A supply-side economist might recommend a large tax cut to revive the economy. How might such a measure affect the *AS* curve? The *AD* curve? The resulting levels of price and real output?

5. Why is it important to be able to forecast the future of business activity? Give business and government examples. How would *you* forecast?

6. Is forecasting a science? An art? How has the availability of large data bases and cheap computing changed the role of qualitative judgments and quantitative equations?

7. Some business cycles originate from the demand side, while others arise from supply shocks.

    (a) Give examples of each. Explain the observable differences between the two kinds of shocks for output, prices, and unemployment.

    (b) State whether each of the following would lead to a supply-side business cycle or a demand-side cycle and illustrate the impact using the *AS-AD* diagram: a wartime increase in defense spending; devastation from wartime bombing of factories and power plants; a decrease in net exports from a debt-induced recession in Latin America; an oil-price increase; a sharp slowdown in the rate of productivity growth.

8. At the beginning of 1981, the Reagan administration forecast that its Economic Recovery Program would increase the growth of potential output to 4.5 percent per year, while actual output would grow at 5.0 percent per year. Skeptical Keynesian economists believed that the Reagan policies would have little effect on potential output, with potential output growing at only 3.0 percent per year. Assuming that the initial unemployment rate was 7 percent in 1980, what would the unemployment rate be for the years 1981–1984 if the optimistic forecast proved correct? What would happen to unemployment if the pessimists were correct about potential-output growth, while the Reagan forecasters were right about actual GNP growth? What would happen if potential-output growth was 3 percent per year while actual-output growth was 0 percent over the period 1980–1982?

9. Advanced problem: In recent years, a new theory of "equilibrium business cycles" has been proposed. This suggests that workers work harder or firms produce more as a result of misperceptions about relative prices. Thus firms are thought to move up their supply curves because they think their prices have risen in booms, when in fact the economy-wide price level *P* has risen. Such a view also holds that people hold "rational" expectations—being excellent forecasters of future events.

    Could such a theory explain: (*a*) why output may rise above potential output (and unemployment may fall below its natural rate) when prices rise unexpectedly? (*b*) how business downturns may persist for many years, as in the 1930s? (Chapter 16's appendix will show the answers to these questions are, respectively, Yes and No.)

10. Advanced problem: Find two dice and use the following technique to see if you can generate something that looks like a business cycle. Record the numbers from 20 or more rolls of the dice. Take five-period moving averages of the successive numbers. Then plot these. They will look very much like movements in GNP, unemployment, or inflation.

One sequence thus obtained was 7, 4, 10, 3, 7, 11, 7, 2, 9, 10. . . . The averages were $(7 + 4 + 10 + 3 + 7)/5 = 6.2$, $(4 + 10 + 3 + 7 + 11)/5 = 7$, . . . and so forth.

Why does this look like a business cycle? [HINT: The random numbers generated by the dice are like exogenous shocks of investment or wars. The moving average is like the economic system's (or a rocking chair's) internal multiplier or smoothing mechanism. Taken together, they produce what looks like a cycle.]

CHAPTER 11

MONEY AND COMMERCIAL BANKING

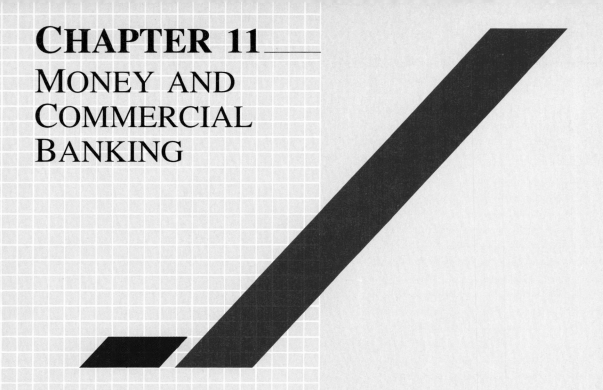

The only thing that has driven more men mad than love is the currency question.

Benjamin Disraeli

OUR SURVEY OF MACROECONOMICS has now toured the provinces of basic macroeconomics, examining how GNP is measured and then analyzing output determination, and then seeing how changes in fiscal policy, foreign trade, and investment affect economic activity and unemployment.

Yet one of the key areas of modern macroeconomics has up to now received only a scant mention. It is time for money to come forward and be introduced. Money has been offstage up to this point but not because it is unimportant. Indeed, as we shall see in the chapters that follow, money is in some ways the most agile and powerful tool that macroeconomic policymakers can employ to affect output, inflation, and unemployment.

This chapter will begin to analyze money's impact upon the economy by focusing on the nature of money itself. We begin with a discussion of different kinds of money, followed by a history of money and banks. The next section of this chapter then explores the demand for money, that is, the reasons why people hold their assets in the form of money.

The final section of this chapter turns to an exami-

CHAPTER OVERVIEW

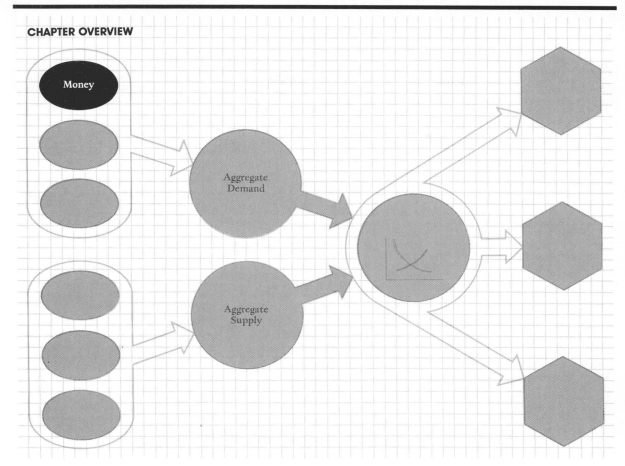

Figure 11-1   We now turn to money: its demand and the role of banks in its supply

Up to now, money's impact upon the macroeconomy has been in the background. In this and the next chapter, we analyze the demand and supply of money, building a foundation for understanding the way monetary policy affects output, inflation, and unemployment.

nation of the supply of money, which will serve as an introduction to the next chapter's analysis of the structure and conduct of our nation's central bank, the Federal Reserve System. Once we have mastered the essentials of the supply and demand for money, we

are prepared to plunge into the fundamental issues concerning inflation, unemployment, and macroeconomic fiscal and monetary policy. Figure 11-1 shows, using our thematic flow diagram, the location of the topics covered in this chapter.

A. HISTORY OF MONEY

Money is so much a part of our daily lives that we pursue it relentlessly yet seldom stop to consider what it is. A modern financial system with $100 bills, checks, Federal Funds, and other sophisticated financial instruments did not spring forth overnight. It has evolved over centuries.

THE EVOLUTION OF MONEY

Definition of Money

Before we analyze how money evolved over time, let us begin by giving a careful definition of money:

Money is anything that serves as a commonly accepted medium of exchange or means of payment. In the earliest days, money took the form of commodities, but over time it evolved into paper currencies and checking accounts. All these have the same essential quality: They are accepted as payment for buying goods and services.

In making use of money, societies have passed through numerous historical stages. The sequence of barter, then commodity, then paper, then bank money illustrates how monies have evolved over time.

Barter vs. the Use of Money When Stanley Jevons, in an early textbook on money, wanted to illustrate the tremendous leap forward when civilization turned from exchange by barter to the use of money, he could not do better than to quote experiences like the following.

Some years since, Mademoiselle Zélie, a singer of the Théâtre Lyrique at Paris, . . . gave a concert in the Society Islands. In exchange for an air from *Norma* and a few other songs, she was to receive a third part of the receipts. When counted, her share was found to consist of three pigs, twenty-three turkeys, forty-four chickens, five thousand cocoa-nuts, besides considerable quantities of bananas, lemons, and oranges. . . . [I]n Paris . . . this amount of live stock and vegetables might have brought four thousand francs, which would have been good remuneration for five songs. In the Society Islands, however, pieces of money were scarce; and as Mademoiselle could not consume any considerable portion of the

receipts herself, it became necessary in the mean time to feed the pigs and poultry with the fruit.

This example shows the nature of barter. **Barter** consists of the exchange of goods for other goods, rather than the exchange of goods for a commonly accepted medium of exchange, or money.

Inconvenient as barter obviously is, as shown by the comical example of exchanging songs for pigs, it actually represents a great step forward from the state of complete self-sufficiency, where each household made everything it needed and where everyone had to be a jack-of-all-trades and a master of none. Nevertheless, barter operates under grave disadvantages. An elaborate division of labor would be unthinkable without the introduction of a great improvement—the use of money.

Once economies leave the most rudimentary stages, people do not directly exchange one good for another. Instead, they sell one good for money, and then use money to buy the goods they wish. At first glance this seems to complicate rather than simplify matters, to replace one transaction by two.

Thus, if I have apples and want nuts, would it not be simpler to trade one for the other rather than to sell the apples for money and then use the money to buy nuts?

Actually, the reverse is true: The two transactions are simpler than one. Ordinarily, there are always people ready to buy apples and always some willing to sell nuts. But it would be an unusual coincidence to find a person with tastes exactly opposite your own, with an eagerness to sell nuts and buy apples. This situation, called the "double coincidence of wants," would be extraordinarily unlikely.

To use a classical economic phrase, instead of there being a double coincidence of wants, there is likely to be a want of coincidence. So, unless a hungry tailor happens to find an undraped farmer who has both food and a desire for a pair of pants, under barter neither can make a trade.

Because societies that traded extensively simply could not overcome the overwhelming handicaps of barter, the use of a commonly accepted medium of exchange, money, sprang up to ensure that farmer could buy pants from tailor, who buys shoes from cobbler, who buys leather from farmer.

Commodity Money Money as a medium of exchange first came into human history in the form of commodities. A great variety of items have served as money at one time or another: cattle, olive oil, beer or wines, copper, iron, gold, silver, rings, diamonds, and cigarettes.

Each of the above has advantages and disadvantages. Cattle are not divisible into small change. Beer does not improve with keeping, although wine may. Olive oil provides a nice liquid currency that is as minutely divisible as one wishes, but it is a bit messy to handle. And so forth.

By the nineteenth century, commodity money was almost exclusively limited to metals. Silver has luster but tarnishes. Gold's high specific gravity makes detection of counterfeiting and adulteration easy. But through most of history, gold's scarcity value has been so great per ounce as to require inordinately minute coins for ordinary purchases.

Most kinds of money tended once to be of some value or use for their own sake. Thus, gold has been used in teeth and jewelry. But the intrinsic value of money is now the least important thing about it.

Paper Money The age of commodity money gave way to the age of paper money. The essence of money is now laid bare. *Money, as money rather than as a commodity, is wanted not for its own sake but for the things it will buy.* We do not wish to use up money directly—rather we use it by getting rid of it. Even when we choose to use it by keeping it, its value comes from the fact that we can spend it later on.

Money is an artificial social convention. If for any reason a substance begins to be used as money, people will begin to value it. A nonsmoker will value cigarettes if they are money in a prisoner of war camp.

This leads to a paradox: Money is accepted because it is accepted.

The use of paper currency (dollar bills, fives, tens, . . .) has become widespread because it is a convenient medium of exchange. Currency is easily carried and stored. By the printing of more or fewer zeros on the face value of the bill, a great or small amount of value can be embodied in a light, transportable medium of little bulk. By the use of decimal points, it can be made as divisible as we wish. By ensuring careful engraving, the value of money can be protected from counterfeiting. The fact that private individuals cannot legally create money keeps it scarce.

Given this limitation in supply, modern currencies have value. They can buy things, independently of any gold, silver, or government backing. The public need not know or care whether its currency is in the form of silver certificates, Federal Reserve notes, or copper or silver coins. So long as each form of money can be converted into any other at fixed terms, the best is as good as the worst.

Bank Money Finally, today is the age of bank money—checks written on a deposit in a bank or other financial institution.

A biologist has her salary paid directly into her bank account. Her rent or dentist bills, clothing or store purchases, are paid by check. Except for petty sums for lunches and movies, she needs little cash.

If we calculate the total dollar amount of transactions, nine-tenths take place by bank money, the rest by paper money.

Continued Evolution Today there is extremely rapid innovation in the kinds of money available. Some financial institutions link a checking account up to a savings account or even to a stock portfolio, so that you can write checks on the value of your IBM stock. Credit cards and traveler's checks can be used for many transactions. Some people believe that the day is near when we will have a personal debit card with a non-counterfeitable signature, hooked up to a central computer, by which we can make all large transactions. The rapid mutation in the nature of money causes difficult problems for central banks, which are charged with measuring and controlling the nation's money supply.

Components of the Money Supply

Let us now look more carefully at the different kinds of money that Americans employ. The major *monetary aggregates* are known today as M_1, M_2, and so on—you can read about their week-to-week movements in the newspaper, along with sage commentaries on the significance of the latest wiggle. Here we will delve into the exact definitions as of 1988.

Transactions Money (M_1) The most important and closely watched measure of money is M_1, which consists of those items that are actually used for transactions, to buy and sell things. M_1 includes such things as coins and currency held outside banks, along with checking accounts.

What are the components of the money supply?

Coins First, there are the *coins* we use for small change: zinc pennies and 5-cent pieces, and silver-looking copper dimes, quarters, and half-dollars.

Paper Currency More significant is the second kind of money: *paper currency*. Most of us know little more about a $1 or $5 bill than that it is inscribed with the picture of an American statesman, that it bears some official signatures, and—most important—that each has a numeral showing its face value.

Examine a $10 bill or some other paper bill. You will probably find it says "Federal Reserve Note." Also, it announces itself as "legal tender for all debts, public and private."

What lies behind this $10 bill? Is it "backed" by gold, silver, or anything? Not a thing. Many years ago, people believed that our currency had value because of "gold backing." There is no such pretense today.

Today, all U.S. coins and paper currency are **fiat money.** This term signifies that something is money because the government decrees it is money. More precisely, the government states that coins and paper currency are *legal tender,* which must be accepted for all debts, public and private. Metallic backing of money is of no practical significance in the United States today.

Coins and paper currency (the sum known as "currency") add up to about one-fourth of total transactions money, M_1.

Checking Accounts There is a third component of transactions money—checking accounts or bank money. These are funds, deposited in banks and other financial institutions, that you can write checks on.

These are technically known as "demand deposits and other checkable deposits."[1]

If I have $1000 in my checking account at the Albuquerque National Bank, that deposit can be regarded as money. Why? For the simple reason that I can pay for purchases with checks drawn on it. The deposit is like any other medium of exchange. Being payable on demand, it serves as money in the same sense that 1000 dollar bills do; i.e., like paper money, the bank deposit can be used to purchase goods or can be converted into cash at fixed terms, dollar for dollar. Possessing the essential properties of money, bank checking-account deposits are counted as transactions money, as part of M_1.

Table 11-1 shows the quantitative importance of the different components of transactions money, M_1.

Other Monetary Aggregates

Broad Money Although M_1 is generally the most closely watched of the money figures, others attract attention from time to time. The most important other aggregate is *broad money,* or M_2 (sometimes called "asset money" or "near-money"). M_2 includes M_1 as well as certain assets that are very close substitutes for transactions money.

Examples of such near-monies in M_2 include a $10,000 deposit in a savings account in your local thrift institution; a $5000 account in a "money market mutual fund" operated by your stockbroker; a $6500 deposit in a "money market deposit account" run by a commercial bank. And so on.

Why are these not transactions money? Because they cannot be used as an unlimited medium of exchange for small and large purchases. They are near-

---

[1]Up till the late 1970s, virtually all checking accounts were "demand deposits" at commercial banks and bore a zero interest rate. Under pressure of advancing technology and high interest rates, the sharp difference between demand deposits and other assets gradually eroded. In 1980 and 1982, Congress passed laws allowing other financial institutions to offer checking accounts (called "negotiable orders of withdrawal," or NOW accounts), and allowed payment of interest on checking accounts. By the late 1980s, interest-rate ceilings on almost all assets were removed. The result of this dismantling of regulatory restrictions between different institutions and assets is a blurring of the distinction between money and other financial assets.

KINDS OF MONEY	BILLIONS OF DOLLARS		
	1959	1971	1988
Currency (outside of financial institutions)	29.0	52.6	207.3
Demand deposits (excludes government deposits and certain foreign deposits)	111.6	176.8	298.3
NOW accounts and other checkable deposits	0.4	1.3	291.0
Total transactions money (M_1)	141.0	230.7	796.6
Savings accounts and small time deposits (includes money market funds)	156.8	482.0	2,278.5
Broad money (M_2)	297.8	712.7	3,075.1
Total credit (D)	692.2	1,569.9	8,670.1

Table 11-1   Alternative concepts of the money supply of the United States

Two concepts of the money supply are widely used: transactions money (M_1) and broad money (M_2). M_1 consists of currency and checking accounts. M_2 adds to these certain "near-monies" such as savings accounts and time deposits. Some economists look at a very broad aggregate known as credit (D). Measures of money and credit are important indicators of policy and of the state of the economy. (Source: Federal Reserve Board.)

monies, however, because you can turn them into cash very quickly.

M_2 has been a useful indicator of trends in money supply growth during the 1980s because it has shown greater stability than M_1. When new kinds of checking accounts were introduced (as in the fall of 1982), M_1 behaved very erratically. M_2 proved a better barometer of economic activity.

Further Refinements Central banks measure yet further near-monies. M_3 is another broad-money concept and includes M_2 plus savings accounts and similar deposits owned by large institutions. Another measure, called L for "liquid assets," includes items such as short-term Treasury securities; they are called liquid assets because they can readily be turned into cash.

A final measure, called D, or *credit,* representing all debt of domestic nonfinancial sectors, is the broad-

est measure of money-type assets. This credit aggregate includes mortgages, bonds, and similar instruments along with all liquid assets.

Why do economists pay close attention to broad money and credit aggregates? They do so because M_2 and total credit move in tandem with overall economic activity; sharp changes in M_2 or credit growth often signal a similar movement in GNP. When credit is plentiful, banks are more generous in making loans for homes or inventories or new factories. Thus a rapid growth in money and credit accompanies booms, and contractions in money and credit are often followed by recessions or worse.

Definitional Problems Fastidious people are driven to distraction by the attempt to define the money supply. Alas, there is no hard-and-fast line in the chain of assets where you can say, "Here and no further lies money." The exact definition of "the" money supply is as much a matter of taste as of scientific necessity. Along with M_1 and M_2, economists have been able to define more than a dozen different money-supply concepts: M_3, M_{1a}, M_{1b}, L, . . . !

Why are economists constantly debating about the "correct" definition of the money supply? Partly because of different economic theories; some feel that only M_1 affects economic activity, while others feel that the whole range of near-monies or credit exerts an influence.

Also, some earlier definitions of the money supply are simply rendered obsolete by financial innovations. With every new asset that is created, the list of what's in and what's out of a particular "M" must be reexamined.[2]

We will stick to this definition in this book:

M is transactions money, or M_1, the sum of coins and paper currency in circulation outside the banks, plus checkable deposits. Less often we will also refer to the broader definition (called M_2), which includes assets such as savings accounts in addition to coins, paper currency, and checkable deposits.

We have now sketched the history and major components of money. But how is the money supply determined? What economic variables cause people to hold money? In short, what forces are behind the demand and supply of money? The next two sections focus on these issues.

B. THE DEMAND FOR MONEY

Before looking into modern theories of the demand for money, it is worthwhile to pause a moment to reflect on why the demand for money is different from the demand for ice cream or movies. Remember that money is not desired for its own sake—you cannot eat nickels, and we seldom hang $100 bills on the wall for the artistic quality of their engraving.

Rather, money is held because it serves us indirectly, as a lubricant to trade and exchange.

Money's Functions

To review what we said earlier, what are the functions of money?

1. By far the most important function of transactions money (M_1) is to serve as a *medium of exchange*. Without money we would be constantly roving around in search of someone to barter with, a hopelessly inefficient system in a modern economy with great specialization and division of labor.

2. Money is also used as the *unit of account*. We de-

[2]Question 11 at the end of this chapter explores further the spectrum of assets from money to capital.

nominate the prices of goods and services, present and future, in terms of dollars (just as foreigners do in British pounds sterling, German deutsche marks, or Japanese yen). The use of a common unit of account simplifies economic life enormously.

3. Money is sometimes used as a *store of value*. By comparison with risky assets like stocks or real estate or gold, money is a relatively riskless asset. In earlier days, people held currency as a safe form of wealth. Today, more and more people are holding high-yield money (such as NOW accounts) as a safe asset. But the vast preponderance of wealth is held in other assets—in near-monies like savings accounts, stocks, bonds, and so forth.

Cost of Holding Money These three functions of money are extremely important to people, so important that they are willing to incur a cost to hold currency or low-yielding checking accounts. What is the *cost of holding money*? The cost is the sacrifice in interest and profit from holding money rather than a higher-yielding asset or investment.

Recall from Chapter 7 that assets have returns or interest rates. An *interest rate* is defined as the yield (in dollars per dollar lent out for a year) to money lent out. For comparison, let's contrast the yield from holding money with the yield on "money funds." A **money fund** is a savings account like a money market mutual fund or a money market deposit account. These savings accounts earn unregulated interest rates that have ranged between 5 and 15 percent annually in recent years.

Say that you put $1000 in a money fund at the beginning of 1988; you would earn about 8 percent interest and would end with $1080 at the end of 1988. This represents an 8 percent money or nominal interest rate.

Now let's return to the cost of holding money. Assume that you had left your $1000 in currency rather than in the money fund for 1988. You would have ended up with only $1000, for currency pays no interest. Thus the cost of holding money as currency is the lost or forgone interest.

Money is useful because it allows easy and quick transactions, unambiguous determination of the price, plus storage of value over time. These services are not free, however. If wealth were held in stocks, bonds, or savings accounts rather than money, it would yield a higher interest rate. The cost of holding money is the interest lost because the money is not invested in these alternative assets.

Let's consider yet another example. You have $1000 in your checking account, or bank money (M_1). The bank pays 5 percent per year on your checking account, or $50 per year.

As an alternative, you can earn 8 percent in a money fund. Thus the net cost (or opportunity cost) of keeping your $1000 in bank money is $30 = ($80 minus $50).

Why might you sacrifice the $30? Because it is worthwhile to keep the money in your checking account to pay for food or a new bike. You are getting "money services" that are worth at least $30 a year.

MOTIVES FOR HOLDING MONEY

Clearly, the main motive for holding money and losing interest is the convenience of being able to buy things. Let us examine this component of the demand for money.

Transactions Demand

People and firms need money as a transactions medium. Households need money to buy groceries and to pay electricity and fuel bills as well as to buy large consumer durables. Firms need money to pay for materials and labor. These needs constitute the *transactions demand for money*.

We can illustrate the mechanics of the transactions demand for money in Figure 11-2. This figure shows the average money holdings of a family that earns $1000 per month, keeps it in money, and spends it all evenly over the month. Clearly, the family holds $500 on average in money balances.

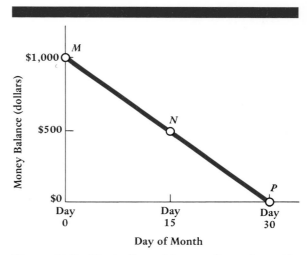

Figure 11-2   Illustration of transactions demand for money

This figure illustrates how much money a typical family might hold. We assume that the family is paid $1000 at the beginning of the month, and spends the whole amount over the course of the month at a constant rate of $33⅓ per day. Moreover, the family does not put any of its money in another asset during the month. Thus the family has $1000 on day 0, $500 on day 15, and nothing at the end of the month. This is illustrated by the line *MNP*.

How much money does the family hold on average? Answer: ½ of $1000 = $500.

To understand the way the demand for money behaves, ask how this figure would change if all prices and incomes doubled? If real incomes doubled? If interest rates on savings accounts went to 20 percent?

This example can help us see how the demand for money responds to economic variables. If all prices and incomes double, then the vertical axis in Figure 11-2 is simply relabelled by doubling all the dollar values. Clearly the nominal demand for *M* doubles. Thus the transactions demand for money doubles if nominal GNP doubles with no change in real GNP or other real variables.

Interest-Rate Effect An extremely important question is, How does the demand for money vary with interest rates? Recall that our family is paying an opportunity cost for its checking account—the interest rate on *M* is less than that on other assets. As interest rates rise, the family might say:

> Let's put only half of our money in the checking account at the beginning of the month, and put the other half in a money fund earning 8 percent per annum. Then on day 15, we'll take that $500 out of the money fund and put it in our checking account to pay the next 2 weeks' bills.

Note the net effect: As interest rates rose, and the family decided to put half its earnings in a money fund, the average money balance of our family fell from $500 to $250. This shows how money holdings (or the demand for money) may be sensitive to interest rates: *Other things equal, as interest rates rise, the demand for money declines.*

You might think that the economic gains from a constant reshuffling of portfolios is such small potatoes that households' money holdings are likely to be largely unaffected by interest-rate fluctuations. How much will people's average bank balance change when they find they can earn 2 or 4 percent more on their money funds? Very little, according to most studies.

Rather, the major impact of interest rates on the demand for money comes in the business sector. Firms often find themselves with bank balances of $100 million one day, $250 million the next day, and so forth. If they do nothing, they could easily lose $20 to $50 million a year in interest payments. The era of high interest rates since the 1970s has ushered in corporate "cash management," in which banks help their corporate customers keep their cash constantly invested in high-yield assets rather than lying fallow

in zero-yield checking accounts. And with higher interest rates, corporations work a little harder to keep their cash balances at a minimum.

Asset Demand

In addition to holding money for transactions needs, people may also hold money as a store of value. As we noted in Chapter 7's discussion of consumption, people save for retirement, for hard times, and for their children's educations. At the end of 1987, households owned about $9 trillion of financial assets of various kinds. Shouldn't money be one of these assets?

Portfolio Theory One of the most important topics of modern economics is **portfolio theory,** which describes how rational investors put their wealth into a "portfolio" (or group of securities). For example, your portfolio might consist of $10,000 worth of Treasury bonds, $5000 in a money market fund, and $14,000 in the stock market.

Portfolio theory begins with the fundamental assumption that people seek high returns on their investments but are averse to risky investments. In other words, people will generally hold risky investments only if their returns are sufficiently high. ("Returns" consist of the annual return per dollar of investment.) Faced with two assets with equal returns, people seek the safer investment. To draw people away from low-risk assets into risky stocks or real estate, the high-risk asset must offer a higher return.

Portfolio theory analyzes how a risk-averse investor should allocate wealth. One important rule is to diversify the portfolio among different assets. "Don't put all your eggs in one basket" is one way of expressing this rule.

In addition, advanced studies of portfolio theory show that an optimal portfolio would generally contain a mixture of low-risk and high-risk assets. The low-risk assets might well include interest-bearing checking accounts. We should not be surprised, therefore, that in today's world many households will hold money as part of their strategy for investing their wealth and not only for transactions purposes.

What of the rest of the portfolio? Calculations show (as we will see in this chapter's appendix) that by diversifying their wealth among a broad group of investments—different companies' common stocks, different kinds of bonds, perhaps real estate—people can attain a good return on their wealth without incurring unacceptable risks.*

The appendix to this chapter provides an overview of modern finance theory with special application to the stock market.

We summarize as follows: The demand for money (M_1) arises from our need for a medium of exchange, that is, from a transactions demand. We hold currency and checking accounts to buy goods and pay our bills. As our incomes rise, the value of the goods we buy goes up and we therefore need more money for transactions, raising our demand for M_1.

The transactions demand for M will be sensitive to the cost of holding money. When interest rates on alternative assets rise relative to the interest rate on money, people and firms tend to economize on their money holdings.

In addition, people sometimes hold money as an asset. They want to protect some of their wealth against the vicissitudes of economic life, avoiding the folly of putting all their eggs in one basket. And one basket that many investors will want to use is that of an ultra-safe asset. This asset may be a high-yield checking account, part of M_1, or it may be a near-money in M_2, perhaps a savings account or a money fund.

C. BANKING AND THE SUPPLY OF MONEY

Next turn to an analysis of the supply of money. Section A showed that transactions money, M_1, is comprised of two major components, currency and checking accounts. In understanding the way that money affects the economy, we need to master the process by which the central bank and the banking sector "produce" money. In this section we begin by surveying some historical and institutional aspects of commercial banking. The last part then analyzes the process by which banks "create" money.

BANKING AS A BUSINESS

We have seen that the bulk of transactions money (M_1) is bank money—checking deposits at financial institutions. What are financial institutions and

banks? What is the mechanism that allows banks to create money? What are its historical roots?

Bank money and many other financial services are today provided by financial intermediaries. **Financial intermediaries** are institutions like banks, insurance companies, and savings and loan associations that take deposits or funds from one group and lend these funds to another group. For example, financial intermediaries take savings from households or firms or foreigners. They then turn around and lend these to households to buy homes, to businesses to build factories, to other countries to finance foreign trade, or to students to finance college.

In performing financial services, intermediaries provide depositors with a wide variety of *financial instruments,* or assets and liabilities. These can take the form of checking accounts, savings accounts,

---

*The theory of portfolio choice is at the center of one of the most exciting and popular fields of intermediate economics: money and banking. This analysis uses a framework similar to that of the utility theory of Chapter 19. It assumes that people like high yields on assets but dislike risk of assets. Work of Harry Markowitz and James Tobin showed that utility-maximizing consumers would spread their wealth (i.e., diversify their portfolios) among many different risky assets.

This line of research has become extremely important in finance theory, pursued by W. Sharpe, E. Fama, S. Ross, and others, and takes its modern form in the "capital asset pricing model." Every good portfolio manager on Wall Street uses these techniques to bolster his or her intuition in choosing stocks and bonds.

For his contribution to portfolio theory and other aspects of monetary theory, Tobin was awarded the Nobel Prize in economics in 1981.

BALANCE SHEET OF ALL COMMERCIAL BANKING INSTITUTIONS, 1988
(Billions of dollars)

ASSETS		LIABILITIES	
Reserves	$ 51	Checking accounts	$ 578
Loans	1,926	Savings and time deposits	1,426
Investments and securities	523	Other liabilities	844
Other assets	348		
Total	$2,848	Total	$2,848

Table 11-2   Checking accounts are liabilities of the commercial banks

Reserves and checking accounts are the two key items of interest to our later economic analysis. Checking accounts are payable on demand and thus can be withdrawn quickly when customers write checks. Reserves are large primarily because of legal requirements and not to provide against possible unexpected withdrawals. (Source: *Federal Reserve Bulletin,* August 1988.)

annuity policies, 3-year certificates of deposit, life-insurance policies, and so forth.

Who are the major financial intermediaries today? The largest class consists of commercial banks, with about 33 percent of the assets of financial institutions. Savings and loan associations and mutual savings banks rank second, with about 19 percent of the assets. Other important groups are life-insurance companies, pension funds, and money market mutual funds. Altogether, at the end of 1985, all such firms had a total of $6.8 trillion of assets and liabilities.

In what follows we will focus on commercial banks, or "banks" for short. We do so because these institutions are still the main source of checking accounts, or the bank-money component of M_1.

In summary:

Financial institutions transfer funds from lenders to borrowers. In doing this, they create financial instruments (like checking or savings accounts). But from a macroeconomic vantage point the most important instrument is bank money (or checking accounts) primarily provided today by commercial banks.

A Business Venture

Banks and other financial intermediaries are much like other businesses. They are organized to earn profits for their owners. A commercial bank is a rela-

tively simple business concern. It provides certain services for customers and in return receives payments from them in one form or another.

A bank's balance sheet shows certain assets, liabilities, and capital ownership.[3] Except for minor rearrangements, the bank's published balance sheet looks much like the balance sheet of any business, although it is a bit simpler than most. The peculiar feature about the bank balance sheet shown in Table 11-2 is an item called "reserves" on the asset side. **Reserves** are funds or assets held by banks in the form of cash on hand or of funds deposited by the bank with the central bank. A small fraction of reserves are for day-to-day business needs, but the bulk is held to meet legal reserve requirements.

How Banks Developed from Goldsmith Establishments

Sometimes a page of history is worth a chapter of analysis. The history of how banking developed from goldsmiths illustrates how modern banks evolved. Commercial banking in England began with the gold-

[3]Balance sheets, assets, and liabilities are extensively discussed in Chapter 20's appendix on accounting. A balance sheet is a listing of assets (those things that have positive value) and liabilities (those items that are owed now or in the future).

smiths, who developed the practice of storing people's gold and valuables for safekeeping. At first, such establishments were simply like baggage checkrooms or warehouses. Depositors left gold for safekeeping, were given a receipt, later presented that receipt, paid a small fee for the safekeeping, and got back their gold.

Note, however, that money has an anonymous quality, making one dollar just as good as another, and one piece of pure gold as good as another. The goldsmiths soon found it more convenient not to have to tag the gold belonging to any one individual so as to return exactly the same piece of gold that the customer had left. Instead, customers were quite willing to accept a receipt for a certain amount of gold, even though they might not get back exactly the same set of molecules that they had left.

This "anonymity" is important. Therein lies a significant difference between a bank and a checkroom or warehouse. If I check my bag at the Denver airport and later see someone walking down the street with it, I place an outraged phone call to the airline. If I mark my initials on a $10 bill, deposit it in my bank account, and later see it in the hands of a stranger, I have no grievance against the bank management. They've only agreed to pay me on demand any old $10.

Returning to the goldsmith establishments, what would balance sheets of a typical establishment look like? Perhaps like Table 11-3.

We assume that First Goldsmith Bank no longer hammers gold bars but is occupied solely with storing people's money for safekeeping. In the past, $1 mil-

lion has been deposited in its vaults, and this whole sum is held as a cash asset (this is the item "cash reserves" in the balance sheet). To balance this asset, there is a demand deposit of the same amount. Cash reserves are therefore 100 percent of deposits.

The bank money would just offset the amount of ordinary money (gold or currency) placed in the bank's safe and withdrawn from active circulation. No money creation has taken place. The process would be of no more interest than if the public decided to convert nickels into dimes. We say that a 100 percent reserve banking system has a neutral effect on money, spending, and prices—not adding or subtracting from total M.

Modern Fractional-Reserve Banking

Let us return to our early goldsmith-banker to see how modern banks gradually evolved. As a keen-eyed profit maximizer, the goldsmith-banker would soon notice that, although his deposits are payable on demand, they are not all withdrawn together. He would soon learn that, although 100 percent reserves are necessary if all depositors suddenly had to be paid off in full at the same time, such an event almost never occurs. On a given day, some people withdraw money while others deposit money. These two pretty much balance out. As a result of deposits and withdrawals being nearly equal, it is estimated that most banks would need only 1 percent of deposits to avoid running out of cash.

The banker also notes that any funds held as re-

BALANCE SHEET

ASSETS		LIABILITIES	
Cash reserves	$1,000,000	Demand deposits	$1,000,000
Total	$1,000,000	Total	$1,000,000

Table 11-3 First Goldsmith Bank held 100 percent cash reserves against demand deposits

In a primitive banking system, with 100 percent backing of demand deposits, no creation of money out of new reserves is possible.

serves are sterile—they earn no interest as vault cash or gold. And today's reserves held with the Federal Reserve are equally barren of interest. Bankers like to keep their money working. Early banks therefore hit upon the idea of using the money entrusted to them to buy bonds or other earning assets. They soon found that investing their deposits was beneficial because depositors were still paid off on demand, and the bank made some extra earnings.

Actually, the banks are making themselves and their customers better off. By getting each customer to agree to the banks' putting most of the money deposited with them in earning assets and keeping only fractional cash reserves against deposits, they maximize their profits. And from these profits they can provide extra services or lower fees to depositors.

The results of First Goldsmith's decision to move to fractional rather than 100 percent reserves against deposits is revolutionary. *The total amount of deposits will now exceed the amount of gold reserves.* Banks can create money. The next section shows exactly how this process works.

What is the lesson of this page of history? Simply that as banks moved from being checkrooms to fractional-reserve depository and lending institutions, banks were no longer neutral. They can literally create money—they turn a dollar of gold reserves (or today's central bank reserves) into several dollars of money.

Legal Reserve Requirements

In banking, reserves are that part of a bank's assets held either as cash on hand or as deposits with the central bank. A prudent banker, concerned only to assure customers that the bank had enough cash for daily transactions, might desire to keep 1 or 2 percent of the bank's assets in reserves. In fact, banks keep more than 10 percent of their checking deposits in reserves, generally in deposits with our central bank, the Federal Reserve System.

Why are reserves so high? The reason is that a financial institution is required by law and Federal Reserve regulations to keep a substantial portion of its assets as reserves. Since 1980, all financial intermediaries are required to hold reserves against different

kinds of deposits. Deposits are divided into two types, checking type and savings type. *Reserve requirements are imposed on each type of deposit, independent of the actual need for cash on hand or of the kind of financial institution that houses the deposit.*[4]

Table 11-4 indicates the level of *required reserve ratios*. They range from 12 percent against checking-type accounts down to nothing for personal savings accounts. For convenience in our numerical examples, we will use 10 percent reserve ratios, with the understanding that the actual ratio required is slightly different from 10 percent.

These legal reserve requirements need to be explained since they are so important a part of the mechanism by which the Fed controls the supply of bank money.

Legal Reserves Set Too High Bankers complain that they must hold barren assets beyond what they think prudent, or even beyond what an objective jury would think needed to meet the ebb and flow of withdrawals and receipts. Why, they say, must we lose valuable earnings? And, indeed, a few economists today argue for complete deregulation of the financial system, abolishing reserve requirements altogether.

While this view has merit from the point of view of bankers, it misses the macroeconomic point: *Legal reserve requirements are set too high in order to help the central bank control the money supply.* That is, by setting reserve requirements well above the level that banks themselves would desire, the central bank can determine the precise level of reserves and can thereby control the money supply. We will explain the logic of how high legal reserve requirements can help the central bank control the money supply in the next section.

We may sum up:

The main function of legal reserve requirements is not to make deposits safe and liquid, or payable on demand. Their vital function is to enable the Federal Reserve to control the amount of checking deposits

---

[4]The pathbreaking legislation that set out the rules for today's financial intermediaries was contained in the "Depository Institutions Deregulation and Monetary Control Act of 1980" and the "Garn–St Germain Depository Institutions Act of 1982." For brevity, we call these the 1980 and 1982 Banking Acts.

TYPE OF DEPOSIT	RESERVE RATIO	RANGE IN WHICH FED CAN VARY
Checking (transaction) accounts		
First $40 million	3	no change allowed
Above $40 million	12	8 to 14
Time and savings deposits		
Personal	0	
Nonpersonal		
Up to $1\frac{1}{2}$ years maturity	3	0 to 9
Maturity $1\frac{1}{2} +$ years	0	0 to 9

Table 11-4   Required reserves for financial institutions

This table shows the pattern of reserve requirements for financial institutions under the 1980 Banking Act (known as the Depository Institutions Deregulation and Monetary Control Act of 1980). The Reserve Ratio column shows the percent of deposits in each category that must be held in non-interest-bearing deposits at the Fed or in cash on hand.

There are three classes of deposits. Checking-type accounts in large banks face required reserves of 12 percent. Business time accounts of short maturity and checking accounts in small banks face a small reserve requirement of 3 percent. Other deposits will have no reserve requirements.

Note as well that the Fed has power to alter the reserve ratio within a given range. It does so only on the rare occasion when economic conditions warrant a sharp change in monetary policy.

that banks can create. By imposing high fixed legal reserve requirements, the Fed can better control the money supply.

THE PROCESS OF DEPOSIT CREATION

In our simplified discussion of goldsmith banks, we suggested that banks turn reserves into bank money. There are, in fact, two steps in the process:

• First, the central bank (the Fed) decides on the reserves of the banking system within the limits set by Table 11-4. The detailed process by which the central bank does this is discussed in the next chapter.

• Second, the banking system takes those reserves as an input and transforms them into a much larger amount of bank money. The currency plus this bank money then is the money supply, M_1.

Can Banks Create Money?

We now turn to the second step in the process, which is known as "multiple expansion of bank deposits." This area is sometimes thought mystical because banks are said to transform a dollar of reserves into many dollars of money. Actually, there is nothing strange about the process. It simply builds upon the fractional-reserve nature of a modern banking system.

Figure 11-3 gives a schematic overview of the process. It shows how $1 of new deposits or reserves, at the upper left, is transformed into $10 of total deposits, or bank money, on the right. Inside the rectangle, which represents the banking system as a whole, Bank 1 receives the initial new deposit. Banks 2, 3, . . . and all other banks are listed below. The red arrows circulating around show how reserves are redistributed while the black lines show new deposits. As the red arrows between the banks show, all the banks get involved in the lengthy secondary chain of money creation. Though the chain has many links,

MULTIPLE-BANK EXPANSION OF MONEY

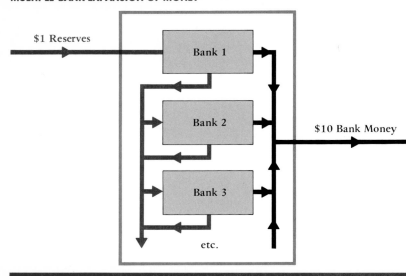

Figure 11-3 All banks can do what one can't do alone

For each dollar of new reserves deposited in a bank, the system as a whole creates about $10 of bank money. The red arrows in the box show that Bank 1 cannot do it alone. As we'll see, the second, third, and other banks will get their share of the expansion.

each is a dwindling fraction and the whole effect does add up to the 10-to-1 total.

The balance of this chapter explains this process of money creation.

How Deposits Are Created: First-Generation Banks

Let us begin our discussion by considering what happens when new reserves are injected into the banking system. The source of the new reserves is not important, but for concreteness assume that the Federal Reserve buys a $1000 government bond from Ms. Bondholder, and she deposits the $1000 in her checking account at Bank 1.

The change in the bank's balance sheet, as far as the new demand deposit is concerned, is shown in Table 11-5(a).[5] Together, Bank 1 and the public "created" $1000 of bank money, or checking deposits.

---

[5]For simplicity, our tables will show only the *changes* in balance sheet items, and we use reserve ratios of 10 percent. Note that when bankers refer to their loans and investments, by "investments" they mean their holdings of securities. They don't mean what economists mean by *I*, where *I* means capital formation for the community.

But as yet there is no multiple expansion, no 10 for 1 or anything else. Moreover, if banks were to keep 100 percent of deposits in reserves, like the old goldsmiths, they could not create any extra money out of a new deposit of $1000 left with them. The depositor's $1000 checking deposit would then just match the $1000 of reserves.

But modern banks do not keep 100 percent reserves for their deposits. As Table 11-4 showed, banks are required by law to keep but a fraction of each $1 of deposits. Current law requires them to hold 3 or 12 percent of deposits as reserves, but in our example we will assume a reserve requirement of 10 percent, for simplicity of calculations.

What can Bank 1 now do? It has $900 more in reserves than it needs to meet the reserve requirement. Because reserves earn no interest, our profit-minded bank will loan or invest the excess $900. The loan might be for a car, or the investment might be in a Treasury bond.

Let's say the bank makes a loan or buys a bond. The person who borrows the money or sells the bond takes the $900 (in cash or check) and deposits it in her account in another bank. Very quickly, then, the $900 will be paid out by Bank 1.

BANK 1 IN INITIAL POSITION

ASSETS		LIABILITIES	
Reserves	+$1,000	Deposits	+$1,000
Total	+$1,000	Total	+$1,000

Table 11-5(a)   **Multiple-bank deposit creation is a story with many successive stages. At the start, newly created reserves get deposited in original first-generation bank**
We begin the process of money expansion by having an initial deposit in Bank 1 that creates $1000 of reserves.

What does the bank's balance sheet look like after all transactions are complete and all investments have been made? After it has loaned or invested $900, Bank 1's legal reserves are just enough to cover its deposits. There is nothing more it can do until the public decides to bring in some more money for deposit. The balance sheet of Bank 1 after it has made all possible loans or investment (but still meets its reserve requirement) is shown in Table 11-5(b).

Before leaving Bank 1, note this important fact: It has created money. How? Clearly there is the original $1000 of deposits shown on the right of Table 11-5(b). But in addition, there is $900 of demand deposits in someone else's account (i.e., in the checking account of the person who got the $900). Hence, the total amount of M is now $1900. *Bank 1's activity has created $900 of new money.*

Chain Repercussions on Other Banks

But the banking system as a whole cannot settle down yet. The people who borrowed the $900 from Bank 1 will soon deposit the proceeds in some other bank or pay someone else who will make such a deposit.

Second-Generation Banks Lump these other banks together and call them "second-generation banks" (or Bank 2). Their balance sheets now appear as shown in Table 11-5(c). To these banks, the dollars deposited are just like any other dollars—they function just like our original $1000 deposit. These banks do not know, and do not care, that they are second in a chain of deposits. But they do know, and they do care, that they are at first holding too much non-earn-

BANK 1 IN FINAL POSITION

ASSETS		LIABILITIES	
Reserves	+$ 100	Deposits	+$1,000
Loans and investments	+ 900		
Total	+$1,000	Total	+$1,000

Table 11-5(b)   **A profit-maximizing bank will lend or invest any excess reserves. Thus Bank 1 has kept only $100 of the original cash deposit (as required reserves) and has lent or invested the other $900**

SECOND-GENERATION BANKS IN INITIAL POSITION

ASSETS		LIABILITIES	
Reserves	+$900	Deposits	+$900
Total	+$900	Total	+$900

Table 11-5(c)

ing cash, or excess reserves. Only one-tenth of $900, or $90, is legally needed against $900 deposits.

Therefore, they will use the other nine-tenths to acquire $810 worth of loans and investments. Hence, their balance sheets will soon reach the equilibrium shown in Table 11-5(d).

So much for the second-generation banks. As shown back in Figure 11-3 by the red arrows connecting Bank 2 to Bank 1, part of the original reserves ends up in these second banks, and they too have created money.

Thus far, the original $1000 taken out of hand-to-hand circulation has now produced a total of $2710 of money. The total of M has increased, and the end's not yet in sight.

Later-Generation Banks The $810 spent by the second-generation banks in acquiring loans and investments will go to a new set of banks called the "third-generation banks." (Again, follow the red arrow below Bank 2 back on Figure 11-3.)

You can now create your own set of balance sheets (initial and final) for third-generation banks. Evi-

dently, the third-generation banks will lend out their excess reserves and will thereby create $729 of new money. A fourth generation of banks will clearly end up with nine-tenths of $810 in deposits, or $729, and so on.

Final System Equilibrium

What will be the final sum $1000 + $900 + $810 + $729 + \cdots$? Table 11-6 shows the complete effect of the chain of money creation is $10,000. We can get the answer by arithmetic, by common sense, and by elementary algebra.

Common sense tells us the process of deposit creation must come to an end only when no bank anywhere in the system has reserves in excess of the 10 percent reserve requirement. In all our examples, no cash reserves ever leaked out of the banking system; the money simply went from one set of banks to another set of banks. The banking system will reach equilibrium when the $1000 of new reserves is all used up as required reserves on new deposits. In other words, the final equilibrium of the banking system

FINAL POSITION OF SECOND-GENERATION BANKS

ASSETS		LIABILITIES	
Reserves	+$ 90	Deposits	+$900
Loans and investments	+ 810		
Total	+$900	Total	+$900

Table 11-5(d)   Next, the money lent out by Bank 1 soon goes to new banks, which in turn lend out nine-tenths of it

MULTIPLE EXPANSION OF BANK DEPOSITS THROUGH THE BANKING SYSTEM

POSITION OF BANK	NEW DEPOSITS	NEW LOANS AND INVESTMENTS	NEW RESERVES
Original banks	$ 1,000.00	$ 900.00	$ 100.00
2d-generation banks	900.00	810.00	90.00
3d-generation banks	810.00	729.00	81.00
4th-generation banks	729.00	656.10	72.90
5th-generation banks	656.10	590.49	65.61
6th-generation banks	590.49	531.44	59.05
7th-generation banks	531.44	478.30	53.14
8th-generation banks	478.30	430.47	47.83
9th-generation banks	430.47	387.42	43.05
10th-generation banks	387.42	348.68	38.74
Sum of first 10 generations of banks	$6,513.22	$5,861.90	$651.32
Sum of remaining generations of banks	3,486.78	3,138.10	348.68
Total for banking system as a whole	$10,000.00	$9,000.00	$1,000.00

Table 11-6   Finally, through this long chain, all banks create new deposits of 10 times new reserves

All banks together do accomplish what no one small bank can—multiple expansion of reserves into M. The final equilibrium is reached when every dollar of original new reserves supports $10 of demand deposits. Note that in every generation each bank has "created" new money in the following sense: It ends up with a final bank deposit 10 times the reserve it finally retains.

will come when 10 percent of new deposits *(D)* equals the new reserves of $1000. What level of D satisfies this condition? The answer is $D = \$10,000$.

We can also see the answer intuitively by looking at a consolidated balance sheet for all banks together—first, second, and hundredth generation. This is shown in Table 11-7. If total new deposits were less than $10,000, the 10 percent reserve ratio wouldn't yet be reached, and full equilibrium would not yet be attained.[6]

The Money-Supply Multiplier We see that there is a multiplier operating on reserves. For every additional dollar in reserves provided to the banking system,

banks eventually create $10 of additional deposits or bank money.

Just as Chapter 8's multiplier made income rise threefold to generate new savings equal to the new dollar of investment, here money must rise tenfold so that 10 percent of it will match the new dollars of reserves that started the chain. Note that the arithmetic of M expansion is like that of the "expenditure multiplier" of Chapter 8. But don't confuse the two. The amplification here is from the stock of reserves to the stock of total M; it does not refer to the extra output induced by investment or money.

The ratio of new deposits to the increase in reserves is called the **money-supply multiplier.** In the simple case analyzed here, the money-supply multiplier is equal to

$$10 = \frac{1}{0.1} = \frac{1}{\text{(required reserve ratio)}}$$

The money-supply multiplier summarizes the logic

[6]The algebraic solution can be shown as follows:

$$\$1000 + \$900 + \$810 + \cdots$$
$$= \$1000 \times [1 + \tfrac{9}{10} + (\tfrac{9}{10})^2 + (\tfrac{9}{10})^3 + \cdots]$$
$$= \$1000\left(\frac{1}{1 - \tfrac{9}{10}}\right) = \$1000 \times \left(\frac{1}{0.1}\right) = \$10,000$$

CONSOLIDATED BALANCE SHEET SHOWING FINAL POSITION

ASSETS		LIABILITIES	
Reserves	+$ 1,000	Deposits	+$10,000
Loans and investments	+ 9,000		
Total	+$10,000	Total	+$10,000

Table 11-7   All banks together end up increasing deposits and *M* by a multiple of the original injection of reserves

of how banks create money. The entire banking system can transform an initial increase in reserves into a multiplied amount of new deposits or bank money.

Deposit Destruction

The process of deposit creation can also work in reverse when a drain in reserves reduces bank money. It is useful to reinforce your understanding of money creation by tracing in detail what happens when the Fed permanently destroys $1000 of reserves by selling a government bond to a woman who withdraws cash from her checking account to pay for it. In the end, the withdrawal of $1000 of reserves from the banking system kills off $10,000 worth of deposits throughout the whole system.

Two Qualifications to Deposit Creation

The real world is somewhat more complicated than our simple banking example. Two qualifications are necessary. We have shown that $1000 of new reserves put into a bank will ultimately result in an increase of $10,000 of bank deposits. This assumed that all the new money remained as checking accounts in the banking system, in one bank or another at every stage, and that no bank would have excess reserves. Let us see what would happen if some money leaked into circulation or if some banks had excess reserves.

Leakage into Hand-to-Hand Circulation It is possible that, somewhere along the chain of deposit expan-

sion, an individual who receives a check will not leave the proceeds in a bank checking account. He might put some cash in a cookie jar.[7]

The effects of such withdrawals on our analysis are simple. When $1000 stayed in the banking system, $10,000 of new deposits was created. If $100 were to leak into circulation outside the banks and only $900 of new reserves were to remain in the banking system, then the new checking deposits created would be $9000 (+$900 × 10). Therefore, the 10-to-1 amplification would occur only when no reserves leak from banks.

Possible Excess Reserves Our description of multiple deposit creation has proceeded on the assumption that the commercial banks stick to their legal reserve requirements. But might not a bank choose to keep more reserves than the legally required amount? Suppose, for example, that the original bank decided to keep $900 as additional reserves rather than lend it out. Then the whole process of multiple deposit creation would stop dead in its tracks, with no expansion of deposits at all.

This decision would of course make no sense for the bank. Because the bank earns no interest on reserves, it would be losing interest payments on the $900. So as long as the interest rate on investments is above zero, banks have a strong incentive to avoid holding any excess reserves.

Interest rates in the Great Depression fell to 0.12 percent per year, so banks during this period often

[7]In Fig. 11-3, pencil in holes at the bottom of the black box. Draw arrows out from them indicating that some part of the original red $1 input will leak into currency held by the public.

held significant excess reserves. Another case that might lead to excess reserves would arise if the Federal Reserve paid interest on bank reserves, as some reformers have proposed. In this case, where both reserves and Treasury bills earned the 4 or 6 or 10 percent per year, banks would have no incentive to invest or loan out their excess reserves.

In sum, when the interest rate on reserves is close to that on market investments, the legal reserve requirement will no longer bind banks tightly. As we will see in the next chapter, monetary policy will thereby become a less useful instrument for control of the economy. For this reason, many economists strenuously oppose paying market interest rates on bank reserves.

In any case, we are far from the world of monetary reformers or of the 1930s where bankers cannot profit from lending out their reserves. Today, banks find it attractive to lend in the Federal Funds market any temporary excess reserves to banks short of reserves. The amount of excess reserves is typically a very small fraction of total reserves.

With a legal reserve requirement of 10 percent, reserves will be multiplied by tenfold into new deposits. However, when some of the increased deposits spill into currency or nonmonetary assets, or where banks hold excess reserves, the deposit creation will depart from the ratio of 1/(legal reserve ratio).

∎ ∎ ∎

We have discussed the essence of money along with the major factors determining the demand for money and the financial system's supply of bank money. In the last section, we saw how an infusion of bank reserves could lead to a multiple expansion of money. What remains for a complete understanding of monetary markets is an analysis of the workings of the Federal Reserve System. We will see in the next chapter how the Federal Reserve can manipulate bank reserves by central-banking operations and thereby increase or decrease the total money supply. Later chapters will then demonstrate how such changes in the money supply can help determine output, inflation, and employment.

SUMMARY

A. History of Money

1. Money, along with fiscal policy, is an important determinant of output, unemployment, and inflation in a modern economy. Money affects the economy in three logical steps: Changes in the money supply affect interest rates and the amount and terms of credit; interest rates and credit conditions affect interest-sensitive items of spending (like housing or business investment or net exports); and changes in aggregate demand leads to changes in equilibrium output and prices.

2. Money is anything that serves as a commonly accepted medium of exchange or means of payment. Before money came into use, people exchanged goods for goods in a process called barter. Then money arose as a lubricant to facilitate trade. Early money was composed of commodities but was superseded by paper and bank money. Unlike other economic goods, money is valued because of social convention. We value money indirectly for what it buys, not for its direct utility.

3. The analysis of monetary aggregates is extremely common today among both economists and policymakers. The most widely used definition of the money supply is transactions money (M_1)—made up of currency and checking deposits. Another widely used concept is broad money (M_2), which includes M_1 plus highly liquid "near-monies" like savings accounts.

4. The definitions of the M's have evolved extremely rapidly over the last decade as a result of rapid innovation in financial markets. This rapid change makes the conduct of monetary policy more difficult because monetary definitions (and thus targets for money growth) are ambiguous when new assets appear.

B. The Demand for Money

5. The demand for money differs from that for other commodities because of money's functions. Money is held by people because of its use as a medium of exchange and as an asset that can store value over time. Unlike other goods, money is held for its indirect rather than its direct value. But money holdings are limited because keeping assets in money rather than in other forms has an opportunity cost: We sacrifice interest earnings when we hold money.

6. The demand for money is grounded in the need to make transactions and the desire to hold assets for the future. The most important—the transactions demand—comes because people need cash or checking deposits to pay bills or buy goods. Such transactions needs are met by M_1 and are chiefly related to the value of transactions, or to nominal GNP. In addition, with today's high-yield checking accounts, some assets are held in checking accounts as a super-safe part of investors' portfolios.

Economic theory predicts, and empirical studies confirm, that the demand for money will be sensitive to interest rates—with higher interest rates leading to a lower demand for M.

C. Banking and the Supply of Money

7. Banks are commercial enterprises in business to earn profits for their owners. One major function of banks is to provide checking accounts to customers. Modern banks gradually evolved from the old goldsmith establishments in which money and valuables were stored. It finally became general practice to hold less than 100 percent reserves against deposits, the rest being put into securities and loans for an interest yield. Fractional-reserve banking was born.

8. If banks kept 100 percent cash reserves against all deposits, there would be no multiple creation of money when new reserves were injected by the central bank into the system. There would be only a 1-to-1 exchange of one kind of money for another kind of money.

9. Today, banks are legally required to keep reserves on their checking deposits, with the rate for large banks rising as high as 12 percent of deposits. These can be held in cash on hand or in non-interest-bearing deposits at the Federal Reserve. For illustrative purposes, we examined a required reserve ratio of 10 percent. In this case, the banking system as a whole—together with public or private borrowers and the depositing public—does create bank money 10 to 1 for each new dollar of reserves created by the Fed and deposited somewhere in the banking system.

10. Each small bank is limited in its ability to expand its loans and investments. It cannot lend or invest more than it has received from depositors; it can lend only about nine-tenths as much.

11. But while no bank alone can expand its reserves 10 to 1, the banking system as a whole can. The first individual bank receiving a new $1000 of deposits lends nine-tenths of its newly acquired cash on loans and investments. This gives a second group of banks nine-tenths of $1000 in new deposits. They, in turn, keep one-tenth in reserves and lend the other nine-tenths on new earning assets; this causes them to lose cash to a third set of banks, whose deposits have gone up by nine-tenths of nine-tenths of $1000. If we follow through the successive groups of banks in the dwindling, never-ending chain, we find for the system as a whole new deposits of

$$\$1000 + \$900 + \$810 + \$729 + \cdots = \$1000 \times [1 + \tfrac{9}{10} + (\tfrac{9}{10})^2 + (\tfrac{9}{10})^3 + \cdots]$$

$$= \$1000 \left(\frac{1}{1 - \tfrac{9}{10}} \right) = \$1000 \left(\frac{1}{0.1} \right)$$

$$= \$10,000$$

12. Only when each $1 of the new reserves retained in the banking system ends up supporting $10 of deposits somewhere in the system will the limits to deposit expansion be reached. Then the system is loaned up; it can create no further deposits until it is given more reserves. The 10-to-1 ratio of increased bank money to increased reserves is called the money-supply multiplier.

13. As a qualification to the above discussion, we must note that there will be some leakage of the new cash reserves of the banking system into circulation outside the banks (indeed, some will go abroad or underground) and into assets other than checking accounts. Therefore, instead of $10,000 of new checking deposits created, as in the previous examples, we may have something less than that—the difference being due to what is withdrawn from the system.

A second qualification results from the fact that a bank may keep excess reserves above the legally required reserves. Excess reserves crop up when the interest rate on reserves is close to that on safe investments. So there is nothing automatic about the money-supply multiplier of 10 to 1 or whatever.

CONCEPTS FOR REVIEW

barter
commodity M, paper M, bank M
coins, paper currency, checking
  accounts
M_1, M_2
reserves (vault cash and deposits with
  Fed)
money's functions
financial intermediaries

motives for money demand: transactions
  demand, asset demand
interest as opportunity cost of holding
  money
money-supply multiplier
goldsmiths and 100% reserves
fractional-reserve banking
legal reserve requirements
chain of generations of banks

QUESTIONS FOR DISCUSSION

1. Define M_1 and M_2. What is included in M_1? What is in M_2 but not M_1? Relate each of the components of M_2 to the factors lying behind the demand for money.

2. List and describe stages of money from barter to bank money. Describe how a typical transaction might occur at each stage. What institutions or laws would be necessary to pass from one stage to the next?

3. Suppose that all banks kept 100 percent reserves. Construct Tables 11-5(a) and 11-7 when $1000 of reserves is added to a banking system that keeps 100 percent reserves. What is the net effect of a reserve addition to the money supply in this case? Do banks ''create'' money?

4. Suppose that banks hold 20 percent of deposits as reserves and that $200 of reserves is *subtracted* from the banking system. Redo Tables 11-5(a) through 11-7. What is the money-supply multiplier in this case? Calculate the money-supply multiplier in a second way by the technique shown in footnote 6.

5. What would be the effect on the demand for money (M_1) of each of the following (holding other things equal):

    (a) An increase in real GNP

    (b) An increase in the price level

    (c) A rise in the interest rate on savings accounts and Treasury securities

    (d) Allowing banks to pay interest on checking deposits

    (e) Doubling all prices, wages, and incomes

[For (e), can you calculate exactly the effect on the demand for money?]

6. In 1937, hoping to increase M, the Federal Reserve provided reserves to banks. Because interest rates were so low (around $\frac{1}{8}$ of 1 percent), excess reserves increased sharply and the money supply hardly changed at all. Explain why low interest rates encourage excess reserves, while high interest rates discourage excess reserves. Explain why changes in reserves might not be tightly linked to money-supply changes when interest rates are near zero.

7. Monetary reformers sometimes propose paying banks market interest rates on reserves. What would the effect of this proposal be on the level of excess reserves? On the level and stability of the money-supply multiplier?

8. Explain whether you think that each of the following should be counted as part of the narrow money supply (M_1) in the United States: traveler's checks, savings accounts, subway tokens, postage stamps, credit-card balances, Mexican pesos.

9. Suppose reserve requirements were abolished. What would determine the level of reserves in the banking system? What would happen to the money-supply multiplier in this situation?

10. Suppose that one giant bank, the Humongous Bank of America, held all the checking deposits of all the people, subject to a 10 percent legal reserve requirement. If there were an injection of reserves into the economy, could the Humongous Bank lend out more than 90 percent of the deposit addition, knowing that the new deposit must come back to it? Would this change the ultimate money-supply multiplier?

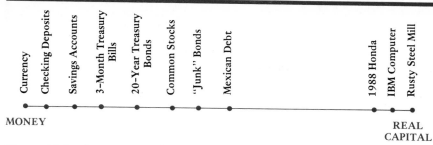

Figure 11-4   A spectrum of assets from money to capital

11. This chapter defines money as an object generally accepted and used as a medium of exchange. Over time, the objects used as money have evolved, and it may be difficult to identify a unique object as "the money supply." Today, assets have differing degrees of "moneyness" depending upon whether they are actually accepted as means of payment and upon the speed with which they can be converted into cash. Consider Figure 11-4's spectrum of assets from money to real capital goods. Where does the Federal Reserve draw the line between money (M_1) and other assets? Where would you draw the line? Devise some new assets and place them on the spectrum.

12. "Because the ratio of reserves to the total of all credit (to the total of D) is very much less than 10 percent, each \$1 of new central bank reserves in effect can create much more than \$10 of new D." Explain why this is true.

13. Advanced problem: Suppose the public always holds $\frac{1}{21}$ of its M in currency and $\frac{20}{21}$ in demand deposits. Then if banks always keep $\frac{1}{10}$ of reserves against their demand deposits, verify that each R of new reserves gives rise to total M as follows:

$$ M = \left(\frac{1}{\frac{1}{21} + \frac{1}{10}\frac{20}{21}} \right) R = \frac{21}{3} R = 7R; \quad \text{deposits} = \frac{20}{21}\frac{21}{3} R = 6\frac{2}{3}R; \quad \text{currency} = \frac{1}{3}R $$

14. Advanced problem: Before the Federal Reserve was in place, gold constituted the bulk of bank reserves. Gold supplies were fixed in the short run. From time to time, people would desire to convert their deposits into currency. Explain why this would lead to difficulties if gold reserves are fixed. Why might it lead to a "banking crisis"? What could be done to cure these crises?

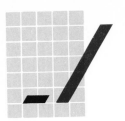

APPENDIX: 11
Stock Market Fluctuations

In the main part of this chapter we examined the nature of money. This asset will be the focus of our attention in subsequent chapters because changing the money supply is the major method by which government monetary policies affect the economy. But households hold assets other than money. Table 11A-1 shows the way households invested their assets in the years 1963 and 1986.

One of the most fascinating assets owned by households is common stocks (or corporate equities). These volatile securities take part in a daily drama in which people's fortunes are made and lost overnight. The 1980s demonstrated well the perils of "playing the market." Beginning in 1982, the stock market surged upward steadily for 5 years, gaining almost 300 percent. Great fortunes were made by those who had the luck or vision to put all their assets into stocks. Then the market peaked in the summer of 1987. In a single day, the "black Monday" of October 19, 1987, the stock market lost 22 percent of its value in 6 hours. The shock to securities markets was a vivid reminder of the risks you take when you invest in stocks.

In this appendix we explore modern theories of the behavior of the stock market. A **stock market** is a place where the shares in publicly owned companies, the titles to American capitalism, are bought and sold. In a recent year, these titles might be worth $1.5 trillion; sales in a single year might total $900 billion. The stock market is the hub of our corporate economy.

The New York Stock Exchange is the main stock market, listing more than a thousand securities. The smaller American Stock Exchange began when brokers met on the street to buy and sell, giving hand signals to the clerks hanging out the windows to record the transactions, and only in the twentieth century did the American Stock Exchange move indoors.

Every large financial center has its stock exchange. Important ones are in Tokyo, London, Frankfurt, Hong Kong, Toronto, and Zurich. More than any other single feature, the stock exchange is the essence of capitalism. Under capitalism, the means of production are privately owned; the stock markets are the places where the ownership rights to these means of production are traded.

Who owns American capitalism? Radicals of the left portray a world in which a handful of super-rich hoard shares like the king in his counting house. At the other extreme is the myth of "people's capitalism," put forth by the New York Stock Exchange; in this dreamworld, everyone owns stock and will vote to protect private property and the interest of capital.

The reality lies somewhere in between. True, 35 million Americans own some stocks. True, 3 million people with incomes less than $10,000 are shareowners. But the fraction of shares owned by the poor is minuscule. Over 50 percent of the value of shares directly held by persons is owned by the top 1 percent of wealthholders. In 1981, the average amount of dividends received by households with income less than $10,000 was $80 per person.

FINANCIAL ASSETS OF HOUSEHOLDS

CLASS OF ASSET	PERCENT OF TOTAL ASSETS IN EACH CLASS	
	1963	1986
Dollar-denominated		
Currency and checking deposits (M_1)	4.6	4.7
Savings accounts	14.3	21.9
Government securities	6.4	7.3
Other	3.3	2.8
Equity in businesses		
Corporate	31.3	20.5
Noncorporate	25.7	22.3
Pension fund and life insurance reserves	13.4	18.8
Other	1.0	1.8
Total	100.0	100.0
Item: Total assets of households (billions)	$1,641	$10,785

Table 11A-1   Savings accounts and corporate equities (common stocks) are the most popular assets

This table shows how the holdings of households were divided among different assets in 1963 and 1986. Note that the share of equities fell sharply, while pension funds and savings accounts rose markedly. (Source: Federal Reserve System.)

THE GREAT CRASH

A study of stock exchanges and financial markets relies upon both economic analysis and a careful reading of the lessons of history. One traumatic event has cast a shadow over stock markets for decades—the 1929 panic and crash in Wall Street. This event ushered in the long and painful Great Depression of the 1930s.

The "roaring twenties" saw a fabulous stock market boom, when everyone bought and sold stocks. Most purchases in this wild "bull" market (one with rising prices) were "on margin"; i.e., the buyer of $10,000 worth of stocks had to put up only $2500 or less in cash and borrowed the difference, pledging the newly bought stocks as collateral for the new purchases. What did it matter that you had to pay the broker 6, 10, or 15 percent per year on the borrowings when, in one day, Auburn Motors or Bethlehem Steel might jump 10 percent in value!

The most wonderful thing about a speculative mania is that it fulfills its own promises. If people buy because they think stocks will rise, their act of buying sends up the price of stocks. This causes people to buy still further and sends the dizzy dance off on another round. But, unlike people who play cards or dice, no one loses what the winners gain. Everybody gets a prize. Of course, the prizes are all on paper and would

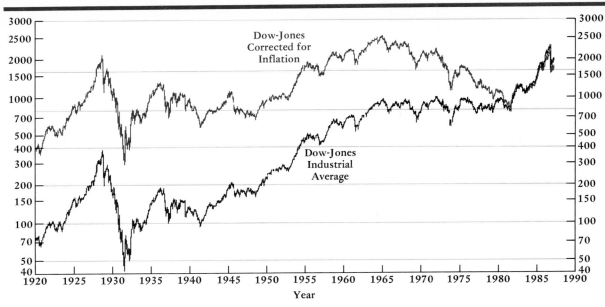

Figure 11A-1   The only guarantee about stock prices is that they will fluctuate

Stock prices in nominal terms, shown in the bottom line, tend to rise with inflation. The Dow-Jones Industrial Average (DJIA) shown here tracks the prices of 30 blue-chip (safe and stable) companies, and that average has risen almost 40-fold since the early 1920s.

The top line shows the "real Dow-Jones," which is the conventional DJIA corrected for movements in the consumer price index. The all-time high came in January 1966, and by year-end 1988 real stock prices were still below the pre-Depression peak of 1929. (Source: *The Media General Financial Weekly,* updated by authors.)

disappear if everyone tried to cash them in. But why should anyone wish to sell such lucrative securities?

The great stock market boom of the 1920s was a classic speculative bubble. Here prices were rising because of hopes and dreams, not because the profits and dividends of companies were soaring. Eventually, like all bubbles, it burst and the crash began in "black October" of 1929. Everyone was caught, the big-league professionals and the piddling amateurs—Andrew Mellon, John D. Rockefeller, the engineer-turned-President in the White House, and Yale's great economics professor Irving Fisher.

When the bottom fell out of the market in 1929, those investors who bought on margin could not put up funds to cover their holdings and the market fell still further. The bull market turned into a "bear" (or declining) market. By the trough of the Depression in 1933, the market had lost 85 percent of its 1929 value.

Finally, after the banking crisis of 1933, the stock market began to recover. Figure 11A-1 shows the history of the well-known Dow-Jones Industrial Average (a stock index that tracks the average price of 30 high-grade stocks) from 1920 to 1988. Note that the stock market did not recover to its 1929 level until 1955.[1]

---

[1] A detailed account of the role of the stock market in the Great Depression is provided in John Kenneth Galbraith, *The Great Crash, 1929* (Avon, New York, 1980); and C. P. Kindleberger, *Manias, Panics, and Crashes* (Basic Books, New York, 1980).

After World War II, the stock market climbed sharply, although every few years saw major downturns, often associated with recessions. In real (or inflation-corrected) terms, the market hit an all-time high in 1966, but then failed to keep up with inflation during the next decade. The pro-business Reagan years witnessed a dramatic bull market. By the summer of 1987, real stock prices again attained the level of 1929. Then a sharp "correction" occurred with the market meltdown of October 19, 1987, pushing stock prices down 22 percent and sending a jolt of fear through stock markets around the world.

Where will it all end? Is there a crystal ball that will foretell the movement of stock prices? This is the subject of modern finance theory.

THE EFFICIENT-MARKET THEORY

Economists and finance professors have long studied prices in speculative markets, like the stock market or markets for commodities such as corn. Their findings have stirred great controversy and have even angered many financial analysts. Here is an area where the facts have largely corroborated the theories. Today, practical investors pay heed, and more, to the professors of finance.

The ideas developed in this area are today grouped under the heading of the **efficient-market theory.**[2] There are many ways of seeing the basic point. One way of expressing the fundamental theory is:

> You can't outguess the market. There are no easy pickings.

We'll see in a minute *why* this proposition is plausible. For the moment, however, turn to its factual basis. There have been numerous studies over the years about rules or formulas for making money. A typical rule is "buy after two days of increases" or "buy on the bad news and sell on the good news." An early study by Alfred Cowles investigated the recommendations of stockbrokers. He examined different brokers' performance—i.e., the return (in dollars of total income per year per dollar invested) on stocks selected by the stockbrokers under examination. He found that, on average, the stockbrokers' stocks did no better than a random "portfolio" (or combination) of stocks. This led to the "dart board theory" of stock selection:

> You can throw a dart at the *Wall Street Journal* as a way of selecting stocks. Better still, buy a little of everything in the market, so that you hold a diversified "index" portfolio of the stock market. This would probably leave you better off than your cousin who follows a broker's advice. Why? Because he would have to pay more broker's commissions and his stocks would on average not outperform yours.

This pessimistic view of the ability of formulas to outperform the market has been generally confirmed in hundreds of studies over the last four decades. Their lesson is not that you will never become rich by following a rule or formula, but that, on average, such rules cannot outperform a randomly selected and diversified portfolio of stocks.

---

[2]"Efficiency" in finance theory here is used differently from in other parts of economics. Here, efficiency means that information is quickly absorbed, not that resources produce the maximal outputs.

Rationale for the Efficient-Market View

Modern finance theory has spent many years analyzing stock and bond markets in order to understand why such a puzzling result might hold. Is there a *reason* why well-functioning financial markets might rule out persistent excess profits? According to the theory of efficient markets, the answer is, Yes.

An efficient market is one where all new information is quickly understood by market participants and becomes immediately incorporated into market prices. For example, say that Lazy-T Oil Company has just struck oil in the Gulf of Alaska. This is announced at 11:30 A.M. on Tuesday. When will the price of Lazy-T's shares rise? Wednesday morning after J. R. Ewing has read the *Wall Street Journal?* Or perhaps after lunch on Tuesday, when the stock analysts have had time to chew it over a bit? Or perhaps a week later, after Grandpa has placed his order to his St. Louis broker?

No, says the efficient-market theory. The news will be at once incorporated into prices. The market participants will react immediately, bidding the price of Lazy-T up by the correct amount. In short, at every point in time, markets have already digested and included in stock prices or corn prices or other speculative prices all the latest available information.

Anything that was announced yesterday is already stale. If you read in the newspaper that a heavy frost in Florida has decimated the orange crop, don't think that you can enrich yourself by buying frozen orange juice futures during your lunch break. The orange juice price went up the minute the news was reported, or even earlier.[3]

The theory of efficient markets holds that market prices contain all available information. It is not possible to make profits by looking at old information or at patterns of past price changes.

A Random Walk

The efficient-market view provides an important way of analyzing price movements in organized markets. Under this approach, the price movements of stocks should look highly erratic, like a random walk, when charted over a period of time.

A price follows a *random walk* when its movements over time are completely unpredictable. For example, toss a coin for heads or tails. Call a head "plus 1" and a tail "minus 1." Then keep track of the running score of 100 coin tosses. Draw it on graph paper. This curve is a random walk. Now for comparison also graph 100 days' movement of IBM stock or of the Dow-Jones Average. Note how similar all three figures appear.

What is the reason for this resemblance of speculative prices to a random walk? Merely a coincidence? No. Economists, on reflection, have come to realize the following truths:

In an efficient market all predictable things have already been built into the price. It is the arrival of *new* news—a freeze in Florida, war in the Persian Gulf, a report that the Federal Reserve has tightened the money supply—that affects stock or commodity

---

[3]Scholars have attempted to measure the speed of price adjustment in such efficient markets. One study found that, if you were willing to put up $100,000, you could make a profit only if you bought stocks within 30 seconds after the information became public.

prices. And the news must be random and unpredictable (or else it would be predictable and therefore not true news).

Is Randomness Rational?

Many people complain that the stock market is nothing more than an enormous casino. Little is accomplished there, critics say. One point in favor of such a viewpoint is that stock prices are so erratic. And there is a good question here: How *could* a rational market behave so erratically?

The answer to this is one of the deepest theories of modern economics. The efficient-market theory states that the prices in a well-functioning speculative market like the stock market should move randomly!

The efficient-market theory explains why movements in stock prices look so erratic. Prices respond to news, to surprises. But surprises are unpredictable events—like the flip of a coin or next month's rainstorm—that may move in any direction. Because stock prices move in response to erratic events, stock prices themselves move erratically, like a random walk.

One point should be reinforced here. The role of news in stock prices suggests why you cannot beat the market. In trying to beat the market, you are trying to forecast the future; even worse, you are trying to forecast the unpredictable events in the future. Little wonder then that stock market forecasts are inherently so unreliable when the events to be forecasted are unpredictable.

Objections

There are four important objections to the efficient-market view of markets.

▪ Suppose everybody accepts the efficient-market philosophy and stops trying to digest information quickly. If everyone accepts that stock prices are correctly valued, then will those prices *stop* being right?

A good question. The point is, everybody won't quit. Indeed, the minute too many people stopped looking ahead, the market would cease being efficient. You'd start to be able to then make profits by acting on old information. So the efficient market is a stable, self-monitoring equilibrium state.

▪ Some people are quicker and smarter than others. Some have much money to spend on digging for information to narrow down the odds on the uncertain future. Doesn't it stand to reason that they'll make higher profits?

Remember, however, there are many such people competing against each other. Donald Trump can buy the best investment counsel there is. But so can the Basses. And the Ford Foundation. And First Bank of Boston. And so on. It is competition that provides the checks and balances of efficiency and ensures minimal excess profits.

Moreover, the efficient-market theory does suggest that a few people with special flair and skills will permanently earn high returns on their skills—just as great quarterbacks and sopranos do. They're hard to identify. When you find them, you must pay them what economists call their "competitive rents." (See Chapter 27.) If you have a flair for spotting such people, *you* will also get a juicy competitive rent.

The point is that competition grinds fine. There are indeed no easy pickings in a well-trodden field.

▪ Economists who look at the historical record ask whether it is plausible that sharp movements in stock prices could actually reflect new information. Consider the 30 percent drop in the stock market from October 15 to October 19, 1987. The efficient-market view would hold that this drop was caused by economic events that depressed the value of future corporate earnings. What were those events? James Tobin, Yale's Nobel Prize–winning economist, commented, ''There are no visible factors that could make a 30 percent difference in the value of stock [prices over these four days].'' Efficient-market theorists fall silent before this criticism.

▪ Finally, the efficient-market view applies to individual stocks but not necessarily to the entire market. Some economists (such as James Poterba and Lawrence Summers) have found evidence of long, self-reversing swings in stock market prices, and others believe that these swings reflect changes in the general mood of the financial community. These long-term swings may lie behind the boom psychology of the 1920s and 1980s or the depression mentality of the 1930s.

Let us say that we believed that the whole stock market was too high in 1987 or too low in 1931. What could we do? We could not individually buy or sell enough stocks to overcome the entire national mood. So, from a macroeconomic perspective, speculative markets *can* exhibit waves of pessimism or optimism without powerful economic forces moving in to correct these swings of mood.

INVESTMENT STRATEGIES

Don't preach this doctrine of the efficient market to your cousin in the securities business. Few in that industry are willing to accept the view that ''passive investment strategies, '' simply buying a share of the market, are the best approach. Some institutions, however, insist upon a passive approach, and some banks, such as Wells Fargo in San Francisco, have adopted this philosophy and now invest billions of dollars in passive accounts.

What are the lessons of the many studies of the behavior of financial markets and investment advisers? A few lessons can be gleaned from the record:[4]

▪ Be skeptical of approaches that claim to have found the quick route to success. You can't get rich by consulting the stars (although, unbelievably, some investment advisers push astrology on their clients). Hunches work out to nothing in the long run. Some advisers, called chartists, claim to see patterns in price movements: ''resistance levels,'' ''head and shoulders,'' and ''pennants.'' Those who have studied the performance of chartism say, ''The chartists generally end up with holes in their shoes. So forget it.''

▪ The best brains in Wall Street rarely do as well as the averages (the Dow-Jones, Standard & Poor's, etc.). We've seen why, on reflection, this is not so surprising. True, the big money managers have all the money needed for any kind of research and digging. But remember, they are all competing with one another.

[4]For amusing, but well-informed, accounts of the modern stock market, the reader might refer to Burton G. Malkiel, *A Random Walk Down Wall Street,* 4th ed. (Norton, New York, 1985).

If there is a bargain for one to see, it is also there for another, and it will already have been wiped out by competitive bidding in efficient markets.

▪ If you want to achieve a good return with the least possible risk, your best bet is to buy a broadly diversified mutual fund of common stocks. You might buy an "index fund," which is a fixed portfolio of stocks with minimal management and brokerage fees. And you might combine this with some diversified bonds or savings accounts. Over the longer run, you will probably earn a return of a few percentage points per year above inflation. But not much more can be said.

▪ You can also increase your expected return if you are willing to bear greater risks. Some stocks are inherently riskier than others. By investing in more cyclical stocks, in ones that move up and down relatively more than the market as a whole, and in small companies, you can on average beat the market. But beware: When the market goes down, you will generally suffer worse-than-average losses in these riskier stocks.

▪ If after reading all this you still want to try your hand in the stock market, be not daunted. But take to heart the caution of one of America's great financiers, Bernard Baruch:

> If you are ready to give up everything else—to study the whole history and background of the market and all the principal companies whose stocks are on the board as carefully as a medical student studies anatomy—if you can do all that, and, in addition, you have the cool nerves of a great gambler, the sixth sense of a kind of clairvoyant, and the courage of a lion, you have a ghost of a chance.

SUMMARY TO APPENDIX

1. Stock markets, of which the New York Stock Exchange is the most important, are places where titles of ownership to the largest companies are bought and sold. The history of stock prices is filled with violent gyrations, such as the Great Crash of 1929. Trends are tracked by the use of stock-price indices, such as the familiar Dow-Jones Industrial Average.

2. Modern economic theories of stock prices generally focus on the role of efficient markets. An efficient market is one in which all information gets quickly absorbed by speculators and is immediately built into market prices. In efficient markets, there are no easy profits; looking at stale news or past patterns of prices or elections or business cycles will not help predict future price movements.

3. Thus, in efficient markets, prices move in response to news, to surprises. Because surprises are inherently random, stock prices and other speculative prices move erratically, as in a random walk.

CONCEPTS FOR REVIEW

New York Stock Exchange
common stocks (corporate equities)
Dow-Jones stock index
efficient market

random walk of stock prices
mutual fund, index fund, passive
  strategies
news, stale information, and speculative
  prices

QUESTIONS FOR DISCUSSION

1. According to the efficient-market theory, what effect would the following events have on the price of GM's stock:

(a) A surprise announcement that the government was going to undertake a new program to contract the economy by raising taxes on next July 1

(b) An increase in tax rates on July 1, six months after Congress had passed the enabling legislation

(c) An announcement, unexpected by experts, that the United States was imposing quotas on imports of Japanese cars for the coming year

(d) Implementation of (c) by issuing regulations on December 31

2. Pick a group of 10 or so of your classmates. Each of you should write down a formula for successful gains in the stock market. Then keep careful track of the performance of each person's rule. Compare the performance of your rules to a broad stock-price average over the same period (the Dow-Jones or the Standard & Poor's 500). How did the rules do relative to the averages?

3. One economist commented as follows on the sharp drop in stock prices during October 1987: "There have been no events over the last few days that can rationally explain the selling frenzy during 'black October.' News about inflation, the trade balance, the budget deficit, or events in the Persian Gulf can be indicted for no more than a few dozen points of the 509 point decline in the Dow-Jones." Explain how this quotation relates to the efficient-market hypothesis. If you agree with this quotation, what would you conclude about the validity of that hypothesis?

4. Flip a coin 100 times. Count a head as "plus 1" and a tail as "minus 1." Keep a running score of the total. Plot it on a graph paper. This is a random walk. (Those with access to a computer can do this using a computer program, a random-number generator, and a plotter.)

Next, keep track of the closing price of the stock of your favorite company for a few weeks (or get it from past issues of the newspaper). Plot the price against time. Can you see any difference in the pattern of changes? Do both look like random walks?

CHAPTER 12____
THE FEDERAL RESERVE AND CENTRAL BANK MONETARY POLICY

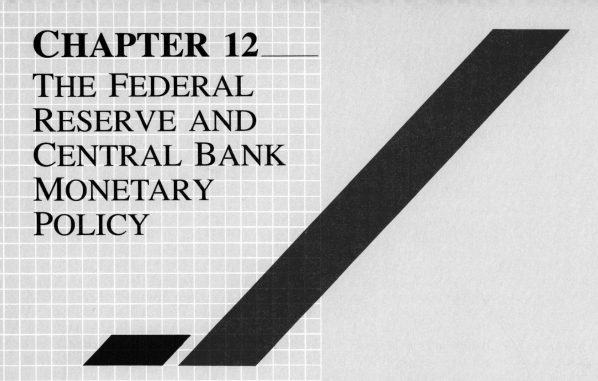

There have been three great inventions since the beginning of time: fire, the wheel, and central banking.

Will Rogers

THE LAST CHAPTER reviewed the functions of money along with the reasons why people hold money. It then began a discussion of the supply of money by seeing how goldsmith banks evolved into modern fractional-reserve commercial banks that literally create money from reserves.

The present chapter continues the discussion of the money supply by analyzing the nature of interest rates and the tasks of central banking. The Federal Reserve System, which is the United States' central bank, is a banker's bank. Its primary function is to control the supply of bank reserves and thereby to regulate the nation's money supply and determine the level of interest rates.

The Federal Reserve's goals are steady growth in national output and low unemployment. Its sworn enemy is inflation. If aggregate demand is excessive, so that prices are being bid up, the Federal Reserve Board may want to slow the growth of the money supply, thereby slowing aggregate demand and output growth. If unemployment is high and business languishing, the Fed may consider increasing the money supply, thereby raising aggregate demand and augmenting output growth.

In a nutshell, this is the function of central banking,

257

which is an essential part of macroeconomic management in all mixed economies.

HOW MONETARY POLICY WORKS TO CONTROL SPENDING

Before we begin our discussion of the exact steps by which the Federal Reserve (often called ''the Fed'') expands or contracts money and credit, we pause to consider the process by which the central bank affects aggregate demand and thereby output and prices. For concreteness, let us assume that the Federal Reserve is concerned about growing inflationary trends. It wishes to slow down the economy and relieve upward pressures on wages and prices. There are five steps in the process.

1. *In the first step, the Fed will need to reduce bank reserves.* Reducing bank reserves will eventually lead to a reduction in the money supply, to higher interest rates, and to an economic slowdown. We will see in this chapter that the Fed changes bank reserves primarily by buying and selling government securities in the open market.

2. *Each dollar reduction in bank reserves produces a multiple contraction in checking deposits, thereby reducing the money supply.* This step was described in the last chapter, where it was shown that changes in reserves lead to a multiplied change in deposits. Since the money supply equals currency plus checking deposits, the reduction in checking deposits reduces the money supply.

3. *The reduction in the money supply will tend to increase the level of interest rates and tighten credit conditions.* Put differently, with a reduced supply of money, the price of money (which is the interest rate) will tend to increase. The amount of credit (loans and borrowing) available to people will be reduced.

Interest rates will rise for mortgage borrowers (builders and home buyers) and for businesses that want to build factories, buy new equipment, or add to inventory. Higher interest rates will also lower the values of people's assets: their bonds, stocks, land, homes, etc. The combination of higher interest rates and reduced wealth will surely discourage many people or businesses who want to borrow to finance their spending.

4. *With higher interest rates and lower wealth, private and public spending—especially investment—will tend to fall.* Why will aggregate demand decline? It does so because people's decisions as to whether it is profitable to build a new plant, order a new machine, and hold more inventory depend on the rate of interest. If they have to pay a high interest rate or find it hard to get loans, they often scale down their investment plans. The same holds for state and local governments. The new road does not get built and the new school gets postponed when a town finds it cannot float its bonds at any reasonable rate. Similarly, consumers decide to buy a smaller house, or to renovate their existing one, when rising mortgage interest rates make monthly payments high relative to monthly income. And in an economy increasingly open to international trade, higher interest rates may raise the foreign exchange rate of the dollar, depressing net exports.

To repeat, a decline in the supply of money will tend to raise interest rates and reduce those components of aggregate demand that are sensitive to interest rates.

5. *Finally, the pressures of tight money, reducing aggregate demand, will reduce income, output, jobs, and inflation.* The aggregate supply-and-demand (or, equivalently, the multiplier) analysis showed how such a drop in investment may depress output and employment sharply. Furthermore, as output and employment fall below the levels that would otherwise occur, prices tend to rise less rapidly or even to fall. Inflationary forces subside. If the Fed's diagnosis of inflationary conditions was on target, the drop in output and the rise in unemployment will help relieve inflationary forces.

Recapitulation

This five-step sequence—from the Fed's changing the commercial banks' reserves, to a multiple change in total M, to changes in interest rates and credit availability, to changes in private and public investment

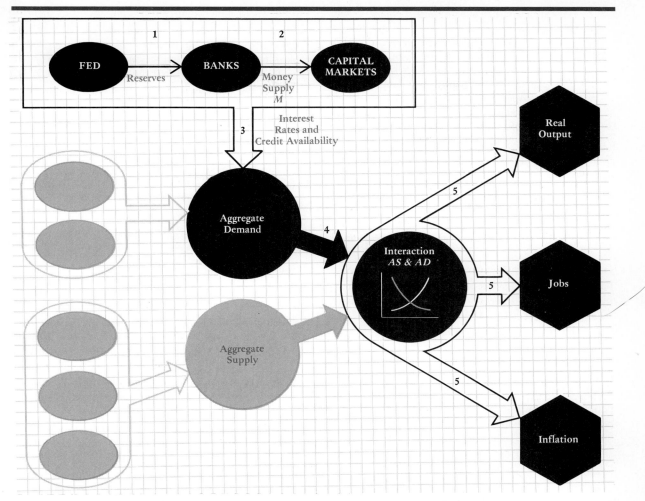

Figure 12-1   A bird's-eye view of how monetary policy affects output and inflation

This diagram shows graphically the steps by which Fed policy affects economic activity. Step 1 is a change in reserves, leading to: step 2, a change in M, leading to: step 3, changes in interest rates and credit conditions. In step 4, AD is changed by a response of interest-sensitive spending. In step 5, changes in output, employment, and inflation follow.

Remember, however, that monetary policy is not the only influence: Fiscal policy enters into the crucial step 4, feeding into the aggregate demand circle.

spending shifting aggregate demand, and finally to the response of lower output, employment, and inflation—is vital.

As a way of deepening your understanding of the monetary mechanism, think through the opposite case of a monetary expansion:

Suppose you are the reigning Chairman of the Fed's Board of Governors at a time when the economy is depressed. You are called to testify before a congressional committee—as a Fed Chairman so often is. Explain to an interrogating senator just how your expansionary acts would operate. Retrace these detailed steps:

The Fed expands reserves; banks then engineer a multiple expansion in checking deposits; an increase in the nation's M is associated with "easier money conditions," i.e., lower interest rates on loans, bonds, and mortgages, and easier credit. All this results in an increase in spending on interest-sensitive items like housing, business investment, and net exports. Consumption also rises in response to the higher income, as the multiplier turns on, so output increases and unemployment falls. Prices firm a bit, and inflation may begin to increase.

Figure 12-1 drives home the sequence by showing the box containing the Fed, the banks, and capital markets in which interest rates and credit availability are determined. This expanded monetary box then links up with our familiar flow diagram to show how M ultimately affects output and inflation.

Be sure you can follow the steps from the far left (where the Fed initiates changes in reserves) to the far right (where real GNP, the rate of unemployment, and inflation are affected by monetary policy).

We now continue our analysis of money and banking. The first section of this chapter analyzes the nature of interest rates, which are sometimes called "the price of money." The second section then analyzes in detail the functioning of the Federal Reserve System.

A. THE NATURE OF INTEREST RATES

Our discussion of the workings of monetary policy has on several occasions alluded to the impact of the money supply on interest rates. What exactly do we mean by interest rates? This section surveys the most important interest-rate concepts.

The primary point is the following: Interest is the payment made for the use of funds. The **interest rate** is the amount of interest paid per unit of time. In other words, in return for the opportunity to borrow funds, people must pay a certain annual amount. The cost of borrowing funds, measured in dollars per year per dollar borrowed, is the interest rate.

Some examples will illustrate how interest works.

▪ When you graduate from college you have $500 to your name. You decide to keep it in currency. If you spend none of your funds, at the end of a year you still have $500 because currency has a zero interest rate.

▪ You place $2000 in a savings account in your local bank, where the interest rate on savings accounts is 5 percent per year. At the end of 1 year, your savings have grown by $100 of interest to $2100.

▪ You land a job with an Atlanta company and need a new car to live there. You need $10,000 to finance your car and will be able to pay it back in a year. Your company offers you a short-term loan at 12 percent per year. You therefore must pay interest of $100 per month (or $1200 per year) and repay the principal of $10,000 at the end of the year.

▪ After a few months in Atlanta, you find a small house to purchase and settle on a price of $100,000. You go to your local bank and find that 30-year, fixed-interest-rate mortgages have an interest rate of 10 percent per year. Each month you make a mortgage payment of $877.58. Note that this payment is a little bit more than the pro-rated monthly interest charge of $\frac{10}{12}$ percent per month. Why so? Because it includes not only interest but also *amortization,* which consists of repayments of *principal,* which denotes the amount borrowed. By the time you have made your 360 monthly payments, you will have completely paid off the loan.

A few facets of interest rates should be appreciated. Note that the interest rate has the dimension of a pure ratio per year, that is, dollars paid per year per dollar borrowed. Read back through the examples just given. You will see that in each case the interest rate was measured as dollars of interest per year per dollar borrowed. Whether in America, Japan, or Europe, interest rates are quoted in terms of money paid back for money borrowed, in percent per year.

You might wonder, Why should anyone pay interest? After all, the person who is lending the money is not doing any work and is simply making the funds available. Indeed, money is just paper and does not even have gold or silver to back it up.

The reasons that the market interest rate is not zero but a positive number are profound and relate not to money but to the real resources that money makes available. Recall that money is the medium of exchange, the instrument with which we buy everything that markets have to offer. When you borrow money, you borrow the right to buy goods, services, capital, land, oil, robots, and the vast array of marketed commodities. Once you acquire such commodities, you can satisfy a craving for consumption. Alternatively, you can buy an investment good that has a high yield in future goods and services. It is the rewards from consumption or investment that induce people to pay interest on borrowed funds.

For example, you might choose to borrow funds from a bank to insulate the attic in your new house. Say that you borrow $1000 at an interest rate of 10 percent per year for an annual payment of $100 (ignoring amortization for this calculation). At the end of the year, a careful check of your fuel bills shows that you have saved $200 over the year. This was clearly a wise investment and shows that your decision to borrow funds, even at an interest rate of 10 percent per year, was prudent.

An Array of Interest Rates

Textbooks often speak of "the interest rate," but a glance at the *Wall Street Journal* or at the financial pages of the newspaper reveals a bewildering array of interest rates in today's complex financial system. There are indeed many varieties of interest rates, but they differ mainly in terms of the characteristics of the loan or of the borrower. Let us review the major differences.

1. *Term or maturity*. Loans differ in their term or maturity, that is, the length of time until they must be paid off. The shortest loans are overnight, such as when a bank lends to an importer who expects to collect on a shipment the next day. Short-term securities are for periods up to a year. Companies often float bonds that have maturities of 10 to 30 years, and mortgages are typically up to 30 years in maturity. Longer-term securities generally command a higher interest rate than do short-term issues because people are willing to sacrifice some yield to retain quick access to their funds.

2. *Risk*. Some loans are riskless while others are highly speculative, and investors require a premium to invest in risky ventures. At the safe end of the spectrum lie the securities of the U.S. government. These bonds and bills are backed by the full faith, credit, and taxing powers of the government. Nobody doubts that interest on the government debt will be paid. Intermediate in risk are borrowings of creditworthy corporations or of states and localities. Risky investments, which bear a significant chance of default or nonpayment, include those in companies close to bankruptcy, farmers with negative net worth, or Latin American countries with large overseas debts and little income with which to pay their debt service.

The U.S. government pays what is called the "riskless" interest rate, which over the last decade has ranged from 5 to 15 percent per year for short-term loans. Riskier securities might pay 1 or 2 or even 6 percent per year more than the riskless rate, with the premium reflecting the amount necessary to compensate the lender for aversion to risk or for the losses in case of default.

3. *Liquidity*. An asset is said to be "liquid" if it can be converted into cash quickly and with little loss in value. Most marketed securities, including common stocks and corporate and government bonds, can be turned quickly into cash at close to their current value—these are therefore highly liquid assets. Illiquid assets include unique assets for which no well-established market exists. If you own a house in a depressed region, you might find it difficult to sell the house quickly or at near its replacement cost. Similarly, it might be difficult to cash in on the full value of a small, privately owned computer-software company. The house and the computer company are illiquid assets. Because of the higher risk and the difficulty of extracting the borrower's investment, illiquid assets or loans usually command considerably higher interest rates than do liquid, riskless ones.

4. *Administrative costs*. Loans differ in terms of the time and diligence needed for their oversight and administration. Some loans simply require cashing interest checks periodically. Others, such as student loans or mortgages or credit-card advances, require ensuring timely payments and sometimes even mean that banks need to hire detectives to track down debt-

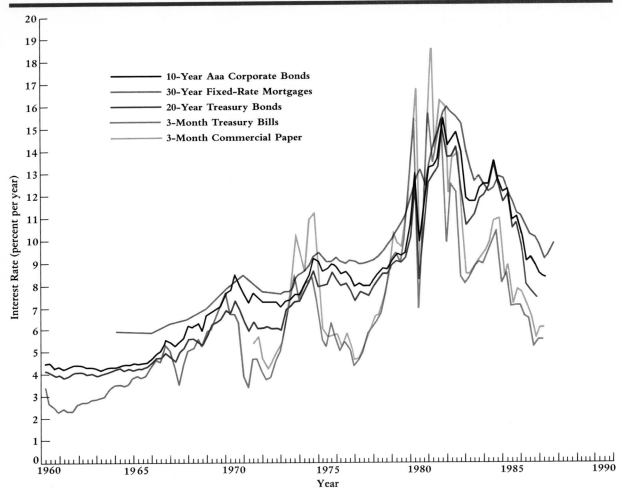

Figure 12-2 Most interest rates move together

This graph shows some of the major interest rates in the U.S. economy: those on government securities like short-term Treasury bills and long-term Treasury bonds, short-term corporate liabilities in commercial paper and long-term corporate borrowings in corporate bonds, and consumer debt for home mortgages. (Source: Federal Reserve System.)

ors or engage lawyers to attach people's wages. Those loans with high administrative costs may command interest rates from $\frac{1}{2}$ to 10 percent per year higher than other interest rates.

When these four factors are put together, it is not surprising that we see so many different financial instruments and so many different interest rates. Figure 12-2 shows the behavior of a few important interest

rates over the last decade. In what follows, when we speak of "the interest rate," this can be taken to be the interest rate on short-term government securities, such as the 90-day Treasury-bill rate. As Figure 12-2 shows, most other interest rates rise and fall in sympathy with the 3-month Treasury-bill rate although the premiums for risk and maturity vary from year to year.

Real vs. Nominal Interest Rates

Up to now we have spoken of interest rates in terms of the dollar returns on dollar loans. But what about inflation? Should we worry that when we get our money back, it might be worth relatively little because inflation has reduced the amount of real goods and services that our dollars can buy? The concepts of real and nominal interest rates allow us to answer these questions.

In the early 1980s, interest rates rose to levels that had not been seen since the Civil War. Short-term interest rates rose to nearly 20 percent, as compared to rates of less than 5 percent in the mid-1970s or even lower in the early 1960s. What was happening? Were investment opportunities arising at an accelerating rate? Was there a capital shortage? Did a large part of the capital stock get destroyed in a war?

None of these events lay behind the increase in interest rates. Rather, the measuring rod of money became severely distorted as inflation rates increased from near-zero in the early 1960s to over 10 percent in the 1979–1981 period.

Let us pursue the relationship between inflation and interest rates a bit further. Recall that interest is measured in dollar terms, not in terms of fish or cars or goods in general. The interest rate measures the yield in dollars per year per dollar invested. But dollars can become distorted yardsticks. The prices of fish or cars or goods in general change from year to year—these days their prices generally rise due to inflation.

Put differently, the interest rate on dollars does not measure what a lender really earns in terms of goods and services. Let us say that you lend $100 today at 5 percent per year interest. You would get back 105 dollar bills at the end of a year. But because prices changed over the year, you would not be able to obtain the same quantity of goods that you could have bought at the beginning of the year with the original $100.

Clearly, we need another concept of interest that measures the return on investments in terms of real goods and services rather than the return in terms of dollars. This alternative concept is called the real interest rate, which measures the quantity of goods we get tomorrow for goods forgone today. The real interest rate is obtained by correcting nominal or dollar interest rates for the rate of inflation.

You can understand the pitfalls of not making an inflation correction during periods of galloping inflation. In Brazil during the 1980s, interest rates often exceeded 100 percent a year. But you could not become rich in real goods and services by investing in Brazilian bonds, for inflation also exceeded 100 percent per year during this period.

Or to take the U.S. experience, say that in 1969 you invested $1000 for 20 years at a nominal interest rate of 5 percent. In this case, you would receive $2653 in 1989. Yet because the average inflation rate over that period was greater than the interest rate, the *real* value of your $2653 would be only $785 in 1969 prices. In other words, the real interest rate on your investment was negative during this period.

These examples emphasize the important concepts of the real and nominal interest rates. The **nominal interest rate** (sometimes also called the "money interest rate") is the interest rate on money in terms of money. When you read about interest rates in the newspaper, or examine interest rates in Figure 12-2, you are looking at nominal interest rates, for they give the dollar return per dollar of investment.

Nominal interest rates are contrasted with **real interest rates,** which are interest rates corrected for inflation and are defined as the nominal interest rate minus the rate of inflation. As an example, suppose the nominal interest rate is 13 percent per year and the inflation rate is 7 percent per year; we can calculate the real interest rate as $13 - 7 = 6$ percent per year. In other words, if you lend out 100 market baskets of goods today, you will next year get back only 106 (and not 113) market baskets of goods as principal and real interest payments.

During inflationary periods, we must use real interest rates, not nominal or money interest rates, to calculate the yield on investments in terms of goods earned per year on goods invested. The real interest rate is the nominal interest rate less the rate of inflation.

Recent Interest-Rate Movements The difference between nominal and real interest rates is illustrated in Figure 12-3. It shows that until 1980 the rise in

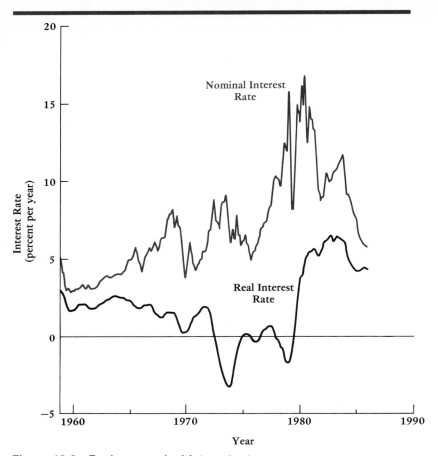

Figure 12-3 Real vs. nominal interest rates

This figure shows in red the nominal interest rates on safe short-term securities (1-year Treasury notes). Note their upward trend over the last 25 years. Most of the upward movement can be seen as the reflection of the increase in inflation. The black curve shows the real interest rate, equal to the nominal or money rate less the realized inflation rate over the prior year. Note that real interest rates drifted downward until 1980. After 1980, however, real interest rates have moved up sharply. (Source: Federal Reserve Board, U.S. Department of Labor.)

nominal interest rates was purely illusory, for nominal interest rates just kept up with inflation. After 1980, however, real interest rates rose sharply, from around zero in the late 1970s to around 5 percent per year in the early 1980s.

What was the reason for the jump in real interest rates? Most macroeconomists believe that the increase was due to a tightening of monetary policy—with the Fed contracting the money supply to combat

inflationary trends of that period much as was illustrated in the five-step sequence at the beginning of this chapter.

This concludes our survey of the important concepts concerning interest rates. In the next section we begin to understand the process by which the Federal Reserve regulates reserves and money with an eye to determining interest rates and affecting output, employment, and inflation.

B. CENTRAL BANKING

THE FEDERAL RESERVE SYSTEM

With this overview of the transmission mechanism by which the Fed affects economic activity, we turn to the first link of the chain. In this section we analyze how the Fed manipulates its instruments—reserves, the discount rate, and other tools—to determine the money supply.

Structure of the Federal Reserve

History The nineteenth century was plagued by banking panics. Panics occurred when people attempted to turn their bank deposits into currency. Because the supply of currency was fixed and smaller than the amount of bank deposits, there ensued bank failures and economic downturns. After the severe panic of 1907, agitation and discussion led to the creation of the Federal Reserve System in 1913.

Legally, the Federal Reserve System consists of 12 regional Federal Reserve Banks, located in major cities like New York, Chicago, Richmond, Dallas, and San Francisco. The sprawling regional structure was originally designed in a populist age to ensure that different areas would have a voice in banking matters and to avoid too great a concentration of central-banking powers in Washington or in the hands of the bankers of the eastern establishment. Each Federal Reserve Bank today manages bank operations and oversees banks in its region.

Who's in Charge? In spite of the formally dispersed structure of the Fed, close observers think that power is quite centralized. The Federal Reserve Board, joined at meetings by presidents of the 12 regional Federal Reserve Banks, operates under the Fed Chairman to formulate and carry out monetary policy. The informal structure of the Federal Reserve System is shown in Figure 12-4.

The core of the Federal Reserve is the *Board of Governors* of the Federal Reserve System, which consists of seven members nominated by the President and confirmed by the Senate to serve overlapping terms of 14 years. Members of the board are generally bankers or economists who work full time at the job; their long terms in office give them considerable independence in setting monetary policy.

The key decision-making body in the Federal Reserve System is the *Federal Open Market Committee (FOMC)*. The 12 voting members of the FOMC consist of the seven governors plus five of the presidents of the regional Federal Reserve Banks. This central group controls the single most important and frequently used tool of modern monetary policy—the supply of bank reserves.

At the pinnacle of the entire system is the *Chairman of the Board of Governors,* currently Alan Greenspan. He chairs the board and the FOMC, acts as public spokesman for the Fed, and exercises enormous power over both the style and substance of monetary policy. He is often, and accurately, called the "second most powerful man in America," reflecting the extent to which he can influence the entire economy through his impact on monetary policy.

Independence On examining the structure of the Fed, one might ask, "In which of the three branches of government does the Fed lie?" The answer is, "None. Legally, the 12 regional banks are private. In reality, the Fed as a whole behaves as an independent government agency."

Although nominally a corporation owned by the commercial banks that are members of the Federal Reserve System, the Federal Reserve is in fact a public agency. It is directly responsible to Congress; it listens carefully to the advice of the President; and whenever any conflict arises between its making a profit and the public interest, it acts unswervingly in the public interest. Because the Fed is allowed to print currency, in return for which it holds interest-bearing government securities, it earns billions of dollars of profits each year. But, to reflect its public mission, every penny of profit above a certain return goes to the U.S. government.

Above all, the Federal Reserve is an *independent* agency. It sets the course of monetary policy according to what it thinks best for the economy. While it listens carefully to Congress and the President (and

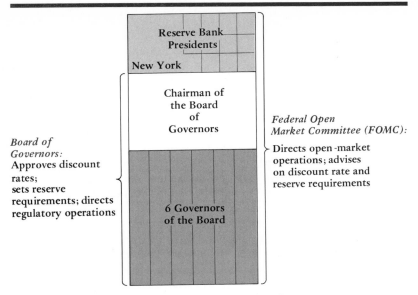

Figure 12-4 The major actors in monetary policy

The major powers of the Federal Reserve are lodged in two bodies. The 7-member Board of Governors approves changes in discount rates and sets reserve requirements. The 12-member FOMC directs setting of bank reserves. The Chairman of the Board of Governors leads both committees.

To show the realities of power within the system, we have made the size of each of the boxes proportional to the power that different groups wield—note the size of the Chairman's box. The relative importance of different people is drawn on the basis of the study by former Fed governor Sherman Maisel, *Managing the Dollar* (New York, Norton, 1973).

even to the election returns), in the end the members of the Board of Governors and the FOMC vote according to their philosophies and forecasts. Sometimes, as a result, the Fed comes into conflict with the executive branch. The Roosevelt, Johnson, Carter, and Reagan administrations all at times had harsh words for Fed policy. The Fed listened politely, but the President could not force the Fed to bend to his wishes. Because Congress can legislate changes in its structure, or even remove its independence, the Fed also listens respectfully to the views of Congress.

From time to time some people argue that the Fed is too independent. ''Isn't it undemocratic to allow a group of private bankers control over monetary policy?'' ask critics. Who, they ask, gave the Federal Reserve the authority to raise interest rates to 20 per-

cent in 1980? Where can we read that the Fed is authorized to create recessions? Shouldn't monetary policy be set by elected representatives in Congress or by the executive branch?

Here is a case where the American practice differs from that of many other countries. For example, in Britain, the Bank of England understands well that it must in the last analysis be subservient to the will of the Cabinet, with a right to protest publicly but a duty to coordinate its policies with those of the Cabinet. The German central bank, by contrast, is even more fiercely independent than the Fed.

There is no right answer to the question of independence for the Fed. On the one hand, the Fed's independence allows it the leeway to undertake policies, such as fighting inflation, that have little popular support. The elected branches will not always sacrifice short-run electability for long-run economic welfare, and an independent Fed may be the best answer to the political business cycle analyzed in Chapter 10.

At the same time, because they are so far removed from the political process, monetary managers at the Fed may lose touch with social and economic realities. Members of Congress are routinely forced to confront unemployed autoworkers and bankrupt farmers—groups seldom encountered in the Federal Reserve building in Washington.

The debate about the Fed's independence is neither new nor frivolous. Proposals to change the composition of the board, to put representatives of the Congress or the Executive on the FOMC, or to let each new President appoint his own Chairman of the Board of Governors are perennial topics for debate about central banking.

We can summarize the structure of the Federal Reserve System this way:

The Federal Reserve Board in Washington, together with the 12 Federal Reserve Banks, constitutes our American central bank. Every modern country has such a central bank—as, for example, the Bank of England and the German Bundesbank.

The primary function of a modern central bank is to control the nation's money supply and credit conditions.

Overview of the Fed's Operations

We turn now to a quick survey of the objectives, tools, and procedures of the Fed. It is useful to start by viewing the "world as seen by the Fed." Figure 12-5 shows the various stages of Federal Reserve operations. The Federal Reserve has at its disposal certain policy instruments (levers like open-market operations, the discount rate, and reserve requirements); these instruments produce certain direct impacts on the economy seen in intermediate targets (such as reserves, the money supply, and interest rates); but all these operations are in the end aimed to affect the ultimate objectives (inflation, real GNP, and unemployment). It is important to keep these three sets of variables distinct in our analysis.

We have already alluded to the three major instruments of monetary policy. They are as follows:

■ *Open-market operations*—buying or selling government bonds

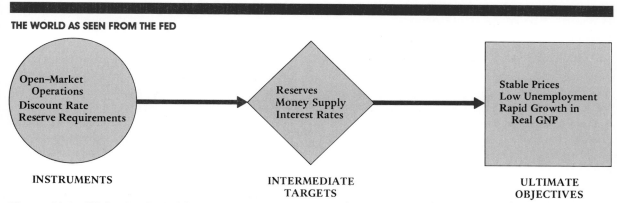

THE WORLD AS SEEN FROM THE FED

| Open–Market Operations Discount Rate Reserve Requirements | → | Reserves Money Supply Interest Rates | → | Stable Prices Low Unemployment Rapid Growth in Real GNP |

INSTRUMENTS   INTERMEDIATE   ULTIMATE
                           TARGETS   OBJECTIVES

Figure 12-5   While the Fed ultimately pursues objectives like stable prices, its short-term operations focus on the intermediate targets

In determining monetary policy, the Fed directly sets instruments or policy variables under its control—open-market operations, discount rate, and reserve requirements. These help determine bank reserves, the money supply, and interest rates—the intermediate targets of monetary policy. Ultimately, the Fed is a partner with fiscal policy in influencing the ultimate objectives of a high level of real GNP, low unemployment, and stable prices.

▪ *Discount-rate policy*—setting the interest rate, called the discount rate, at which member banks can borrow reserves from the Fed

▪ Changing the *legal reserve ratio requirements* on deposits with banks and other financial institutions

In addition, the Federal Reserve must keep its eye on a set of variables known as *intermediate targets*. These are economic variables that are neither Fed policy instruments nor true policy objectives but instead stand intermediate in the transmission mechanism between Fed instruments and goals. Looking back at Figure 12-1, we see that when the Fed wants to affect its ultimate objectives, it *first* changes one of its instruments and this change *next* affects intermediate variables like interest rates or the money supply.

Why is the Fed so concerned with its intermediate targets? It is concerned because the ultimate objectives are logically quite far removed from the Fed's own policy actions—for example, there are numerous intervening steps between open-market operations and GNP. Hence, much as a doctor interested in the health of a patient will monitor pulse and blood pressure, so will the Federal Reserve keep a careful watch on intermediate targets like the money supply, credit conditions, and interest rates even though its ultimate concerns are output and inflation.

Balance Sheet of the Federal Reserve Banks

Now that we have reviewed the basic structure and objectives of the Federal Reserve, let us study exactly how the Fed sets bank reserves and thereby controls the supply of money. Begin with a look at Table 12-1. This shows the consolidated balance sheet of the Federal Reserve Banks. The first asset consists mostly of gold certificates, i.e., warehouse receipts from the Treasury to the Fed for official gold. United States government securities (e.g., bonds) make up most of the rest of the assets.

The small items, loans and acceptances, are primarily loans or advances to commercial banks. The interest rate the Fed charges banks for such loans, or "discounts," is called the *discount rate*, which is another of the Fed's tools.

The right-hand side lists the usual capital accounts: original capital paid in by the member banks plus retained earnings or accumulated surplus.

Federal Reserve notes are the Fed's principal liabilities. These are the $1, $5, and other bills we carry in our wallets. Little comment is needed on several of its deposit liabilities: U.S. government deposits, foreign central bank deposits, and miscellaneous.

Of vital importance, though, are the *bank reserves,* or balances kept on deposit by commercial banks with the Federal Reserve Banks and shown as Fed liabilities. Taken along with small amounts of banks' vault cash, these are the reserves we have been talking about. They provide the basis for multiple deposit creation by the nation's banking system.

We shall see that the Fed, *by altering its holding of government securities,* can change bank reserves and thereby trigger the five-step sequence discussed at the beginning of this chapter. In other words, by varying its holdings of government bonds and other assets, the Fed determines the reserves of the banks. Because it determines the total quantity of bank reserves, the Fed thereby determines the total supply of money.

THE NUTS AND BOLTS OF MONETARY POLICY

Open-Market Operations

The Fed's most important tool is "open-market operations."

By selling or buying government securities in the open market, the Fed can lower or raise bank reserves. These so-called open-market operations are a central bank's most important stabilizing instrument.

Every month the FOMC meets to decide whether to pump more reserves into the banking system by buying Treasury bills (i.e., short-term bonds) and longer-term government bonds, or whether to tighten monetary policy by selling government securities.

To see how an open-market operation changes reserves, let us suppose that the Fed thinks the economic winds are blowing up a little inflation. The FOMC holds its secret meeting. The committee decides "Let's sell $1 billion of Treasury bills from our portfolio to contract reserves and tighten overall money and credit." The motion is unanimously ap-

COMBINED BALANCE SHEET OF 12 FEDERAL RESERVE BANKS, 1988
(in billions of dollars)

ASSETS		LIABILITIES AND NET WORTH	
Gold certificates and other cash	$ 11.5	Capital accounts	$ 4.6
U.S. government securities	230.5	Federal Reserve notes	215.2
Loans and acceptances	3.3	Deposits:	
Miscellaneous other assets	24.7	Bank reserves	38.8
		U.S. Treasury	2.9
		Foreign and other	0.7
		Miscellaneous liabilities	7.8
Total	$270.0	Total	$270.0

Table 12-1   Federal Reserve notes and deposits underlie our money supply

By controlling its earning assets (government securities and loans), the Fed controls its liabilities (deposits and Federal Reserve notes). It controls the economy's money supply (currency and demand deposits, M_1), and thereby affects GNP, unemployment, and inflation. (Source: *Federal Reserve Bulletin*.)

proved by vote of the seven Washington governors and five regional Bank presidents.

To whom are the bonds sold? To the open market: to dealers in government bonds, who then resell them to commercial banks, big corporations, and other financial institutions.

The purchasers usually buy the bonds by writing checks to the Fed, drawn from an account in the purchasers' commercial banks. Take one of the many transactions, in which the Fed sells $10,000 worth of bonds to Ms. Smith, who writes a check on the Farmers' Bank of Denver. The Fed presents the check at the Farmers' Bank. When the Farmers' Bank pays the check, it will debit its account with the Fed for the $10,000 check. At the end, the Farmers' Bank, and the entire commercial banking system, will lose $10,000 in reserves to the Federal Reserve System.

When all such transactions are completed, Table 12-2(a) shows the all-important effects of a $1 billion open-market operation on the Federal Reserve balance sheet. The open-market sale changes the Federal Reserve balance sheet by reducing both assets and liabilities by $1 billion: the Fed has sold $1 billion of government bonds, and its liabilities have declined by exactly the same amount, $1 billion of bank reserves.

Effects on Money What happens to the money supply? Reserves go down by $1 billion, and that tends to set off a contraction of deposits. Using our simple example of a 10 percent reserve requirement, the $1 billion sale of government bonds will result in a $10 billion cut in the community's money supply. We've seen why—in Chapter 11. Table 12-2(b) shows the banks' ultimate position after $1 billion of reserves have been extinguished by the open-market operation. In the end, the Fed's open-market sale has caused a $10 billion contraction in the money supply.

To test your understanding of open-market operations, consider the reverse process. Suppose the economy is depressed, or M is below the target level. What will the FOMC want to do? What will be the effect on the Fed's assets and liabilities? What will happen to the money supply?

The Fed will buy government bonds on the open market; this step creates new reserves for the banks and produces a multiple expansion in M, thus making credit cheaper for investors. Consequently, investment and aggregate demand will increase.

Finally, to make sure you understand the reasoning, show where in Figure 12-1 the open-market operation enters in the logical chain from policy to effects.

FEDERAL RESERVE ASSETS (billions)		FEDERAL RESERVE LIABILITIES (billions)	
U.S. securities	−$1.0	Bank reserves	−$1.0
	−$1.0		−$1.0

BANK ASSETS (billions)		BANK LIABILITIES (billions)	
Reserves	−$ 1.0	Checking deposits	−$10.0
Loans and investments	− 9.0		
	−$10.0		−$10.0

Table 12-2(a) Open-market sale cuts reserves initially

Table 12-2(b) . . . and ultimately cuts deposits 10 to 1

This crucial set of tables shows how open-market operations affect the Fed's balance sheet and the balance sheet of banks.

In Table 12-2(a), the Fed has sold $1 billion of securities. The funds used to pay for the securities are deposited in the Fed, reducing bank reserves by $1 billion. Bank reserves thus decline by $1 billion as a result of the open-market operation.

Then in Table 12-2(b), we see the effect on the balance sheet of banks. With a required reserve ratio of 10 percent of deposits, the banks will be content only when they have no excess or deficit reserves. Thus deposits must fall by $10 billion for the banking system to be back in equilibrium.

In the end, an open-market operation in which the Fed sells $1 billion of securities leads to an eventual decline of $10 billion in bank money and in the money supply.

Operating Procedures

The FOMC meets eight times a year to give instructions to its operating arm, the Federal Reserve Bank of New York. The instructions are contained in an "FOMC policy directive." The directive has two parts: First comes a general assessment of economic conditions; second, the general objectives of monetary policy. As an example, consider the statement of August 1982—in the midst of the deepest recession of the postwar period the FOMC began with its review of the economy:[1]

> The information reviewed at this meeting suggests only a little further advance in real GNP in the current quarter, following a relatively small increase in the second quarter, while prices on the average are continuing to rise more slowly than in 1981.

What did the Fed plan for the objectives of monetary policy? It stated:

> The Federal Open Market Committee seeks to foster monetary and financial conditions that will help to reduce inflation, promote a resumption of growth in output on a

sustainable basis, and contribute to a sustainable pattern of international transactions.

The most important part of the procedure comes where the FOMC tells the New York Fed what to do—instructing its front-line troops about how to manage financial markets on a day-to-day basis.

Before the 1970s, the FOMC used to give such vague instructions as, "Keep credit conditions and interest rates as tight as they have been." Or, "Loosen credit a little to help expand GNP." The result was a great preoccupation with "keeping the bond market orderly" and keeping interest yields from bouncing around. This earlier obsession with keeping interest rates stable sometimes slowed the Fed's reaction to changing business-cycle conditions. Rather than allowing interest rates to rise quickly when inflation threatened, the Fed would move interest rates up in a slow and orderly fashion. This tendency was reinforced by political pressures, for few people like high interest rates.

Targeting In the late 1970s, in part because of the prodding of the monetarist school,[2] the Federal Reserve altered its operating procedures to pay closer attention to movements in the money supply. Before

---

[1]The quotations from the FOMC are from the *Federal Reserve Bulletin,* which contains monthly reports on Federal Reserve activities and other important financial developments.

[2]Monetarism is fully discussed in Chapter 16.

the 1970s, the Fed had no discernible targets. It would explain to Congress that it desired to "lean against the wind" or "control excesses of the business cycle." During the 1970s, however, the Fed came under a barrage of criticism. It was accused of contributing to the political business cycle and helping to reelect President Nixon in 1972; this was followed by a tardy response to the boom conditions of 1973; shortly afterward, the Fed was accused of overreacting to the sharp recession of 1974–1975 and of allowing unemployment to rise too sharply.

Economists criticized and administrations fumed. While the Fed temporized and explained, the patience of Congress wore thin and it decided to assert its power over the Fed. Congress passed a concurrent resolution in 1975 and the Humphrey-Hawkins Act of 1978, directing the Fed to state explicit targets for its monetary policy and to set target growth rates for the major monetary aggregates.

From October 1979 until late 1982, the Federal Reserve undertook a major experiment by concentrating almost exclusively upon the growth of M_1, M_2, and bank reserves. It hoped that a clear and decisive strategy of targeting the monetary aggregates would help reduce an annual inflation rate that was surging beyond 10 percent. An example of the operational directive given by the FOMC dates from August 1982:

> In the short run, the Committee continues to seek behavior of reserve aggregates consistent with growth of M_1 and M_2 from June to September [1982] at annual rates of about 5 percent and about 9 percent respectively.

Note the carefully crafted words: The FOMC seeks *behavior of reserve aggregates* consistent with its *M* targets. It is telling the portfolio managers to undertake open-market operations, pumping or draining reserves from banks, needed to hit certain monetary targets.

The shift to targeting reserves and the money supply in 1979 was highly controversial. The immediate result was a major reduction in the growth of the money supply and a consequent tightening of monetary policy. This led to an increase of market interest rates to levels not seen since the Civil War, followed shortly thereafter by the deepest recession since the 1930s. The policy was definitely successful in reducing inflation to 3 to 4 percent per year by the mid-1980s.

Retreat from Targeting In the political hue and cry surrounding the sharp recession of 1982, the Fed concluded that its monetary policy had become overly restrictive. In addition, the definitions of the monetary aggregates became confused at this time because of the addition of a number of new assets (such as interest-bearing checking accounts) to M_1 and M_2. The Fed therefore retreated from its strict reserve and monetary targeting in the fall of 1982. Figure 12-6 shows the history of monetary targeting and the results during the controversial period of 1980–1983. This figure illustrates the difficulty that the Fed experienced in keeping monetary aggregates inside its targets.

After 1982, the Fed began to downplay the use of monetary aggregates in its decisions about monetary policy. In 1987, it ceased stating explicit targets in terms of M_1, although it continued to publish monitoring ranges for other aggregates. In 1988, the vice chairman of the Fed stated that, because the money supply had become so unreliable, the Fed was instead using a combination of variables (such as the exchange rate, commodity prices, and interest rates) as an early-warning indicator of inflationary forces.

Choice of Policies How does the Federal Reserve choose its money and interest-rate targets? The process is shrouded in mystery, but firsthand accounts and memoirs of Fed governors and staff members boil down to something like the following.

The Fed staff and the FOMC have certain macroeconomic objectives, including goals for inflation, the foreign exchange rate of the dollar, real GNP, unemployment, and the trade balance. The Fed makes regular projections on variables outside its control (such as fiscal policy, oil prices, foreign economic growth, and so forth) and then forecasts the behavior of the economy using a number of different assumptions about monetary policy.

The FOMC then debates the proper course for monetary policy. If the economy was performing satisfactorily, it might decide to leave interest rates and money-supply growth at their current levels. Or, if the FOMC thought that the current setting was en-

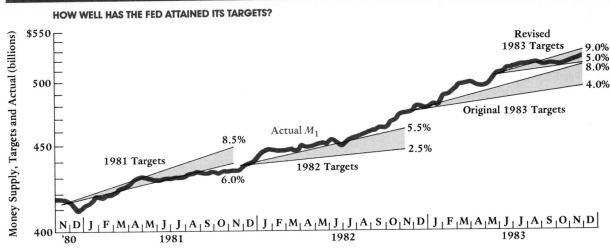

Figure 12-6   Monetary targeting, 1980–1983

From 1979 to 1983, the Fed pursued explicit monetary targets. The most closely tracked aggregate was transactions money, M_1. This figure shows the actual targets adopted by the Fed, as well as the actual money-supply movements over the period around the deep recession of 1982.

Note that the Fed undershot its M_1 target in 1981. Many feel that this action led to higher interest rates and a deep recession. Also observe that in early 1983 M_1 was way above the target cone.

Because of difficulties in attaining monetary targets, the Fed abandoned targets for M_1 in 1987. (Source: *Federal Reserve Bulletin*.)

couraging inflation, it might choose to tighten monetary policy a notch. Alternatively, if the Fed thought that a recession loomed ahead, it might inject reserves into the system, increasing the money supply, and lowering interest rates.

Every time the Fed sets monetary policy, it must deal with agonizing choices: What is the best forecast for investment? Will a severe drought fuel inflation? Will the fall in the value of the dollar raise inflation and produce a major increase in net exports? How will Congress react to a tighter monetary policy in an election year? How will financial markets respond to a looser monetary policy right after a new President has been installed? These and many other questions confront those who decide the nation's monetary policies.

It is not always easy to understand the exact chain of reasoning that led to a particular monetary-policy step. Nonetheless, historians who sift through the decisions usually find that the Fed is ultimately concerned with preserving the integrity of our financial institutions, combating inflation, defending the exchange rate of the dollar, and preventing excessive unemployment.[3]

Discount-Rate Policy: A Second Instrument

The Federal Reserve Banks also make loans to banks. These were included under the asset heading "Loans and acceptances" in the Fed balance sheet in Table 12-1. We will call these loans *borrowed reserves*. When borrowed reserves are growing, the banks are borrowing from the Fed, thereby increasing total bank reserves (borrowed plus unborrowed reserves). When borrowed reserves are dropping, that helps total bank reserves to contract.

Although borrowed reserves get multiplied into

[3]For a careful analysis of political and economic forces operating on the Federal Reserve, see Donald Kettl, *Leadership at the Fed* (Yale University Press, New Haven, Conn., 1986).

bank money just as much as the unborrowed reserves we discussed in the last section, they are not a precise instrument under the control of the Fed. It's like the old saying, "You can lead a horse to water, but you can't make him drink." The Fed can induce or discourage bank borrowings, but it cannot set a precise level of borrowed reserves.

If the Fed thinks borrowings are low, it cannot send sales agents out to drum up more borrowing. All it can do is lower the "discount rate," which represents the interest rate charged on bank borrowings from the 12 regional Federal Reserve Banks. The Fed can expect to get more takers by lowering the discount rate, or it can discourage borrowing by raising the discount rate. But the relationship between the discount rate and bank borrowings is not very precise.[4]

However, the Fed does not allow completely free use of the "discount window" (the name given to the place where the Fed lends banks money). Sometimes, the discount rate is below the interest rate that banks can earn on safe assets. Thus in the spring of 1982, short-term interest rates were 15 percent, while the discount rate was 12 percent. Banks would be tempted to borrow from the Fed and make a big profit by investing in short-term securities.

Such behavior is not tolerated. The Fed "frowns" on excessive use of the discount window; that is, it may publicly reprimand banks that borrow too much or too often, and there are limits on how much big banks are allowed to borrow. According to the Fed, borrowing is a privilege, not a right.

Because the Federal Reserve regulates borrowing at the discount window, bank borrowings are typically a small fraction of bank reserves.

Changing the Discount Rate For many years, the discount rate was the bellwether of monetary policy.

For example, in 1965 when the Fed wanted to send a signal to markets that the Vietnam war boom was becoming ominously strong, it raised the discount rate. So powerful was this signal that Chairman Martin of the Fed was called to the LBJ ranch for a dressing down by President Johnson, who was afraid the higher discount rate would slow the economy.

During the period in which the Federal Reserve targeted the money supply, the discount rate played a passive role. It was then set to follow the market and to make sure banks could not profit from borrowing at the discount window and lending at a higher market interest rate. In the most recent period, as the U.S. economy has become more integrated with other countries, the discount rate has occasionally been used to signal major changes in economic policy or to coordinate monetary policies with other countries.

Some economists would like the Federal Reserve to make the discount rate a market-based interest rate. One reform proposal would tie the discount rate directly to short-term interest rates—in principle removing any need for the Fed to ration borrowing by banks. Other economists fear that such a move would make the money supply more unpredictable. It is unlikely that such a change is in the wind today.

Reserve Requirements

We noted in the last chapter that, but for government rules, banks would probably keep only about 1 percent of their deposits in the form of reserves. In fact, today American banks are required to keep substantially more reserves. Table 11-4 showed current reserve requirements along with the Fed's discretionary power to change reserve requirements.

In principle, the Fed can change reserve requirements if it wants to change financial conditions very quickly. For instance, if the Fed wants to make money tight very quickly, it can raise the required reserve ratios for the big banks to the 14 percent statutory limit. It might even raise reserve requirements on time deposits. And if the Fed wants to ease credit conditions, it can do the reverse. It can cut legal reserve ratios.

Exactly how does an increase in required ratios operate to tighten credit? Suppose the banks had built up their deposits in a 10-to-1 ratio with their reserves

[4]When the Federal Reserve System was started, it was thought that discount policy would be most important of all. The idea was to have banks buy their customers' promissory notes at a "discount," sending them over to the Reserve Banks in return for new cash. That way, the neighborhood banks would never run out of money to accommodate worthy farm and business borrowers. It did not work out that way. Why not? Largely because the last thing a healthy economy wants is an elastic money supply that will *automatically* expand when business is good and contract when it is bad. That way lies disastrous reinforcement of business cycles and inflation.

as a result of the required ratio having been 10 percent, with excess reserves being negligible. Now suppose the Fed decides to tighten credit and Congress allows it to raise the required reserve ratio to 20 percent. (This fantastic figure is for algebraic simplicity. The Fed cannot and would not take such a drastic step today.)

Even if the Fed does nothing by way of open-market operations or discount policy to change bank reserves, banks now have to contract their loans and investments greatly—and their deposits as well. Why? Because (as Chapter 11 showed) bank deposits can now be only 5 times reserves, not 10 times reserves. So there must be a drop by one-half in all deposits!

This painful cut will start to take place quickly. As soon as the Federal Reserve Board signs the new rule raising requirements to 20 percent, banks will find that they have insufficient reserves. They will have to sell some bonds and call in some loans. The bond buyers and borrowers will drain their checking accounts. The process ends only after banks have brought down their deposits to 5 rather than 10 times their reserves.

This enormous change in so short a time would result in very high interest rates, in credit rationing, in large declines in investment, and in great reductions in GNP and employment. So this fantastic example warns that this powerful tool of changing reserve requirements has to be used with great caution.

While changing reserve requirements is a potential tool of monetary policy, changes are made extremely sparingly because they present too large and abrupt a change in policy. Open-market operations can achieve the same results in a less disruptive way.

Interest-Rate Regulation

In addition to the three major instruments discussed above, the Federal Reserve (with the help of Congress and other government agencies) has historically regulated financial markets by limiting interest rates. Until the 1980s, most interest rates paid by commercial banks were controlled. Banks were not allowed to pay interest on checking accounts, and there were ceilings on interest rates on savings accounts and time deposits. These regulations were the product of the 1930s, a period in which Congress acted on the dubious notion that many banks had failed because they offered excessively high interest rates to depositors in an attempt to compete.

How could such a situation survive in competitive markets? It could not. Financial institutions began to offer new kinds of instruments, and these began to lure funds out of low-yield deposits. The high interest rates of the late 1970s and early 1980s put further pressure on the system, for banks (which paid 5 percent per year on their savings accounts) had to compete with money market mutual funds (which paid 10 or 15 percent on their deposits). Eventually the regulatory edifice constructed during the Great Depression began to crumble. Congress reacted with the Banking Acts of 1980 and 1982, which largely deregulated interest rates.

The New Regulatory Structure The Banking Acts of 1980 and 1982 created a new regulatory structure that has largely decontrolled interest rates in financial markets. The analytical basis of the new approach was to separate out transactions accounts from non-transactions accounts. A *transactions account* is one (like currency or checking accounts) whose primary purpose is to serve as a means of payment. A *non-transactions account* is an asset (like a savings account) whose primary purpose is to put aside funds for the future, not to pay bills.

Once this separation was made, the 1980 and 1982 acts effectively deregulated non-transactions accounts. This legislation phased out interest-rate ceilings for non-transactions accounts in 1986, and reserve requirements on these deposits are set at zero for personal accounts and at minimal levels for business accounts. As of the late 1980s, non-transactions accounts earn market interest rates and are effectively outside the regulatory structure of the Federal Reserve.

The remaining assets—transactions assets like checking accounts—have been largely deregulated. These accounts are subject to substantial reserve requirements (currently amounting to 12 percent of transactions deposits for large banks). However, personal transactions accounts are no longer subject to interest-rate ceilings. In a competitive financial market, the interest rate on transactions accounts will hence be bid up to about 88/100 of open-market interest rates.[5]

International Reserve Movements

Because the dollar is the world's most important currency, it is widely held abroad by those who export and import with the United States, by foreign and American investors, by those who finance trade and investments between other countries, by speculators and dealers in the Euro-dollar markets, by foreign governments, central banks, and international agencies like the International Monetary Fund. These entities own hundreds of billions of dollars in U.S. dollar-denominated assets.

Because currency itself yields no interest return, foreigners prefer to hold interest-bearing assets (bonds, stocks, etc.). However, as a medium for buying and selling such earning assets, foreigners do hold some transactions dollars in M_1.

Why are we concerned about international money holdings at this point? Because deposits by foreigners in the banking system increase the total amount of bank reserves just as do domestic residents' deposits. Thus changes in dollar money holdings of foreigners can set off a chain of expansion or contraction of the U.S. money supply.

For example, say Germans decide to deposit $1 billion of U.S. currency in U.S. banks. What happens? There is a $1 billion increase in reserves in the domestic banking system, just as was illustrated in Table 11-5(a) in the last chapter. As a result, the banking system can expand deposits tenfold, in this case to $10 billion.

Another way of seeing the point is to go back to Figure 12-1. Pencil in a new arrow showing bank reserves coming in from abroad, and you will see that this new input gets amplified in the same way as the input from the Fed's domestic open-market operations.

[5]This number is obtained as follows. Ignoring the costs of providing checking services, banks will earn free-market interest rates on 88/100 of the funds obtained by checking accounts; plus 0 percent on the 12/100 that are kept as reserves with the Federal Reserve. Thus if open-market interest rates are 10 percent, the competitive rate on checking accounts will be 8.8 percent (again, neglecting any charges for banking services, which might lower the 8.8 percent rate).

Thus the Fed's control of the nation's M is modified by international disturbances to bank reserves. Is there nothing the Fed can do about this? Clearly, the Fed does have the power to offset any change in reserves coming from abroad. It can engage in what is called "sterilization." *Sterilization* occurs when a central bank undertakes open-market operations to offset international reserve flows.

To summarize:

The central bank's control over reserves on which M is based must contend with disturbances from international changes in those reserves. But, if it wants to do so, the central bank does have the power to offset or sterilize any such disturbances.

In practice, the Fed today routinely sterilizes international disturbances to reserves. Other countries, with less well-developed financial markets and central banking systems, sometimes have trouble fully sterilizing international reserve flows.

Other Activities

At this point, you probably have concluded that the Fed is pretty busy. But we have up to now described only the money market functions of the Fed—those relating to control of the money supply. There are, in addition, a number of subsidiary tasks delegated to the Fed and other federal agencies:

- *Manage official exchange-rate operations.* The Fed buys and sells different currencies on foreign exchange markets on behalf of the government. While this task is generally light, from time to time foreign exchange markets become erratic and the Fed (under orders from the Treasury) steps in. (A full discussion of the way that central banks can intervene to affect currency values is given in Chapter 40.)

- *Regulate banks.* Since the Great Depression, the federal government has stood behind the banks. To instill confidence in banks, the government insures bank deposits, inspects the books of banks, and (when crises hit) manages bank insolvency. The important task of insuring the deposits of commercial banks is handled by the Federal Deposit Insurance Corporation (the F.D.I.C.).

The deregulation in financial markets over the last decade, along with much greater volatility in interest rates, has made banking a risky business. Hundreds of savings and loan associations, along with a score of commercial banks, have become insolvent. When that happens, the federal government takes charge of the bank, finds a solvent bank to take it over, and occasionally pays back depositors out of insurance funds.

Occasionally a really big bank gets in trouble, as in the summer of 1984 when the Continental Illinois Bank (with $41 billion in assets) looked shaky. Foreigners and others started withdrawing deposits by the billions of dollars. In this case, the federal government became alarmed and guaranteed *all* the deposits of this giant bank.

From 1984 to 1988, the Federal government devoted billions of dollars to bailing out financial institutions that had made unwise investments in real estate or energy. Giant banks such as First RepublicBank (Texas) were taken over by the government or sold off to the highest bidder. In response to the excessive risk-taking of many banks, in 1988 the Federal Reserve, along with other central banks, imposed new regulations to require exposed banks to maintain higher levels of net worth.

▪ *Coordinate international financial policy.* The Federal Reserve has taken the lead during the 1980s in working with foreign countries and with international agencies to alleviate the problems of large debt burdens. The debt crisis, which appeared in 1981 and 1982, found many middle-income and poor countries, such as Mexico and Brazil, burdened with extremely high levels of interest payments relative to their export earnings. At an early stage, the Fed understood that the debt crisis could lead to a crisis of confidence in the financial system, because some large American banks had portfolios of shaky foreign loans that were as large as their net worth. Working together with other agencies, the Fed helped manage the crisis, so that by 1988 the debt burdens of most countries, along with the risks to the international financial system, had been significantly reduced.

In short, the task of central bankers is never finished.

▪   ▪   ▪

We have now completed our tour through the supply of money. It can be summarized as follows:

The money supply is ultimately determined by the policies of the Fed. By setting reserve requirements, the discount rate, and especially open-market operations, the Fed determines the level of reserves and the money supply.

Banks and the public are cooperating partners in this process. Banks create money out of reserves by multiple expansion of reserves; the public agrees to hold money in depository institutions.

Putting these together, the Fed can (within a small margin of error) determine the money supply on a medium-term basis.

We now turn to some major policy issues of today. The next three chapters survey inflation and unemployment. Subsequently, we move to a discussion of the major issues of monetary and fiscal policy along with an analysis of the impact of government deficits and debt on the economy.

SUMMARY

A. The Nature of Interest Rates

1. The Federal Reserve helps determine market interest rates. Interest rates are the price paid for borrowing money and are measured in dollars per year paid back per dollar borrowed or in percent per year. People willingly pay interest of 5 or 10 or even 15 percent per year because the borrowed funds allow them to buy goods and services to satisfy consumption needs or make profitable investments.

2. Markets grind out a wide array of interest rates. These differ because of the term or maturity of the loans, because of the risk and liquidity of the investment, and because of the associated administrative costs.

3. Interest rates generally rise during inflationary periods to reflect the fact that the purchasing power of money declines as prices rise. To calculate the interest yield in terms of real goods and services, we use the real interest rate, which equals the nominal or money interest rate minus the rate of inflation.

B. Central Banking

4. The Federal Reserve System is a central bank, a bank for bankers. Its function is to control the amount of bank reserves, thereby determining the nation's supply of money. If the Fed wished to slow down the economy, the five-step sequence goes thus: (1) It contracts bank reserves; which (2) causes multiple contractions in total M deposits; which (3) makes interest rates high and credit hard to get, and reduces the market value of wealth; all of which (4) depress private and public investment spending; which (5) finally, after a decline in aggregate demand, puts a damper on output and prices (see Figure 12-1).

5. The Federal Reserve System (or "Fed" as it is often called) was created in 1913 to control the nation's money and credit. The important bodies are the Board of Governors, headquartered in Washington, and the Federal Open Market Committee (or FOMC). The Fed acts as an independent government agency, setting the instruments of monetary policy with a great deal of discretionary power.

6. The Fed has as its major policy instruments: *(a)* open-market operations, *(b)* the discount rate on bank borrowing, and *(c)* reserve requirements on depository institutions. Using these three instruments, the Fed can pursue intermediate targets: the level of bank reserves, market interest rates, and the money supply. All these operations aim to improve the economy's performance with respect to the ultimate objectives of monetary policy: achieving the best combination of low inflation, low unemployment, rapid GNP growth, a sustainable trade balance, and stable exchange rates with the rest of the world.

In addition, the Fed (along with other federal agencies) must backstop the domestic and international financial system in times of crisis.

7. The most important instrument of monetary policy is open-market operations. Sales by the Fed of government securities in the open market reduce the Fed's assets and liabilities and thereby reduce the reserves of banks. The effect is to reduce banks' reserve base for deposits. People end up with less M and more government bonds. Open-market purchases do the opposite, ultimately expanding M by increasing the reserves of banks.

8. Outflows of international reserves can reduce reserves and M unless offset by central-market purchases of bonds. Inflows have opposite effects unless offset. The process of offsetting international flows is known as "sterilization." In recent years, the Fed has routinely sterilized international reserve movements.

CONCEPTS FOR REVIEW

the five-step sequence
bank reserves
Federal Reserve balance sheet
open-market purchases and sales
discount rate, borrowings from Fed
real and nominal interest rates
riskless interest rate

interest-rate premiums due to:
  maturity, risk, illiquidity,
   administrative costs
legal reserve ratio requirements
FOMC, Board of Governors
policy instruments, intermediate targets,
  ultimate objectives

QUESTIONS FOR DISCUSSION

1. List the policy instruments of the Fed. Explain how each changes bank reserves and the money supply. How powerful is each for controlling: *(a)* reserves, *(b)* M_1, *(c)* interest rates, *(d)* output, *(e)* prices?

2. Trace the effects of a $1 billion open-market purchase by the Fed; a $1 billion open-market sale. In terms of Figure 12-1, pencil in open-market operations and discount borrowing at (1) on the reserves input branch. Pencil in legal reserve ratio changes as gearing changes at (2) on the output-of-M branch.

3. Trace the effects of a doubling of reserve requirements; a halving. Which alters bank profits more: open-market or reserve-requirement action?

4. Consider the balance sheet of the Fed in Table 12-1. Construct a hypothetical corresponding balance sheet for banks (like the one in Table 11-2) assuming that reserve requirements are 10 percent on checking accounts and zero on everything else.

  (a) Construct a new set of balance sheets, assuming the Fed sells $1 billion in government securities by open-market operations.

  (b) Construct a new set of balance sheets if the Fed increases reserve requirements to 20 percent.

  (c) Assume banks borrow $1 billion of reserves from the Fed. How will this change the balance sheets?

5. Start with a set of balance sheets of the Federal Reserve System and of the banking sector similar to Tables 12-1 and 11-2. Assume that reserve requirements are zero for savings accounts and 10 percent for checking accounts. Trace through the impact of the following on the balance sheets and upon the money supply (M_1):

  (a) The Fed buys $1 billion of government bonds.

  (b) Banks borrow $0.1 billion from the Fed.

  (c) The required reserve ratio is increased to 11 percent.

  (d) Households move $2 billion from their savings accounts to their checking accounts.

  (e) The Japanese withdraw $3 billion of checking deposits and buy common stocks.

6. Discuss the following Federal Reserve statement: "The Federal Reserve System can see to it that banks have enough reserves to make money available to commerce, industry, and agriculture at low rates; but it cannot make the people borrow, and it cannot make the public spend the deposits that result when the banks do make loans and investments."

7. The "opportunity cost" of holding money is equal to the yield on safe short-term assets (such as Treasury bills) minus the interest rate on money. What is the impact of the following on the opportunity cost of holding money in checking deposits (assume that reserve requirements are 10 percent of deposits):

(a) In the pre-1980 world, where checking deposits had zero yield, of an increase in market interest rates from 8 to 9 percent?

(b) In a 1984 world, where NOW accounts have a maximum yield of 5 percent, of an increase of interest rates from 3 to 4 percent? From 8 to 9 percent?

(c) In a 1989 world, where the interest rates on NOW accounts are deregulated, of an increase in market interest rates from 3 to 4 percent? From 8 to 9 percent?

How would you expect the demand for money to respond to the change in market interest rates in each of the above cases if the elasticity of demand for money with respect to the opportunity cost of money is 0.2?

8. Interest-rate problems (which may require a calculator):

(a) You invest $2000 at 13.5 percent per year. What is your total balance after 6 months?

(b) Interest is said to be "compounded" when you earn interest on whatever interest has already been paid; most interest rates quoted today are compounded. If you invest $10,000 for 3 years at a compound annual interest rate of 10 percent, what is the total investment at the end of each year?

(c) Consider the following data: The consumer price index in 1977 was 181.5 while in 1981 it was 272.4. Interest rates on government securities in 1978 through 1981 (in percent per year) were: 7.2, 10.0, 11.5, and 14.0. Calculate the average nominal and real interest rates for the 4-year period, 1978–1981.

(d) Treasury bills (T-bills) are usually sold on a discounted basis; that is, a 90-day T-bill for $10,000 would sell today at a price such that collecting $10,000 at maturity would produce the market interest rate. If the market interest rate is 6.6 percent per year, what would be the price on a $10,000 90-day T-bill?

9. "Gold movements affected prices only because we used them as a barometer, signaling us to expand or contract total M supply. Of course, the gold standard was a defective system; but it was wiser to tie ourselves to such an imperfect system than to trust corrupt and politicking legislatures whose tendency is always to print inflationary paper money." Discuss.

10. In recent years, some have written: "We cannot trust the autonomous Fed, a group of bankers and economists, to set monetary policy. It is too important a determinant of our economic fate to leave to such an undemocratic group." Think back to what you know about American government, about the political business cycle from Chapter 10, and about the composition of the FOMC and Federal Reserve Board. Do you feel that the structure of the Fed should be changed?

11. Advanced problem: Define *high-powered money* as currency and bank reserves. Before the creation of the Fed, the total amount of high-powered money was fixed or "inelastic." From time to time, however, the public would become concerned about bank failures and would want "safer" money—i.e., it would form long lines to convert bank money into currency. What will happen to the money supply in such a case if high-powered money is fixed?

Now, imagine the creation of the Federal Reserve. What actions could the Fed take to prevent a contraction in the money supply if a crisis of bank confidence occurred? Work this through using the balance sheet for the Fed and for banks (in Table 12-2).

PART THREE

MACROECONOMIC POLICY

CHAPTER 13___
UNEMPLOYMENT

*Be nice to people on your way up because you'll
meet them on your way down.*

Wilson Mizner

WE NOW TURN to one of the central social concerns of
modern capitalism: How can millions of people be
unemployed when there is so much work to be done?
What flaw in a modern mixed economy forces so
many who want work to remain idle? These questions, and their relationship to inflation, concern
workers, policymakers, and economists more than
any other economic problem.

The present chapter is a tour of concepts, facts, and
policy problems that relate to unemployment. In the
following sections, we first discuss the reason that the
topic is of such importance; we review the official
definition of unemployment; and we describe the economic interpretation of unemployment, particularly
involuntary unemployment. In the final two parts of
this chapter, we examine in detail the microeconomic
foundations of unemployment and then end with a
review of the key questions about unemployment policy facing the nation today.

Before we launch into our unemployment discussion, Figure 13-1 reminds us where it fits into the
logical structure of macroeconomics. Earlier chapters
showed, in both classical and Keynesian approaches,
how aggregate demand and supply are determined,
and how these interact to affect output and prices.

283

CHAPTER OVERVIEW

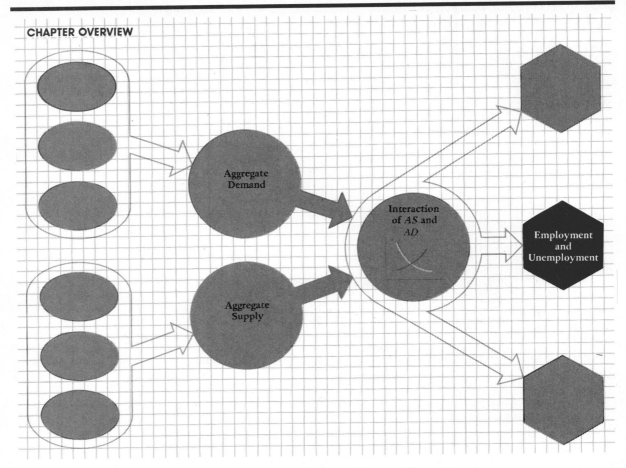

Figure 13-1 Chapter 13 analyzes the sources and nature of unemployment

Earlier chapters have examined how output is determined. We now turn to a detailed discussion of the definition and economic impact of unemployment.

Chapter 10 introduced Okun's Law, which shows that every 2 percent fall in output from its potential leads to a 1-percentage-point increase in the overall unemployment rate.

We now survey the definitions of unemployment along with the patterns of labor-force participation among different groups. Our survey will allow us to understand why policies to create jobs or reduce the burden of joblessness are among the most controversial topics of modern macroeconomics.

IMPORTANCE OF UNEMPLOYMENT

Unemployment is a central problem in modern societies. When unemployment is high, resources are wasted and people's incomes are depressed; during such periods, economic distress also spills over to affect people's emotions and family lives.

Economic Impact

The economic importance of employment, and the serious losses from unemployment, are facets that we reviewed in Chapter 10's analysis of business cycles. According to Okun's Law, periods of high unemployment are times in which actual GNP is below its potential. High unemployment is a symptom of waste—for during recessions, when unemployment is high, the economy is not producing up to par. During these times, it is as if vast quantities of automobiles, housing, clothing, and other commodities were simply dumped into the ocean.

How much waste occurs because of high unemployment? Table 13-1 gives a calculation of how far output fell short of potential GNP during the major periods of high unemployment over the last half-

century. The largest economic loss occurred during the Great Depression, but the stagnant 1970s and 1980s also witnessed more than a trillion dollars of lost output.

The losses during periods of high unemployment are the greatest documented wastes in a modern economy. They are many times larger than the estimated inefficiencies from monopoly (of Chapter 24) or than the waste induced by tariffs and quotas (to be discussed in Chapter 39).[1]

---

[1]At the same time, the estimated output losses shown in Table 13-1 may overestimate the true economic cost of recessions. As Chapter 6's estimates of NEW show, some of the idle time can be usefully put to work around the house, insulating walls, or tuning up your engine. Careful estimates by Northwestern University's Robert J. Gordon suggest, however, that this offset is only about 25 percent of the output loss due to the gap between actual and potential output. Even after these corrections, the macroeconomic losses from recessions appear very large relative to other microeconomic inefficiencies.

THE COST OF STAGNATION

		LOST OUTPUT	
PERIOD	AVERAGE UNEMPLOYMENT RATE (percent)	GNP LOSS in billions (1988 prices)	OF AVERAGE ANNUAL GNP DURING THE PERIOD
Great Depression (1930–39)	18.2	$2,850	385
Sluggish fifties (1954–60)	5.2	46	2
Stagnant seventies and eighties (1975–84)	7.6	1,333	35

Table 13-1   Economic costs from periods of high unemployment

The three major periods of high unemployment since 1929 occurred during the Great Depression, the sluggish fifties, and the stagnant period from 1975 to 1984. The amount of lost output shown above is calculated as the cumulative difference between potential GNP and actual GNP. Note that the Great Depression showed losses relative to GNP more than 10 times that of recent stagnant periods. (Source: Authors' estimates on the basis of official GNP and unemployment data.)

Social Impact

However large the economic costs of unemployment, a recounting of dollars lost does not adequately convey the human, social, and psychological toll that periods of persistent involuntary unemployment bring.

The personal tragedy of unemployment is conveyed by two personal reminiscences. The first depicts the futility of job search in San Francisco during the Great Depression.

> I'd get up at five in the morning and head for the waterfront. Outside the Spreckles Sugar Refinery, outside the gates, there would be a thousand men. You know dang well there's only three or four jobs. The guy would come out with two little Pinkerton cops: "I need two guys for the bull gang. Two guys to go into the hole." A thousand men would fight like a pack of Alaskan dogs to get through. Only four of us would get through.[2]

And here is the recollection of an unemployed construction worker:

> I called the roofing outfits and they didn't need me because they already had men that had been working for them five or six years. There wasn't that many openings. You had to have a college education for most of them. And I was looking for *anything*, from car wash to anything else.
>
> So what do you do all day? You go home and you sit. And you begin to get frustrated sitting home. Everybody in the household starts getting on edge. They start arguing with each other over stupid things 'cause they're all cramped in that space all the time. The whole family kind of got crushed by it.[3]

It would be surprising if such experiences did not scar their victims. And recent studies indicate that unemployment leads to a deterioration of both physical and psychological health—higher levels of heart disease, alcoholism, and suicide. The leading expert on the subject, Dr. M. Harvey Brenner, estimates that a 1-percentage-point rise in the unemployment rate

[2]Studs Terkel, *Hard Times: An Oral History of the Great Depression in America* (Pantheon, New York, 1970).

[3]Harry Maurer, *Not Working: An Oral History of the Unemployed* (Holt, New York, 1979).

STRESS ASSOCIATED WITH JOBLESSNESS AND OTHER EVENTS

LIFE EVENT	LEVEL OF STRESS ASSOCIATED WITH EVENT
Death of spouse	100
Went to jail	66
Fired from job	**49**
Close friend died	47
Laid off from job	**40**
Failed school	37
Child left home	29
Major change in working conditions	20

Table 13-2 Losing a job is a traumatic event
Social scientists have surveyed people to determine the amount of stress that occurs after important events. The scale here is set such that "death of spouse" equals 100. Note that involuntary separations from work rank high on the list. [Sources: T. H. Holmes, "The Social Readjustment Rating Scale," *Journal of Psychosomatic Research,* 1967; B. S. Dohrenwend, L. Krasnoff, A. R. Askenasy, and B. P. Dohrenwend, "The Psychiatric Epidemiology Research Interview Life Events Scale," in L. Goldberger and S. Breznitz, *Handbook of Stress* (Free Press, New York, 1982).]

sustained over a period of 6 years would lead to 37,000 early deaths in the United States. Table 13-2 shows an index of the stress caused by different "life events," ranging from death of family and friends to changing working conditions. These and other studies indicate that involuntary joblessness is a highly traumatic event for many people.

MEASURING UNEMPLOYMENT

Changes in the unemployment rate make monthly headlines. What lies behind the numbers? Data on work and unemployment are among the most carefully designed and comprehensive economic data the nation collects—as is appropriate to such an important issue. The data are collected monthly in a procedure known as *random sampling* of the

DEPLOYMENT OF THE POPULATION

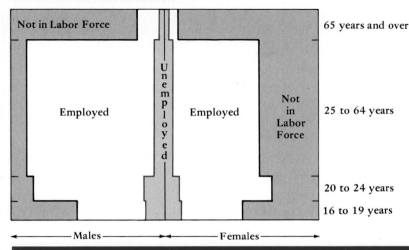

Figure 13-2 Labor-force status of the population, 1988

How do Americans spend their time? This figure shows how males and females of different ages are divided among employment, unemployment, and not in the labor force. The size of each block shows the relative proportion of the population in the designated category. Note the continuing difference in labor-force behavior of men and women. (Source: U.S. Department of Labor, *Employment and Earnings*.)

population.[4] Each month about 60,000 households are interviewed—with questions asked about their recent work patterns.

The survey divides the population 16 years and older into three groups:

- **Employed.** These are people who perform any paid work, as well as those with jobs but absent from work because of illness, strikes, or vacations.

- **Unemployed.** This includes people who are not employed but are actively looking for work or waiting to return to work. More precisely, a person is unemployed if he or she is not working and *(a)* has made specific efforts to find a job during the last 4 weeks, *(b)* is laid off from a job and is waiting to be recalled, or *(c)* is waiting to report to a job in the next month. To be counted as unemployed a person must do more than simply think about work or, for example, contemplate the possibility of writing a novel. A person

must report specific efforts (like visiting local firms or answering want ads) to find a job. Those who are either employed or unemployed are in the **labor force.**

- Everyone else is *not in the labor force*. This includes the 36 percent of the adult population that is going to school, keeping house, retired, too ill to work, or is simply not looking for work.

Thus the government's rule is the following:

People with jobs are employed; people without jobs but looking for work are unemployed; people without jobs who are not looking for work are outside the labor force. The *unemployment rate* is the number of unemployed divided by the total labor force.

Figure 13-2 shows how the male and female populations in the United States are divided among the three categories.

Criticisms of Official Estimates

The official data on employment and unemployment have proven valuable tools for understanding economic behavior over the half-century since they were first developed. Yet critics have pointed to a number of shortcomings of these data. The most important is that the official rate underestimates the extent of un-

---

[4]Random sampling is an extremely useful technique for estimating the behavior or characteristics of the population as a whole without visiting 250 million people. It consists of choosing a subgroup of a population at random (say, by selecting telephone digits by a computer-generated series of random numbers) and then surveying the selected group. Random sampling is used in market research, TV ratings, public-opinion polling, and many other areas.

employment because it excludes "discouraged workers." Thus at the trough of the 1981–1982 recession, November 1982, there were estimated to be 1.8 million workers who wanted jobs but were not looking because they thought none were available. In addition, the official index does not count workers whose jobs have been downgraded or who must work shorter hours. In 1982, there were over 2 million workers who usually worked full time but worked part time because the demand for labor was depressed. Neither the discouraged workers nor the part-time workers were counted as unemployed.

Should the definition of unemployment be revised to incorporate discouraged workers and involuntary part-time workers? Should the unemployment rate be changed into an index of "hardship," with those suffering the most weighted more heavily? Numerous commissions have considered these issues, but the questions have always been resolved in favor of the current approach. The reason against changing the definition is that attempting to measure "discouragement" or "hardship" would require inherently subjective and highly controversial judgments about a person's motivation or reliability. How do we measure distress or hardship? How do we tell that a person is really too discouraged to look for work? Statisticians are naturally reluctant to risk tainting objective data on people's activities with subjective data on their attitudes.

ECONOMIC INTERPRETATION OF UNEMPLOYMENT

Turn now from the way the government counts the unemployed to the economic analysis of unemployment. Some of the important questions we address are: What are the different reasons for being unemployed? What is the distinction between "voluntary" and "involuntary" unemployment? What is the relationship between different kinds of unemployment and the business cycle?

Three Kinds of Unemployment

In sorting out the structure of today's labor markets, we can usefully identify three different kinds of unemployment: frictional, structural, and cyclical.

Frictional unemployment arises because of the incessant movement of people between regions and jobs or through different stages of the life cycle. Even if an economy were at full employment, there would always be some turnover as people search for jobs when they graduate from school or move to a new city. Women may reenter the labor force after having children. Because frictionally unemployed workers are often moving between jobs, or looking for better jobs, it is often thought that they are "voluntarily" unemployed.

Structural unemployment occurs when there is a mismatch between the supply of and the demand for workers. Mismatches can occur because the demand for one kind of labor is rising while the demand for another kind is falling, and supplies do not quickly adjust. Thus we often see imbalances across occupations or regions as certain sectors grow while others decline. If wages adjusted smoothly to changing supplies and demands, then imbalances across labor markets would disappear as wages fell in areas of labor surpluses while rising in areas of labor shortages. But wages do not respond quickly to economic shocks; rather, they take years to adjust to shortages or surpluses. For example, even though an acute shortage of nurses arose in the mid-1980s, nurses' salaries rose only a little bit faster than other salaries; some hospitals were forced to leave beds vacant for want of nurses. By contrast, the demand for steelworkers has been depressed since the mid-1970s, yet those workers' wages hardly fell relative to others, and unemployment among steelworkers continued above average for more than a decade. In extreme cases, such as in coal-mining regions of Appalachia, unemployment can reach rates of 25 percent in individual states or even 75 percent in isolated communities.

Cyclical unemployment exists when the overall demand for labor is low (rather than demand for labor being low in certain pockets like coal or auto towns). As total spending and output fall, we see unemployment rising virtually everywhere. Thus in the recession year 1982, the unemployment rate rose in 48 of the 50 states. This rise in unemployment in virtually every region was a signal that the increased unemployment was largely cyclical.

The distinction between cyclical and other kinds of joblessness helps economists diagnose the general health of the labor market. High levels of frictional or structural unemployment can occur even though the overall labor market is in balance, for example, when turnover is high or when geographical imbalances are large. Cyclical unemployment arises when employment falls as a result of insufficient aggregate demand.

Microeconomic Foundations

No topic has generated more puzzlement or controversy among economists than the reasons for unemployment in a market economy. Economics teaches that prices rise or fall to clear competitive markets. At the market-clearing price, buyers willingly buy what sellers willingly sell. But something is gumming up the workings of the competitive labor market, for many hospitals are searching for nurses but cannot find them while thousands of steelworkers want to work at the going wage but cannot find a job. Nor is this strictly an American phenomenon. Unemployment in Europe today is almost 10 times what it was two decades ago, and a whole generation of workers in Britain is growing up in an economy of high unemployment. Just what is causing this market breakdown?

Economists have looked to microeconomics to help understand the existence of unemployment. In their search for answers, no universally accepted theory has emerged. But most analyses share a common theme: the inflexibility of wages. We therefore explore the reasons why inflexible wages lead to involuntary unemployment along with the reasons why wages are inflexible.

Employment under Flexible and Inflexible Wages

We begin our analysis of the microeconomic foundations of unemployment theory by considering a typical labor market. A group of workers has a labor supply schedule shown as *SS* in Figure 13-3 on the next page. The supply curve becomes completely inelastic at labor quantity L^* when wage levels are high. We will call L^* the labor force. For low wage levels, the quantity of labor supplied declines.

Voluntary Unemployment

The left-hand panel of Figure 13-3 at the top of the next page shows the usual picture of supply and demand, with a market-clearing intersection at point *E* with a wage of *W*. At that competitive, market-clearing equilibrium, the going wage ensures that firms willingly hire all qualified workers who wish to work at that wage. The number of employed is represented by the line from *A* to *E*. Some members of the labor force, shown by the segment *EF,* would like to work, but only at a higher wage rate. *The workers represented by the segment from E to F are "voluntarily" unemployed in the sense that they do not want to work at the going market wage rate.*

The existence of voluntary unemployment points to an important misconception about unemployment. An economy may well be performing at the peak of efficiency even though it generates a certain amount of unemployment. The voluntarily unemployed workers might prefer leisure or school or other activities to working at the going wage rate. Or they may be frictionally unemployed and moving from college to their first job. Or they might be mothers or fathers who decided to take home leave to care for young children. They might actually have a job offer but be busily scurrying around to find a better or higher-paying job. They might decide to retire early and move to California. Or they might be low-productivity workers who prefer leisure to low-paid work. There are countless reasons why people might voluntarily choose not to work at the going wage rate, and some of these people would be officially counted as unemployed.

It is important to note that voluntary unemployment might well be economically efficient. Having some unemployment might help maximize the nation's net economic welfare or GNP, even though a philosopher or politician might bemoan the fact that everybody cannot obtain high-paying jobs. The fact is that, even when it is operating at the peak of its productivity, a complex modern economy—with thousands of different skills and jobs—may produce a considerable volume of unemployment. That fact reinforces a point often made about competitive markets: They are alert to efficiency but blind to equity.

In summary, a labor market characterized by perfectly flexible wages cannot underproduce or have involuntary unemployment. Prices and wages simply float up or down until the markets are cleared. In any

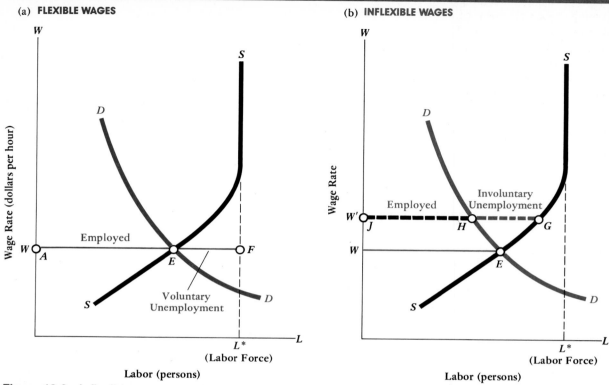

Figure 13-3   Inflexible wages can lead to involuntary unemployment

We can depict different kinds of unemployment using the supply-and-demand framework of Chapter 4. In **(a)**, wages move up or down to clear the labor market. There is never any involuntary unemployment.

Part **(b)** shows what happens if wages do not adjust to clear the labor market. At the too high wage at *W'*, *JH* workers are employed, but *HG* workers are involuntarily unemployed.

economy with perfectly flexible wages, the kind of unemployment that the world was experiencing as Keynes wrote the *General Theory* in the 1930s, or that Europe saw in the 1980s, would simply not exist.

Involuntary Unemployment Go back to read the quotations from unemployed workers at the beginning of this chapter. No one would say that these workers are carefully balancing the value of work against the value of leisure, or that they are asking themselves if they should continue to be unemployed while they search for a better job. The theory of voluntary unemployment cannot cope with such facts. Keynes' great breakthrough was to let the facts oust a beautiful but

irrelevant theory. He began to explain why we see occasional bouts of involuntary unemployment, periods in which qualified workers are unable to get jobs at the going wage rates.

Keynes argued that wages in reality do not adjust to clear labor markets. Rather, wages tend to respond sluggishly in response to economic shocks. If wages do not move to clear markets, there can arise a mismatch between job seekers and job vacancies. This mismatch may lead to the patterns of unemployment that we see today.

To understand the way inflexible wages lead to involuntary unemployment requires an analysis of *non-market-clearing economies*. An illustration of this analysis is shown in Figure 13-3(b). This figure assumes that, in the wake of an economic disturbance, the labor market finds itself with too high a wage rate. Labor's price is at W' rather than at the equilibrium or market-clearing wage of W.

What is the result? At the too high wage rate, there are more qualified workers desiring to work than there are jobs looking for workers. The number of workers willing to work at wage W' is found at point G on the supply curve, but firms only want to hire H workers, as shown by the demand curve. Because the wage is above the market-clearing level, there is a surplus of workers. The quantity JH indicates the number who ultimately find jobs. The group of unemployed workers represented by the dashed line segment HG is *involuntarily unemployed,* signifying that they are qualified workers who wish to work at the prevailing wage but cannot find jobs. When there is a surplus of workers, firms will set more stringent skill requirements, add to the workload, and hire the most qualified or most experienced workers.

You can also see the opposite case, where the wage is too low. This is the case of the labor-shortage economy, where employers cannot find enough workers to fill the existing vacancies. Firms put "Help Wanted" signs in their windows, advertise in the newspaper, and even recruit people from other towns.

Sources of Inflexibility The theory of involuntary unemployment rests on inflexible wages. But why do wages not move up or down to clear markets? Would not the economy function better if labor markets were more like auction markets?

The answers to these questions are among the deepest unresolved mysteries of modern economics. Few economists today would argue that wages move quickly to erase labor shortages and surpluses. Yet no one completely understands the reasons for the sluggish behavior of wages and salaries. We can therefore provide no more than a tentative assessment of the sources of wage inflexibility.

The major distinction that should be made is the difference between auction markets and administered markets. An *auction market* is a highly organized and competitive market where the price floats up or down to balance supply and demand. At the Chicago Board of Trade, for example, the prices of "number 2 stiff red wheat delivered in St. Louis" or "dressed 'A' broiler chickens delivered in New York" change every minute to reflect market conditions—market conditions that are seen in the buy and sell orders of farmers, millers, packers, merchants, and speculators.

But 90 percent of all goods, as well as 100 percent of all labor, is sold in administered markets and not in competitive auction markets. Nobody grades labor into "number 2 sheet steelworker" or "class 'AA' assistant professor of economics." No specialist is worked into a frenzy trying to make sure that steelworkers' wages or professors' salaries are set at just the level where all qualified workers are placed into a job.

Rather, most firms *administer* their wages and salaries, setting fixed pay scales and hiring people at an entry-level wage or salary. These wage scales are generally fixed for a year or so, and when they are adjusted, the pay for almost all categories goes up by the same percentage. For example, a bank might have 15 different categories of staff: three grades of secretaries, two grades of tellers, one class of courier, and so forth. Each year, the bank managers will decide how much to increase wages and salaries—say 5.5 percent in 1989—and the compensation in each category will then move up by that same percentage. On infrequent occasions the bank might decide to move one category up or down more than the average. Given the procedure by which wages and salaries are determined, there is little room to have major adjustments when the firm finds shortages or gluts in a particular area. Except in extreme cases, the firm will tend to adjust the minimum qualifications required for a job rather than its wages when it finds labor market disequilibrium.[5]

For unionized labor markets, the wage patterns are even more rigid. Wage scales are typically set for a 3-year contract period; during that period, wages are

---

[5]The example of college admissions will illustrate the kind of adjustment that takes place when shortages or gluts occur. Many colleges found that applications for places soared in the 1980s. How did they react? Did they raise their tuition enough to choke off the excess demand? No. Instead, they raised their admission standards, requiring better grades in high schools and higher average SAT scores. This process of upgrading the requirements rather than changing wages and prices is exactly what happens in the short run when firms experience excess supply of labor.

not adjusted for excess supply or demand in particular areas. Moreover, unionized workers seldom accept wage cuts even when many of their workers are unemployed. It is a costly and divisive task—pitting senior against junior workers, hurting morale and productivity—when firms and unions renegotiate existing contracts to cut wages in the hope of increasing employment. Little wonder that union contracts are so rarely reopened in mid-contract.

To summarize, a careful look at wage setting in America today finds a highly administered process. Wages and salaries are generally set infrequently, usually no more than once a year, and relative wages tend to change very slowly. *Wages and salaries adjust to reflect shortages or surpluses in a particular market only over an extended period of time.*

What is the economic reason for the sluggishness of wages and salaries? Most economists believe that the inflexibility arises because of the costs of administering compensation. To take the example of union wages, a long process, requiring much management time, is needed every time a new collective bargaining agreement is settled. The process is so costly that such agreements are only negotiated once every 3 years.

Setting compensation for nonunion workers is less costly, but it nevertheless requires considerable scarce management time. Every time wages or salaries are set, every time fringe benefits are changed, previous understandings are changed as well. Some workers will become upset, others complain about unjust procedures, and grievances may be triggered. Personnel managers have therefore moved to a system in which wages are adjusted infrequently and most workers in a firm get the same pay increase, even though the market conditions may differ for different skills or categories. While this system may appear inefficient to economists, because it does not allow for a perfect reflection of market supply and demand, this process in fact economizes on scarce managerial time and helps promote a sense of fair play and equity in the firm. In the end, it is much cheaper to recruit workers more actively or to change the cutoff for qualifications than it is to upset the entire wage structure of a firm simply to hire a few new workers.

We emphasize that the fundamental reason for involuntary unemployment lies in the administered nature of wages: Labor markets do not clear instantaneously, so we see surpluses and shortages appearing in individual labor markets. But labor markets do eventually respond to market conditions, and wages of high-demand occupations move up relative to low-demand occupations. Labor markets look very much like the non-market-clearing example of Figure 13-3(b) in the short run. But in the long run, wages tend to move to balance supply and demand, so major pockets of unemployment or of job vacancies tend to disappear as wages and quantities adjust to market conditions. In between the long run and the short run, however, periods of unemployment can persist for many years.

LABOR MARKET ISSUES

Having analyzed the functioning of labor markets, we turn next to major labor market issues for today. Which groups are most likely to be unemployed? How long are they unemployed? What is the natural rate of unemployment, and why is this natural rate rising over time?

Who Are the Unemployed?

In attempting to understand who the unemployed workers are, it will be useful to track labor market conditions in periods when unemployment is low (as in 1973) as well as in recession years (such as 1982).

Several features of labor markets are seen from a careful reading of Table 13-3, which shows figures on unemployment statistics for boom and recession. The first two columns of numbers are the unemployment rates by age, race, and sex. These data show that the unemployment rate of every group tends to rise during recession. The last two columns show how the total pool of unemployment is distributed among different groups; observe that the distribution of unemployment across groups changes relatively little across the business cycle.

Note also that nonwhites tend to experience unemployment rates twice those of whites. The relative unemployment rates of males and females, on the other hand, have reversed over the last decade.

LABOR MARKET GROUP	UNEMPLOYMENT RATE OF DIFFERENT GROUPS (percent of labor force)		DISTRIBUTION OF TOTAL UNEMPLOYMENT ACROSS DIFFERENT GROUPS (percent of total unemployed)	
	BOOM (1973)	RECESSION (1982)	BOOM (1973)	RECESSION (1982)
By age:				
16–19 years	14.5	23.2	28.5	18.5
20 years and older	3.8	8.6	71.5	81.5
By race:				
White	4.3	8.6	79.2	77.2
Black and other	8.9	17.3	20.8	22.8
By sex (adults only):				
Male	3.3	8.8	51.8	58.5
Female	4.8	8.3	48.2	41.5
All workers	**4.9**	**9.7**	**100.0**	**100.0**

Table 13-3   Unemployment by demographic group

This table shows how unemployment varies across different demographic groups in boom and recession years. The first set of figures shows the unemployment rate for each group in 1973 and 1982. The last two columns show the percent of the total pool of unemployed that lies in each group. (Source: U.S. Department of Labor, *Employment and Earnings*.)

Women have generally faced higher unemployment rates than men, but this was not the case in 1982.

Finally, note that the importance of teenagers to unemployment is much greater in boom than in recession. In the boom period of 1973, teenagers were more than one-quarter of all unemployed workers. In deep recession they were less than one-fifth.

Duration Another key question concerns duration. How much of the unemployment experience is long-term and of major social concern, and how much is short-term as people move quickly between jobs?

Figure 13-4 shows the duration of unemployment in boom and recession, again using 1973 and 1982 data. A surprising feature of American labor markets is that a very large fraction of unemployment is of very short duration. Thus in the boom year of 1973, less than one-fifth of unemployment lasted more than 14 weeks. In recessions, however, it takes considerably longer to find jobs, and long-term unemployment becomes a serious social problem. The number of workers out of a job for more than 6 months rose from 340,000 in 1973 to 2,600,000 at the end of 1982. And in Europe, with lower mobility and greater institutional rigidity, long-term unemployment in the mid-1980s reached 50 percent of unemployed. Long-term unemployment poses a problem because the resources that families have available—their savings, unemployment insurance, and goodwill toward one another—begin to run out after a few months.

Source of Joblessness A final question we ask is: Why are people unemployed? Figure 13-5 shows how people responded when asked the source of their unemployment, again for 1973 and 1982.

There is always some unemployment that results from changes in people's residence or from the life cycle—moving, entering the labor force for the first time, and so forth. The major changes in the unemployment rate over time arise from the increase in job losers. This source swells enormously in recession for two reasons: First the number of people who lose their jobs increases, and then (as shown in Figure 13-4) it takes longer to find a new job.

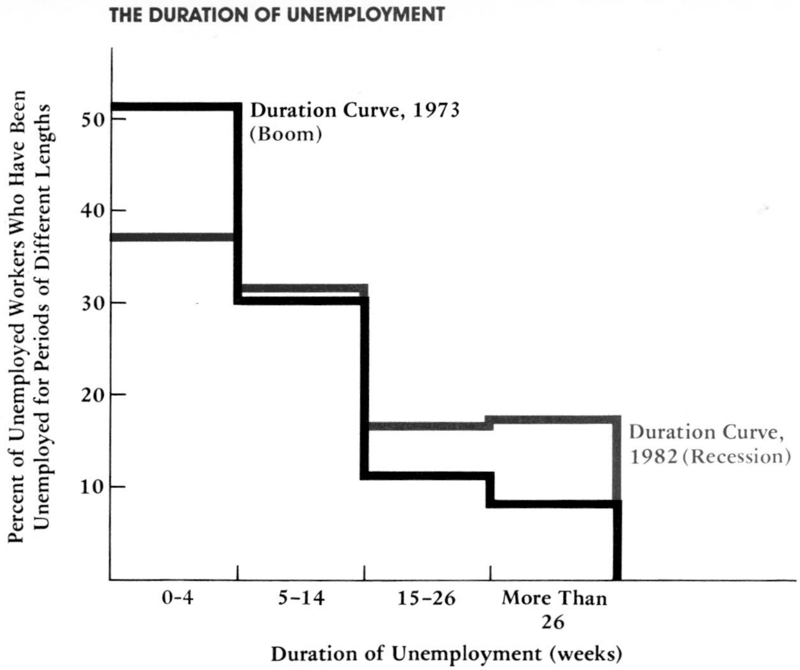

THE DURATION OF UNEMPLOYMENT

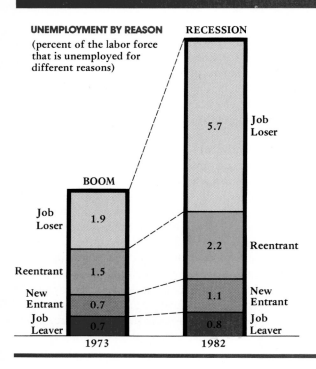

Percent of Unemployed Workers Who Have Been Unemployed for Periods of Different Lengths

Duration Curve, 1973 (Boom)

Duration Curve, 1982 (Recession)

Duration of Unemployment (weeks)

0-4   5-14   15-26   More Than 26

Figure 13-4   Most unemployment in the United States is short-term, but long-term unemployment increases in recessions

How long does it take workers to find jobs? The "duration curves" in the figure show what percent of the unemployed have been unemployed for different periods. Thus in the boom year 1973, only 8 percent of the unemployed were unemployed for more than 26 weeks. In the deep-recession year of 1982, the incidence of very long-term unemployment (over 26 weeks) had increased to 1.8 million, or 17 percent of the unemployed. Thus the duration curve in recession tends to flatten, with more people having to wait longer to find jobs and therefore with fewer people daring to quit jobs they don't like. (Source: U.S. Department of Labor, *Employment and Earnings*.)

UNEMPLOYMENT BY REASON
(percent of the labor force that is unemployed for different reasons)

RECESSION

BOOM

Job Loser   1.9

Reentrant   1.5

New Entrant   0.7

Job Leaver   0.7

1973

Job Loser   5.7

Reentrant   2.2

New Entrant   1.1

Job Leaver   0.8

1982

Figure 13-5   Distribution of unemployment by reason

Why did people become unemployed? Less than 1 percent of the labor force are unemployed because they left their jobs, and another 2 to 3 percent are new entrants into the labor force (say, because they just graduated from college) or reentrants (people who had earlier left the labor force and are back looking for a job). The major change from boom to recession, however, is found in the number of job losers. From 1973 to 1982 the fraction of the labor force unemployed because they lost their jobs rose by a factor of 3. (Source: U.S. Department of Labor, *Employment and Earnings.*)

Teenage Unemployment Primarily Frictional

Teenagers generally have the highest unemployment rate of any demographic group, and black teenagers in recent years have experienced unemployment rates between 40 and 48 percent. Is this unemployment frictional, structural, or cyclical?

Recent evidence indicates that, particularly for whites, teenage unemployment has a large frictional component. Teenagers move in and out of the labor force very frequently. They get jobs quickly and change jobs frequently. The average time spent unemployed by teenagers (the duration of their unemployment) is only half the period of adults; the average length of a typical job is 12 times greater for adults than teenagers. In most years, half the unemployed teenagers are "new entrants" who have never had a paying job before. All these phenomena suggest that teenage unemployment is largely frictional—that is, it represents the job search and turnover necessary for young people to find out their personal skills and to learn what working is all about.

But teenagers do eventually learn the skills and work habits of experienced workers. Table 13-4 shows the unemployment rate for white males by age in 1987. The acquisition of experience and training, along with a greater desire and need for full-time work, leads middle-aged workers to have much lower unemployment rates than teenagers.

Black Teenage Unemployment While the description of teenage unemployment as largely frictional applies reasonably well to white teenagers, the situation among black youths has been a major puzzle to analysts. After World War II, the labor market data for black teenagers was virtually identical to that for white teenagers. The labor-force participation rates and unemployment rates of black and white teenagers were virtually identical until 1955. Since that time, however, unemployment rates for black teenagers have risen relative to other groups while their labor-force participation rates fell. By 1988, 35 percent of black teenagers (16 to 19 years of age) were unemployed as compared to 13 percent of white teenagers. The employment rate (equal to the ratio of total em-

UNEMPLOYMENT BY AGE, 1987

AGE	UNEMPLOYMENT RATE (percent of labor force)
16–17	16.7
18–19	12.7
20–24	8.0
25–34	5.1
35–44	4.0
45–54	3.7
55–64	3.2
65 and over	2.4

Table 13-4   Unemployment rate for white males, 1987

As workers search for jobs and gain training, they settle on a particular occupation; they tend to stay in the labor force; and they find a preferred employer. As a result, the unemployment rate of mid-life males falls to one-fourth that of teenage males. (Source: U.S. Department of Labor, *Employment and Earnings*, January 1988.)

ployment to total population) was only 27 percent for black teenagers as opposed to 51 percent for white teenagers.

What could explain this extraordinary divergence in the experience of the two groups? One explanation might be that labor market trends have worked against black workers in general. This explanation does not tell the whole story. While adult black workers have always suffered higher unemployment rates than adult white workers—because of lower education levels, fewer contacts with people who can provide jobs, less on-the-job training, and racial discrimination—the ratio of black to white adult unemployment rates has not increased since World War II.

Numerous studies of the sources of the rising black teenage unemployment rate have turned up no clear explanations of the trend. One possible source is discrimination, but for the black-white unemployment differential to rise would require a rising intensity of discrimination—for which there is no evidence. One study finds that many black teenagers have little interest in low-paying jobs in the service sector. Another study points to the decline of agriculture, historically an important source of jobs for southern black youths, as a factor.

Another theory holds that a high minimum wage tends to drive low-productivity black teenagers into unemployment. The change in the relation of the minimum wage to average wages would allow a test of this hypothesis. From 1981 to 1988, the ratio of the minimum wage to average wages in nonfarm establishments fell from 46 percent to 35 percent, yet no improvement in the relative unemployment situation of black teenagers occurred. That no improvement took place casts doubt on the minimum wage as the prime suspect. One conservative critic of the modern welfare state, Charles Murray, blames high unemployment of blacks on the culture of dependency that is nurtured by government aid to the poor; analysts find little concrete evidence to support Murray's theory.[6] Taken as a whole, existing studies explain but a small fraction of the puzzle of rising black teenage unemployment.

Does high teenage unemployment lead to long-lasting labor market damage, with permanently lower levels of skills and wage rates? This question has been a topic of intensive research over the last decade. The tentative answer is: Yes, there are long-run effects of high unemployment, particularly for black teenagers. It appears that when youths are unable to develop on-the-job skills and work attitudes, they experience lower wages and higher unemployment when they are older. To the extent that this research is validated, it suggests that public policy has an important stake in devising programs to reduce teenage unemployment among minority groups.

THE NATURAL RATE OF UNEMPLOYMENT

Why is the unemployment rate so high? And can society do anything to reduce the waste and misery caused by periods of high unemployment?

---

[6]A fuller discussion of Murray's theory of America's "losing ground" to poverty and dependency is contained in Chapter 34.

Concepts and Estimates

To understand these issues, we turn to the concept of the natural rate of unemployment.[7] The natural rate is the unemployment rate at which labor and product markets are in balance. More precisely:

The **natural rate of unemployment** is that rate at which upward and downward forces on price and wage inflation are in balance. At the natural rate, inflation is stable, with no tendency to show either accelerating or declining inflation. In a modern economy, concerned with preventing high inflation rates, the natural rate of unemployment is the lowest level that can be sustained; it thus represents the highest sustainable level of employment and corresponds to a nation's potential output.

Natural Rate above Zero There are two important points to be understood about the natural rate. First, the natural rate is not zero—a substantial number of people are unemployed in a high-employment economy. Why is this? Because in a large country, with high levels of mobility, diversity in tastes and talents, constant change in the demand for and supply of the myriad goods and services, there will be substantial frictional and structural unemployment. Recall from Figure 13-5 that 2 to 3 percent of the labor force usually are unemployed new entrants or reentrants into the labor force, and another 1 percent or so are unemployed because they have quit work. Thus in the highly mobile United States of the 1980s, we would see 3 or 4 percent of the labor force unemployed even if no one ever lost a job.

Relation to Inflation Second, the natural rate is intimately related to the process of inflation. Societies prefer low to high unemployment. Why should we not have an unemployment rate of 2 or 3 percent, as we did in World War II or during the Korean conflict, rather than the 5 to 10 percent that we suffered during the 1970s and 1980s? The only clear reason not to

---

[7]Some economists prefer the more descriptive term, the "non-accelerating-inflation rate of unemployment" or "NAIRU."

allow the economy to attain such low unemployment rates is concern for the inflationary consequences: Such low rates would lead to an accelerating spiral of inflation rates past 10 or 15 or 20 percent per year. The natural rate is the lowest unemployment rate the nation can enjoy without risking an unacceptable acceleration of inflation.

The natural rate is the golden mean between too high and too low, that level at which inflation neither rises from excess demands nor falls from excess supplies. It comes at the unemployment threshold below which pressures in labor and product markets tend to lead to wages and prices rising faster and faster every year.

Societies are extremely averse to accelerating inflation (for reasons to be plumbed in the next chapter). Responsible and farsighted policymakers therefore generally do not intentionally aim the economy at utilization rates above potential GNP, or unemployment rates below the natural rate. To do so would lead to rising inflation.

This discussion also shows why the level of output that corresponds to the natural rate of unemployment is a nation's potential output. Recall from Chapters 5 and 10 that potential output is the highest sustainable level of GNP. Why does the highest sustainable level of GNP come with unemployment at the natural rate? The reason is that, were unemployment to be lower and output to be higher, inflation would spiral upward. Because nations are unwilling to allow inflation to gallop ever faster, they cannot permanently operate their economies at unemployment rates lower than the natural rate; hence, a nation's potential output comes at its natural rate of unemployment.

Because inflation acts as a constraint on economic policy, the natural rate of unemployment is the lowest unemployment rate that can be indefinitely sustained.

Quantitative Estimates Although many economists find the concept of the natural unemployment rate highly useful, precise numerical estimates of the natural rate have proven elusive. One of the leading experts on the subject, Northwestern University's Robert J. Gordon, estimates that the natural rate was around 6 percent of the labor force in the 1980s. His estimates, along with the actual unemployment rate, are shown in Figure 13-6 on the next page. Other economists, such as those on President Reagan's Council of Economic Advisers, believed that the natural rate was higher, somewhere in the 6 to 7 percent range. Most economists agree that, with today's price-and-wage-setting institutions, the United States could not maintain an unemployment rate well below 6 percent without experiencing rising inflation.

Why so High? Why can the nation not guarantee good jobs to all without accelerating inflation? One reason is simply that in America the amount of turnover, or frictional unemployment, is high when job opportunities are plentiful. Thus in the last year in which the economy was near its natural rate, 1988, one-third of the unemployed workers were young (less than 25 years old). Only $2\frac{1}{2}$ percent of the labor force were unemployed job losers. There were $2\frac{1}{4}$ times as many quits as layoffs in manufacturing.

In addition to the frictional component of unemployment, there is normally a great deal of structural and involuntary unemployment. Even when the unemployment rate is low, a substantial fraction of the unemployed are job losers and long-term unemployed. Labor markets do not quickly match up job vacancies and the unemployed.

In sum, the natural rate is high in the United States in part because mobility of workers is so great, and in part because the labor market is unable to match up quickly job vacancies with unemployed workers.

Doubts about the Natural Rate The concept of the natural rate of unemployment, along with its output twin, potential GNP, forms the central core of modern macroeconomics. Yet, many economists have some lingering doubts about the validity of the natural-rate concept. One major concern revolves around whether the natural rate is a stable magnitude. Will an extended period of high unemployment lead to a deterioration of job skills, loss of on-the-job training and experience, and thereby to a higher natural rate of unemployment? Might not slow growth of real GNP, with investment low because of the accelerator mechanism, leave the country with a diminished capital

THE NATURAL RATE OF UNEMPLOYMENT

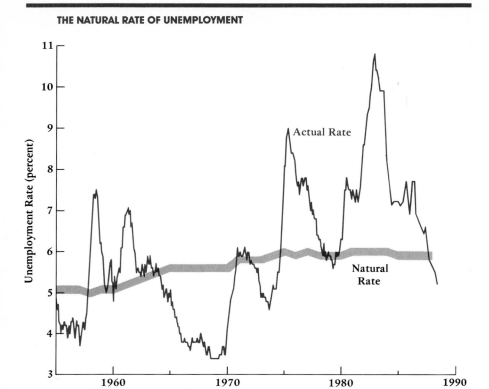

Figure 13-6   Actual and natural rate of unemployment, 1955–1988

The natural rate of unemployment is that level at which forces on wages and prices are in balance. Below that rate, inflation generally tends to rise; above it, inflation tends to subside.

Note that the natural rate has risen substantially over the last quarter-century. Today, it appears to be around 6 percent. Also note that the natural rate is given as a wide band to reflect the fact that it is difficult to estimate the natural rate precisely. (Source: Actual unemployment rate from U.S. Department of Labor, *Employment and Earnings;* natural unemployment rate from Robert J. Gordon, "Understanding Inflation in the 1980s," *Brookings Papers on Economic Activity,* 1985, pp. 263–302, for 1954–1984, with other years from estimates by the authors.)

stock, so that a capacity shortage could produce rising inflation at unemployment rates above the natural rate?

Experience in Europe over the last two decades appears to confirm some of the doubters' concerns. In the early 1960s, labor markets in Germany, France, and Britain appeared to be in equilibrium with unemployment rates between 1 and 2 percent. By the mid-1980s, after a decade of stagnation and slow job growth, labor market equilibrium seemed to be in balance with unemployment rates in the 7 to 12 percent range. On the basis of recent European experience, some economists have questioned the utility of the natural-rate concept, pointing to its instability and dependence upon the actual history of unemployment.

The Rising Natural Rate

One of the most disturbing trends of recent years has been the upward drift in the natural rate. In the early 1960s, President Kennedy's economists concluded that at full employment of the labor force, the unemployment rate would be below 4 percent; the number was estimated to be 5 percent in the early 1970s. By the 1980s, as we have just seen, the natural rate was thought to be 6 percent or even higher. What is the reason for this trend? Economists point to three factors: demographic changes, government policy, and structural change.

Demographic Changes A first factor originates in the changing demographic structure of the labor force, particularly in the rising labor-force participation of teenagers, minorities, and women. Recall that adult males normally have the lowest unemployment rate of any group. Over the period 1950 to 1988, the share of adult men in the total labor force declined from 66 to 52 percent.

This changing composition of the labor force would raise the overall natural unemployment rate even though the natural unemployment rate for each group stayed the same. To see how a changing composition of the labor force affects the natural rate, suppose that in 1950 one-tenth of workers were youths with unemployment rates of 20 percent, and the rest were adults with unemployment rates of 4 percent.

The average unemployment rate would be $0.1 \times 20\% + 0.9 \times 4\% = 5.6\%$. Now in 1990 assume a proportion of one-fifth young and four-fifths adults. Then if each group had the same unemployment rate as before, the overall rate would be $0.2 \times 20\% + 0.8 \times 4\% = 7.2\%$. In the example, the changing composition of the labor force toward high-turnover, high-unemployment workers increases the natural rate by 1.6 percent.

Effects of Policy? Some analysts are fearful that humanitarian government policies have also led to an upward shift in the natural rate. One often-cited example is unemployment insurance (UI). In most states, a worker who is fired or laid off qualifies for UI and, for up to 26 weeks, the unemployed person can collect around 50 percent of prior wages.

As a result, workers search somewhat less assiduously for a new job when they are collecting UI. They are also understandably more likely to refuse a low-paying job. Consequently, the unemployment rate is higher. Similar effects are thought to occur because of welfare, food stamps, and other government transfer programs. A final factor is the minimum wage, which is thought to increase unemployment among low-paid workers.

How large is this "disincentive" effect of these government policies on the natural rate? The estimates range from a few tenths of a percentage point to more than a percent. Defenders of government transfer programs wonder, however, whether UI and other government programs could really have had a significant effect upon the natural rate in recent years. They point out that these programs were introduced in the 1930s. Moreover, the ratio of unemployment benefits paid to total wages and salaries has been unchanged since 1955, and the average benefit per unemployed worker, as a share of average wages, has declined in recent years. How much of the recent rise in the natural rate can then be attributed to social programs is, therefore, hotly contested.

However, not even the harshest critics recommend abolition of programs designed to alleviate the ravages of unemployment. Instead they usually point to reforms, such as raising taxes for those employers that have high turnover, cutting the benefit levels, and getting tougher on fraud and abuse.

Rising Structural Unemployment? In addition to the effects of demographic change and government programs, some economists believe that the natural rate is even higher than conventional estimates because of increasing structural unemployment. They point to the fact that the 1970s and 1980s produced severe shocks to industries and regions dependent on energy or exposed to international trade—auto and steel were depressed, oil drilling grew and then collapsed, and electronics boomed. In the 1970s, the sun belt prospered while the frost belt stagnated, but a decade later the northeast was again thriving.

Why would an increased *divergence* of labor markets or industries raise the natural rate? Recall that the natural rate is high because a dynamic economy is in constant flux. Firms, industries, and regions rise and fall, and it takes time for workers and firms to match up, much as it takes time for men and women to find the right mate. If, as a result of oil shocks and foreign competition, the unemployed workers are in Detroit or Pittsburgh while the job vacancies are in Boston or San Diego, the amount of dispersion in the economy rises—and so does the natural rate.

Examination of different markets does indeed suggest a rising pattern of structural unemployment over the last two decades. The divergences among regions have grown, as is demonstrated by a rising dispersion in unemployment rates across regions or demographic groups, as well as by increasing differences among regions in the ratio of help wanted to unemployment. Studies by David Lilien and James Medoff suggest that the natural rate in the 1970s and 1980s may have increased as much as 1 percentage point because of increasing structural unemployment.

There may be some grounds for optimism, however. As the labor force ages over the coming decade—and if the frequency and severity of oil, food, and external shocks to the economy abate—then the upward drift of the natural rate may reverse itself in the coming years.

Lowering the Natural Rate

As we see the natural rate of unemployment go from 4 to 5 to 6 percent and beyond, important public-policy questions arise: Is the natural rate the optimal level of unemployment? If not, what can we do to lower it toward a more desirable level?

We must start by noting that, although it has become common parlance among macroeconomists, the term "natural rate" is misleading. The natural rate is in no way natural; as we have seen above, it is influenced by the pattern of demographic change, by the kinds of shocks the economy experiences, by government's labor market policies, and perhaps even by the past history of unemployment itself.

Moreover, the natural rate is not necessarily the optimal unemployment rate. An optimal level of unemployment would come where net economic welfare was maximized. Theorists who have studied the relationship of unemployment to economic welfare find two reasons to think that the optimal unemployment rate is lower than the natural rate. First, if output were

maximized at the natural rate, then we would find that Okun's Law were repealed at very low unemployment rates. This is not the case. A glance back at Figure 10-3, p. 205, indicates that output continues to rise as unemployment falls below the natural rate.

A second reason to question the optimality of the natural rate comes from the spillovers involved in the social costs of unemployment. As we noted at the beginning of this chapter, when an employer lays off a worker, the worker suffers from a variety of social and economic hardships. Yet the employer does not pay the costs of unemployment; most of the costs spill over and are absorbed by the worker or by the government (in unemployment insurance, in welfare payments, in health costs, in family distress, and so forth). Causing unemployment is a bit like causing an externality such as pollution: The firm gets the benefits in lower costs but does not pay the full social costs. To the extent that unemployment has external costs, the natural unemployment rate is likely to be higher than the optimal rate.

The natural rate of unemployment is likely to be above the optimal unemployment rate, above that level of unemployment where net economic welfare is maximized.

If the natural rate is neither natural nor optimal, why can the nation not achieve a lower level of unemployment? The reason is, as we have stressed above, that such a step would lead to rising, and unacceptable, inflation. An enormous social dividend, therefore, awaits the economist who discovers how to reduce the natural rate by 1 or 2 percentage points.

What are the possible measures that might lower the natural rate?

• *Improve labor market services.* Some unemployment occurs because job vacancies are not matched up with unemployed workers. If better information, computerized job lists, and more training opportunities are provided, the amount of frictional and structural unemployment can be reduced.

• *Bolster government employment programs.* If you read the "Help Wanted" section of your Sunday newspaper, you will find that most of the job vacancies call for skills held by few people. Conversely, most of the unemployed are unskilled or semiskilled workers, or find themselves in the wrong job or in a depressed industry. Many believe that government training programs can help unemployed workers retool for better jobs in growing sectors. If successful, such programs provide the double bonus of allowing people to lead productive lives and of reducing the burden on government transfer programs.

■ *Remove government obstacles.* We noted above that, in protecting people from the hardships of unemployment and poverty, the government has at the same time removed the sting of unemployment and reduced incentives to seek work. Some economists call for reforming the unemployment-insurance system; reducing the disincentives for work in welfare, disability, and social security programs; adding work requirements to welfare programs; and reducing the minimum wage, or instituting a "sub-minimum wage" for teenagers.

■ *Create a high-pressure economy.* Having seen how prolonged European recessions seem to have increased the European natural rate, some economists believe that the United States should maintain a "high-pressure" economy, i.e., keep GNP high and drive the unemployment rate as low as possible. This would provide more secure jobs for low-skilled workers, help upgrade the labor force, reduce labor turnover, and allow workers to develop a permanent attachment to the labor force. A high-pressure economy that is operating with a full head of steam is particu-larly beneficial to female and minority workers, who tend to be the last hired and the first fired.

■ *Create public jobs.* A more radical proposal is for the government actually to create jobs for unemployed workers; under this approach, the government is "the employer of last resort." This policy would be particularly attractive if the public jobs were targeted principally at high-unemployment groups (especially minority teenagers). The result could be a long-lasting improvement of the skills and productivity, and a consequent lowering of the natural unemployment rate, of these groups. Many economists are skeptical of public-employment programs. They believe that the government jobs would simply displace private-sector jobs as the government spent its funds on public jobs rather than on privately produced goods and services. Studies of the effectiveness of public-service employment show mixed results.

Having reviewed the options for reducing the natural rate, we must enter a cautionary note: Three decades of research and labor market experiments on this subject have led objective analysts to be extremely modest in their claims. Short of solutions that force the unemployed to go hungry in the cold, most proposals would probably have but a very modest effect on the natural rate. It seems unlikely that a reduction of more than a few tenths of a percentage point could be accomplished by a set of politically acceptable reforms of the kinds outlined above.

SUMMARY

1. Although unemployment has plagued capitalism since the Industrial Revolution, understanding its causes and costs has been possible only with the rise of modern macroeconomic theory. It is now apparent that recessions and the associated high unemployment are extremely costly to the economy. Major periods of slack like the 1970s and 1980s cost the nation almost two-fifths of a year's GNP; additionally, they scar people as the unemployment spills over into stress, loss of skills, and heightened illness.

2. The monthly statistics on unemployment, employment, and the labor force are gathered in a sample survey of the population. People with jobs are employed; people without jobs but looking for work are unemployed; people without jobs who are not looking for work are outside the labor force. Over the last decade, 64 percent of the population over 16 was in the labor force, while 7 percent of the labor force was unemployed.

3. It is useful to classify unemployment into three classes:

(a) Frictional—workers who are simply moving between jobs

(b) Structural—workers who are in regions or industries that are in a persistent slump

(c) Cyclical—workers laid off when the overall economy suffers a downturn

4. Understanding the sources of unemployment has proved one of the major challenges of modern macroeconomics. Some unemployment, often called voluntary, would occur in a flexible-wage, perfectly competitive economy when qualified people chose not to work at the going wage rate. Voluntary unemployment might be the efficient (but not necessarily fair) outcome of competitive markets. A recession would be interpreted as a mass vacation or an epidemic of laziness.

Most economists believe that some unemployment, particularly the high unemployment that occurs in recessions, does not reflect the voluntary decisions of qualified workers not to work at going wages. Rather, cyclical unemployment occurs because wages are inflexible, failing to adjust quickly to labor surpluses or shortages. If a wage is above the market-clearing level, some workers are employed, but others (qualified ones who would willingly toil at the going wage rate) cannot find work. Such unemployment is involuntary and also inefficient in that both workers and firms could be made better off by a renegotiation of labor contracts.

5. The key element to understanding involuntary unemployment is the inflexibility of wages in the face of economic shocks. Inflexibility arises because of costs involved in administering the compensation system. These costs are seen in the long duration of union contracts—which typically last 3 years. In nonunion settings, wages and salaries are generally set no more than once a year. Too frequent adjustment of compensation would command too large a share of management time and might upset feelings of fairness or hurt worker morale and productivity.

6. A careful look at the unemployment statistics reveals several surprises.

(a) Recessions hit all groups in roughly proportional fashion—that is, all groups see their unemployment rates go up and down proportionally to the overall unemployment rate.

(b) A very substantial part of unemployment is very short-term. In low-unemployment years (such as 1973) more than 90 percent of unemployed workers are unemployed less than 26 weeks. The average duration of unemployment, particularly the number of very long-term unemployed, rises sharply in deep and prolonged recessions.

(c) A substantial amount of unemployment is simple turnover, or frictional—people entering the labor force for the first time or reentering. Only in recessions is the pool of unemployed composed primarily of job losers.

7. One of the key concepts in modern macroeconomics is the natural rate of unemployment. The natural rate is that level at which the nation's diverse and differentiated labor markets are, on average, in balance. Some show excess demand (or vacancies) while others show excess supply (or unemployment). Taken together, the sum of the forces acts so that pressure on wages and prices across all markets are in balance.

The natural rate is not necessarily the optimal rate of unemployment. Rather, it is the lowest sustainable rate that the nation can enjoy without risking an upward spiral of inflation.

8. The natural rate of unemployment has crept inexorably upward in recent decades. In the early 1960s, many macroeconomists thought that unemployment could be 4 percent without triggering inflation. Most estimates place the natural rate around 6 percent in the late 1980s.

The upward creep in the natural rate arises mainly because of demographic trends— particularly the higher proportion of teenagers in the labor force. In addition, some part of the high natural rate may be due to government policies (such as unemployment insurance) and to increased turbulence in the economy as a result of oil, foreign-trade, and other shocks in the last decade.

9. Economists have put forth many proposals for lowering the natural unemployment rate: improve labor market information and training programs; refashion government programs so that workers have greater incentives to work; operate a high-pressure economy so as to make finding jobs easier; and make government the employer of last resort. Sober analysis of politically viable proposals leads most economists to expect at best a modest improvement from such labor market reforms.

CONCEPTS FOR REVIEW

unemployed, employed, labor force, not
  in labor force, unemployment rate
flexible-wage (market-clearing)
  unemployment vs. rigid-wage (non-
  market-clearing) unemployment
frictional, structural, cyclical
  unemployment

voluntary vs. involuntary unemployment
natural rate of unemployment
rising natural rate of unemployment:
  demographics, government policies,
  shocks
natural vs. optimal rate of
  unemployment

QUESTIONS FOR DISCUSSION

1. What is the labor-force status of each of the following:
(a) A teenager searching for a first job
(b) An autoworker who has been dismissed and has given up hope of finding work but would like to work
(c) A retired person who moved to Florida, but reads the want ads to find a part-time job
(d) A parent who works part time, wants a full-time job, but doesn't have time to look
(e) A teacher who has a job but is too ill to work
2. Think about the last 2 or 3 years in your life. For each month, decide what your labor-force status was (employed, unemployed, not in labor force). Then for the periods you were unemployed, classify your unemployment into the three categories (frictional, structural, cyclical). What has been your personal unemployment rate? What does your experience tell you about the sources of teenage unemployment? Compare notes with your classmates.

3. Do you think that the economic costs or stress of a teenager unemployed for 1 month of the summer might be less or more than a head-of-household unemployed for a year? Do you think that this suggests that public policy should have a different stance with respect to these two groups?

4. What is the natural rate of unemployment? Why is it not zero? Why is it so high in the United States? What would you expect the natural rate to be in a country like Japan that has a "lifetime employment system," a kind of permanent job tenure for most of its workers?

5. Can the government set policies that will put the actual unemployment rate below the natural rate for a year or two? For several decades?

6. Explain why policymakers might have a hard time deciding whether to increase the level of unemployment insurance. What are the costs and benefits to the nation of an increase? Is there any objection to setting unemployment insurance equal to 100 percent of the last wage rate?

7. The following policies or phenomena affected labor markets during the 1980s. For each, explain its likely effect upon the natural rate of unemployment:

(a) The minimum wage fell 40 percent relative to the average wage rate.

(b) Unemployment insurance became subject to taxation.

(c) Funds for training programs for unemployed workers were cut sharply by the federal government.

(d) Because of high cyclical unemployment, many minority-group teenagers received little on-the-job training.

(e) Because of the decline of labor unions, a smaller fraction of the work force operated under 3-year collective bargaining agreements.

(f) The severity of supply or demand shocks to individual markets was higher than during earlier periods.

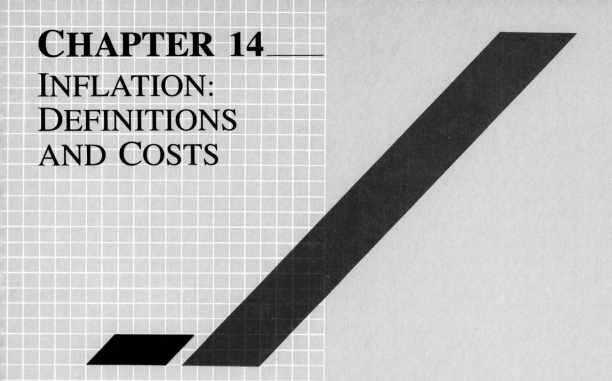

CHAPTER 14____
INFLATION:
DEFINITIONS
AND COSTS

Lenin is said to have declared that the best way to destroy the capitalist system was to debauch the currency. By a continuing process of inflation, governments can confiscate, secretly and unobserved, an important part of the wealth of their citizens.

J. M. Keynes

EARLIER CHAPTERS analyzed the macroeconomic forces that expand or contract output. For the most part, however, we have pushed issues concerning the determination of the price level and inflation into the background. The discussion of the Keynesian multiplier model showed how changes in investment or government spending would affect aggregate demand. An expansion of aggregate demand would then expand production and lower unemployment as long as the economy had unemployed resources. The Keynesian multiplier model focuses on the impact of changes in aggregate demand on output and employment, and the reaction of prices is largely ignored.

Perhaps an approach that downplayed the importance of price changes was adequate back in the Great Depression of the 1930s. But today we are living in an economy in which prices tend to rise year in and year out, and sometimes the price increases are very rapid. Whenever nominal GNP rises, the price component goes up with the output component. Moreover, prices tend to rise even though the economy has a substantial amount of unemployment and excess capacity. Even in the deep recession year of 1982, when output fell sharply and unemployment rose to almost 10 percent of the labor force, the overall price level was rising at 6 percent per year.

In this and the next chapter, we direct our attention to the determination of the aggregate price level and inflation. We will begin to understand why prices rise even in periods of high unemployment. We will study the pages of history to examine a particularly virulent form of inflation called hyperinflation, which occurs when a disorganized nation is printing new paper currency by the bale, causing prices to rise by a factor of 100 or 10,000 or 1,000,000 during a year. We will ask ourselves, Why are nations so concerned about galloping inflation? And what steps can be taken to keep inflation in the barn rather than running wild? Answers to these questions must be found if we are to understand why nations take stern measures, and sometimes even tolerate high unemployment, to beat down high inflation rates.

Figure 14-1 provides an overview of this chapter's content. We survey here the definition, measurement, and history of the price level and inflation. The next chapter analyzes current theories of inflation along with policy measures that a nation can use to keep inflation under control.

WHAT IS INFLATION?

Surprisingly, inflation is widespread but widely misunderstood. Let us begin with a careful definition of inflation:

Inflation occurs when the general level of prices is rising. The **rate of inflation** is defined as the rate of change of the price level (as measured, say, by the consumer price index, or CPI) and is measured as follows:

Rate of inflation (year t)

$$= \frac{\begin{array}{c} \text{price level} \\ \text{(year } t) \end{array} - \begin{array}{c} \text{price level} \\ \text{(year } t-1) \end{array}}{\text{price level (year } t-1)} \times 100$$

Inflation measures the trend in the average level of prices. As an example, take the year 1980, during which the CPI rose 13 percent. In that year, the prices of all major product groups rose: food, beverages, shelter, apparel, transportation, medical care, and so forth. It is this general upward trend in prices that we call inflation.

You should not, however, infer that all prices rise by the same amount during inflationary periods. During 1980, some prices rose more than 13 percent while others rose less, but the increase in the average price level was the stated amount.

Inflation measures the rate of change in the "price level." But how is that measured? We measure the trend in the overall price level by constructing price indexes, which are averages of consumer or producer prices.

Deflation The opposite of inflation is **deflation,** which occurs when the general level of prices is falling. Deflations have been rare in the late twentieth century. In the United States, the last time consumer prices actually fell from one year to the next was 1955. Sustained deflations, where prices fall steadily over a period of several years, are associated with periods of deep depression, such as the 1930s or the 1890s. The advent of active government stabilization policies, which has wiped out deep and sustained depressions in most advanced industrial countries, has also eliminated deflations from the economic scene.

Another term often encountered is **disinflation,** which denotes a decline in the rate of inflation.

Price Indexes

When the newspaper headlines state that "Inflation has fallen" or "The Federal Reserve reacted to increased inflationary tendencies," we are reading about the movement of a price index. A **price index** is a weighted average of individual prices, where the weight on each commodity's price reflects the economic importance of that commodity. The most important price indexes are the consumer price index, the producer price index, and the GNP deflator.

The Consumer Price Index (CPI) The most widely used measure of inflation is the consumer price index, also known as the CPI. The CPI measures the cost of a market basket of consumer goods and services. It is

CHAPTER OVERVIEW

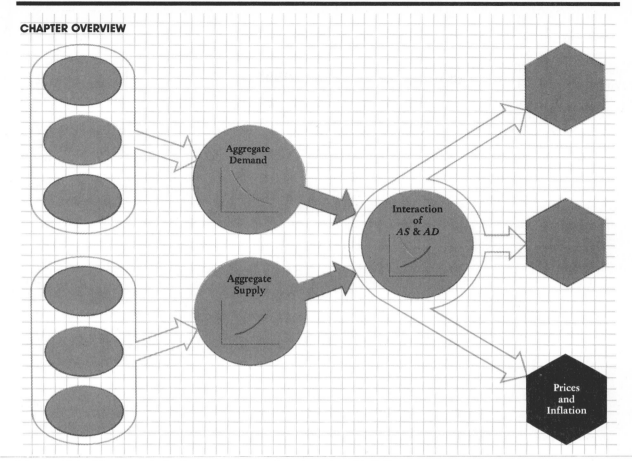

Figure 14-1 We now study the measurement and costs of inflation

Having analyzed the essence of money and the forces affecting output and employment, we now examine the determination of changes in the overall price level. How do we measure the overall price level and the rate of inflation? What are the major kinds of inflations? And why are people so averse to high and variable inflation rates? These questions will be addressed in this chapter.

based on prices of food, clothing, shelter, fuels, transportation, medical care, college tuition, and other commodities purchased for day-to-day living. Prices on 364 separate classes of commodities are collected from over 21,000 establishments in 91 areas of the country.

A basic question for any price index concerns how to *weight* the different prices. It would clearly be silly merely to add up the different prices or to weight them by their mass or volume. Rather, we construct a price index by *weighting each price by the economic importance of the commodity*.

In the case of the CPI, each item is assigned a *fixed* weight proportional to its relative importance in consumer expenditure budgets; the most recent weights for each item are proportional to the total spending on that item as derived from a 1982–1984 survey of consumer expenditures.

Numerical Example To get a concrete idea of how inflation is measured, we can use an illustrative numerical example. Let us assume that consumers buy three commodities: food, shelter, and medical care. A hypothetical budget survey finds that consumers spend 20 percent of their budgets on food, 50 percent on shelter, and 30 percent on medical care.

Using 1992 as the base year, we set the price of each commodity at 100, so the CPI is also 100 [= (0.20 × 100) + (0.50 × 100) + (0.30 × 100)]. Next, calculate the consumer price index and the rate of inflation for 1993. In 1993, food prices rise 2 percent to 102, shelter prices rise 6 percent to 106, and medical care prices are up 10 percent to 110. We recalculate the CPI for 1993 as follows:

$$CPI\ (1993) = (0.20 \times 102) + (0.50 \times 106) + (0.30 \times 110)$$

$$= 106.4$$

In other words, if 1992 is the base year in which the CPI is 100, then in 1993 the CPI is 106.4. The rate of inflation in 1993 is then [(106.4 − 100)/100] × 100 = 6.4 percent per year.

This example captures the essence of how inflation is measured. The only difference between this simplified calculation and the real one is that the CPI in fact contains many more commodities. Otherwise, the arithmetic and the concepts are exactly the same.

The Producer Price Index (PPI) This index, dating from 1890, is the oldest continuous statistical series published by the Labor Department. It measures the level of prices at the wholesale or producer stage. It is based upon approximately 3400 commodity prices and includes prices of foods, manufactured products, and mining products. The fixed weights used are the net shipments (or sales) for the commodity. This index is important because of its great detail and is widely used by businesses.

GNP Deflator We met the GNP deflator in Chapter 6's discussion of national income and output accounting. Recall that the GNP deflator is the ratio of nominal GNP to real GNP and can thus be interpreted as a comprehensive price index; in other words, it is the price of *all* GNP (consumption, investment, government purchases, and net exports) rather than of a single sector. This index is a variable-weight rather than a fixed-weight index. The national income accounts also construct deflators for components of GNP, such as for investment goods, personal consumption, and so forth, and these can sometimes be used to supplement the CPI or the PPI.

Index-Number Problems While price indexes like the CPI are enormously useful, they are not without their faults. Some problems are intrinsic to price indexes. One problem is the notorious "*index-number problem,*" which concerns the appropriate period to use as a base year. Recall that the CPI uses fixed weights for each good. As a result, the true cost of living is overestimated when consumers substitute relatively inexpensive for relatively expensive goods. For example, the weighting in the CPI neglects the fact that the amount of gasoline bought by consumers declined after gasoline prices rose sharply in the early 1970s. One could change the base year, or use other fancier weighting schemes, but there is no way of solving the index-number problem perfectly.

Another set of difficulties is imposed by limited research budgets: the CPI does not accurately capture changes in the quality of goods—no correction to the CPI is made for the fact that sound reproduction is becoming more faithful in phonographic equipment, that computers are becoming smaller and faster, that ski bindings are becoming safer, or that watches have more features. Studies indicate that if quality change were properly incorporated into price indexes, the CPI would have risen less rapidly in recent years.

Misconceptions People often get confused about inflation. Here are some questions that reflect common misconceptions along with the correct answers.

Doesn't inflation mean that goods are expensive? No, inflation means that the average price level is rising.

Doesn't inflation mean that we are getting poorer?

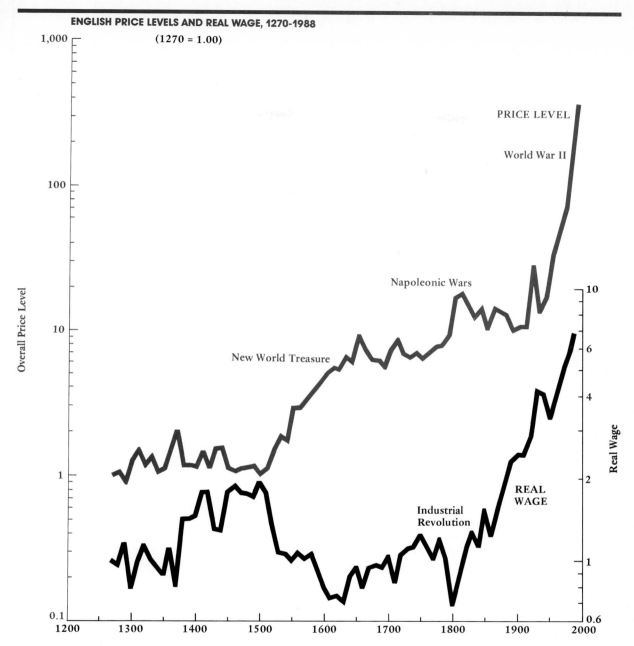

Figure 14-2 Price inflation has dogged the history of capitalism

This figure shows England's history of prices (in red) and real wages (in black) back to the Middle Ages. Note that the price of a market basket of food, clothing, and other goods has risen almost 400-fold since 1270. In early years, price increases are associated with increases in the money supply such as from discoveries of New World treasure and printing of money during the Napoleonic Wars.

   Note the meandering of the real wage (money wage divided by the price level) prior to the Industrial Revolution. Then see how real wages have risen sharply and steadily from 1800 to today. (Source: E. H. Phelps Brown and S. V. Hopkins, *Economica,* 1956, updated by authors.)

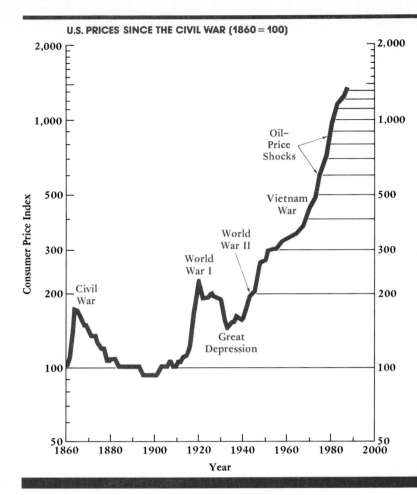

U.S. PRICES SINCE THE CIVIL WAR (1860 = 100)

Figure 14-3   Inflations came with wars, but now they don't go away afterward

This figure shows the history of American consumer prices since 1860. Prices go up with each war, then drift down afterward. Thus prices in 1940 were at almost the same level as in 1870. But since 1940, the trend has been upward, both here and abroad. The only changes today are in the *rate* of inflation, not in the *fact* of inflation. (Source: U.S. Department of Labor, Bureau of Labor Statistics.)

Not necessarily. Our incomes tend to rise rapidly during inflationary periods, so our real incomes (incomes corrected for the cost of living) may go up or down during inflationary times.

Don't companies get rich and workers get poor during inflationary times? Not necessarily. The effect of inflation on the distribution of income depends on the type of inflation.

You will hear many more misconceptions about inflation, but you can avoid adopting them if you remember the definition of inflation given above.

Inflation's Long History

Inflation is as old as market economies. Figure 14-2 on p. 309 depicts the history of English inflation since the thirteenth century. Over the long haul, prices have risen steadily, as the red line reveals. Look as well at the black line, which charts the path of *real wages* (the wage rate divided by consumer prices). Real wages meandered along until the Industrial Revolution. Comparing the two lines shows that inflation is not necessarily accompanied by a decline in real incomes. See also how real wages have climbed steadily since around 1800, rising more than tenfold.

Figure 14-3 above focuses on the behavior of consumer prices in the United States since the Civil War. Until 1945, the pattern was regular: prices would double or so during wartime, then fall back during the postwar slump. But the pattern changed ominously after World War II. Prices and wages now travel on a one-way street. They rise rapidly in periods of eco-

THREE KINDS OF INFLATION

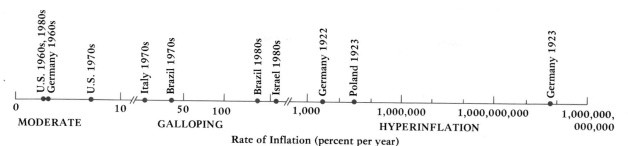

Figure 14-4   **Inflations come in many varieties, sometimes mere annoyances, at other times highly destructive**

The figure shows the three kinds of inflation that occur. Moderate inflations are typical today in most industrialized countries. In galloping inflation, such as that seen in Brazil and Israel during recent years, inflation jumps around from year to year, but does not explode. Hyperinflations occur when runaway printing presses allow a tremendous increase in the money supply, leading prices to rise at a thousand, million, or trillion percent annually. Hyperinflation is not sustainable, and leads generally to a currency reform or a major economic collapse.

nomic expansion; in recessions they do not fall but merely rise less rapidly. Prices and wages show a major structural change after 1940: they are now inflexible downward.

Three Strains of Inflation

Like diseases, inflations exhibit different levels of severity. It is useful to classify them into three categories: moderate inflation, galloping inflation, and hyperinflation. A pictorial description is shown in Figure 14-4 above. The distinction between these three categories is blurred. There is no clear point that marks the boundaries. Rather, it is the qualitative distinctions that should be understood.

Moderate Inflation Moderate inflation occurs when prices are rising slowly. We might arbitrarily classify this as single-digit annual inflation rates. When prices are relatively stable, *people trust money.* They are willing to hold on to currency because its value will not depreciate rapidly. People are willing to keep money in the bank, in checking accounts, or in low-yielding savings deposits because their money will be almost as valuable when they withdraw it in a month

or a year as it is today. People are willing to write long-term contracts in money terms (or in nominal terms), because they are confident that the price level will not get too far out of line with the good they are selling or buying. People do not waste time or resources trying to put their wealth into ''real'' assets rather than ''money'' or ''paper'' assets because they believe their money assets will retain their real value. In short, the monetary system is functioning well.

Galloping Inflation This occurs when prices start rising at double- or triple-digit rates of 20, 100, or 200 percent a year. At the low end of this spectrum we find advanced industrial countries like Italy (see Figure 14-4). Many Latin American countries, such as Argentina and Brazil, have experienced inflation rates of 50 to 700 percent per year in the 1970s and 1980s.

Once galloping inflation becomes entrenched, serious economic distortions arise. Generally, most contracts become indexed to a price index or to a foreign currency, like the dollar. Because money loses its value so quickly—with real interest rates of minus 50 or 100 percent per year—people avoid holding any more than the bare minimum. Financial markets wither away, and funds are generally allocated by rationing rather than by interest rates. People hoard goods, buy houses, and never, never lend money at low nominal interest rates.

The surprising fact, indeed, is that economies with 200 percent annual inflation manage to perform so well. Countries like Brazil and Israel grew rapidly, for a time, even though prices were galloping along.[1]

Hyperinflation While economies seem to survive, and sometimes even to thrive, with galloping inflation, a third and deadly strain takes hold when the cancer of hyperinflation strikes. Nothing good can be said about the extraordinary price increases that took place in Germany in 1920–1923 or after World War II in China and Hungary.

The most carefully documented case of hyperinflation took place in the Weimar Republic of Germany.

[1]Brief surveys of the inflations and stabilization policies in middle-income countries suffering from galloping inflation are contained in articles by Stanley Fischer, Jeffrey Sachs, Daniel Heymann, Eliana Cardoso, and Rudiger Dornbusch in *American Economic Review* (May 1987), pp. 275–292.

The picture of German hyperinflation is shown in Figure 14-5 below. There we see how the government unleashed the monetary printing presses, driving both money and prices to astronomical levels. From January 1922 to November 1923, the price index rose from 1 to 10,000,000,000. If a person had owned $300 million worth of bonds in early 1922, this amount would not have bought a piece of chewing gum 2 years later.

Hyperinflations are particularly interesting to students of inflation because they highlight its effects. Pathology illustrates anatomy. Just as we feed massive doses of substances to rats in the hope that we can understand the effects of smaller amounts on humans, so we study hyperinflations for the light they cast on less virulent strains of inflation.

Consider this description of hyperinflation in the Confederacy during the Civil War:

We used to go to the stores with money in our pockets and come back with food in our baskets. Now we go with

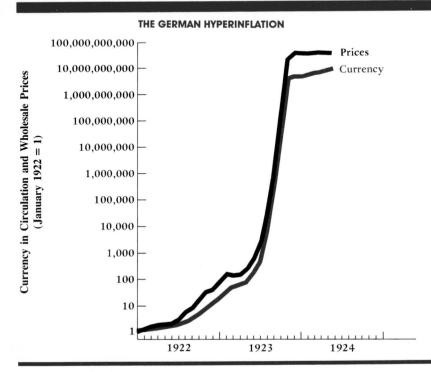

THE GERMAN HYPERINFLATION

Figure 14-5 The incredible shrinking reichsmark

In the early 1920s, the young Weimar Republic of Germany was struggling to meet harsh reparations payments and satisfy creditors. It could not borrow or raise enough taxes to pay for government spending, so it turned on the printing press. The stock of currency rose 7 billionfold from early 1921 to December 1923, and prices spiraled upward as people frantically tried to dump their money like hot potatoes. The result of this was as if the value of a reichsmark shrank from the size of a battleship to that of a pea.

money in baskets and return with food in our pockets. Everything is scarce except money! Prices are chaotic and production disorganized. A meal that used to cost the same amount as an opera ticket now costs twenty times as much. Everybody tends to hoard "things" and to try to get rid of the "bad" paper money, which drives the "good" metal money out of circulation. A partial return to barter inconvenience is the result.

Germany Careful studies find several common features in hyperinflations. First, the velocity of money (how quickly it is spent once received) increases enormously. By the end of the German hyperinflation, currency was turning over 30 times more quickly than at the beginning. Second, relative prices become highly unstable. Usually, the real wages of a person move only a percent or less from month to month. During 1923, German real wages changed on average one-third (up or down) each month. Indeed, this enormous variation in relative prices and real wages—and the inequities and distortions caused by these fluctuations—illustrates the major costs imposed by inflation.

Perhaps the most profound effects are on wealth distribution. The distinguished British economist Lionel Robbins summarized the impact:

> The depreciation of the mark . . . destroyed the wealth of the more solid elements in German society; and it left behind a moral and economic disequilibrium, apt breeding ground for the disasters which have followed. Hitler is the foster-child of the inflation.[2]

Do Inflations Accelerate?

Many people fear inflation, even moderate inflation rates of 6 or 9 percent, because they worry that prices will begin to gallop upward, or perhaps that the moderate inflation will degenerate into a hyperinflation. Is this concern warranted? Does creeping inflation inevitably become a trot? A trot become a canter? A canter become a gallop?

The history of inflations suggests that there is no

[2]The history of the German hyperinflation is told in detail in C. Bresciani-Turroni, *The Economics of Inflation: A Study of Currency Depreciation in Post-War Germany,* 3d ed. (Augustus M. Kelley, London, 1968). The quotation from Professor Robbins is from the introduction to the book.

such inevitable sequence. Fortunately, hyperinflations are extremely rare. They occur mainly during wartime or in the backwash of war and revolution. Indeed, only one hyperinflation has occurred in the past four decades—12,000 percent annual inflation occurred in Bolivia in 1985.

Galloping inflation, on the other hand, is not rare. Like periods of prolonged unemployment, galloping inflation breaks out occasionally even in advanced economies. Since the oil shock of 1973, the advanced economies of France, Italy, and Britain have experienced bouts of galloping inflation.

The tendency in advanced economies like the United States is, however, toward moderate inflation. By using the tools of modern macroeconomics, responding to signs of inflation by tightening the monetary and fiscal screws, nations are able to keep inflation at a moderate creep and hold its costs down to tolerable levels.

THE IMPACT OF INFLATION

Politicians and central bankers pronounce daily on the dangers of inflationary expectations. Public-opinion polls often find that inflation is economic enemy number one. Such behavior suggests that a well-defined "cost of inflation" has been clearly identified, measured, and labelled as a hazardous substance. What then are the costs of inflation?

In fact, identifying the costs of inflation has proven one of the most difficult tasks for modern macroeconomics. A comparison with unemployment is useful here. The economic and social costs imposed by unemployment are obvious and clear to all as we saw in the last chapter. By contrast, the costs of inflation are elusive and clear to few. The costs of inflation do not confront you the way a visit to high-unemployment areas in Detroit or the South Bronx would. We must therefore carefully weigh the true costs of rising prices.

We noted above that during periods of inflation all prices and wages do not move at the same rate; that is, changes in *relative prices* occur. As a result of the diverging relative prices, two definite effects of inflation are:

- A *redistribution* of income and wealth among different classes

- *Distortions* in the relative prices and outputs of different goods, or sometimes in the output and employment for the economy as a whole.

But remember that all inflations are not created equal. There are moderate inflations, galloping inflations, and hyperinflations. The economic impacts of these differ enormously and could be compared to catching a cold, having the flu, or being hit by a truck.

Impacts on Income and Wealth Distribution

The major distributional impact of inflation arises from differences in the kinds of assets and liabilities that people hold. When people owe long-term fixed-interest-rate debts (like conventional home mortgages), a sharp rise in prices is a windfall gain for them. Suppose you borrow $100,000 to buy a house and your annual mortgage payments are $10,000. Suddenly, a great inflation appears and doubles wages and prices. Your dollar income doubles, although the amount of food, clothing, medical care, and so forth that your income can buy is unchanged. But what has happened to the real cost of your mortgage? Although your mortgage payment is still $10,000 per year, you will need to work only half as long as before to make your mortgage payment. The great inflation has increased your wealth by halving the real value of your mortgage debt.

From time to time, as in the late 1970s, this kind of thinking leads people to borrow heavily to buy houses or farmland. Then, when inflation slows and recession hits, as happened in the early 1980s, the mortgage payments are so burdensome that thousands of people end up in bankruptcy court.

If you are a lender and have assets in mortgages or long-term bonds, the shoe is on the other foot. A sudden rise in prices will leave you the poorer because the dollars you are repaid are worth less than you originally expected.

Real-Interest-Rate Adjustment Once an inflation has gone on for a long time and people come to antici-

pate it, markets begin to adapt. An allowance for inflation will gradually get built into the market interest rate. Say the economy starts out with interest rates of 3 percent and stable prices. Once people expect prices to rise at 9 percent per year, bonds and mortgages will tend to pay 12 percent rather than 3 percent. The 12 percent nominal interest rate reflects a 3 percent real interest rate plus a 9 percent inflation premium. There are no longer major redistributions of income and wealth once interest rates have so adjusted.

This adjustment of interest rates to chronic inflation has been observed in Brazil, Chile, and indeed in almost all other countries with a long history of rising prices. In the 1980s, we have seen a similar inflation premium built into American and European interest rates.[3]

The major redistributive impact of inflation occurs through its effect on the real value of people's wealth. In general, unanticipated inflation redistributes wealth from creditors to debtors (that is, unanticipated or unforeseen inflation helps those who have borrowed money and hurts those who have lent money). An unanticipated decline in inflation has the opposite effect.

Special Cases Some examples will illustrate the process. Governments find that the burden of their debt shrinks during inflation. Someone who invests money in real estate or gold will make a large profit during unforeseen inflation. It used to be thought that common stocks were a good inflation hedge, but they proved disappointing during the post-1965 inflation. Only when inflation declined in the early 1980s did stock prices take off.

Because of institutional responses to inflation, some old myths are no longer applicable. Widows and orphans receive social security pensions that are "indexed" to the CPI—they are insulated from inflation because benefits automatically increase as the CPI increases. Also, many debt instruments (like "floating-rate" mortgages) have interest rates that move up and down with market interest rates, so unanticipated inflation hurts lenders less than before.

There has been a vast volume of research on the

---

[3]Figure 12-3 shows movements in nominal and real interest rates for the United States in recent years.

redistributional impacts of inflation. The summary wisdom of these studies indicates that the overall impact is highly unpredictable. Those who live on capital income tend to lose from inflation, while younger wage earners tend to gain. Contrary to stereotypes, statistics indicate that poor families often gain from inflation at the expense of the affluent.

But the main conclusion is that inflation simply churns income and assets, randomly redistributing wealth around the population without any significant impact on any single group.

Effects on Output and Employment

In addition to redistributing incomes, inflation affects the real economy. Indeed, there are two separate effects: on total output and on the allocation of resources and economic efficiency.

Macroeconomic Impacts The first impact is on the level of *output as a whole*. Periods of unexpectedly rising inflation are usually ones of high employment and output. Until the 1970s, with its supply shocks, rising inflation had occurred when investment was brisk and jobs were plentiful. Periods of unanticipated declines in inflation—the 1930s, 1954, 1958, and 1982—were times of high unemployment of labor and capital. Indeed, periods where declining inflation supposedly left banks and other creditors ''better off'' actually left them with uncollectible debts—whether owed by farmers in the 1930s or by Brazilians in the mid-1980s.

But these observations raise the question: In the observed association between inflation and output, which was cause, which effect? Was the rising output caused by the rising prices? Or were the rising prices the result of rising output? Or were both the result of a third factor that moved both?

In the long run, there is no necessary relationship between prices (or inflation) and output. And in the short run, the association is ambiguous: a rightward shift in the aggregate demand curve may lead to higher output and/or inflation, but, a supply shock, shifting up the aggregate supply curve, could lead to inflation and lower levels of output. (These two cases are actually shown in Figures 5-9 and 5-10, respectively.)

Modern macroeconomic theory concludes, therefore, that there is no necessary relationship between inflation and the level of output and employment.

Microeconomic Impacts A second and more subtle effect of inflation is the microeconomic impact on the *allocation of resources*. Recall that inflation distorts relative prices; generally the higher the inflation rate, the greater are the relative price distortions. One asset whose return is severely distorted by inflation is currency (coins and paper money). By its nature, currency does not receive interest; that is, the nominal or money interest rate on currency is zero. But recall that the real interest rate (the interest rate in terms of real goods) is defined as the nominal interest rate minus the rate of inflation. It follows that the real interest rate on currency is equal to minus the inflation rate. For example, those who held currency in 1980 earned a real return equal to minus 12.4 percent (since 12.4 percent was the inflation rate). The upshot here is that the real interest rate on currency is dramatically affected by inflation; we should not be surprised, therefore, if people begin to unload their currency and acquire other assets when prices begin to rise rapidly.

Also, the prices of inputs or goods that are priced under long-term arrangements (labor contracts and prices in regulated or state-owned industries) tend to become more out of line with the general price level during inflationary periods. We will analyze these and other inefficiencies below.

ANALYSIS OF INFLATION'S COSTS

We have seen that inflation imposes costs on an economy, redistributing income and reducing efficiency by distorting relative prices. We can now apply earlier concepts to the different strains of inflation experienced in the United States and abroad.

In the discussion that follows, we will find that two key elements determine the economic impact of an inflation: whether or not it is *anticipated* by people, and whether or not it is *balanced*. In this discussion, a ''balanced'' inflation is one that leaves relative prices unchanged.

Balanced, Anticipated Inflation

It will help to understand inflation's costs if we begin with the case of inflation that is both balanced and fully anticipated. Suppose that all prices are rising at 10 percent each year. Nobody is surprised by the price changes. Food and clothing, wages and rents are all rising at 10 percent each year, and all real interest rates (that is, interest rates after correcting for inflation) are just the same as they would be if all prices were stable. (This example is used not for realism but to illustrate a polar case in which the effects are more easily seen.)

Would anyone care about such an inflation? Would the efficiency of resource use or real GNP be a bit smaller or larger? The answer to both questions is, No. *There is no effect on real output, efficiency, or income distribution of an inflation that is both balanced and anticipated.* My income is rising 10 percent faster than it would be with stable prices; my cost of living is also rising 10 percent faster. There is no gain or loss to different kinds of assets. Prices are, in this case, simply a changing yardstick to which people completely adjust their behavior.

This polar case raises an unsettling thought: Is the social cost of inflation an optical illusion? Do people dislike inflation because they see their cost of living rise but forget that their incomes are rising in step with costs?

No doubt, there is incomplete understanding of inflation in many people's minds. People often confuse high *inflation* with high *prices*. Sometimes people think that high inflation lowers their standard of living or their real wages.* But neither of these is intrinsic to inflation, as the case of balanced inflation shows.

Unbalanced Inflation: Inflation-Induced Distortions

Let us take a step toward realism by recognizing that inflation affects relative prices, costs, and tax burdens. For the moment, let us stay with the case of anticipated inflation.

One inefficiency resulting from unbalanced inflation arises because some prices do not adjust to reflect inflationary trends, with money and taxes being two important examples. Currency is a form of money that bears a zero nominal interest rate. If the inflation rate rises from 0 to 10 percent annually, then the real interest rate on currency falls from 0 to -10 percent per year. There is no easy way for a central bank or government to correct this distortion.

How does the negative real interest rate on currency or other kinds of money lead to inefficiency? Studies show that when inflation rises, people devote real resources to reducing their money holdings. They go to the bank more often—using up "shoe leather" and valuable time. Corporations set up elaborate "cash management" schemes. Real resources are thereby consumed to cope with the changing monetary yardstick. Empirical studies indicate, however, that this cost is modest.[4]

The impact of inflation on taxes is potentially more significant. Under progressive taxation (a "progressive" tax being one that taxes high-income people at a higher rate than low-income people), inflation raises

[4]This "shoe leather" effect is, surprisingly, the only well-documented cost of inflation. One study found that each 1-point rise in the inflation rate would in 1977 induce people to spend $1 billion of extra resources to economize on cash balances. This compares to a 1977 GNP of $1900 billion.

*In 1978, when Robert Strauss was appointed President Carter's "inflation czar," he received letters of advice that give a nonscientific sample of how people think about inflation. Examples are: "Why should my labor be sucked dry by postal clerks?" Or "Grocery prices are advancing far above the inflation rate and with no reason." Or "The culprit is ill-managed voluntary nonprofit hospitals." Or "Budget deficits are the problem." One writer even complained that Strauss's $66,000 salary was a problem because she thought it a "rip-off." Another man used a vivid physical analogy: "The great American dream is like a balloon. Don't inflate it too much or it will blow up." (These and other views can be found in *U.S. News & World Report*, June 26, 1978, and *Newsweek*, May 29, 1978.) Discussion question 3 pursues the meaning of these statements further.

people's average tax rates. It thus allows the government to collect more taxes without passing laws. Such "taxation without legislation" has led many countries to "index" their tax laws against inflation. Parts of the U.S. tax code were indexed beginning in 1985.

Indexing alone will not purge the tax system of the impacts of inflation. Inflation distorts the measurement of income. For example, if you collected an interest rate of 8 percent on your funds in 1988, half of this simply replaced the loss of purchasing power of your funds from inflation; yet the tax code does not distinguish between real return and the interest that just compensates for inflation. Similar components of income whose measurement is distorted by inflation dot the pages of the income-tax code. No country has succeeded in completely correcting its tax system for inflation.

Other distortions are more subtle. In regulated industries, firms come to regulatory agencies to ask approval for changes in their prices. They must come more often during periods of inflation, and they are more likely to be turned down in such periods. As a result, regulated prices are often depressed during inflationary periods.

Inflation Destroys Information Many economists stress the fact that prices contain information that is valuable to consumers. We may remember that Elm City sells gas for $1.10 a gallon; with this in mind, it is easy to compare Elm City's prices with those of Exxon or Arco.

Inflation, however, destroys information. In rapid inflations, price tags are changed frequently. Consumers will have difficulty comparing prices when last week's price has already changed when they shop this week; consequently, consumers may mistakenly pay more than necessary for goods.

An analogy shows how a rapid change in prices destroys valuable information. Imagine that every year telephone numbers were increased a bit as we experience "telephone-number inflation." Think of how much trouble it would cause you if telephone-number inflation were rapid, and you had to find out the number for your home every day. What if the number for the operator and directory assistance also changed daily?

Unanticipated Inflation

We turn next to unanticipated inflations, for changes in inflation are usually a big surprise even to professional forecasters. We discussed above the way that inflationary surprises affect the economy. People who have long-term, money-fixed arrangements—whether they own assets like mortgages or enjoy contracts like labor-union agreements—find that the real value or cost of these arrangements is different from what they had originally expected. If prices double, the real value of a bond is halved.

Generally, the economic impact of an unanticipated moderate inflation is mainly on the distribution of income and wealth, and less on the efficiency of the system. An unexpected jump in prices will impoverish some and enrich others, but will have little effect on how effectively farms and factories are run. Unanticipated inflation may greatly affect the distribution of income and wealth (the *for whom*) while leaving the economy's efficiency (the *how* and *what*) virtually untouched.

How costly is this redistribution? Perhaps "cost" does not describe the problem. The effects may be more social than economic. An epidemic of burglaries may not lower GNP, but it causes great distress. Similarly, the random redistributions from inflation are like forcing people to play a lottery they would prefer to avoid.

Moreover, the effect of a redistribution due to inflation depends on how big the inflation is. There is no doubt that galloping inflation or hyperinflation saps the morale and vitality of an economy, as the German case attests. On the other hand, an inflation rate of 2 to 4 percent, such as that in the United States in the mid-1980s, probably has but a minor impact on the distribution of income and wealth.

Unbalanced and Unanticipated Inflation

In reality, most inflations are both unbalanced and unanticipated, as can be seen in the last major U.S. inflation, which began in 1979. Most forecasters thought inflation would be around 7 percent for 1979, and few foresaw an increase in oil prices. In early

1979, the Iranian revolution led to a spurt of oil prices, and the CPI for 1979 rose 11 percent over 1978. The inflation was definitely unbalanced, for energy prices rose 12 percent faster than the general price level while real wages fell 3 percent.

In the end, much random redistribution occurred. Fortune smiled on those lucky enough to own oil wells, oil-bearing land, or oil companies. By contrast, people who owned gas-guzzling cars, airplanes, or airline companies suffered economic losses.

A careful reading of the history of this period suggests that much of the perceived cost of inflation did not stem from the inflation per se. Rather, social frictions arose from the changes in relative prices. Real incomes fell because people had to pay more for oil products, not because the general price level rose. And even if the inflation rate had been zero, the rising relative price of oil would still have hurt oil-consuming households and nations.

Recapitulation

We can summarize this discussion in the accompanying Table 14-1. In addition to the size of the inflation, two facets of inflation will determine the severity of its impact: whether it is balanced, and whether it is anticipated. The mildest impacts will be found when inflations are at a low rate; these are in the upper left corner of this table—small, anticipated, and balanced. Major social and economic impacts arise for galloping inflations or hyperinflations, at the lower right—high inflation rates that are unanticipated and unbalanced.

The Macroeconomic Reaction

But whatever the real or perceived costs of inflation, nations today will not long tolerate high inflation rates. Sooner or later, they take steps to reduce inflation—by restraining the growth of real output and raising unemployment, or sometimes by putting controls on prices and wages. The result is almost always a painful period of stagnation, as workers are pinched by layoffs, short hours, and poor job prospects. Indeed, it was primarily the decision by governments to contain inflation that lay behind the long stagnation in Europe and North America that followed the 1979

TWO DIMENSIONS OF INFLATION'S COSTS

	BALANCED INFLATION	UNBALANCED INFLATION
ANTICIPATED INFLATION	Inflation has no cost	Efficiency losses
UNANTICIPATED INFLATION	Income and wealth redistribution	Efficiency losses and redistribution

Table 14-1 The impacts of inflation are governed by two main factors: whether it is balanced and whether it is anticipated

The costs of inflation depend on two different factors. First, is it a balanced inflation, where no relative prices are being changed and there are no inflation-induced distortions? Second, is it anticipated? If the answer to both questions is yes, then we are in the upper left part of the table, and the costs are negligible. On the other hand, if the inflation has led to a severe and unanticipated misalignment of relative prices, then both the efficiency losses and the redistribution may be severe, as in the lower right corner of the table.

oil-price increase and lasted until the end of the 1980s in Europe.

Thus, whatever economists may conclude about the "shoe leather" or other microeconomic costs of inflation, the reaction of monetary and fiscal policy in a democracy must be counted as one of the costs of inflation. And that reaction has generally been to contain inflation by high unemployment and low GNP growth; as the next chapter shows, the quantity of output and the number of jobs that must be lost to curb inflation is very large.

Final Appraisal

This chapter's analysis shows that inflation is a complex phenomenon, with many different kinds of costs. Can we make a final estimate of inflation's burdens? Does inflation markedly lower a nation's real output? Are the measurable costs to GNP or the unmeasured costs to morale and social stability great or small?

A careful sifting of the evidence suggests that moderate inflation like that seen recently in the United States has only a modest impact on productivity or real output. It is difficult to find studies that can point to yearly impacts of more than a few billion dollars in a $5 trillion economy. Even during the German hyperinflation, output and employment fell less than in the Great Depression.

On the other hand, the impact of sudden inflation-induced distortions or changes in income and wealth undoubtedly is severe and unpleasant for many individuals, not unlike the experience of being mugged.

And, finally, even though economists have been unable to find large costs of moderate inflations, the electorate responds forcefully to an upsurge in prices. People vote for leaders who will take measures to reduce inflation, and the leaders in turn take measures to curb inflation by slowing output growth and raising unemployment. This reaction is the most visible and dramatic effect of inflation in a modern economy.

SUMMARY

1. While earlier chapters analyzed the determinants of output and employment, this chapter begins a survey of changes in the overall price level. In today's economy, changes in aggregate demand lead to changes in prices as well as output. Indeed, because of the inflexibility of wages, prices may be rising even though the economy still has high unemployment and unutilized capacity.

2. Inflation occurs when the general level of prices is rising (and deflation occurs when they are generally falling). Today, we calculate inflation by using "price indexes"— weighted averages of the prices of thousands of individual products. The most important price index is the consumer price index (CPI), which measures the cost of a market basket of consumer goods and services relative to the cost of that bundle during a particular base year.

3. Until World War II, prices rose during wartime and fell afterward. Today, we see that inflation rises during booms and subsides during recessions. But the overall price level almost never declines these days.

4. Like diseases, inflations come in different strains. We generally see moderate inflation in the United States (a few percent annually); sometimes, inflations turn into the galloping variety, with rates of 50 or 100 or 200 percent each year. A third and deadly virus takes over when the printing presses spew out currency and prices start rising many times each month—hyperinflation. Many people fear that moderate inflations inevitably start to gallop, and then tend toward hyperinflation. Historically, hyperinflations almost always occurred in association with war and revolution.

5. Inflation affects the economy in two ways: by redistributing income and wealth and by changing the level and pattern of production. Inflations and deflations are rarely of the balanced and anticipated type, in which all prices and all wages are anticipated to move by the same percentage, with no one helped and no one hurt by the process. Unforeseen inflation usually favors debtors, profit seekers, and risk-taking speculators. It hurts creditors, fixed-income classes, and timid investors.

6. In a modern economy, containing inflation is one of the prime targets of macroeconomic policy. What are the costs of inflation that lead policymakers to pay such careful attention to movements of inflation?

If all inflations were balanced and perfectly anticipated, inflation would impose no major economic burden. But real-world inflations are seldom fully balanced or anticipated. When inflations are unbalanced, relative prices, tax rates, and real interest rates get distorted. People take more trips to the bank, taxes may creep up, and measured income may become distorted. Also, when inflations are unanticipated, they lead to mistaken investments and to demoralizing and random income redistributions. And when society determines to take steps to lower inflation, the real costs of such steps in terms of lower output and employment can be painful.

CONCEPTS FOR REVIEW

inflation, deflation
price index (consumer, producer, GNP
  deflator)
strains of inflation (moderate,
  galloping, hyperinflation)
impacts of inflation (redistributional, on
  output and employment)

disinflation
costs of inflation: ''shoe leather,''
  income and tax distortions, loss of
  information
balanced and unbalanced inflation
anticipated and unanticipated inflation
macroeconomic reaction to inflation

QUESTIONS FOR DISCUSSION

1. If you were sure that an inflation were coming, what would you expect to be the effect on your personal situation? What steps could you take to protect yourself?
2. The following statements have been made about inflation. Which ones correctly describe a cost of inflation and which are misdiagnoses? Explain.
  (a) Inflation is just big oil companies ripping off the little people.
  (b) Inflation is theft. Governments can increase their taxes without passing a tax bill.
  (c) Inflation lowers our living standards by raising the cost of living.
  (d) The main cost of inflation is the unemployment that follows as governments attempt to lower inflation.
  (e) The 1988 drought drove up food prices, increased the CPI, and triggered COLA clauses in many labor contracts. Paradoxically, farmers as a whole were better off while workers were disadvantaged.
3. Reread the special footnote on page 316. For each of the quotations, decide whether the statement is genuinely a lament about inflation, or if instead the statement confuses inflation with other economic issues. For those that refer to inflation, decide whether the inflation is balanced or unbalanced and whether it was anticipated or unanticipated. Does this list of concerns about inflation help you understand why inflation is so unpopular among voters?
4. Imagine that you were in an economy where prices were rising 10 percent each month. What kinds of changes in the economy would you expect to occur? Which of these changes impose serious economic costs and which are simply minor nuisances?
5. The following are data on the CPI and nominal interest rates:

YEAR	CONSUMER PRICE INDEX (1967 = 100)	NOMINAL INTEREST RATE (percent per annum)
1979	217.4	10.0
1980	246.8	11.4
1981	272.4	13.8
1982	289.1	11.1
1983	298.4	8.8
1984	311.1	9.8
1985	322.2	7.7
1986	328.4	6.0
1987	340.4	5.8
1988	354.3	6.5

Calculate the rate of inflation for each year from 1980 to 1987. Then calculate the real rate of interest. Do you see any major shift in the level of the real interest rate over this period? (Chapter 16 will pursue this question further.)

6. Consider an economy that starts out with money wages rising 2 percent each year while prices are stable. Describe whether each of the following would be balanced or unbalanced, and anticipated or unanticipated inflation:

(a) There is a sharp upturn in wage settlements so that wages are rising at 4 percent annually, while prices remain stable.

(b) Prices soon catch up, so that workers are surprised to find that prices are now rising at 2 percent per annum.

(c) A decade later, wages are still rising at 4 percent each year, and prices are climbing at 2 percent annually.

7. This chapter speaks of the impact of inflation, but unanticipated deflation also produces serious social costs. For each of the following, describe the deflation and analyze the associated costs:

(a) During the Great Depression, prices of major crops fell along with the prices of other commodities. What would happen to farmers who had large mortgages?

(b) Many students have borrowed $20,000 to pay for their college education, hoping that inflation would allow them to pay off their loans in depreciated dollars. What would happen to these students if wages and prices began to *fall* at 5 percent per year?

CHAPTER 15 ___
INFLATION AND UNEMPLOYMENT

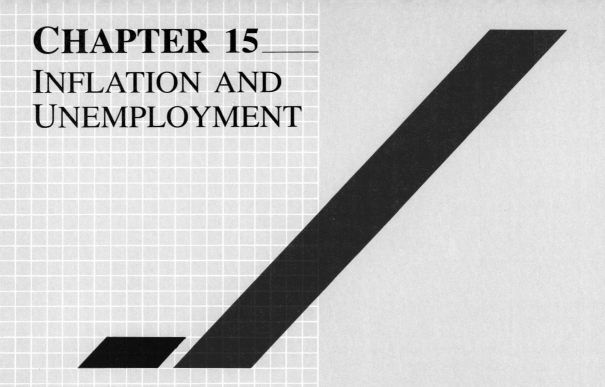

In no period during the past forty years has the American economy been free of excessive unemployment and inflationary tendencies simultaneously. Nor has any other industrial nation found the happy combination. Hitting the dual target of high utilization and essential price stability remains the most serious unsolved problem of stabilization policy throughout the Western world.

Arthur Okun
The Political Economy of Prosperity (1970)

THE LAST CHAPTER described the way we measure the price level and the rate of inflation, surveyed inflation's long history, and examined the costs of different kinds of inflation. We now turn to the specter haunting economies everywhere: Can we simultaneously enjoy the blessings of full employment and price stability?

Do we face a fundamental dilemma in choosing between full employment and price stability? Must the promise of good jobs for all inevitably be paid for by creeping inflation? Or even by inflation which gallops upward ever faster? Is there no way to control inflation other than by economic slowdowns that keep unemployment undesirably high?

And if the nation thinks that recessions are too high a price to pay for the control of inflation, do we need "incomes policies" that can lower inflation without raising unemployment? Are such policies to be found in direct wage-price controls, in voluntary guidelines, in more competitive markets, or in profit sharing? Or is the goal of effective incomes policies a snare and a delusion?

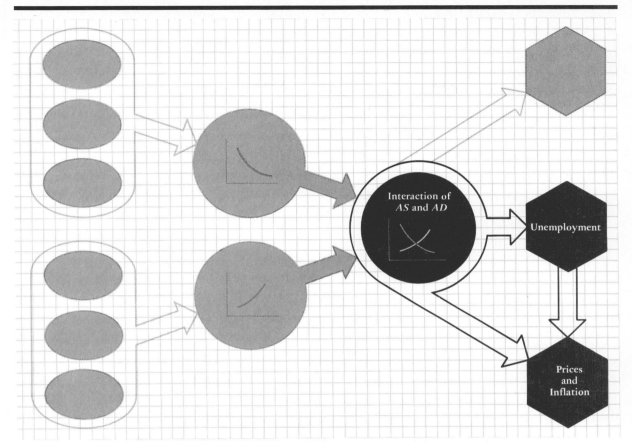

Figure 15-1   Aggregate supply and demand interact to determine prices and inflation

In this chapter, we study how *AS* and *AD* interact to determine the rate of inflation. We will see, as well, that there is a close connection between the overall unemployment rate and upward or downward movements in the inflation rate.

Questions, questions, questions. Yet answers to these are critical to the economic health of modern mixed economies. To some of these questions—such as how economists today view the inflation-unemployment tradeoff—we will be able to provide clear answers. But the fundamental dilemma remains. Just as no responsible physician can today tell you the cure

for cancer, no jury of economic experts can today agree on a satisfactory cure for the modern disease of stagflation—inflation and stagnation. All the proposed cures are controversial, and many have side effects that are worse than the disease itself. Figure 15-1 above shows the road map for the present chapter.

ALTERNATIVE SOURCES OF INFLATION

Before we begin our analysis of different theories of inflation, we must emphasize that there is no single kind of inflation. Like illnesses, inflations come in many different forms and sizes with some more damaging than others. Moreover, economists do not always agree about the sources of a particular inflationary episode; some may stress the importance of monetary forces while others point to expectations or to commodity prices. A final complication in our analysis of inflation is that the economy itself changes over time in response to external forces and economic events. We should not be surprised, therefore, that inflation has been a fertile ground for controversy.

Armed with this caution, we begin our analysis of theories of inflation. The first section notes that inflation tends to be highly "inertial," that is, inflation tends to remain at a given rate until shocked. We next analyze the kinds of shocks that move inflation up or down: demand shocks and supply shocks. We then conclude our analysis with the "Phillips curve," which is a device for representing the dilemmas facing the macroeconomy.

Inertial Inflation

In a modern industrial economy, inflation is highly *inertial;* i.e., it tends to stay at its prior rate until shocked by economic events. We can compare inertial inflation to a sleepy old dog. If the dog is not "shocked" by the push of a foot or the pull of a stray cat, it will stay where it is. Once shocked by the foot or cat, the dog may move around a bit, but then it eventually lies down in a new spot where it stays until the next shock.

In a modern economy like the United States, inflation shows similar inertial behavior. During the mid-1980s, prices rose steadily at around 4 percent annually, and most people came to expect that inflation rate. This expected rate of inflation was built into the economy's institutions. Labor and management wrote contracts designed around a 4 percent inflation rate; government monetary and fiscal plans assumed a 4 percent rate; interest rates included a 4 percent infla-

tion premium. Nominal GNP could grow at 7 percent (3 percent growth of potential output and 4 percent inflation) without any major surprise. We then say that 4 percent was the *inertial rate of inflation;* other names sometimes heard for this concept are the expected, anticipated, underlying, or core inflation rate.

The rate of inflation that is expected and built into contracts and informal arrangements is the inertial or expected rate of inflation.

The important point to note about inertial inflation at moderate rates is that it can persist for a long time. As long as the same inflation rate is expected and accommodated by economic policymakers, by investors, consumers, labor, and management, there is no reason why inflation cannot continue for years at 4 percent. Or at 2 percent. Or at 8 percent. A fully built-in inflation represents a *neutral* equilibrium, able to sustain itself at 2 or 4 or 8 percent for an indefinite period of time.

But inflation does not always proceed at a constant rate. The economy is not a sleeping dog for long because it receives frequent shocks. What kicks inflation off its inertial path and pushes it up or down? The shocks include high or low demand, sharp oil-price changes, poor harvests, movements in the foreign exchange rate, productivity changes, and countless other economic events. When such shocks affect the economy, inflation moves above or below its inertial rate.

To sum up:

In a given year, the economy has inherited a given rate of inflation (4 percent in our example), and people's expectations have adapted to this rate. This expected rate is called the inertial rate of inflation. Once built in, the inertial rate tends to persist until a new shock arrives. When a shock occurs, the inertial rate moves up or down.

Shocks to Inflation

In a tranquil world, we would expect inflation to chug quietly along at its inertial rate. In reality, just as the weather gets incessantly worse or better, inflation is constantly shocked by economic forces. The major forces are demand-pull and cost-push inflation.

Demand-Pull Inflation

We saw in earlier chapters that changes in investment or government spending or net exports can increase aggregate demand and propel output beyond its potential. We also studied how, by creating more money, a central bank can stimulate the economy. And we examined the case of the German hyperinflation, where the monetary printing presses ran amok and prices rose a billionfold over a year.

Whatever the source, if aggregate demand rises rapidly and exceeds the economy's productive potential, prices will begin to rise more and more rapidly. Demand dollars will beat against the limited supply of commodities and will bid up their prices. Because the labor market also becomes very tight at such times, the bidding up of wages is also part of the inflationary process.

Here the direction of causation is clear-cut. It proceeds *from* demand *to* inflation. Thus, if the German central bank prints billions and billions of paper marks in 1922 and these come into the marketplace in search of bread or housing, it is no wonder that the German price level would rise a billionfold as the marks become worthless. This is demand-pull inflation with a vengeance. But the matter would not be essentially different if there were an 1849 gold discovery in California. Or if the war-swollen boom during the Vietnam conflict drove the economy well above its potential GNP.

Figure 15-2 illustrates the process of demand-pull inflation using our earlier *AS-AD* framework. Suppose the economy is in an initial equilibrium at the intersection of the *AS* and *AD* curves at point *E*. The price level at that point is *P* on the vertical axis.

Suppose there is an expansion of spending that pushes the *AD* curve to the right. The economy's equilibrium moves from *E* to *E'*. At this higher level of demand, prices have risen from *P* to *P'*. Demand-pull inflation has taken place.

Major schools of macroeconomics today do not disagree much about the general nature of demand-pull inflation. Keynesians, monetarists, and classical economists all agree that the essence of demand-pull inflation is too much spending beating against a limited supply of goods.

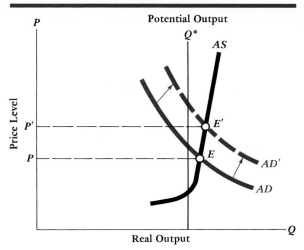

Figure 15-2 Demand-pull inflation occurs when too much spending chases too few goods

When the economy is at or above potential output, a demand increase leads to demand-pull inflation. As aggregate demand increases, the rising spending is competing for a limited supply of goods. With a steep *AS* curve, much of the higher aggregate spending ends up in higher prices. Prices rise from *P* to *P'*. Hence, it is higher demand that pulls up the prices—demand-pull inflation.

Cost-Push Inflation

If only the world of the twentieth century were more like the classical vision with its simple demand-pull inflation! A more realistic description notes that no country has for long enjoyed full employment, free markets, and stable prices.

A glance back at the history of prices on page 310 reminds us that prices today travel a one-way street— up in recession, up faster in boom. And this is true for all the mixed economies of the world—the United States, Germany, Britain, France, and Japan.

What differentiates modern inflation from the simple demand-pull theories is that prices and wages begin to rise before full employment is reached. They rise even when 30 percent of factory capacity lies idle and 10 percent of the labor force is unemployed. Prices rise in recessions because the cost of labor,

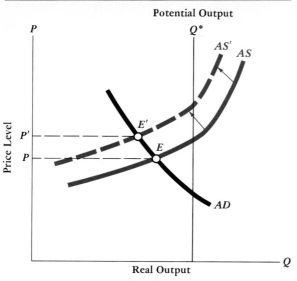

Figure 15-3 Cost-push inflation

In a modern economy, inflation often occurs even though output is well below potential. In periods of slack, wages or commodity prices rise, the *AS* curve shifts up, and final-goods prices tend to rise.

Suppose a terrible drought or a big wage increase occurs when the economy is in recession. These cost increases shift up the *AS* curve from *AS* to *AS'*. Consequently, prices rise from *P* to *P'*. Cost-push inflation has taken place.

capital, and materials tends to rise even in a slack economy.

When costs push prices up during periods of high unemployment and slack resource utilization, we call this cost-push inflation.

Who Is Pushing Up Costs? Cost-push inflation does not appear to have been present in the early stages of market economies. Rather, it first appeared during the 1930s and 1940s, leading to the dramatic change in the pattern of price behavior after World War II shown in Figure 14-3.

It is natural to look for culprits, and wage behavior is clearly an important part of cost-push inflation. In 1982, when the unemployment rate was almost 10 percent, wages rose 5 percent. Some point to unions as the responsible parties because they force money

wages to rise even though many of their members are out of work.

This view of unions as the clear-cut villains of cost-push inflation does not fit the complex historical facts. Take as an example the depressed year 1982, when unemployment averaged 9.7 percent of the labor force. During that year, labor costs for union workers rose 7.2 percent, and the cost of nonunion labor rose 6 percent. Both union and nonunion wages rose smartly in spite of high unemployment.

During the 1970s another set of players entered the cost-push fray: oil and other primary products. In 1973 and again in 1979, countries were minding their own macroeconomic business when severe shortages in oil and other markets occurred. These arose largely from political events, such as the Arab-Israeli war in 1973 and the fall of the Shah of Iran in 1978. In each case, when the sand had settled in the Mideast, a gigantic cost-push inflation had occurred. The producer price index (defined in the last chapter) for crude materials like oil and wheat rose 54 percent from 1972 to 1974.

In response to the sharp jump in commodity prices, the *AS* curve shifted up and inflation rose from 3 percent in 1972 to 11 percent in 1974. A similar cost-push inflation occurred from 1978 to 1980. Then, during the early 1980s, the prices of oil and other commodities fell while the rising foreign exchange rate of the dollar lowered import prices. These factors led to a sharp downward or *disinflationary* supply shock, pushing inflation below its inertial level.

Figure 15-3 illustrates the mechanism of cost-push inflation. In our *AS* and *AD* framework, cost-push occurs when a rise in costs shifts up the *AS* curve; in Figure 15-3, this is shown as an upward shift from *AS* to *AS'*. As a result, prices are pushed up, even though the economy may be well below full employment. Note that if the *AS* curve moves enough, we get what is called a *supply shock:* output may decline sharply (as is illustrated in Figure 15-3) as rising costs shift the *AS* curve up the downward-sloping aggregate demand curve.

Expectations and Inertial Inflation

Now that we have analyzed the major reasons why inflation tends to rise or fall, let us focus on the reasons that inflation has strong inertial tendencies. We noted above that, if there are no cost or demand shocks, inflation tends to continue at its historical rate. This is so because many prices and most wages are set with an eye to future economic conditions. When prices and wages are rising rapidly and are expected to continue doing so, firms and labor unions will tend to build the rapid rate of inflation into their price and wage decisions. High or low inflation expectations tend to be self-fulfilling prophesies.

An example will clarify the role of expectations in inertial inflation. Say that in November 1988, Brass Mills Inc., a nonunionized light manufacturing firm, was contemplating its annual wage and salary decisions for 1989. Its sales were growing well, and it was experiencing no major supply or demand shocks. Brass Mill's chief economist reported that, in the 1987–1988 period, both prices and wages were rising in the range of 3 to 4 percent per year, and the major forecasting services were expecting national wage growth of 4 percent in 1989. Brass Mills has conducted a survey of local companies and found that most employers were planning on increases in compensation of $3\frac{1}{2}$ to $4\frac{1}{2}$ percent during the next year. All the signals, then, pointed to wage increases of around 4 percent for 1989 over 1988.

In examining its own "internal labor market," Brass Mills determined that its wages were in line with the local labor market. The managers did not want to fall behind local wages, so Brass Mills decided that it would try to match local wage increases. It therefore set wage increases at the expected increase of the market and implemented an average 4 percent wage increase for 1989.

The process of setting wages and salaries with an eye to expected future economic conditions can be extended to virtually all employers. This kind of reasoning applies as well to many prices—such as automobile model prices or long-distance telephone rates or college tuitions—that cannot be easily changed after they have been set. Because of the long time delays required to modify inflation expectations and to affect most wages and prices, once inflation has been established and most economic participants expect it, it takes major supply or demand shocks and a considerable period of time to move inertial or expected inflation to a different rate.

We can illustrate the process of inertial inflation using our *AS-AD* framework in Figure 15-4 on the next page. For this simple example, assume that there is no growth in productivity or potential output and that there are no supply or demand shocks. When everyone expects wages and prices to rise at 4 percent each year, average costs will rise at that rate, and the *AS* curve will be shifting upward at 4 percent per year. If there are no demand shocks, the *AD* curve will also be shifting up at that rate. Therefore the intersection of the *AD* and *AS* curves will be 4 percent higher each year. We thus see a pattern of equilibria first at *E*, then at *E′*, then at *E″*—where prices are rising 4 percent from one year to the next: inertial inflation at 4 percent has set in.

Inertial inflation occurs, then, when the *AS* and *AD* curves are moving steadily upward at the same pace.

Price Levels vs. Inflation

Up to now we have not distinguished carefully between movements in the price level and movements in inflation. Figure 15-4 will help us clarify that distinction.

In general, a rightward shift of the *AD* curve will raise prices from what they would otherwise be, other things equal. Similarly, an upward shift in the *AS* curve will raise prices, other things equal.

Generally, however, we must analyze phenomena in the context of other things changing. In particular, the *AD* and *AS* curves are almost always moving over time. In Figure 15-4, for example, we see the *AS* and *AD* curves marching up together from year to year as the economy experiences inertial inflation of 4 percent per year.

What if there was an unexpected shift in the third period's *AS* or *AD* curve? How would prices and inflation be affected? If we were to shift the third period's *AD″* curve to the left and cause a recession, the equilibrium might be at *E‴* on the *AS″* curve. At this point, output would have fallen below potential; prices and the inflation rate would be lower than at *E″*, but the economy would still be experiencing inflation because the price level at *E‴* is still above the previous period's equilibrium *E′* with its price of *P′*.

Keep in mind that economic forces may reduce the price level below the level it would otherwise have

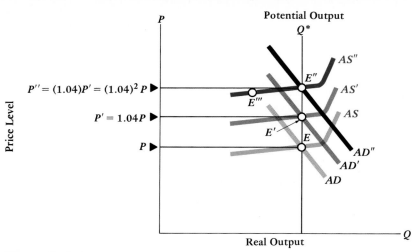

CHANGING PRICES, UNCHANGING INFLATION

Figure 15-4 **Inertial inflation shifts up the *AS* curve, leading to an upward spiral of prices and wages**

How does inertial inflation lead to an upward spiral of prices? Assume that the costs of production are rising by 4 percent each year. Thus, for every level of output, the *AS* curve will be 4 percent higher next year; another 4 percent higher the year after; and so on.

As long as the *AD* curve is moving up at the same pace, output will stay close to potential, and prices will also rise by 4 percent. As the macroequilibrium moves from *E* to *E'* to *E"*, prices march up steadily because of inertial inflation.

Using this framework, can you see what would happen if the inertial inflation rate were 2 (or 8) percent a year?

attained. Nonetheless, costs and prices may tend to rise in an inertial way, and the economy may continue to experience inflation even in the face of these contractionary (or disinflationary) shocks.

Stagflation This point is central for understanding the phenomenon of stagflation, or high inflation in periods of high unemployment. As long as the inertial elements driving up costs are powerful, a recession may still occur simultaneously with high inflation. Thus, if we again examine Figure 15-4, we see that the recessionary point E''' has output well below potential. But prices are still rising since the price level corresponding to E''' is perhaps 3 percent above the previous period's price level at P'.

THE PHILLIPS CURVE

Although aggregate supply and demand are crucial for understanding the inflationary process, this framework does get quite complicated when inertial forces shift the curves upward each period in the way shown in Figure 15-4. Economists therefore searched for a simpler device for capturing inflation theory. In the late 1950s and early 1960s, a striking innovation radically changed the way economists analyzed inflation. This was the Phillips curve.

The Phillips curve emerged from a pioneering study by the New Zealand-born economist A. W. Phillips, who attempted to quantify the determinants of wage inflation. After careful study of more than a century's worth of data on unemployment and money wages in the United Kingdom, Phillips found an inverse relationship between unemployment and the changes in money wages.

Early Approaches

Figure 15-5 portrays the typical Phillips curve as drawn by writers in the 1960s. On the diagram's horizontal axis is the unemployment rate. On the black left-hand vertical scale is the annual rate of price inflation. As you move leftward on this early Phillips curve by reducing unemployment, the rate of price and wage increase indicated by the curve becomes higher.

Underlying modern views of inflation is an important piece of inflation arithmetic. Let us assume for simplicity that labor productivity (output per worker) rises at a steady rate of 2 percent each year. And further, assume that firms set (or "mark up") prices on the basis of average labor costs, so prices are always 120 or 140 percent of average labor costs.

The arithmetic connecting prices and wages is then simple: if wages are rising at 6 percent, and productivity is rising at 2 percent, then average labor cost will rise at 4 percent. Consequently, in our simple example, prices will also rise at 4 percent.*

Using this inflation arithmetic, we can see the relation between wage and price increases in Figure 15-5. On the right-hand side, the red scale shows the percentage change in money wage rates while the left-hand side shows the rate of price inflation. These two scales differ only by the assumed rate of productivity growth (so that the price change of 6 percent per year would correspond to a wage change of 8 percent per year if productivity grew by 2 percent per year and if prices always rose as fast as average labor costs).

Where do the theories of the determination of output and income fit into this simple "tradeoff" view?

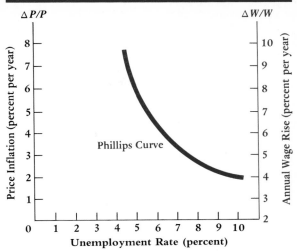

Figure 15-5   An early Phillips curve: tradeoff between inflation and unemployment

The Phillips curve depicts the relationship between unemployment and inflation. The red wage-change scale on the right-hand vertical axis is higher than the black left-hand inflation scale by the assumed 2 percent rate of growth of average labor productivity.

The key assumption here is that inflation and unemployment are inversely related. This means that more unemployment is required if you want to hold down inflation.

They are backstage, so to speak. Monetary and fiscal policy, along with other determinants of aggregate spending, sets the overall level of total dollar or nominal GNP in ways we have described in earlier chapters. But we need a relationship like the Phillips curve—whether the simple relationship shown in Figure 15-5 or a more complex relationship used in realistic macroeconomic models—to explain how the increase in nominal GNP is divided between higher real GNP and higher prices.

---

*This important piece of arithmetic can be formalized as follows. We assume firms set prices as a constant "markup" on average labor costs per unit of output. This means that P is always proportional to (WL/X), where P is the price level, W is the wage rate, L is labor-hours, and X is output. Further, assume that average labor productivity (X/L) is growing smoothly at 2 percent per year. Hence, if wages are growing at 6 percent annually, prices will grow at 4 percent annually ($= 6$ growth in wages minus 2 growth in productivity). More generally,

$$\begin{pmatrix} \text{Rate} \\ \text{of} \\ \text{inflation} \end{pmatrix} = \begin{pmatrix} \text{rate} \\ \text{of wage} \\ \text{growth} \end{pmatrix} - \begin{pmatrix} \text{rate of} \\ \text{productivity} \\ \text{growth} \end{pmatrix}$$

THE TRADEOFF IN EDEN

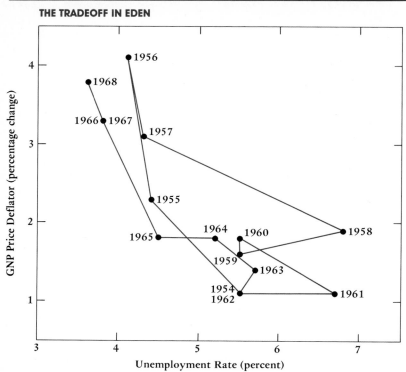

Figure 15-6   Phillips curve of 1969

This figure is taken from the 1969 *Economic Report of the President*. There was widespread belief at that time that the Phillips curve was relatively stable, providing a menu for choice between inflation and unemployment. The *Report* wrote that the chart "reveals a fairly close association of more rapid price increases with lower rates of unemployment. . . . Upward pressures on prices and wages are likely to be intensified when the economy is operating at high utilization of manpower and capital. *In a slack economy, rising prices are rarely a problem.*" (Source: *Economic Report of the President, 1969;* lines have been drawn in to connect the dots for ease of comparison with the next figure. Emphasis added.)

This simple early Phillips curve was christened the "tradeoff theory of inflation." According to this view, a nation could buy a lower level of unemployment if it were willing to pay the price of a higher rate of inflation. Moreover, this tradeoff was thought to hold for the long run as well as for the short run. Economists believed that there was a fundamental *tradeoff* between inflation and unemployment as represented by the downward-sloping Phillips curve.

Applications of Early Phillips Curves

Many economists were incautious in their interpretation of the Phillips curve when it was first introduced. Sometimes people thought that an economy could buy *permanently* lower unemployment by accepting a high but stable inflation rate. Figure 15-6 shows the Phillips curve that appeared in the influential *Economic Report of the President* of 1969. This figure, along with the accompanying discussion given in Figure 15-6, suggested that the major unfortunate consequence of low unemployment would be *high* inflation. How can we understand this empirical curve?

When people first examined the data shown in Figure 15-6, they were surprised that prices began to rise before the economy reached full employment. Thus look at the dots representing 1961 to 1964, a period in which there was considerable unemployment and many factories were idle. Why did prices creep up 1 or 2 percent per year during this period? Why were they not falling, as might the price of wheat or tin when excess supply appears?

The answer lies in the fact that prices and wages are not set in competitive auction markets; rather, as we have stressed, they are set or administered by economic agents like firms and unions. At any point in time, some regions or industries will be experiencing slack while others will be enjoying booms. In sectors experiencing slack, wages and prices will be relatively stable. In booming areas, prices will be moving up. Thus, on average, prices will be moving up even in the face of moderate slack.

Note that as the overall level of unemployment declines, the fraction of sectors that are experiencing excess demand increases—so the rate of upward creep in prices increases. The more we move to the left along the horizontal axis of Figure 15-6, the higher the inflation rate.

The Phillips Curve Shifts

The Phillips curve was sometimes described as a ''menu for choice between inflation and unemployment.'' Alas, the prices changed as the diners were enjoying their meal. Figure 15-7 on p. 332 illustrates what happened to the optimistic Phillips-curve trade-off after 1968: the points circled clockwise to the northeast—indeed, a skeptical observer might conclude that the Phillips curve has an upward slope!

A careful examination of history reveals a more complicated but fascinating story. In tracing through events, it is crucial to distinguish between actual and inertial inflation. There are always surprises (such as an oil-price change or a change in the foreign exchange rate on the dollar). When surprises occur, the actual rate of inflation may then diverge from the inertial or expected rate.

But inertial inflation responds to inflationary surprises. The process is illustrated in Figure 15-8. During the early 1960s, inflation was at low levels. The rapid growth and low unemployment during the Vietnam war led to bidding up of prices and wages—a demand shock occurred. This drove actual inflation above inertial or anticipated inflation. But inertial inflation followed in the tracks of the rising actual inflation. So by the early 1970s, inertial inflation was 5 percent rather than the 1 percent of the early 1960s.

Things were quiet until 1974, when rising oil prices propelled actual inflation up to 11 percent. Again, inertial inflation followed, rising to 9 percent. In 1979, a rerun of the first oil shock occurred, driving inertial inflation up to 8 or 9 percent. In 1979–1980, however, policymakers decided to pay almost any price in a crusade against inflation. The subsequent recession did restrain the economy. Under the pinch of tight money, actual inflation fell from 13 percent in 1980 to 4 percent in 1984, and inertial inflation crept down behind it. In the absence of major shocks in the mid-1980s, actual and inertial inflation remained near 4 percent per year.

The narrative points to the crucial flaw in the early Phillips curve:

The tradeoff between inflation and unemployment remains stable only as long as the inertial or expected inflation rate remains unchanged. But when the inertial inflation rate changes, the short-run Phillips curve will shift.

The Natural Rate of Unemployment

How can we make sense of the unstable-looking Phillips curve shown in Figure 15-7? After sifting through the data, many macroeconomists put forth a different hypothesis about the way unemployment and the utilization of capacity affects wage and price inflation. This view, sometimes called ''the natural-rate hypothesis'' or the ''accelerationist Phillips curve,'' distinguishes the long-run Phillips curve from the short-run Phillips curve. Moreover it puts forth the bold proposition that the only unemployment rate consistent with a steady rate of inflation is the natural rate of unemployment, implying that the long-run Phillips curve is vertical.

The basis of the natural-rate hypothesis is the following: At any point in time, the economy has inherited a given inertial or expected rate of inflation. If *(a)* there is no excess demand and if *(b)* there are no supply shocks, then actual inflation will continue at the inertial rate. What do these conditions signify? Condition *(a)* means that unemployment is at that level—the natural rate of unemployment—at which the upward pressure on wages from vacancies just matches the downward wage pressure from unemployment. Condition *(b)* denotes the absence of unusual changes in the costs of materials like food and oil and imports, so that the aggregate supply curve is rising at the inertial rate of inflation. Putting conditions *(a)* and *(b)* together leads to a state in which inflation can continue to rise at its inertial or expected rate.

By contrast, what would happen in the presence of either demand or cost shocks? If unemployment is driven far below the natural rate, as it was during the Vietnam war, then inflation will be pushed above its inertial rate as we move along the short-run Phillips curve. Or, if unemployment rises to levels far in excess of the natural rate, as when it approached 10 percent of the labor force during 1982–1983, then inflation will begin to decline below its earlier inertial rate as we move down the short-run Phillips curve. But the story does not end here.

Once actual inflation rises above its inertial or expected level, people begin to adapt to the new level of

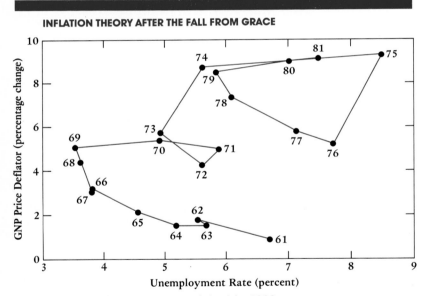

Figure 15-7 Phillips curves revisited in 1982

Thirteen years after the report shown in Fig. 15-6, the CEA under President Reagan produced the above figure and pronounced the stable Phillips curve a relic for the junkyard: "There are those who argue that a permanent reduction in the rate of inflation brings about a permanent rise in the unemployment rate. But the lesson [of history is that there] is no reason to expect a systematic association between the average unemployment rate and the average rate of price-level change. The average rate of unemployment and the average rate of inflation are best regarded as unrelated in the long term. The failure of previous policymakers to accept this conclusion is one of the principal reasons we have had a decade of stagnation." (Source: *Economic Report of the President, 1982;* the price index here is the GNP deflator.)

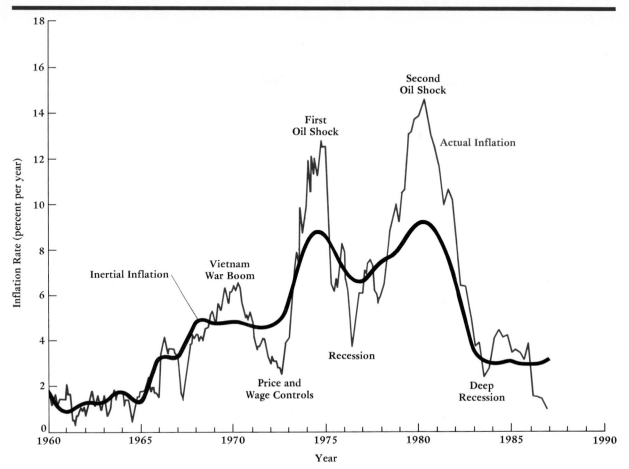

Figure 15-8   How inflation shocks affect the inertial inflation rate

The Phillips curve may become unreliable when inertial or expected inflation shifts. Thus, the Vietnam war, the first oil shock, and the second oil shock all propelled the inertial inflation rate upward. Then the period of tight money after 1979 led to "disinflation," or a reduction in the rate of inflation, and the inertial rate declined. What is happening now to change the inertial rate of inflation? (The price index shown here is the CPI.)

inflation and to expect higher inflation. The inertial rate of inflation then adjusts to the new reality. And the Phillips curve shifts.[1]

The Shifting Phillips Curve

The way in which shocks to demand or supply tend to change the inertial inflation rate and to shift the Phil-

[1]Macroeconomists have described several mechanisms by which inertial inflation adapts to the actual inflation rate. An early explanation was "adaptive expectations," which means that your expectations for the future reflect your experience in the past. More recent discussions have focused on the role of long-term contracts, such as the 3-year contracts typically negotiated in unionized indus-

tries. Such contracts can respond to inflation only after their expiration. Some economists hold to the theory of "rational expectations," examined in the appendix to Chapter 16. In this view, people are sensitive and accurate forecasters, so the short run turns into the long run with great rapidity.

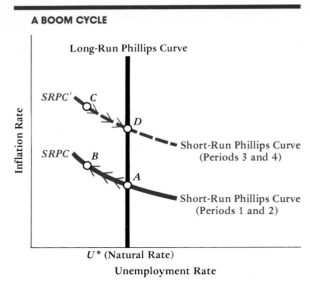

Figure 15-9   How shocks move the Phillips curve

This figure shows how a period of low unemployment shifts the short-run Phillips curve. The economy starts at point *A*. The economy then expands, with unemployment falling below the natural rate at point *B* in period 2. As a result, inflation rises above the inertial rate.

As time passes, however, the higher inflation becomes anticipated and gets built into the new short-run Phillips curve *SRPC'*; so at the same low unemployment rate as at point *B* the inflation rate is higher. When the economy comes back to the natural rate at point *D* in period 4, it is now saddled with a higher inertial and actual inflation rate.

Note that if points *A*, *B*, *C*, and *D* represent different years, you can connect the dots. A surprise is in store because the shifting curve has produced a clockwise loop like that seen in Fig. 15-7.

lips curve is an important part of modern macroeconomic theory. The process can be understood as a sequence of steps, illustrated by a "boom cycle" described here and in Figure 15-9.

Period 1. In the first period, unemployment is at the natural rate. There are no demand or supply surprises, and the economy is at point *A* on the lower short-run Phillips curve in Figure 15-9.

Period 2. A rapid increase in output during an economic expansion lowers the unemployment rate. As unemployment declines, firms tend to recruit workers

more vigorously, and some firms decide to increase their compensation more rapidly than they did in the previous period. Wages and prices begin to accelerate. In terms of our Phillips curve, the economy moves up and to the left to point *B* on its short-run Phillips curve (along *SRPC* in Figure 15-9). Inflation expectations do not change, but the lower unemployment rate raises inflation during the second period.

Period 3. With the higher rate of wage and price inflation, firms and workers begin to *expect* higher inflation. The higher expected rate of inflation gets incorporated into wage and price decisions. The inertial or expected rate of inflation thus increases.

How does higher expected inflation show up in the Phillips-curve framework? The short-run Phillips curve shifts upward. The new Phillips curve (labelled *SRPC'* in Figure 15-9) lies above the original Phillips curve, indicating that at every level of unemployment the inflation rate is higher. For example, the unemployment rate at point *C* on the shifted Phillips curve is the same as the unemployment rate at point *B*. But the inflation rate at point *C* is higher than at point *B*, reflecting the fact that the expected rate of inflation has risen between period 2 and period 3. Each short-run Phillips curve is drawn for a given inertial or expected rate of inflation.

Period 4. In the final period, the unemployment rate returns to the natural rate. This happens because the economy slows, say because policymakers take actions to contract the economy or because an investment boom runs out of steam. The contraction in economic activity brings output back to its potential, and the unemployment rate returns to the natural rate.

What is the outcome? The answer is shown at point *D* in Figure 15-9. Because the expected or inertial inflation rate has increased, the rate of inflation at the natural rate is higher than during period 1. Even though aggregate supply and demand are in balance, firms and workers have come to expect a higher inflation rate. The economy will experience the same *real* GNP and employment as it did in period 1, even though the *nominal* magnitudes (prices and nominal GNP) are now growing more rapidly than they did before the expansion raised the expected rate of inflation.

We can depict the sequence of unemployment and

inflation rates over time in Figure 15-10. This shows the unemployment rate starting in period 1 and ending in period 4 at the natural rate of unemployment, with the unemployment rate below the natural rate during the intervening periods. As a result of the tight labor markets during this cyclical upturn, wages and prices tend to rise more rapidly, so that by the end of the boom, the actual and inertial inflation rates have settled down at a new and higher level.

This hypothesis about the relationship between unemployment and inflation—which states that prices and wages tend to *accelerate* when unemployment is below the natural rate—is known as the natural-rate hypothesis.

The cycle will also work in the opposite direction when the economy experiences an "austerity cycle." In this case, unemployment rises; the actual inflation rate then falls below the inertial rate; the inertial rate of inflation finally falls; and the economy enjoys a lower inflation rate when it returns to the natural unemployment rate. Something like this painful cycle of austerity was exemplified by the Carter and Reagan wars against inflation during 1979–1988.

The Vertical Long-Run Phillips Curve

We have seen that when the unemployment rate diverges from the natural rate of unemployment, the inflation rate will tend to change. For example, say that the natural rate is 6 percent, while the actual unemployment rate is 4 percent. Consequently, inflation will tend to rise from year to year, as shown in Figure 15-10. Inflation might be 6 percent in the first year, 7 percent in the second year, 8 percent in the third year, and continue to move upward thereafter.

When would this upward spiral stop? According to the natural-rate theory, it will never stop until unemployment moves back to its natural rate. Put differently, as long as unemployment is below the natural rate, inflation will tend to increase.

The opposite behavior will be seen at high unemployment. In that case, inflation will tend to fall as long as unemployment is above the natural rate.

Only when unemployment is *at* the natural rate will inflation stabilize; only then will the forces of excess supply and demand in different labor markets be in balance; only then will inflation—at whatever is its

inertial rate—tend neither to increase nor decrease.

Therefore, according to the natural-rate theory, the only level of unemployment consistent with a stable inflation rate is the natural rate of unemployment. The long-run Phillips curve must, in this theory, be drawn as a vertical line, rising straight up at the natural unemployment rate, as shown by the vertical *DA* line in Figure 15-9.

The natural-rate theory of inflation has two important implications for economic policy. First, it implies that there is a minimum level of unemployment that an economy can sustain in the long run. According to this view, a nation cannot push unemployment below the natural rate for long without igniting an upward spiral of wage and price inflation.

Second, a nation may be able to ride the short-run Phillips curve. An expansionist President can drive the unemployment rate below the natural rate and the nation can temporarily enjoy low unemployment, but at the expense of rising inflation. Conversely, when a nation thinks that its inertial inflation rate is too high, as was the case in 1979–1982, it can steel itself for a

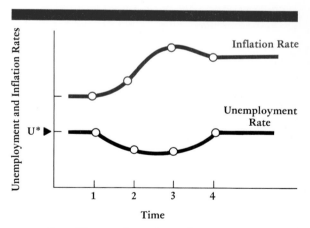

Note: U* = natural rate of unemployment

Figure 15-10   Low unemployment tends to drive up the inertial inflation rate

This figure shows the temporal sequence of inflation and unemployment rates graphed in Fig. 15-9. As unemployment declines below the natural rate, the actual rate of inflation rises. According to the natural-rate hypothesis, when unemployment comes back to the natural rate in period 4, the expected and actual inflation rates have reached a new plateau.

period of austerity, induce a recession, and thereby reduce inflation to a lower level.

Review

It will be useful to review the highlights of this section:

- Inflation is highly inertial. It tends to continue at its previous rate until shocked either by demand or by costs.

- In the short run, a positive demand shock which lowers the unemployment rate below the natural rate will tend to increase the inflation rate (and conversely for a negative shock). In the short run, while the Phillips curve is stable, there is a tradeoff between inflation and unemployment.

- In the long run, Phillips curves tend to be unstable. A period of low unemployment and increasing inflation will lead people to expect higher inflation and will tend to shift up the short-run Phillips curve.

- According to the natural-rate theory, the long-run Phillips curve is completely vertical at the natural unemployment rate; as long as the unemployment rate is below the natural rate, inflation will tend to rise continually.

OPEN ISSUES

The economy changes in response to policy and external events. Our economic theories, concerned with issues like inflation and unemployment, must also adapt. No sooner has one set of issues been resolved than others arise to confound economists.

In the area of inflation, numerous questions remain controversial. In this final section on inflation theory, we turn to four questions that concern modern inflation theory and policy.

Is the Phillips Curve Dead?

In response to the incoherent scatter of dots shown earlier in Figure 15-7, many skeptics claim that the Phillips curve is stuff and nonsense. Are they right?

A closer look reveals that the theory of the *simple*

and stable Phillips curve is indeed dead. The earlier view has, for many macroeconomists, been replaced by the more subtle natural-rate theory explained in the last section. The latest test of the theory came over the last decade in Thatcher's Britain and Reagan's United States. Both countries suffered deep recessions as means of reducing unacceptably high inflations. Both countries subsequently found clear and substantial declines in inflation, much as predicted by the modern inflation theory just outlined.

We must, however, add a note of caution about the new orthodoxy of the natural-rate theory. This theory has been the subject of numerous theoretical and empirical studies and is widely accepted among today's macroeconomic thinkers and policymakers. Nonetheless, it remains at best imprecise and approximate. No economist has succeeded in measuring the natural rate with precision. Moreover, as was sketched in Chapter 13, the behavior of unemployment and inflation in Europe during the last decade has led some economists to wonder whether a stable natural rate and long-run Phillips curve exist. Some economists believe that the natural rate is not a precise number but a broad band of unemployment rates.

These reservations are important reminders of the tentative and evolutionary nature of economic theory. We should be prepared, in inflation theory as elsewhere, for surprises and prediction errors. But for the moment, the prevailing view is that the central insight of the Phillips-curve approach—with a tradeoff between unemployment and inflation in the short run—is a fruitful way of viewing today's macroeconomy.

How Long Is the Long Run?

The natural-rate theory holds that in the long run the Phillips curve is vertical. How long is the long run in such a world?

The length of time that it takes the economy to adjust to a shock is not precisely known. Recent studies suggest that most of the adjustment takes place in 5 to 10 years, after labor contracts have been renegotiated and the effects of such adjustments have percolated through the economy. The length of time probably depends upon the type and novelty of the shock. Therefore, a politician might be able to count on enough slope to the Phillips curve to engineer a political business cycle, but it would be unwise to count on the Phillips-curve tradeoff for much more than a half dozen years.

Liquidation or Adaptation?

When inflation heats up, we naturally ask, should we attempt to liquidate inflation by austerity and other hard-hearted strategies? Or, should we adapt our economy to inflation, and live with inflation as the lesser evil?

For the most part, since 1980 the major industrial economies have opted for eradicating inflation. Thatcher in Britain and Reagan in the United States elevated inflation control to the top of their macroeconomic priorities.

Some countries have chosen "indexation" and other adaptive techniques. **Indexing** or indexation is a mechanism by which a contract or an economy is partially or wholly immunized from changes in the general price level.

Examples are seen in labor contracts, such as those between a union and a company, where workers receive cost-of-living adjustments or *COLA*s. These typically say: The firm will next year give the worker a 2 percent wage increase if there is no inflation. However, if prices rise 10 percent over the next 12 months, the firm will add another 4 (or 6 or 8) percent as a cost-of-living adjustment. Such clauses were rare before the inflationary 1970s, but 30 percent of labor contracts today contain COLAs.

Also, in 1981, the Congress partially "indexed" the personal income tax. For every 5 percent that prices rise, the income-tax brackets (shown in Table 33-3) will move out by 5 percent. Thus, people's real taxes (taxes in dollars of constant purchasing power) will rise only when their real taxable incomes rise.

Why don't we simply insulate the entire economy by indexing everything? In such a world, inflation will not matter for anything "real," and we can presumably ignore inflation and concentrate on reducing unemployment.

This sounds like a good idea. But on closer look it turns out that the more you insulate the economy from inflation by indexation, the more unstable inflation becomes. Assume that wages, rents, interest rates, and public-utility prices are all 100 percent indexed to

the CPI. Say a bad harvest drives food prices up enough to increase the CPI by 10 percent. The shock will rage through the economy like an epidemic. Everything indexed to the CPI goes up 10 percent. But since all costs are indexed, the next month the CPI goes up almost 10 percent again. And the third month, prices rise almost 10 percent again. By the time the cost-price spiral has ended, prices would be up many times.

A high rate of indexation is like a big multiplier in our output-determination model of Chapter 8—it amplifies outside price shocks. Perhaps this is why the German government—which has been highly averse to inflation since the hyperinflation of the 1920s—prohibits COLAs, the prohibition acting as a kind of inflation stabilizer.

Adaptation to inflation thus contains a paradox: The more a society insulates its members from inflation, the more unstable inflation is likely to become. Countries that have thoroughly indexed their economies (such as Israel or Brazil) have not found much solace there.

How Much Does It Cost to Reduce Inflation?

A final question is: How much does it cost to squeeze inflation out of the economy? How costly is *disinflation,* the policy of lowering the rate of inflation?

Another way of viewing this question is to ask, What is the shape of the short-run Phillips curve? If the Phillips curve is relatively flat, this means that reducing inflation will require a big increase in unemployment; if the Phillips curve is steep, then a small rise in unemployment will bring down inflation quickly and relatively painlessly.

There have been numerous studies of the cost of reducing inflation, and the answers vary depending upon the country, the initial inflation rate, and the policy used. Studies of the cost of disinflation for the United States give a reasonably consistent answer. These studies indicate that using unemployment to reduce the underlying inflation rate by 1 percentage point (e.g., from 6 percent per year to 5 percent per year) will cost the nation between 2 and $4\frac{1}{2}$ percent of 1 year's GNP. In terms of the level of GNP in the late 1980s, this would amount to between $100 and $225

THE COSTS OF DISINFLATION, 1980–1984

Inertial rate of inflation:

1979	9 percent
1984	4 percent
Change:	minus 5 percentage points

Difference between potential and actual GNP (1982 prices):

1980	$ 85 billion
1981	105
1982	270
1983	235
1984	105
Total:	$800 billion

Cost of disinflation = $800 billion/5 percentage points

= $160 billion per percentage point

Table 15-1   Illustration of the cost of disinflation, 1980–1984

This table illustrates the costs of reducing the inertial rate of inflation from around 9 percent in 1979 to around 4 percent in 1984. Over that period the inertial rate declined 5 percentage points, while the economy produced $800 billion less than its potential GNP. Dividing these two figures provides an estimate of $160 billion of output lost per percentage-point reduction in inflation. This figure is close to the estimate based on behavior of the U.S. economy during the 1960s and 1970s. (Source: Authors' estimates.)

---

billion (in current prices for the late 1980s) to reduce the inflation rate by 1 percentage point.[2]

Numerical Estimates Let us indicate how the estimates of the cost of disinflation are obtained. This calculation is based on the statistical finding that when the unemployment rate is raised 1 percentage point above the natural rate of unemployment for 1 year, and then returns to the natural rate, the inflation

rate will decline about $\frac{1}{2}$ percentage point. Therefore, to reduce inflation by 1 full percentage point, unemployment must be held 2 percentage points above the natural unemployment rate for 1 year.

Recall that Okun's Law (discussed in Chapter 10) states that when the unemployment rate is 2 percentage points above the natural rate, this entails an actual GNP that is 4 percent below potential GNP. In terms of 1989, with a potential GNP (in 1982 prices) of $4000 billion, reducing inflation by 1 percentage point would require about 2 percentage points on the unemployment rate (U) for 1 year. In dollars, then, a disinflation of 1 percentage point would cost 2 (U points) × (2 percent of GNP per U point) × ($4000 billion of GNP) = $160 billion.

This statistical estimate of the cost of disinflation can be compared to the American experience in the deep recession of the early 1980s. Table 15-1 shows a calculation of the estimated output loss from the recession (compared to producing at potential output), along with the estimated decline in the inertial inflation rate. This calculation indicates that the disinflation of the 1980–1984 period cost the nation approximately $160 billion of lost output (in 1982 prices) per percentage-point reduction in inflation. Clearly the experience of the early 1980s corroborates the earlier estimates of the cost of disinflation.

Credibility and Inflation Recent experience in the United States can help address another important issue. In the last decade, many economists argued that the Okun analysis cited above was too pessimistic. The dissenters held that credible and publicly announced policies—for example, adopting fixed monetary rules or the gold standard—might lead to a much more rapid and less painful reduction in inflation. These economists pointed to "regime changes," such as monetary and fiscal reforms, that ended Austrian and Bolivian hyperinflations at relatively low cost in terms of unemployment or lost GNP.

Other economists argued that, while such policies might work in countries torn by hyperinflation, war, or revolution, no realistic policy could hope to work miracles in today's stable United States.

The bold experiment of 1980–1984 provides a good laboratory in which to test Okun's view of the costs of disinflation. During this period, unemploy-

---

[2]Several studies reviewed by Arthur Okun in "Efficient Disinflationary Policies," *American Economic Review* (May 1978), produce a range of estimates of the disinflationary impact of higher unemployment. This figure used here takes into account Okun's review along with more recent studies by R. J. Gordon and others.

ment was deliberately increased as a means of curbing inflation. Studies indicate that the price tag for using economic slack to slow inflation is as high as Okun and other pessimists have argued. Moreover, using tough preannounced policies to enhance credibility did not appear effective in lowering the cost. More formal studies, with essentially the same conclusions, are found in papers by Robert Gordon, the late Otto Eckstein, George Perry, and Olivier Blanchard.

The thought that disinflation costs the nation $100 to $225 billion per point of disinflation is surprising. Upon hearing this people often have two responses: First, is it worth it? Second, aren't there cheaper ways of lowering inflation?

On the question of "Is it worth it?" people are deeply divided. We reviewed the costs of inflation in the last chapter. We saw a wide variety of costs, although none of the quantifiable costs appeared to be quite large. We noted, however, that to say the costs are difficult to identify with precision does not mean that they are small (consider the case of freedom of speech).

The second question, on the feasibility of less costly ways of reducing inflation, has been the topic of continual discussion and debate over the last three decades. This is the issue of incomes policies.

WANTED: AN EFFECTIVE ANTI-INFLATION POLICY

Concerns about inflation rise and ebb with the rate of inflation itself. In periods of high inflation, such as in 1973–1974 or 1979–1981, combating inflation became the nation's highest economic priority. When inflation declined and unemployment rose, inflation was quickly forgotten and policymakers turned their attention to more pressing issues. President Reagan came into office riding the crest of a wave of popular anger with the "Carter inflation," yet the 1988 presidential candidates debated trade policy and national defense while ignoring the perils of inflation.

But economists cannot ignore inflation. They know that supply or demand shocks can ignite a roaring inflation in a few months. They recall that the inflationary monster appeared from nowhere in 1950, in 1956, in 1973, and in 1978. They know that when

inflation appears, policymakers will wrestle with the devil, trying to decide whether to allow inflation to continue or to induce a recession to slow inflation. And, in inflationary circumstances, economists will search for policies to slow inflation without raising unemployment.

How can nations resolve the dilemma of inflation versus unemployment? Policies that attempt to lower inflation without raising unemployment are sometimes called "incomes policies." **Incomes policies** are government actions that attempt to moderate inflation by direct steps, whether by verbal persuasion, legal controls, or other incentives. In terms of our economic analysis, they are attempts to shift the Phillips curve inward and to the left.

What are some of the approaches to anti-inflation policies in recent decades? And how successful have they been? Here are some examples:

- *Peacetime wage-price controls* have been extensively used in Scandinavia, the Netherlands, and elsewhere. Although in the short run they have sometimes been effective—Finland in 1967–1971 being a notable case, and America in 1951–1952 perhaps another—in the longer run such controls have either blown up or been allowed to become ineffective as people evaded them. And in some cases, such as the United States during 1971–1974, price-and-wage controls appear to have been totally ineffective in the struggle to slow the wage-price spiral.

- *Voluntary wage-price guidelines* proved modestly better than nothing in the Netherlands, and also in the United States during the Kennedy, Johnson, and Carter years. But with time they tended to become ineffective and inequitable—particularly when accompanied by excessively stimulative fiscal and monetary policies that ignited demand-pull price pressures.

- A *free-market* strategy has been urged by many economists, particularly by those of a conservative bent. This approach would rely on the natural discipline of markets to restrain price and wage increases. Advocates would attempt to make market forces work more forcefully. How? Speed the deregulation of industries like natural gas, utilities, telecommunications, transportation, and finance; remove market impediments to competition in perverse antitrust laws or in retail-price maintenance; repeal government laws that inhibit competition (such as foreign-trade quotas or minimum-wage laws); even consider banning labor-union monopolies. By making markets behave more competitively, this approach argues, the inflationary bias of markets could be at least partially removed.

• *Tax-based incomes policies* (sometimes dubbed ''TIP'') have been proposed as a way of harnessing the market mechanism to attain macroeconomic objectives. TIP would use fiscal carrots and sticks to encourage anti-inflationary actions by taxing those whose wages and prices are rising rapidly and subsidizing those whose wages and prices are rising slowly. At this time, TIP is no more than a bright idea—it has not been tested. Some activist economists think it is worth a try during inflationary periods; conservative economists answer that there is no substitute for the discipline of the market mechanism as a means of containing inflation.

• *Profit sharing* has been advocated by Martin Weitzman of MIT as a way of giving firms an incentive to hire and retain workers during recessions. His argument is that a profit-sharing arrangement lowers the incremental or marginal cost to the firm of keeping its workers, so the firm will tend to keep employment up in bad times, with a consequent decline in the natural unemployment rate. He believes that part of the success of the Japanese economy comes from a ''bonus'' system, whereby workers are paid a certain amount of their compensation in end-of-year lump sums. Critics of the Weitzman proposal counter that the Japanese system is in fact not a profit-sharing system; that profit sharing would do little to induce firms to retain workers; and that the overall impact on the natural rate would be negligible. A decisive test of profit sharing has yet to be constructed.

The search for an effective and durable incomes policy has, alas, been futile up to now. As a thorough study of the subject summarized:

> Incomes policy, to generalize from the experience of the [seven] countries studied in this account, has not been very successful. . . . [A]ccumulation of experience . . . suggests that in none of the variations so far turned up has incomes policy succeeded in its fundamental objective, as stated, of making full employment consistent with a reasonable degree of price stability.[3]

The Cruel Dilemma

This and the preceding chapter covered the important and complex phenomenon called inflation. In the end, we cannot escape the conclusion that the control of inflation in a modern industrial economy poses one of the cruelest dilemmas that must be faced by economic policymakers.

Many economists today think that there is a natural rate of unemployment below which our economies can go only at the risk of spiraling inflation. Moreover, the natural rate of unemployment is judged by many economists and policymakers to be excessively high and to lie well above the rate necessary for frictional migration of young and untested workers looking for jobs. Critics of capitalism, indeed, find the high unemployment that prevails in North America and Europe to be the central flaw in modern capitalism. The search for a way to resolve the cruel dilemma of needing high unemployment to contain inflation continues to be one of the most pressing concerns of modern macroeconomics.

[3]Lloyd Ulman and Robert J. Flanagan, *Wage Restraint: A Study of Incomes Policies in Western Europe* (University of California Press, Berkeley, 1971).

SUMMARY

1. Back in the days of laissez-faire, when Queen Victoria reigned from Windsor Castle and William McKinley dozed in the White House, there may have been some validity to the fear that capitalism would intermittently suffer from economic crises and extended depressions. But, whatever the merits of such theories then, the theories discovered by Keynes allowed mixed economies to use their fiscal and monetary powers to raise spending and lower unemployment. Once successful, such policies led to an expectation of greater stability and then produced a different kind of problem: cost-push inflation and stagflation.

2. Today's inflations come in many varieties. At any time, an economy has inherited a given *inertial* or expected inflation rate. This is the rate that people have come to anticipate and that is built into labor contracts and other agreements. The inertial rate of inflation can chug along at 2, or 6, or 10 percent each year without a strong tendency to rise or fall. The inertial rate of inflation is a short-run equilibrium, and persists until the economy is shocked.

3. In reality, the economy receives incessant price shocks. The major kinds of shocks that propel inflation away from its inertial rate are demand-pull and cost-push.

Demand-pull inflation occurs when there is too much spending chasing too few goods, when the aggregate demand curve shifts up and to the right. The result is that wages and prices get bid up in markets.

Cost-push inflation is a new phenomenon of modern industrial economies. It arises when the costs of production rise even though there is no excess demand for goods or inputs. In graphical terms, cost-push inflation occurs when the aggregate supply curve pushes up. Cost-push pressures dominate when labor unions or businesses exercise market power by raising wages or prices despite high unemployment or excess capacity.

4. The modern Phillips curve is a device for showing the way that inertial inflation and shocks affect the economy.

In the short run, the economy faces a tradeoff between unemployment and inflation. Suppose in a given year the inertial inflation rate is 4 percent and the natural rate of unemployment is 6 percent. Then if unemployment declines below the natural rate, inflation will rise above the inertial rate, to an inflation rate of 5 or 6 percent or more. Similarly, if unemployment rises above the natural rate (as it did during the 1980–1984 period), inflation will tend to fall below the inertial rate.

5. But the Phillips curve has proven an unstable relationship, shifting over time as expected inflation and productivity growth change. If inflation persists above the expected or inertial inflation rate, people's expectations adapt, and the inertial inflation rate itself changes. Under the natural-rate theory, there is no permanent tradeoff between unemployment and inflation, and the long-run Phillips curve is vertical. If policymakers attempt to hold unemployment below the natural rate for long periods, according to the natural-rate theory, inflation will tend to spiral upward until the employment rate rises to the natural rate. While many macroeconomists accept the natural-rate theory, it leaves many questions unanswered, such as the reasons for the upward drift in unemployment rates in Europe over the last decade.

6. Even as economic science evolves from the early Phillips-curve theory to the new natural-rate theory, new issues and debates emerge. A central question for policymakers is how much damage must be done to output and employment in order to reduce a stubbornly imbedded inertial inflation—i.e., what are the costs of disinflation? Current estimates indicate that a substantial recession, reducing GNP by $100 to $225 billion below its potential, is necessary to slow inertial inflation by 1 percentage point. Such a large cost gives many people pause as they contemplate inducing a recession to curb a moderate inflation.

7. Because of the high costs of reducing inflation through recessions, nations have often turned to other approaches. These are incomes policies such as wage-price controls or voluntary guidelines. Many would rely on strengthening market forces. A new but untested approach is tax-based incomes policies (TIP), which would use the tax system to discourage inflation much as it imposes excise taxes to curb consumption of alcohol and tobacco. A recent proposal for profit sharing holds that such arrangements would induce firms to hold on to their employees in recessions.

CONCEPTS FOR REVIEW

inertial inflation, shocks to inflation
  from demand or costs
sources of shock to inflation (demand-
  pull, cost-push)
demand-pull and cost-push in the *AS*
  and *AD* framework
early Phillips curves, modern natural-
  rate theory
natural rate of unemployment and the
  long-run Phillips curve

boom cycle, austerity cycle, Phillips-
  curve loops
costs of disinflation
incomes policies: wage-price controls
  and guidelines, competition, TIP,
  profit sharing
indexing, COLA adjustments
stagflation

QUESTIONS FOR DISCUSSION

1. ''Unemployment in 1988 is 9 percent in the steel industry, yet wage rates in the steel industry are rising at 6 percent per year.'' Show that this is cost-push and not demand-pull inflation in the labor market. What reasons might exist for this phenomenon?

2. What is a short-run Phillips curve? What is on its horizontal axis? On its vertical axis? What can cause the short-run Phillips curve to shift up or down?

3. The following data describe inflation and unemployment in the United States in the 1980s:

YEAR	UNEMPLOYMENT RATE (PERCENT)	INFLATION RATE, CPI (PERCENT PER YEAR)
1979	5.8	11.3
1980	7.1	13.5
1981	7.5	10.4
1982	9.6	6.2
1983	9.4	3.2
1984	7.4	4.3
1985	7.1	3.5
1986	7.0	1.9
1987	6.3	3.7
1988	5.5	4.1

Source: *Economic Report of the President, 1988,* updated by authors.

Note how the economy started out near the natural rate of unemployment in 1979 and ended near the natural rate in 1988. Can you explain the decline of inflation over these years? Do so by drawing the short-run and long-run Phillips curves for each of the years 1979–1988.

4. Many economists argue as follows: "Because there is no long-run tradeoff between unemployment and inflation, there is no point in trying to shave the peaks and troughs from the business cycle." Think about this view. Does this view suggest that we should not care if the economy is stable or fluctuating widely as long as the average level of unemployment is the same? Would you agree?

5. Is unemployment above or below the natural rate today? What are the arguments for leaving the unemployment rate where it is? For moving it toward the natural rate? How do you resolve these two views?

6. A leading economist has written: "If you think back to our discussion of the social costs of inflation, at least of moderate inflation, it is hard to avoid coming away with the impression that they are minor compared with the costs of unemployment and depressed production." What do you think about this critical question?

7. A gaggle of Phillips curves is shown in the accompanying figure. The U^* point is the natural rate of unemployment, and the dots are such that 1 is for year 1, 2 for year 2, and so forth.

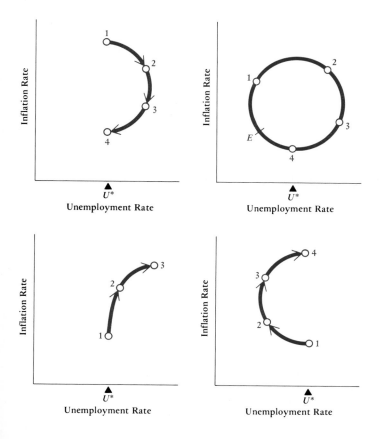

The figures correspond (in jumbled order) to boom cycle, austerity cycle, supply shock, and political business cycle. Identify each. Explain why the illustrated shape occurs in each case. Identify periods of history that would be represented by each case.

8. Examine the data on inflation and unemployment in question 3. Plot a series of short-run Phillips curves along with a long-run Phillips curve that might be consistent with that data.

9. Incomes policies are attempts to shift the Phillips curve in a favorable direction. Choose two examples of incomes policies given in the text. For each, describe the policy and show how it might affect the short-run and the long-run Phillips curves.

10. Consider the following anti-inflation policies: high unemployment, wage-and-price controls, voluntary wage-price guidelines, and tax-based incomes policies. For each, list the advantages and disadvantages in terms of inflation control and other economic objectives. Which would you choose if the President asked for your recommendation?

11. Recall the discussion of policies to lower the natural rate in Chapter 13. Describe the impact of those policies upon the Phillips curve of this chapter.

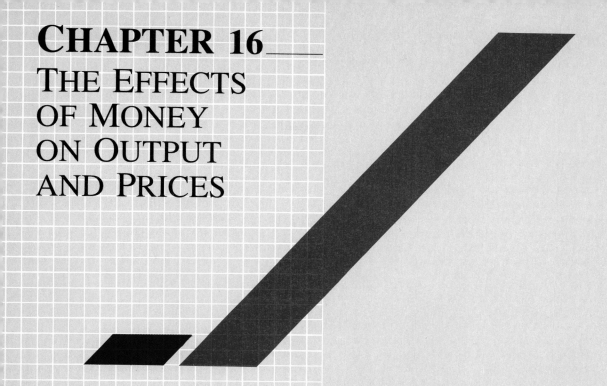

CHAPTER 16___
THE EFFECTS
OF MONEY
ON OUTPUT
AND PRICES

EARLIER CHAPTERS surveyed the essence of money and prices. The time has now come to describe the *monetary mechanism,* the route by which changes in the supply of money get translated into changes in output, employment, prices, and inflation.

The first section of this chapter begins by reviewing the major themes of the earlier chapters on money. We then describe the modern mainstream view of the transmission mechanism from monetary changes to money's impact upon output and prices. This analysis of monetary forces shows that there is another route, parallel to government spending and taxation, by which economic policy can affect the macroeconomy.

The second section of this chapter turns to a discussion of the classical tradition formerly known as the quantity theory of money and today called monetarism. This influential view stresses the primacy of the money supply in determining nominal GNP; it will be explained and contrasted with the modern mainstream view of monetary macroeconomics. Figure 16-1 depicts the path followed by this chapter.

345

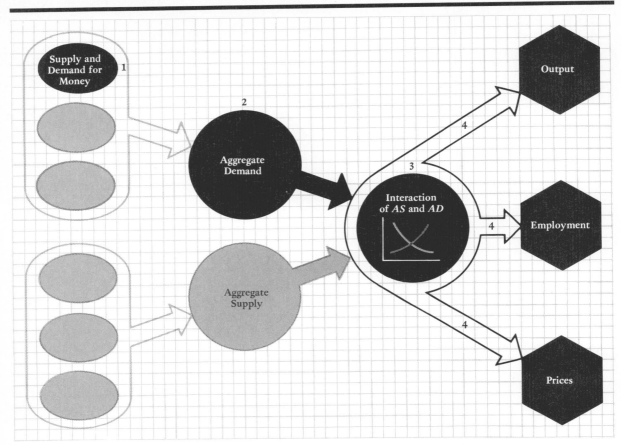

Figure 16-1 This chapter studies the impact of money on output and prices

Having analyzed the forces affecting the supply and demand for money, we now analyze the overall impact of money on the macroeconomy. We begin at 1 by reviewing forces determining the demand and supply of money. We see how money affects the level of aggregate demand at 2, interacts with AS at 3, and then determines the levels of output, employment, and prices at 4.

A. HOW MONEY AFFECTS OUTPUT

THE MONEY MARKET

Before analyzing the transmission mechanism from money to economic activity, we pause to recapitulate the elements of the supply and demand for money

surveyed in Chapters 11 and 12. To begin with, recall that money is a unique economic commodity. It is demanded not for its own sake but for what it will buy. As the French economist Frederic Bastiat remarked, "People are not nourished by money. They do not clothe themselves with gold; they do not warm themselves with silver.'' Instead, money is held because it serves people indirectly by facilitating trade and exchange.

To understand the *demand for money,* we need to recall its three special functions. It serves as:

1. a *medium of exchange,* the thing used to buy and sell all manner of goods and services.

2. the *unit of account,* the way we keep our books, the universal yardstick by which the values of goods and services are measured.

3. a *store of value,* a riskless asset that can be used to hold wealth from one period to another.

To understand the functions of money is to understand the nature of demand for it. The demand for money is derived primarily from the need to undertake transactions. Households, businesses, governments—all these economic agents demand money so they may buy goods, services, and other items. In addition, some part of the demand for M_1 derives from the need for a super-safe and highly liquid asset.

The *supply of money* is jointly determined by the private banking system and the nation's central bank. The central bank, through open-market operations and other instruments, provides reserves to the banking system; these reserves take the form of cash-in-the-vault and non-interest-bearing bank deposits with the Federal Reserve. Commercial banks then create deposits out of the central bank reserves. The banks must hold a legally fixed fraction of deposits in reserves, while they then lend out the rest of their funds. By manipulating reserves, the central bank can determine the money supply within a narrow margin of error.

Supply and Demand for Money

We now break new ground by combining the supply and demand for money and seeing how they jointly determine the market interest rates. Figure 16-2 shows the total quantity of money (M_1) on the horizontal axis and the nominal interest rate *(i)* on the vertical axis. The supply curve is drawn as a vertical line on the assumption that the Federal Reserve sets

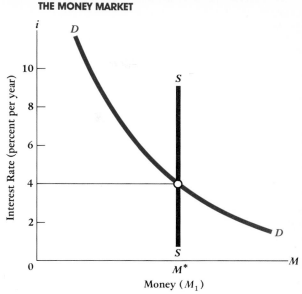

THE MONEY MARKET

Figure 16-2   Demand and supply of money determine the interest rate

This figure illustrates the determination of interest rates. The Fed has a money target at M^*, represented by the vertical supply-of-money schedule, *SS*. The public (households and businesses) desires to hold different amounts of M_1 at different levels of interest rates—with lower interest rates inducing larger desired money balances. The example given produces a demand for M_1 equaling the supply at an equilibrium nominal interest rate of 4 percent per year.

Note, also, that the *DD* curve assumes a given level of output and prices (or nominal GNP). If real GNP or the price level increased, this would shift the *DD* curve to the right.

its instruments (open-market operations, discount rate, etc.) to keep the money supply at a given level, shown as M^* in Figure 16-2. Put differently, the money supply curve is drawn as vertical because the money supply is assumed to be fixed at M^* for any interest rate.

In addition, we show the money demand schedule as a downward-sloping line in Figure 16-2. The demand curve slopes down because the holdings of money decline as the level of interest rates rise: At higher interest rates, people and businesses shift more of their assets to interest-bearing accounts from non-interest-bearing money. This is accomplished by shifting funds to high-interest assets more often, by holding less currency on average and replenishing their cash supply more often, by trying to synchronize income and expenditures, and by similar cash-management schemes.

The intersection of the supply and demand schedules in Figure 16-2 determines the market interest rate. Recall that interest rates are the prices paid for the use of money. That is, in return for the ability to borrow money, people must pay a certain amount of money annually as interest. In the **money markets,** which are the markets where short-term funds are lent and borrowed, the important interest rates include short-term rates such as the rates on 3-month Treasury bills, short-term commercial paper (notes issued by large corporations), and the Federal Funds rate that banks pay each other for the overnight use of bank reserves. Longer-term interest rates include 10-year or 20-year government and corporate bonds and mortgages on real estate. (See Figure 12-5 for a graph of recent behavior of interest rates.)

In the example shown, the equilibrium interest rate is 4 percent per year. Only at 4 percent is the level of the money supply that the Fed has targeted consistent with the desired money holdings of the public. At a higher interest rate, there would be excessive money stocks, and people would be unwilling to hold all the $M*$. People would get rid of their excessive money holdings by buying bonds and other financial instruments and thereby lowering market interest rates toward the equilibrium 4 percent rate. What would happen at an interest rate of 2 percent?

How would changes in the supply or demand for money affect the money market? First consider a change in monetary policy. Say that the Federal Reserve spots an inflationary gust on the horizon, as it did in mid-1988. Because the Fed believes its most important task is to maintain stable prices by containing inflation, the Fed tightens monetary policy a notch. It slows down the growth of reserves and thereby contracts the money supply somewhat. Similar episodes of monetary tightening occur frequently.

The impact of a monetary tightening is shown in Figure 16-3(a). The leftward shift of the money supply schedule means that at the going 4 percent interest rate there are insufficient money balances to meet people's transactions and asset needs. The gap between E and N shows the extent of excess demand for money at the old interest rate. People start to sell off some of their assets and convert them into money. Interest rates rise until the new equilibrium is attained, shown in Figure 16-3(a) at point E' with a new and higher interest rate of 6 percent per year.

Another disturbance might come from inflation itself. Suppose that in the face of the threatening inflation, the Federal Reserve held firm to its money target at $M*$. It might do this under the influence of the "monetarist" school (described in section B of this chapter), which believes the money supply should grow at a constant, predetermined rate through foul and fair economic weather. Say that because of the increase in food and import prices in the beginning of 1989, prices rose a few percent with no impact upon real GNP. Then people would need more money to finance their transactions. In this case, shown in Figure 16-3(b), the demand for money would increase, shifting the money demand curve to the right from DD to $D'D'$.

Immediately after the demand shift, people find that their money balances are too small. Again, they attempt to move out of their nonmonetary assets and into money. As this occurs, interest rates rise and continue to climb until the new quantity demanded of money equals the old supply of $M*$, at point E''. As shown in Figure 16-3(b), the inflation has led to an increase of interest rates from 4 percent per year to 7 percent. A similar increase in money demand and an upward rise of interest rates would occur if real GNP increased or if people decided to hold a larger fraction of their wealth in money.

Opposite cases arise when the Federal Reserve becomes concerned about a recession and expands the money supply, or when there is a contraction in the demand for money because of a slowdown in inflation, a decline in real output, or a shift in the public's desire to hold money.

To check your understanding, make sure you can work through the following cases using Figure 16-2: (1) The Federal Reserve has decided that unemployment is rising too sharply and wishes to reverse this by expanding the money supply. What steps must the

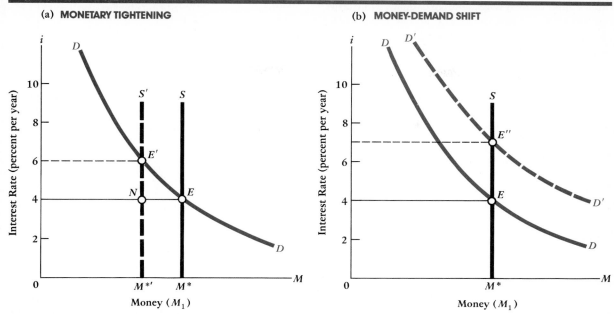

Figure 16-3   Changes in monetary policy or prices affect interest rates

In **(a)**, the Federal Reserve has contracted bank reserves and the money supply in response to fears of increased inflation. The lower money supply produces an excess demand for money shown by the gap *NE*. As the public attempts to attain the desired money stock, interest rates rise to the new equilibrium at *E′*.

In **(b)**, the demand for money has increased because of a run-up in the price level with real output held constant. The higher demand for money forces market interest rates upward until they in turn force the quantity of money demanded back down to *M**.

Fed take to expand money? What will be the impact on the money supply curve? What is the reaction in money markets? (2) As a result of a falling foreign exchange rate on the dollar, exports rise and real GNP increases. What happens to the demand for money? What is the impact upon the market interest rate? (3) As banks introduce new interest-bearing checking accounts, people decide to put more of their assets into these accounts and less in savings accounts at every level of GNP and of interest rates. The Fed is uncertain about what is going on and therefore keeps its money-supply targets unchanged. What will be the impact of the asset switch on money supply and demand? On market interest rates?

Let's summarize our findings about the money market:

The money market is affected by a combination of

(1) the public's desire to hold money (represented by the *DD* curve) and (2) the Fed's monetary policy (which is shown in Figure 16-3 as a fixed money supply or a vertical *SS* curve at point *M**). Their interaction determines the market interest rate, *i*. A tighter monetary policy shifts the *SS* curve to the left, raising market interest rates. An increase in the nation's output or price level shifts the *DD* curve to the right and raises interest rates. Monetary easing or a money-demand decline have the opposite effects.

THE MONETARY MECHANISM

Every day, the newspapers and television report on developments in money markets and monetary policy, providing analyses of the impacts of monetary affairs upon interest rates, foreign exchange rates, the trade and budget deficits, output, employment, inflation, and virtually every macroeconomic variable. If you read the news in the late 1980s, you would have found the following statements:

The Fed clearly is using the opportunity of a stronger dollar [and] reduced inflationary concerns . . . to ease credit. *(Wall Street Journal)*

The vice chairman of the Federal Reserve Board warned that passage of protectionist trade legislation or a higher minimum wage would unleash inflationary forces . . . that the Fed would have to counter by tightening credit, perhaps severely. *(New York Times)*

Analysts . . . contend that [current Fed Chairman Alan Greenspan] will take an even tougher anti-inflation stance than [former Chairman] Paul Volcker in an effort to underscore the Fed's independence. . . . The one thing any central banker wants to avoid at all costs is to be labeled as soft on inflation. That is death. *(Wall Street Journal)*

Behind all these statements lie views about the way the Federal Reserve operates, the way that money affects the economy, and the way that political leaders and the populace want to shape monetary policy. In this section we will analyze the monetary mechanism, the route by which changes in the supply of money get translated into changes in output, employment, prices, and inflation.

Let us start with a preview of the monetary mechanism:

When the Federal Reserve undertakes open-market purchases, buying government securities in the open market, this increases bank reserves and increases the money supply. The higher money supply tends to drive down interest rates and make credit more plentiful. As a result, the interest-sensitive components of spending tend to rise: business investment increases as the cost of capital falls, home building rises as mortgage rates fall, consumers buy more cars and other consumer durables as credit conditions loosen, and net exports may rise if the foreign exchange rate on the dollar falls. These shifts all tend to increase aggregate demand, increasing real GNP, employment, and the price level. (The sequence is reversed when monetary policy is tightened.) In this simplest case, the sequence is this:

$$M \text{ up} \longrightarrow i \text{ down} \longrightarrow I, C, X \text{ up} \longrightarrow$$
$$AD \text{ up} \longrightarrow \text{real GNP}, P \text{ up}$$

We first show how this sequence works using the 45° diagram of the multiplier model with the components of aggregate demand; we then examine this proposition in the aggregate demand-and-supply framework.

Graphical Analysis of Monetary Policy

Let us begin our discussion by using our earlier analysis of the impacts of money, investment, and the expenditure-output or multiplier model. Figure 16-4 shows the impact of a monetary expansion; we first describe each of its three parts.

Figure 16-4 shows three different relationships: *(a)* the money market in the lower left, *(b)* the determination of investment in the lower right, and *(c)* the determination of aggregate demand and GNP by the multiplier mechanism in the upper right. We can think of the causality moving counterclockwise from the money market through investment to the determination of aggregate demand and GNP as a whole.

Let's start at the lower left in Figure 16-4*(a)*. In this we show the demand and supply for money just described in Figures 16-2 and 16-3. For purposes of the present discussion, assume that in the initial state the money supply schedule was S_A and the interest rate was 8 percent per year. If the Fed was concerned about a looming recession, it might increase the money supply by open-market purchases, shifting the curve to S_B. In the case shown in Figure 16-4*(a)*, market interest rates would thereby fall to 4 percent.

Figure 16-4*(b)* picks up the story to show how lower interest rates increase spending on interest-sensitive components of aggregate demand. We saw in Chapter 7 that a decline in interest rates would induce businesses to increase their spending on plant, equipment, and inventories. One of the most reliable effects of eased monetary policy is on the housing market, where lower interest rates mean lower monthly mortgage payments on the typical house, encouraging households to purchase more and larger houses.

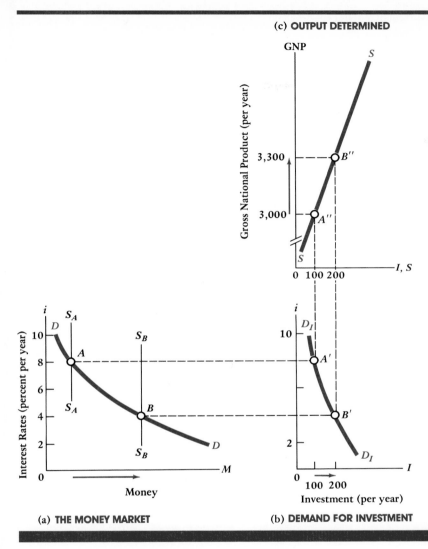

(c) OUTPUT DETERMINED

Figure 16-4   Central bank determines the money supply, changing interest rates and investment, and thereby affecting GNP

When the Fed raises the money supply, from S_A to S_B, this step reduces interest rates as people hold more money. That is, the economy moves down the money demand schedule in **(a)**.

Lower interest rates reduce the cost of investment, thus encouraging business purchases of plant and equipment and consumer purchases of houses. The economy moves down the demand-for-investment schedule D_1D_1 from A' to B' in **(b)**.

By the multiplier model in **(c)**, the higher investment raises aggregate demand and GNP from A'' to B''.

Can you trace the reverse process in which open-market sales by the Fed will contract M, I, and GNP?

(a) THE MONEY MARKET

(b) DEMAND FOR INVESTMENT

In addition, consumption spending increases, both because lower interest rates generally increase the value of wealth—as stock, bond, and housing prices tend to rise—and because consumers tend to spend more on automobiles and other big-ticket consumer durables when interest rates are low and credit is plentiful. Lower interest rates also induce state and local governments to increase the size of their capital budgets for items such as roads and bridges, mass transit and public housing. And, as we have seen in Chapter 9, lower interest rates tend to lower the foreign ex-

change rate on the dollar, thereby increasing the level of net exports. We see then how lower interest rates lead to increased spending in many different areas of the economy.

The graphical depiction is shown in Figure 16-4(b), where the drop in interest rates (which was induced by the increase in the money supply) leads to a rise in investment from A' to B'. In thinking about the effect shown in panel (b), we should construe investment in the very broad sense sketched a moment ago: it includes not only business investment but also consumer durables and residences, government capital programs, and net foreign investment in the form of net exports.

Finally, Figure 16-4(c) shows the impact of changes in investment in the multiplier model. This upper diagram is simply Figure 8-11 turned on its side. Recall from Chapter 8 that, in the simplest multiplier model, equilibrium output is attained when desired saving equals desired investment. In Figure 16-4(c), we have shown this relationship by drawing the savings schedule as the SS schedule; this line represents the desired level of saving (measured along the horizontal axis) as a function of GNP on the vertical axis. Equilibrium GNP comes at that level where the investment demand from panel (b) equals the desired saving from the SS schedule.

The initial level of investment was 100, as read off at A' in panel (b), producing a level of GNP of 3000. After monetary loosening has lowered the interest rate from 8 to 4 percent, investment rises to 200 at point B'. This higher level of investment raises aggregate spending to the new equilibrium at B'' in panel (c) with a new equilibrium GNP of 3300.

What has occurred? The rise in the money supply from S_A to S_B lowered the interest rate from A to B; this caused investment to rise from A' to B'; and this in turn, acting through the multiplier, led GNP to rise from A'' to B''.

Such is the route by which monetary policy acts through intermediate targets like the money supply and interest rates to affect its ultimate targets.

Monetary Policy in the *AD-AS* Framework

The three-headed diagram in Figure 16-4 has shown how an increase in the money supply would lead to an increase in aggregate demand. We can now show the effect on the overall macroeconomic equilibrium by using our AS and AD curves in Figure 16-5.

We have seen how a money-supply increase would produce higher investment and thereby increase aggregate demand. This is seen as a rightward shift of the AD curve in Figure 16-5, which illustrates a monetary expansion in the presence of unemployed resources, with a relatively flat AS curve. Here, the

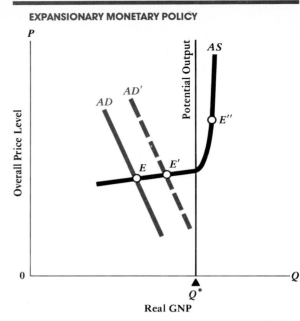

EXPANSIONARY MONETARY POLICY

Figure 16-5   An expansionary monetary policy shifts *AD* curve to the right, raising output and prices

Earlier discussion and Fig. 16-4 showed how an increase in the money supply would lead to an increase in investment and thereby to a multiplied increase in aggregate demand. This results in a rightward shift of the *AD* curve.

In the Keynesian region where the *AS* curve is relatively flat, a monetary expansion has its primary effect on real output, with only a small effect on prices.

In the classical region the *AS* curve is relatively vertical (shown at point *E''*) and a monetary expansion will primarily raise prices and nominal GNP and will have little effect on real GNP. Can you see why in the long run money may have little impact on real output?

monetary expansion shifts aggregate demand from AD to AD', and the overall equilibrium moves from E to E' in Figure 16-5. This case illustrates how monetary expansion can increase aggregate demand and have a powerful impact on real output.

But what would happen if the economy were operating near its capacity? This is illustrated by point E'' on the steeply sloping (or classical) segment of the AS curve in Figure 16-5. In this case, monetary changes would have little impact on real output. Rather, in the classical region of the *AS* curve, the higher money stock, chasing the same amount of output, would primarily end up raising prices.

To clinch your understanding of this vital sequence, work through the opposite case of a monetary contraction. Say that the Federal Reserve decides, as it did in 1979, to contract reserves, slow the economy, and reduce inflation. The sequence is:

Monetary contraction bids up market interest rates. This depresses interest-sensitive spending on business investment, housing, consumer durables, and the like. Via the multiplier mechanism, aggregate demand declines, lowering output and prices below the levels they would otherwise attain. The basic sequence is therefore:

$$M \text{ down} \longrightarrow i \text{ up} \longrightarrow I, C, X \text{ down} \longrightarrow$$
$$AD \text{ down} \longrightarrow GNP \text{ and } P \text{ down}$$

You can trace this sequence in Figure 16-4 by reversing the direction of the monetary policy, thereby seeing how money, interest rates, investment, and aggregate demand interact when monetary policy is tightened. Then see how a leftward shift of the *AD* curve in Figure 16-5 would reduce both output and prices.

Monetary Effects in the Long Run Many economists (including non-monetarists) believe that in the long run changes in the supply of money will increase the price level proportionally with little or no impact upon real output. We can understand this point by analyzing the impact of monetary changes with different-shaped *AS* curves. As shown in Figure 16-5, monetary changes will affect aggregate demand and will tend to change real GNP in the short run, particularly when there are unemployed resources and the *AS* curve is relatively flat.

However, as prices and wages adjust over the longer run, the output effects will diminish, and the price effects will tend to dominate. Recall that the *AS* curve tends to be vertical or near-vertical in the long run as all sticky or contractual elements of wages and prices adapt to the higher expected levels of prices and wages. As the *AS* curve becomes more and more vertical, more and more of the effect of the *AD* in-

crease turns up in prices and less and less shows up in real output.

What is the intuition behind this difference between the short run and the long run? We can construct a highly simplified example to see the difference. Suppose we start out as in Figure 16-4 with a nominal GNP of 3000 and stable prices; then a monetary expansion that increases the money supply by 10 percent might increase nominal GNP by 10 percent to 3300. Studies by Robert J. Gordon and others indicate that, in the short run, "nominal GNP changes have been divided consistently, with two-thirds taking the form of output change and the remaining one-third the form of price change." Consequently, we would expect the short-run impact of a monetary change to show real GNP increasing around 7 percent and prices increasing around 3 percent.

As time passes, however, wages and prices begin to adjust more completely to the higher price and output levels. Demand inflation in both labor and product markets would raise wages and prices; wages would be adjusted to reflect the higher cost of living; cost-of-living provisions in contracts would raise wages and prices even further. After a second year, prices might rise another 1 or 2 percent, with output then being only 5 or 6 percent above its original level. In the third year, prices might rise again while output falls somewhat. Where would it end? It might continue over a period of years and decades until prices had risen by fully 10 percent and output was back to the original level. If this occurred, the monetary policy would have raised prices and wages by about 10 percent but would have left real output unchanged.

In this example, finally, all nominal magnitudes are increased by 10 percent, while all real magnitudes are unchanged. Nominal magnitudes like the GNP deflator, the CPI, nominal GNP, wages, the money supply, currency, checking deposits, dollar consumption, dollar imports, the dollar value of wealth, and so forth are 10 percent higher. But real GNP, real consumption, the real money supply (equal to the money supply divided by the price level), real wages, real incomes, and the real value of wealth are all unchanged by the monetary policy. When this occurs, we say that money is "neutral" in the long run, meaning that monetary changes have no impact upon real magnitudes in the economy.

A word of caution is in order: The scenario of money changes leading to proportionate changes in all nominal magnitudes with no changes in real variables is both generally plausible and supported by certain empirical evidence. But it is not a universal law. The long run may be a period of many decades; intervening events may throw the economy off the long-run trajectory; and interest-rate changes along the path might have an irreversible impact upon the ultimate outcome.[1] The long-run neutrality of money is therefore only a tendency and not a universal law.

Monetary Policy and Real Interest Rates

Our discussion showed how a tight monetary policy would tend to raise interest rates and lower investment. But we nowhere mentioned whether this monetary shift involved real or nominal interest rates.

Recall that the nominal interest rate is the dollar return on dollar assets (such as the 5 percent return earned per dollar in your savings account). The real interest rate, by contrast, measures an asset's yield in terms of real goods, not in terms of the shrinking dollar yardstick; it corrects for the amount that inflation has shrunk the amount of goods that the money yield can buy.

In our discussion of the way money affects output, we have up to now assumed that prices were stable. Consider instead a situation where inflation prevailed, with prices rising at 5 or 10 percent a year. How would our analysis be modified?

First consider the effect of inflation on the demand for money. We found earlier that the demand for money is governed by the level of nominal interest rates. This is true even if prices are rising, for people will compare money to other interest-bearing assets—

and the comparison will be between the nominal interest rate on money and the nominal interest rate on the other assets.

Next, consider the way that inflation affects investment demand. We saw in Chapter 7 that the relevant interest rate for investment decisions is the real interest rate. Why? Because when you buy a capital good, you get not only the rentals on that good but also an automatic return as the value of that asset rises with the general price level. Thus, if you own and rent out a building, you get a certain amount of rental payments from your tenants every year. But the value of your building is increasing over time because of inflation.

For example, assume the interest rate and the inflation rate are both 10 percent per year. Then you can buy a $10,000 asset, pay $1000 interest for a loan on it, and get back the interest from the higher asset price (or ''capital gains'') when you sell the asset for $11,000 at the end of the year. In essence, the real cost (or real interest rate) of holding this asset is equal to the nominal interest rate less the inflation rate, or zero.

From this simple example we see that the demand for investment goods like buildings or equipment is primarily determined by the real interest rate rather than the nominal interest rate. This insight will explain why investment was quite high in 1979 even though nominal interest rates in the United States were also unusually high. The high rate of inflation in that period meant that the *real* interest rate faced by investors was unusually low. Similar reasoning will suggest why investment in Brazil continued to be high in the 1970s even though nominal interest rates were as high as 100 percent per year.

Long-Run vs. Short-Run Effects on Interest Rates Once we recognize the way real and nominal interest rates enter our analysis, we can see why the long-run effects of monetary policy may be the opposite of the short-run effects. Let's say there is a monetary contraction, such as occurred in 1979. This would drive up nominal and real interest rates. Investment would fall, and as a result output and employment would decline.

But in the long run, the economic slowdown would tend to lower inflation. With less inflation, nominal

[1] An example will show how interest-rate changes might knock the economy off a neutral trajectory. When the Federal Reserve contracted the money supply and raised interest rates in 1979, the intention was to push the economy onto a low-inflation path by slowing the economy and even causing a recession. The dramatic rise of interest rates, with short-term Treasury securities rising from 7 percent in 1978 to 14 percent in 1981, led to an appreciation of the dollar, to a massive foreign-trade deficit by the mid-1980s, and to a ''debt crisis'' among middle-income countries. By 1990, the United States will be saddled with a foreign debt of around $1 trillion, which will affect its economy for the foreseeable future.

GNP would rise more slowly, and the demand for money would thereby also grow at a reduced rate. This would allow nominal interest rates to fall. When the economy returned to a more normal state, real interest rates would return to their usual levels, and nominal interest rates (equal to the lower inflation rate plus the usual real interest rate) would now have declined as a result of tight money.

Thus if a monetary contraction succeeds in slowing price inflation, nominal interest rates may eventually decline.

The paradox of tight money leading to lower interest rates is often stressed by those who advocate stringent monetary policies. We must not forget, however, that this analysis refers to lower nominal interest rates, for real interest rates may not decline at all. And, even more important, the lower interest rates may arrive only after a period of higher nominal and real interest rates, low output, high unemployment, and recession.

This point is well illustrated by the tight-money policies of 1979–1982. This period began with a dramatic increase in nominal and real interest rates, a painful recession, and high unemployment. Because inflation slowed sharply, nominal interest rates also came down. By 1986, real interest rates were still somewhat higher than in 1978, but nominal short-term interest rates had fallen to 6 percent, which was *below* the level of nominal interest rates before the period of tight money.

B. ISSUES IN MONETARY POLICY

Inflation is always and everywhere a monetary phenomenon in the sense that it is and can be produced only by a more rapid increase in the quantity of money than in output.

Milton Friedman
The New Palgrave (1987)

Having seen how money affects economic activity, we move on to an assessment of important issues in the conduct of monetary policy. Money cannot manage itself. Rather, people in the central bank must make the crucial decisions about how fast the money supply should grow, how high interest rates should rise, and how tight credit should be. And different schools of thought have different philosophies about the best way to manage monetary affairs. Some believe in the active conduct of policy, trying to ''lean against the wind'' by slowing money growth when inflation threatens. Others are skeptical about the ability of policymakers to use monetary policy to ''fine-tune'' the economy. At the far end of the spectrum are the monetarists, who believe that discretionary monetary policy should be replaced by a fixed rule.

In this section, we will analyze the major competing views about the conduct of monetary policy. We begin by sketching the monetarist approach and end this chapter with some current controversies revolving around the appropriate targets of monetary policy.

THE ROOTS OF MONETARISM

What is monetarism? As its name implies, this theory views the role of money as central to macroeconomic theory and policy. More precisely, **monetarism** holds that the money supply is the major determinant of short-run movements in nominal GNP and is the prime determinant of prices in the longer run.

Monetarism, like mainstream macroeconomics, emphasizes careful attention to the determinants of aggregate supply and demand. The main difference between monetarists and others lies in their approaches to the determination of aggregate demand. While mainstream theories point to a number of different forces that influence aggregate demand—monetary and fiscal policies, investment spending, net exports, and so forth—monetarists hold that changes in the money supply are far more important than all other forces in affecting nominal GNP in the short run and prices in the long run.

In addition, under the influence of the conservative

economist Milton Friedman, monetarists have generally espoused maximal reliance on market forces. In their view, governments should avoid interfering with free markets and should never fine-tune the economy with monetary or fiscal steps. This forceful philosophy had an important influence upon the economic policies of the Reagan government in the United States from 1981 to 1988 and on the Thatcher government in the United Kingdom after 1979.

In order to understand monetarism, we need to introduce a new concept—the velocity of money—and describe a new relationship—the quantity theory of prices.

The Velocity of Money

One of the most important concepts in modern macroeconomics is the velocity of money. This concept, introduced at the turn of this century by Cambridge University's Alfred Marshall and Yale's Irving Fisher, measures the speed at which money is turning over or circulating through the economy. We first provide a careful definition of velocity and then explain its usefulness.

Definition Sometimes money is turning over very slowly, sitting in cookie jars or people's bank accounts for long periods between transactions. At other times, particularly during rapid inflation, people get rid of money like hot potatoes, with money circulating rapidly from hand to hand. In the first case, when the quantity of money is large relative to people's incomes, the velocity of circulation is low, while in the second case money's velocity is high.

More precisely, we define the **income velocity of money** as follows: The income velocity of money is the ratio of total nominal GNP to the stock of money. Velocity measures the rate at which the stock of money turns over relative to the total income or output of a nation. The formal definition of income velocity is:[2]

---

[2] The definitional equations have been written with the three-bar identity symbol rather than with the more common two-bar equality symbol. This is to drive home the fact that they are ''identities''— statements which tell us nothing about reality but which hold true by definition even if the United States experienced a hyperinflation or if its M were halved while its GNP grew tenfold.

$$V \equiv \frac{\text{GNP}}{M} \equiv \frac{p_1 q_1 + p_2 q_2 + \cdots}{M} \equiv \frac{PQ}{M}$$

Here P stands for the average price level and Q stands for real GNP. Velocity (V) is simply defined as the amount of nominal GNP each year divided by the money stock.

Intuitively, we can think of the income velocity of money as the speed at which money changes hands in the economy. As a simple example, assume that the economy produces only bread, and GNP consists of 48 million loaves of bread each selling at a price of $1, so GNP = PQ = \$48 million per year. If the money supply is \$4 million, then by definition V = \$48/\$4 = 12. This means that money turns over once a month, as if people's earnings are used only once a month to buy their monthly bread.

What determines the level and changes in the velocity of money? A quick look at the definition of velocity shows that it is another way of writing the demand for money; it measures the GNP per dollar of money. Anything that changes the GNP/money ratio will affect velocity. In our discussion of the demand for money we found that important influences include interest rates and the availability of other assets (such as savings accounts).

Figure 16-6 shows the recent history of the income velocity of transactions money (M_1). This shows that nominal GNP has been rising faster than the money supply over the last four decades. We can thus conclude that the income velocity of money has been rising over time. The question of the stability and predictability of money's velocity is a central issue of modern macroeconomics, as we will shortly see.

The Quantity Theory of Prices

So far we have not learned anything about the economy; we simply defined an interesting new variable called velocity. But now let us move on to analyze how some economists use the concept of velocity to help explain movements in the overall price level.

The key assumption here is that *the velocity of money is relatively stable and predictable*. Put differently, though the money supply, the price level, and nominal GNP might change dramatically over time,

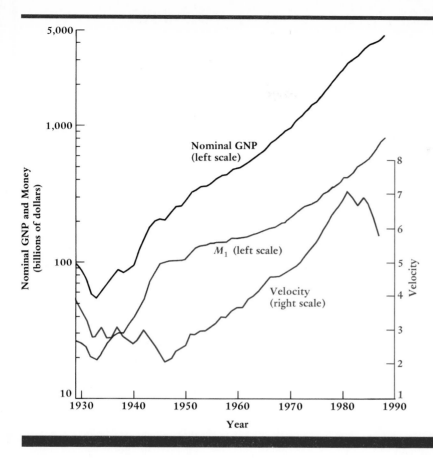

Figure 16-6   Velocity and its components, 1929–1988

Income velocity for transactions money is the ratio of nominal GNP to M_1. Over the period since 1929, money has grown 32-fold while nominal GNP has grown 45-fold.

One of the tenets of monetarism is that V is relatively stable and predictable. How stable does V appear? Can you think of some reasons why V has grown over time? HINT: Think of the determinants of the demand for money. (Source: V constructed by the authors from data of the Federal Reserve Board and the Department of Commerce.)

the velocity of money changes relatively little from year to year.

Why might the velocity of money be relatively stable? The reason, according to monetary economists, is that velocity mainly reflects patterns in the timing of income and spending. If people get paid once a month and tend to spend all their incomes evenly over the course of the month, income velocity will be 12 per year. Incomes could double, prices might rise 20 percent, and total GNP may be up many times—yet with unchanged spending patterns the income velocity of money would remain unchanged. Only as people or businesses modify the way they hold their assets or the manner of paying their bills does the velocity of income change.

Using this insight about the relative stability of ve-

locity, some early writers, particularly the classical economists, used velocity to explain changes in the price level. This approach, called the **quantity theory of prices,** starts by rewriting the definition of velocity as follows:

$$P \equiv \frac{MV}{Q} \equiv \left(\frac{V}{Q}\right)M \equiv kM$$

In this equation, we first rearrange the earlier equation for the definition of velocity and then substitute the variable k as a shorthand for V/Q. We write the equation this way because many classical economists believed that k would be constant or relatively stable in the short run. Why so? First, the classical economists believed, as noted above, that velocity would be near-constant because of the stable nature of transactions patterns. In addition, they generally assumed full employment, which meant real output would be equal to its potential and be growing smoothly along its trend. Putting these two assumptions together, $k = V/Q$ would be near-constant in the short run and a smoothly growing trend in the long run.

What are the implications of the quantity theory? As can be seen from the equation, if k is constant the price level would then move proportionally with the supply of money. A stable money supply would produce stable prices; if the money supply grew rapidly, so would prices; if the money supply was multiplied by 10 or 100, the economy would experience galloping inflation or hyperinflation. Indeed, the most vivid demonstrations of the quantity theory of prices can be seen in hyperinflations. Turn back to Figure 14-5, p. 312, which shows how prices rose a billionfold in Weimar Germany after the central bank unleashed the monetary printing presses. This is the quantity theory with a vengeance.

To understand the reasoning behind the quantity theory of prices, it is essential to recall that money differs fundamentally from ordinary goods like bread or cars. We want bread to eat and cars to drive. But we want money only for the work it does in buying us bread or cars. If prices in Brazil today are 50 times what they were a decade ago, then it is natural that people will need about 50 times as much money as they did 10 years ago. Here lies the valid core of the quantity theory of money: that the demand for money rises proportionally with the price level.

The quantity theory of prices holds that prices move proportionally with the supply of money. Although the quantity theory of prices is only a rough approximation, it does help explain why countries with low money growth have moderate inflation while others with rapid money growth find their prices galloping along at 20 or 50 percent, or more, each year.

MODERN MONETARISM

Having analyzed classical monetary economics, we now turn to its modern variant. This important doctrine was developed after World War II by Chicago's Milton Friedman and his numerous colleagues and followers.[3] The school started by challenging the tendency of many early Keynesians to overemphasize fiscal policy in the 1935–1960 period. Under Friedman's leadership, monetarists also put forth a coherent set of views about macroeconomic theory and policy that challenged the reigning Keynesian orthodoxy of the 1960s. In the 1970s and early 1980s, the monetarists recruited many academics, political figures, and members of the financial community. At its high-water mark, in the 1979–1981 period, monetarist thinking dominated economic policymaking in many of the advanced industrial countries.

During the last two decades, the monetarist approach branched. One fork continued along the older tradition that we will now describe. The younger offshoot became the powerful "rational-expectations" school that is analyzed in this chapter's appendix.

The monetarist approach emphasizes the importance of money in determining nominal GNP in the short run and prices in the long run. This analysis operates in the framework of the quantity theory of prices and relies on the analysis of trends in velocity. Monetarists argue that the velocity of money is relatively stable (or in extreme cases constant). If correct, this is an important insight, for the quantity equation shows that if V is constant then movements in M will affect PQ (or nominal GNP) proportionally. Thus velocity plays a central role in monetarist analysis.*

[3] A highly influential landmark was the empirical study by M. Friedman and A. Schwartz, *A Monetary History of the United States 1867–1960* (Princeton University Press for the National Bureau of Economic Research, Princeton, N.J., 1963). A lively debate on monetary vs. fiscal policy took place between Walter Heller (President Kennedy's chief economist) and Friedman in *Monetary vs. Fiscal Policy* (Norton, New York, 1969).

*Eclectic Keynesians of the 1980s, using the language of "the demand-for-money function," regard velocity as a rising function of interest rates. Many who call themselves monetarists, but who do not share Friedman's view that velocity is negligibly affected by changes in interest rates, are very hard to distinguish from today's Keynesian economists. This kind of convergence, from disagreement into the synthesis of modern mainstream macroeconomics, is a common phenomenon in the history of science.

The Essence of Monetarism

Like all serious schools of thought, monetarism has differing emphases and degrees. The following points are central:

1. *The money supply is the major systematic determinant of nominal GNP growth.* Monetarism, like Keynesian multiplier theory, is basically a theory of the determinants of aggregate demand. It holds that aggregate demand is affected primarily by changes in the money supply. Fiscal policy is important for some things (like the fraction of GNP devoted to defense or public consumption), but the major macroeconomic variables (aggregate output, employment, and prices) are affected mainly by money and only slightly and temporarily by fiscal policy. This was put neatly in the following oversimplified way: "Only money matters."

What is the basis for monetarists' belief about the primacy of money? It is based on two central propositions: First, as Friedman has stated, "There is an extraordinary empirical stability and regularity to such magnitudes as income velocity that cannot but impress anyone who works extensively with monetary data."[4] In addition, many monetarists have in the past held the view that the demand for money is completely insensitive to interest rates; this view has, however, fallen out of favor in recent years.

Why do these two assumptions lead to the monetarist view? Return to the quantity equation of exchange, which says $PQ \equiv MV$. Note that if velocity V is stable, then M will determine $PQ \equiv$ nominal GNP. Put differently, if velocity does not change, money and only money affects nominal GNP.

If, on the other hand, M changes lead to V changes, the PQ will not be proportionally affected by M. Similarly, if V is extremely unstable, changing erratically from one year to the next, then knowledge about M changes will be of little help in predicting PQ movements.

Why is fiscal policy irrelevant according to the monetarists? Simply because, if V is stable, the only force that can affect PQ is M. With constant V, there is simply no door by which taxes or government expenditures can enter the stage. By contrast, if fiscal deficits can raise interest rates and thereby raise velocity, then even without money-supply changes fiscal policy does have independent effects on inflation, output, and unemployment.

2. *Prices and wages are relatively flexible.* Recall that one of the fundamental insights of Keynes was that prices and wages do not move quickly to clear product and labor markets. Prices and wages are "sticky." An economy with sticky wages and prices has a sloping rather than a vertical short-run Phillips curve. Equivalently, an economy with sticky wages and prices will have an upward-sloping (but not vertical) short-run aggregate supply curve.

Monetarists disagree with the idea that prices and wages move like January molasses. While generally accepting the view that there is *some* inertia in wage-price setting, monetarists tend to think that Keynesians made too much of the inertia. Monetarists tend to think the Phillips curve is relatively steep even in the short run, and, led by Friedman, they have insisted that the long-run Phillips curve is vertical.[5] In the *AS* framework, monetarists hold that the short-run *AS* curve is quite steep.

Next, put these first two items together. Since money affects nominal GNP, and since prices and wages are fairly flexible around potential output, this implies that money moves real output only modestly and for a short time. The main effect of M is on P.

Accordingly, money can affect both output and prices in the short run, but in the long run money's main impact is on prices because output gravitates toward its potential. Fiscal policy affects output and prices negligibly in both the short run and the long run. This is the essence of monetarist doctrine.

---

[4] See Milton Friedman, "The Quantity Theory of Money—A Restatement," in M. Friedman (ed.), *Studies in the Quantity Theory of Money* (University of Chicago Press, Chicago, 1956).

[5] Some writers see the new classical economics or rational-expectations school of Lucas, Sargent, and Barro as an extreme version of monetarism. The appendix shows why this school argues that the *short-run* Phillips curve is vertical (or that the *AS* curve is vertical in the short run). While there are common elements between monetarism and the rational-expectations school, we find it useful to treat them as distinct. The essential difference between monetarists and mainstream economists concerns the role of money in aggregate demand; by contrast, the central contention of rational-expectationists is that aggregate supply is classical.

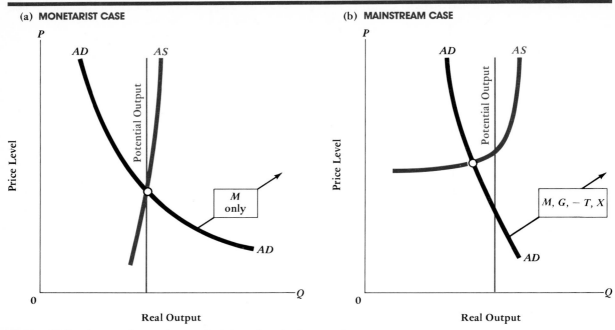

Figure 16-7   Comparison of monetarist and mainstream views

The figure compares monetarist and mainstream (or neo-Keynesian) views of the functioning of the macroeconomy. Two major differences are seen.

First, monetarists emphasize the primacy of the money supply in determining aggregate demand. This is seen by the box, next to the *AD* curve, that contains only *M* in it. Mainstream macroeconomists are more eclectic, believing that a wide variety of variables affect the economy—money, government spending, taxes, net exports, and so forth are included in the box. To simplify, monetarists say, "Only money matters." Mainstream macroeconomists say, "Money matters, but so does fiscal policy."

The second difference revolves around aggregate supply. Mainstream economists stress that the *AS* curve is relatively horizontal in the short run, particularly in the presence of underutilized resources. Monetarists hold that prices and wages are relatively flexible, so that the short-run *AS* curve is near-vertical. For monetarists, *AD* changes mainly affect prices; for mainstream economists, *AD* changes affect both prices and output, at least in the short run.

3. *The private sector is stable*. Finally, monetarists believe that the private economy is relatively stable. What does this mean? Simply that since *V* is stable, most fluctuations in nominal GNP have been caused by changes in the money supply—and the money supply, in turn, is determined by monetary policy or external events like gold discoveries, movements on and off the gold standard, the twists and turns of Fed policy, the political business cycle, and so forth.

Comparison with Mainstream Macroeconomics

How do monetarist views compare with modern mainstream (sometimes called neo-Keynesian) approaches? Although the shrill debate between monetarists and Keynesians might suggest profound differences, in fact the disputes are ones of emphasis rather than of fundamental beliefs. Indeed, monetarists and mainstream Keynesians have much more in common than either group has with more radical groups like supply-side economists.

We can depict the major differences between monetarists and mainstream Keynesians in Figure 16-7, which deserves careful study. This figure shows both views in terms of the behavior of aggregate supply and demand. Two major differences stand out.

First, the two schools disagree about the forces that operate on aggregate demand. Monetarists believe that aggregate demand is affected only (or primarily) by the money supply and further that the impact of money on aggregate demand is stable and reliable. They also believe that fiscal policy or autonomous changes in spending, unless accompanied by monetary changes, will have negligible effects upon output and prices.[6]

Mainstream economists, by contrast, hold that the world is more complex. They believe that money has an important effect upon aggregate demand, output, and prices, as described in the first section of this chapter. But factors other than money also matter. If government spending rises in wartime, if new technologies lead to a surge of spending on investment, if growth abroad leads to rapid growth of net exports— all these would, in the mainstream view, lead to an increase of aggregate demand even with unchanged money growth. In other words, mainstream macroeconomists hold that money enters into output determination *along with* spending variables like fiscal policy and net exports.

The second major difference between monetarists and mainstream economists concerns the behavior of aggregate supply. Mainstream economists emphasize the inertia in prices and wages; in other words, they believe that the *AS* curve is quite flat in the short run, and some think that the short run extends a long time. Monetarists think that mainstream economists exaggerate the economy's wage-price stickiness and believe that the short-run *AS* curve is therefore quite

steep—not vertical, probably, but much steeper than a mainstream economist would allow.

Because of differing views about the slope of the *AS* curve, mainstream economists and monetarists differ on the short-run impact of changes in aggregate demand. Mainstream economists believe that a change in spending will significantly change output with little effect on prices in the short run. Monetarists think that a shift in demand will primarily end up changing prices rather than quantities.

In sum, the essence of monetarism in macroeconomic thinking centers on the importance of money in determining aggregate demand and on the relative flexibility of wages and prices.

The Monetarist Platform

Over the last two decades, monetarism has played an important role in shaping economic policy. The monetarist platform contains three distinguishing features: (1) a belief in small government and free markets; (2) emphasis on containing inflation rather than reducing unemployment; and (3) a desire to avoid active government policies, preferring ''rules of law'' rather than ''discretion of people.''

1. *Laissez-faire.* Monetarists have generally favored markets free of government intervention. They believe that markets are sufficiently competitive that *how* and *what* will be efficiently solved without the visible hand of government. Governments are often viewed as inefficient, venal, and destructive of personal liberty.[7]

2. *Role of price stability.* A second part of the monetarist economic approach is its emphasis on the desirability of stable prices. Monetarists tend to believe that a large part of unemployment is either voluntary or induced by ill-designed government policies. Indeed, Friedman invented the term ''natural rate of

---

[6] Note as well that the *AD* curve is drawn as a ''rectangular hyperbola'' for the monetarist case. Recall that an equation $xy = constant$ describes a rectangular hyperbola in a graph of x and y. For given M and V, the aggregate demand curve is described by $PQ = constant$, so the *AD* curve is a rectangular hyperbola.

[7] See particularly Friedman's *Capitalism and Freedom* (University of Chicago Press, Chicago, 1962). We examine the role of this view in the context of the history of economic thought when we review libertarianism in Chapter 35.

unemployment,'' implying that most unemployment is the normal outcome of market forces and is acceptable and even optimal. The voluntary nature of unemployment is much more explicit in the rational-expectations school (see this chapter's appendix).

Inflation, rather than unemployment, is the enemy of economic efficiency. Monetarists have devoted considerable time to the study of hyperinflations and their resulting turmoil in countries like Germany and Brazil. For these reasons, monetarists are more inclined than mainstream macroeconomists to risk high unemployment in order to prevent high inflation.

3. *Policy rules.* The most important contribution of monetarists to macroeconomic policy has been the insistence upon rules rather than discretion in the conduct of macroeconomic policy.

In principle, a monetarist might recommend the use of monetary policy to fine-tune the economy. After all, if a decline in investment or net exports threatened to raise unemployment, then a swift and decisive increase in *M* might be just what is needed to maintain full employment.

But this road was not followed by the monetarists. Instead, they held that the private economy is stable but for government actions; that governments are unreliable, prone to pursue their self-interest rather than the general welfare, likely to generate political business cycles; that *M* affects *PQ* only with long and variable lags; and that whatever shocks occur are quickly corrected by relatively flexible prices and wages.

Thus rather than recommending that governments use monetary policy to lean against the prevailing economic winds, monetarists put forth as a central part of their economic philosophy a *monetary rule:* The optimal monetary policy is to set the growth of the money supply at a fixed rate and to hold to that policy through all economic conditions.

What is the rationale for this view?

Monetarists believe that a fixed growth rate of money (at 3 or 4 percent annually) would eliminate the major instability in a modern economy—the capricious and unreliable shifts of monetary policy. If we replace the Federal Reserve with a computer program that always produces a fixed *M* growth rate,

there will be no bursts in *M* growth. With stable velocity, money GNP will grow at a stable rate. And as long as *M* grows at about the growth rate of potential GNP, we will soon attain price stability. In short, the Fed must not ''lean against the wind.'' It must not fine-tune the economy. It must not try to second-guess developments in financial markets. We must have a rule of law, not of the men and women at the Federal Reserve. This is the essence of the argument for a monetary rule.

The Monetarist Experiment Monetarist views gained widespread influence in the late 1970s. In the United States, many thought that Keynesian stabilization policies had failed to contain inflation, and the Carter administration seemed to vacillate between concern about unemployment and tough anti-inflation rhetoric. As oil prices rose and commodity prices soared in 1978 and 1979, inflation moved up into the double-digit range. Many economists and policymakers believed that monetary policy was the only hope for an effective anti-inflation policy.

In October 1979, a new Chairman of the Federal Reserve, Paul Volcker, launched a fierce counterattack against inflation in what has been called a *monetarist experiment.* In a dramatic change in its operating procedures, the Fed decided to stop smoothing interest rates and instead focused on keeping bank reserves and the money supply on predetermined growth paths. The Fed hoped that a strict quantitative approach to monetary management would accomplish two things: First, it would allow interest rates to rise sharply enough to brake the rapidly growing economy, raising unemployment and slowing wage and price growth through the Phillips-curve mechanism. In addition, some believed that a tough and credible monetary policy—with low money-growth targets enforced by a no-nonsense Federal Reserve—would deflate inflationary expectations, particularly in labor contracts, and demonstrate to workers and firms that the high-inflation period was over. Once people's expectations were deflated, the economy could experience a relatively painless reduction in the underlying rate of inflation.

The monetarist experiment was largely successful in reducing inflation. As a result of the high interest rates induced by slow money growth, interest-sensitive spending slowed and the foreign exchange rate on the dollar rose sharply, producing a contractionary decline in net exports. The high interest rates were a particularly unwelcome shock to many middle-income countries that had high levels of foreign indebtedness. Their debt-service burdens (the ratio of interest and repayment of principal to exports or GNP) doubled overnight. The resulting shock led to severe recessions and contractions of foreign trade in many Latin American countries.

As a result, real GNP stagnated from 1979 to 1982, and the unemployment rate rose from under 6 percent to a peak of $10\frac{1}{2}$ percent in late 1982. Inflation began to fall as the recession took hold, with the inflation rate for the CPI falling from 13 percent in 1980 to 4 percent in 1984. The monetarist experiment brought the roaring inflation of the 1970s virtually to a dead stop. Any lingering doubts about the effectiveness of monetary policy were stilled. Money works.

But what of the monetarist claim that a tough and credible monetary policy would reduce inflation at lower economic cost than less forceful measures? Numerous economic studies of this question have been made, and these were reviewed in the last chapter. The conclusion of these studies is the following: the economic costs of reducing inflation through the monetarist approach in the United States in the 1979–1982 period do not appear appreciably different from the costs experienced during other periods of recession. In terms of unemployment or output losses, the economic sacrifices of the monetarist disinflation policy were about as large, per point of inflation, as anti-inflation policies of earlier periods. Money works, but it does not work miracles.

But the use of monetary policy to slow inflation produced some surprising and unwelcome side effects. As a result of targeting the money supply rather than interest rates, interest rates became much more volatile. Month-to-month changes in interest rates increased by a factor of 4 to 8 during the monetarist period. Long-term bonds, which had in an earlier era been thought safe investments, became more risky and less desirable assets during this period. On the technical side of monetary policy, it proved quite difficult to control the money supply. Even though the

Fed attempted to produce smooth money-growth paths, money growth was just as erratic during the monetarist period as it had been in earlier years.

One of the paradoxes of this period lay in the behavior of velocity. Recall that the monetarist doctrine stems from a belief that velocity is relatively stable and predictable. Given stable velocity, changes in the money supply would get smoothly translated into changes in nominal GNP. But just as the monetarist doctrine was adopted, velocity became extremely unstable. Indeed, M_1 velocity changed more in 1982 than it had in several decades (see Figure 16-6). Some believe that the instability in velocity was actually produced by the heavy reliance placed upon monetary policy during this period.

BEYOND MONETARISM: CURRENT ISSUES IN MONETARY POLICY

At the end of 1982, the Federal Reserve called a halt to its monetarist experiment. This abrupt end came for a number of reasons: because of the perceived need to loosen monetary policy during the deep recession, because of growing political opposition to the Federal Reserve's tight-money policies, because of confusion about the definition of the money supply in light of changes in banking law and practices, and because of the extraordinary drop in velocity. Although the Fed did not revert completely to its earlier operating procedures, after 1982 it no longer attempted to keep the money supply within the monetarist straitjacket. Rather, monetary policy was operated in a more eclectic fashion, based on economic conditions (such as unemployment, inflation, and the foreign exchange rate on the dollar), trends in velocity, and other events.

Once the simple monetarist operating procedures were put aside, the Federal Reserve was forced to confront the same dilemmas that central banks have faced here and abroad for decades: How effective is monetary policy? What targets should the Federal Reserve follow? What are the relative merits of rules and discretion? How should monetary policy take into account the growing importance of foreign trade? What is the best interaction between monetary and

MONEY, OUTPUT, AND PRICES

	RESPONSE OF AFFECTED VARIABLE TO 4 PERCENT CHANGE IN MONEY SUPPLY (percent change in affected variable from baseline path)				
AFFECTED VARIABLE	**YEAR 1**	**YEAR 2**	**YEAR 3**	**YEAR 4**	**YEAR 5**
Real GNP	0.9	1.1	1.2	1.1	0.8
Consumer prices	0.2	0.7	1.1	1.5	1.8
Nominal GNP	1.1	1.8	2.3	2.5	2.7

Table 16-1   Estimated effect of monetary policy on output and prices

A survey studied the impact of a change in monetary policy upon the macroeconomy in eight different econometric models. In each case, a baseline run of the model was "shocked" by adding 4 percent to the money supply in year 1 and holding the money supply 4 percent above the baseline in all years thereafter. Estimates in the table show the average calculated response of the models.

See how the output response of a monetary-policy shift is relatively rapid, with the peak response coming in year 3. Further, the impact upon the price level builds up gradually because of the inertial response of price and wage behavior estimated in most models. Note that the impact on nominal GNP is less than proportional to the money growth even after 5 years.

[Source: Ralph C. Bryant, Peter Hooper, and Gerald Holtham, "Consensus and Diversity in the Model Simulations," in Ralph Bryant and others, eds., *Empirical Macroeconomics for Interdependent Economies* (Brookings, Washington, D.C., 1988).]

fiscal policy? In this final section, we will sketch current thinking on these crucial questions.

Effectiveness of Monetary Policy

In the first section of this chapter, we examined the qualitative impacts of money on output. But in implementing policy, the central bank must go beyond qualitative discussion to quantitative estimates. For example, say that in November 1991 the Federal Reserve forecasts that current monetary and fiscal policy will produce an expansion with real GNP growth of 5 percent in the coming year; further, the FOMC believes that a growth rate of 4 percent is the most that the economy can sustain for 1992 without risking an unacceptable inflation. The FOMC asks the staff how much money growth must be slowed to bring real GNP growth down to the target level.

Economic modelers have attempted to estimate the quantitative impacts of monetary policy using statisti-

cal techniques. The results of a recent study of a number of macroeconomic models are shown in Table 16-1. This study estimates the impact of increasing the money supply by 4 percent above the money supply of a "baseline" projection, with the money supply remaining 4 percent higher than the baseline for the indefinite future.

The results indicate a relatively rapid response of real GNP in the United States to an increase in the money supply. By contrast, the increase in the price level builds up slowly over time, with less than one-fifth of the increase in nominal GNP in year 1 coming in prices. At the end of five years, according to the model simulations, most of the increase in nominal GNP comes in prices rather than in real output. The models tend to confirm the belief of mainstream economists who point to the sluggish reaction of wages and prices (that is, to the relatively flat shape of the short-run *AS* curve).

What then might the staff of the Federal Reserve say when asked about the change in the money supply needed to slow the economy by 1 percentage point? According to Table 16-1, the money supply would have to be slowed by somewhat more than 4 percent to produce a 1-percentage-point decrease in real GNP.

Targets: Interest Rates or Money Stocks?

What intermediate targets should the Federal Reserve pursue? In its day-to-day and month-to-month operations, should the Fed keep its eye on interest rates, on money targets, on reserves, on the dollar, on the price of gold, on the price level, or what?

As we have noted above, the Federal Reserve has changed its operating procedures on numerous occasions. During World War II, the Federal Reserve acceded to the Treasury's requests to ''peg'' interest rates on government bonds at fixed levels. This policy effectively emasculated monetary policy: as a glance at Figure 16-3(a) shows, fixing interest rates with a given money demand curve effectively determines the money supply.

Starting in 1951, the Federal Reserve stopped pegging interest rates and developed an independent monetary policy. During most of the 1960s and 1970s, the Fed pushed interest rates upward or downward to slow or speed the economy, but the interest-rate movements were smoothed to avoid upsetting markets. As a result, monetary policy often reacted too little and too late for the needs of countercyclical economic policies. Then caution was thrown to the winds during the monetarist experiment of 1979–1982, a period in which interest rates moved more in a single month than they had during the entire 1950s.

Today, most economists believe that the Federal Reserve should use multiple indicators in formulating policy. The basic tenet is that movements in money, interest rates, and other variables serve as a kind of barometer of future economic conditions. By reacting to these leading indicators, the Federal Reserve can lean against the wind more effectively. But any single policy indicator is inadequate: the narrow money supply (M_1) may change either because of changes in nominal GNP or because of the addition of new kinds of deposits, so it is best to look at a wide variety of money measures; short-run interest rates may change because of shifts in the demand for money due to a recession or because of temporary changes in preferences among assets; and so forth. By looking at the entire array of monetary aggregates, of interest rates, and of economic forecasts, the Federal Reserve can be poised to react to adverse economic events quickly and appropriately.

Rules vs. Discretion

In our earlier discussions of monetarism, we laid out the role for fixed policy rules. Advocates of fixed rules argue that, because the private economy is relatively stable, active policymaking is likely to destabilize rather than stabilize the economy. In addition, stable rules help reinforce expectations—so that a money-growth rule at a low rate (3 to 5 percent per year) will help convince people that prices will be essentially stable. Furthermore, stable policies will help insulate the economy from the temptation of politicians to manipulate economic policy for purposes of reelection. Finally, libertarian economists sometimes argue that discretion may interfere with political freedom.

Other economists answer by arguing that discretionary policies, within a rational framework, can improve upon a fixed rule. The major economic argument against a constant-money-growth rule is that velocity may change in unforeseeable ways; when it does, the economy may be thrown into recession or inflation. It would be better to allow the central bank to adjust monetary policies to large and small changes in velocity or to other structural changes. Critics point to the sobering experience with constant-money-growth rules during the 1979–1982 period as evidence of the realistic disadvantages of following such an approach.

Some critics of fixed rules point out that they may actually lead to large discrete changes in policy regimes as the fixed rules are abandoned from time to time. To take the most recent experience, the economy was jolted by the Federal Reserve's decision to move to the rule of monetary targeting in 1979 and then went through another period of confusion when targeting was abandoned in 1982. The same ultimate economic outcome might have been accomplished less painfully with more gradual changes in economic policy.

On the political level, some critics question whether rigid rules are feasible in a democratic society. A rule is set up by discretion, followed by discretion, interfered with by discretion, and abandoned by discretion. Any policy, whether a fixed rule or a discretionary one, will inevitably become unpopular at some point. What Federal Reserve is strong enough to withstand congressional threats to reduce the Fed's monetary powers or to subjugate the central bank to the executive branch? What Federal Reserve is so self-confident as to believe that a fixed rule should be adhered to in the face of great inflations or deep recessions that threaten political unrest?

The debate over rules versus discretion is one of the oldest debates of political economy. No single answer is likely to persuade economists or policymakers for all time. Perhaps the dilemma between rules and discretion is incorrectly posed. In most cases, the real issue is between short-run expediency to support partisan political needs and long-run desires to enhance the general welfare. What is needed is not rigid adherence to rules, but farsighted dedication to the public good. Ironically, the most acclaimed economic policymaker of the postwar period has been Federal Reserve Chairman Paul Volcker (served 1979–1987), whose tenure was marked by sharp, discretionary changes in policies set with an eye to protecting the integrity of the nation's financial system and to keeping inflation in check. His success in both goals is testament to the power of wise and disinterested discretionary policies.

Monetary Policy in an Open Economy

In recent years, the interaction between the domestic economy and foreign economies has come to dominate economic policy. The relationship between monetary policy and foreign trade has always been a major concern for smaller and more open economies like Canada, Britain, and Japan. However, after the introduction of flexible exchange rates in 1973, with a growing share of imports and exports in the U.S. economy, and in the presence of increasingly closely linked financial markets, international trade and finance have come to play a central role in U.S. monetary policy during the 1980s.

Recall briefly the route by which monetary policy affects trade and then output. Suppose the Federal Reserve decides to slow money growth to fight inflation. This process drives up interest rates on assets denominated in U.S. dollars. Large institutional investors will compare interest rates in U.S. dollars with interest rates for assets in other currencies. Attracted by higher dollar interest rates, they will buy dollar securities, driving up the foreign exchange rate on the dollar. The high exchange rate on the dollar encourages the United States to import and hurts U.S. exports. Net exports fall, decreasing aggregate demand. This has the impact of both lowering real GNP and lowering prices or the rate of inflation.

Note that the direction of the effect of monetary policy is the same for the trade impact as for the impact on domestic investment: tight money lowers output and prices. The trade impact *reinforces* the domestic-economy impact.

If the foreign-trade impact simply augments the domestic response, why do open-economy ties pose additional problems for monetary policymakers? They complicate the life of the Federal Reserve both because the open-economy impacts of policy are not precisely understood and because our economic relations with the rest of the world pose a whole new set of dilemmas for economic policymakers.

The first complication arises because the quantitative relationships between monetary policy, the exchange rate, foreign trade, and output and prices are complicated and imperfectly understood. The weak point in our understanding comes at the very first link: our economic models cannot accurately predict the impact of monetary-policy changes on exchange rates. Further, even if we knew the money–exchange-rate relationship, the impact of exchange rates on net exports is not a firm one. As an example of the infirmity of our understanding, economic modelers in 1979 and 1980 failed to predict the major swing in the exchange rate and in net exports that followed upon the movement toward tight money in 1979. On balance, then, because of the uncertainties of the impacts of monetary policy upon foreign trade, confidence in our understanding of the timing and impact of monetary policies has eroded in recent years.

On the second point, foreign economic relations add another dimension to economic policy. In addition to domestic economic policies, the Federal Reserve must also concern itself with the exchange rate of the dollar, for a rapidly falling dollar value is taken as a sign of loss of confidence in the nation's financial system while a rapidly rising dollar augurs a decline in the nation's net exports. Furthermore, over the last decade, the Federal Reserve has taken a special interest in the fortunes of heavily indebted countries, such as Mexico and Brazil. These countries owe billions of dollars to New York banks, and default on those loans could cause untold damage to the U.S. financial system. Finally, the nation cares not only about the total of its GNP; the composition of output matters as well. Because of shifting patterns of foreign trade, the United States has witnessed stagnation in its "tradable" sectors (manufactures, mining, and agriculture), while the "non-tradable" sectors (services, retailing, and communications) have blossomed. This pattern of a withering away of the U.S. capacity to produce manufactured goods has troubled not only those who work in the steel or automobile industries, but also those who worry about the U.S. capacity to compete with other countries in the important new technologies of the future.

Open-economy macroeconomics is one of the most exciting areas of modern economics. Economists clearly have much to learn about the interactions between monetary policy and economic performance in a world increasingly open to foreign trade and financial flows.

Monetary vs. Fiscal Policy

As we conclude this chapter, we note that the discussion of the role of monetary policy has taken place without reference to fiscal policy. In reality, whatever the philosophical predilections of the government, every advanced economy constantly operates both fiscal and monetary policies. Each policy has its strengths and its weaknesses. The next chapter will begin by considering the role of fiscal policy in today's economy and will then analyze the roles that fiscal and monetary policy play in managing the ever-present business cycle.

SUMMARY

A. How Money Affects Output

1. Central bank monetary policy affects output by changing aggregate demand, which interacts with aggregate supply to determine output and prices. The process by which money affects output can be seen in a three-step analysis.

(a) In the money market, changes in the money supply induce changes in interest rates by moving along an unchanged money demand schedule. An increase in the money supply will lower interest rates enough to persuade people to hold all the new money.

(b) Along the downward-sloping demand-for-investment schedule, lower interest rates make it profitable for firms to start new investment projects.

(c) Along the familiar saving-investment multiplier relation, the induced increase in I leads to higher aggregate demand. Thus the rightward shift of the AD curve, along an upward-sloping AS curve, raises output and prices. In summary,

$$M \text{ up} \longrightarrow i \text{ down} \longrightarrow I \text{ up} \longrightarrow AD \text{ up} \longrightarrow \text{real GNP}, P \text{ up}$$

2. Although the three-step process speaks of money affecting "investment," in fact the monetary mechanism is an extremely rich and complex process whereby changes in interest rates and asset prices affect a wide variety of elements of spending. Affected sectors include: housing, affected by changing mortgage interest rates and changing housing prices; business investment, affected by changing interest rates and stock prices; spending on consumer durables, influenced by interest rates and credit availability; state and local capital spending, affected by interest rates; and net exports, determined by the effects of interest rates upon foreign exchange rates.

3. Monetary policy may have differential effects upon real and nominal interest rates. A tight-money policy will drive up nominal and real interest rates. However, in the long run, as a slack economy lowers the inflation rate, the lower inflation premium resulting from tight money may lead to lower nominal interest rates along with unchanged or higher real interest rates.

B. Issues in Monetary Policy

4. Monetarism relies upon the analysis of trends in the velocity of money to understand the impact of money on the economy. The income velocity of circulation of money (V) is defined as the ratio of the dollar GNP flow to the stock of M. While V is definitely not a constant—if only because it rises with interest rates—V's movements are subject to some regularity and predictability. From its definition as $V \equiv \text{GNP}/M \equiv PQ/M$ comes the quantity theory of prices $P \equiv kM$, where $k = V/Q$. The quantity theory of prices regards P as almost strictly proportional to M. Useful as this view is for understanding hyperinflations and certain long-term trends, few would today uphold it in its literal form.

5. Modern monetarism has grown into a major economic school today. It rests on three economic propositions: *(a)* the growth of the money supply is the major systematic determinant of nominal GNP growth; *(b)* prices and wages are relatively flexible; and *(c)* the private economy is stable. These propositions suggest that macroeconomic fluctuations arise primarily from erratic money-supply growth.

6. In addition, modern monetarism is generally associated with a laissez-faire and anti-big-government political philosophy. Because of their desire to avoid active government, along with a belief in the inherent stability of the private sector, monetarists often propose that the money supply grow at a fixed rate of 3 or 4 percent annually. Some monetarists believe that this will quickly and painlessly lead to stable prices and in the long run produce steady growth with stable prices.

7. The Federal Reserve conducted a full-scale monetarist experiment from 1979 to 1982. The experience from this period convinced most observers that *(a)* money is a powerful determinant of aggregate demand, *(b)* most of the short-run impacts of money changes are on output rather than on prices, *(c)* a firm and credible monetary policy did not appear to reduce inflation at lower cost than earlier anti-inflation episodes, and *(d)* velocity appears to have become quite unstable when a monetarist approach was followed.

8. When the Federal Reserve rejected the monetarist approach after 1982, monetary-policy analysts turned their attention to other central concerns:

(a) How effective is monetary policy? Econometric models use statistical estimates to gauge the impact of monetary-policy changes on the macroeconomy. Most models today find that money-supply changes have their primary impact upon output in the short run, with a larger and larger share of the impact on nominal GNP coming in inertial prices and wages as time proceeds.

(b) A major question for the conduct of monetary policy revolves around the appropriate targets: Should policy stabilize the money supply, reserves, interest rates, or what? After the disappointing experience with targeting money and reserves in 1979–1982, most experts now favor an eclectic approach with the Federal Reserve keeping its eyes on monetary aggregates, interest rates, and other financial variables, as well as upon economic forecasts.

(c) Should the Fed follow fixed rules or its discretion? This debate concerns both political views on the appropriate level of active government involvement in the economy—with conservatives often espousing rules and liberals advocating active fine-tuning of monetary policy to attain economic goals. More basic is the question of whether active and discretionary policies stabilize or destabilize the economy. Increasingly, economists point to the importance of *credible* policies, whether credibility is generated by rigid rules or by wise leadership.

(d) One of the major challenges for monetary policy has been the increasing importance of trade and financial interactions between the United States and other countries. In a regime of flexible exchange rates, changes in monetary policy can affect the exchange rate and net exports, adding yet another complication to the monetary mechanism. This influence led to a major shift in the composition of GNP away from tradable goods to non-tradable goods in the early 1980s. Open-economy considerations complicate the life of central banks both because the links between money and net exports are imprecise and because of the added political and economic concerns raised by the value of the dollar, the composition of GNP, and third-world debt.

CONCEPTS FOR REVIEW

demand and supply of money
three-step monetary transmission
 mechanism:
  money to interest rates; interest rates
   to investment; investment to GNP
interest-sensitive components of
 spending
monetary policy in the *AS-AD*
 framework
monetary effects on real, nominal
 interest rates
M down $\rightarrow$ i up $\rightarrow$ I down $\rightarrow$ AD
 down $\rightarrow$ GNP, P down

velocity of circulation of money:
 $MV \equiv PQ$
quantity theory of prices:
 $P \equiv kM$
modern monetarism
1979–1982 monetarist experiment
current issues of monetary policy:
 effectiveness of monetary policy
 targets for policy
 rules vs. discretion
 open-economy issues

QUESTIONS FOR DISCUSSION

1. Define income velocity *(V)*. For the following data, calculate the level and annual growth rates of the money supply and of velocity:

YEAR	NOMINAL GNP (billions)	MONEY SUPPLY, M_1 (billions, lagged 6 months)
1981	$3,053	$416.6
1982	3,166	443.2
1983	3,406	481.3
1984	3,772	526.9
1985	4,015	557.5
1986	4,240	627.0
1987	4,527	730.5
1988	4,853	753.2

2. Using Figure 16-4, explain the way the tight-money policies after 1979 lowered GNP. Also explain each of the steps in words.

3. In the discussion of the demand for money, and in the demand-for-money schedule in Figure 16-2, it was shown that the demand for money would be sensitive to interest rates. What would be the impact of higher interest rates on velocity for a given level of nominal GNP? What are the implications of interest-sensitive demand for money on monetarist arguments that rely upon constant velocity of money?

4. Marxists sometimes argue, ''War is necessary for full employment.'' How would an increase in military expenditures help cure a depression? Are there any other fiscal or monetary steps that might serve equally well to reduce unemployment and raise output?

5. Monetarists say, ''Only money matters.'' Eclectic Keynesians answer, ''Money matters, but other things, like fiscal policy, matter too.'' Explain and evaluate each position.

6. ''Tight-money policies to fight inflation will raise real and nominal interest rates in the short run, but will lower nominal interest rates in the long run.'' Explain the reasoning behind this statement. Explain why this statement holds for the period 1979 to 1986.

7. Movement to flexible exchange rates in the last 15 years has opened up a new route by which monetary policy can affect the economy. To illustrate this route, assume that interest-rate changes affect exchange rates positively and that net exports move inversely with exchange rates. With this assumption, we can create a new diagram, to replace Figure 16-4*(b)*, with interest rates on the vertical axis and net exports on the horizontal axis. Draw the new schedule, substitute it for the one used in Figure 16-4*(b)*, and show the impact of monetary-policy changes on GNP through foreign trade. Explain the diagrams in words.

8. Using a diagram like Figure 16-2, provide answers for the three examples in the paragraph at the bottom of p. 348.

9. If, in boom times, we printed and spent $100 trillion in new greenbacks, what would happen to prices? Is there some truth, then, to the crude quantity theory? What might happen to prices if M were increased 1 percent in a depression?

10. Although he was a passionate advocate of rules instead of discretion, Henry Simons of the University of Chicago also wrote the following about the use of gold as backing for a monetary system: "The utter inadequacy of the old gold standard . . . as a system of rules . . . seems beyond intelligent dispute." Is there a contradiction here? How can we establish a firm and credible rule that can be abandoned when it is beyond intelligent dispute? How does this problem apply to the monetarist experiment of 1979–1982?

11. What are the various arguments for and against a fixed-money-growth rule? Consider specifically questions such as the inherent stability of the private economy, the ability to forecast the economy, stability of the demand-for-money schedule, and the validity of the political-business-cycle theory.

12. Consider what monetarists and modern mainstream macroeconomists would predict to be the impacts of each of the following on the course of prices, output, and employment (in each case, hold taxes and the money supply constant unless specifically mentioned):

    (a) A large tax cut

    (b) A large cut in the money supply

    (c) An increase in oil prices

    (d) A wave of innovations that increase potential output by 10 percent

    (e) A burst of exports

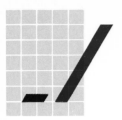

APPENDIX: 16

The Rational-Expectations Approach

The sciences do not try to explain, they hardly even try to interpret, they mainly make models. By a model is meant a mathematical construct which . . . describes observed phenomena. The justification of such a mathematical construct is solely and precisely that it is expected to work.

John von Neumann

In previous chapters we reviewed the major approaches to macroeconomic theory and policy, which emphasize stabilizing the economy through changes in monetary and fiscal policy. These ideas were applied time and again over the last four decades in countries from Japan to the United States to West Germany. And there can be little doubt that, for the period from the end of World War II until the early 1970s, these policies were accompanied by rapid growth and great prosperity.

But the structure of the economy evolved while countries engaged in stop-and-go policies. Policymakers grew accustomed to thinking of the Phillips curve as representing the "menu of choice" between inflation and unemployment. But if the Phillips curve was the menu, then the prices were constantly changing as the diners enjoyed the meal. The stable tradeoff between unemployment and inflation broke down. Economists saw the rightward-shifting Phillips curve and christened the worsening tradeoff as "stagflation." Soon they were hard at work trying to understand the mystery of the unstable Phillips curve.

The solution to the puzzle of the shifting Phillips curve soon focused on the natural-rate theories in which the long-run Phillips curve is vertical. This view—radical, heretical, unacceptable to many when introduced by Edmund Phelps and Milton Friedman in 1967—is widely accepted among macroeconomists today.

One school went further and argued that the Phillips curve is vertical even in the short run. This radical theory was put forth by "rational-expectations" macroeconomics (REM), sometimes also called the new classical economics, of which the principal practitioners are Robert Lucas of Chicago, Thomas Sargent of Stanford, Neil Wallace of Minnesota, and Robert Barro of Harvard.

The rational-expectations school believes that there is no slope in the *short-run* Phillips curve on which the policymaker can get a toehold. Any systematic attempt to stabilize the economy is self-defeating; in trying to expand the economy, policymakers only succeed in raising inflation. Believers in this new approach argue that understanding the phenomena of the 1970s and 1980s requires a completely different approach to macroeconomics from that of Keynes and his followers.

In this appendix we will take a tour of the rational-expectations approach. We will look at its view of the economy, and how it contrasts with mainstream views. We will see its striking implications for policy. And we will examine the criticism that skeptics cast at this new doctrine.

THE RATIONAL-EXPECTATIONS POSTULATES

Rational-expectations macroeconomics has a view of the economy that resembles that of the classical economists. It holds that (I) people use all available information and that (II) prices and wages are flexible. These two postulates are the essence of the rational-expectations revolution and will be explored in depth below. A quick summary will help prepare the ground.

Hypothesis (I) holds that people make their economic decisions on the basis of the best available information. Their expectations are formed using the latest available data and the best available economic theory. Such a postulate assures us that the government cannot "fool" the people, for people have access to the same information as the government.

Hypothesis (II)—that prices and wages are flexible—is familiar. This simply means that prices and wages adjust rapidly to balance supply and demand.

Putting (I) and (II) together will lead to striking results. But first we will explore the significance of each assumption.

Assumption I—Rational Expectations

We have already seen that expectations are important in economics. They influence how much investors will spend on investment goods and whether consumers buy a new car or save. But what should we assume about expectations? This is a big subject inside and outside economics, but the rational-expectations theorists cut through the thicket with a very powerful assumption called the *rational-expectations hypothesis:*

According to rational expectations, forecasts are unbiased and are based on all available information.

In simple language, a forecast is "unbiased" if it contains no systematic forecasting errors. Clearly a forecast cannot always be perfectly accurate—you cannot foresee how a coin flip will come up on a single toss. But you should not commit the statistical sin of *bias* by predicting that a fair coin would come up tails 90 percent of the time. By contrast, predicting that 50 percent of tosses come up tails would be an *unbiased* forecast.

But the rational-expectations hypothesis goes even further. It postulates that people use all available information and economic theory. Consequently, Los Angelenos make their economic decisions fully knowledgeable about all relevant macroeconomic and microeconomic data. Floridians know about the linkages between M_1 and GNP just as well as the Fed Chairman. New Mexicans have mastered rational-expectations macroeconomics and know exactly how true or untrue it is.

The critical assumption of rational-expectations macroeconomics is that people understand any systematic policy rules or strategies employed by the government. Thus, say the Fed always cuts its M targets when inflation reaches 10 percent, or that Congress always cuts taxes in election years. Rational-expectations theorists assume that people have learned these regularities and make their economic decisions fully informed about the systematic behavior of governments.

A first corollary of the rational-expectations hypothesis, then, is that people quickly learn about policymakers' behavior: you cannot fool the people about systematic economic policies.

Assumption II—Flexible Prices and Wages

The second central assumption is that prices and wages are flexible, so that supply and demand are in equilibrium at all times. This assumption holds that every price and wage—for apples, oranges, calculators, students, professors—moves quickly to balance supply and demand.

The rational-expectations theorists assume that prices move quickly enough so that markets are always in equilibrium. In other words, prices are flexible, and all markets clear at all times.

The assumption of flexible wages and prices is central to rational-expectations macroeconomics. Many economists also believe that this assumption contains its fatal flaw. Critics argue that many markets, particularly those for labor, do not balance supply and demand quickly.

RATIONAL EXPECTATIONS AND THE LABOR MARKET

The rational-expectations approach can be applied to many places. One important application concerns speculative markets, discussed in Chapter 11's appendix on the stock market.

But for macroeconomics, the most important application comes in labor markets, where the nature of unemployment is a most controversial issue. Is unemployment involuntary, with people willing and able to work at going wages but unable to find jobs? Or are they voluntarily unemployed—electing not to work even though jobs are available?

We can visualize these questions in Figure 16A-1. Point E shows the market-clearing equilibrium, with no involuntary unemployment. Some workers are not employed, as shown by the segment EG. The reason for this voluntary unemployment is that the market-clearing wage is insufficient to draw all workers out of retirement or back from extended vacations.

Involuntary Unemployment   Involuntary unemployment occurs in this example when labor demand declines and wages are inflexible. As shown in Figure 16A-1, if the demand for labor declines while the real wage remains at V, the segment HE represents involuntarily unemployed workers—people who would like to work at the going wage but cannot find jobs.

The distinction between involuntary and voluntary unemployment lies at the heart of the dispute between the rational-expectations school and modern mainstream macroeconomists. The latter group thinks that a sizable fraction of unemployment, particularly in recessions, is involuntary. By contrast, the rational-expectations school thinks that labor markets clear quickly after shocks, as wages move to balance supply and demand. Unemployment, in their view, increases because more people are hunting around for better jobs during recessions. People are unemployed because they think that their real wages are too low, not because wages are too high as in the case of sticky-wage unemployment.

To summarize:

Rational-expectations macroeconomics holds that prices and wages are sufficiently

RIGID WAGES PRODUCE INVOLUNTARY UNEMPLOYMENT

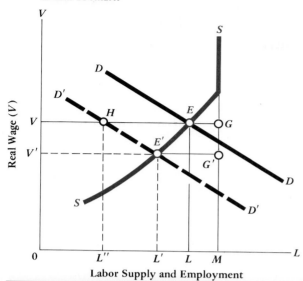

Labor Supply and Employment

Figure 16A-1   Supply and demand for labor

In a representative labor market, the original equilibrium is at point *E*. Even at that perfectly competitive equilibrium, employment (*L*) is less than the total labor force (*M*). So *EG* people are voluntarily unemployed. What happens if the demand for labor suddenly shifts downward to *D'D'*? If wages are perfectly flexible, the real wage moves swiftly downward to clear the market at *E'*. Unemployment rises to *E'G'*, but the higher unemployment is "voluntary."

If wages are sticky, remaining at *V* after the downward shift in demand, then *HE* workers will become "involuntarily" unemployed.

flexible so as to ensure continuous clearing of all markets, including the labor market. This implies that almost all unemployment is voluntary. People are unemployed because they think that real wages are too low to induce them to work.

Why High Unemployment?

So far, rational-expectations macroeconomics has told us little about macroeconomics. We want to know why the unemployment rate rose from 4 percent in 1929 to 25 percent in 1933, or from 6 percent in 1979 to almost 10 percent in 1982. Clearly, to provide a persuasive macroeconomic theory, rational-expectations macroeconomics needs to find a mechanism explaining such swings in unemployment.

One possible explanation for these large swings in unemployment lies in people's decisions to work or not. Was there an epidemic of idleness in the 1930s? Did the American people take a $300 billion vacation in 1982? Few economic historians could swallow such notions.

Instead, rational-expectations macroeconomics looks to people's *misperceptions* as the key to business cycles. They believe that high unemployment arises because workers are confused about economic conditions, quitting their jobs to look for better ones and thereby swelling the ranks of the unemployed.

A simple example will illustrate the process. Suppose I am a worker and I think that prices will not change next year. I am currently working for $10 an hour, and am satisfied to work 40 hours a week. My employer offers me $11 an hour; delighted, I move up my labor supply curve and offer to work 50 hours a week for the coming year. The higher expected real wage has induced me to increase my labor supplied. Other

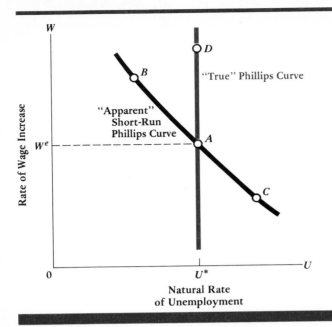

Figure 16A-2 The rational-expectations Phillips curve

According to rational-expectations macroeconomics, the true Phillips curve is vertical. But we may observe an "apparent short-run Phillips curve," drawn through points *B*, *A*, and *C*.

Point *B* arises when an inflationary shock hits the economy, raising money wages above their expected levels. Workers are confused, thinking that their real wages were raised, so they decide to work more, and unemployment falls. Thus the economy moves from point *A* to point *B*. (Trace through the opposite pathway to *C*.)

As a result, economic historians see a scatter of points that look like *A*, *B*, and *C*—and erroneously conclude that a stable short-run Phillips curve exists.

workers, who were previously unemployed, decide to take jobs because of the expectation of the coming higher real wage.

When next year comes, workers are chagrined to learn that *everybody* got a 10 percent wage increase. Prices rise 10 percent. So my money wage gain is wiped out: I get no real wage increase. I was induced to work harder by a misperception about my real wage.

If such misperceptions were widespread, unemployment would fall when money wages moved up unexpectedly. Workers would work more in the mistaken belief that real wages had risen. Conversely, unemployment would rise when money wages fell as workers quit their jobs thinking that prospects were better elsewhere.

We can illustrate this analysis with a natural-rate Phillips curve, as shown in Figure 16A-2. Denote the expected rate of change of money wages as W^e, and assume prices rise as fast as wages. If the actual rate of increase of wages (W) is equal to the expected rate (so $W = W^e$), then nobody is surprised or disappointed, and unemployment is equal to the natural rate. Thus point *A* represents the no-surprise, natural-rate outcome.

How do we get to points *B* and *C*? Each case arises from some kind of economic shock. To generate point *B*, assume that the Federal Reserve has unexpectedly increased the money supply. As a result, wages and prices rise unexpectedly; that is, employers offer their workers wages growing more rapidly than W^e. Workers misperceive economic events, not knowing that prices are rising as rapidly as wages; they supply more labor; unemployment falls; thus the economy goes to point *B*. You should trace through how we can generate point *C* by an unexpected cut in wages and prices.

Note the surprising result. If we connect the points of surprise, they are apparently a short-run Phillips curve, downward-sloping and well behaved. Thus the downward-sloping "apparent short-run Phillips curve" arises as the result of misperceptions of real wages or of relative prices.

This summarizes the rational-expectations theory of unemployment and inflation.

POLICY INEFFECTIVENESS

At this point you might say to yourself: "Okay, so rational-expectations economists believe that the Phillips curve is downward-sloping because people are fooled about what is happening to their real wages. But what do we care if you have to fool people a little bit to get them off the vertical Phillips curve? It's all for their own benefit anyway because unemployment will be lower. And no less an authority than Abe Lincoln told us you can fool all the people some of the time, so it looks as if such a strategy might work pretty well for a while, right?"

Wrong, say the rational-expectations theorists. They show that the two postulates—rational expectations and flexible wages and prices—imply that the government cannot use economic policy to affect output and employment.

To understand the argument, imagine the government saying, "Election time is coming. Let's pump up the money supply a little." But people would say to themselves, "Aha, elections are coming. From past experience, I know that the government always pumps up the money supply before elections. They can't fool *me* and get me to work any harder."

To see what will happen, look back at the Phillips curve of Figure 16A-2. The government is trying to move the economy to point *B*. But instead, as people anticipate the government's actions, the economy ends up at point *D*—with unemployment equal to the natural rate, but with inflation higher.

Thus rational-expectations macroeconomics says that the short-run Phillips curve is vertical when policy is anticipated. This is the *policy ineffectiveness theorem:*

With rational expectations and flexible prices and wages, anticipated government policy cannot affect real output or unemployment.

It is important to note that the policy ineffectiveness theorem depends on both assumptions, rational expectations and flexible prices. The assumption of flexible prices implies that the only way that economic policy can affect output and unemployment is by surprising people and causing misperceptions. But you can hardly surprise people if your policies are predictable. Hence predictable policies cannot affect output and unemployment.

Fixed Rules Optimal

We studied in the main part of this chapter the monetarists' case for fixed rules, that is, for avoiding discretionary policy changes. We can now understand the argument for fixed rules. An economic policy is composed of two parts, a predictable part (the "rule") and an unpredictable part ("discretion"). Rational-expectations macroeconomists argue that discretion should be avoided like the plague.

Why so? They reason that policymakers have no monopoly upon forecasting ability and cannot see economic shocks before markets can. Therefore, by the time policymakers act on the news—an oil embargo, a declining dollar, a corn blight—flexibly moving prices in markets populated by well-informed buyers and sellers have already incorporated the news. The market prices and wages have been announced. People have returned to their supply and demand curves. Unemployment has gravitated to its natural rate. There is simply nothing discretionary economic policy can do to improve the outcome or prevent the brief spells of involuntary unemployment that are caused by transient misperceptions.

Government policy can make things worse, however. If the government attempted to take a corrective action, people might for a time be confused, think their supply or demand curves had shifted, and therefore actually end up off them. But being off the curves would lead to temporary inefficiencies—just as monopolies can lead to wasteful resource allocation.

Thus the ''noise'' of unpredictable discretionary policies can confuse and mislead people, distort their economic behavior, and cause waste. Rather than risk such confusing noise, say the rational-expectations economists, governments should completely avoid any discretionary macroeconomic policies.

We have here a powerful case against discretionary policies. Because discretion may mislead and confuse people, stick to rules. Better yet, stick to simple rules, for they are even less likely to confuse. Do not attempt to fine-tune the economy into a nirvana of full employment, for it simply cannot be done. Such is the rigorous logical argument for fixed monetary and fiscal rules in a rational-expectations economy.

Monetarist Rules and the Lucas Critique

One of the ironies of the rational-expectations revolution is that, while it has lent support to the monetarists' advocacy of fixed rules, it also has raised a devastating point against a key monetarist argument. Monetarists note that the velocity of money has shown a surprising amount of stability. From this stability they conclude that we can stabilize $MV \equiv PQ \equiv$ nominal GNP by imposing a fixed-money rule.

A student of the rational-expectations movement should scold monetarists, saying: ''Ah, but you have forgotten the most important contribution of our new school, the *'Lucas critique.'* Robert Lucas pointed out that people will change their behavior when policy changes. Just as the apparent short-run Phillips curve crumbled in the hands of Keynesians when they attempted to manipulate it, so will the apparently constant velocity fall apart when you attempt to run the economy by keeping money on a fixed-growth-rate track. If a nation clamps down hard on money—as the United States did in the 1979 to 1982 period—you should expect that velocity will behave differently from the era when monetary policy was more passive.''

And such a scolding would be correct. Velocity became extremely unstable during the 1979–1982 period, when the Fed followed a monetarist operating rule. Indeed, 1982 showed the biggest decrease in velocity since the Federal Reserve began collecting the data. Monetarists, no less than Keynesians, have stumbled over the Lucas critique.

STATE OF THE DEBATE

We now end with our summary of the state of the debate between the rational-expectations and mainstream macroeconomists. Which side has had the best of the argument?

The debate has centered principally around the issue of flexible prices and wages. Firsthand observation, buttressed by reams of empirical studies, suggests that prices in many markets move slowly in response to shocks. Few economists believe that labor markets are in constant supply-demand equilibrium. Many workers faced long periods of unemployment in the 1930s, in the 1970s, and in the 1980s because of the inability of wages and contracts to adjust flexibly to new economic conditions.

What happens to the rational-expectations theory when the assumption of perfectly flexible wages and prices is abandoned? In general, policy will regain its power to affect the real economy—at least for the short run.[1]

A second set of criticisms aims at the rational-expectations assumption. This criticism denies the assertion that humans are agile computers, incorporating the latest forecast or outpouring of data. A psychologist would become apoplectic at the notion that the average wage earner is an unbiased and efficient information processor. Any student of economics can recount, chapter by chapter, the trials of learning economic theory. Several careful studies of people's actual behavior have uncovered significant elements of non-rational expectations, even among the most sophisticated professional economic forecasters.

Perhaps the most powerful criticisms of rational-expectations macroeconomics are targeted at the predictions of the theory. The theory forecasts that misperceptions lie behind business-cycle fluctuations. But can misperceptions about wages and prices really lie behind deep depressions and persistent bouts of unemployment? Did it really take people a full decade to learn how hard times were in the Great Depression? Like Rip van Winkle, did people fall asleep on the job in 1929 and not wake up until full employment returned in 1943? Few mainstream economists take such ideas seriously.

Another prediction is that unemployment rises because people quit their jobs; i.e., people quit because they misperceive real wages, thinking that jobs are more plentiful than they actually are. This proposition would suggest that the quit rate would rise in periods of high unemployment—while in reality quits *fall* in recessions.

The rational-expectations theorists have not fallen silent in the face of these criticisms, but the off-the-mark predictions of rational-expectations macroeconomics are a sobering reminder that the ultimate test of a theory is fit rather than elegance.

A New Synthesis

After almost two decades of analysis and econometric testing of the rational-expectations approach to macroeconomics, elements of a synthesis of old and new theories are beginning to appear. What are some of the lessons? To begin with, economists realize that they must pay careful attention to the formation and role of expectations in economic activity. Earlier approaches—ones assuming that expectations react mechanically to events or to policies—will no longer survive careful scrutiny. Rather, particularly in auction markets like those selling stocks, bonds, foreign exchange, and

---

[1] Perhaps the best example is work that maintains the rational-expectations framework except for one modest change. Studies of "overlapping wage contracts," particularly by Stanford's John Taylor, recognize that a substantial part of the labor force works under long-term contracts that are written in *nominal* (rather than real) terms. A typical labor contract will specify a fixed money-wage rate. During the period of the contract, anticipated macroeconomic policy can affect unemployment. Put in terms of the expectational view, the macroeconomic policymakers can use information that comes available *after* the contract is written but was unavailable when workers agreed to a particular money wage path.

commodities, market participants are extremely well informed and often base their information on detailed studies and sophisticated analysis. In such situations, people's expectations are generally forward-looking, as people attempt to forecast future events on the basis of careful analysis of future policies and external events.

Some macroeconomists have begun to fuse together the new view of expectations with the modern mainstream (or neo-Keynesian) view of product and labor markets. This synthesis is embodied in macroeconomic models that assume that *(a)* labor and goods markets display inflexible wages and prices, *(b)* the prices and quantities in money and other financial auction markets adjust rapidly to economic shocks and expectations, and *(c)* the expectations in auction markets are formed in a rational, forward-looking way.

A recent survey compares the behavior of macroeconomic models that incorporate the old ("adaptive, backward-looking") approach to expectations with models that incorporate the new ("forward-looking, rational") approach. The adaptive assumption holds that people form their expectations on the basis of limited information and using an oversimplified model of the economy's structure. For example, an adaptive assumption about next period's unemployment rate might be that it is the average of this period's and last period's unemployment rate. The forward-looking approach, as explained in this appendix, holds that people form their expectations by taking into account all available information, including information about the structure of the economy. An example of a rational forecast would be one based on a large econometric model (such as the DRI model of the U.S. economy).

A review of the forward-looking and the adaptive models finds a number of important differences. One salient feature is that forward-looking models tend to have large "jumps" or discontinuous changes in interest rates, stock prices, or exchange rates when large changes in policy or external events occur. For example, an election of an expansionist president or prime minister might lead people to think that inflation was on the horizon and might therefore produce a sharp rise in interest rates along with a fall in the stock market and exchange rates. The prediction of "jumpy" prices replicates one characteristic of auction markets and thus suggests where forward-looking expectations might be important in the real world.

Figure 16A-3 shows the differences in impact of fiscal policies between forward-looking and adaptive models. This graph compares the expenditure multipliers of four forward-looking models with the multipliers of seven adaptive-expectations models. Note that the multipliers of the forward-looking models are significantly smaller than those in the adaptive models.

The smaller multipliers in forward-looking models occur for two reasons: First, after a fiscal expansion, interest rates generally rise more rapidly in forward-looking than in adaptive models. This is so because forward-looking market participants predict a future expansion of output after an increase in government spending; this higher expected future output tends to increase interest rates *today,* and reduced investment (called "crowding out") therefore occurs rapidly in forward-looking models.

Second, as interest rates rise quickly in response to a fiscal stimulus in forward-looking models, the flexible exchange rate on the dollar tends to rise. A rise in the exchange rate of the dollar leads to a reduction in net exports and tends to retard economic activity. Overall, therefore, crowding out of investment (both of domestic investment by higher interest rates and of net exports or net foreign investment by a

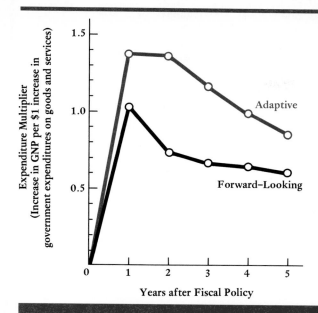

Figure 16A-3 Comparison of multipliers in forward-looking and adaptive models.

This graph shows the difference in expenditure multipliers of models using two different approaches to expectations: adaptive (which uses simple backward-looking rules for forecasting) and forward-looking (or "rational," which incorporates all information and knowledge about the structure of the economy).

Because crowding out (from the impact of interest rates on domestic investment and of exchange rates on net exports or net foreign investment) takes place more rapidly in forward-looking models, the forward-looking expenditure multipliers are considerably smaller than those in adaptive models. [Source: Ralph C. Bryant, Gerald Holtham, and Peter Hooper, "Consensus and Diversity in the Model Simulations," in Ralph C. Bryant and others (eds.), *Empirical Macroeconomics for Interdependent Economies* (Brookings, Washington, D.C., 1988), Fig. 3-33.]

higher exchange rate on the dollar) occurs more rapidly in forward-looking models, with the consequence of a lower expenditure multiplier.

Although this discussion touches on only two of the many differences between the rational-expectations approach and more traditional macroeconomics, it does point to an important set of results that every serious macroeconomist must study carefully. Economic behavior with forward-looking expectations produces different behavior from that seen under adaptive expectations. The reaction of markets to external events, and even to policies and policymakers themselves, cannot be ignored. The credibility of policy comes to the fore.

SUMMARY TO APPENDIX

1. Rational-expectations macroeconomics rests on two fundamental hypotheses: (I) people's expectations are efficiently and rationally formed and (II) prices and wages are flexible. Under these two assumptions, the striking policy ineffectiveness theorem holds: Predictable government policies cannot affect real output and unemployment.

This theory states that, while we may *observe* a downward-sloping short-run Phillips curve, we cannot *exploit* the slope for the purposes of lowering unemployment. If economic policy makes systematic attempts to increase output and decrease unemployment, economic agents will soon come to understand and to anticipate the policy. Once such a policy is anticipated, prices and wages will adjust in advance. People will remain on their supply and demand curves, and unemployment will stay at the natural rate.

2. Critics point to several weaknesses in the rational-expectations view. The assumptions of flexible prices and rational expectations are not borne out by empirical studies. And the predictions—particularly that business cycles are caused by misperceptions— seem farfetched as an explanation of downturns, like those of the 1930s or after 1979, that lasted as much as a decade.

CONCEPTS FOR REVIEW

rational (forward-looking) expectations
adaptive (backward-looking)
  expectations
flexible prices and wages
policy ineffectiveness theorem
Lucas critique

criticism of rational-expectations
  macroeconomics
synthesis of rational-expectations
  macroeconomics and modern
  mainstream macroeconomics

QUESTIONS FOR DISCUSSION

1. Assume that the Federal Reserve is targeting the money-supply growth, and that on Friday of each week the Fed and the public learn what the money supply was. Further assume that there are significant random elements to the money demand, but not to the money supply. Can you understand why an announcement of a large money-supply increase in a given week will quickly drive *up* market interest rates? (HINT: Trace through how the Fed will have to shift the upward-sloping money supply curve when it learns about a shock to money demand.)

2. Consider the effect of rational expectations on consumption behavior. Say the government proposes a temporary tax cut of $20 billion, lasting for a year. Irrational consumers might expect that their disposable incomes would be $20 billion higher every year. What would be the impact on consumption spending and GNP in the simple multiplier model of Chapter 9?

Next suppose that consumers have rational expectations. They rationally forecast that the tax cut is for only 1 year. Being ''life-cycle'' consumers (see p. 133), they recognize that their average lifetime incomes will increase only $2 billion per year, not $20 billion per year. What would be the reaction of such consumers? Analyze, then, the impact of rational expectations on the effectiveness of temporary tax cuts.

3. Look at the cobweb model of the appendix to Chapter 23. Assume that farmers have rational expectations. What does this imply about farmers' views of future prices? Once farmers develop the correct rational expectation, what happens to their supply behavior? What happens to the cobweb?

CHAPTER 17___
FISCAL POLICY, DEFICITS, AND THE GOVERNMENT DEBT

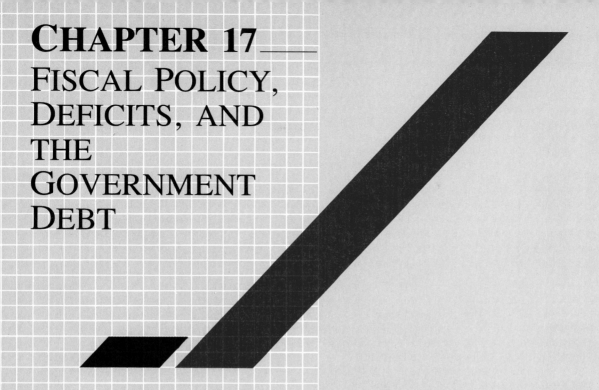

The only good rule is that the budget should never be balanced—except for an instant when a surplus to curb inflation is being altered to a deficit to fight recession.

Warren Smith of Ann Arbor (1965)

FOR MOST OF THE TIME since the Revolutionary War, the federal government of the United States balanced its fiscal budget. Wars, with their heavy military spending, were customarily financed by borrowing, so the government debt tended to soar in wartime. In peacetime, the government would pay off some of the debt, shrinking the debt burden.

During the 1980s, this pattern changed. President Reagan announced in 1981 a new economic program that promised to cut taxes, sharply increase America's military spending, and balance the budget. Only the first two promises were kept, and the federal government began to spend far more than it taxed. Government deficits soared to over $200 billion a year in the mid-1980s; the government debt grew from $620 billion when President Reagan was inaugurated to nearly $2000 billion when he left office.

What were the causes of the surging deficits in the 1980s? How did the large deficits affect the economy's pattern of investing and saving? Did government deficits "crowd out" investment? How did the expansionary fiscal policy interact with the Federal Reserve's monetary policy? And what will be the long-lasting impact of the large and growing govern-

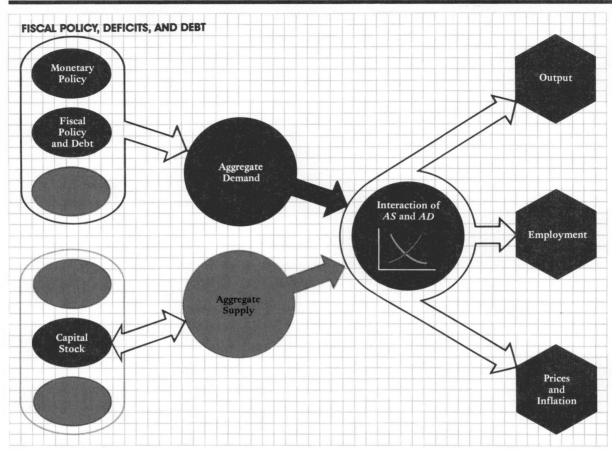

Figure 17-1   This chapter explores fiscal policy, deficits, and the burden of government debt
This final chapter on macroeconomics studies the economic impact of fiscal policy, deficits, the mix of fiscal and monetary policies, and the government debt. Note how the causal arrows point both toward and away from the capital stock, reminding us that monetary and fiscal policies leave a significant mark on investment and capital.

ment debt upon economic activity? These crucial questions will be addressed in this chapter.

Figure 17-1 shows the topics to be studied in this last chapter on macroeconomics.

A. BUDGETS AND FISCAL POLICY

Before analyzing the economic effects of deficits and the government debt, we cover the major institutional features and concepts of government budgeting.

Basic Definitions

Governments use budgets to control and record their fiscal affairs. A budget shows, for a given year, the planned expenditures and expected receipts that government spending and tax programs would yield. The budget typically will contain a list of specific programs (education, welfare, defense, etc.), as well as tax sources (individual income tax, social-insurance taxes, etc.).[1]

In a given year, governments generally run either budgetary surpluses or budgetary deficits. A **budget surplus** occurs when all taxes and other revenues exceed government expenditures. A **budget deficit** is run when expenditures exceed taxes. When taxes and expenditures are equal, the government has a **balanced budget.**

As an example, consider President Reagan's budget for fiscal year 1989. This was submitted to Congress in February 1988 and proposed taxes and expenditures for the 1989 fiscal year, which stretched from October 1, 1988, to September 30, 1989. Reagan's budget called for receipts of $1029 billion and expenditures of $1146 billion. The planned deficit was thus $117 billion.

When the government incurs a budget deficit, it must either print money or borrow from the public to pay its bills. The **government debt** (sometimes called the public debt) consists of the total or accumulated borrowings by the government; it is hence the total dollar value of government bonds owned by the public, i.e., by households, banks, businesses, foreigners, and other non-federal entities. In the pages that follow, we study the impact of government deficits and debt upon the economy.

THE MAKING OF FISCAL POLICY

The simple Keynesian multiplier analysis led many early enthusiasts to believe that fiscal policy was the philosopher's stone, the answer to all prayers for curbing business cycles. If unemployment strikes, simply raise spending or cut taxes; if inflation threatens, do the opposite. In such a simple world of Keynesian multipliers, the life of a macroeconomic manager would surely be an easy one.

Or so some perhaps believed two or three decades

---

[1] Details on the budgets of federal, state, and local governments are provided in Chapters 32 and 33.

ago. Today, none hold such naively optimistic views about banishing the business cycle to history books. The business cycle is still with us, and the use of fiscal policy is not so easy in practice as in theory. This section reviews why it has proven difficult to employ countercyclical fiscal policy effectively.

By *fiscal policy,* we mean the process of shaping taxation and public expenditure in order *(a)* to help dampen the swings of the business cycle, and *(b)* to contribute toward the maintenance of a growing, high-employment economy, free from high and volatile inflation.

Suppose the economic system in a particular year is threatened with a deep and prolonged recession. What action might people call for? The Federal Reserve, the U.S. central bank, might use monetary policy to try to stimulate investment. Additionally, Congress and the President might alter fiscal policy, changing tax and public expenditure programs to help reachieve their output and inflation targets. Alternatively, if inflation is unacceptably high, Congress might raise tax rates and trim expenditure programs, or the Federal Reserve might reduce the growth of the money supply and raise interest rates.

In summary, fiscal policies dealing with taxes and public expenditure, in cooperation with monetary policies, have as their goals rapid economic growth with high employment and stable prices.

Automatic vs. Discretionary Policy

You might get the impression that only *discretionary fiscal policies,* those involving the explicit making and changing of taxes and expenditures, can affect the economy. Discretionary (sometimes called "active") policies occur when policymakers carefully watch trends, forecast future developments, and change policies when the economy is not performing in a satisfactory manner. These policies are important, but they are only part of the story.

The modern fiscal system has, as well, great inherent *automatic stabilizing* properties. All through the day and night, whether or not the President is awake, the fiscal system is helping keep our economy stable. If a recession gets under way while Congress is out of session in 1990, powerful automatic forces will instantly begin to counter the recession before any committees meet or any discretion is exercised.

Automatic Stabilizers

What are the automatic stabilizers? They are primarily the following:

▪ *Automatic changes in tax receipts.* Our federal tax system depends on progressive personal and corporate income taxes. (Progressive taxes are those whose rates rise as income rises.) What does progressive taxation mean for stability? It means that as soon as income begins to fall off, even if Congress makes no change in tax rates, the government tax receipts begin to fall off. Today, for each $10 billion drop in GNP, total tax receipts drop by about $3½ billion.

Why are such tax changes useful? They may be the right medicine for an unexpected change in the economy. If output drops, tax receipts will automatically fall and thereby help maintain personal incomes and spending; output may not fall as much as it otherwise would have. In inflationary times, an increase in tax revenues will lower personal income, dampen consumption spending, reduce aggregate demand, and slow the upward spiral of prices and wages.

A century ago, writers thought that *stability* of tax revenue was a good thing. Today many economists believe exactly the opposite. We may be lucky, therefore, that our present tax system has almost unintentionally come to possess a high degree of automatic flexibility, with its receipts tending to rise in inflationary times and to fall in times of recession. This is a powerful factor stabilizing the economy and moderating the business cycle.

▪ *Unemployment insurance, welfare, and other transfers.* In the last 50 years we have built up an elaborate system of transfer payments, such as unemployment insurance (UI). Soon after employees are laid off, they begin to receive UI; when they go back to work, the payments cease. Thus UI pumps funds into or out of the economy in a countercyclical, stabilizing way.

Similar features are seen in many income-support programs. Food stamps, aid to families with dependent children, and medicaid are examples of public transfer payments that help to shave the highs and lows from the business cycle.

Limitations of Automatic Stabilizers

Before leaving the subject of automatic stabilizers, we must stress that built-in stabilizers are a first line of defense but are not by themselves sufficient to maintain full stability. Let's see why, using the example of taxes.

The automatic tendency for taxes to take away a fraction of each extra dollar of GNP means that the size of the "multiplier" is cut down. Each dollar change in autonomous spending—investment, net exports, or defense spending, for example—will have its destabilizing effect on the economy reduced but not completely wiped out. Instead of such disturbances having their effects on GNP multiplied 3 or more times, there will now—because of the automatic stabilizing effect of taxes—be a multiplier effect of only 2 to 2.5.[2]

In short, automatic stabilizers act to reduce part of any fluctuation in the economy, but they cannot wipe out 100 percent of the disturbance. Whether to reduce the balance of a disturbance, and how, remains the task of discretionary monetary and fiscal policy.

Discretionary Fiscal Policy

Even after automatic stabilizers have done their job, fluctuations in economic activity remain. The principal weapons of discretionary fiscal policy—programs which involve explicit public decision making—are:

▪ Public-works and other expenditure programs
▪ Public employment projects
▪ Tax rates

Public Works When governments first began to counter depressions actively, they often relied on

---

[2]The explanation for the partial stabilizing effect can be illustrated as follows: Assume that without any taxes, government, foreign sector, etc., the *MPC* is $\frac{9}{10}$; this implies that the multiplier is 10. Now assume that 33⅓ percent of any additional income goes to taxes, so for every dollar of increase in GNP, $\frac{1}{3}$ goes to taxes and $\frac{2}{3}$ goes to disposable income *(DI)*. And of the $\frac{2}{3}$ going to *DI*, 90 percent (or 60 cents) is spent. The multiplier is now only 2.5.

public investment projects to create jobs for the unemployed. Some public-works investments, including rural electrification or water projects like the Tennessee Valley Authority, proved of enormous utility to underdeveloped areas. Others were no more than inefficient ''make-work'' for people and added little of value (e.g., raking leaves during the Depression). The extreme make-work case was a program to dig holes and fill them up again.

Today, we understand a great deal about the economic impacts of countercyclical programs, and we seldom rely on public-works projects to combat recessions. Why have policy makers turned away from public works as a recession cure? Planners now realize that it takes a long time to get a post office started or to put into effect a road-building or slum-clearance program. Plans must be made; blueprints drawn; land acquired by purchase or court condemnation; buildings razed; new structures built.

All these steps may take 4 or 6 or 10 years. It may take 2 or 3 more years before a significant part of the funds is spent and people are employed. Given the difficulty of forecasting more than a year or two into the future, we might find that the anti-recession public-works project is just coming on stream as the economy is recovering sharply from the recession or even when the government has turned its concerns to fighting inflation. Like generals fighting the wrong war, countercyclical public-works programs may fight the wrong phase of the business cycle.

Public Employment Projects At the other extreme from highly capital-intensive, long-duration public-works projects are a recent tool of stabilization policy—public employment projects or public-service employment (PSE) jobs. These are projects to hire unemployed workers for periods of a year or so. After the 1975 recession, 700,000 adults and 1 million teenagers found work through this route.

PSE jobs avoid one of the major shortcomings of public-works projects, for they can be started up and phased out very quickly. Critics of such programs think they are wasteful however. Often the projects are of secondary importance (otherwise they would already have been done). In addition, the transition from PSE jobs to regular jobs has been a rocky one; most studies indicate that getting a PSE job does not markedly improve one's chances of holding a regular job later.

Variation of Tax Rates If there is good reason to think that an economic downturn will be brief, a temporary cut in income-tax rates can be one way of keeping disposable incomes from falling and of preventing a decline from snowballing. Under our withholding system, shortly after Congress and the executive branch decide the economy needs stimulus through tax reduction, employers begin to withhold less from salary paychecks. Varying tax rates can be used to either stimulate or restrain an economy.

Many advocates of active stabilization policy see varying tax rates as the ideal weapon. Once taxes have been changed, consumers react quickly; a tax cut is spread widely over the population; and it stimulates spending on consumption goods, which then stimulates an upturn in the economy.

Unfortunately, experience has pointed to important shortcomings to varying taxes countercyclically. It often takes Congress a long time to debate and enact tax proposals. During the Vietnam war boom, it took Congress $1\frac{1}{2}$ years to pass a surtax proposal. A second problem is the political fact of life that when there is a ''temporary'' suspension of tax rates to counter a recession, democracies often find it hard to increase taxes after the emergency is over. Political sentiment to fight unemployment is often easier to mobilize than sentiment to fight inflation.

And, finally, as we have seen in Chapter 7, if people know tax changes are to be temporary and will not alter their permanent incomes much, they may not vary their consumption very much and the countercyclical impact may be small.

From the time when countercyclical fiscal policy was analyzed by J. M. Keynes in 1936 until the late 1970s, many macroeconomists believed that fiscal policy could play a major role in stabilizing the business cycle. A deep skepticism arose in the last decade, however, partly because of the fiscal-policy shortcomings just discussed and partly because monetary policy seemed to work much more quickly and effectively. Today, most economists would relegate fiscal policy to the backseat and leave the primary short-run stabilization task to monetary policy. Fiscal policy would, in this view, aim to determine the investment-saving balance and perhaps to counter any deep recessions or great inflations that cannot be handled by monetary policy alone.

With this overview of the major concepts of fiscal policy behind us, we now turn to an analysis of the role of fiscal deficits in the economy.

FISCAL DEFICITS: CONCEPTS AND TRENDS

Old-Fashioned Public Finance

Sixty years ago, economic textbooks dealing with public finance read much as they had in Adam Smith's time. From 1776 to 1929 there was little discernible progress. The Democratic President Grover Cleveland differed not a bit in his ideology of public finance from Republican William McKinley—or for that matter from Calvin Coolidge and Herbert Hoover.

What were the classical precepts of public finance, the doctrines our grandparents were taught and preached to us in turn?

- Public finance is simply an application of family finances. If a husband and wife spend more than their monthly income, they go bankrupt and misery follows. The same is true for Uncle Sam.
- The budget should be balanced in every year; the budget should be small, with expenditure prudent and purposes strictly limited.
- The government debt is a burden on the backs of our children and grandchildren; every dollar of debt is like a heavy rock that we must carry on our shoulders. Debt corrupts; government debt corrupts absolutely.

Although economic thinking about public finance has advanced a great deal, these simple homilies resurface periodically. Particularly during the 1980s, with surging deficits and the rapid buildup of government debt, people hark back to these early views about the virtues of having a balanced budget and of retiring the public debt. But few experienced public-finance specialists today agree completely with the three precepts of our forbears. Our task is to understand the logic and experience behind modern views about budgets.

Modern Public Finance

Our earlier analysis of appropriate fiscal policy focused on the need to stabilize the economy: higher deficits combat recession while lower deficits or even surpluses curb inflation (see the quotation from Michigan economist Warren Smith at the beginning of this chapter). But what if the needs of stabilization policy drive deficits and government debt ever upward? Or down to zero? Should we be concerned about the deficits and debt as our grandparents were?

There are no simple answers to these questions. Rather, the answers depend upon the impact of the deficits and debts upon the economy. We focus in the balance of this chapter on the consequential questions that will determine whether deficits and debts are for good or for ill:

- Are the deficits recession-induced or policy-induced? This is the issue discussed next in the analysis of structural and cyclical deficits.
- What is the appropriate mix of monetary and fiscal policies?
- Do deficits "crowd out" investment or do they "encourage" it?
- What is the true economic burden of the government debt?

Structural vs. Cyclical Deficits

One of the most important distinctions in modern public finance is that between structural and cyclical deficits.[3] The idea is simple. Part of the budget is *structural* or active—determined by discretionary policies (such as setting tax rates, social security benefits, or the size of defense spending). But an uncomfortably large fraction of the budget is *cyclical*—determined passively by the state of the business

---

[3] The following discussion analyzes government deficits in light of the prevalent budgetary imbalance of the 1980s; the principles apply equally to a budget surplus with the appropriate change in sign.

cycle, that is, by the extent to which national income and output are high or low.

To make this distinction clear, economists measure structural and cyclical budgets:

The **actual budget** records the actual dollar expenditures, revenues, and deficits in a given period.

The **structural budget** calculates what government revenues, expenditures, and deficits would be if the economy were operating at potential output.

The **cyclical budget** calculates the effect of the business cycle on the budget—measuring the changes in revenues, expenditures, and deficits that arise because the economy is not operating at potential output but is in boom or recession.

The cyclical budget is the difference between the actual budget and the structural budget.

In practice, the distinction between structural and cyclical budgets is closely related to the difference between discretionary and automatic stabilizers. For the most part, structural spending and revenues consist of the discretionary programs enacted by the legislature; cyclical spending and deficits consist of those taxes and spending that adjust automatically to the state of the economy.

For example, during a recession, every percentage-point increase in the unemployment rate raises government spending and decreases tax revenues by a total of about $40 billion as of 1989. This increase in the deficit—in the cyclical deficit—comes as unemployment insurance increases, as welfare payments rise, and as tax revenues fall. And all these occur even if Congress is in recess and does not pass a single bill.

By contrast, say that Congress cuts tax rates or increases military spending. These steps would add to the structural deficit, which denotes the budget deficit at full employment or potential output. Or suppose that Congress decides to enact a $25 billion program reimbursing older Americans for large medical expenses. This would add $25 billion to structural expenditures and would therefore increase the structural deficit by that amount.

Generally, fiscal-policy actions change both the structural and the cyclical deficits (at least for the short run). If the government were to sign an arms-control agreement that cut $30 billion from defense spending, this would cut the structural deficit by $30 billion. If nothing else happened, such a cut would also tend to contract the economy, thereby increasing the cyclical deficit.

Statistical studies indicate that the net effect of a measure that changes the structural budget deficit is to change the actual budget deficit in the same direction.

Applications of Cyclical and Structural Budgets

By distinguishing cyclical deficits from structural deficits, we get a better reading of the true impact of fiscal policy. If the deficit increases in a given year, one might be tempted to say, "The deficit is up, therefore the government is stimulating the economy."

But this reaction would not necessarily be correct. If the higher deficit came because Congress cut tax rates or raised defense spending (i.e., because the structural deficit rose), this would indeed tend to increase aggregate demand. On the other hand, if the budget deficit increased because of an economic downturn, then the higher actual deficit would not be a sign of fiscal expansion; a downturn would not be signaled by an increase in the structural budget deficit, but by an increase in the cyclical budget deficit.

Hence to gauge the direction in which fiscal policy is leading the economy, one should watch the structural budget, not the actual budget.

Figure 17-2 on the next page illustrates this central lesson well. Note how the structural budget moved sharply toward deficit during the Vietnam war, again before the 1972 election, and once again after 1982. These were periods of strong fiscal expansion.

But the figure also indicates that movements in the actual deficit can provide misleading indicators of the direction of fiscal policy. From 1979 to 1982, the cyclical budget moved sharply into deficit while the structural budget changed little. What was happening? What occurred was simply that, as the economy went into recessions in these years, tax receipts fell off. Fiscal policy did not become more expansionary until after 1982; the deficit increase was largely cyclical, not structural.

The structural budget is one of the most important analytical tools of macroeconomics. It allows us to separate changes in policy from the effects of the

ACTUAL, STRUCTURAL, AND CYCLICAL DEFICITS

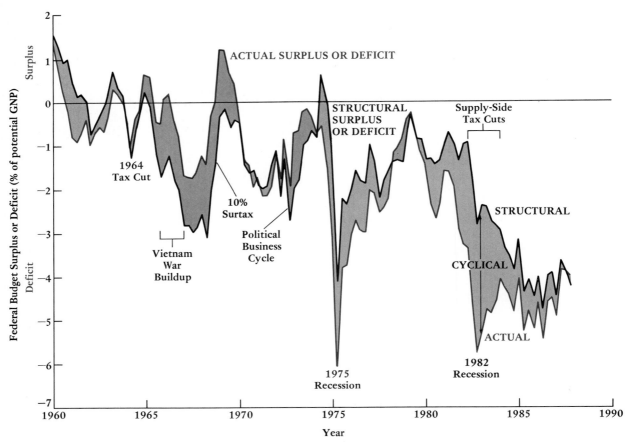

Figure 17-2 Structural, actual, and cyclical budget deficits

The red line shows the actual budget deficit or surplus over the last 3 decades (as a percentage of potential GNP). The black curve depicts the structural component, i.e., what the budget deficit or surplus would have been if the economy had been at potential output.

The difference between the actual and structural deficits or surpluses is the cyclical deficit or surplus. Where the shaded area is red, the economy had high unemployment and the cyclical budget was in deficit. Where the gap is shaded gray, output was above potential and the cyclical budget showed surplus. (Source: U.S. Department of Commerce, modified by authors to reflect the definition of potential output used in this text.)

business cycle, enabling us to make a better diagnosis of where fiscal policy is leading the economy.

The Soaring Fiscal Deficits after 1979

The most perplexing macroeconomic issue of the 1980s revolved around the mounting federal budget deficit. Deficits were not new to the American economy; indeed, the federal government incurred deficits through the entire 1970s. But after 1979, the size of the federal deficit jumped sharply both absolutely and as a fraction of GNP. The federal deficit rose from $16 billion in 1979 to $204 billion in 1986.

From 1982 on, the federal deficit became a central

concern of economic policymakers. Every year, Congress passed laws attempting to slow the rising sea of red ink, but deficits climbed throughout this period. Early in his first term, President Reagan downplayed the importance of deficits and blamed their growth on 50 years of poorly designed, Democratic welfare programs; during his second term, President Reagan proposed a constitutional amendment to balance the budget and supported the Gramm-Rudman bill to mandate a balanced budget through legislative means. Democrats attacked the President, blamed his supply-side policies, and insisted that Reagan's economic policies were solely to blame.

What indeed were the sources of the rising deficit? No simple analysis can resolve this complex question, but a few facts, shown in Table 17-1, illustrate the problem. This table shows the actual, structural, and cyclical deficits in 1979 (a high-employment year), 1982 (at the trough of a deep recession), and 1986 (a year of stable macroeconomic conditions). In addition, in part C of the table, we show how much each of four contributing factors changed from 1979 to the reference year. For these benchmark comparisons, we examine the change in each factor as a share of GNP. For example, from 1979 to 1982, federal net interest payments rose from 1.69 percent to 2.67 percent of nominal GNP; the difference between these shares is $31 billion $[= \frac{1}{100}(2.67 - 1.69) \times 1982$ GNP of $3166 billion].

What conclusions can we draw from this table and other studies?[4] We see the following:

[4] A particularly useful source of information on federal budget trends is the Congressional Budget Office.

DEFICIT OR CONTRIBUTING FACTOR	AMOUNT, BILLIONS OF DOLLARS		
	YEAR		
	1979	1982	1986
A. Budget deficit			
Actual	$16	$146	$204
Cyclical	0	91	26
Structural	16	55	178
B. Increase in budget deficit from 1979			
Actual	0	130	188
Cyclical	0	91	26
Structural	0	39	162
C. Contributing factor			
Increased defense spending	0	40	72
Increased interest payments	0	31	64
Increased transfer payments	0	58	44
Decreased taxes	0	5	26
Total, Contributing Factors	0	134	206

Table 17-1   Sources of the rising deficit

From 1979 to 1986, the federal budget deficit rose from $16 billion to $204 billion. In the early period, from 1979 to 1982, most of the increase was due to the recession and rising cyclical deficit. In the second part of the period, structural factors were at work.

Part C of the table shows the major contributing factors. In each case, we have taken as a baseline the ratio of spending or taxes to 1979 GNP. By this test, the most important factors were the increase in defense spending and the rise of interest payments. Tax cuts and larger transfer payments contributed as well. (Source: U.S. Department of Commerce.)

▪ During the early 1980s, most of the increase in the deficit was due to the deep recession, with only a modest increase in the structural deficit. After 1982, the structural deficit rose sharply as the cyclical deficit shrank.

▪ The deficit rose because all four contributing factors moved toward deficit: taxes were cut, while defense spending, interest payments, and transfer payments increased.

▪ The two largest increases came in defense spending and in interest payments. The former was due largely to the Reagan military buildup and was a conscious and announced policy step; the latter was inadvertent and resulted from the high interest rates which accompanied the tight monetary policies after 1979 along with the increase in the government debt stemming from the large government deficits.

▪ In the end, no single source can be pointed to as the culprit. Rather, it was the combination of policies and events, all interacting and moving in the same direction, that led to the soaring deficits. In other words, it was a combination of tight monetary policy, tax cuts, recession, and military buildup *all operating at the same time* that left the United States with budget deficits higher than at any period of peacetime prosperity.

B. THE INTERACTION OF MONETARY AND FISCAL POLICIES

Now that we have analyzed the tools and recent trends of fiscal policy, we turn to an evaluation of the principles that lie behind the setting of monetary and fiscal policies. Should monetary policy be loose or tight? Should fiscal or monetary policy, or both, or neither, be used to fight inflation and unemployment? What should be the division of labor between monetary and fiscal policies—the fiscal-monetary mix?

There are no simple answers to these questions. No magic formulas will come to the rescue of governments trying to find the best policies. Rather, the best setting for monetary policy, taxes, and spending will depend upon (a) demand management, which refers to policies that stimulate or contract the overall economy and (b) the desired fiscal-monetary mix, which concerns the relative strength of fiscal and monetary forces in the economy.

Demand Management

The first consideration in determining the appropriate setting for monetary and fiscal policies is the overall state of aggregate demand. When the economy is stagnating, fiscal and monetary policies can be used to stimulate the economy and promote economic recovery. When inflation threatens, monetary and fiscal policies can help to slow the economy and dampen inflationary fires. These are examples of *demand management,* which refers to the use of monetary and fiscal policies to set aggregate demand at the desired level.

Let us consider a concrete example. Suppose that we have entered a period of stagnation, in which overall aggregate demand is depressed relative to potential output. This might have occurred because businesses and households are pessimistic about the future or perhaps because a high exchange rate on the dollar has reduced the level of net exports.

What can the government do to revive the lagging economy? It can manage aggregate demand by increasing the structural budget deficit, or raising money growth, or both. After the economy has responded to the monetary and fiscal stimulus, output growth and employment would increase and unemployment would fall.

What about the opposite case of a period of excessive economic expansion? For example, after World War II, capital was so scarce that investment demand threatened to propel aggregate demand way beyond potential output. In such a condition, the government might decide to take demand-management steps to slow the economy, either by tightening monetary policy or by fiscal restraint. Indeed, we find that the government did run a structural fiscal surplus after World War II, which had the effect of restraining a booming economy.

We see, then, that the first consideration in setting monetary and fiscal policies is the need for demand management, that is, for ensuring that aggregate demand is at the appropriate level so that neither unemployment nor inflation is unacceptably high.

The Policy Mix

The second factor affecting the optimal fiscal deficit or surplus and the best monetary policy is the desired **fiscal-monetary mix,** which refers to the combination of fiscal and monetary policies used to influence macroeconomic activity. Monetary and fiscal policies can be used to affect not only the *level* of GNP but also the *composition* of GNP. Put differently, by varying the mix of taxes, government spending, and monetary policy, the government can change the fraction of GNP devoted to business investment, consumption, net exports, and government purchases of goods and services.

Example 1. Let's say that the people empower a President to start a big defense buildup, leaving overall output unchanged by having housing and other investment contract to provide the necessary resources. What could be done? The President could increase defense spending, leave taxes alone, and tighten money, thereby raising interest rates enough to squeeze investment and net exports to make room for the added government purchases. This policy would also lead to an increase in the structural budget deficit. Such a fiscal course was followed by President Reagan from 1981 to 1988.

Example 2. Suppose that a President thinks that the top priority is to increase investment so as to increase the capital stock and raise the growth rate of potential output. And he feels this should be done without any change in the overall level of GNP; higher investment should come at the expense of private consumption. What policy mix should be pursued?

Undertake an expansionary monetary policy to lower interest rates and raise investment; keep government spending on goods and services unchanged; raise taxes and squeeze transfer payments so as to reduce disposable income and thereby lower consumption. The point of this policy mix is to encourage investment by increasing public saving (taxes less spending). Such a change in the policy mix was proposed by Democratic presidential aspirants in 1984 and 1988.

The Mix in Practice

These real-world examples show how the mix of monetary and fiscal policies can be just as important as the overall setting of policies. A nation is not indifferent between a tight monetary–loose fiscal policy or a loose monetary–tight fiscal policy, for those two options will lead to different compositions of GNP.

In reality, an examination of postwar American history shows little resemblance to the reasoned analysis of the optimal fiscal-monetary mix. Ironically, while most economists and political leaders have urged the nation to take steps to increase investment and reduce consumption, in fact policies moved steadily in the opposite direction; the fiscal-monetary mix in the United States has increasingly tended toward high deficits and high real interest rates. This combination tends to increase consumption and government spending at the expense of private domestic investment and net exports with the overall national rate of saving and investment declining over time.

How did it come to pass that the fiscal-monetary reality moved divergently from the desired policies? One major reason is that monetary and fiscal policies have not been coordinated in the United States. Rather, they combat each other and lead to a macroeconomic policy that neither fiscal experts nor the Federal Reserve would recommend. Let us see why.

Fiscal policy marches to different drummers; indeed, the tune tends to change with every new President. During the Kennedy-Johnson administrations (1961–1968), fiscal policy was used first to take up economic slack and then to finance a war in Vietnam. In the Nixon-Ford years (1969–1976), the winding down of the Vietnam war allowed many new domestic programs to get started. Moreover, frequent recessions drove up cyclical deficits. The Carter presidency (1977–1980) was one of fiscal austerity, with rising taxes and few new spending programs. We have seen how the Reagan years produced a combination of military buildup, higher interest payments, lower taxes, and continued growth in transfer spending.

What common thread runs through all these years? It is that changes in spending and taxing tend to be highly asymmetric. Congress delights in lowering taxes or increasing spending on new transfers or other programs. On the other hand, increasing taxes or reducing entitlements or other spending programs has proven extremely difficult to accomplish. The net effect is that it is easy to increase, but hard to reduce, structural deficits.

This results in a tug of war between monetary policy and fiscal policy. Over time, fiscal policy has produced greater deficits, while the Federal Reserve has responded to the loosening of fiscal policy by progressively tightening monetary policy, continually raising real interest rates higher and higher. The dynamics of the uncoordinated fiscal-monetary mix left the United States in the mid-1980s with the highest real interest rates and the largest budget deficit in decades. The consequences, as we will shortly see, are a curtailment of domestic investment and a gaping foreign-trade deficit while consumption and government spending on goods and services take a growing share of GNP.

THE CROWDING-OUT CONTROVERSY

Often, politicians and business analysts argue that government spending undermines the economy. They argue, ''Government spending saps our nation's vitality. When the government spends money on giant public-works projects or pours money into poorly maintained housing projects, these funds simply crowd out private investment projects with higher yields and greater social utility.''

This argument invokes the **crowding-out hypothesis,** which holds that government spending tends to reduce private investment. In its extreme form, this hypothesis suggests that when government spends $100 more on public goods, private investment falls by $100. Let's investigate this idea.

Crowding Out and the Money Market

What is the crowding-out mechanism? Suppose that the government starts a road-building project, increasing government spending on goods and services. Operating through the multiplier, GNP will then rise by 2 or 3 times the increase in G.

But we must also take into account the reaction of the money market. Because GNP is higher, the trans-actions demand for money rises. As a result, for a given money supply interest rates rise. *But the rising interest rates will choke off some investment.*[5] (You should trace through how a tax cut would lead to the same outcome.)

We see, then, that as money markets, interest rates, and investment respond indirectly to the rise in government spending, the fiscal-policy measures will reduce (or crowd out) investment.

How does this relate to deficits? Recall that our example assumes that there is a discretionary increase in G or cut in T. This implies that the structural deficit is increased. We can therefore also say that, when interest rates rise in response to a larger structural deficit, the deficit crowds out investment.

Crowding out occurs when the effectiveness of fiscal policy is reduced because of money market reactions. An increase in the structural deficit (through tax cuts or higher government spending) may lead to rising interest rates thereby lowering investment. Thus some of the induced increase in GNP may be offset as the higher structural deficit crowds out investment.

Crowding Out in Recessions? Before we analyze the issue of crowding out, one preliminary comment is necessary. Crowding out is primarily concerned with the effects of structural rather than cyclical deficits. If the deficit rises because of a recession—this being a cyclical deficit—the logic of crowding out simply does not apply. Why not? Because a recession causes a *decline* in the demand for money and leads to *lower* interest rates. The relationship between deficits, interest rates, and investment in recessions shows why there is no automatic crowding out of investment by higher deficits.

Impacts of Structural Deficits

Turn then to the impact of higher structural or discretionary deficits upon investment. Most macroeconomists agree that at least some investment is crowded

---

[5] In the discussion that follows, we will proceed under the simplifying assumption that investment is the only interest-sensitive component of spending. In fact, consumption (particularly spending on housing services and consumer durables), net exports, and state and local government spending are also sensitive to interest rates. This should be kept in mind after the general points are understood, for these items will also be crowded out by fiscal policy.

out by government deficits. The dispute revolves around *how much* investment is reduced. Is investment reduced by only a small fraction of the government deficit? Or by virtually the whole amount?

We can understand the logic of crowding out using our earlier aggregate supply-and-demand analysis. Consider an economy that behaves in both a classical and monetarist way, as seen in Figure 17-3. Here the *AS* curve is vertical and only money affects aggregate demand. When the government increases its goods purchases, the *AD* curve does not shift because only money affects total spending. Thus, total GNP is unchanged by the fiscal measure, so the new equilibrium E' is at the old equilibrium E.

What has happened behind these curves? As the fiscal policy stimulated the economy, the demand for money rose; faced with a fixed supply of money, interest rates rose; and in the end interest rates had to rise enough so that investment declined by just the amount of the *G* increase. *Hence, in the classical-monetarist case, investment is 100 percent crowded out by an increase in government spending.*

Investment Encouragement

Many economists think that the classical-monetarist view is too extreme, particularly for the short run in an economy with underemployed resources. Some, indeed, point out that when the economy is in recession, investment may actually be *encouraged* (or "crowded in") by larger deficits.

Investment encouragement is shown in Figure 17-4 on the next page. We allow for a variant of the accelerator to operate on output; here, investment may be higher at higher levels of GNP because businesses buy more plant and equipment as their current plant and equipment are more intensively used. Assume as well that monetary policy accommodates fiscal expansion, meaning that the Fed increases or decreases the money supply to keep interest rates from changing when output increases.

We can see how investment is encouraged in Figure 17-4(a) using the aggregate spending diagram of earlier chapters. Note one major difference here. The investment line (*II*) in this case is shown at the bottom of Figure 17-4(a) as *upward-sloping*, indicating that investment rises as real output rises. Equilibrium still

CLASSICAL-MONETARIST CROWDING OUT

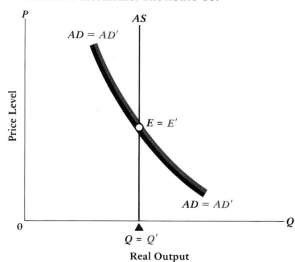

Figure 17-3   When fiscal policy does not affect demand, government spending or tax cuts are completely offset by investment decline

Crowding out occurs in a monetarist world because money demand is invariant to interest rates. An increase in *G* (with no *M* change) raises interest rates enough to crowd out interest-sensitive spending dollar-for-dollar. The *AD* curve therefore does not shift; *P* and *Q* are unaffected. (Similar reasoning will show why a tax cut will crowd out investment almost dollar-for-dollar.)

occurs where the total spending line (the $C + I + G + X$ line) intersects the 45° line.

So what is the effect of higher *G* in the investment-encouragement case? As fiscal policy raises spending from *G* to G', the structural deficit rises: the spending line shifts upward to the new aggregate spending line $(C + I + G' + X)$. The equilibrium level of output moves from *Q* to Q'. *Because output is higher, investment is actually encouraged,* moving from *I* to I' in Figure 17-4(a).

The effect of the investment-encouragement case can also be seen in the right-hand panel of Figure 17-4, using the *AS* and *AD* framework. Note that the *AS* curve is here shown as upward-sloping to reflect the assumption that the economy could be in equilibrium with underemployed resources. Further, spend-

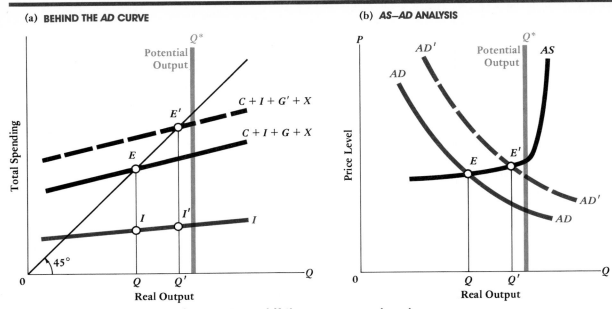

Figure 17-4   Investment may be encouraged if there are unemployed resources

Investment may be encouraged by higher deficits when there are unutilized resources and when investment responds to higher output. Panel **(a)** shows that an increase in G shifts up the $C + I + G + X$ curve. Equilibrium output rises from Q to Q'. But because investment responds positively to the higher level of output, it increases as a result of the higher government spending.

Panel **(b)** shows what happens in the $AS-AD$ framework. Fiscal expansion shifts the AD curve to the right, up the non-vertical AS curve, increasing output and investment.

ing is affected by both monetary policy and fiscal policy—which shows why the AD curve shifts to the right with a fiscal expansion.

This example shows that in an underemployed economy a fiscal expansion with accommodating monetary policy may actually raise investment.

Empirical Evidence

Such are the theories about deficits encouraging or crowding out investment and other interest-sensitive components of GNP. Which of these extremes is closer to the truth? What has been the experience in the United States when structural deficits have increased or decreased?

History provides no clear answer. During the 1960s, the fiscal expansion appears to have encouraged investment, partly because there were ample unutilized resources and partly because the Federal Reserve allowed the economy to expand without raising interest rates.

During the 1980s, the pattern appears to have been quite different, although few economists foresaw the way that the growing fiscal deficits would affect both the level and the composition of investment. The conventional view of the mechanism by which crowding out would occur was described above. If pressed further, most macroeconomists would have predicted (and most forecasting services did forecast) that the investment decline would occur in residential housing, business investment, and state and local governments.

The historical record shows two major surprises, as demonstrated in Table 17-2. First, personal saving did not rise in response to lower tax rates and higher interest rates; rather, personal saving fell despite the lower tax rates and the higher post-tax real returns on saving. Second, the major component of investment that was affected was net exports (which equals net foreign investment). The mechanism by which this occurred was discussed in earlier chapters: the higher interest rates after 1979 led to a major appreciation of the dollar, which in turn led to higher imports and lower exports and depressed real net exports from a surplus of $4 billion in 1979 to a deficit of $138 billion in 1986.[6]

Some economists accept the decline in net exports as preferable to lowering domestic business investment; they point out that lower net exports mean that the nation owes more to foreigners; i.e., a foreign trade deficit leaves the nation ''paper poor,'' with fewer assets abroad and more investments in the United States by the Japanese and others. The alternative would have been to squeeze investment in housing, plant, and equipment by $138 billion, which would have led to a painful reduction in the nation's capital stock. Others point out, however, that the negative net investment will require the United States to pay back the loans to foreigners through higher exports in the future, reducing the consumption possibilities for future generations.

What can we conclude about the extent of crowding out? The events of the last decade would seem to confirm the views of those who argue that interest rates and other financial forces tend to offset the impact of government spending. Moreover, the extent of the crowding out will surely depend upon the stance of the Federal Reserve, with an aggressive anti-inflation Fed producing more crowding out than a feeble and passive central bank. But the central lesson is that there are a number of different channels through which crowding out can occur—through changes in savings behavior, through domestic investment, and through foreign trade and investment. It may be diffi-

IMPACT OF DEFICITS ON SAVING AND INVESTMENT, 1979–1986

SECTOR	1979	1986	CHANGE
Gross saving (as percent of GNP)			
Personal	4.7%	2.9%	−1.8%
Business	13.1	13.9	0.8
Government			
Federal	−0.6	−4.9	−4.3
State and local	1.1	1.3	0.2
Gross investment (as percent of GNP)			
Private investment			
Residential housing	5.5%	5.1%	−0.4%
Business	12.6	10.6	−2.0
Net foreign investment (net exports)	0.1	−2.5	−2.6

Table 17-2   Increase in fiscal deficit produced surprising results

The increase in deficits of the Reagan era produced a test of the crowding-out hypothesis. From 1979 to 1986, the federal government deficits (or dissaving) increased from 0.6 percent to 4.9 percent of GNP. This was reinforced (rather than offset) by lower personal saving.

What was the impact upon investment? Only a small part of the decline in total saving came in residential housing; the share of business investment declined modestly. But the largest part of the investment decline came as a rising exchange rate on the dollar led to an enormous shift toward deficit in net exports. (Source: U.S. Department of Commerce.)

cult to predict in advance which route crowding out will follow in the next fiscal expansion.

A New Discipline?

We have seen that modern macroeconomics has destroyed the shibboleth of the balanced budget. But this does not mean that government can go wild, with legislators' pet projects hungrily gobbling up an ever-increasing portion of the national pie. Resources are limited, so some new discipline must replace the budget-balancing maxim. But what new discipline?

Many people, particularly conservatives, believe

---

[6] We cannot say, however, that the increase in the federal deficit *caused* the changes in personal saving, business investment, and net foreign investment. To make that claim without showing the causal linkage would be to commit the *post hoc, ergo propter hoc* fallacy. While many analysts believe that the change in the federal deficit was the major force causing the changes shown in Table 17-2, other forces—such as the monetarist experiment of 1979–1982 and the debt crisis after 1982—also exerted important influences on saving and investment during this period.

that Congress lacks the self-control to prevent the continued growth of transfer programs and public works. They see our legislators as pious spendoholics who preach budget balance by day and spend wildly by night. During the early 1980s, fiscal conservatives called for a constitutional amendment to balance the budget and contain the growth in federal spending. President Reagan periodically campaigned for a balanced-budget amendment during his second term.

A dramatic turn came when Congress passed the *Gramm-Rudman bill,* which mandated a decline in the budget deficit. This bill required Congress to reduce the deficit to no more than a specified numerical target each year (e.g., $136 billion in fiscal year 1989). If Congress was unable to meet the quantitative budget target, an automatic across-the-board cut in expenditures would be required.

The Gramm-Rudman bill went into effect in late 1985, and $10 billion of automatic cuts took place in 1986. The bill was amended in 1987 to correct some constitutional infirmities, and new budget deficit targets were set, as follows:

REVISED GRAMM-RUDMAN TARGETS
(as of 1987 Act)

FISCAL YEAR	MAXIMUM DEFICIT (billions)
1988	$144
1989	136
1990	100
1991	64
1992	28
1993	0

Hence, the amended Gramm-Rudman bill requires that Congress achieve a balanced budget by 1993. Congress' determination to meet this ambitious timetable will be severely tested in the years to come.

C. ECONOMIC CONSEQUENCES OF GOVERNMENT DEBT

We have reviewed the principles underlying modern fiscal policy. Some will say that, while useful for normal times, these principles must be revised for the 1980s and 1990s, which are the era of deficits and debt.

As a result of wars, recessions, and the increasing trend toward a loose fiscal policy shown in Figure 17-2, the debt of the federal government held by the public at the end of 1988 stood at $1790 billion.

What are the various economic problems created by such a debt? What are the analogies between public and private debt? What are the important noneconomic factors that must be reckoned with in any discussion of this vital political issue?

Analyzing the "burden of the debt" is important and difficult. At one extreme, we must avoid the customary practice of assuming that public debt is bad because private debt is burdensome. On the other hand, we must not belittle possible problems because they are thought to be rendered obsolete by an enlightened view of deficits and debt. There are real burdens in a large debt, but there is also a large oversupply of myths.

MEANING AND HISTORY OF GOVERNMENT DEBT

Definitions

When governments run budget deficits, they must either print money or borrow from the public to pay their bills. The accumulated borrowed amounts are called the *government* or *public debt*. Most government debt is short-term interest-bearing securities, such as Treasury bills or notes.

The government debt is simply related to the government deficit: *the change in the government debt over a given year is equal to the budget deficit.* Put differently, the projected $1790 billion of public debt owed at the end of 1988 represents the sum total of deficits minus surpluses since the founding of the republic.

An example will show the relationship between deficits and government debt. At the beginning of fiscal year 1989, $1790 billion of federal debt was held by the public. The total budget deficit for 1989 (including so-called off-budget items) was estimated to be $130 billion. Then, ignoring any changes in the government's bank balances or in the Federal Reserve's holdings, borrowing requirements for 1989 would be $130 billion. So at the end of 1989, federal debt would be $1790 + $130 = $1920 billion. (These figures have been rounded to facilitate calculations.)

The government debt is largely held domestically by banks, state and local governments, and so forth. These groups receive interest on the government debt (at an average rate of 8 percent per year in 1987).

Historical Trends

To assess the importance of the present public debt, it is always useful to start by placing the problem in historical perspective.[7]

Do interest payments on the debt swallow up much of the GNP? How does the total of all public interest payments compare with past years and with the experience of other countries?

To see how America's present debt compares with the past and with Britain's debt, look at Table 17-3 on the next page. This shows each nation's government debt in relation to size of gross national product and interest payments.

Thus, in 1988 our national debt of about $1790 billion represented 37 percent of our annual $4743 billion GNP. The debt's interest payments represented 3.2 percent of that GNP.

How "large" are these numbers? Note that England in 1818 had an internal debt estimated at double its GNP, and interest on its debt as a percentage of

GNP far exceeded anything that we can look forward to; yet the century from 1818 to World War I was England's greatest century in terms of power and material progress. By contrast, Britain's modest-sized debt of the 1970s was accompanied by stagnation. With an eye to history, we can see that there are no magic ratios linking a nation's debt to its glory or decline.

Longer-run data for the United States appear in Figure 17-5 on page 401, which shows the ratio of federal debt to GNP since 1789. We see dramatically how wars drove up the ratio of debt to GNP, but rapid growth with roughly balanced budgets in peacetime normally reduced the ratio of debt to GNP. Studies also show that government debt has grown more slowly than private debt (items like bonds and mortgages) from 1945 to 1980.

After 1980, the historical patterns changed. Because of the Reagan fiscal policies, government deficits climbed well above those seen in earlier periods of peace and prosperity. The debt/GNP ratio rose sharply. Economists began to worry that America was entering a period when high debt levels would constrain the growth of government programs and would require heavy taxes to service the debt. The unprecedented increase in the peacetime federal debt gives added importance to a careful analysis of the burdens of a large government debt, a topic we take up next.

Some Old Myths

Before we turn to the genuine burdens of the debt, let us first dispose of some ancient but hardy myths.

- "How can the government go on running up debt? If my spouse and I lived beyond our means and ran a debt, we'd soon learn what trouble is." This person has assumed that what is folly for an individual is therefore necessarily folly for a nation.

- "Why do conservatives always complain about the size of the government debt? Private debt has grown even faster than public debt, and business leaders never complain about that! If people are to invest, they must be able to borrow, and the devil take the squeamish." The speaker here is also using an anal-

---

[7] In measuring the federal government debt, we exclude debt held by government agencies (which the government owes itself) and debt held by the Federal Reserve System (which is effectively part of the monetary base and costs the government no interest since the Federal Reserve does not pay interest on bank reserves). Debt held by government agencies and the Fed at the beginning of fiscal year 1989 adds another $670 billion to the federal debt, the total known as the "gross federal debt" as opposed to the "debt held by the public" analyzed here.

ogy to private finance, but in this case assumes that the advantages of private debt carry over to government debt.

These are but two common myths about the government debt. Both cases result from the fallacy of composition—which holds that what is true for individuals is also true for the entire economy. But the analogy does not necessarily hold. We cannot simply assume that private vices are public vices. We must instead carefully analyze the facts and theories and decide whether or not a nation is benefited by a large government debt.

GENUINE DEBT BURDENS

What then are the real problems posed by a large government debt? We discuss three here: the need to service an external debt; the efficiency losses from taxes

GOVERNMENT DEBT AND INTEREST CHARGES RELATIVE TO GROSS NATIONAL PRODUCT

(1) YEAR	(2) FEDERAL GOVERNMENT DEBT (billions)	(3) INTEREST CHARGES ON GOVERNMENT DEBT (billions)	(4) GNP (billions)	(5) DEBT/GNP (5) = (2)/(4)	(6) INTEREST CHARGES AS A PERCENTAGE OF GNP (6) = 100 × (3)/(4)
United States					
1988	$1,790	$153.	$4,843	0.37	3.2
1980	594	53.3	2,732	0.22	2.0
1945	211	4.1	213	0.99	1.9
1940	33.3	0.86	100.4	0.33	0.9
1930	16.0	0.61	90.8	0.18	0.7
1920	24.1	1.02	91.9	0.26	1.1
1915	0.97	0.02	40.2	0.02	0.05
1868	2.60	0.13	6.8	0.38	1.9
Britain					
1985	£158	£14.0	£355	0.45	3.9
1975	46.4	2.8	106	0.44	2.6
1945	21.4	0.4	9.9	2.16	4.3
1925	7.6	0.3	4.9	1.55	6.3
1915	1.1	0.0	3.3	0.33	0.6
1818	0.8	0.0	0.4	2.00	7.5

Table 17-3   **Alternative measures of the size of the debt**

The absolute size of the government debt is always frighteningly large. From an economic perspective, it is important to compare the size of the debt to GNP [in column (5)], or to measure the amount of GNP that must go to cover interest payments [in column (6)].

Note how Britain's debt burden in the past was many times larger than it is today. Also, see how American fiscal policies of the 1980s led to a dramatic increase in U.S. debt burdens.

(Source: U.S. Departments of Commerce and Treasury; Great Britain, Central Statistical Office, *Annual Abstract of Statistics;* authors' updating. For the United States, government debt is defined to be all federal interest-bearing debt held outside the federal government and outside the Federal Reserve System.)

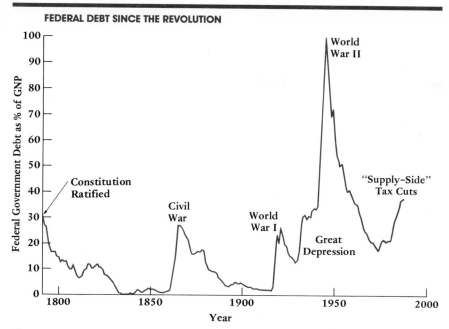

FEDERAL DEBT SINCE THE REVOLUTION

Figure 17-5   The ratio of government debt to GNP rose in wars, then declined afterward—but rose sharply after 1980

Until recently, the federal government ran large deficits during wartime, which led to a ballooning government debt and debt/GNP ratio. Then in peacetime, budgets were close to balance and the debt/GNP ratio declined.

However, the Reagan fiscal policies of the 1980s reversed this trend, with large tax cuts accompanied by expenditure increases. As a result, the United States more than tripled its government debt in 8 years. (Source: U.S. Department of Treasury for debt; historical data on GNP from U.S. Department of Commerce and private scholars. Note that GNP data before 1900 are approximate, but the debt/GNP ratio is reasonably accurate. Holdings of government debt by the federal government or the Federal Reserve are excluded.)

to pay interest and principal; and the displacement of capital when people hold public debt rather than capital-based assets.

External vs. Internal Debt

The first distinction to be made is between an internal and an external debt. An *internal debt* is owed by a nation to its own citizens. Many argue that an internal debt poses no burden because "we owe it all to ourselves." While this statement is oversimplified, it does represent a genuine insight. If every citizen owned $10,000 of government bonds and all were equally liable for the taxes to service that debt, it would not make sense to think of a heavy load of debt that each citizen must carry.

An *external debt*, one owed by a nation to foreigners, does involve a net subtraction from the goods and services available to people in the debtor nation. Many nations in the 1980s—Poland, Brazil, and Mexico being prime examples—labored under severe economic hardships after they incurred large external debts. They were forced to export more than they imported—to run trade surpluses—in order to service their external debts, that is, to pay the interest and principal on their past borrowings. In the mid-1980s, countries like Brazil and Mexico needed to pay one-fourth to one-third of their export earnings to service their external debts. The debt-service burden on an external debt represents a reduction in the consumption possibilities of a nation.

In the late 1980s, the United States was added to the list of debtor countries. Because the large federal budget deficit was financed by negative net foreign investment (that is, by borrowing from abroad), the United States turned from a creditor nation to a debtor nation. Economists project that by 1990 the United States will owe $750 billion to foreigners. What will be the impact of this debt on the U.S. economy? The United States will eventually need to run a trade surplus to pay the interest on its foreign loans, exporting many billions of dollars more in aircraft, food, and manufactured goods than it imports. Indeed, just to pay the real interest rate on the $750 billion of foreign debt would require an export surplus of around $30 billion. The difficulties of making this adjustment will be studied in the final chapters of this text.

Efficiency Losses from Taxation

An internal debt requires payments of interest to bondholders, and taxes must be levied for this purpose. But even if the same people are taxed to pay on the average the same amounts they receive in interest, there will still be the *distorting effects on incentives* that are inescapably present in the case of any taxes. Taxing Paula's interest income or wages to pay Paula interest will introduce microeconomic distortions. Paula may work less hard and may save less—and either of these outcomes may be reckoned a distortion of efficiency and well-being.[8]

Displacement of Capital

Perhaps the most serious consequence of a large public debt is that it displaces capital from the nation's stock of wealth.

How could this happen? To provide for old age or for whatever reason, people hold their wealth in a variety of assets: housing, stocks and bonds of corporations, savings accounts (which are often re-lent to companies to finance their investment), and government bonds. We can separate the assets into two piles: (a) government debt and (b) those assets that ultimately represent ownership of private capital, land, and similar items.

Let's say for simplicity that people want to hold a fixed amount of wealth in stocks, bonds, real estate, and so forth; say the desired holdings are 1000 units. Then as the government bonds increase, people's holdings of other assets must be reduced since total desired wealth holdings are fixed. But recall that these assets ultimately represent private capital and other real private assets. If the government debt goes up 100 units, we would see that people's holdings of capital and other private assets fall by 100 units. We thus say that *private capital may be displaced by government debt.*

The case where 100 units of government debt displace 100 units of capital is extreme and unlikely to occur in practice. Rather, as the next section's supply-and-demand analysis shows, it is more likely that the displacement will be partial; that is, 100 units of government debt are likely to displace somewhere between 0 and 100 units of capital. The exact amount of displacement will depend on the conditions of production and on the savings behavior of households.

A Geometric Analysis[9] The process by which capital is displaced in the long run is illustrated in Figure 17-6.[10] In the left panel we show the supply and demand for capital as a function of the real interest rate or return on capital. As interest rates rise, firms demand less capital, while individuals may want to supply more. The equilibrium shown is for a capital stock of 4000 units with a real interest rate of 4 percent.

Now say that the government debt rises from 0 to 1000—because of war, recession, expansionary fiscal policies, or whatever reason. We can analyze the

---

[8] The efficiency losses of taxes are reviewed in the second half of Chapter 33.

[9] The balance of the discussion of displacement is somewhat more technical and can be omitted in short courses.

[10] This supply-and-demand diagram is explained at greater length in Chapter 30.

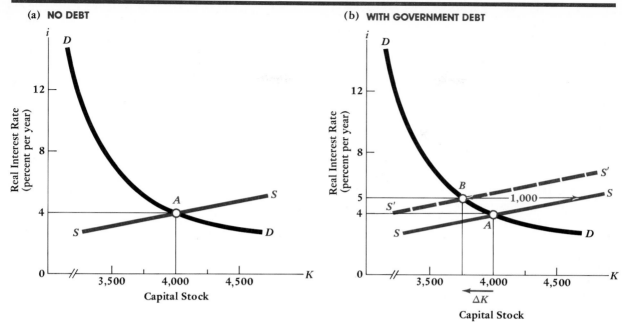

Figure 17-6   Government debt displaces private capital

We show here the supply and demand for capital. Capital is demanded by firms—they need capital for inventories, factories, trucks, and computers. Households supply capital by saving in stocks, bonds, real estate, and so forth. Thus the *DD* curve is the downward-sloping business demand for *K* and the *SS* curve is the upward-sloping household supply of *K*. Both of these are assumed to respond to the real interest rate.

Panel **(a)** shows the equilibrium without government debt. *K* is 4000 and the real interest rate is 4 percent.

Panel **(b)** shows what happens if the government debt is 1000 units. The 1000 units of government debt will be sold off for what it will yield, so that is the bedrock of households' portfolios. Thus the curve showing the *net* supply of *K* shifts to the left by the 1000 units of the government debt. The new equilibrium arises northwest along the demand-for-*K* curve, moving from point *A* to point *B*. The interest rate is higher (5 instead of 4 percent), firms are discouraged from holding *K*, and the capital stock falls from 4000 to 3750, as is shown by the little red arrow under **(b)**.

Thus the 1000 units of government debt in the long run displace 250 units of society's capital stock, and output is therefore smaller.

(These numbers are only illustrative, for we do not know the extent to which public debt displaces private capital.)

impact of the increase in debt in the right-hand diagram of Figure 17-6. This figure shows the 1000-unit increase in debt as a shift in the supply of capital (or *SS*) curve. As depicted, the households' supply-of-capital schedule shifts 1000 units to the left, to the new *S'S'* curve.

Why do we represent an increase in government debt as a leftward shift in the households' supply-of-capital schedule? Because the *SS* curve represents the amount of capital that people willingly hold at each interest rate, the capital holdings are equal to the total wealth holdings minus the holdings of government debt. Since the amount of government debt (or assets aside from capital) rises by 1000 and the government debt must be sold, the amount of private capital that people can buy after they own the 1000 of government debt is 1000 less than total wealth at each interest rate. Therefore, if *SS* represents the total wealth held by people, *S'S'* (equal to *SS* less 1000) represents the total amount of capital held by people. In short, the new supply-of-capital schedule after 1000 units of government debt are sold is $S'S'$.[11]

What is the net impact of a 1000-unit increase in government debt? As the supply of capital dries up—with national saving going into government bonds rather than into housing or into companies' stocks and bonds—the market equilibrium moves northwest along the demand-for-K curve. Interest rates rise. Firms slow their purchases of new factories, trucks, and computers.

In the new long-run equilibrium, the capital stock falls from 4000 to 3750. Thus, in this example, the 1000 of government debt has displaced 250 of private capital. Such a reduction has significant economic effects, of course. With less capital, potential output, wages, and the nation's income are lower than they would otherwise be.

The diagram shown in Figure 17-6 is purely illustrative. How large is the displacement effect in reality? Does the $1790 billion of government debt at the beginning of 1989 displace $1790 billion of capital? Or $1000 billion? Or none? In fact, economists have little precise information about the size of the displacement effect. Looking at the long trends of history, particularly at the postwar period in the United States, the best evidence is that some capital is indeed displaced by government debt but that the displacement is only a fraction of the added debt. The precise answer is one for future generations of economists to determine. It is clear, however, that the possibility of capital displacement is extraordinarily important for the United States as the debt continues to climb in the next few years.

Valediction

With the debate about the government debt and its impact upon future economic growth, we come to the end of our chapters on macroeconomics. Before we end, pause a moment to consider the sobering fiscal facts that will face the generation that will study economics, or make economic policies, in the 1990s. They will confront a large external debt, significant potential efficiency costs from the need to service the public debt, and possibly large capital displacement effects. The need to reduce the fiscal and the trade deficits will haunt the nation for many years to come. But in the midst of today's tempest, it is well to keep in mind the words of the great English historian, Lord Macaulay, written more than a century ago on growth and debt:

> At every stage in the growth of that debt, the nation has set up the same cry of anguish and despair. At every stage in the growth of that debt, it has been seriously asserted by wise men that bankruptcy and ruin were at hand. Yet still the debt went on growing; and still bankruptcy and ruin were as remote as ever. . . .
>
> The prophets of evil were under a double delusion. They erroneously imagined that there was an exact analogy between the case of an individual who is in debt to another individual and the case of a society which is in debt to a part of itself. . . . They made no allowance for the effect produced by the incessant progress of every experimental science, and by the incessant efforts of every man to get on in life. They saw that the debt grew; and they forgot that other things grew as well.

What can the wisdom of Macaulay teach us for the 1980s and 1990s? We can hardly doubt that the high fiscal deficits are producing an unprecedented growth in peacetime debt in the United States. Because much of the debt is flowing abroad to finance a large trade deficit, the nation will face rising interest payments, debt burdens, and taxes to service the debt. At some point, the trade deficit will have to turn to a surplus as we export our future production to pay for current consumption. It is possible that the transition from today's low-saving economy to the future high-saving economy may be accompanied by turmoil in financial markets or even by reductions in living standards for consumers.

But it would be unwise to forecast economic collapse. The specter of national bankruptcy or financial ruin is remote for the United States in the 1990s.

---

[11] An argument by Robert Barro of Harvard suggests that, because of future taxes, people may act as if government bonds have no net value. For every dollar of government bonds there is an equal amount in the present value of taxes (for which they feel liable now or in the future). If people are very farsighted and take their heirs' well-being into account, then they may simply reduce their consumption by just the present value of taxes—completely offsetting the wealth effect of the bonds. In such a case, there will be no shift in the SS curve of Fig. 17-6(b).

SUMMARY

A. Budgets and Fiscal Policy

1. Fiscal policy refers to taxation and expenditure policies, to budget surpluses and deficits. In this connection, the modern economy is blessed with important "built-in stabilizers." Requiring no discretionary action, tax receipts change automatically when income changes. This reduces the multiplier and wipes out part of any disturbance. The same stabilizing effect is created by unemployment compensation and other welfare transfers that automatically grow as income falls.

2. Automatic stabilizers never fully offset the instabilities of an economy. They reduce the multiplier, but do not make it zero. Scope is left for discretionary programs. Discretionary policies include public works, jobs programs, and various tax programs. Public works involve such long time lags in getting under way as to make their use to combat short recessions impractical. Discretionary variations in tax rates have greater short-run flexibility but suffer from severe political complications in the United States.

3. When people began to drop the notion that the government's budget had to be balanced in every year or month, they first thought it would be in balance over the business cycle—with boom-time surpluses matching depression deficits. Today, it is realized that only by coincidence would the surpluses in prosperous years just balance deficits in the recession years.

4. To get a better measure of changes in discretionary fiscal policy, economists supplement knowledge of the budget by separating the actual budget into its structural and cyclical components. The structural budget calculates how much the government would collect and spend if the economy were operating at potential output. The cyclical budget calculates the impact of the business cycle on tax revenues, expenditures, and the deficit. For measuring the impact of fiscal policy on the economy, we should pay close attention to the structural deficit; changes in the cyclical deficit are a result of changes in the economy rather than a cause of changes in the economy.

B. The Interaction of Monetary and Fiscal Policies

5. In setting the optimal monetary and fiscal policies, we face two considerations: the appropriate level of aggregate demand and the best monetary-fiscal mix. The mix of fiscal and monetary policies helps determine the composition of GNP. A high-investment strategy, for example, would call for a budget surplus along with an expansionary monetary policy. The mix in practice has evolved toward a very loose fiscal and tight monetary policy—a sure recipe for a low ratio of investment to GNP and for slow growth of potential output.

6. A pervasive concern has been that government deficits "crowd out" investment. This statement only makes sense for structural deficits (i.e., for policies that raise the structural deficit). Even then, there is mixed evidence on the extent of crowding out. Evidence from the high-deficit era of the 1980s points to a complex set of reactions to deficits, including lower domestic and foreign investment.

The extent to which active fiscal policy will crowd out investment also depends upon the state of the business cycle. Crowding out becomes important and damaging when output and employment are high and total resources are limited. But active fiscal policy, if introduced at a time of deep-recession shock, may on balance encourage rather than crowd out investment. Why? Because business may be induced to spend on plant and equipment when its sales have been elevated—and this "accelerator" effect can outweigh interest-rate crowding-out effects until the system begins to approach high employment.

C. Economic Consequences of Government Debt

7. The public debt does not burden the shoulders of a nation as if its citizens were forced to carry rocks on their backs. To the degree that we borrow from abroad for consumption and pledge posterity to pay back the interest and principal on such external debt, we do place upon that posterity a net burden. Our descendants will indeed find a subtraction from what they can consume.

8. To the degree that we bequeath to posterity an internal debt but no change in capital stock beyond what would otherwise have been given them, there are various internal effects. The process of taxing Peter to pay Paula, or taxing Paula to pay Paula, can have definite costs: these involve various distortions of production and efficiency but should not be confused with owing money to another country.

9. In addition, there may be a serious cost if the public debt displaces capital in people's portfolios. This arises because firms' bonds and common stocks are good substitutes for government bonds. Hence, an increase in government debt may reduce the economy's capital stock.

10. It is important, also, to keep in perspective the size of the federal debt in relation to gross national product and interest charges. The growth of the debt must be appraised in terms of the growth of the economy as a whole. From 1945 to 1980 the ratio of government debt to private debt and to gross national product fell substantially, but the ratio of debt to GNP has risen sharply during the 1980s.

CONCEPTS FOR REVIEW

budget deficit, surplus
government debt
discretionary policies vs. automatic
  stabilizers
automatic stabilization and the reduced
  multiplier
tools of discretionary policy
budget: actual, structural, cyclical
demand management

fiscal-monetary mix
crowding out vs. investment
  encouragement
internal vs. external debt
Gramm-Rudman bill
real debt burdens: distortions from
  taxation, displacement of capital
ratios of debt to GNP over space and
  time

QUESTIONS FOR DISCUSSION

1. Define automatic and discretionary stabilizers. What would be your preferred discretionary stabilizer for fighting inflation? For fighting recessions? Which discretionary stabilizers seem least useful? Why?

2. From the early 1870s to the middle 1890s, depressions were deep and prolonged, booms were short-lived and relatively anemic, and the price level was declining. What long-run fiscal policy would have been appropriate then? Would your answer be the same for the following 20 years leading up to the First World War, a period of chronic, demand-pull inflation?

3. Recall the definition of the structural and cyclical deficits. For each of the following, analyze the effects on the actual, structural, and cyclical deficits:

    (a) A permanent tax cut
    (b) A sharp decrease in private investment
    (c) A tightening of monetary policy
    (d) An increase in exports
    (e) An increase in welfare benefit levels
    (f) An increase in tax evasion

4. Explain why, in a classical and monetarist world (such as shown in Figure 17-3), a tax cut would crowd out investment slightly less than dollar for dollar. (HINT: Remember the *MPC* is less than 1.)

5. In year 0, GNP is 1000, taxes are 200, and government spending is 250. Output is equal to potential output. In year 1, the government undertakes a fiscal expansion that increases G to 270. If taxes are unaffected by changes in income, and the expenditure multiplier is 2, what is the impact of the fiscal expansion upon the structural and cyclical budgets? How would your answer change if tax revenues rise 20 cents for every dollar increase in GNP?

6. What phase of the business cycle is the country now in? What is the current fiscal-monetary mix? What tax and expenditure policies seem appropriate? How would you vary the relative mix of policy (expenditures, taxes, and the money supply) to fight unemployment or inflation?

7. J. M. Keynes wrote, "If the Treasury were to fill old bottles with banknotes, bury them in disused coal mines, and leave it to private enterprise to dig the notes up again, there need be no more unemployment and the real income of the community would probably become a good deal greater than it actually is" (*The General Theory*, p. 129, edited from the original). Explain why Keynes' analysis of the utility of a discretionary public-works program might be correct during a depression. Can you think of fiscal or monetary policies that would have the same macroeconomic impacts and while producing a larger quantity of useful goods and services?

8. Is it possible that government *promises* might have a displacement effect along with government debt? Thus, if the government were to promise large future social security benefits to workers (i.e., larger than the workers would pay in as taxes) could workers feel richer? Could they reduce saving as a result? Could the capital stock end up smaller? Illustrate using Figure 17-6.

9. Trace the impact upon the government debt, the nation's capital stock, and real output of a government program that borrows abroad and spends the money on the following:

(a) Grain to feed its population (as did Poland in the 1970s)

(b) Capital to drill for oil, which is sold for exports (as did Mexico in the 1970s)

10. Professor Robert Eisner of Northwestern University wrote as follows: "Significant cuts in our budget deficits, whether by slashing expenditures or raising taxes, pose a serious danger. They will . . . hold down consumption, but in the process they are likely to drag down investments and along with them GNP, employment, and profits." Analyze the reasoning behind this statement in terms of the crowding-out debate. What do the lessons of history suggest about Eisner's contention?

11. Explain how a change in the mix of monetary and fiscal policies could reduce the budget deficit, increase domestic investment, and maintain the same level of real GNP and inflation.

12. The following table shows the major components of federal spending and revenues, along with the deficit, for 1987. Although most economists and policymakers agreed that reducing the federal budget deficit was the top economic priority of the late 1980s, there was no agreement on how the deficit should be reduced. Among the major proposals for deficit reduction were the following:

(a) Reduce defense spending

(b) Raise taxes on personal incomes and on personal consumption

(c) Lower interest rates to reduce the interest component of federal spending

Comment on the economic impacts of each of these proposals on GNP as a whole and on the different components of GNP. What change in the fiscal-monetary mix could be taken to offset the impacts of each on aggregate demand?

COMPONENT OF BUDGET	AMOUNT (billions), 1987
Expenditures	
Defense spending	$295
Other purchases	87
Net interest paid	143
Transfer payments	414
Other	136
Revenues	
Personal taxes	406
Corporate profits taxes	106
Social-insurance taxes	351
Sales, excise, and other indirect taxes	54
Deficit	**158**

(Source: U.S. Department of Commerce.)

13. Advanced problem on debt dynamics: The "primary budget" is defined as the budget excluding interest payments (i.e., it includes all payments and receipts except interest). Assume that the primary budget is balanced. Denote the ratio of government debt to nominal GNP as d, while q represents the growth of nominal GNP, and i is the nominal interest rate.

What is the relationship between i and q that will lead to an exploding debt/GNP ratio? To a d ratio that tends to zero? Refer to a recent copy of the *Economic Report of the President* to calculate i and q. What can you conclude about the trends in d shown in Figure 17-5 from the data you have collected?

14. Advanced problem. Figure 17-7 shows a recent estimate of the accumulation of assets by the social security trust fund (which is, in effect, the opposite of government debt) over the next seven decades, as a percent of GNP. Assuming that the Gramm-Rudman bill succeeds in balancing the rest of the budget after 1992, what would be the impact of the buildup of the trust fund on the capital stock and national output:

    (a) Assuming that the trust fund retires government debt?

    (b) Assuming that the Barro hypothesis (in footnote 11, p. 404) is correct?

    (c) Assuming that people change their private pension contributions to offset on a dollar-for-dollar basis payments to social security?

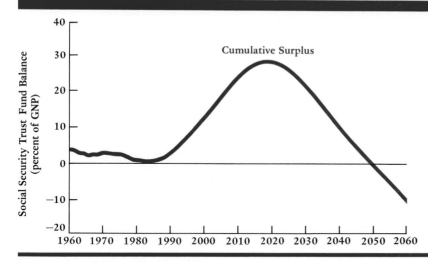

Figure 17-7   Estimated accumulation of assets in social security trust fund

Estimates show the extent to which cumulative social security taxes plus interest on balances exceed cumulative benefits. Because tax rates are relatively high in the next 3 decades, social security trust fund is projected to reach around one-fourth of GNP. What will be the effect on the capital stock and national output? [Source: Henry Aaron, Barry Bosworth, and Gary Burtless, *OASDI Trust Fund Policy, National Saving, and the Economy* (Brookings, Washington, D.C., 1988).]

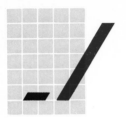

APPENDIX: 17

Advanced Treatment of Monetary and Fiscal Policy

CLASSICAL THEMES

Before Keynes wrote the *General Theory,* the major economic thinkers generally adhered to the classical view of the economy. As incredible as it may seem, the early economists were little concerned with unemployment. Rather, they were fascinated with the Industrial Revolution that was lifting the Western world out of muddy fields and into dusty factories.

Early discussion revolved around *Say's law of markets.* This theory, named for the French writer J. B. Say and put forth in 1803, states that overproduction is impossible by its very nature. In more approachable language, this is today expressed as ''supply creates its own demand.''

What is the rationale for Say's Law? It rests on a view that there is no essential difference between a monetary and a barter economy—that if factories can produce more, workers will be there to buy the output.

The durable and valid core of Say's Law is shown in Figure 17A-1. This is a world where prices and wages are determined in competitive markets, moving flexibly up and

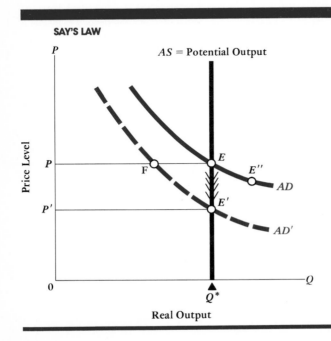

SAY'S LAW

Figure 17A-1 According to Say's Law, supply creates its own demand as prices move to balance demand with aggregate supply

Many early classical economists thought that persistent periods of glut could not occur. If *AD* or *AS* shifted, prices would flexibly react to ensure that full-employment output was sold. Here we see how flexible prices ensure that prices move down enough to increase spending to full-employment output. (What would happen if *AD* were unchanged, but full-employment output increased? What forces would move the economy to *E″*? Why might sticky wages and prices lead to a situation where supply cannot create its own demand, with the economy stuck at *F*?)

down to eliminate any excess demand or supply. Thus if aggregate demand declines (because of a monetary contraction or other factors), the equilibrium will rapidly travel down the vertical AS curve from E to E'. In this valid version of Say's Law, supply creates its own demand because prices and wages adjust upward or downward to ensure that aggregate spending equals potential output.

A long line of the most distinguished economists—D. Ricardo, J. S. Mill, and A. Marshall—subscribed more or less firmly to the macroeconomic view that overproduction is impossible. For example, as late as 1933, with an unemployment rate of 25 percent in the United States, with Hitler's Third Reich rising from the ashes of the inflation-torn Weimar Republic, with fascism spreading across Europe—the eminent classical economist A. C. Pigou could still write from Cambridge, England (in *The Theory of Unemployment*): "With perfectly free competition there will always be a strong tendency toward full employment. Such unemployment as exists at any time is due wholly to the frictional resistances [that] prevent the appropriate wage and price adjustments being made instantaneously."

MODERN TREATMENTS: *IS-LM* ANALYSIS

As we have seen, modern mainstream macroeconomists have learned much since the days of the classical economists. We now know that, if prices and wages are inflexible, the economy can suffer extended spells of unemployment or inflation or both. Look again at Figure 17A-1, and ask what would happen if wages and prices were firmly frozen at level P and the aggregate demand curve shifted from AD to AD'. Supply no longer could create its own demand. Rather, the equilibrium would move to F, and output would fall below the full-employment level. This case is exactly the critique that Keynes and others launched against the early believers in Say's Law. Moreover, fiscal and monetary policies are now known to have rather different and subtle effects on the economy—affecting interest rates and the level and composition of output.

The tools of the main text can show some of the ways that monetary and fiscal policies affect the economy. But a deeper understanding can be achieved by use of an important tool known as *IS-LM analysis,* which summarizes concisely the main features of modern mainstream macroeconomics. It shows the interaction between output, money, and interest rates, and highlights some central points of current macroeconomic debates.

We proceed by making the simplifying assumptions that prices are constant and that the central bank holds the money supply fixed (or on a predetermined trajectory).

The *IS* Curve

Start by examining the IS curve (which stands for "investment equals saving") in Figure 17A-2. The IS curve depicts in a single line the relationship between interest rates and output that our more complex three-quadrant diagram showed back in Figure 16-4. The IS curve shows that, at lower levels of the interest rate, investment, and hence equilibrium GNP, will be higher. It is called the IS curve because it is the combinations of interest rates and outputs for which planned investment (I) equals planned saving (S).

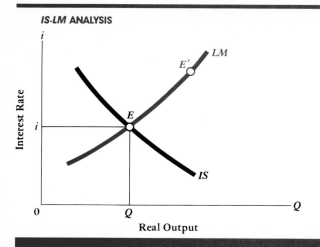

Figure 17A-2   The *IS-LM* approach depicts investment-saving equilibrium in *IS* curve, and money market equilibrium in *LM* curve

The *IS* curve represents the combinations of interest rates and outputs where planned saving equals planned investment. The *LM* curve shows the *(i, Q)* combinations where the supply and demand for money are equal.

Where both goods and money markets are in equilibrium, we have *IS* and *LM* intersection. Thus at point *E*, demand and supply of money are equal, and planned saving equals planned investment. Point *E* hence represents the macroeconomic equilibrium levels of output and interest rates.

The *LM* Curve

Next turn to examine the *LM* curve, which shows the supply and demand in money markets. Figure 17A-3 shows how the *LM* curve is derived. This figure is similar to Figure 16-2, showing a vertical supply-of-money schedule (reflecting the assumption that the central bank has a fixed-*M* target) and a demand for money that responds negatively to interest rates. The equilibrium interest rate comes at the intersection of supply and demand, shown at point *E* in Figure 17A-3.

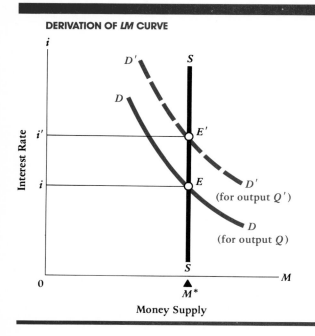

Figure 17A-3   Supply and demand in the money market lead to *LM* curve

The vertical line at *M** is the money supply, fixed by the Federal Reserve. It is vertical to represent the fact that the Fed sets a fixed money supply no matter what the interest rate.

The demand for money is represented by *DD*. It slopes downward (as in Fig. 16-2) because higher interest rates lead people and firms to economize on their cash balances.

But we can also see how a higher level of GNP changes the equilibrium in the money market. As GNP rises (from *Q* to *Q'*) the demand-for-money curve moves from *DD* to *D'D'*. Interest rates must rise to induce people to hold the same amount of *M*. Hence, *(i, Q)* and *(i', Q')* are two different points (*E* and *E'*) on Fig. 17A-2's *LM* curve.

But recall that the demand-for-money graph pushes into the background one very important feature—that people hold money largely for transactions purposes. As output and income rise, the demand for money increases at each interest rate. So if we want to consider the effect of a higher level of GNP, we must shift the demand-for-money schedule to the right in Figure 17A-3, from DD to $D'D'$. The new money market equilibrium with higher output hence is shown at point E' in Figure 17A-3, with a higher equilibrium interest rate.

We are now ready to derive the LM curve, so called because it gives us the set of interest-rate–output combinations that ensure that money demand (known in earlier days as ''liquidity preference,'' hence L) is equal to the fixed supply of money. Simply put, each point on the LM curve represents a couplet of interest rates and output levels for which the demand and supply of money are equal.

Why does LM slope upward? Say GNP increases; as the level of GNP increases, transactions demand for M also increases. But the supply of M did not increase. So, the excess demand for M was choked off by higher interest rates, as was illustrated in Figure 17A-3. To put it in a somewhat oversimplified way, transactions needs for M drive out interest-sensitive holdings of M. The higher transactions M is found by coaxing some people into bonds or savings accounts and out of money.

To see the relationship between the LM curve and the money market, examine points E and E' in Figures 17A-2 and 17A-3. Note how higher output Q' is seen at the upper right of the LM curve in Figure 17A-2, at E'—along with a higher interest rate. (Work through the relationship between points E and E' in Figures 17A-2 and 17A-3.)

Interaction

Now that we have derived the IS and LM curves, go back to Figure 17A-2. Remember that the IS curve is the combination of output and interest rates for which spending is at equilibrium because planned investment equals planned saving and that the LM curve represents money market equilibrium.

Therefore, at the intersection of the IS and LM curves, *both* the goods market and the money market are in equilibrium. So the macroeconomic equilibrium of output and interest rates is jointly determined by the IS curve's spending relation and the LM curve's money market equilibrium. Only at point E is the money supply just sufficient to produce an interest rate that balances planned saving and planned investment.

A Monetarist *LM* Curve

One of the most important applications of *IS-LM* analysis is to highlight aspects of the monetarist debate. Recall that many monetarists believe that velocity is constant or stable, and that the demand for money is insensitive to interest rates. In terms of the quantity equation, $Q \equiv MV/P$, where V is velocity. We take M and P to be fixed, while velocity is thought by many monetarists to be near-constant, so output is simply equal to MV/P. Thus the LM curve is precisely vertical at output level MV/P.

If the demand for money is completely insensitive to interest rates, the LM curve is vertical.

EFFECT OF POLICY SHIFTS

Monetary Policy

We now put our *IS-LM* apparatus to work by examining the effect of monetary and fiscal policies. What if the Fed engineers an increase in *M*? What will that do to the *LM* curve? This case is shown in Figure 17A-4. After the policy change, at the old interest rate, the supply of money exceeds the demand for money. In order for people to be willing to hold the extra money, output would have to be higher to induce a higher transactions demand for money. Equilibrium in the money market thus requires a higher level of output at every interest rate. A money-supply increase therefore shifts out the *LM* curve.

What is the impact of monetary policy on the *IS* curve? In this case, the *IS* curve is unchanged because the monetary shift was not accompanied by changes in spending.

Note the impact of an increase in *M*: the rightward shift of *LM* moves the economy to point E^M, increases equilibrium GNP, and decreases equilibrium interest rates. *Expansionary monetary policy moves the economy to a new equilibrium, with a higher level of output and a lower interest rate.*

Fiscal Policy

In contrast to monetary policy, fiscal policy shifts the *IS* curve. What would be the impact of a change in *G* with unchanged *M*? An increase in government purchases (or indeed an increase in any component of aggregate demand or a tax cut which tends to increase spending) will shift the *IS* curve rightward to a new position such as *IS′*.

This shift occurs because a *G* increase leads to a higher level of GNP at each interest rate. Thus, *expansionary fiscal policy leads to a new equilibrium at E^F, up and to the right on the unshifted LM curve, with GNP and i both higher.*

Crowding Out

One of the important controversies of modern macroeconomics concerns the extent to which government spending will crowd out investment. The mechanism is easily visualized in Figure 17A-4. A fiscal expansion shifts the *IS* curve to *IS′*, producing a new equilibrium at E^F. Interest rates are seen to rise. Depending on the degree to which interest rates rise and on the interest-sensitivity of investment, investment will decline and hence be *crowded out* by the fiscal expansion. A rough index of the degree to which investment is crowded out is the extent to which the new equilibrium is to the left of the equilibrium that would come if interest rates were constant.

Note that if the *LM* curve is relatively flat, then little investment is crowded out. On the other hand, if the *LM* curve is very steep, the extent of crowding out is large.

How does this analysis differ from the simple multiplier in Chapter 9? There we showed the effect of fiscal policy on output for a *given* interest rate (as well as a given price level). The simple multiplier there calculated the magnitude of the rightward shift in the *IS* curve at each interest rate. But that earlier analysis was incomplete, for it ignored the impact of the money market; it ignored the fact that the higher output would increase interest rates and thereby crowd out some investment. Once we examine both *IS* and *LM* curves, we can see the complete effects of fiscal policy.

POLICY CHANGES SHIFT *IS* OR *LM* CURVE

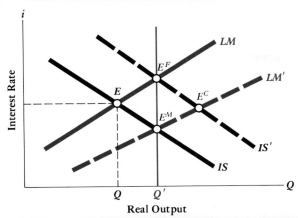

Figure 17A-4   Shifting *IS* and *LM* curves depict macroeconomic-policy changes

Start out at equilibrium *E*. A monetary expansion shifts the *LM* curve to the right, to *LM'*. This leads to lower interest rates and a higher equilibrium GNP.

A fiscal expansion shifts the *IS* curve to the right at every interest rate, to *IS'*. Tax cuts or spending increases thus lead to higher interest rates and higher GNP.

What does a combined fiscal and monetary expansion do? It unambiguously increases GNP, as at E^C, but the effect on interest rates is unclear.

Up to now we have discussed "pure" fiscal or monetary policies. However, governments often change fiscal and monetary policies at the same time. For example, an increased budget deficit may be financed partly by an increase in the money supply. This implies both an expansionary fiscal and an expansionary monetary policy.

Such a case is shown in Figure 17A-4. There we shift both the *IS* curve (to show the change in fiscal policy) and the *LM* curve (to show the change in monetary policy). In our example of the budget deficit financed through monetary expansion, the new equilibrium would be established at a point like E^C.

Monetarist Case   We noted above that in the monetarist case with a fixed velocity of money, the *LM* curve would be vertical. In this case, the basic monetarist propositions can be easily verified. This case is discussed in question 5 at the end of this appendix.

The Monetary-Fiscal Mix

In the main part of this chapter we introduced the concept of the monetary-fiscal mix, which refers to the extent to which monetary and fiscal policies are expansionary or contractionary. The mix is important because the same level of output can be attained by different mixes of monetary and fiscal policies—tight money and loose fiscal policy; loose money and tight fiscal policy; or something in between.

We can see the effect of the monetary-fiscal mix easily by using the *IS-LM* analysis. Look again at Figure 17A-4. Let's say we want output level *Q'*. We see that there are actually two different policy packages that yield output level *Q'*: one at E^F and one at E^M. The upper one at E^F occurs when the mix is tight money and loose fiscal. How do we know this? Because the *LM* curve is relatively high or to the left (indicating that the money supply is relatively low), while the *IS* curve is relatively far to the right (as would occur when the structural budget deficit is high).

We saw that exactly this fiscal-monetary mix was pursued in the early 1980s. Interest rates were relatively high, and investment was pinched. Many observers called for reducing the structural budget deficit. Such a step would be a prelude to changing the monetary-fiscal mix. By tightening fiscal policy (shifting the *IS* curve to the left) while loosening monetary policy (shifting the *LM* curve to the right), the equilibrium would be shifted to E^M in Figure 17A-4. The economic impact would be to reduce the structural budget deficit, lower interest rates, and promote investment and economic growth.

This appendix only skims some of the most important definitions and applications of *IS-LM* analysis. Intermediate textbooks pursue these issues in greater depth.

SUMMARY TO APPENDIX

1. Say's Law held that "supply creates its own demand." Such a view—held by classical economists—cannot stand up to historical evidence or modern analysis.
2. Today, Say's Law is replaced by the *IS-LM* analysis, which synthesizes money-output-interest interdependencies and thus allows a richer discussion of the effects of fiscal and monetary policies than was possible with the simplest tools. The effectiveness of fiscal and monetary policies in changing output—as well as the extent to which expansionary fiscal policy "crowds out" private investment—is seen to depend on the exact shapes of the *IS* and *LM* curves.
3. Monetarists argue that the *LM* curve is practically vertical. In this view fiscal policy is unable to affect output or inflation, while money is all-powerful. Mainstream macroeconomists today tend to be intermediate, believing that both the *IS* and *LM* curves have slope, so that both monetary policy and fiscal policy are potent weapons of macroeconomic control. But all now agree that monetary policy has a powerful effect on output and inflation.
4. The fiscal-monetary mix changes when there are offsetting changes in the *IS* and *LM* curves—keeping output at the same level while changing its composition.

CONCEPTS FOR REVIEW

Say's Law
IS and *LM* curves
effectiveness of fiscal and monetary
  policies

full and partial crowding out
fiscal-monetary mix

QUESTIONS FOR DISCUSSION

1. Show that a rise in *G* or a lowering of taxes will shift *IS* rightward in Figure 17A-2, raising GNP. What will *M* contraction do to the *LM* curve, to GNP, and to *i*?
2. The President says that the Fed's tight-money policies cause big deficits. The Fed says the big budget deficits cause high interest rates. Using the *IS-LM* apparatus, see if you can figure out why both are partly right.
3. Recall the discussion of crowding out in the text of this chapter. Use the *IS-LM* curves to show the following: *(a)* a budget deficit induced by a defense buildup will crowd out investment; (b) a budget deficit induced by a slump in investment (and a leftward shift in the *IS* curve) will *not* crowd out investment.

4. In the 1980s, many economists and public figures were concerned about the tight money and loose fiscal policy.

(a) Draw a set of *IS* and *LM* curves depicting this fiscal-monetary mix.

(b) What would happen to output if the structural budget deficit were cut (say, by cutting defense spending)? Depict such a step in a second diagram. What would you think of taking such a step during a deep recession?

(c) Next assume that the President and Congress say, ''Look here, Federal Reserve, we want you to expand the money supply by just enough to offset the economic contraction induced by our deficit-reducing measures.'' Assuming the Fed complies, draw a third *IS-LM* diagram.

(d) Now carefully list the differences in the macroeconomy between the first and third situations (or diagrams). Make sure you analyze the impact of the change in the fiscal-monetary mix on interest rates, government expenditures, the deficit, taxes, output, and prices.

5. Figure 17A-5 shows a monetarist *LM* curve along with a conventional *IS* curve. Using this diagram show why ''only money matters'' for the determination of GNP. That is, show that changes in the money supply affect GNP. Why does an increase in investment or government spending (unaccompanied by changes in money) shift *IS* to *IS'* but not affect output? Further show that government spending fully crowds out investment and other interest-sensitive spending components.

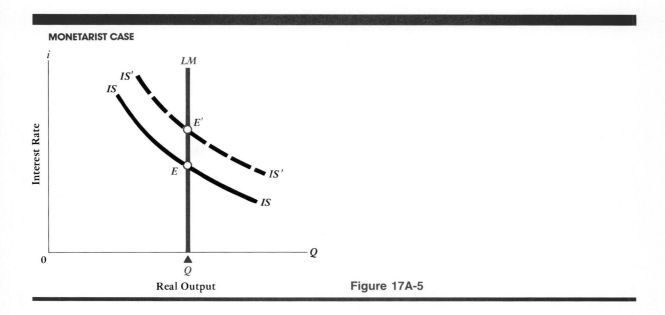

MONETARIST CASE

Figure 17A-5

6. Consider the impact of a rise in the foreign exchange rate of the dollar in the *IS-LM* analysis. When the dollar rises and net exports contract, what impact does this have upon the position of the *IS* curve? Assuming that the *LM* curve is unchanged, what is the impact upon GNP? Using this analysis, can you explain why the rise of the dollar in the early 1980s had a contractionary impact upon the U.S. economy? What would the impact be on foreign economies?

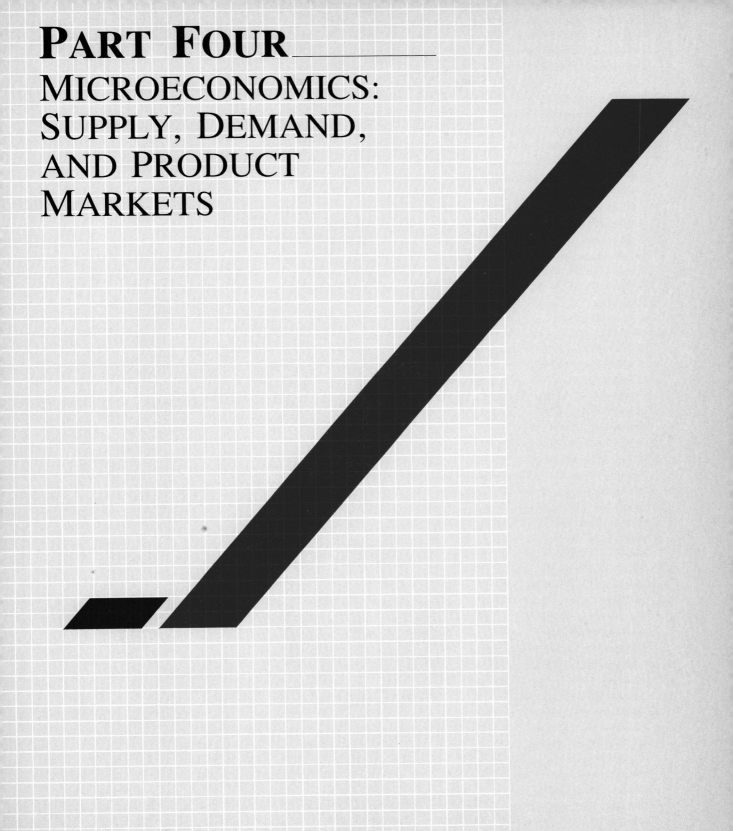

PART FOUR

MICROECONOMICS: SUPPLY, DEMAND, AND PRODUCT MARKETS

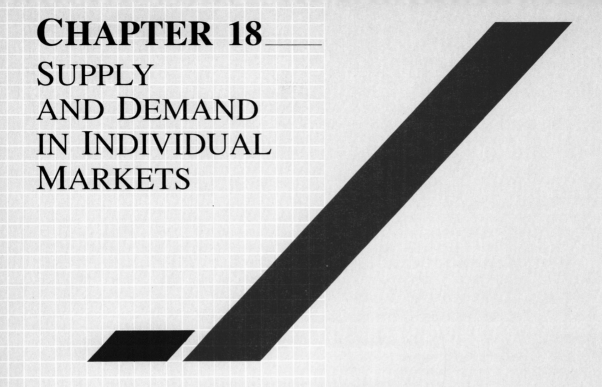

CHAPTER 18____
SUPPLY AND DEMAND IN INDIVIDUAL MARKETS

The end is easily foretold,
When every blessed thing you hold
Is made of silver, or of gold,
You long for simple pewter.

When you have nothing else to wear
But cloth of gold and satins rare,
For cloth of gold you cease to care
Up goes the price of shoddy.

Gilbert and Sullivan
The Gondoliers

IN THE CHAPTERS that follow, we develop the foundations for microeconomics—the study of individual consumers, firms, and markets. Chapters 18 through 25 analyze the workings of product markets—supplies and demands for final goods like food, clothing, and recreation. The subsequent chapters analyze the functioning of factor markets—wages of labor, interest on capital, and rent of land.

Preview

This chapter begins with a review of the tools of supply and demand presented in Chapter 4, presents the important economic concept of elasticity, then ends with some applications of supply and demand. Among the pertinent questions that supply-and-demand analysis can help answer are: Do consumers or producers end up paying a gasoline tax? Why is good weather bad for farmers? What is the effect of a quota or tariff on Japanese automobiles on the price and quantity of automobiles purchased in the United States?

421

After the analysis of product markets in the next several chapters, Part Five follows with a closely related analysis of the determinants of incomes and the prices of factors of production. These chapters examine such issues as: Why have real wages grown 700 percent over the last hundred years? Why do doctors of medicine earn five times more than doctors of divinity? Why does the average woman earn only 65 percent of the average man's wages? Why do the forces determining the salary of a baseball star like Darryl Strawberry parallel those determining the price of a choice plot of Fifth Avenue real estate?

Such questions about the distribution of income require a mastery of the principles of supply and demand as developed in this chapter and beyond. Indeed, understanding virtually all the major microeconomic questions—whether about equity and efficiency, government's economic role, economic growth, or international trade—requires the vital tools we now survey.

Are you concerned about the rising toll of poverty on children and minority groups? If so, you must first study carefully the economic basis of income inequality before you can hope to design lasting and efficient programs for raising the incomes of the poor.

Perhaps you have heard that the low energy prices of the mid-1980s will eventually lead to dangerous levels of dependence on insecure foreign sources of oil. How can we reduce our energy dependence? A thorough study of the supply and demand for oil, as well as of the economics of quotas and tariffs, will clarify the costs and benefits of energy independence.

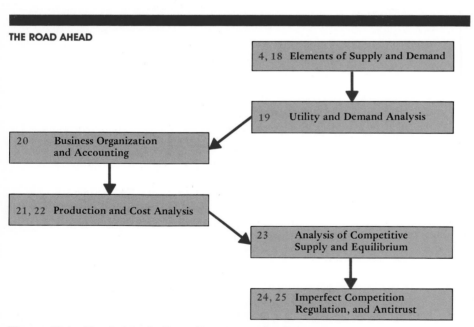

THE ROAD AHEAD

Figure 18-1 Road map to the microeconomic chapters

This flow chart shows the road we will follow in our study of the microeconomics of product markets. We begin with an analysis of the elements of supply and demand and then probe in detail the building blocks of the demand curve. Chapter 20 then surveys the essentials of business organization and accounting.

The next topic involves production and cost analysis, which describes the factors entering production and the way cost is measured. The final three chapters of this Part analyze perfect and imperfect competition along with the fundamentals of regulatory and antitrust policy.

You have undoubtedly heard of the distress of American farmers as farm incomes have fallen to disastrously low levels. Whether you are a farm-state senator, a budget analyst for the White House, or a concerned citizen, you cannot choose sound policies to help farmers until you understand the impact of subsidies or acreage-planting restrictions. Supply-and-demand analysis is essential for determining the impacts of such policies.

Insight into these and other questions is the reward for studying the foundations of microeconomics presented in the chapters that follow. Figure 18-1 previews the microeconomics chapters that follow in this Part.

A. ELASTICITY OF DEMAND AND SUPPLY

Review

The chapters of Part One discussed the general principles behind the determination of prices and quantities by markets. What are the key elements of that analysis? Glance back to the supply-and-demand diagram, Figure 4-5. Recall that the demand curve represents the different quantities that consumers are willing to buy at each price, while the supply curve shows the different quantities that firms are willing to sell at each price. The intersection of the two curves represents the competitive equilibrium—the price and quantity at which buyers willingly buy exactly the amount that sellers willingly sell.

If price lay above the competitive price, this would create an oversupply, with firms wishing to produce and sell more than consumers were willing to purchase. In a competitive market, such a glut would lead to a fall in price back toward equilibrium. Similarly, if price stood below the equilibrium price, the eager buyers would want to buy more than sellers were producing, and price would be driven up by the spirited bidding of buyers, until finally price arrived back at its equilibrium.

Turn also to Figure 4-6(a), which illustrates a shift in supply. This decrease in supply might occur because of unfavorable weather or a rise in costs of production. Recall that in this case demand was unchanged, so that the shift in supply caused a rise in price which in turn induced a decrease in quantity demanded. Remember not to confuse this sequence with a decrease in demand; restoring equilibrium required a movement along the demand curve, not a shift of the demand curve. After the supply shift and the response of quantity demanded, a new equilibrium was reached at E'.

As an exercise, describe the movement from one equilibrium to another in the case of the demand shift displayed in Figure 4-6(b).

In addition to these examples, refresh your memory about important concepts such as the assumption that other things are held equal; the diverse forces that lie behind the supply and demand curves; and the nature of equilibrium. Recall as well the law of downward-sloping demand, which states that the demand curve slopes down and to the right, reflecting the observation that quantity demanded tends to increase as the price of a commodity falls.

We now leave our review and proceed to break new ground.

Price and Revenues

Our supply-and-demand analysis shows clearly that an increase in supply, say arising because of an abundant harvest, will tend to depress price. So it is no surprise that early economists like Gregory King should have remarked on this fact. But King also observed a less obvious point. His statistical studies convinced him that farmers as a whole receive less total revenue when the harvest is good than when it is bad. Paradoxically, then, good weather is bad for farmers as a whole.

This fact, that large harvests (high Q) tend to be associated with low revenue (equal to $P \times Q$), has dogged every American president who has reckoned with low incomes of farmers. The relationship between price and revenue introduces a new and important economic concept, price elasticity of demand. Any business firm tempted to cut its price in order to sell more and increase its profits must consider its price elasticity of demand.

PRICE ELASTICITY OF DEMAND

We know that, according to the law of downward-sloping demand, quantity demanded tends to vary inversely with price: quantity demanded falls when price rises, and quantity demanded rises when price falls. We here consider *how much* quantity demanded will change in response to a change in price.

The **price elasticity of demand** (or the "elasticity of demand" for short) is a concept that measures how much the quantity demanded of a good changes when its price changes. Elasticity is analogous to responsiveness; a good is "elastic" when its quantity demanded responds greatly to price changes. Demands for goods differ in their elasticities. Demand for food generally responds little to price changes and is inelastic, while airline travel is highly price sensitive and is therefore elastic.

The concept of price elasticity allows us to attach a precise number to the degree of price responsiveness of the demand for different goods. Price elasticities are classified in three categories depending upon the response of quantity demanded to price change.

1. When a 1 percent rise in price calls forth more than a 1 percent decline in quantity demanded, this is **price elastic demand.**

2. When a percentage rise in price results in an exactly compensating decline in quantity demanded (so that total revenue remains unchanged), this is **unit-elastic demand.**

3. When a 1 percent rise in price evokes less than a 1 percent fall in quantity demanded, this is **price inelastic demand.**

These definitions refer to rising prices and declining quantities. They could just as well refer to falling prices and rising quantities. Moreover, as we shall see, we can calculate elasticities for price changes other than 1 percent.

Price Elasticity in Diagrams

Figure 18-2 illustrates the three cases of elasticities. In each, price is cut in half as we move from point *A* to point *B*. The easiest to begin with is the borderline case of unitary elasticity of demand shown in Figure 18-2(b). In this example, the doubling of quantity demanded exactly matches the halving of price, so revenue received remains unchanged.

In Figure 18-2(a), a halving of price has produced a tripling of quantity demanded, so demand is price elastic. In Figure 18-2(c), the halving of price led to only a 50 percent increase in quantity demanded, so this is the case of price inelastic demand.

Measurement of Elasticity

The actual numerical definition of price elasticity of demand follows naturally from its definition. The coefficient of demand elasticity, E_D, between two different points on a demand curve is:

Price elasticity of demand $= E_D$

$$= \frac{\text{percent increase in } Q}{\text{percent decrease in } P}$$

Note that P and Q move in opposite directions because of the law of downward-sloping demand. Also, the use of percentages brings in the property that the units of goods or of prices—bushels or tons, dollars per bushel or francs per ton—do not affect elasticity.[1] Note also that we follow the convention of measuring demand elasticity as a positive number simply for convenience.

Numerical Measurement We pause to examine the details of numerical measurement of E_D. You may have noticed that there is always a slight ambiguity

---

[1]Before moving on, note that the units or scale will affect the slope of the demand diagram, and we can make a curve look steep or flat by changing the scale of one of the axes (see the appendix to Chapter 1 for a discussion of this point). Further, it is important not to confuse slope and elasticity. As Fig. 18-2(b)'s curve with $E_D = 1$ shows, a curve of constant elasticity is not a straight line with constant slope, but rather one whose slope varies in order to keep the percentage changes of price and quantity in the same ratio. So the purpose of a later section is to help you avoid confusing slope and elasticity.

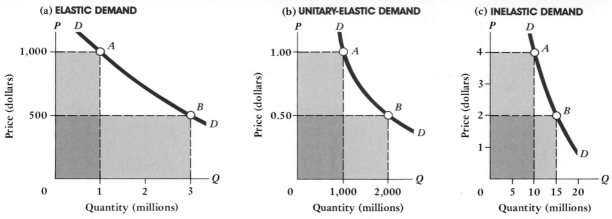

Figure 18-2 **Price elasticity of demand falls into three categories, depending on how strongly quantity demanded responds to a change in price**

about percentage changes. This ambiguity concerns whether the change is measured against the initial or the final quantity. Suppose a record shop buys a record for $6 and sells it for $9. Is this $3 markup a 50 percent change, $3 being 50 percent of the lower base of $6? Or is it a $33\frac{1}{3}$ percent change, $3 being one-third of the larger $9 base? Both these approaches to calculating percentage changes are correct.

Fortunately, when it comes to very small percentage changes, as from 100 to 99, the difference between $\frac{1}{100}$ and $\frac{1}{99}$ becomes hardly worth talking about. But for larger ones, it may make quite a difference, and the chosen method must be used consistently.

To resolve this ambiguity, we choose a third option for calculating percentage change: we relate the price change to neither the higher nor the lower of the two Ps, but to their *average*. The same averaging method will be used here for Q. Hence, we say that a cut from 101 to 99 is a change of $\frac{2}{100}$, because the average of 99 and 101 is 100. This is the method we will use in calculating demand elasticity. It is shown in the formula:

$$ E_D = -\frac{Q_2 - Q_1}{(Q_1 + Q_2)/2} \div \frac{P_2 - P_1}{(P_1 + P_2)/2} $$

where P_1 and Q_1 represent the original price and quantity and where P_2 and Q_2 stand for the new price and quantity.

Table 18-1 at the top of the next page is self-explanatory: it shows how to calculate E_D for three movements along a straight-line DD curve. We shall see that such DD curves start out elastic at high P and end up inelastic at low P, passing through unitary elasticity at an intermediate position where total revenue $P \times Q$ is at its maximum.

Elasticity and Revenue

An understanding of price elasticity is crucial for many business and economic decisions because elasticity determines the effect of price changes on the total revenue gained from a commodity's sale. Let us look at the relationship between price elasticity of demand and total revenue.

Total revenue is by definition equal to price times quantity (or $P \times Q$). If consumers buy 5 units at $3 each, total revenue is $15.

The three cases of elasticity correspond to three different relationships between total revenue and price changes. If a price decrease leads to a decrease in total revenue, this is a case of inelastic demand; if a price decrease leads to an increase in total revenue, this is the case of elastic demand; and if a price de-

NUMERICAL CALCULATION OF ELASTICITY COEFFICIENT

Q	ΔQ	P	$-\Delta P$	$\dfrac{Q_1 + Q_2}{2}$	$\dfrac{P_1 + P_2}{2}$	$E_D = \dfrac{\Delta Q}{(Q_1 + Q_2)/2} \div \dfrac{-\Delta P}{(P_1 + P_2)/2}$
0		6				
	10		2	5	5	$\dfrac{10}{5} \div \dfrac{2}{5} = 5 > 1$
10		4				
	10		2	15	3	$\dfrac{10}{15} \div \dfrac{2}{3} = 1$
20		2				
	10		2	25	1	$\dfrac{10}{25} \div \dfrac{2}{1} = .2 < 1$
30		0				

Table 18-1   Dividing percentage response of quantity demanded by percentage change in price gives price elasticity of demand

ΔP denotes the change in P, i.e., $\Delta P = P_2 - P_1$, and similarly $\Delta Q = Q_2 - Q_1$. Each P cut, $-\Delta P$, is related to the average P, namely $(P_1 + P_2)/2$; each Q rise, ΔQ, is related to the average Q, namely $(Q_1 + Q_2)/2$. The resulting ratio gives the elasticity coefficient, E_D, a measure which is unitless (or without dimensions), not expressed in absolute units. Can you see the relationship between the elasticity and the effect of a price cut on total revenue ($P \times Q$)?

crease leads to no change in total revenue, this is the borderline case of unit-elastic demand.

We can return to Figure 18-2 to illustrate the three cases. Recall that in each case price was cut in half as we moved from point A to point B. In the borderline case in (b), the quantity reduction just matched the price increase, with total revenue unchanged at $1000 million. So we know that this is the unit-elastic case.

Is it possible to read off the revenue response in the diagram itself? Yes, as long as we recall that total revenue is the arithmetic product of price times quantity, P times Q. Further, the area of a rectangle is always equal to the product of its base times its height. Total revenue at any point on a demand curve can thus be found by examining the area of the rectangle formed by the P and Q at that point. You can check that the shaded rectangle at A in Figure 18-2(b) does have a base equal to Q and a height equal to P. Hence, if we watch how the area of each point's rectangle changes as we cut price and move down the demand curve, we can determine whether demand is elastic, inelastic, or unit-elastic.

Clearly, in the middle diagram of Figure 18-2, the shaded areas are remaining the same because of offsetting changes in the Q base and the P height. This is what we would expect for the borderline case of unitary price elasticity of demand.

We can also see that Figure 18-2(a) corresponds to elastic demand. In this figure, the revenue rectangle expands from $1000 million to $1500 million as price is halved from $1000. Here, total revenue goes up when P is cut, so demand is elastic.

Figure 18-2(c) corresponds to the case of inelastic demand. In this case, the revenue rectangle falls from $40 million to $30 million when price is halved, so demand is inelastic.

Which diagram represents Gregory King's finding that a bumper harvest means lower total revenues for farmers? Clearly Figure 18-2(c). Which represents MCI Communications' belief that a reduction in its long-distance telephone rates would induce such a large volume of calls as to increase its total sales? Surely Figure 18-2(a).

An Example Suppose you are a firm operating a baseball franchise. Your team, the Albuquerque Dukes, usually operates with a half-empty stadium. Your business manager comes in and says, "We would like to increase ticket revenues for the Dukes' games as much as possible, and I estimate that the price elasticity for our tickets is 0.5 between $5 and $10 a ticket, 1.2 between $10 and $12 a ticket, and 2 between $12 and $15 a ticket. Our current price is $10 a ticket. What should we do?"

By application of the elasticity formula, you see that if price is lowered below $10 a ticket, total revenues will go down because demand is price inelastic. If price is raised above $10, total revenues will fall because demand is price elastic in that range. Therefore, the ticket price of $10 will bring in the maximal revenues of the four ticket prices under consideration.

Graphical Measurement of Price Elasticity

Beware a very common mistake. Often the slope of a curve is confused with its elasticity. You might think a steep slope for *DD* must mean inelastic demand, and a flat slope must mean elastic demand. This is not quite true. Why not? Because the slope of *DD* depends upon the *absolute* change in *P* and *Q*, whereas the elasticity depends upon the *percentage* changes.

The straight line *DD* in Figure 18-3(*a*) illustrates the pitfall of confusing slope and elasticity. A straight line has the same slope everywhere. But at the top of the line, near *A*, the change in *P* is divided by a large *P* and the change in *Q* is divided by a small *Q*. Elasticity at that point is a very large percentage change in *Q* divided by a very small change in *P* and is hence almost infinitely large. So our numerical formula for E_D gives a very large E_D when you are high on the *DD* curve.

Further, above the midpoint *M* of any straight line, demand is elastic, with $E_D > 1$. At the midpoint, demand is of unitary elasticity, with $E_D = 1$. Below the midpoint, demand is inelastic, with $E_D < 1$.

When many students make the same mistake, there is usually a reason. The limiting cases of completely vertical and completely horizontal demand curves, shown in Figure 18-3(*b*) and (*c*), do validly portray the limiting cases of completely inelastic demand (0 elasticity) and infinitely elastic demand (∞ elasticity).

But do not think that the in-between cases, where

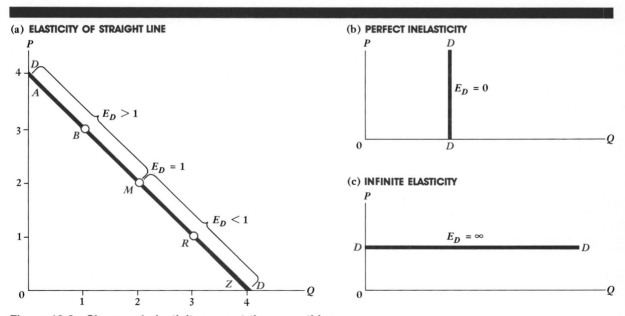

Figure 18-3   Slope and elasticity are not the same thing

All points on *DD*'s straight-line demand in **(a)** have the same absolute slope. But above the midpoint price, demand is elastic; below it, demand is inelastic; at the midpoint, demand is unitary elastic. Only in the case of perfectly vertical or perfectly horizontal curves as in **(b)** and **(c)** can you infer inelasticity and elasticity from slope alone.

most of reality falls, can have their elasticities depicted by slope alone.*

Reasons for Elasticity Differences

Our analysis has concentrated solely on the measurement of elasticity. But why are the demands for some goods elastic while other demands seem quite unresponsive to price? A fuller discussion will be postponed to next chapter's analysis of the foundations of demand, but let us take a first look at the answer.

For necessities like food, fuel, and shelter, demand tends to be relatively unresponsive to price changes. Such items are the staff of life and cannot easily be forgone when their prices rise. By contrast, you can perhaps abstain from luxuries like vacations, 17-year-old Scotch whiskey, and designer clothing in response to rising prices without a major decline in satisfactions.

In addition, those goods that have ready substitutes tend to have higher price elasticities than those that have no substitutes. If the price of gasoline rose 20 percent tomorrow, most workers and shoppers could hardly ride horses for their transportation needs, so the demand for gasoline would tend to be quite inelastic in the short run. On the other hand, if hoof-and-mouth disease decimates cattle herds and drives up beef prices, people can turn to lamb or poultry for their meat needs, so beef shows a high price elasticity.

Other factors also affect the size of price elasticities. Those goods that consume a large fraction of

income tend to be more responsive to price than those that are a trivial part of spending. Compare the effect of a doubling of automobile prices to a doubling of shoelace prices: you might not even notice a shoelace price inflation, so the demand for shoelaces will be price inelastic. Similarly, as we discuss later in this section, the response of demand to price depends upon the length of time since the price change. Studies have shown that the doubling of gasoline prices in the 1970s had little effect on demand for a year or so. But as people began to replace their gas-guzzling behemoths with efficient Japanese subcompacts, the demand for gasoline declined sharply relative to earlier trends.

This brief survey of the determinants of the price elasticity of demand reveals that important economic factors lie beneath the price elasticities for individual goods.

Other Demand Elasticities

Elasticities turn up in many other areas and indeed are among the concepts essential for mastery of elementary economics. The next section extends price elasticity to the supply side of the market, but first we mention two other types of elasticities that relate to the demand for a commodity.

The first is the income elasticity of demand for a good. We saw in Chapter 4 that one of the important determinants of a person's or country's demand for a good is the level of income of the person or country. For normal goods, demand responds positively as income rises. The responsiveness of demand to income

---

*A simple device will allow us to calculate E_D at any point on a straight line. This device will provide the same number for elasticity as the formula given above: E_D equals "the length of the line segment below the point divided by the length of the line segment above it." Since M in Fig. 18-3(a) is halfway, the formula there gives $E_D = 1$, unitary elasticity. At B, it gives 3/1 = 3.0; at R, $E_D = 1/3 = 0.33$.

Knowing how to calculate E_D for a

straight line enables you to calculate it for any point along a curved DD. (1) Draw the straight line tangent to the curve at your point (e.g., at B in Fig. 18-4); (2) calculate the E_D for the straight line at that point (e.g., E_D at $B = 3$); (3) identify your resulting ratio as the correct elasticity for the DD curve at your chosen point. Question 12 at the end of this chapter shows how to prove this rule for calculating the elasticity of a straight line.

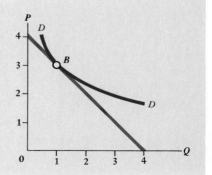

Figure 18-4

is the **income elasticity,** which measures the percentage response in demand for every 1 percent increase in income. High income elasticities, such as are found for airline travel or VCRs, indicate that the demand for these goods rises rapidly as income increases. Low income elasticities, such as for food or shoes, denote a weak response of demand as income rises. We present a fuller discussion of income elasticities in the next chapter.

Another type of elasticity arises when we want to determine the effects of the price of one good on the demand for other goods. Say that the prices of oil and oil products rise sharply. What will happen to the consumption of oil? From the law of downward-sloping demand, we know that the demand for oil-based products like gasoline or heating oil will decline. But what of goods like natural gas and automobiles? People will probably substitute other fuels like natural gas for oil, so that the cross effect of oil price on natural gas demand will be positive. Moreover, studies have found that as the prices of oil and gasoline rise, consumers drive fewer miles and the demand for cars falls, so the cross effect of oil prices on car demand is negative. These cross effects are technically called **cross elasticities of demand** and measure the percentage increase or decrease in the demand for a good in response to changes in the prices of other goods. Chapter 19 will explore the different kinds of cross elasticities.

PRICE ELASTICITY OF SUPPLY

What we did for demand, we can also do for supply. Economists introduce the concept of price elasticity of supply to measure the responsiveness of the quantity supplied of a good to its market price. More precisely, the **price elasticity of supply** measures the percentage change in quantity supplied in response to a 1 percent change in the good's price.

Suppose the amount supplied is perfectly fixed, as in the case of perishable fish brought to today's market for sale at whatever price it will fetch. Then we face the limiting case of perfectly inelastic supply or a vertical supply curve.

Now, suppose instead that we have a horizontal supply curve. Here a tiny cut in P will cause Q to

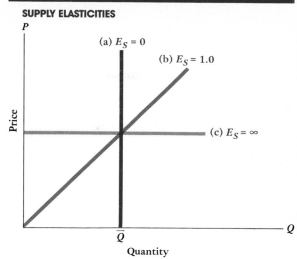

SUPPLY ELASTICITIES

Figure 18-5   Supply elasticity depends upon supply response to price

When supply is fixed, supply elasticity is zero as in curve **(a)**. Curve **(c)** displays an indefinitely large quantity response to price changes. Intermediate case **(b)** arises where quantity response is equal to price change.

become zero and the slightest rise in P will coax out an indefinitely large supply. Put differently, the ratio of the percentage change in quantity supplied to percentage change in price is extraordinarily large. Thus for the horizontal supply curve, we find ourselves at the extreme of infinitely elastic supply.

Between such extremes, we call supply elastic or inelastic depending upon whether the percentage rise in Q is respectively greater than or less than the percentage rise in P that brought it about. And the borderline unit-elastic case, where price elasticity of supply equals 1, indicates that the percentage increase of quantity supplied is exactly equal to the percentage increase in price.

Define the numerical coefficient of supply elasticity, E_S, as follows:

$$E_S = \frac{\text{percentage rise in quantity supplied}}{\text{percentage rise in price}}$$

Figure 18-5 draws three important cases—the vertical supply curve showing perfectly inelastic supply; the horizontal supply curve displaying perfectly elastic supply; and an intermediate case of a straight line, going through the origin, illustrating the borderline case of unitary elasticity.[2]

What determines supply elasticity? One of the key factors is the time period under consideration: A given change in price tends to have greater and greater effects on amount supplied as the time for suppliers to respond increases, a point we explore further in the next section. The other factor influencing supply elasticity is the extent to which production in the industry can be increased. If, as in the case of textiles, looms, textile labor, fibers, and factories are plentiful at the going prices, then output can be sharply increased without a major increase in price. On the other hand, if, as in the case of South African gold, the mining capacity and ore deposits are severely limited, then even sharp increases in the price of gold will call forth but a small response in production of South African gold.

MOMENTARY, SHORT-RUN, AND LONG-RUN EQUILIBRIUM

We can advance our understanding of supply behavior by analyzing the time element in supply as it applies to the microeconomics of competitive equilibrium. At the turn of the century Cambridge University's great economist Alfred Marshall helped forge the supply-and-demand tools we use today. In addition, Marshall distinguished three time periods for supply:

- *Momentary* equilibrium, when supply is fixed

- *Short-run* equilibrium, when firms can increase their output even though plant and equipment are fixed

- *Long-run* equilibrium, when firms can abandon old plants or build new ones and when new firms can enter the industry or old ones leave it

---

[2]You can determine the elasticity of a supply curve which is not a straight line in the fashion described for the demand curve in the footnote on page 428 by drawing the straight line that lies tangent to the curve at a point and measuring the elasticity of the tangential straight line.

Consider the demand for a perishable good, such as fish that cannot be preserved. Let demand increase from DD to $D'D'$. With the amount of fish supplied unchanged, the stronger demand sharply bids up the momentary price of fish. This is shown in Figure 18-6(a), where the vertical supply curve S_mS_m runs up to the new demand curve $D'D'$ to determine the new, sharply higher momentary equilibrium price shown at E'. The price has had to rise greatly in order to ration the fixed supply of fish among the now more eager demanders.

But with so high a price prevailing in the market, skippers of the fishing boats will soon be motivated to hustle around to increase their catch. They do not, in the short run, have the time to get new boats built, but they can hire more hands and work longer hours. They will in the short run begin to bring to the market a greater quantity of fish than they did at the old momentary equilibrium. Figure 18-6(b) shows the new S_SS_S short-run supply schedule. It intersects the new demand curve at E'', the point of short-run equilibrium. Note that this equilibrium price is lower than the momentary E' price in Figure 18-6(a). Why? Because of the extra quantity of fish induced in the short run by more intensive use of the same number of boats.

Figure 18-6(c) shows the final long-run equilibrium price. The higher prices that long prevailed have coaxed out more shipbuilding and attracted more sailors into the industry. Seeing the high price of fish and the potential for high profits, new firms entered the industry. Where the long-run supply curve S_LS_L intersects the demand curve $D'D'$ at E''' is the final equilibrium reached after *all* economic conditions (including the number of ships and shipyards) have adjusted to the new level of demand.

Note that the long-run equilibrium price is lower than the short-run equilibrium price, and much lower than the momentary equilibrium price. Yet it is still a little bit higher than the price that prevailed previously when demand was lower. We call this case, where the long-run supply curve is upward-sloping, an "increasing-cost industry." Marshall regarded this as the usual one in most large competitive industries.

Why usual? Because when a large industry such as fishing expands, it must coax workers, ships, ice, and other productive inputs away from other industries. It

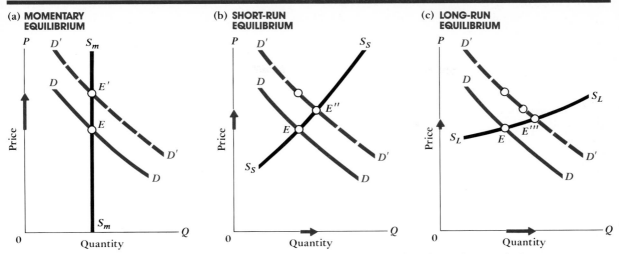

Figure 18-6   Effect of increase in demand on price varies in Marshall's three time periods

We distinguish between periods in which supply elements have time to make **(a)** no adjustments (momentary equilibrium), **(b)** some adjustments of labor and variable factors (short-run equilibrium), **(c)** full adjustment of all factors, fixed as well as varying (long-run equilibrium). The longer the time for adjustment, the greater the elasticity of supply response and the less the rise in price.

does so by bidding up their prices, which increases its costs of producing output. Therefore, the long-run supply curve for a competitive industry will usually slope gently upward, as it does in Figure 18-6(c). Only when the industry is small, and it employs but a tiny fraction of the specialized inputs like sailors or ice, will the long-run supply curve be horizontal, as in the perfectly elastic supply curve in Figure 18-5. Such an industry is said to experience "constant cost."

Test your understanding of this discussion by now assuming a downward shift in the demand curve back to *DD*. Show what happens in the new momentary run, in the short run, and in the long run.

Time Element in Demand

Demand will show a time-varying pattern of response as well. A good example is that of gasoline. Let's say you are on a long trip when the price of gasoline suddenly shoots up. You are unlikely to sell your car or abandon your vacation; thus in the momentary case, the elasticity of demand may be near zero.

In the short run, with no change in the stock of cars, you may have somewhat more flexibility. You can ride your bike, take the train, or carpool with other people. This increased flexibility in the short run will produce some noticeable demand elasticity over a year or so. Studies indicate that the demand elasticity for gasoline for a short period might be 0.1 or so.

In the very long run, contrary to what many people believe, the price elasticity for gasoline is quite large, perhaps as large as 1. Why? Primarily because when they are faced with much higher gasoline prices, people buy smaller cars that have much better fuel economy. By replacing their gas guzzlers that get 10 miles per gallon with sleek front-wheel-drive subcompacts getting 30 mpg, people can reduce their demand for gasoline, other things equal, by two-thirds.

When we consider how the time element affects both supply and demand, we often find that in the very short run, prices move violently and quantities move modestly. In the very long run, however, prices move little and quantities move substantially. This pattern can be seen as a result of the phenomenon of small supply and demand elasticities in the short run and larger ones in the long run.

We now end our analysis of the technical aspects of elasticity and return to the mainstream of supply and demand.

B. APPLICATIONS OF SUPPLY AND DEMAND

Supply-and-demand analysis is one of the most useful tools that economics has to offer. Like a Swiss Army knife, it can perform many simple tasks. But, as with any tool, proper employment of supply and demand curves requires a great deal of practice—being mindful to keep other things equal and to distinguish shifting curves from movements along curves—lest you stumble into one of the common pitfalls of economic analysis.

We now move on to some important applications of supply and demand. Supply and demand help us understand the plight of farmers and analyze the kind of measures that the government can take to boost farm incomes. We then examine the incidence of a tax, review how governments intervene in markets, and finish with an investigation of the efficiency of market equilibrium.

THE ECONOMICS OF AGRICULTURE

Supply and demand apply strictly speaking only to perfectly competitive markets—where a homogeneous product is auctioned off in markets served by large numbers of buyers and sellers. Although perfect competition does not accurately describe most of American life, it does apply closely to the agricultural sector. Farming is also a valuable area to examine because it dominates the politics of many states, and its products are a vital export resource.

Long-Run Relative Decline of Farming

Farming was once our largest single industry, and it remains so in most developing countries. A hundred years ago, half the American population lived and worked on farms, while today only 3 percent of our work force tend crops. What lies behind this relative shift away from agriculture? In part, people sought the higher incomes and more active social life of cit-

ies, and in part many black families left the south in search of what they thought to be greater opportunity in the large northern cities.

In addition, technological progress has enormously reduced the number of farmers needed to feed the population. Mechanization with tractor, combine, cotton picker; fertilization and irrigation; selective breeding and miracle hybrid seeds—all these innovations vastly increased the productivity of agricultural inputs.

Finally, as we saw earlier, the demand for food tends to grow relatively slowly as incomes expand. The low income elasticity for food products, revealed by almost every statistical study of food demand, means that the demand for food has grown more slowly than has national income.

Decline of the Farm: Graphical Analysis

A single diagram can explain the sagging trend in farm prices better than libraries of books and editorials. Figure 18-7 shows an initial equilibrium with high prices at point E. Observe what happens to agriculture as the years go by. We know that demand shifts to the right with the increase in the American population. But because foods are necessities with low income elasticities, the demand shift is small over time in response to growing average incomes.

What about supply? Although many people mistakenly think that farming is a backward business, statistical studies show that productivity (output per unit of input) has grown more rapidly in agriculture than in most other industries. So as new machinery, technologies, and seeds have been introduced, the supply curve has shifted a great deal to the right, as shown from SS to $S'S'$ in Figure 18-7.

What must happen at the new competitive equilibrium at point E'? Sharp increases in supply outstrip modest increases in demand to produce a downward

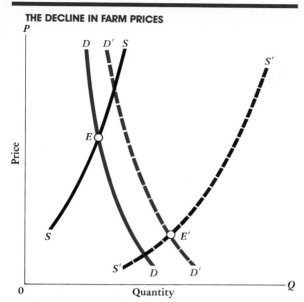

Figure 18-7   Agricultural distress results from expanding supply and price inelastic demand

Start at initial equilibrium at *E*. The increase in demand for farm products tends to be far less than the vast increase in supply generated by technological progress. Hence competitive farm prices tend to fall. Moreover, with price inelastic demand, farm incomes are reduced with increases in supply.

One of the most common government farm programs requires farmers to restrict the planted acreage. Figure 18-8 shows the economics of this policy. If the Department of Agriculture requires every farmer to "set aside" 20 percent of the last year's planted area of corn, this has the effect of shifting the supply curve of corn up and to the left. Because the demands for corn and most other agricultural products are inelastic, such crop restrictions not only raise the price of corn and other crops; they also tend to raise the total revenues earned by farmers and total farm incomes.

Of course, consumers are hurt by the crop restrictions and higher prices—just as they would be if a flood or drought created a scarcity of foodstuffs. But this is the price society must pay when it chooses artificially to idle productive farm resources.

trend in farm prices. And this is precisely what has happened in recent decades: from 1951 to 1986, the prices of crops have fallen 62 percent relative to the overall price level. And with demand being inelastic, as prices fell, what happened to farm incomes? They tended to decline as well.

Crop Restrictions   Farmers have not taken their plight fatalistically. In response to falling incomes, they invaded Washington and surrounded the White House with a brigade of tractors. Governments over the ages have taken many steps here and abroad to help farmers: they have raised prices through price supports; they have curbed imports through tariffs and quotas; in the 1980s the Treasury simply mailed a subsidy payment to farmers for every bushel of wheat or corn harvested.

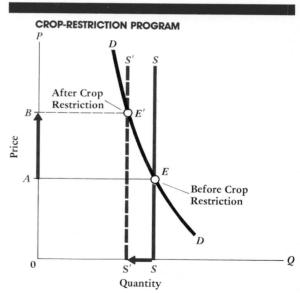

Figure 18-8   Crop restriction programs raise both price and farm income

Before the government program, the competitive market produces an equilibrium with low price at *E*. When farmers persuade the government to restrict production, the supply curve is shifted leftward to *S'S'*, moving equilibrium to *E'* and raising price to *B*. With inelastic demand, confirm that new revenue rectangle *0BE'S'* is larger than original revenue rectangle *0AES*.

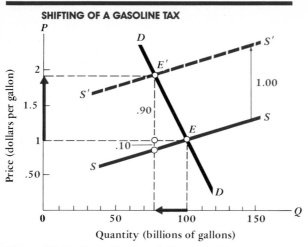

SHIFTING OF A GASOLINE TAX

Figure 18-9 Gasoline tax falls on both consumer and producer

A $1 tax shifts *SS* up $1 everywhere to give parallel *S'S'*. This new supply curve intersects *DD* in new equilibrium at *E'*, where price to consumers has risen 90 cents above old equilibrium and where price to producers has fallen by 10 cents. The red arrows show changes in *P* and *Q*. (Had *DD* been very elastic while *SS* was inelastic, most of the $1 tax would have fallen on the producer. Had *SS* been completely elastic, all the $1 tax would have shifted forward onto the consumer.)

FURTHER EXAMPLES OF SUPPLY-AND-DEMAND ANALYSIS

How does supply and demand apply outside of agriculture? We begin with an important example that concerns the effect of a tax on price and quantity. After reviewing a common fallacy, we then examine briefly four applications of supply and demand from different areas of economics.

Incidence of a Tax

Governments levy taxes on a wide variety of commodities—on cigarettes and alcohol, on payrolls and profits. Can we use our analysis to examine the microeconomic impact of a tax—its incidence on a particular industry?

Yes. An important case is the gasoline tax. Most

European countries set gasoline taxes at $1 or $2 per gallon, while in America the federal tax is but a few pennies per gallon. Advocates of higher gasoline taxes point out that the country would benefit twice from a tax of as high as $1 per gallon: The tax would not only bring in precious revenues to reduce our budget deficit, but it would also curb our growing oil consumption and reduce our dependence on insecure foreign sources of supply.

Let us use supply and demand to analyze the **incidence** of a $1 tax on gasoline. By "incidence" we mean the ultimate economic impact of a tax. Is its burden shifted back completely onto the oil industry? Or will it be shifted forward in part to the consumers? The answer can be determined only from supply and demand curves. Figure 18-9 shows the original equilibrium to be at *E*, the intersection of the *SS* and *DD* curves, with gasoline price of $1 a gallon and total consumption of 100 billion gallons per year.

We represent the imposition of a $1 tax as an upward shift of the supply curve with the demand curve remaining unchanged. To understand this approach, consider first the demand curve. There is no reason for a $1-per-gallon tax to have shifted the demand curve. Holding other things like income and automobile prices equal, consumers will still be willing to buy the same amounts of gasoline at the prices given by the original demand curve. Consumers may not even know whether the price they pay goes to the government, the oil companies, or Saudi Arabia.

But the whole supply curve is shifted upward and leftward: leftward, because at each market price the producers will now supply less as a result of the tax; upward, because to get the producers to bring any given quantity to market (say, 100 billion gallons), we must give them a higher market price than before—$2 rather than $1, which is higher by the exact amount of the $1 tax the producers must pay.

To reinforce your understanding, first construct a table that shows the original supply curve in Figure 18-9 (similar to that in Figure 4-3, page 60). Then put in a second column the new supply curve after the $1 tax has been imposed.

To repeat, in Figure 18-9 the demand curve *DD* is unchanged, but the *SS* supply curve has been shifted up everywhere by $1 to a new *parallel* supply curve *S'S'*.

Where will the new equilibrium price be? The answer is found at the intersection of the new supply and demand curves, or at E', where $S'S'$ and DD meet. Because supply has decreased, the price is higher. Also, the quantity bought and sold is reduced. If we read the graph carefully, we find that the new equilibrium price has risen from $1 to about $1.90. The new equilibrium output, at which purchases and sales are in equilibrium, has fallen from 100 billion to about 77 billion gallons.

Who ultimately pays the tax? What is its incidence? Clearly the oil industry pays a small fraction, for it receives only 90 cents ($1.90 − $1 tax) rather than $1. But the consumer bears most of the burden, with the retail price rising 90 cents. The incidence lies most heavily on the consumer because supply is relatively price elastic while demand is quite price inelastic.

More generally, the incidence of a tax will fall most heavily on consumers or on producers depending upon the relative elasticities of demand and supply. A tax is shifted forward onto consumers if the demand is inelastic relative to supply; a tax is shifted backward to producers if supply is relatively more inelastic than demand. (To test your understanding of these points, work through the alternative assumptions in the legend to Figure 18-9.)

The supply-and-demand analysis of taxes can apply to many other kinds of taxes as well. Using this apparatus we can understand how cigarette taxes affect both the prices and consumption of cigarettes; how taxes or tariffs on imports affect foreign trade; and how taxes on inputs like labor, capital, and land will affect wages, interest rates, and land rents.

A Common Fallacy

By now you have mastered supply and demand. Or have you? You know that a tax will have the effect of raising the price that the consumer will have to pay. Or do you? Consider the following argument often seen in the press and heard from the political platform:

> The effect of a tax on a commodity might seem at first sight to be an advance in price to the consumer. But an advance in price will diminish the demand. And a reduced demand will send the price down again. Therefore it is not certain, after all, that the tax will really raise the price.

Will the tax raise the price or not? According to the paper's editorial and the senator's oratory, the answer is, No.

We have once again encountered the confusion of movements along curves versus shifts of curves. (Recall a similar example given in Chapter 4, page 66.) The second sentence in the quotation is incorrect: the speaker has confused a downward shift with a movement along the demand curve. Since the demand curve remains unchanged after the tax increase, there cannot be any shift in demand. Generally, then, the tax really will raise the price.

Four Examples of Supply and Demand at Work

Everyday life offers countless problems and issues that can be completely understood only by a careful analysis of supply and demand. Here are four:

▪ *Deregulation and airfares.* Until the late 1970s, the federal Civil Aeronautics Board limited competition among airlines by restricting the entry of both new and established airlines into most cities. Ticket prices were high and many flights were virtually empty. Criticisms led to a complete deregulation by 1980, and the industry saw the growth of many upstart airlines like Continental Airlines and Texas Air along with the bankruptcy of poorly managed airlines.

Figure 18-10(*a*) illustrates the effect of deregulation on airfares: the entry of new airlines and the expansion of established carriers increased supply, shifted out the supply curve, drove down the average price of air travel, and greatly increased the volume of air travel. Those who benefited most were people who bought discount fares and people living in hub cities, such as New York and Chicago, where intense competition drove prices in the late 1980s well below those of the 1970s.

▪ *Restriction of the supply of doctors.* The number of candidates for medical school is many times greater than is the number of places. For every medical school slot, two people take the required entrance

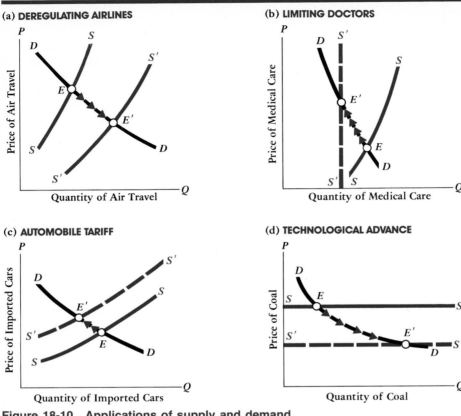

Figure 18-10 Applications of supply and demand

Supply-and-demand analysis can illustrate many important economic processes. Panel **(a)** shows how deregulation of the airline industry led to lower prices and more air travel; **(b)** shows how limitation on the number of doctors can raise the price of medical care along with the income of doctors; **(c)** shows how an import tariff lowers the quantity and raises the price of imported cars; **(d)** provides an example of how technical advance lowers costs and price and may increase the demand for labor in the coal industry.

examination. This limitation is enforced by stringent certification of medical schools imposed by the American Medical Association.

The restriction effectively decreases the supply of doctors, shifting the supply curve of physicians to the left in Figure 18-10(*b*). Proponents of this and similar certification procedures defend them as necessary to maintain high standards of quality.

Because the demand for medical care is inelastic, this restriction raises the price of medical care and the incomes of doctors. The higher quality comes at the expense of more costly medical care.

▪ *A tariff on automobiles.* From the era of Henry Ford until the 1950s, the United States dominated the world automobile market. Then, with the rapid growth and technological sophistication of Europe and Japan, imports made large inroads in American markets, attaining a 25 percent market share by the 1980s. Automobile companies and unions, hard hit by excess capacity and unemployment, lobbied for restrictions on foreign-made cars.

One proposed solution was to put a tariff on autos. A $2000 tariff would reduce supply of imported autos, shifting the supply curve to the left. The price of imports would rise, and the quantity demanded would fall. See Figure 18-10(c).

Also, the demand for domestic autos would shift to the right and upward. Why? The demand for domestic autos would increase because the price of a close substitute for domestic autos (i.e., the price of imported autos) was higher after the tariff. Thus both the price and quantity of domestic autos would rise, as the demand curve moves northeast along a given supply curve for domestic autos.

▪ *Technological advance.* One of the recurring dilemmas of labor is how to react in the face of technological change. Should laborers welcome innovation, as did the United Mine Workers under John L. Lewis? Or should they attempt to sabotage new machinery, as did the Luddites in nineteenth-century England, and as some labor unions today might desire?

This is a somewhat involved question, but it can be simplified as follows: Assume that a commodity (say, coal or haircuts) is competitively produced at constant costs by labor alone. Thus the supply curve for coal or haircuts is horizontal at a price given by the average labor cost per unit of output. A technological improvement that doubles labor productivity will halve costs and price. What will happen to the demand for labor? It depends simply on the demand elasticity for the industry's product. Since all revenues go to pay wages, total wages will rise or decline as demand is elastic or inelastic. If demand elasticity is 2, then Figure 18-10(d) shows how the technical advance will raise total revenues. It will also double total wages, and will therefore shift the demand curve for labor to the right.

By using supply and demand, we can predict that workers in an industry might be hostile to technological advance in industries where demand is inelastic.

GOVERNMENT INTERVENTION IN MARKETS

Is the Law of Supply and Demand Immutable?

The applications above show how supply and demand work to determine the competitive price and quantity of different goods. But do not costs or tastes or incomes also affect price? Surely we have overlooked the role of government taxes and spending along with the impact of foreign trade.

Actually, price does depend on these and other factors. But they do not *add to* the forces of supply and demand; rather, they are among the numerous forces that *act through* supply and demand. Hence if government spends more money on road-building or mine-sweepers, this will shift out the demand for different products and raise their prices. But competitive price is still determined by supply and demand. In sum, supply and demand are not the ultimate explanations of price. They are merely useful catchall categories for analyzing and describing the multitude of forces, causes, and factors impinging on price. Rather than final answers, supply and demand represent the beginning of economic understanding.

Once we understand that important forces lie behind supply and demand, we can recognize the confusion of novices who utter, "You can't repeal the law of supply and demand. King Canute knew he could not command the ocean tide to retreat from his throne on the seashore. Likewise, any wise government knows it cannot evade, or interfere with, the workings of supply and demand."

It would be better not to have learned any economics than to be left with this opinion. Of course the government can affect price. Governments affect price by influencing supply or demand, or both.

Indeed, governments over the ages have used cartels to fix prices or restrict outputs. The Organization of Petroleum Exporting Countries (OPEC) limited production in the 1970s and again in 1986, thereby raising prices manyfold. Brazil has burned coffee to raise its price. Countries limit sugar production to keep prices high. And so forth.

These governments have not violated the law of supply and demand. They have worked through the law of supply and demand. The state has no secret economic weapons. What is true for the state is also true for individuals. Anyone can affect the price of wheat who has either sufficient money to throw on the market or wheat to hold off the market.

Prices Fixed by Law

There is one genuine government interference with supply and demand whose effects we must analyze.

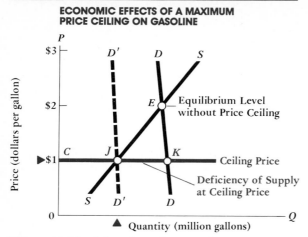

ECONOMIC EFFECTS OF A MAXIMUM PRICE CEILING ON GASOLINE

Figure 18-11   A legal maximum price, without rationing, leaves a gap between demand and supply

Without a legal price ceiling, price would rise to *E*. At the artificial ceiling price, supply and demand do not balance and some method of rationing, formal or informal, is needed to allocate the short supply and bring the actual demand down to *D'D'*.

The government sometimes legislates maximum or minimum prices. Thus, in 1988, a floor of $3.35 in the form of a minimum hourly wage applies to most workers. In war or in peace, wage and price controls may be enacted by the government—the last example of wage and price controls in the United States coming under President Nixon in the early 1970s.

These interferences with the laws of supply and demand are genuinely different from governments acting through supply and demand. Let's see why.

Price Ceilings Consider market gasoline, which has ordinary curves of supply and demand such as we have repeatedly met in this chapter. Let's say we start out in a situation where the price of gasoline is $1 a gallon. Then, because of a war or revolution, a drastic cut in oil supply occurs—that is, the supply curve of oil shifts far to the left. Imported gasoline rises to $2 a gallon, and prices of domestic oil start to climb.

Senators rise to denounce the situation. Oil companies are called "profiteers." The poor are subject to a

heavy "tax" from offshore and domestic gougers. And the rising prices surely threaten to add to an inflationary spiral in the cost of living. So goes the argument of price controllers (as the United States saw in the 1970s).

As a result, the government might choose to control prices (as it did in 1973–1981 for oil and still does for natural gas). It passes a law putting a maximum price on gasoline at the old level of $1 a gallon. The ceiling-price line *CJK* in Figure 18-11 represents the legal ceiling price. Now what will happen?

At the legal ceiling price, supply and demand do not match. Consumers want billions of gallons of gasoline in excess of what producers are willing to supply. This is shown by the gap between *J* and *K*. This gap is so large that before long there will not be enough fuel in dealers' pumps or storage tanks to make up the difference. Somebody will have to go without. If it were not for the maximum-price law, this somebody would gladly bid the price up to $2 or more, rather than do without gas.

But it is against the law for the producer to accept a higher price. There follows a period of frustration and *shortage*—a game of musical cars in which somebody is left without gasoline when the pump runs dry. The inadequate supply of gasoline must somehow be rationed. At first, this may be done by "first come, first served," with or without limited sales to each customer. Lines form, and much time has to be spent foraging for fuel.

Rationing Eventually, some kind of *non-price rationing mechanism* evolves. In the case of gasoline, it is often rationed by making people wait in line.

Nobody is happy, least of all the harassed dealer. Were it not for the community's elementary sense of fair play the situation might soon become intolerable. It is no wonder that black markets (or illegal sales) occasionally develop; the real surprise is that they do not occur sooner.

If for political or social reasons market price is not to be permitted to rise high enough to bring quantity demanded down to the level of quantity supplied, ultimately some kind of non-price rationing develops. Governments generally turn to formal allocation or coupon rationing during periods of extreme shortages.

Under *coupon rationing,* each customer must have a coupon as well as money to buy the goods—there are two kinds of money. Once rationing is adopted and tickets are handed out according to family size, occupational need, or other criteria, many people heave a sigh of relief, because now sellers need not turn people away and now buyers can count upon getting their fair quota of the limited supplies.

Just how do ration coupons work out in terms of supply and demand? Clearly, one must try to issue just enough of them to lower the demand curve to $D'D'$ in Figure 18-11, where supply and the new demand balance at the ceiling price. If too many coupons are issued, demand is still too far to the right and we encounter the old difficulties, but to a lesser degree. If too few coupons are issued, stocks of fuel will pile up and P will fall below the ceiling price. This is the signal for liberalizing the gasoline ration.

Coupon rationing has fallen out of favor in most market economies. But the lessons of the history of rationing and price controls extend far beyond the problems of war or energy crises for, like the breakdown of price mechanisms in hyperinflation, such abnormalities illuminate the function of prices in normal times.

The point to recall is that goods are always scarce; society can never fulfill everyone's wishes. In normal times, price itself rations out the scarce supplies—rising to choke off excessive consumption and to encourage production; falling to encourage consumption, discourage production, and work off excessive inventories. When governments step in to interfere with supply and demand, something besides money fills the role of rationer, and studies indicate that serious waste and inefficiency are a certain companion of these interferences.

Minimum Floors and Maximum Ceilings

When there arises any kind of emergency or state of general shortage and inflation, political pressures develop for wage and price controls. Experience has taught that such extreme measures may work in short emergencies. But detailed sector-by-sector price and wage controls tend to create greater and greater distortions and inefficiencies the longer they are in ef-

fect. Economists therefore generally recommend that such blanket controls be reserved for emergency periods.

Nevertheless, as Adam Smith well knew when he protested against the devices of the mercantilist advisers to the earlier kings, most economic systems are plagued by inefficiencies stemming from well-meaning but inexpert interferences with the mechanisms of supply and demand. We can analyze three kinds of government intervention as a way of understanding the impact of keeping price from equating supply and demand. The examples shown in Figure 18-12—the minimum wage, rent controls on housing, and interest-rate ceilings—illustrate how surprising side effects often arise when governments attempt to interfere with market determination of price and quantity.

▪ *Minimum wage rates.* Governments sometimes legislate a minimum wage rate that sets a floor for most jobs, this rate having been frozen at $3.35 per hour since 1981 under federal law. Although almost everyone would agree that a living wage requires even higher pay, studies show that a high minimum wage often hurts those it is designed to help. What does it profit an unskilled youth to know that a job will pay $3.35 an hour if no jobs are available?

▪ *Rent controls.* No one likes to pay rent. Moreover, houses and apartments look so durable that people sometimes forget that they must be built and maintained. It is quite natural, therefore, that governments sometimes impose rent controls as a way of keeping rents down.

The supply-and-demand analysis shown in Figure 18-12 shows the effects of rent controls. At the controlled rental price, there is a large group of buyers who cannot find an apartment. People hang on to too large apartments because they are cheap. Non-price rationing occurs, as people have to bribe landlords or pay enormous security deposits to obtain a rental apartment. New building—along with maintenance and upgrading of existing rent-controlled dwellings—suffers.

Historical experience in New York, Berkeley, Paris, and other cities shows that just such problems have arisen when effective rent-control measures were adopted. New York has seen tens of thousands

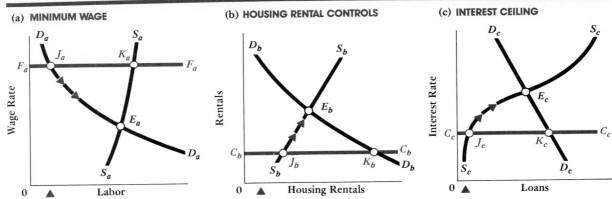

Figure 18-12   When government by fiat sets maximum or minimum prices, troublesome gaps may arise

(a) Setting minimum-wage floor at F_aF_a, high above free-market equilibrium rate E_a, results in forced equilibrium at J_a. The too high floor freezes workers into unemployment from J_a to K_a. Lowering the minimum wage moves us down along D_aD_a, as shown by red arrows, raising employment. (If DD is elastic, total wage payrolls rise though hourly rate falls!)
(b) Setting maximum rental ceiling at C_bC_b, far below free-market equilibrium at E_b, causes fringe of unsatisfied renters between forced equilibrium at J_b and K_b. Raising the ceiling rate moves the system up S_bS_b as shown by red arrows: new construction provides more living space, and old quarters are used more efficiently.
(c) Setting maximum interest rates at C_cC_c, far below free-market equilibrium rate E_c, results in drying up of available funds. Desperate borrowers between J_c and K_c turn to loan sharks. Raising interest ceiling moves system toward more loans, as shown by red arrows on S_cS_c.

of buildings abandoned because the controlled rents were too low to cover expenses and taxes. In the wry words of one European critic, ''Nothing is as efficient at destroying a city as rent controls—except for bombing.''

▪ *Interest-rate ceilings.* Interest rates are the price paid when people borrow money. That is, when you borrow $5000 to buy a car or to finance your education, you might have to pay 10 percent (or in this case, $500) per year as interest on the borrowed funds.

Since biblical times, the charging of interest has been an object of suspicion, for people wonder why a borrower need pay a lender anything for the use of funds when the lender performs no visible service. In earlier times, lending at interest was a crime, and even today some states place a legal maximum on interest rates.

Unfortunately, the ceiling is sometimes far below the interest rate that would be determined by supply and demand. While 18 percent per year might seem high for a credit-card or a car loan, this high rate

might barely cover administrative costs and the risk of default. What is the result of too low a ceiling on interest rates? Funds dry up. Banks or other financial institutions refuse to make unprofitable loans at the legal rate. Those who are the intended beneficiaries find that they cannot get loans from anyone but a loan shark, and the interest rate might be as high as 50 or 75 or 100 percent per year. The inexpensive loan you cannot get does you no good.

EFFICIENCY AND EQUITY OF SUPPLY-DEMAND PRICING

We do not study supply and demand for the beauty of the subject. We study it for the light it throws on the organization of an economy's resources. The pathologies that arise when markets break down help to emphasize the remarkable efficiencies produced by perfect competition—when it is able to operate.

Why, then, do politicians and the populace keep interfering with the mechanism? Primarily, because people cannot live on efficiency alone. We must ask the questions: Efficiency *for what?* And *for whom?*

Most interferences in supply and demand are attempts to promote equity or to protect particular groups against the impersonal forces of supply and demand. Those helped are sometimes poor, sometimes affluent. The minimum wage probably raises the income of some low-wage workers at the expense of others who cannot find work or of consumers who must pay higher prices. Agricultural programs, such as those helping sugar farmers, aid some who are among the richest Americans. In each case, the legislature was persuaded to pay the costs of the market interference in order to protect a group of workers, firms, or consumers.

Evaluation of Government Intervention

Can we render final judgment on government interventions? Are all such interferences with the price system to be condemned?

Probably not. Careful analysis will find a role for government in markets. As noted in Chapter 3, markets sometimes fail to perform properly. Spillovers sometimes cause harm or good that is not included in the calculations of free and unregulated markets. Monopolies may take over industries. And the income distribution churned out by the invisible hand may be socially unacceptable. In each case, governments may guide the economy toward outcomes that society prefers.

Some market interventions by government are designed to override consumer preference. Is it possible that Congress knows better than consumers what is really good and evil? Take heroin as an example. Governments do not treat consumers as sovereigns who can decide how much heroin they will spend their dollar votes on. Where heroin is concerned, the state adopts a paternalistic attitude, treating consumers like children. Society also controls people's behavior regarding cigarettes and other cancer-causing substances.

But where computer games and designer jeans are concerned, consumers are allowed to spend their dollars in their own ways. Perhaps advertising has given us one set of tastes, which may not be intrinsically better than another set. But in the interests of freedom, the consumer is treated as sovereign in most areas.

The rationale for government interference is particularly complicated when the sellers or the buyers in a market happen to be especially rich, especially poor, especially "deserving," or especially "undeserving." For example, suppose that 100 very wealthy oil drillers sold oil in competitive markets to 10 million very poor people. Would you be tempted to say, "Let's control oil prices, not allowing the producers to get rich at the expense of the poor"? When oil prices were raised by OPEC in 1973, Congress took this view, and domestic oil prices were put under price controls. The result, as would be predicted by supply-and-demand analysis, was that oil imports grew rapidly. By 1979, a consensus developed that the equity gains from oil-price controls were not worth the efficiency losses, and domestic oil prices were gradually decontrolled.

Equity through Taxes; Efficiency through Markets

These and many other lessons lead many economists to take the following cautious approach toward government intervention:

Interfering with the competitive supply-and-demand mechanism is often an inefficient way of correcting the income distribution. Whatever distribution you want to end up with can often be more efficiently attained by using the tax system to redistribute income than by narrow interferences in a single market.

Having put forth this cautious statement, we must emphasize that such a view is highly controversial. There is no unassailable answer as to how much government interference is right. And partisan politics intrudes to muddy the analysis. In fact you can see that some forms of government intervention occur in virtually all societies. Doctors often charge rich patients more than poor ones, subsidizing the latter from revenues of the former. Milk and other basic foods are subsidized in almost all countries. Basic education is universally available at highly subsidized prices. Do you see any pattern here?

■   ■   ■

This concludes our detailed introduction of supply-and-demand analysis. In the next few chapters we will be looking carefully behind supply and demand curves to see why some cost curves are flat and some steep, why vital necessities like water are cheap while luxuries like diamonds are expensive, and why competitive markets lead to an efficient (although possibly inequitable) allocation of resources.

SUMMARY

A. Elasticity of Demand and Supply

1. Microeconomics deals with the detailed working of the market mechanism. It grapples with how the economy solves *what, how,* and *for whom* in each market. The supply and demand curves in Chapter 4 explain what goes on in each competitive market.

2. Price elasticity of demand determines what happens to total revenue as price is cut. Demand is elastic, inelastic, or unitary elastic, according to whether a reduction in price increases, decreases, or does not change total revenue. The numerical coefficient of price elasticity of demand is defined as "the percentage increase in quantity demanded divided by the percentage cut in price." Depending upon whether the percentage rise in Q exceeds or falls short of the percentage fall in P, we have $E_D > 1$ or $E_D < 1$, with $E_D = 1$ in between. Price elasticity is a pure number, involving percentages; it is not to be confused with absolute slope, as numerical tables and graphs can show.

3. Price elasticity of demand tends to be low for necessities like food and shelter and high for luxuries like snowmobiles and air travel. Other factors affecting price elasticity are the extent to which a good has ready substitutes and the length of time that consumers have to adjust to price changes. Additional elasticities relating to demand are: income elasticities, which indicate the response of demand to changes in consumer incomes; and cross elasticities of demand, which relate the quantity response of one good to the price change of another good.

4. Elasticity of supply measures percentage responsiveness of output supplied by producers when market P is raised by a given percentage.

5. Marshall stressed the time element in the supply curve: *(a)* momentary equilibrium of fixed supply; *(b)* short-run equilibrium with output varying within fixed plants and firms; *(c)* long-run equilibrium, when numbers of firms and plants, and all other conditions, adjust completely to the new demand conditions.

B. Applications of Supply and Demand

6. The apparatus of supply and demand enables us to analyze the effects of shifts in either curve, or in both simultaneously. In using this apparatus, we should avoid the pitfall of confusing the expression "an increase in demand" (i.e., an outward *shift* of the whole demand curve) with "an increase in quantity demanded" (i.e., a movement *along* an unchanged demand curve because price has changed). Similar cautions apply to increases in supply and increases in quantity supplied.

7. One of the most useful arenas for application of supply and demand lies in agriculture. Improvements in agricultural technology mean that supply increases greatly, while demand for food rises less than proportionately with income. Hence free-market prices for foodstuffs tend to fall. No wonder that government has adopted a variety of programs, like crop restrictions, to maintain farm incomes.

8. A tax of so many dollars per unit of a good will shift the supply-and-demand equilibrium. The tax's burden will be shifted forward to consumers rather than backward to the producers to the degree that the demand is inelastic relative to supply.

9. A thousand forces affect price. But in a freely competitive market, they do so only by acting *through* supply and demand. Governments usually affect price and quantity in individual markets by operating through supply and demand, but on occasion government affects price and quantity by setting maximum ceilings or minimum floors that interfere with the workings of competitive markets. Then quantity supplied need no longer equal quantity demanded. And some producers or consumers may wish to sell or buy more than they are able to at the legal price. Distortions and inefficiencies result. Unless the discrepancies between supply and demand are removed by legislation (rationing, etc.), disorder and black markets may result.

10. Interferences with supply and demand will often lead to inefficient pricing and allocations. Thus when the government interferes with supply and demand for the purpose of protecting one group or redistributing income, hidden costs may crop up because the protective or redistributive devices are inherently so inefficient. Often the same goal could be better accomplished by the simultaneous use of the tax system to promote equity and market pricing to preserve efficiency.

CONCEPTS FOR REVIEW

price elasticity of demand, supply
total revenue, $P \times Q$
elastic, inelastic, unitary elastic
$E_D = (\% \ Q \text{ rise})/(\% \ P \text{ cut})$
$E_S = (\% \ Q \text{ rise})/(\% \ P \text{ rise})$
demand versus quantity demanded
income elasticity
momentary, short-run, long-run
  equilibrium

shift of vs. movement along a curve
rationing required by price ceilings
time element in supply, demand
incidence of a tax: forward-shifting
  onto consumers, backward-shifting
  onto producers
efficiency vs. equity

QUESTIONS FOR DISCUSSION

1. List a number of factors that would increase the demand for concerts. Make another list of those factors increasing the supply of concerts.

2. For each pair of commodities, state which you think is the more price elastic and give your reasons: perfume and salt; penicillin and ice cream; cigarettes and books; ice cream and chocolate ice cream.

3. What will a rise in price do to total revenue when demand is elastic, inelastic, or unit-elastic? What will higher quantity do in the three cases?

4. "*P* drops by 1 percent, causing *Q* to rise by 2 percent. Demand is therefore *elastic*, with $E_D > 1$.'' If you change 2 to $\frac{1}{2}$ in this sentence, what two other changes will be required?

5. Consider a competitive market for apartments. What would be the effect on the equilibrium output and price after the following changes (other things held equal)? In each case, explain your answer using supply and demand curves.

(a) A rise in the income of consumers.

(b) A $10-per-month tax on apartment rentals.

(c) A government edict saying apartments could not rent for more than $200 per month.

(d) A new construction technique allowing apartments to be built at half the cost.

(e) A 20 percent increase in construction workers' wages.

6. A recent study concluded, ''It is one of the ironies of the apartment market in New York that, although there are three times more rent-regulated apartments than free-market apartments, yet it is much easier to find a vacant, unregulated apartment.'' Using supply-and-demand analysis, explain this apparent paradox.

7. ''A good harvest will generally lower the income of farmers.'' Illustrate this proposition using a supply-and-demand diagram.

8. After studying the economics of gasoline taxation similar to that shown in Figure 18-9, the city of Washington, D.C., decided to pass a high gasoline tax. The city was surprised to find that the demand for gasoline sold within its city limits was highly elastic, as people simply went to the suburbs to buy gasoline, so that revenue collections were far under forecasts. Explain this situation verbally and graphically.

9. In response to low farm prices, governments have often purchased grains and other foods for government stockpiles. Explain the impact of this step on food prices and on farm incomes.

10. Elasticity problems:

(a) Consider the baseball-ticket price example given on page 426. Assuming you sell 15,000 tickets at a ticket price of $10, calculate the revenues collected for ticket prices of $5, $10, $12, and $15.

(b) Demand studies find that the price elasticity of demand for heroin is 0.1. Say that half the heroin users in New York City support their habit by criminal activities. Using supply-and-demand analysis, show the impact on crime in New York City of a tough law-enforcement program that cuts off the supply of heroin into the New York market by 50 percent. What would be the effect on criminal activities and on drug use of legalizing heroin (as was done in the late nineteenth century) if that lowered the price of heroin products by 90 percent?

(c) The short-run demand for oil is estimated to have a price elasticity of 0.05. If the initial price of oil were $3 per barrel, what would be the effect on oil price and quantity of an embargo that curbed world oil supply by 5 percent?

(d) To show that elasticities are independent of units, refer back to Table 18-1. Change the price units from dollars to pennies; change the quantity units from bushels to tons, using the conversion of 30 bushels equals 1 ton. Then calculate the first two elasticity rows.

11. Examine the diagram below, which shows demand and supply curves for wheat for different years. Identify historical intersection points. Fill in columns at right showing the P and Q of wheat for each of the 4 years. Use this example to explain why it may be difficult to estimate or "identify" the supply and demand curves from time-series data on P and Q alone. Are there circumstances where the data do indeed trace out SS or DD curves?

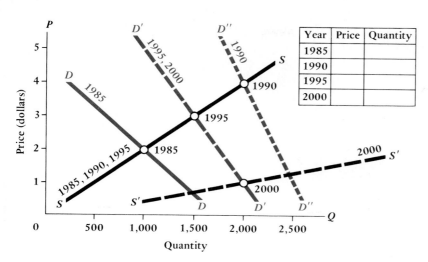

Year	Price	Quantity
1985		
1990		
1995		
2000		

12. Advanced problem for those who like simple geometry and algebra: Justify the E_D rule given in the footnote on page 428 for a straight line. In the triangle below, the DD has the equation $Q = b - (b/a)P$, where b is the Q intercept and a the P intercept. The absolute inverted slope of DD is $-(dQ/dP) = -(\Delta Q/\Delta P) = b/a$. Now apply the formula $E_D = -(dQ/dP)(P/Q)$ to get $E_D = (b/a)\{P/[b - (b/a)P]\} = P/(a - P)$—the ratio of the lower vertical bracket to the upper. Can you show, by the property of similar triangles, that $E_D = P/(a - P) = bC/aC$ equals "the length of the straight line below the point divided by its length above the point," as stated in the footnote on page 428?

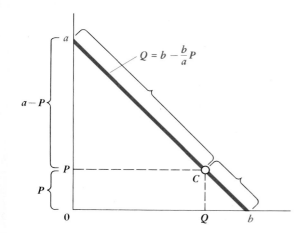

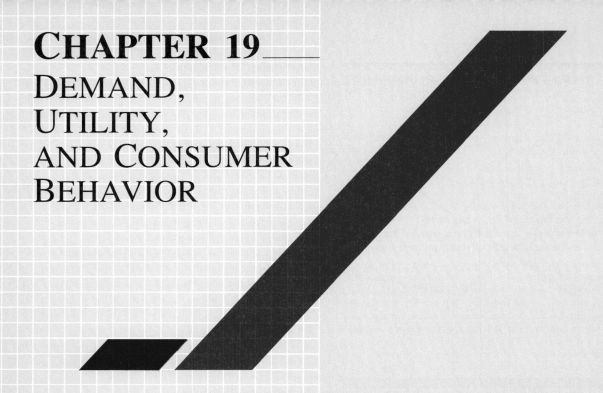

CHAPTER 19 ___
DEMAND, UTILITY, AND CONSUMER BEHAVIOR

What is a cynic? A man who knows the price of everything and the value of nothing.

Oscar Wilde

EACH OF US makes dozens, even hundreds, of choices every day: Should we eat breakfast or sleep late? Drink coffee, tea, or milk? Buy a new shirt, a second-hand coat, or a fancy hat? Spend our time studying economics or talking to friends? Buy a new car or fix our old one? These kinds of decisions, which form consumption choices or consumer behavior, are the stuff of our daily existence.

One of the major tasks of economics is to help us understand the principles of consumer behavior. We have encountered the law of demand and know that people tend to buy more of a good when it is inexpensive than when it is costly. And in the preceding pages we learned that necessities have low price elasticities while luxuries are often price elastic. This chapter examines the reasons underlying such observations. We shall see that the economic principles of total utility and marginal utility can help explain consumer behavior and market demands.

The theory of utility and consumer behavior will help unravel certain mysteries. People sometimes wonder why the source of all life, water, is so cheap while useless frivolities like furs are so expensive.

The concept known as consumer surplus will help explain this paradox. The appendix presents an alternative approach to the theory of consumer behavior called indifference curves.

CHOICE AND UTILITY THEORY

In explaining the behavior of consumers, we rely on the fundamental premise that people tend to choose those goods and services they value most highly. To describe this, economists a century ago developed the notion of utility, and with the help of this concept, they were first able to derive the demand curve and explain its properties.

What do we mean by utility? In a word, **utility** denotes satisfaction. More precisely, it refers to the subjective pleasure or usefulness that a person derives from consuming a good or service. We should not identify utility with any precise neural action that psychologists can measure. Rather, utility is a scientific construct that economists use to understand how rational consumers divide their limited resources among the commodities that provide them satisfaction.

Marginal Utility and the Law of Diminishing Marginal Utility

How does utility apply to the theory of demand? Say that consuming the first unit of a good (ice cream, concerts, or movies) provides you a certain level of utility. Now imagine consuming a second unit. Your total utility goes up because the second unit of the good gives you some additional or *marginal* utility. What about adding a third and fourth unit of the same good?

The effect of adding units of consumption involves the notion of marginal utility. What do we mean by ''marginal''? Marginal is used in the sense of ''additional'' or ''extra.'' Thus when you eat an additional ice cream cone, you receive a certain increment to your psychic utility, and that increment is called **marginal utility.** We will encounter the term ''marginal'' many times in the chapters that follow, and it is always used in the sense of extra.

A century ago economists formulated an important

relationship quite analogous to the law of diminishing returns. Recall that the law of diminishing returns says that the extra output declines as a firm adds extra doses of inputs (see Table 2-2).

When economists thought about utility, they established the **law of diminishing marginal utility.** This law postulates that the amount of extra or marginal utility declines as a person consumes more and more of a good.

Utility tends to increase as you consume more of a good. However, according to the law of diminishing marginal utility, as you consume more and more, your total utility will grow at a slower and slower rate. Growth in total utility slows because your marginal utility (the extra utility added by the last unit consumed of a good) diminishes as more of the good is consumed. The diminishing marginal utility results from the fact that your appreciation or taste for a good drops off as more of the good is consumed.

The law of diminishing marginal utility states that, as the amount of a good consumed increases, the marginal utility of that good tends to diminish.

A Numerical Example

Column (2) of the table with Figure 19-1 shows that total utility enjoyed increases as consumption *(Q)* grows, but at a decreasing rate. Column (3) measures marginal utility as the increment of total utility when one more unit of the good is added.

The fact that marginal utilities in the table are declining exemplifies the law of diminishing marginal utility.

Figure 19-1*(a)* pictures how total utility increases, but at a decreasing rate. Figure 19-1*(b)* depicts marginal utilities—increments of utility (not the total of utility itself). Whether we work with sizable units of the good and measure utilities by blocks and steps, or whether we smooth the drawings by use of the black and red curves to reflect continuously divisible units, the law of diminishing marginal utility means that the curves in Figure 19-1*(b)* must slope downward; in other words, the total utility relations in Figure 19-1*(a)* must look concave (like a dome). The shape of the curves in Figure 19-1*(a)* and *(b)* reflects the law of diminishing marginal utility.

(a) TOTAL UTILITY

(b) MARGINAL UTILITY

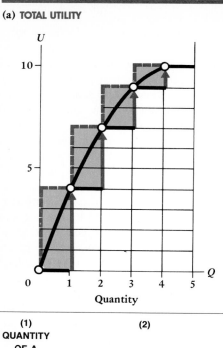

(1) QUANTITY OF A GOOD CONSUMED	(2) TOTAL UTILITY	(3) MARGINAL UTILITY
0	0	
		4
1	4	
		3
2	7	
		2
3	9	
		1
4	10	
		0
5	10	

Figure 19-1   Curves as well as numbers can show law of diminishing marginal utility

Although total utility rises with consumption, the table shows it rises at a decreasing rate. This means that marginal utility—the extra utility added by the last extra unit of the good—will decrease. From this observation, earlier economists prepared their demonstration of the law of downward-sloping demand. (Note the similarity to Chapter 2's law of diminishing returns.)

The red blocks show the extra utility added by each new unit. The fact that total utility increases at a decreasing rate is shown in **(b)** by the declining steps of marginal utility. If we make our units smaller, the steps in total utility are smoothed out and total utility becomes the smooth black curve. Moreover, smoothed marginal utility, shown in **(b)** by the red downward-sloping smooth curve, becomes indistinguishable from the slope of the smooth curve of **(a)**.

Relationship of Total and Marginal Utility Using Figure 19-1, we can easily see that the total utility of consuming a certain amount is equal to the sum of the marginal utilities up to that point. For example, assume that 3 units are consumed. Column (2) of the table shows that the total utility is 9 units. In column (3) we see that the sum of the marginal utilities of the first 3 units is also 4 + 3 + 2 = 9 units.

Examining Figure 19-1(*b*), we see that the total

area under the marginal utility curve at a particular level of consumption—as measured either by blocks or by the area under the smooth *MU* curve—must equal the height of the total utility curve shown for the same number of units in Figure 19-1(*a*).

Whether we examine this relationship using tables or graphs, we see that total utility is the sum of all the marginal utilities that were added from the beginning.

Historical Sketch of Utility[1]

Its association with utilitarianism marks utility theory as one of the intellectual landmarks of the last two centuries. The notion of utility arose soon after 1700 among students of mathematical probability. Thus Daniel Bernoulli, a member of the brilliant Swiss family of mathematicians, observed in 1738 that people act as if the dollar they stand to gain in a fair bet is worth less to them than the dollar they stand to lose. This means they are averse to risk and successive new dollars of wealth bring them smaller and smaller increments of true utility.

An early introduction of the utility notion into the social sciences was accomplished by the English philosopher Jeremy Bentham (1748–1831). After studies devoted to legal theory, and under the influence of Adam Smith's doctrines, Bentham turned to the study of the principles necessary for drawing up social legislation. He proposed that society should be organized on the "principle of utility," which he defined as the "property in any object . . . to produce pleasure, good or happiness or to prevent . . . pain, evil or unhappiness."[2] All legislation, according to Bentham, should be designed on *utilitarian* principles, to promote "the greatest happiness of the greatest number." Among his other legislative proposals were quite modern-sounding ideas about crime and punishment in which he suggested that raising the "pain" to the criminal by harsh punishments would deter crimes; these ideas have recently been pursued by economists of the Chicago School.

Bentham's views about utility seem crude to many people today. But 200 years ago they were revolutionary, as they began to focus on the practical results of economic and social policies, whereas earlier justifications were based on tradition or on religious doctrine. Today, many political thinkers defend their legislative proposals on utilitarian notions of what will make the most people better off.

The next step in the development of utility theory

came when the neo-classical economists—such as William Stanley Jevons (1835–1882)—extended Bentham's utility concept to explain consumer behavior. Like Bentham, Jevons thought economic theory was a "calculus of pleasure and pain" and showed how rational people would base their consumption decisions on the extra or marginal utility of each good. Many utilitarians of the nineteenth century believed that utility was a psychic reality—directly and cardinally measurable, like length or temperature. They looked to their own sentiments for affirmation of the law of diminishing marginal utility.

Ordinal Utility Most economists today reject the notion of a cardinal, measurable utility that is attached to consumption of ordinary goods like shoes or coffee. Indeed, it is possible to derive demand curves without being able to measure utility. What counts for modern demand theory is whether a consumer prefers certain bundles of commodities more than others, an approach represented by statements like "A is preferred to B." No more than this "ordinal utility" statement is required to establish firmly the general properties of market demand curves described in this chapter and in its appendix.[3]

EQUILIBRIUM CONDITION: EQUAL MARGINAL UTILITIES PER DOLLAR FOR EVERY GOOD

What is the condition under which I, as a consumer, am most satisfied with my market basket of consumption goods? We say that a consumer attempts to maximize his or her utility, or the amount of satisfaction or

---

[1]This section on the history of the development of utility theory can be omitted in short courses.

[2]*An Introduction to the Principles of Morals* (1789). Note that the term "utility" was used by Bentham in quite a different way from the more common usage today as something that is useful.

[3]A statement that "situation A is preferred to situation B"—which does not require that we know *how much* A is preferred to B—is called "ordinal," or dimensionless, meaning that different situations are ranked in order, but there is no measure of the quantitative difference between the situations. We might rank pictures in an exhibition in terms of the order of their beauty, but not have a quantitative measure of beauty.

Some economists rely on "cardinal," or dimensional, measurement of utility, in which the quantitative differences in preference are measured. An example of a cardinal measure comes when we say that a substance at 100° kelvin is twice as hot as one at 50° kelvin. These economists examine the way people behave in uncertain situations as a way of measuring utilities; the topic of behavior under uncertainty is pursued in the appendix to Chapter 24.

happiness produced by purchases of consumer goods. Can we see what a rule for such an optimal decision would be? Certainly I would not expect that the last egg I am buying brings exactly the same marginal utility as the last record album I am buying, for records cost much more per unit than eggs. On reflection, it would seem more reasonable that I should keep buying a good which costs twice as much per unit as another good until it brings me just twice as much in marginal utility.

In short, if I arrange my consumption so that every single good is bringing me the same marginal utility per dollar of expenditure, then I am assured that I am attaining maximum satisfaction or utility from my purchases. At such a point I am in consumer equilibrium. This fundamental condition can now be stated. A consumer with a fixed income and facing given market prices of goods can come to a point of maximum satisfaction or utility, or be at a consumer equilibrium, when the following condition is satisfied:

The law of equal marginal utilities per dollar states that each good is demanded up to the point where the marginal utility of the last dollar spent on it is exactly the same as the marginal utility of the last dollar spent on any other good.

Why must this law hold? If any one good gave more marginal utility per dollar, I would gain by taking money away from other goods and spending more on that good—up to the point where the law of diminishing marginal utility brought its marginal utility per dollar down to equality with that of other goods. If any good gave less marginal utility per dollar than the common level, I would buy less of it until the marginal utility of the last dollar spent on it had risen back to the common level.[4] The common marginal utility per dollar of all commodities in consumer equilibrium is called the "marginal utility of income," which measures the additional utility that would be gained if the consumer enjoyed the consumption from one additional dollar of income.

This fundamental condition of consumer equilibrium can be written in terms of the marginal utilities (MU) and prices (P) of the different goods in the following compact way:

$$\frac{MU_{\text{Good 1}}}{P_1} = \frac{MU_{\text{Good 2}}}{P_2}$$
$$= \frac{MU_{\text{Good 3}}}{P_3} = \cdots$$
$$= MU \text{ per } \$ \text{ of income}$$

Why Demand Curves Slope Downward

Using this fundamental rule for consumer behavior, we can easily see why demand curves slope downward. For simplicity, hold the common marginal utility per dollar of income constant. Then increase the price of good 1. With no change in quantity consumed, the first ratio (i.e., $MU_{\text{Good 1}}/P_1$) will be below the MU per dollar of all other goods. The consumer will therefore have to readjust the consumption of good 1. How? By (a) lowering the consumption of good 1; (b) thereby raising the MU of good 1; until (c) at the new reduced level of consumption of good 1, the new marginal utility per dollar spent on good 1 is again equal to the MU per dollar spent on other goods.

Hence, we see why a higher price for a good reduces the consumer's optimal consumption of that commodity and therefore why demand curves slope downward.

Economizing on the Use of Time

The principles of stretching a budget so as to maximize satisfaction need not apply only to our use of money but, as emphasized by Chicago's Gary Becker, to our use of time as well. Our "time budget" is limited to 24 hours a day whether we are rich or poor in dollars. We can therefore apply the same concepts to time budgets that we applied earlier to dollar budgets.

Suppose that, after satisfying all your obligations,

[4]At a few places in economics the indivisibility of units is important and cannot be glossed over. Thus, Cadillacs do not come like juice, and their indivisibility may matter. Suppose I buy one but definitely not two Cadillacs. Then the marginal utility of the first car is enough larger than the marginal utility of the same number of dollars spent elsewhere to induce me to buy this first unit. The marginal utility that the second Cadillac would bring is enough less to ensure I do not buy it. When indivisibility matters, our equality rule for equilibrium can be restated as an inequality rule.

you have 3 hours a day of free time and can devote it to playing cards, listening to music, or reading. What is the best way to allocate your time? Let's ignore the possibility that time spent on some of these activities might be an investment that will enhance your earning abilities in the future. Rather, assume that these are all pure consumption or utility-yielding pursuits. The principles of consumer choice would suggest that you will make the best use of your time when the marginal utilities of the last minute spent on each activity in which you engage are equal.

To take another example, suppose you want to maximize your learning or your grade-point average but you have only a limited amount of time available. Should you study each subject for the same amount of time? Surprisingly, the answer is, Not necessarily. You may find that an equal study time for economics, history, and chemistry will not yield the same amount of learning in the last minute. If the last minute produces a greater marginal grade advantage in chemistry than in history, then you would raise your grade-point average by shifting additional minutes from history to chemistry, and so on until the last minute yields the same incremental learning in each subject.[5]

The same rule of maximum utility per hour can be applied to many different areas of life. It is not merely a law of economics. It is a law of rational choice.

Are Consumers Wizards?

A word of caution is in order about how we view consumers. We consumers are not expected to be wizards. We may make most of our decisions unconsciously or just out of habit. What is assumed is that consumers are fairly *consistent* in their tastes and actions; that they do not flail around in unpredictable ways, making themselves miserable by persistent errors of judgment or arithmetic. If enough people act

---

[5]Does this result suggest that you will end up with the same grades in each subject? Surely not. You might end up with a 90 in economics, an 80 in history, and an 85 in chemistry, but with the last hour of studying adding one grade point to your grade in each subject.

Economists have found many kinds of behavior to be consistent with the economics of time sketched here. For example, the theory correctly predicts that, other things equal, women with high-paying jobs will tend to have fewer children than those with low-paying jobs. Can you explain this result in terms of the monetary value of time?

consistently, avoiding erratic changes in buying behavior, our scientific theory will provide a tolerable approximation to the facts.

AN ALTERNATIVE APPROACH: SUBSTITUTION EFFECT AND INCOME EFFECT

The concept of marginal utility has been a valuable way of understanding the fundamental law of downward-sloping demand. But over the last few decades, economists have developed an alternative approach to analysis of demand—one that makes no mention of marginal utility. This alternative approach uses "indifference curves" and is thoroughly explored in the appendix to this chapter. We can easily summarize here the main features of this alternative approach. The alternative approach does lead rigorously and consistently to the desired result, and it does provide an interesting insight into the factors that tend to make the responsiveness of quantity demanded to price—the price elasticity of demand—be very large or very small.

This alternative approach asks: What are the income effect and substitution effect of a change of price? By looking at these, we can see why the quantity demanded of a good declines as its price rises.

Substitution Effect

The first factor explaining diminishing consumption when price rises is an obvious one. If the price of tea goes up while other prices do not, then tea has become relatively more expensive.

When tea becomes a relatively more expensive source of stimulation than before, less tea and more coffee or cocoa will be bought. Similarly, a rise in the price of movies relative to concerts may cause us to seek more of our amusement in the cheaper diversion. More generally, the **substitution effect** says that it pays to substitute other goods for goods whose prices have risen (like tea) in order to maintain one's standard of living most cheaply.

Consumers are doing here only what businesspeople do when rises in the price of one productive factor cause them to adjust their production methods so as to substitute cheap inputs for the more expensive input.

By this process of substitution, businesses can produce the same output at least total cost. Similarly, when consumers substitute less expensive goods, they are buying satisfaction at least cost.

Income Effect

In the second place, when your money income is fixed, being forced to buy a good at a higher price is just like experiencing a decrease in your real income or purchasing power (particularly if you have been buying a great deal of the commodity). More generally, the **income effect** says that, when a price rises, your real income falls and you are likely to buy less of almost all goods (including the good whose price has risen). With a lower real income, you will now want to buy less tea. Thus, the income effect will normally reinforce the substitution effect in making the demand curve downward sloping.*

Income and substitution effects combine to determine the major characteristics of different commodities. Under some circumstances the resulting demand curve is very price-elastic, as where the consumer has been spending a good deal on the commodity and where ready substitutes are available. But if a commodity, such as salt, requires only a small fraction of the consumer's budget, is not easily replaceable by other items, and is needed in small amounts to complement more important items, then demand will tend to be price inelastic.

Estimates of Price and Income Elasticities

The previous chapter discussed the concept of elasticity, while this chapter has so far explored the foundations of demand curves and described income and substitution effects. For many applications, it is essential to have numerical estimates of demand elasticities. For example, when installing costly pollution-control equipment, an automobile manufacturer will want to know the impact on sales of the now-higher car prices; a college needs to know the impact of higher tuition rates on its applications; a publisher will calculate the impact of higher textbook prices on its sales. All these questions require a numerical estimate of price elasticity.

Similar decisions depend on income elasticities. A state planning its road network will estimate the impact of rising incomes on automobile travel; the federal government must calculate the effect of higher incomes on beef consumption in planning quotas on beef imports; in planning the necessary additions to generating capacity, electrical utilities require income elasticities for estimating electricity consumption. In each of these and many other goods and services, knowledge of income elasticities is essential.

Economists have devoted considerable time to estimating price and income elasticities. Estimates are derived from data on quantities demanded, prices, incomes, and other variables. Tables 19-1 and 19-2 provide selected estimates of elasticities.

FROM INDIVIDUAL TO MARKET DEMAND

Up to now we have discussed the principles underlying a single individual's demand for tea or coffee or concerts. How can we pass from the individual to the entire market? The demand curve for a good is obtained for the whole market by summing up the

---

*Income and substitution effects explain not only the downward slope of demand but also a rare exception to that law. A perverse case may arise for an "inferior good," one on which people spend less when their incomes rise; examples of inferior goods are bologna, margarine, and pig products.

What happened when the 1845 Irish famine greatly raised the price of potatoes? Consider the case of a poor family that consumed some meat and a lot of potatoes in 1844. After the potato blight, potato prices rose so sharply that the family's real income actually fell. As a result, they ended up consuming more rather than fewer of the high-P potatoes. Why? Because now they had to spend so much on potatoes, the necessity of life, as to make it quite impossible to afford any meat at all; hence, they were forced to become even more dependent than before on potatoes. In brief, the substitution effect was here overcome by the perverse income effect applicable to a peculiar inferior good, such as the potato, whose consumption tends to decrease in the poor person's budget when incomes rise.

This curiosity is attributed to Sir Robert Giffen, a Victorian economist. Note that in the case of inferior goods on which we spend little money, the perverse income effects will not outweigh the substitution effects to produce the odd Giffen case.

COMMODITY	PRICE ELASTICITY
Tomatoes	4.6
Green peas	2.8
Legal gambling	1.9
Marijuana	1.5
Taxi service	1.2
Furniture	1.0
Movies	0.87
Shoes	0.70
Legal services	0.61
Cigarettes	0.51
Medical insurance	0.31
Bus travel	0.20
Electricity, residential	0.13

Table 19-1   Selected estimates of price elasticities of demand

Estimates of price elasticities of demand show a wide range of variation. High elasticities are generally found for goods like tomatoes or peas where ready substitutes are available. Low price elasticities exist for those goods like electricity which are essential to daily life and which have no easy substitutes. [Source: Heinz Kohler, *Intermediate Microeconomics: Theory and Applications,* 2d ed. (Scott Foresman, New York, 1986).]

amounts of the good that will be demanded by each consumer. Each consumer has a demand curve along which the quantity demanded can be plotted against the price. It generally slopes downward and to the right. If all consumers were exactly alike in their demands and if there were 1 million consumers, then we could think of the market demand curve as a millionfold enlargement of each consumer's demand curve.

But people are not all exactly alike. Some have high incomes, some low. Some greatly desire tea; others prefer coffee. What must we do to the demand schedules or curves of each consumer to arrive at the total market curve?

All we have to do is calculate the sum total of what all the different consumers will consume at any given price; we then plot that total amount as a point on the market demand curve. Or if we like, we may set the total down in a demand table like that first seen in Chapter 4.

We sum individual demands at each price to end up with the market demand curve. Figure 19-2 adds individual *dd* demand curves horizontally to get the market *DD* demand curve.

Demand Shifts

Factors other than changes in the price of tea can change the quantity of tea demanded. We know this from budget studies, from historical experience, and from examining our own behavior. We discussed briefly in Chapter 18 some of the important non-price determinants of demand. We now review the earlier analysis using our principles of consumer behavior.

An increase in income is a factor normally tending to increase the amount we are willing to buy of any good. Goods that are necessities tend to be less responsive to income changes. Goods that are luxuries tend to be more responsive. Indeed, as we saw in the footnote on page 452, for a few abnormal goods, known as inferior goods, purchases may shrink as

COMMODITY	INCOME ELASTICITY
Automobiles	2.5
Housing, owner-occupied	1.5
Furniture	1.5
Books	1.4
Restaurant meals	1.4
Clothing	1.0
Physicians' services	0.75
Tobacco	0.64
Eggs	0.37
Margarine	−0.20
Pig products	−0.20
Flour	−0.36

Table 19-2   Income elasticities for selected products

Income elasticities are high for luxuries, whose consumption grows rapidly relative to income. Negative income elasticities are found for "inferior goods," whose demand falls as income rises. Demand for many staple commodities like clothing grows proportionally with income. [Source: Heinz Kohler, *Intermediate Microeconomics: Theory and Applications,* 2d ed. (Scott Foresman, New York, 1986).]

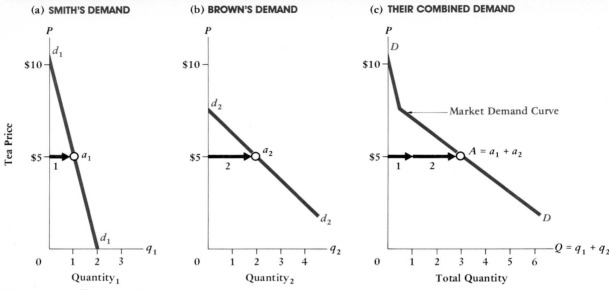

Figure 19-2   To get market demand, we add all consumers' demand curves

At each price, such as $5, we add quantities demanded by each person to get market quantity demanded. For example, at a price of $5, we add horizontally Smith's 1 unit demanded to Brown's 2 units to get the market demand of 3 units.

incomes increase because people can afford to replace them with other, more desired goods.

Bologna, soup bones, and potatoes might be examples of inferior goods for many Americans today. Fortunately, the species called inferior goods is so rare that we can usually neglect it in our discussions.

Let us now show what all this means in terms of the demand curve. This curve, you will recall, shows how the quantity of a good demanded responds to a change in its own price.

But quantity bought may change also as a result of changes in the prices of other goods or as a result of a change in the consumer's income. The demand curve was drawn on the assumption that these other things were held constant. But what if they change? Then the whole demand curve will shift to the right or to the left.

Figure 19-3's curves show such changes. Given people's incomes and the prices for other goods,

we can draw the demand curve for tea as DD.[6] First assume that price and quantity are at the point A. Suppose that incomes rise. Even though the price of tea is unchanged, because tea is a normal good, people will increase their purchases of tea. Hence the demand curve for tea will shift to the right, say to $D'D'$, with A' indicating the new quantity demanded of tea. If incomes should fall, then we may expect a reduction in demand and in quantity bought. This downward shift we illustrate by $D''D''$ and by A''.

Income is only one of many factors that affect the position of the demand curve. An increased taste or fashion for tea would also shift the demand to the right. A decreased taste would have the opposite effect. Advertisement shifts out the DD curve. Even if each individual consumed the same amount of a

[6]In this and in other chapters, we label *individual* demand or supply curves in lowercase letters (*dd* and *ss*), while uppercase letters (*DD* and *SS*) pertain to the *market* demand and supply curves.

good, a growth in population would have the effect of increasing the total market demand for a product. If people think that an inflation is about to get under way, they may increase their purchases now in order to beat the gun.[7] Still other factors operate all the time to shift demand.

Cross Relations of Demand

Everyone knows that raising the price of tea will decrease the amount of tea demanded. We have seen that it will also affect the amounts demanded of other commodities. For example, a higher price for tea will lower the demand for a commodity such as lemon; i.e., it will shift the whole demand schedule of lemon downward. But it will also increase the demand for coffee. It will probably have little effect on the demand curve for salt.

We say, therefore, that tea and coffee are rival or competing products; they are **substitutes** because an increase in the price of good A will increase the demand for substitute good B. Tea and lemon, on the other hand, are cooperating or complementary products; they are called **complements** because an increase in the price of good A causes a decrease in the demand for its complementary good B. In between are **independent goods,** such as tea and shoes, for which a price change for one has no effect on the demand for the other. You might classify such pairs as turkey and cranberry sauce, automobiles and gasoline, oil and coal, college and textbooks, salt and shoelaces.

Besides showing effects of income changes, Figure 19-3 also illustrates how changes in other goods' prices affect demand. A fall in the price of coffee may well cause consumers to buy less tea; the demand curve shifts to, say, $D''D''$. But what if the price of lemon were to fall? The resulting change on this DD

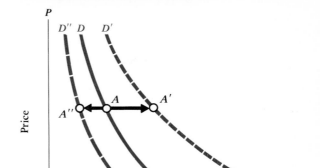

SHIFTS IN THE DEMAND CURVE

Figure 19-3   Demand curve shifts with changes in income or in other goods' prices

As incomes increase, consumers want more of a good, thus shifting DD to $D'D'$ (explain why lower incomes shift DD to $D''D''$). Similarly, a rise in the price of a substitute good like coffee shifts out tea's DD to $D'D'$. (What would be the effect of a large increase in the price of a complementary good like lemon?)

may not be very large. But if there is any change, it will be in the direction of increased tea purchases—a rightward shift of DD. Why this difference in response? Because coffee is a rival or substitute product for tea; lemon, on the other hand, is a complementary commodity to tea.

THE PARADOX OF VALUE

The principles outlined here can help explain a famous question that troubled Adam Smith. He wondered how it could be that water, which is so useful that life itself is impossible without it, has no value, while diamonds, which are quite unnecessary, command such an exalted price.

Unlike Adam Smith, you can give a correct answer

[7]In fact, when I see in today's paper that the price of heating oil is going up, I may rush out to buy more. This may seem to be an exception to the law of downward-sloping demand, but it can be reconciled with that law when we realize that I am buying more now because I want to be able to buy less of it tomorrow when its price is higher. Despite this dynamic effect of changing prices, it remains true that at a steady high price for oil I shall consume less than at a steady low price.

to the problem, as follows: "The supply and demand curves for water intersect at a very low price, while supply and demand for diamonds are such that the equilibrium price of diamonds is very high."

Adam Smith could not have given it because supply and demand curves as descriptive tools had not yet been invented, and were not to be for 75 years or more. But after he had mastered the new tools, Adam Smith would naturally ask the question, "But *why* do supply and demand for water intersect at such a low price?"

The answer is that diamonds are very scarce and the cost of getting extra ones is high, while water is relatively abundant, with its cost low in many areas of the world.

This would all have seemed reasonable even to the classical economists of the last century, who would probably have let it go at that. But they would not have known how to reconcile the facts about cost with the equally valid fact that the world's water is more useful than the world's supply of diamonds.

Today, we should add to the above cost considerations a second truth: The utility of water as a whole does not determine its price or demand. It is the marginal utility of the *last* glass of water that determines water's price. Because there is so much water, its price falls to a very low level. Even though the first few drops are worth life itself, the last few are only needed for watering the lawn, or washing the car. We thus find that an immensely valuable commodity like water sells for next to nothing because its last drop is worth next to nothing.

As one student put the matter: The theory of economic value is easy to understand if you just remember that in economics the tail wags the dog: it is the tail of marginal utility that wags the dog of prices and quantities.

We can resolve the paradox of value as follows: The more there is of a commodity, the less the relative desirability of its last little unit becomes, even though its total usefulness grows as we get more of the commodity. So, it is obvious why a large amount of water has a low price, or why an absolute necessity like air could become a free good. In each case, it is the large quantities that pull the marginal utilities so far down, and thus reduce the prices of these vital commodities.

CONSUMER SURPLUS

The paradox of value emphasizes that the recorded money value of a good (measured by price × quantity) may be very misleading as an indicator of the total economic value of that good. The measured economic value of the air we breathe is zero, yet air's contribution to welfare is immeasurably large.

The gap between the total utility of a good and its total market value is called **consumer surplus.** The surplus arises because we "receive more than we pay for"; it is rooted in the law of diminishing marginal utility.

It is easy to see how this consumer surplus arises. We pay the same price for each egg or glass of water. Thus we pay for *each* unit what the *last* unit is worth. But by our fundamental law of diminishing marginal utility, the earlier units are worth more to us than the last. Thus, we enjoy a surplus of utility on each of these earlier units.

Figure 19-4 illustrates the concept of consumer surplus for an individual who consumes water. Say that the price of water is $1 per gallon. This is shown by the horizontal black line at $1 in Figure 19-4. The consumer considers how many gallon jugs to buy at that price. The first gallon is highly valuable, slaking extreme thirst, and the consumer is willing to pay $9 for it. But this first gallon costs only $1—the market price—so the consumer has gained a surplus of $8.

Consider the second gallon. This is worth $8 to the consumer, but again only costs $1, so the surplus is $7. And so on down to the ninth gallon, which is worth only 50 cents to the consumer, and so it is not bought. The consumer equilibrium comes at a point E, where 8 gallons of water are bought at a price of $1 each.

But here comes the important finding: Even though the consumer has paid only $8, the total value of the water is $44. This is obtained by adding up each of the marginal utility columns (= $9 + $8 + \cdots + $2). Thus the consumer has gained a surplus of $36 over the amount paid.

In our example of Figure 19-4, we took the case of a single consumer purchasing water. But we can apply the concept of consumer surplus to a market as a whole. The market demand curve in Figure 19-5 is

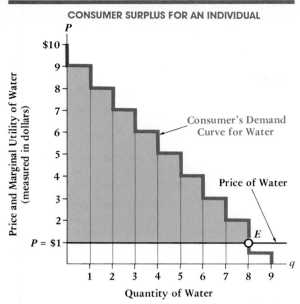

CONSUMER SURPLUS FOR AN INDIVIDUAL

Figure 19-4   Because of diminishing marginal utility, consumer's satisfaction exceeds what is paid

The downward-stepping demand for water reflects the diminishing marginal utility as the consumer is satiated with water consumption. Note how much excess or surplus satisfaction occurs from the earlier units. Adding up all the red surpluses ($8 of surplus on unit 1 + $7 of surplus on unit 2 + ⋯ + $1 of surplus on unit 8), we obtain the total consumer surplus of $36 on water purchases.

In the simplified case seen here, the area between the demand curve and the price line is the total consumer surplus.

the horizontal summation of the individual demand curves (of which that shown in Figure 19-4 is but one). The logic of the individual consumer surplus carries over to the market as a whole.

The area of the market demand curve above the price line, shown as *NER* in Figure 19-5, represents the total consumer surplus. It shows the extra utility that consumers received over what they paid for the commodity.

Applications of Consumer Surplus

The concept of consumer surplus is extremely useful in making many decisions about public goods—it has

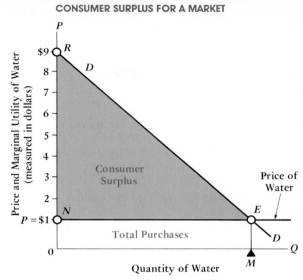

CONSUMER SURPLUS FOR A MARKET

Figure 19-5   Total consumer surplus is the area under the demand curve and above the price line

The demand curve measures the amount consumers would pay for each unit consumed. Thus the total area under the demand curve (*0REM*) shows the total utility attached to the consumption of water. By subtracting what the water costs consumers (equal to *0NEM*), we obtain the consumer surplus from water consumption as the triangle *NRE*.

been employed in decisions about airports, roads, dams, subways, and parks.

Suppose a new highway is being considered. Being free to all, it will bring in no revenues. Any utility to users will be seen only in individual consumer surplus. To avoid difficult issues of interpersonal utility comparisons, assume that there are 10,000 users, all identical in every respect.

By careful experimentation, we determine that each individual's consumer surplus is $350 for the highway. Consumers should vote for the road if its total cost is less than $3.5 million (10,000 × $350). And economists performing "cost-benefit analysis" generally recommend that the road should be built if its total consumer surplus ($3.5 million) exceeds its costs.

Aside from helping societies understand when it pays to build bridges or highways, consumer surplus explains why people are justifiably suspicious when price is equated with value. We have seen that water or air may have little monetary value (price times quantity) even though their total economic value swamps that of diamonds or furs. The consumer surplus of air and water is huge, while diamonds and furs may have little value over purchase price.

The concept of consumer surplus also points to the enormous privilege enjoyed by citizens of modern societies. It is easy for a consumer to overlook the vast array of enormously valuable goods that can be bought at low prices.

This is a humbling thought. If you know a person who is becoming arrogantly proud of his economic productivity and his level of real earnings, suggest that he pause and reflect. If he were transported with all his skills and energies intact to a desert island, how much would his money earnings buy? Indeed, without capital machinery, without rich resources, without other labor, and above all without the technological knowledge which each generation inherits from society's past, how much could he produce? It is only too clear that all of us reap the benefits of an economic world we never made. As L. T. Hobhouse said:

> The organizer of industry who thinks that he has "made" himself and his business has found a whole social system ready to his hand in skilled workers, machinery, a market, peace and order—a vast apparatus and a pervasive atmosphere, the joint creation of millions of men and scores of generations. Take away the whole social factor and we [are] but . . . savages living on roots, berries, and vermin.

■　■　■

We have now completed our analysis of the forces that lie behind the demand curve. Key to the economic theory of demand is that consumers must stretch their limited incomes to meet many different needs and wants, and that they do so by allocating their incomes so that the utilities of the last dollars spent are equal for all goods. Such an allocation generates the vast array of demand curves for different commodities.

But what of business? What of the production and supply of the goods that consumers demand? The next three chapters turn to this other partner in the dance of supply and demand. We begin in the next chapter with an understanding of different kinds of businesses, from tiny food shops to giant corporations. Chapters 21 and 22 focus more carefully on the analysis of production and costs, concepts which will be shown to determine business supply decisions.

Once our survey of costs and businesses is complete, we can return to analyze supply and demand—but at that point with a fuller understanding of the forces that lie behind each of the two fundamental curves that dance through the pages of textbooks and indeed through economic life itself.

SUMMARY

1. Economists explain consumer demand by the concept of *total utility* and with the *law of diminishing marginal utility*. Utility is a concept that represents the amount of usefulness or satisfaction that a consumer obtains from a commodity. The additional satisfaction obtained from consuming an additional unit of a good is given the name *marginal utility,* where "marginal" means the extra or incremental utility.

The law of diminishing marginal utility states that as the amount of a commodity consumed increases, the marginal utility of the last unit consumed tends to decrease.

2. Economists assume that consumers allocate their limited incomes so as to obtain the greatest satisfaction or utility. To get maximal utility, a consumer must equate the marginal utilities of the last dollars spent for each and every good. Only when the marginal utility per dollar is equal for bread and butter and shoes and records and concerts will the consumer attain the greatest satisfaction from the limited dollar incomes. (But be careful to note that the marginal utility of a \$25-per-ounce bottle of perfume is not equal to the marginal utility of a 25-cent glass of cola. Rather, their marginal utilities divided by price per unit—that is, their marginal utilities per last dollar, MU/P—are all to be equalized in the consumer's optimal allocation.)

This is a fundamental rule of logic that transcends demand theory: If you want to allocate any limited resource among competing uses, whenever the marginal advantage in one use happens to be greater than in another, you can benefit by transferring from the low-marginal-advantage use to the high—until a final equilibrium is reached at which all marginal advantages have become equal.

3. The market demand curve for all consumers is derived by adding horizontally the separate demand curves of each consumer. A demand curve can shift for many reasons. For example, a rise in income will normally shift DD rightward, thus increasing demand; a rise in the price of a substitute good (coffee for tea, and so forth) will also create a similar upward shift in demand; a rise in the price of a complementary good (such as lemon in its relation to tea) will represent a cross effect that shifts the DD curve downward and leftward. Still other factors—changing tastes, population, or expectations—can increase or decrease demand.

4. Without using the marginal utility concept explicitly, we can gain new insight into the factors making for downward-sloping demand by dividing the effect of a price rise into *(a)* its *substitution effect* component and *(b)* its *income effect* component. When P for a good rises, you tend to maintain the same level of well-being by substituting other goods for the good that has just become more expensive. Reinforcing this decrease in a good's Q that arises out of substitution is the income effect: since you ordinarily buy less of the good in question when your family income is lower, the rise in its price—which has produced a drop in your real income or real purchasing power—thus induces a further cut in consumption as the result of your now having a lower real income.

5. Adam Smith's paradox of value—that a commodity important for welfare may sell for less in the market than one less important—is clarified by the distinction between the concepts of marginal and total utility. The scarcity of a good, as determined by its cost (i.e., supply conditions), interacts with the market demand for the good as determined by the usefulness of its marginal unit (not the usefulness of the total stock of the good). It is not paradoxical that total U is high when marginal U is low.

6. The fact that market price is determined by marginal rather than total utility is dramatized by the concept of *consumer surplus*. We pay the same price for each quart of milk that we buy in the market. Moreover the price is equal to the marginal utility of the last unit bought. But this means that we reap a surplus of utility over price on all earlier units, for the marginal utilities of earlier units are greater than that of the last unit by the law of diminishing marginal utility. This surplus of utility over price is called consumer surplus. Consumer surplus reflects the benefit we gain from being able to buy all units at the same low price. In simplified cases, we can measure consumer surplus as the area between the demand curve and the price line. It is a concept relevant for many social decisions—such as deciding when the community should incur the heavy expenses of a road or bridge.

CONCEPTS FOR REVIEW _____

utility, marginal utility
utilitarianism
law of diminishing marginal utility
equating marginal utility of last dollar
  spent on each good: $MU_1/P_1 =$
  $MU_2/P_2 = \cdots = MU$ per $ of income
market demand versus individual
  demand

demand shifts from income and other
  sources
substitutes, complements, independent
  goods
substitution effect and income effect
paradox of value
consumer surplus

QUESTIONS FOR DISCUSSION _____

1. Explain the meaning of utility. What is the difference between total utility and marginal utility? Explain the law of diminishing marginal utility and give a numerical example.

2. Each week, Jean Jones buys two hamburgers at $2 each, eight cokes at $0.50 each, and eight slices of pizza at $1 each, but buys no hot dogs at $1.50 each. What can you deduce about Jean's marginal utility for each of the four goods?

3. Which pairs of the following goods would you classify as complementary, substitute, and independent goods: beef, ketchup, lamb, cigarettes, gum, pork, radio, television, air travel, bus travel, taxis, and paperbacks? Illustrate the resulting shift in the demand curve for one good when price of another good goes up. How would a change in income affect the demand curve for air travel? The demand curve for bus travel?

4. Why is it wrong to say, "In equilibrium, the marginal utilities of all goods must be exactly equal"? Correct the statement and explain.

5. If you wanted to avoid using the marginal utility concept, show that you can still justify the law of downward-sloping demand through reasoning that employs (a) substitution effect and (b) income effect.

6. How much would you be willing to pay rather than give up *all* movies? How much do you spend on movies? Estimate roughly your consumer surplus.

7. Consider the following table showing the utility of different numbers of days skied each year:

NUMBER OF DAYS SKIED	TOTAL UTILITY (dollars)
0	0
1	30
2	55
3	73
4	88
5	98
6	103
7	103
8	100

Construct a table showing the marginal utility for each day. Assuming that there are 1 million people with preferences shown in the table, what would the market demand for ski-days be? If lift tickets cost $20 per day, what is the equilibrium price and quantity of days skied?

8. For each of the commodities in Table 19-1, calculate the impact of a doubling of price on quantity demanded. Similarly, for goods in Table 19-2, what would be the impact of a 50 percent increase in consumer incomes?

9. As you add together the identical demand curves of more and more people (in a way similar to the procedure in Figure 19-2), the market demand curve becomes flatter and flatter on the same scale. Does this fact indicate that the elasticity of demand is becoming larger and larger? Explain your answer carefully.

10. Suppose that you have 10 hours a week available for recreation. You very much like bowling, dancing, and reading, but dislike golf and rock-climbing. What would the equilibrium condition be for your allocation of time across these five activities (i.e., the marginal utility per hour)?

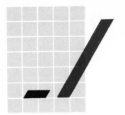

APPENDIX: 19
Geometrical Analysis of Consumer Equilibrium

The main part of this chapter showed how consumer demand relations could be derived using the concepts of utility and marginal utility. Almost a century ago, the economist Vilfredo Pareto (1848–1923) discovered that all the important elements of demand theory could be analyzed without what he viewed as the dubious utility concept, needing only what are today called indifference curves. This appendix presents the modern theory of indifference analysis, and then proceeds to derive the major results of consumer behavior with that new tool.

THE INDIFFERENCE CURVE

It is instructive to show graphically, and without using the language of numerical utility, exactly what the consumer's equilibrium position looks like.

We start out by considering you as a consumer who buys only two commodities, say, food and clothing, at definite quoted prices. We suppose you can tell us whether (1) you prefer a given combination or batch of the two goods, say, 3 units of food and 2 of clothing, to some second combination or batch, say, 2 units of food and 3 of clothing, or (2) you are "indifferent" as between the two combinations.

Let us suppose that, actually, these two batches happen to be equally good in the eyes of our consumer—that you are indifferent as to which of them you receive. Let us go on to list in the table for Figure 19A-1 some of the other combinations of goods between which you are likewise indifferent.

Figure 19A-1 shows these combinations diagrammatically. We measure units of clothing upon one axis and units of food upon the other. Each of our four combinations or batches, *A, B, C, D,* is represented by its point. But these four are by no means the only combinations among which you are indifferent. Another batch, such as $1\frac{1}{2}$ units of food and 4 of clothing, might be ranked as equal to any of *A, B, C,* or *D* above, and there are many others not shown.

The curved contour of Figure 19A-1, linking up the four points, is an **indifference curve.** Every point thereon represents a different combination of the two goods; and the indifference curve is so drawn that you, our consumer, are indifferent between any two points on it. All would be equally desirable to you, and you would be indifferent as to which batch is received.

Law of Substitution

Indifference curves are drawn as convex to the origin, meaning that as we move you downward and to the right along the curve—a movement which implies increasing the quantity of food and reducing that of clothing—the curve becomes more nearly horizontal. The curve is drawn in this way because this illustrates a property that seems most often to hold true in real life and which we may call the "law of substitution":

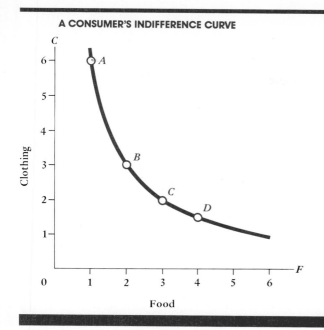

A CONSUMER'S INDIFFERENCE CURVE

INDIFFERENCE COMBINATIONS

	FOOD	CLOTHING
A	1	6
B	2	3
C	3	2
D	4	$1\frac{1}{2}$

Figure 19A-1

Getting more of one good compensates for giving up some of the other. The consumer likes situation A exactly as well as B, C, or D.

The food-clothing combinations that yield equal satisfaction can be plotted as a smooth indifference curve (or so-called equal-utility contour). This is convex (from below) in accord with the law of substitution, which says: As you get more of a good, its substitution ratio, or indifference-curve slope, diminishes.

The scarcer a good, the greater its relative substitution value; its marginal utility rises relative to the marginal utility of the good that has become plentiful.

Thus, when you are the consumer at A in the table for Figure 19A-1, you would swap 3 of your 6 clothing units in exchange for 1 extra food unit. But when you've moved to B, you would sacrifice only 1 of your remaining clothing supply to obtain a third food unit—a 1-for-1 swap. For a fourth unit of food, you would sacrifice only $\frac{1}{2}$ unit from your dwindling supply of clothing.

If we join the points A and B of Figure 19A-1 or 19A-2, we find that the slope of the resulting line (neglecting its negative sign) has a value of 3. Join B and C, and the slope is 1; join C and D, and the slope is $\frac{1}{2}$. These figures—3, 1, $\frac{1}{2}$—are the "substitution ratios" (sometimes called the "marginal rates of substitution") between the two goods. Moreover, as the size of the movement along the curve becomes very small, then the closer the substitution ratio comes to the actual slope of the indifference curve.

The slope of the indifference curve is the measure of the goods' relative marginal utilities, or of the substitution terms on which—for very small changes—the consumer would be willing to exchange a little less of one good in return for a little more of the other.

An indifference curve which is convex in the manner of Figure 19A-1 conforms to the law of substitution noted earlier. As the amount of food you consume goes up— and the clothing goes down—food must become relatively cheaper and cheaper in order for you to be persuaded to take a little extra food in exchange for a little sacrifice of clothing. The precise shape and slope of an indifference curve will, of course, vary from one consumer to the next, but the typical shape will take the form shown in Figures 19A-1 and 19A-2.

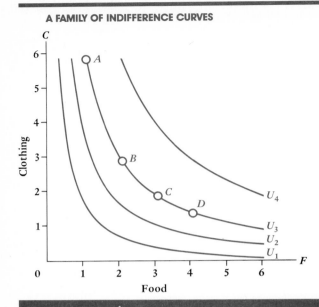

A FAMILY OF INDIFFERENCE CURVES

Figure 19A-2

The curves labeled U_1, U_2, U_3, and U_4 represent indifference curves, or equal-utility contours. (Which of the indifference curves is preferred by the consumer?)

The Indifference Map

Our previous table is one of an infinite number of possible tables. We could have started with a still higher level of satisfaction or utility and listed some of the different combinations that would bring the consumer this higher level of satisfaction. One such table might have begun with 2 food and 7 clothing; another with 3 food, 8 clothing. Each table could be portrayed graphically; each has its corresponding indifference curve.

Figure 19A-2 shows four such curves; the old curve of Figure 19A-1 is now labelled U_3. This diagram is analogous to a geographical contour map. A person who walks along the path indicated by a particular height contour on such a map is neither climbing nor descending; similarly, the consumer who moves from one position to another along a single indifference curve enjoys neither increasing nor decreasing satisfaction from the change in the flow of goods consumed. Only a few of the possible indifference curves or equal-utility contours are shown in Figure 19A-2.

Note that as we increase both goods and hence move in a northeasterly direction across this "map," we are crossing successive indifference curves; we are reaching higher and higher levels of satisfaction. This assumes that I would be enjoying increasing satisfaction from receiving increased quantities of both goods. Hence, curve U_3 stands for a higher level of satisfaction than U_2; U_4, for a higher level of satisfaction than U_3; and so forth.

BUDGET (OR CONSUMPTION-POSSIBILITY) LINE

Now let us set a particular consumer's indifference map aside for a moment and give him a fixed income. He has, say, $6 per day to spend, and he is confronted with fixed

THE BUDGET LINE

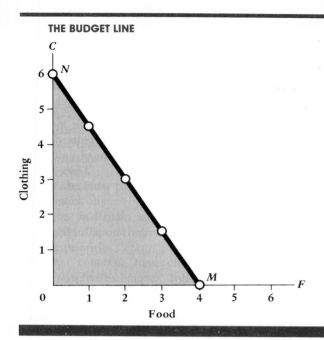

ALTERNATIVE CONSUMPTION POSSIBILITIES

	FOOD	CLOTHING
M	4	0
	3	$1\frac{1}{2}$
	2	3
	1	$4\frac{1}{2}$
N	0	6

Figure 19A-3

The budget limit on expenditures can be indicated by a numerical table. The total cost of each budget (reckoned as $1.50F + $1C) adds up to exactly $6 of income.

The budget constraint plots on a diagram as a straight-line tradeoff, whose absolute slope equals the P_F/P_C ratio. NM is the consumer's budget line. When someone spends, say, just $6 daily, with food and clothing prices $1.50 and $1, he can choose any point on this line. (Why is its slope $1.50/$1 = 3/2?)

prices for each food and clothing unit—$1.50 for food, $1 for clothing. It is clear that he could spend his money on any one of a variety of alternative combinations of food and clothing. At one extreme, he could buy 4 food units and no clothing; at the other, 6 clothing units and no food. The table with Figure 19A-3 illustrates some of the possible ways in which his $6 could be allocated.

Figure 19A-3 shows these five possible positions. Each position is marked by a point. Note that they all lie on a straight line, labelled *NM*. Moreover, any other attainable point, such as $3\frac{1}{3}$ food units and 1 clothing unit, lies on *NM*. The straight black budget line *NM* sums up all the possible positions the consumer could occupy in spending $6 of budget income.[1]

The slope of *NM* (neglecting its sign) is $\frac{3}{2}$, which is necessarily the ratio of food price to clothing price, and the common sense of line *NM* is clear enough. Given these prices, every time our consumer gives up 3 clothing units (thereby dropping down 3 vertical units on the diagram), he can gain 2 units of food (i.e., move right 2 horizontal units).

We call *NM* the consumer's "budget" (or "consumption-possibility") line.

---

[1]This is so because, if we designate quantities of food and clothing bought as F and C, respectively, total expenditure on food must be $1\frac{1}{2}F$ and total expenditure on clothing, $1C$. If daily income and expenditure is $6, the following equation must hold: $6 = $1\frac{1}{2}F + $1C$. This is a linear equation, the equation of the budget line *NM*. Note:

$$\text{Arithmetic slope of } NM = \$1\frac{1}{2} \div \$1$$
$$= \text{price of food} \div \text{price of clothing}$$

THE EQUILIBRIUM POSITION OF TANGENCY

Now we are ready to put our two parts together. The axes of Figure 19A-3 were the same as those of Figures 19A-1 and 19A-2. We can superimpose the black budget line *NM* upon this red consumer indifference map, as in Figure 19A-4. The consumer is free to move anywhere along *NM*. Positions to the right and above *NM* are barred to him unless he has more than $6 of income to spend; and positions to the left and below *NM* are unimportant, since we assume that he will want to spend the full $6.

Where will the consumer move? Obviously, to that point which yields the greatest satisfaction; or, in other words, to the highest available indifference curve, which in this case must be at the red point *B*. At *B*, the budget line just touches—but does not cross—the indifference curve U_3.

At this point of tangency—of the budget line to an indifference contour—is found the highest utility contour the consumer can reach.[2]

Geometrically, the consumer is thus at equilibrium where the slope of his budget line is exactly equal to the slope of his indifference curve. Moreover, the slope of the budget line is the price ratio of food to clothing.

We may say, then, that equilibrium is attained when the consumer's substitution ratio (or ratio of relative marginal utilities) is just equal to the ratio of food price to clothing price.

Put differently, the substitution ratio, or slope of the indifference curve, is the ratio of the marginal utility of food to the marginal utility of clothing. So our tangency condition is just another way of stating that a good's price and its marginal utility must be proportional in equilibrium—the consumer there getting the same marginal utility

---

[2]At any point on *NM* other than *B*, *NM* is crossing indifference curves. And as long as the consumer can keep crossing indifference curves, he can keep moving to higher ones.

CONSUMER'S EQUILIBRIUM

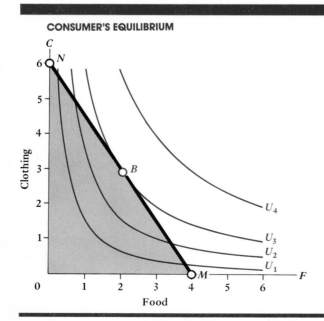

Figure 19A-4   Consumer's most preferred and feasible consumption bundle is attained at *B*

Now we combine the budget line and indifference contours on one diagram. At *B* the consumer reaches highest indifference curve attainable with fixed income. *B* represents tangency of budget line with highest indifference curve. (Why? If slopes were unequal, *NM* would intersect a *U* contour and the consumer could cross over onto higher satisfaction levels.)

At tangency point *B*, substitution ratio equals price ratio P_F/P_C. This means that all goods' marginal utilities are proportional to their prices, with marginal utility of the last dollar spent on every good being equalized—as demonstrated in the chapter's main text.

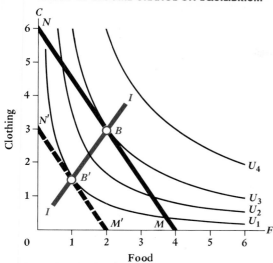

EFFECT OF INCOME CHANGE ON EQUILIBRIUM

Figure 19A-5

An income change shifts the budget line in a parallel way. Thus, halving income to \$3 shifts NM to $N'M'$, moving equilibrium to B'. (Show what raising income to \$8 would do to equilibrium. Estimate where the new tangency point would come.)

from the last penny spent on food as from the last penny spent on clothing. Therefore, we can derive the following equilibrium condition:

$$P_F/P_C = \text{substitution ratio} = MU_F/MU_C$$

This is exactly the same condition as we derived for utility theory in the main part of this chapter.

CHANGES IN INCOME AND PRICE

Our understanding of the process will be furthered by considering the effects of *(a)* a change in money income and *(b)* a change in the price of one of the two goods.

Income Change

Assume, first, that the same consumer's daily income is halved, the two prices remaining unchanged. We could prepare another table, similar to the table for Figure 19A-3, showing the consumption possibilities that are now open to him. Plotting these points on a diagram such as Figure 19A-5, we should find that the new budget line occupies the position $N'M'$ in Figure 19A-5. The line has made a parallel shift inward.[3] The consumer is now free to move only along this new (and tighter) budget line. Again, he will move to the highest attainable indifference curve, or to the point B'. A similar tangency condition for consumer equilibrium again applies. The red curve through $B'B$ depicts what are called "Engel curves," showing how consumption changes when income changes.[4]

[3] The equation of the new $N'M'$ budget line is now $\$3 = \$1\frac{1}{2}F + \$1C$.
[4] Recall the important budgetary income-expenditure patterns of Fig. 7-2 of Chapter 7.

Single Price Change

Now return our consumer to his previous daily income of $6, but assume that the price of food rises from $1.50 to $3 while the price of clothing is unchanged. Again we must examine the change in the budget line. This time we find that it has pivoted on the point N and is now NM'',[5] as in Figure 19A-6.

The common sense of such a shift is clear. Since the price of clothing is unchanged, the point N is just as available as it was before. But since the price of food has risen, point M (which meant 4 food units had been purchasable) is no longer attainable. With food costing $3 per unit, only 2 units can now be bought with a daily income of $6. So the new budget line must very definitely still pass through N, but it must pivot around N and pass through M'', which is to the left of M. (The new line has a slope of $\frac{3}{1}$. Why?)

Equilibrium is now at B''; we have a new tangency situation in that equilibrium. Higher food price has definitely reduced food consumption; higher P_F may change clothing consumption in either direction.

To clinch understanding, you can work out the cases of an increase in income, and of a fall in the price of clothing or food.

DERIVING THE DEMAND CURVE

We are now in a position to show how the demand curve arises. Look carefully at Figure 19A-6. Note that as we increased the price of food from $1.50 per unit to $3 per unit, we kept other things constant—tastes as represented by the indifference curves did not change, while money income and the price of clothing stayed constant. Therefore, we are in the ideal position to trace out the demand curve for food. Thus at a price of $1.50, the consumer buys 2 units of food, shown as equilibrium point B. When price rises to $3 per unit, the food purchased is 1 unit, at equilibrium point B''. If you draw in the budget line corresponding to a price of $6 per unit of food, the equilibrium occurs at point B''', and food purchases are 0.45 unit.

Now plot the price of food against the purchases of food, again holding other things equal (this is taken up in the third question at the end of this appendix). You will have derived a neat downward-sloping demand curve from indifference curves. Note that we have done this without ever needing to mention the term "utility"—basing the derivation solely on measurable indifference curves.

BALANCED PRICE CHANGES AND THE QUANTITY THEORY

Suppose all prices exactly double. It is easy to see that this is exactly like a halving of income. Hence when all prices double, this can be seen as a movement from NM to $N'M'$ in Figure 19A-5. But then double income; this returns the consumer exactly to the original budget line NM. Thus doubling income and all prices leaves the budget line unchanged. And as a result we have:

Changing all prices *and* income in exactly the same proportion leaves equilibrium quantities demanded completely unchanged.

This provides the theoretical rationale for the quantity theory of money discussed at

---

[5]The budget equation of $N'M'$ is now $6 = $3F + $1C$.

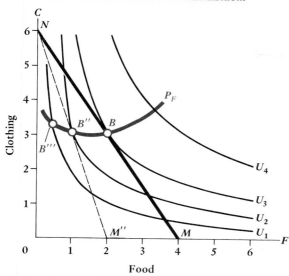

EFFECT OF PRICE CHANGE ON EQUILIBRIUM

Figure 19A-6

A rise in the price of food makes the budget line pivot on *N*, rotating from *NM* to *NM″*. New tangency equilibrium is at *B″*, with less food and either more or less clothing. (Can you handle a change in P_C?)

length in Chapter 16. Why? If all prices double and income doubles, then I will buy exactly the same quantities of goods and services. I will need exactly twice the money balances to buy exactly twice the value of transactions. Thus demand for money (*M*) exactly doubles. The velocity of money is defined as the ratio of the value of purchases $(p_1q_1 + p_2q_2 + \cdots)$ divided by the amount of money (*M*). In our example, the *p*'s all double, the quantity of *M* exactly doubles, so velocity is unchanged.

This very important property of demand systems is the core of the quantity theory of money. Because prices and incomes tend to move together during periods of galloping inflation, it is not surprising that the velocity of money is close to constant, so that the aggregate price level moves with the money supply. Such has been the experience of many Latin American countries with inflation rates of 100 or 200 percent per annum.

SUMMARY TO APPENDIX

1. An *indifference curve* or *equal-utility contour* depicts the points of equally desirable consumption. The indifference contour is usually drawn convex (or bowl-shaped) in accordance with the empirical law of diminishing relative marginal utilities (or of substitution ratios).

2. When a certain consumer has a fixed money income, all of which he spends, and is confronted with market prices of two goods, he is constrained to move along a straight line called the *budget* (or *consumption-possibility*) line. The steepness of the line's slope will depend on the ratio of the two market prices; how far out it lies will depend on the size of his income.

3. The consumer will move along this budget line until reaching the highest attainable indifference curve. At this point, the budget line will touch, but not cross, an indifference curve. Hence, equilibrium is at the point of *tangency,* where the slope of the budget line (the ratio of the prices) exactly equals the slope of the indifference curve (the substitution ratio or relative-marginal-utility ratio of the two goods). This gives additional proof that, in equilibrium, marginal utilities are made to be proportional to prices.

4. A fall in income will move the budget line inward in a parallel fashion, usually causing less of both goods to be bought. A change in the price of one good alone will, other things being equal, cause the budget line to pivot so as to change its slope. In any case, whatever change has occurred, a new equilibrium point of highest satisfaction will be reached. It is at a new point of tangency, where the marginal utility per dollar has become equal in every use. By comparing the new and old equilibrium points, we trace out the usual downward-sloping demand curve.

CONCEPTS FOR REVIEW

indifference curves or equal-utility
  contours
slope or substitution ratio
budget or consumption-possibility line,
  NM
convexity and law of diminishing
  relative marginal utilities

optimal tangency equilibrium:
  P_F/P_C = substitution ratio
      = MU_F/MU_C
parallel and pivoted shifts of *NM* to
  new tangency equilibrium as income
  changes or price changes

QUESTIONS FOR DISCUSSION

1. Explain why one, and only one, indifference curve will go through any point on an indifference map, i.e., why two such curves never cross.

2. If a consumer is at a point on her budget line where it crosses an indifference curve, explain why she cannot have reached equilibrium. What will she do to attain her equilibrium?

3. Use a table to list the price and quantity combinations that arise from shifting the price of food in Figure 19A-6. Then plot these on a graph. This will be the demand for food. Why does it slope downward? What would happen to the demand curve if the consumer's income increased?

4. In Figure 19A-4, label the indifference contours with the utility numbers 1, 2, 3, 4. Show that any other four numbers would give the same demand equilibrium, provided only that they are ordinal, or in the same more-or-less relationship. Infer from this that only "ordinal utility" rather than numerically measurable, or "cardinal," utility is needed for demand economics.

5. Draw the indifference curves for a consumer who consumes each of the following pairs of goods under the listed conditions:
  (a) Pepsi and Coke are always enjoyed equally.
  (b) Pizza is desired, while water is neither desired nor loathed.
  (c) I always need both a left and a right shoe.
  (d) Chocolate is tasty while celery makes me sick.

CHAPTER 20___
BUSINESS
ORGANIZATION

The business of America is business.

Calvin Coolidge

MOST OF THE economy's goods and services, from automobiles to zithers, are produced in business firms—in tiny proprietorships, in partnerships, or in giant corporations. This and the next five chapters explain how business supply decisions interact with the consumer preferences described in the last chapter to produce the array of goods we enjoy.

But to understand our business civilization, we must first understand the organization and functioning of business enterprise. Using an extended case study, the first part of this chapter describes small business before turning to an analysis of the modern corporation. The second part deals with the financial structure of corporations and mentions some of the current issues surrounding corporate control of the economy.

The appendix presents a brief introduction to the fundamentals of accounting, for a grasp of accounting is essential to an understanding of the economics of enterprise.

471

A. BIG, SMALL, AND INFINITESIMAL BUSINESSES

There are more than 17 million different businesses in America in the late 1980s. The majority of these are tiny units owned by a single person—the individual proprietorship. Some others are partnerships, owned by two or perhaps two hundred partners. The largest businesses tend to be corporations.

In terms of numbers, the tiny self-owned individual proprietorships are overwhelmingly the dominant business form. But in dollar value, in political and economic power, and in size of payroll and employment, the few hundred largest corporations occupy the strategically dominant position. Figure 20-1 shows how businesses are divided according to size, number, and economic importance.

The Role of the Firm

Before we examine the different kinds of business enterprises, we might well ask, Why do we need large organizations to produce our daily bread rather than producing everything ourselves? Why does business activity generally take place in firms? Why do people need to gather into small or large organizations to produce goods? As we shall see, firms exist for many reasons, but the most important are to exploit economies of scale in production, to raise funds, and to organize the production process.

The most compelling factor leading to the organization of production in firms arises from *economies of scale*. In production analysis, economies of scale occur when the cost of production declines with larger and larger volumes of output. Studies indicate that efficient production of automobiles requires annual production of at least 300,000 units per year. We could hardly expect that workers would spontaneously gather to perform each task correctly and in the right sequence; rather, workers gather under the coordination of firms to produce cars and most other goods of an industrial economy. To put this differently, if there were no economies of scale and specialization, then we could each produce our own car and digital watch and stereo system and finespun shirt in our backyard. It is obvious that we cannot perform such feats and therefore that we gain enormously because production is organized in large firms.

A related function of firms is to *raise the resources* for large-scale production. It costs $1 billion to build a new integrated steel mill; the research and development expenses for a new line of aircraft might be even greater. Where are such funds to come from? Perhaps a few large investments could be financed by rich individuals, as when nineteenth-century tycoons built empires in steel or railroads. But the days of such fabulously wealthy captains of industry are past. Today, in a private-enterprise economy, most funds for production must come from company profits or when firms borrow from large numbers of individual savers. Indeed, privately financed production would be virtually unthinkable without the ability of corpo-

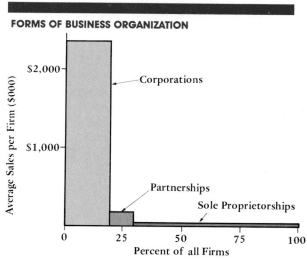

FORMS OF BUSINESS ORGANIZATION

Figure 20-1   The three kinds of business firms

This figure shows the major economic organizations in the American economy. The horizontal axis indicates the percent of firms that are corporations, partnerships, or proprietorships. The vertical axis shows the average size (as measured by annual sales in dollars) per firm. The area (number × sales) indicates the share of total economic activity represented by each segment. Note that even though corporations are few, they represent the bulk of economic activity. (Source: U.S. Department of Treasury, Internal Revenue Service.)

rations to raise billions of dollars each year for new projects.

A third reason for firms is the necessity of *management*. The manager is the person who organizes production, introduces new ideas or products or processes, makes the business decisions, and is held accountable for success or failure. After all, production cannot organize itself. Someone has to decide whether to build a new factory, to redesign a computer program, or to start a new line of business. Someone has to negotiate with labor unions and make commitments about materials and supplies. Someone has to hire baseball players, find a baseball field, hire umpires, and sell tickets. Once all these factors of production are engaged, someone has to monitor their daily activities to ensure that the job is being done effectively and honestly. In today's economy, with its legal framework, such managerial decisions are made by firms, or more precisely by people on behalf of firms.

Production is organized in firms because efficiency generally requires large-scale production, the raising of significant external resources, and careful management and monitoring of ongoing activities.

Now that we have seen why productive activities are organized in firms, we can proceed to study different varieties of business organizations—from the tiniest individual proprietorships to the giant corporations that dominate the economic life of a capitalist economy.

TINY BUSINESS

Let us glance briefly at the role in our economy of "infinitesimal businesses." There are 240,000 food-shop owners in the United States, all trying to make a living. There are 135,000 gas stations, 50,000 drugstores, and so on. All told, there are almost 10 million tiny businesses making less than $50,000 per year.

Some of these ventures are highly successful. But it is still true to say that most do not earn for their owners much more than they could get with less effort and lower risk by working for somebody else. The classic small business is the "Mom and Pop" grocery store—

doing a few hundred dollars of business per day, having too small a store, and barely earning a minimum wage for its owners' efforts.

The major obstacle to starting a small business is obtaining the start-up funds for initial capital. Businesses differ greatly in the amount of financial investment required. For example, to build a modern service station costs more than $300,000, but to lease one from an oil company brings the initial investment down to around $20,000.

Aside from the capital necessary to open a business, there is the tremendous amount of personal effort required. Self-employed farmers work from 55 to 60 hours per week during the peak summer months. Still, people will always want to start out on their own. *Theirs* may be the successful venture, and people are always attracted by the opportunity to make their own plans and undertake the variety of tasks that a small business calls for.

THE SINGLE PROPRIETORSHIP

We gain insight into the principal forms of business organization by following the hypothetical history of one business venture as it grows from a small beginning into a good-sized corporation.

Let us suppose you decide to start a business to make computer software. Perhaps you learned how to program at an early age and have now come up with an exciting video game or a way to write company accounts more easily. To be a single proprietor you need not get anybody's permission. You merely say, "Today, I am in business."

You can hire as few or as many people as you wish, and borrow whatever capital you can. At the end of the month, whatever is left over as profits—after all costs have been met—is yours to do with as you like. The losses of the business are all yours, too. If your sales fail to cover the costs you have incurred, your creditors can ask you to dig deeper into your personal assets: your car, the family home, and the rest.

In legal terms, an individual proprietor has unlimited liability for all debts contracted by the business. All your property, with the exception of a small minimum, is legally available to meet those debts.

Business Growth and the Need for Capital

You are pleasantly surprised to find that your software business is a big success as your first device—an accounting package—has been snapped up by a number of small businesses. Although you are making more money than you expected, you find yourself harder pressed for cash than ever before.

Why? Because you are not paid in advance for your sales; you must, however, pay your computer programmers and suppliers promptly on receipt of their services. But developing new software takes time. For the moment, you are putting out money and getting nothing for it—that is, nothing except the likelihood of future payment when your next software package is marketed. You look around for an infusion of funds.

Why can't the local banker be called upon for a commercial loan at 10, 13, or 16 percent? Ordinarily, a commercial bank will not provide "venture capital" (investment funds available for highly speculative or risky projects). Even an innovative bank would hesitate before providing capital to a business like yours. To the bank you are only one of numerous would-be entrepreneurs. And most, it knows, are destined for failure even in the best of times; certainly many would be wiped out if a serious recession should come along. For banks or investors to be willing to undertake the risk and bother of putting venture capital into your firm, they would need an expected return of 20 or 30 percent per year.

Despite your makeshift attempts to raise capital, the business is still suffering from growing pains. You have exhausted all possibilities of raising further loan capital.

Perhaps the time has come to look for a partner.

THE PARTNERSHIP

Any two or more people can get together and form a partnership. Each agrees to provide some fraction of the work and capital, to share some percentage of the profits, and of course to share the losses or debts. A purely oral agreement will do, but it is more businesslike and makes for fewer misunderstandings if you have a lawyer draw up some sort of formal partnership agreement. Partnerships are the least popular of the major business forms. There are $1\frac{1}{2}$ million partnerships, but they account for only 4 percent of all business sales. (See Figure 20-1.)

For your software business, you find that a college friend has an interest in computers and has inherited $80,000. After looking at your disks, he agrees to join fortunes. Your partner contributes $80,000 in return for one-third of the firm's *equity,* which represents your partner's stake or claim on the profits and losses of the business. Like you, he is to work for his fair market wage. You receive two-thirds of all profits or losses, and he gets one-third.

Your partner has put up $80,000 in cash. What have you brought into the venture? Only a few blank floppy disks and an IBM personal computer. This doesn't seem like much.

Actually, you bring much more to the partnership in the form of what accountants call "goodwill." This represents intangible but valuable assets such as trade secrets, know-how, skills, trademarks, and reputation. In your case, your goodwill comes in a copyrighted computer-software package and as specialized knowledge about devising business software. More concretely, you have built up a firm with an earnings potential (after all costs) of $30,000 per year. Moreover, for your partner's investment of $80,000, he is purchasing one-third of the $30,000 annual earning power.

To get this much per year from a common-stock investment would cost him more than $80,000. He would have to buy $100,000 worth of 10 percent government bonds to get such a return. So, aside from the risk element, your partner is getting a fair buy for his $80,000, since he will collect some $12\frac{1}{2}$ percent annually on his investment. Hence your two-thirds share is justified by the goodwill that you supply.

A Small Business Matures

And your business continues to prosper and grow. Each year, both partners agree to take out only their stipulated drawings (which are like wages) and about a fifth of their share of profits, plowing the rest of the profits back into the business. Why do new businesses like yours grow? Here are some reasons:

- Sales of your product have risen as a result of your trade name being advertised and becoming better known, and from your hiring more salespeople.

- As more units are produced, economies of large-scale production are realized. You are able to cut your price and generate more sales.

- A new factor of growth results from "vertical integration": you decide to open a chain of retail outlets, thus operating two stages rather than only one stage of production.

- The company also grows by "horizontal integration": you take advantage of a profitable opportunity to buy out a number of competitors who sell popular competing software packages.

- New complementary products such as video monitors, printers, and a data service are added. You feel that bringing in these new lines under the same roof will help to spread the overhead expenses, and your salespeople feel that they might just as well get many orders as few when making a call.

- You might even become a baby "conglomerate," growing by adding unrelated activities to your business (e.g., machine tools, car repairs, golf balls).

- You may grow because your costs are lower. Many of your competitors have been unionized and have high labor costs. You undercut them with a non-union-wage scale that is only two-thirds that of your rivals.

- But most likely of all, your business may grow simply because you had a good idea, embodied it in a well-made product, worked hard most weekends, managed your company well, and marketed your product skillfully.

New Needs and Sources of Capital

Once again, the enterprise finds itself in a bind: the more successful it is and the faster it grows, the hungrier it is for capital. The $80,000 of new equity capital brought into the business did not stay long in the form of cash. It was quickly transformed into working capital, such as office supplies. Part of it went to pay off the most pressing liabilities.

The remainder was used as a down payment on a factory building, a big new computer, and other equipment. The difference between the down payment and the purchase price of the capital good was secured by a mortgage loan on the property.

But your success only produces more fruitful uses for capital and leaves your firm even more strapped for funds. You must find new owners and new sources of equity capital. This will involve letting even more people into the firm, people willing to contribute capital and share in the profits and losses.

Disadvantages of the Partnership Form

Why not admit more partners? There is no limit to the number you can admit, and partnerships in the brokerage and banking fields often involve more than 100 people. But the partnership poses certain disadvantages that make it impractical for large businesses. First, most partnerships have **unlimited liability.** General partners are liable without limit to the full extent of personal fortune for all debts contracted by the partnership. If you own 1 percent of the partnership and the business fails, then you will be called upon to foot 1 percent of the bills and the other partners will be assessed their 99 percent. But suppose they cannot pay any part of their assessment. Then you, as the 1 percent partner, may be called upon to pay for all, even if it means selling off your prize possessions.

This problem with unlimited liability reveals why partnerships tend to be confined to small, personal enterprises like agriculture and retail trade. Partnerships are simply too risky for most situations.

In addition, partnership agreements require complicated legal maneuvering to buy or sell shares. A partnership can be dissolved whenever any party finds the existing arrangement unsatisfactory and wishes to withdraw. The law of partnerships also makes it impossible for old partners to sell their shares to a new party without the consent of all partners. If agreement cannot be secured, the partnership will have to be dissolved. Finally, because of the red tape and unlimited liability, partnerships are incapable of raising capital from large numbers of people. Only through incorporation can our largest enterprises raise sufficient funds for the needs of modern industry.

B. THE CORPORATION

We have up to now traced the birth and infancy of your small computer-software firm, beginning as a single proprietorship and expanding into a partnership. As your firm's capital needs outgrow its resources, you decide the time has come to form a corporation.

What is a corporation? Some history will illustrate its nature. Centuries ago, corporate charters were awarded on very rare occasions by special acts of the king or legislatures. Parliament or Congress would permit a railroad or canal line or munitions company to organize and perform certain specific functions.

The British East India Company was a privileged corporation and as such it practically ruled India for more than a century. In the nineteenth century, railroads here and abroad often had to spend as much money in getting a charter through the legislature as in preparing their roadbeds. Gradually, over the past century, this procedure began to seem unfair and inefficient, and it became the practice to pass general incorporation laws granting almost anyone the privilege of forming a corporation for almost any purpose, without having to get a special vote of approval from the state legislature or from Congress.

Today, a **corporation** is a form of business organization, chartered in one of the 50 states and owned by a number of individual stockholders. The corporation has a separate legal identity, and indeed is a legal "person" that may on its own behalf buy, sell, borrow money, produce goods and services, and enter into contracts. In addition, the corporation enjoys the right of limited liability, whereby each owner's investment in the corporation is strictly limited to a specified amount.

This capsule description of the status of a corporation can be fleshed out by continuing the hypothetical case study of your growing software firm as it becomes a corporation and expands further.

Incorporation

To incorporate, or form a corporation, you begin by hiring a lawyer to draw up the necessary papers. Your state automatically grants the corporate charter for a fee of a few hundred dollars.

Let us see how the incorporating procedure works in the case of your computer company. A central question is, Who will own your corporation? Ownership is determined by who holds the shares or common stock of the company. (More details on stocks and other securities are given later in this chapter.) You and your partner want to retain control of the corporation, so you issue 10,100 shares to yourselves and decide to sell another 10,000 to outside interests.

A careful audit leads you to believe that a fair market value of the 10,000 shares is at least $300,000—so you set the value conservatively at $25 per share. You expect that your firm will be able to pay dividends of $2 per share each year (growing with inflation), so the new co-owners of your company will receive a fair return on their investment.

Who will buy the 10,000 shares? You don't know enough potential purchasers so you decide to market the 10,000 shares through a local investment banking firm. These firms are merchandisers of securities; like any merchant, they profit from the difference between their buying and selling prices. Because your firm is an unknown and risky enterprise, you agree that they will pay you $20 and resell your company's shares at $25 per share.

Corporate Structure

The stock offering is a big success as all the shares are sold and you receive $200,000 in cash for them. You need not concern yourself with the people who bought the shares or with the fact that they may resell their shares. The names of the owners of the shares, the new co-owners of the corporation with you, are registered with the company or its bank agent, so that you will know where to send the dividend checks and the announcements of stockholders' meetings. Shares in the corporate earnings and voting privileges are in direct proportion to the number of shares owned. Those with 1000 shares get 1000 votes and 1000 times higher dividends than those with 1 share.

The outside owners of 10,000 shares have paid in $200,000 cash to the company. What have you and your partner paid in? Obviously not cash, but rather a sizable amount of earning assets: plant, computers, software, equipment, goods in process, and goodwill.

Does anybody watch over the sale of securities to protect potential investors against fraud and abuse? Back in the old days before 1929, you and your investment bankers might have puffed up the value of stocks with wild claims about fabulous real-estate ventures in Florida or overestimates of future earnings.

Such practices are curbed today. You have to submit any sizable new interstate issue of stocks to the Securities and Exchange Commission (SEC), a regulatory agency set up during the Great Depression in 1934. The SEC would have to satisfy itself that your statements regarding the stock offering were not misleading before it allowed you to sell the new shares. However, it does not pretend to pass judgment on, or attest to, the value of the stock. *Caveat emptor*—let the buyer beware—still prevails as a doctrine in judging the value of stocks.

ADVANTAGES AND DISADVANTAGES OF THE CORPORATE FORM

Private Advantage

The corporation has solved most of the problems that bothered you about the partnership. To begin with, as we noted above, the corporation is an almost perfect device for raising large sums of capital.

In addition, all corporate stockholders enjoy *limited liability,* which protects shareholders from incurring the debts or losses of the corporation beyond their initial contribution. In our example, after paying $25 per share, stockholders need never be liable for additional funds or worry about their personal fortunes being in jeopardy. If worse comes to worst and the business goes bankrupt, the most investors can lose is their original payment of $25 per share. They cannot be assessed further.

Of secondary importance is the fact that the corporation is a convenient form for doing business. It is a separate legal entity created by the state. The corporation can be sued in court and can sue in its own name (without needing to gather the agreement of its thousands of owners).

Also, the corporation may have "perpetual succes-

sion" or existence, regardless of how many times the shares of stock change hands by sale or bequest and regardless of whether there are 10 or 10,000 different stockholders.

No group of shareholders can force any other group to sell or retain their holdings. Only a majority vote is needed to reach business decisions, which include making investments, setting salaries, buying or selling lines of business, and approving budgets. Normally, the stockholders will be too many to meet for every decision. They will prefer to elect a board of directors consisting of a dozen or so members to represent them between annual meetings, in much the same way that democratic electorates select legislative representatives to act for them. As we shall see, however, the problem of keeping large corporations truly democratic is a hard one to solve.

Corporate Taxes You will, however, face one major disadvantage when you incorporate: an extra tax on corporate profits. For an unincorporated business, any income after expenses would be taxed as ordinary personal income. The corporation is treated differently in that corporate income is doubly taxed, first as corporate profits and then as individual income.

As an example, say that your computer company has net taxable profits (revenue minus costs) of $1 million in 1988. You will pay 34 percent ($340,000) of federal corporate income tax on these profits, and there may be additional state taxes as well, but state taxes will be ignored in this example. Of the $660,000 left over, say the firm distributes to shareholders $500,000 in dividends. The dividends are then taxed at the tax rate of the individual, which would be 28 percent for very wealthy shareholders, for another $140,000 of federal taxes. Hence the total federal tax rate on the income from your computer company might be as high as 48 percent in this simple example. These two layers are sometimes called "double taxation of corporate income."

This taxation of corporate income has been severely criticized in recent years. It is a high price to pay for the privilege of limited liability and the ease of raising capital. One proposal recommends "integration" of corporate and individual income tax— treating corporate income as if it were income from an unincorporated business, allocating all such income to the owners, and taxing the income only once. Proponents of this approach believe that it would lead to more even-handed taxation of people and of capital income in different sectors of the economy.

Economic Advantages

When British Prime Minister Gladstone was shown electricity on a visit to Michael Faraday's laboratory, he asked, "What is the use of electricity?" To this Faraday gave the ironic reply, "I suppose some day, Sir, you may come to put a tax on it." Surely the advantage to society of the corporate form lies not merely in the fact that the state can tax it.

Because many production processes require large-scale enterprises, with millions or billions of dollars of capital, investors need a way to pool their funds. Corporations, with limited liability and a convenient management structure, provide the way to attract large supplies of private capital, produce a variety of related products, pool risks, and utilize the economies of sizable research units and managerial know-how.

This is the economic rationale of the legal entity called the corporation.

HOW A CORPORATION CAN RAISE CAPITAL

We have noted that one major advantage of a large corporation is that it can raise large sums of money to engage in efficient large-scale production. How does it do this? What forms of financing are available? Table 20-1 shows the sources of all funds raised by domestic U.S. corporations during the year 1986. Note that this refers to funds raised for total investment, including replacement of capital. A surprising finding is that most funds raised are *internal;* that is, they are paid for out of depreciation and retained earnings. Raising these funds simply requires the firm to decide not to pay out all its earnings.

Some funds are raised externally, or from outside the company. These come from bonds and mortgages, from bank debt, and from stocks. These are

SOURCE	AMOUNT (billions of dollars)	PERCENT OF TOTAL
Internal:		
Depreciation	$321	82%
Retained earnings	10	3
		85%
External:		
Bonds	$117	30%
Stocks	−57	−15
Bank credit and other debt	1	0
		15%
Total funds for gross investment	$392	100%

Table 20-1 Sources of funds for U.S. corporations, 1986

How do American corporations raise the funds necessary for expansion? The table shows the funds raised to finance gross investment, both new and replacement plant and equipment. The bulk of the funds are internal, from depreciation, which measures the amount of funds set aside to replace capital used up during the year. Securities and mortgages represent most of the external financing. Stocks or equity financing was negative, indicating that firms bought back $57 billion of their own or other companies' stock. (Source: Data Resources Inc., March 1988.)

different kinds of *securities,* which are legal forms of indebtedness.

Common Stocks or Equities

We discussed above the nature of **common stocks,** sometimes called equities. These represent shares of ownership in a corporation and are held by individuals, pension funds, and other companies. For publicly owned corporations, the most important stocks are traded on stock exchanges, such as the New York or American Stock Exchanges.

In principle, the shareholders control the companies they own, and they elect directors and vote on many important issues by mail ballot. In practice, the notion of shareholder control is a fiction, for no single person or organization owns a sufficient number of shares to control behemoths like IBM, GM, or Exxon. A controlling interest might require 20 percent of the stock, yet for the largest corporations this would amount to $5 or $10 billion. It is the managers, not the owners, who directly control large publicly owned corporations today.

Until recently, corporations raised a modest amount of funds, $10 billion to $30 billion each year, from new stock offerings. Then, suddenly in 1984, equity began to disappear, with a $77 billion loss of equity (or stocks) in 1984, $82 billion disappearing in 1985, a $67 billion loss in 1986, and $57 billion evaporating in 1987. Where was the equity going? Some was bought back by companies hoping to boost their share prices; part was absorbed in complicated financial maneuvers like "leveraged buyouts." Financial analysts are today concerned that corporate America is too leveraged, with too much debt relative to levels of equity: the higher levels of debt might leave some companies in shaky financial condition if a serious economic downturn were to occur.

Bonds

A second important form of security is **bonds.** These are special kinds of promissory notes, nicely printed on gilt paper, issued in $1000 or other denominations to be readily marketable for resale. A bond promises to pay a certain number of dollars in interest, every 6 months or so, for a number of years until it matures.

At maturity, the borrowing company promises to pay off the principal of the bond at its face value.

Ordinarily, payments for interest and principal must be made on time, regardless of whether the company has been making profits or not. Otherwise the company is in default of its obligations and can be taken to bankruptcy court like any debtor.

Hybrids

In addition, there are numerous hybrid or combination securities, combining the features of bonds and stocks. Thus "preferred stocks" have a fixed yield like a bond, but dividends can go unpaid without triggering bankruptcy.

A major new hybrid that has become very popular in recent years is an *option.* This represents the right to buy a security or commodity at a specified price within a specified period of time. For example, we might be offered the option of buying 100 shares of IBM stock at $120 each at any time in the next 3 months. If IBM is now selling for $110, would such an option be of value? Indeed it would, for IBM's price might rise. If you thought that IBM had a 50 percent chance of rising to $130 during the period, then the expected value of the option would be $5 per share $[= \frac{1}{2} \times (\$130 - \$120)]$. You can buy options on many stocks, on Treasury bills and bonds, on foreign currencies, on pork bellies and French francs—enjoying the thrills of Las Vegas from your own home.

Bank Credit

Bank credit has been a traditional source of finance. Unlike stocks and bonds, bank debt is not traded in financial markets. Rather, it is a loan negotiated between a company or a country and banks, usually commercial banks. Moreover, bank debt is usually of a short-term nature, maturing in a few months or sometimes a few years. Often it has a variable interest rate, moving up and down with market interest rates. The major advantage of bank debt is that firms employing it can avoid cumbersome and expensive legal requirements, such as registering with the SEC (see the earlier discussion in this chapter). Bank debt has become less popular in recent years, as investors have come to prefer liquid marketed securities over illiquid non-marketed loans.

Advantages of Different Securities

Common stocks have been the preferred investment vehicle for many investors in recent decades because of their high yields over the long run. Taking the period from the mid-1920s through 1987, common stocks have yielded an average real return (i.e., the return after correcting for inflation) of around 6 percent per year as opposed to an average real return of 1 percent per year for long-term bonds and around 0 for short-term bonds. These yields are calculated to include both annual return (in interest or dividends) and capital gains. The returns on common stocks were even higher during the mid-1980s, and many young investors became fabulously wealthy on their gains during the great bull market from 1982 to 1987. The euphoric bubble of the gilded 1980s burst on October 19, 1987, however, when stock prices fell by a record 23 percent, wiping out $600 billion of assets in a single day. Some economists believe that common stocks will long be tarnished in the eyes of investors as too risky for their golden nest egg.

It would be a mistake to think that bonds are perfectly safe investments. As recently as 1983, $2 billion of bonds from the state of Washington defaulted because the nuclear power plants under construction became too costly and were scrapped. In addition, aside from risk that the corporation won't pay its bond interest and principal, every time general interest rates change, bond prices bob up and down. In the last 15 years of inflation and soaring nominal interest rates, investors have learned that they could lose money and *real* purchasing power in bonds. Indeed, since 1979, bonds have fluctuated in price almost as violently as common stocks.

In recent years, companies have become much more *leveraged*. That is, they have developed much higher ratios of bonds to stocks (or debt to equity) than in earlier periods. Why is that? One major factor pushing companies toward debt is that interest payments are tax-deductible, while dividend payments are not. Offsetting this advantage of debt finance is, however, a big risk in moving to a more leveraged position: a business downturn would deplete profits

AMERICA'S LARGEST CORPORATIONS

COMPANY	SALES, 1986 (millions)
1. General Motors (automobiles)	$101,782
2. Exxon (petroleum)	76,416
3. Ford Motor (automobiles)	73,145
4. IBM (computers)	54,217
5. Mobil (petroleum)	51,223
6. Sears, Roebuck (retailing)	48,440
7. General Electric (electrical equipment)	39,315
8. Texaco (petroleum)	34,372
9. AT&T (telecommunications)	33,598
10. du Pont (chemicals)	30,224
11. Citicorp (banking)	27,519
12. Chrysler (automobiles)	26,277
13. Chevron (petroleum)	26,015
14. K-Mart (retailing)	25,864
15. Philip Morris Cos. (beverages)	22,279
16. Aetna Life and Casualty (insurance)	22,114
17. Amoco (petroleum)	20,174
18. ITT (conglomerate)	19,525
19. Procter & Gamble (consumer products)	17,892
20. American Express (finance and services)	17,768

Source: *Forbes 500s*, Annual Directory, April 25, 1988.

Table 20-2   The largest U.S. corporations dominate economic life

so much that the company could not meet its interest obligations. This is the risk that sent many companies to bankruptcy courts in the early 1980s.

THE GIANT CORPORATION

While one should not infer that all corporations go through these stages, we have now carried our successful computer-software company far enough up the ladder of success. The rest of this chapter will be concerned with the economic position and power of the very large modern corporation and the problems that it creates for the American economy. It is these giant corporations, often multinational, that play the dominant role in today's economy.

A selection of the largest corporations is shown in Table 20-2. This list reads like an honor roll of American business, with almost every name a household word. The largest companies include not only industrial giants like General Motors, IBM, and Exxon, but also service companies: banks like Citicorp, insurance companies like Aetna, retailers like Sears, and utilities like AT&T.

Large size breeds success, and success breeds further success. But there are also economic and political barriers to largeness. The statistical evidence on profits suggests that the rate of profit increases with size. But the very biggest firms in an industry seem to show a slight dropping off of relative profits compared with the next to the largest.

Moreover, just because large corporations rarely go bankrupt, this does not imply that the corporate pecking order is absolutely fixed. Just as a hotel may always be full—but with different people—so the list of the biggest corporations is a changing one. Thus, if we look at the list of the 10 largest U.S. companies in 1909, not a single one remained in the top 10 by 1988.

Divorce of Ownership and Control in the Large Corporation

Let us examine the internal working of one of these giant corporations. The first point to note about our large corporations is that they are all publicly held. The shares can be bought by anyone, rather than being "privately held," or owned by a family. The most striking feature is the diversification of ownership among thousands and thousands of small stockholders.

Take a company like AT&T. In 1987, more than 2 million people owned its shares, but 92 percent of these people had fewer than 500 shares and no single person owned as much as 1 percent of the total. Such dispersed ownership is typical of our large publicly owned corporations.

In a classic study,[1] Berle and Means pointed out

that the wide diversification of stockholding has resulted in a separation of ownership from control. Because ownership is so dispersed, owners have great difficulty affecting the actions of large corporations.

A Managerial Revolution Who makes corporate decisions? Primarily, it is the increasingly important class of *professional managers*—John Kenneth Galbraith called it the "technostructure."[2] The old-time captain of industry, for all his creativeness and ability to calculate the risks necessary to build up a great enterprise, often had something of the buccaneer in his makeup and the "public-be-damned" attitude. In company after company, the original founders have been replaced by new types of executives. They are less likely to be self-made and more likely to be graduates of the Harvard, Stanford, or other leading business schools. They will probably have acquired special training and management skills. The new professional executive is more adept at public relations and the handling of people—is necessarily more the "bureaucrat," often interested as much in preserving the status quo as in taking risks.

Typically, the dominant person will be the chairperson of the board of directors, often called the "chief executive officer," or CEO, of the corporation. Legally, however, the corporation is run by its board of directors—a group of insiders and knowledgeable outsiders, often with a dash of prestige. On the whole, it would be going too far to say that most boards of directors act simply as rubber stamps to approve the decisions already made by the officers of the company. But it is true that so long as management possesses the confidence of the board, that body will usually not actively intervene to dictate specific policies.

This is the same administrative procedure usually followed by the board of trustees of a private college or university, and it is not too unlike the parliamentary system of ministerial responsibility used in Great Britain and elsewhere.

Conflicts of Interest Generally speaking, there will be no clash of goals between the management and

[1] A. A. Berle, Jr. and Gardner C. Means, *The Modern Corporation and Private Property* (Commerce Clearing House, New York, 1932). R. J. Larner, in a 1966 *American Economic Review* study, suggested that the Berle-Means thesis on separation of ownership and control has been reinforced since 1929: whereas 6 of the 200 largest corporations were privately owned (80 percent or more of stock) in 1929, in 1963 there were none; 84.5 percent of the largest firms had no group of stockholders owning as much as 10 percent.

[2] See Chapter 35 for a more detailed discussion of Galbraith's critique of American capitalism.

stockholders. Both will be interested in maximizing the profits of the firms or in raising the growth in earnings and market price per share. But in two important situations there may be a divergence of interests, often settled in favor of management.

First, insiders may vote themselves and friends or relatives large salaries, expense accounts, bonuses, and fat retirement pensions at the stockholders' expense.

A second conflict of interest may arise in connection with undistributed profits. Like kings or emperors, the managers of firms have an understandable tendency to try to make firms grow and perpetuate. The psychological reasons are subtle and by no means always selfish. Still, when profits are plowed back into a company, there is sometimes reason to suspect that the same capital could be more profitably invested by the stockholders elsewhere or spent upon consumption. Indeed, a company would often be well advised to wind itself up, pay back its capital, or agree to merge with another corporation. But few are the occasions when management gladly votes itself out of jobs and the firm out of business.

Takeover! Managers are not complete corporate autocrats, however, for this is the age of the takeover battle.

What might be the typical scenario? Let's say that Lazy-T Oil is sitting on a rich oil deposit, worth millions of dollars. But its management has become fat and happy, so Lazy-T is simply letting the oil field lie fallow.

Another firm, say a tobacco company called Lucky Smoke, feels that its own sector has poor future prospects and is looking for greener fields. It sees a rich prospect in Lazy-T, which is currently selling for $30 per share whereas a careful analysis indicates that Lazy-T's oil assets would bring $60 per share if the firm were liquidated. Lucky Smoke makes a "tender offer" for, or formal offer to purchase, Lazy-T's shares at $45 per share, using Lucky Smoke's cash or credit. The shareholders of Lazy-T hungrily accept, and Lucky Smoke purchases the assets and liabilities of Lazy-T. After taking control, the new owners might begin an intensive drilling program to gain a handsome return on their investment.

Another technique that became popular in the late 1980s is the "leveraged buyout." In this variant, a small group of investors might buy out Lazy-T owners by issuing "junk bonds," or highly speculative bonds, of Lazy-T itself.

The example of Lazy-T suggests that takeovers are a kind of market for corporate control, and as such they might provide a useful check to inefficient practices of entrenched managers. And in some cases new managers do indeed shake up a firm's practices, cut costs, and improve productivity and profits. Studies indicate that takeovers are not always followed by improved profitability, and in many cases takeovers seem more motivated by the possibility of a quick paper profit. Most experts believe, however, that the possibility of a takeover does at least somewhat rein in management inefficiencies.

THE CONSERVATIVE 1980s

The distinguished American historian Arthur Schlesinger, Jr., has written that American political beliefs swing back and forth between periods of liberalism, marked by introduction of innovative new programs, and conservatism, in which the earlier reforms are digested and refined. During the 1930s, President F. D. Roosevelt introduced programs that many businesspersons labelled as "socialistic." Distrust of business lingered into the Kennedy administration, and Kennedy himself is reported to have reacted to a rise in steel prices by saying, "My father told me all businessmen were SOBs, but I never believed it till now."

The pendulum swung in the conservative direction during the 1980s. President Reagan championed the free market, attempted to roll back government regulation of business, and reduced taxes sharply for the rich. The supply-side policies of the Reagan administration glorified entrepreneurship and vilified the role of government. Business schools were besieged by eager applicants, and the salaries of newly minted business-school graduates reached $60,000 or even $70,000. The "yuppie" mystique appeared, heralding the young urban professionals, usually depicted as investment bankers who toured the countryside in their BMWs and found it difficult to make ends meet on $500,000 a year. Once again, many joined Calvin Coolidge in proclaiming that "the business of America is business."

Toward the end of the 1980s, the pendulum began to swing away from these unabashed probusiness views. Many date the end of the gilded era with the stock market crash of October 19, 1987, a day when many a young fortune was lost. Others say that the supply-side excesses became apparent with the budget and trade deficits and the fall of the U.S. dollar after 1985. Another critical point came when arbitragers like Ivan Boesky were convicted of criminal violations of securities laws. As the 1980s come to a close, many commentators wonder whether the excesses of the recent era have propelled America into a new radical age in which Congress will legislate against businesses and in which governments will overturn market forces.

This chapter has taken a whirlwind tour through the world of small, medium, and giant business. We saw how individuals can start, finance, and run their own small firms. But today's economy is increasingly populated by publicly owned corporations, each fueled with funds raised from thousands of investors. And for those who want a closer look at the way that company accounts are reckoned, the appendix to this chapter delves into business accounting.

Having concluded this survey of business organization, we go on to economic analysis of firms. We turn in the next chapters to an analysis of production and cost and then to an analysis of the way competitive firms make their supply decisions.

SUMMARY

A. Big, Small, and Infinitesimal Businesses

1. In our market economy, production is organized in firms—some in tiny one-person proprietorships, some in partnerships, and the bulk of economic activity in corporations.

2. The different kinds of enterprise have different advantages and disadvantages. Small businesses are flexible, can start new products, acquire other firms, and disappear quickly. But they suffer from the fundamental disadvantage of being unable to accumulate large amounts of capital from a dispersed group of investors. Today's large corporation, granted limited liability by the state, is able to amass billions of dollars of capital by borrowing from banks, bondholders, and owners of its common stock.

3. Production takes place in firms because: *(a)* economies of scale necessitates that output is produced at high volumes; *(b)* the financial requirement of production requires much more capital than a single individual would willingly put at risk; and *(c)* efficient production requires careful management and coordination of the tasks by a centrally directed entity.

B. The Corporation

4. Modern corporations have a wide variety of sources from which they can draw funds. Most important is internal financing—funds raised by reinvesting profits or depreciation. External financing comes primarily from common stocks (which are titles of ownership to the company), bonds (which are promises to pay interest and principal over a fixed period of time), and bank debt (a newer form of debt obtained from financial institutions).

5. As public corporations grow, and their owners become numerous and dispersed, we see the phenomenon of the separation of ownership from control. Such a trend can introduce conflicts of interest between shareholders and managers—such as when managers shun risk or pay themselves overly generous compensation. Takeovers today may help curb the most inefficient practices.

CONCEPTS FOR REVIEW

reasons for firms: scale economies,
   financial needs, need for coordination
single proprietorship
partnership
corporation
unlimited, limited liability

bonds
common stocks
goodwill earning power
separation of ownership from control
takeovers as constraint on managerial
   discretion

QUESTIONS FOR DISCUSSION

1. What are the major reasons that production of goods like automobiles or steel takes place in large corporations? Can you think of reasons why certain goods or services are *not* produced in business firms?

2. Compare the advantages and disadvantages of the *(a)* single proprietorship, *(b)* partnership, and *(c)* corporate form of business organization.

3. List ways of raising capital for small and large businesses.

4. Since interest on bonds is tax-deductible (and therefore avoids ''double taxation''), why is a corporation ever ''foolish'' enough to raise capital through common stocks?

5. Recently Robert Reich, Lester Thurow, and others have claimed that America's stagnation is partly due to poor management being overwhelmed by Japanese managers who are more innovative. Are there any forces other than foreign competition that might force American managers to become more efficient? Examples might be: recession, rivals in product markets, takeovers, deregulation, exposure to ridicule. Explain.

6. What is meant by calling ours the age of the ''managerial or bureaucratic revolution''? How does this apply to corporations?

7. Give examples of conflict of interest between stockholders and management; of coincident interests.

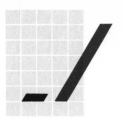

APPENDIX: 20

Elements of Accounting

In this age of accounts, familiarity with the key concepts of accounting is a necessity. Indeed, it is one of the most practical tools you learn in economics, whether as a manager, professional, or investor. If you operate a business, you will depend on your accounts and accountants to tell you whether you are making or losing money and which lines of business are thriving. Or if you are thinking of buying a business, or buying a share of a business, you and your financial advisers will want to pore over the firm's accounts if you want to understand its financial strengths and weaknesses.

We begin with the two fundamental accounting statements: the balance sheet and the statement of profit and loss (or the so-called income statement).

The balance sheet represents a snapshot of the financial condition of the enterprise on some particular day, usually the last day of the year.

The income statement that is discussed next records the flow of resources in and out of a firm during, say, a year. We will emphasize that the balance sheet, like the amount of water in a bathtub, represents a stock of dollars, while the income statement shows a flow of dollars in and out of a firm, like the stream of water coming out of the bathtub drain or spout.

THE BALANCE SHEET

We begin our discussion of accounting with the **balance sheet.** This is a statement that records what a firm, person, or nation is worth at a given point in time. On one side of the balance sheet are the **assets** (valuable properties or rights owned by the firm). On the other side are two items, the **liabilities** (money or obligations owed by the firm) and **net worth** (or net value, equal to total assets less total liabilities).

The fundamental identity or balancing relationship of the balance sheet is this: The total assets are balanced by total liabilities plus the value of the firm to its owners. That is,

$$\text{Total assets} = \text{total liabilities} + \text{net worth}$$

This states that the assets of the firm must be balanced by its liabilities plus the net worth, or "owner's equity." Sometimes, it is useful to think of the fundamental identity by rearranging terms as follows:

$$\text{Net worth (or owner's equity)} = \text{assets} - \text{liabilities}$$

Let us illustrate this by considering a simple balance sheet, as shown in Table 20A-1. On the left are assets, and on the right liabilities and net worth for a new company—say, Snack-Man Computers, Inc.—whose operations have just begun.

A blank space (black dots) has been deliberately left next to the common-stock net worth item because the only correct entry compatible with our fundamental balance

BALANCE SHEET OF SNACK-MAN COMPUTERS, INC. *(December 31, 1989)*

ASSETS		LIABILITIES AND NET WORTH	
		LIABILITIES	
Current assets:		**Current liabilities:**	
Cash	$ 20,000	Accounts payable	$ 20,000
Inventory	80,000	Notes payable	30,000
Fixed assets:		**Long-term liabilities:**	
Equipment	150,000	Bonds payable	100,000
Buildings	100,000		
		NET WORTH	
		Stockholders' equity:	
		Common stock	. . . .
Total	**$350,000**	**Total**	**$350,000**

Table 20A-1 The balance sheet records the stock of assets and liabilities, plus net worth, of a firm at a given point in time

sheet identity is $200,000. *A balance sheet must always balance*—because net worth is a residual defined as assets minus liabilities.

To illustrate how net worth always balances, suppose a fire burns up one-half the inventory. Your accountant reports to you: "Total assets are down $40,000; liabilities remain unchanged. This means total net worth has decreased by $40,000, and I have no choice but to write net worth down from the previous $200,000 to only $160,000." That's how accountants keep score.

Here is one further general point about a balance sheet:

Although its two sides must balance in total, no single item on one side is necessarily matched by an item on the other side.

Thus, bonds do not correspond in value to the equipment or buildings, nor do capital items correspond to cash. The only correct statement about a balance sheet is that creditors (bondholders, banks, etc.) have a general claim of a definite value against the enterprise, and owners have a residual claim against the rest.

Accounting Conventions

In examining the balance sheet in Table 20A-1 you might well ask, How are the values of the different items measured? How do the accountants know that the buildings are worth $100,000, the equipment worth $150,000, and so forth?

The answer lies in the conventions used by accountants. Accountants use a set of agreed-upon rules that answer most questions. The most important assumption used in a balance sheet is that assets are valued at their *historical costs*. (As noted below, this differs from the economist's concept of "value"; also, there are exceptions.) Thus land enters the balance sheet at its purchase price; equipment and buildings enter the balance sheet at their purchase price less depreciation. While there are exceptions to this central accounting rule, the historical cost principle lies behind most valuations.

Why use historical cost, even when it may be inappropriate? Largely because any other convention would involve arbitrary and manipulable judgments—ones that would inevitably make it much more difficult for an outsider to interpret the economic meaning or the financial viability of a firm.

A number of interesting facts are revealed by the simple balance sheet of Table 20A-1. First, it is often customary to divide up assets according to whether they will normally be convertible into cash within a year or in more than a year; the first category being called current assets and the second, fixed assets. The liabilities also subdivide into current and long-term liabilities, depending on whether they must be paid in less than a year or more than a year.

Most of the specific items listed are more or less self-explanatory. Cash consists of coins, currency, and money on deposit in the bank. Cash is the only asset whose value is exact rather than an estimate.

Inventories and Depreciation

Two elements of a balance sheet require discussion: inventories and fixed assets. In both cases the difficulties arise because these assets are used up or consumed over time.

Inventory—consisting in the case of our computer company of floppy disks, computer paper, and pencils—can be valued in many different ways. Especially difficult problems arise when the costs of materials vary over time. Should we figure the cost of the floppy disks at the original cost, which is different from today's price? Or should we figure cost at today's cost, the price that is now being paid for the disks to replace those being used up? [Accounting texts refer to these two alternatives of valuing inventory changes respectively as "first-in, first-out" (FIFO) and "last-in, first-out" (LIFO), and analyze them in detail.]

The other slippery item on the balance sheet is fixed assets—buildings and equipment. If we assume that the equipment and buildings items were bought just at the end of 1989, the date of the balance sheet, then their balance sheet values will be listed as equal to their purchase price. This follows a fundamental accounting rule or convention: At time of purchase a thing is presumed worth what the enterprise pays for it. However, as we shall see in connection with the income statement and next year's balance sheet, difficult questions are involved in deciding exactly how to evaluate equipment and buildings that have been used up (or "depreciated") through wear and tear.

On the liabilities side, accounts payable are the sums owed for goods bought but not yet paid for, while notes payable might represent bank debt. The bonds payable are a long-term loan, bearing a 12 percent interest rate, due in 15 years.

The last item on the balance sheet is net worth, or stockholders' equity. The net worth must equal $200,000.

This completes our first glance at a simple balance sheet.

THE INCOME STATEMENT, OR STATEMENT OF PROFIT AND LOSS

Now let time march on. In the months following the balance sheet shown in Table 20A-1, the firm is profitably engaged in producing and selling computer software. To show its flow of income over the 12 months of the year, we must turn to its **income statement,** or—as many companies prefer to call it—the statement of profit and loss, shown in Table 20A-2.

This is a statement which reports the following: (1) Snack-Man's revenues from sales in 1990, (2) the expenses to be charged against those sales, and (3) the net income (or profits remaining after expenses have been deducted). That is,

$$\text{Net income} = \text{total revenue} - \text{total expenses}$$

which is the fundamental identity of the income statement.

Look first at the figures in the right-hand column. Sales were $242,000; the total cost of goods sold came to $170,000. After deducting another $14,000 for selling and administrative costs, $58,000 remained in net operating profit. A total of $8500 plus $15,000 in interest and various taxes had to be paid out of this, leaving $34,500 in net

INCOME STATEMENT OF SNACK-MAN COMPUTERS, INC.
(January 1, 1990, to December 31, 1990)

Net sales (after all discounts and rebates)		$242,000
Less:		
Materials	$ 50,000	
Labor cost	90,000	
Depreciation	20,000	
Miscellaneous operating cost	10,000	
Equals: Cost of goods sold	$170,000	170,000
Gross profit (or gross margin)		$ 72,000
Less: Selling and administrative costs		14,000
Net operating profit		$ 58,000
Less: Fixed interest charges and state and local taxes		8,500
Net income before income taxes		$ 49,500
Less: Corporation income taxes		15,000
Net income after taxes		$ 34,500
Less: Dividends paid on common stock		14,500
Addition to retained earnings		$ 20,000

Table 20A-2   The income statement shows total sales and expenses for a period of time, say, a year

income after taxes (or profit). Dividends of $14,500 on the common stock were paid, leaving $20,000 to be plowed back as retained earnings in the business.

Now turn back to the manufacturing cost of goods sold. Most of these items are self-explanatory: material, labor, and miscellaneous. But, as with the balance sheet, there are two particularly tricky items on the income statement—inventories and depreciation. In our simple example shown in Table 20A-2, Snack-Man had no inventories, so no problem of valuing inventories arose. If there had been a change in the stock of finished software disks, we would have to ask, "Which units of inventory were sold, the software disks produced in 1989 or in 1990? Were the units sold the last ones produced (the LIFO method) or the first ones (the FIFO method)?"

Depreciation

Turn next to the $20,000 charge for depreciation shown in Table 20A-2. This represents the charge for the cost of using fixed assets like buildings and equipment. Let's see how it is calculated.

Most companies own their own capital goods—buildings, computers, equipment, trucks, and so forth—using these capital goods in various ways in the production process. But these assets do not last forever. Trucks wear out, computers become obsolete, and buildings eventually begin to deteriorate.

The accountant naturally insists that an appropriate charge or cost be made for fixed assets along with all other costs, and the difficulty arises in determining how much of an asset is "used up" in a given year. Indeed, you might wonder why any depreciation charge at all has been made for 1990 since the buildings and equipment were bought brand new at the beginning of the year and surely they have not worn out already. Your engineer might advise you that the machines will operate perfectly for 10 years and then fall apart at that time. How much, then, should you charge each year for the expense of the machines? Should you charge it all in the year of purchase? In the year when they collapse?

Here is where the farseeing wisdom of the accountant comes to the fore. It would be poor management to charge nothing for depreciation for 9 years, persuade yourself that you are earning a nice profit, and then incur a great loss when you have to replace the entire machine in the tenth year. Much more realistic is to recognize that the machines are being used up all the time—used up in the economic sense that their value declines because of wear and tear, obsolescence, and age. To account for this decline in the value of fixed capital buildings and equipment, then, accountants reduce their value, or depreciate them, by using a depreciation formula.

What kind of formula is used to calculate the depreciation on a capital good? There are a number of different ones, as will be explained in the next section, but the essentials are easily sketched. The major principles are two: *(a)* The total amount of depreciation must equal the capital good's historical cost or purchase price; *(b)* the depreciation is taken in annual accounting charges (even if no money ever leaves the firm) over the asset's accounting lifetime, which is usually related to the actual economic lifetime of the asset.

We can now understand how depreciation would be charged for Snack-Man Computers. The equipment is depreciated according to a 10-year lifetime, so that the $150,000 of equipment has a depreciation charge of $15,000 per year. The $100,000 of buildings, carrying a 20-year lifetime, shows an annual depreciation charge of $5000. The total depreciation charge for 1990 is then $20,000—just as is shown in Table 20A-2.

A Further Look at Depreciation

The last section touched upon the most essential elements of calculating depreciation. For those who wish to understand better the different depreciation formulas, along with the policy issues involved, this section contains an advanced treatment.

Tax vs. Accounting Treatment   Depreciation comes in two different forms, because depreciation for tax purposes may differ from that for normal accounting purposes. There is no rule that requires firms to report the same numbers to the Internal Revenue Service as to their stockholders. We first discuss standard accounting techniques, then cover tax treatment.

Of the methods used by accountants to calculate depreciation, two have been widely used for decades; the third, required for tax purposes, was introduced in 1981 and modified in 1986.

Straight-Line and Accelerated Depreciation   The first technique is called "straight-line depreciation" and is the technique employed by Snack-Man in its accounts shown here. We suppose that the $150,000 of equipment will last 10 years (that is, has a 10-year accounting lifetime) and has no scrap value. According to the straight-line method, you will recognize that each year one-tenth of the life of the machine has been used up, and you will figure in as depreciation expense for the year one-tenth of the lifetime decline in its total value—one-tenth of $150,000 (new price minus zero scrap value). Thus, $15,000 will be entered every year in depreciation charges for the equipment. Similarly, if the buildings valued at $100,000 have a 20-year life and no scrap value, the depreciation charge will be $5000 each year. Adding these two together gives us the $20,000 of depreciation charges on Snack-Man's income statement.

A second widely used technique is called the "double-declining-balance method." This technique allows most depreciation charges to be taken in early years and is thus "accelerated depreciation"; here, the depreciation charges decline over time rather than being constant as in the straight-line method. For example, under the double-declining-balance method, you take double the amount of straight-line depreciation in the first year; with a 10-year lifetime, you take 2×10 percent = 20 percent depreciation in the first year.

Clearly, you cannot go on charging off that amount for each year of life since that would leave you with zero value by the halfway point, at the end of 5 years. Rather, what the double-declining-balance method does is to let you take off 20 percent of the *remaining* value or balance each year. Thus, consider a $10,000 truck. In the first year you take $0.20 \times \$10,000 = \$2000$ of depreciation. In the second year, $8000 of value is left, so depreciation equals $0.20 \times \$8000 = \$1600$. So the process goes. It can be calculated that by the time the asset has reached half the length of its useful life, you have been permitted to write off more than two-thirds of its value—rather than one-half, as under the straight-line method. (There are other kinds of declining-balance methods as well, such as 150-percent-declining balance.)

Although depreciation is usually figured by some apparently exact formula, all accountants know that the estimates are really very rough, being subject to large and unpredictable errors and involving arbitrary corrections and assumptions. Accountants comfort themselves with two thoughts: (1) A rough method of depreciation, like an imperfect watch, is often better than none at all. (2) Mistakes in estimates of depreciation will ultimately "come out in the wash."

Let us see why a mistake in depreciation ultimately tends to correct itself for a given investment. Suppose that the truck lasts 15 years rather than the predicted 10. We have then been overstating our depreciation expenses during the first 10 years. But in the eleventh and later years there will be no depreciation charged on the truck at all, since it has already been written down to its scrap value by the end of the tenth year. Our profits in these later years tend, therefore, to be overstated exactly as much as they were understated in the earlier years. After 15 years, the pluses and minuses cancel out.

Depreciation and Taxes   Given that the total depreciation (plus scrap value) must equal the purchase price of the capital good, why would anyone care about the depreciation method? One reason is that the depreciation charge affects the time profile of profits, and this in turn affects a company's taxes. Generally, firms prefer to have a depreciation method that allows very fast depreciation *for tax purposes*. Why? Because by postponing tax payments, a firm can put the money it would have paid as taxes to work earning more money. In an economic sense, accelerated depreciation reduces the cost to a firm of buying capital goods because a firm can offset against the price of the truck or building some tax savings from the quicker depreciation.[1]

In order to stimulate investment, the United States over the last 25 years has taken a number of steps to speed up the rate at which depreciation can be calculated for tax purposes. The high point was the 1981 Accelerated Cost Recovery System (ACRS), passed as part of the Reagan administration's "supply-side" tax cuts. These changes were modified in the 1986 Tax Reform Act, which repealed the investment tax credit, lowered the corporation tax rate, and tended to equalize the tax burden on corporate equity capital in different sectors.

RELATIONSHIP BETWEEN THE INCOME STATEMENT AND THE BALANCE SHEET

A full year has passed, and the firm's successes are recorded in the income statement of Table 20A-2. At year-end, we will want to take another financial snapshot of the firm by looking at its new balance sheet, so we turn to Table 20A-3.

Snack-Man has prospered. Net worth has increased between the beginning and end of the accounting period by $20,000: from $200,000 to $220,000. This amount, as we saw at the bottom of the income statement in Table 20A-2, is just equal to $34,500 minus $14,500, or to $20,000 of undistributed profits.

Some net worth item has recognizably risen by $20,000. Conceivably, one

---

[1] Problem 7 at the end of this appendix provides a detailed example of how accelerated depreciation increases the after-tax profits of firms.

BALANCE SHEET OF SNACK-MAN COMPUTERS, INC. *(December 31, 1990)*

ASSETS			LIABILITIES AND NET WORTH	
			LIABILITIES	
Current assets:			**Current liabilities:**	
Cash		$ 27,000	Accounts payable	$ 10,000
Inventory		80,000	Notes payable	23,000
			Taxes payable	15,000
Fixed assets:			**Long-term liabilities:**	
Equipment	$150,000		Bonds payable	100,000
Less: Depreciation	15,000			
		135,000		
Buildings	$100,000			
Less: Depreciation	5,000			
		95,000		
			NET WORTH	
Intangible assets:			**Stockholders' equity:**	
Patents		10,000	Common stock	200,000
Goodwill		21,000	Retained earnings	20,000
Total		$368,000	Total	$368,000

Table 20A-3   The balance sheet after a year of operations

could add the $20,000 to the common-stock capital account. However, this is not done.

Retained Earnings

Instead, accountants create a new account called ''retained earnings'' in the business— to show how much of the increase in net worth has resulted from accumulated undistributed earnings plowed back through the years.

We must once more warn against trying to link specific items on the balance sheets. Only the final totals correspond. It is not even possible to say exactly how the $20,000, plowed back into the business as retained earnings, was used. An addition to retained earnings must be associated with an increase in assets or a decrease in liabilities, or both—that is all we can say.

Summary of Elementary Accounting Relationships

Before taking a last look at the new complexities introduced in the 1990 balance sheet over that of 1989, we may briefly summarize the relationship between balance sheets and income statements:

- The balance sheet indicates an instantaneous financial picture or snapshot. It is like a measure of the stock of water in a lake.

- The income statement shows the flow of sales, cost, and revenue over the year or accounting period. It measures the flow of water in and out of the lake—the progress of the firm over the year.

- The change in total net worth between the beginning and end of the period—as shown by comparing the new and old balance sheets—can be derived from changes in retained earnings as appended to the income statement in Table 20A-2: the change in the lake's level over the year is equal to the flow-in minus the flow-out during the year.

There do remain, however, certain changes in the balance sheet items from their levels in the earlier period to which the intervening income statement gives no clue. A closer look at the December 31, 1990, balance sheet will therefore prove instructive.

The New Balance Sheet

The new balance sheet looks much like the old. But some new items are present for the first time. The last of these new items, retained earnings in the business, we have already explained. Among the liabilities there is another new item, called "taxes payable," of $15,000. The taxes that the corporation will have to pay the government are as much short-term liabilities as the accounts payable or notes payable.

Turning to the fixed assets, we find that they are treated in a somewhat roundabout way. From the income statement, we know that $20,000 of depreciation has been charged against income; on the balance sheet, therefore, the original cost of $250,000 should be written down to a new value of $230,000.

Instead, this is done in a three-stage procedure: First, the balance sheet lists the original cost of fixed assets. Then the allowance for depreciation is subtracted. Then the fixed assets are entered on the books at original cost less total depreciation allowances to date.

Why do accountants use such a strange language, writing "5 minus 3" where the rest of us would write "2"? There are good reasons. Accountants know their depreciation estimate is only the roughest of estimates. Were they simply to estimate and put down the final figure of $135,000 for equipment, the public would not know how much reliance to place upon the figure. So they put down $150,000 of original value, which is firmly rooted in the solid fact of original cost; they then isolate their own calculated allowance for depreciation. Then the public is in a better position to evaluate the reliability of the final $135,000 figure. The roundabout procedure does no harm, and it may do some good.

Now we know the precise meaning of allowances for depreciation. They are not sums of money sitting in the bank. They are subtractions from deliberately overstated asset figures. Thus, the allowance for depreciation of buildings of $5000 is an explicit correction of the original cost of buildings.

Intangible Assets

One further new category of assets can be found on the December 31, 1990, balance sheet. In addition to tangible items like trucks or computers, firms own *intangible* but nonetheless valuable assets like patents, trademarks, or goodwill. To illustrate that an asset need not be a tangible commodity, we can introduce a patent into the picture. Suppose it is a patent on a profitable new printing device giving Snack-Man an exclusive production right for 17 years.

Such a patent is obviously worth money. Of course, as 5, 10, and 16 years pass, the patent will be nearing the end of its 17-year life and will be declining in value. Therefore, some amortization formula (analogous to a depreciation allowance) will be applied to it, much as if it were a truck.

As another example of an intangible asset, let us suppose that, at the same time Snack-Man bought the patent, it also took over a rival computer company. This horizontal combination will presumably add to its market power and earnings. Therefore, Snack-Man was willing to buy the company for more than its net worth. In such a case, the value today (or present value or capitalized value) of the earning power is called *goodwill*.

How much are the new assets valued for? The careful accountant will reply: ''If you paid a certain sum of money for a concern, it must be worth that much to you. If its balance sheet doesn't show what you paid, we must recognize the excess of price paid over net worth as goodwill. And goodwill shall be entered as an asset on your balance sheet.''

The intangible asset, goodwill, is thus the difference between what a company pays in buying another company and the accounting or book value of the acquired firm's identifiable assets less liabilities.

Accounting Abuses

Before we complete our discussion of accounting, we should note that accounting entries, like other magnitudes in economics, cannot be measured with great precision. When a firm's auditors certify a company's accounts, they are not really swearing that all measurements are 100 percent accurate. Rather, they perform spot checks of many transactions, audit financial assets, and check the conformity of the firm's accounting practices with generally accepted practices.

However, sometimes a company can fool the public and its accountants so much as to distort the firm's financial picture in a material way. Sometimes the distortion arises from shady accounting practices, sometimes from plain dishonesty. A recent fraud occurred when a company stated it had many millions of grams of gold bullion stored deep in the Rocky Mountains. When auditors came to look, however, the cupboard was bare.

The accounting profession and government agencies are working to reform some of these abuses. But, again, *caveat emptor*—let the buyer beware—must still prevail.

ECONOMICS AND ACCOUNTING

Up to now we have stressed the logic of the accountant's language and conventions. We now step back to ask whether these conventions all make good economic sense.

The major difference between the viewpoints of the economist and the accountant is the following: The accountant generally prefers actual historical cost as a technique for measuring the value of goods; the economist prefers to use the *market value* of a good in measuring its value. The market value measures the value of a good in its highest and best use.

Three important examples of this discrepancy can be seen in our simple example. First, the owner of Snack-Man is also its manager; she pays herself no salary, but she takes out her share of the profits at year-end. If she were to work for the local chemical plant, she could earn $50,000 a year—that is her market value as a manager. Thus, the income statement understates the "true" economic cost of management by $50,000.

A second example arises from the capital contributed to start up the firm, along with the retained earnings. If these funds were invested in a stock of equivalent risk, they might yield 10 percent annually. Yet the accountant does not record any charge to the firm for use of this financial investment. As a result, again, the firm's true profit is overstated: a firm can make an accounting profit yet not earn a rate of return on its net worth that equals the market rate of return on investments of equivalent risk.

A third area of divergence between accounting and economics concerns the effect of inflation. When prices are rising rapidly, the historical cost of items, particularly capital goods, can diverge sharply from their market value. Such divergences are minor during periods of low inflation, such as in the mid-1980s. But during periods of galloping inflation, accounts can become grossly distorted. In the high-inflation year of 1974, for example, profits of American companies were overstated by 40 percent because accounts were not corrected to reflect inflation.

To point out that accountants do not use the same concepts as economists does not imply any criticism of the accounting profession, for there are good reasons why accountants might be reluctant to use the economist's approach. To take the first of the differences cited above, the accountant would say: "Of course, we could allow for the value of the firm's owner in other occupations. But what salary should I use? And how would I know that the accounts were not being manipulated from year to year? I prefer to stay with actual historical or market transactions so as to assure the public that the accounts are being honestly kept."

Economics Based on Accounts

Finally, some interesting relationships between economics and accounting can be briefly mentioned.

▪ All balance sheets depend on valuation of assets, which is one of the basic questions of the capital and interest theory discussed in Part Five.

■ National-income statistics depend on the accounting data of sales, cost, etc., as Chapter 6 shows.

■ An understanding of a nation's balance of payments in Chapter 38 will be aided by knowing how to read a balance sheet.

■ Finally, a discussion of banking and the Federal Reserve depends critically on understanding balance sheets.

You will be amply rewarded both in studying economics and in your later economic life by a thorough understanding of accounting.

SUMMARY TO APPENDIX

Instead of summarizing the appendix, we give a checklist of accounting concepts that you should understand:

1. The fundamental balance sheet relationship between assets, liabilities, and net worth; the breakdown of each of these into current and fixed assets, current and long-term liabilities, capital, and retained earnings in the business.

2. The character of the income statement (or profit-and-loss statement) and how retained earnings relate to changes on the new balance sheet.

3. The whole problem of depreciation, both in its income-statement aspect as a necessary expense (which need not be an expenditure) and in its balance sheet treatment as a deduction from a purposely overstated asset.

4. The relationship between economics and accounting.

CONCEPTS FOR REVIEW

fundamental balance sheet identity
income statement
assets, liabilities, and net worth
current vs. fixed assets
market value vs. historical cost

dividends, retained earnings
sales, cost, net income
depreciation
intangible assets—patents, goodwill
accounting conventions

QUESTIONS FOR DISCUSSION

1. Describe the right-hand side of the balance sheet. Its left-hand side. Because of the basic accounting identity, what items must match?

2. You are a banker deciding whether to lend money to the computer company described in this appendix. Examine carefully the balance sheet and income statement for 1990. Decide how much money the firm could safely borrow at an interest rate of 10 percent per year.

3. Write out a list of many different business assets. Give the nature of each in a few lines. Do the same for liabilities.

4. A company has $10 million of net sales and $9 million of costs of all kinds (including taxes, etc.) and rents its equipment and plant. Its inventory doesn't change in the year. It pays no dividends. Draw up its simplified 1991 income statement.

5. The same company as in question 4 owes no money, having been completely financed by common stock. Fill in the year-end balance sheet for 1990 using the data in the table below. Then, using the data and income statement from question 4, complete the balance sheet for 1991.

ASSETS (end of year)			LIABILITIES AND NET WORTH (end of year)		
	1990	1991		1990	1991
			Liabilities	0	0
			Net worth	. . . .	. . . .
Total	$50 million	. . . .	Total	. . . .	. . . .

6. Redo questions 4 and 5, making the following changes: In addition to the other expenses, the firm bought in 1991 a $20 million building that depreciated by $2 million. Draw up an income statement showing its loss. If the building was bought by a long-term bond, adjust its 1991 balance sheet accordingly.

7. Advanced problem on depreciation: Many people are puzzled about the idea that acceleration of depreciation will be valuable to firms even though the total amount of depreciation does not change.

To see the effect of acceleration, assume the following: A firm is thinking of buying a $10,000 truck. The tax-free interest rate is 10 percent per year. The firm will earn before-tax profits of $50,000 each year on its total operations. The tax rate on company profits is 50 percent.

The truck is assumed to have a lifetime of 10 years. Under straight-line depreciation, the firm would deduct $1000 per year from profits, thus reducing its taxes by how much? Now say that each year it puts its tax savings into a tax-free savings account yielding 10 percent per year. How much would the firm have accumulated in tax savings from the straight-line depreciation method at the end of the 10-year period, including interest?

Next consider an accelerated depreciation scheme known as "expensing," where all the depreciation on the truck is charged in the first year. How much is the tax saving in the first year? How does it compare with the total tax saving (excluding interest) in the straight-line case? (HINT: It is equal.)

Finally, put the tax savings under expensing in the tax-free savings account for 10 years. What is the value of the tax savings under expensing (or accelerated depreciation) at the end of 10 years? Show that this value will be considerably larger than the accumulation under straight-line depreciation. Explain with the help of this example why firms prefer accelerated depreciation.

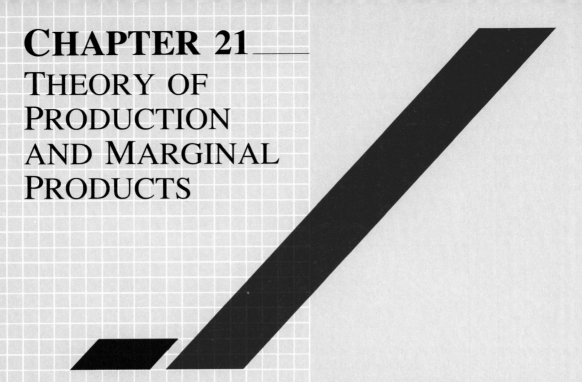

CHAPTER 21

THEORY OF PRODUCTION AND MARGINAL PRODUCTS

We have no more right to consume happiness without producing it than to consume wealth without producing it.

George Bernard Shaw

THE LAST CHAPTER examined the face of American business—the different forms of organizations, the financing of firms, and the role of giant corporations. We now begin to explore some of the critical decisions made by business enterprises: What goods should firms produce—steel or computers or haircuts? What combination of inputs of land, labor, and capital should be employed? How much does it cost a firm to produce a given bundle of goods? At what prices should the goods and services be sold? These and many similar questions must be answered by every firm, large and small, and in the next five chapters we examine the major factors entering into these decisions.

A study of the firm begins with an analysis of production. The essence of a firm is to buy inputs, use these inputs to produce outputs, and then to sell the outputs. This is true of competitive firms as well as monopolies, under capitalism as well as communism. We devote this chapter, therefore, to an analysis of production theory. The next chapter follows with the closely related topic of cost analysis. Only after we have begun to understand the essential elements of production theory can we master the cost concepts that underpin business decisions for perfect and imperfect competitors.

BASIC CONCEPTS

Let us begin by considering the case of production of food by a farmer. The farmer will use a number of inputs, or factors of production, such as land, labor, machinery, and fertilizer. These inputs will be applied over the planting and growing season, and at harvest time the farmer will reap certain outputs, such as wheat.

In what follows, we will assume that the farmer always strives to produce efficiently, or at lowest cost. That is, he will always attempt to produce the maximum level of output for a given dose of inputs, avoiding waste whenever possible. Later on, when our farmer decides what crops to produce and sell, we will also assume that he acts to maximize economic profits.

The Production Function

We have spoken of inputs like land and labor and outputs like wheat. But if you have a given quantity of land and labor, how much output can you get? In practice, the answer depends on the state of technology and engineering knowledge. At any point in time, given available technical knowledge and available labor, machinery, and fertilizer, only so much wheat can be obtained from a given plot of land. The relationship between the amount of input required and the amount of output that can be obtained is called the "production function."

The **production function** is the technical name given to the relationship between the maximum amount of output that can be produced and the inputs required to make that output. It is defined for a given state of technical knowledge.

Here are some examples.

An agronomist lists in a book of agricultural production functions the various combinations of land and labor that will produce various quantities of corn. On one page of the book, the alternative combinations of land and labor needed to produce 100 bushels of corn are listed; another page lists the alternative input combinations that will produce 200 bushels of corn; and so forth.

Another production function is that for generating electricity. A book of technical specifications shows the combination of plant, turbines, cooling ponds, fuel, and labor needed to produce 1 million kilowatts of power. On one page is a blueprint for an oil-fired plant—whose capital costs are low and whose fuel costs are high. On the next page would be the blueprint for a coal-fired plant: high capital costs (in part to remove sulfur emissions), but much lower fuel costs. On yet other pages are the techniques for building nuclear power plants, hydro stations, solar power stations, and so forth. When all the different blueprints for 1989 are put together, these form the production function for electricity generation for 1989.

A third example of a production function, which will be used extensively in this chapter, is the volume of crude oil that can be delivered through a pipeline. Engineers know that the amount of output (tons of oil pumped per day) depends upon the diameter of the pipe as well as the horsepower of the pump. Other factors such as the viscosity of the oil and the slope of the terrain also enter into the production function. The list of different pipe diameters, pump sizes, and other factors, along with the associated throughputs of oil, represents the production function for oil pipelines.

There are thousands of different production functions in the American economy: at least one for each firm and product. We will see in the next chapter how a firm's production functions will help determine its cost curves. And, when we discuss the determination of the demand for labor, land, and capital in Part Five, we will again find that the contribution of each factor to production will determine that factor's price in competitive markets.

Note how, in making its decisions, the firm is poised between two markets: it is a demander in factor markets, buying inputs that enter into the production process, while simultaneously appearing as a supplier in goods markets, where it adjusts its production to the demand curve of its customers.

Total, Average, and Marginal Product

Once a firm's production function has described how inputs are transformed into outputs, we can calculate important production concepts. We begin by computing the total physical product, or **total product,** which designates the total amount of output pro-

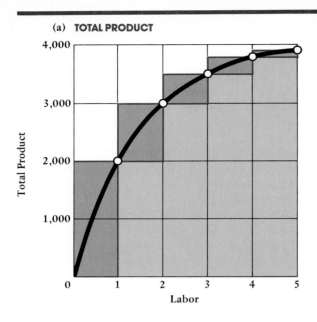

(a) **TOTAL PRODUCT**

(1) UNITS OF LABOR	(2) TOTAL PRODUCT	(3) MARGINAL PRODUCT	(4) AVERAGE PRODUCT
0	0		
		2,000	
1	2,000		2,000
		1,000	
2	3,000		1,500
		500	
3	3,500		1,167
		300	
4	3,800		950
		100	
5	3,900		780

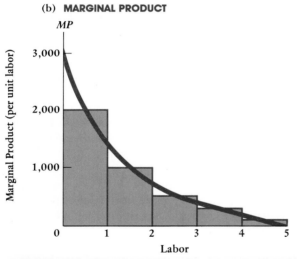

(b) **MARGINAL PRODUCT**

Figure 21-1   Marginal product is derived from total product

Marginal product is calculated as the additional units of total output produced by 1 extra unit of input (as when the fourth worker adds 300 = 3800 − 3500 units of product). Each new worker adds diminishing marginal product.

The upper diagram **(a)** shows that total product increases by smaller and smaller steps as more input units are added.

The lower diagram **(b)** shows the declining steps of extra or marginal product. Smoothing the steps gives the red declining curve of smoothed marginal product. The area in **(b)** under the red marginal product curve (or of the red rectangles) adds up to the total product shown in **(a)** above. (For example, 2000 + 1000 + 500 = total product of 3500 for three workers. What gives total product for four, or five, workers?)

duced, in physical units such as bushels of wheat or barrels of oil pumped. Figure 21-1(a) and column (2) of the accompanying table illustrate the concept of total product. In that case, we examine a farmer producing wheat on a given plot of land and show how total product responds as the amount of labor applied

is increased. For the illustrated production function, the total product starts at zero for zero labor, then increases as additional units of labor are applied, reaching a maximum of 3900 units of wheat when 5 units of labor are used.

We can use the numerical example here to define

more carefully the production concepts first introduced in Chapter 2. In earlier chapters we have used the term "marginal" to mean extra units. Here, "marginal product" (sometimes also called marginal physical product) means the additional units of output that are obtained for each additional unit of input.

The **marginal product** of an input is the extra product or output added by 1 extra unit of that input while other inputs are held constant.

For example, assume that we are holding land, machinery, fertilizer, and all other inputs constant. Then labor's marginal product is the extra output the farmer harvests when adding 1 unit of labor. The third column of the table in Figure 21-1 calculates the marginal product in our farming example. The marginal product of labor starts at 2000 for the first unit of labor, then falls to only 100 units for the fifth unit. This declining marginal product will in the next section be associated with the law of diminishing returns.

A final concept is the **average product,** sometimes called average physical product; this measures total output divided by total units of input. The fourth column of the table in Figure 21-1 shows the average product for our farming example, with the average product being 2000 units per worker with one worker, 1500 units per worker with two workers, and so forth. Note that, in our farming example, the average product falls through the entire range of increasing labor input.

Marginal Products and Diminishing Returns

The marginal product of labor is shown graphically in Figure 21-1(b). The marginal products are calculated from the total product curves in (a), or from the accompanying table, by calculating the additional amounts of output added by each extra unit of input. Note that each increment of labor adds less and less output, as is shown by the diminishing size of the added-output slabs. Figure 21-1(b) has also included a smoothed marginal product curve as a heavy red line, and that continuous curve shows a smooth downward-sloping marginal-product relationship.

The phenomenon of declining marginal product is Chapter 2's law of diminishing returns.

The **law of diminishing returns** holds that the marginal product of each unit of input will decline as the amount of that input increases, holding all other inputs constant.

Figure 21-1 illustrates the law of diminishing returns for labor, holding land and other inputs constant. What is true for labor is also true for land and any other input. We can interchange land and labor, now holding labor constant and varying land. Land's marginal product is the change in total harvested output that results from 1 additional unit of land, with all other inputs held constant. We can calculate the marginal product of each input (labor, land, machinery, water, fertilizer, etc.); and the marginal product would apply to any output (wheat, corn, steel, soybeans, and so forth). We would find that other inputs also tend to obey the law of diminishing returns.

Why do production functions generally obey the law of diminishing returns? The rationale for diminishing returns is quite straightforward: As more and more of an input like labor is added to a fixed amount of land, machinery, and other inputs, the labor has less and less of the other factors to work with. The land gets more crowded, the machinery is overworked, and the jobs done become less important. Or, to take another input, we can easily see that diminishing returns to water will soon set in. The first units of water are essential to plant life; the next units will keep the plant healthy and growing smartly; but as more and more water gets added, the soil becomes waterlogged, and most crops will actually die as more water is added.

In describing the law of diminishing returns, we must emphasize that it is really a widely observed empirical regularity rather than a universal truth like the law of gravity. It has been found in numerous empirical studies, but exceptions have also been uncovered. Moreover, diminishing returns might not hold for the entire range of outputs. The very first inputs of labor might actually show increasing marginal products, since a few minutes are needed just to get the machinery running and to transport the workers to the field. And the last units might actually show negative marginal products as workers begin to interfere with one another or as plants suffocate from too much water. Therefore, we should always remember that the law of diminishing returns is an empirical regularity subject to exceptions and not a universally valid finding.

AN ENGINEERING EXAMPLE: OIL PIPELINES[1]

Critics of economics sometimes say that the subject deals with abstractions rather than with real-world situations. To dispel this notion and to illustrate that production theory is an essential part of modern business life, we present a short case study of the economics of transporting oil by pipelines. This example has the advantage of resting on extremely simple physical principles while constituting a critical lifeline in our economic system.

Recall that we gave as an example of a production function the relationship between the quantity of crude oil transported each day through a pipeline (the output or "throughput") and the inputs, represented by the size of the pipe and the power of the pumping machinery. Engineers studying this technology have made measurements and have discovered a numerical relationship between the inputs and the outputs. We can use these studies to show the nature of the production function along with the total and marginal products for pipelines.

Table 21-1 lists the inputs and outputs for this engineering example. The output, measured in throughput (in barrels of oil per day) is shown to be a function of two different sizes of pipes—12 inches and 24 inches—and of a variety of different horsepower settings for the pumps. Pipes come in other sizes, of course, and each would have different outputs, but two will be sufficient to illustrate the point.

Examining the table, we can determine the effect on total output of an increase of one of the two inputs. By reading down column (2) in Table 21-1, we see the effect of increasing the amount of horsepower inputs. In this calculation, as we move down from one row to the next, the use of horsepower increases in increments of 10,000 units. An estimate of the marginal product can be computed as the ratio of the increase in

throughput (output) to the increase in horsepower (input). If, for example, pumping horsepower were to increase 10,000 units from 10,000 to 20,000, then throughput would climb from 43,000 barrels per day to 57,000 barrels per day for the 12-inch pipe. The marginal product of horsepower would, as a result, equal

$$MP = \frac{57,000 - 43,000}{20,000 - 10,000} = \frac{14,000}{10,000} = 1.4$$

(measured in barrels per day per horsepower) for the interval from 10,000 to 20,000 units of horsepower. Moving down one row, we see that the marginal product of horsepower is 1.0 barrel per day per horsepower as power moves from 20,000 to 30,000 units. We see that our engineering study has confirmed the law of diminishing returns.

Notice that, when horsepower is constant, output rises as the size of the pipe increases. For example, if 10,000 horsepower is applied, moving from a 12-inch pipe to a 24-inch pipe increases the throughput from 43,000 barrels per day to 141,000 barrels per day. This result is sensible because you can force more fluid through a larger pipe without increasing the power. In economic terms, this shows that the marginal product of piping size is positive, for employing a larger pipe increases the total output when other inputs are held constant.

Similar engineering studies have been made for many other areas of the economy, including ones for agriculture, power plants, chemical factories, communications systems, and mines. These studies are essential for firms who wish to design their productive processes efficiently and compete effectively.

RETURNS TO SCALE

Diminishing returns and marginal products refer to the response of output to an increase of a *single* input when all other inputs are held constant. For example, we saw that increasing labor while holding land constant would increase food output by ever-smaller increments. Similarly Table 21-1 showed that increasing the pumping power while holding pipe size constant would increase output by smaller and smaller quantities.

[1]This section contains illustrative material that can be omitted in courses pressed for time.

TOTAL AND MARGINAL PRODUCTS FOR OIL PIPELINES

(1)	(2)	(3)	(4)	(5)	(6)	(7)
	12-INCH PIPE			24-INCH PIPE		
PUMPING HORSEPOWER	TOTAL PRODUCT (bbl per day)	AVERAGE PRODUCT	MARGINAL PRODUCT (bbl per day-hp)	TOTAL PRODUCT (bbl per day)	AVERAGE PRODUCT	MARGINAL PRODUCT (bbl per day-hp)
10,000	43,000	4.3		141,000	14.1	
			1.4			4.4
20,000	57,000	2.85		185,000	9.25	
			1.0			3.3
30,000	67,000	2.23		218,000	7.27	
			0.8			2.7
40,000	75,000	1.88		245,000	6.13	
			0.7			2.3
50,000	82,000	1.64		268,000	5.36	
			0.6			2.0
60,000	88,000	1.47		288,000	4.80	
			0.5			1.8
70,000	93,000	1.33		306,000	4.37	

Table 21-1 Engineering production function for oil pipelines

Studies of the design of oil pipelines provide the table's empirical data on the relationship between the flow of oil (in barrels per day) and the size of pipe and horsepower. The data show diminishing returns to horsepower sets in quickly, as marginal product of horsepower declines at higher levels of horsepower. [Source: L. Cookenboo, *Crude Oil Pipe Lines and Competition in the Oil Industry* (Harvard University Press, Cambridge, Mass., 1955).]

But sometimes we are interested in the impact on output when *all* inputs are increased. What would happen to corn production if all inputs—land, labor, machinery, and water—were increased by the same amount? Or what would happen to production of automobiles if the quantity of labor, computers, robots, steel, and factory space were all doubled? These questions refer to the returns to scale, or the effects of scale increases of inputs on the quantity produced. Put differently, the returns to scale reflect the responsiveness of total product when *all* the inputs are increased *proportionately*. Three important cases should be distinguished:

▪ **Constant returns to scale** denote a case where a change in all inputs leads to an equally large increase in output. For example, if inputs of labor, land, capital, and other inputs are doubled, then under constant returns to scale output would also double. Many handicraft industries (such as handlooms operated in a developing country) tend to show constant returns.

▪ A situation of **decreasing returns to scale** occurs when a balanced increase of all inputs leads to a less-than-proportional increase in total output. For example, say that a farmer's cornland, seed, labor, machinery, etc., were increased by 50 percent. If as a result total output increased by only 40 percent, then this situation is one of decreasing returns to scale. Many productive activities involving natural resources, such as growing wine grapes or forestry, show decreasing returns to scale.

▪ A final category is **increasing returns to scale.** Such a case arises when an increase in all inputs leads to a more-than-proportional increase in the level of output. For example, an engineer planning a small-

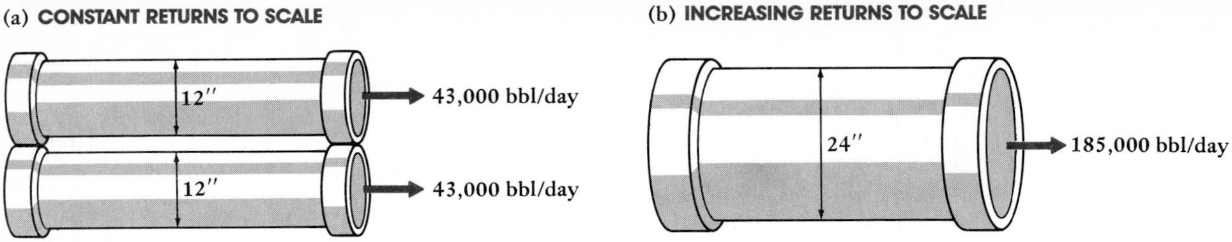

(a) CONSTANT RETURNS TO SCALE

12″ → 43,000 bbl/day

12″ → 43,000 bbl/day

(b) INCREASING RETURNS TO SCALE

24″ → 185,000 bbl/day

Figure 21-2   Constant and increasing returns to scale

By replicating projects such as pipelines, a firm can double output by doubling inputs, thus enjoying constant returns to scale, as shown in **(a)**. Building a larger-diameter pipe along with doubling horsepower, as in **(b)**, allows increasing returns to scale. (Source: Table 21-1.)

scale chemical plant would generally find that increasing the inputs of labor, capital, and materials by 10 percent will increase the total output by more than 10 percent. Engineering studies have determined that many manufacturing processes enjoy modestly increasing returns to scale for plants up to the largest size used today.

Production shows increasing, decreasing, or constant returns to scale when a balanced increase in all inputs leads to a more-than-proportional, a less-than-proportional, or a just-proportional increase in output.

Economists tend to think that most production activities should be able to attain constant returns to scale. They reason that if production can be adjusted by simply replicating existing plants over and over again, by building one steel plant or textile mill next to another, then the producer would simply be multiplying both inputs and output by the same number. In such a case, you would observe constant returns to scale for any level of output.[2]

In some cases, however, we should be able to improve upon constant returns and achieve increasing returns to scale. To take our pipeline example, Table 21-1 shows that one 12-inch pipe with 10,000 horsepower of pumping can transport 43,000 barrels of oil each day. If we were to place a second 12-inch pipe alongside the first, adding an additional 10,000 horsepower, the total throughput would increase to 86,000 barrels per day, showing how replication will lead to constant returns to scale. Figure 21-2(a) shows schematically the case of constant returns to scale from replication of identical 12-inch pipelines.

Consider, however, a 24-inch pipe with 20,000 horsepower of pumping capacity, shown in Figure 21-2(b). This new investment would double the power and double the amount of pipe. What would be its effect on total output? A glance at Table 21-1 shows that throughput increases from 43,000 barrels per day to 185,000 barrels per day, which is much more than doubled and therefore displays increasing returns to scale. This example, which is typical of many manufacturing processes, shows that by efficiently redesigning a process, doubling inputs may lead to a considerably larger than proportional increase in outputs.

While the pipeline example emphasizes the role of expanding the physical scale, other reasons may be equally important in contributing to increasing returns. Chapter 3 described how, as output increases, firms may break down production into smaller steps, taking advantage of specialization and division of

[2]Suppose as an example that a steel plant were capable of producing 100,000 tons of steel each year using 10 acres of land, 100 million Btu of power, 1500 person-hours, and 120,000 tons of steel scrap. Then an identical plant could ideally be built next door; and another next door; and so on. Hence two plants could produce 200,000 tons of steel with double the inputs; 10 identical plants could produce 1 million tons with 10 times the inputs; and so on for any mix which represented a certain number of plants. Constant returns to scale would then be ensured because multiplying all inputs by any number K by constructing K duplicate plants necessarily would result in total output equal to K times the output of one single plant.

labor. In addition, mass production allows intensive use of specialized capital equipment, of automation, even of robots, to perform simple and repetitive tasks quickly.

The question of returns to scale is of great importance for the economic growth of nations. Most countries have experienced steady increases in their population, capital stock, available land, and other resources. In the course of growth, firms have expanded, with production levels of typical firms today many times larger than those of large firms a half-century or century ago. What would be the effect of a general increase in the scale of economic activity of most firms? If increasing returns prevailed, then the larger scale of inputs and production would lead to greater productivity—where **productivity** is a concept measuring the ratio of total output to a weighted average of inputs. If, for example, the typical firm's inputs increased by 100 percent and output consequently increased by 120 percent, then productivity (output per unit of input) would rise by 20 percent. This example suggests that increases in a nation's per capita output and living standards may result in part from exploiting economies of scale in production as the nation grows.[3]

While the potential scale economies are great in many sectors, at some point decreasing returns to scale may take hold. As firms become larger and larger, the problems of management and coordination become increasingly difficult. In relentless pursuit of greater profits, a firm may find itself expanding into a greater number of geographic markets or into more and more product lines. But a firm can have only one chief executive officer, one chief financial officer, one board of directors. With less time to study each market and spend on each decision, top managers may become insulated from day-to-day production and begin to make business mistakes. Like empires that have been stretched too thin, such firms find themselves liable to invasion by smaller and more agile rivals. In sum, while technology might ideally allow constant or increasing returns to scale, the needs for management and supervision may eventually lead to decreasing returns to scale for giant firms.

[3]Further analysis of production, economic growth, and productivity trends is contained in Chapter 36.

MOMENTARY RUN, SHORT RUN, AND LONG RUN

The discussion of production has up to now ignored the time needed to build production facilities and to make management decisions. But production and planning take time. Pipelines cannot be built overnight, and once built they last for decades. Farmers cannot change crops in mid-season, nor can new land be cleared quickly. Nuclear power plants take a decade or more to plan, construct, test, and commission. Moreover, once capital equipment has been put in the concrete form of a power plant on the Tennessee River or a petrochemical factory in Galveston, the investment cannot be economically dismantled and moved to another location or transferred to another use.

In Chapter 18 we discussed three different lengths of time over which a market would reach equilibrium. We can use the same distinctions to understand the dynamics of production response. In these discussions, we call the *momentary run* a period so short that production is fixed, the *short run* a period in which firms can adjust production by changing variable factors such as materials and labor but cannot change fixed factors such as capital, and the *long run* a period sufficiently long so that all factors including capital can be adjusted.

To understand these concepts more clearly, consider the way the production of steel might respond to changes in demand. Say that Republic Steel is operating its furnaces at 70 percent of capacity when a sudden and unexpected increase in the demand for steel occurs because of a breakdown in a competitor's plant. In the momentary run of a day or so, the steel firm cannot adjust its production at all. It takes time to check and recheck the order books, to call customers to confirm their needs, to recalculate the optimal production level, to stoke up the furnaces, to reschedule worker-hours, and to order the necessary materials. During the period in which such actions are taken, production will remain unchanged. Therefore, in this shortest of time periods, the momentary run, output is essentially fixed or predetermined.

As time passes, Republic Steel can begin to adjust its production to the new level of demand. The firm can increase production by asking its workers to work overtime, by hiring more workers, and by operating its plants and machinery more intensively. The factors which are increased in the short run are called *variable* factors, for they can easily be changed in a short period of time. Hence, the level of production can be increased within the limits of existing plant capacity during the short run.

Suppose that the increase in steel demand persisted for an extended period of time, for 2 or 3 years or even for a decade. Republic Steel might then examine its plant and equipment and decide that it should increase its productive capacity. More generally, it might examine all its *fixed* factors, those being ones that cannot be changed in the short run because of physical conditions or legal contracts. The period of time over which all inputs, fixed and variable, can be adjusted is called the long run. In the long run, Republic might add new and more efficient production processes, introduce robots to perform new tasks, computerize additional steps, or build a plant in Mexico. These additions to Republic's capital equipment would allow a greater increase in production than simply adding more workers, and they would also allow more efficient use of the existing labor force.

To recapitulate our definitions:

Planning and implementing production decisions may take long periods of time. We therefore distinguish three different time periods in production and cost analysis:

- The **momentary run** is the period of time so short that no change in production can take place.

- The **short run** is the period of time in which variable inputs, such as materials and labor, can be adjusted, but of insufficient length for all inputs to be changed. In the short run, fixed factors, such as plant and equipment, cannot be fully modified or adjusted.

- The **long run** is the period such that all fixed and variable factors employed by the firm can be changed, including labor, materials, and capital.

TECHNOLOGICAL CHANGE

The production processes analyzed above consider situations of a given state of technology. The study of

pipeline production possibilities in Table 21-1 represents the best engineering practice at a point in time, whereas the production data in Figure 21-1 might show the wheat output that was producible with the prevailing agricultural technology of 1988. *A production function represents the relationship between inputs and outputs for a given state of engineering and technical knowledge.*

But technologies do change. Even the most casual historical observation finds that today's array of goods and services is far different from what prevailed a century ago. Today we see digital watches, synthetic fibers, electronic computers, airplanes, electric lights, automobiles, and similar products that were unavailable in 1890. Indeed, you would be hard-pressed to find a commodity or production process that has not changed dramatically over the last few decades. Changes in technology—invention of new products, improvements in old products, or changes in the processes for producing goods and services—are what we mean by **technological change.**

Expressing this differently, technological change occurs when new or improved engineering and technical knowledge allows more output to be produced from the same inputs, or when the same output can be produced with fewer inputs. In terms of our production terminology, technological change occurs when the production function changes. The following examples illustrate recent technological changes:

- Introduction of new hybrid-corn seeds increased the productivity of corn farming by over 25 percent within a decade.

- Introduction of continuous casting of steel increased the output per unit of input by 20 percent.

- Wide-body jets increased the number of passenger-miles per unit of input by almost 40 percent.

- Miniaturization and laser-etching allows, for the same inputs of capital and labor, 100 times more information to be stored in computer memories compared to two decades ago.

These examples can be multiplied manifold in manufacturing, telecommunications, mining, agriculture, and other spheres of economic life. Figure 21-3 illustrates the impact of technological change on the total product curve of Figure 21-1. The lower line might represent the producible output, or production function, for the year 1985. If we return to the same industry or firm a decade later, changes in technical and engineering knowledge in this example have led to a 50 percent improvement in output per unit of input, or productivity. The technological change is represented by an upward shift in the total product curve to the dashed line in Figure 21-3.

This discussion raises the natural question, Can there ever be technological regress? In a well-functioning market economy, firms will introduce only technological advances. If, for example, someone discovered a new photocopying machine that cost as much as the old one and copied at only half the rate, no sensible, profit-oriented firm would introduce the new machine. Inferior technologies would tend to be discarded in a market economy, while superior technologies—ones with higher productivity levels—would tend to be introduced because they will increase the profits of the innovating firms.

In perverse cases, particularly those involving market failures, technological regress might occur. An unregulated electricity-generating company might introduce a socially wasteful process, say one using high-sulfur coal instead of low-sulfur coal, because the former was much cheaper to buy. The company would introduce the environmentally inferior process because it did not include the pollution costs in its calculations of costs of production. Another example might occur if government regulation mandated that a company adopt an inefficient technology.

Instances of technological regress are clearly in the minority, however, for economic history shows a clear preponderance of technological advance over technological regress. The next section shows the overall impact of technological improvements in the United States.

THE AGGREGATE PRODUCTION FUNCTION FOR THE UNITED STATES

Now that we have examined the principles of production theory, we can apply these theories to measure the aggregate performance of the U.S. economy. We might investigate the behavior of total output, of different inputs (like labor, capital, and land), and total

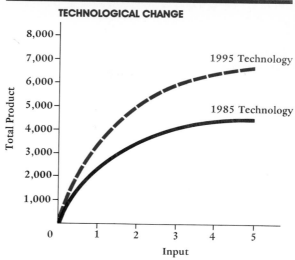

Figure 21-3 Technological advance shifts production function upward

The solid line at the bottom represents maximum producible output, for each amount of input, given the state of technical knowledge in 1985. As a result of computerization, new processes, better quality control, and similar factors, improved technical knowledge in 1995 allows 50 percent more output to be produced for each quantity of input.

productivity. Because they involve serious problems of measurement, all such magnitudes must be calculated with great care. Yet they are useful in giving a broad description of an overall economy's behavior.

Empirical studies of the aggregate production function date back to the 1920s, when Paul Douglas (Chicago professor, later a U.S. senator) analyzed data for manufacturing. In the 1950s and 1960s, others pursued this approach further, including Robert Solow, John Kendrick, and Edward Denison. The goal of these studies was to find how economic growth depended upon capital, labor, and productivity growth. Recall from our earlier discussion that productivity measures the total quantity of output per unit of input. **Productivity growth** denotes the rate of growth of the level of productivity. For example, if output per worker is 100 units in 1990, and it grows to 102.5 units in 1991, then we say that productivity growth was 2.5 percent per year.

In measuring productivity, we denote labor productivity as the amount of output per unit of labor; capital productivity as output per unit of capital; and total factor productivity as output per unit of total inputs of capital and labor.

Empirical Findings What have economic studies found? Here are a few of the important results:

- Total factor productivity has been increasing throughout this century because of technological progress and higher levels of worker education and skill. The average rate of total productivity growth has been slightly under $1\frac{1}{2}$ percent per year during the twentieth century.
- The capital stock has been growing faster than the number of worker-hours. As a result, labor has a growing amount of capital goods to work with; hence labor productivity and wages have tended to rise even faster than the $1\frac{1}{2}$ percent per year attributable to productivity growth alone.
- The rate of return on capital (the ''rate of profit'') might have been expected to encounter diminishing returns because each capital unit now has less labor to cooperate with it. Yet capital's rate of return has in fact remained about the same. Why? Because the increased capital per worker has been offset by the impact of technological progress on the productivity of capital. Just as a greater number of machines might have led to a lower rate of return on machines, there appear new and improved machines that once again make capital highly profitable.
- In the last two decades, all measures of productivity have shown a marked growth slowdown.

Whereas the first seven decades of this century witnessed total factor productivity growth of almost $1\frac{1}{2}$ percent per year on average, the decades of the 1970s and 1980s experienced productivity growth of only $\frac{1}{2}$ percent per year. This productivity growth slowdown has produced a markedly slower growth in real wages and in living standards in the United States.

Similar statistical measurements all over the globe help to put flesh on the bare bones of the microeconomic theory of production. They serve as factual tests of the validity of economic principles—principles that Chapter 36 will use for explaining the economic growth of nations.

From Production to Cost

This analysis of trends in the aggregate production function ends our survey of the basic elements of the theory of production and marginal products. Production theory is of great importance in its own right, helping us to understand how firms manage their internal activities and to analyze underlying behavior of productivity and living standards. But production theory is also an important building block in understanding business costs, which are the central determinants of supply. In the next chapter, then, we turn to an analysis of different cost concepts; the appendix to Chapter 22 will also provide a more complete analysis of the theory of production and cost. Mastery of these analytical tools is a prerequisite to understanding businesses' supply of goods and services and the behavior of markets in the remaining chapters of this part.

SUMMARY _____

1. In understanding the functioning of business enterprises, we begin by analyzing a firm's production behavior. The relationship between the quantity of output (such as wheat, steel, or automobiles) and the quantities of inputs (of labor, land, and capital) is called the production function.

2. Total product refers to the total output produced. Average product equals total output divided by the total quantity of inputs. By varying the inputs of one factor of production, while holding all other inputs constant, we can calculate the marginal product of a factor, which is equal to the extra output added for each additional unit of input. The law of diminishing returns holds that the marginal product of each input will decline as the amount of that input increases, when all other inputs are held constant. The law of diminishing returns is a widely observed empirical regularity and is seen in many engineering examples, such as that of oil pipelines.

3. Because decisions take time to implement, and because capital and other factors are often very long-lived, the reaction of production may change over different time periods. The momentary run is the brief period in which output cannot be changed. The short run is a period in which variable factors, such as labor or material inputs, can be easily changed. In the long run, all factors, fixed and variable, can be adjusted; the capital stock, a firm's machinery and factories, can depreciate and be replaced.

4. The returns to scale refer to the impact on output of a balanced increase in all inputs. A technology in which doubling all inputs leads to an exact doubling of outputs is one of constant returns to scale. When doubling inputs leads to less than double the quantity of output, this situation is one of decreasing returns to scale. Conversely, when doubling inputs leads to greater than double the quantity of output, we have increasing returns to scale. When processes can be replicated, as when one 12-inch pipeline is nestled next to another one, constant returns to scale will generally prevail. In many manufacturing processes, where a larger scale of operations allows redesign of capital equipment, studies indicate that increasing returns to scale prevail. As firms become larger and larger, difficulties of control and management may produce decreasing returns to scale.

5. Technological change refers to a change in the underlying techniques of production, as when a new product is invented, an old product is improved, or a process of production is made more efficient. In such situations, the same output is produced with fewer inputs, or more output is produced with the same inputs. In technical terms, technological change shifts the production function.

6. Ambitious attempts to measure an aggregate production function for the American economy tend to corroborate theories of production and marginal products. In this century, technological change has increased the productivity of both labor and capital. Total factor productivity (measuring the ratio of total output to total inputs) has averaged almost $1\frac{1}{2}$ percent per year over the twentieth century although the rate of productivity growth has slowed markedly since 1970.

CONCEPTS FOR REVIEW

inputs, outputs, production function
total, average, marginal product
diminishing marginal product and the
 law of diminishing returns
momentary, short, and long run

constant, increasing, and decreasing
 returns to scale
technological change
productivity (labor, capital, total factor)
aggregate production function

QUESTIONS FOR DISCUSSION

1. Explain the concept of a production function. Describe the production function for hamburgers, concerts, and education.

2. For the following table, fill in the missing values for marginal products and average products.

(1)	(2)	(3)	(4)
		18-INCH PIPE	
PUMPING HORSEPOWER	TOTAL PRODUCT (bbl per day)	MARGINAL PRODUCT (bbl per day-hp)	AVERAGE PRODUCT (bbl per day-hp)
10,000	86,000		_____
20,000	114,000	_____	_____
30,000	134,000	_____	_____
40,000	150,000	_____	_____
50,000	164,000	_____	_____

3. For the data in question 2, plot the production function of output against horsepower. On the same chart, plot the curves for average product and marginal product.

4. For the data given in question 2, say that technological change in the form of a new pipe material allows 20 percent more output to be produced for each level of horsepower. Plot the original production function and the new production function after the technological change.

5. Give some examples of important technological advances of the twentieth century. Explain for each how it would change the production function for the given product or process.

6. ''If it were not for the law of diminishing returns, it would be possible to grow all the world's food in a single flowerpot.'' Explain this statement.

7. Refer back to Table 21-1. Calculate the marginal product of ''pipe'' at each level of horsepower; that is, what is the additional output obtained when the diameter of the pipe increases from 12 inches to 24 inches?

8. Refer back to Table 21-1. Calculations will show that the numerical production function for throughput of oil is given by the following formula:

$$Q = 43,000\left(\frac{H}{10,000}\right)^{0.4}\left(\frac{P}{12}\right)^{1.7}$$

where Q is throughput in barrels per day, H is horsepower, and P is pipeline diameter in inches. Calculate the marginal product of additional horsepower for increments of 10,000, and calculate the marginal product of adding an additional 12 inches of pipe for the first five horsepower settings.

9. Consider a firm producing automobiles. If the demand for the firm's output declines, what steps could it take to reduce output in the short run? In the long run?

10. Consider the following changes in a firm's behavior. Which represent substitution of one factor for another with an unchanged technology, and which represent technological change?

(a) When the price of oil increases, a firm replaces an oil-fired plant with a coal-fired plant.

(b) With the introduction of laser-operated scanning machinery, a steel manufacturer improves the guarantee on the thickness of its steel plate to a tolerance of 0.01 inch from 0.05 inch in the prior year.

(c) Over the period 1970–1985, a typesetting firm decreases its employment of typesetters by 60 percent and increases its employment of computer operators by 150 percent.

(d) After a successful unionization drive for clerical workers, a university buys personal computers for its faculty and reduces its secretarial work force.

11. Consider a firm that produces wheat with land and labor inputs. Contrast diminishing returns and decreasing returns to scale. Is it possible to have diminishing returns to one input and constant returns to scale for both inputs?

12. Advanced problem: Show that if the marginal product is always decreasing, then the average product is always above the marginal product.

13. Advanced problem: Let output be Q and inputs be L (for labor) and A (for acres of land). Show that the arithmetic mean of L and A, namely $Q = \frac{1}{2}L + \frac{1}{2}A$, would not make an accurate production function because it does not show diminishing marginal products. (HINT: Each equal increment of L by 1 always increases Q by the same increment of $\frac{1}{2}$.) But the Cobb-Douglas production function $Q = \sqrt{LA} = \sqrt{L}\sqrt{A}$ is a good production function with diminishing returns. (HINT: The square roots of 1, 2, 3, . . . are 1, 1.41, 1.73, . . . which do show decreasing increments of Q, namely, 0.41, 0.32, ...)

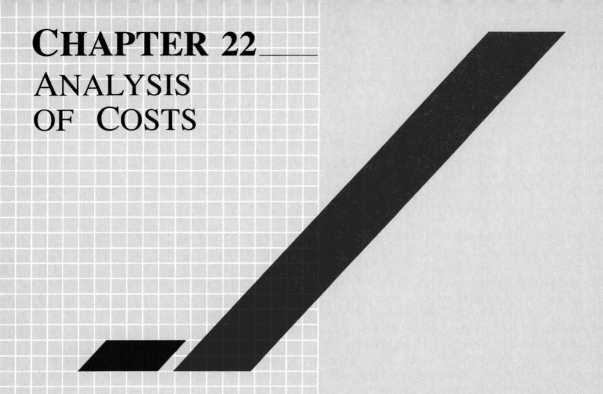

CHAPTER 22

ANALYSIS OF COSTS

Costs merely register competing attractions.

Frank Knight,
Risk, Uncertainty, and Profit (1921)

THE LAST CHAPTER analyzed physical production by firms, examining such questions as marginal products and the relationship of production concepts to the law of diminishing returns. We now translate issues of production into analysis of cost, laying the groundwork for a full analysis of the supply decisions of firms and of the price and output determination in markets.

Why do firms care about costs? Clearly they must pay careful attention to costs because every dollar of cost reduces the firm's profits. But costs are important in economics for a deeper reason: firms will decide how much of a good to produce and sell depending on the price and cost of the good. More precisely, supply depends upon incremental or marginal cost. And the dependence of supply decisions on cost is true not only for perfect competitors but also for firms in the vast terrain of imperfect competition. We thus devote the present chapter to a thorough analysis of different economic concepts of cost, including broader opportunity costs as well as dollar costs.

Once the major cost concepts have been mastered we can move on to Chapter 23's analysis of the supply decisions of competitive firms and industries. Whatever the market structure, whether perfectly or imperfectly competitive, marginal cost is a key concept for understanding a firm's behavior.

TOTAL COST: FIXED AND VARIABLE

Consider a firm that produces a quantity of output denoted by q. As described in the last chapter, this output is produced according to some production function with capital, labor, and other inputs. The firm must of course buy these inputs in the factor markets. A profit-minded firm will keep an eagle-eye on its costs so as to maintain its profits, and it is to the firm's accountants that the task is given to calculate the total dollar costs incurred at each level of q.

Table 22-1 shows the simplified total cost *(TC)* for each different level of output q. Columns (1) and (4) are the crucial ones, showing that *TC* goes up as q goes up. This is natural because it takes more labor and factor inputs to produce more of a good; these extra factors involve an extra money cost. It costs $110 in all to produce 2 units, $130 to produce 3 units, and so forth.

As an aside, note that when we write down a cost schedule like that in Table 22-1 or draw a cost curve

later in this chapter, we make the firm's job look altogether too simple. Why so? Because much hard work lies behind the figures in Table 22-1. To attain the lowest level of costs, the firm's managers have to make sure that they are paying the least possible amounts for necessary materials (like oil or iron ore); that wages are neither so costly as to raise the firm's costs unnecessarily nor so low as to increase labor turnover and vacancies; that the latest engineering techniques are incorporated into the factory layout; and that countless other decisions are made in the most economical fashion.

As a result of such managerial effort, the fixed and variable costs shown in Table 22-1 are the firm's *minimum costs* necessary to produce that level of output. A poor manager could, of course, do worse. But a good manager can do no better than attain the minimum costs shown in the table.

Fixed Cost

Columns (2) and (3) break total cost into two components: total fixed cost, *FC*, and total variable cost, *VC*. Figure 22-2(a) later in this chapter will show these components graphically.

What are a firm's **fixed costs**? Sometimes called "overhead" or "sunk costs," they consist of items like contractual payments for building and equipment

(1) QUANTITY q	(2) FIXED COST FC	(3) VARIABLE COST VC	(4) TOTAL COST TC
0	55	0	55
1	55	30	85
2	55	55	110
3	55	75	130
4	55	105	160
5	55	155	210
6	55	225	280

Table 22-1   Fixed, variable, and total costs

The major elements of a firm's costs are its fixed costs (that do not vary at all when output changes) and variable costs (that increase as output increases). Total costs are equal to fixed plus variable costs: $TC = FC + VC$.

rents, interest payments on debts, salaries of long-term employees, and so forth. These must be paid even if the firm produces no output, and they will not change if output changes. Hence, *FC* is the amount of cost that must be paid independently of the level of output; that is why *FC* stays constant at $55 in column (2).

Variable Cost

Column (3) of Table 22-1 shows variable cost *(VC)*. **Variable costs** are those costs that vary with the level of output. Examples include materials required to produce output (such as steel to produce automobiles); production workers to staff the production lines; fuel, light, and power to operate factories; and the like.

By definition, *VC* begins at zero when *q* is zero. It is the part of *TC* that grows with output; indeed, the jump in *TC* between any two outputs is the same as the jump in *VC*. Why? Because *FC* stays constant at $55 throughout and cancels out in the comparison of costs between different output levels. Let us summarize these cost concepts:

"Total cost" represents the lowest total dollar expense needed to produce each level of output *q*. *TC* rises as *q* rises.

"Fixed cost" represents the total dollar expense that is paid out even when no output is produced; fixed cost is unaffected by any variation in the quantity of output.

"Variable cost" represents expenses that vary with the level of output—including raw materials, wages, and fuel—and includes all costs that are not fixed.

Always, by definition,

$$TC = FC + VC$$

DEFINITION OF MARGINAL COST

The key to understanding how much a firm will want to produce and sell is its marginal cost of producing goods and services. What do we mean by marginal cost? **Marginal cost** denotes the extra or additional cost of producing 1 extra unit of output.

Say a firm is producing 1000 hard disks for a total

(1) OUTPUT *q*	(2) TOTAL COST *TC*	(3) MARGINAL COST *MC*
0	$ 55	
		$30
1	85	
		25
2	110	
		20
3	130	
		30
4	160	
		50
5	210	

Table 22-2   Calculation of marginal cost

Once we know total cost, it is easy to calculate marginal cost. Thus to calculate the *MC* of the fifth unit, we subtract the total cost of the fourth unit from the total cost of the fifth unit, i.e.,

$$MC = \$210 - \$160 = \$50$$

cost of $10,000. If the total cost of producing 1001 disks is $10,015, then the marginal cost of production is $15 for the 1001st disk.

Table 22-2 uses the example from Table 22-1 to illustrate how we calculate marginal costs. Begin by recalling that in economics the term "marginal"—whether applied to utility, cost, production, consumption, or whatever—means "incremental" or "extra." The red *MC* numbers in column (3) of Table 22-2 come from subtracting the *TC* in the adjacent column from the *TC* of the earlier unit. Thus the *MC* of the first unit is $30 = $85 − $55. The marginal cost of the second unit is $25 = $110 − $85. And so on. Verify that the marginal cost of the fifth unit of output is $50.

Instead of getting *MC* from the *TC* column, we could as easily get the *MC* figures by subtracting each *VC* number of column (3) of Table 22-1 from the row below it. Why? Because variable cost always grows exactly like total cost, the only difference being that *VC* must—by definition—start out from 0 rather than from the constant *FC* level. (Check that 30 − 0 = 85 − 55, and 55 − 30 = 110 − 85, ...)

(a) TOTAL COST

(b) MARGINAL COST

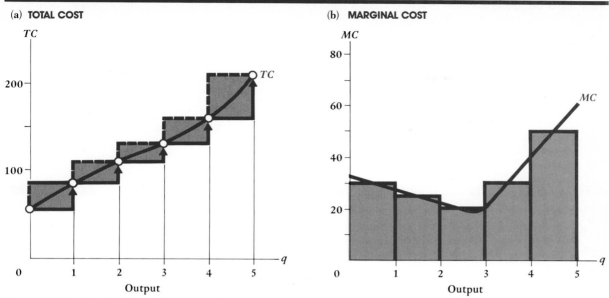

Figure 22-1   Marginal cost is to total cost exactly as marginal product is to total product

Marginal cost in **(b)** is found by calculating the extra cost added in **(a)** for each unit increase in output. Thus to find the *MC* of producing the fifth unit, we subtract $160 from $210 to get *MC* of $50. A smooth curve has been drawn through the points of *TC* in **(a)**, and the smooth *MC* curve in **(b)** links the discrete steps of *MC*. (Source: Table 22-2.)

At each output level, the marginal cost of production is the additional cost incurred in producing 1 extra unit of output. It is calculated in Table 22-2 by comparing the total costs of producing adjacent output levels.

Marginal Cost in Diagrams Figure 22-1 illustrates total cost and marginal cost. It shows that *TC* is related to *MC* in the same way that Figure 21-1 related total product to marginal product (or as Figure 19-1 related total utility to marginal utility).

What kind of shape would we expect the *MC* curve to have? Empirical studies have found a wide variety of *MC* curves in practice, with the shape of the *MC* curve depending upon the type of industry and the time period under consideration. A typical marginal cost curve for the short run is the U-shaped one shown in Figure 22-1(*b*). This U-shaped curve falls in an initial phase, then reaches a minimum point, and fi-

nally begins to rise. Such a U-shaped cost curve would be appropriate for calculating the short-run marginal costs for many firms—that is, costs for a period of time in which the firm's plant and equipment are fixed.

The cost curves can have other shapes as well. The reasons behind the shape of the cost curves will be covered later in this chapter where we describe the relationship between cost analysis and production analysis.

COST CONCEPTS

We can complete our catalogue of cost concepts important in economics and business with a discussion of different kinds of average or unit cost. Table 22-3 extends the figures of Table 22-1 to include three new measures: average cost, average fixed cost, and average variable cost.

Average or Unit Cost

One of the most important cost concepts is average cost, which, when compared with price or average revenue, will allow a business to determine whether or not it is making a profit. **Average cost** is the total cost divided by the number of units produced, as is shown in column (6) of Table 22-3. That is,

$$\text{Average cost} = \frac{\text{total cost}}{\text{output}} = \frac{TC}{q} = AC$$

In column (6), when only 1 unit is produced, average cost has to be the same as total cost, or \$85/1 = \$85. But for $q = 2$, $AC = TC/2 = \$110/2 = \$55$, as shown. Note that average cost is, at first, falling lower and lower. (We shall see why in a moment.) But AC reaches a minimum of \$40 at $q = 4$, and then slowly rises.

Next, we plot carefully the different concepts of cost as they are shown in Table 22-3. The top half of Figure 22-2 is the total, fixed, and variable cost shown at different levels of output. The bottom half

IMPORTANT COST CONCEPTS

(1) QUANTITY q	(2) FIXED COST FC	(3) VARIABLE COST VC	(4) TOTAL COST $TC = FC + VC$	(5) MARGINAL COST PER UNIT MC	(6) AVERAGE COST PER UNIT $AC = \dfrac{TC}{q}$	(7) AVERAGE FIXED COST PER UNIT $AFC = \dfrac{FC}{q}$	(8) AVERAGE VARIABLE COST PER UNIT $AVC = \dfrac{VC}{q}$
0	55	0	55	33	Infinity	Infinity	Undefined
				30			
1	55	30	85	27	85	55	30
				25			
2	55	55	110	22	55	$27\frac{1}{2}$	$27\frac{1}{2}$
				20			
3	55	75	130	21	$43\frac{1}{3}$	$18\frac{1}{3}$	25
				30			
4*	55	105	160	40*	40*	$13\frac{3}{4}$	$26\frac{1}{4}$
				50			
5	55	155	210	60	42	11	—
				—			
6	55	225	280	80	$46\frac{4}{6}$	$9\frac{1}{6}$	$37\frac{3}{6}$
				90			
7	55	—	370	100	$52\frac{6}{7}$	$7\frac{6}{7}$	45
				110			
8	55	—	480	120	60	$6\frac{7}{8}$	$53\frac{1}{8}$
				130			
9	55	555	610	140	$67\frac{7}{9}$	$6\frac{1}{9}$	$61\frac{6}{9}$
				150			
10	55	705	760		76	$5\frac{5}{10}$	$70\frac{5}{10}$

*Minimum level of average cost.

Table 22-3 From schedule of firm's total cost, all other costs can be computed

All the costs can be calculated from the *TC* in column (4). Columns (5) and (6) are the important ones to concentrate on: Incremental or marginal cost is calculated by subtraction of adjacent rows of *TC* and is shown in red. The light red numbers of smoothed *MC* come from Figure 22-2(b). In column (6) note the point of minimum cost of \$40 on the U-shaped *AC* curve in Figure 22-2(b). (Can you see why the starred *MC* equals the starred *AC* at the minimum? Also, calculate and fill in all the missing numbers.)

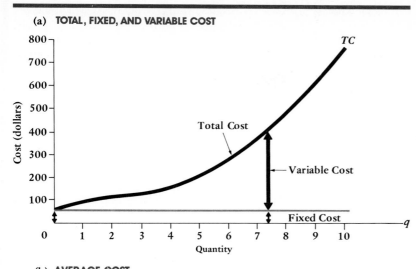

(a) TOTAL, FIXED, AND VARIABLE COST

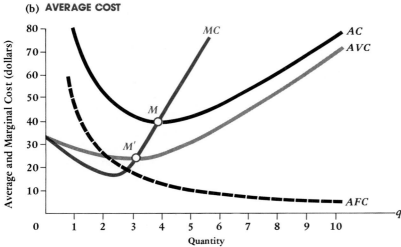

(b) AVERAGE COST

Figure 22-2   Total cost curve gives rise to all the other curves

(a) Total cost is made up of fixed cost and variable cost. **(b)** The red curve of marginal cost falls and then rises, as indicated by the light red *MC* figures given in column (5) of Table 22-3. The three average cost curves in **(b)** are calculated by dividing total, fixed, and variable cost by total output, so

$$AC = TC/q \qquad AVC = VC/q \qquad \text{and} \qquad AFC = FC/q$$

Also, $$AC = AVC + AFC$$

Note that *MC* intersects *AC* at its minimum. This key fact is not a coincidence, but is due to the important relationship between marginal and average costs.

shows the different average cost concepts, along with a smoothed marginal cost curve.

The top half of Figure 22-2 is self-explanatory. You can see how total cost moves with variable cost while fixed cost stays fixed.

Now turn to the bottom half. This gives a careful plotting of U-shaped AC, correctly aligned below the TC it came from. We can now break down average cost into its two components, fixed and variable—just as earlier we had the breakdown of TC into FC and VC. By dividing each of the last two by q, we get average fixed cost, $AFC = FC/q$ of column (7), and average variable cost, $AVC = VC/q$ of column (8).

Average Fixed Cost

Since total fixed cost is a constant, dividing it by an increasing output gives a steadily falling average fixed cost curve in column (7) of Table 22-3. The dashed black AFC curve in Figure 22-2(b) looks like a hyperbola, approaching both axes: it drops lower and lower, approaching the horizontal axis as the constant FC gets spread over more and more units. If we allow fractional and zero units of q, AC starts infinitely high, as finite FC is spread over ever tinier q.

Average Variable Cost

Average variable cost *(AVC)* equals variable cost divided by output, or $AVC = VC/q$. In our numerical example of Table 22-3 and Figure 22-2(b), AVC first falls and then rises. As we will see in the next section, this shape for *AVC* can be predicted from the behavior of marginal cost.

Minimum Average Cost

Figure 22-2(b) is a crucial economic diagram. Study it carefully and fix it in your mind's eye. Note the relationship between the MC curve and the AC curve—particularly the way that the MC curve cuts the minimum point of the AC curve: *The* AC *curve is always pierced at its minimum point by the rising* MC *curve.*

This is no coincidence, and we will now explain why this has to be the case. The basic point to see is that if MC is below AC, then AC must be falling. Why

is this so? Because if MC is below AC, then the last unit produced costs less than the average of all the earlier units produced. If the last unit costs less than the earlier ones, then the new AC (i.e., the AC including the last unit) must be less than the old AC, so AC must be falling. To put this in terms of our cost curves, this shows that if the MC curve is below the AC curve, then the AC curve must be falling.

What if MC is above AC? In this case, the last unit costs more than the average of the earlier units. Hence the new average cost (the AC including the last unit) must be higher than old AC. Therefore, when MC is above AC, AC must be rising.

Finally, if MC is just equal to AC, this means that the last unit costs exactly the same as the average cost of all earlier units. Hence the new AC, the one including the last unit, is equal to the old AC; the AC curve is flat when AC equals MC.

From this discussion, we can see why a rising MC curve must cut the AC curve at its minimum point. To the left of the minimum point of the AC curve, MC is below AC, so the AC curve is falling. To the right of the AC minimum, MC is above AC, so the AC curve is rising. At the point where MC equals AC, the AC curve is flat. Hence, the MC curve cuts the AC curve at the minimum average cost.

A Classroom Example Here is an explanation of the MC and AC relationship in terms of college grade averages. Let AG be your average grades (or cumulative grade average up to now), and MG is your marginal or incremental grade average for this year. When MG is below AG, it will pull the new AG down. Thus if your AG for the first 2 years is 3, while your MG for your junior year is 2, then the new AG (at the end of junior year) is $2\frac{2}{3}$. Similarly, if your MG in your third year is higher than your AG up to then, your new AG will be pulled up. Where MG equals AG, AG will be flat over time, or is unchanged. The same relation holds for average and marginal cost.

To better understand the relationship between MC and AC, you should study carefully the curves in Figure 22-2(b) and the numbers in Table 22-3. Note that for the first 3 units, MC is below AC; AC is thus declining. At exactly 4 units AC equals MC. Above 4 units, *MC* is above *AC* and pulling *AC* up steadily.

To summarize:

So long as marginal cost is below average cost, it is pulling average cost down; when *MC* gets to be just equal to *AC*, *AC* is neither rising nor falling and is at its minimum; when *MC* is above *AC*, it is pulling *AC* up. Hence:

At the bottom of U-shaped *AC*, *MC* = *AC* = minimum *AC*.

Finally, note as well that a rising *MC* cuts *AVC* at its lowest point or minimum. You can again verify this fact in Table 22-3. The reasoning about why it cuts *AVC* at the minimum is exactly the same as why it cuts *AC* at its minimum.*

THE LINK BETWEEN PRODUCTION AND COSTS

At this point, we should pause to consider the source of the cost curves that have appeared in this chapter. In truth, cost curves are not the beginning of the story. Rather, they are grounded in the production techniques employed by the firm and in the prices the firm pays for the inputs. Now that both production and cost concepts have been presented, we bring the

linkage between the two out of the background.

The essence of the link between costs and production is simple: for each level of output, firms must choose the least costly combination of inputs. A profit-oriented firm will always strive to choose the bundle of labor, capital, land, and materials that produces the output at lowest cost. Hence, for given wage rates, land rents, machinery rentals, and materials prices, the firm will seek that combination of inputs that can produce the output in the least expensive way. When the total cost of this least-cost bundle of inputs is calculated, we have the total cost shown in Tables 22-1 through 22-3.

We can show the derivation of cost from production data through a simple numerical example. Suppose Farmer Jones rents 10 acres of land and can hire farm labor to produce wheat. Per period, land costs $5.5 per acre and labor costs $5 per worker. Using up-to-date farming methods, Jones can produce according to the production function shown in the first three columns of Table 22-4. In this example, land is a fixed cost (because Farmer Jones operates under a 10-year lease), while labor is a variable cost (because labor can be easily hired and dismissed in the local labor market).

Using the production data and the input-cost data, we can for each level of output calculate the total cost

---

*One other important relation can be seen by looking at the total cost graph. In our example up to now, we have seen large jumps in *MC* as output goes from one level to the next. Instead, focus a microscope on the total cost curve. This we can do if the units of *q* are in thousands, so we can examine the cost of going from 3.999 (thousand) *q* to 4.000 (thousand) *q*. This smoothed total cost curve was used to give the light red *MC*s in Table 22-3.

Recall that marginal cost is the slope of the total cost curve. We saw how the slope of curved lines is measured back in the appendix to Chapter 1, and *MC* is an excellent illustration of the technique. Figure 22-3 helps to clarify the distinction between (1) *MC* as an increment of cost for a finite step between two points

of *q*, and (2) *MC* as a smoothed-out instantaneous rate depicting the tangential slope at which *TC* is rising at one given *q* point. The *a* to *b* distance represents 1 extra unit of output. The *b* to *a'* distance represents the resulting increase in total cost, which is the first and simplest definition of marginal cost. The second definition is given by the slope of the total cost curve at point *a*—and what mathematicians call *d(TC)/dq*—or what is the same thing numerically, by the distance from *b* to *c* divided by the unit distance *a* to *b*. In the limit, as the size of the extra units becomes small and we reexamine the ratios in the new smaller triangle, the discrepancy between the two definitions becomes relatively negligible. (That is, *ba'* ÷ *bc* approaches 1 as *a'* approaches *a*.)

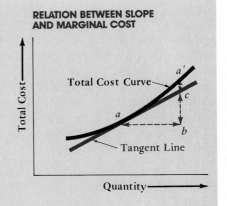

RELATION BETWEEN SLOPE AND MARGINAL COST

Figure 22-3

(1)	(2)	(3)	(4) LAND RENT (dollars per acre)	(5) LABOR WAGE (dollars per worker)	(6)
OUTPUT (tons of wheat)	LAND INPUTS (acres)	LABOR INPUTS (workers)			TOTAL COST (dollars)
0	10	0	5.5	5	55
1	10	6	5.5	5	85
2	10	11	5.5	5	110
3	10	15	5.5	5	130
4	10	21	5.5	5	160
5	10	31	5.5	5	210
6	10	45	5.5	5	280
7	10	63	5.5	5	370
8	10	85	5.5	5	480
9	10	111	5.5	5	610
10	10	141	5.5	5	760

Table 22-4 Costs are derived from production data and input costs

Farmer Jones rents 10 acres of wheat land and employs variable labor. According to the relevant production function, careful use of labor and land allows inputs and yields shown in columns (1) to (3) of the table. At input prices of $5.5 per acre and $5 per worker, we obtain Jones' cost of production shown in column (6). All other cost concepts (such as those shown in Table 22-3) can be calculated from the total cost data.

of production shown in column (6) of Table 22-4. As an example, consider the total cost of production for 3 tons of wheat. Using the given production function, Jones can produce this quantity with the 10 acres of land and 15 farmhands. The total cost of producing 3 tons of wheat is (10 acres × $5.5 per acre) + (15 workers × $5 per worker) = $130. Similar calculations will give all the other total cost figures in column (6) of Table 22-4.

Note that these total costs are identical to the ones shown in Tables 22-1 through 22-3, so that the other cost concepts shown in the tables (i.e., MC, FC, VC, AC, AFC, and AVC) are also applicable to the production-cost example of Farmer Jones.

Diminishing Returns and U-Shaped Cost Curves

Once the relationship between cost and production is understood, we can explain why the U-shaped cost curves so prevalent in economics are grounded in the law of diminishing returns.

Momentary, Short, Long Run The reasons for a U-shaped cost curve are best understood in terms of the time factor in production and cost. Economists recognize that planning and implementing decisions may take long periods of time. They therefore distinguish three different time periods in production and cost analysis. Recall our definitions of the momentary period, short run, and long run from Chapter 21 and apply those concepts to costs:

■ The momentary run is the period of time so short that no change in production can take place, so costs are fixed in this period.

■ The short run is the period of time in which variable inputs, such as materials and labor, can be adjusted, but which is of insufficient length for all inputs to be changed. In the short run, overhead factors such as plant and equipment cannot be fully modified or adjusted. Therefore, in the short run, labor and materials costs are variable costs, while capital costs are fixed.

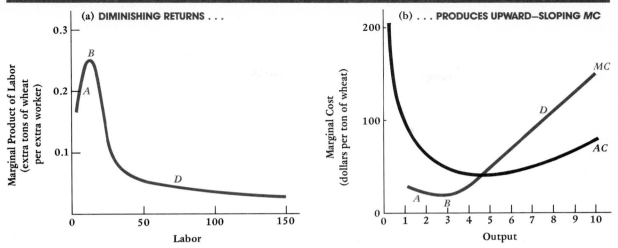

Figure 22-4   Diminishing returns and U-shaped cost curves

The U-shaped marginal cost curve in **(b)** arises from the shape of the marginal product curve in **(a)**. With fixed land and variable labor, the marginal product of labor in **(a)** first rises to the left of B, peaks at B, and then falls at D as diminishing returns set in.

The marginal product curve is reflected in the marginal cost schedule. In the region to the left of B in **(b)**—such as at point A—rising marginal product means that marginal cost is falling; at B, peak marginal product occurs at minimum marginal cost; in the region to the right of B, say at D, as marginal product of labor falls, the marginal cost of producing output increases.

Overall, increasing and then diminishing returns to variable factor produces a U-shaped marginal cost curve.

▪ In the long run, all inputs can be adjusted—including labor, materials, and capital; hence, in the long run, all costs are variable and none are fixed.[1]

Returning to our analysis of cost curves, suppose some factor such as capital is fixed in the short run under consideration. Further suppose that output varies when different amounts of the variable factor labor are hired. In a competitive labor market, where the firm can buy all the labor it wants at the going wage rate per unit of labor, the marginal cost of output would only rise because the extra output produced by each extra labor unit was going down. Put differently, if there is diminishing returns to the variable factor in the short run, then the short-run marginal cost will increase as the marginal product decreases. We can therefore see why diminishing returns would naturally lead to rising marginal costs after some point.

[1]For a more complete discussion of momentary, short, and long runs, see Chapter 21.

Figure 22-4, which contains exactly the same data as Table 22-4, illustrates the point. In that figure, point B in part *(a)* is the point where diminishing returns to the variable factor labor sets in. To the right of point B in *(a)*, diminishing returns means that the marginal product of labor is declining. Turning to part *(b)* of Figure 22-4, point B corresponds to the minimum marginal cost of output. For higher levels of output, as the marginal product in *(a)* declines, the marginal cost of output rises.

The data in Table 22-4, along with the left-hand part of the marginal cost curve in Figure 22-4(b), show that MC often declines at first. Why might this happen? Recall that the law of diminishing returns tends to hold as output increases with a fixed capital plant or capacity. However, at very low levels of inputs, there may be a strong tendency toward increasing marginal product of labor, owing to economies of large-scale production associated with indivisibility of manufacturing processes. You need a minimum of people to field a baseball team or to fly a large commercial aircraft. For the first few workers, therefore, we may have a period of increasing marginal product rather than decreasing marginal product. For that period, illustrated in Figure 22-4 at point A in both (a) and (b), marginal costs will be declining.[2]

We can summarize the relationship between the productivity laws and the cost curves as follows:

In the short run, when some factors like capital are fixed, variable factors tend to show an initial phase of increasing returns followed by diminishing returns. The corresponding cost curves show an initial phase of declining marginal costs followed by increasing MC after diminishing returns has set in.

THE LONG-RUN ENVELOPE CURVE[3]

We have seen how a firm's short-run cost curves tend to look U-shaped when a fixed factor such as capital or land limits the firm's production capacity. But what will happen when firms can replace their worn-out capital, adjust the size of their plants, or even move to new regions? What is the relation between the short-run cost curves and those holding for the long run?

Suppose that a petroleum refinery located on the Gulf Coast has a plant of so much capacity (perhaps 100,000 barrels per day of refining capacity). For this size plant, it has a short-run U-shaped AC curve (call it SAC in order to emphasize its short-run nature). If

the firm builds a larger refinery, its cost-minimizing output will be larger, so the new SAC curve must be drawn farther to the right. Now, suppose the firm is still in the planning stage, with no obligations, not having decided exactly what size plant to build. The firm's engineers can estimate different U-shaped SAC curves. For each design capacity, or planned output level, the firm would choose a different plant size and a different SAC curve.

Figure 22-5(a) shows how, in the long run, the firm would select an SAC' at the left if it needs but a low q. For intermediate q, it does better to plan to use SAC''. For still larger q, SAC''' leads to lowest costs. The heavy black curve of long-run average cost (LAC) is composed of the three lowest branches of the three SAC curves.

Figure 22-5(b) shows the same lower limit in the case where the firm has a choice of infinitely many smooth short-run AC curves. The long-run average cost (LAC) curve is the smooth lower boundary of the many SAC curves. It is called an "envelope curve" because it wraps around the outside of all the curves. The long-run LMC envelope curve provides the firm's long-run marginal cost curve and can be derived from the LAC. As with all AC and MC curves, the LMC goes through the minimum point of the LAC, and the LMC has a gentler slope than the short-run SMC at the minimum point.

This concludes our discussion of cost curves and their relationship to production. We turn now to further applications of cost concepts.

CHOICE OF INPUTS BY THE FIRM

Our major tasks are nearly completed. We now must apply our production and cost analysis to the firm's need to select the best combination of inputs. More precisely, this section completes the link between production and cost by using the marginal product concept to illustrate how firms select the least-cost combinations of inputs for a given set of input prices.

Marginal Products and the Least-Cost Rule

One of the most important questions that every firm must decide is how much of each input it should em-

[2]Later we shall examine the behavior of marginal cost in the long run. Suppose we consider so extended a period of time that *nothing* can be regarded as fixed. Old plants can wear out and be replaced. New plants can be designed and built. Old land obligations can expire. New land contracts can be made. And so forth. In the long run, as a small firm, we may be able to buy *all* the factors of production at unchanged input prices. Now what will happen to long-run costs, particularly long-run MC, if the firm has no fixed factors and can enjoy "constant returns to scale"? (This is defined as a state where there is no reason for diminishing returns to operate, since all factors grow in balance, and where all economies of large-scale production have already been realized.)

Answer: If long-run constant returns to scale holds, then doubling all inputs will exactly double their total dollar costs and will at the same time exactly double total output. Hence, there will be constant marginal cost, MC being horizontal rather than rising or falling. (In the next sections of this chapter we analyze the longest-run "planning" or envelope cost curves.)

[3]This section may be skipped in brief courses.

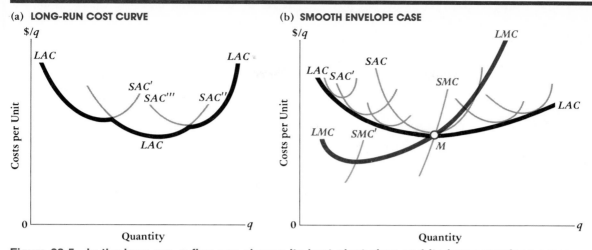

Figure 22-5 In the long run, a firm can choose its best plant sizes and its lower-envelope curve

(a) LAC is the black "envelope" or lower frontier of the three possible choices of plant. **(b)** There is now an infinite number of choices, and we get LAC as a smooth black envelope. In the usual way we derive from the black LAC curve its red marginal curve, LMC.

ploy: how much labor, capital, land, and materials. In making this decision, we start with a fundamental assumption, called the assumption of cost minimization: *Firms are assumed to choose their combination of inputs so as to minimize the total cost of production.*

This cost-minimization assumption actually makes good sense not only for perfectly competitive firms but for firms in imperfect competition and indeed for nonprofit entities like colleges or hospitals. It simply states that, whatever the level of output, the firm should strive to produce that output at the lowest possible cost and thereby have the maximum amount of revenue left over for profits or other objectives of the firm.

A simple example will show how a firm might decide between different input combinations. The firm's engineers have calculated that the desired output level of 9 units could be produced with two possible options. In both cases, fuel *(F)* costs $2 per unit while labor *(L)* costs $5 per hour. Under option 1, the input mix is $F = 10$ and $L = 2$. Option 2 has $F = 4$ and $L = 5$. Which is the preferred option? At the going input prices, total production costs for option 1 are ($2 × 10) + ($5 × 2) = $30, while total costs for

option 2 are ($2 × 4) + ($5 × 5) = $33. Therefore, option 1 would be the desired or least-cost combination of inputs.

Can we generalize to a case where there is a large number of possible input combinations? Is there a general rule for picking the least-cost combination? The general procedure is to begin by calculating the cost per unit of each input of labor, fuel, capital, and so forth. Then calculate the marginal product of each input. The cost-minimizing combination of inputs comes when the marginal product per dollar of input is equal for all inputs. That is to say, the marginal contribution to output of each dollar's worth of labor, of land, of oil, and so forth must be just the same.

What is the rationale for this rule? Let's say that land costs $800 an acre and labor costs $8 per hour. No one of sound mind would expect to achieve least cost if land and labor were chosen so that their marginal *physical* products were equal. Since land costs 100 times as much as labor, the least-cost combination arises when land's *MP* is 100 times labor's *MP*.

Following this reasoning, a firm will minimize its total cost of production when the marginal product per dollar of input is equalized for each factor of production. This is the least-cost rule.

Least-cost rule: To produce a given level of output at least cost, a firm will hire factors until it has equalized the marginal product per dollar spent on each factor of production. This implies that

$$\frac{\text{Marginal product of } L}{\text{Price of } L} = \frac{\text{marginal product of } A}{\text{price of } A} = \cdots$$

This rule for firms is exactly analogous to what consumers do when they maximize utilities, as shown in Chapter 19. In that chapter we saw that maximizing utility comes when the marginal utility per dollar spent on consumer goods is equalized for all commodities.

One way of understanding the least-cost rule is the following: Break each factor into units worth $1 each (in our earlier fuel-labor example, $1 of labor would be one-fifth of an hour, while $1 of fuel would be one-half unit). Then the least-cost rule states that the marginal product of each dollar-unit of input must be equalized.

To understand the least-cost rule, we can use a common method of analysis by supposing that it is not true and showing a contradiction. Assume, for example, that a dollar-unit of labor had a marginal product of 1 bushel of wheat, and a dollar-unit of fuel had a marginal product of 3 bushels of wheat. Since dollar-units of fuel have higher marginal products than those of labor, reorganize production by expanding the employment of fuel by 1 dollar-unit and contracting that of labor by 3 dollar-units. By assumption, total production would remain unchanged, but the cost of production would go down by $2. Therefore the original state, in which marginal products per dollar-unit of input were not equal, was not a least-cost situation.

Substitution Rule A corollary of the least-cost rule is the substitution rule. If the price of one factor, say labor, falls while all other factor prices remain the same, firms will benefit by substituting the now-cheaper factor for all the other factors. Why will this happen? It occurs because a fall in the price of labor will raise the ratio MP_L/P_L above the MP/P ratio for other inputs. By raising the employment of L, which by the law of diminishing returns lowers MP_L and therefore lowers MP_L/P_L, we bring the marginal prod-

uct per dollar for labor back into equality with that ratio for other factors.

OPPORTUNITY COST

This chapter has concentrated on the treatment of many kinds of business costs. But what kinds of costs are included in these calculations? Monetary costs only? Or do they include costs, like pollution damage, that are social costs but do not enter into a firm's accounts?

Chapter 2 introduced the notion of opportunity cost. Here we will consolidate our earlier understanding by relating opportunity costs to the dollar costs measured by firms and analyzed in this chapter. We have observed on numerous occasions (such as in our treatment of accounting in the appendix to Chapter 20) that the world of the businessperson or the accountant often differs from that of the economist. And right here—with the concept of cost—is where a major distinction arises.

Where does the difference lie? In essence, the economist generally includes more items in cost than do accountants or businesspeople. Economists include all costs—whether they reflect monetary transactions or not; business accountants generally exclude nonmonetary transactions.

We have already encountered in Chapter 20 examples of true economic costs that do not show up in business accounts. The return to an owner's effort, the normal return on contributed capital to a firm, the risk premium on highly leveraged owner's equity—these are all elements that should figure into a broadly conceived set of economic costs but do not enter business accounts. An economist would insist that the wages of management or the return on contributed capital are real economic costs: they use real, live managers and tangible capital.

The concept that can help us understand this distinction between money costs and true economic costs is **opportunity cost.** The opportunity cost of a decision consists of the things that are given up by making that particular decision rather than the best alternative decision.

Let's illustrate the concept of opportunity cost by considering the owner of a small business, such as the computer-firm proprietor in Chapter 20. The owner puts in 60 hours a week but earns no "wages." At the end of the year, the firm earns a profit of $20,000—pretty good for a neophyte firm.

Or is it? The economist would disagree, saying that the return to a factor of production is economically important regardless of how the factor happens to be owned. We should count the owner's own labor as a cost even though the owner does not get paid directly but instead receives compensation in the form of profits.[4] We should take into account that the owner has alternative opportunities for work and reckon that lost opportunity as a cost.

Thus, by looking around the town, we see that the firm's owner could find a similar and equally interesting job working for someone else and earning $45,000. This represents, then, the opportunity cost or earnings forgone because the owner decided to become the unpaid owner of a small business rather than the paid employee of another firm.

Therefore, the economist continues, let's calculate the true profits of the computer firm. If you take the measured profits of $20,000 and subtract the $45,000 opportunity cost of the owner's labor, you find a net *loss* of $25,000. Thus while the accountant might conclude that such a typical small business was an economically viable enterprise, the economist would pronounce the firm an unprofitable loser.

Another example of an opportunity cost not included in the firm's accounts is the return on the capital contributed by the owners. Suppose that the firm's owners put $30,000 of equity capital into the firm—perhaps in the form of computer equipment. The standard financial accounts do not deduct an opportunity cost for these funds. If investments of similar risk normally earn 14 percent, then another $4200 (= 0.14 × $30,000) should be deducted from earnings to account for the opportunity costs of these funds.

Or if you own some special factors of production—like rich ore land, exceptional know-how, or fertile soil—your accounts may show a high profit. But we should recognize the opportunity costs of these factors and realize that this high return is in fact not a genuine profit but rather a rent return to that special factor of production you are lucky enough to own.[5]

Opportunity Cost and Decisions

The concept of opportunity cost is actually even broader and more useful than the examples of unpaid factors used by a firm. It can be applied in economics to the real economic cost or consequence of making decisions in a world where goods are scarce.

Life is full of choices. In choosing one thing we must give up something else. When we go to a movie, we cannot read a book. When we go to college, we forgo for a time the opportunity of getting a full-time job. When a nation drafts people into the army, it loses the time they might otherwise spend reading poetry or writing computer programs. Every time a firm or a nation makes a decision, it incurs costs by discarding alternative courses of action.

When we are forced to choose between scarce goods, we incur opportunity costs. The opportunity cost of a decision is the value of the best available alternative.

One of the best ways of seeing the concept of opportunity cost is to return to the production-possibility frontier of Chapter 2. Let's say the nation wants to gird up its loins and increase the size of the army. It proposes to draft 1 million young men, increasing the army's size from 2 million to 3 million. Critics fume, claiming that the economic vitality of the nation will be sapped. The Pentagon rebuts by pointing to the small budgetary cost of the larger army. Who is right?

From an economic vantage point, the best way to answer this question is to examine the opportunity cost of the action. Figure 22-6 provides an illustrative production-possibility frontier between the size of the army and the production of civilian goods and services. In an efficiently organized society, the military expansion would be represented by a movement from point A to point B in the figure. As the boot camps fill

---

[4]Economists call these unpaid factors of production *implicit costs,* which is a somewhat narrower concept than opportunity cost.

[5]If you happen to own very fertile land and persist in cultivating it by uneconomical methods, you will be paying for your folly or stubbornness by forgoing the high return such land is capable of yielding. In dollars, the land is worth more to others than to you, and if you refuse to rent or sell, you are as surely spending your sustenance to please your own tastes as you would be doing if you sold the land and spent the proceeds on wine, skiing, or song.

OPPORTUNITY COST

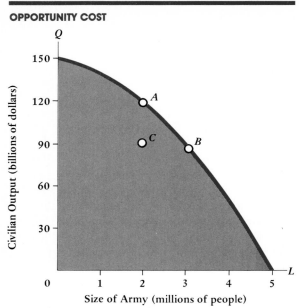

Figure 22-6   In a world of scarcity, a larger army requires giving up food, clothing, or other civilian goods

The nation starts at *A* with a peacetime army of 2 million men. It decides to draft 1 million more people and moves to point *B*. What is the true economic or opportunity cost? Not the few extra dollars in the defense budget. Rather, the opportunity cost is the amount of civilian output forgone, shown here as $30 billion.

up, fewer resources are available for civilian production, and, in this example, adding 1 million men to the army would reduce civilian production by $30 billion. In other words, whatever the *budget* cost might be, the *opportunity* cost of the army expansion is $30 billion.

This example presumes that the economy is operating efficiently. The military expansion is compared with the best or most efficient alternative use of the resources. It is not appropriate for the Pentagon to say "Well, the cost is not really $30 billion, because we start with a lot of unemployment and therefore move from a point of unemployed resources (such as point *C* in Figure 22-6) to an efficient use of resources (such as point *B*). So in fact there are no real costs of a larger army."

This reasoning, which is extremely common in such debates about federal spending, is not correct economic analysis. If in fact there is unemployment, then this can be corrected without necessarily increasing the size of the army. In using the concept of opportunity cost, we should make comparisons of points on the *PPF*, or with constant levels of unemployment, so as to calculate the economic effects of the decision relative to the best or most efficient alternative.

Opportunity Costs in Markets You might naturally say, "Well, now I'm totally confused. First I learn that the market price is the measure of the social value of a good. Now I read that opportunity cost is the right concept. There seems to be an inconsistency here."

Actually not, for when we examine a competitive market, it is easily seen that the price equals opportunity cost. Assume that a commodity like coal is bought and sold on a competitive market. If I bring my ton of coal to market, I will receive a number of bids from prospective buyers: $25.02, $24.98, $25.01. These represent the values of my coal to, say, three utilities. I pick the highest—$25.02. The opportunity cost of this sale is the value of the best available alternative—that is, the second-highest bid at $25.01—which is almost identical to the price that is accepted. As the market approaches absolutely perfect competition, the bids get closer and closer until in the limit the second-highest bid (which is our definition of opportunity cost) exactly equals the highest bid (which is the price). This example shows that in competitive markets, the price that will be generated equals the best available alternative and is therefore equal to the opportunity cost.

Opportunity Costs outside Markets The concept of opportunity cost is particularly crucial when analyzing transactions that take place outside markets. How do you measure the cost of a college education? The value of a dam or a park? Of a draft army? Of a health or safety regulation? For these we need to turn to opportunity cost for sound economic analysis.

▪ What is the opportunity cost of going to college? For a public university, tuition, room, board, books, and expenses in 1988 were around $5000. So the opportunity cost is $5000, right? No. You must include as well the opportunity cost of the *time* spent studying and going to classes. A 20-year-old high school graduate holding a full-time job would on an average earn about $14,000 in 1988. Thus the opportunity cost of college is $19,000 per year rather than $5000 per year.

■ The notion of opportunity cost might explain why students watch more TV the week after exams than the week before exams. Watching TV right before an exam has a high opportunity cost, for the alternative use of time (studying) would have high value in improving grade performance. After exams, time has a lower opportunity cost.

■ Say the federal government is thinking of drilling for oil at Yosemite National Park. A storm of complaints is heard. The secretary of energy says, ''What's all the ruckus about? There's valuable oil under there, and the land's not worth two bits an acre.''

In fact, the opportunity cost might be very high. If oil drilling brought lots of noise and new roads, it might spoil the park for hikers and bear watchers. The opportunity cost might not be easily measured, but the recreational value of the land is as real as is the energy value of the barrels of oil under the soil.

The Road Not Traveled Opportunity cost, then, is a measure of what has been given up when we make a decision. Consider what Robert Frost had in mind when he wrote

> Two roads diverged in a wood, and I—
> I took the one less traveled by,
> And that has made all the difference.

What other road did Frost have in mind? An urban life? An avocation where he would not be able to write of roads and walls and birches? Imagine the immeasurable opportunity cost to all of us if Robert Frost had taken the road more traveled by.

But let us return from the poetic to the practical concepts of cost. The crucial point to grasp is this:

Cost includes, in addition to explicit money outlays, those opportunity costs that arise because factors might be used in alternative ways. If my labor or capital in computer programs could have been used in coal or wheat, or even in some other person's computer firm, then my true costs must include the best alternative opportunity costs.

Preview

We have now completed a discussion of the economic meaning of production and cost, along with the important total, average, and marginal cost concepts. The appendix pursues those issues in greater depth. In the next chapter, we show how a firm's and an industry's supply decisions are directly derived from their marginal cost curves.

SUMMARY

1. Total cost *(TC)* can be broken down into fixed cost *(FC)* and variable cost *(VC)*. Fixed costs are unaffected by any production decisions, while variable costs are incurred on items like production labor or materials which increase as production levels rise.

2. Marginal cost *(MC)* is the extra total cost resulting from 1 extra unit of output. Average total cost *(AC)* is the sum of ever-declining average fixed cost *(AFC)* and average variable cost *(AVC)*. Short-run average cost is generally represented by a U-shaped curve that is always intersected at its minimum point by the rising *MC* curve.

3. Useful rules to remember are

$$TC = FC + VC \qquad AC = \frac{TC}{q} \qquad AC = AFC + AVC$$

At the bottom of U-shaped *AC*, *MC* = *AC* = minimum *AC*.

4. Trends of costs and of productivity returns are like mirror images. When the law of diminishing returns ultimately holds, the marginal product falls and the *MC* curve rises. When there is an initial stage of increasing returns, *MC* initially falls. If all factors of production could be bought at unchanged prices and output were to show constant returns to scale, long-run marginal costs would be horizontal forever.

5. In the long run, when all fixed commitments expire and a firm is free to plan to operate any number of plants, the long-run cost curve *LAC* (and *LTC*) must be the lower-envelope frontier of best choice of plant for each level of output. If potential plant sizes are smoothly continuous, this frontier will be a smooth envelope, containing at any point a tangential short-run cost curve.

6. We can apply cost and production concepts to understand a firm's choice of the best combination of factors of production. Firms that desire to maximize profits will want to minimize the cost of producing a given level of output. In this case, the firm will follow the least-cost rule: different factors will be chosen so that the marginal product per dollar of input is equalized for all inputs. This implies that $MP_L/P_L = MP_A/P_A = \cdots$. This rule has the important corollary that when the price of an input falls (or rises) relative to other inputs, the employment of that factor will rise (or fall) relative to other factors of production.

7. The economic definition of costs is broader than the accountant's. Economic cost includes not only the obvious out-of-pocket purchase of fuel and labor. It also includes the more subtle implicit or opportunity costs, such as the implicit return to labor supplied by the owner of a firm. These opportunity costs are tightly constrained by the bids and offers on competitive markets, so that price is usually close to opportunity cost for marketed goods and services. The most important application of opportunity cost arises for non-market goods—those like clean air or health or recreation—where the services may be highly valuable even though they are not bought and sold in markets.

CONCEPTS FOR REVIEW

total costs: fixed and variable
$TC = FC + VC$
$AC = TC/q = AFC + AVC$
marginal cost (incremental and
  smoothed)
least-cost rule:

$$\frac{MP_L}{P_L} = \frac{MP_A}{P_A} = \frac{MP_{\text{any factor}}}{P_{\text{any factor}}} = \cdots$$

economists' and accountants' cost
  concepts
opportunity costs
diminishing returns, rising *MC*
long-run envelope curve

QUESTIONS FOR DISCUSSION

1. Make a list of cost elements: wages, salaries, fuel, rentals, etc. Divide them into fixed and variable categories.

2. Explain the difference between marginal cost and average cost. Why should AVC always look much like MC? Why is MC the same when computed from VC as from TC?

3. To the $55 of fixed cost of Table 22-3, add $90 of additional FC. Now calculate a whole new table, with the same VC as before but new $FC = \$145$. What happens to MC, AVC? To TC, AC, AFC? Can you verify that minimum AC is now at $q^* = 5$ with $AC = \$60 = MC$?

4. Explain why MC cuts AC and AVC at the bottom of their U's.

5. Explain how the long-run envelope cost curve is defined as the lower frontier of all short-run curves. Illustrate with *(a)* the case of a few plant sizes, and *(b)* the case of many and continuously varied plant sizes.

6. Relate the rising MC curve to the law of diminishing returns. Contrast the falling part of the curve with that law.

7. Consider the data in the following table, which contains a situation similar to that in Table 22-4.

   (a) Calculate the TC, VC, FC, AC, AVC, and MC. On a piece of graph paper, plot the AC and MC curves.

   (b) Assume that the price of labor doubles. Calculate a new AC and MC. Plot the new curves and compare them with those in (a).

   (c) Now assume that productivity doubles (i.e., that the level of output doubles for each input combination). Repeat the exercise in (b). Can you see two major factors that tend to affect a firm's cost curves?

(1)	(2)	(3)	(4)	(5)
			LAND	LABOR
OUTPUT	LAND	LABOR	RENT	WAGE
(tons	INPUTS	INPUTS	(dollars	(dollars
of wheat)	(acres)	(workers)	per acre)	per worker)
0	15	0	12	5
1	15	6	12	5
2	15	11	12	5
3	15	15	12	5
4	15	21	12	5
5	15	31	12	5
6	15	45	12	5
7	15	63	12	5

8. Explain the fallacies in each of the following:

   (a) Average costs are minimized when marginal costs are at their lowest point.

(b) Because fixed costs never change, average fixed cost is a constant for each level of output.

(c) Average cost is rising whenever marginal cost is rising.

(d) The opportunity cost of spilling oil in the Atlantic Ocean is zero because no one pays to sail or swim there.

(e) A firm minimizes costs when it spends the same amount on each input.

9. Say you are considering whether to fly or take the bus from Atlanta to New Orleans. The airfare is $100, and the flight takes 1 hour. Bus fare is $50 and takes 6 hours. Which is the most economical way to travel for: *(a)* a businessperson whose time costs $40 per hour, *(b)* a student whose time is worth $4 per hour, *(c)* you? Show how the concept of opportunity cost is crucial here.

10. Advanced problem: With the help of the adjoining graphs, explain the meaning of the following rules. *First rule:* If a marginal cost curve is below its associated average cost curve, it is pulling the *AC* curve down; if *MC* is above *AC*, it is pulling *AC* up; if *MC* = *AC*, *AC* must be horizontal. *Second rule:* If *AC* is a straight line, as in (a), (b), or (c), *MC* will be a straight line starting from the same vertical intercept point but with twice the slope of *AC*. [NOTE: This tells us how to find the *MC* point above or below the *AC* point on any nonstraight-line *AC* curve. At a chosen *q* in (d), merely draw the straight line tangent to *AC*; from the vertical intercept of that line, draw an *MC* line with twice the slope; read off from the last line the *MC* value at your chosen *q* level. Of course, you must draw two new straight lines for every different *q* level.]

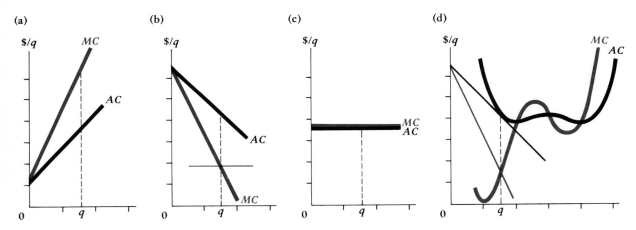

(a)   (b)   (c)   (d)

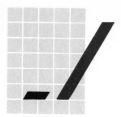

APPENDIX: 22

Production, Cost Theory, and Decisions of the Firm

The production theory described in Chapter 21 and the cost analysis of this chapter are among the fundamental building blocks of microeconomics. A thorough understanding of production and cost is necessary for an appreciation of how economic scarcity gets translated into prices in the marketplace. In this appendix, therefore, we develop these concepts further and introduce the concept of a production-indifference curve, or isoquant.

A Numerical Production Function

Production and cost analysis have their roots in the concept of a production function. Recall that a production function is the relation showing the maximum amount of output that can be produced with various combinations of inputs. Table 22A-1 starts with a numerical example of a hypothetical, constant-returns-to-scale production function, showing the amount of inputs along the axes and the amount of output at the grid points of the table.

Along the left-hand side are listed the varying amounts of land, going from 1 unit to

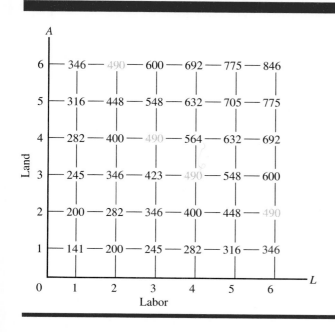

Table 22A-1 A tabular picture of a production function relating amount of output to varying combinations of labor and land inputs

When you have 3 land units and 2 labor units available, the engineer tells you your maximum obtainable output is 346 units. Note the different ways to produce 346. Do the same for 490. (The production function shown in the table is a special case of the "Cobb-Douglas production function," one given by the formula $Q = 100\sqrt{2LA}$.)

531

6 units. Along the bottom are listed amounts of labor, which also go from 1 to 6. Output corresponding to each land row and labor column is listed inside the table.

If we are interested in knowing exactly what output there will be when 3 units of land and 2 units of labor are available, we count up 3 units of land and then go over 2 units of labor. The answer is seen to be 346 units of product. (Can you identify some other input combinations to produce $q = 346$?) Similarly, we find that 3 units of land and 6 of labor produce 600 units of q.

Thus, for any combination of labor and land, the production function shown in Table 22A-1 tells us exactly how much output we can produce. Remember, also, that this is the *maximum* output given engineering skills and technical knowledge available at a given point in time. Also, note that the example given in Table 22A-1 displays *constant returns to scale:* a proportional increase in both factors of production (increasing them both by a factor of 2 or $\frac{1}{2}$ or 1.5) will increase output by exactly the same factor (2 or $\frac{1}{2}$ or 1.5).

THE LAW OF DIMINISHING MARGINAL PRODUCT

Table 22A-1 can nicely illustrate the law of diminishing returns.

First recall that we have given the name "marginal product of labor" to the extra production resulting from 1 additional unit of labor, land being held constant. At any point in Table 22A-1, the marginal product of labor can be derived by subtracting the given number (representing product at that point) from the number on its right lying in the same row. Thus, when there are 2 units of land and 4 units of labor, the marginal product of an additional laborer would be 48, or 448 minus 400 in the second row.

By the "marginal product of land" we mean, of course, the extra product resulting from 1 additional unit of land, labor being held constant. It is calculated by comparing adjacent items in a given column. Thus, when there are 2 units of land and 4 units of labor, the marginal product of land is shown in the fourth column as $490 - 400$, or 90.

We can easily find the marginal product of each of our two factors by comparing adjacent entries in vertical columns or horizontal rows of Table 22A-1.

Having defined the concept of marginal product of an input, we now can easily define the law of diminishing returns: The law of diminishing returns states that as we increase one input and hold other inputs constant, the marginal product of the varying input will, at least after some point, decline.

To illustrate this, hold land constant in Table 22A-1 by sticking to a given row—say, that corresponding to land equal to 2 units. Now let labor increase from 1 to 2 units, from 2 to 3 units, and so forth. What happens to q at each step?

As labor goes from 1 to 2 units, the level of output increases from 200 to 282 units, or by 82 units. But the next dose of labor adds only 64 units, or $346 - 282$. Diminishing returns has set in. Still further additions of a single unit of labor give us, respectively, only 54 extra units of output, 48 units, and finally 42 units. You can easily verify that the law holds for other rows, and that the law holds when land is varied and labor held constant.

We can use this example to verify our intuitive justification of the law of diminishing returns—the assertion that the law holds because the fixed factor decreases relative to the variable factor. According to this explanation, each unit of the variable factor has less and less of the fixed factor to work with. So it is natural that extra product should drop off.

If this explanation is to hold water, there should be no diminishing returns when both factors are increased in proportion. When labor increases from 1 to 2 and land *simultaneously* increases from 1 to 2, we should get the same increase in product as when both increase simultaneously from 2 to 3. This can be verified in Table 22A-1. In the first move we go from 141 to 282, and in the second move the product increases from 282 to 423, an equal jump of 141 units.

LEAST-COST FACTOR COMBINATION FOR A GIVEN OUTPUT

The numerical production function shows us the different ways to produce a given level of output. But which of the many possibilities should the firm use? Which way should goods be shipped or houses be built or electricity be generated? If the desired level of output is $q = 346$, there are no less than four different combinations of land and labor shown as A, B, C, and D in Table 22A-2.

As far as the engineer is concerned, each of these combinations is equally good at producing an output of 346 units. But the accountant, interested in keeping profits of the firm at a maximum and costs at a minimum, knows that only one of these four combinations will give least cost. Just which one will depend, of course, on the respective factor prices.

Let us suppose that the price of labor is $3 and the price of land $2. The total costs when input prices are at this level are shown in the third column of the red row of numbers in Table 22A-2. For combination A, the total labor and land cost will be $20, equal to $(1 \times \$2) + (6 \times \$3)$. And costs at B, C, and D will be, respectively, $13, $12, $15. At these stated input prices, there is no doubt that C is the least costly way to produce the given output.

If either of the input prices changes, the equilibrium proportion of the inputs will also change so as to use less of the input that has gone up most in price. This is just like the substitution effect of Chapter 19's discussion of consumer demand.

Thus, if labor stays at $2 per unit but land falls to $1 per unit, the new optimal

	(1)	(2)	(3)	(4)
	INPUT COMBINATIONS		TOTAL COST WHEN $P_L = \$2$ $P_A = \$3$	TOTAL COST WHEN $P_L = \$2$ $P_A = \$1$
	LABOR L	LAND A		
A	1	6	$20	—
B	2	3	13	$7
C	3	2	12	—
D	6	1	15	—

Table 22A-2   Inputs and costs of producing a given level of output

Assume that the firm has chosen 346 units of output. Then it can use any of the four choices of input combinations shown as A, B, C, and D. As the firm moves down the list, production becomes more labor-intensive and less land-intensive.

The firm's choice among the different techniques will depend on input prices. When $P_L = \$2$ and $P_A = \$3$, verify that the cost-minimizing combination is C. Show that lowering the price of land from $3 to $1 leads the firm to a more land-intensive combination at B.

combination will be B, where more land is substituted for reduced labor and where total cost is only $7. Verify this by computing the new total expense of all other combinations and seeing that they are higher. (Pencil in missing costs in Table 22A-2.)

Exactly the same exercise can be performed for every level of output. As soon as input prices are known, the least-cost method of production can be found by calculating the costs of different input combinations and choosing the one that costs the least.

Equal-Product Curves

The common-sense numerical analysis of the way in which a firm will combine inputs to minimize costs can be made more vivid by the use of diagrams. We will take the diagrammatic approach by putting together two new curves, the equal-product curve and the equal-cost line.

Looking back at Table 22A-1, imagine how that could be turned into a smooth curve. More precisely, let us draw a smooth curve through all the points that yield $q = 346$. This smooth curve, shown in Figure 22A-1, indicates all the different combinations of labor and land that yield an output of 346 units. It could be called a "production-indifference curve" by analogy with the consumer's indifference curve of the appendix to Chapter 19. But a more expressive name would be an *equal-product curve*. (You should be able to draw on Figure 22A-1, as a light red curve, the corresponding equal-product curve for output equal to 490 by getting the data from Table 22A-1. Indeed, an infinite number of such equal-product contour lines could be drawn in, just as a topographical or weather map could be covered with an indefinitely large number of equal-altitude or equal-pressure contour lines.)

Equal-Cost Lines

Given the price of labor and land, the firm can evaluate the total cost for points A, B, C, and D or for any other point on the equal-product curve. The firm will minimize its

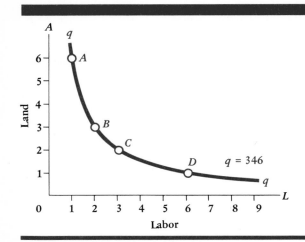

Figure 22A-1 Equal-product curve

All the points on the equal-product curve represent the different combinations of land and labor that can be used to produce the same 346 units of output.

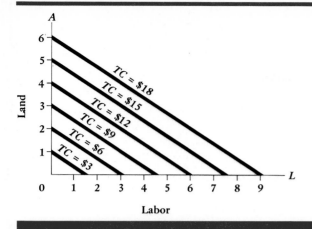

Figure 22A-2   Equal-cost lines

Every point on a given equal-cost line represents the same total cost. The lines are straight because factor prices are constant, and they all have a negative slope equal to the ratio of labor price to land price, $2/$3, and hence are parallel.

costs and maximize its profits when it selects that point on its equal-product curve that has the lowest total cost.

An easy visual device for finding the least-cost method of production is to construct *equal-cost lines*. This is done in Figure 22A-2, where the family of parallel straight lines represents a number of equal-cost curves when the price of labor is $2 and the price of land $3.

To find the total cost for any point, we simply have to read off the number appended to the equal-cost line going through that point. The lines are all straight and parallel because the firm is assumed to be able to buy all it wishes of either input at constant prices. The lines are somewhat flatter than 45° because the price of labor P_L is somewhat less than the price of land P_A. More precisely, we can always say that the arithmetic value of the slope of each equal-cost line must equal the ratio of the price of labor to that of land—in this case $P_L/P_A = \frac{2}{3}$.

Equal-Product and Equal-Cost Contours: Least-Cost Tangency

Combining the equal-product and equal-cost lines, we can easily determine the optimal, or cost-minimizing, position of the firm. Recall that the optimal input combination comes at that point where the given output of $q = 346$ can be produced at least cost. To find such a point, simply superimpose the single red equal-product curve upon the family of black equal-cost lines, as is shown in Figure 22A-3. The firm will always keep moving along the red convex curve of Figure 22A-3 as long as it is able to cross over to lower cost lines. Its equilibrium will therefore not be at A, B, or D. It will be at C, where the equal-product curve touches (but does not cross) the lowest equal-cost line. This is, of course, a point of tangency, where the slope of the equal-product curve just matches the slope of an equal-cost line and the curves are just kissing.

We already know that the slope of the equal-cost curves is P_L/P_A. But what is the slope of the equal-product curve? Recall from Chapter 1's appendix that the slope at a point of a curved line is the slope of the straight line tangent to the curve at the point in

**SUBSTITUTING INPUTS TO
MINIMIZE COST OF PRODUCTION**

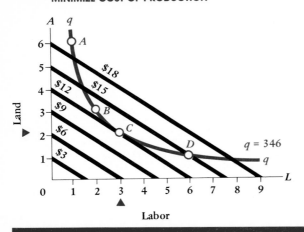

**Figure 22A-3   Least-cost input combination
comes at C**

The firm desires to minimize its costs of producing a given output of 346. It thus seeks out the least expensive input combination along its red equal-product curve. It looks for the input combination that is on the lowest of the equal-cost lines. Where the equal-product curve touches (but does not cross) the lowest equal-cost curve is the least-cost position. This tangency means that factor prices and marginal products are proportional, with equalized marginal products per dollar.

question. For the equal-product curve, this slope is a kind of "substitution ratio" between the two factors, and it depends upon the relative marginal products of the two factors of production, namely, MP_L/MP_A—just as the rate of substitution between two goods along a consumer's indifference curve was earlier shown to equal the ratio of the marginal, or extra, utilities of the two goods (see the appendix to Chapter 19).[1]

Least-Cost Conditions

Using our graphical apparatus, we have therefore derived the conditions under which a firm will minimize its costs of production:

1. The ratio of marginal products of any two inputs must equal the ratio of their factor prices.

$$\text{Substitution ratio} = \frac{\text{marginal product of labor}}{\text{marginal product of land}} = \begin{array}{c} \text{slope of} \\ \text{equal-product} \\ \text{curve} \end{array} = \frac{\text{price of labor}}{\text{price of land}}$$

[1]The careful reader will notice the parallel between the geometry of this section and that of the analysis of consumer equilibrium in the appendix to Chapter 19. Each equal-cost line indicates all the possible different quantities of labor and of land that the firm might buy for any given cost outlay. Each line is straight since its equation is $TC = \$2L + \$3A$. In the appendix to Chapter 19, the consumer is buying goods, not factor services; otherwise the "budget line" exactly parallels the equal-cost lines we are now discussing. We can explain, similarly, why the slope of an equal-cost line equals the ratio of the two prices involved.

But note this difference: the consumer was assumed to have a fixed budget, and had but one budget line. The firm is not limited to any particular level of costs, so it must consider many equal-cost lines before discovering its least-cost equilibrium.

2. The marginal product per dollar received from the (last) dollar of expenditure must be the same for every productive factor.

$$\frac{\text{Marginal product of } L}{\text{Price of } L} = \frac{\text{marginal product of } A}{\text{price of } A} = \cdots$$

Relation 2 is discussed in detail in the main body of this chapter. (It could also be derived from relation 1 by transposing terms from one numerator to the other denominator, i.e., by going from $a/b = c/d$ to $a/c = b/d$.)

But you should not be satisfied with abstract explanations. Always remember the common-sense economic explanation which shows how a firm will redistribute its expenditure among inputs if any one factor offers a greater return for each last dollar spent on it.

SUMMARY TO APPENDIX

1. A production-function table lists, for each labor column and each land row, the output that is producible. Diminishing returns to one variable factor applied to a fixed factor can be shown by calculating the decline of marginal products in any row or column.

2. An equal-product curve depicts the alternative input combinations that produce the same level of output. The slope, or substitution ratio, along such an equal-product curve equals relative marginal products (e.g., MP_L/MP_A). Curves of equal total cost are parallel lines with slopes equal to factor-price ratios (P_L/P_A). Least-cost equilibrium comes at tangency point, where an equal-product curve touches but does not cross the lowest TC curve. There, marginal products are proportional to factor prices, with equalized marginal product per dollar spent on all factors (i.e., equalized MP_i/P_i).

CONCEPTS FOR REVIEW

equal-product curves
parallel lines of equal TC
substitution ratio = MP_L/MP_A
P_L/P_A as the slope of parallel
  equal-TC lines

least-cost tangency:
  $MP_L/MP_A = P_L/P_A$ or
  $MP_L/P_L = MP_A/P_A$

QUESTIONS FOR DISCUSSION

1. Show that raising labor's wage while holding land's rent constant will steepen the black equal-cost lines and move tangency point C in Figure 22A-3 northwest toward B with the now-cheaper input substituted for the input which is now more expensive. Should union leaders recognize this relationship?

2. What is the least-cost combination of inputs if the production function is given by Table 22A-1 and input prices are as shown in Figure 22A-3, where $q = 346$? What would be the least-cost ratio for the same input prices if output doubled to $q = 692$? What has happened to the "factor intensity," or land/labor ratio? Can you see why this result would hold for any output change under constant returns to scale?

3. Advanced problem for those trained in geometry and elementary calculus: The famous statistical equation of Senator Douglas related Q output to L labor and K capital by the Cobb-Douglas production function $Q = 1.01\ L^{.75}K^{.25}$. Ignoring the 1.01 scale factor and identifying marginal products with partial derivatives, show that labor's relative share is necessarily given by $WL/PQ = L(W/P)/Q = L(\partial Q/\partial L)/Q = L(0.75L^{.75-1}K^{.25})/L^{.75}K^{.25} = 0.75$. Show also that capital's share is $K(\partial Q/\partial K)/Q = 0.25$. Instead suppose $Q = [(3L)^{-1} + K^{-1}]^{-1}$, a weighted harmonic mean. Verify that $MP_K = \partial Q/\partial K = [\frac{1}{3}(K/L) + 1]^{-2}$, and hence capital's share, $K(\partial Q/\partial K)/Q$, declines as K increases relative to L, as a calculation shows.

4. Advanced problem: Using the same Cobb-Douglas production function as in problem 3 show that, if both K and L are paid their marginal products, the sum of wages and payments to capital exactly equals output. This proves the "exhaustion of product" theorem of the neoclassical economists for the Cobb-Douglas production function.

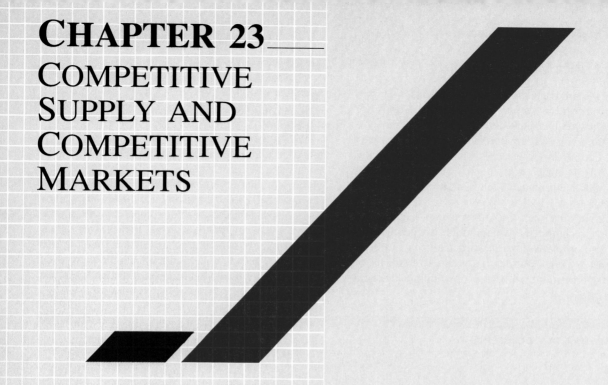

CHAPTER 23

COMPETITIVE SUPPLY AND COMPETITIVE MARKETS

Cost of production would have no effect on competitive price if it could have none on supply.

John Stuart Mill

THE LAST TWO CHAPTERS analyzed the pivotal concepts of production and cost. We are now prepared to see how the cost of production determines the supply behavior of competitive firms and industries.

In the first part of this chapter, we show how the desired production level of profit-maximizing firms depends upon the cost of production. We will then see that the competitive firm's supply curve corresponds to its marginal cost curve.

After we have explored the individual firm's supply behavior, the second half of the chapter analyzes the behavior of a competitive industry and shows that the marginal cost of production plays a central role for the industry as well as for the firm. We also study how a competitive industry behaves in an efficient fashion, allocating resources so that there is no reorganization of production that can make everyone better off.

Throughout this chapter, we will see that marginal cost is not an arid piece of economic terminology. Rather, it is a central economic concept with a crucially important role to play in any society or organization trying to allocate its resources in the most efficient manner.

539

A. SUPPLY BEHAVIOR OF THE COMPETITIVE FIRM

This first part concentrates on the behavior of perfectly competitive firms. The central questions we address are, How much output should the firm produce given market conditions? How much wheat should Farmer Jones produce if wheat sells at $3 per bushel? How many tons of coal should Pittsburgh Coal and Coke produce if the market price of coal is $25 per ton?

In answering such questions about supply, we begin by recalling the assumptions we are making about firm behavior. First, we are analyzing perfectly competitive firms. While the essential elements of perfect competition will be described in greater detail

in the next section, recall for now that a perfectly competitive firm is one that is so small relative to the market that it cannot affect the market price.

The other major assumption we will maintain is that our competitive firm maximizes profits. This means that the firm will buy inputs, select production processes, manage its operations, choose goods to produce, set its output level, and make all business decisions so that profits (the arithmetic difference between revenues and costs) are at their highest attainable level. Put differently, a profit-maximizing firm must both manage its internal operations (prevent waste, encourage worker morale, and choose efficient

REVIEW OF COST CONCEPTS

(1) QUANTITY q	(2) FIXED COST FC	(3) VARIABLE COST VC	(4) TOTAL COST $TC = FC + VC$	(5) MARGINAL COST PER UNIT MC	(6) AVERAGE COST PER UNIT $AC = \dfrac{TC}{q}$	(7) AVERAGE FIXED COST PER UNIT $AFC = \dfrac{FC}{q}$	(8) AVERAGE VARIABLE COST PER UNIT $AVC = \dfrac{VC}{q}$
0	55,000						
1,000	55,000	30,000	85,000	27	85	55	30
2,000	55,000	55,000	110,000	22	55	27.5	27.5
3,000	55,000	75,000	130,000	21	43.33	18.33	25
3,999	55,000	104,960.01	159,960.01	39.98 ⟍ 39.99	40.000+	13.753	26.247
4,000	55,000	105,000	160,000	40 ⟨ 40.01	40	13.75	26.25
4,001	55,000	105,040.01	160,040.01	40.02	40.000+	13.747	26.253
5,000	55,000	155,000	210,000	60	42	11	31

Table 23-1   Cost of production for a competitive firm

This table reiterates the important cost concepts analyzed in the last chapter (see Table 22-3). We have changed units so that these now are in thousands. We also made a tiny adjustment in output to find the cost levels around the point of minimum average cost at 4000 units. The dark red marginal cost figures in column (5) are the numbers that are read off the smoothed *MC* curve. The light red *MC* numbers in column (5) between the lines are the exact *MC*. Note that at 4000, *AC* is minimized and *MC = AC*.

production processes) and make external decisions (buy the correct quantity of inputs at least cost and choose the optimal level of output) so that profits are at the highest possible level.

Why would a firm want to maximize profits? Profits are like the net earnings or take-home pay of a corporation. They represent the amount a firm can reinvest in new plant and equipment, use to buy other firms or make financial investments, or pay out to owners in dividends. All these actions increase the value of the firm to its owners. We see then why a firm primarily interested in serving its owners will desire to maximize its profits.[1]

Competitive Supply and Marginal Cost

Before we turn to the derivation of the individual firm's supply curve, we quickly review marginal cost.

Marginal Cost Review In Chapter 22 we first encountered the important concept of marginal cost. Recall that marginal cost is defined as the increment to total cost that comes from producing an additional unit of output. Table 23-1 repeats the basic cost table used in the last chapter. The only change we have made is to measure q in thousands of units. Take a moment to review the important concepts: total, fixed, and variable cost; marginal cost; and the different varieties of average cost.

Perfect Competition

This chapter analyzes the supply behavior of perfectly competitive firms and markets. Recall the definition of perfect competition:

Perfect competition occurs when no producer can affect the market price. More specifically, under perfect competition, there are many small firms, each

producing an identical product and each too small to affect the market price. Under such conditions, each producer faces a completely horizontal demand (or *dd*) curve.

The world of perfect competition is the world of "price-takers," where firms produce and sell their output at given market prices. Just as most households must accept the prices that are charged by grocery stores or movie theaters, so must competitive firms accept the market prices of the wheat or oil or coal that they produce.

Using the concept of a perfect competitor, we can see how the market looks to a competitive firm. Figure 23-1 shows the contrast between the industry demand curve (the *DD* curve) and the *dd* demand curve facing a single competitive firm. Because a competitive industry is populated by a multitude of small firms, the firm's segment of the demand curve is but a tiny segment of the curve. Graphically, the competitive firm's portion of the demand curve is so small that, to the lilliputian eye of the perfect competitor, the firm's *dd* demand curve looks completely horizontal or infinitely elastic. Figure 23-1 illustrates

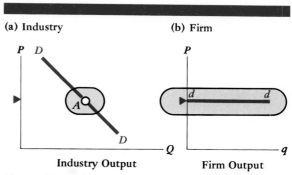

(a) Industry   **(b) Firm**

Industry Output   Firm Output

Figure 23-1   Demand curve looks horizontal to a perfect competitor

Industry demand curve is on the left, showing price elasticity somewhat less than one at point *A*. However, the perfect competitor is such an insignificant part of the market that at its level of output, the demand curve looks completely flat. The perfect competitor can sell all it wants at the market price.

---

[1]Chapter 20 discussed situations where the divorce of ownership from control may lead firms to choose not to maximize profits, focusing instead on the firm's sales or upon managers' compensation. We return to this issue in Chapter 25.

how the elasticity of demand for a single competitor appears very much greater than that for the entire market.

Competitive Supply

How does a competitive firm decide on the amount that it will supply? Recall that we are concerned with the decisions of profit-maximizing firms. Clearly, then, the amount of output supplied must have a great deal to do with the costs of production. Take the supply of bicycles as an example. No sane firm would supply bicycles at a dollar a dozen, for that price would not even cover the cost of the seats. On the other hand, if bicycles were selling at $10 million apiece, a rush of businesses would enter to start up new bicycle firms. But under normal circumstances, a firm's output decision is not so obvious and will involve the marginal cost of producing output. Let's see how.

A typical perfect competitor will be able to sell any amount of output it wishes at the going market price. Under perfect competition, a profit-maximizing firm will set its production at that level where marginal cost equals price.

Why? Because the firm can always make additional profit so long as the price (which is the extra revenue brought in from the last unit sold) is greater than the extra or marginal cost which that last unit entailed. Total profit reaches its peak—is maximized—when there is no longer any extra profit to be earned by selling extra output; the last little unit the perfect competitor produces and sells is then just in balance as far as extra cost and extra revenue are concerned. What is that extra revenue? It is price per unit. What is that extra cost? It is marginal cost.

This point can be seen in the numerical example shown in Table 23-1. Assume that the market price for the good is $40 per unit. Looking at the firm's costs in Table 23-1, ask why it would not want to sell 1 unit more than 4000 units. If it did, that unit would bring a price of $40, but the marginal cost of that unit is $40.01. So the firm would lose money on the 4001st unit.

Let's go in the other direction, asking whether it would make sense for the firm to sell 1 unit less than 4000. It would save the *MC* on the last unit (which is

$39.99), but it would lose $40 in revenue. Thus *P* is greater than *MC,* and it does not pay to reduce output. So best-profit output comes at exactly $q = 4000$ where $P = MC$.

Deriving the Firm's Supply Curve from Its *MC* Curve

We have now demonstrated that a profit-maximizing competitive firm will set output so that all units it is producing have marginal cost less than or equal to price and so that it is not producing units for which *MC* is greater than price. Hence, a competitive firm's maximum-profit equilibrium comes when it follows the rule

$$\text{Price} = \text{marginal cost} \qquad \text{or} \qquad P = MC$$

We can illustrate a firm's supply decision diagrammatically in Figure 23-2. This shows the firm's upward-sloping *MC* curve. When the market price of output is $40, the firm can consult its cost schedule in Table 23-1 and find that the production level corresponding to that marginal cost is 4000 units. Hence, for a market price of $40, the firm will wish to produce and sell 4000 units, an amount that corresponds to the intersection of the price line at $40 and the *MC* curve at point *B* in Figure 23-2. Note as well that at a production level of 4000, Table 23-1 shows that total average or unit cost is also $40, so the firm just breaks even there, with total revenues just covering total costs.

If the market price were $50, then the profit-maximizing firm would be at intersection point *A* in Figure 23-2. (We can calculate the loss of profit if the firm mistakenly produced at *B* when price was at $50 by the shaded gray triangle in Figure 23-2. This depicts the surplus of price over *MC* for the last few units. Draw in a similar shaded triangle above *A* to show the loss from producing too much.)

Alternatively, suppose the firm were faced with a market price of $35.00, shown by the horizontal *d"d"* line in Figure 23-2. At that price the firm has *MC* equal to price at point *C*. But note that the price is actually less than the average cost of production. Would the firm want to keep producing even though it was incurring a loss? Or would it want to shut down? We might say that the firm should in this situation

FIRM'S SUPPLY

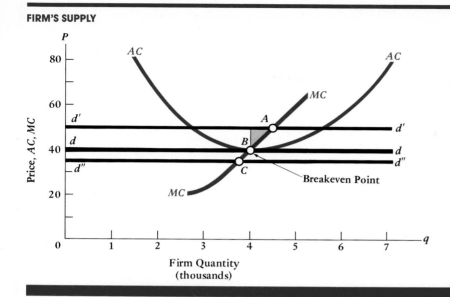

Figure 23-2 **Profit-maximizing firm's supply curve is its rising marginal cost curve**

For a profit-maximizing competitive firm, the upward-sloping marginal cost *(MC)* curve is the firm's supply curve. For market price at *d'd'*, firm will supply output at intersection point at *A*. Explain why intersection points at *B* and *C* represent equilibria for prices at *d* and *d''* respectively.

minimize its loss. Shutting down would lead to a loss of the fixed cost of $55,000. A careful calculation shows that producing at point *C* would produce a loss of only $20,000. Therefore, in this situation, the firm would continue to produce where price equals marginal cost because it would lose less money than if it were to shut down completely.

The general rule then is:

A profit-maximizing firm will set its output at that level where marginal cost equals price. Diagrammatically, this means that a firm's marginal cost curve is also its supply curve.

Total Cost and the Shutdown Condition

Our general rule for a firm's supply condition leaves open one possibility—that the price will be so low that the firm will want to shut down. When would this occur? Generally, a firm will want to shut down in the short run when it can no longer cover its variable costs.

Recall that the "short run" is defined as that period of time in which certain equipment, resources, and commitments of the firms are fixed. Because of these frozen elements, a firm has certain fixed costs in the short run, costs that must be incurred at every level of

output, even zero. Examples of fixed costs include bond interest, rentals, and directors' salaries.

The balance of the firm's total cost is called variable cost. This consists of costs that vary with output. Examples are cost of materials, wages for workers on the production line, and so forth. Chapter 22 discussed all these in detail.

Returning to our firm, consider what happens as it faces lower and lower *P*. It has the option of producing nothing at all. How much will it then lose? With its revenue zero and all its fixed costs going on anyway, its loss would exactly equal its fixed costs.

This reasoning suggests a rule governing when the firm should shut down: When the price falls so low that total revenues are less than variable cost, the firm will minimize its losses by shutting down.

The critically low market price at which revenues just equal variable cost (or at which losses exactly equal fixed costs) is called the **shutdown point.** For prices above the shutdown point, the firm will produce along its marginal cost curve. (Why so? Because, even though the firm might be losing money, it would lose more money by shutting down.) For prices below the shutdown point, the firm will produce nothing at all, i.e., will shut down. (Why so? Because by shutting down, the firm will lose only its fixed costs. If it were to produce at the point where *MC* equals the very low price, it would lose even more than fixed costs.)

Figure 23-3 shows the important *shutdown* and *breakeven* points for a firm. The breakeven point comes where price is equal to *AC,* while the shutdown level of output comes where price is equal to *AVC.* Thus the firm's supply curve is the solid red line in Figure 23-3. It goes up the vertical axis to the price corresponding to the shutdown point; jumps to the shutdown point at *M′,* where *P* equals the level of *AVC;* then continues up the *MC* curve for prices above the shutdown price.

The analysis of shutdown conditions leads to the surprising conclusion that profit-maximizing firms may in the short run continue to operate even though they are losing money. Such a paradox occurs, particularly for firms that own a great deal of capital and therefore have high fixed costs, because it is often less costly to continue producing at a loss than to shut down and still be forced to pay the high fixed costs.

We have completed our analysis of the supply behavior of competitive firms. The essential point is that profit-maximizing competitive firms will decide how much to produce and sell depending upon their costs of production: the optimal level of output will be such that the marginal cost of the last unit is just equal to the price of that unit.

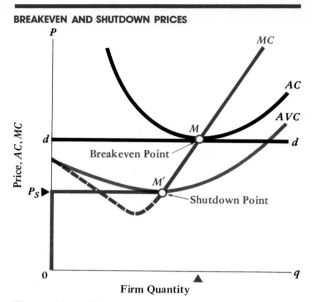

BREAKEVEN AND SHUTDOWN PRICES

Figure 23-3   Firm's supply curve travels down the *MC* curve to the shutdown point

The firm's supply curve corresponds to its *MC* curve as long as it is covering its variable costs. Once price falls to below P_S, the shutdown point, revenues no longer cover variable costs, so the firm gives up the ghost. Thus the solid red curve is the firm's supply curve.

B. SUPPLY BEHAVIOR IN COMPETITIVE INDUSTRIES

We now move from the firm to the industry, beginning with a description of how the supply decisions of individual firms are added together to get total industry supply. We then proceed to a discussion of long-run supply and examine the implications of decreasing costs. The discussion concludes with an analysis of the efficiency of competitive markets.

Summing All Firms' Supply Curves to Get Market Supply

Figure 19-2 showed how we add horizontally all individual demand curves to get the market demand curve. The same horizontal addition also applies to supply.

Suppose we are dealing with a competitive market for fish. How much of this commodity will be brought to market at each different level of market price? Firm A will bring so much to market at a particular price. Firm B will bring so much at this price. Firms C, D, and so forth will also bring quantities of fish as shown by their supply curves. The total quantity that will be brought to market at a given market price will be the sum of the individual quantities that firms supply at that price. This reasoning leads to the following relationship between individual and market supplies:

To get the market supply curve for a good, we must add horizontally the supply curves of the independent producers of that good.

Figure 23-4 below illustrates this for two firms, both in the short run and for momentary supply. Recall that the firms' momentary supply curves are defined as the inelastic supplies in a time period so short that no change in output is possible. Thus, to get the industry's momentary supply curve S_mS_m, add horizontally, at the same P, all firms' momentary supply curves s_ms_m. If the firms' supply curves are all vertical, so will be the industry's S_mS_m curve.

Recall next from Chapter 21 that the short run is defined as that period of time in which variable factors of production (like materials or production labor) can be changed, but during which the firm is stuck with certain fixed commitments like capital. In the short run, then, the firm can produce more output if the price is higher, so we see the short-run supply curves for firms A and B as s_ss_s in Figure 23-4. Again, to obtain the short-run supply curve for the industry, we add horizontally the individual short-run supply curves, as is shown in Figure 23-4(c).

The Long Run for a Competitive Industry

We know that firms might stay in business for a time even though they are losing a great deal of money. This would occur when losses are less than fixed costs, which is most likely when fixed costs are very high. The logic of continuing to produce while covering fixed costs helps explain why, in the business downturn in the early 1980s, many of America's large companies—General Motors, U.S. Steel, International Harvester—stayed in business even though they incurred staggering losses in the billions of dollars.

But do such losses suggest a troubling conclusion? Might capitalism tend toward a state where chronic losses are the normal condition? For this question, we need to turn to the long run.

The shutdown point arises when firms no longer can cover their variable costs. But in the long run, *all* costs are variable. I can pay off my bonds, let go my managers, decide not to renew my franchise or fac-

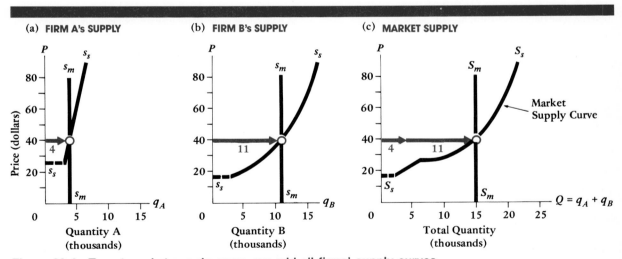

Figure 23-4   To get market supply curve, we add all firms' supply curves
The diagrams show how the market momentary supply curve (S_m) is composed of two individual momentary supply curves (s_m), while the market short-run curve (S_s) is made up of two short-run supply curves. In each case, at every price, such as $40, we horizontally add quantities supplied by each firm to get total market supply. This applies to any number of firms. If there were 1000 identical firms, the market supply curve could be made to look just like the supply curve of each firm by a careful, thousandfold change of horizontal scale in the third diagram.

tory lease. Thus in the long run, when all commitments are once again options, firms will produce only when price is at or above the long-run breakeven point. Consider the average cost curve *(AC)* in Figure 23-3. (Since this is a long-run situation, *AC* is long-run average costs.) Hence, price must be at or above the *dd* curve—the intersection must be at point *M* or above—for the firm to stay in business in the long run.

There is, then, a critical *breakeven point* below which long-run price cannot remain if I am to stay in this business. If every other firm were exactly like me, the long-run supply would dry up completely below this critical breakeven level which covers all costs of staying in business.

Now let us suppose further that entry into the industry is absolutely free in the long run, so that any number of firms can come into the industry and manage to produce in exactly the same way and at exactly the same costs as the firms already in the industry. When firms can be freely replicated, the long-run price cannot remain above this same critical breakeven point at which they all cover their long-run total costs. That is, long-run price must just cover (1) all labor, materials, equipment, taxes, and other expenses; (2) all wages payable to the identical managers at the level determined competitively by the bidding in all industries for people of such talents and industriousness; and (3) the interest yield that the firms' owners could get on the amounts of capital that they tie up here instead of investing it elsewhere.

The long-run breakeven condition comes at a critical *P* where identical firms just cover their full competitive costs. Below this critical long-run *P*, firms would leave the industry until *P* had returned to the critical equilibrium level. At higher than this long-run *P*, new firms would enter the industry, replicating what existing firms are doing and thereby forcing market price back down to the long-run equilibrium *P* where all competitive costs are just covered.

Thus, as Figure 23-3 shows, the long-run equilibrium condition of a competitive market with free entry and exit is as follows:

When an industry is supplied by competitive firms with identical cost curves, and when firms can enter

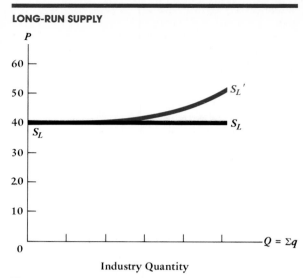

LONG-RUN SUPPLY

Figure 23-5 Long-run industry supply depends on cost conditions

With entry and exit free and any number of firms able to produce on identical, unchanged cost curves, the long-run $S_L S_L$ curve will be horizontal at each firm's minimum average cost or breakeven price. If the industry uses a specific factor, like scarce beachfront property, the long-run supply curve must slope upward as higher production employs less-well-suited inputs.

and leave the industry freely, the long-run equilibrium condition is that price equals marginal cost equals the minimum average cost point for each identical firm. Thus:

$$P = MC = \text{minimum } AC = \text{breakeven price}$$

Figure 23-5 shows the long-run supply curve for an industry. If this industry uses general factors, such as labor, that can be attracted from the vast ocean of other uses without affecting the overall level of wage rates, we get the case of constant costs as shown by the horizontal $S_L S_L$ supply curve.

By contrast, suppose the labor readily attracted from other industries must be applied to fixed factors specific to this industry alone—e.g., rare vineyard land for the wine industry or scarce beachfront properties for ocean swimming. Then higher demand for wine or swimming must intersect a rising supply curve, shown as $S_L S_L'$ in Figure 23-5.

Why must the long-run supply curve of industries with specific factors be rising? Because of the law of diminishing returns. To take the case of the rare vineyard land, varying labor, applied to fixed land, produces smaller and smaller increments of wine products; but each dose of labor costs the same in wages—and, hence, MC of wine rises. This long-run rising MC means the long-run supply curve must be rising.

An interesting phenomenon occurs in industries with rising long-run MC. In such cases, owners of productive factors peculiar to this industry—vineyards, beachfront property, ski mountains, productive oil fields—will earn a higher income from their properties as the industry expands. (This return to scarce resources will be examined in Chapter 27, where such earnings will be identified as "rents.")

What can we conclude about the long-run profitability of competitive capitalism? While no precise conclusions can be drawn, we may note that the forces of competition tend to push firms and industries toward a zero-profit long-run state. Those industries that are profitable tend to attract entry of new firms, thereby driving down prices and reducing profits toward zero. By contrast, those industries which are suffering losses tend to repel firms, as firms seek industries with better profit opportunities. Prices and profits then tend to rise. The long-run equilibrium hence is one with no pure profits.

But note that we are discussing *economic profits,* that is, profits after all implicit and opportunity costs are accounted for. This proviso is especially important when we examine the profits of today's large corporations. Recall from Chapters 20 and 22 that a substantial amount of the funds in a publicly owned company is contributed by the stockholders (mainly through retained earnings). The zero-profit condition should clearly hold only after allowing for the appropriate cost of capital on shareholders' invested funds. Once we have taken into account that the company's shareholders expect a 6 or 8 or 10 percent real return on their equity capital, then a competitive firm should

in the long run make zero economic profits. And, as we shall see in Chapter 30, American corporations have earned on average no more than their cost of capital over the last two decades.

Decreasing Costs and the Breakdown of Perfect Competition

At the beginning of this century, textbooks used to supplement the cases of horizontal and upward-sloping supply curves with a third case in which marginal costs of the firms were falling rather than rising. This was thought to create a long-run supply curve for the competitive industry that sloped gently downward.

Today, we know such reasoning is incorrect. If we review our argument of page 542 (which tells us why a profit-maximizing firm will want to produce where $MC = P$), we find the competitive argument fails completely in the case where the firm's MC declines with greater output, i.e., when the firm's MC curve is downward-sloping. For, if you move to the right of a point on a falling MC curve, you find that your additional price per unit is in excess of the now lower MC. Hence, in the case of decreasing marginal cost, the perfectly competitive firm can increase its profits indefinitely by expanding its output.

Under decreasing marginal cost, the first firm to get a head start will find its advantage increasing the larger this firm grows. Other firms must contract their outputs, resulting in a competitive disadvantage as they are forced to travel back up their falling MC curves.

What is the result? Under persisting decreasing costs for the firms, one or a few of them will so expand their outputs as to become a significant part of the market for the industry's total Q. We then end in one of the following three cases:

1. A single monopolist who dominates the industry

2. A few large sellers who together dominate the industry and who we will call "oligopolists"

3. Some kind of imperfect competition that, either in a stable way or in a series of intermittent price wars, represents an important departure from the economist's model of "perfect" competition

The case of decreasing costs is not an isolated phenomenon. Numerous detailed econometric and engineering studies confirm that a wide range of manufacturing industries show declining average costs—their *AC* curves are more like elastic demand curves than like U-shaped cost curves. The case of the U-shaped cost curves, with the bottom of the U coming at a negligible percent of industry output, appears to hold mainly in agriculture. Given the prevalence of decreasing *AC* in many industries, we should not be surprised to find that perfect competition is the exception rather than the rule outside agriculture.

The case of decreasing costs is of great importance to economics. Once cost curves are seen to be generally decreasing, we see the role that imperfect competition plays.

THE EFFICIENCY OF COMPETITIVE MARKETS

We have now completed our basic analysis of how competitive markets function, of the way supply and demand solve the basic economic problems in a market economy. The appendix to this chapter provides a number of cases of supply and demand in competitive markets—including constant-cost industries, inelastic supply, backward-bending supply, and shifts in supply. These cases will help illustrate the analytical power and versatility of our supply-and-demand theory.

In this final section, we go beyond the descriptive analysis of the determinants of price and quantity in competitive markets to ask how well these markets perform. Do competitive markets fail to satisfy people's economic needs and desires? Or do they deserve high grades in terms of using society's scarce resources to provide high living standards?

To answer these questions, we proceed as follows: First, we review the meaning of efficiency, which will turn out to be the key concept in analyzing the performance of competitive markets. We then turn to see how competitive markets behave in a simplified economy of identical individuals. Finally, we turn to the realistic case of an economy with many goods, consumers, and firms. At the end of this section, important qualifications concerning competitive markets

are presented as a reminder that—however elegant and ideal perfect competition may be—the market economy of the 1980s is a blend of competitive and monopolistic forces.

The Concept of Efficiency

We have seen how competitive markets grind out thousands of prices and quantities as supply and demand interact in the marketplace. We have looked behind these forces in this and earlier chapters to try to understand what forces determine supply and demand. From Chapter 19, we found that marginal utility determines how much consumers will pay for different quantities of a commodity. And in the early pages of this chapter, we saw that the supply curve for a commodity reflects the horizontally summed marginal cost curves of the supplying firms.

But the critical question for those judging a competitive economy—and perhaps thinking whether to turn production over to the government or to a cooperative movement—is, How efficient is such an outcome? Is society getting much guns and butter for a given amount of inputs? Or is the butter melting on the way to the store, while the guns have crooked barrels?

To answer this we must introduce the concept of **allocative efficiency** (or **efficiency,** for short). An economy is efficient if it is organized so as to provide the consumers the largest possible combination of commodities, given the resources and technology of the economy. More precisely:

Allocative efficiency occurs when no possible reorganization of production can make anyone better off without making someone else worse off. Under conditions of allocative efficiency, therefore, one person's utility can be increased only by lowering someone else's utility.[2]

We can think of the concept of efficiency intuitively. One clear example of inefficiency occurs when society is inside its production-possibility frontier. If we move out to the *PPF,* no one need suffer a decline in utility.

---

[2]This concept of efficiency is also called "Pareto efficiency," after Vilfredo Pareto (1848–1923), the Italian economist who first devised the concept.

Efficiency of Competitive Equilibrium

Let us examine the performance of a competitive economy in terms of the standard of allocative efficiency. We begin with a simplified example to illustrate the general principles.

Consider an idealized situation where all individuals are identical. Further simplify by assuming: *(a)* Each person works at growing food. Moreover, as leisure hours dwindle, each additional hour of work becomes increasingly tiresome. *(b)* Each extra unit of food consumed brings diminished marginal utility *(MU).*[3] *(c)* Because the food production takes place on fixed plots of land, the law of diminishing returns tells us that each extra minute of work brings less and less extra food.

Figure 23-6 represents the outcome for such a simplified competitive market. When we add the identical supply curves of our identical farmers, we get the upward-sloping *MC* curve. We learned in this chapter that this is also the industry's supply curve (hence note that Figure 23-6 shows *MC = SS*). In addition, we see the downward-stepping *MU = DD* curve for food in Figure 23-6. This *DD* curve is the horizontal summation of the identical individuals' marginal utility and demand-for-food curves.

The intersection of the *SS* and *DD* curves provides the competitive equilibrium for food. At point *E*, farmers supply just what consumers will purchase. Each person will be laboring up to the critical point where the declining marginal-utility-of-consuming-food curve intersects the rising marginal-cost-of-growing-food curve.

A careful analysis of this competitive equilibrium will show a remarkable truth: The competitive outcome has allocative efficiency. More precisely, at competitive equilibrium point *E* in Figure 23-6, the representative consumer will have higher utility than for any other feasible allocation of resources. This is so because at competitive equilibrium *E*, the marginal utility of the consumed good *(MU)* equals the price *(P)*, which in turn equals the marginal cost of produc-

---

[3]To simplify the analysis, we adjust our utility yardstick so that the marginal utility of an additional hour of leisure replacing an hour of work is always constant (say, having 10 utils per hour of increased leisure). If we go further and define \$1 as the value of 1 unit of leisure, we can express all prices in these dollar-units.

EFFICIENCY OF COMPETITIVE EQUILIBRIUM

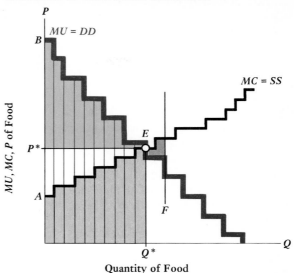

Figure 23-6 At competitive equilibrium point *E*, the marginal costs and utilities of food are balanced

Many identical farmer-consumers bring their food to market. The upward-stepping *MC = SS* curve adds together the marginal cost curves, while the downward-stepping *MU = DD* curve represents the consumer valuation of food. At competitive market equilibrium *E*, the marginal gain from the last unit of food is exactly equal to the marginal cost in terms of the labor required to produce the last unit of food.

Cost of producing the food is shown by the gray slices, showing the utils lost from the labor needed to produce food. Vertical slices of red under *MU* show excess of food utils over their cost. The red area is thus the consumer surplus. It is maximized at *E*: the dark gray area to the right of *E* shows the loss from producing too much food.

---

ing the good *(MC)*. As the following three-step process shows, if *MU = P = MC*, then the allocation is efficient.

1. *P = MU.* Consumers choose food purchases up to the amount *P = MU*. As a result, every person is gaining *P* utils of satisfaction from the last unit of food consumed.

2. *P = MC.* As producers, each person is supplying sweaty labor up to the point where the price of food exactly equals the *MC* of the last unit of food supplied (the *MC* here being the cost in terms of the utility of leisure forgone and the disutility of sweaty labor that is needed to produce the last unit of food). To repeat, the price is equal to the utils of satisfaction lost by working that last bit of time needed to grow that last unit of food.

3. Putting these two equations together, we see that $MU = MC$. This means that the utils gained from the last unit of food consumed exactly equals the utils lost from the sweaty labor required to produce that last unit. It is exactly this condition—that the marginal gains to society from the last unit consumed equal the marginal costs to society of that last unit produced—which guarantees that a competitive equilibrium is efficient.

Consumer Surplus

An alternative way to understand the efficiency of competitive markets is through the concept of consumer surplus. Recall from Chapter 19 that consumer surplus is the difference between the amount that a consumer would be willing to pay for a good and the amount actually paid for that good. Clearly an economy is performing well when it generates much consumer surplus, and an efficient situation is one in which the maximum amount of consumer surplus is squeezed out of the system.

Figure 23-6 shows the consumer surplus at *E* as the red shaded area between the *MU* line and the *MC* line. Each slab represents the difference between the *MU* of that unit and the *MC* (in terms of utility lost from sweaty work) of producing that food unit. At point *E*, the total surplus from the economy is maximized (that is, the red area is maximized).

Indeed, we can also see why any point other than the competitive equilibrium point *E* in Figure 23-6 will be inefficient. Assume that, by some mistake, the level of output rose from *E* to the level indicated by the thin line at *F*. Because the *MC* curve is above the *MU* curve for outputs beyond *E*, people will be putting in more sweaty labor and losing more from that labor than they will be gaining from extra food consumption. The dark gray area between the *MC* and *MU* curves and between *E* and line *FF* is a measure of

the loss in consumer welfare resulting from too high a level of output.

Equilibrium with Many Markets

Let us now turn from parables about identical farmer-consumers. What about an economy populated by millions of different firms, hundreds of millions of people, and endless numbers of commodities? Can a perfectly competitive economy still achieve allocative efficiency in such a situation?

Qualifications The answer is, ''Yes,'' or better still, ''Yes, if.'' The most complex competitive economy is efficient if certain conditions are met: atomistic competition, true demand curves, and no externalities.

First, the markets must be perfectly competitive; we must rule out monopolies and oligopolies. As the next chapter will show, when imperfect competition reigns, prices will be too high and output will be too low.

Second, we must rule out cases where people's demand curves deviate from true utility. That is, don't apply the theory to heroin consumption. Or, if you believe that television advertising has manipulated consumers into demanding worthless gadgets that don't deserve to have the word ''utility'' applied to them, don't apply the theory to that area.

Third, we must rule out externalities. If some firms pour dioxin or arsenic into the local dump and do not pay for the social cost of that activity, then we have an oversupply of dioxins and other such commodities. In this case, the price equals the firm's marginal costs but not society's marginal costs. So, as we will see in Chapter 32, perfect competition doesn't behave efficiently when uncorrected spillovers take place.

If there remains a group of goods and industries—say, shoes, beef, or bowling—where there are many reasonably informed consumers, many mutually competing producers, and negligible externalities, then you may hope to achieve efficiency by means of market pricing along perfectly competitive principles.

Market Synthesis Now turn to Figure 23-7 to see how a competitive system does bring out a balance

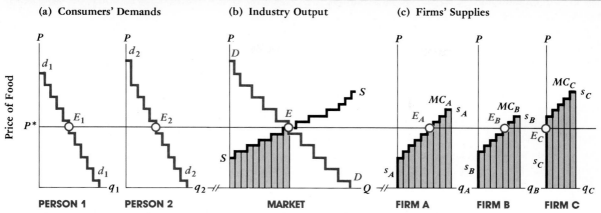

Figure 23-7   Competitive market integrates consumers' demands and producers' costs

(a) Individual demands are shown on the left. We add the consumers' *dd* curves horizontally to obtain the market demand *DD* curve in the middle.

(b) The market brings together all consumer demands and firm supplies to reach market equilibrium at *E*. The horizontal price-of-food line shows where each consumer on the left and each producer on the right reaches equilibrium. At *P**, see how each consumer's *MU* is equated to each firm's *MC*, leading to allocative efficiency.

(c) For each competitive firm, profits are maximized when the supply curve is given by the rising *MC* curve. The gray area depicts each firm's cost of producing the amount at *E*. At prices equal to marginal cost, the industry produces output at the least total cost.

---

between utility and cost for a single commodity with nonidentical firms and consumers.

On the left, we add horizontally the demand curves for all consumers to get the market *DD* curve in the middle. On the right, we add all the separate firms' *MC* curves to get the industry *SS* curve in the middle.

Note what the equilibrium price at the *E* intersection achieves: it gives people on the left what they are willing to purchase of the good at the price reflecting efficient social *MC*. On the right, we see how the equilibrium market price does allocate production most efficiently. (That is, the gray area under *SS* in the middle represents the minimized sum of gray cost areas on the right.)

One of the key points to understand is that each firm is producing output at *MC = P*. Production efficiency is achieved because there is no reorganization of production that would allow the same level of industry output to be produced at lower cost. (Note also that firm C is not producing at all. Is this efficient? Is this fair? Question 7 at the end of this chapter addresses these issues.)

The perfectly competitive market is a device for synthesizing *(a)* the willingness of people possessing dollar votes to pay for goods as represented by demand with *(b)* the marginal costs of those goods as represented by supply. Under ideal conditions, the outcome guarantees allocative efficiency, in which no consumer's utility can be raised without lowering another consumer's utility.

Many Goods A final situation would be where there are many consumer goods. A real economy has not only food, but also clothing, movies, concerts, vacation trips, haircuts, and many other commodities. How does our analysis apply when consumers must also choose among many products?

The principles are exactly the same, but now we add one further condition: that utility-maximizing consumers spread their dollars among different goods until the marginal utility of the last dollar is equalized for each good consumed. In this case, as long as the three qualifications discussed in the last subsection are met, we determine that a competitive economy is efficient with a multitude of goods and factors of production.

In a multiproduct and multifactor world, when individual and social costs and demands coincide, a perfectly competitive economy is efficient. Each industry must balance MC and MU. If movies have two times the MC of hamburgers, then the P and the MU of movies must also be twice those of hamburgers. Only then will the MUs, which are equal to the Ps, be equal to the MCs. Thus by equating price and marginal cost, competition guarantees that an economy can attain allocative efficiency.

We must emphasize that our conclusion about the efficiency of perfect competition does not depend on any of the simplifying assumptions discussed here. It is a general conclusion subject only to the three qualifications discussed above.

The Central Role of Marginal-Cost Pricing

This chapter has stressed the importance of competition and marginal cost in attaining an efficient allocation of resources. But the centrality of marginal cost extends far beyond perfect competition. The idea that the marginal benefit of an action should equal its marginal cost is a vital concept for any society or organization trying to make the most effective use of its resources—whether that entity is a capitalist or socialist economy, a profit-maximizing or not-for-profit corporation, a university or a church, or even a family.

What is the essential role of marginal cost in a market economy? It is this: Only when prices are equal to marginal costs is the economy squeezing the maximum output from its scarce resources of land, labor, and capital. Only when each firm has its own marginal cost equal to each other firm's MC—as will be the case when each MC has been set equal to a common price—will the industry be producing its total output at minimum total cost. Only when price is equal to marginal cost for all firms will society be out on its production-possibility frontier and not inefficiently inside this frontier.

The use of marginal cost as a benchmark for efficient resource allocation is as applicable to a communist, socialist, or fascist society as to a capitalistic

society. Unless wheat cultivation has been pushed in different parts of the Soviet Union so as to equalize marginal costs (including transportation), the planners there will fail to achieve the abundance of wheat and other goods that could be theirs with a more efficient allocation of resources. Given such a hard-headed result, it is not surprising to learn from recent debates in Soviet economic journals that they are considering ways to use marginal costs in their economic decisions.[4]

Because marginal cost has this efficiency property, it can with some care be used as a yardstick to detect inefficiency in any organization or society. Even if perfectly competitive industries did not exist at all, we would still derive great benefit from defining and studying the concept of marginal cost.

Two Cheers for the Market, but Not Three

But we must not leave the subject of efficient pricing without a warning. We have not proved that laissez-faire with perfect competition maximizes the greatest good for the greatest number. We have not proved that it produces a maximum of social utility. We have not proved that it results in the best attainable level of social welfare.

Why not? Because people are not equally endowed with purchasing power. Some are very poor through no fault of their own. Some are very rich through luck or inheritance rather than skill or talent. So the weighting of dollar votes, which lie behind the individual demand curves on the left in Figure 23-7, is not necessarily equitable or even tolerable.

For Maximal Bread Alone? How does a modern society respond to the tension between efficiency and fairness? Is society satisfied with outcomes where the maximal amount of bread is produced? Or will modern democracies take loaves from the wealthy and pass them out to the poor? And if they do, what residual role remains for the market mechanism to play?

---

[4]The Soviet mathematician, Academician L. V. Kantorovich, shared the 1975 Nobel Prize in economics for his original and deep research into the use of optimal pricing mechanisms in a centrally planned economy. Chapter 35 explores this topic further.

Will society want to have the maximal bread produced out of which to distribute a small fraction to the poor? Or will society tolerate a large reduction in the total bread output in order to ensure a more equal distribution of bread consumption? These issues—of the importance of the distribution of income and consumption, as well as the tradeoffs between equality and efficiency—are ones that will occupy us at length in Parts Five and Six.

∎   ∎   ∎

This completes our discussion of the relationship between marginal cost and industry supply, and of marginal-cost pricing in its relationship to efficient allocation of resources. In the next chapter, we extend our analysis by examining the way monopolists behave, the inefficiencies they cause, and public-policy remedies for monopoly.

SUMMARY

A. Supply Behavior of the Competitive Firm

1. A perfectly competitive firm is one that can sell all the output it wants at the going market price. Competitive firms are assumed to maximize their profits (or minimize their losses). To maximize profits, the competitive firm will choose that output level at which price equals the marginal cost of production, i.e., $P = MC$. Diagrammatically, the competitive firm's equilibrium will come where the rising MC curve intersects its horizontal demand curve.

2. Variable (or avoidable) costs must be taken into consideration in determining a firm's short-run shutdown point. Below some critical shutdown point, the firm will not even recover in revenues the variable cost that could be saved completely if it shut down. Rather than end up losing more than its fixed cost, it will shut down and produce nothing when price falls below the shutdown price.

3. A competitive industry's long-run supply curve, $S_L S_L$, must take into account the entry of new firms and exodus of old ones. In the long run, all the commitments of any firm will expire. It will decide to stay in business only if price at least covers all its long-run costs. These costs may be "explicit" out-of-pocket payments to labor, lenders, material suppliers, or landlords; or opportunity costs, such as implicit returns on the property assets owned by the firm (and whose opportunity costs are measured by what they will yield in other equally risky uses).

B. Supply Behavior in Competitive Industries

4. The rising MC curve of each firm is its supply curve. To obtain the supply curve of a group of independent competitive firms, we add horizontally their separate supply curves. The supply curve of the industry hence also represents the marginal cost curve for the competitive industry as a whole.

5. In the long run, when firms are free to enter and leave the industry, and where no one firm has any particular advantage of skill or location, competitors will compete away any excess profits earned by existing firms in the industry. So, just as free exit means P cannot fall below the breakeven point, free entry means P cannot persist above that point in long-run equilibrium. Where an industry can expand by replication without pushing up the prices of any factors peculiar to it or used in especially large proportions by it, the resulting long-run supply curve will be horizontal. More likely, any but the smallest industry will generally use some factors of production in large enough amounts to force up their prices slightly. As a result, the long-run supply curve of a competitive industry will slope upward, at least gently.

6. When firms' marginal costs are declining, and firms enjoy decreasing costs as output increases, marginal cost curves cannot serve as supply curves. With decreasing MC, competitive firms could increase their profits by expanding output indefinitely, so one or a few firms will tend to expand and the remaining firms will tend to contract. Thus forever-decreasing cost curves lead to destruction of perfect competition.

7. The analysis of competitive markets sheds light on the efficient organization of a society. Allocative efficiency occurs when there is no way of reorganizing production and distribution such that everyone's satisfactions can be improved. A different way of defining allocative efficiency is to say that no single individual can be made better off without making another individual worse off.

8. Under ideal conditions, a competitive economy attains allocative efficiency. This occurs because of a three-step condition: *(a)* First, when consumers buy goods in markets, they buy that amount such that the marginal utility just equals the price. *(b)* But when competitive producers supply goods, this chapter shows how the output is chosen so that marginal cost just equals price. *(c)* Since $MU = P$ and $MC = P$, it follows that $MU = MC$. Thus the social cost of producing a good under competition just equals its marginal-utility valuation.

9. Ideal competitive markets must meet three tests before they are socially optimal. First, there must not be any imperfect competition—no producers should be able to affect the price of output. Second, there must be no spillover effects or externalities—processes where one firm imposes a social cost (or causes a benefit) without the affected party being compensated (or paying). Finally, for a competitive outcome to be optimal, the distribution of dollar votes must correspond to the society's concepts of justice. Competitive markets by themselves cannot ensure that the resulting distribution of income and consumption corresponds to the society's ethical ideals.

CONCEPTS FOR REVIEW

marginal cost
characteristics of perfect competition
$P = MC$ as maximum-profit condition
firm's ss supply curve and its MC
  curve
breakeven point where $P = MC = AC$
shutdown point where $P = MC = AVC$
summing ss curves to get SS
decreasing costs and the breakdown of
  competition

long-run zero-profit condition
horizontal and rising $S_L S_L$
allocative (Pareto) efficiency
conditions for allocative efficiency:
  $MU = P = MC$
efficiency of competitive markets
three qualifications on efficiency of
  perfect competition

QUESTIONS FOR DISCUSSION

1. Explain why each of the following statements about profit-maximizing competitive firms is incorrect. Restate each one correctly.

(a) A competitive firm will produce output up to the point where price equals average variable cost.

(b) A firm's shutdown point comes where price is less than minimum average cost.

(c) A firm's supply curve depends only on its marginal cost. Any other cost concept is irrelevant for supply decisions.

(d) The $P = MC$ rule for competitive industries holds for upward-sloping, horizontal, and downward-sloping MC curves.

2. Why would a firm ever supply goods at a loss?

3. One of the most important rules of economics, business, and life is: "Let bygones be bygones." This means that fixed costs (which are bygone in the sense that they are unrecoverably lost) should be ignored when making decisions. Only future costs, involving marginal and variable costs, should count in making rational decisions.

To see this, ask the following: What is the profit-maximizing level of output for the firm in Table 23-1 if price is $40 while fixed costs are $0? $55,000? $100,000? $1,000,000,000? Minus $30,000?

How does the bygones rule apply to the price you should ask for your house as compared to the price you paid?

4. Examine the cost data shown in Table 23-1. Calculate the supply decision of a profit-maximizing competitive firm when price is $21, $40, and $60. What would the level of total profit be for each of the three prices? What would happen to exit or entry of firms in the very long run at each of the three prices?

5. For the cost data shown in Table 23-1, calculate the price elasticity of supply between $P = 40$ and $P = 40.02$ for the individual firm. If there are 2000 firms identical to that shown in Table 23-1, construct a table showing the industry supply schedule. What is the *industry* price elasticity of supply between $P = 40$ and $P = 40.02$?

6. Consider a world where goods are allocated by ideal planning rather than by markets. Assume that the planners wish to maximize the total consumer surplus (shown as the light red slabs in Figure 23-6); in addition, however, the planners wish to allow consumers to have free choice, so they set planning prices and allow consumers to pick their consumption bundles. Show why the rule of $P = MU = MC$ holds in such an idealized planned economy.

7. Examine Figure 23-7 to see that competitive firm C is not producing at all. Explain the reason why the profit-maximizing (or loss-minimizing) output level for firm C is at $q_C = 0$. What would happen to total industry cost of production if firm C produces 1 unit while firm B produces 1 less unit than the competitive output level?

Say that firm C is "Mom and Pop's" grocery store. Why do chain grocery stores A and B drive C out of business? How do you feel about keeping C in business? What would be the impact of legislation that divided the market in three equal parts between "Mom and Pop's" store and chain stores A and B?

8. Interpret this dialogue. *A:* "How can competitive profits be zero in the long run? Who'll work for nothing?" *B:* "It is only *excess* profits that are wiped out by competition. Managers get paid for their work; owners get a normal return on capital in competitive long-run equilibrium—no more, no less."

9. Advanced problem: A firm can generate power from two generators; the newer one has lower *MC* at first. Show that only at peak loads should the firm use the older generator, only after the new generator's *MC* rises above the beginning *MC* of the older generator. At high loads, it should charge high *P*, equal to the common *MC*s of the two.

10. Advanced problem: Interpret the accompanying diagrams. *(a)* The first three depict Adam Smith's labor theory of value. Each 1 hour's labor catches 1 beaver; each 2 hours' labor catches 1 deer. Long-run supply curves are constant or horizontal, and the production-possibility frontier is a straight line, with relative prices or exchange values set by embodied labor requirements of 2 to 1. *(b)* The second three diagrams depict a case where scarce cornland and diminishing returns (to labor producing corn) destroy the labor theory of value and produce cornland rent. As people demand more corn, the corn industry moves up its rising *MC* or $S_c S_c$ curve. The rising corn receipts are divided between variable labor costs (the dark gray area under the *MC* curve) and competitively bid-up land rent (the light red area, often called "rent" or "producer surplus"). By contrast, since haircuts need labor only, $S_h S_h$ is horizontal.

Describe why Smith's labor theory of value is correct in his beaver-deer economy. Explain why the addition of a fixed factor, land, destroys Smith's (or Marx's) labor theory of value. Further describe the efficient distribution of income between wages and rent in the two economies.

Finally, explain why the *PPF*s are linear for Smith's economy and concave for Ricardo's economy.

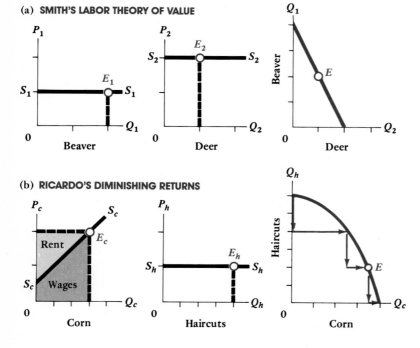

(a) **SMITH'S LABOR THEORY OF VALUE**

(b) **RICARDO'S DIMINISHING RETURNS**

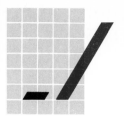

APPENDIX: 23 _____

Special Cases of Competitive Markets: Supply and Demand at Work

Chapters 18 through 23 have laid out the foundations of competitive, supply-and-demand analysis. This treatment put together the building blocks of utility and demand analysis for consumers, along with production, cost, and supply behavior for competitive firms. Supply-and-demand analysis is the most important item in the economist's tool kit, and it will reappear in many guises in the chapters that follow.

Before moving on to study imperfect competition, however, we pause in this appendix to probe more deeply into supply-and-demand analysis. We first consider certain general propositions about competitive markets and then continue with some special cases. A careful study of this appendix will pay valuable dividends in understanding the functioning of competitive markets.

GENERAL RULES

We begin with two general rules about the impact of demand and supply shifts in competitive markets. These rules apply to virtually any competitive market, whether it is for codfish, brown coal, Douglas fir, Japanese yen, IBM stock, or petroleum. In the propositions that follow, we investigate the impact of shifts in supply or demand upon the price and quantity bought and sold. Recall always that by a shift in demand or supply we mean a shift in the demand or supply curve or schedule, not a movement along the curve.

Proposition 1. (a) As a general rule, an increase in demand for a commodity (supply being constant) will raise the price of the commodity. *(b)* For most commodities, an increase in demand will increase the quantity demanded as well. A decrease in demand will have the opposite effects.

We will see that Proposition 1*(b)* is phrased cautiously because the case of "backward-bending supply" (see Case 4 below) provides an exception to the rule that increased demand raises quantity demanded.

Proposition 2. An increase in supply of a commodity, demand being constant, will almost certainly lower the price and increase the quantity bought and sold. A decrease in supply has the opposite effects.

These two central propositions summarize the *qualitative* effects of shifts in supply and demand. But the *quantitative* effects on price and quantity depend upon the exact shapes of the supply and demand curves. In the cases that follow, we will see the response for a number of important cost and supply situations.

CASE 1. CONSTANT COST

Imagine a manufactured item, like pencils, whose production can be easily expanded by merely duplicating factories, machinery, and labor. To produce 100,000 pencils per

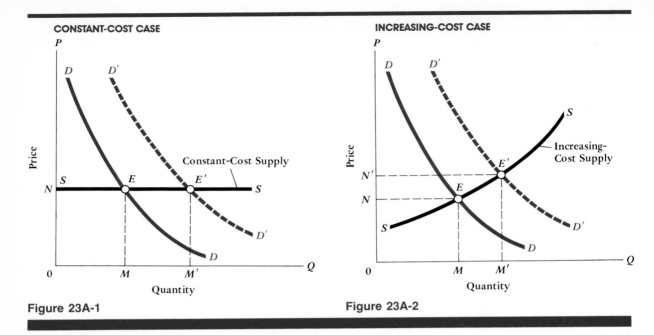

Figure 23A-1

Figure 23A-2

day simply requires us to do the same thing as when we were manufacturing 1000 per day, but on a hundredfold scale. (Also, the pencil industry must be assumed to use land, labor, and other inputs in the same proportions as the rest of the economy.)

In this case the long-run supply curve *SS* in Figure 23A-1 is a horizontal line at the constant level of unit costs. A rise in demand from *DD* to *D'D'* will shift the new intersection point to *E'*, raising *Q* but leaving *P* the same.

CASE 2. INCREASING COSTS AND DIMINISHING RETURNS

Suppose an industry like wine-grape growing requires a certain kind of soil and location (sunny hillsides, etc.). Such sites are limited in number. The annual output of wine can be increased to some extent by adding more labor and fertilizer to each acre of land. But as we saw in Chapter 21, the law of diminishing returns will begin to operate if variable factors of production, like labor and fertilizer, are added to fixed amounts of a factor like land. Why is that? Because each new addition of labor and fertilizer has a smaller proportion of land to work with. By the same token, each fixed unit of land has more labor and fertilizer cooperating with it. Therefore productivity and earnings from the land are higher.

The result: Getting extra amounts of wine sends total cost up more than proportionately. Therefore the cost per unit of wine is rising. The supply curve rises because at higher market prices, more will be supplied.

Figure 23A-2 shows the rising supply curve *SS*. What will be the effect on price of an increase in demand? How will an increase in demand affect quantity supplied? The figure illustrates the answers.

CASE 3. COMPLETELY INELASTIC OR FIXED SUPPLY AND ECONOMIC RENT

Some goods or productive factors are completely fixed in amount, regardless of price. There is only one *Mona Lisa* by da Vinci. Nature's original endowment of the "natural and indestructible" qualities of land can also often be taken as fixed in amount. Raising the price offered for land cannot create more than four corners at State and Madison in Chicago. Highly paid artists and business executives who love their work would continue to work at their jobs even at low pay.

In all such cases the supply curve is vertical in the relevant region. In Figure 23A-3, a higher price cannot elicit an increase in Q. Nor is the higher price necessary to coax out the existing Q, for even at lower prices the same Q will still be forthcoming. If the commodity is land, then our example shows that the supply of land is fixed no matter what its rent. Because the same amount of land is forthcoming no matter what its price, the price of such a factor of production is called a "pure economic rent."

If demand now shifts upward, the whole effect is to raise price. Quantity supplied is unchanged. And the rise in price exactly equals the upward shift in demand. (More on this topic will be found in the section on rents and costs in Chapter 27.)

Likewise, when a tax is placed upon the commodity, its whole effect is to reduce the

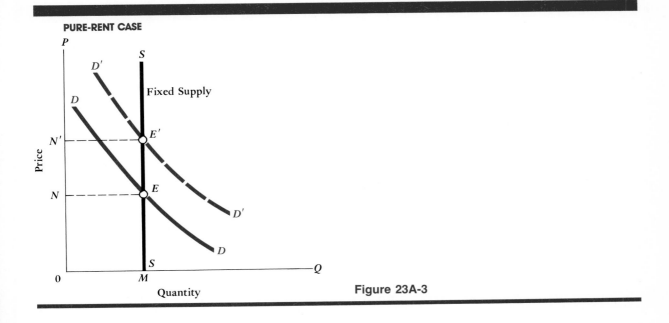

Figure 23A-3

price received by the supplier by exactly the amount of tax. The tax is completely paid by the supplier (say, the landowner); the tax is ''shifted'' completely to the supplier, who absorbs it all out of economic rent. The consumer buys exactly as much of the good or service as before and at no higher price.

CASE 4. BACKWARD-BENDING SUPPLY CURVE

Firms in poor regions often noted that when they raised the wages of workers, they received *less* rather than more labor. When the wage was doubled, instead of working 6 days a week for this minimum of subsistence, the workers might go fishing for 3 days. The same has been observed in high-income countries. As improved technology raises real wages, people feel that they want to take part of their higher earnings in the form of more leisure and less work. Chapter 19's discussion of income and substitution effects explained why a supply curve might bend backward. Chapter 28 explores the empirical evidence on this issue for labor supply.

Figure 23A-4 shows how a supply curve for labor might appear. At first it rises as higher wages coax out more labor, but beyond point *T* higher wages lead people to work fewer hours and to take more leisure. An increase in demand does increase the price of labor, as was stated in Proposition 1 at the beginning of this appendix. But note why we were cautious to add ''for most commodities'' to Proposition 1*(b)*, for now the increase in demand decreases the quantity of labor supplied.

Verification of backward-bending supply can be found in many areas. One of the most important came when many oil-rich countries curbed their production of oil after

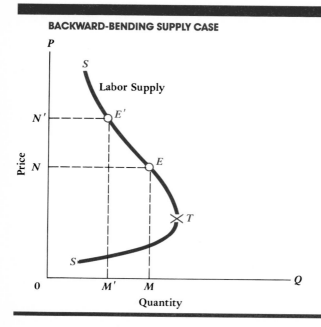

BACKWARD-BENDING SUPPLY CASE

Figure 23A-4

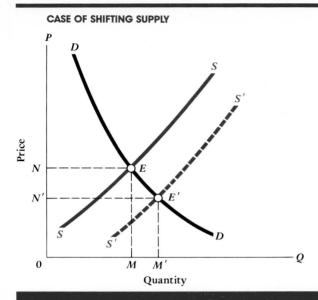

CASE OF SHIFTING SUPPLY

Figure 23A-5

the price of oil quadrupled in the early 1970s. The higher oil prices in effect induced countries like Kuwait to move from point E to point E' in Figure 23A-4.

CASE 5. SHIFTS IN SUPPLY

All the above discussions dealt with a shift in demand and no shift in supply. To analyze Proposition 2, we must now shift supply, keeping demand constant. This is done in Figure 23A-5.

If the law of downward-sloping demand is valid,[1] then increased supply must send us down the demand curve, decreasing price and increasing quantity. You may verify, by drawing diagrams, the following quantitative corollaries of Proposition 2:

(a) An increased supply will decrease P most when demand is inelastic.
(b) An increased supply will increase Q least when demand is inelastic.

What are common-sense reasons for these rules? Illustrate with cases of elastic demand for autos and of inelastic demand for electricity.

[1]In Chapter 19 we found the legitimate exception to the law of downward-sloping demand in the case of the Irish peasants who might be forced by higher potato P to consume *more* of such necessities. Another exception is provided by items such as diamonds or Gucci shoes, which are valuable not so much for their intrinsic qualities as for their ''snob appeal'' and expensiveness, and which may therefore fall off in demand if their price is cut. What appears to be another exception is the case in which a short-run rise in P may make people expect future P to be still higher, thus causing them to buy more rather than less now and thereby leading to destabilizing speculation; but this is more properly interpreted as a case where the whole demand curve is dynamically shifting, rather than as a northeast move along a fixed DD curve.

DYNAMIC COBWEB

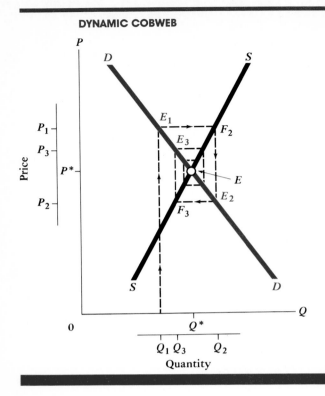

Figure 23A-6

This period's P and Q are given by the DD curve. But now the SS curve is dynamic: it gives the amount of Q supplied in the next period for each P of this period. So if you start at E_1, you move to F_2, down to E_2, over to F_3, up to E_3—and so forth along the converging cobweb, until E is reached.

CASE 6. DYNAMIC COBWEB

A famous economic case shows that tools of supply and demand are not restricted to handling static and unchanging situations but can also be used fruitfully to analyze dynamic situations of change.

Suppose that a competitive crop—let us take the conventional example of hogs for pork production—is auctioned off in the market in the usual way so as to fetch the P given by running vertically up from any given Q to the DD demand.

But now we want to make the supply side dynamic. Suppose farmers look at today's P and use it to determine the Q they will bring to market in the *next* period. Specifically, if today's P is high, they begin to breed many new pigs, to feed and fatten them, and finally to bring them to market some months from now. The farmers do have an upward-sloping supply curve, but it acts with a time lag and connects the next period's Q with this period's P. (We define a period as the time involved in producing hogs.)

If the market price were at the intersection of SS and DD in Figure 23A-6, this would represent an unchanging equilibrium in exactly the same way that it did in the nondynamic cases. Today, tomorrow, and in the period after that, the farmers would be on their SS curve producing the amount shown by E, and the amount consumers would gladly demand at that P would just match what farmers will gladly supply. As yet, then, there is no difference.

But suppose that for some reason, such as hog cholera, the crop initially drops to Q_1, which is below the equilibrium amount Q^*. We run up to E_1 on the demand curve and see that we get the higher P_1 corresponding to the reduced crop. But that is not the end of the story. We are not at long-run equilibrium. To see why, ask, How much will the farmers produce tomorrow at this higher P_1? They will move rightward on their supply curve and produce in the second period at the point marked F_2. We can see that this amount of Q is above the equilibrium Q^*. What will it sell for in the competitive market? We run down to the demand curve and see that P_2 will have to fall to the level shown at E_2. But we are not yet in final equilibrium. At this low price, farmers will plan to cut down tomorrow's production by going leftward to their SS curve, ending up at F_3. From there we move upward to the DD curve, to find the P_3 given at the E_3 point. (Study Figure 23A-6 and its accompanying legend.)

And thus it goes on and on. First Q is low and P is high. But high P makes next period's Q high and next period's P low. So—like an acrobat on a tightrope who goes too far on one side, then compensates by going too far on the other—market price oscillates in successive periods above and below equilibrium, tracing out a spidery cobweb.

What is the final outcome? Figure 23A-6 was drawn with the supply curve's slope at E *steeper* than the demand curve's falling slope. So, as can be seen from the diagram, the oscillations finally do dampen and die out: the cobweb winds inward to E. We are then back at equilibrium, where we can stay forever. Forever? Well, until the next outside disturbance comes to set off another dying-out oscillation.

Not all equilibrium points are so dynamically stable. Figure 23A-7 puts a microscope on the region around E in a number of other possible situations. Thus, in its first

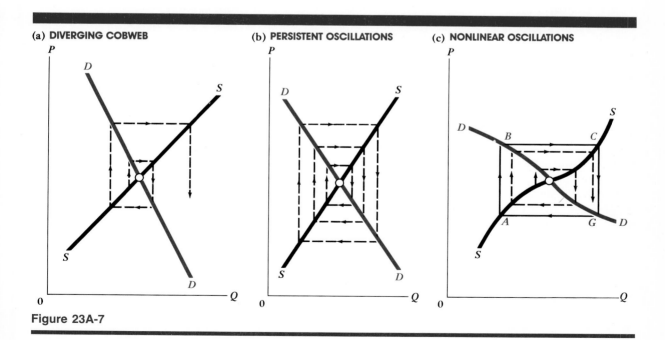

(a) DIVERGING COBWEB

(b) PERSISTENT OSCILLATIONS

(c) NONLINEAR OSCILLATIONS

Figure 23A-7

diagram, *SS* has been made flatter than *DD*, and the cobweb diverges outward in an explosive oscillation.

In the middle diagram, the straight lines are of the same absolute slope and we get a perfect cobweb: Depending upon how severely it is disturbed, the market will oscillate endlessly around equilibrium, getting neither more nor less violent in its swings. (This is like the case of an ideal frictionless pendulum which would repeat its swings forever.)

The final diagram is designed to show that there is no need to stick with straight lines. Because its *SS* is flatter than *DD* at the equilibrium point, any small disturbance will at first send the system into increasing oscillations. But no explosion can go on forever in real life; the curvature of the schedules finally brings the system to the stable "box," indicated by the letters *ABCG*. Ultimately, then, the system oscillates repeatedly, and the amplitude or degree of the oscillation will be determined by the curvatures of *DD* and *SS*.

After any new disturbance, the system tends to come back to this box from inside or outside; even if stationary equilibrium were restored at *E* by accident, the slightest new shock would send the market away from such an unstable equilibrium point.

Rational Speculation

A little thought leads to the following concerns: Could prices swing forever in this regular way without some shrewd speculators beginning to notice the pattern? Wouldn't they soon rationally come to expect that prices were caught in some kind of regular pendular motion? Would they not then tend to buy at low *P*, store, and resell later at a profitable high price? Would not this speculative activity tend to wipe out the price differentials?

More advanced analysis, using the tools of "rational expectations" and dynamic analysis, shows that such effects would indeed occur under ideal speculation. The appendix to Chapter 24 shows how speculators tend to even out price fluctuations over time. And this important theory has been extended to macroeconomics by the "rational-expectations school," analyzed in detail in the appendix to Chapter 16.

SUMMARY TO APPENDIX

By way of summarizing the appendix, you should

1. Review Propositions 1 and 2 along with their corollaries.
2. Make sure you understand important cases, such as constant and increasing costs, completely inelastic supply, backward-bending supply, and shifts in both supply and demand.

CONCEPTS FOR REVIEW

price rise from *DD* increase and
  probable quantity rise
constant costs, horizontal supply
increasing costs, rising *SS*
inelastic supply, vertical *SS*, rent
backward-bending supply
increased *SS* lowering *P*

dynamic supply and demand:
  cobweb oscillations
  lagged supply
  unlagged demand
every-other-period oscillation of *P*
effects of rational speculation

QUESTIONS FOR DISCUSSION

1. For each of the following examples, decide which of the cases in this appendix apply. Use a supply-and-demand diagram to explain each of the observations.

  (a) When the federal individual income tax rate fell after 1981, a top movie star did not thereby change her labor supplied.

  (b) When a faster integrated circuit was made, computer prices fell as sales increased.

  (c) As wine became more popular, wine prices rose sharply.

  (d) Even though real wages have increased manyfold in recent decades, hours of work have fallen.

2. What is the effect of a specific tax (i.e., $X per unit) when supply is as described in each of Cases 1 through 4?

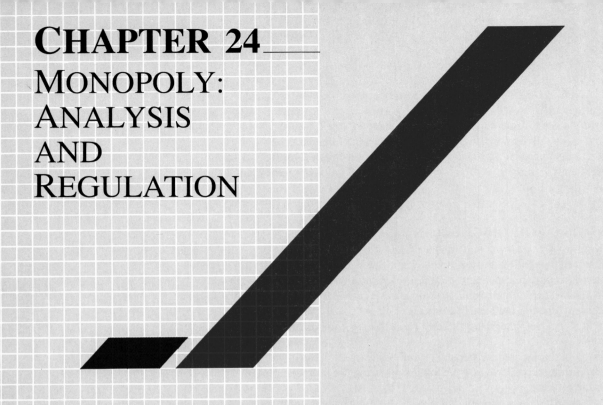

CHAPTER 24

MONOPOLY: ANALYSIS AND REGULATION

The monopolists, by keeping the market constantly understocked, . . . sell their commodities much above the natural price, and raise their emoluments, whether they consist in wages or profit . . .

Adam Smith
The Wealth of Nations

THE PRECEDING CHAPTERS analyzed the workings of competitive markets—those in which many small firms produce and sell a standardized product. Perfect competition receives a great deal of attention from economists because competitive markets achieve a remarkable degree of economic efficiency. Moreover, competitive structures are relatively easy to understand, and the supply-and-demand analysis of competition allows us to study the impact of taxes, demand changes, bad harvests, and a multitude of other real-world disturbances.

But the time has come to push beyond the world of perfect competition. We cannot act like the man who looks for his lost wallet under a lamppost because the light is better there. Most markets—whether in America, Europe, or Asia—contain significant mixtures of monopoly along with competitive elements.

This and the next chapter show how pricing and resource allocation behave in the different types of market structures—monopolistic competition, monopoly, and oligopoly. We shall see that prices are higher and outputs are lower under imperfect competition than under perfect competition. In addition, two major forms of government control of imperfect competition—regulation of business and antitrust policies—will be discussed.

A. PATTERNS OF IMPERFECT COMPETITION

Our strict definition of perfect competition is a market in which every firm is too small to affect the market price. Think of any commodity that comes to mind: automobiles, computers, electricity, cigarettes, aluminum, beer, refrigerators, wheat, or cotton. Which will fit into our strict definition of perfect competition? Certainly not beer or computers or cigarettes. Who ever heard of thousands of brewers or computer firms auctioning off their goods at the competitive Chicago Board of Trade?

Nor does the market in electricity meet the definition of perfect competition. In most towns, a single company, a monopoly, generates and markets all the electricity used by the populace.

What about aluminum or automobiles? Until World War II there was only one aluminum company, Alcoa. Even today, the four largest U.S. firms produce three-quarters of U.S. aluminum output. Aluminum would therefore be called an oligopoly, or an industry characterized by a small number of sellers. And the automobile industry is today served by a handful of giant manufacturing firms—General Motors, Ford, Toyota, and Nissan being the most important oligopolists in this industry.

Looking at the list above, you will find that only wheat and cotton fall within our strict definition of perfect competition. All the other goods, from autos to refrigerators, fail the competitive test for a simple reason: there are firms in the industry (General Motors for automobiles, IBM for computers, and so forth) that can affect the market price by selling less or more output in the market.

Imperfect Competition Defined

If a firm finds that it can appreciably affect the market price of its output, then the firm is classified as an "imperfect competitor."

Imperfect competition prevails in an industry whenever the individual sellers have some measure of control over the price of the good in that industry.

Imperfect competition does not imply that a firm has absolute control over the price of its product. To call Pepsi an imperfect competitor means that it may be able to set the price of a can at 40 or 50 cents and still remain a viable firm. The firm could hardly set the price at $40 or 0.5 cents, or it would go out of business. But an imperfect competitor has at least some discretion in its price decisions.

Moreover, the amount of discretion over price will differ from firm to firm. In some industries, the degree of monopoly power is very small. In the retail gasoline business, for example, more than a few pennies difference in price will usually have a significant effect upon a firm's sales. In the monopolistic electricity distribution business, on the other hand, changes of 10 percent or more in the price of electricity will have only a small effect on a firm's sales in the short run.

Note that the word "imperfect" does not in any way reflect upon the business ethics of the owner of such firms. Nor is there an implication that such firms are not keen rivals in the marketplace. Intense rivalry should be distinguished from perfect competition. Rivalry encompasses a wide variety of behavior, from advertising that attempts to shift out one's demand curve to inventing better products. Perfect competition says nothing about rivalry but simply denotes that every firm in the industry can sell all it wants at the prevailing market price.

Graphical Depiction Figure 24-1 shows graphically the difference between perfect and imperfect competition. Figure 24-1(a) reminds us that a perfect competitor faces a horizontal demand curve, indicating that it can sell all it wants at the going market

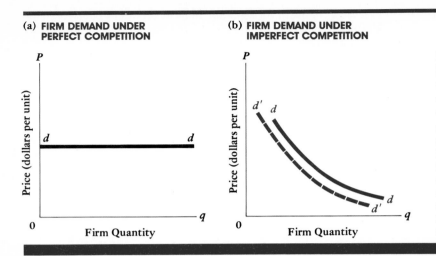

(a) FIRM DEMAND UNDER PERFECT COMPETITION

(b) FIRM DEMAND UNDER IMPERFECT COMPETITION

Figure 24-1   Acid test for imperfect competition is downward tilt of firm's demand curve

The perfectly competitive firm can sell all it wants to along its horizontal *dd* curve, never depressing market price. But the imperfect competitor will find that its demand curve slopes downward as its increased *q* forces down the *P* it can get. And unless it is a sheltered monopolist, a cut in its rivals' *P*s will appreciably shift its own demand curve leftward to *d'd'*.

price. An imperfect competitor, by contrast, faces a downward-sloping demand curve. As we see in Figure 24-1(*b*), if an imperfectly competitive firm throws more output on the market, it definitely can depress the market price of its output.

BEHAVIOR OF IMPERFECT COMPETITORS

In analyzing imperfect competition, we will examine the different kinds of market imperfections, the sources of these imperfections, and the most commonly used measures of market power.

Varieties of Imperfect Competition

Let's begin by surveying the principal kinds of market structures. The *market structure* of an industry denotes the organizational characteristics of an industry, of which the most important are the number and size of the sellers, the extent of concentration and collusion among the firms, and the degree of homogeneity or heterogeneity of their products.

Monopoly How imperfect can imperfect competition get? The extreme case would be that of a single seller with complete control over an industry. (It is called a "monopolist," from the Greek words *mono* for

"one" and *polist* for "seller.") It is the only one producing in its industry, and there is no industry producing a close substitute for its good.

Exclusive monopolies are rare today. Only in the case of franchised local services—local telephone, gas, water, and electricity being the major examples—is there truly a single seller of a service with no close substitutes. But even these isolated examples must reckon with competition from other industries—with cellular telephone for cable phones, with other fuels for electricity or gas. No firm is completely secure from attack by competitors in the long run.

Oligopoly We have seen that this word means "few sellers." Oligopolists are of two types.

First, an oligopolist may be one of a few sellers that produce an identical (or almost identical) product. If A's steel delivered in the Pittsburgh area is much the same as B's, then the smallest price cut by B will drive the consumer from A to B. Neither A nor B can be called a monopolist. Yet, if the number of sellers is few, each can have a great effect on market price.

This first kind of oligopoly is common in a number of the basic industries where the product is fairly homogeneous and the size of enterprise is large—as in the aluminum and oil industries. The airline industry today is oligopolistic, for only a few carriers travel between most cities. In this unregulated market, there are periodic price wars in which one airline undercuts the other in an attempt to gain more of the market in this relatively homogeneous product.

The second kind of oligopoly is typified by the industry where there are few sellers of differentiated products. Goods are said to be *differentiated* when their valued characteristics or qualities vary. The automobile industry sells differentiated products because cars have numerous distinguishing characteristics (size, power, fuel economy, durability, and safety). Indeed, we can say that every distinct automotive product (e.g., Buick Regal) is differentiated from every other product (e.g., Nissan Maxima). Differentiation of products occurs in virtually all consumer commodities, including refrigerators and ice creams, shirts and jeans, pop singers and baseball teams, medical care and legal advice.

While the differentiated products of oligopolists are distinct, they are nonetheless close substitutes. Without being identical, Buicks compete sharply with Lincolns in the luxury-car market while Canon and Minolta vie for market shares in cameras. Oligopoly is competition among the few, but the competition can be very brisk indeed.

Many Differentiated Sellers In this last category of imperfect competition, usually called **monopolistic competition,** a large number of sellers produce differentiated products. This case resembles perfect competition in that there are many sellers, none of whom have a large share of the market. It differs from perfect competition in that the products are differentiated rather than identical.

The classic case of monopolistic competition is the retail gasoline market. I may go to the local Exxon station because it is a bit more convenient and clean or because I think its tanks are free of dirt and water. But it is only one of a number of gas stations, and I am sensitive to the gasoline prices at Exxon and other neighboring stations. If the price at Exxon gets more than a few pennies above the competition, I'll move to the unbranded station a short distance away.

We see here, then, imperfect competition among the many. The only difference between this industry and one in perfect competition is that the commodity here is slightly differentiated. What are the sources of product differentiation in these monopolistically competitive industries? Generally, these industries tend to

be populated by retail outlets doing small volumes of business and serving many customers. The major source of differentiation arises from location: because people want to economize on the time it takes to drive to a store, they prefer nearby locations. In addition, there are differences in quality (as in the crispness of French fries), in brands or trademarks (as in soft drinks), or in styling (as in clothing). Often, custom, familiarity, or inertia leads customers to prefer one seller over another.

We must emphasize that, while the forces of differentiation may be powerful, the product's price will ultimately play a pivotal role in consumer choice. Even though Pop's Grocery Store has a loyal clientele, if Pop's prices are much higher than those of other stores, for an equivalent quality of service, Pop's customers will eventually become disaffected and will move to a lower-priced store. Many a firm has come to ruin because it neglected the fact of business life that the best service a firm can perform is to provide high-quality goods at low prices.

Table 24-1 gives a picture of the various possible categories of imperfect and perfect competition; this table is vitally important and warrants careful study. Note, however, that all these many categories of market structure overlap. They range from perfect competition to monopolistic competition to oligopoly to pure monopoly, and the exact point on the spectrum where an industry falls may be unclear. Often, particularly when legal disputes arise, lawyers will disagree as to whether a particular market is monopolistic or oligopolistic, or whether the degree of product differentiation is high or low. In some important antitrust cases, the answers to these questions have determined the fate of a giant firm.

Sources of Market Imperfections

Why do certain industries display near-perfect competition while others are dominated by a handful of large firms? Fundamentally, imperfect competition arises when an industry's output is supplied by a small number of firms. The two major sources of imperfect competition are cost conditions and barriers to competition. When there are significant economies of large-scale production, the large firms can simply produce more cheaply and undersell small firms so

TYPES OF MARKET STRUCTURES

STRUCTURE	NUMBER OF PRODUCERS AND DEGREE OF PRODUCT DIFFERENTIATION	PART OF ECONOMY WHERE PREVALENT	FIRM'S DEGREE OF CONTROL OVER PRICE	METHODS OF MARKETING
Perfect competition	Many producers; identical products	A few raw agricultural products (wheat, corn, . . .)	None	Market exchange or auction
Imperfect competition				
Many differentiated sellers (monopolistic competition)	Many producers; many real or perceived differences in product	Retail trade (food, gasoline, . . .)		
Oligopoly	Few producers; little or no difference in product	Steel, chemicals	Some	Advertising and quality rivalry; administered prices
	Few producers; some differentiation of products	Autos, computers		
Complete monopoly	Single producer; product without close substitutes	Local telephone, electricity, and gas utilities ("natural monopolies")	Considerable, but usually regulated	Advertising and service promotion

Table 24-1   Most industries are imperfectly competitive—a blend of monopoly and competition

the latter cannot survive. Thus when pervasive economies of scale exist, we may find few sellers.

Similarly, when a product receives patent protection (Polaroid), when a firm has a well-established brand image (Coke), or when regulatory barriers preclude competition (Duke Light and Power)—in such cases, imperfect competition may arise.

Let's examine both sources of imperfection.

Cost Patterns and Structure of Market Imperfection

If every product could be made by every person at equal and constant costs, we would all be able to provide our entire basket of consumables, and we would have no need for giant industrial firms. But the world is not made that way. If you imagine how much time it would take you to build the simplest car or television—starting from nothing more than iron ore, copper, and sand—then you can quickly understand the importance of large-scale production, large firms, and imperfect competition.

Our first hint as to the reasons behind imperfect competition lies in the existence of economies of scale or declining average costs. The interaction between costs and markets is illustrated in Figure 24-2.

In Figure 24-2(a), the firm is shown to have average and marginal costs that fall forever. It displays perpetual increasing returns to scale. As q grows, the firm finds more elaborate ways of specializing its equipment; it organizes its work teams in larger and more efficient units; it can afford ever-larger boilers and machines, which display greater net efficiency. All this without end.

No matter how big is the demand for its product—

no matter how far out the industry demand curve *(DD)* happens to lie—the most efficient operating size for this one firm would be greater still. And so peaceful competitive coexistence of thousands of perfect competitors will be quite impossible. This is the case of natural monopoly (to be further analyzed later in this chapter).

A second case would occur when all the economies of scale have been used up and a firm's cost curves level out or turn up; Figure 24-2(*b*) shows such a case. Note, however, that the *AC* curve did not turn up soon enough to avoid the breakdown of perfect competition: the industry total demand curve *DD* does not provide a big enough market to enable numerous firms to coexist at the efficient level of operation called for by the indicated cost curve. We shall still end up in a situation in which few sellers compete, which is called oligopoly.

In Figure 24-2(*c*) the outlook is more favorable for perfect competition. Why? This industry is character-ized by a demand and cost structure in which the industry can support the large number of efficiently operating firms that are needed for perfect competition.

The relationship between scale economies and imperfections has been intensively studied by industrial-organization economists over the last three decades. Table 24-2 shows the results of one particularly careful study of six U.S. industries. It suggests that economies of scale lie behind some of the concentration of industry today. But economies of scale are only part of the reason for the current concentration of American firms today; a large margin of imperfection is still unexplained by such studies.

Barriers to Competition

Although cost differences are the most important factor behind market structures, other forces enter as

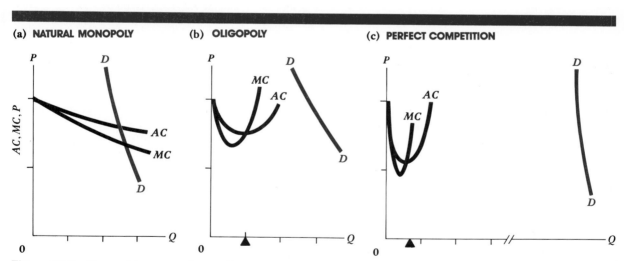

Figure 24-2 To avoid monopoly or oligopoly, average costs must turn upward soon enough

Different cost and demand conditions lead to different market structures. When costs fall indefinitely, as in the case of natural monopoly in **(a)**, one firm can expand to monopolize the industry. In **(b)**, costs eventually turn up, but not soon enough relative to total industry demand *DD*. Coexistence of numerous perfect competitors is impossible; some kind of few-seller oligopoly is likely. In **(c)**, total industry demand *DD* is so vast relative to efficient scale of any one seller as to permit viable coexistence of numerous perfect competitors. Here we have perfect competition. [What if firms contrive to differentiate their product in **(c)**, fragmenting the market and moving *DD* far to the left? They may end up in some kind of imperfect competition—like **(b)** or **(a)**.]

INDUSTRY	(1) SHARE OF U.S. OUTPUT NEEDED BY A SINGLE FIRM TO EXPLOIT ECONOMIES OF SCALE (%)	(2) ACTUAL AVERAGE MARKET SHARE OF TOP THREE FIRMS (%)	(3) MAIN REASON FOR ECONOMIES OF LARGE-SCALE OPERATIONS
Beer brewing	10–14	13	Need to create a national brand image and to coordinate investment
Cigarettes	6–12	23	Advertising and image differentiation
Glass bottles	4–6	22	Need for central engineering and design staff
Cement	2	7	Need to spread risk and raise capital
Refrigerators	14–20	21	Marketing requirements and length of production runs
Petroleum refining	4–6	8	Spread risk on crude oil ventures and coordinate investment

Table 24-2   Economies of scale drive many industries toward concentration

In a path-breaking study, a number of products were studied to see whether the nature of the technology could lie behind existing concentration patterns. Column (1) shows the estimate of the point where the long-run average cost curve begins to turn up, as a share of output. Compare this with the average market share of the top three firms in column (2). [Source: F. M. Scherer, Alan Beckenstein, Erich Kaufer, and R. D. Murphy, *The Economics of Multi-Plant Operation: An International Comparisons Study* (Harvard University Press, Cambridge, Mass., 1975).]

well, particularly barriers to competition.[1] We can illustrate the point with reference to Table 24-2. According to those estimates, the top three cigarette firms would each need 6 to 12 percent of the national market to attain the minimum efficient scale of operation. But the actual market share of the top three firms was, on average, 23 percent of the national market. Aside from cost factors, what could account for the large actual share of the top firms?

One important answer lies in barriers to competition:

A **barrier to competition** arises when legal restrictions or product differentiation reduces the number of

---

[1] Another term often encountered is "barriers to entry." We have chosen to stress barriers to competition because the restrictions on the intensity of competition discussed below do not always relate to entry. The treatment here emphasizes the distinction between cost-based forces (declining average costs) and noneconomic (legal or psychological) factors leading to concentration of industry.

competitors below the number that would survive on the basis of efficient cost structures alone.

Legal Restrictions In many situations, governments undertake to restrict competition in certain industries. Important legal restrictions include patents, entry restrictions, and foreign-trade tariffs and quotas.

Patents are a very special form of legal restriction to entry. A patent is granted to an inventor to allow a temporary exclusive (or monopoly) use of the product or process that is patented. Thus Polaroid has an absolute monopoly over the market for instant cameras because of patent protection. Why would governments grant patent monopolies? Patents are granted to encourage inventive activity and are particularly beneficial to small firms and individuals. Without the prospect of monopoly protection, a lone inventor might despair of ever profiting from years devoted to the endless search for better products or processes.

Governments also impose *entry or exit restrictions* on many industries. As we will see in section C below, franchise monopolies are often granted to local utilities in water, electricity, natural gas, and telephone. Governments believe that these franchises are useful in industries that have sharply falling average costs; in return for such a franchise monopoly, firms allow governments to regulate their prices and business operations. As in the case of patents, such restrictions may be a net plus for the economy, but they are undoubtedly very powerful barriers to competition and support concentration. Thus for many years AT&T used government-authorized entry barriers to prevent competitors from entering the long-distance telephone industry—a practice we will return to in next chapter's discussion of antitrust.

The final example of legal restrictions has less economic rationale. Suppose an industry will support perfect competition, the case illustrated in Figure 24-2(c), but all governments impose high tariffs or quotas on foreign producers. Exclusion of many foreign suppliers and buyers from the market will prevent perfect competition from taking hold. The new industry DD curves in each country will reflect only domestic and not world markets, so the DD curves move far to the left. A protectionist regime moves us from Figure 24-2(c) to 24-2(b) or even to 24-2(a). American historians know this point well, as is shown by their saying, "The tariff is the mother of trusts." A classic example of broadening the market was the European Common Market, which lowered tariffs, encouraged market integration, and thereby promoted vigorous and effective competition.

This brief discussion just touches on a key topic in public policy. The concept of barriers to competition is widely used in areas outside economics, particularly modern antitrust practice.

Product Differentiation In addition to legally imposed barriers to competition, there are economic barriers as well. The major hurdle for potential competitors is the pervasive presence of product differentiation that we discussed above.

Consider as an example the case of automobiles. The major industrial countries currently have among them more than a dozen large companies producing automobiles. Moreover, because transportation costs are low relative to selling prices, we might expect nearly perfect competition in this market.

In fact, because of product differentiation, the barriers to competition are relatively high. Some sources of product differentiation are natural: British cars, with steering wheels on the right side, have a hard time attracting American drivers. Similarly, giant American cars sell poorly in countries with narrow streets and tiny parking spaces. Other sources of product differentiation appear quite contrived. In the 1950s, cars with enormous tail fins, boosted by advertising that associated horsepower with manliness and power, were the darling of consumers. Today, German luxury cars command a premium, as do their look-alikes.

How does product differentiation, whether natural or contrived, impose a barrier and increase the degree of monopoly? The impact is that the DD curves of Figure 24-2(c)'s model of perfect competition are contracted so far to the left as to become like those of the models of monopoly or oligopoly shown in Figure 24-2(a) and (b). That is, the total demand for a product like autos or soft drinks will be fragmented into many smaller markets for differentiated products. The demands for these differentiated products will be so small that they will not be able to support a large number of firms operating at the bottom of their U-shaped cost curves. Hence, differentiation, like tariffs, leads to greater concentration and more imperfect competition.

To summarize, when an industry shows pervasive economies of scale, so that the most efficient scale of a firm's production comes at a significant fraction of industry demand, perfect competition is in peril. In such situations, a few firms will supply most of the industry's output. Imperfections rising from declining costs are accentuated by barriers to competition, such as legal restrictions on competition or product differentiation.

Measuring Market Power

In terms of market organization, industries fall along a spectrum from perfect competition to pure monopoly. In many situations, particularly in assessing whether public-policy steps are needed to curb market power, it is useful to have a quantitative measure of

**CONCENTRATION MEASURED BY VALUE OF SHIPMENTS
IN MANUFACTURING INDUSTRIES, 1982**

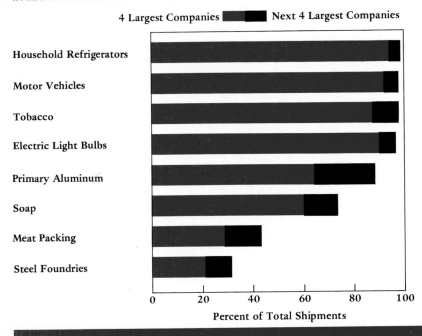

Figure 24-3 **Numerous industries are dominated by a very few sellers: the case of oligopoly**

For refrigerators, motor vehicles, and many other industries, a few firms get most of the business. Compare this with the ideal of perfect competition, in which each firm is too small to affect the market price. (Source: U.S. Bureau of the Census, 1982 data.)

the extent of market power, or the degree of monopoly. **Market power** signifies the degree of control that a single firm or a small number of firms has over the price and production decisions in an industry.

Concentration Ratios The most commonly used measure of market power is the "concentration ratio" for an industry, illustrated in Figure 24-3. The **four-firm concentration ratio** is defined as the percent of total industry·output (or shipments) that is accounted for by the largest four firms. Similarly, the eight-firm concentration ratio is the percent of output shipped by the top eight firms. In a pure monopoly, the four- or eight-firm concentration ratio would be 100 percent, while for perfect competition, both ratios would be close to zero.

How concentrated is American manufacturing? For 1977, data show that about one-fifth of manufacturing output takes place in highly concentrated industries (those with four-firm concentration ratios above 60

percent), while another fifth resides in unconcentrated industries (those with four-firm concentration ratios less than 20 percent).

Economists keep an eye on the historical trends in overall concentration. Data for the 1947–1972 period suggest that there has been a very slight increase in the average four-firm concentration ratio for domestic manufacturing output, from 37 percent in 1947 to 38 percent in 1972. These figures certainly overstate the trends in the growth of concentration, however, for they exclude the increasingly intense foreign competition in American markets. Recent studies of many industries indicate that, when foreign firms are included in concentration measures, concentration ratios have been declining in recent years.

The Herfindahl Index[2] Some economists believe that the traditional concentration ratios do not adequately measure the impact of firm size on market

[2] Short courses may skip to the next section.

power. Suppose industry T, call it long-distance telecommunications, has a 100 percent four-firm concentration with one giant monopoly. A second industry, A, call it airlines, also has a 100 percent concentration ratio, but this is made up of four equally large firms. Most economists believe that the extent of market power would be much greater in industry T than in industry A.

A measure which attempts to reflect the effect of the size differences is the **Herfindahl index,** or *H,* which is equal to the sum of the squared market shares in percentage terms:

$$H = \sum_{i=1}^{n} S_i^2 = S_1^2 + S_2^2 + \cdots$$

where S_i is the percentage market share of the ith firm. When the industry is a pure monopoly, the Herfindahl index is $H = 100^2 = 10,000$, while if an industry is perfectly competitive, the Herfindahl index is $H = 0$. (In the example of the last paragraph, show that the Herfindahl index is much greater for the industry with one large firm than for the industry with four small firms. More precisely, the *H*-index for industry T is 10,000 while that of industry A is 2500.)

The Herfindahl index is sometimes used in examining the impacts of mergers and acquisitions. In 1982, the U.S. Department of Justice proposed a set of merger guidelines that depended heavily upon the Herfindahl index for determining whether a proposed merger was acceptable. We will discuss these rules further in section C of Chapter 25.

Although the measures of concentration discussed here are widely used in economic and legal analysis, they are not infallible indicators of market power. Such indexes are customarily applied to a narrow industry definition, such as microcomputers (personal computers). Sometimes, however, the industry definitions are inappropriate, and strong competition can come from other narrow industries, as when minicomputers compete with microcomputers. Sometimes the threat of entry of foreign competition will keep the firms in a concentrated industry from exercising market power. Care must therefore be used to interpret quantitative indexes of market power appropriately.

B. ANALYSIS OF MONOPOLY

Now that we have described the different species of imperfect competitors, this section analyzes the behavior of a monopolist—i.e., one that sells the entire output of an industry. In undertaking this analysis, we will find a new concept, marginal revenue, essential for describing the equilibrium output and price. But this new concept will also apply more broadly to the analysis of oligopoly in the next chapter, as well as to our understanding of public policies toward big business, such as regulation and antitrust laws.

Price, Quantity, and Total Revenue

Let's say that a firm finds itself in possession of a complete monopoly in an industry. The firm might be the fortunate owner of a patent for a new anticancer drug, or it might have an exclusive franchise to sell a service like cable television. If the monopolist wishes to maximize its profits, what price should it charge? What output level should it produce?

To answer these questions, we need to compare the costs of production with the revenues from production. More precisely, we need to calculate the change in profits that occurs when production increases; we will see that this calculation is made by comparing the marginal cost of additional output with the marginal revenue of additional sales.

As far as analysis of costs is concerned, we have developed all the relevant concepts in Chapter 22, where we met *TC, AC, MC,* and so forth. We now develop an analysis of the major revenue concepts. From the firm's demand curve, we know the relationship between price *(P)* and quantity sold *(q):* Table 24-3 shows the relationship for a hypothetical monopolist in column (2), while Figure 24-4 depicts, in black, the demand curve *(dd)* for the monopolist.

We now extend that analysis to estimate the impact of quantity sold on total revenue $(P \times q)$. Column (3) of Table 24-3 shows how to calculate the **total revenue** *(TR),* which is simply *P* times *q.* Thus 0 units

TOTAL AND MARGINAL REVENUE

(1) QUANTITY q	(2) PRICE P = AR = TR/q	(3) TOTAL REVENUE TR = P × q	(4) MARGINAL REVENUE MR
0	$200	$ 0	+$200
			+180
1	180	180	+160
			+140
2	160	320	+120
			+100
3	140	420	+80
			+40
4	120	480	+20
			0
5	100	500	−20
			−40
6	80	480	−60
			−80
7	60	___	−100
			−140
8	40	320	−160
			−180
9	___	180	
10	0	0	

Table 24-3   Marginal revenue numbers can be derived from demand-schedule P and q data

First, total revenue comes from multiplying P times q. To get marginal revenue, we increase q by a unit and calculate the difference in total revenue it brings. Note MR is at first positive, but after demand turns inelastic, MR becomes negative even though price never becomes negative. MR lies below P because of loss due to the necessity to lower price on previous units if the new unit of q is to get sold. [Light red data of marginal revenue come from smoothed MR curve in Fig. 24-4(a).]

bring in TR of 0; 1 unit brings in TR = $180 × 1 = $180; 2 units bring in $160 × 2 = $320; and so forth.

In this example of a straight-line or linear demand curve, total revenue at first rises with output, since the reduction in P needed to sell the extra q is moderate in this first elastic range of the demand curve. But when we reach the midpoint of the straight-line demand curve, TR reaches its maximum. This comes at q = 5, P = $100, with TR = $500. Increasing q beyond this point brings you into inelastic demand regions, and now the percentage cut in P needed to sell

1 percent more q is so much greater than 1 that a price cut lowers TR. Figure 24-4(b) shows TR to be dome-shaped, rising from zero to a maximum of $500 and falling back to zero when P has become vanishingly small.

Already Table 24-3 illustrates an important fallacy: "A firm out to maximize its profits will always charge what the traffic will bear. That means charging the highest possible price." This statement is incorrect. As a profit maximizer you may not be an altruist. But that does not mean you are a fool. To

(a) MARGINAL REVENUE

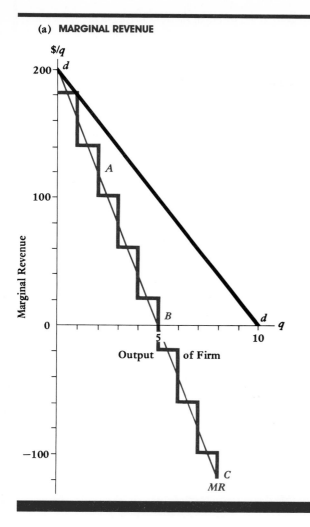

(b) TOTAL REVENUE

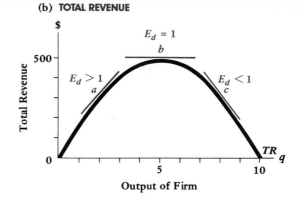

Figure 24-4   Marginal revenue curve comes from demand curve

(a) The red steps show the increments of total revenue from each new unit of output as calculated from Table 24-3 [or from the *TR* of Fig. 24-4(*b*)]. *MR* falls below *P* from the beginning, actually dropping twice as fast as the straight-line *dd* curve. *MR* becomes negative when *dd* turns inelastic. Smoothing the incremental steps of *MR* gives the smooth, thin red *MR* curve, which in the case of straight-line *dd* will always have twice as steep a slope as *dd*. [NOTE: These values from smoothed *MR* are the same as the light red numbers in column (4) of Table 24-3.]
(b) Total revenue is dome-shaped—rising from zero (where *q* = 0) to a maximum (where *dd* has unitary elasticity), and then falling back to zero (where *P* = 0). *TR*'s slope gives instantaneous smoothed *MR* just as jumps in *TR* give steps of incremental *MR*.

charge the highest possible price is to sell no *q* at all and to get no revenue at all.

Even if we reinterpret this doctrine to mean charging the highest price at which anything at all can be sold, it is obvious that selling but 1 unit even at a high price is not the way to maximize your profit. If we neglect for a moment all costs, the correct interpretation of charging what the traffic will bear must mean that we find the best compromise between a high *P* and a high *q*.

Back in Table 24-3, it is at *q* = 5 that $P \times q = TR$ is at a maximum. This is the point where demand elasticity turns into demand inelasticity. Thus, if a

monopolist had no costs of production, it would sell, not at the maximum price, but at the price where *TR* is maximal, or where the demand elasticity turns from greater than one to exactly one.

Before proceeding to introduce the important concept of marginal revenue, we can note the fact that the price per unit can be called average revenue *(AR)* to distinguish it from total revenue. Thus, we get *P* = *AR* by dividing *TR* by *q* (just as we earlier got *AC* by dividing *TC* by *q*). Verify that if column (3) had been written down *before* column (2), we could then have filled in column (2) by division. To test your understanding, fill in the blanks of columns (2) and (3).

Marginal Revenue and Price

To find the highest-profit equilibrium of the monopolist, we need to measure the impact of selling an extra unit of output on total revenue. Marginal revenue is the convenient concept for this purpose.

Marginal revenue is the increment in total revenue (plus or minus) that comes when output increases by 1 unit.

The red numbers of marginal revenue are shown in column (4) of Table 24-3. Here is how they are calculated. Subtract the *TR* we get by selling *q* units from the *TR* we get by selling *q* + 1 units. The difference will be our extra revenue or *MR*. Thus, from *q* = 0 to *q* = 1, we get *MR* = $180 − 0. From *q* = 1 to *q* = 2, *MR* is $320 − $180 = $140.

MR is positive until we arrive at *q* = 5, and negative from then on. That does not mean you are giving goods away at a negative price. Actually, average revenue—which is another name for *P*—continues to be positive. It is merely that in order to sell the sixth unit of *q*, you must reduce the price so much on the first 5 units as to end up getting less *TR* than before—which is what the negative *MR* is telling you.

This warns us not to confuse marginal revenue with average revenue or price. The table shows they are different. Scrutinize Figure 24-4(*a*) to note that the plotted red steps of *MR* definitely lie below the black *dd* curve of *AR*. In fact, *MR* will have already turned negative when *AR* is only partway down toward zero.

Let's review why *MR* is definitely less than *P* (or *AR*) for the imperfect competitor. True, I sell my last unit of output at *P*. But what did I have to do to coax out that last unit of sale? Clearly, I had to lower my price, since I didn't face a perfect competitor's horizontal demand curve. But in lowering my price for the last new buyer, I also had to lower the price for all the previous buyers. So my extra revenue, my *MR*, is evidently less than price by this loss on previous units from the price drop.

To summarize:

With demand sloping downward,

$$P > MR \ (= P - \text{loss on all previous } q)$$

In column (4) of Table 24-3, the light red numbers of *MR* are also seen to be less than the *P*s in column (2).

Only under perfect competition, where the sale of extra units will never depress price, is the term "loss on all previous *q*" equal to zero. Only then will price and marginal revenue be identical. Hence a perfect competitor's *dd* curve and its *MR* curve coincide as horizontal lines.

Elasticity and Marginal Revenue What is the relationship between the price elasticity of demand and marginal revenue?

Marginal revenue is positive when demand is elastic, zero when demand is unit-elastic, and negative when demand is inelastic.

This result is really a different way of restating the definition of elasticity we used in Chapter 18. Recall that demand is elastic when a price decrease leads to a revenue increase. In such a situation, a price decrease raises output demanded so much that revenues rise, so that marginal revenue is positive. For example, in Table 24-3, as price falls in the elastic region from *P* = $180 to *P* = $160, output demanded rises sufficiently to raise total revenue, so marginal revenue is positive.

What happens when demand is unit-elastic? A price cut is then just matched by an increase in output so marginal revenue is zero. Can you see why marginal revenue is always negative in the inelastic range? Why is the marginal revenue for the perfect competitor's infinitely elastic demand curve always positive?

This completes our analysis of marginal revenue and equips us for the task of finding the maximum-profit equilibrium of the monopolist.

Point of Maximum Profit

Suppose that the monopolist wants to maximize its total profits *(TP)*. By definition total profits = total revenues − total costs. In symbols, *TP = TR − TC = (P × q) − TC*.

To maximize its profits, the firm must find the equilibrium price and quantity, *P** and *q**, that give the largest profit, or the largest difference between *TR* and *TC*. Some reflection will tell us that this *maximum profit will occur when output has expanded to just the point where the firm's marginal revenue is equal to its marginal cost.*

SUMMARY OF FIRM'S MAXIMUM PROFIT

(1) QUANTITY q	(2) PRICE P	(3) TOTAL REVENUE TR	(4) TOTAL COST TC	(5) TOTAL PROFIT TP	(6) MARGINAL REVENUE MR	(7) MARGINAL COST MC	
0	200	0	145	−145	+200	34	
					+180	30	$MR > MC$
1	180	180	175	+5	+160	27	
					+140	25	
2	160	320	200	+120	+120	22	
					+100	20	
3	140	420	220	+200	+80	21	
					+60	30	
4*	120	480	250	+230	+40	40	$MR = MC$
					+20	50	
5	100	500	300	+200	0	60	
					−20	70	
6	80	480	370	+110	−40	80	
					−60	90	
7	60	420	460	−40	−80	100	
					−100	110	$MR < MC$
8	40	320	570	−250			

*Maximum-profit equilibrium.

Table 24-4   Equating marginal cost to marginal revenue gives firm's maximum-profit q and P

Total and marginal cost of production is now brought together with total and marginal revenue. The maximum-profit decision is where $MR = MC$, with $q^* = 4$, $P^* = \$120$, and maximum profit $TP = \$230 = (\$120 \times 4) - \$250$. (NOTE: For convenience, the light MR and MC numbers are put in to give the smoothed instantaneous values at each q point itself.)

The first way to see this maximum-profit condition is in a table of costs and revenues, Table 24-4. What quantity and price will maximize total profit? The easiest way to solve this problem is to compute total profit in column (5). This column tells us that the optimal quantity, which is 4 units, requires a price of $120 per unit. This produces a total revenue of $480, and, after subtracting total costs of $250, we calculate total profit to be $230. A glance at other prices and quantities shows that no other combination has as high a level of total profit.

A second way of arriving at the same answer is to compare marginal revenue, column (6), and marginal cost, column (7). (Recall that MR is computed from the TR data in Table 24-3, while MC is calculated from TC in the manner shown in Chapter 22.)

As long as each additional unit of output provides more revenue than it costs—that is to say, as long as MR is greater than MC—the firm's profit is increasing. So the firm would continue to increase its output as long as MR is greater than MC. By contrast, suppose that at a given level of output MR is less than MC. This means that increasing output would lead to *lower* profits, so the profit-maximizing firm should at that point cut back on output. Clearly the best-profit point then comes at the point where marginal revenue exactly equals marginal cost, as is shown by the data in Table 24-4.

The maximum-profit price and quantity of a monopolist comes where its marginal revenue equals its marginal cost:

$MR = MC$, at the maximum-profit P^* and q^*

This second way of finding the optimum point, by

comparing marginal cost and marginal revenue, is neither better nor worse than the first way of examining total profits. They give exactly the same answer.

We see from the examples the logical correctness of the $MC = MR$ rule as a guide to maximizing profits. What is the intuition? Look for a moment at Table 24-4 and suppose that the monopolist is producing $q = 2$. At that point, its MR for producing 1 full additional unit is $+100$, while its MC is 20. Thus, if it produced one additional unit, the firm would make additional profits of $MR - MC = 100 - 20 = 80$. And, indeed, if we look at column (5) of Table 24-4, we see just that same figure for the amount of extra profit gained by moving from 2 to 3 units.

Thus when MR exceeds MC, additional profits can be made by increasing output; when MC exceeds MR, additional profits can be made by decreasing q. Only when $MR = MC$ are there no potential profits to be made by changing output, so the firm is at the level of output that maximizes profits.

Graphical Depiction of Monopoly

We first derived the major tools needed for analysis of a monopolist's behavior. Then we examined the conditions for profit maximization. Turn now to a graphical depiction of monopoly equilibrium.

Figure 24-5 shows monopoly equilibrium. In Figure 24-5(a), MC intersects MR at E, the maximum-profit point, where $q^* = 4$. We run up vertically from E to the DD curve at G, where $P = \$120$. The fact that G lies above F, the point on the AC curve at $q^* = 4$, guarantees a positive profit. [We cannot read directly the amount of total profit unless we calculate the red shaded area in Figure 24-5(a).]

The same story is told in Figure 24-5(b) with total curves. Total revenue is dome-shaped. Total cost is ever rising. The vertical difference between them is total profit, which begins negative and ends negative. In between, TP is positive, reaching its maximum of $\$230$ at $q^* = 4$, where the red slopes of TR and TC are equal and parallel. If these MR and MC slopes were pointing outward in a nonparallel fashion (as at $q = 2$), we should gain a little extra profit by expanding q. At $q^* = 4$, marginal cost and marginal revenue are balanced. At that point total profit (*TP*) reaches its

maximum as an additional unit adds exactly equal amounts to costs and revenues.

In sum, a monopolist will maximize its profits by setting output at the point where $MC = MR$. Because the monopolist has a downward-sloping demand curve, this means that $P > MR$, reflecting the fact that, to sell the last unit, the monopolist had to lower the price on earlier units. In maximizing profits, the monopolist reduces output below the competitive level; price is therefore above marginal cost.

Perfect Competition as a Polar Case of Imperfect Competition

We have now completed our analysis of the concept of marginal revenue; we have seen that the equality of MC and MR is the key rule for a monopolist who desires to maximize profits.

Actually, this rule extends in importance far beyond the analysis of monopoly. A little thought shows that the $MC = MR$ rule applies with equal validity to a profit-maximizing perfect competitor. Here is why:

For a perfect competitor, marginal revenue works out to be exactly the same thing as price. With no need to cut your P to sell an extra unit of q, the marginal revenue it brings you is precisely the P received for that last unit, with no loss on previous units being subtracted. Hence, $P = MR$ does lead to the special rule for profit maximizing by a perfect competitor:

Because a perfect competitor can sell all it wants at the market price,

$$P = MR$$

at the maximum-profit point.

You can see this result visually by redrawing Figure 24-5(a). If this applied to a perfect competitor, then the DD curve would be horizontal and it would coincide with the MR curve. Proceed to find the profit-maximizing $MR = MC$ intersection, which would also come at $P = MC$.[3] We see then how the general

---

[3] If you redraw Fig. 24-5(a) for a perfect competitor, make dd horizontal and coinciding with MR. Then proceed to find the MR and MC intersection as usual (which gives the old MC supply story of Chapter 23). In this new version, Fig. 24-5(b)'s TR merely becomes a straight line, rising from the origin. But the slopes of TR and TC must still match at the maximum-profit equilibrium point.

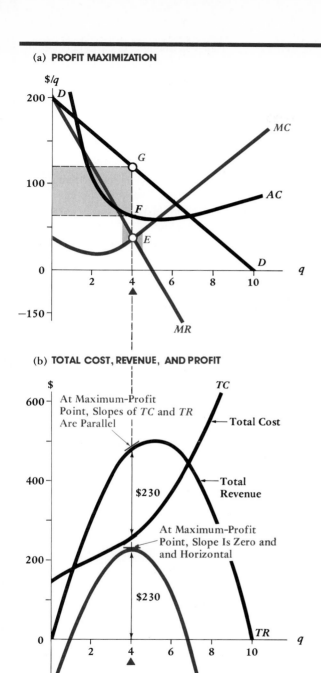

(a) **PROFIT MAXIMIZATION**

(b) **TOTAL COST, REVENUE, AND PROFIT**

Figure 24-5   Profit-maximizing equilibrium can be shown using either marginal or total curves

(a) At *E*, where *MC* intersects *MR*, equilibrium position of maximum profit is found. Any move from *E* will lose some profit. Price is at G above *E*; and since *P* is above *AC*, the maximized profit is a positive profit. (Can you understand why the shaded red rectangle measures total profit? And why the gray triangle of shading on either side of *E* shows the reduction in total profit that would come from a departure from *MR = MC*—i.e., the greater loss of extra revenue in comparison with extra cost?)

(b) This tells the same story of maximizing profit as above, but uses *total* concepts rather than *marginal* concepts. Total profit is given by vertical distance from *TC* up to *TR*. This is at a maximum where the two black total curves have equal and parallel slopes, *MR = MC*. This is necessary if red total profit curve is to be at a maximum, with its red slope horizontal as *MR* cancels out *MC*.

rule for profit maximization applies to perfect as well as imperfect competitors.

Let Bygones Be Bygones

While economic theory doesn't necessarily aim to make you a successful business executive, it does introduce you to some new ways of thinking. Here is one instance.

Economists stress the "extra," or "marginal," costs and benefits of a decision, saying:

> Let bygones be bygones. Don't look backward. Don't moan about your sunk costs. Look forward. Make a hard-headed calculation of the extra costs you'll incur by

any decision and weigh these against its extra advantages. Forget all the good things and bad things that will go on anyway, and make a decision based on future costs and benefits.

This disregarding of bygones is extremely important. Most successful decision makers practice it intuitively, even if they have not had a formal course in economics.*

C. THE COST AND CONTROL OF MONOPOLY

Section B of this chapter examined the way that profit-maximizing monopolists set their prices and quantities. It showed that the ability to control the entire market would allow a monopolist to raise its price above marginal cost, thereby reducing output below the most efficient level.

We now turn to an assessment of the practical importance of monopoly in today's economy. We begin by showing how monopoly distorts resource allocation and then provide quantitative estimates of the waste due to monopoly. We also review how public regulation of monopoly can control the price and quantity decisions of monopolists, and we conclude with a history and analysis of regulatory practices in America.

ECONOMIC COSTS OF MONOPOLY

Begin by recapitulating the major points about monopoly behavior. Monopolists face a downward-sloping demand curve and have no close competitors in the market they control. They set output at that level where the MC of production equals the MR from further sales. But MR is less than price, and so thus is MC. It is just because price exceeds MC that the monopolist will produce inefficiently—that the monopolist will not be led by an invisible hand to produce the optimal level of output. In this section, we describe in detail why a monopolist who sets price above MC causes economic inefficiency.

Deficient Output of Monopoly

To see how and why monopoly keeps q too low, imagine that all money votes are distributed properly while Monopoly Inc. is the only imperfect competitor in the system. All other industries are perfectly competitive, with MC equal to P. In this world, price is the correct economic standard or measure of scarcity: price measures both the marginal utility of consumption to households and the marginal cost of producing

---

*An important recent example of this principle related to nuclear power. In the late 1980s, about two dozen partially completed nuclear power plants dotted the landscape. Some had already absorbed billions of dollars of investment but were not yet ready to operate.

One particularly difficult case was the Shoreham plant on Long Island Sound, New York. By 1987 the owner had spent $5.5 billion on bricks, mortar, fuel rods, and interest, but the operating license had not been granted. You might ask, from a rational economic point of view,

should the plant be opened? And, more particularly, how should the $5.5 billion of past investments be weighed?

The *bygones principle would state that the $5.5 billion of past cost is irrelevant.* From an economic point of view, the only relevant issue concerns *future* costs and benefits. That is, what are the economic benefits of the electricity that Shoreham would produce? And what are the opportunity costs of producing that electricity? (To skirt the safety issue, assume that all sources of power are equally risky.)

The key to observe in making this calculation is that the sunk cost of $5.5 billion is irrelevant to future costs and benefits. Studies indicated that, if the $5.5 billion were ignored, the *future* costs of the nuclear power plant would be slightly less than the next-best alternative, even though the *total* cost (with the $5.5 billion) was far higher than the alternative. A pure economic analysis (again ignoring safety questions) would conclude that the most efficient outcome would be to open the Shoreham nuclear power plant.

goods by firms. Costs, and particularly marginal costs, are the indicators of how much of society's valuable resources each good utilizes. (If you are unsure on this, flip back to Figure 23-7 to refresh your understanding.)

Now the monopolist enters the picture. What is Monopoly Inc. doing? It is not a wicked firm—it does not force consumers to buy from it, nor does it rob old people. Rather, Monopoly Inc. exploits the fact that it is the sole seller of a good and faces a downward-sloping demand curve. It produces where MR equals MC, and consequently produces less output than where MC equals P.

In other words, Monopoly Inc. does not produce output up to the point where the social cost (as measured by MC) is equal to the value of the good to consumers (as measured by $P = MU$). Rather, the monopolist is keeping its output a little scarce. It does not produce up to the point of $P = MC$ because to do so would require lowering P to all consumers, which would lose the monopolist some profit. So society does not get as much of the monopolist's output as it wants in terms of the good's marginal cost and marginal value to consumers.

Having seen qualitatively how monopolists impose economic costs, we next turn to an analysis of the quantitative measurement of these costs.

Measure of the Waste from Monopoly

Using the tools of this and earlier chapters, we can see graphically how large the efficiency losses from monopoly turn out to be. Figure 24-6 is a simplified version of our earlier Figure 24-5(*a*). If the industry could be competitive, then the equilibrium would be reached at the point where $MC = P$, that is, at point E. Under the strict conditions of universal perfect competition and identical consumers, this industry's quantity would be 6 while the price was 100.

Now let a monopolist enter the scene, perhaps aided by tariffs, regulations, or an important patent. It would set MC equal to MR (not to industry P), displacing the equilibrium to $Q = 3$ and $P = 150$ in Figure 24-6. Thus, price is higher and quantity restricted relative to a perfectly competitive industry.

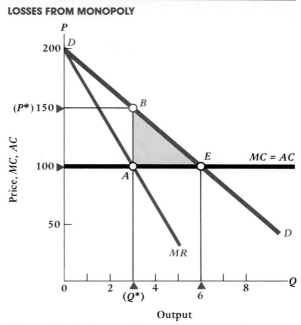

LOSSES FROM MONOPOLY

Figure 24-6   Monopolists cause economic waste by restricting output

This figure illustrates the economic loss from monopolistic pricing. Assume that all other industries and factor markets are perfectly competitive and that all consumers are alike.

Then at competitive output point E, social MC equals social MU, so welfare is maximized. At monopolist's output at point B ($Q^* = 3$ and $P^* = 150$), social MU is above social MC, and consumer surplus is lost. Adding together all the consumer-surplus losses between $Q = 3$ and $Q = 6$ leads to economic waste from monopoly equal to the red shaded area ABE.

Using our tools of consumer surplus (see Chapter 19), we can measure the loss from such an exercise of monopoly power. Recall that for each unit of quantity reduction below E, the net social loss is the vertical distance between the demand curve and the MC curve. The total loss in consumer surplus in this case is the sum of all such losses, represented by the triangle ABE in Figure 24-6. Why? Because the DD curve represents consumers' marginal utility at each level of output, while the MC curve represents the lost utility from not producing the goods of other industries. Thus at $Q = 3$, the vertical difference between B and A represents the utility that would be gained from a small increase in the output of Q. Adding up all the lost social utility from $Q = 3$ to $Q = 6$ gives the shaded region ABE.[4]

Empirical Studies of Costs of Monopoly Not content to stop with purely theoretical exercises, economists have in recent years pushed on to attempt to measure the overall costs of imperfect competition in the United States. In essence, these studies try to estimate the size of the ABE area illustrated in Figure 24-6, which represents the deadweight or net losses to society from monopoly.

An early study by Arnold Harberger calculated the costs of monopoly in manufacturing by estimating (a) the difference between MC and P and (b) the output restriction. The welfare loss is given by the area ABE, which is approximately $\frac{1}{2} \times (P - MC) \times (Q$ change as a result of monopoly). By summing the triangular welfare losses across industries, Harberger obtained an estimate of the total welfare loss from monopoly power.[5]

Harberger's finding shocked the economics community. He found the welfare loss from monopoly was slightly less than 0.1 percent of GNP. In today's economy, it would total about $5 billion. One economist quipped that, if we believe this study, economists would make a larger social contribution fighting fires and eradicating termites than attempting to curb monopolies.

Many studies have refined and criticized Harberger's original findings. Economists have questioned whether the parameters of the supply and demand curves were correctly estimated. After reviewing all these subsequent analyses, a careful recent survey concludes:

> It appears that the deadweight welfare loss attributable to monopolistic resource misallocation in the United States lies somewhere between 0.5 and 2 percent of gross national product, with the estimates nearer the lower bound inspiring more confidence than those on the high side.[6]

In addition, some critics of Harberger's approach argue that his estimates ignored the potential impact of market structure upon technical advance or "dynamic efficiency." The deadweight efficiency loss measured in Figure 24-6 assumes that the cost curves are the same for competitors and for monopolists. But studies, such as those discussed in Chapters 21 and 36, show that most of the growth in living standards arises from dynamic invention and technological change. Are sheltered monopolists the geese that lay the golden eggs of invention? Or do monopolists stifle ingenious would-be inventors? We return to this central question in next chapter's discussion of the Schumpeterian hypothesis. At this point, we simply foreshadow that discussion by observing that the impact of monopoly on dynamic innovation and technical change is likely to far outweigh any deadweight losses of the kind displayed in Figure 24-6 and analyzed by Harberger and others.

Excess Profit of Monopoly

A second aspect of imperfect competition arises because a monopolist may be earning more than it would if it were forced to compete like a perfect competitor. If so, is that excess profit a good or a bad thing? Is the monopolist more or less worthy than other firms?

When people think of the monopoly problem, they give most weight to the issue of monopoly profits—to the way that monopolists are supposed to enrich

---

[4]The loss from monopoly must be used with caution, however. First, our calculations must recognize that consumers and monopolists have divergent interests. Second, in almost all cases, monopolies arise when perfect competition would not be viable, that is, when cost curves are falling and the minimum efficient scale of plant is a sizable fraction of industry output (see pages 570–571 above). Competition would thus not be viable. When an industry is subject to declining costs, then the comparison is not with perfect competition but with a regulated monopolist, discussed later in this chapter.

[5]Arnold C. Harberger, "Monopoly and Resource Allocation," *American Economic Review* (May 1954), pp. 771–787.

[6]F. M. Scherer, *Industrial Market Structure and Economic Performance* (Rand McNally, Chicago, 1980), p. 464.

themselves at the expense of hapless consumers. The distortions of income arising from monopoly are thus the second major economic problem growing out of imperfect competition, along with distortion of prices and quantities.

INTERVENTION STRATEGIES

What are the possible ways that government can intervene to curtail the costs of monopoly? There are many, some effective, some not. The following are important approaches that have been used over the years:

1. *Taxes* have sometimes been used to alleviate the income-distribution effects. By taxing monopolies, a government can reduce monopoly profits, thereby softening some of the socially unacceptable effects of monopoly. But if taxation overcomes the objections to monopoly based on equity, it does little to reduce the distortion of output. Recall that monopolies tend to raise price too high and produce too little. A nondistorting tax drains profits but has no effect on output. If the tax is less than ideal, it is likely to push the monopolist even further from the efficient level of output—raising price and lowering output even more.

2. *Price controls* have been used in wartime (and by the Nixon administration during the early 1970s), partly as a way of containing inflation, partly as a way of keeping down prices in concentrated industries. Studies indicate that these controls are a very blunt instrument. During the 1970s, profit margins of large corporations did indeed shrink during the period of price controls. But most economists feel that numerous distortions and subterfuges undermined the overall impact of the price controls: the period of price controls during the 1970s witnessed shortages of gasoline when its price was set too low, and shortages also cropped up for beef, natural gas, and even indispensables like toilet paper. To place the entire economy under price controls to curtail a few monopolists is like destroying the entire garden to kill a few chinch bugs. Few economists today advocate general price controls to curtail the economic power of monopoly.

3. *Government ownership* of monopolies has been an approach widely used outside the United States, but infrequently used here. In some industries (telephone, water, gas, electricity), it is thought that efficient production can occur only when firms have a monopoly or near-monopoly. In such cases, the real dilemma is whether to impose government ownership or government regulation on such firms. Studies of these industries indicate that, in Western countries, both approaches work well—the quality of nationalized Swedish or Japanese telephone service approached that of the privately owned system in the United States before the breakup of the Bell System's monopoly; and state-owned railroads in Western Europe are models of efficiency compared to private U.S. lines that are often run-down and behind schedule. The choice between regulation and public ownership, then, may depend more on a nation's history and institutions than on clear economic advantage.

The first three approaches to the monopoly problem are rarely used in the United States. Instead, the United States has developed two particular forms of public policy: regulation and antitrust policy.

4. Over the last 100 years, American government has evolved a new tool for government control of industry in the form of *regulation*. Economic regulation allows specialized regulatory agencies to oversee the prices, outputs, entry, and exit of firms in regulated industries; it pervades public utilities, transportation, and financial markets. It is, in effect, government control without government ownership, socialism in capitalist garb. This very important tool for containing monopoly and for establishing government controls over many business decisions will be discussed in the final section of this chapter.

5. The final means by which government can curtail monopoly power is *antitrust policy*. Antitrust policies are laws that prohibit certain kinds of behavior (such as firms joining together to fix prices) or curb certain market structures (such as pure monopolies). Such laws are useful for curbing abuses not only of monopolies but also of the oligopolies that dominate the American economy. Unlike regulation, which tells business what to do and how to price products, antitrust policies are passive in that they tell businesses what *not* to do. This important policy approach will be explored in section C of the next chapter.

THE NATURE OF REGULATION

The previous section outlined the major approaches that a mixed economy could follow in controlling the costs of imperfect competition. We now focus on a single one of these—government regulation. This discussion first outlines the scope and nature of government regulation, then turns to an analysis of the purpose and effect of economic regulation.

In attempting to control or influence economic activity, governments can use incentives or commands. Market incentives, such as tax or expenditure programs, coax people or firms to do the state's will. Or governments can simply command people to undertake or desist from certain activities. The latter course is the function of regulation, to command and control economic activity.

Regulation consists of government rules or laws issued to alter or control the operations of economic enterprises.

It is customary today to distinguish between two forms of regulation. **Economic regulation** refers to the control of prices, kinds of products, entry and exit conditions, and standards of service in a particular industry. Prominent examples are regulation of public utilities (telephone, electricity, natural gas, or water) as well as a miscellany of regulations in utility-type industries (transportation, finance, radio, and TV). This is the species of regulation that will be examined in this chapter.

In addition, there is a newer form of regulation, arising from concerns about the health and safety of workers and consumers, so-called **social regulation.** This denotes rules aimed at correcting a wide variety of side effects or externalities that attend economic activity. Programs to clean our air and water, or to ensure the safety of nuclear power or drugs or cars or toys, are the most prominent examples of social regulation. These will be addressed in Chapter 32.

Economic Regulation of Imperfect Competition

Economic regulation of American industry goes back just a century to the founding of the Interstate Commerce Commission in 1887. The ICC was designed as much to prevent price wars and to guarantee service to small towns as it was to control monopoly. Since that time, federal regulation spread to banks in 1913, to electric power in 1920, and to communications, securities markets, labor, trucking, and air travel during the 1930s. There was little legislation authorizing further economic regulation after World War II.

How much of the private economy is under government economic regulation? At its peak, in 1978, industries under some kind of price or other economic regulation comprised somewhat more than 15 percent of national income. This percentage has declined since 1978 because of the deregulation movement we will discuss later in this chapter.

Why Regulate Industry?

Regulation restrains the unfettered market power of firms. What are the reasons that the land of free enterprise shackles the invisible hand? Two major reasons underlie traditional economic regulation: First, economists stress the importance of containing market power. A second reason, deriving from public-choice theories, is that the regulators are "captured" by the regulated. Let's look at each.

Containing Market Power The traditional economic view of regulation is normative: that regulatory measures should be taken to correct major market failures. More specifically, the targeted failures are breakdowns of competition or, in extreme cases, natural monopoly.

Natural monopoly arises when the entire output of an industry can be most efficiently produced by a single firm. This situation would occur when the technology of the industry has significant economies of scale, and average costs therefore decline at all levels of output. This case is shown in Figure 24-2(*a*). An important example of a natural monopoly is local telephone service. The cost of sending wires into every home and gathering the wires in a local telephone exchange is sufficiently great that it would not pay to have more than one firm provide such local telephone service, so this is a natural monopoly.

Another source of natural monopoly is *economies of scope,* which occur when a number of different products can more efficiently be produced together than by separate firms. For example, transport equipment firms show economies of scope—a firm producing cars and trucks has a cost advantage in producing buses and tanks. Why? Because specialized knowledge and machinery is shared across the different products. These firms have economies of scope in production of ground-based transport systems.

We know from our discussion of declining costs in Chapter 23 that pervasive economies of scale are inconsistent with perfect competition; we will see oligopoly or monopoly in such cases. But the point here is even more extreme: *When there are such powerful economies of scale or scope that only one firm can survive, we have a natural monopoly.*

In this case, section B of this chapter shows how a monopolist could jack up its price, gain enormous monopoly profits, and induce economic waste. Just such a situation is what economic regulation of monopoly prices and output is intended to curb.

There are other reasons often tendered for economic regulation, but these are less easily justified on economic grounds. A traditional argument is that regulation is needed to prevent cutthroat competition. This was one argument for continued control over the railroads, trucks, airlines, and buses, as well as for regulating the level of agricultural production. Economists generally feel that these arguments are a smoke screen behind which vested interests can lobby to maintain their entrenched market power.

Interest-Group Theories of Regulation A second theory of regulation holds that economic regulation results from the interplay of political forces and economic interests in regulated industries. This view, first put forth by economists from the University of Chicago, runs as follows:[7] Regulation creates an economic return for some firms or groups. This happens, for example, because regulators limit entry into the regulated industry, as when the FCC limited entry into the telecommunications market or when the government limited entry into the airline market. Limiting entry or otherwise controlling the terms of doing business raises the profits of those firms who are established in the regulated industry. Hence, once an industry is regulated, it becomes in the economic interest of the regulated to perpetuate regulation. Put differently, the vested interests of the regulated firms create a demand for regulation; this demand asks for legislated market power. In terms of our discussion in section A, established firms want to maintain regulatory barriers to keep out competitors, raise prices, and keep profits high.

What about the supply of regulation? The supply is provided by legislators or administrators who operate in the political marketplace; these suppliers want to gain votes or political support to maintain themselves in office. Sometimes the currency for supporting politicians is campaign contributions and sometimes it is support on other issues. As long as regulated firms outbid other interest groups, providing ample support for political decision makers, the latter will maintain the regulatory cartel.

In effect, the interest-group theorists say, "You may say that regulation is in the interest of consumers and is necessary for maintaining low prices and curbing monopoly power. Don't believe it. Rather, regulation is a political activity like paying veterans benefits or agricultural support payments. It is designed to boost the incomes of producers by limiting entry and preventing competition in the regulated industry."

While this theory may seem far-fetched, it is supported by numerous studies of economic regulation. It has been shown that regulation often held prices *up* (in trucking, in airlines, in brokerage firms, in insurance), while the economic rationale for regulation was to prevent monopoly pricing abuses by holding prices *down.* Moreover, these findings are consistent

---

[7] The seminal work in this area is by University of Chicago's Nobel laureate, George Stigler, "The Theory of Economic Regulation," *Bell Journal of Economics* (Spring 1971), pp. 3–21. The theory has been formalized and refined by law professor (now Circuit Court Judge) Richard Posner, "Theories of Economic Regulation," *Bell*

Journal of Economics (Autumn 1974), pp. 356–358. James Buchanan won the 1986 Nobel Prize in economics for his studies of public-choice economics in regulation, taxation, expenditures, and other areas. These topics are pursued in depth in Chapter 32.

with the burgeoning public-choice literature explored in Chapter 32.

At the same time, while consumers have often been poorly served by economic regulation, people generally voted to regulate industries out of a sincere belief that regulation was in the public interest. Legislators long on intuition and short on economic understanding often promoted a regulatory approach with a firm conviction that it would better prevent price discrimination among customers or would ensure universal or regular service. The road to waste is paved with good intentions.

Public-Utility Regulation of Natural Monopoly

A review of the reasons for regulation suggests that the major economic argument is to prevent monopoly pricing by natural monopolists. Let us see exactly how regulators control the activities of monopolists. Recall that a natural monopoly is an industry in which the most efficient way of organizing production is through a single firm. Figure 24-7 shows the way the *AC*, *MC*, and industry demand curve might look for a typical natural monopoly. Note that the industry demand curve *(DD)* intersects the firm's *MC* curve

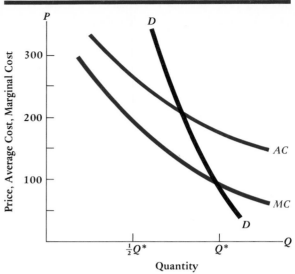

Figure 24-7   Cost curves for a natural monopolist

For a typical natural monopolist, the *AC* curve is still falling at the point where it cuts the industry's *DD* curve. Thus efficient production at that level of output requires output to be concentrated in a single integrated firm. (Can you estimate from the diagram how much more expensive it would be if Q^* were to be produced by two firms each producing $\frac{1}{2}Q^*$?)

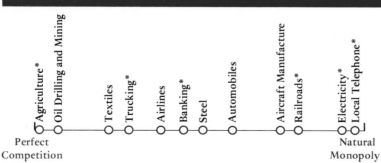

Figure 24-8   Degree of natural monopoly in different industries

This figure arrays several regulated and unregulated industries by their inherent degree of natural monopoly or of perfect competition. Perfectly competitive industries are ones in which the minimum efficient scale of firm is minuscule relative to the market, while a natural monopoly is one where *AC* is still falling sharply at the level of total industry output. Agriculture and mining are inherently quite competitive, while local telephone and electric utilities are close to polar natural monopolies. The asterisk (*) indicates industries where prices are significantly affected by government regulation.

where *AC* is falling. If two similar firms were to produce the industry output, the average cost for the two firms would be considerably higher than that for a single firm.

How prevalent are natural monopolies in today's American economy? Figure 24-8 shows some representative examples from regulated and unregulated industries. Note that many industries that are still regulated or were recently deregulated (airlines, trucks, banks) have a low degree of natural monopoly. This low degree of natural monopoly in many regulated industries lends support to the public-choice theory of economic regulation—that regulation has long outlived its usefulness for consumers and lives on because of political contributions from protected firms in regulated industries.

Suppose that the legislature decides to impose *public-utility regulation* on a particular industry. How would it proceed? It would first set up a public-utility commission to oversee prices, service, and entry into and exit from the industry. The most important decision would be to determine the pricing of the monopoly firm.

Traditionally, regulation imposes *average cost pricing* on regulated firms. For example, an electric utility would take all its costs (fixed as well as variable) and distribute them to each product sold (say, electricity and steam). Then each class of customer would be charged the *fully distributed average cost* of that type of service.

Figure 24-9 illustrates public-utility regulation. Point *M* (associated with output Q_M) is the unregulated profit-maximizing output of the monopolist—sky-high price, tiny quantity, and handsome profits (as shown by the difference between price and average cost).

In traditional regulation, the monopolist is allowed to charge a price only high enough to cover average cost. In this case, the firm will set its price where the demand curve *DD* intersects the *AC* curve. Hence, the equilibrium is at point *R*, with output Q_R in Figure 24-9.

How good is the solution? Economically speaking, it probably does represent something of an improvement over unregulated monopoly. First, the owners of the monopoly are presumably no more deserving, or poorer, than the consumers. So there is no reason to

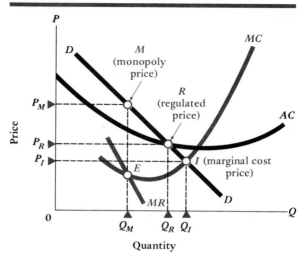

Figure 24-9   Ideal and practical regulation of monopolists

Maximum-profit equilibrium for the unregulated monopolist is at *M*, directly above the intersection of *MR* and long-run *MC*, with *P* above *MC*.

Public-utility commissions customarily require prices to be at *R*—where the demand curve intersects the long-run average cost curve. This wipes out excess profit. More important, it brings price down closer to marginal cost.

Ideally, *P* should be forced all the way down to *I*, where *P* = *MC* and hence marginal social costs and benefits are appropriately balanced. At point *I*, there is no efficiency loss from price being above marginal cost.

let them extract monopoly profits from consumers. By wiping out monopolistic profit, we may end up with what most people feel to be a more equitable distribution of income. (But beware that value judgments beyond technical economics are involved in such a conclusion.)

Second, the regulators have lowered the discrepancy between price and marginal cost in making the monopolist cut its price from P_M to P_R. Why is this deemed an improvement? Because the higher output is worth more to consumers in marginal utility than their extra or marginal cost. The proof of this proposition was given in Figure 24-6: there we showed that at the monopoly equilibrium the social valuation of a monopolist's *Q* was above the forgone leisure or output in other industries.

Ideally Regulated Pricing If $P = MC$ is such a good thing, why shouldn't the regulators go all the way and make the monopolist lower P until it is at the intersection point of the DD and MC curves (at I)?

Actually, requiring $P = MC$ or *marginal-cost pricing* is the ideal target for economic efficiency. But one serious problem arises. A firm that has declining cost, and produces where price equals marginal cost, will be incurring a chronic loss. Why so? The reason is illustrated in Figure 24-7: If AC is falling, then $MC < AC$, so setting $P = MC$ implies having $P < AC$. When price (or average revenue) is less than average cost, the firm is losing money.

Firms of course will not operate for long when they are running at a loss. Hence the ideal regulatory solution requires the government to subsidize the decreasing-cost producer, presumably by funneling tax revenues to the firm. The requirement to raise taxes to pay for the ideal regulatory solution has prevented this approach from becoming a popular one, and it is only rarely employed.

The Deregulation Movement

For the last two decades, many economists have argued that the regulatory process was in reality creating monopoly power rather than curbing it. This idea occurred to economists partly based on the public-choice view of regulation analyzed above. In addition, observers noted that economic regulation had spread far beyond the local natural monopolies. By the mid-1970s, regulators were issuing their orders to railroads and trucks, airlines and buses, radio and TV broadcasting, oil and natural gas, to pecans and milk, and to virtually all financial markets. Most of these industries were closer to the pole of perfect competition than of natural monopoly, as is suggested in Figure 24-8.

Economists thus argued that the time was ripe for dismantling most of the existing economic regulation, and since 1975 the federal government has loosened constraints on many regulated industries. The deregulation of the airlines is one of the most dramatic examples.

From its creation in the New Deal of the 1930s, the Civil Aeronautics Board (CAB) viewed its role as deterring competition. No new trunk air carriers were allowed to enter the interstate market from 1938 to 1978. When innovative, low-cost and no-frills airfares were proposed, they were slapped down. The CAB was (as the public-choice view of regulation predicted) devoted to keeping airfares up, not down.

In 1977, President Carter appointed Alfred Kahn chairman of the CAB. A distinguished economist and critic of regulation, Kahn set out to allow more competition by entry and fare flexibility.* In 1978, legislation was passed to allow free entry and exit on all air routes. Airlines were freed to set whatever fares the traffic would bear. Many noneconomists fretted that there would be massive layoffs and loss of service without regulation—a forecast that proved far from correct.

After several years of experience, it is clear that competition has changed the entire structure of the airline industry. Studies indicate that (after correcting for inflation) average fares fell sharply over the years after deregulation; that utilization of aircraft increased; that there was minimal loss of service to small communities, with many others experiencing better service by small airlines; and that airlines have become extraordinarily innovative in their design of pricing strategies. Moreover, the vision of vigorous competition has certainly been borne out, with four bankruptcies among major airlines in the first 8 years of deregulation. Economists can be justly proud of their accuracy in forecasting the effects of airline deregulation.

---

*Kahn is known for his wit as well as his wisdom. He once admitted to a group of airline executives that he knew nothing about the business, saying that for him an airplane was simply marginal cost with wings. In 1978, Kahn left the CAB to become President Carter's chief inflation fighter. In that post he furthered deregulation of the trucking industry. Kahn also predicted that, without an effective anti-inflation policy, the economy would soon be in a deep recession. But because White House aides seemed allergic to the word, he relabelled the recession a "banana" and spoke of the need for "bananas" to fight inflation.

A similar history occurred in the oil industry after its complete deregulation in February 1981. Oil companies began to introduce new forms of marketing to compete for the dwindling gasoline market. Many companies expanded self-service, abolished use of credit cards, and introduced electronic high-speed pumps. These innovations forced the price margin between gasoline and crude oil to shrink sharply after early 1981. Instead of gouging consumers, oil companies were competing with one another.

Many specialists feel that the successes of airline and oil deregulation can be applied to ocean shipping, agriculture, natural gas production, electricity generation, railroads, and communications. Political obstacles often prevent deregulation, however, for regulated industries have often secured positions sheltered from competition and prefer to continue the easy, regulated life.

SUMMARY

A. Patterns of Imperfect Competition

1. Most market structures in the real world fall somewhere on a line between the limiting poles of perfect competition and natural monopoly. Under imperfect competition, a firm has some control over its price, a fact seen as a downward-sloping demand curve for the firm's output.

2. Important kinds of market structure are *(a)* natural monopoly, where a single firm produces all the output in a given industry; *(b)* oligopoly, where a few sellers of a similar or differentiated product supply the industry; *(c)* monopolistic competition, where a large number of small firms supply related but somewhat differentiated products; and *(d)* perfect competition, where a large number of small firms supply an identical product. In the first three cases, firms in the industry face downward-sloping demand curves.

3. Economies of scale, or decreasing average costs, are the major source of imperfect competition. When firms can lower costs by expanding their output, this tends to destroy perfect competition, since one or a few companies can kill off the numerous sellers required for competition. When the minimum efficient size of plant is large relative to the national or regional market, then cost conditions produce imperfect competition.

4. In addition to declining costs, other forces leading to imperfections are barriers to competition in the form of legal restrictions (such as patents or government regulation) and natural or contrived product differentiation (such as left- versus right-hand drive in cars or similar products made to seem different by advertising).

5. Major measures of market power are concentration ratios (such as the four-firm measure which calculates what percent of the market is served by the four largest firms) and the Herfindahl index (which calculates the sum of the squares of market shares).

B. Analysis of Monopoly

6. From the firm's demand curve, we can easily derive its total revenue curve. From the schedule or curve of total revenue, we can easily derive its marginal revenue—the extra revenue resulting from the sale of an extra unit of output. For the monopolist, marginal revenue will fall short of price because of the loss on all previous units of output that will result when it is forced to drop its price in order to sell an extra unit of output.

7. A firm will find its maximum-profit position where the last unit it sells brings in extra revenue just equal to its extra cost. This same *MR* = *MC* result can be shown graphically by intersecting *MR* and *MC* curves, or by the equality of the slopes of the total revenue and total cost curves. In any case, *marginal revenue = marginal cost* must hold at the equilibrium position of maximum profit, always.

8. Economic reasoning leads to an emphasis upon *marginal* advantages and disadvantages—to a disregard of bygones and of activities that go on no matter how you make a decision.

C. The Cost and Control of Monopoly

9. Exercise of monopoly power leads to economic waste when price rises above marginal cost. Empirical studies indicate that the actual waste or efficiency losses from imperfect competition are small relative to national output.

10. There is a spectrum between perfect competition and natural monopoly. Natural monopoly occurs when average costs are falling for every level of output, so that the most efficient organization of the industry requires a single firm. Few industries come close to this condition today—perhaps only local utilities like telephone, water, or electricity.

11. In conditions of natural monopoly, the state has several strategies. Taxation, price controls, and nationalization are little used today in the United States. The two major tools in American policy are currently regulation and antitrust laws.

12. Regulation consists of government rules commanding firms to alter their business conduct. While control of natural monopoly is often the stated goal of economic regulation, a new view holds that regulation is desired by regulated firms whose interests are furthered by exclusion of potential rivals. Moreover, the actual experience of deregulation over the last decade supports the interest-group view.

CONCEPTS FOR REVIEW _____

perfect versus imperfect competition
monopoly, oligopoly, product
  differentiation (natural or contrived)
marginal (or extra) revenue, *MR*
MR = *MC* at maximum-profit output
barriers to competition (costs, legal
  restrictions, product differentiation)
economic vs. social regulation
natural monopoly

three price outcomes under monopoly
  (unregulated, regulated, ideal)
economic vs. interest-group theories of
  regulation
$P > MR = (P -$ loss on previous units)
  for imperfect competition
$MR = P$, $P = MC$, for perfect
  competitor
inefficiency of $P > MC$

QUESTIONS FOR DISCUSSION

1. List the distinguishing features of perfect and imperfect competition. What are the main varieties of imperfect competition? In which category would you place: General Motors? Your local telephone company? Sears? Farmer Jones? Your college or university?

2. "A corporation charges what the traffic will bear." Explain the error here, and suggest a correct statement in terms of marginal revenue and marginal cost.

3. What is MR's numerical value when dd has unitary elasticity?

4. Figure 24-5(a) and (b) describes the maximum-profit equilibrium position. Explain in detail that it really shows two different ways of describing exactly the same fact: namely, that a firm will stop expanding its production where the extra cost of further output just balances its extra revenue.

5. The market shares in the U.S. airline industry for 1986 were the following:

United	17 percent	Northwest	9 percent
American	14	TWA	8
Delta	12	Pan Am	7
Eastern	12	Eight others	2 each

Source: U.S. Department of Transportation, *Air Carrier Financial Statistics* (December 1986).

Calculate the four-firm and eight-firm concentration ratios and the Herfindahl index. What would be the change in these indexes if Delta merged with United?

6. Pear Computer Company has fixed costs of production of $100,000, while each unit costs $600 of labor and $400 of materials and fuel. At a price of $3000, consumers would buy no Pear computers, but for each $10 reduction in price, sales of Pear computers increase by 1000 units. Calculate marginal cost and marginal revenue for Pear Computer, and determine its monopoly price and quantity.

7. Explain in words and with the use of diagrams why a monopolistic equilibrium leads to economic inefficiency relative to a perfect competitor. Why is the condition $MC = P = MU$ of Chapter 23 critical for this analysis?

8. Review the three pricing outcomes in Figure 24-9. Can you think of the difficulties of implementing the ideal regulated price? (HINT: Where does the country get the revenues? Is MC easy to measure?) Similarly, can you think of reasons why many economists would prefer the unregulated to the regulated outcome? (HINT: What if P_M is not much above P_R? What if you worried about the interest-group theories of regulation?)

9. Why is the interest-group theory of regulation's analogy of votes and dollars only an imprecise one?

10. Make a list of the industries that you feel are candidates for the title of "natural monopoly." Then review the different strategies for intervention. What would you do about each industry on your list?

11. Show that a profit-maximizing, unregulated monopolist will never operate in the price inelastic region of its demand curve. Show how regulation can force the monopolist onto the inelastic portion of its demand curve. What will be the impact of an increase in the regulated price of a monopolist upon revenues and profits when it is operating on *(a)* the elastic portion of the demand curve, *(b)* the inelastic portion of the demand curve, and *(c)* the unit-elastic portion of the demand curve?

12. Advanced problem: Firm A has *dd* demand function, $P = 15 - 0.05q$, and hence $TR = qP = 15q - 0.05q^2$. Its $TC = q + 0.02q^2$. Verify: $MR = d(TR)/dq = 15 - 0.1q$, $MC = d(TC)/dq = 1 + 0.04q$. So $d(\text{profit})/dq = 0$ at $MR = MC$ or at $15 - 0.1q = 1 + 0.04q$ or at $q^* = 100$. Then $P^* = \$15 - \$5 = \$10 > MC^* = \$5$. You can show that maximum profit $= \$1000 - (\$100 + \$200) = \$700$. Can you show that a tax of \$1/unit will add $1q$ to TC, cutting q^* by 100/14 units and raising P by 5/14 units? Were A a perfect competitor, with horizontal *dd* at \$5, its maximum profit on $q^* = 100$ would have been $\$500 - \$300 = \$200$; now a \$1/unit tax would cut competitor's q^* by more than monopolist's—namely, by 100/4 = 25 units. Show all this.

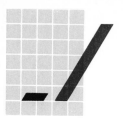

APPENDIX: 24_____

Economics of Risk and Uncertainty

We have seen that supply and demand are versatile tools for economic analysis. In Chapter 23's analysis of competitive markets and in Chapter 24's extension to monopoly, we examined the functioning of markets with no risk or uncertainty. In those discussions, costs and demands were known for certain, and every economic actor was able to foresee how other firms would behave.

The reality is that business life is rife with risk and uncertainty. Demand fluctuates from month to month; input prices of labor, land, machines, and fuels are often quite variable; the behavior of competitors cannot be seen in advance. In some businesses, like farming or oil and gas, people make investments now and produce the output in the future, putting their profits as hostage to future price movements. And all of us are subject to random catastrophic losses from fire, hurricanes, earthquakes, or illness. Life is a risky affair.

Modern economics has recently begun to incorporate uncertainty into the analysis of business and household behavior. Although some elements of the economics of uncertainty must be reserved for advanced treatments, this appendix presents the basic ingredients. We here examine the role of markets in spreading risks over space and time, present the theory of gambling and individual behavior under uncertainty, and provide the essential theory underlying insurance markets. These topics are but a brief glimpse into the fascinating world of risk and economic life.

THE ROLE OF SPECULATION

We begin our discussion by considering the role of speculators. Who are **speculators**? They are people who buy (or sell) a commodity with an eye to selling (or buying) it later for a profit. The commodity might be grain or eggs or foreign currencies or government securities. Speculators are not interested in using the product or making something with it. Rather, they want to buy low and sell high, and the last thing they want is to see the egg truck roll up to their door.

You might wonder what kind of benefit this activity brings. Surprisingly, as we will see, even though speculators never once see a carton of eggs or a bushel of wheat, they may help even out the price differences among regions, or over time, or even between good and bad harvests.

Arbitrage and Geographical Price Patterns

Begin with the case of arbitrage between regional price differences. **Arbitrage,** which is closely related to speculation, occurs when a commodity is simultaneously bought in one market and sold in another market at a higher price. Let's say that the price of wheat is 50 cents a bushel higher in Chicago than in Kansas City. Further say that it costs 10 cents a bushel to insure and ship the wheat from one market to another. Then an arbitrager (a person engaged in arbitrage) can purchase wheat in Kansas City, ship it to Chicago, and make a profit of 40 cents a bushel. As a result of arbitrage, the price differential between Chicago and Kansas City must always be less than 10 cents a bushel.

The frenzied activities of arbitragers—talking on the phone simultaneously to several brokers in several markets, searching out price differentials, trying to eke out a tiny profit every time they can buy cheap and sell high—tend to align the prices of identical products in different markets. Once again, we see the invisible hand at work, with the lure of profit acting to smooth out price differentials across markets and make markets function more effectively.

Nobody legislates prices to be equal in different markets. That follows from supply and demand.

SPECULATION AND PRICE BEHAVIOR OVER TIME

In an ideal competitive market there tends to be a definite pattern of prices over time just as there is over space. But the difficulties of predicting the future make this pattern a less perfect one: we have an equilibrium that is constantly being disturbed but is always in the process of re-forming itself—rather like a lake's surface under the play of the winds.

Stabilizing Seasonal Patterns

Consider the simplest case of a grain, like corn, that is harvested at one period of the year. This crop must be made to last all year long if shortages are to be avoided. Since no one passes a law regulating the storage of grain, how is this desirable state of affairs brought about? Through the attempts of speculators to make a profit.

A well-informed speculator who is a specialist in this grain realizes that if all the grain is thrown on the market in the autumn, it will fetch a very low price because there will be a glut on the market. On the other hand, months later, with almost no grain coming on the market, price will tend to skyrocket. Speculators realize that by (1) purchasing some of the autumn crop while it is cheap, (2) withholding it in storage, and (3) selling it later when the price has risen, they can make a profit. This they do. But in doing so, they increase the autumn price, and they increase the spring supply of grain and lower its spring price. At the same time that they are equalizing the price over the year, they are also equalizing the supply coming on the market in each month—which is as it should be.

Moreover, if there is brisk competition among speculators, none of them will make an excessive profit over the costs that they incur (including, of course, the wages necessary to keep them in this line of activity). The speculators themselves may never touch a kernel of corn or a bag of cocoa, nor need know anything about storage, warehouses, or delivery. They merely buy and sell bits of paper. But the effect is exactly as described.

Now there is one and only one monthly price pattern that will result in neither profits

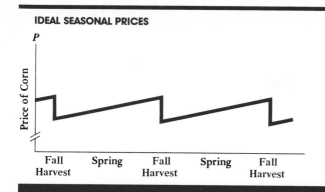

IDEAL SEASONAL PRICES

Figure 24A-1 Speculators even out the price of a commodity over time

For a good to be stored, expected price rise must match storage cost. Ideally, *P* is lowest at harvest time, rising gently with accumulated storage, insurance, and interest costs until the next harvest. This flexible pattern tends to even out consumption over the seasons—as compared with a harvest glut's causing very low autumn price and summer scarcity's causing sky-high price.

nor losses. A little thought will show that it will not be a pattern of constant prices. Rather, the ideal price pattern will produce lowest prices in the autumn glut; then prices gradually rise until the peak is reached just before the new corn comes in. The price must rise from month to month to compensate for the storage and interest costs of carrying the crop in storage—in exactly the same way that the price must rise over space from one mile to the next to compensate for the cost of transportation. Figure 24A-1 shows the behavior of prices over an idealized yearly cycle.

Spreading of Risks, or Hedging

In addition to their help in stabilizing prices, speculators have another important function. They can take risk on their own shoulders, thereby enabling others to avoid unwanted risks.

For example, the owner of a warehouse must carry large inventories of grain in the course of her business. If the price of grain rises, she makes a large windfall gain, but if grain prices fall, she incurs a large and unwelcome loss. But the warehouse owner might want to earn her living by storing grain; she has no interest in speculating on the price of grain. She can avoid grain-price risk by a process of *hedging*.

What is **hedging**? This is the process of avoiding a risk by making a counteracting sale or investment. In our warehouse example, the firm hedges by selling today the amount of grain that is in the warehouse but will not be shipped for a number of days or months.

To get a notion of how the process of hedging works out, here is a simplified example. Suppose I am buying and storing corn in the late fall. I am a specialist in running a warehouse and wish to stick to my job rather than become involved in the risky business of making speculative bets as to whether the price of corn will change between now and next spring, when I expect to stop storing corn and to sell it. In effect, I would really like to sell it now for an agreed-upon price that will compensate me for my storage expenses between now and later delivery time (amounting, let's say, to 15 cents per bushel). If a speculative market exists, that is precisely what I can do by the device of hedging.

Here is where the speculator enters: He agrees to buy the corn now for future delivery. (Technically, the speculator might in September buy a 5000-bushel May corn-future contract from me at, say, $4 a bushel.) Now I am hedged. No matter what happens to the price of corn over the next few months, I have netted the same amount and I bear no corn-price risk. The hedge protects me from all corn-price fluctuations, for the speculator who bought my future corn took the price risk off my shoulders.

UNCERTAINTY AND DIMINISHING MARGINAL UTILITY[1]

Moralists often attack speculators, charging that they are simply riverboat gamblers, no better than people who bet on the horses or enjoy cockfights.

Defenders of speculation resent these charges. They emphasize that an uncertain world necessarily involves risk and that someone must bear these risks. They claim that the knowledge and the venturesomeness of the speculator are chained to a socially useful purpose, thereby reducing fluctuations and risks to others.

Chance and the Law of Diminishing Marginal Utility

To understand the way that speculators (or, later in this appendix, insurance) can spread risks and raise economic welfare, we must return to the concepts of utility and marginal utility. Why is it that I, as a grain merchant or a farmer or a worker, find that large uncertainties about prices or about my consumption might be economically harmful?

One answer is to be found in the widely held belief that the gain in utility achieved by an extra $1000 of income is not so great as the loss in utility of forgoing $1000 of income. Where that is the case, a bet at fair odds involves an economic loss. The money you stand to win balances the money you may lose, but the satisfaction you stand to win is less than the satisfaction you stand to lose.

For example, as a farmer, I must contend not only with the risks of the weather on my farm; I must, as well, contend with price risks. Let's say that I expect that the price will be $4 per bushel, but this expectation arises from two equally likely outcomes with prices of $3 and $5 per bushel. In essence, unless I can shed the price risk, I am forced into a lottery where I can sell my 10,000-bushel crop for either $30,000 or $50,000.

But by the principle of diminishing marginal utility, I would far prefer a sure thing—to be able to hedge my price risk by selling my grain for the expected-value price of $4, yielding $40,000. Why? Because the loss of $10,000 is more painful than the gain of $10,000 is pleasant. If my income is cut to $30,000, I will have to cut back on important consumption, like my daughter's first-choice college or the family food budget. On the other hand, the extra $10,000 may only go into a new set of furniture or a second tractor.

Thus activities that reduce the uncertainty or risk about people's consumption lead to improvements in economic welfare.

---

[1] This discussion leans on and illustrates our earlier discussion of marginal utility (Chapter 19).

WHY STABILIZATION BY SPECULATORS CAN INCREASE UTILITY

We can now use the tools of marginal utility to show how ideal speculation would maximize total utility over time. Suppose every consumer has a utility schedule that holds for each year independently of any other year. Now suppose that in the first of 2 years there was a big crop—say, 3 units per person—and in the second a small crop of only 1 unit per person. If this crop deficiency could be foreseen, how should the consumption of the 2-year 4-unit total be spread over the 2 years?

Agree, for simplicity, to neglect all storage, interest, and insurance costs and all questions of the interpersonal and intertemporal comparison of utility. Then we can prove this:

Total utility for the 2 years together will be maximized only if consumption is equal in each year.

Why is uniform consumption better than any other division of the available total? Because of the law of diminishing marginal utility. Here is the reasoning: "Suppose I consume more in the first year than in the second. My last unit's marginal utility in the first year will be low, and then in the second it will be high. So if I carry some crop from the first to the second year, I shall be switching from low to high marginal utilities—and that will maximize my total utility."

But is not that exactly what the ideal speculation pattern would accomplish? Yes, it is. If speculators can neglect interest, storage, and insurance charges and happen to forecast accurately next year's low crop, what will they do? They will figure it pays to carry goods over from this year's low price resulting from the bumper crop, hoping instead to sell at next year's higher price. But as each speculator subtracts from this year's supply and adds to next year's, what must finally happen? Equilibrium can be reached only when the two prices have been equalized. Then there will be no further incentive to carry over more crop. (Of course, a small payment for the speculator's effort might have to be included—but we can ignore all costs just to keep the example simple.)

A graph can illuminate this argument. If utility could be measured in dollars, with each dollar always denoting the same marginal utility, the demand curves would look just like the marginal utility schedule of Figure 19-1 on page 448. The two curves of Figure 24A-2(a) show what would happen if there were no carryover—with price first determined at A_1, where S_1S_1 intersects DD, and second at A_2, where the lower supply S_2S_2 intersects DD. Total utility of the red shaded areas would add up only to $(4 + 3 + 2) + 4$, or \$13 per head.

But with optimal carryover to the second year of 1 unit by speculators, as shown in Figure 24A-2(b), Ps and Qs will be equalized at E_1 and E_2, and now the total utility of the shaded areas will add up to $(4 + 3) + (4 + 3)$, or \$14 per head. A little analysis can show that the gain in utility of \$1 is measured by E_2's dark block, which represents the excess of the second unit's marginal utility over that of the third. Hence, one can show that equality of marginal utilities is optimal.

We thus see that ideal speculation serves the very important function of reducing the variation in consumptions, and (in a world with individuals who display diminishing marginal utility) increases total utility.

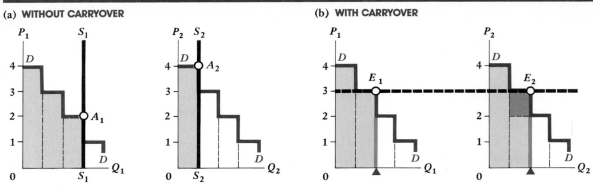

Figure 24A-2

The red areas measure total utility enjoyed each year. Carrying 1 unit to the second year equalizes Q and also P, and increases total utility by amount of dark red block. This diagram will, as the next section shows, apply equally to a number of situations. It could be labelled "**(a)** without insurance" and "**(b)** with insurance." Or equally "**(a)** without arbitrage across regional markets" and "**(b)** with arbitrage across markets." Some would even propose an extension by assuming all individuals are the same, so that it could be labelled "**(a)** without redistributive taxation" and "**(b)** with redistributive taxation."

The example in Figure 24A-2 assumed perfect foresight about future events. Moreover, to the extent that flesh-and-blood speculators forecast accurately, they perform a useful stabilizing function, as do government agencies that help collect and disseminate data on which these intelligent private forecasts are made. And even if a few forecasters are pigheadedly using astrological data for their million-dollar bets, they will get eliminated as fast as their capital is depleted.

Speculative Bubbles   Having seen how ideal speculation can increase economic welfare, we must note the possibility of less happy outcomes. From time to time, investors lose sight of fundamentals and fall prey to rumors, hopes, and fears. Sometimes, speculation gets caught in the grip of a mass contagion, like the inexplicable dancing crazes that swept medieval villages, like the Dutch tulip mania that sent the price of a single bulb higher than that of a house, like the South Sea Bubble in which companies sold stock at fabulous prices for enterprises which would "later be revealed."

While economic science may have difficulty explaining why "rational" investors would buy into such *speculative bubbles,* history documents numerous cases. Moreover, such destabilizing speculation serves the economy poorly; it is as if speculators take consumers from the "with carryover" to "without carryover" phases of Figure 24A-2. Destabilizing speculation leads to a deterioration in economic welfare.

ECONOMICS OF INSURANCE

We are now in a position to see why insurance, which appears to be just another form of gambling, actually has exactly opposite effects. For the same reasons that introducing useless risks or destabilizing speculation is bad, insurance is economically advantageous. Whereas the weather creates risks, insurance helps to lessen and spread risks.

In buying fire insurance on their house, the owners seem to be betting with the insurance company that the house will burn down. If it does not—and the odds are heavily in favor of it not burning—the owners forfeit the small premium charge. If it does burn down, the company must reimburse the owners to the tune of the agreed-upon loss. (For the obvious reason of removing temptation from hard-up homeowners who like fire engines and excitement, or technically to avoid such a "moral hazard," the face values of the insurance policies are often somewhat less than the money value of the property insured.) What is true of fire insurance is equally true of life, accident, automobile, or any other kind of insurance.

The function of the insurance company is to *spread risks*. It does this by pooling many different risks (millions of houses or lives or cars, thousands of factories or hotels). Note that what is unpredictable and subject to chance for the individual is highly predictable and uniform in the mass. Whether Joan Brown, age 50 and in good health, will live for 30 more years is a matter of chance. But Chapter 1's law of large numbers guarantees that out of 100,000-odd 50-year-old females in good health, one definite proportion will still be alive at the end of the period. The life-insurance company can easily set a premium which will earn the company a profit and at the same time lead to a gain in the prospective utility of individuals.

Where does the gain come from? It arises from the law of diminishing marginal utility, which holds that the gain from winning is less valued than the pain from an equal-sized loss.[2]

UNINSURABLE EVENTS AND SOCIAL INSURANCE

While insurance is undoubtedly a useful device for spreading risks across the population, the fact is that we cannot buy insurance for all the risks of life. The reason for incompleteness of insurance markets lies in the stringent conditions that must be met before insurance can be profitably marketed.

What are these conditions? First, there must be a large number of events. Only then will companies be able to pool different events and rely upon the law of large numbers. Moreover, the events must be relatively independent. No prudent insurance company would sell all its fire-insurance policies in the same building or sell only earthquake insurance in Palo Alto. Rather, insurance companies strive to spread their coverage around to different and independent risks. Finally, the insurance must not be contaminated by excessive moral hazard, which occurs when the insured individual can markedly affect the likelihood of the insured event. When all these conditions are met—when there are many risks, all more or less independent, and where the probabilities can be accurately gauged—in such conditions private-market insurance will flourish.

---

[2] Figure 24A-2 can show why risk spreading is economically advantageous. Label the left-hand pair of diagrams "without insurance" and the right-hand set "with insurance." Without insurance, people are faced with very different supplies of housing (or cars or health). Because of diminishing marginal utility, this will lower their total expected utility relative to a situation where they pay a fair insurance premium to be assured the same level of housing (or cars or health) no matter how the dice of life turn up.

Social Insurance   But what about cases where the conditions for private insurance do not hold? In that situation, there may be a role for social insurance. Many important contingencies are ones for which insurance either is unavailable or is priced at unfavorable terms because of moral hazard or selection problems (the latter arise, for example, when health insurance is bought predominantly by sick people, thus driving the cost of insurance for healthy people way above its expected value). Market failures arise in unemployment insurance, health insurance, and to some extent old-age annuities.

In these circumstances, the government may be able to step in and provide broader coverage. The huge financial reserves of government, plus the ability to avoid selection bias through universal coverage, may make government insurance a welfare-improving measure.

SUMMARY TO APPENDIX

1. The intelligent profit-seeking action of speculators and arbitragers tends to create certain definite *equilibrium patterns of price over space and time*. To the extent that speculators moderate price and consumption instability, they perform a socially useful purpose. To the extent that they provide a market and permit others to hedge against risk, they also help to spread out social risk. But to the extent that speculators cause great fluctuations in stock and commodity prices (or in foreign exchange rates) they do social damage.

2. The economic principle of diminishing marginal utility shows why the stability of consumption is economically beneficial, and why insurance is sound: when consumption is equalized across different uncertain states, the average of expected level of utility rises. But all events are not insurable, and many risks remain.

CONCEPTS FOR REVIEW

spatial P equality

ideal seasonal price pattern

law of diminishing marginal utility

speculation, hedging

consumption stability vs. instability

arbitrage

insurable and uninsurable risks

social vs. private insurance

QUESTIONS FOR DISCUSSION

1. How does ideal speculation stabilize seasonal prices?

2. Early social reformers believed that people had essentially the same utility functions. Assuming that the parts of Figure 24A-2 represent different individuals before and after income redistribution, explain how equalization of incomes would lead to the maximum total utility.

3. List some important differences between private and social insurance.

4. In the early nineteenth century, markets for agricultural crops carried little of the nation's agricultural output. Transport costs were very high. What would you expect to have been the degree of variation of prices across regions and across time?

5. Assume that a single risky event is undertaken by a firm (say, introduction of a $1 million minisupercomputer). Can you see how the widely diversified ownership of this firm could allow near-perfect risk spreading on the computer investment?

6. In the late 1980s, arbitragers who became rich upon the illegal use of inside information gave a bad name to speculation and arbitrage. Say that arbitrage were made a criminal offense. Explain the economic damage that could ensue.

7. Advanced problem for students of statistics: Suppose each of four cab companies faces accidents "normally distributed," with a standard deviation, $\sigma_i = \$3000$, around a mean loss of $50,000. Let them now pool risks through mutual reinsurance. Show that this gives a total mean loss of $200,000 [or still $50,000 for each one's fair share; but now total variance is only $4 \times (\$3000)^2$, or $\sigma^2 = 4\sigma_i^2 = 36,000,000 = (6000)^2$]. So each ends up with a standard deviation of only $1500 = \$6000/4$—halving the risk through quadrupling the size. Can you use the same reasoning to see the following? *(a)* Diversifying your wealth into four independent stocks, each with the same mean return and same (independent) variability, will halve the expected variability of your portfolio. *(b)* Pooling the independent peak-load demand of two utility systems will reduce the need to have twice the stand-by capacity. *(c)* A company's needed inventory tends to grow only like the square root of the number of its independent customers. Hence, a firm four times as big has only half the inventory cost per unit of sales.

CHAPTER 25___
IMPERFECT COMPETITION AND ANTITRUST POLICY

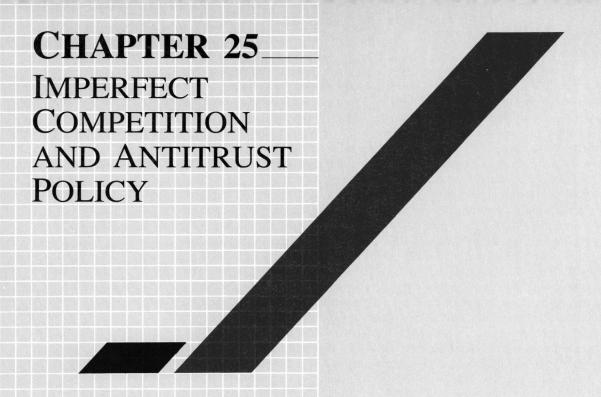

Both monopolistic and competitive forces combine in the determination of most prices.

Edward H. Chamberlin

EARLIER CHAPTERS surveyed the poles of monopoly and perfect competition. But many industries in today's American economy lie between these two extremes. Most markets exhibit imperfect competition among a handful of firms. We see such oligopolistic markets in manufacturing industries like automobiles, computers, and aircraft; in communications industries like telephone or TV broadcasting; in transportation areas like railroads and airlines; and so forth. So in this final chapter on product-market structures, we focus on the world of competition among the few.

Section A begins the survey by examining different theories of imperfect competition, with particular attention to markets with collusion, with a single dominant firm, and with many firms selling slightly differentiated products. Section B then explores the behavior of the giant corporation, moving beyond marginal revenue and cost curves to examine exactly how large companies affect our economy. We want to know just what motivates big firms. Do they fine-tune their prices so as to equate marginal cost and marginal revenue, or are they more likely to follow rules of thumb? And is there a relation between the size of a firm and its inventiveness?

Finally, section C provides an introduction to the antitrust laws of the United States. These pages give a brief history and analysis of these laws—which are so important for maintaining competition and curbing the anticompetitive behavior of large firms.

A. PATTERNS OF IMPERFECT COMPETITION

A modern industrial economy like the United States contains many varieties of market structures. Glance back at Table 24-1, which shows the following major species:

- *Perfect competition* is found when a large number of firms produce an identical product—so many firms, indeed, that none of them can affect the market price. This species thrives mainly on farms.

- *Monopoly,* in which a single firm produces the entire output of an industry, was analyzed in depth in the last chapter. Such cases are rare in American capitalism today.

- Between the two poles lie intermediate forms of imperfect competition. In this chapter we first investigate *oligopoly,* in which an industry is dominated by a few firms, and then turn to *monopolistic competition,* in which a large number of firms produce slightly differentiated products.

Salient Characteristics

Different market structures exhibit different patterns of behavior. Table 25-1 selects four groups of industries (those with high, moderate, and low concentration along with perfect competition) and examines historical data on major characteristics. What do these data show?

As we see in column (3), there is little relationship between the degree of concentration and an industry's rate of profit: more concentrated industries tend to have only slightly higher profits than unconcentrated ones. This finding has been a surprise to critics of capitalism, who expect supernormal monopoly profits in giant firms.

Concentrated industries tend to have much higher levels of advertising and research and development (R&D) spending per unit of sales. In perfect competition, by contrast, advertising and research are absent.

Column (6) in Table 25-1 displays the degree of price flexibility in different market structures. From studies of individual firms, we know that firms in concentrated industries tend to be price setters, who engage in *administered pricing*. Administered pricing occurs when firms set or administer the prices of their goods and then hold those prices fixed for weeks or even months. For example, automobile manufacturers set the sticker prices on new cars at the beginning of the model year and adjust them only infrequently during the next 12 months. The price setting by oligopolists contrasts with *auction pricing* in perfectly competitive markets—markets like those for wheat or corn, where prices are determined by the hurly-burly of auctions and sometimes fluctuate more in an hour than administered prices change in a month.

OLIGOPOLY: COMPETITION AMONG THE FEW

An economic theory of oligopoly must account for the patterns of behavior shown in Table 25-1. In devising explanations for the origins and behavior of oligopolistic markets, economists stress three key factors: cost conditions, barriers to competition, and collusion.

Costs

The major factors determining market structure are the cost conditions and underlying technology of an

CHARACTERISTICS OF MARKET STRUCTURES

(1) INDUSTRIAL STRUCTURE (with examples)	(2) FOUR-FIRM CONCENTRATION RATIO, 1982 (percent)	(3) RATE OF PROFIT, 1960–1979 (as percent of stockholders' equity)	(4) RESEARCH AND DEVELOPMENT, 1980–1982 (as percent of sales)	(5) ADVERTISING SPENDING, 1982 (as percent of sales)	(6) DEGREE OF PRICE FLEXIBILITY, 1960–1983 (100 = flexibility for competitive industry)
High concentration (motor vehicles, tobacco, non-ferrous metals)	79	13	2.7	2.3	38
Moderate concentration (paper, stone, clay, glass, chemicals)	42	12	2.1	2.2	25
Low concentration (apparel, printing, furniture)	26	11	0.6	1.3	14
Perfectly competitive (corn and wheat farming)	~0.01	Not available	~0	~0	100

Table 25-1   Different patterns of research, advertising, and price flexibility are found in different market structures

We can distinguish four major groupings: industries with high, moderate, and low levels of concentration, and perfectly competitive industries. In each category, a small number of important representative industries have been selected.

The table suggests some key characteristics: (1) profit rates are only slightly higher in more concentrated industries; (2) research and development and advertising are more prevalent in concentrated industries; and (3) more concentrated industries tend to have much stickier prices than competitive industries that sell their products in auction markets. (Sources: U.S. Bureau of the Census, *Census of Manufacturing;* National Science Foundation; Federal Trade Commission, *Quarterly Financial Report; Economic Report of the President;* Internal Revenue Service, *Corporation Income Tax,* 1982.)

industry. We saw above (recall page 572 and Table 24-2) that the technology of many industries dictates that the point of minimum average cost occurs at a sizable fraction—10 or 20 or even 50 percent—of industry output. When an efficient plant for petroleum refining, automobiles, or aircraft manufacturing must produce a large fraction of market output, that industry will tend to be oligopolistic, with but a few large producers.

Barriers to Competition

The last chapter analyzed the role of barriers to competition, which are forces that prevent the full force of rivalry among firms from operating in an industry. Important barriers are legal restrictions (like patents on inventions, tariffs and quotas on foreign trade, and government regulation) and product differentiation (arising from natural effects like linguistic barriers, from trademarks, and from perceived differences in quality of products). When such barriers are high, an industry may have few firms and limited rivalry.

Because of economies of scale and barriers to competition, oligopoly is the norm in manufacturing. In petroleum refining, the smallest efficient plant would cost almost $1 billion, while an automobile manufacturer would need to produce at least 300,000 units per year to attain an efficient scale of production. It is in the same manufacturing industries that we meet the highest concentration ratios in Germany and Japan and the United States.

Collusion

A final factor influencing a market's structure is the extent to which firms engage in **collusion,** which occurs when two or more firms jointly set their prices or outputs, divide the market, or make other business decisions.

The impetus to collude arises when firms realize that their prices and profits are closely interrelated. Each oligopolist learns from experience that, when it cuts its price, its rivals tend to meet or to exceed its price cut. Keen price rivalry and occasional economic warfare tend to lower everyone's prices, and everyone's profits as well. Sooner or later, the few sellers realize that they are in the same boat.

During the early years of American capitalism, oligopolists often merged or formed a trust or cartel. A **cartel** is an organization of producers in an industry who gather jointly to make business decisions, set prices, or divide up the market. Meeting at celebrated dinners, such as those that Judge Gary of U.S. Steel held around 1910, the sellers' cartel would engage in *explicit collusion*. This practice involved setting price well above the competitive level, sometimes attempting to drive it up to or near the monopoly price.

Today, however, it is strictly illegal in the United States and most other advanced market economies for companies to collude by jointly setting prices or dividing markets. (The antitrust laws pertaining to such behavior are discussed in section C of this chapter.) Nonetheless, if there are but a few large firms in an industry, they may engage in *tacit collusion*, setting

prices at inflated levels or dividing markets among oligopolists through implicit agreement, by refraining from competitive measures, and without leaving any traces of meetings or joint actions or decisions. Under tacit collusion, firms refrain from using prices as a competitive tool and tend to quote rather similar prices—prices which come nowhere near the competitive level of price equal to MC.

MODELS OF IMPERFECT COMPETITION

There are myriad possible combinations of cost differences, barriers to competition, and degrees of tacit or explicit collusion. To describe them all would require an advanced treatise on industrial organization. For an introductory taste, we will serve up three of the most important cases of imperfect competition—collusive oligopoly, dominant-firm oligopoly, and monopolistic competition. This appetizer will just hint at the great richness of the subject of industrial organization.

Collusive Oligopoly

The simplest case of oligopoly arises when all the rivals sell similar products and fully recognize that they are all in the same boat. They realize that their fortunes depend on the extent to which joint decisions on prices and outputs drive prices down to unprofitable levels or allow a comfortable monopoly profit. In this case, oligopolists are sure to recognize their *mutual dependence*. They will see that any initial advantage A gets in undercutting B's price will be lost when B is induced to cut its price in return.

When a few firms produce a very similar product, therefore, they soon learn that the prices of all firms in the industry are likely to end up at the same level. For industrial chemicals, sold in open markets between sophisticated buyers and sellers, no major price differences can long persist, so we see products like petrochemicals or bulk acids quoted at identical prices by different sellers. To examine these kinds of markets analytically, assume that there are four firms of equal size—call them A, B, C, and D—each taking

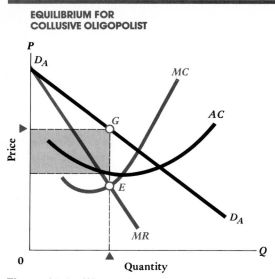

EQUILIBRIUM FOR COLLUSIVE OLIGOPOLIST

Figure 25-1   When oligopolists collude or recognize interdependence, outcome is much like monopoly

After experience with disastrous price wars, each of the few rivals that dominate a given market is almost sure to recognize that each price cut is canceled by competitors' price cuts. So oligopolist A may estimate its demand curve $D_A D_A$ by assuming others will be charging similar prices. In the extreme, firms may illegally collude to set a jointly profit-maximizing price. In both cases, the price will be very close to the level that a single monopolist would choose.

one-quarter of the market. Figure 25-1 illustrates the situation for oligopolist A. Here, A's demand curve, $D_A D_A$, is drawn assuming that all firms have the same cost curves and that other firms' prices follow firm A's price upward and downward. Thus the firm's demand curve is about as inelastic as the entire industry's DD curve, for firm A will always get its pro-rated one-fourth of the shared market as long as all firms charge the same price.[1]

---

[1]Why is a collusive oligopolist's demand curve about as inelastic as the industry demand curve? Recall from Fig. 23-1 that when firm A takes other firms' prices as given, then A's demand responds powerfully to a change in A's price. If firm A's price is a little above other firms' prices, it will get *none* of the market; if firm A undercuts other firms, it gets *all* the market. Thus demand looks much more elastic to the firm in the non-collusive than in the collusive case. (Indeed, can you see why if there are *n* equal-sized competitive firms, demand to the firm looks *n* times more elastic than to the industry?)

In this case, firms may decide to cooperate and seek the **collusive oligopoly** equilibrium, a situation in which firms collude to set the monopoly price and maximize their joint or collective profits. What is the maximum-profit equilibrium for the collusive oligopolist? It is shown in Figure 25-1 at point E, the intersection of the firm's MC curve with the MR curve derived from the $D_A D_A$ demand curve (i.e., the demand curve with mutual dependence recognized). The price for the collusive oligopolist is shown at point G on $D_A D_A$, just above point E. Note that the price is well above MC, just as it is for the monopolist, indicating that output will be depressed below the efficient level where $P = MC$.

Thus when oligopolists can collude completely and maximize their joint profits, taking into account their mutual interdependence, the price and quantity will be close to that of a single monopolist.

While a successful collusive oligopolist would raise price and lower output much as would a monopolist, in reality many obstacles hinder effective collusion. First, collusion is illegal, as we will see in section C of this chapter. Second, firms can "cheat" on the other members of an agreement by cutting their price to selected customers and thereby increasing their market share. This outcome is particularly prevalent in markets where prices are secret, where goods are differentiated, where there is more than a handful of firms, or where the technology is changing rapidly. Moreover, once the trust among rivals breaks down, it is as hard to put back together again as was Humpty-Dumpty, and non-collusive behavior is likely to take over.

How prevalent, then, is collusive oligopoly? According to Adam Smith, writing in 1776:

> People of the same trade seldom meet together, even for merriment and diversion, but the conversation ends in a conspiracy against the public, or in some contrivance to raise prices.

Undoubtedly Smith exaggerated—but only a bit. An examination found that of 1043 major corporations, 94 have recently admitted to or been convicted of illegal price fixing.

On the other hand, we should avoid seeing conspiring businesses behind every bush. Most industries experience vigorous competition from both domestic and foreign firms. Moreover, the attempt to raise prices does not always succeed. And the low rates of profit of concentrated industries shown in Table 25-1 suggest that, however much rivals would *like* to behave collusively, successes are the exception rather than the rule.

Two failures at collusion can be cited. First, the Organization of Petroleum Exporting Countries (OPEC) has again and again attempted to set a monopoly price for oil. This would require member countries to curtail production to keep prices high. On several occasions, however, countries inside and outside OPEC have refused to cut production. The most dramatic collapse of collusion for the oil cartel came temporarily in 1986, when an outbreak of price cutting by Saudi Arabia drove oil prices from $28 per barrel down to below $10.

An even more dramatic example is the following tape-recorded conversation between the heads of Braniff and American Airlines (with expletives deleted):

Putnam (Braniff): Do you have a suggestion for me?

Crandall (American): Yes, I have a suggestion for you. Raise your . . . fares 20 percent. I'll raise mine the next morning. . . . You'll make more money and I will, too.

Putnam: We can't talk about pricing.

No one knows how frequent are such abortive attempts to rig prices.*

Dominant-Firm Oligopoly

Often an industry is composed of one large and dominant firm surrounded by a number of smaller rivals. Early in this century this pattern was exemplified by Standard Oil, U.S. Steel, and Alcoa. More recently IBM, Xerox, General Motors, and AT&T dominated their markets.

Where the largest firm controls 60 to 80 percent of the market, that firm has a number of possible strategies. The most profitable is often to cede part of the market to the competitive fringe and then to behave as a monopolist for the remaining 60 or 80 percent of the market that the firm controls. Such a market is called a *dominant-firm oligopoly,* which is illustrated in Figure 25-2. Here, the demand curve for the entire industry is shown as the black *DD* curve, while the demand for the dominant firm is *dd*.

Consider first the competitive fringe. We have not shown the competitors' supply curve directly; rather, we show the competitive firms' supply as the horizontal distance from the black *DD* curve to the dominant firm's red *dd* curve. Thus way up at price P', the competitive fringe is supplying all the industry demand. Similarly at price P^D, the competitive fringe supplies the quantity between L and C (or Q^C on the horizontal axis).

The key to understanding how prices are set in dominant-firm markets is the derivation of the dominant firm's demand curve, which is the red *dd* curve. How is this derived? We find the dominant firm's *dd* curve by subtracting the competitive fringe's supply from market demand. Hence, at the price P^D, the

---

*Business life is full of strategic bargaining like that between Putnam and Crandall. A century of theorizing by economists about what mind A thinks mind B will do if B thinks A will do such-and-such culminated in the pathbreaking work by J. von Neumann and O. Morgenstern, *The Theory of Games and Economic Behavior,* 3d ed. (Princeton University Press, Princeton, N.J., 1953). While this mathematical theory, cannot clear up all the philosophical problems of how two omniscient minds will act against each other in an interdependent world, it does offer many incisive insights for political warfare as well as economics. Some examples of game theory at work are: A teacher picks quiz questions at random from a book of test questions. A security guard makes rounds at random, not in a discernible pattern. Facing you as a smart rival, I work hard to maximize my most vulnerable defense, knowing you will find out the weakest link in my chain. I bluff at poker, not simply to win a pot with a weak hand but rather, to ensure that all players do not drop out when I bet high on a good hand.

Game theory is also key to understanding the dynamics of the arms race. It can help us understand why, when the United States develops a new weapons system (A-bomb, H-bomb, cruise missile, Star Wars), the military advantage is only temporary. Why? Because the Soviet Union *reacts* to minimize the potential damage from each new weapons system or to imitate the system itself.

The principles of game theory, along with applications to economic behavior, are sketched in the appendix to this chapter.

DOMINANT-FIRM OLIGOPOLY

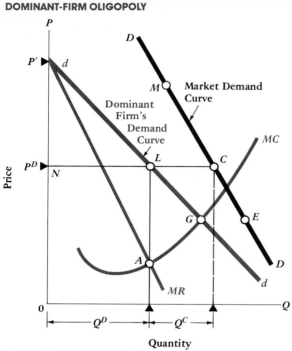

Figure 25-2 A competitive fringe reduces price and raises output

This figure illustrates how the competitive fringe exercises restraint on the dominant firm. The *DD* curve is the industry demand. The competitive fringe has an upward-sloping supply curve. We represent the fringe's supply response as the horizontal difference between black *DD* and red *dd* at each price. After subtracting the fringe's supply response from the industry *DD* demand curve, we find the *dd* demand curve of the dominant firm; this is the industry demand curve less the competitive fringe's output.

Next the dominant firm sets *MC* = *MR*. We see that the equilibrium price is at point *L*. This outcome is more efficient than the outcome at monopoly point *M*, but less efficient than the ideal outcome at *E*.

market demand is shown by the segment *NC*, while the competitive fringe is supplying *LC*, so the demand for the dominant firm's product is *NL*. By calculating at each price the difference between the market demand and the competitive fringe's supply, we derive the dominant firm's *dd* demand curve. Note that at every price the dominant firm's demand curve is somewhat flatter and more elastic than the market *DD* demand curve—the difference reflecting the fact that, as the dominant firm's price rises, the firm will lose more and more business to the competitive fringe.

We can understand price and output decisions in this market by examining cost and demand conditions for the dominant firm. In Figure 25-2, red *dd* is its demand curve, of which red *MR* is the applicable marginal revenue curve. In addition, red *MC* is the dominant firm's marginal cost curve. The profit-maximizing price is found by applying our monopoly analysis to the dominant firm's *MC* and *MR* curves. Equilibrium occurs at the intersection of the dominant firm's marginal cost and marginal revenue schedules at point *A*. At equilibrium price P^D, the dominant firm is supplying Q^D (from point *N* to point *L*), while the competitive fringe is supplying Q^C (from point *L* to point *C*).

The price and quantity under dominant-firm oligopoly will differ markedly from either the monopolistic or the competitive outcomes. If the dominant firm were to behave competitively, it would set its output where its marginal cost intersects its demand curve, at point *G*, leading to total industry output at point *E* on the demand curve. Note how much lower is price and how much higher is output in the competitive case.

What if the industry were suddenly monopolized and the dominant firm wiped out the competitive fringe? Elimination of the fringe would present the dominant firm with a different *MR* curve (the new monopoly *MR* curve would be derived from the total market demand curve, *DD*). Drawing in such an *MR* curve will help show that the monopoly equilibrium without the fringe will come way up the *DD* demand curve at point *M* of Figure 25-2, with a higher price and lower quantity than the dominant-firm oligopoly equilibrium.

For most of its history, OPEC has behaved as a dominant-firm monopolist. Saudi Arabia and its close neighbors (Kuwait and smaller Gulf countries) control approximately 60 percent of the productive capacity of OPEC. The Saudi group has been unable to persuade some of its members to limit production as a way of maintaining OPEC's control on world oil markets. Since 1982 (with the exception of the 1986 price war) Saudi Arabia has allowed the other countries to produce a given amount, while Saudi production was set in order to maintain the cartel's official price.

In terms of Figure 25-2, then, OPEC has agreed upon the price P^D. Shifts in market demand *(DD)* and the competitive fringe's supply *(DD* minus *dd)* were absorbed by changes in the output of the dominant producer (Saudi Arabia).

There are variants of the dominant-firm model. One important case is *price leadership* by the dominant firm. Here the largest firm performs a signaling role, showing other firms what it thinks the collusive oligopoly price should be. Steel, cigarettes, automobiles, and cereals were industries in which a dominant firm at times during past decades acted like a pilot, attempting to steer prices upward from competitive levels.

As a result of price leadership, an oligopoly might well have high prices without a telephone call like that of American Airlines' Crandall. Collusion can be tacit. But the increased pressure of foreign competition and deregulation has probably made tacit collusion more difficult during the last decade or so. As a result we may have witnessed a sharp reduction in the power of dominant firms to be price leaders. The reduced rate of profit in American industry since the 1960s may indicate the extent to which increased domestic and foreign competition has eroded dominant-firm profit margins.[2]

Monopolistic Competition

A third important type of imperfect competition occurs when many firms sell similar but not identical products. This variety, first analyzed by Edward Chamberlin, is called **monopolistic competition.**

Monopolistic competition resembles perfect competition in three ways: there are many buyers and sellers, entry and exit is easy, and each firm takes other firms' prices as given. What is the difference? The distinction is that products are identical under perfect competition (as, for example, the red winter wheat sold in the Chicago Board of Trade), while products are differentiated under monopolistic competition.

[2]Another important approach is the "limit pricing model." This is explored in question 9 at the end of this chapter.

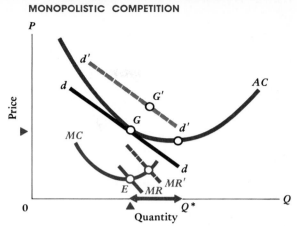

MONOPOLISTIC COMPETITION

Figure 25-3   Free entry of numerous monopolistic competitors wipes out profit

The typical seller's original profitable *d'd'* curve will be shifted downward and leftward by entry of new rivals. Entry ceases only when each seller has been forced into a long-run, no-profit tangency such as at *G*. At long-run equilibrium, price remains above *MC*, and each producer is on the left-hand declining branch of its long-run *AC* curve.

Examples of such differentiated products are different brands of gasoline or soft drinks or prescription drugs or apartments. Within each product group, products or services are closely related but different in some way. (What are the similarities and differences among some colleges that you know?)

The sources of product differentiation are not important at this point. What is important is that *product differentiation leads to a downward slope in each seller's demand curve.*

Figure 25-3 shows a grocery store in short-run equilibrium at G'. Its *d'd'* demand curve is sloped because its product is a little different from anyone else's. Price is at G', and the firm is making a handsome profit (because price at G' is above *AC*).

But our grocery store has no monopoly on land or lettuce. Entry is free, so new firms can produce their own differentiated products. For simplicity, assume that costs are the same for new and existing firms (so all firms have the same *AC* curve). Since the industry is profitable, new firms are drawn into the market.

These new entrants cut into the demand curve of old firms, and our firm's $d'd'$ curve moves leftward to dd.

What is the ultimate economic outcome? Grocery stores will continue to enter the market until all economic profits have been beaten down to zero. Thus, final long-run equilibrium for the typical seller ends up at the tangency point G where the dd curve just touches (but never goes above) the firm's AC curve. Point G is a long-run equilibrium for the industry because profits are zero and no one is tempted to enter or forced to exit the industry.

The monopolistic competition model describes many important features of American capitalism. The first feature, noted at the beginning of this chapter in Table 25-1, is that the rate of profit in many concentrated industries seems low relative to what a monopolist, or even a crafty oligopolist, should be able to earn. Figure 25-3 suggests that monopoly profits will be competed away as new firms create new differentiated products—Pepsi competes with Coke, Newport with Kools, Hondas and Toyotas drive down prices of Fords and Chevrolets.

Some economists go on to a second point, that monopolistic competition is inherently inefficient. Look back at the long-run equilibrium point G of Figure 25-3.[3] At that point, price is above marginal cost; hence, output is reduced below the ideal competitive level.

In light of its inefficiency, critics of monopolistic competition go on to a third point: "These industries are the quintessence of what capitalism doesn't need. We have hundreds of thousands of retail outlets, hundreds of virtually identical soaps or aspirins—all selling at prices well above marginal costs. If we could somehow get rid of a quarter or a half of these products, and standardize on just a few designs, wouldn't the economy gain enormously?"

Modern analysts find that the answer to this question is not clear-cut. They respond: "By decimating the monopolistic competitors, you might well lower prices. But you might also lower ultimate consumer welfare as people would no longer have the desired diversity of goods. The efficiency losses from too high prices are small, while people appear willing to pay a great deal for diversity rather than all going around in identical gray shirts or box-like cars."

Where can we look to see an illustration of monopolistic competition in action? Perhaps the most familiar example is the retail gasoline market. There are 140,000 gasoline stations in the United States, each selling to an infinitesimal part of the national market. But each one has a little bit of market power, or slope to its demand curve. Its product differentiation comes from location (being near one's normal travel route), the type of gasoline sold, cleanliness of the station, and ancillary services (like windshield cleaning or a convenience store at the same location).

You might think that with a bit of slope to their demand curve, gasoline stations would make a profit over the normal return to capital and management. In fact, they don't. Entry and exit tend to regulate the level of profits so that, over the long run, gas stations earn but a normal economic return on their invested capital.

Again and again the same story is told—how in markets like retailing or wholesale trade, where barriers to entry are low and products are differentiated, numerous firms produce inefficiently small quantities and have no economic profits to show for their efforts.

B. BEHAVIOR OF LARGE CORPORATIONS

The first part of this chapter presented the major elements of the theory of imperfect competition—describing how the price and quantity in oligopolistic markets depend upon the number of firms and upon the degree of their successful collusion.

We now turn to a discussion of three of the central controversies surrounding large firms. We begin by asking whether firms really maximize profits. A careful review of principles of markup pricing will suggest limitations on firms' profit-seeking tendencies.

---

[3]Question 11 at the end of the chapter investigates the difference between the perfectly competitive and the monopolistically competitive tangencies.

We then examine the Schumpeterian defense of monopoly as the major source of innovation of new products and processes. We conclude by summarizing the pros and cons of imperfect competition.

Do Firms Maximize Profits?

To what degree do business firms actually try to maximize their profits? To what extent do they succeed when they try?

We cannot give a precise answer to these questions, but this much is certainly true: If a firm is reckless in making its cost, revenue, and profit decisions, then competitive forces will eventually eliminate that firm, or its managers, from the scene. And these forces operate more powerfully in more competitive markets. Hence, to survive, a firm must pay some attention to the profitability of its actions.

But this does not necessarily mean that every oligopolist or monopolist is seeking desperately to squeeze the last ounce of profit from every transaction. As soon as a firm gains some market power, it begins to have the ability to seek other objectives than pure profit maximization. For example, if a dominant firm decides to set its price a bit below the profit-maximizing level, it can sell more output without going bankrupt. Or if its price is set a bit above the profit-maximizing price, it will still sell enough output to make a tidy profit.

Why might a firm deviate from pure profit maximization? There are two general classes of reasons—bounded rationality and alternative goals.

Bounded rationality denotes behavior in which firms or consumers do not attempt to squeeze the last drop of profit or utility out of their actions. Why not? In reality, people have limited time, resources, and information and are therefore forced to make imperfect decisions. Consumers cannot spend all day looking for the lowest-priced head of lettuce. Searching for low prices or for the absolute optimum requires scarce time and resources. And decision making, like all other valuable commodities, must be rationed out.

Because perfect rationality is too costly, people and firms must settle for fairly good decisions. Moreover, in some repetitive situations, the use of a "rule of thumb"—or simplified decision rule—is a way of making decisions that greatly economizes on time. Markup pricing, to be discussed in a moment, is an example of a rule of thumb that has its roots in bounded rationality.

A second reason that firms do not single-mindedly maximize profits is that they sometimes pursue *alternative goals*. We saw in Chapter 20 that ownership is separated from control in today's giant corporations. Won't managers therefore have different incentives from shareholders? Shareholders are mainly interested in high dividends and stock-price increases. But managers may be motivated by the desire to run a large firm—much as kings want large empires. Further, they may shun risky investments for fear that if the firm loses money on some project the managers may lose their jobs. And directors may want to siphon large salaries and bonuses out of stockholders' earnings.

While some alternative goals may be innocuous, one particular conflict between management and owners raises a serious economic concern. If firms avoid worthwhile but risky investments because their managers fear the possibility of large losses, the pace of invention and innovation could be slowed. On a large scale, excessive aversion to risk could retard productivity growth and thereby hurt a nation's living standard. The best way to guarantee adequate investment and risk taking is to encourage the coexistence of different varieties of firms—small firms, foreign firms, and privately held firms—that are waiting in the wings to pounce on a market should the leaders show excessive caution or technical sloth.

Markup Pricing

One of the classical instances where firms deviate from pure profit maximization is in their price setting. Observation shows that firms rarely sit down to calculate marginal revenues and marginal costs and set price on that basis. Most firms have only a vague idea of the shape of their demand curve or of the price elasticity for their products. They cannot determine their optimum price and output with neat exactitude. Yet prices must be set.

Here is where average cost plays an important role. If you were to discuss pricing with a management consultant, she might tell you the following:

Put yourself in the seat of the president of a company producing hundreds of products. You have a rough forecast of this year's sales and costs, but only a hazy idea of the demand elasticities for your various products.

You might start with your sales forecasts. Then you turn to the cost experts to determine the average cost of producing each product in question at some standard or normal level of sales. There will be plenty of headaches in arriving at any sort of figure, but the accountants provide an estimate of the average costs.

Here is where the surprise comes:

Armed with the information about sales and costs, you will almost surely never set your price by an *MR* and *MC* comparison. Rather, you will generally take the calculated average cost of a product and *mark it up* by adding a fixed percentage—5 or 10 or 20 or 40 percent of the average cost. This cost-plus-markup figure then becomes the selling price. Note that if all goes as planned, the price will cover all direct and overhead costs and allow the firm a solid profit.

Investigators of actual business pricing policies have testified that corporations often do follow the above-described practice of quoting prices on a ''cost-plus-markup'' basis. Case after case shows that markup pricing is the norm in imperfectly competitive markets.

However realistic, this analysis is incomplete. It stops tantalizingly short of telling us *why* the average markup is 40 percent in one industry and 5 percent in another. It cannot tell us why the average markup in 1984 was 13 percent in pharmaceuticals and minus 1 percent in metals. To explain the level of the markup requires an analysis of the market structure, along with demand and costs.

Does the prevalence of markup pricing suggest that firms do not maximize profits? Or, worse, that managers are simply inert slugs who follow the same markup pricing rules that their predecessors used? In a few cases, this conclusion is probably warranted. More often, however, markup pricing should be seen as a rule of thumb—a management tool produced by the requirements of bounded rationality. In a large company producing tens of thousands of products, it is simply not possible to set every price every day. By the use of markup pricing, and adjustment of markups from time to time, firms can move in steps toward their desired profit-maximizing outcome. Just as a baseball pitcher may not calculate the equations of motion for every pitch, so managers in search of excellence may not always have *MC* and *MR* in mind as markups are adjusted up and down in the search for higher profits.

Markup pricing is only one example of how we can better understand seemingly irrational economic behavior when we remember the principle of bounded rationality—that decision makers' time is scarce and information is imperfect.

The Schumpeterian Hypothesis

The last chapter has contained a litany of complaints about imperfect competitors. They tend to set prices too high and quantities too low, they may earn supernormal profits, and so on. But we must now turn to one point of defense—and a powerful one. In a line of argument originating with Joseph Schumpeter, many have argued that the wellspring of innovation and technical change is found in giant corporations and in imperfect competition. While it is true that imperfect competitors cause inefficiencies because their prices lie above marginal costs, Schumpeter thought monopolies to be the engines of dynamic invention and technological growth in a capitalist economy.

We have already seen in Table 25-1 that research and development (R&D) is more intensively pursued in concentrated than in competitive industries. The classical case in point is the Bell Telephone Labs. This giant research organization operated with the support of the world's largest monopoly—AT&T. Over the four decades before the breakup of the Bell System, Bell Labs invented or made major contributions to transistors and semiconductors, microwave and fiber optics, bubble memory and programming languages, satellites and electronic switching. Over the 1970s fully 10 percent of all American industrial basic research was conducted by Bell Labs.

Powerful R&D efforts have shown similar results in du Pont, RCA, IBM, GE, GM, and many other large companies.

Where does the imperfection of competition enter? R&D and invention are quite distinct from other economic activities. They are important examples of externalities, which, as Chapter 3 described, arise when firms or people impose costs or benefits on others without paying the appropriate costs or receiving the proper benefits. When Bell Labs invented the transistor, the benefits (in terms of new, improved, or cheaper products) spread widely around the globe. Japanese TVs, German cars, American microcomputers, everyone's digital watches—all these goods benefited enormously from transistors and semiconductors. But the inventor, Bell Labs, received only a tiny monetary reward in the form of royalties on the inventions. Most of the benefit from these inventions flowed to consumers in the form of less expensive and higher-quality goods and services.

The inability of firms to capture the full monetary value of their inventions is called *inappropriability*. The example of the transistor, where the inventor reaped but a tiny fraction of the value of the invention, is quite typical. Careful studies by Edwin Mansfield and others have found that the social return to invention (that is, the value of inventions to all consumers and producers) has been around 3 times the private return to invention (that is, the monetary value to the inventor alone).

To the extent that the rewards to invention are inappropriable, we would expect that private research and development is underfunded and that the nation invests too little in industrial R&D. Moreover, the most significant underinvestment is likely to lie in basic research, and this tendency has led most governments to subsidize most basic research in health and science.

The inappropriability of invention also explains why large firms are much more likely to undertake R&D than are small firms. If IBM sells 65 percent of the nation's computers, then any computer invention is likely to benefit IBM in a major way. It has a strong incentive to invest in R&D. Small inventors have a much smaller incentive: if I were to invent a new disk drive, since I sell only a negligible fraction of the nation's computers it would be much more difficult for me to profit from my invention. Moreover, only if I can receive an enforceable patent can I as an individ-

ual or small firm collect the fruits of my inventive activity.[4] Finally, only large firms can afford the substantial development and marketing costs for new products, thereby gaining a head start on the competition in the race for a large market share.

It was just this view that led Joseph Schumpeter to advance his bold hypothesis.

> The modern standard of life of the masses evolved during the period of relatively unfettered ''big business.'' If we list the items that enter the modern workman's budget and, from 1899 on, observe the course of their prices not in terms of money but in terms of the hours of labor that will buy them—i.e., each year's money prices divided by each year's hourly wage rates—we cannot fail to be struck by the rate of the advance which, considering the spectacular improvement in qualities, seems to have been greater and not smaller than it ever was before. . . .

> Nor is this all. As soon as we go into details and inquire into the individual items in which progress was most conspicuous, the trail leads not to the doors of those firms that work under conditions of comparatively free competition but precisely to the doors of the large concerns—which, as in the case of agricultural machinery, also account for much of the progress in the competitive sector—and a shocking suspicion dawns upon us that big business may have had more to do with creating that standard of life than keeping it down.[5]

An even greater enthusiasm was expressed by J. K. Galbraith:

> A benign Providence . . . has made the modern industry of a few large firms an almost perfect instrument for inducing technical change. . . . There is no more pleasant fiction than that technical change is the product of the matchless ingenuity of the small man forced by competition to employ his wits to better his neighbor. Unhappily,

---

[4]Countries have long recognized the need for public protection for inventions. Today, the United States awards patents to the inventor of an original product or process. The holder of a patent has the monopoly right to use or profit from the patented invention for 17 years. By award of such a monopoly in well-defined circumstances, the government increases the degree of appropriability for the invention and thus increases the incentive to invent, especially for small inventors. Examples of successful patents include those for the telephone, the Xerox machine, and the Polaroid camera.
[5]J. A. Schumpeter, *Capitalism, Socialism and Democracy* (Harper, New York, 1942), p. 81.

it is a fiction. Technical development has long since become the preserve of the scientist and the engineer. Most of the cheap and simple inventions have, to put it bluntly, been made.[6]

Because economists had been taught about the evils of monopoly and the wastes of imperfect competition, this bold pronouncement of *the Schumpeterian hypothesis* came as a profound shock to the economics profession. Perhaps imperfect competition is the major source of our high living standards rather than an impediment to rapid economic growth.

This hypothesis has been subject to careful scrutiny for over four decades. How well have these views survived in the academic marketplace? To begin with, everyone grants the basic truth in the Schumpeterian hypothesis. We hardly see our local grocery store, gasoline station, or tomato farmer supporting a large R&D establishment. Thus, in 1982, firms with more than 5000 employees accounted for 87 percent of privately financed R&D. In the quarter-million manufacturing firms with less than 1000 workers, only 4 percent had a formal R&D program, as compared to 91 percent of the large firms.

While most will concede that tiny firms do little research, some will go no further. Skeptics concerning the Schumpeterian hypothesis note that many firms with low market shares have substantial and successful R&D programs. Moreover, when John Jewkes and his colleagues traced the history of the most important inventions of this century, they found that less than half came from the laboratories of large corporations. The importance of small inventors has been confirmed in recent years as major new products seem to arise from nowhere—as occurred when Apple Computer, Inc. launched the microcomputer revolution in the early 1980s.

To summarize, the relationship between innovation and market power is complex. Because large firms have made a major contribution to research and innovation, we should be cautious about claims that bigness is unmitigated badness or about plans to subdivide firms into tiny establishments. At the same time, we must recognize that small businesses and individuals have made some of the most revolutionary technological breakthroughs. To promote rapid innovation, a nation must preserve a variety of approaches and organizations.

[6]*American Capitalism* (Houghton Mifflin, Boston, 1952), p. 91.

A Balance Sheet on Imperfect Competition

Now that we have completed our survey of the major theories and key controversial issues of monopoly and oligopoly, let us sum up the positive and negative points about imperfect competition.

- *Output restrictions*   Imperfect competitors produce economic waste when they set prices too high relative to marginal cost. Thus consumers in the monopolistic or oligopolistic industry are paying more than the good is costing in terms of goods forgone in other industries.

- *Economies of scale*   In many industries, there are pervasive economies of scale. To make the car or steel or aircraft industries atomistic would be to push firms far up their average cost curves. Where concentration of industry is driven by scale economies, consumers may face prices above marginal costs—but prices are probably still far below what they would be in an economy where every town had its own steel mill and every state its aircraft manufacturer.

- *Dynamic research and development*   Similarly, the Schumpeterian hypothesis argues that monopolies and oligopolies are the major source of innovation and technological progress. If we atomized our large firms, dividing them into many small firms, we might at the same time pulverize the nation's great private R&D laboratories.

Policies toward Large Firms

In weighing this assessment of the strengths and weaknesses of markets characterized by imperfect competition, experts point to three important conclusions for economic policy:

- *Keep barriers low*   Barriers to competition should be at a minimum. Nothing slows the pace of innovation as quickly as walling off firms and markets from actual or potential rivalry. Remember that ''the tariff is the mother of trusts.'' When rivals are present, they will drive prices down and quality up and increase the pace of introduction of better products.

■ *Respect scale economies* Many technologies exhibit significant economies of scale or scope. In these industries, efficiency may require large firms that produce a sizable share of the entire market. The best policy here is to allow large firms to compete vigorously and to keep regulatory or trade barriers as low as possible.

■ *Curb collusion* Remember that firms may be tempted to collude in raising prices or dividing markets; firms with market power may also engage in predatory or exclusionary activities. No serious economic defense has been made of these collusive practices, and most governments today condemn anticompetitive practices.

The goal of preventing anticompetitive collusive practices is the subject of antitrust policy, to which we now turn.

C. ANTITRUST POLICY

Large firms have long been viewed as unwelcome agglomerations of economic power and undesirable sources of economic inefficiency. Just a century ago, legislatures began to pass antitrust laws that attempted to contain monopolies. Antitrust policies attack anticompetitive abuses in two different ways: first, by prohibiting certain kinds of *business conduct,* such as price fixing, and second by curbing some *market structures,* such as monopolies, that are thought most likely to restrict commerce and to abuse their power in other ways.

This area of public policy has been a fruitful arena for interactions of law and economics for decades. So as we turn to the study of antitrust policy, we will examine one of the most critical parts of business law, and at the same time see how the tools of microeconomic analysis extend beyond the textbooks into economic life itself.

A study of American antitrust policy must include the following:

■ The history of *legislative acts*—e.g., the Sherman Act (1890), the Clayton Act (1914), and the Federal Trade Commission Act (1914), plus later amendments.

■ The evolution of *case law on structure and conduct*—the definition of different forms of illegal conduct, changing views on the role of size and structure in finding antitrust violations, and the outcomes of the major antitrust cases from Standard Oil in 1911 to IBM in 1982.

■ *The new approach to antitrust of the 1980s*—one that stresses the intrinsic rivalry of oligopolists and is skeptical of the ability of government to use antitrust policies to improve the performance of large multinational enterprises.

The balance of this chapter explores these three aspects of antitrust policy.

THE FRAMEWORK STATUTES

Antitrust law is like a huge forest that has grown from a handful of seeds. The statutes on which the law is based are so straightforward that they are shown in Table 25-2; it is astounding how much law has grown from so few words.

Sherman Act (1890)

Monopolies had long been illegal under the common law. But these laws proved ineffective against the mergers and trusts that began to grow in the 1880s. Populist sentiments then led to the Sherman Act.

The Sherman Act made it illegal to "monopolize trade" and outlawed all "combination or conspiracy in restraint of trade." But beyond an antipathy toward "monopolizing" there is no evidence that anyone had clear notions as to which actions were to be regarded as legal or illegal.

Clayton Act (1914)

To spell out the vague intent of the Sherman Act and to strengthen it, the Clayton Act was passed. It outlawed *tying contracts* (in which a customer is forced to buy product B if she wants product A); it ruled

THE ANTITRUST LAWS

Sherman Antitrust Act (1890, as amended)

§1. Every contract, combination in the form of trust or otherwise, or conspiracy, in restraint of trade or commerce among the several States, or with foreign nations, is declared to be illegal.

§2. Every person who shall monopolize, or attempt to monopolize, or combine or conspire with any other person or persons, to monopolize any part of the trade or commerce among the several States, or with foreign nations, shall be deemed guilty of a felony. . . .

Clayton Antitrust Act (1914, as amended)

§2. It shall be unlawful . . . to discriminate in price between different purchasers of commodities of like grade and quality . . . where the effect of such discrimination may be substantially to lessen competition or tend to create a monopoly in any line of commerce. . . . *Provided,* That nothing herein contained shall prevent differentials which make only due allowance for differences in the cost. . . .

§3. That it shall be unlawful for any person . . . to lease or make a sale or contract . . . on the condition, agreement, or understanding that the lessee or purchaser thereof shall not use or deal in the . . . commodities of a competitor . . . where the effect . . . may be to substantially lessen competition or tend to create a monopoly in any line of commerce.

§7. No [corporation] . . . shall acquire . . . the whole or any part . . . of another [corporation] . . . where . . . the effect of such an acquisition may be substantially to lessen competition, or to tend to create a monopoly.

Federal Trade Commission Act (1914, as amended)

§5. Unfair methods of competition . . . and unfair or deceptive acts or practices . . . are declared unlawful.

Table 25-2 The basis of American antitrust law is contained in these statutes

price discrimination and exclusive dealings illegal; it banned *interlocking directorates* and *mergers* formed by acquiring common stock of competitors. In each case, such actions were illegal when they might substantially lessen competition.

The Clayton Act emphasized prevention before the fact as well as punishment after. In contrast to the early common law, which had been used particularly against organized labor, the Clayton Act specifically provided antitrust immunity to labor unions.

Federal Trade Commission

In 1914 the Federal Trade Commission (FTC) was established. The FTC's primary functions are to prohibit "unfair methods of competition" and to warn against anticompetitive mergers. In 1938, the FTC also acquired one of its most important functions—the power to ban false and deceptive advertising. In order to enforce these powers, the FTC is empowered to investigate, hold hearings, and issue cease-and-desist orders.

BASIC ISSUES IN ANTITRUST: CONDUCT, STRUCTURE, AND MERGERS

In the century since passage of the Sherman Act, economists and jurists have developed a body of thinking about the proper role of large enterprises. Modern antitrust theory emphasizes the role of structure and conduct in analyzing market structures.

Illegal Conduct

Among the earliest antitrust decisions were those concerning illegal behavior. The courts have ruled that certain kinds of collusive behavior are illegal per se (in themselves); these acts are illegal in that no defense is permitted. The offenders cannot defend themselves by pointing to some worthy objective (such as product quality) or mitigating circumstance (such as low profits).

The most important set of per se illegal conduct is agreements among competing firms that fix prices, restrict output, or divide markets. Such actions have the effect of raising prices and lowering output. Even the severest critics of antitrust policy can find no redeeming virtue in price fixing.

Other forms of conduct have also been limited by antitrust laws. These include:

■ Retail price maintenance, where retailers agree not to sell below or above a price specified by manufacturers.

■ Predatory pricing, in which a firm sells its goods for less than production costs (usually interpreted as marginal cost or average variable cost).

■ Tying contracts or arrangements, where a firm will sell product A only when the purchaser buys product B.

■ Price discrimination, in which a firm sells the same product to different customers at different prices for reasons not related to cost or meeting competition.

As you read over this list, as well as the previous paragraph, note again that these practices relate to a firm's *conduct*. They might take place in monopolies or in smaller firms, but it is the acts that are illegal and not the size of the firm that undertakes them.

Although conduct-related cases receive less public attention than structural cases, they are an important part of antitrust. Perhaps the most celebrated example is the great electric-equipment conspiracy.

In 1961, the electric-equipment industry was found guilty of collusive price agreements. Executives of the largest companies—such as GE and Westinghouse—conspired to raise prices and covered their tracks, in a manner reminiscent of a spy novel, by meeting in out-of-the-way hunting lodges, using code names, and making telephone calls from public phone booths. Although the top executives in these companies apparently were unaware of what the vice-presidents just below them were doing, they had put much pressure on the vice-presidents for increased sales. The companies agreed to pay extensive damages to their customers for overcharges; some of the executives involved spent time in jail on criminal charges.

While extreme, such practices are not infrequent. There are on average 50 federal cases and hundreds of private cases each year that attack price fixing and other illegal behavior.

Structure: Is Bigness Badness?

The most visible antitrust cases were those relating not to conduct but to structure. These come either as attempts to *break up* large firms, or in *anticipatory* cases brought against the proposed mergers of large firms. We will review each of these two themes.

The early 1900s witnessed the first surge of activity under the Sherman Act. In 1911, the Supreme Court ordered the American Tobacco Company and Standard Oil to be broken up into many separate companies.

In condemning these flagrant monopolies, the Supreme Court enunciated the important ''rule of reason'': Only *unreasonable* restraints of trade (mergers, agreements, and the like) came within the scope of the Sherman Act and were considered illegal.

The rule-of-reason doctrine virtually repealed the antitrust law's attack on monopolistic mergers, as shown by the U.S. Steel case (1920). Although J. P. Morgan had put this giant together by merger, and it did in the beginning enjoy 60 percent of the market, the court held that mere size per se was no offense. Courts in that period, as today, focused more on anticompetitive *conduct* than on pure monopoly *structure* as the legal offense.

The New Deal and Alcoa Congress passes laws. But nothing happens unless private parties or the Department of Justice brings suit to enforce them. During the roaring twenties, antitrust went into hibernation. Not until the late 1930s, when F. D. Roosevelt put Thurman Arnold in charge of antitrust, was there a real burst of federal prosecutions in this area. Arnold tackled the building industries, glass, cigarettes, cement, and many others.

The Alcoa case (1945) represents the culmination of New Deal activism, as well as the furthest boundary of trust-busting judicial findings. Alcoa had gained a 90 percent market share, but by means that were not in themselves illegal: installing capacity ahead of demand, keeping prices *low* to prevent potential competition, and so forth. The court nonetheless found Alcoa had violated the Sherman Act. Monopoly power, even if lawfully acquired, could constitute an evil and be condemned. This period was one in which the courts came to emphasize market *structure* along with market *conduct: monopoly power, even without otherwise illegal conduct, was declared illegal.*

Recent Developments

Since the high-water mark in 1945, the pattern of judicial findings and economic theory has steadily retreated from the hostility to market power seen in the Alcoa case. Only two major structural cases (brought under section 2 of the Sherman Act) have been pursued in the last two decades: the IBM and the AT&T cases, to be discussed in detail below, ended in 1982. Since 1982, federal antitrust policy has lain dormant, with the late 1980s marking the first time in a half-century that no major government antitrust case was being conducted.

A review of the latest two cases will reveal some of the flavor of modern thinking about antitrust policy.

The AT&T Case Until 1983 AT&T had a virtual monopoly on the telecommunications market. It provided more than 95 percent of all long-distance calls and 85 percent of all local lines and sold most of the nation's telephone equipment. The complex of companies owned by AT&T included Bell Telephone Labs, Western Electric Company, and 23 Bell Operating Companies. This complex was often called the Bell System.

Since the invention of the telephone in 1876, the company Alexander Graham Bell founded has spent almost as many years fighting antitrust suits as making telephones. Two earlier government antitrust suits had had limited effect on the company.

In 1974, the Department of Justice filed yet another and more far-reaching suit. It complained that AT&T had (a) prevented competing long-distance carriers (like MCI) from connecting to local exchanges, and (b) obstructed other equipment manufacturers from selling telecommunications equipment to subscribers or to Bell Operating Companies. The important legal and economic argument was that Bell had used its local telephone monopoly to project monopoly into the long-distance and the telephone-equipment markets.

Bell took two lines of defense. It first (as defendants often do) denied many factual charges or rebutted their relevance. Its second rebuttal was that the U.S. telephone system was the best in the world precisely *because* Bell owned and operated virtually the entire U.S. telephone system. In a line of argument similar to the Schumpeterian hypothesis, AT&T argued that the size and scope of the Bell System made its monopoly a "reasonable" way to conduct the telephone business.

The result was bizarre and surprised everyone. Fearful of the outcome of the case and hoping to be freed to compete more effectively, Bell's management settled with the government in a *consent decree* that essentially met every point of the government's proposed remedy. Bell's local telephone operating companies were divested (or legally separated) from AT&T and in 1984 were regrouped into seven large regional telephone holding companies. AT&T held on to its long-distance operations as well as Bell Labs (the research organization) and Western Electric (the equipment manufacturer). But its size, in terms of assets, was reduced by 80 percent.

In some respects, the AT&T settlement is a victory for competition. Local telephone companies are free to select their equipment. Consumers are free to choose among alternative long-distance providers. AT&T is no longer able to take advantage of its local franchise monopoly to block the entry of rival companies.

But many economists raised questions about the wisdom of the consent decree. What will happen to the quality of telephone service in a more fragmented industry? Will Bell Labs maintain its technological virtuosity? In a world where many companies are responsible for the electric and acoustic properties of telecommunications, will cross talk and buzz return to the levels of the 1920s and 1930s, as "everybody's business becomes nobody's business"? These questions, and that of the overall economic wisdom of the outcome, will be answered only in the years to come.

The IBM Case The second major antitrust case in recent years was the government suit to dismember IBM. The government filed suit in 1969, charging that IBM "has attempted to monopolize and has monopolized . . . general purpose digital computers." The government charged that IBM had a dominant market share, with 76 percent of the market in 1967. Moreover, the government claimed that IBM had used many devices to prevent others from competing; the listed anticompetitive steps included tie-in pricing, such low prices as to discourage entry, and introduction of new products that tended to reduce the attractiveness of the products of other companies.

IBM contested the government case (along with a host of private cases) with tenacity and vigor. The government case dragged on for 13 years. IBM's major defense was that the government was penalizing success rather than anticompetitive behavior. The fundamental dilemma in such cases was crisply stated in the Alcoa case: "the successful competitor having been urged to compete must not be turned on when he wins." IBM claimed that the government was doing just that—penalizing the firm that had accurately foreseen the enormous potential in the computer revolution and had dominated the industry through its "superior skill, foresight, and industry."

The case was dragging along inconclusively when the Reagan administration's antitrust chief, William Baxter, undertook a careful review and then landed a bombshell on the legal community. In 1982, the government dismissed the case as "without merit." The government's reasoning was that the computer industry, unlike the telecommunications industry, was unregulated and subject to the full force of market competition. Relying on the Chicago view of antitrust (see below), Baxter held that this industry was intrinsically competitive and that government attempts to restructure the computer market were more likely to harm than promote economic efficiency.

Private Antitrust Up to now we have considered government antitrust actions. One of the remarkable developments in recent years has been the privatization of antitrust enforcement. Under the law, private parties can bring damage suits. If the private party wins, it gets *triple damages* plus reasonable costs.

Spurred by the gains from triple damages, private parties have been increasingly active in bringing antitrust suits. In the first decades of this century, the number of government and private antitrust suits were approximately equal. But by the late 1970s, private parties were bringing more than a thousand cases a year, compared to the government's fifty or so. Awards as high as $1.8 billion (in a preliminary judgment against AT&T) have made this a lucrative hill to mine.

The issues raised by the privatization of antitrust

law are just beginning to be debated. On the one hand, the prospect of a billion-dollar lawsuit must surely give pause to a potential conspiracy—so in this respect the antitrust laws are probably better enforced. But to the extent that the present antitrust laws are inefficiently designed, as many economists now believe, the army of private litigators will only help enforce poorly designed laws more strictly. Some thoughtful scholars now think that the reward of triple damages is too powerful and should be reduced.

Mergers: Law and Practice

Companies can gain market power through growth (plowing back earnings and building new plants). But a much easier way to gain market share, or simply to get bigger, is to merge with another company.

Horizontal mergers—in which companies in the same industry combine—are forbidden under the Clayton Act when the effect may be to reduce competition substantially. Case law and the Department of Justice's 1982 and 1984 merger guidelines clarified the meaning of this vague statutory language. Thus, under the guidelines, industries are divided into unconcentrated, moderately concentrated, and highly concentrated. Mergers in the latter two types of industries will be challenged even in cases where the firms involved have small market shares. For example, in a highly concentrated industry, if a firm with a market share of 10 percent acquires one with a share of 2.5 percent or more, the Department of Justice is "likely to challenge" the merger.[7]

Vertical mergers occur when two firms at different stages of the production process come together. In recent decades, the courts took a hard line toward vertical mergers. They looked mainly at the fact that a merger might lead to exclusive dealings; they worried less about whether vertical integration was driven by true efficiencies of joint operations.

As part of its changes in antitrust policy (discussed more fully in the next section), the Reagan administration changed the guidelines on mergers in 1982 and 1984. The guidelines greatly relaxed enforcement with respect to both vertical and horizontal mergers.

[7]Question 12 at the end of this chapter provides an illustration of how such guidelines operate in practice.

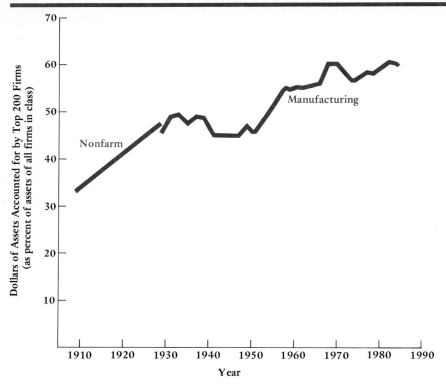

Figure 25-4 Share of assets in top 200 firms

Since the turn of the century, industrial assets have become more and more concentrated in fewer giant companies. The data are not always comparable, but they show a sharp increase during the 1920s and 1930s, as well as during the early 1950s. [Source: F. M. Scherer, *Industrial Market Structure and Economic Performance*, 2d ed. (Houghton Mifflin Company, Boston, 1980); Clair Wilcox and William G. Shepherd, *Public Policies toward Business* (Irwin, Homewood, Ill., 1975); U.S. Bureau of the Census, *Concentration Ratios in Manufacturing*; and *Statistical Abstract of the United States*. The break in the series indicates a change in the method of calculating shares.]

Many believe that these changes brought on the great wave of mergers and acquisitions of the 1980s.

Yet a third kind of combination, called **conglomerate mergers,** involves unrelated businesses. In a conglomerate merger, a chemical or steel company might buy an oil company, or a firm (like ITT) that has many lines of business might add yet more strings to its bow (hotels, rental cars, or whatever).

The critics of conglomerates make two points. First, they note that, in part because of merger activity, the concentration of assets in the top companies has grown steadily over this century. Figure 25-4 shows an estimate of the share of assets accounted for

by the 200 largest corporations. While incomplete, the data show that the asset share of the top 200 has apparently risen from about one-third around 1910 to 61 percent in 1984. The increasing trend in asset concentration alarms many economists and policymakers, as evidenced by the Federal Trade Commission, which wrote a few years ago that "the giant corporations will ultimately take over the country." In every era when a large number of conglomerate mergers occur, critics in Congress and elsewhere propose a moratorium on further acquisition.

The data shown in Figure 25-4 can mislead casual observers. The rise in concentration of assets depicted there does not necessarily imply that the degree of effective monopoly power is also increasing: the asset share may increase as large firms poach in other firms' markets. When du Pont acquired the large oil firm, Conoco, or when the cigarette firm Philip Morris acquired General Foods, the concentration of assets increased but the degree of effective competition rose in the affected industries. The data in Figure 25-4 do indicate, however, that fewer people are making the central decisions for American industry, and this centralization of power and decision making distresses many analysts.

The second point made by the critics of conglomerates is that these combinations serve no economic purpose. They are simply a brand of boardroom poker to entertain managers bored with supervising their tiresome steel or chemical operations. And, indeed, there is a point here: What does the airplane business have in common with meat-packing? Or typewriters with birth-control pills? Or computer leasing with passenger-bus operations?[8]

Conglomerates are not without defenders, who argue that conglomerates bring good modern management to backward firms and that takeovers, like bankruptcy, represent the economy's way of eliminating deadwood in the economic struggle for survival. Economists have reached no consensus on the merits or demerits of conglomerate mergers. No study has found major gains or costs, so perhaps the best policy is to keep a watchful eye.

ANTITRUST LAWS AND EFFICIENCY

The dismissal of the federal antitrust case against IBM and the revision of merger guidelines of the early 1980s marked a new chapter in American antitrust policy. With these steps, antitrust law has shed most of its early populist concern "to put an end to great aggregations of capital because of the helplessness of the individual before them" (to quote from the 1945 Alcoa decision). Under the Reagan administration, the antitrust laws were directed solely toward the goal of improving economic efficiency. If big is efficient, big shall reign.

---

[8]An exciting, blow-by-blow account of an unfriendly takeover is told by the chief executive officer (CEO) of an acquired firm in Dorman Commons, *Tender Offer* (Penguin, New York, 1985).

What led to the changing attitude toward antitrust policy? In part, the change grew out of technical developments in economics proper. Economists found that performance was not always closely associated with structure. Some large firms (IBM, AT&T, Boeing) and some highly concentrated markets (computers, telecommunications, aircraft manufacture) proved to be among the industries with the highest performance with respect to innovation and productivity growth. Whereas economic theory held that monopoly keeps prices high, these industries had prices declining relative to less concentrated industries. At the same time, some unconcentrated industries, such as agriculture, exhibited outstanding performance. No iron law could be found linking structure and performance.

How can we explain this paradox? Some economists invoke the Schumpeterian hypothesis: Firms in concentrated industries garner monopoly profits only to reinvest them in research and development, thereby attaining a more rapid rate of cost reduction. If, as Schumpeter claimed, technological change originates in large firms, then it would be foolish to slay these giant geese who lay such golden eggs. This view has been well expressed by Lester Thurow, dean of the MIT Sloan School of Management: "The millions spent on the IBM [antitrust] case would have been better spent if they had been plowed back into research and development on keeping America No. 1 in computers."

A second buttress of the new antitrust policy arose from revised views of the nature of competition. Considering both experimental evidence and observation, many economists have come to believe that intense rivalry will spring up even in highly concentrated markets, as long as collusion is precluded. Indeed, in the words of one scholar (now federal judge), Chicago's Richard Posner:

> The only truly unilateral acts by which firms can get or keep monopoly power are practices like committing fraud on the Patent Office or blowing up a competitor's plant, and fraud and force are in general adequately punished under other statutes.[9]

---

[9]Richard A. Posner, *Antitrust Law: An Economic Prospectus* (University of Chicago Press, Chicago, 1976), p. 212. This book—along with writings of Robert Bork, William Baxter, and William Landes—has been highly influential in determining the new climate of antitrust thinking.

In this view, the only valid purpose of the antitrust laws should be to replace existing statutes with a simple prohibition against *agreements*—explicit or tacit—that unreasonably restrict competition.

Third, the swing of the pendulum against strict antitrust enforcement came from the movement toward laissez-faire economic views, stemming particularly from proponents of the Chicago School, during the Reagan era. This school held that monopoly power is derivative of government interventions. The major pools of monopoly power, in this view, lie in areas protected by government fiat: important examples include the exemption of labor unions from antitrust laws, government regulation of interstate trucking rates, barriers to entry into the professions, rate setting and restrictions in medical care, and state limitations on the cable television or the taxicab industry. Advocates of the laissez-faire view, including FTC chief James Miller, who often wore an Adam Smith necktie, argued that relaxing government regulation would enhance competition.

The new approach to antitrust was largely adopted by the Reagan administration during the 1981–1988 period. The major items included dismissal of the IBM case, with its attack on a large unregulated firm, promulgation of a set of permissive merger guidelines, failure to challenge a single conglomerate merger, and a sharp drop in the number of litigated cases.

In addition, in 1986, the Reagan administration proposed the biggest overhaul of the antitrust laws in decades. The major provisions included: (1) removing restrictions on interlocking directorates of large corporations, (2) removing jurisdiction of American courts over antitrust violations that take place outside the United States, (3) removing triple damages for antitrust violations, (4) putting into legislative form the Reagan merger guidelines, and (5) exempting from the antitrust laws distressed industries (defined as ones seriously injured by increased imports).

Will the relaxation of antitrust policies persist beyond the Reagan era? No one can predict the direction of future attitudes toward big business. Nonetheless, because many of the arguments supporting the efficiency-oriented view are shared by economists and lawyers across the political spectrum, a quick return to the trust-busting fervor of earlier years appears unlikely in the near future.

SUMMARY

A. Patterns of Imperfect Competition

1. Between the polar extremes of pure monopoly and perfect competition lies a variety of species of imperfect competition. Which of these species thrives in a particular location will depend on three central factors: *(a)* the production and cost structure of the market; *(b)* the barriers to competition; and *(c)* the extent to which firms in the market collude.

2. If barriers to competition are high and complete collusion exists, we have the collusive oligopoly outcome: this market structure produces a price and quantity relation similar to that in a monopolistic industry.

3. A more common pattern is dominant-firm oligopoly. Here, a single large firm maximizes its profits assuming that the competitive fringe of firms will each individually seek non-collusively to maximize profits. This structure produces a lower price and larger output than the pure-monopoly equilibrium.

4. A final pattern is the monopolistic competition characterizing many retail industries. Here we see many small firms, with slight differences in the quality of products (such as different kinds of gasoline or cigarettes). The existence of product differentiation leads each firm to face a downward-sloping *dd* demand curve. In the long run, free entry extinguishes profits as these industries show an equilibrium in which firms' *AC* curves are tangent to their *dd* demand curves. In this tangency equilibrium, prices are above marginal costs but the industry exhibits greater diversity than under perfect competition.

B. Behavior of Large Corporations

5. A careful study of the actual behavior of oligopolists shows certain kinds of behavior at variance with standard economic assumptions. Firms are assumed to maximize profits. Moreover, under perfect competition, those who stray from competitive pricing will be eliminated. But under imperfect competition, there is elbow room for greater discretion.

One limit on profit maximization is bounded rationality. This principle recognizes that it is costly to make decisions, so managers may make less-than-perfect decisions, often employing "rules of thumb," to economize on their time. In addition, large corporations may pursue goals other than profits, and a divergence may therefore appear between the interests of owners and of managers. The latter may be averse to large risks or may desire to expand their empires, earn large managerial bonuses, or simply live the good life at the expense of profits.

6. An important example of an action that appears not to maximize profits is the process of markup pricing. Firms seldom explicitly calculate prices on the basis of *MC* and *MR*. Rather, they use markup pricing—a rule of thumb that adds a percentage increase on top of costs of production.

7. While monopoly and oligopoly lead to price above marginal cost, and thus to short-run economic inefficiency, the Schumpeterian hypothesis holds that this traditional theory ignores the dynamics of technological change. Monopolies and oligopolies are the chief source of innovation and growth in living standards; to break up large firms, in this view, might lower prices in the short run but would risk raising prices in the long run as the fragmentation of industry slowed technological progress.

C. Antitrust Policy

8. Antitrust policy is the primary way that public policy limits possible abuses by large firms. This policy grew out of legislation like the Sherman Act (1890) and the Clayton Act (1914). The primary purposes of antitrust are: *(a)* To prohibit anticompetitive activities. These include agreements to fix prices or divide up territories; price discrimination; and tie-in agreements. *(b)* To break up monopoly structures. These structures are, in today's legal theory, ones that both have excessive market power (a large share of the market) and engage in anticompetitive acts like excluding competitors.

9. In addition to limiting the behavior of existing firms, antitrust law prevents mergers that would lessen competition. Today, horizontal mergers (between firms in the same industry) are the main source of concern, while vertical and conglomerate mergers tend to be tolerated.

10. Antitrust policy has been heavily influenced by economic thinking during the last two decades. As a result, antitrust policy during the 1980s focused almost exclusively on improving efficiency, while ignoring earlier populist concerns with bigness itself. Moreover, in today's economy—with intense competition from foreign producers and in deregulated industries—many believe that antitrust policy should be focused mainly on preventing collusive agreements like price fixing.

CONCEPTS FOR REVIEW

imperfect competition:
    collusive oligopoly
    dominant-firm oligopoly
    monopolistic competition
barriers to competition
tacit and explicit collusion
no-profit equilibrium in monopolistic
  competition
markup pricing
Schumpeterian hypothesis

limits on profit maximization:
    bounded rationality
    alternative goals
Sherman, Clayton Acts
mergers:
    vertical
    horizontal
    conglomerate
efficiency-oriented antitrust policy

QUESTIONS FOR DISCUSSION

1. Review the three theories of oligopoly analyzed in the first section of this chapter. Draw up a table that compares perfect competition, monopoly, and the three oligopoly theories with respect to the following characteristics: *(a)* number of firms; *(b)* extent of collusion; *(c)* price vs. marginal cost; *(d)* price vs. long-run average cost; *(e)* efficiency.

2. Suppose you ran a computer company. How could you go about maximizing profits? Would you use a "marginal approach" (trying to estimate your *MC* and *MR*)? Or would you lean to "markup pricing" (setting price as average cost plus a percentage markup)? Outline the strengths and weaknesses of each approach.

3. "The tragedy of most industries characterized by monopolistic competition is not at all excessive profits. Rather, there are no profits, and prices are excessive as resources are frittered away in low levels of production." Explain what this writer might mean in terms of the long-run equilibrium shown in Figure 25-3. Defend monopolistic competition by showing how it might lead to greater diversity of products.

4. "It is naive to try to break up monopolies into even a few effectively competing units, because the basic cause of monopoly is the law of decreasing cost with mass production, and, in any case, a few competitors are not enough to duplicate the pricing patterns of perfect competition." Discuss both parts of this statement.

5. "IBM is not bad just because it is big." Discuss, particularly with reference to the Schumpeterian hypothesis.

6. Explain the following statements:

(a) In the retail drug-store business, each store has a little market power but fails to earn any economic profit on its activities.

(b) According to the theory of bounded rationality, it is truly efficient for IBM not to adjust the price of its computers so that $MC = MR$ each and every day.

(c) The purpose of antitrust policy is to prevent oligopoly from functioning like monopoly.

7. Firms often lobby for tariffs or quotas to provide relief from import competition. Suppose that the dominant firm in Figure 25-2 was the sole domestic supplier of a good, while the competitive fringe was composed entirely of foreign firms (a case that held for aluminum before World War II). What would be the effect on the price and quantity if a prohibitive tariff were levied on the foreign good? (A prohibitive tariff is one that is so high as to effectively wall out all imports.) Use your analysis to explain the statement, ''The tariff is the mother of trusts.''

8. The Justice Department attempted to prosecute Mr. Crandall of American Airlines for his proposal to raise prices (page 609). It failed because his attempt was unsuccessful and prices were not raised. Do you agree that only successful price-fixing conspiracies (and not aborted ones) should be illegal?

9. Often, established oligopolists or monopolists must keep an eye on *potential* as well as *actual* rivals. The following problem will show how such considerations may impose constraints on monopoly. Figure 25-5 below is a conventional monopoly problem, in which the solution without rivals would be with a price of P_M and a quantity of Q_M.

Now assume that potential entrants could produce and sell with constant costs at a price P_L. Can you see how that would affect the *net* demand for the monopolist's output (the *dd* curve in Figure 25-2)? What is the profit-maximizing price for the monopolist, given the threat of entry? Or, put differently, is there a *limit price* to or above which the monopolist dare not go for fear of losing every penny of profits? Why will the monopolist keep price below P_L and output above Q_L?

LIMIT PRICE MODEL

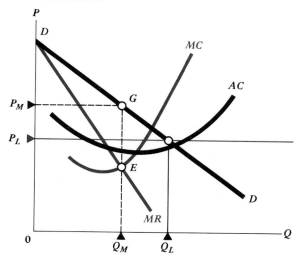

Figure 25-5

10. Two important approaches to antitrust are "structure" and "conduct." The former looks only at the structure of the industry (such as the concentration of firms); the latter at firm conduct (e.g., price fixing).

Review the various statutes and cases to see which are related to conduct and which to structure. What about the new merger guidelines?

What are the advantages and disadvantages of each approach?

11. In long-run equilibrium, both perfectly competitive and monopolistically competitive markets achieve a tangency between the firm's *dd* demand curve and its *AC* average cost curve. Figure 25-3 shows the tangency for a monopolistic competitor, while Figure 25-6 below displays the tangency for the perfect competitor. Discuss the similarities or differences in the two situations with respect to:

(a) The elasticity of the demand curve for the firm's product.

(b) The extent of divergence between price and marginal cost.

(c) Profits.

(d) Economic efficiency.

PERFECT COMPETITION

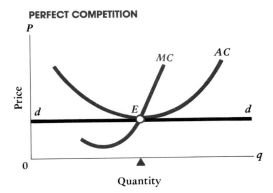

Figure 25-6

12. According to the 1982 guidelines, mergers may be challenged if they significantly decrease competition in moderately concentrated or highly concentrated industries. The Antitrust Division of the Justice Department has adopted the Herfindahl index of concentration for merger policy (see page 575 and question **5** in Chapter 24 for an explanation of the Herfindahl index). The Antitrust Division is "likely to challenge" a merger if it adds more than 100 points to the Herfindahl index when the Herfindahl index is between 1000 and 1800 and is also likely to challenge if a merger adds more than 50 points to the index for an industry whose index is more than 1800.

Consider an industry with a Herfindahl index of 1400 before a merger. Four firms are considering possible combinations of mergers: American with a market share of 20 percent; United with 10 percent; Continental with share of 6 percent; and Piddly with share of 4 percent. Which pairs of companies could merge without running the risk of an antitrust challenge?

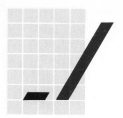

APPENDIX: 25

Game Theory

Economic life is filled with situations in which two or more people or firms or countries jockey for dominance. The oligopolies that we analyzed in the body of this chapter sometimes break out into economic warfare. Such rivalry was seen in the last century when Vanderbilt and Drew used to cut and recut shipping rates on their parallel railroads. In recent years, Continental Air tried to lure customers from its bigger rivals by offering fares far under prevailing levels. And the larger airlines like American or United had to decide how to react, and how Continental would react when they reacted, and so forth. These situations typify an area of economic analysis known as game theory.

Game theory analyzes the way that two or more entities, who interact in a structure such as a market, choose actions or strategies that jointly affect each participant. This theory, which may sound frivolous in its terminology borrowed from chess, bridge, and war, is in fact fraught with significance and was largely developed by John von Neumann (1903–1957), a Hungarian-born mathematical genius. Here we can only sketch the general notions involved in game theory. Let's begin by analyzing the dynamics of price cutting, shown in Figure 25A-1.

The New York–based department store Macy's used to advertise, "We sell for 10 percent less." But its rival, Gimbel's, advertised, "We will not be undersold." The

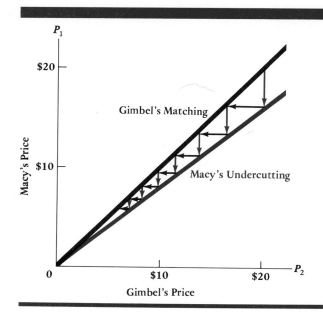

Figure 25A-1   What happens when two firms insist on undercutting each other?

You can trace through the steps by which dynamic price cutting leads to ever-lower prices for two rivals.

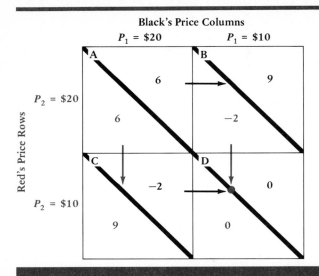

Black's Price Columns

Figure 25A-2   A profit-payoff matrix for the price-cutting game

vertical red arrows show Macy's price cuts; the black horizontal arrows show Gimbel's responding strategy of matching each price cut.

By tracing through the pattern of reaction and counterreaction, you can see that this kind of rivalry will end in mutual ruin, at a zero price. Why? Because the only price compatible with both strategies is a price of zero: 90 percent of zero is zero.

But finally Macy's gets wise and realizes that when it cuts its P_1, Gimbel's P_2 will not stay constant but will follow it downward. Only if it is shortsighted does it think it can undercut its rival for long. Soon Macy's will realize that the two firms are sharing a market. Indeed, if there were but two sellers and no antitrust laws to worry about, the two might collusively raise price to the monopoly level that maximized joint profits.

Once firms begin to worry about the effects their actions will have on the other firms, we have entered the realm of game theory.

Basic Concepts

A useful way of representing the interaction between two firms or people is shown by a two-way table known as a *payoff matrix,* shown in Figure 25A-2. Red picks her price strategy by selecting a row. Black's price strategy involves his choosing a column. Then in each of the four cells A, B, C, D, the red number represents Red's profit-payoff at those prices and the black number gives Black's profit or payoff. For example, in cell A, joint profits $6 + 6$ (thousand dollars) are maximized at the common monopoly price, $\$20 = P_1 = P_2$. But A is not "stable," in that if Red knew Black would really stay in his first column, Red would gain by cutting P_2 down to $10 in cell C, getting the lion's share of the business there with profit of 9. But, of course, Black will now prefer to match Red's P_2 of $10, taking us from cell C to D.

In cell D, where the profits are just zero, the competitive solution is stable. Technically, it is called a *Nash equilibrium* (after economist John Nash). A Nash equilibrium has the characteristic that, given Red's strategy Black can do no better, and given Black's strategy Red can do no better.[1]

That is, 0 is the largest red number in the column Black has picked, and 0 is the largest black number in the row Red has picked. Verify that this red dot cell is a Nash equilibrium.

But note a very important fact. A competitive solution or Nash equilibrium may lead to an efficient zero-profit outcome. Moreover, it is stable against non-collusive moves by a single player or firm. But it is not stable when the two players *collude* and decide to move to cell A. This might come about by overt agreement or by tacit agreement. Or if Black were reluctant to follow suit, Red might threaten him by promising mutual ruin through cutting P far below any cost levels. The only safe guarantee of competition is thus the potential pressure of numerous sellers.

Applications   Game theory brings insights to many areas of economics. Our price-cutting example suggests the instabilities that can be generated by myopic rules like, "I will always have a lower price or a better quality than my rival." Game theory can also explain the dangers of trade wars (see question 4 at the end of this appendix) as well as the risks of an arms race (see question 1 at the end of this appendix). Some believe as well that the phenomenon of "sticky" prices may be rooted in game theory: according to this theory, firms have reached a kind of tacit agreement about the prevailing level of price (say, in the auto or steel industry). Once this agreement has been reached, firms are reluctant to change prices lest other firms interpret this as a declaration of economic war.

Game theory can also suggest why foreign competition may lead to greater price competition. What happens when a Japanese or European firm enters a market which had earlier reached a tacit agreement on the oligopolistic price? The foreign firms may "refuse to play the game." They did not agree to the rules, so they may cut prices to gain market shares. Collusion may break down.

The Prisoner's Dilemma

Game theory can also shed light on the need for cooperation in economic life. Looking back to our price-cutting game in Figure 25A-2, we saw that competition among firms led to cell D, the competitive outcome with low prices. Moreover, we have learned that, by an almost miraculous accident of economic life, Adam Smith's invisible hand produces in perfectly competitive markets a kind of social optimum out of individual utility or profit maximization.

But the lucky outcome of the invisible hand is unlikely to arise in all social circum-

---

[1]More precisely, let player Red pick strategy P_2 while player Black picks strategy P_1. Then the pair of strategies (P_1^*, P_2^*) is a Nash equilibrium if no player can find a better strategy to play under the assumption that the other player sticks to his or her original strategy. That is, as long as Black sticks to strategy P_1^*, Red cannot do better than to stick with strategy P_2^* and similarly for Black.

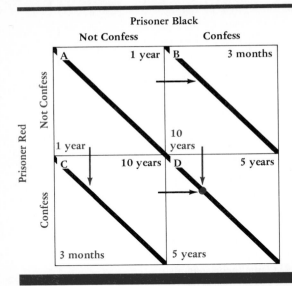

Figure 25A-3   To confess or not to confess, that is the prisoner's dilemma

No matter what the other person does, it is always better at first for each prisoner to confess. Thus cell D is an equilibrium when each prisoner acts selfishly (technically, it is a Nash equilibrium). By cooperating or acting altruistically, the pair can move to cell A with better outcomes for both.

stances. The case of the "prisoner's dilemma" illustrates this basic truth in game-theoretic language. Figure 25A-3 is like Figure 25A-2; here it refers to prisoners Red and Black, who have been caught in a joint crime. The district attorney interviews each separately, saying, "I have enough on both of you to send you to jail for a year. But if you *alone* will confess to the 10-year crime, I'll make a deal with you: you'll get off with a 3-month sentence, while your partner will serve 10 years. If you *both* confess, you'll both get 5 years."

What should Red do? Should she confess and hope to get a really short sentence? That's better than the year she gets from not confessing. But wait. There is an even better reason for confessing. For suppose Red doesn't confess and, unknown to her, Black does confess. Red stands to get 10 years! Better than *that* is to confess and get no worse than 5 years.

Black is in the same dilemma: if only he knew what Red is thinking, or what Red thinks Black thinks Red is thinking. . . .

The important result here is that when both prisoners act selfishly by confessing, they both end up in cell D with long prison terms. Only when they act collusively and altruistically will they end up in cell A with short prison terms.

We see many social and economic situations that resemble the prisoner's dilemma. Replace "confess" with "pollute" each place it appears in Figure 25A-3. This would then be much like a world of unregulated air pollution. In such a world, if a firm is the sole altruist who cleans up every particle of *its* sulfur or waste, that firm will soon go bankrupt. Pressure to move down to cell *D* can lead to social and economic ills in the many cases where the invisible-hand mechanism of efficient perfect competition breaks down. In these cases, the role of government is to get firms cooperatively to move to cell A, the "not-pollute/not-pollute" world.

Can Benevolence Survive?

The prisoner's dilemma and similar games show how self-interest may lead to a world of noncooperation, pollution, and militarism—a nasty, brutish, and short life.

But how can we account for the high degree of benevolence and cooperation within families as well as among friends, communities, and even nations? What happens when a prisoner's dilemma game like that in Figure 25-3 is played again and again? Studies indicate that people are well-advised to cooperate (and often do cooperate) in repeated prisoner's dilemma games.

How might cooperation evolve? Let's say one player plays a *tit for tat* strategy, saying in effect, "If you're nice to me, I'll be nice to you. If you're nasty to me, I'll return the nastiness." In the game shown in Figure 25A-3, this means that Red will always start by cooperating. If Black cooperates by not confessing, Red will continue to play the cooperative strategy of not confessing. If Black double-crosses Red by confessing, the next time they play, Red will sting Black by confessing.

Recent studies show that cooperative strategies like tit for tat are the most profitable *selfish* strategies in many repeated prisoner's dilemma games. This suggests that a watchful golden rule may serve people well in many situations: "Do unto others what you would have them do unto you, but only as long as they act as you do."

But cooperation can also be harmful to society. Tit for tat may lead to tacit collusion in otherwise-competitive markets when firms play a game that says, "Don't invade my market and I won't invade yours." Cooperation among firms may hurt consumers. (The way that collusion can sometimes be harmful was shown in Figure 25A-2, where collusion raised profits; its helpful side was seen in Figure 25A-3, where pollution was reduced by collusion.)

These few examples provide a small tasting from the wide variety of fruits produced by the theory of games. This area has been enormously useful in helping economists and other social scientists think about situations where small numbers of people are well informed and interact in markets, politics, or military affairs.

CONCEPTS FOR REVIEW

game theory
economic warfare, price cutting
payoff matrix
payoff from different strategies
non-collusive and collusive strategies
Nash equilibrium (or stable point)
prisoner's dilemma
competition vs. altruism
tit for tat

QUESTIONS FOR DISCUSSION

1. Superpower A wants superiority over superpower R; R wants parity with A. Hence, A in year t installs 10 percent more missiles than R had in year $t - 1$; while the next year R matches A's missiles. Show how such a strategy leads to an endless arms race, using an approach like that of Figure 25A-1. What is the function of an arms-control agreement that limits each side to 1000 missiles? Show graphically how an arms-control agreement changes the picture.

2. "In a world with no spillovers or externalities, collusion harms the public interest. In a world full of pollution, crime, and pestilence, cooperation is essential." Interpret in light of Figures 25A-2 and 25A-3.

3. Show that for the prisoner's dilemma shown in Figure 25A-3, the outcome in cell D is a Nash equilibrium. Also show that it is the only Nash equilibrium.

4. Consider the payoff matrix in Figure 25A-4, which gives total real national incomes of two regions as a function of foreign-trade policies. The red numbers are Japan's real incomes while the black numbers are America's real incomes.

(a) List the four outcomes and calculate each region's national income and world income.

(b) Show how countries acting uncooperatively (without agreements and in their own selfish national interest) will be led to a trade war at the Nash equilibrium at D in the lower right-hand corner of the matrix. What is the effect of the trade war on total world income?

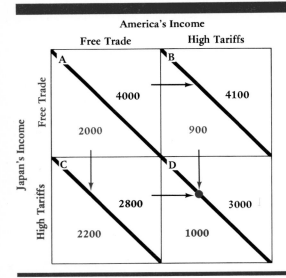

Figure 25A-4   Countries gain from trade, lose from trade wars

(c) What is the impact on incomes of a trade agreement that abolishes all trade restrictions and produces free trade? Relate this result to the prisoner's dilemma.

(d) Is there an incentive for each country to ''cheat'' on the trade agreement? What happens if the cheating leads to retaliation and to the high-tariff outcome?

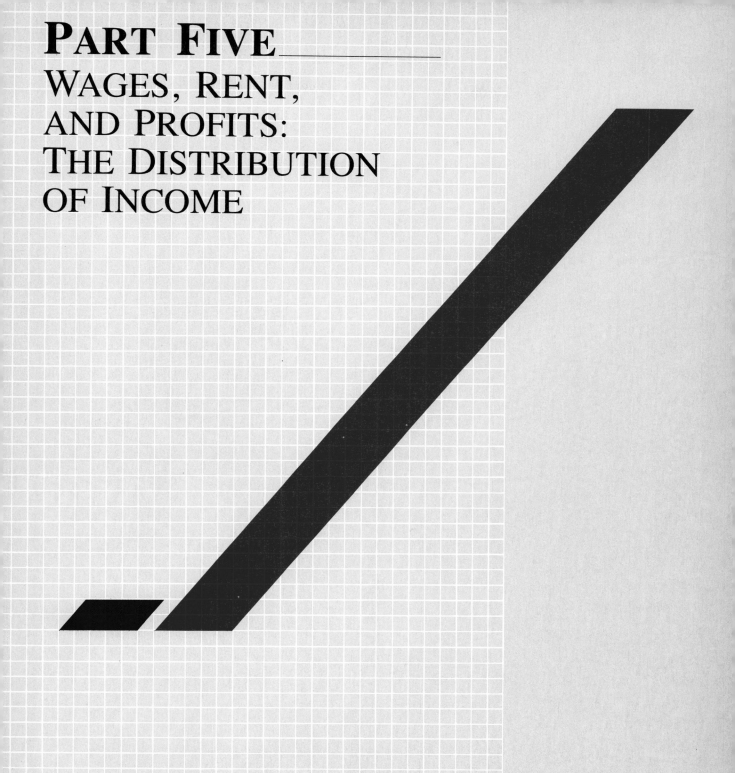

PART FIVE

WAGES, RENT, AND PROFITS: THE DISTRIBUTION OF INCOME

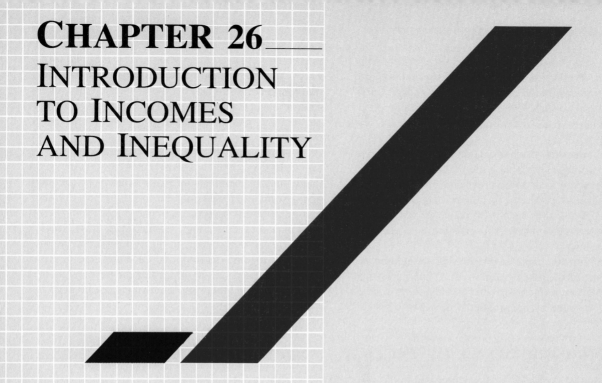

CHAPTER 26

INTRODUCTION TO INCOMES AND INEQUALITY

You know, Ernest, the rich are different from us.

F. Scott Fitzgerald

Yes, I know. They have more money than we do.

Ernest Hemingway

HAVING STUDIED THE WAY that output is produced and priced, we want to understand who enjoys the fruits of economic activity. This question, which concerns the distribution of income, has fascinated economists since classical days. David Ricardo first analyzed the distribution of income among classes:

> The produce of the earth . . . is divided among three classes of the community; namely, the proprietor of the land, the owner of the . . . capital necessary for its cultivation, and the laborers by whose industry it is cultivated.

In the coming pages we will examine the classical questions posed by Ricardo and his followers: What are the sources of the wages of labor, the rents of land, and the interest and profits of capital? Why are some people paid a million dollars a year, while others have trouble landing a job at the minimum wage? Why are the rents on Manhattan real estate worth hundreds of dollars a square foot, while land in the desert may sell for but a few dollars an acre? And what is the source of the billions of dollars of profits earned by giant enterprises like Ford or Exxon?

639

These are the topics discussed in the following chapters. We begin by sketching how income and wealth are distributed today. The next chapters analyze the prices of factors of production, with applications to labor, land (including natural resources), and capital.

Economists call these topics the *theory of distribution*. Distribution deals with the problem of *for whom* goods are produced. More precisely, distribution theory analyzes the pricing of factors of production by supply and demand; once the prices of factors of production are determined, it is possible to understand people's incomes.

Issues surrounding the distribution of income are among the most controversial in all economics. Some argue that high incomes are the result of market power—boosted by the monopoly power of labor unions or large firms. Others think that wages and profits are simply the result of the workings of competitive markets. And many would say that, whoever is right, the state should exercise its power to redistribute incomes from the rich to the poor by taxes and transfers.

The purpose of this chapter is to present the essential facts; to explain what is meant by income and inequality; to examine the major sources of income and wealth; and to see how the social pie gets divided among different people, here and abroad.

This is not the last time we shall meet these issues. After we have mastered the analytical questions involved in income distribution, we return to a discussion of the causes of and remedies for poverty, along with the conflict between equity and efficiency, in Chapter 34.

A. MEASUREMENT OF INCOMES AND INEQUALITY

The centuries before the Industrial Revolution experienced very slow changes in income levels and in class divisions in most areas of the world for which we have statistical records. The advent of technological and social changes associated with the Industrial Revolution brought, starting around 1770, sharp changes in wages and the division of society along clear class lines between capitalists and workers.

This phenomenon was identified by many early critics of capitalism, particularly by Karl Marx. He and Friedrich Engels wrote in 1848:

> The modern laborer . . . , instead of rising with the progress of industry, sinks deeper and deeper below the condition of his own class. He becomes a pauper, and pauperism develops more rapidly than population and wealth.[1]

While some of Marx's predictions about the future of industrial capitalism were proven correct in the intervening years, his prediction about the fortunes of the working class proved to be wrong. His assertion that the rich would become richer and the poor poorer cannot be sustained by careful historical and statistical research.

In Europe and America, there has definitely been a steady, long-term improvement in minimum standards of living, when measured by the consumption of food, clothing, and housing, as well as by the health and longevity of the population. This fact about industrial market economies is clear from statistics presented below. The highlights are shown graphically in Figure 26-1.

The Fruits of Industrialization

Historians sometimes dwell on the evils of the Industrial Revolution and on the poverty-ridden condition of the masses in polluted cities. In point of fact, no Dickens novel did full justice to the dismal conditions of child labor, length of the working day, workplace dangers, and poor sanitation in early nineteenth-century factories. A workweek of 84 hours was the prevailing rule, with time out for breakfast and sometimes supper. A good deal of work could be squeezed out of a 6-year-old child, and if a woman lost two fingers in a loom, she still had eight left.

---

[1] K. Marx and F. Engels, *The Communist Manifesto* (1848), widely reprinted.

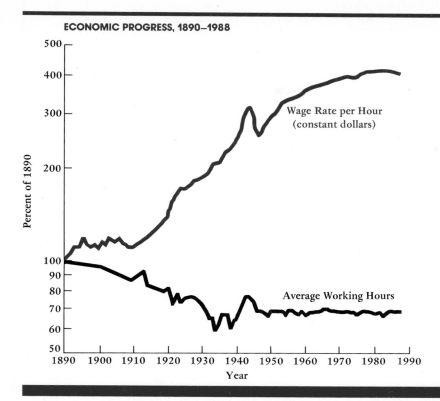

ECONOMIC PROGRESS, 1890–1988

Wage Rate per Hour
(constant dollars)

Average Working Hours

Figure 26-1   Wages have improved as hours of work declined

With advancing technology and improved capital goods, American workers enjoy higher wages while working shorter hours. Marx's prediction of impoverishment of the working class has proved far from the historical truth.

Such a lurid picture often led people to believe that the Industrial Revolution was a step backward for the working class. Weren't people better off on the farms than in the factories? Probably not. Poverty was simply more visible in the cities. The idyllic picture of the healthful, jolly countryside peopled by stout yeomen and happy peasantry is a mirage in most parts of the world. Even today, New York's Hell's Kitchen or Harlem, Roxbury, or Los Angeles' Watts district hardly overshadow the poverty and squalor of our rural slums: the Tobacco Road of the upper south, border towns of the southwest, hill towns of Appalachia, or Indian reservations of Arizona and New Mexico.

Modern historians therefore emphasize that the conditions of the industrial present, inadequate as they may seem, are nevertheless great improvements in living standards over earlier centuries of agrarian feudalism or unregulated laissez-faire. Real wages tended to meander up and down for the four centuries before the Industrial Revolution; since that time, wages have shown enormous gains. Today's average wage earner commands a volume and variety of goods that would dazzle the princes and princesses of medieval times.

Income and Wealth

In measuring a person's economic status, the two yardsticks most often used are income and wealth. Before turning to the shape of economic inequality, therefore, we define these two key concepts and examine the components of income and wealth.

Income refers to the total amount of money re-

TYPE OF INCOME	AVERAGE INCOME PER HOUSEHOLD, BEFORE TAXES, 1988	EXAMPLES
Labor income		
Wages and supplements	$26,700	Autoworker's wages Teacher's salary
Other labor income	2,400	GM's contribution to pension fund
Proprietors' income	3,700	Lawyer's share of partnership earnings Farmer's net income
Property income		
Rent	200	Landlord's rental from apartments
Dividend	1,000	Dividend from IBM
Interest	6,000	Interest paid on savings account
Transfer payments		
Government	3,200	Social security
	3,100	Other (unemployment insurance, welfare, etc.)
Total	**$46,300**	

Table 26-1   Major sources of personal income, 1988

American households earn most of their incomes from wages and salaries, but property income and government transfers are supplements especially for the rich and the poor, respectively. (Source: U.S. Department of Commerce, Bureau of the Census, *Current Population Reports*, Series P-60.)

ceived by a person or household during a given time period (usually a year). Income consists of wages or labor earnings; property income such as rents, interest, and dividends; and transfer payments, or receipts from the government, such as social security or unemployment insurance.

Table 26-1 shows the average income of Americans, or more precisely the total personal income for the United States divided by the number of households, for the year 1988. (Personal income was defined in more detail in Chapter 6.) Labor income constitutes about two-thirds of personal income, while property income is particularly important for high-income groups. The poorer tenth of the population benefits substantially from government transfer payments such as social security and welfare payments.

Wealth consists of the net dollar value of assets owned at a point in time. Note that wealth is a stock of dollars (like a lake) while income is a flow of dollars (like a stream). We generally include in a household's wealth its tangible items (like houses, cars and other consumer durable goods, and land) and its financial assets (like cash, savings accounts, bonds, and stocks). The total items that are of value are called *assets,* while those that are owed are called *liabilities,* and the difference between assets and liabilities is called wealth or net worth.

Table 26-2 presents a breakdown of the wealthholdings of Americans. The single most important asset of most households is the family home: 65 percent of families own houses, as compared with 55 percent a generation ago. Most households own a modest amount of financial wealth, such as savings accounts and corporate stocks. As we will see below, the ownership of the nation's financial wealth is concentrated in the hands of a small fraction of the population.

MEASUREMENT OF INEQUALITY

Having defined income and wealth, we now review the extent of inequality of economic status.

Distribution of Income in the United States

A poll of students will show that many are not very sure what their own family incomes really are. Usually it turns out they have a slightly exaggerated notion of their parents' earnings. Indeed, some people are so casual with their financial records that they do not themselves know how much they make.

In the absence of statistical knowledge, it is understandable that one should form an impression of the American standard of living from TV commercials showing a healthy white family standing in front of a split-level house, both parents about to rush off to work in their brand-new luxury compacts, with a garage full of boats and power lawn mowers in the background. Actually, this sort of picture is highly unrepresentative of the kind of life that 90 percent of Americans lead.

The Sober Truth What are the facts? In reality, during the moderately prosperous year of 1988, the per capita disposable income of Americans was approximately $265 per week. **Disposable income** (or total income after taxes and transfer payments) equals the personal income shown in Table 26-1 less taxes paid.

But of course the nation's income is unequally distributed. To understand the *distribution of income,* consider the following experiment. Suppose each member of a group—or of the entire nation—writes down his or her yearly family income on an index card. We can then sort these cards into *income classes.* Some of the cards will go into the lowest class, the group with under $5000 of income. Some

WHAT AMERICAN HOUSEHOLDS OWN

TYPE OF ASSET	PERCENTAGE OF TOTAL WEALTH, 1984
Tangible:	
Own home	41.3
Rental property	9.0
Motor vehicle	6.0
Other real estate	4.4
Financial:	
Checking account	0.6
Interest-earning accounts (savings accounts, time deposits, etc.)	17.5
Stocks and mutual funds	6.8
Equity in businesses	10.3
Other	4.1
Total	100.0
Median dollar value of household assets per household, 1984	$32,667

Table 26-2 Tangible and intangible assets of households, 1984

Households hold a wide variety of assets: tangibles such as houses and cars and intangibles such as savings accounts and stocks. Even though the average assets per household totalled almost $80,000, much of this was concentrated in a few hands, so the median value was only $32,667. (Source: U.S. Department of Commerce, Bureau of the Census, "Household Wealth and Asset Ownership: 1984," Series P-70.)

go into the next class. A few go into the income class over $75,000.

The actual distribution of income for the United States in 1985 is shown in Table 26-3. Column (1) shows the different income-class intervals. Column (2) shows the percentage of families in each income class. Column (3) shows the percentage of the total of all income that goes to the people in the given income class.

Columns (4) and (5) are computed from (2) and (3), respectively. Column (4) shows what percentage of the total number of families belongs to each income class or below. Column (5) shows what per-

(1)	(2)	(3)	(4)	(5)
INCOME CLASS	PERCENTAGE OF ALL FAMILIES IN THIS CLASS	PERCENTAGE OF TOTAL INCOME RECEIVED BY FAMILIES IN THIS CLASS	PERCENTAGE OF FAMILIES IN THIS CLASS AND LOWER ONES	PERCENTAGE OF INCOME RECEIVED BY THIS CLASS AND LOWER ONES
Under $5000	4.8	0.4	4.8	0.4
$5,000–$9,999	8.5	2.0	13.3	2.4
$10,000–$14,999	10.2	3.9	23.5	6.3
$15,000–$19,999	10.5	5.5	34.0	11.8
$20,000–$24,999	10.3	7.0	44.3	18.8
$25,000–$49,999	37.4	40.4	81.7	59.2
$50,000–$59,999	7.2	11.8	88.9	71.0
$60,000–$74,999	5.5	11.1	94.4	82.1
$75,000 and over	5.6	17.9	100.0	100.0
Total	100.0	100.0		

Table 26-3   Distribution of total incomes of American households, 1985

This table shows how total incomes were distributed among households. Half of households received less than the median income of $26,400 while half received more. (Source: U.S. Bureau of the Census, "Money Income of Households, Families, and Persons in the U.S., 1985," *Current Population Report,* 1987.)

centage of total income goes to the people who belong in the given income class or below.

A glance at the income distribution in the United States shows the wide spread of incomes. "There's always room at the top" because it is *hard* to get there, not because it is easy. If we made an income pyramid out of a child's blocks, with each layer portraying $500 of income, the peak would be far higher than Mt. Everest, but most people would be within a few feet of the ground.

How to Measure Inequality among Income Classes

How great is the dispersion of disposable incomes, and how shall we measure the degree of inequality of income distribution? A useful way to analyze inequality is to ask: What percent of all income goes to the lowest 10 percent of the population? What to the lowest 20 percent? The lowest 50 percent? The lowest 95 percent? And so forth. Such data can be derived from the data underlying Table 26-3.

At one pole, if incomes were absolutely equally distributed, the lowest 20 percent of the population would receive exactly 20 percent of the total income; the lowest 80 percent would receive 80 percent of the income; and the highest 20 percent would also get only 20 percent of the income.

The actual degree of inequality, shown in the first two columns of Table 26-4, indicates that the lowest 20 percent of the families get only 4.6 percent of the total income; the most affluent 20 percent of the families get 43 percent. The second-lowest 20 percent get only 11 percent of income, and the third 20 percent only 17 percent. But the fourth 20 percent get 24 percent, and the upper 5 percent get no less than 17 percent—more than what the bottom two-fifths of the population get all together.

In order to plot the degree of inequality, we use a diagram known as the **Lorenz curve.** This shows graphically in Figure 26-2 the amount of inequality listed in the columns of Table 26-4; that is, it contrasts the patterns of *(a)* absolute equality, *(b)* absolute inequality, and *(c)* actual 1985 American inequality.

Absolute equality is depicted by the gray column of numbers in column (4) of Table 26-4. When they are plotted, these become the diagonal line of Figure 26-2's Lorenz diagram (shown as a broken line).

(1)	(2)	(3)	(4)	(5) CUMULATIVE PERCENTAGE OF INCOME		(6)
FAMILY INCOME BY RANK	PERCENT SHARE OF 1985 INCOME	CUMULATIVE PERCENTAGE OF PEOPLE	ABSOLUTE EQUALITY	ABSOLUTE INEQUALITY		ACTUAL 1985
		0	0	0		0
Lowest fifth	4.6	20	20	0		4.6
Second fifth	10.9	40	40	0		15.5
Third fifth	16.9	60	60	0		32.4
Fourth fifth	24.2	80	80	0		56.6
Highest fifth*	43.4	100	100	100		100.0

*Top 5 percent receive 17 percent of total income.

Table 26-4   By grouping the population into fifths, we can compare actual and polar cases of inequality

We group the population into the fifth with the lowest income, the fifth with the second-lowest income, and so forth. Column (2) shows what fraction of total income each fifth receives. Then, by cumulating the income of each quintile (or fifth), we can compare the actual distribution with polar extremes of complete inequality and equality. (Source: U.S. Bureau of the Census, "Money Income of Households, Families, and Persons in the U.S., 1985," *Current Population Report,* 1987.)

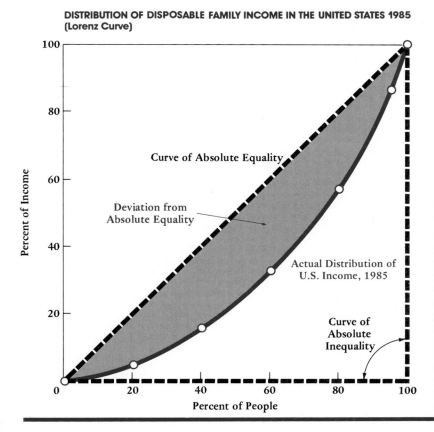

DISTRIBUTION OF DISPOSABLE FAMILY INCOME IN THE UNITED STATES 1985 (Lorenz Curve)

Curve of Absolute Equality

Deviation from Absolute Equality

Actual Distribution of U.S. Income, 1985

Curve of Absolute Inequality

Percent of Income

Percent of People

Figure 26-2   Lorenz curve measures degree of income inequality between opposite polar cases

By plotting from Table 26-4's column (6), we see that the red actual distribution-of-income curve lies between the two extremes of absolute equality and absolute inequality. The shaded area of this Lorenz chart (as a percentage of the triangle's area) measures relative inequality of income. (How would the curve have looked back in the roaring 1920s when inequality was greater? In a Utopia where all have equal inheritances and opportunities?)

At the other extreme, we have the hypothetical case of absolute inequality, where everybody (say, 99 out of 100 people) has no income, except for one person, who has all the income. This is shown in column (5) of Table 26-4. What lies behind the numbers shown there? The zeroes reflect the assumption in this case that the lowest 0, 20, 80, and 99 people have no income at all. But the lowest 100 do include the last person, and all the people have all the income. The lowest curve on the Lorenz diagram—the dashed, right-angled line—gives this limit of absolute inequality.

Any actual income distribution, such as that of 1985, must fall between these extremes. The red column in Table 26-4 presents the data derived from the first two columns in a form suitable for plotting as an actual Lorenz curve. This actual Lorenz curve is given in Figure 26-2 by the solid red intermediate curve, with the shaded area indicating the deviation from absolute equality, hence giving us a measure of the degree of inequality of income distribution.[2]

This concludes our discussion of the Lorenz curve. This useful device is widely used in analyzing income and wealth inequality and will be met many times in economic studies.[3]

Trends of Inequality

What is happening to the degree of inequality of incomes in modern industrial economies like the United States? Is it getting greater, as the Cassandras of the last century believed? By calculating Lorenz and other curves, scholars find that inequality has definitely declined since the beginning of this century.

[2] Two times the shaded area represents the "Gini coefficient," discussed in question 6 at the end of this chapter.

[3] There are still other ways of measuring the degree of inequality of income. One of the most interesting of these, employed by the Italian economist Vilfredo Pareto, used a certain logarithmic chart called the "Pareto chart." He found that the "upper tail" of the income data of many different countries and many different times fell along straight lines of almost the same slopes. He came to believe this to be a fundamental natural law. According to *Pareto's Law,* there is an inevitable tendency for income to be distributed in the same way—regardless of social and political institutions and regardless of taxation. In the past 80 years, many careful studies have refuted the universality and inevitability of Pareto's Law.

But there appears to have been a turn toward greater inequality and poverty over the last decade. Between the mid-1970s and 1986, the share of income going to the upper-income groups increased, while the lowest-income group lost ground.

The trends in inequality can be gauged as follows: According to historical studies, the share of total income going to the poorest fifth (or quintile) of the households stood around 3.6 or 3.8 percent in the late 1920s. The share of the bottom quintile rose to 5.0 percent after World War II, as many people from low-income agricultural jobs migrated into industry. There was some increase in the income share of the bottom fifth of households until the mid-1970s, after which this share declined sharply in the 1980s. (A graphical display of several indexes of inequality and poverty is provided in Figure 34-1.)

What lay behind the changing extent of inequality? In part, inequality has been substantially reduced by government actions. Government programs like welfare and food stamps for the indigent, social security for the elderly, and unemployment insurance take the worst edge off abject poverty. Moreover, our income-tax system tends to tax high incomes more heavily than low incomes, thereby tending to reduce the degree of inequality.

The rising inequality over the last decade has several sources. Among the important ones are a rise in female-headed households, an increase in low-wage jobs, and an erosion of government transfer programs—all of which depressed the incomes of the poorest part of the population. In addition, rising interest rates and lower income-tax rates at the top raised the relative incomes of the richest groups.

Inequality in Different Regions Which countries show great, which less, inequality? Lorenz curves of four countries are shown in Figure 26-3(a). We see that Britain and Sweden have less income inequality than does the United States. The reason for this lies partly in the high levels of redistributive taxation in the European countries. In addition, the United States has larger proportions of its population in low-income minority groups and larger numbers of single-headed households.

It is extremely difficult to compare the inequality in

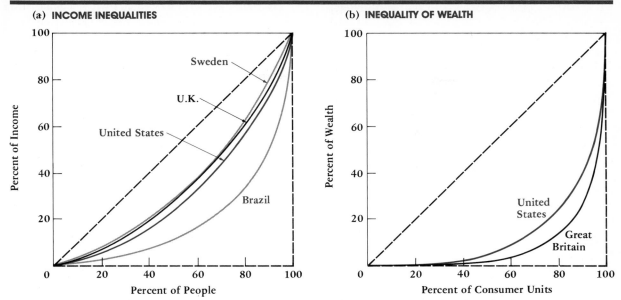

(a) INCOME INEQUALITIES

(b) INEQUALITY OF WEALTH

Figure 26-3 Inequality differs in different societies, and is greater for wealth than for income

(a) Advanced economies show less inequality of income distribution than do industrializing economies. Contrary to predictions of many socialists that the rich get richer and the poor get poorer under capitalism, the mixed economy shows increasing equality over time.

(b) Holdings of wealth tend to be more concentrated than do annual incomes. The United States and the United Kingdom have similar income distributions, but British wealth is much more concentrated than American. Socialist countries like China and the Soviet Union would show much less concentration of private wealth. [Source: James D. Smith and Stephen D. Franklin, "The Concentration of Personal Wealth, 1922–1969," *American Economic Review* (May 1974); A. B. Atkinson and A. J. Harrison, "Trends in the Distribution of Wealth in Britain," in A. B. Atkinson (ed.), *Wealth, Income and Inequality* (Oxford University Press, Great Britain, 1980).]

the Soviet Union[4] or China with that of advanced market economies. If we confine ourselves to the ad-

[4] Our survey of different economic systems in Chapter 35 finds that the distribution of earnings in the Soviet Union looks about as unequal as that in the United States (see Chapter 35). Top scientists or composers in the Soviet Union probably make about as much as similar persons in the United States. Government officials in communist countries probably have a higher economic status than do leaders of democracies, although the exact earnings and economic privileges of Soviet party chiefs, military leaders, and ministers are not susceptible to precise numerical measurement.

Even if the structure of wages were similar in communist and capitalist countries, one major difference remains: in capitalist countries, perhaps a tenth of national income goes to upper-income groups as property income (interest, dividends, capital gains, etc.). In the Soviet Union or China, by contrast, there are no Rockefellers or Gettys.

vanced market economies, the greatest income equality is found in Japan and West Germany. The most unequal income distributions come in the United States, Canada, and France.

Effects of Industrialization on Equality

Historians have examined the patterns of inequality as nations follow the road from isolated traditional societies through the first phases of development into advanced industrialized countries. What does the fragmentary evidence indicate?

Firsthand reports suggest a pattern first of greater, then of lesser inequality. The extremes of inequality—with conspicuous opulence appearing alongside the most abject poverty—occur in industrializing countries.

Recent studies by the World Bank and scholars confirm this casual observation. Those countries with the greatest inequality tend to be the middle-income countries—particularly Latin American countries like Peru, Panama, Brazil, or Venezuela. In these countries, it is not uncommon for the bottom fifth to gain only 2 percent of total income, while the top 10 percent may get 40 or even 50 percent of income.

These data suggest that economic development itself temporarily increases original inequality. Then, as the share of labor rises in the mixed economy, inequality is reduced.

Distribution of Wealth

Up to now we have seen how incomes differ across income classes and nations. One important determinant of differences in income lies in differences in wealth. By *wealth* we mean the net ownership of financial claims or tangible property, assets minus liabilities. In terms of our accounting definitions in the appendix of Chapter 20, wealth strictly means the net worth of a household.

One of the sources of inequality of income lies in inequality of ownership of wealth. Those who are fabulously wealthy—whether because of inheritance, skill, or luck—start with incomes far above the average household. Those with no wealth start with an income handicap.

By and large, wealth is much more unequally distributed in market economies than is income, as Figure 26-3 shows. In the United States, 1 percent of the people own about 19 percent of all wealth, and the richest $\frac{1}{2}$ percent own fully 14 percent of the nation's wealth. To take the latest year for which extensive data are available, 1983, American households owned a total of approximately $5700 billion of net worth. The top $\frac{1}{2}$ percent owned $1001 billion of assets, representing one-sixth of total household net worth. The distribution of wealth in the United Kingdom is even more lopsided than in the United States. In part this is because certain peers and tycoons in Britain own tremendous amounts of land and other property. But study of the data shows that much of the difference comes from the fact that many Americans of quite modest incomes have positive net worth (i.e., assets in excess of liabilities), whereas this is less common among the lower-income British.

The visible differences in ownership of wealth have spurred levellers over the ages to propose heavy taxation of property incomes, wealth, or inheritances, and radicals have agitated for expropriation by the state of great accumulations of property. In recent years, however, increased emphasis on private capital accumulation for economic growth has muted the call to increase the tax burden on high-income or wealthy individuals.

We have now concluded the discussion of the measurement of income and wealth inequality in the United States and other countries. The balance of this chapter discusses the roots of economic inequality.

B. THE SOURCES OF INEQUALITY

One of the most profound aspirations of a modern democracy is to promote equality—equality of opportunity, of education, and of political freedoms. Direct attempts to reduce inequality of income prove much more controversial. People disagree strongly about whether taxation should be used to redistribute incomes and whether government welfare programs should do more than prevent starvation. Philosophers debate whether it is ethically right that those who earn the most should keep most of their earnings.

Economics can provide no right answers to these normative questions; they must be answered by our political institutions. However, we must explore the facts before informed choices can be made. What are the sources of poverty and wealth? Are the poor lazy or unlucky? Does most wealth come from hard work and thrift or from inheritance? How do savings and work respond to the tax system? The answers to such questions will inevitably influence our attitudes toward political steps to reduce inequality.

In this section we review the roots of inequality of incomes in a market economy. Because we determined that labor incomes and property incomes are the two major categories of income, we focus on these sources of inequality.

INEQUALITY IN LABOR INCOME

Labor earnings constitute 80 percent of factor incomes. Even if property incomes were equally distributed, much inequality would remain. Let us begin then by examining the factors that produce inequalities in earnings: differences in abilities and skills of labor, differences in occupation and intensity of work, differences in level of education, and finally the effect of discrimination.

Abilities and Skills

People differ enormously in their abilities; such differences lead to different skills of workers and hence to different wage rates or salaries. The differing abilities may be physical, mental, or temperamental. They may be associated with biological inheritance or, as scientific evidence increasingly shows, with social and economic environment.

However, these personal differences provide us with very little of the answer to the puzzle of income dispersion. Physical traits (such as strength or height or girth) and measured mental traits (such as intelligence quotient or tone perception) appear to be less varied among people than the differences in income distribution.

This paradox is illustrated in Figure 26-4. The bell-shaped red curve shows how commonly measured abilities are distributed. The much flatter black curve shows how much more unequally distributed are incomes.

This difference between the distribution of measured abilities and of incomes suggests that superficial traits like strength or measured IQ can easily be overemphasized in trying to explain income differences. Instead, the important sources of income differences should be sought in peculiar talents, risk taking, luck, strokes of genius, and hard work—none of which tend to turn up in standardized tests.

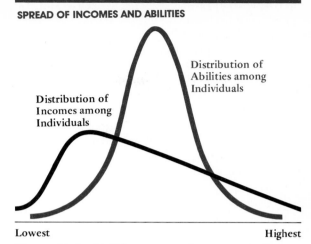

SPREAD OF INCOMES AND ABILITIES

Distribution of Abilities among Individuals

Distribution of Incomes among Individuals

Lowest   Highest

Figure 26-4   Abilities are much more equally distributed than are incomes

Human characteristics such as measured intelligence, height, weight, or strength are much more equally distributed than are incomes. While human traits seldom differ by more than a factor of 3, high incomes today are more than 100 times greater than the lowest.

Intensity of Work

The intensity of work differs enormously among individuals. The workaholic may log 70 hours a week on the job, never take a vacation, and forgo retirement. Those who enjoy leisure might work just enough to pay for life's material necessities. The difference in incomes might be a factor of 2 or 3 from effort alone, yet no one would say that economic opportunity was therefore genuinely unequal.

Differences among Occupations

One important source of income inequality lies in people's occupations. At the low end of the scale we find domestic servants, fast-food personnel, and similar service workers. A full-time, year-round job at McDonald's or at a car wash might earn $8000 a year in 1988.

At the other extreme are the high-earning professionals. What single profession seems to make the most money? In recent years it has without question been doctors. Physicians working in medical corporations had median earnings of $155,000 in 1988. Doctors have forged well ahead of lawyers, who had median earnings of $52,000 in 1988.[5]

Dentists, engineers, and schoolteachers are estimated to have 1988 median incomes of $80,000, $48,000 and $27,000, respectively. University teachers as a class have an average salary of about $38,000 for a 9-month academic year. Full professors at the largest universities get about twice that amount; professors of computer science and finance average higher incomes than do professors of education and English; supply and demand decrees that medical school professors average the highest salaries of all.

Figure 26-5 shows how professions differ in their inequality of earnings. What is the source of such vast differences among occupations? Part of the difference comes from the years of training needed to become a doctor or lawyer (this point is developed in the discussion of human capital in the next section). Abilities also play a role, for example, in limiting engineering jobs to those who have some quantitative skills. Some jobs pay more because they are dangerous or unpleasant. And in most cases (recall Chapter 18's discussion of limiting the number of doctors), limiting the supply of its members drives up the income potential of a profession.

Differences in Education (Is College Worthwhile?)

How do education and training affect lifetime incomes? Are they worth the cost? This question is addressed by the study of **human capital,** which represents investments of time and money in improving the quality of workers through training and education. We are used to the idea of tangible investments in housing or equipment, but investment in improving human skills, as economists like Chicago's Theodore Schultz and Gary Becker have emphasized, may benefit society and individuals just as much as new steel mills.

[5]Top New York law firms bill their giant corporate clients at more than $500 per hour. In 1988, top graduates of the best law schools *started out* with the big New York firms at $80,000 per year.

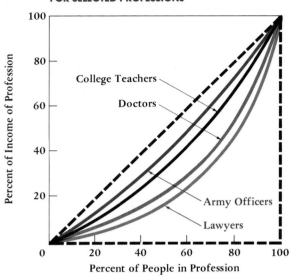

Figure 26-5   Lawyers and doctors show more inequality than salaried professors or army officers

Income inequality is highest in law. How would the curve look for clerical workers? For government janitors? Why would the curve for oil drillers and speculators on the stock exchange be the most unequal of all? [Source: G. J. Stigler, *Employment and Compensation in Education* (National Bureau of Economic Research, New York, 1950).]

How does such an investment occur? When a student goes to college, he or she might pay $10,000 in tuition and $15,000 in opportunity costs of earnings forgone. In return for this substantial investment, the earnings of the college graduate might be a job paying $10,000 per year more than a high school graduate could land. The higher earnings are the return on the investment in human capital.

Does college actually pay off? The evidence suggests that it does, but college is not as profitable an investment as it used to be. Those who never finished high school had median incomes of $16,800 in 1988. Those who completed 12 years of schooling earned $29,000 in 1988. By contrast, college graduates had a median income of $44,000 in 1988, earning 52 percent more than those who only finished high school. Moreover, the unemployment rate of college graduates tends to be about one-half that of less educated groups. How does education affect the incomes of men versus women and of minority groups? Studies indicate that the earnings of women and minorities are lower than those of white males, but the relative contribution of education to earnings is similar for all groups.

Even if you have to borrow at 10 percent interest, put off years of gainful employment, live away from home, and pay for food and books, your lifetime earnings in the professions that are open only to college graduates will probably more than compensate you for the costs.

Recent data show that an 18-year-old male who goes on to graduate from college will earn about $3,100,000 (at 1988 price and income levels) before the age of 65. Those of the same generation who only graduate from high school will earn about $2,100,000. Those who do not finish high school will earn an average of only $1,500,000. What about postgraduate education? Going on to graduate or professional schools adds an average of 10 percent to earnings, thus paying a modest return.

Other Factors

In addition to ability, occupation, and education, other factors affect the inequality of wage earnings. We will see in Chapter 28 that discrimination and exclusion from certain occupations have played an important role in keeping down the incomes of many minority groups. And we should not underestimate the role of pure chance or luck in affecting our economic circumstances.

INEQUALITIES IN PROPERTY INCOME

While the differences in incomes among wage earners are large, it is the disparities in wealth and in property incomes that have produced the most vitriolic attacks from capitalism's critics. "Property is theft!" wrote the nineteenth-century socialist Proudhon. Before deciding whether to agree, however, let's examine the statistics.

By comparison to income, the ownership of wealth is extremely concentrated. In 1983, the top 1 percent of wealthholders owned 23 percent of all personal wealth; the top $\frac{1}{2}$ percent owned 18 percent. While the average person in the bottom 99 percent had net worth of around $52,000, the top $\frac{1}{2}$ percent averaged $2.3 million per household.

What are the sources of this vast gulf between the super-rich and the poor? Have the rich become kings of the mountain by their own virtue, saving, and risk taking? Or by their ancestors' virtue? Or by sheer luck?

Inheritance

Many wealthy people inherited a great deal of their property from their parents or grandparents. The progeny of the tycoons of an earlier era—Rockefeller, Ford, Getty, and du Pont—are among today's top wealthholders. According to surveys, two-thirds of the top 1 percent of wealthholders in America inherited a substantial fraction of their property.

Saving and Risk Taking

Economic mythology spins tales of modern-day Horatio Algers, poor children who toil, take risks, save their entire earnings, and end up in a fabulous San Francisco penthouse. To what extent, in fact, does America's accumulated wealth result from people saving over their working lives (the so-called life-cycle model of saving behavior described in Chapter 7)?

A recent study by Laurence Kotlikoff and Lawrence Summers suggests that only a small fraction of personal wealth, perhaps 20 percent, can be explained by life-cycle savings. The balance, it appears, is gained from other sources, such as inheritances or gifts.

Another theory is that today's wealth is the reward for yesterday's risk taking. We cannot expect someone to drill a 25,000-foot oil well, to spend years hunting for the genetically engineered cure for cancer, to slave for years over the word processor hoping to write a best-selling Gothic novel—without some lure of exceptional reward.

AMERICA'S 100 RICHEST PEOPLE

		AMOUNT OF NET WORTH	
SOURCE OF WEALTH	NUMBER OF PERSONS	(billions of $)	(percent)
Inheritance	37	48.7	35
Financial acumen	7	9.6	7
Entrepreneurship	56	80.7	58
Of which:			
Oil	9	11.8	9
Real estate	12	13.0	9
Retailing	9	17.1	12
Electronics	4	8.5	6
Candy	4	4.6	3
Other	18	25.7	19
Total	**100**	**139.0**	**100**

Table 26-5 How did the richest Americans reach the summit?

In 1987, 100 Americans had net worth of at least $740 million, according to *Forbes* magazine. Most gained their wealth by entrepreneurship—putting together shopping centers, oil-drilling schemes, computer companies, or even candy-bar firms. A minority represent the beneficiaries of *earlier* entrepreneurship (like the Rockefellers). A tiny fraction gained wealth by stock market speculation or by inventing radically new products. [Source: *Forbes* (October 26, 1987).]

And markets *do* reward such risk taking with higher-than-average returns. No one has succeeded in quantifying how much of the inequality of wealth is due to such extraordinary risk taking, but data on top wealthholders indicate that much of the great inequality of wealth is due to the fact that very few are destined to make the innovations upon which great fortunes are built.

What is the relative importance of inheritance and other factors for the very wealthy? Table 26-5 displays the experience of the top 100 wealthholders in 1987 (as collected by *Forbes* magazine). These data suggest that entrepreneurship has been the surest route to great wealth. Those who put together new organizations—oil-drilling companies, shopping center complexes, even candy-bar firms—most often gained great wealth; somewhat more than one third of the 100 wealthiest got there by birth; while a handful were financial wizards.

Markets and Inequality

After this brief review of the forces leading to inequality of income, the next chapter starts the more complete analysis of the determination of wages, rents, and interest rates. As we turn to that subject, the central properties of markets should be kept in mind. Remember that competitive markets are particularly adept at solving the *what* and *how* problems—questions about allocation of resources among industries and choice of the best technique for producing particular commodities. But markets have no particular talent for finding the best solution to the *for whom* question. The most efficient economy in the world may produce a distribution of wages and property that would offend even the staunchest defender of free markets.

We can therefore shout two cheers for the market but not three. We can reserve our judgment about the way markets solve the *for whom* question until Chapter 34, where we will trace the incidence of poverty in America and see how a society might tackle the problem of reducing inequality while preserving the remarkable efficiency properties of markets.

SUMMARY

A. Measurement of Incomes and Inequality

1. Distribution theory refers to the way that income and wealth are distributed in an economy—to the initial allocation of factors of production (land, labor, and capital), and to the prices that these factors receive in markets. The major concepts studied are income (the flow of wages, salaries, property returns, and transfers received during a period) and wealth (the net stock of assets owned at a point in time).

2. The view that the poor are becoming poorer in modern industrial nations will not stand up under careful factual examination. Since the Industrial Revolution, living standards in Western Europe and America have shown a rising long-term trend.

3. The Lorenz curve is a convenient device for measuring the spreads or inequalities of income distribution. It shows what percentage of total income goes to the poorest 1 percent of the population, to the poorest 10 percent, to the poorest 95 percent, and so forth. The distribution of American income today appears to be less unequal than in the early part of this century or than in less developed countries now. But it still shows a considerable measure of inequality and even a slight increase of inequality over the last decade. Wealth is even more unequally distributed than is income, both in the United States and in other capitalist economies.

B. The Sources of Inequality

4. In explaining the inequality in income distribution, we can look separately at labor income and property income. Labor earnings differ because of differences in abilities, in intensity of work (both hours and effort), and because occupational earnings differ, due to divergent amounts of human capital, among other factors.

5. Property incomes are more unevenly distributed than labor earnings, largely because of the great disparities in wealth. Inheritance helps the children of the wealthy begin ahead of the average person; only a small fraction of America's wealth can be accounted for by life-cycle savings. Entrepreneurship appears prominently as a source of the net worth of the 100 richest Americans.

CONCEPTS FOR REVIEW

income and wealth
trends of income distribution
Lorenz curve of income and wealth
human capital

labor and property income
relative roles of luck, life-cycle savings,
 risk taking, inheritance
sources of inequality

QUESTIONS FOR DISCUSSION

1. Let the members of the class each anonymously write down on a card an estimate of their families' annual income. From these, draw up a frequency table showing the distribution of incomes. What is the median income? The mean income?

2. Many people believe that incomes should be more equally distributed. How unequal do *you* think incomes should be for people of different abilities? If you desired less inequality, what methods would you propose to equalize incomes? (Choose between redistributive taxation and government transfers.)

3. What effect would the following have on the Lorenz curve of after-tax incomes? (Assume that the taxes are spent by the government on a representative slice of GNP.)

   (a) A proportional income tax (i.e., one taxing all incomes at the same rate)

   (b) A progressive income tax (i.e., one taxing high incomes more heavily than low incomes)

   (c) A 5 percent national sales tax

   (d) A deep recession

Draw five Lorenz curves to illustrate the original income distribution and the income distribution after each of actions (a) to (d).

4. How does the fact that different cities and regions have different costs of living affect comparisons of incomes? Thus, in Anchorage (Alaska) and Honolulu, living is a third to a quarter more expensive than in the average city. Boston, New York, and San Francisco are also expensive places. Austin, Atlanta, and Dallas run 10 percent below average. Small towns run 10 to 20 percent below big cities.

5. Consider two ways of supplementing the income of the poor: *(a)* cash assistance (say, $500 per month) and *(b)* categorical benefits such as subsidized food, medical care, or housing.

   List the pros and cons of using each strategy. Can you explain why the United States tends to use mainly strategy *(b)*? Do you agree?

6. Instead of using the Lorenz curve to measure inequality, calculate the area between the actual curve of inequality and the curve of equal incomes (i.e., the red shaded region in Figure 26-2). Two times this ratio is called the "Gini coefficient."

   What is the Gini coefficient for a society with absolute equality of income? For one in which one person gets all the income? Estimate the Gini coefficients for the different Lorenz curves in Figure 26-3.

7. In a country called Econoland, there are 10 people. Their incomes (in thousands) are $3, $6, $2, $8, $4, $9, $1, $5, $7, and $5. Construct a table of income quintiles like Table 26-4. Plot a Lorenz curve. Calculate the Gini coefficient defined in question 6.

8. The following table shows the per capita incomes of 12 major countries for 1985. These are converted from the national currencies into U.S. dollars using "purchasing-power" exchange rates that measure actual buying power.

PER CAPITA INCOMES, 1985

United States	$16,700	South Korea	$2,150
Japan	11,300	Mexico	2,080
West Germany	10,900	Hungary	1,950
France	9,540	Brazil	1,640
United Kingdom	8,460	Kenya	290
Italy	6,520	India	270

Source: World Bank, *World Development Report, 1987.*

Use an encyclopedia to obtain populations of each country. Then, assuming that each person in a given country received exactly that country's per capita GNP, construct a Lorenz curve for the 12 countries. Does this Lorenz curve show more or less inequality than the Lorenz curves for individual countries shown in Figure 26-3(a)?

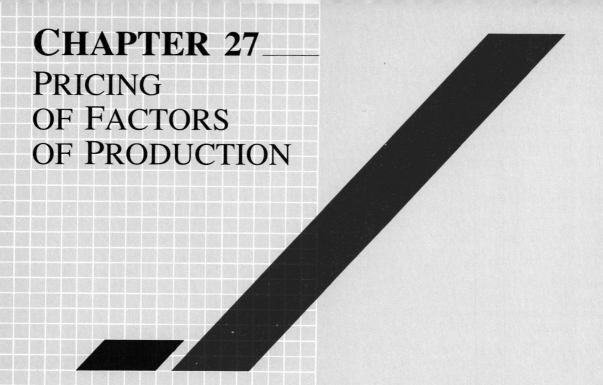

CHAPTER 27

PRICING
OF FACTORS
OF PRODUCTION

[The price of] corn is not high because a rent is paid, but a rent is paid because [the price of] corn is high.

David Ricardo

THE THEORY of income distribution in competitive markets is simply a special case of the theory of prices. Wages are the price of labor, rent is the price of land, and interest is the price of capital. But within this general rule, many controversial and important questions are left unanswered: Why are pleasant professions like law paid many times more than are unpleasant tasks like garbage collection? Why are land rents in Manhattan sky-high while those in the desert are negligible? Why are women paid on average only 65 cents for every dollar earned by men? Is labor exploited by capital? What determines the interest and profit rates on capital? All these topics are addressed by the theory of income distribution.

We might ask from a macroeconomic perspective, Why are wages three-quarters of GNP? To answer this question, we must understand the forces that determine all the factor prices—the factors lying behind the supply and demand for labor, land, and capital. In short, economics analyzes the distribution of income by focusing on the markets where factors of production get priced.

The key to factor pricing is found in the marginal-productivity theory of the firm. We therefore begin by reviewing the theory of production first introduced in Chapter 21. We see that factor prices relate closely to the familiar law of diminishing returns. Indeed, the demand curves for the various factors of production— the demand for labor, land, and so forth—can be expressed in terms of the revenues earned on their mar-

ginal products. Putting the demand curves together with the supplies of each factor, we obtain the market price and quantity of each factor. This chapter ends by applying the theory of distribution to the important case of land rents.

A. MARGINAL-PRODUCTIVITY THEORY OF DISTRIBUTION

DEMANDS FOR FACTORS ARE INTERDEPENDENT

The basic peculiarity about the demand for inputs stems from the technological fact that inputs usually do not work alone. A shovel by itself is worthless to me if I want a garden. A worker with empty hands is equally worthless. Together, the worker and shovel can dig my garden. In other words, the productivity of one factor, such as labor, depends upon the amount of other factors available to work with.

Sir William Petty put the matter in this striking way: Labor is the father of product and land the mother. We cannot say which is more important in producing a baby—a mother or a father. So, too, it is generally impossible to say how much output has been created by any one of the different inputs taken by itself. The different inputs interact with one another.

It is this *interdependence* of productivities of land, labor, and capital goods that makes the distribution of income a complex topic. Suppose we had to distribute at one time the entire output of a nation. If land had by itself produced so much, and labor had alone produced so much, and machinery had by itself produced the rest, distribution might seem easy indeed. Under supply and demand, if the separate factors could produce goods by themselves, each factor would produce output alone and enjoy the undivided fruits of its own work.

But reread the above paragraph and underline such words as ''by itself produced'' and ''had alone produced.'' They refer to a fantasy, to an independence of productivities which simply does not exist in reality. If an omelette is produced by labor and fuel and

eggs, how can you unscramble the separate contributions of each input?

How then is the puzzle of income distribution resolved? It gets resolved by the interaction of supply and demand, operating in perfectly or imperfectly competitive markets.

MARGINAL PRODUCTIVITY

Before turning to the determination of the demand for factors of production, we will review the essentials of Chapter 21's production theory.

The theory of production begins with the notion of the *production function*. If you have given quantities of land, labor, and capital, what is the maximum output of a particular good that you can produce? In technical language, we represent the relationship by the production function, which states the maximum amount of output that can be produced, with a given state of technical knowledge, for each combination of factor inputs. A specific production function might tell you that you can produce 1 ton of steel with 1.2 tons of iron ore, 150,000 Btu of energy, and 1.2 hours of labor.

Using the production-function concept, we provided a rigorous definition of *marginal product*.[1] Table 27-1 is a reminder of the way marginal products

---

[1]Note that the marginal product of a factor is expressed in *physical* units of product per unit of additional input. So economists sometimes use the term ''marginal physical product'' rather than marginal product, particularly when they want to avoid any possible confusion with a concept we will soon encounter called ''marginal revenue product.'' For brevity, we will skip the word ''physical'' and abbreviate marginal product as *MP*.

DIMINISHING RETURNS REVIEWED

(1) UNITS OF LABOR (workers)	(2) TOTAL PRODUCT (bu)	(3) MARGINAL PRODUCT OF LABOR (bu per worker)
0	0	
		20,000
1	20,000	
		10,000
2 (initial input)	30,000	
		5,000
3	35,000	
		3,000
4	38,000	
		1,000
5	39,000	

Table 27-1   Diminishing returns is seen as diminishing marginal product

Marginal product of labor is calculated by adding 1 additional unit of labor while holding all other inputs constant. If the initial input is 2 units of labor, then adding a third produces 5000 additional bushels of corn. Diminishing returns is seen as a fall in the marginal product of labor as the number of workers increases.

are calculated. Say we start out with 2 units of labor, plus a given dose of land and machinery, and this combination produces 30,000 bushels of corn. How much additional corn would be produced if we added 1 extra unit of labor, holding all other inputs constant? Table 27-1 provides an answer of 5000 extra bushels. We then say that the marginal product of labor at that initial point is 5000 bushels of corn.

As a final element of review, recall what is meant by *diminishing returns*. Column (3) of Table 27-1 displays the marginal product of labor. Note how each successive unit of labor adds less and less output—i.e., has a declining marginal product.

Declining marginal product is another name for the law of diminishing returns. Moreover, a similar calculation of marginal product can be made for any input: we can interchange land for labor, varying the amount of land while holding constant labor and other inputs. And we would observe the law of diminishing returns at work for land as well as for labor.

Marginal Revenue Product

With this review of production theory behind us, we are prepared to break new ground in understanding the behavior of factor markets. We can use the tools of production theory to devise a new key concept in distribution theory, marginal revenue product.

Suppose we are operating a firm making laser disks. We know how much extra output each additional worker brings in. But ultimately as managers we are concerned with maximizing profits measured in dollars, for we buy our daily bread with money, not with disks. And workers too want to be paid with dollars rather than with disks. Exactly how much additional revenue does each additional unit of input produce?

Economists give the name ''marginal revenue product'' to the extra money brought in by selling the output generated by an additional worker or unit of input.

The **marginal revenue product** of input A is the additional revenue produced by an additional unit of input A.

Competitive Case It is easy to calculate marginal revenue product when product markets are perfectly competitive. In this case, the marginal product that the worker brings in (MP_L) can all be sold at the competitive output price (P). Moreover, since we are considering perfect competition, the output price is unaffected by the firm's output, and price therefore equals marginal revenue (MR). If we have MP_L of 10,000 bushels and a price and MR of \$3, the dollar value of the output produced by the last worker—the marginal revenue product of labor (MRP_L)—is \$30,000 (equal to 10,000 × \$3). This is shown in column (5) of Table 27-2. More generally, under perfect competition, each worker is worth to the firm the dollar value of the last worker's marginal product; the value of each acre of land is the marginal product of land times the output price; and so forth for each factor.

Imperfect Competition Perfect competition is but one polar case, that of a horizontal demand curve for each single firm's product. Where the individual firm's demand curve is downward-sloping, then the marginal revenue received from each extra unit of output sold is less than the price (recall that this is so because to sell an additional unit the firm must lower its price and therefore lose revenue on previous units). Hence with $MR < P$, each unit of labor's marginal product will be worth the MR to the firm.

To pursue our previous example, say that the MR was \$2 while price was \$3. Then the MRP of the second worker in Table 27-2 would be \$20,000 (equal to the MP_L of 10,000 times the MR of \$2), rather than the \$30,000 of the competitive case.

To summarize, the additional revenue gained by a firm from an additional unit of input (such as labor) is called the marginal revenue product. It is measured in dollar terms by the marginal revenue (MR) multiplied by the marginal product of the input (MP_L in the case of labor).

Marginal revenue product represents the additional

MARGINAL REVENUE PRODUCT

(1) UNITS OF LABOR (workers)	(2) TOTAL PRODUCT (bu)	(3) MARGINAL PRODUCT OF LABOR (bu per worker)	(4) PRICE OF OUTPUT (dollars per bu)	(5) MARGINAL REVENUE PRODUCT OF LABOR (dollars per worker)
0	0			
		20,000	3	60,000
1	20,000			
		10,000	3	30,000
2	30,000			
		5,000	3	15,000
3	35,000			
		3,000	3	9,000
4	38,000			
		1,000	3	3,000
5	39,000			

Table 27-2   Calculation of marginal revenue product for perfectly competitive firm

Using the production data in Table 27-1 along with the price of output, we can easily calculate the marginal revenue product of labor. Marginal revenue product of labor shows how much additional revenue the firm receives when an additional unit of labor is employed. It equals the marginal physical product in column (3) times the competitive output price (equal to marginal revenue) in column (4).

revenue gained by a firm from employment of an additional unit of an input, with other inputs held constant. It is defined as the marginal product of the input multiplied by the marginal revenue obtained from selling an extra unit of output. This holds for labor *(L)*, land *(A)*, capital *(K)*, and other inputs:

Marginal revenue product of labor *(MRP$_L$)*
$$= MR \times MP_L$$
Marginal revenue product of land *(MRP$_A$)*
$$= MR \times MP_A$$

and so forth.

THE DEMAND FOR INPUTS

Now that we have analyzed various underlying concepts, we turn to the determinants of the demand for inputs. We first note that the demand for inputs is a derived demand rather than an ultimate demand. We then show how profit-maximizing firms decide upon the optimal combination of inputs, which then allows us to describe the demand curve for inputs.

Demand for Factors Is a Derived Demand

At the outset, we must note that there is an essential difference between the demand by households for consumer goods and the demand by firms for inputs.

Why do households demand final goods like movies or muffins? They do so because of the direct enjoyment or utility these consumption goods provide. But does this also hold for a business buying an input such as fertilizer or sulfur or unskilled labor or land? Surely a business does not buy these for the direct satisfaction it hopes to get. Rather, it buys inputs because of the production and revenue that it hopes to secure from employment of those factors.

Satisfactions are in the picture—but at one stage removed. The satisfactions that consumers get from eating muffins help determine how many muffins the firm must make and therefore how many ovens and how much wheat are needed for the muffins. An accurate analysis of the demand for inputs must, therefore, recognize that consumer demands do *ultimately*

determine the baker's demand for wheat inputs. The firm's demand for labor and wheat and other inputs is derived indirectly from the consumer demand for its final product.

Economists therefore speak of the demand for productive factors as a "derived demand."

The demands for inputs or factors of production are **derived demands.** This means that when profit-seeking firms demand an input, they do so because that input permits them to produce a good which consumers are willing to buy now or in the future. The demand for the input is thus derived ultimately from consumer demands for final goods.

Figure 27-1 shows how the demand for a given input, such as fertile cornland, must be regarded as derived from the consumer demand curve for corn.

Factor Demands for Profit-Maximizing Firms

Where did the demand for cornland shown in Figure 27-1 come from? For that matter, what determines the demand for any factor of production? To understand these issues, we must analyze how a profit-oriented firm chooses its optimal combination of inputs.

Imagine that you are a profit-maximizing farmer. In your area, you can hire all the farmhands you want at $20,000 per year. Your accountant hands you a spreadsheet with the data in Table 27-2. You must decide how many workers to hire. How would you proceed?

You could try out different possibilities. If you hire one worker, the additional revenue (the *MRP*) is $60,000 while the marginal cost of the worker is $20,000, so your profit is $40,000. A second worker gives you an *MRP* of $30,000 for an additional profit of $10,000. However, the third worker produces extra output yielding revenues of only $15,000 as compared to a cost of $20,000 so it is not profitable to hire the third worker. The maximum profit in Table 27-2 is earned by hiring two workers. Note that by trial and error we have found an interesting rule. Our firm will maximize profits by hiring labor (or indeed any factor) as long as the *MRP* of that input exceeds the extra cost of that input.

(a) COMMODITY DEMAND   **(b) DERIVED FACTOR DEMAND**

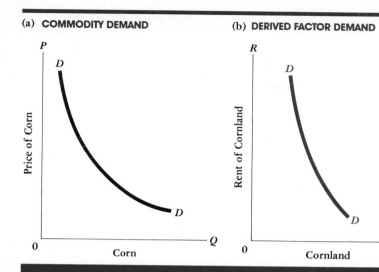

Figure 27-1   Demand for factors is derived from demand for goods they produce

The red curve of derived demand for cornland comes from the black curve of commodity demand for corn. Shift the black curve out, and out goes the red curve. Make the black commodity curve more inelastic, and the same tends to happen to the red input-demand curve.

By using this reasoning, we can derive the rule for choosing the optimal combination of inputs: To maximize profits, inputs should be added as long as the marginal revenue product of the input exceeds the marginal cost or price of the input.

In the case of perfectly competitive factor markets, we have an even more striking rule. Recall that under competition the marginal revenue product equals price times marginal product ($MRP = P \times MP$). In other words, a profit-maximizing competitive firm will always want to compare the costs and revenues from hiring more labor or land. The extra cost is the wage rate of labor or the rental on land. The extra revenue is the price of output times the marginal product of labor or land.

We therefore see that for perfectly competitive firms, maximum profits are earned when:

Marginal product of labor × output price
= the price of labor = the wage rate

Marginal product of land × output price
= the price of land = the rent

and so forth.

Least-Cost Rule We can use the profit-maximizing conditions on input choice to describe how all inputs

should be combined. If our firm desires to maximize profits, it will follow the conditions just listed for all inputs. But we can easily solve the equations to obtain an important new set of equations for perfectly competitive firms:

$$\frac{\text{Marginal product}}{\text{of labor}} = \frac{\text{marginal product}}{\text{of land}}$$
$$\frac{}{\text{Price of labor}} = \frac{}{\text{price of land}}$$

$$= \cdots = \frac{1}{\text{output price}}$$

What does this condition say? We find that profits are maximized when the marginal product per dollar of input is equalized for each input. If an acre of land costs $800 while an hour of labor costs 100 times less at $8, then no rational person would decide to equalize the marginal products of the two factors. Rather, as the equation shows, costs are minimized when the marginal products *per dollar of input* are the same. Since land costs 100 times as much as labor, land's *MP* must be 100 times labor's *MP*. (Recall that this rule is identical in spirit to Chapter 19's rule for maximum consumer satisfaction—that rule states that maximum satisfaction comes when the marginal utility per dollar is equalized for each good consumed.)

Demand for Labor and Marginal Revenue Product

We can now provide an exact description of the demand for factors of production. The last section showed how a profit-maximizing firm would choose input quantities such that the price of each input equalled the *MRP* of that input. This implies that, once we have found the *MRP* schedule for an input, we can immediately determine the demand for that input.

Glance back at Table 27-2. This table shows in the last column the *MRP* of labor for our corn farm. By the profit-maximizing condition, we know that at a wage of $60,000 the firm would choose 1 unit of labor; at a $30,000 wage, 2 units of labor would be sought; and so forth. Hence the *MRP* schedule *is* the demand schedule for the firm.

Figure 27-2 uses this result to draw a demand curve for our corn farm using the data shown in Table 27-2. In addition, we have drawn a smooth curve through the individual points to show how the demand curve would appear if fractional units of labor could be purchased.

An obvious corollary of the above is this:

Substitution Rule If the price of one factor, like labor, rises while other factor prices remain fixed, it will generally benefit the firm to substitute more of the other inputs for the now-more-expensive factor. A rise in P_L will reduce MP_L/P_L and cause labor to be fired and land rented until equality of marginal products per dollar of input is restored—thus lowering the amount of needed L and increasing the demand for land acres. A fall in P_L will do the reverse. A rise in P_A alone will, by the same logic, cause labor to be substituted for now-more-expensive land.

DETERMINATION OF FACTOR PRICES BY SUPPLY AND DEMAND

Let's now move on to a full analysis of the determination of factor prices by supply and demand. The last section provided the underpinnings for analysis of demand. We showed there that, for given factor prices, profit-maximizing firms would choose input

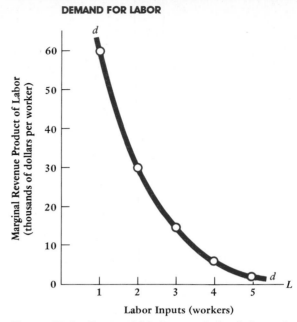

DEMAND FOR LABOR

Figure 27-2   **Demand for inputs derived through marginal revenue products**

The demand for labor arises from the marginal revenue product of labor. This figure uses the data for the competitive firm displayed in Table 27-2.

combinations according to their marginal revenue products. As the price of land falls, each farmer would substitute land for other inputs like labor, machinery, and fertilizer. Each farmer therefore would show a demand for cornland inputs like that on the right of Figure 27-1.

How do we obtain the *market demand* for inputs (whether cornland, unskilled labor, or fertilizer)? We add together the individual demands of each of the firms. Thus at a given price of land, we add together all the demands for land of all the firms at that price; and we do the same at every price of land. Put differently, we add *horizontally* all the individual firms' demand curves to obtain the market demand curve for an input.[2] We follow the same procedure for any

[2]Note that this process of adding factor demand curves horizontally is exactly the same procedure that we followed in obtaining market demand curves for consumers in Chapter 19.

input, summing up all the derived demands of all the businesses to get the market demand for each input. And in each case, the derived demand for tractors or unskilled labor or any input is based on the marginal revenue product of the input under consideration. Figure 27-3 shows a general demand curve for a factor of production as the *DD* curve.

Along with the demand curve we must also have a supply curve for the input, shown as *SS* in Figure 27-3. The general principles of supply will differ from input to input. Later in this chapter we will investigate the special case of land, while the next three chapters will discuss the supply of labor and capital goods.

Can we say anything about the slope of the supply

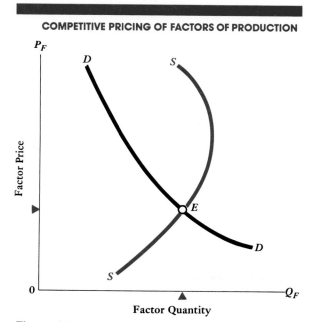

COMPETITIVE PRICING OF FACTORS OF PRODUCTION

Figure 27-3 Factor supply and derived demand interact to determine factor prices and income distribution

Factor prices are determined by the interaction of factor supply and demand. If the demand for a factor such as land rises, then that factor's share of national income will rise. Similarly, supplies and demands for trucks or computer programmers or office buildings will affect their prices and quantities sold. Supply curve may bend backward in special cases, such as for labor.

curve of inputs? Actually, the supply curve may slope positively or negatively or even be vertical. Land's supply is usually thought to be unaffected by price, as we will shortly see. Alternatively, if the factor of production were labor, people might feel that they could afford to work fewer hours when wages rise, so that the *SS* curve might eventually bend backward and northwestward from the vertical, rather than rising. (The case of backward-bending supply of a factor is discussed at greater length in Chapter 28.)

Whether the slope is positive or negative, a competitive market will have a supply curve such as the *SS* curve shown in Figure 27-3. The market price of the input will be set where the derived demand curve for a factor intersects its supply curve. And if the demand curve for the factor shifts up, its equilibrium price will tend to rise. On the other hand, if the supply offered of a factor increases, so that the supply curve shifts rightward, the factor price will tend to fall.

In a competitive market economy, therefore, factor prices and people's incomes are not determined at random. There are definite forces of supply and demand operating to create high returns to scarce factors that are very useful in producing the things wanted by people with purchasing power. And, of course, any factor's earnings tend to drop if more of it becomes available, or if other close substitutes for it are found, or if people stop wanting the goods that the factor is best suited to make. Competition gives, and competition takes.

MARGINAL-PRODUCTIVITY THEORY OF DISTRIBUTION

We can now use marginal-productivity theory to solve the riddle of the sphinx: How do markets allocate national output among two or more factors of production?

John Bates Clark, a distinguished Columbia University economist, provided a simplified theory of distribution around 1900. It can be applied to competitive price-and-wage determination when there are any number of goods and factor inputs. But it is most easily grasped if we consider a simplified world with only one product in which all accounts are kept in real terms. The product could be corn or a basket of

DISTRIBUTION OF NATIONAL PRODUCT

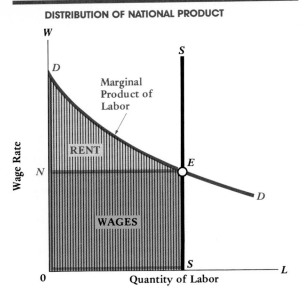

Figure 27-4 Marginal product principles determine traditional factor distribution of income

Each vertical slice represents the marginal product of that unit of labor. Total national output is found by adding all the vertical slices up to the total supply of labor at *S*.

The distribution of output is determined by marginal product principles. Total wages are the dark red area (equal to the wage rate *ON* times the quantity of labor *OS*). Land rents get the residual light red triangle *NDE*.

goods, but we will call it *Q*. Moreover, by setting the price equal to 1, we can conduct the entire discussion in real terms, with the value of output being *Q* and with the wage rate being the real wage in terms of goods or *Q*. In this situation, a production function tells how much *Q* is produced for each quantity of labor-hours, *L*, and for each quantity of acres of homogeneous land, *A*.

Clark reasoned as follows. A first worker has a large marginal product because there is so much land to work with. (Note that because *P* = 1, and given the assumption of perfect competition, *MP* = *MRP* and the wage = *MP*.) Worker 2 has a slightly smaller marginal product. But the two workers are alike: they must get exactly the same wage. Which wage? The *MP* of worker 1? The lower *MP* of worker 2? The average of these?

Under perfect competition, where landowners are free to employ as few or many workers as they like, the answer is plain: Landlords will never freely hire that second worker if the market wage they must pay exceeds the new marginal product received. So the demand curve for labor will ensure that *all* the workers who get hired do receive as a wage rate the marginal product of the last worker.

What happens to the excess of *MP* produced by the first worker and all the earlier workers up to the very last? The excess stays with the landlords as their residual earning; we will later analyze in detail the residual earnings of landowners and call these earnings *rent*. In free competitive markets, no one can take it away from them. Are they "profiteering"? Not in the usual sense of the word. Each landowner is but one of thousands: each has acres no better and no worse than the acres of the rest. Just as worker competes with worker for jobs, landowner competes with landowner for workers. There are no conspiracies, no employer associations, and no unions in Clark's competitive world.

Figure 27-4 shows that the marginal product curve of labor gives the *DD* demand curve of all employers in terms of real wages (in corn, or market baskets of goods, or *Q* units). The population or labor force provides us with the supply of labor (shown as *SS*), and the equilibrium wage comes at *E*. The total wage share of labor is given by *W* × *L* (for example, if *W* = 5 and *L* = 1 million, total wages = 5 million); this is shown by the dark red area of the rectangle, 0*SEN*.

We have determined not only the distributive share of labor but also that of land. The indicated light red rent triangle simply measures all the "excesses over final marginal product that the early workers brought and never got paid in wages." Whether fair or unfair, all the workers are alike; all landlords are free competitors who can hire labor or not as they like; so it is inevitable under competition that all workers get paid the *MP* of the last worker and, because of diminishing returns, that there be left the residual triangle of rent that goes to the landowners.

This completes the marginal-productivity theory of distribution. Note that labor wages exceed property rents in this example: the wage rectangle of *MP* is about 3 times as large as the residual rent triangle. This 3-to-1 relationship between labor income and non-labor income reflects the fact that wages and salaries constitute about three-quarters of national income. Labor's share of national income has been remarkably stable over the twentieth century, a topic we return to in Chapter 36.

If mass immigration or a rise in the birth rate increased labor supply so much as to move society down the labor demand curve to a lower wage, the rectangular share of labor might or might not fall relative to the rent triangle of land. Here is the explanation:

An increase in labor supply down the labor demand curve must always raise the absolute total of land's rent triangle. (Try it.) What about the absolute total of labor's rectangle? The elasticity discussion of Chapter 18 reminds us that labor's total wage rectangle will most certainly increase if DD has more-than-unitary elasticity. But can labor's rectangle grow as great in percentage as land's triangle, or even greater? Although not obvious until you experiment with drawing in labor demand curves, the answer is definite: Yes, the relative share of wage's rectangle can increase and the relative share of land's triangle can decrease if the marginal product curve slopes downward slowly enough.

We noted above that labor's share of national income has varied surprisingly little over the last century. This suggests that the elasticity of the labor demand curve has been close to one.

Marginal-Productivity Theory with Many Inputs

The marginal-productivity theory discovered by J. B. Clark was a great step forward in understanding the pricing of different inputs. David Ricardo had grasped the essence of Figure 27-4 in the early 1800s. But Clark saw that the position of land and labor could be reversed to get a complete theory of distribution.

You can switch the roles of labor and land. Hold labor constant and add successive units of variable land to fixed labor. Calculate each successive acre's marginal product. Draw a $D'D'$ curve showing how many acres labor-owners will demand of land at each rent rate. In the new version of Figure 27-4 that you draw, find a new E' point of equilibrium. Identify

land's rectangle of rent as determined by its *MP*. Identify labor's residual wage triangle. And note the complete symmetry of the factors. This new graph shows that we should think of the distributive shares of each and every factor of production as being simultaneously determined by their interdependent marginal products.

That is not all. Instead of labor and land, suppose the only two factors were labor L and some versatile capital goods K. Suppose a smooth production function relates Q to L and K, with the same general properties as in Figure 27-4. Then you can redraw Figure 27-4 and get an identical picture of income distribution between L and K.[3]

Profit-maximizing employers in competitive factor markets will have their demand curves for inputs determined by the additional output produced by successive units of each factor, i.e., by marginal products. In the simplified case of a single output (with $P = 1$) we get

Wage = marginal product of labor

Rent = marginal product of land

and so forth for any factor.

This distributes 100 percent of output, no more and no less, among all the factors of production.

To summarize, we see that Clark's aggregate theory of the distribution of income is compatible with the realistic pricing of any number of goods produced by any number of factors. But, while it is a rigorous theory, marginal productivities provide only one-half of the answer to income distribution—they determine the demand blade but omit the supply blade of the scissors of supply and demand.

A complete theory of income distribution must, then, include a pair of forces: (1) the forces of demand for factors, influenced by both the production function and the demands for final goods that lie behind the derived demands for factors; and (2) factor supplies, as determined by nature's endowment, the size and quality of the work force, and the accumulated stock of capital goods.

---

[3] That is still not all. If there are three or more factors of production, we can calculate each individual factor's *MP* and supply curve and Figure 27-4 still holds.

B. FACTOR PRICING: THE CASE OF LAND RENTS

Land is a good investment: they ain't making it no more.

                                                    Will Rogers

Having developed the concepts necessary for the analysis of demand for factors of production, we now apply those theories to factors that are fixed in supply like land and natural resources. We pay particular attention to analyzing how markets determine *rents* to factors that are fixed in supply. We shall also see that, when rents are not charged, society may overuse common property resources, like air or fisheries.

Rent as Return to Fixed Factors

One of the peculiarities of land is that, unlike other factors, its total supply is fixed by nature and in general cannot be augmented in response to a higher price for it or diminished in response to lower land prices.

Pure Economic Rent While land can sometimes be created by drainage, and the fertility of existing land can be depleted by overcropping, we can accept the complete fixity of land's supply as its characteristic feature. The classical economists referred to land as the "original and inexhaustible gift of nature" whose total supply is by definition fixed or completely inelastic. It was the price of such a fixed factor that the classical economists of the last century called **rent,** or sometimes "pure economic rent."

The concept of rent applies equally well to other factors that are fixed in supply. There is only one Mona Lisa, and if you could pay for its temporary use, you would pay rent. If you were hiring the services of unique individuals like Whoopi Goldberg or James Taylor, you would be paying a rent for their talents. Any payments for the use of such unique commodities are rents.

Market Equilibrium In Figure 27-5, the supply curve for land is completely inelastic because of the fixity of its supply. The demand and supply curves intersect at

the equilibrium point *E*. It is toward this factor price that the rent of land must tend. Why?

Because if rent rose above the equilibrium price, the amount of land demanded by all firms would be less than the existing amount that would be supplied. Some property owners would be unable to rent their land at all; therefore they would offer their land for less and thus bid down its rent. By similar reasoning, the rent could not remain below the equilibrium intersection for long. If it did, you should be able to show how the bidding of unsatisfied firms would force the factor price back up toward the equilibrium level.

Only at a competitive price where the total amount of land demanded exactly equals the total supply will

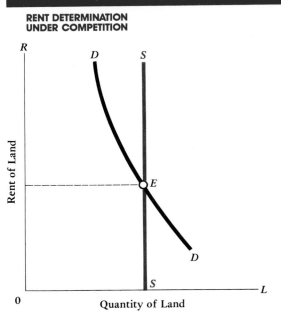

RENT DETERMINATION UNDER COMPETITION

Figure 27-5   Fixed land must work for what its demanders bid

Perfect inelasticity of supply characterizes the case of "rent," sometimes also called "pure economic rent." We run up the *SS* curve to the factor demand curve to determine rent. (Aside from land, we can apply rent considerations to rich oil and gold properties, 7-foot basketball players, and anything else in fixed supply.)

the market be in equilibrium. It is in this sense that supply and demand determine any factor price.

A factor of production like cornland is said to earn a pure economic rent (1) when its total supply is fixed or perfectly inelastic; and (2) when the factor has no other uses, such as land in the production of cotton. Adam Smith's great follower in England, David Ricardo, noted in 1815 that the case of such an inelastically supplied factor could be described as follows:

It is not really true that the price of corn is high because the price of cornland is high. Actually the reverse is more nearly the truth. The price of cornland is high because the price of corn is high. Because the supply of land is inelastic, land will always work for whatever is given to it by competition. Thus the value of the land is completely derived from the value of the product, and not vice versa.

Rent and Costs[4]

Some economists go so far as to say: "Rent does not enter into the cost of production." The last section shows that there is a grain of truth in this, but still it is very dangerous terminology. If you were a farmer trying to go into the corn-raising business, you would certainly find that the landlord has to be paid like anybody else. You would certainly include rent in your costs of production, and if you did not pay your rent, you would get taken to court.

Relativity of Viewpoint   What then are economists saying when they claim that rent does not enter into society's cost of production? They are reminding us that rent is the return to a factor that is completely inelastic in supply, so that the same quantity would be supplied even if price were much lower. Therefore, the prices of goods really determine land rent—rather than land rent determining the prices of goods.

But at this point we must avoid our old enemy "the fallacy of composition." What appears as a cost of production to each and every small firm using a particular kind of land may, as we have seen, to the whole community be merely a derived, price-determined rent expense rather than a price-determining one.

[4]This theoretical section may be skipped in brief courses.

This point can be most easily seen when the land is specialized and can be used only for the production of one industry. If a piece of land is inelastically supplied to one industry and has no place else to go, it will always work for whatever it can earn there; its return thus will appear to every small firm as a cost like any other. But as observers of the whole industry, we still must recognize that the land return is a price-determined rent and not a price-determining cost.

In conclusion:

Whether rent is or is not a price-determining cost depends upon the viewpoint. What looks like a price-determining cost to a single firm or industry may for the entire economy be a pure economic rent paid to an inelastically supplied factor.

Henry George's Single-Tax Movement: Taxing Land's Surplus

In the last part of the nineteenth century, America's population grew rapidly as people migrated here from all over the world. As the population grew, land gradually became more heavily utilized. Competitive land rents tended to rise. This created handsome profits for some of those who were lucky or farsighted enough to get in on the ground floor and buy land early.

Why, some people asked, should lucky landowners be permitted to receive these "unearned land increments"? Henry George (1839–1897), a printer who thought a great deal about economics, crystallized these sentiments in the single-tax movement. This movement, which agitated for heavy taxation of land rents, had a considerable following a century ago and still has some adherents today. But it is unlikely that anyone will soon come forward and write so persuasive a bible for the single-tax movement as did Henry George in his best-selling *Poverty and Progress*.

Taxing Land's Rents   This is not the place to attempt a full assessment of the merits and demerits of George's political movement. But one important principle of distribution and taxation can be illustrated by his central tenet:

Pure land rent is in the nature of a "surplus" that can be taxed heavily without distorting production incentives or impairing productive efficiency.

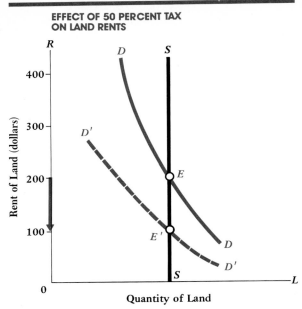

EFFECT OF 50 PERCENT TAX ON LAND RENTS

Figure 27-6   Tax on fixed land is shifted back to landowners, with government skimming off pure economic rent

A tax on fixed land leaves prices paid by users unchanged at *E* but reduces rent retained by landowners to *E'*. (What can the landowners do but accept a lower return?) This provides the rationale for Henry George's single-tax movement, which aimed to capture for society the increased land values that result from urbanization and conversion of agricultural land to higher-value uses.

Let us see why. Suppose that supply and demand create an equilibrium land rent, as in Figure 27-6 at *E*. Now what would happen if we were to introduce a 50 percent tax on all land rents? Mind you, we are not taxing buildings or improvements because that certainly would affect the volume of construction activity. All we are taxing is the return to the naturally fixed supply of agricultural and urban land sites.

After the tax, the total demand for the land's services will not have changed. At a price (*including* tax) of $200 in Figure 27-6, people will continue to demand the entire supply of land. Hence, with land fixed in supply, the market price of land services (including the tax) must be at the old intersection point *E*.

What about the rent received by the landowners? The pretax price is unchanged, and the quantity supplied is the same. Therefore, the tax must have been completely paid by the landowner.

The situation can be visualized in Figure 27-6. What the farmer pays and what the landlord receives are now two quite different things. As far as the landlords are concerned, once the government steps in to take its 50 percent share, the effect is just the same as if the net demand to the owners had shifted down from *DD* to *D'D'*. Landowners' equilibrium return after taxes is now only as high as *E'*, or only half as high as *E*. *The whole of the tax has been shifted backward onto the owners of the factor in inelastic supply*.

The landowners will not like this. But under perfect competition there is nothing they can do about it, since they cannot alter the total supply and the land must work for whatever it can get. Half a loaf is better than none.

No Distortion from Tax on Rent But, you might ask, what about the effects of such a tax on economic efficiency? The striking result is that *a tax on rent will lead to no distortions or economic inefficiencies*. Why not? Because a tax on pure economic rent does not change anyone's economic behavior. Demanders react not at all because (as we just saw) the price to those who buy such services is unchanged. The behavior of suppliers is unaffected because, by supposition, the supply of land is fixed and cannot react. Hence, the economy operates after the tax exactly as it did before the tax—with no distortions or inefficiencies arising as a result of the tax.

Ramsey Taxes

As in many areas of economics, we hear today in modern taxation theory strains from earlier times. In the 1920s, the English economist Frank Ramsey asked the natural sequel to George's inquiry: What are the most efficient kinds of taxes? Modern theorists have now developed a complete theory much along lines first suggested by George and Ramsey.

The modern theory of *Ramsey taxes* asks, How can the government raise the necessary taxes most efficiently, that is, with least loss in consumer surplus? The answer is simple and is called the "Ramsey tax rule,'' after its discoverer: Put the heaviest taxes on those inputs and outputs that are most price inelastic in supply or demand. Thus if land and food have very price-inelastic supply and demand curves, tax them heavily. If airline travel and cars are very price elastic, tax them lightly.

The rationale for the Ramsey tax rule is basically the same as that shown in Figure 27-6: if a commodity is very price inelastic in supply (or demand), then a tax on that commodity will produce relatively little change in consumption and production. In some circumstances, Ramsey taxes may constitute a way of raising revenues with a minimum of economic inefficiency.

Fairness? Both the single-tax and the Ramsey-tax analyses present powerful arguments for certain kinds of taxes as the most efficient way to organize our fiscal structure. But economies and politics do not run on efficiency alone. While stiff taxation of land rents or food might be efficient, many would think them unfair. More generally, since the necessities of life often show the lowest price elasticities, efficient taxation would mean placing the greatest tax burden on the poor. Here we see a central dilemma of a modern society, the need to choose between efficiency and fairness in design of economic policy.

FACTOR PRICING AND EFFICIENCY: RENT AND FACTOR PRICES AS DEVICES TO RATION SCARCE RESOURCES

Clearly, the supply and demand for factors of production help determine the distribution of income or solve the *for whom* problem. We might or might not like the particular solution produced by markets. But whether or not we like the competitive distribution of income—and in the case of land rent, Henry George certainly did not—we must recognize that competitive pricing does contribute to an efficient solution to questions of *how* goods are to be produced; it plays a role in the choice of the most efficient combination of factors of production.

Thus, as a result of supply and demand in markets for goods and for factors, in America, where land is plentiful and labor scarce, we find high land-labor ratios. In Japan, where people are plentiful relative to land, we find high labor-land ratios. Why? Because of government planning? No. Rather, it is through the signals transmitted by prices that the efficient land-labor combinations get induced. Land has to be auctioned off at a low price in America; labor, auctioned off at a high price. So the American farmer, seeking the least-cost combination, substitutes land for labor. Abroad, by contrast, labor gets substituted for land.

We thus see the role of prices as indicators of scarcity: they provide signals to producers as to the relative scarcity of different inputs and thereby help producers select the combination of inputs most appropriate for a society's factor endowments.

The Tragedy of the Commons

These examples show how charging rents on scarce resources helps an economy use its resources efficiently. This point extends as well to vital questions of the environment. Many of our natural resources are owned by no one. Such resources are *common property resources,* like the town commons of New England villages. As has been eloquently described by the eminent biologist Garrett Hardin, a tragic outcome occurs when common land is overgrazed:

> Picture a pasture open to all. Each herdsman tries to keep as many cattle as possible on the commons. This works well for centuries because wars, poaching, and disease keep the numbers well below the carrying capacity of the land. But eventually the day of reckoning arrives. Each herdsman seeks to maximize his personal gain; he concludes that the only sensible course is for him to add another animal to his herd. And another. But this is the conclusion reached by each and every rational herdsman sharing a commons. Herds are increased without limit— in a world that is limited. Therein is the tragedy: Freedom in a commons brings ruin to all.[5]

Hardin uncovered a key point: When no rent is (or can be) charged on a scarce good, severe misallocation or even abuse of resources can occur. In his ex-

[5]This slightly simplified paraphrase is further developed in Garrett Hardin, ''The Tragedy of the Commons,'' *Science* (December 13, 1968).

ample, no rent was charged to those who graze their cattle on common ground, leading to overgrazing and even to destruction of the fertility of the soil. Consider these other cases:

- The oceans are open to all. So everyone fishes and overfishes. Whales are threatened, and many lakes or oceans are depleted. Without an adequate fish population, breeding and maintenance of the fish schools are not possible. There would be a better use of fish resources if rents were charged to those who use fisheries—better for consumers and for those in the fishing industry.

- During peak periods, many airports get very congested, with flights stacked up in the air and lined up on the runways. Economists like Alfred Kahn have proposed the use of peak-load "congestion fees" to ration out the scarce landing rights. These would raise ticket prices during peak periods enough to persuade some people to reschedule their flights to off-peak times.[6]

- Factories that make power or chemicals often pump pollution into water and air. They are treating clean air and water as commons, whose disposal services they can use without paying. Why shouldn't firms be charged for use of clean air and water just as they are for scarce capital and labor? By charging rents on the environment, we can ration out its use to those firms for whom dumping a ton of particulates or sulfur dioxide is most valuable.

Externalities in the Commons Note that there is a shared feature in each of these three examples. The act of fishing, flying, or dumping imposes costs on other members of society. These are *externalities,* or external diseconomies of production or consumption, such as we encountered in Chapter 3 and will discuss in greater detail in Chapter 32. Careful observation suggests that the use of common property resources often exhibits important externalities, and that these externalities can be reduced by "scarcity rents" attached to the common property resource.

---

[6]Question 10 below analyzes the problem of congestion and congestion tolls in terms of the supply and demand for road use.

Why Rents Are Absent It is natural to ask, Why are rents not charged on these scarce resources? The lack of rents can be attributed to two general sources.

First, in some cases, there are no owners or the owners are not interested in maximizing their profits. Nobody owns the air or the oceans, so there is no one to charge and collect the appropriate rent. Or sometimes, governments may own roads or waterways, but through collective choice they may decide to underprice the resource (as occurs in the case of crowded highways). Everybody's land is nobody's land, and people are often free to dump or pollute at no private cost.

A second reason for abuse of common property resources is that it may be extremely costly to monitor use and collect rents. Can you imagine a meter on every tailpipe or car or fishing rod—calculating the item's contribution to pollution, crowding, or overfishing? Because the cost of such metering is extraordinarily high, governments often choose to allow common property resources to be used free of charge.

The Commons Enclosed But changes in the treatment of our common property resources have taken place. The English enclosure movement turned most land over to private hands in the eighteenth century. Air and water pollution regulation has limited the ability of firms to dump wastes. The Law of the Sea Convention allows nations to regulate ocean resources as far as 200 miles from their shores. While not perfect mechanisms for charging the appropriate scarcity rents, these devices help to reduce the worst abuses of the commons.

Conclusions

The same general principles determining land rent also determine the prices of all inputs: capital goods, natural resources, or labor. Thus the rentals of computers or of trucks are determined in essentially the same way.

One can even say that wages are the rentals paid for the use of a person's services for a day or a week or a year. This may seem a strange use of terms, but on second thought, one recognizes that every agreement to hire labor is really for some limited period of time. By outright purchase, you might avoid ever renting any kind of land. But in our society, labor is one of the few productive factors that cannot legally be bought outright. Labor can only be rented, and the wage rate is really a rental.

The next chapter deals with the peculiar issues involved in analyzing wages and labor markets. Chapter 29 then focuses on the special institution of labor unions and collective bargaining. Finally, in Chapter 30 we examine interest and profits—the return to capital.

SUMMARY

A. Marginal-Productivity Theory of Distribution

1. Distribution is concerned with the determination of different people's incomes—or with the basic question of *for whom* economic goods are to be produced. To understand what determines labor's and property's share in national product, and to understand forces acting on the degree of equality of income, distribution theory studies the problem of how the different factors of production—land, labor, capital, entrepreneurship, and risk taking—get priced in the market. Thus it must study how supply and demand interact to set all kinds of wages, rents, interest rates, and profits.

2. To understand the demand for factors of production, we must analyze the theory of production and the derived demand for factors. The demand for inputs is a derived demand: we demand ovens and wheatlands and wheat not for their own sake, but for the muffins and bread that they can produce for consumers. Hence we must understand the production and revenue relationships between inputs and outputs.

3. We met in earlier chapters the concepts of a production function and marginal products. The demand for a factor is drawn from the marginal revenue product *(MRP)*, which is defined as the extra revenue earned by the firm from employing an extra unit of a factor. For all firms, *MRP* equals the marginal revenue earned by the sale of an additional unit of the product times the marginal product of an input *(MRP = MR × MP)*. For competitive firms, because price equals marginal revenue, this simplifies to *MRP = P × MP*.

4. A firm maximizes profits (and minimizes costs) when it sets the *MRP* of each factor equal to that factor's marginal cost or factor price. This can be stated equivalently as a condition in which the *MRP* per dollar of input is equalized for each input. Why must this hold in the maximum-profit equilibrium? Because any employer with common sense will stop hiring any factor at the point where what its marginal product will return in dollars of marginal revenue begins to fall short of the factor price.

5. Unlike consumer goods, inputs are bought for what they produce, not for their ability to satisfy wants. Factor demand curves are derived from commodity demand curves. An upward shift in the latter causes a similar upward shift in the former, and inelasticity in commodity demand makes for inelasticity of derived factor demand.

6. To obtain the market demand for a factor, we add horizontally all firms' demand curves. This, along with the particular factor's own supply curve, determines the supply-and-demand intersection. At the equilibrium market price for the factor of production, the amount demanded and supplied will be exactly equal—only at equilibrium will the factor price have no tendency to change. Anywhere above the equilibrium price, suppliers will tend to undercut the market and will cause the price to fall; anywhere below the equilibrium price, shortages will cause demanders to bid the price upward, restoring the equilibrium.

7. J. B. Clark's marginal-productivity theory of income distribution analyzes the way total national output gets distributed among the different factors. Competition of numerous landowners and laborers drives factor prices to equal their marginal products. That process will allocate exactly 100 percent of the product. Any factor, not just labor alone, can be the varying factor. Because each unit of the factor gets paid only the *MP* of the *last* unit hired, there is enough of a residual surplus left (from the triangle of excess-of-early-over-last-*MP*s) to pay the other factors their exact marginal products. Hence, Clark's neoclassical theory of distribution, though simplified, is a logically complete picture of the distribution of income under perfect competition.

B. Factor Pricing: The Case of Land Rents

8. The unchangeable quantity of land is an interesting special case where the supply curve happens to be perfectly vertical and inelastic. In this case of pure economic rent, competition will still determine an equilibrium market price. But rent here is more price-determined than price-determining; the land rent is more the result of the market prices for the finished commodities than their cause. (Yet we must not forget that, to any small firm or industry, rent will still enter into the cost of production just like any other expense. To such a small firm or industry, rent reflects the opportunity cost of using land elsewhere and appears to be as much price-determining as any other cost element.)

9. A factor like land that is inelastically supplied will continue to work the same amount even though its factor reward is reduced. For this reason, Henry George pointed out that rent is in the nature of a ''surplus'' rather than a reward necessary to coax out the factor supply. This provides the basis for his single-tax program, proposing to tax the unearned increment of land value—without any shifting forward of the tax to the consumer or distorting effects on production.

Modern public finance finds some enduring truth in George's analysis: the theory of efficient (or Ramsey) taxes shows that the amount of economic inefficiency is minimized when taxes are levied on goods or factors that are most inelastically supplied or demanded.

10. Many of today's environmental problems occur because rents are not (perhaps cannot be) charged on scarce resources. The ''tragedy of the commons'' arose when too many herds grazed common land at a zero rent, thereby destroying the vegetation. Grazing, fishing, or dumping of wastes can produce externalities, or costs on society not paid for by the grazer, fisher, or dumper. In these cases, common property resources are scarce, but no rents are charged to limit their use. Why are rents not charged? Sometimes because no one owns the resource; sometimes because owners choose not to charge a fee for use; but most often because the cost of monitoring use and charging rents would be astronomically high.

11. The general principles of supply and demand can be used to explain the competitive price determination of all services. The rental of all inputs—including the wages that have to be paid for the use of the services of human beings and the rentals of durable machines—is determined in a competitive system by supply and demand.

CONCEPTS FOR REVIEW

distribution theory
marginal product, marginal revenue
 product
factor prices, rents
Clark's aggregate distribution theory
MP rectangle, residual rent triangle
equalizing marginal revenue product per
 dollar spent on each factor under
 perfect competition:
   marginal product of labor × output price = wage rate
   marginal product of land × output price = rent
   and so forth

or

$$\frac{\text{marginal product of labor}}{\text{price of labor}} = \frac{\text{marginal product of land}}{\text{price of land}} = \frac{1}{\text{output price}}$$

derived demand
efficient or Ramsey taxes
"tragedy of the commons"
scarcity rents for common property
 resources
inelastic supply of land

QUESTIONS FOR DISCUSSION

1. Define marginal product and marginal revenue product for a corn farmer. What are the units of each? Give a common-sense explanation of why maximization of profits requires that each factor price must be equal to the factor's marginal revenue product.
2. For each of the following factors, name the final output for which the item is a derived demand: wheatland, gasoline, barber, machine tool for skis, wine press.
3. In Clark's theory shown in Figure 27-4, let land rather than labor be the varying input. Draw a new figure and explain the marginal-productivity theory with this new diagram.
4. Explain the mistake in each of the following statements:
   (a) Marginal product is calculated as output per worker.
   (b) Distribution theory is no problem. You simply figure out how much each factor produced, and then give it that part of output.

(c) Under competition, workers get paid the amount of output produced less the costs of raw materials.

(d) Marginal revenue product is simply the price times the marginal product.

5. Suppose GNP grows faster than labor supply in every decade. If, contrary to Karl Marx's predictions, wage share stays about the same fraction of GNP, show that real wage rates must rise.

6. Define the "pure economic rent" case. Explain the sense in which rent of such a factor is "output-price-determined" rather than "output-price-determining." Show that, nonetheless, an increase in supply of the rent-earning factor will depress its return and lower prices of goods that use much of it.

7. What would you expect to be the result of a tax on the wage of championship tennis players or baseball stars?

8. Labor leaders used to say, "Without any labor there is no product. Hence labor deserves *all* the product." Apologists for capital would reply, "Take away all capital goods, and labor scratches a bare pittance from the earth; practically all the product belongs to capital."

Analyze the flaws in these arguments. If you were to accept them, show that they would allocate 200 or 300 percent of output to two or three factors, whereas only 100 percent can be allocated. How does Clark's marginal-productivity theory resolve this dispute?

9. It is sometimes argued that, because housing is fixed in supply, price controls on apartment rentals will do no damage to the housing market. Assume (contrary to fact) that housing is completely inelastic in supply. What would happen if a rent control board of New York or Berkeley decreed that rents should be 20 percent below the market price? (Recall the discussion of government interferences in Chapter 18.) Compare the effects on renters and landlords of rent control and taxes on the incomes from rental properties. (Supply-and-demand analysis will help answer both parts of this question.)

10. Our highways have limited traffic capacity, as is illustrated by the vertical line *CS*

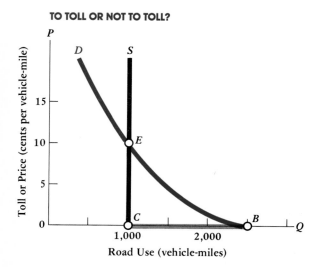

TO TOLL OR NOT TO TOLL?

Road Use (vehicle-miles)

Figure 27-7

in Figure 27-7. During peak periods, the demand curve *(DEB)* is far to the right. Explain what happens when society charges no tolls for road use, so the demand for highway use is at point *B* on the demand curve. Interpret segment *CB*.

Some have suggested using ''congestion tolls'' to keep demand within the available supply. What would the equilibrium congestion toll be? Explain how demand is restrained. Who would be made better off, who worse off by such a scheme?

11. Advanced problem: Using supply-and-demand analysis, along with the concept of consumer surplus, see if you can understand the notion of Ramsey (or efficient) taxes as follows. Construct the supply and demand curves for two markets, one with an inelastic demand, another with a very elastic demand. Both sell 1000 units at $100 each before the tax. For simplicity, use horizontal supply curves for each. Then impose a $2-per-unit tax on each product. Compare the revenues raised and the size of the deadweight losses (or consumer-surplus losses) in each case. Can you see that the consumer surplus lost per dollar of revenue raised is much smaller in the case of the product with inelastic demand? Does this suggest a rationale for Ramsey taxes?

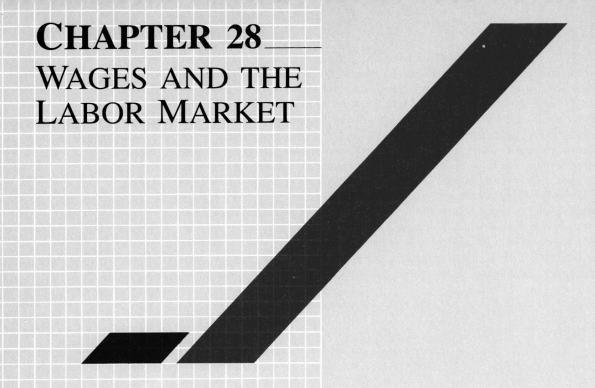

CHAPTER 28

WAGES AND THE LABOR MARKET

The laborer is worthy of his [or her] hire.

Luke 10:7

FOR THE VAST majority of households, labor earnings are the only significant source of income. Wages and salaries, along with the earnings of self-employed people, today constitute 80 percent of national income. As a result of its importance, the labor market is a constant source of controversy and political struggle. The pitched battles between labor and capital of the last century and today's struggles by women and minorities to gain pay equity are only two examples.

This and the next chapter explore how wages are set in a market economy. Section A of this chapter reviews the determination of wages under competitive conditions, while the second section discusses the thorny problem of discrimination in labor markets. The next chapter then turns to an analysis of imperfect competition in labor markets, with particular attention to the ways that unions limit the supply and raise the wages of labor.

A. WAGE DETERMINATION UNDER PERFECT COMPETITION

Wage rates differ enormously. The average wage is as hard to define as the average person. An auto executive may earn $3 million a year at the same time that a clerk earns $13,000 and a farmhand $10,000. In the same factory, a skilled machinist may earn $450 a week, while an unskilled janitor gets $240. Experienced women may be paid $300 a week at the same time their younger brothers are starting at $400. Any complete theory of wages must explain these differentials.[1]

But important as these wage differences are, we must not overlook the general wage level. Wages of virtually every category of labor are higher than they were a century ago. As Table 28-1 demonstrates, wages are higher in North America than in Latin America; higher in Japan than in South Korea; higher in Europe than in India. By using the analytical tools of economics—particularly the supply and demand for labor—we can go far in understanding these important facts.

THE GENERAL WAGE LEVEL

Why is the wage level in the United States $5\frac{1}{2}$ times that in South Korea and 25 times that in India? We can understand this phenomenon by examining the simplified case of wages paid in competitive markets to identical workers with identical jobs.

Begin by recalling what we mean by competition. A *perfectly competitive labor market* is one in which there is a sufficiently large number of workers and employers so that no one has the power to affect wage rates appreciably. This definition rules out labor unions or labor markets dominated by a large firm. In reality, few labor markets show complete perfection, but some labor markets—like a large city's market for inexperienced teenagers or clerical workers or

REGION AND YEAR	WAGE RATE IN MANUFACTURING (dollars per hr, 1988 wage levels)
United States	
1890	2.61
1988	11.22
Great Britain	
1890	2.66
1988	8.22
West Germany (1988)	10.96
Japan (1988)	13.54
South Korea (1988)	2.06
Mexico (1988)	1.40
India (1988)	0.45

Table 28-1   General wage levels vary enormously across space and time

The United States is a high-wage country while Indian hourly wages are a tiny fraction of American levels. General wage levels are determined by supply and demand, but behind supply and demand lie relative scarcity of labor, high levels of capital, and sophisticated technology in advanced industrial countries. (Source: International Labor Organization, Federal Reserve System.)

sales personnel—resemble the competitive concept tolerably well.

In a market of identical jobs and similar people, competition will cause the hourly wage rates to be exactly equal. No employer would pay more for the work of one person than for that person's identical twin; no class of such workers would be able to get more for their services than others get.

How is this single market wage determined? If we know the supply and demand curves for these workers—such as those shown in Figure 28-1(a)—then we can see that the competitive equilibrium wage rate must be at E_n. Put differently, E_n represents the intersection of the supply of and demand for homogeneous labor. If the wage were lower than E_n, then shortages of labor would occur and employers would bid up wages to E_n, restoring the equilibrium.

---

[1]In this chapter, we will generally use the term "wages" as a shorthand expression for "wages, salaries, and other forms of compensation." The theories here apply to the salaries of engineers and lawyers as well as to the wages of blue-collar workers like auto mechanics or carpenters.

COMPARATIVE WAGE RATES

(a) North America

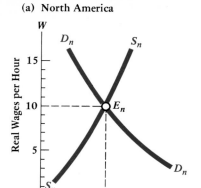

(b) South America

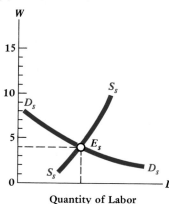

Figure 28-1 Favorable resources, skills, management, capital, and technology explain high North American wages

Supply and demand determine a higher competitive wage in North America than in South America. The major forces leading to high North American wages are a better-educated and more skilled work force, a larger stock of capital per worker, and more up-to-date technologies.

We are interested in real wages—in what the wage will buy—and not just in the money wage. Therefore, in our illustrations, we express wages in terms of the purchasing power of an hour's work. By definition, an index of the **real wage** represents an index of money wages divided by an index of the cost of living (such as measured by the consumer price index, which measures the cost of a fixed market basket of consumer goods). The illustrative case shown in Figure 28-1 measures real wages in terms of how large a quantity of goods the wages would buy.

Imagine that Figure 28-1(a) represents the state of affairs in North America while Figure 28-1(b) describes South America. Why are the general levels of wages so different? Is it because labor unions are so powerful in North America? Or because minimum wages are so low in South America? Surely not. Rather, real wages differ among regions or in a given region over time through the operation of the supply and demand for labor.

Of course, pointing to supply and demand provides no ultimate answer. Why is the demand for labor so high in the north? Why did Europe catch up with the United States in the 1980s, while Africa lagged behind? To answer these questions, we must look at the forces underlying the supply and demand for labor.

DEMAND FOR LABOR

We begin our analysis of the general wage level by examining the demand for labor, illustrated in Figure 28-1 by the high demand curve for North America and the low curve for South America. Why are the demands so different? The answer was provided in a general way in the last chapter, where we saw that the demand for a factor reflects the marginal productivity of that input.

Figure 28-2 reiterates the marginal-productivity theory. At a given time and with a given state of technology, there exists a relationship between the quantity of labor inputs and the amount of output. By the law of diminishing returns, each additional unit of labor input will add a smaller and smaller slab of output. In the example shown in Figure 28-2, at 10 units of labor, the competitively determined, general wage level will be $20 per unit.

We can probe deeper and ask what lies behind labor's marginal productivity. A complete analysis of productivity is provided in Chapters 36 and 37, but a preview at this point will illustrate the important issues. Labor's marginal product depends upon the quality of labor inputs, upon the quantity and quality of cooperating factors of production, and upon the level and utilization of technical and engineering knowledge.

The quality of labor inputs refers to the literacy, education, training, and skills of the labor force. An illiterate country can hardly hope to enjoy widespread use of sophisticated computers and machinery. Years of education are necessary to produce an engineer capable of designing precision equipment. A decade of training must precede the ability to perform successful brain surgery. Such accumulations of human

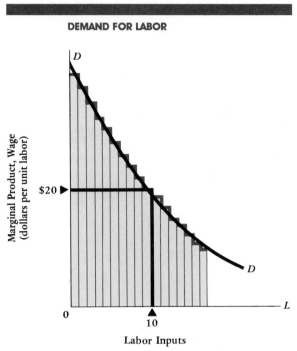

DEMAND FOR LABOR

Figure 28-2   Demand for labor reflects marginal productivity

The demand for labor as a general factor is determined by its marginal productivity in producing national output. The light red vertical slices represent the extra output produced by the first, second, . . . unit of labor. The competitively determined general wage level at 10 units of labor is $20 per unit, equal to the marginal productivity of the tenth unit. The labor demand curve shifts up and out over time with improvements in labor quality, capital accumulation, and technological advance.

capital provide a substantial boost to the productivity of labor.

The quantity and quality of cooperating factors will also affect labor's productivity. Wages are high in the United States in part because the nation is well endowed with fertile land and other resources. Advanced countries have accumulated substantial capital stocks—dense road and rail networks, substantial amounts of plant and equipment for each worker, and adequate inventories of spare parts. In poor countries, by comparison, roads are often unpaved and narrow, factories are generally crowded and hot, and equipment is old and about to fall apart.

But the quantity and quality of inputs does not tell the whole story. Two regions may have similar resources and labor inputs, but if one uses superior managerial and technological methods, its productivity may be much higher than the other's. Britain has ample resources and a highly educated labor force, but poor management and labor strife have so hobbled Britain in the industrial race that its productivity is less than one-half that of North America. Superior technological methods arise from better basic and applied science, advanced engineering designs, and better management.

Ultimately, the combination of higher-quality labor, capital accumulation, and technological advance produces an enormous surge in labor's productivity and in the demand for labor. More than anything else, these factors lie behind the high wages of advanced regions shown in Table 28-1.

SUPPLY OF LABOR

Determinants of Supply

Now turn to the supply side of the labor market. Labor supply refers to the number of hours worked in gainful activities in factories, farms, other businesses, government, or not-for-profit establishments.[2] The

---

[2]Chapters 5 and 13 analyze concepts and trends in the labor market. The important terms defined there include: the *labor force,* consisting of workers who are either working or unemployed, and the *labor-force participation rate,* which is the ratio of employed plus unemployed workers to the population (either of a nation or of a group, such as adult women).

major determinants of labor supply are the size of the population and the way the population spends its time.

Population Population is determined both by natural births and deaths and by immigration. Begin with the second. You might wonder, if wages are so high in North America, why foreigners don't move from their low-wage area to our high-wage area. People did migrate to this country in great numbers during the three centuries prior to World War I. A few came to seek religious freedom, many because they wanted to start new lives, but by far the greatest number came to better their economic condition.

After World War I, however, laws were passed severely limiting immigration. Only a trickle of legal immigrants has been admitted since then. Illegal entry is another thing, and in recent years it has grown in volume across the United States' southern borders.

Restricting the flow of labor is a first example of interference with the free play of competition in the wage market. By keeping labor supply down, restrictive immigration policy tends to keep wages high. Let us emphasize this basic principle: Limitation of the supply of any grade of labor relative to all other productive factors can be expected to raise its wage rate. An increase in labor supply will, other things being equal, tend to depress wage rates.

Given the downward-sloping demand for labor, it is understandable that labor unions are opposed to relaxed immigration and would like to close the borders to illegal immigration. Why might businesses be more favorable to immigration than workers are?

What about the natural increase in population? For the most part, population growth in advanced economies responds to a wide variety of religious, social, and economic factors. As a result of social trends such as the higher labor-force participation rate of women, along with the smaller families and later marriages that these trends produce, the natural growth of population in the United States and many advanced countries today is close to zero.

Labor-Force Participation and Hours Worked
What is the effect of economic conditions on the number of hours worked per year or the number of years worked per lifetime? There are many complex social

and political forces at work here, in addition to the economic ones.

One of the most dramatic developments in recent decades is the rise in women's labor-force participation. Why did the labor-force participation rate of women (i.e., the fraction of women over 15 in the labor force) jump from 40 percent in the mid-1960s to 55 percent in the late 1980s? This explosion cannot be explained by economic analysis alone. To fully understand such a significant change in working patterns, one must look outside the narrow scope of economics—to changing social attitudes toward the role of women as mothers, homemakers, and workers.

"Substitution Effect" vs. "Income Effect" In analyzing labor supply, one of the most important issues is how labor responds to higher wages. What will be the effect of higher wages on the number of hours worked per lifetime? Figure 28-3 illustrates the is-

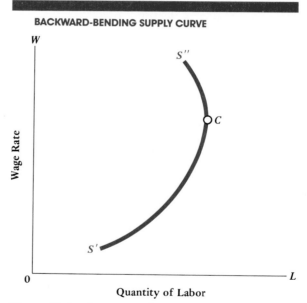

BACKWARD-BENDING SUPPLY CURVE

Figure 28-3 As wages rise, workers may work fewer hours

Above the critical point C, raising the wage rate reduces the amount of labor supplied as the income effect outweighs the substitution effect. Why? Because at higher wages we can afford more leisure even though each extra hour of leisure costs more in wages forgone.

sues; it shows a hypothetical supply curve of total hours that a group of people will want to work at each wage rate. Note how the supply curve rises at first in a northeasterly direction; then at the critical point *C*, it begins to bend back in a northwesterly direction. How can we explain why higher wages may first increase and then decrease the quantity of labor supplied?

Put yourself in the shoes of a worker who has just been offered higher hourly rates and is free to choose the number of hours worked. You are tugged in two different directions. On the one hand, you are tempted to work some extra hours because now each hour of work is better paid. Each hour of leisure has become more expensive, and you are therefore tempted to substitute extra work for leisure.

But acting against this "substitution effect" is an opposing "income effect."[3] With the wage higher, your income is higher. With a higher income, you will want to buy more clothes, better food, more of other consumer goods. But you'll also want more leisure time. Now you can afford to take a week's vacation in the winter or an extra week in the summer, or take your retirement a couple of years earlier.

Which will be more powerful, the substitution effect or the income effect? There is no single correct answer. It depends upon the individual and the situation faced. In the case shown in Figure 28-3, for all wage rates up to point *C*, labor supplied increases with a higher wage: the substitution effect outweighs the income effect. But from point *C* upward, the income effect outweighs the substitution effect, and labor supplied declines as wage rates climb higher.[4]

Empirical Findings

It is all well and good to find that labor supply can bend forward or backward. But for many purposes we

need to know exactly which way it does bend. Will tax cuts on wages increase or decrease labor supply? Will more generous welfare payments encourage or discourage work? These questions have hounded public-policy economists attempting to advise legislatures and Presidents.

Table 28-2 presents a summary of numerous studies of the subject. This survey shows that the labor supply curve for adult males appears to be slightly backward-bending, while the response of other demographic groups looks more like a conventional upward-sloping supply curve. For the population as a whole, labor supply appears to respond very little to a change in real wages.

WAGE DIFFERENCES ACROSS GROUPS

Having studied the problem of the general wage level, we turn now to the vital problem of wage differentials among different categories of people and jobs. Why is it that doctors earn 15 or 20 times more than lifeguards when both are saving lives? Why do workers in Alaska earn 25 percent more than those working in the same jobs in the lower 48 states?

We can start by examining patterns of wages and compensation in different industries. As is shown in Table 28-3, there is a wide range of wage rates among broad industry groups. Smaller, nonunionized sectors like farming or services tend to have low wages, while the larger firms in manufacturing and communications have wage levels 2 or 3 times higher.

How can we explain the wage differences across industries or individuals? To do so, we must examine the influence of four factors: compensating differentials, differences in labor quality, unique elements, and labor market segmentation.

Compensating Wage Differentials

Some of the tremendous wage differentials observed in everyday life arise because of differences in the quality of jobs. Jobs differ in their attractiveness; hence wages may have to be raised to coax people into the less attractive jobs.

Wage differentials that serve simply to compensate

---

[3]See Chapter 19 for a discussion of substitution and income effects in connection with consumption.

[4]Supply-side economists (see Chapter 10) contend that high tax rates reduce output because they discourage the supply of labor and capital. This might occur because higher tax rates produce lower after-tax returns. Paradoxically, however, we can see in Figure 28-3 that a tax cut might *decrease* labor supplied if the after-tax wage lay above point *C*. In that region a reduction in the tax on wages would increase the after-tax wage and decrease the amount of labor supplied.

LABOR-SUPPLY PATTERNS

GROUP OF WORKERS	LABOR-FORCE PARTICIPATION RATE (percent of population)		RESPONSE OF LABOR SUPPLY TO INCREASE IN REAL WAGES
	1960	1988	
Adult males	86	78	Supply curve found to be backward-bending in most studies. Thus income effect dominates the substitution effect. Supply elasticity is relatively small, in the order of minus 0.1 to minus 0.2. Thus a 10 percent increase in real wage would lead to a 1 to 2 percent reduction in labor supplied.
Adult females	38	57	Considerable uncertainty about response. Most studies find positive effect of labor supplied in response to higher real wage.
Teenagers	46	55	Wide variety of findings. Weight of evidence is that labor supply responds positively to higher wages.
Entire population 16 years & over	59	66	Total labor supply close to vertical, with income effects just balancing out substitution effects. Estimated labor supply elasticity for entire population is in the range from 0 to 0.2.

Table 28-2 Empirical estimates of labor-supply responses

There have been numerous studies of the response of labor supply to real wages. For males, the supply curve looks firmly backward-bending, while for teenagers and adult females, the supply curve appears positively sloped. For the economy as a whole, the labor supply curve is close to vertical. [Sources: George Borjas and James Heckman, "Labor Supply Estimates for Public Policy Evaluation," *Proceedings of the Industrial Relations Research Association,* 1978, pp. 320–331; Ronald G. Ehrenberg and Robert S. Smith, *Modern Labor Economics,* 3rd ed. (Scott, Foresman and Company, Glenview, Ill., 1988), Chap. 6; Don Fullerton, "Can Tax Revenues Go Up When Tax Rates Go Down?" in Bruce Bartlett and Timothy P. Roth (eds.), *The Supply Side Solution* (Chatham House, Chatham, N.J., 1983), pp. 140–157.]

for the nonmonetary differences among jobs are called **compensating differentials.**

Window washers must be paid more than janitors because people do not like the risks of climbing skyscrapers. Workers often receive 5 percent extra pay on the 4 P.M. to 12 P.M. "swing shift" and 10 percent extra pay for the 12 midnight to 8 A.M. "graveyard shift." For hours beyond 40 per week or for holiday and weekend work, $1\frac{1}{2}$ to 2 times the base hourly pay is customary. And when you read that doctors earn $150,000 a year, note that a part of this is a compensating differential needed to induce people to incur tuition costs and endure the lack of pay during schooling and training.

Jobs that involve dirt, tedium, low social prestige, irregular employment, seasonal layoff, short working life, and much dull training all tend to be less attractive. No wonder, then, that companies must pay $50,000 or $80,000 a year to recruit people to work on dangerous and lonely jobs on offshore oil platforms. Similarly, for jobs that are especially pleasant and psychologically rewarding, like park rangers and life guards, pay levels tend to be modest.

To test whether a given difference in pay between two jobs is a compensating differential, ask people who are well qualified for both: "Would you take the higher-paying job in preference to the lower?" If they are not eager to make such a choice, then it is fair to conclude that the higher-paid job is not really more attractive when due weight is given to all considerations, nonmonetary and monetary.

Differences in Labor Quality

We have just seen that some wage differentials arise to compensate for the differing degrees of attractiveness of different jobs. But look around you. Clearly most high-paying jobs are more pleasant, not less pleasant, than low-paying work. We must look to fac-

tors beyond compensating differentials to explain existing wage differentials.

A key to wage disparities lies in the tremendous qualitative differences among people—traceable to differences in innate mental and physical abilities, in education and training, and in experience. A zoologist might label us all as members of the species *Homo sapiens,* but a personnel officer would insist that people differ enormously in their abilities to contribute to a firm's profits.

Many of the differences in labor quality are determined outside the labor force, by genetic nature or family nurture. Much also is affected by investment in "human capital," a term that designates the stock of useful and valuable knowledge built up in the process of education and training. Doctors, lawyers, and engineers invest many years in their formal education and on-the-job training. They spend vast sums on tuition and wages forgone, invest $100,000 to $200,000 in college and graduate training, and often work late at night and on weekends. Part of the high salaries of these professions should be viewed as a return on their investment in human capital—a return on the

COMPENSATION BY INDUSTRY, 1986

INDUSTRY	AVERAGE COMPENSATION PER FULL-TIME EMPLOYEE	AVERAGE HOURLY EARNINGS
Farming	$13,300	—
Mining	40,400	12.45
Manufacturing	31,200	9.73
Steel mills	—	14.53
Communication	42,000	12.11
Retail trade	16,200	6.02
Services	22,300	8.16
Laundries	—	5.99
Government	29,200	—

Table 28-3   Wages and compensation in different sectors, 1986

Compensation during a particular year varies widely across industries. Average compensation per full-time employee (which includes wages, health benefits, pensions, etc.) varied by broad industry groups from a high of $42,000 in communication to a low of $13,300 in farming. Among narrow industry groups, we see that average hourly earnings vary by a factor of 2.5 between the steel industry and laundries. (Source: U.S. Department of Labor, Bureau of Labor Statistics, *Employment and Earnings;* U.S. Department of Commerce.)

education that makes these highly trained workers a very special kind of labor.

Rent Elements in Wages of Unique Individuals

For the lucky few, fame has lifted incomes to levels far above those of the average worker. Reported annual earnings for these stars include such astronomical figures as $57 million for entertainer Bill Cosby, $1.5 million for baseball's Dave Winfield, and $1.4 million for football's John Elway and for tennis's Martina Navratilova. Former Secretary of State Henry Kissinger is reported to bill at least $25,000 per appearance. And the lecture fee of Murray Weidenbaum, President Reagan's former chief economist, now at Washington University (St. Louis), soared into the five-digit range.

These extremely talented people have a particular skill that is highly prized and priced in today's economy. Outside their specialization, they might earn only one-tenth as much; moreover, their labor supply may be completely unaffected by their wage rate, indicating that their labor supply curve is completely inelastic or vertical for wages 20 or 80 or 120 percent of their high compensation levels. Economists term the excess of such wages above their best available incomes in other occupations a *pure economic rent,* for they are logically the same as the rent to fixed land discussed in the last chapter. Because the labor supply of these top consultants or baseball players or musicians is completely inelastic, their efforts will respond little to tax rates of 50 or 60 or 70 percent. Even when the net reward for their services is reduced by taxes or by market forces, they will continue to consult or play or sing.

Noncompeting Groups in the Labor Market

We see then that, even in a world of perfect competition where people could move easily from one occupation to another, substantial wage differentials would appear. These differentials would be necessary to reflect differences in the costs of education and training or in the unattractiveness of certain occupations or as rewards for unique talents.

But after accounting for all these reasons for wage differentials, we still find a large disparity in wage rates. The major reason for the difference is that labor markets are segmented and we therefore find *noncompeting groups* in the labor market. This fact was first pointed out by J. E. Cairnes a century ago when he wrote:

> What we find, in effect, is not a whole population competing indiscriminately for all occupations, but a series of industrial layers, superimposed on one another, . . . while those occupying the several strata are, for all purposes of effective competition, practically isolated from each other.[5]

In other words, instead of being a single factor of production, labor is many different, but closely related, factors of production. Doctors and mathematicians, for example, are noncompeting groups because it is difficult and costly for a member of one profession to enter into the other market. Just as there are many different kinds of computers, each commanding a different price, so are there many different occupations and skills that compete only in a general way.

Once we recognize that there are many different kinds of labor operating in different submarkets of the labor market, we can see why wages may differ greatly among groups.

Why is the labor market divided into so many noncompeting groups? The major reason arises from the fact that, for professions and skilled trades, it takes a large investment of time and money to become proficient. Economists can hardly hope to become cardiovascular surgeons overnight. Nor are surgeons trained to frame a house or lay a neat row of bricks. Hence, once people specialize in a particular occupation, they become part of a particular labor submarket. They are thereby subject to the supply and demand for that skill and will find that their own labor earnings rise and fall depending upon events in their own occupation and industry. Moreover, once the different submarkets are segmented, the wages for one occupation can diverge substantially from wages in other areas.

The theory of noncompeting groups takes on great importance in understanding labor market discrimina-

[5]J. E. Cairnes, *Some Leading Principles of Political Economy* (London, Macmillan, 1874), p. 72.

tion. We will see in the second section of this chapter that much discrimination arises because, by custom, law, or prejudice, workers are separated by gender, race, or ethnic background into noncompeting groups. We find otherwise-equal people put into separate noncompeting labor pools, with the favored group receiving higher wages than the other group.

While the theory of noncompeting groups highlights an important aspect of labor markets, we must nonetheless recognize that some competition always exists. Just as you decide whether to hire a horse or rent a tractor to plough your field, so you must choose between hiring a high-paid professional and a low-paid, less skilled worker. Similarly, if welders' wages become $200,000 per year, I might study the craft and quit being a teacher. We see, then, that different categories of labor are neither 100 percent identical nor completely different. They are partial substitutes rather than perfect substitutes, so the true situation is generally one of partially competing groups.

General Equilibrium in the Labor Market

We have seen that several forces tend to create wage differentials—those needed to compensate for differ-ent levels of unpleasantness, returns on human capital, differences in skill and talents, and segmentation of the market into noncompeting groups.

Studies of wage behavior indicate that wage differentials are surprisingly persistent. Whether we examine the relative wages of men and women, blue-collar versus white-collar workers' wages, or differentials in particular industries like construction or autos—we see that the relative wages change very slowly from year to year.

But wage differentials are not cast in concrete. As people move into high-paying occupations and leave those that pay less, as the barriers to equal access for all groups slowly erode—as these slow-moving forces come into play, we see some tendency for wages to converge.

But for such differentials as remain, how exactly are they determined? The answer is provided by supply and demand: The market will tend toward that equilibrium pattern of wage differentials at which the total demand for each category of labor exactly matches its competitive supply. Only then will there be general equilibrium with no tendency for further widening or narrowing of wage differentials. Table 28-4 sums up our conclusions about competitive wage determination.

SUMMARY OF COMPETITIVE WAGE DETERMINATION

LABOR SITUATION	WAGE RESULT
1. People all alike—jobs all alike.	No wage differentials.
2. People all alike—some jobs differ in unpleasantness.	Compensating wage differentials.
3. People differ, but each type of labor is in unchangeable supply ("noncompeting groups").	Wage differentials that are "pure economic rents" or "surpluses."
4. People differ, but there is some mobility among groups ("partially competing groups").	General-equilibrium pattern of wage differentials as determined by general demand and supply (includes 1–3 as special cases).

Table 28-4 **Market wage structure shows great variety of patterns under competition**

TWO CLASSICAL VIEWS[6]

Modern labor economics pays a great deal of attention to wage differentials and the presence of race or gender discrimination. The classical economists, on the other hand, were fascinated by the general trend of wages and by the impacts of social legislation upon wages. Two important theories shaped views about social and economic policy during the nineteenth century and continue to have relevance today, so we review them here.

The Iron Law of Wages: Malthus and Marx

In Chapter 37, we will study in detail the Malthusian theory of population. According to this doctrine, the size of population will grow very rapidly whenever wages rise above the subsistence level (*subsistence wages* being the minimal level needed to support a person's life). In this approach, then, the labor supply curve should be horizontal at the subsistence wage level: such was the dismal science's *iron law of wages*.

A brief look at economic history shows how unrealistic for the West is this notion that people inevitably reproduce so rapidly that their incomes are relentlessly forced back to a bare minimum, and how misleading it would be as a basis for any predictions about the long-term "laws of motion of the capitalistic system."

The Reserve Army of the Unemployed A quite different version of the iron law of wages was provided by Karl Marx. He put great emphasis upon the "reserve army of the unemployed." In effect, employers led their workers to the factory windows and pointed to the unemployed workers outside, eager to work for less. This, Marx thought (or is interpreted by some Marxists to have thought), would depress wages to the subsistence level.

Let us show this on our diagrams. Figure 28-1(a) is redrawn as Figure 28-4. Suppose that the wage is

[6]This historical excursion may be skipped in short courses.

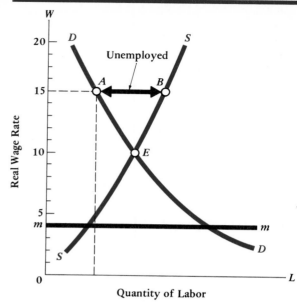

Figure 28-4   Marxists exaggerate power of "reserve army of unemployed" to depress wages

The "reserve army of the unemployed"—as shown by *AB*—is not able to depress real wages to the minimum-subsistence level at *mm*. It can only depress competitive wages to equilibrium level *E*. If labor supply became so abundant that *SS* intersected *DD* at *mm*, the wage would be at a minimum level, as in many underdeveloped regions.

pegged at $15 per hour. Employment is at the level indicated by the point *A*. At this high wage, there would indeed be unemployment; the amount of unemployment would be represented by the distance *AB* between the labor supplied and demanded. In our simple, idealized model of competition, such unemployment could certainly be expected to put downward pressure on wages.

But does the basic Marxian conclusion follow? Is there any tendency for real wage rates to fall to a minimum-subsistence level such as *mm* in Figure 28-4? None at all. There is no reason why wage rates should ever fall below the equilibrium level at *E*. In a country well endowed with technology, capital, and natural resources, this competitively determined equilibrium wage might be a very comfortable one indeed. Thus we reach an important principle: If competition in the labor market were really perfect, there would be no necessary tendency in an advanced country for wages to fall toward the minimum-subsistence level.

Employers might prefer to pay low wages, but that would not matter. In a competitive market, they are unable to set wage rates as they would like. As long as employers are numerous and do not act in collusion, their demands for any grade of labor will bid its wage up to the equilibrium level at which the total forthcoming labor supply is absorbed. The workers may aspire to still higher wages, but under competition they do not get what they would like; as long as they do not act collusively to limit the labor supply, their wishes will not serve to make wages rise above the competitive level.

The Lump-of-Labor Fallacy

In periods of high unemployment, people often think that a solution lies in spreading the existing amount of work more evenly. In Europe today, for example, many labor unions are proposing that the workweek be reduced so that more people will be able to have jobs at the reduced hours. This view—that the total amount of work to be done in the short run is fixed—is sometimes called the ''lump-of-labor fallacy.''

To begin with, we must give this notion its due. To a particular group of workers, with special skills and stuck in one region, a reduction in the demand for labor may indeed pose a threat to their jobs. As long as wages and prices adjust slowly, these workers may face prolonged spells of unemployment. Viewed from their personal standpoint, the lump-of-labor notion may not be so fallacious. Moreover, in a great depression, when there is mass and chronic unemployment, one can understand how workers generally may yield to a lump-of-labor philosophy.

But the lump-of-labor argument implies that there is only so much useful remunerative work to be done in any economic system, and this is indeed a fallacy. It is more correct to say that an economy can adjust to create jobs for willing workers. In the longer run, as prices and wages adjust to changes in technology and tastes, to supplies and demands, jobs will come to workers or workers will move to jobs. And in the short run, this process can be lubricated by appropriate macroeconomic policies (discussed in Parts Two and Three). A look at history or across countries shows that there is no fixed lump of labor to be distributed—there is no need to ration out scarce work among the army of unemployed workers.

■   ■   ■

We have now completed our analysis of the basic forces driving wages—both their overall levels and wage differentials among different groups. In the next section we apply these concepts to one of the most important issues of labor market policy—discrimination.

B. Discrimination by Race and Gender

Most of the world is nonwhite. But the white minority controls most of the economic power and enjoys a disproportionately high standard of living. Within the most advanced economic society, the United States, the one in eight citizens who is black has long experienced a measurably lower level of income and wealth. Many other minority groups also earn markedly less than do white Americans.

Half the population is female. How is it that a woman who has the same amount of schooling as a man, who also has two eyes and hands, the same tested IQ and aptitude scores, the same parental background, nonetheless ends up getting paid for full-time work only two-thirds what her brother of similar abilities gets?

Some earnings differentials arise from differences

in education, work experience, and other factors. But even after correction for such differences, a large gap remains between the wages of white males and those of other groups—at least part of which is due to discrimination. In this section, we see how discrimination affects labor markets and incomes.

Earnings differentials between groups will always be present in a market economy. But when a difference in earnings arises simply because of an irrelevant personal characteristic—such as race, gender, or religion—we call this **discrimination.**

Historical Roots

In the United States, discrimination has its roots in the early beliefs and institutions of society. British settlers became the dominant elite in New England 300 years ago. When other nationalities arrived, they were resented and were often kept out of the best jobs. A frequently observed sign in lodging houses and job advertisements was, "No dogs or Germans need apply." Yet with time the descendents of Germans and many other nationalities mixed in a grand melting pot, became assimilated and accepted, and prospered, working their way up from Ellis Island to corporate boardrooms and the halls of Congress.

This cheerful view of American history cannot, however, apply to all ethnic groups. American Indians resided in America long before the British; Spanish conquistadores were the first European settlers; more than 100 years have elapsed since the Emancipation Proclamation freed the slaves. Yet for these ethnic groups, discrimination in the labor market, housing, and other community activities remains a barrier to economic and social advancement.

The history of black Americans will illustrate the way their incomes and economic status were kept low. There is no economic puzzle about how nineteenth-century slavery in America, or twentieth-century apartheid in South Africa, persisted and thrived. The ruling groups made "colored people" a second class of citizen, endowed with few inalienable rights, and subject to harsh laws and discipline if any of its members attempted to gain the freedoms enjoyed by others.

After slavery was abolished here, the black population in the south quickly fell into a caste system of peonage under "Jim Crow" legislation. Even though legally free and subject to the laws of supply and demand, black workers found their wages far below those of whites. Why? Because, as we will see shortly, they were shunted off into menial, low-skilled occupations—into low-wage noncompeting groups. Most of the well-paid jobs were simply not open to blacks—partly by custom and partly because they did not have the necessary education to qualify.

Graphical Analysis of Discrimination

We can use our supply-and-demand apparatus to illustrate how exclusion lowers the incomes of groups that are targets of discrimination—whether the groups be blacks in the apartheid system of modern South Africa, or women and minorities in many professions and managerial positions in America today.[7] In such systems, certain jobs are reserved for the privileged group, as is depicted in Figure 28-5(a). In this labor market, the supply of privileged white workers is shown by $S_w S_w$, while the demand for such labor is depicted as $D_w D_w$. Equilibrium wages occur at the high level shown at E_w.

Meanwhile, Figure 28-5(b) shows what is happening in the low-paid service sector or in unskilled jobs. Because black workers live in areas with poor schools or because they cannot afford the best private education, they do not receive training for the high-paying jobs. Rather, with low levels of skills, they have low marginal revenue products in the low-skilled jobs, so their wages are depressed to the low-wage equilibrium at E_b.

Note the differential between the two equilibria. Exclusion has discriminated against the earning power of black workers. Once black workers were forced into unskilled jobs, market forces decreed that blacks would earn much lower wages than the privileged white workers. An ignorant observer might even argue that blacks "deserve" lower wages be-

---

[7]One of the pathbreaking analyses of discrimination is found in Gary Becker, *Economics of Discrimination* (The University of Chicago Press, Chicago, 1957), which showed the economic costs that result if people insist on indulging their prejudices against hiring or working with certain groups.

EFFECTS OF DISCRIMINATORY EXCLUSION

(a) Market for Whites

(b) Market for Blacks

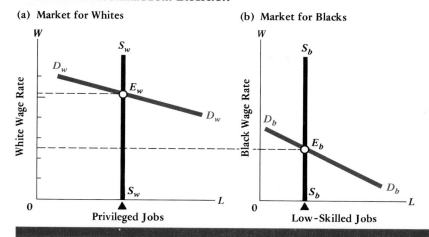

Figure 28-5   Discrimination by exclusion lowers the wage rates of blacks

Discrimination is often enforced by excluding certain groups from privileged jobs. If blacks are excluded from good jobs in market **(a)**, they must work in inferior jobs in **(b)**. Whites then end up with high wage rates at E_w while blacks earn low wage rates at E_b in market **(b)**.

cause their competitive marginal revenue products are lower. But this observer would overlook the genuine source of the wage differentials: they arose because certain groups were excluded from the good jobs by force of custom, law, or collusion.

ECONOMIC DISCRIMINATION AGAINST WOMEN

The largest group to suffer from economic discrimination is women. Even year-round, full-time female workers on average earn only 65 percent of the earnings of men of comparable education and background.

The pattern of earnings is clear. Female college graduates earn about the same amount as male high school graduates. Although white males, for the most part, receive increases in annual earnings as they grow older, income profiles show that women in their late twenties earn as much on the average as do older women.[8]

[8]A recent presentation and analysis of the position of women in the labor market is contained in *Economic Report of the President 1987*, Chap. 7.

Changing Occupational and Industrial Patterns by Gender

Before turning to economic analysis, let us review some history of the role of women in economic activity. Among human societies, men and women have devised many alternative patterns of specialization with respect to hunting, foraging, herding, planting, and sowing. Only in the art of warfare have men shown any unique talent.

As economies developed, work became more specialized. Men and women tended to cluster in separate roles and jobs, although, aside from biologically differentiated roles like childbearing, there was no single pattern of gender specialization in all cultures. Sometimes women hunted, often they carried water, and on rare occasions they held the scepters of power. Modern Anglo-American cultures were influenced by a curious twist of history when nineteenth-century Victorian Britain developed a caricature of a "lady" who was incapable of performing any economic functions outside the home. This was ironically noted by Thorsten Veblen in his *Theory of the Leisure Class* when he wrote that status in an affluent society was proved by the uselessness, except for display, of chattels and women. Such a social pattern found little

LABOR MARKET SEGMENTATION

OCCUPATION	PERCENT FEMALES, 1981
High-paid occupations:	
Sales agents, wholesale	10.7
Stock and bond salespersons	17.2
Engineering technicians	17.8
Managers and administrators	28.4
Low-paid occupations:	
Nurses' aides	84.4
Hairdressers and beauticians	84.9
Childcare workers outside home	86.7
Sewers and stitchers	96.7
Practical nurses	97.7

Table 28-5 Many high-paid occupations are reserved for men

Discrimination today seldom occurs because women get lower wages for the same job. Rather, women have been limited to lower-paying occupations. Overall, such factors drive the average earnings of women down to only 65 percent of those of men. (Source: U.S. Department of Labor, Bureau of Labor Statistics, "Analyzing 1981 Earnings Data from the Current Population Survey," September 1982.)

EARNINGS DIFFERENTIALS, 1970

GROUP	EARNINGS OF GROUP (as a percentage of earnings of white males)	
	MALES	FEMALES
White	100	49
Japanese-American	99	52
Chinese-American	85	46
American Indian	68	42
Mexican-American	67	36
Black	64	40
Puerto Rican	63	45

Table 28-6 Minorities and women earn substantially less than white males

Data were examined on the total annual earnings of men and women of different minority groups in the United States. These data do not correct for education, labor-force status, or previous work experience.

The most disadvantaged minority-group males earn only 63 to 68 percent of white male earnings. Females earn even less, partly because of low wages, partly because of fewer hours worked.

[Source: J. D. Gwartney and J. E. Long, "The Relative Earnings of Blacks and Other Minorities," *Industrial and Labor Relations Review* (April 1978).]

room for women in top positions in education, business, or government.

By the middle of the twentieth century the Victorian ethic began to decay. Because of smaller families and better health care, women could look forward to many years in which they could participate fully in the labor force. Moreover, improvements in technology now allow household tasks—ones that a century ago required one full-time person—to be performed much more expeditiously. Female labor-force participation rates have soared (see Table 28-2). More and more, women in advanced economies are employed virtually all their adult lives, with some taking a brief time off to raise young children. But as women enter the labor force today, they find traces of earlier discriminatory practices and sex-based job stereotypes.

Gender Discrimination

As we have emphasized above, women typically earn less than men not primarily because they are paid less for the same job. Rather, the main bar to equality of incomes is that the best jobs have historically been reserved for men. Until recently, few women were ever elected to the boards of directors of large corporations, to senior partnerships in major law firms, or to tenured professorships in top universities.

Like minority groups, then, women are often found in low-paying noncompeting groups (see Figure 28-5 above). The extent of labor market segmentation is shown in Table 28-5. In this, we see the fraction of women in selected high-paying and low-paying occupations. The labor market segmentation apparent in

Table 28-5 shows that discrimination is much more subtle than the picture of employers simply beating down the wage demands of women or blacks or Hispanics.

Empirical Evidence

Now that we have seen the mechanisms by which the political process and the market economy enforce discrimination against women and minority groups, let's examine the size of earnings differentials. Table 28-6 shows the ratio of total annual earnings of males and females of different minority groups relative to white males. On average, earnings differentials are greatest for women and for black and Indian men as well as for men of Hispanic background. Note that women are generally penalized in the labor market only once— for many minority women show earnings close to those of white women.

Discrimination vs. Personal Characteristics It is

important to understand that all differentials among different groups are not necessarily based on discrimination. The first part of this chapter noted that there are differences in quality of labor. Black workers have historically received less education than have whites; women customarily spend more time out of the labor force than do men. Since both education and continuing work experience are linked to higher pay, it is not surprising that *some* earnings differentials exist.

Economists in recent years have conducted numerous empirical studies attempting to separate out the earnings differentials due to measurable characteristics (education, experience, etc.) from discrimination and other factors. For women, studies by Jacob Mincer, Haim Ofek, Solomon Polacheck, and others indicate that from one-half to three-quarters of the male-female wage gap can be explained by differences in education and job experience—leaving from one-quarter to one-half to be explained by discrimination and other non-measured sources.*

*The technique of accounting for personal characteristics is one of the most powerful tools of modern economics. To illustrate how this works, take the first column of numbers in Table 28-6. Gwartney and Long deploy statistical techniques to estimate what part of observed differentials is due to observed and clearly relevant characteristics (like education, age, native language, and so forth), and what fraction is due to discrimination and unobserved characteristics.

We can calculate "uncorrected" differentials as shown in Table 28-6. Or we can calculate "corrected" differentials, which account for the average worker characteristics in different groups. More precisely, the "corrected" ratio here calculates what a minority worker would earn if he had the average education, age, language background, etc., of the average white male worker. For example, this table indicates that black men as a whole earned 64 percent as much as white men. However, when the worker characteristics of black men were taken into account (i.e., their education, age, marital status, residence, and so forth), then black men were estimated to earn 79 percent as much as white men. Expressed in different words, a black male with the average worker characteristics of black males earned but 64 percent of the wages of a white worker with the average worker characteristics of white males. On the other hand, a black male who happened to have the worker characteristics of the average white male would generally earn 79 percent of the wages of the average white male. What accounts for the remaining 21 percent? Discrimination and other unmeasured factors.

RATIO OF MINORITY-GROUP MALE WAGES TO WAGES OF WHITE MALES

GROUP	UNCORRECTED	CORRECTED
White	100	100
Japanese-American	99	89
Chinese-American	85	83
American Indian	68	81
Mexican-American	67	91
Black	64	79
Puerto Rican	63	87

Source: See Table 28-6.

REDUCING LABOR MARKET DISCRIMINATION

Governments have over the last 25 years taken numerous steps to end discriminatory practices. Even today, however—although few defend discrimination—the United States has been unable to eradicate discrimination on the basis of race, sex, and many other characteristics.

What approaches are available to combat discrimination? The major steps were legal landmarks, such as the Civil Rights Act of 1964 (which outlaws discrimination in hiring, firing, and employment) and the Equal Pay Act of 1963 (which requires employers to pay men and women equally for the same work).

Such laws helped to dismantle the most blatant discriminatory practices, but more subtle barriers (and sometimes even unconscious attitudes) remain to exclude minorities and women from the best jobs. Policies to promote "affirmative action" were promulgated: these required employers to show that they were taking extra steps to locate and hire underrepresented groups. This approach, labelled by some as "reverse discrimination," has always been highly controversial, but it has apparently increased the representation of women and minority groups in some sectors.

Comparable Worth

In the mid-1980s, a new approach to reducing the male-female wage gap was put forward: comparable worth. This idea goes beyond the idea of "equal pay for equal work" to "equal pay for comparable worth." To understand the issue, we begin by analyzing wage structures and then see how comparable worth would attempt to equalize wages for different jobs.

Wage Structures Most large firms administer their internal labor market by setting up a number of different job categories or grades—say, 10 grades of clerical workers, 15 grades of craft workers, 12 grades of technicians, and so forth. Each category carries a job description that varies in terms of characteristics like skill, experience, training, working conditions, etc.

Generally, firms try to set the wage levels with reference to the compensation for similar jobs in the relevant external labor market. Hence beginning secretaries will be paid more or less what other beginning secretaries earn in the same city, while the salaries of newly minted college professors in economics are determined relative to the national market for new economists.

Where no external comparison can be easily made, firms tend to set wages for particular jobs at the level earned by similar jobs. As we will shortly see, firms sometimes assign numerical "point scores" to the skill, experience, and working conditions of jobs and then use these scores to help set wages of noncomparable jobs. Putting the external comparisons and internal evaluations together provides a firm with a wage structure for its different job categories.

Using the notion of a wage structure, we can now understand the difference between jobs of "equal worth" and those of "comparable worth." Table 28-7 shows three jobs—A, B, and C—in a particular company. Jobs A and B are assigned equal ratings on the four job characteristics (skill, training, responsibility, and working conditions). They are hence designated as "equal jobs," and under the 1963 Equal Pay Act they must receive the same pay. To pay $250 per week for job A while job B pays $300 per week would represent unlawful discrimination even if the weekly market wages for A and B differed by $50.

Many advocates of breaking down discriminatory practices argue that comparable jobs should also receive equal pay. The last two columns of Table 28-7 show two jobs with an equal number of total points but with differing individual characteristics. Job A might be a technician with major responsibilities over blood samples working in pleasant surroundings, while job C could be a forklift operator with little skill or training but working in harsh and noisy conditions. The market wage rate in the local area, driven by ample supply of technicians and sparse supply of forklift drivers, might produce weekly wage rates of $250 for technicians and $400 for forklift operators. And under current law and practice, it would be perfectly legal for a firm to pay those differing market-based wages for comparable but dissimilar jobs.

Enter comparable-worth doctrine. This holds that pay should be based on what a job is worth. Jobs that

EQUAL AND COMPARABLE JOBS

	POINT SCORES ASSIGNED TO DIFFERENT JOBS			
	EQUAL JOBS		COMPARABLE JOBS	
JOB CHARACTERISTIC	JOB A	JOB B	JOB A	JOB C
Skill	80	80	80	80
Training	90	90	90	60
Responsibility	150	150	150	60
Working conditions	30	30	30	150
Total points	350	350	350	350

Table 28-7   Should comparable jobs receive equal pay?

Jobs A and B have similar levels of skill, training, responsibility, and working conditions and are treated as "equal jobs." Under federal laws, because they are equal jobs, A and B must earn equal pay. Jobs A and C have different characteristics, but by a company's point rating system they have the same total points and are hence treated as "comparable" jobs. Under comparable-worth doctrine, comparable but different jobs should earn equal pay even though market supply and demand dictate different wages.

have comparable worth—such as A and C in Table 28-7—should be paid equally, and employers' failure to do so, according to this view, should constitute immoral and illegal discrimination. Under this approach, by equalizing wages on jobs that have comparable overall job characteristics, society can reverse decades of discrimination and eliminate the male-female wage gap.

Analysts have often been critical of basing compensation on a comparable-worth system, such as that shown in Table 28-7, rather than on the market. Critics argue that the point system is not an adequate basis for determining wages. Among potential defects in using a point system are: that the factors entering the point scores are incomplete, subjective, and prey to manipulation; that there are many attributes, such as responsibility, that cannot be precisely measured; that different attributes are worth differing amounts in different jobs; and that people's disutilities of work (and therefore their required compensating differentials) may differ for different people.

Most damaging, perhaps, is that thorough investigation of the effect of these measured attributes on wages finds much left to be explained. Even when studies are confined to a single race and sex, they seldom explain more than one-third of the variations of earnings across different people. Using such point scores to predict an employee's worth is like predicting individual baseball batting averages on the basis of a player's height, weight, age, and education. Because of the inherent difficulty in determining the correct scores for different jobs, many economists and labor experts would be loath to use such an imperfect yardstick for measuring a job's true economic value.

What would be the likely outcome of introducing comparable worth to determine wages in today's labor markets? The major impact would be that wages are set in a way that shuts out considerations of supply and demand. If the wages of truck drivers and telephone operators were equalized, we might find a glut of operators with too few willing to deliver the goods. Moreover, wage patterns would be frozen, locking the economy into a wage structure that was relatively unresponsive to economic shocks. If a sudden energy crisis drove up energy prices, companies would be unable to raise the relative wages of oil-drilling roustabouts and coal miners. While wage rates and pay structures tend to show considerable short-run sticki-

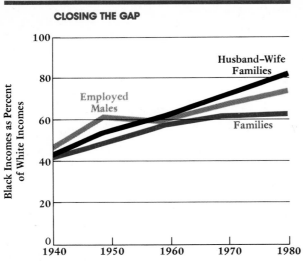

CLOSING THE GAP

Figure 28-6   Black family income and male earnings as a percent of white earnings

The gap between whites and blacks has closed slowly in recent decades in the United States. Intact families have made the most progress, but the average family income of blacks has not succeeded in closing the gap in recent years because of the growing number of one-adult black families. (Source: RAND Corporation.)

ness in a modern economy, no one can doubt that over the long run wages do adjust to major gluts and shortages in particular markets. In short, comparable worth would gum up an already sticky wage structure.

It should be emphasized that comparable worth is not an arcane idea confined to economics textbooks. Eleanor Holmes Norton, as chair of the Federal Equal Employment Opportunity Commission, attested that comparable worth would be the employment and discrimination issue of the future. Many unions, particularly those in which women are heavily represented,

have raised the banner of comparable worth as a negotiating issue. And the courts have sometimes ruled that comparable worth is an appropriate solution to the stubborn male-female wage gap. Comparable worth is likely to persist for many years as a central public-policy issue for labor markets.

Slow Progress

Discrimination is a complex social and economic process. Its roots took hold as discrimination was enforced by laws that kept disadvantaged groups from education and jobs. After legal equality was attained, separation of races and sexes perpetuated social and economic stratification.

But progress is being made. Members of disadvantaged groups are entering the best educational institutions and the highest-paying professions in large numbers. For example, among those under 35 years of age, women now constitute 41 percent of mathematicians and computer scientists, 29 percent of lawyers and judges, and half of managerial and professional workers. As people observe that women or minority groups are equally able, they begin to revise notions about what these groups can and should do in life. Figure 28-6 shows the slow progress that has been made in recent decades in closing the earnings gap between black and white members of the population. But substantial differences in incomes, wealth, and jobs persist.

In sum, careful studies have convinced most analysts that objective differences explain only a part of the income differentials between white men and other groups. Under such circumstances, beating down the walls of occupational protection, allowing noncompeting groups to compete, enforcing laws of equal opportunity—all these measures may help remove the stigma and economic losses of discrimination.

SUMMARY

A. Wage Determination under Perfect Competition

1. In perfectly competitive equilibrium, if all people and jobs were exactly alike, there would be no wage differentials. The equilibrium wage rate would be determined by supply and demand.

2. The demand for labor, as for any factor of production, is determined by labor's marginal product. A country or region will show a higher marginal product of labor and higher wages when the quality of labor inputs is higher, when the quality and quantity of cooperating inputs is greater, and when that area has access to more advanced knowledge and production techniques.

3. The supply of labor has four dimensions: population size, percentage of people gainfully employed, average number of hours worked, and quality of productive effort.

4. As wages rise, there are two opposite effects on the supply of labor: the substitution effect tempts each worker to work longer because of the higher pay for each hour of work. The income effect exerts influence in the opposite direction. Higher wages mean that workers can now afford more leisure time along with more commodities and other good things of life. At some critical wage, the supply curve may bend backward. The labor supply of very gifted, unique people is quite inelastic: their wages are largely pure economic rent.

5. Once we drop unrealistic assumptions concerning the uniformity of people and jobs, we find substantial wage differentials even in a perfectly competitive labor market. Compensating wage differentials, which compensate for nonmonetary differences in the quality of jobs, explain some (but by no means all) of the differentials. But differences in the quality of various grades of labor are probably the most important cause of wage differences. Although it cannot be claimed that labor consists of wholly noncompeting groups, it is nonetheless true that there are innumerable categories of partially competing groups. The final pattern of wages would, in a perfectly competitive labor market, be determined by the general equilibrium of the interrelated schedules of supply and demand, as shown in Table 28-4.

6. Fear of unemployment often leads to acceptance of the lump-of-labor fallacy. This belief, that there is only a fixed amount of useful work to be done, may arise from experiencing technological unemployment or depression. It lies behind much of the agitation for a shorter workweek and "work-sharing" proposals. But excessively high unemployment calls for macroeconomic policies to expand employment, not for policies to decrease the supply of labor.

B. Discrimination by Race and Gender

7. By accident of history, the minority of white males in the world has enjoyed the greatest affluence. Even a century after slavery, inequality of opportunity and economic, racial, and sex discrimination can be shown, by the tools of competitive supply and demand, to lead to loss of income by the underprivileged classes and for society.

8. There are many routes to discrimination, but the most important may be to create noncompeting groups. By segmenting labor markets, reserving managerial positions for white men while relegating women and blacks to menial, dead-end jobs, an economy can allow inequality of earnings to persist for decades.

9. Steps to reduce labor market discrimination have been taken in many directions. Early approaches focused on outlawing discriminatory practices, while later controversial steps imposed the requirement to take affirmative actions. Recently, advocates of comparable worth have argued that jobs with similar value but different job characteristics should receive equal pay even if supply and demand dictate otherwise. Critics of comparable worth foresee gluts and shortages if the externally imposed comparable-worth wages differ markedly from the equilibrium of supply and demand.

CONCEPTS FOR REVIEW

elements in demand for labor: labor
  quality, other inputs, technology
elements in supply of labor: population,
  labor-force participation, hours, quality
equal jobs vs. comparable worth
backward-bending supply curve
income vs. substitution effect

rent element in wages
compensating differentials in wages
segmented markets and noncompeting
  groups
earnings differentials due to education
  vs. discrimination

QUESTIONS FOR DISCUSSION

1. Make sure you understand the concepts of compensating differentials, pure economic rent, and noncompeting groups. Give examples of each from history or today's world.

2. Earnings in the United States average $450 per week, while in India workers earn but $20 per week. What forces lie behind the supply and demand for labor in the two countries that would produce such a large difference? What might India do to raise its wage level?

3. Explain what would happen to wage differentials as a result of: *(a)* less imperfect competition among people with similar labor skills; *(b)* free migration among regions in a country; *(c)* introduction of free public education into a country where education had previously been private and expensive; *(d)* a drop in popularity of television sports and entertainment programs featuring prominent stars.

4. Using supply and demand, explain the impact of immigration on labor supply, quantity of labor supplied, and wage rates. Can you use this analysis to help explain why labor leaders often oppose higher levels of immigration? Also use a similar line of reasoning to explain the old labor jingle:

    Whether you work by the week or the day
    The shorter the work the better the pay.

5. Modern economic theory of discrimination states that disadvantaged groups like women or blacks have lower incomes or poor jobs because they are segmented into low-wage markets. Explain how each of the following practices, which prevailed in some cases into the 1970s, helped perpetuate discriminatory labor market segmentation: Many state schools would not allow women to major in engineering; elite colleges like Princeton, Yale, and Stanford would not admit women; blacks and whites received schooling in separate school systems; elite social clubs would not admit women, blacks, or Catholics; many high-paid jobs (coal mining, fire fighting, construction, etc.) were thought too "tough" for women.

6. What steps could be taken to break down the segmented markets shown in Table 28-5?

7. In Europe of the 1980s, many labor groups pushed for lowering the average work-week because of the prevalence of high unemployment. What fallacy is at work here? If they succeeded, what would you expect to happen to the real wage?

8. What are the pros and cons of comparable worth? Why might it attract unions representing female workers yet find traditional male-dominated unions unsympathetic?

9. Figure 28-7 shows the effect of removing restrictions to entry into the segmented labor markets displayed in Figure 28-5. In panel *(a)*, the privileged jobs are open to all workers. The disadvantaged group is now free to take jobs in either market. Describe the new equilibrium and compare it with the equilbrium shown in Figure 28-5. Who gains and who loses? Can you show why the shaded region is the gain in total national income—with losers losing less than gainers gain?

DISCRIMINATION REMOVED

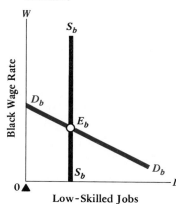

Figure 28-7

10. Advanced problem: Many people would charge a very high compensating differential to run the risk of working in an underground coal mine or in a nuclear power plant. A few people are relatively indifferent to such risks. Can you use this set of facts to explain (perhaps with the use of supply and demand) why actual compensating differentials may be surprisingly low?

CHAPTER 29___
LABOR UNIONS AND COLLECTIVE BARGAINING

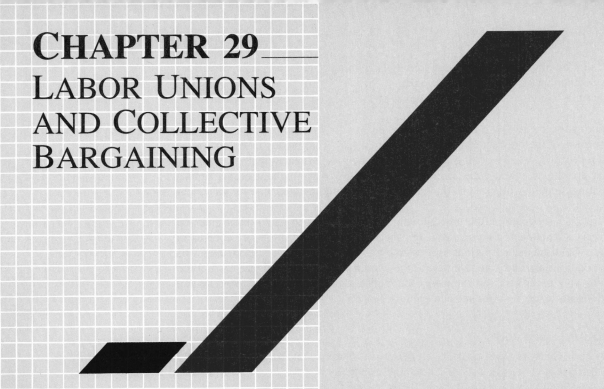

The function of unions, broadly considered, is to maintain purchasing power The function of unions, broadly considered, is to maintain purchasing power at a high enough level to absorb the products of business competition. Business competition and national unions are the indispensable blades of our twin scissors of supply and demand.

Robert F. Wagner,
Address at the Institute of Social Order, 1947

MOST PEOPLE work for the bulk of their adult lives. A third of our waking hours are spent on the job, and labor earnings constitute 80 percent of national income. No wonder that some say that ours is a laboristic rather than a capitalistic economy.

This chapter extends the analysis of labor markets to include important legal and institutional features of the workplace. We devote so much space to labor not only because labor is important but also because it is a unique commodity. After all, the economy is ultimately organized to enhance the well-being of laborers. Since the Civil War, workers cannot be bought, only "rented" for wages. Moreover, workers vary enormously in their characteristics, their strength, intelligence, skill, cheerfulness, industry, and reliability.

The fact that workers are rented by firms has one extraordinarily important implication. There must be some kind of understanding or contract between workers and employers. Sometimes the agreement is extremely casual, such as "If you work out well, the job's yours. Pay's $7.50 an hour." At the other extreme are tediously negotiated collective bargaining agreements between a group of firms and a union representing several thousand workers. Whether formal or casual, explicit or implicit, it is useful to think of labor "rental" in terms of contracts.

It is difficult, however, to study the process of determining casual agreements. In the first half of this chapter, therefore, we focus on the more formal agreements that are hammered out between labor unions and management. This discussion of the institutions of the American labor market will serve as a prelude to the analytical issues of labor market imperfections in section B.

A. THE AMERICAN LABOR MOVEMENT

Some 19 million Americans belong to unions. One-sixth of the labor force is made up of union members. If we exclude white-collar workers, supervisors, and executives, the proportion would be higher still. Practically all eligible workers belong to unions in important industries such as rail, steel, autos, mining, and clothing. Few large firms avoid being organized by unions.

Growth and Decline

Figure 29-1 shows the growth of union membership since 1900 measured as a percent of the labor force. Note the slow, steady advance up to World War I, the upsurge during that war and immediately thereafter, and the rather sharp decline and leveling off during the 1920s. Then see the explosive acquisition of new members during the New Deal and the continued rapid growth during World War II. United States unions are no longer in a strong growth phase. Since around 1950, there has been a gradual decline in the fraction of the labor force belonging to unions.

Membership statistics understate the influence of unions. Many nonunion employees are covered by union agreements on wages, hours, and work conditions. In many areas or industries, nonunion wages and benefits parallel those in union firms, so that if you work for a nonunion firm you will enjoy many of the benefits of the union sector.

BRIEF HISTORY OF THE AMERICAN LABOR MOVEMENT

How did labor unions first begin? What are the functions of unions? We begin with a brief history of the American labor movement.

Although the first stirrings of American labor unions predate the Civil War, it was not until the last third of the nineteenth century that labor began to revolt against "big interests." The first national movement was the Knights of Labor, which began as a secret society that all but "lawyers, bankers, gamblers or liquor dealers, and Pinkerton detectives" could join. Secrecy was dropped and by 1886, the high-water mark of the movement, 700,000 members had joined the Knights. The Knights represented an attempt to form one great labor union that would speak for all labor; it was more interested in political reform and social "uplift" than in bread-and-butter issues like hourly wages. After a few unsuccessful strikes, the Knights declined in membership as rapidly as it had grown. But the lesson of the Knights was not lost on key strategists of the American labor movement: to thrive, unions must concentrate on the economic betterment of their members rather than on reforming society.

In the face of labor organizations like the Knights, employers fought back. They too learned that strength came from cooperation; they backed up one another by drawing up "blacklists" of union sympathizers and refusing to hire labor "agitators." Generally, employers were able to invoke the law on their side to "keep labor peace," and the police or the National Guard was brought in to protect company property. Some companies even hired gunmen and spies to fight unions.[1]

---

[1] The chief weapons used by employers to fight unions have been (1) discriminatory discharge of union members, (2) the blacklist, (3) the lockout, (4) the "yellow-dog" contract (requiring agreement in advance not to join a union), (5) the labor spy, (6) the strikebreaker and armed guards, (7) conspiracy of town merchants, police, and judges against organizers and would-be union joiners, (8) the "company union," and (9) court injunctions.

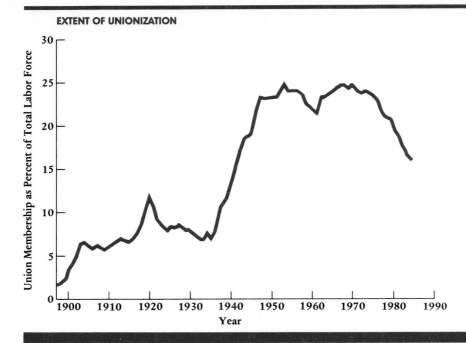

EXTENT OF UNIONIZATION

Figure 29-1   Union membership is a declining share of labor force

Of all workers, one-sixth now belong to unions—as against a fourth in 1955. Organized labor is no longer in a stage of vibrant growth. There has been a decline in relative importance of production workers in manufacturing, mining, and transport—the groups most prone to join unions. (Source: U.S. Department of Labor.)

The American Federation of Labor

In 1881, the present-day labor movement took its form in the birth of the American Federation of Labor (AFL). For almost half a century until his death in 1924, Samuel Gompers dominated this organization and gave the movement its characteristic pattern. Though early interested in socialist movements, he soon concluded that no movement opposed to capitalism would flourish on American soil.

Gompers' main principles were simple:

▪ He committed the AFL to the principle of *federalism*—with each national union to have sovereignty and "exclusive jurisdiction" over its craft specialty. This meant that the AFL would not tolerate "dual unionism": two unions could not try to organize the same workers, and no group of workers could break away from a recognized national union.

▪ He insisted on *voluntarism*—with labor and firms bargaining over wages, but with government staying out of collective bargaining.

▪ Gompers insisted on *business unionism*. Under this principle, American unions were to exist primarily for economic improvement of workers, rather than to engage in a class struggle to alter the form of government or to promote socialism. By and large, American labor unions since Gompers' time have focused on the struggle for higher wages, shorter hours, more vacations, easier work rules, and better fringe benefits in items such as pensions and health insurance. American unions thus were the opposite of the labor movements in many foreign countries—which, like Britain's Labour party, have come to run major political parties and have waged the class struggle for major political reforms.

During the early part of this century, labor unions met bitter repression from business groups. Opposed by business and battered by the high unemployment of the Great Depression, union membership fell to only 7 percent of the labor force. In addition, the AFL's old insistence on organizing unions on the basis of crafts, like carpentry or bricklaying, prevented the organization of the huge mass-production industries like steel in a single union. The defect of craft unionism was vividly demonstrated when Judge Gary of United States Steel crushed the great 1919 steel strike by outmaneuvering an unwieldy committee of some two-score craft unions set up to conduct the strike.

Astute observers saw the handwriting on the wall: *industrial unions* (those organizing an entire industry, like steel) were the wave of the future; *craft unions* (organizing workers of a particular skill, like carpentry) were a relic of the past. Industrial unions were introduced in 1935 with the formation of the Congress of Industrial Organizations (CIO). Helped by new government attitudes during the New Deal period, legislation (especially the Wagner Act of 1935), and court decisions, a whirlwind organizing campaign followed. The important mass-production industries—such as automobiles, steel, rubber, and oil—were organized, despite the bitter opposition of the principal companies in these industries.

By this time, the AFL had learned the important lesson of industrial unionism. It, too, began to organize workers on an industrial basis, but its craft unions remained dominant. The AFL and CIO lived in healthy rivalry for two decades. Finally, in 1955, they merged into the AFL-CIO, which is today the major national labor organization in the United States.

National and Local Unions and the AFL-CIO

There are three layers in the structure of American unions:

- The *local* union
- The *national* union
- The *federation* of national unions

To members, the local is the front line of unionism. Members join the local in their plant or town. They pay dues to it. Usually, the local union negotiates the collective bargaining agreement determining their wages and work conditions.

But the local is only a single chapter of the national union. Thus, an autoworker in Pontiac belongs to the local union there, which is one of hundreds of local chapters of the United Auto Workers.

Most unions belong to the federation of unions called the AFL-CIO. Although the public thinks of the federation as the most important element of the labor movement, in reality, the AFL-CIO is the public-relations and lobbying arm for its individual unions and depends on its members for financial support. The AFL-CIO's power is strictly limited. Like members of the Security Council of the United Nations, each national union insists upon its "sovereignty," "right of veto," and "exclusive jurisdiction" over workers in its sphere. Because national unions retain so much power, the AFL-CIO is today mainly a figurehead.

HOW COLLECTIVE BARGAINING WORKS

The wages and fringe benefits of unionized workers are determined by **collective bargaining.** This is the process of negotiation between firms and workers' representatives for the purpose of establishing mutually agreeable conditions of employment.

Let us examine how collective bargaining is conducted. First comes union certification. Consider a production-line worker in a factory that is being organized. An AFL-CIO union has petitioned the National Labor Relations Board (NLRB) for an election to determine who will represent workers in this plant. The worker marks a secret ballot in favor of the union, and the union wins a majority. The NLRB then certifies the new union as the collective bargaining agent for the plant, prohibiting any other union from negotiating directly with management.

A day is set for the new union representatives to meet with management at the bargaining table. Seated at the table will probably be a company vice-president in charge of industrial relations; with her will be attorneys from a law firm that specializes in labor law. On the union side will be the local business agent of the union, a small committee of union officers, and an expert on negotiations from union headquarters.

What Are the Issues?

We have all heard of the last-minute, all-night sessions before a labor agreement is reached. What is actually in this agreement?

The central part, of course, is the *economic package*. This includes the basic wage rates for different job categories, overtime rates, along with the rules for holidays and coffee breaks. In addition, the agreement will contain provision for "fringe benefits," such as a pension plan, coverage for health care, and similar items. During periods of high inflation the agreement will generally contain a COLA (cost-of-living-adjustment) clause, which adjusts wages upward when consumer prices rise rapidly.

A second important and often controversial issue is *work rules*, which concern work assignments and tasks, job security, and workloads. Particularly in declining industries, the staffing requirements are a major issue because the demand for labor is falling. Thus in railroads, there were decades of disputes about the number of people needed to run a train. Airlines are currently battling unions over the size of the cockpit crew.

Finally, the agreement has *procedural* features. These include rules of seniority—who gets laid off first or last—as well as a grievance procedure for handling discharges or disputes.

At last the contract, covering many pages of fine print, is signed. Everything is set down in black and white. Generally there are provisions for the arbitration of issues that arise under it, each side agreeing in advance to accept the decision of an impartial outside arbitrator. The usual life of a contract is 3 years.

Collective bargaining is a complicated business—a matter of give-and-take. Much effort is spent negotiating purely economic issues, dividing the pie between wages and profits. Sometimes agreements get hung up on issues of management prerogatives, such as the ability to reassign workers or change work rules. In addition, some provisions pertain to issues which are cooperative rather than antagonistic, such as the design of education or drug-abuse programs for workplace health and safety. In the end, both workers and management have a large stake in ensuring that workers are both satisfied and productive on their jobs.

GOVERNMENT AND COLLECTIVE BARGAINING

The history of labor unions tells a story of their gradual political acceptance and freedom from restrictive laws. Two hundred years ago, when labor first tried to organize in England and America, the common-law doctrines against "conspiracy in restraint of trade" were used against union members. Well into this century, unions and their members were convicted by courts, fined, and harassed by various injunctive procedures. Repeatedly the Supreme Court struck down acts designed to improve work conditions for women and children and other reform legislation on hours and wages.

In 1890, the Sherman Antitrust Act made monopolistic restraints of trade illegal. It did not mention labor unions, but in the next 20 years the Sherman Act was used increasingly by the courts to curb the activities of unions. If a union struck for ends that a judge thought undesirable, the court might rule against it. And many traditional weapons used by unions were declared illegal.

Finally the AFL was forced into the political arena. By 1914, labor was successful in getting the Clayton Antitrust Act passed. Although hailed as "labor's Magna Carta" and designed to remove labor from antitrust prosecution under the Sherman Act, this act did not end legislative and judicial opposition to the labor movement.

Prolabor Laws

Gradually the pendulum swung toward support of union collective bargaining. Major landmarks were the Railway Labor Act (1926), which accepted the basic premise of collective bargaining; the Norris-LaGuardia Act (1932), which virtually wiped out injunctive interference by the federal courts in labor disputes; and the Fair Labor Standards Act (1938), which barred child labor, called for time-and-a-half pay for weekly hours over 40, and set a federal minimum wage for most nonfarm workers (currently $3.35 per hour for 1988).

The biggest landmark of all was the National Labor Relations (or Wagner) Act (1935). Its section 7 stated clearly:

Employees shall have the right to self-organization, to form, join, or assist labor organizations, to bargain collectively through representatives of their own choosing, and to engage in concerted activities, for the purpose of collective bargaining or other mutual aid or protection.

Moreover, it set up the National Labor Relations Board (NLRB) to make sure that employers do not engage in "unfair labor practices" against labor.[2] The NLRB also goes into plants and holds elections to see what organization is to be regarded as the collective bargaining representative for all workers. It can, and does, issue cease-and-desist orders against employers, enforceable by the courts after appeal. And it often makes employers reinstate, with back pay, employees unjustly discharged.

Without doubt, this flurry of pro-union legislation helped propel unionism to its preeminent position on the eve of World War II.

Postwar Legislation

After World War II, many felt that the pendulum had swung too far in labor's direction, and Congress passed legislation aimed at both sides of labor disputes. The most important statute was the 1947 Taft-Hartley Act. This two-edged labor relations law prescribes standards of conduct for unions as well as employers.

Among its principal features are the following: Strikes which "imperil the national health or safety" may be suspended for an 80-day "cooling off" period, which may be imposed by a court injunction requested by the attorney general.

Unfair union labor practices are defined, and union's behavior limited. Unions can be sued and held responsible for acts of their agents. The "closed shop," which requires employees to be members of the union before they are hired, is declared illegal,

and states are given a free hand to pass "right-to-work" or open-shop laws. Secondary boycotts and jurisdictional strikes are illegal. Political activity and financial contributions by unions to political candidates or public officials are restricted. The free-speech rights of the employer are reaffirmed and strengthened.

With the passage of the Taft-Hartley Act, the framework for collective bargaining was in place. Although labor and business have from time to time proposed modifications of current law—a major goal of labor, for example, being the repeal of Taft-Hartley's section 14(b) allowing state right-to-work laws—no side has mustered the strength to change the status quo in a significant way since 1947.

CURRENT LABOR ISSUES

The issues facing labor unions in the 1990s are not dissimilar to those of the last century. These include strikes, competition from nonunion labor, and productivity restraints.

Strikes

Unions devote their bargaining efforts to improving the wages, fringe benefits, and working conditions of their members. Only by threatening to strike can unions force concessions from management. It is not surprising, therefore, that work stoppages provide the major headlines in labor relations.

Contrary to common impressions, power to strike is used sparingly, as is shown in Figure 29-2. The number of days lost from work on account of the common cold is far greater than that from all work conflicts.

The second half of this chapter points out that, without the right to strike, a union's powers to bargain would be substantially altered. Time and again concessions have been wrung out of employers only by the realistic threat of forcing upon them the heavy financial losses involved in a prolonged shutdown. Workers, too, suffer grievous financial losses and demoralization from a long shutdown. And many a time employers have successfully refused union de-

---

[2]The term "unfair labor practices" as used in the Wagner Act refers to employers' activities that interfere with employees' rights to self-organization. Examples of such employer practices are (1) firing people for joining a union, (2) refusing to hire people sympathetic to unions, (3) threatening to close an establishment if employees join a union, (4) interfering with or dominating the administration of a union, or (5) refusing to bargain with the employees' designated representatives.

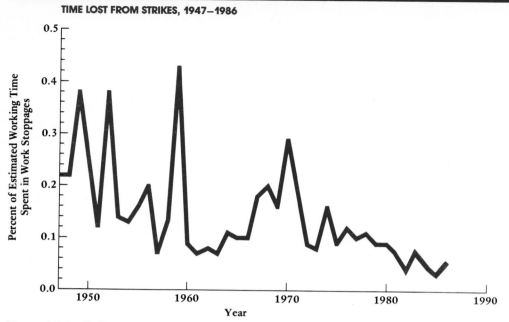

TIME LOST FROM STRIKES, 1947–1986

Figure 29-2   Strike activity has declined in recent years

Time lost from strikes, as a percent of total labor days worked, never reached ½ percent and has declined to under 0.1 percent per year. In a typical recent year, Switzerland, West Germany, and Japan have had less strike activity than the United States; Italy and Canada are more strike-prone than the United States. (Source: U.S. Department of Labor.)

mands by a determined willingness to withstand a painful strike.

Generally, the government stays out of individual strikes, allowing unions and firms to battle it out. But, when strikes involve key functions (such as coal mining or shipping) or take place on a nationwide scale in an important sector (like autos), many feel that the public interest dictates intervention. Just as the rights of private property and of personal freedoms are not absolute, so the rights of "free collective bargaining" are subject to limitation and coordination with social necessities.

These are not academic questions. In 1919 Massachusetts Governor Calvin Coolidge said in connection with the Boston police strike, "There is no right to strike against the public safety, by anybody, anywhere, any time." The government has often had to decide whether to intervene in order to stop what

might be a damaging strike. In railroads, steel, and coal, Presidents often turned to Taft-Hartley or other injunctive procedures during the 1950s and 1960s. Over the last decade, however, as strikes have become less prevalent and as the federal government has taken a less active role in economic management, direct government involvement in private labor disputes has all but disappeared.

Attitudes toward strikes have also changed among businesses and the public. In part because of favorable interpretations of labor law by the courts, and partly because of successful experience in breaking strikes, firms increasingly have decided to resist union strike threats. An important public demonstration was provided by President Reagan in 1981 when he refused to accept the demands of the union during an illegal strike by the air controllers. After the firing of 11,400 air-traffic controllers, the nation suffered a painful slowdown in air traffic and years of delayed service at major airports. But the government's willingness to pay the price for rebuffing the controllers' union provided a demonstration of the possible benefits to management of a tough bargaining stance.

During the 1980s, then, a new management attitude toward strikes arose. Managers began to think about the unthinkable: that they could endure a strike, perhaps by hiring nonunion workers as temporary or permanent replacements, without facing financial ruin or public censure. The increased prevalence of anti-labor views both inside and outside government has led to a major reduction in union bargaining power over the last decade.

Increasing Competitiveness

The greatest threat to unions comes from nonunion workers who supply the same product. Sometimes, as in textiles and coal mining, the nonunion workers are in right-to-work states, where companies have successfully resisted union drives. In the last decade, however, the greatest threat to unions arose from deregulation of domestic industries and from foreign competition. As a result of import penetration, American unions no longer have a monopoly on labor supply in autos, steel, rubber, or communications equipment. Foreign workers from Toyota, Mitsubishi, and Ericsson now openly compete with domestic workers through foreign goods imported into American markets.

Similarly, the deregulation of many industries has opened them up to the entry of nonunionized firms. In an earlier era, a few established firms controlled most of the output in regulated industries. Once these firms had been unionized, unions in regulated industries like trucking, airlines, telephone, and shipping gained a virtual monopoly on labor sold in those sectors. After those industries were deregulated, nonunionized firms could enter and undercut established firms with lower-cost labor, thereby eroding the labor monopoly of unions.

A vivid example of competition undermining unions is the deregulation of the airlines in the early 1980s. As a result of deregulation, new carriers were allowed to enter the airline industry for the first time in decades, and low-cost airlines expanded into new markets without burdensome government constraints. A new firm like People Express or an expanding firm like Continental Airlines could hire nonunion pilots at $40,000 a year as compared to the $80,000 a year or more paid to unionized pilots of the major airlines. Hence, because new nonunionized firms could enter the airline market, the market power of unions was eroded and the average wages of union employees in the airline industry declined.

A second assault on union power came from the inroads on manufacturing industries made by foreign competitors in the early 1980s. From 1980 to 1985, the volume of imported goods rose 45 percent. Our markets were flooded with foreign steel, chemicals, autos, and capital equipment. The embodied labor in imported goods posed a threat to American unions because foreign labor could undersell domestic labor in exactly the way nonunionized workers could undercut unionized workers. In response to the threat from foreign manufacturing workers, many unions reopened their labor contracts. Indeed, for the first time in modern history, steelworkers accepted a pay cut, while the Teamsters' Union froze the wages of truck drivers. The high unemployment and foreign competition of the 1980s stood as major obstacles to large wage gains by unions in manufacturing.

We see then how deregulation and foreign competition both undermine the strength of unions and put downward pressure on wages in unionized industries. This may be one reason why "big labor" has turned restrictionist and protectionist—to insulate its monopoly power from offshore workers and from deregulated firms.

Productivity Restraints

In an age of rapid technical change and at a time when there is much talk of "automation and robotization," union members are often as concerned about job security as about wage gains. What good is a pay raise for a job that no longer exists? This is not a new concern. The word "sabotage" was coined when laborers threw their wooden shoes (sabots) into the works of the new machines brought in by the Industrial Revolution to replace workers. *Featherbedding* refers to rules imposed on employers merely for the purpose of keeping up the demand for workers: use of small shovels, limitation on number of bricks laid per day, requirement that use of music recordings be accompanied by a standby orchestra that does nothing but draw pay, a requirement for fire stokers (i.e., coal shovelers) for diesel engines.

Entrenched unions do have power to enforce such uneconomical arrangements, since unions have a monopoly over the labor supplied to the affected firms or industries. Railroads must bargain in good faith over work rules with their unions because they cannot legally employ nonunion workers to run the locomotives. Perhaps the most extreme example is that of the dockworkers of New York. Since 1966, senior dockworkers have received a guaranteed annual income. The result is that many longshoremen simply punch the clock, drive back home, and collect $33,000 a year. Some of them haven't hauled a line for a decade. But the recent deep recession, foreign competition, competition from nonunion states or firms, and deregulation have undermined many featherbedding practices. And unions are beginning to see that in the long run featherbedding may so hamper

efficiency and drive up prices that the jobs of union members become imperiled.

A study of the history of unionism will show that the controversial issues change little from decade to decade. From their infancy, unions relied upon strikes to force employers to raise wages. Once unions had gained recognition, they then labored to exclude nonunion workers and to maintain their traditional work rules. But success has been gained by skillful negotiations, as the great English economist Alfred Marshall wrote at the beginning of this century:

> Trade unionism has enabled . . . workers to enter into negotiations with the same gravity, self-restraint, dignity, and forethought as are observed in the diplomacy of great nations. It has led them generally to recognize that a simply aggressive policy is a foolish policy, and that the chief use of military resources is to preserve an advantageous peace.[3]

How advantageous an economic arrangement have unions brought to their members? We turn to that issue in the next section.

B. IMPACT OF IMPERFECT COMPETITION ON WAGES

The last chapter analyzed the determination of wages in perfectly competitive markets. We have seen, however, that labor unions definitely lead to monopolistic influences in labor markets. In this section we analyze the impact on wage and employment patterns of market imperfections due to unions and other forces.

Imperfections in Labor Markets

To begin with, we emphasize that labor markets are not the competitive auction markets that we see for grains and common stocks. While wheat can be graded into neat categories, that cannot be done for human beings. No auctioneer allocates workers to the highest bidders. Rather, labor markets tend to display signs of imperfect competition; that is, some firms or groups of workers can affect the wages of individual categories of labor. Most important, workers are extremely heterogeneous. Who could dream of putting

all workers into 12 different grades and pretend that each labor grade would command exactly the same price on competitive labor markets?

Wage Stickiness Two tests indicate that the labor market is imperfect. When there is a considerable increase in unemployment—as in 1982—do wage rates drop as they would in the corn market when a glut occurs? The answer is clearly, No. Money wages rose almost 5 percent in 1982 even though one-tenth of the labor force was unemployed.

Why do wages continue to rise when labor is in excess supply? This phenomenon, known as *sticky wages,* means that wages and salaries tend to respond slowly to economic shocks rather than adjusting instantaneously to balance the supply and demand for labor and clear the labor market.

[3]*Principles of Economics,* 8th ed. (Macmillan, London, 1920), p. 703.

Why don't unemployed workers quickly drive down the equilibrium wage? Just imagine going to General Motors or any other large corporation when the next recession comes, brandishing your degrees and certificates of IQ and excellence, and offering to work for less than GM is paying. GM would not think of changing its entire wage policy just to save a few dollars. Indeed, if you were a blue-collar worker, GM would have to renegotiate its entire contract with the United Auto Workers just to hire you at a reduced wage rate.

Remember that workers are not like machines: a machine cares not a bit about its price, but workers care a great deal about their wages. So when you tried to reduce wage rates, existing workers would probably resent you, call you a "union-busting scab," and pelt you with eggs. These factors, and others as well, have led all but the smallest firms to construct a wage structure to rationalize and administer the compensation of their workers.

Wage Structures of Firms The fact that firms must have wage structures is additional evidence of labor market imperfections. Recall from the end of Chapter 28 that large firms tend to set up classification systems as a means of organizing and paying their workers. In a perfectly competitive market, a firm need not make decisions on its pay schedules. Instead, it would turn to the morning newspaper to learn what the reigning market wage rate was that week. Any firm, by raising wages ever so little, could get all the extra help it wanted. If, on the other hand, it tried to pay less than the competitive wage, it would find no labor to hire at all.

But few labor markets approach perfect competition; rather, they are a blend of competitive and monopoly elements. For most firms, if wages are set too low, at first nothing much happens; but eventually workers quit a little more rapidly than would otherwise be the case. Recruitment of new people of the same quality will get harder and harder, and slacking off in the performance and productivity of those who remain on the job will become noticeable.

How do firms deal with the peculiarities of imperfect competition in labor markets? If you have but a few employees, you might bargain and haggle with each one to avoid paying more than you have to. But if you have more than a hundred employees, you will want to set up an internal wage structure; you will group jobs into different classes, name a wage for each class of job, and then decide how many applicants you will accept for each job opening. Moreover, this wage structure will remain relatively stable in the face of changing labor market conditions.

Hence, these two features of labor markets—wage stickiness and the need for an internal wage structure—are the hallmarks of labor markets today. Moreover, it would be a mistake to think that these peculiarities arise only because of unions. Wage stickiness and wage structures are features of all large organizations, private or public, union or nonunion. Large companies have standard wage scales to help simplify wage decisions and promote a sense of fairness. Also, nonunion firms generally have an annual wage period, adjusting wage rates only once a year. In years of high unemployment, nonunion wages grow more slowly than do union wages, but not by a wide margin. And even in the most competitive labor markets, we seldom see actual money wage cuts in recession years. The phenomenon of sticky wages and wage structures responding slowly to economic shocks is intrinsic to a world of imperfectly competitive labor markets.

FOUR WAYS UNIONS SEEK TO RAISE WAGES

Let's now use our economic theory to analyze how unions operate. For example, how can steelworkers raise their wages above competitive levels? There are four main methods by which a union might raise wages in a particular industry:

1. Unions can reduce the supply of labor.

2. They can use their collective bargaining power to raise standard wage rates directly.

3. They can cause the demand for labor to increase.

4. Unions can resist employers who possess monopoly bargaining power.

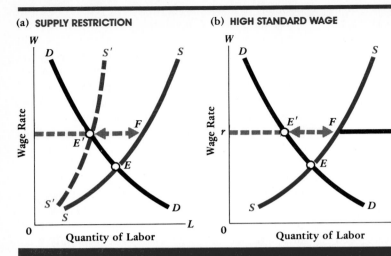

(a) SUPPLY RESTRICTION   **(b) HIGH STANDARD WAGE**

Figure 29-3   To raise pay, unions restrict supply or merely enforce standard wage rate

If the supply of workers is restricted from *SS* to *S'S'* in **(a)**, wages rise and employment declines. Raising the standard wage to *rr* in **(b)** has exactly the same effect on wages and employment as restricting supply. In either case, wages rise and the workers from *E'* to *F* are excluded from employment.

Restricting the Supply of Labor

We have already seen that a union may restrict the supply of labor in order to travel upward on the demand curve for labor. Immigration barriers, maximum-hour legislation, long apprenticeships, racial and sex barriers, refusal to admit new members into the union or to let nonunion members hold jobs—all these strategies are restrictive devices to reduce the supply of labor.

Figure 29-3(*a*) displays the effect of a direct restriction of labor supply. Say that unions persuade the government to pass a law (such as the Davis-Bacon Act) that effectively prohibits government contractors from hiring nonunion construction workers. The effect of this law would be to restrict the supply of construction workers from *SS* to *S'S'*. The supply restriction would lower total employment and raise wages in this labor market. (What would happen if a union imposed long apprenticeships on new carpenters in such a framework?)

Raising Standard Wage Rates

Most union bargains do not directly restrict labor supply. Rather, they attempt to force employers to pay a standard wage higher than prevailing market wages. For example, if nonunion plumbers earn $12 per hour

in Alabama, a union might bargain with a large construction firm to set the wage at $15 per hour for that firm's plumbers.

Such an agreement is valuable to the union only if access to alternative labor supplies can be restricted, however. Hence, under a typical collective bargaining agreement, a firm cannot hire nonunion plumbers; nor can it contract out plumbing services; nor can it subcontract to nonunion firms. Each of these provisions helps prevent erosion of the union's monopolistic lock on the supply of plumbers to the firm. In some industries, like steel and autos, unions will even try to unionize the entire industry so that firm A's unionized workers need not compete with firm B's nonunion workers. All these steps are necessary to protect high union wage rates.

Figure 29-3(*b*) shows the impact of agreed-upon high standard wages, where the union forces employers to pay wages at the standard rate shown by the horizontal line *rr*. As in panel (*a*), the equilibrium is at *E'*, where *rr* intersects the employers' demand curve. The workers from *E'* to *F* are as effectively excluded from jobs as if the union had directly limited entry.

Note that the union has not directly reduced supply when it sets high standard wage rates. What then limits employment? At the above-equilibrium wage rates, employment is limited by the firms' demand for labor. The number of workers who seek employment exceeds the demand by the segment $E'F$. These excess workers might be unemployed and waiting for vacancies in the high-paying union sector, or they might become discouraged and look for jobs in other sectors. The unemployment stemming from too-high wages is called classical unemployment and will be discussed further at the end of this chapter; some economists believe that it is quantitatively important in Europe today.

Increasing the Demand for Labor

A third way to increase wages is by a policy that increases the demand for union labor. Figure 29-4 shows how a shift in the demand for unionized labor will shift up both wage rates and employment from E to E'.

Numerous techniques exist to shift the labor demand curve. Labor may help industry advertise its products. Or it may agitate for an import quota on the product, thereby raising the demand for domestic workers in the industry.

In addition, unions can sometimes take measures that raise demand through increasing the efficiency (and therefore the marginal productivity) of labor. For example, a century ago, workers were being paid so little that they were malnourished and inefficient. Higher wages might then have made them more efficient and thus resulted in lower rather than higher production costs. Today, in this country, few workers are still physiologically undernourished.

But psychological elements can be as important as physiological ones. Many an employer has found that too low wages are bad business even from a hard-boiled, dollars-and-cents standpoint. The quality and contentment of the workers fall off so much that the company is losing, rather than gaining, from trimming the last few dollars of its wage bill. Recently, economists have begun to stress the impact of wages on worker efficiency (sometimes called *efficiency wages*). Some analysts argue that farsighted employers will raise wages above competitively determined levels to attract more efficient workers, boost morale, and improve worker productivity. Recent analyses by Harvard's Richard Freeman and James Medoff have thrown new light on this question. They find evidence

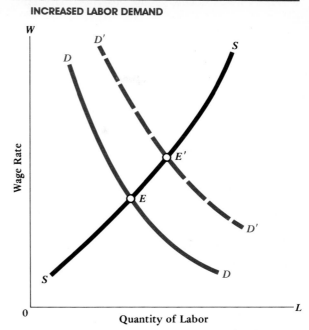

INCREASED LABOR DEMAND

Figure 29-4   **Shifting labor demand increases wage rates**

Labor unions also increase wages by increasing the demand for labor. This occurs either because of increases in labor's marginal product, or through means that increase the derived demand for labor by shifting the demand for the final product toward the output of union-made goods.

that unions, by serving the role of a collective voice of workers, may have actually increased labor productivity.[4]

Some economists question the plausibility of these findings, asking why employers are so resistant to unions if they raise productivity so much. This bold new thesis will be heartily debated in the coming years.

Combating Monopsony Power of Businesses

When union organizers first began to agitate for combinations of workers, they argued that unions were

[4]Richard B. Freeman and James L. Medoff, *What Do Unions Do?* (Basic Books, New York, 1984).

necessary as a "countervailing power" to large employers. In essence, the union's market power was necessary to offset the employers' market power. Let us understand the reasoning behind this contention.

Suppose you live in a company town. The dominant firm hires most people who have jobs. You must take what the employer offers or go without work; your only alternative is to move to another region.

In this case, the employer is a **monopsonist,** which designates a single buyer of a commodity (just as "monopoly" means a single seller). Consider how a profit-maximizing monopsonist would calculate its costs and make its hiring decisions. The monopsonist will no longer behave as a perfectly competitive purchaser of labor. Rather, it will recognize that it can have an effect upon wages in its town, paying higher wages as it hires additional workers. In effect, because the firm is so large, it moves up the town's labor supply curve as it employs more workers.

As a result of the higher wages paid as more workers are employed, the firm finds that its *marginal cost of labor is greater than the wage rate*. Why so? Because when the monopsonist hires an additional worker, it must raise the wage rate paid to all workers. Therefore the marginal cost of a new worker is equal to the wage rate of the new worker plus the higher wages paid to already-hired workers, and this sum is clearly higher than the wage rate. The profit-maximizing monopsonist realizes then that it should not hire labor up to the point where the wage equals the marginal revenue product of labor (recall from the last chapter that this is the condition for profit maximization when firms face perfectly competitive factor markets). Instead, the firm should hire an additional worker only when its marginal revenue product is equal to the marginal cost of labor (which is greater than the wage rate). The monopsonist therefore both depresses wages and restricts employment relative to perfectly competitive labor markets.

Enter the labor union. After organizing the workers, it settles with the employer for a standard wage that is above the depressed monopsonistic wage level. At that higher standard wage, the employer can hire all the workers it needs at a given wage rate; the firm becomes a "wage taker" rather than a "wage maker." It will then become like the competitive firm that hires workers up to the point where the marginal

revenue product equals the going standard wage. A union that exercises countervailing power may produce higher wages *and* higher employment.[5]

The role of unions in combating business monopsony power proved important in their early history, particularly in isolated locations like the tin mines of Bolivia or the lumber camps of the American west. In periods when business trusts behaved like monopsonists by keeping wages low, union countervailing power may have improved wages and employment in labor markets. Countervailing power is less relevant in today's America, where labor mobility is great and where few communities are dominated by a single firm.

Theoretical Indeterminacy of Collective Bargaining

Having seen how unions raise wages, can we devise a theory that accurately predicts the outcome of a bargain between labor and management? Unions sometimes realize it would not be in their interest to ask for higher wages; management sometimes takes the view that a wage increase would improve long-run corporate earnings. But both these views are exceptional. Usually, at any collective bargaining negotiation, the workers are pressing for higher wages while management holds out for a leaner wage bill.

What will be the terms of the final agreement? Unfortunately, this is one important question that no economic theory can answer with precision. This is a situation known as "bilateral monopoly"—where two sides have strong bargaining power. The result depends on psychology, politics, and countless other intangible and unpredictable factors. As far as the economist is concerned, however, the final outcome of bilateral monopoly is in principle indeterminate—as indeterminate as the haggling between two millionaires over the value of a fine painting.[6]

---

[5]The analysis of monopsony and countervailing power is pursued in question 10 at the end of this chapter.

[6]Situations like labor-management bargains are the subject of game theory, analyzed in Chapter 25's appendix. The theoretical indeterminacy of collective bargaining is equivalent to the following result from game theory: that a two-person noncooperative game does not generally have a unique outcome. Rather, like wars or strikes, the outcome of such a two-person game depends on many factors like the bargaining power, prestige, bluffing ability, and even the perceptions on each side of the strength of the other side.

The Importance of Controlling Entry

The control of potential competitors is as important to a labor monopoly as to a product-market monopoly. If you go back to review how unions raise wages, it quickly becomes clear that in many cases *control of entry* is critical. Thus by forming a union that comprises all the workers in a particular group, the union is able to set a monopoly price for its members. To succeed, however, it must fight off competition from nonunion labor.

This need to prevent nonunion competition is behind many of the central policies supported by labor unions. It explains why unions want to limit immigration; why unions support protectionist legislation which would limit foreign goods, that is, goods made by workers who are not members of American unions; and why unions sometimes oppose deregulation in industries like trucking, communications, or airlines, since deregulation allows entry of nonunionized firms.

EFFECTS ON WAGES AND EMPLOYMENT

The advocates of labor unions claim that they have raised real wages, at least for their members. Critics argue that although unions have done just that, the result is high unemployment, inflation, and distorted resource allocation. Despite the agreement about the effects of unions on real wages, the facts are hard to pin down.

Has Unionization Raised Wages?

Let's start by reviewing the effects of unions on relative wages. Economists have first estimated the economic impacts of unions by examining wages in unionized and nonunion industries. This has led most analysts to conclude that union workers receive on average a 10 to 15 percent wage differential over nonunion workers. The effects range from a negligible effect for hotel workers and barbers to 25 to 30 percent higher earnings for skilled construction workers or coal miners. The pattern of results suggests that where unions have the greatest difficulty monopoliz-

ing labor supply and controlling entry (as for barbers), they will be least effective in raising wages.

A second approach examines the wages of individual workers, correcting for worker characteristics and taking into account whether the worker is in a union or nonunion job. Orley Ashenfelter of Princeton examined a panel of workers over the period 1967–1975. Correcting for the influence of each worker's sex, race, education, and other personal characteristics, he found that those workers who belonged to unions in the mid-1970s had wages 17 percent above those of nonunion workers. In addition, Ashenfelter found that black males who belong to unions got even higher wage differentials than other groups: 23 percent higher wages as compared to 16 percent for white males.

Yet a third approach, pioneered by Wesley Mellow, compares the wage received by the same worker as he or she moves from union to nonunion jobs or vice versa. This study found that those becoming union workers experienced an average wage increase of 7.5 percent in 1977–1978 while those leaving unions experienced a wage reduction of the same magnitude. Mellow also found a much smaller impact of unionism on the wages of black workers than have other studies, his study estimating gains of black workers moving into union jobs of only 2 percent. This small figure suggests that the large impact of unions on wages of black workers found by other studies may be attributable to unmeasured worker quality differences of unionized black workers.

Overall Impacts But can unions bootstrap the entire economy to a higher real wage? Most evidence suggests not. The share of national income going to labor (including self-employment) has changed little over the last six decades. Once cyclical influences on labor's share are removed, we can see no appreciable impact of unionization on the level of real wages in the United States. The evidence from heavily unionized European countries suggests that, when unions succeed in raising money wage rates, the main impact is to trigger an inflationary wage-price spiral with little or no permanent effect upon real wages. Moreover, macroeconomic history shows that when inflation heats up, governments and central banks often apply contractionary macroeconomic policies, such

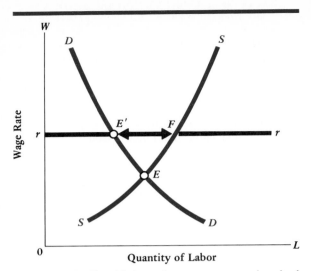

Figure 29-5   Too-high real wages cause classical unemployment

If unions push real wages too high for an entire economy, firms will demand E' while workers will supply F. Thus the black arrow from E' to F represents the amount of classical unemployment. This source of unemployment is particularly important when a country cannot affect its price level or exchange rate, and differs from the unemployment caused by insufficient aggregate demand analyzed in Parts Two and Three.

as raising interest rates and slowing the growth of government spending, resulting in higher unemployment rather than higher real wages.

Effects on Employment

If unions do not affect overall wage levels, this suggests that their major impact would fall upon relative wages. Wages in unionized industries would rise relative to those in nonunionized industries. Moreover, employment would tend to be reduced in unionized and expanded in nonunionized industries.

Waiting for Recall Some economists think that the artificial wage differentials across sectors created by unions are a major cause of unemployment.[7] They

[7]A more complete description of the economics of unemployment is provided in Chapter 13.

point to two mechanisms. The first is *wait unemployment*. As workers from high-paid jobs are laid off, they can collect unemployment insurance or supplemental benefits. In fact, these benefits may well exceed the take-home pay for jobs in other sectors of the economy, such as in service industries. The workers may prefer to wait for a recall from the auto firm or steel firm; they are unemployed but do not wish to work at going rates in the low-paying industries.

Classical Unemployment A second concern, particularly prevalent in Western Europe today, is that unions and government policies have raised real wages to artificially high levels, resulting in excess supply of labor and what is called *classical unemployment*.

This case is illustrated in Figure 29-5. Let us say that *all* workers belong to unions—which is close to accurate for many Western European countries. Say unions succeed in raising wages above the market-clearing wage at E to a higher real wage at r. Then, if supply of and demand for labor in general are unchanged, the arrow between E' and F will represent the number of workers who want to work at wage r but cannot find work. This variety is called classical unemployment because it results from too high real wages, as opposed to Keynesian unemployment, which results from insufficient aggregate demand.

The diagnosis and prescription for classical unemployment belongs more in the macroeconomics sections than here in our microeconomic analysis of wages and marginal products. But it does suggest that when a country gets locked into too high real wages, the high level of unemployment may be primarily a result of inappropriate relative prices rather than insufficient aggregate demand for goods and services.

The Consequences of Decline

We have traced in this chapter how labor unions became legal during this century; how they thrived during the New Deal period; and how their economic strength has eroded slowly as blue-collar jobs became less numerous and as deregulation and foreign competition spurred businesses to fight union power.

What does this eclipse of labor unions portend for labor markets of the 1990s? Harvard's Richard Freeman has the following reflections upon the social implications of the decline of the labor movement:

What are the economic effects of a proportionately smaller trade union movement? From the perspective of the monopoly "face" of unionism the decline can be expected to reduce the monopoly misallocation of resources resulting from unionism and . . . also reduce the union wage advantage. On the other hand, however, reduced unionism can be expected to affect adversely many of the positive effects of strong unionism—lower dispersion of earnings among workers; lower quit rates; and

higher productivity due to pressures on management to reduce costs in organized firms. As the United Mine Workers organization and industrial relations in coal have deteriorated, productivity in union mines has fallen sharply. The broader social effects of a diminished trade union movement remain to be seen.[8]

[8]Richard B. Freeman, "The Evolution of the American Labor Market, 1948–80," in Martin Feldstein (ed.), *The American Economy in Transition* (The University of Chicago Press, Chicago, 1980), p. 372.

SUMMARY

A. The American Labor Movement

1. Labor unions occupy an important but diminishing role in the American economy, in terms of both membership and influence. Their present structure is in three layers: *(a) local* unions, *(b) national* unions, and *(c)* a *federation* of unions (AFL-CIO), the first two being the most important.

2. By the 1900s, the typical American pattern of federated, nonpolitical business unionism had been established. Since 1935, the CIO and finally the AFL have modified the pattern in the direction of *industrial* unionization of whole mass-production industries rather than relying solely upon *craft* unionization of skilled workers.

3. After a union has been recognized by an NLRB election as the exclusive bargaining agent for a group of workers, management and labor representatives meet together in collective bargaining to negotiate a contract. Such agreements typically contain provisions for wages, fringe benefits, and work rules, along with a dispute-resolution mechanism.

4. Until the mid-1930s there was bitter opposition to unions. But the pendulum of government swung to support collective bargaining, and since the Wagner Act (1935), most manufacturing industries have become unionized. The result has been less violence but still vigorous collective bargaining between unions and management. In 1947, Congress felt the law had become one-sided in favor of labor and passed the Taft-Hartley Act to correct the balance.

5. Strikes have become less prevalent since World War II. Featherbedding (or work-slowing practices) are a major obstacle to productivity growth in many declining industries. The biggest threat to unions today is the competition from nonunionized firms, from imported products, and from new firms in newly deregulated industries. These forces, together with a more probusiness political environment, have led to a significant decline in the economic and political power of unions.

B. Impact of Imperfect Competition on Wages

6. Labor markets are not perfectly competitive in real life. With unions or without them, employers usually have some control over wages. The imperfectly competitive nature of labor markets is seen in the stickiness of wages and the existence of wage structures.

7. Unions affect wages by *(a)* restricting labor supply, *(b)* bargaining for standard rates, *(c)* following policies designed to shift productivity or the demand schedule for labor upward, and *(d)* countering monopoly bargaining power of employers (i.e., of so-called monopsonists).

The different techniques show an important common feature: in order to raise real wages above prevailing market-determined levels, unions generally must prevent entry or competition from nonunion workers. This involves pushing for foreign-trade restrictions, regulation, and occupational licensing.

8. Economic theory states that there is no unique outcome of a collective bargaining session: bilateral monopoly or management-union bargaining (like war or two-person games) has a theoretically indeterminate solution.

9. Unions do appear to have raised the wages of union members relative to nonunionized workers. Studies estimate that, on average, union members have earned wages 7 to 17 percent higher than nonunion members for workers with the same characteristics. This union differential may have eroded in the last decade's period of high unemployment and competition from nonunion labor.

10. While unions may raise the wages of their members, they probably do not increase real wages or labor's share for an entire nation. They are likely to increase unemployment among union members who would prefer to wait for recall from layoff of their high-paid job rather than move or take a low-paying job in another industry. And for a nation with inflexible prices, too high real wages may induce classical unemployment.

CONCEPTS FOR REVIEW

AFL-CIO
business vs. political unionism
Wagner and Taft-Hartley Acts, NLRB
collective bargaining agreement
standard wage rates
featherbedding
four ways unions raise wages

unions as monopolies
monopsony
control of entry by unions
effect of unions on real wages of union
  members, of nation
wait and classical unemployment

QUESTIONS FOR DISCUSSION

1. Discuss the economic structure of unions. How are unions able to exercise monopoly power?

2. Describe the swing of the pendulum in the attitude of legislature and courts toward organized labor before and after the Wagner Act.

3. Should the police have the right to strike? Coal workers? Soldiers? Everyone? Anyone?

4. Unions favor minimum-wage laws that apply mostly to the poorer, unorganized workers. Using Chapter 28's concept of discrimination in segmented markets, would less or more union labor be demanded with a higher minimum wage? Might the poor and unskilled be hurt—be priced out of the market—by a minimum wage that is set too high?

5. Collective bargaining contains both cooperative and antagonistic elements. List the elements of a contract that might be cooperative. Also list the antagonistic ones. Does the existence of cooperative elements in labor-management agreements suggest a reason why compulsory arbitration of labor contracts by outside arbitrators might not always be a good solution?

6. Labor unions are the major entities in the economy that are exempt from antitrust laws. Review antitrust legislation in Chapter 25. Review this chapter's discussion of how labor unions became exempt. What are the effects of the exemption? Do you think the exemption is justified?

7. Explain, both in words and using supply and demand, the impact of each of the following upon the wages and employment in the affected labor market:

(a) Upon union bricklayers: the bricklayers' union negotiated a lower standard work rule from 26 bricks per hour to 20 bricks per hour.

(b) Upon airline pilots: after the deregulation of the airlines, nonunion airlines like Continental or People Express increased their market share by 20 percent.

(c) Upon M.D.s: many states begin to allow nurse practitioners to be given more of physicians' responsibilities.

(d) Upon American autoworkers: Japan agreed to limit its exports of automobiles to the United States.

(e) Upon steelworkers: through negotiations, the United Steelworkers raised its members' standard wage rates 30 percent relative to the average manufacturing worker.

8. If you were a union leader, would you focus your attention on: *(a)* an industry with many small firms with easy entry and exit; *(b)* a regulated monopolist, with highly inelastic demand for its output, that is allowed to use average cost pricing? Justify your reasoning in terms of the ways that unions raise wages.

9. In addition to formal unions, there are many "near-unions," which have the effect of limiting employment to their members. For example, state licensure limits the practice of medicine and law to those who pass stringent examinations; some universities limit faculty appointment to those who have a Ph.D.; social workers in some states are pressing for limitation of practice to those who have state certificates; doctors have attempted to limit the medical practice of chiropractors.

Using supply and demand analysis, explain how such practices tend to limit supply and raise the prices of the affected professions. What are the conditions on the demand curve that would lead to such limitations increasing the incomes of the affected professions?

10. Advanced problem: J. K. Galbraith wrote of the "countervailing power" of unions. The reasoning might have been as follows. In a company town, an employer had monopsony buying power over unorganized labor. The outcome is shown as wage rate *mm* in Figure 29-6.

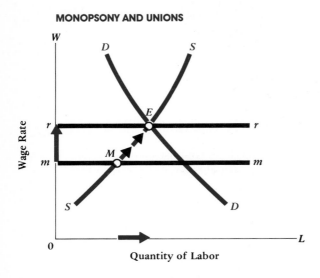

MONOPSONY AND UNIONS

Figure 29-6

Question A: Why would a profit-minded monopsony employer be at point *M* rather than at the competitive equilibrium point *E*?

Now let a union step in. It raises the standard wage rate from *m* to *r* by collective bargaining.

Question B: What has happened to the efficiency of the outcome? What has happened to employment and real wages? Does this analysis suggest conditions in which Galbraith's theory of countervailing power is likely to be valid or invalid?

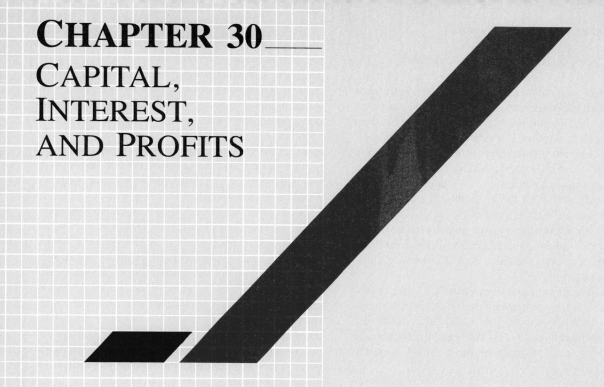

CHAPTER 30
CAPITAL, INTEREST, AND PROFITS

You can have your cake and eat it too:
Lend it out at interest.

Anonymous

PREVIOUS CHAPTERS have analyzed the determination of the rents on land and the wages of labor. This chapter turns to the third broad factor of production, capital. Capital (or capital goods) consists of durable goods that are both produced and used as inputs in the productive process—items like factories and trucks and roads and computers and inventories. A complete understanding of any modern economy, whether it be capitalist or socialist or communist, requires an appreciation of the role of capital in economic growth.

Capital theory is one of the deeper subjects in microeconomics—but many of the basic ideas can be visualized using the elementary tools of supply and demand. In developing the central concepts in capital theory, the main part of this chapter analyzes interest, profits, and production over time. The appendix then presents certain special topics of capital theory in more detail.

CONCEPTS IN CAPITAL THEORY

Economic analysis traditionally divides factors of production into three categories: land, labor, and capital. The first two of these are called *primary* factors of production—where "primary" means "original" factors that are available before production takes place. To them we add a produced factor of production, capital or capital goods.

Capital consists of those durable produced goods that are in turn used as productive inputs for further production. Some capital goods might last a few years while others might last for decades. But the essential property of a capital good is that it is both an input and an output.

There are three major categories of capital goods: structures (such as factories and residences), equipment (consumer durable goods like automobiles and producer durable equipment like machine tools), and inventories (such as groceries on the shelf or cars in dealers' lots).

Rentals on Capital Goods

Capital goods are bought and sold in capital-goods markets. For example, IBM sells capital goods to businesses in the form of mainframe computers—these computers are used by firms to help improve the efficiency of their payroll systems or production management.

Most capital goods are owned by the firm that uses them. Some capital goods, however, are rented out by their owners for short or long periods. Payments for the temporary use of capital goods are called *rentals*. An apartment that is owned by Ms. Landlord might be rented out for a year to a student, with the monthly payment of $200 constituting a rental.

Rate of Return on Capital Goods

One of the most important tasks of any economy, business, or household is to decide how to allocate its capital across different possible investments. Should the United States invest in steel mills or in computers? Should IBM build a new plant to produce microcomputers or add to its productive capacity in mainframe processors? Should the Valdez family, hoping to improve its accounting records, put its dollars in an IBM personal computer or buy an Apple or a Leading Edge? All these questions involve costly investments, spending money today that might yield handsome dividends in the future.

In deciding upon the best investment, we need a measure for that yield or return on capital. One important measure is the **rate of return on capital,** which denotes the net dollar return per year for every dollar of invested capital.

Let's consider an example of a rental car company. Ugly Duckling Rental Company buys a used Ford for $10,000 and rents it out for $2500 per year. After calculating all expenses (maintenance, insurance, depreciation, etc.), and ignoring any change in car prices, Ugly Duckling earns a net rental of $1200 each year.[1] We then say that the rate of return on the Ford was 12 percent per year (= $1200 ÷ $10,000). Note also that the rate of return is a pure number per unit of time. That is, it has the dimensions of (dollars/dollars) per period of time and is usually calculated as percent per year.

You might be considering different investments: rental cars, oil wells, apartments, computer disks, and so forth. Your financial advisers tell you that you do not have sufficient cash to invest in everything, so how can you decide which ones to invest in?

One common approach is to compare the rates of return on capital on the different projects. For each one, you first calculate the dollar cost of the capital good. Then estimate the annual dollar receipts or rentals yielded by the asset. The ratio of the annual rental to the dollar cost is the rate of return on capital: it tells you the amount of money you get back for every dollar invested, measured as dollars per year per dollar of investment.

The rate of return on capital is the annual net return (rentals less expenses) per dollar of invested capital. It is a pure number—percent per year.

Of Wine, Trees, and Drills Here are some examples of rates of return on investments:

- I buy grape juice for $10 and a year later sell it as

---

[1] Depreciation is an estimate of the loss in dollar value of a capital good due to obsolescence or wear and tear during a period of time.

wine for $11. If there are no other expenses, the rate of return on this investment is $1/$10, or 10 percent per year.

■ I plant a pine tree with labor cost of $100 paid in advance. At the end of 25 years the grown tree sells for $430. The rate of return on this capital project is then 330 percent per quarter-century, which, a calculator will show, is equivalent to a return of 6 percent per year.

■ I buy a $20,000 piece of oil-drilling equipment. For 10 years it earns annual rentals of $30,000, but I incur annual expenses of $26,000 for fuel, insurance, and depreciation. What is the rate of return on the drill? It is the same as the annual percentage yield of an investment of $20,000 which pays $4000 per year for 10 years and then self-destructs. Interest tables show this drill's yield to be 15 percent per year.

Profits as Return on Capital Where would you look to find the return on capital in the American economy? Generally, when companies own capital, the return is included in business profits. *Profits* are a residual income item equal to total revenues minus total costs. When you own shares in corporate capital, you get your return as your part of the overall profits of the firm. While the return has a different name and is more risky than many other investments, it is nonetheless a return on capital and has the dimensions of dollars of earnings per year per dollar invested. Business profits are the largest part of the return on capital in the U.S. economy today.

We will further examine the nature of profit at the end of this chapter.

Financial Assets and Interest Rates

We have spoken so far of capital goods like automobiles. But where do the resources needed to produce capital come from? Someone must be *saving* to provide funds for buying the capital goods. Someone must be abstaining from current consumption, thereby releasing resources needed to produce new capital goods. In a complex modern economy, with a sophisticated financial system like that of the United States, households and firms channel funds into capital goods by saving money in various financial assets.

People buy bonds and stocks; they put money in savings accounts; they put money away for retirement in their pension funds. All these are vehicles that carry funds from savers to the firms or people who actually buy capital goods.

But people do not save for nothing. They lend money in the market for funds. What is the "price of funds" or the return on financial assets? It is the *interest rate,* or the annual return on borrowed funds.

Examples abound. When you put your money in a time deposit at a commercial bank, you might receive an 8 percent interest rate. This means that if you deposit $1000 on January 1, 1990, you will end up with $1080 on January 1, 1991.

You will usually see interest rates quoted as *x* percent per year. This means that the interest would be paid at that rate if the sum were borrowed for an entire year; for shorter or longer periods, the interest payment is adjusted proportionately.

Interest comes in many guises. There are long-term and short-term interest rates, depending on the length of the loan or the bond; there are fixed interest-rate loans and variable interest-rate loans; there are interest rates on super-safe bonds (like U.S. government securities) and there are interest rates on highly risky "junk bonds."

To summarize: Households and other savers provide financial resources or funds to those who want to purchase physical capital goods. The rate of interest represents the price that a bank or other financial intermediary pays a lender for the use of the money for a period of time and interest rates are quoted as a certain percent yield per year.

Present Value of Assets

We have seen that capital goods are durable assets that produce a stream of rentals or receipts over time, much as a fruit tree produces a series of harvests. If you owned an apartment building, you would collect a series of rental payments over the life of the building.

But say you became weary of tending the building and decided to sell the capital good. To determine a fair price for the building, you would be interested in determining the value today of the entire stream of future income. The value of that stream is called the

present value of the capital asset. The present value is obtained by calculating how much money invested today would be needed, at the going interest rate, to generate exactly the same stream of receipts as the asset under consideration.

Let's start with a very simple example. Let's say somebody offers to sell you a bottle of wine that matures in exactly 1 year and will then be worth exactly $11. Assuming the market interest rate is 10 percent per year, what is the present value of the wine—that is, what should you pay for the wine today? Pay exactly $10, for $10 invested today at the market interest rate of 10 percent will be worth $11 in 1 year, and that is just what the wine will be worth.

Present-Value Formula We can provide an exact formula for calculating present value for a perpetuity (an asset that lasts forever, like land) that will pay you $N every year from now to eternity. What is its present value *(V)* if the interest rate is *i* percent per year?

To answer this, find the amount of money invested today that would yield exactly $N each year. The answer is simply:

$$V = \frac{\$N}{i}$$

where *V* = the present value of the land

$N = permanent annual receipts

i = interest rate in decimal terms (e.g., 0.05, or $\frac{5}{100}$, for 5 percent per year)

Put differently, if the interest rate is always 5 percent per year, then an asset yielding a constant stream of income will sell for exactly 20 (= 1 ÷ $\frac{5}{100}$) times its annual income. In this case, what would be the present value of a perpetuity yielding $100 every year? At a 5 percent interest rate its present value would be $2000 (= $100 ÷ 0.05).[2]

Note how important is the role played by the interest rate in determining the market value of assets. When the interest rate drops from a high to a low level, the present value of existing machines, land, bonds, stocks, or any other assets yielding a stream of

future returns must rise considerably. Thus in our example of the last paragraph, if the interest rate fell from 5 percent per year to 2 percent, the present value of the land yielding $100 per year would rise from $2000 to $5000. There may, then, be a large impact on people's wealth when interest rates move sharply, as they often have in the last few years.

Review

Let's review quickly the terms we have learned before turning to apply them:

- The economy today has accumulated large stocks of *capital,* or capital goods. These are the machines, buildings, and inventories that dot the landscape.

- The annual dollar receipts on capital are called *rentals.* When we divide the net receipts (rentals less costs) by the dollar value of the capital generating the rentals, we obtain the *rate of return on capital* (measured in percent per year). NOTE: These must be *net* receipts, after appropriate allowance for expenses such as depreciation of assets has been subtracted from *gross* rentals.

- Capital is financed by savers who lend *funds,* getting financial assets in return. The dollar yield on these financial assets is the *interest rate,* measured in percent per year.

- *Profits* are a residual income item, equal to total revenues minus total costs. For large corporations that own their own capital, business profits are the earnings after payment of wages, rents, and other direct factor costs.

- Capital goods and financial assets generate a stream of income over time. This stream can be converted to a *present value,* i.e., a value that the stream of income would be worth today. This conversion is made by asking what quantity of dollars today would be just sufficient to generate the asset's stream of income at going market interest rates.

THEORY OF CAPITAL

Now that we have surveyed the major concepts in capital theory, we turn to an analysis of the *classical*

---

[2]The appendix to this chapter deals at greater length with the concepts and measurement of present value.

theory of capital. This approach was developed about a century ago by the Austrian economist E. V. Böhm-Bawerk, the Swede Knut Wicksell, and Irving Fisher in the United States.

Roundaboutness

As we saw in our introduction to capital in Chapter 3, investing in capital goods involves indirect or roundabout production. Instead of catching fish with our hands, we find it ultimately more worthwhile first to build nets and boats—and then to use the nets and boats to catch many more fish than we could by hand.

Put differently, we frequently forgo present consumption to increase future consumption. Fewer fish caught today frees up labor for making nets to catch many more fish tomorrow. Society thus invests, or abstains from present consumption, and by waiting obtains a yield or return on that investment. In the most general sense, this yield—more future consumption in return for forgone present consumption—is the return on capital.

To see this, imagine two islands exactly alike. Each has exactly the same amount of labor and land. Island A uses these primary factors directly to produce consumption goods like food and clothing; it uses no produced capital goods at all. Island B, on the other hand, for a preliminary period sacrifices current consumption; it uses some of its land and labor to produce capital goods, such as plows, shovels, and looms. After this preliminary period of sacrificing current consumption pleasures in the interest of net capital formation, B ends up with a varied stock of capital goods.

Figure 30-1 shows the way that Island B forges ahead of A. For each island, measure the amount of consumption per person that can be enjoyed while keeping up the existing capital stock. Because of its thrift, Island B, using roundabout, capital-intensive methods of production, will enjoy more future consumption than Island A. B gets more than 100 units of future consumption goods for its initial sacrifice of 100 units of present consumption.

We conclude that investment takes place because it allows an economy that sacrifices present consumption to get more consumption in the future.

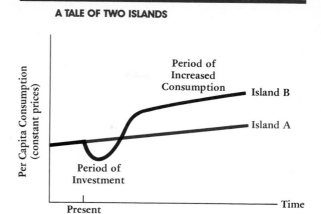

A TALE OF TWO ISLANDS

Figure 30-1   Investments today yield consumption tomorrow

Two islands begin with equal endowments of land and labor. Spendthrift Island A invests nothing and shows a modest growth in per capita consumption. Thrifty Island B devotes an initial period to investment, forgoing consumption, and then enjoys the harvest of much higher consumption in the future.

Diminishing Returns and the Demand for Capital

But what happens as society invests in more and more capital goods? As a nation transfers more and more of its consumption toward capital accumulation? As production becomes more and more roundabout or indirect?

The answer is that we would expect the law of diminishing returns to set in. As we add more fishing boats or nets or power plants or steel mills or chemical factories or computers or trucks, the extra product or return on even more roundabout production begins to fall. The first few fishing boats yield many fish, but too many fishing boats simply deplete the fish stock. Eventually, as capital is accumulated, the rate of return on the investments would fall from, say, 20 percent per year to 10 percent or even to 2 percent.

Unless offset by technological change, therefore, rapid investment would produce diminishing returns, which would drive down the rate of return on investment. But then, why have rates of return on capital not fallen markedly over the course of the last 150 years, even though our capital stocks have grown manyfold? Because innovation and technological change have created profitable new opportunities as rapidly as past investment has annihilated them.

Determination of Interest and the Return on Capital

What determines the return on capital and the level of interest rates? We can now provide the classical explanation based on the supply of and demand for capital.

Households *supply* funds for investment by their accumulation of saving over time (that is, by abstaining from current consumption). In the long run, people may decide to supply more saving if the return on their saving is higher. At the same time, firms and other entities *demand* capital goods—in the form of trucks, buildings, and inventories—to combine with labor, land, and other inputs. In the end, firms' demand for capital is driven by their desire to make profits by producing goods.

Or as Yale's great Irving Fisher put the matter at the beginning of this century:

> Supply-and-demand determination of the amount of capital and return on capital is determined by interaction between (1) people's *impatience* to consume now rather than accumulate more capital goods for future consumption (perhaps for old-age retirement or for that proverbial rainy day); and (2) *investment opportunities* that yield higher or lower returns to such accumulated capital.

A Riskless World To understand how interest rates and the return on capital are determined, consider an idealized world without risk, monopoly, or inflation. A profit-maximizing firm, when deciding whether to undertake an investment, will always compare its cost of funds with the rate of return on capital.[3] If the rate of return is higher than the market interest rate at which the firm can borrow funds, it will undertake the investment. If the interest rate is higher than the rate of return on investment, the firm will decline to invest.

---

[3]An example of the way that firms alter their investment choices at different interest rates is provided in Chapter 7.

Where will this process end up? Eventually, firms will undertake all investments whose returns are higher than the market interest rate. Hence, the equilibrium is reached in our idealized world when competition among firms beats down the return on investment to the level of the market interest rate.

Hence, in a world free of risk, inflation, and monopoly, the competitive rate of return on capital would be equal to the market interest rate.

Note that the market rate of interest has two functions: it rations out society's scarce supply of capital goods into the uses that have the highest rates of return; and it induces people to sacrifice current consumption and add to the stock of capital.

Graphical Analysis of the Return on Capital

We can illustrate capital theory using supply-and-demand diagrams. In doing so, we must drastically simplify economic conditions—concentrating on an elementary case in which all physical capital goods are alike. In addition, we consider a stationary economy in which there is no population growth or technological change.

Figure 30-2 illustrates how the interest rate is determined. Curve *DD* shows the demand curve for the stock of capital; it shows the relationship between the quantity of capital demanded and the rate of return on capital. Where does the demand for capital come from? Remember how the demand for labor was formed from the marginal productivity curve for labor. Similarly, the demand for capital is a "derived demand"—derived ultimately from the *marginal product of capital,* that is, from the extra output yielded by additions to the capital stock.

Diminishing Returns We see that the law of diminishing returns applies to capital as well as to other factors. This is shown by the fact that the demand-for-capital curve is downward-sloping. When capital is very scarce, there are some very profitable roundabout projects that yield 15 percent per year or more. Gradually, as capital is accumulated and the community has exploited all the 15 percent projects, with total labor and land fixed, diminishing returns to capital has set in. The community must then invest in 12

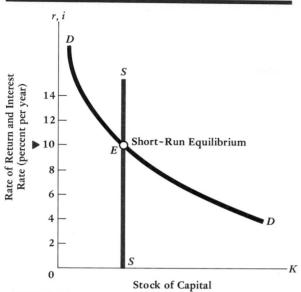

Figure 30-2   Short-run determination of interest and returns

In the short run, the economy has inherited a given stock of capital from the past, shown as the vertical *SS* supply-of-capital schedule. Intersection of the short-run supply with the demand-for-capital schedule determines the short-run return on capital, and the short-run real interest rate, at 10 percent per year.

and 10 percent projects as it moves down the demand-for-capital curve.

Short-Run Equilibrium

We can now see how the supply and demand interact. In Figure 30-2, past investment has bequeathed a given stock of capital, shown as the vertical short-run supply curve, *SS*. Firms will demand capital goods in a manner shown by the downward-sloping demand curve, *DD*.

At the intersection of supply and demand, at point *E*, the amount of capital is just rationed out to the demanding firms. At this short-run equilibrium, firms are willing to pay 10 percent a year to borrow funds to buy capital goods. At that point, the lenders of funds are satisfied to receive exactly 10 percent a year on their supplies of capital.

Thus, in our simple riskless world, the rate of return on capital exactly equals the market interest rate.

Any higher interest rate would find firms unwilling to borrow for their investments; any lower interest rate would find firms clamoring for the too scarce capital. Only at the equilibrium 10 percent rate are supply and demand equilibrated.

But the equilibrium at *E* is sustained only for the short run. Why? Because, even though capital is scarce enough to keep the economy temporarily at *E*, people want to go on saving. Figure 30-3 shows how interest rates are determined in the long run. The long-run supply of capital or wealth, shown as $S_L S_L$ in Figure 30-3, slopes upward to indicate that people are willing to supply more funds at higher real interest rates. At an interest rate of 10 percent, the long-run supply of wealth or capital exceeds the demand for capital at *E*. People thus desire to accumulate more capital, i.e., to continue saving. This means that net capital formation is taking place at point *E*. So each year, the capital stock is a little higher as net investment occurs. As time passes, the community moves slowly down the *DD* curve as shown by the black arrows in Figure 30-3.

The March toward Equilibrium

We move rightward down the *DD* curve because positive investment means that the capital stock is increasing; the short-run supply curve is consequently being pushed further and further to the right each year. You can actually see a series of very thin short-run supply-of-capital curves in Figure 30-3—*S*, *S'*, *S''*, *S'''*, ... These curves show how the short-run supply of capital marches to the right with capital accumulation.

Why do the rate of return and interest rate move downward? Because of the law of diminishing returns. As capital increases, while other things such as labor, land, and technical knowledge remain unchanged, the rate of return on the increased stock of capital goods falls to ever-lower levels.

Long-Term Equilibrium

Where does long-run equilibrium occur? It comes at *E'* in Figure 30-3, the intersection of the long-run supply of capital (shown as $S_L S_L$) with the demand for capital. The long-run equilibrium is attained when the interest rate has fallen to the point where the capital stock held by firms has expanded so as to match the amount of funds or financial capital that people desire to supply. At that

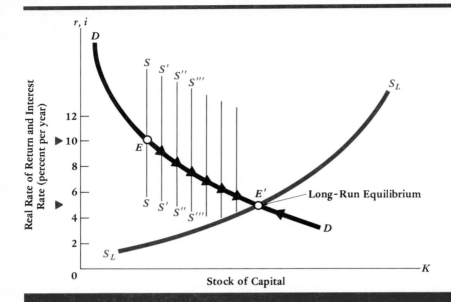

Figure 30-3   Long-run equilibration of the supply of and demand for capital

In the long run, society can accumulate capital, so the supply curve is no longer vertical. As here pictured, the supply of wealth is responsive to higher interest rates. At the original short-run equilibrium at *E* there is net investment, so the economy moves down the *DD* demand curve as shown by the black arrows. Long-run equilibrium comes at *E'*, where net saving ceases.

point, net saving and net capital accumulation are zero.

When net saving is zero, the capital stock is no longer growing; the vertical short-run supply curve no longer shifts rightward. The long-run equilibrium interest rate and rate of return on capital come at the point where the value of financial assets that people want to hold in the long run exactly matches the amount of capital the firms want to hold at that interest rate.[4]

■   ■   ■

We can now summarize the results of the classical view of interest and the return on capital.

There are two forces that drive the accumulation of capital and its return. First, the demand for capital is grounded in the fact that indirect or roundabout production processes are productive; by abstaining from consumption today, society can raise consumption in the future. Second, people must be willing to abstain from consumption; they must be willing to accumulate financial assets, lending funds to firms who will make the productive investments in roundabout productive processes.

These two forces of technology and impatience are brought into balance by the interest rate, which ensures that the society's accumulation of capital just matches the amount that people are willing to hold back from consumption in the form of saving.

SOME MAJOR QUALIFICATIONS

Now our main task is done. But the classical capital theory needs some amplifications and qualifications.

Technological Disturbance

Real life does not remain unchanged while the economy proceeds to accumulate capital and travel down the road of diminishing returns. Inventions and discoveries are constantly being made. Such technological changes will often raise the return on capital and thereby affect equilibrium interest rates. Historical studies suggest that, for America and the West gener-

[4]More advanced and realistic cases are considered in the appendix and in later chapters. More specifically, see the appendix's Fig. 30A-1 for a further discussion of interest determination, including Irving Fisher's illuminating analysis. Chapter 36 considers the process of economic growth, in which both population and technology are changing over time.

ally, the tendency toward falling interest rates via diminishing returns has been just about canceled out by inventions and technological progress.

Some economists (such as Joseph Schumpeter) have likened the investment process to a plucked violin string: In a world of unchanging technology, the string gradually comes to rest as capital accumulation drives down returns on capital. But before the economy has settled into a steady state, an outside event or invention comes along to pluck the string and set the forces of investment into motion again.

Uncertainty and Expectations

Our exposition of capital theory has proceeded without a discussion of uncertainty in the investment decision. This is a serious oversimplification. In real life no one has a crystal ball to read the future. All evaluations of capital and all investment decisions, resting as they do on estimates of future earnings, must necessarily be guesses—accurate guesses based on much thought and information in some cases, wild guesses in other cases, but in every case uncertain guesses. Each day we wake up to learn that our expectations were not quite accurate and have to be revised. Each night we go to bed realizing that the next morning will have some surprises for us.

How does the presence of uncertainty affect capital theory? Recall that we carried out our classical analysis assuming that there were no risks. But what, in this troubled world, is safe? Generally, people treat loans to the U.S. federal government as the safest of risks. It is hard to think of a situation short of nuclear holocaust in which the government could not pay off its obligations.

But almost any other loan or investment has an element of risk. Machines break down; an oil well may turn out to be a dry hole; your favorite computer company may go belly up. So unless you leave your money in 3-month Treasury bills, you must face up to the inherent riskiness of your investment.

Investors are generally averse to holding risky assets. They would rather hold an asset that is sure to yield them 10 percent than an asset that is equally likely to yield 0 or 20 percent. Thus, you must offer an extra return, or *risk premium,* to get them to hold risky investments.

For example, raising cattle involves risks due to weather, while production of telephones does not. Suppose that investments in service industries are riskless and the normal return for such riskless investments is 10 percent per year. By contrast, owning cattle is a highly risky investment—because of bad weather, disease, and other factors you could with equal chances double your money or lose half of it. Your average return in cattle is then 25 percent per year.[5] The extra 15 percent return, over and above the riskless 10 percent return, is a risk premium required to coax cattle ranchers to endure the extra risks and sleepless nights in such an uncertain business.

In summary, the high rates of return on risky assets or ventures include risk premiums that investors require before they will hold such risky investments.

Real vs. Nominal Interest Rates

We have up to now banished inflation from the picture. But in a world of changing prices we need to correct interest rates for the changes in the monetary yardstick caused by inflation.

Recall that interest rates are measured in dollar terms and not in terms of trees or fish or wine. Interest is the yield on an investment measured in dollars per year per dollar of capital. But dollars can become distorted yardsticks. The price of fish, trees, wine, and other goods changes from year to year—these days the overall level of prices tends to rise, showing inflation. Thus we need to derive a *real* return on capital, a genuine measure of the quantity of goods we get tomorrow for goods forgone today. In short, we need to correct money yields and interest rates for inflation to obtain real interest rates.

As an example, say that you obtain a 10 percent nominal or money yield on your investment, obtaining $110 next year for $100 invested this year. Over the course of the year, however, prices have risen 6 percent. In real terms, that is, in terms of the amount of goods you could buy, your real yield is not 10 percent but $10 - 6 = 4$ percent. In other words, if

---

[5]The average, or expected value, of the return is equal to the return in each state weighted by the probability of that state's occurring. Since in one state the return is 100 percent and in the other minus 50 percent, with each state having probability of one-half, the expected return is $\frac{1}{2}(100) + \frac{1}{2}(-50) = 25$ percent.

you were to lend 100 market baskets of goods today, you could obtain only 104 market baskets of goods next year.

Thus, during inflationary periods, we must use real interest rates, not money or nominal interest rates, to calculate the true yield on investments. The *real interest rate* is the nominal interest rate less the rate of inflation.

The difference between real and nominal interest rates is most dramatic during periods of high inflation. During the inflationary period of 1979–1980, nominal interest rates in the United States soared to 12 percent per year. After inflation was subtracted, however, these proved to be real interest rates of around zero. This difference shows the importance of keeping in mind the distinction between real and nominal returns when making investments. (The recent history of real and nominal interest rates is shown in Figure 12-3, page 264.[6])

Macroeconomic Shocks and Policies[7]

Perhaps the most significant shortcoming in the classical theory of capital is its neglect of modern macroeconomic theory. Changes in the level of real income and output profoundly affect the demand for investment and the supply of savings. The interaction between aggregate spending and the level of saving and investment was analyzed thoroughly in the macroeconomic chapters, especially Chapters 7, 8, and 17. We showed there how investment and saving would be affected by the level of income and of output. Moreover, that analysis indicated that macroeconomic policies (such as the level of taxation or the rate of growth of the money supply) could change the national savings and investment rates.

The possibility of shifts in capital's supply and demand schedules, arising from shifting levels of GNP, is absent from the classical theory. Many classical economists were unaware of this possibility because they held that chronic unemployment was impossible and that output would not fluctuate. They didn't always know why they believed full employ-

ment was inevitable. But they did hold to Say's Law that "supply always creates its own demand: general overproduction is an impossibility."

Today, mainstream macroeconomic theory holds otherwise. We see that saving and investment respond not only to interest rates, but also to the levels of output and income. A deep and prolonged depression can leave a country with a smaller supply of capital—thus lowering potential GNP and raising real interest rates.

The economic policies of the 1980s illustrate the way that macroeconomic policies can affect the accumulation of capital. As a result of tax cuts, a defense buildup, and other policy measures, the United States found itself saddled with high federal budget deficits and unusually high real interest rates. This policy effectively shifted Figure 30-3's supply-of-capital schedule to the left. Real interest rates rose while the net accumulation of domestic and foreign capital dropped sharply. At decade's end, the United States inherited a smaller stock of capital and lower potential output than it would have enjoyed with a macroeconomic policy that produced lower real interest rates.[8]

Many economists and public officials call for a reversal of the current policy stance—arguing that the nation would benefit from a policy that would increase the aggregate supply of capital by lowering the amount of government dissaving. While not questioning the importance of the goals, others tend to discount the long-run costs of public deficits, questioning whether in fact any major shift in the supply of capital has occurred. Such debates are a reminder that the need to forge policies affecting the nation's saving and investment—moving the capital stock and interest rates in desired directions—remains one of the most sobering tasks of governments today.

PROFITS

In addition to wages, interest, and rent, economists often talk about a fourth category of income called profits. What are profits? How do they differ from interest and the returns on capital more generally?

---

[6]A further discussion of the determination of real interest rates is provided in Chapter 12.
[7]This section can most profitably be read after the macroeconomic tools of Parts Two and Three have been mastered.

[8]The impact of such policies is analyzed along with the burden of the public debt in Chapter 17.

In this section we will look carefully at the definition of profits, then explore different sources of profit income.

Reported Profit Statistics

When statisticians calculate profits, what do they usually include? This issue was discussed in detail in Chapter 6's analysis of national-income accounts and in Chapter 20's appendix on firm accounting, but let's review the definition here.

Profits are defined as the difference between total revenues and total costs. Thus, start with total revenues from sales. Subtract all expenses (wages, salaries, rents, materials, interest, excise taxes, and the rest). What is left over is the residual called profits.[9]

The profit figures reported in the national-income accounts are limited to profits of corporations. In 1987, corporate profits before taxes were $310 billion. Companies paid $134 billion in taxes, distributed $96 billion in dividends to shareholders, and retained the balance.

How large are corporate profits? In the United States in the 1980s, corporate profits after taxes are significantly below 8 percent of total GNP. The rate of return on American corporate capital (defined as profits divided by the current dollar cost of capital goods) has averaged about 8 percent per year in the last 15 years. This return is well above the real interest rate on safe assets, which averaged around 4 percent per year over the last decade. Why is the rate of profit so high? Or is it? We now turn to this issue.

Determinants of Profits

What determines profits? The following list provides some of the explanations that have been given over the years.

---

[9]In analyzing profits, it is important to distinguish *business profits* from *economic profits*. Business profits are the residual income, equal to sales less costs, measured by accountants. Business profits include an implicit return on the capital owned by firms. By economic profits we mean the earnings after all costs—both money and implicit—are subtracted. In large corporations, therefore, economic profits would equal business profits less an implicit return on the capital owned by the firm along with any other costs (such as unpaid management time) not fully compensated at market prices.

1. *Profits as implicit returns.* To the economist, business profits are a hodgepodge of different elements. Obviously, part of reported business profits is merely the return to the owners of the firm for their own labor or their own invested funds, i.e., for factors of production supplied by them.

For example, part may be the return to the personal work provided by the owners of the firm—by the doctor or lawyer who works in a small professional corporation. Part may be the rent return to self-owned natural resources. In large corporations, most profits are the implicit return on invested capital. (Recall Chapter 22's discussion of implicit costs and opportunity costs.)

Thus some of what is ordinarily called profit is really nothing but rentals, rents, and wages under different names. *Implicit* rentals, *implicit* rent, and *implicit* wages are the names economists give to the earnings on factors that the firm itself owns.

2. *Profits as reward for risk bearing.* If the future were perfectly certain, there would be no opportunity for a bright young person to come along with a revolutionary innovation. Everything would already be known. A half-century ago, Chicago economist Frank Knight suggested that all true profit is linked with uncertainty or imperfect information. By this he meant that, once the implicit returns—the pure interest on capital, implicit wages on managerial labor, and so forth—are subtracted, what remains is a reward for a willingness to undertake investments with uncertain returns.

Default In examining this theory, modern economics specifies three kinds of risks that lead to profits. The first kind of risk that leads to profits is *default risk*. Because there is a possibility that an enterprise will go into bankruptcy—this even applies to giants like First Republic Bank (Texas), the Penn Central Railroad, or the Public Service Company of New Hampshire—the return on invested capital must include a premium for default. This default premium should add enough to the return on capital to cover the risk of an enterprise going bankrupt.

Pure Risk A second kind of risk that must be considered in profit calculations is the *pure risk* (or statistical risk) associated with different investments. A company may have good and bad years, just as a farmer may face good or bad weather. Even though two firms may have the same average net revenues year in and year out, one may show highly volatile earnings (like a steel or auto firm) while another may be very stable (like telephone or beverage firms). Investors are averse to risky situations; when they are unable to insure or diversify their risks, investors require a risk premium added to returns to offset their risk aversion.

How does the presence of uninsurable risk relate to profits? Profits are the most volatile component of national income—indeed, they turned negative during the Great Depression. Moreover, investors cannot buy an insurance policy to protect themselves from the fluctuations of corporate profits. As a result, corporate capital must contain a significant risk premium to attract investors. How large is this risk premium? We do not know for sure, and the premium probably changes over time. Recent studies suggest, however, that between 3 and 6 percentage points of the annual return on corporate capital is a risk premium that serves as a reward for the willingness to bear risks.

Innovation A third kind of risk contributing to profits is the *reward for innovation and enterprise*. Let us subtract from measured profits the implicit return for owners' labor, capital, and land. Subtract a default premium. Even subtract an estimate of the reward for risk bearing. Would there be nothing left?

In a world of perfect competition and no economic evolution, there would be no further profits at all. Let's see why. Firms might still be reporting some profit figures to the press, but under these ideal conditions, the implicit returns on the labor and property supplied by owners, along with the reward for risk bearing, would exactly swallow up all the profits reported. Why? Because owners would be getting for their owned factors and risk incurred exactly what those services were worth in competitive markets.

In other words, free entry of numerous competitors would, in a static world of perfect knowledge, bring price down to cost. The only sustainable profits in a static world would be the competitive wages, rentals, rent, and return for risk bearing.

We do not live in such a dreamworld. In the world

as we know it, there is a chance for someone with a brand-new idea to invent a revolutionary medicine or computer or software program—to promote a new product or find a way to lower costs of an old one. Let's call the person who does any of these things an *innovator* or *entrepreneur*. We can identify "innovational profits" as the temporary excess return to innovators or entrepreneurs.

What do we mean by "innovators"? Such people should not be confused with managers, who are the people who run large and small companies but do not own a significant part of the equity. These managers are talented at oiling the wheels of industry; like any other factor of production, they move into those jobs where they will receive the highest prices.

Innovators are different. They are always trying to carry out new activities. Here is the person with vision, originality, and daring. Although not always the inventor of the new process or device, the innovator is the one who successfully introduces it. Maxwell developed the scientific theory of radio waves, Hertz discovered them experimentally, but Marconi and Sarnoff made them commercially profitable. Carlson invented xerography, made a personal fortune, and launched a great firm, Xerox. The 1980s saw innovators like Steven Jobs launch Apple Computers, Dr. Herbert Boyer help found Genentech, and Mitch Kapor become wealthy through spreadsheets he developed at Lotus Corporation. For every one of these successful innovators, others fail on the road to fame and fortune. Many try; few succeed.

Every time there is a successful innovation, a temporary pool of monopoly is created. For a short time, innovational profits are earned. These profit earnings are temporary and are soon competed out of existence by rivals and imitators. But just as one source of innovational profits is disappearing, another is being born. So these innovational profits will continue to exist.

3. Profits as monopoly returns. Innovational profits shade off into our last category. Many people are downright suspicious of profit. The critics of profits do not see them as implicit rentals or return for risk bearing in competitive markets. Their image of the profiteer is more likely that of someone with a penchant for sly arithmetic who somehow exploits the rest of the community. What critics have in mind is a third quite different meaning of profit: *profit as the earnings of monopoly*.

How are monopoly profits generated? Once a market departs appreciably from perfect competition, firms in the industry can earn extra or super-normal profits by raising prices. If you are the sole owner of a valuable patent or if you have acquired the sole franchise to lease cable television in a city, you can raise prices above marginal cost, restrict supply, and earn monopoly profits on your investment.

What does this all add up to? It means that part of what is called profit is the return to market or monopoly power.

Awash with Profits?

This brief survey of different theories reveals many sources of profits. Which is most important? No definitive answer can be given. But given all the ways that firms can extract profits in a modern economy— implicit returns; rewards for default, risk bearing, and innovation; and returns to monopoly power—we would expect to see the coffers of American corporations awash in cash.

Surprisingly, however, they are not. Over the last 15 years, corporations earned a modest rate of return on their investments—only about 8 percent in real terms. And for the last decade the ratio of the market value of corporations (i.e., the value of their stocks and bonds) to the value of their land, plant, and equipment (called "Tobin's Q") has been substantially less than 1. On average, from 1980 to 1987 every $100 worth of corporate tangible assets sold for only $76 on stock and bond markets.

This low level of corporate profitability is a puzzle to many observers. It does suggest, however, that some of the arguments about extraordinary monopoly power of large companies are exaggerated, and that the forces of competition among American corporations are powerful.

The Next Steps

With this discussion of the return on capital, our treatment of pricing of factors of production is completed. We are now ready to move on to Part Six, where we will weigh the major issues of design of an economic system: How do the prices and quantities in all the markets interact in a general equilibrium of markets? How does government intervene to change the allocation of resources? What are the possible conflicts between equity and efficiency? What are the alternative economic systems and how do they compare with modern mixed capitalism?

SUMMARY

1. Recall the definitions of key terms given on page 720:
   - *Capital goods:* durable produced goods used for further production
   - *Rentals:* net annual dollar returns on capital goods
   - *Rate of return on capital:* net annual receipts on capital divided by dollar value of capital (measured as percent per year)
   - *Interest rate:* yield on funds, also measured in percent per year
   - *Present value:* value today of a stream of future returns generated by an asset
   - *Profits:* a residual income item equal to revenues minus costs

2. In addition to the two primary factors of production, labor and land, capital is a third factor, a produced good that is used in further production. In the most general sense, capital is roundabout production, postponing consumption today by producing buildings or equipment, which increase consumption in the future. It is a technological fact that roundabout production yields a positive rate of return.

3. Assets generate streams of income in future periods. By calculating the present

value, we can convert the stream of returns into a single value today. This is done by asking what amount of dollars today will generate the stream of future returns, when invested at the market interest rate.

4. Interest is a device that serves two functions in the economy. It provides an incentive for people to save and accumulate wealth—for retirement, for a rainy day, for heirs. But the interest rate is also a rationing device; it allows society to select only those investment projects with the highest rates of return. However, as more and more capital is accumulated, and as the law of diminishing returns sets in, the rate of return on capital and the interest rate will be beaten down by competition. As interest rates fall, this is a signal to society to adopt projects that have lower rates of return.

5. Saving and investment represent waiting for future consumption rather than consuming today. Such thrift interacts with the net productivity of capital to determine interest rates, the rate of return on capital, and the capital stock. The funds or financial assets needed to purchase capital are provided by households who are willing to sacrifice consumption today in return for larger consumption tomorrow. The demand for capital comes from firms that have a variety of investment projects. In long-run equilibrium, the interest rate is thus determined by the net productivity of capital and the extent to which households are willing to postpone consumption today for consumption tomorrow.

6. Important qualifications of classical capital theory include the following: Lack of perfect foresight means that capital's return is highly volatile as expectations, technology, and income levels change. Also, classical theory ignores deviations from full-employment output. Finally, to get the real rate of interest, one must subtract the rate of inflation from the nominal rate of interest.

7. Profits are revenues less costs. Reported business profits are chiefly corporate earnings. Economically, we must distinguish three different categories. Perhaps the most important source is profits as an implicit return. Firms generally own many of their own nonlabor factors of production—land, capital, patents. Sometimes, the labor earnings of the owners are included in profits. In these cases, the implicit return on unpaid or owned land, labor, or capital is part of profits.

8. A second source of profits arises from uncertainty—associated with the extra return to cover default, the return to cover uninsurable risks, and the profits earned by entrepreneurs who introduce new products or innovations.

9. Finally, profits may result from firms exercising monopoly power—on their patents, from special privileges, or due to regulation.

CONCEPTS FOR REVIEW

capital, funds
rate of return on capital, interest rate
indirect, roundabout production methods
present value by $V = \$N/i$
implicit rewards to factors in profits
real vs. nominal interest rate

twin elements in interest determination:
  returns to roundaboutness and
  impatience
uncertainty and profits: default risk,
  return to risk bearing, innovation

QUESTIONS FOR DISCUSSION

1. Give some examples of efficient roundabout processes; of "produced" or "intermediate" outputs that serve in their turn as inputs.

2. Contrast three "prices" of capital: *(a)* rental of a capital good, *(b)* rate of return on a capital good, and *(c)* interest rate. Give an example of each.

3. Using the supply-and-demand analysis of interest, explain how each of the following would affect interest rates in the classical analysis:

(a) An innovation that increased the marginal product of capital at each level of capital.

(b) A decrease in the desired wealthholdings of households.

(c) A 50 percent tax on the return on capital.

4. Define "implicit" factor earnings. Contrast with other profit concepts.

5. Consider each of the following sources of reported profits. Decide into which of the three categories (or subcategories) of profits each falls:

(a) The profit earned by a medical corporation in a perfectly competitive industry.

(b) The profits earned by a firm that has relatively little invested capital but is extremely cyclical.

(c) A firm that is making $100,000 a year on a new video game, but whose competitors are expected to invade the field and wipe out the profits.

(d) The profit of a farm that owns a prime vineyard in California.

6. Looking back to Figures 30-2 and 30-3, review how the economy moved from a short-run equilibrium interest rate at 10 percent per year to the long-run equilibrium. Now explain what would occur in both the long run and the short run when innovations shifted *up* the demand-for-capital curve. What would happen if the government debt became very large and part of people's supply of capital was reduced by their holdings of government debt?

7. Explain the rule for calculating present discounted value of a perpetual income stream. At 5 percent, what is the worth of a perpetuity paying $100 per year? Paying $200 per year? Paying $*N* per year? At 6 or 8 percent, what is the worth of a perpetuity paying $100 per year? What does doubling of the interest rate do to the capitalized value of a perpetuity—say, a perpetual bond?

8. Many states offer a "Million Dollar Prize" in their lotteries. These generally pay $50,000 per year for 20 years. What would be the present value of a "consol" lottery that pays you and your heirs $50,000 each year forever if the interest rate is 8 percent per year? Explain why its present value is not infinite. Can you see why the "Million Dollar Prize" is worth less than the consol lottery? (For those who wish to estimate the exact value of the "Million Dollar Prize," consult the formula given in the appendix.)

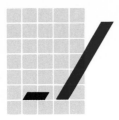

APPENDIX: 30

Advanced Analysis of Capital and Interest

Capital theory and the theory of interest form one of the most exciting topics of microeconomics. They underpin discussions of modern finance theory and monetary economics, and they constitute a central core for understanding the growth of nations. In this appendix we elaborate upon this chapter's introductory analysis.

PRODUCTIVITY OR IMPATIENCE?

Some people like to find a single cause for everything, and they ask: "Is interest caused by the productivity of capital? Or by the fact that savers must be paid for the unpleasant task of 'abstinence' or 'waiting'? Which is more important, opportunity to invest or impatience to spend?"

Our previous argument shows this is a false antithesis. *Both* factors operate to determine the time path of interest rates: the impatience to spend, or the tendency to prefer the present to the future, limits the accumulation of capital, and the productivity of capital tells us what interest rate can be earned for any given level of the capital stock.

Just as both blades of a scissors are needed to cut—so that you cannot say that one blade rather than the other is doing the actual work—both factors, impatience and productivity, interact to determine the behavior of the interest rate.

Determination of the Interest Rate

Can our account of interest determination avoid the use of Figure 30-2's and Figure 30-3's simplifying concept of a stock of homogeneous capital? Yes.

Thus, we may work with various different physical capital goods and processes, being careful never to add their heterogeneous units together and never forgetting that it is machines and not dollars which enter into physical production functions. Advanced treatises can show rigorously how an equilibrium interest-rate pattern can be defined in such a heterogeneous world.

The key to an understanding of the deeper theory of interest rates lies in the *Fisher diagram* in Figure 30A-1, named after the American economist who first used this approach. We start with a production-possibility frontier showing how consumption today can be transformed into consumption tomorrow (this is the black curve in Figure 30A-1). We also put on this same diagram a set of indifference curves, like those described in Chapter 19. These indifference curves reflect the struggle of impatience—showing how society or representative individuals trade off consumption today against consumption tomorrow.

In this more complete analysis, the interest rate is determined by the equilibrium at *E* in Figure 30A-1. At that point, the *PPF* is tangent to the highest indifference curve.

FISHER'S INTEREST DIAGRAM

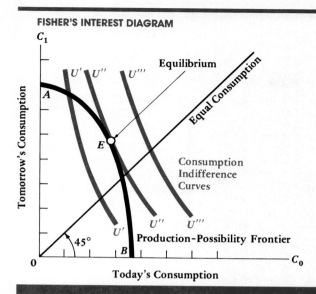

Figure 30A-1 Impatience and technology interact to determine interest rate

The red indifference curves represent society's or the representative individual's degree of impatience about tomorrow's consumption. The black production-possibility frontier shows how the economy can transform consumption today into consumption tomorrow. At the tangential equilibrium of point E, satisfaction is maximized. The slopes of the two curves at E are equal to minus $(1 + r)$, where r is the real interest rate, or the return in consumption goods tomorrow for a sacrifice of consumption goods today.

The slope of both curves at point E (changing the sign from negative to positive) represents how many future goods are equivalent to today's consumption goods—the slope is $(1 + r)$ where r is the real interest rate. This is then a more complete theory of interest determination. But note that we have not had to make any mention of capital goods or mobility of factors or homogeneity of capital. We simply need the *PPF* and indifference curves to derive the market interest rate.

We thus derive the following fundamental proposition about the theory of interest:

Society can exchange present consumption goods for future consumption goods at a tradeoff rate depicted by the real rate of interest.

Figure 30A-1 makes an additional interesting point. Note that there is no need for the intersection at E to show a slope greater than 1. It could be relatively flat. But because the slope is equal to $(1 + r)$—where r is the real interest rate—if for some reason the tangency came with a slope less than 1, *the real interest rate would be negative*. Such an outcome might result if people were very patient or if the *PPF* showed no net return to sacrificing current consumption.

PRESENT VALUE EXTENDED

The chapter presented a simple case of present value for perpetual income streams. We here consider the more general case of the present value of an asset with income streams that vary over time, as would be the case for the yield on a computer that tended to become obsolete as it got older.

The main thing to remember about present value is that future payments are worth

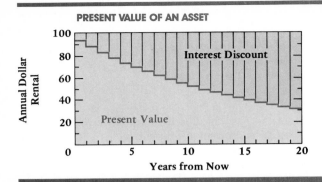

Figure 30A-2   Present value of an asset

The present value of a machine giving net annual rentals of $100 for 20 years (with the interest rate prescribed at 6 percent) is shown by the lower red area. The upper gray area has been discounted away. (Show that raising the interest rate depresses the market price of an asset such as a machine or bond. It does so by enlarging the gray discount area subtracted.)

less than current payments—they are *discounted* relative to the present. Why are future payments discounted? Because a positive interest rate means that today's dollars will become more valuable in the future; hence future payments are worth less now, just as a distant building looks tiny.

The interest rate produces a similar shrinking of time perspective. Even if I knew you would pay $1 million to my heirs 999 years from now, I would be foolish to pay you as much as a cent today. To see why, let us review the arithmetic of discounting.

At 6 percent interest I can set aside about 94 cents today, and it will grow to $1 after 1 year. Hence, the present value of $1 payable a year from now is today only 94 cents (or, to be exact, $100/1.06 = 94\frac{36}{106}$ cents).[1] The present discounted value of $1 payable in 2 years' time is about 89 cents, or $\$1/(1.06)^2$.

More generally, to arrive at any asset's present value, let each dollar stand on its own feet. Evaluate the present value of each part of the stream of future receipts, giving due allowance for the discounting required by its payment date. Then simply add together all these separate present values. This summation will represent the asset's present value.

The exact formula for present value is the following: Let i be the one-period market interest rate. Further, let N_1 be the net receipts (positive or negative) in period 1, N_2 the net receipts in period 2, N_t the net receipts in period t, and so forth. Then a stream of payments $(N_1, N_2, \ldots, N_t, \ldots)$ will have the present value, V, given by the following formula:

$$V = \frac{N_1}{1 + i} + \frac{N_2}{(1 + i)^2} + \cdots + \frac{N_t}{(1 + i)^t} + \cdots$$

[1]The general rule for present values is the following: To figure out the value today of $1 payable t years from now, ask yourself how much must be invested today at compound interest to grow into $1 at the end of t years. We know that at 6 percent compound interest any principal grows in t years proportionally to $(1 + 0.06)^t$. Hence, we need only invert this expression to arrive at the final answer: the present value of $1 payable t years from now is only $\$1/(1 + 0.06)^t$. What if the interest rate were 8 percent? Replace 0.06 by 0.08 and recalculate.

For example, assume that the interest rate is 10 percent per year, and that I am to receive $100 next year and $470 in 3 years. The present value of this stream is:

$$V = \frac{100}{(1.10)^1} + \frac{470}{(1.10)^3} = 444.03$$

Figure 30A-2 shows this graphically for a machine that earns steady net annual rentals of $100 over a 20-year period and has no scrap value at the end. Its present value is not $2000, but only $1147. Note how much the later dollar earnings are scaled down or discounted because of our time perspective. The total area remaining after discounting (the red shaded area) represents the total of the machine's present value—the value today of the stream of all future incomes.

Acting to Maximize Present Value

Our formula tells us how to calculate the value of any asset once we know what the earnings on that asset are. But note that an asset's future receipts usually depend on our business decisions: Shall we use a truck 8 or 9 years? Overhaul it once a month or once a year? Replace it with a cheap, nondurable truck or an expensive, durable one?

There is one rule that gives correct answers to all investment decisions: Calculate the present value resulting from each possible decision. Then always act so as to achieve the maximum present value. That way you will have more wealth, to spend whenever and however you like.

SUMMARY TO APPENDIX

1. Investment opportunities (to swap present consumption for future consumption goods) interact with people's subjective time preferences (about how much to consume today or in the future) to determine the interest rate. As in all markets, *both* supply and demand factors interact.

2. Avoiding the device of homogeneous stock of physical capital, we can still have a complete interest theory using the Fisher diagram. The real interest rate equals the terms of trade at which we can get next year's consumption goods for today's sacrificed goods—106 meals next year for 100 given up today means a 6 percent annual real interest rate.

3. The formula for calculating the present value of an asset can be extended when receipts are neither constant nor perpetual. Each dollar payable t years from now is worth only its "present value" *(V)* of $1/(1 + i)^t$. So for *any* net receipt stream $(N_1, N_2, \ldots, N_t, \ldots)$ where N_t is the dollar value of receipts t years in the future, we have:

$$V = \frac{N_1}{1 + i} + \frac{N_2}{(1 + i)^2} + \cdots + \frac{N_t}{(1 + i)^t} + \cdots$$

CONCEPTS FOR REVIEW

abstinence, impatience, waiting
opportunity to invest
present value
Fisher diagram
tradeoff between consumption today
  and consumption tomorrow

QUESTIONS FOR DISCUSSION

1. After nuclear weapons were developed, people's time preference for present over future consumption increased. After having learned that my uncle will bequeath me a fortune a decade from now, my time preference changed in the same way. Was this rational? Thinking of a steak dinner tonight, I offer you $15 on next Monday for $10 now. Is this irrational?

2. Two communities have the same technological production functions. Why might they show different patterns of nominal interest rates? (HINTS: impatience; wealth inequality; inflation.)

3. Give reasons why lower real interest rates might increase investment.

4. Recall the algebraic formula for a convergent geometric progression:

$$1 + K + K^2 + \cdots = \frac{1}{1 - K}$$

for any fraction K less than 1. If you set $K = 1/(1 + i)$, can you verify the present-value formula for a permanent income stream, $V = \$N/i$? Provide an alternative proof using common-sense economics.

5. Advanced problem: If a doubling of i halves the present value of a perpetuity, can you show that the stream of income shown in Figure 30A-2 will *less* than halve in present value? (HINT: The perpetuity has a rectangle that goes on forever, with its red area getting less and less. The finite stream in Figure 30A-2 lacks this infinite tail off to the right. The early years' receipts hardly change in value at all, since, say, 0.96 is not much changed when it becomes 0.92. So the average change in all the red area is less than that for the perpetuity.) By similar reasoning, establish the rule: Interest changes have their biggest effects on the value and prices of *long-term* bonds; their least effects are on the prices of *short-term* bonds—whose principal will be repaid soon and is therefore barely affected by any discounting.

6. Advanced problem: Figure 30A-1 showed that real interest rates can be negative in certain conditions. (Review the reasons.) But the nominal interest rate can never be negative (Why not? Because storable currency bears a zero nominal interest rate, and other assets cannot have yields below super-safe currency.) How could an economy ever generate an equilibrium with negative real interest rates? (As a hint, consider the impact of inflation.)

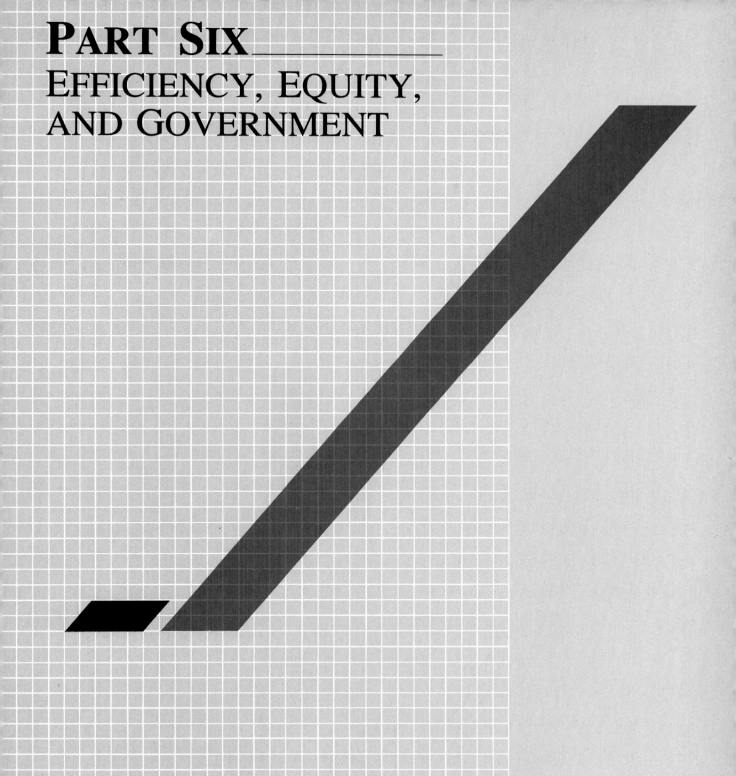

PART SIX

EFFICIENCY, EQUITY, AND GOVERNMENT

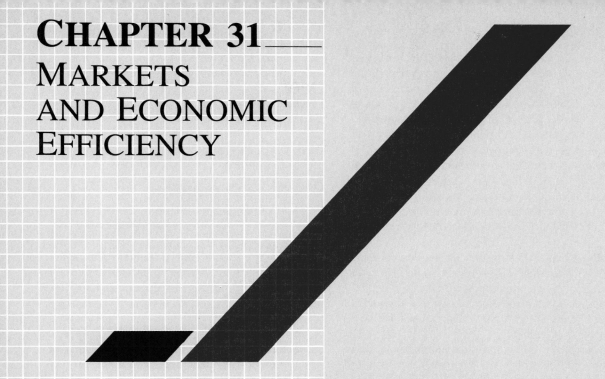

CHAPTER 31
MARKETS AND ECONOMIC EFFICIENCY

The delicate, invisible web you wove . . .

T. S. Eliot

OUR STUDY OF microeconomics has afforded us a better understanding of how technological opportunities interact with consumer tastes to determine millions of prices and quantities in a market economy. The market mechanism sends out factor-price signals in the form of rents of land and wages of labor along with the prices of a multitude of commodities like guitars, textbooks, and concrete. We have seen that perfectly competitive markets have the remarkable efficiency properties of the invisible hand but that monopolistic influences can drive up prices and restrict production below the most efficient level.

In the chapters of Part Six that follow, we take a more careful look at the efficiency and equity of market economies. We begin in this chapter by examining how the different markets interact to reach an overall or general equilibrium of all the products and factors together. It may be true that individual competitive markets display the invisible-hand property of efficiency, but does this hold when all the markets are put together? And what are the failures that sometimes prey on market economies, leading to business cycles, monopolies, and environmental pollution?

This chapter's review of the general functioning of markets is followed by two chapters investigating the role of government in an advanced industrialized economy. There we examine the nature of public choice, study the patterns of government taxation and expenditure systems, and explore the ways government can cope with spillovers or externalities.

Chapter 34 then analyzes further a key potential flaw in the invisible hand—poverty in today's society. In addition, it examines the conflict between efficiency and equity, asking how much output a nation must sacrifice if it wishes to reduce or eradicate poverty.

Finally, Chapter 35 turns to the biggest economic issue of all—alternative economic systems. Here we tour different views on the most efficient and equitable economic system and then review how alternative systems like the Soviet Union are organized and how they perform in reality.

This part, then, is devoted to the thorniest and most controversial issues of microeconomics: How well or badly does the market perform? How much should government intervene in economic activity? How much, if any, should the state tax the rich to boost the living standards of the poor? Are socialism and communism superior to capitalism as ways of organizing economic activity?

Modern positive economics cannot, by itself, provide crisp "yeses" or "nos" to these perennial questions. But it can throw light on some factual and analytical questions that must be answered before reasoned value judgments can resolve such enduring political dilemmas.

GENERAL EQUILIBRIUM AND THE INVISIBLE-HAND THEORY

Let's review the path we have followed in understanding the behavior of individual markets:

1. Competitive supply and demand operate to determine price and quantity in a single market.

2. The marginal utilities of different goods lie behind the market demand curves.

3. The marginal costs of different commodities lie behind their competitive supply curves.

4. Firms calculate marginal costs of products and marginal revenue products of factors and then choose inputs and outputs so as to maximize profits.

5. These marginal revenue products, summed for all firms, provide the derived demands for the factors of production.

6. These derived demands for land, labor, or capital goods interact with their market supplies to determine factor prices such as rent, wages, rentals, and interest rates.

7. The factor prices and quantities determine incomes, which then close the circle back to steps 1 and 2 by helping to determine the demand for different commodities.

Each of these relationships is the subject of *partial-equilibrium analysis,* which analyzes the behavior of a single market, household, or firm, taking the behavior of other markets, individuals, or firms as given. In this chapter we examine the properties of a *general equilibrium,* which analyzes the simultaneous interaction of all households, firms, and markets.

Simultaneous General Equilibrium

Notice how, in the listing of the seven steps above, each follows from the preceding one—from step 1 to step 2 and then step 3—until finally we come to step 7. In the textbook chapters, they follow in almost the same order.

But in real life, which comes first? Is there any order and sequence which determines prices in single markets on Monday, evaluates consumer preferences on Tuesday, and reckons business costs on Wednesday and marginal products on Thursday? Obviously not. All these processes are going on at one and the same time.

That is not all. These different processes do not go on independently, each in its own little groove, careful not to get in the way of the other. All the processes of supply and demand, of cost and preference, of factor productivity and demand are really different aspects of one vast, simultaneous, interdependent process.

Thus, the supply curve for wheat is the result of the cost calculations, of the production considerations, and of the wage, rent, and interest determinations. Actually, you can take any one of the seven steps in the outline and draw arrows connecting it causally with every other step.

Nor is the interdependence limited to the seven steps outlined above. There are as well linkages across different products. Thus wheat supply and demand, and wheatland supply and demand, depend upon tastes for cornbread and oatmeal; upon how many people want to sacrifice traditional food purchases for innovations like VCRs or personal computers; and upon the demand for fertile land as biologists develop new, genetically engineered strains of corn.

A Circular Flow Like an invisible web, the many input and output markets are connected in an interdependent system we call a general equilibrium. Figure 31-1 depicts the general structure of the web of a general equilibrium.[1] The outer loops show the demands and supplies of goods and factors. We speak here not of a single good or factor but of all different products (corn, medical care, concerts, pizzas, etc.), which are made by a vast array of factors of production (cornland, surgeons, studios, trucks, etc.).

Each good or factor is exchanged in a market, and the equilibrium of supply and demand determines the price and quantity of the item. That marriage of supply and demand is occurring thousands of times every day, for all kinds of commodities from albums to zinc. Note in Figure 31-1 that the upper loop carries the supplies and demands for products, while the lower loop matches the supplies and demands for factors of production. See how consumers demand products and supply factors; indeed, consumers buy their consumption goods with the incomes they earn from the factors they supply. Similarly, businesses buy factors and supply products, paying out factor incomes and profits with the revenues from the products that businesses sell.

Thus we see a logical structure behind the millions of prices and outputs: (1) households with supplies of factors and preferences for products interact with (2) firms that, guided by the desire to maximize profits, transform factors bought from households into products sold to households. The logical structure of a general-equilibrium system is complete.

Properties of a Competitive General Equilibrium

In earlier chapters, using partial-equilibrium analysis, we analyzed the behavior of individual competitive markets for factors and products. We now consider, using general-equilibrium analysis, the properties of an ensemble of competitive markets. Such a general equilibrium contains thousands of different kinds of labor, machines, and land, and these serve as inputs to produce dozens of different kinds of computers, hundreds of different specifications of automobiles, thousands of different items of clothing, and so on.

What are the characteristics of a general economic equilibrium? Do the efficiency properties of perfect competition in individual markets carry over to all markets together? Do prices play an important role as indicators of scarcity for the overall economy? Do the equations of supply and demand actually lead to an equilibrium, or is the overall outcome indeterminate? These questions are addressed by general-equilibrium analysis.

In this section we proceed as follows. We first describe the assumptions of our general economic equilibrium. We then describe in a summary fashion the properties of a general equilibrium. Next, in a more technical section, we sketch the properties of a general equilibrium in more detail. Finally, we show why a perfectly competitive general equilibrium will be efficient.

The Basic Principles To simplify the analysis, we will consider an economy in which all markets are

---

[1]This picture is similar to two earlier ones. Figure 3-1 showed a simplified version of the circular flow, while the aggregate flow of dollars was presented in our discussion of national-output accounting in Chapter 6's Figure 6-2.

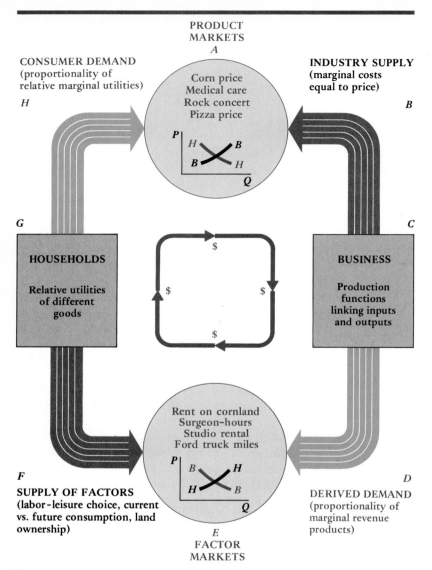

PRODUCT
MARKETS
A

CONSUMER DEMAND
(proportionality of
relative marginal utilities)

H

Corn price
Medical care
Rock concert
Pizza price

INDUSTRY SUPPLY
(marginal costs
equal to price)

B

G

HOUSEHOLDS

**Relative utilities
of different
goods**

BUSINESS

**Production
functions
linking inputs
and outputs**

C

F

SUPPLY OF FACTORS
(labor-leisure choice, current
vs. future consumption, land
ownership)

Rent on cornland
Surgeon-hours
Studio rental
Ford truck miles

E
FACTOR
MARKETS

DERIVED DEMAND
(proportionality of
marginal revenue
products)

D

**Figure 31-1   General-equilibrium pricing determines *what, how,* and
for whom for the overall economy**

The circular flow of economic life is described by the general economic
equilibrium. Observe how profit-maximizing firms and utility-maximizing households
interact in product markets at *A* and factor markets at *E*, determining the prices
and quantities of each. Note that the flow of money inside the figure moves in the
opposite direction from the physical flow of goods and factors.

perfectly competitive and are subject to the relentless competition of many buyers and sellers. Firms maximize profits, while consumers choose their most preferred market baskets of goods. Further, there are no natural monopolies—rather, each good is produced under conditions of constant or decreasing returns to scale. No pollution, entry-limiting regulation, or monopolistic labor unions mar the competitive landscape. Finally, each price, whether for an input or output, moves flexibly enough to equilibrate supply and demand at all times. Such an economy, were it to exist, would be one in which Adam Smith's invisible hand could rule without any impediment from imperfect competition.

For this economy, we can describe consumer and producer behavior and then show how they dovetail to produce an overall equilibrium. First, consumers will allocate their incomes across different goods so as to maximize their satisfactions. They thereby choose goods such that the marginal utilities per dollar of expenditure are equal for the last unit of each commodity. Put differently, for each individual consumer, each dollar's worth of consumer purchase has exactly the same marginal utility.

What are the conditions for the profit maximization of producers? In product markets, each firm will set its output level so that the marginal cost of production equals the price of the good. Since this is the case for every good and every firm, it follows that the competitive market price of each good reflects the marginal cost of that good to society as a whole. (A second set of conditions concerns inputs; consideration of these conditions will be postponed to the fuller treatment in the next section.)

Putting together the conditions for perfectly competitive producers and consumers, we see that, for each consumer, the marginal utility per dollar of consumption equals that good's social cost of production. Further, the marginal utility per dollar of consumption of each good is equal to the social cost of every other good.

This is the central result of general-equilibrium theory: that the marginal utilities per dollar of all consumer goods are all equal and are also equal to the social costs of production of those goods.

A simple example will clarify this result. Say that we have two individuals, Ms. Smith and Mr. Ricardo, and two kinds of goods, corn and clothing. Under consumer equilibrium, and with an appropriate adjustment of her utility scale, Ms. Smith buys corn and clothing until the *MU* per dollar of each good is 1 (Smith) util. Similarly, we could adjust the utility scale of Mr. Ricardo so that his purchases are also each worth 1 (Ricardo) util per dollar of spending. The corn and clothing producers set their output levels such that price equals marginal cost, so a dollar-bundle of corn will have a marginal cost of production of $1 for each producer, and similarly for clothing. If society were to produce one more dollar-bundle of corn, this would cost society exactly 1 dollar's worth of scarce resources of labor, land, and capital.

Putting these conditions together, we see that each extra dollar of consumption, by either Smith or Ricardo, yields exactly 1 extra util of satisfaction, whether that extra spending is on clothing or on food. Similarly, each extra unit of spending will have a marginal or additional cost to society of 1 extra dollar of resources, and this is so whether that extra dollar is spent by Smith or Ricardo or on food or clothing. We see, then, that the general equilibrium of markets ties together the value of purchases to consumers with the economic cost to society so that the satisfaction value of goods to consumers equals the economic cost of goods to society. This linkage of social cost and satisfaction value will play a crucial role in the analysis of allocative efficiency later in this chapter.

Detailed Analysis of General Equilibrium[2]

In this section we will present a more complete analysis of the conditions of general equilibrium for those students who wish to see how our general-equilibrium analysis relates to the partial-equilibrium analysis of Chapters 19 through 23. We have seen in earlier chapters that perfectly competitive markets lead to a number of important results. Before we investigate how those results lead to an efficient allocation of resources, we reiterate the *conditions of a competitive general equilibrium*. These conditions break naturally into two categories corresponding to the upper and

---

[2]The balance of this section is more technical and may be omitted in courses pressed for time.

lower loops of Figure 31-1: those relating to consumers and those relating to production.

1. *Consumer equilibrium.* Our analysis of consumer behavior in Chapter 19 showed that consumers would maximize their utility when choosing among goods by equalizing the marginal utility per dollar of spending. Using this rule, we then see that the ratio of the marginal utilities of two goods, known technically as the "marginal rate of substitution" between the two goods (or $MRS_{1,2}$ for the substitution relation between goods 1 and 2), satisfies the condition:

$$MRS_{1,2} = \frac{MU_1}{MU_2} = \frac{P_1}{P_2}$$

In words, the ratio of marginal utilities of two goods, or the relative satisfactions derived from the two goods, is equal to the ratio of the goods' relative prices. This condition must hold for an individual consumer who buys the two goods in question; further, because all consumers face the same competitive prices, the consumer condition must hold in exactly the same way for all consumers.

2. *Producer equilibrium.* The behavior of profit-maximizing firms leads to an analogous but somewhat more complex set of conditions, as we described in Chapters 21 to 23. In those chapters we found that competitive firms choose input and output levels as follows:

(a) The first and most fundamental *output condition* for producers is that the level of output is set so that the price of each good equals the marginal cost of that good. By rearranging terms in this equation, we then find that

$$\frac{MC_1}{MC_2} = \frac{P_1}{P_2}$$

Putting this equation into words, we say that, in a competitive economy, the ratio of the marginal costs of two final products is equal to their price ratio. The equality holds for all goods that are produced and for all firms that produce these goods. We can also interpret the ratio of marginal costs as the rate at which society can transform one good into another (sometimes the ratio of marginal costs is called the "mar-

ginal rate of transformation of goods'' or the *MRT*). If corn's *MC* is \$1 and a haircut's *MC* is \$10, then, by transferring resources from barbers to farmers, society can transform one haircut into 10 units of corn.

The fundamental point to understand about a competitive economy is that the competitive prices reflect social costs or scarcities. We just noted that the ratio of marginal costs, or the *MRT* between two goods, tells us the rate at which society can substitute or trade off one good for another. But since the price ratio of the two goods equals the *MRT* between the two goods, it follows that relative prices reflect social scarcities under perfect competition. It is just this surprising fact, that competitive prices provide an accurate signal of the relative scarcity of different goods, that demonstrates the validity behind the invisible-hand principle that perfectly competitive markets lead to allocative efficiency.

(b) In addition to the first condition, competition leads to certain relationships concerning input use. We have seen that profit-maximizing firms choose the amount of each input so that the value of its marginal product is equal to its price. Hence

Marginal product of land in good 1
    × price of good 1 = rent on land
Marginal product of land in good 2
    × price of good 2 = rent on land
Marginal product of labor in good 1
    × price of good 1 = wage of labor

And so forth.

These conditions have several important implications. First, because each firm faces the same prices for inputs and output, the marginal product of input A for output X is the same for each firm. Under perfect competition, we will not find that some firms have low values of marginal products of labor while other firms have high ones. All producing competitive firms will have the same values of marginal products of each input.

By rearranging the terms in the above equations, we can see that the ratio of marginal products of inputs is equal to the ratio of their prices:

Marginal product of land in good 1

Marginal product of labor in good 1

$$= \frac{\text{price of land}}{\text{price of labor}}$$

In addition, this condition holds for all firms that use land and labor to produce good 1. Moreover, it holds for all factors of production (capital, oil, unskilled labor, etc.) and for all produced goods.

The importance of this *input condition* comes from the fact that it implies that the ratios of marginal products of factors are the same for all inputs and all firms in all uses. If labor is scarce in America, then all firms will operate with low ratios of land-to-labor marginal product. Moreover, the price ratio of land to labor, the rental-wage ratio, will be low in America, thereby providing a signal to producers to substitute land for labor. For inputs, as for outputs, competitive prices are an accurate index of the economic scarcity of different factors of production.

To summarize, under competitive conditions, with utility-maximizing consumers and profit-maximizing firms, the general-equilibrium conditions provide:

■ that the ratios of marginal utilities of goods for all consumers are equal to the relative prices of those goods;

■ that the ratios of marginal costs of goods produced by firms are equal to the relative prices of those goods;

■ that the relative marginal products of all inputs are equal for all firms and all goods and are equal to those inputs' relative prices.*

PERFECT COMPETITION AND ALLOCATIVE EFFICIENCY

Once a system of competitive markets overcomes the first hurdle of actually solving the *what, how,* and *for whom* issues for an economy, we can next ask how efficiently the system performs. We have repeatedly seen for individual markets—that is, in partial equilibrium—that a competitive market mechanism serves to allocate resources with remarkable efficiency. Does an ensemble of markets in general equilibrium also allocate resources efficiently?

Allocative Efficiency

We encountered the concept of allocative efficiency in Chapter 23. This concept measures the extent to which society is providing consumers the largest possible bundle of commodities, in the desired proportions, given society's endowment of inputs and technology. More precisely, **allocative efficiency** (sometimes also called "Pareto efficiency," or "efficiency" for short) occurs when there is no other reorganization of production or consumption that will increase the satisfaction of one person without reducing the satisfaction of another person. More informally, efficiency means that no one can be made better off without making someone else worse off.

The Utility-Possibility Frontier We have defined efficiency as a state in which the maximum amount of goods and satisfaction is squeezed out of society's resources. This definition sounds very much like the

---

*A careful reader might here ask: "Are you sure that you have *exactly* the right number of equations to solve all the unknown prices and quantities? That they will actually have supply-and-demand equilibria? Is nothing left to chance or to the state?"

Economists have pondered these profound questions for almost a century. Léon Walras, a French economist of the last century, is usually credited with discovery of the theory and equations of general equilibrium. He was, however, unable to provide a rigorous proof that

there is an equilibrium of the competitive system. Only in the middle third of the twentieth century was a complete proof of the existence of a solution given, using high-powered mathematical tools such as topology and set theory, by J. von Neumann, A. Wald, and American Nobel Prize–winning economists Kenneth Arrow and Gerard Debreu. This revolutionary discovery showed that there will always exist at least one set of prices that will exactly balance the supplies and demands for all inputs and outputs—even if there are millions of inputs

and outputs, in many different regions, and even if goods are produced and sold at different times.

But before writing home to announce the final victory of the invisible-hand doctrine, we should pause to consider the stringent assumptions that are used to prove the theorems about the competitive model: no increasing returns anywhere, no externalities, perfectly flexible wages and prices, no uninsurable risks, no monopolies or oligopolies, and other assumptions as well.

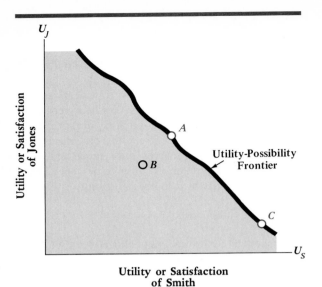

U_J

Utility or Satisfaction of Jones

A

○ *B*

Utility-Possibility Frontier

C

U_S

Utility or Satisfaction of Smith

Figure 31-2   Outcomes on the utility-possibility frontier are efficient

An economy is operating efficiently when no person's satisfaction can be improved without lowering someone else's satisfaction. Efficient points are on the utility-possibility frontier *(UPF)*. Moving from outcome *A* to outcome *C* can improve Smith's position only by hurting Jones; point *A* is therefore efficient. Point *B* is inside the *UPF*; it is thereby inefficient because Jones or Smith or both can be made better off without hurting anyone else.

economy is on a frontier. And indeed it is—the *utility-possibility frontier* (or the *UPF*). This curve shows the outer limit of utilities or satisfactions that an economy can attain. Such a concept is very similar in spirit to the production-possibility frontier. The major difference here is that the *UPF* places utilities or levels of satisfaction on the two axes, as is shown in Figure 31-2.

Note as well that we have drawn the *UPF* as somewhat wavy. This unevenness indicates that we do not have a clear way of measuring or comparing different people's utilities. But it must be emphatically stated that the lack of a precise scale of measurement is completely irrelevant. All that matters here is that a person's level of satisfaction rises as the utility index increases. Because of this positive relation between utility and desired levels of consumption, we are

guaranteed that each person will want to move out as far as possible on his or her utility axis.

Return now to allocative efficiency. This central concept was introduced by Vilfredo Pareto in 1906 and forms the core of modern welfare economics, public-choice theory, and the burgeoning discipline of theoretical political science. An economic outcome is defined as having allocative efficiency (or Pareto efficiency) when it is on the frontier of the utility-possibility curve. Such a Pareto-efficient point is shown at point *A* in Figure 31-2.

Why is point *A* Pareto-efficient? Because there is no feasible economic reorganization that makes anyone better off without making someone else worse off. We can, of course, move to point *C*. Such a move would certainly delight Smith, whose consumption and satisfaction are increased. But Smith's gain comes only at Jones' expense. When all possible gains to Smith must come at Jones' expense, this implies that the economy is on its *UPF* and that the economy is operating efficiently.

Efficiency, Competition, and Welfare Economics

As we examine the relationship between perfect competition and allocative efficiency, we are traveling in the realm of **welfare economics.** This is the general term for the normative analysis of economic systems: for the study of what is right and what is wrong, what is desirable and what is undesirable about the economy's functioning. Welfare economics has nothing to do with the welfare system, which provides income to poor people. Rather it is concerned with the best way to organize economic activity, with the best distribution of income, and with the best tax system. In each case, however, the analysis should rest upon clearly stated value judgments about economic organization, income distribution, or tax policy.

One of the central subjects of welfare economics concerns the efficiency of a perfectly competitive economy. Two centuries ago, Adam Smith proclaimed that, through the workings of the invisible hand, those who pursue their own self-interest would most effectively promote the public welfare. But it took almost two centuries for economists to prove the kernel of truth in Smith's intuition. Today, this result is known as the *first theorem of welfare economics:*

A perfectly competitive, general-equilibrium market system will display allocative efficiency. Such a system has all goods prices equal to marginal costs, all factor prices equal to the value of their marginal products, and contains no externalities. In such an economy, when each producer selfishly maximizes profits and each consumer selfishly maximizes utility, the economy as a whole is efficient in the sense that you cannot make anyone better off without making someone else worse off.

What does this mean? It means that even the most skilled planner or engineer cannot come along with a computer or an ingenious reorganization scheme and find a solution superior to the competitive marketplace; no reorganization can make everyone better off. And this result is true whether the economy has one or two or 2 million competitive markets for goods and factors.

Rationale What is the reason for this most surprising result? Advanced treatises can prove this result rigorously with the use of modern mathematics, but we can easily see the logic using an example.

Suppose some wizard comes forth and says, "Aha, I have found a way of reorganizing the perfectly competitive economy to make everyone better off. Simply give everyone more pizzas and fewer shirts and everyone will be better off."

You would explain that the wizard is *necessarily* sadly mistaken. Suppose the current price of shirts is $15, while the price of pizzas is $5. On the consumer's side, each individual has allocated his or her budget so that the marginal utility per dollar of the last pizza is just one-third that of the last shirt. So consumers would certainly not want to have more pizzas and fewer shirts unless they could get more than three pizzas for each shirt given up.

Can the economy squeeze out more than three pizzas for each forgone shirt? Not if the economy is competitively organized. Under perfect competition, the ratio of the price of shirts to the price of pizzas is the ratio of the marginal costs of the two goods. Hence if their price ratio is $15/$5 = 3, producers can eke out only three more pizzas for each shirt not produced. Indeed, if the production-possibility frontier is bowed

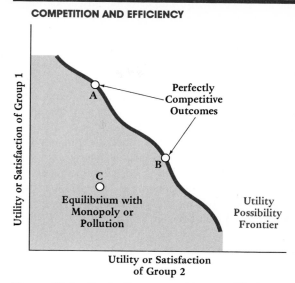

COMPETITION AND EFFICIENCY

Utility or Satisfaction of Group 1 (vertical axis)

A — Perfectly Competitive Outcomes

B

C — Equilibrium with Monopoly or Pollution

Utility Possibility Frontier

Utility or Satisfaction of Group 2 (horizontal axis)

Figure 31-3   Perfectly competitive equilibria are efficient

A fundamental result of general-equilibrium theory is that perfectly competitive economies perform efficiently. Hence all competitive outcomes are on the production-possibility and utility-possibility frontiers. Market failures like monopoly or pollution push the economy inside both frontiers.

out, producers will actually get somewhat less than three pizzas for every shirt forgone.

So we see why our wizard is wrong. Consumers are willing to eat more pizzas and have fewer shirts only if they can improve their satisfactions, which means that they must get more than three pizzas for every shirt forgone. Profit-maximizing producers cannot get more than three pizzas by producing one less shirt. Therefore the proposed reorganization will not improve everybody's economic satisfaction.

The reasoning, of course, extends far beyond pizzas and shirts. With a little thought you can see that it works as well for all consumer goods. With a lot of thought, or with the help of an intermediate textbook, you can even see how it will extend to include reorganizations of inputs and production across firms. The basic point to see is that, because prices serve as signals of economic scarcity for producers and social utility for consumers, a competitive price mechanism allows the maximum output to be produced from a society's resources and technology.

The efficiency of perfect competition is illustrated in Figure 31-3. We have divided the population into two groups, group 1 and group 2, and have shown the satisfaction of the two groups on the two axes. Points *A* and *B* represent alternative competitive equilibria. As perfectly competitive economies, both operate efficiently. By contrast, point *C* shows an economy laboring with much pollution or inefficient monopolies; economy C operates well inside its frontier, with groups 1 and 2 both losing consumption relative to efficiently operating economy B. We see, therefore, that all perfectly competitive economies operate efficiently and are somewhere on their utility-possibility frontiers.[3]

QUALIFICATIONS TO THE INVISIBLE-HAND THEORY

Our discussion has proceeded on the basis of some abstract assumptions: no monopolies, no spillovers or externalities, no unforeseen innovations or disturbances, no government policy failures, and so forth. The perfectly competitive world of the economist is like the frictionless model of the physicist. It is not a picture of the real world as we know it when we step outside the library and rub elbows with real, live, breathing people on the street. Moreover, even if perfect competition ruled everywhere, people still might not be satisfied with the distribution of incomes generated by competition.

Let's review, then, the two qualifications of the

invisible-hand theory—market failures and unacceptable income distribution.

Market Failures

In reality, a pair of market failures spoils the idyllic picture of perfect competition assumed in the invisible-hand theory: imperfect competition and externalities. Issues of imperfect competition have been analyzed in depth in Chapters 24 and 25, while externalities will occupy us in Chapter 32.

The key problem in both sources of market failure is similar: the market outcome is one in which the prices do not reflect true social marginal costs and social marginal utilities.

Monopoly   Say that a firm has a monopoly over a particular market—a patented drug, a local electricity franchise, or a brand name on a soft drink. In these cases it can raise the price of the drug, electricity, or drink above its marginal cost. Consumers buy less of these goods than they would under competition, and wasteful distortions are created. Such distortions are typical of the inefficiencies created by imperfect competition.

Externalities   The other key market failure is externalities. Recall that externalities arise when all the side effects of production or consumption are not included in markets. Thus when a utility pumps sulfurous fumes into the air, neighboring homes suffer property damage and people experience illnesses. But the utility does not pay for these impacts—the sulfur is external to the circular flow of Figure 31-1.

Not all externalities are harmful. There are *positive externalities*, such as those that rise when knowledge is generated. Chester Carlson invented xerography, but he received scant compensation when the world's secretaries and scribes were relieved of billions of hours of drudgery. Inventors are on the whole drastically undercompensated for their work—their incomes are far less than their social marginal products—and society therefore tends to underinvest in inventive activity.

Economics in a Vacuum?   In the last 13 chapters, we have encountered many, many other examples of

[3]The text discussion has described what is known as the "first theorem of welfare economics." In addition, a second theorem of welfare economics is the converse of the first theorem. Consider an economy in which preferences and technology are "regular"—that is, with diminishing marginal utilities of consumption and non-increasing returns in production. Under these and a few other conditions, any efficient allocation of resources can be reached by some perfectly competitive equilibrium. Put differently, if the government wishes to reach some particular efficient outcome, such as point *A* in Figure 31-3, it can do so by redistributing initial incomes (say by lump-sum taxes and transfers) and then allowing the invisible hand to guide the economy to the desired point. In such regular economies, a combination of efficient income redistribution plus competition is enough to reach any efficient allocation of resources.

market failure or breakdown of competition. We have seen that prices are often rigid in contrast to the minute-to-minute flexibility of competitive auction prices seeking their equilibria. We have seen that two people may work in the same city for different wage rates at similar jobs. We have seen how oligopolies and monopolies can restrain quantities to raise prices and profits.

We found that discrimination and segmented labor markets may lead to unequal employment opportunity, generating economic inefficiencies and social inequities. And we have seen how government interferences in markets can lead to unemployment or unavailability of credit or apartment shortages.

After reading this list of qualifications, you might naturally wonder whether they vitiate the whole notion of the efficient invisible hand. When we consider the wide range of actual market failures, should we believe that the real-world economy bears any resemblance to the idealized general-equilibrium analysis of the textbooks?

Taken literally, there is no doubt that a perfect and absolutely efficient competitive mechanism differs markedly from the real-world economy. But in a broader sense, the insights of the competitive theory retain a great deal of validity. Even though engineers know that they can never create a perfect vacuum, they still find the analysis of behavior in a vacuum extremely valuable for throwing light on many complicated problems. So it is with our competitive model. In the long run, many imperfections turn out to be transient as monopolies are eroded by competing technologies. While oversimplified, the competitive model points to many important hypotheses about economic behavior, and these hypotheses appear especially valid in the long run.

Suppose, for example, that an invention cuts the cost of computer-memory devices. Competitive analysis says that the price of such devices will fall and the quantity demanded will rise. Sophisticated students of imperfect competition aver that the real world is not perfectly competitive and that no hard-and-fast conclusions can be drawn. But put your money with the competitive model—betting that prices will fall in the long run—and you will probably end up wealthier than the sophisticated skeptics.

Initial Distribution of Income

But let us for the moment close our eyes to monopolies, pollution, labor unions, and other market failures. Let us ignore unemployment, inflation, and the business cycle. What do ideal competitive markets mean for the distribution of incomes? Is there an invisible hand in the marketplace that ensures that the most deserving people will obtain their necessities? No. In fact, competitive markets do not guarantee that income and consumption will necessarily go to those who are thought most needy or deserving. Rather, the distribution of income and consumption in a market economy reflects initial endowments of inherited talents and wealth along with a variety of factors such as discrimination, effort, health, and luck.

Perfect competition under laissez-faire could lead to massive inequality, to malnourished children who grow up to produce malnourished children, and to the perpetuation of inequality of incomes and wealth for generation after generation. Or, if the initial distribution of wealth, genetic abilities, education, and training happened to be spread quite evenly, perfect competition might lead to a society characterized by near-equality of wages, incomes, and property.

In short, Adam Smith, in the famous passage quoted on page 37, was not wholly justified in asserting that an invisible hand successfully channels individuals who selfishly seek their own interest into promoting the "public interest"—where the public interest is defined to include the socially acceptable distribution of income and property. Smith proved nothing of this kind, nor has any economist since 1776.

A Final Word on Welfare Economics

In Part Six of this book, we will be traveling extensively in the land of welfare economics, confronting some of the major ethical and political issues of modern society. We will consider whether government should intervene in certain markets and whether the tax system should redistribute income from rich to poor or from farm to city. We will continue to apply the results of our analysis of perfect competition, recalling the important results of the great master Adam

Smith along with the refined analyses of his twentieth-century counterparts.

But even Adam Smith cannot have the final word on these controversial problems. For underlying all these issues lie normative assumptions and value judgments about what is good and right and just. What a modern-day Adam Smith does, therefore, is try very hard to keep positive science cleanly separated from normative doctrines. Recall from the very first chapter that we defined positive statements as ones that are confined to description, while normative statements concern what society ought to do.

For the most part in science, scholars discuss what is and what will be under this or that situation. The task of positive description is kept as free as is humanly possible from the taint of wishful thinking and ethical concern about what ought to be. Why? Because scientists are cold-blooded robots? No. Rather, because experience shows that a more accurate job of positive description will be achieved if one tries to be objective.

Birds or Antelopes? Experience also shows that, try as we may, we humans never succeed in separating completely the objective and subjective aspects of a discipline. Indeed, the very choice of what scientists decide to measure, the perspective from which they observe and measure it, and the reactions the observer produces in that which is observed—all these conspire against totally objective analysis and observation. Recall Chapter 1's bird-antelope paradox (page 9) and be warned that one's unconscious attitudes can color one's seemingly objective perceptions.

The citizens of a nation are, of course, mainly interested in the final outcomes, not in the fine points of economic theory or macroeconomic modeling. But citizens are best served by scientists who can give the most accurate description of what is relevant, and of what the consequences of different policy actions will be.

The issues of welfare economics studied in the chapters that follow are highly controversial and subjective ones that cannot be settled within positive science. Conservatives may legitimately interpret the above principles in terms of their version of the good society. Middle-of-the-roaders may do the same for theirs. And radicals may call for small or large reforms of the present structure of a mixed economy by giving their interpretation of fundamental economic laws.

Economic science does not determine the final conclusion. It arms us for the great debate.

SUMMARY

1. Earlier chapters examined the functioning of individual markets—for labor and land, for wheat and baking machines, for final goods such as bread and muffins. But the economic system must reach a *general equilibrium* of all these markets. This general equilibrium of *what, how,* and *for whom* is interrelated in a competitive market by a web of price connections. Households supply factors of production and demand final goods; businesses buy factors of production and transform and sell them as final goods.

2. The general-equilibrium competitive price system is a logically complete one. There is a sufficient number of relationships (i.e., a sufficient number of supply and demand curves) to determine all relative prices and all quantities.

3. Under certain conditions, a competitive general equilibrium will display *allocative efficiency*. Allocative efficiency (sometimes called Pareto efficiency) signifies that no one person can be made better off without someone else being made worse off. In such a situation, the economy is on both its production-possibility frontier and its utility-possibility frontier. But there are severe limits on the conditions under which an efficient competitive equilibrium will be attained: there may be no externalities, no monopolies or economies of scale, and no uninsurable risks. The presence of such imperfections leads to a breakdown of the *price = marginal cost = marginal utility* conditions, and hence to inefficiency.

4. Even if the world were one in which the ideal conditions for efficient perfect competition were to hold, a major reservation about the outcome of competitive laissez-faire would remain: we have no reason to think that the dollar votes under laissez-faire will be justly distributed. The outcome might be one with enormous disparities in income and wealth that persisted for generations. Or, conceivably, the outcome might be one in which there was a virtual equality of outcomes—one that some might even feel to be a dull gray sameness of personal fortunes.

CONCEPTS FOR REVIEW

partial equilibrium vs. general
  equilibrium
allocative (or Pareto) efficiency
utility-possibility frontier *(UPF)*
invisible-hand theory: in Adam Smith
  and in today's general-equilibrium
  theory

qualifications to the invisible-hand
  doctrine: market failures and arbitrary
  distribution of dollar votes
welfare economics
two theorems of welfare economics

QUESTIONS FOR DISCUSSION

1. Summarize how a competitive pricing system solves the three fundamental economic problems. Illustrate the price mechanism for the seven steps (page 742) where the economy produces outputs of food and clothing with inputs of labor and land.

2. List the qualifications to the invisible-hand theory. In terms of the economy as you know it, illustrate each of the qualifications with a real-world example.

3. State carefully the two theorems of welfare economics. How would they apply to the following quotations:

(a) "Perfect competition affords the ideal condition for the distribution of wealth." (Francis Walker, 1892)

(b) "The invisible hand, if it is to be found anywhere, is likely to be found picking the pockets of the poor." (Edward Nell, 1982)

(c) Adam Smith's quotation on the invisible hand (see the beginning of Chapter 3).

(d) "Pareto . . . suggested that competition brought about a state in comparison to which no consumer's satisfaction can be made higher, within the limitations of available resources and technological know-how, without at the same time lowering at least one other consumer's satisfaction level." (Tjalling Koopmans, 1957)

(e) "Perfect competition can achieve anything that can be achieved by socialism."

4. The analysis of efficiency of competitive economies assumes that there is no technological advance by innovations and inventions. Recall the Schumpeterian hypothesis from Chapter 25. How does this elaboration qualify the view of economic efficiency of the competitive mechanism? In a world of rapid potential technological advance, use production-possibility curves to illustrate how in the long run an innovative economy with imperfect competition might produce higher consumption than an efficient but technologically stagnant competitive economy.

5. "You say that the competitive general-equilibrium system is complete, and that there are enough equations to determine economic equilibrium. But it looks like a circular argument to me. Suppose that I say, 'My age, Y, is twice yours, X. Your age, X, is 25 years less than mine.' What a swindle: to know X, I must first know Y; but to know Y, I must first know X!" Show that the logical circle is not circular. The only solution to $Y = 2X$ and $X = Y - 25$ is $X^* = 25$ and $Y^* = 50$. So it is with supply and demand determining wheat's P and Q. And so it is with general equilibrium involving 1 million P's and 1 million Q's. Comment.

6. Advanced problem: "The second theorem of welfare economics (page 750, fn. 3) means that all the debates about socialism vs. capitalism are vacuous. Anything that can be done by ideal, centrally planned socialism can, by the second welfare theorem, be done by competitive markets plus the proper dose of redistributive taxation." Comment on the logic behind this statement. State whether you agree or not and why.

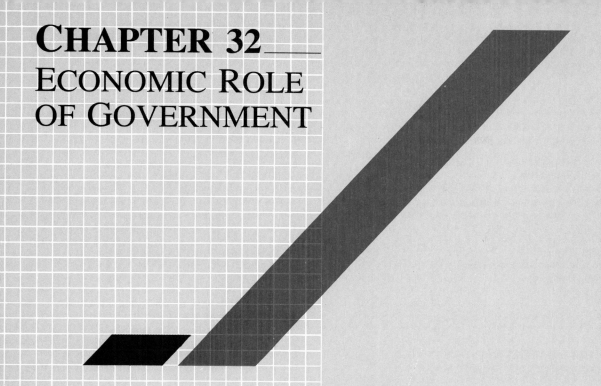

CHAPTER 32___
ECONOMIC ROLE OF GOVERNMENT

Democracy is the recurrent suspicion that more than half the people are right more than half the time.

E. B. White

OVER THE SPAN of the last century, the governments of most advanced economies have steadily increased their control and influence over economic activity. This trend is reflected in the growth of government expenditure and taxation, in the increasing share of national income devoted to transfers and income-support payments, and in the increase in legal and regulatory controls over economic life. Governments have not exercised a continuous encroachment on the private sector; rather, reflecting the cycle of politics, capitalist economies take two steps forward, then one step backward, on the road to greater government involvement. During the most recent era, under the inspiration of political leaders like President Reagan in the United States and Prime Minister Thatcher in Britain, most industrial countries have witnessed a retrenchment in the activities of government during the 1980s.

In this and the next chapter we survey the economics of government activity. This chapter begins with an analysis of the central economic functions performed by governments. It then turns to the topic of public choice, which describes how governments actually choose among the alternatives open to their societies. The final section of the chapter applies the analysis to externalities like pollution. After this chapter's analysis of the economic theory of government's role, the next chapter analyzes taxation and government expenditure.

Of course, the economic role of government cannot be neatly divided up and placed in two chapters. The study of macroeconomics, along with an analysis of how government's monetary and fiscal policies affect overall economic activity, was contained in Parts Two and Three; in those chapters we saw how government could affect unemployment, economic growth, and inflation. And we saw in Parts Four and Five on microeconomics how governments use economic regulation and antitrust policy to control monopoly. But in this chapter, we want to take a more comprehensive look at the norms and realities of government economic policy.

However, be warned at the beginning. The electorate is divided. Some people want to continue expanding the scope of government; others take up the banner of the Reagan revolution and strive to further reduce government's role. Whether you tend to agree with liberals or conservatives, or even if you have not developed your own political philosophy, you will benefit from a cool analysis of factual trends and modern theories.

A. GOVERNMENT'S ROLE IN A MODERN ECONOMY

THE INSTRUMENTS OF GOVERNMENT POLICY

How do governments affect the economy? They cannot have a durable impact by simply exhorting the populace to save more or pollute less. Rather, attaining public-policy objectives requires that governments raise revenues, spend money, or issue regulatory commands over economic activity.

The major instruments with which governments affect economic activity are: (1) *taxes* that reduce private expenditure (such as for automobiles or restaurant food) and thereby make room for public expenditure (on goods like trucks or food for the army); (2) *expenditures* that induce firms or workers to produce certain goods or services, along with *transfers* (like welfare payments) that provide income support; and (3) *regulations* or controls that direct people to perform or desist from certain economic activities. Governments have come to rely on each of these three kinds of instruments increasingly over the last century.

Taxing and Spending

For more than a century, national income and production have been rising. At the same time, in most countries, the trend of governmental expenditure has been rising even faster. Each period of emergency—each war, each depression, each wave of enhanced concern over poverty and inequality—expands the activity of government. But after the urgency has passed, expenditures never seem to go back down to previous levels.

Before World War I, all federal, state, and local government expenditure or taxation combined amounted to little more than one-tenth of our entire national income. During World War II, the war effort compelled government to consume about half the nation's greatly expanded total output. In the 1980s, expenditure of all levels of government in the United States ran around 35 percent of GNP.

Figure 32-1 shows the trend in government taxes and expenditures (for all levels of government in the United States). The rising curves indicate that the shares of taxes and spending have grown steadily upward over the course of this century.

Figure 32-2 shows how government spending as a percent of GNP varies among countries. High-income countries tend to tax and spend a larger fraction of GNP than do poor countries. Can we discern a pattern among wealthy countries? Note that highly productive and efficient countries are not uniformly high-spending or low-spending areas. West Germany—a country whose conservative economic pronouncements have made it the darling of those longing for

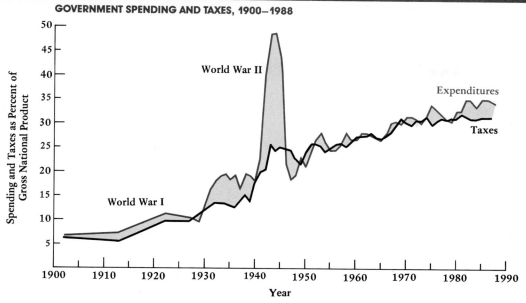

GOVERNMENT SPENDING AND TAXES, 1900–1988

Figure 32-1   The size of government has grown sharply over the twentieth century

Government expenditures include federal, state, and local spending on goods, services, and transfers. Note how the share of spending and taxing jumped sharply during World Wars I and II, but the size of government did not return to prewar levels after these wars. The difference between the tax and spending curves represents the overall government deficit. (Source: U.S. Department of Commerce.)

reduced government interference in the economy—actually has a higher tax burden than the United States. No simple law relating tax burdens and the citizenry's well-being can do justice to the true diversity of the fiscal facts of nations.[1]

The Growth of Government Controls and Regulation

The increase in collective expenditures is only part of the story. Besides the rapid growth in spending and

[1]Figures 32-1 and 32-2 show the total expenditures of governments. Such expenditures include "exhaustive" expenditures on goods and services (like missiles and teachers) as well as "nonexhaustive" transfer payments (like social security and interest on the government debt). Exhaustive expenditures make a direct claim upon the productive capacity of a country by using commodities like steel, microcomputers, and labor; transfer payments, by contrast, increase people's incomes and allow them to purchase goods and services but do not directly reduce the quantity of goods and services available for private consumption and investment.

taxing, there has also been a vast expansion in the laws and regulations governing economic affairs.

Nineteenth-century America came as close as any economy has to being a pure laissez-faire society—the system that the British historian Thomas Carlyle dubbed "anarchy plus the constable." This extreme permitted people great personal freedom to pursue their economic ambitions, and indeed it was a century of rapid material progress. But critics saw many flaws in this laissez-faire idyll. They witnessed periodic business crises, extremes of poverty and inequality, slavery followed by deep-seated racial discrimination, and poisoning of water, land, and air by pollution. Muckrakers and progressives called for a bridle on capitalism so that the people could steer this wayward beast in more humane directions.

Gradually, beginning in the 1890s, the United States turned away from the belief according to which "that government governs best which governs least." Presidents Theodore Roosevelt, Woodrow Wilson,

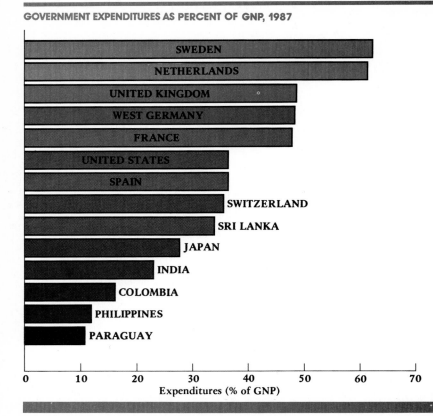

GOVERNMENT EXPENDITURES AS PERCENT OF GNP, 1987

SWEDEN
NETHERLANDS
UNITED KINGDOM
WEST GERMANY
FRANCE
UNITED STATES
SPAIN
SWITZERLAND
SRI LANKA
JAPAN
INDIA
COLOMBIA
PHILIPPINES
PARAGUAY

0 10 20 30 40 50 60 70
Expenditures (% of GNP)

Figure 32-2 Government's share of GNP is biggest in wealthy lands

Governments of poor countries show a tendency to tax and spend less, relative to national product, than advanced countries. With affluence come greater interdependence and the desire to meet social needs, along with less need to spend on private necessities. (Source: International Monetary Fund.)

Franklin Roosevelt, and Lyndon Johnson—in the face of strenuous opposition—pushed out the boundaries of federal control over the economy, devising new regulatory and fiscal tools to suit their purposes.

Constitutional powers of government were interpreted broadly and used to "secure the public interest" and to "police" the economic system. Utilities and railroads came under state regulation. In 1887, the federal Interstate Commerce Commission (ICC) was set up to regulate rail traffic across state boundaries. The Sherman Antitrust Act and other laws were invoked after 1890 against monopolistic combinations in "restraint of trade."

Economic regulation of banking became increasingly pervasive: after 1913, the Federal Reserve System was established to serve as a central bank, controlling commercial banks; since 1933 most bank deposits have been insured by the Federal Deposit Insurance Corporation (FDIC). As we saw in Chap-

ter 24, during the New Deal a whole set of industries came under *economic regulation,* where government sets the prices, conditions of exit and entry, and safety standards. Regulated industries included the airlines, trucks, barge and water traffic; electric, gas, and telephone utilities; financial markets; oil, natural gas, as well as pipelines. The mid-1970s recorded the high-water mark of economic regulation, with many conservatives portraying the United States as a planned economy run by regulatory agencies.

In addition to regulating the prices and standards of business, the nation attempted to protect health and safety through increasingly stringent *social regulation.* Pure food and drug acts were passed following the revelations of the muckraking era of the early 1900s. Then, during the 1960s and 1970s, a series of acts were passed that regulated mine safety and then worker safety more generally; set the framework for federal regulation of air and water pollution and of hazardous substances; authorized safety standards for automobiles and consumer products; controlled strip mining; and regulated nuclear power safety and toxic wastes.

So great was the proliferation of regulation by the late 1970s that many saw in the regulatory agencies a "fourth branch" of government. So powerful was the opposition to new regulatory programs that further growth of regulation was abruptly halted during the Reagan years (1981–1988), a time when the stringency of social regulation was abated, when enforcement was relaxed, and when the amount of antipollution spending by business fell sharply.

Political Evolution

How does it come to pass that the nation adopts such radically new doctrines? Looking back, we see how each new policy produced violent reactions on both sides. The social security system introduced by Franklin Roosevelt was espoused as essential to protecting the well-being of older citizens, as a kind of public pension system. Opponents denounced social security as an ominous victory of socialism during the troubled 1930s. Newspapers of the day recorded similar sentiments about public subsidies for medical care, regulation of factory conditions, legal protection for unions, and antipollution laws.

With the passage of time, as the old generation passes away and is replaced by new ideas and experiences, political attitudes evolve. The radical doctrines of one era become accepted as the gospel of the next. The much-criticized social security system of the 1930s was defended by conservative President Ronald Reagan in the 1980s as part of the "social safety net." The public has come to accept government constraints on laissez-faire capitalism, constraints that changed the very nature of capitalism. Private property is less and less wholly private. Free enterprise has become progressively less free. Irreversible evolution is part of history.

THE FUNCTIONS OF GOVERNMENT

Philosophers since the time of Plato have debated the role of the state, and political thinkers have proposed different approaches to government. In recent years economics has developed a new field called **public choice.** This is the study of how governments make choices and direct the economy. It asks *what* goods are bought by governments, *for whom* are the benefits of government programs distributed, and *how* government goods and services are produced.

Our survey of public-choice theory begins in this section with an analysis of the *normative* role of government; that is, of the kind of economic functions that government ought to perform. The next section presents the *positive* or descriptive analysis of government behavior, describing the actual behavior of governments and legislatures. We then end with an application of these principles to the important public-policy problem of externalities.

We are beginning to get a picture of how government directs and interacts with the economy. What are the major economic functions that government performs in a modern mixed economy? In fact there are four:

- Establishing the legal framework for the market economy
- Determining macroeconomic stabilization policy
- Affecting the allocation of resources to improve economic efficiency
- Establishing programs that affect the distribution of income

Let's look at each.

The Legal Framework

The government's first function, setting the legal framework, establishes the rules of the economic game played by households, firms, and even governments. Such rules include the definition of property (just how "private" is private property?), the laws of contracts and business enterprise, the mutual obligations of labor and management, and a multitude of statutes constraining the way different members of the society interact. If red lights mean stop and green lights mean go, it is because these and countless other rules are woven into the fabric of our society by laws.

Although the legal framework profoundly affects

economic behavior, most laws are not set on the basis of a finely honed economic cost-benefit analysis. Rather, some came from Roman times, others grew from English common law, while modern law is often driven by feelings about what is fair or right or, sometimes, by what will sell in the political marketplace.

Whatever the source of our laws and customs, the legal framework strongly influences economic activity. For example, in the nineteenth century, firms were not responsible for workers who became ill while working in unsafe or unhealthful factories; also, consumers had little recourse if they bought a defective product. What were the results? There were thousands of occupational illnesses and millions of dollars spent on ''snake-oil remedies'' that purported to cure all ailments.

Over the twentieth century, the legal system evolved to make businesses legally responsible for their actions and products. Firms can now be sued if workers become ill from their work. Recently, thousands of workers have sued asbestos manufacturers after they contracted cancer, and one giant firm, Manville Corporation, filed for bankruptcy under the weight of these claims. Firms are more and more held responsible for faulty products. In many states, you can return a car that turns out to be a ''lemon.''

As a result of these legal changes, firms now pay much closer attention to the safety of their products and workplaces. Managers must constantly ask themselves, ''What can go wrong with this product? Will we be sued if there is an accident? Should we buy insurance? Or should we scrap the whole venture and take on a less risky line of work?'' The net effect is to reduce the dangers from products. In addition, businesses have become averse to undertaking many risky activities, as was recently seen when vaccines were unavailable because there was no insurance coverage for product liability.

Macroeconomic Stabilization

Now that we have seen how government sets the legal framework, we turn next to a discussion of the three central economic functions of government: stabilization, allocation, and income distribution.

The first economic function of the federal government is macroeconomic. As we can see in Chapters 5 to 17, modern governments generally try to smooth out the business cycle—preventing chronic unemployment, economic stagnation, and rapid price inflation. Two principal weapons are used: monetary policy and fiscal policy.

A central bank is a governmental bank for banks which is given the power to issue currency and control bank reserves. Our central bank, the Federal Reserve, exercises money and credit policies designed for high employment, production growth, and price stability.

Governments have controlled the supply of money since Roman times. But only in the last 50 years have governments attempted to employ fiscal policies—variations in government spending and taxation—to influence the levels of employment and output along with the rate of inflation. Well-designed stabilization policies can help moderate the cycles of unemployment and contain excessive inflation. But bad stabilization policy can make the business cycle worse.

Allocation

The second central economic purpose of government is to assist in the socially desirable allocation of resources. This is the *microeconomic* side of government policy, tending to the *what* and *how* of economic life. Microeconomic policies might emphasize a hands-off, laissez-faire approach, leaving all questions to the market. Or they might lean toward central planning, with decisions about steel and car and computer production made by government planners.

Ours is fundamentally a market economy. On any microeconomic issue, the first presumption is that the market will be allowed to solve the economic problem at hand. But sometimes our government chooses to override the allocational decisions of market supply and demand. Let us see why.

Hypothetical Laissez-Faire In the first place suppose all goods could be produced efficiently by perfectly competitive enterprise at any scale of operations. And assume that all goods were like loaves of bread, the total of which could be cut up into separate consumptions of different individuals, so that the more I consumed out of the total, the less you consumed. And further, suppose there were no spillovers or externalities like air pollution and that each person had equal initial access to human and natural resources, had equal opportunity in every sense, and could carry on any activity independently of others, much as in frontier days.

If all these idealized conditions were met, would there be any need whatsoever for government intervention in the market? Couldn't the invisible hand provide a perfectly efficient and equitable production and distribution of the economic fruits? Why should there be any government functions at all? Indeed, why speak of "a society" at all, since we could then be regarded as an array of independent atoms with absolutely no organic bonds among us?

Yet even in this case, if there were to be a division of labor among people and regions, and if a price mechanism were to work, the need would soon grow for the legal framework described above: for government courts and police forces to ensure honesty, fulfillment of contract, nonfraudulent and nonviolent behavior, and freedom from theft and external aggression, and to guarantee the legislated rights of property.

This is the case for laissez-faire with minimal government—and indeed, it might be a good system if the idealized conditions listed above were truly present.

Real Interdependencies Each and every one of the idealized conditions enumerated above is violated to some extent in all human societies. The market is not ideal. There are market failures.

Abilities, opportunities, and ownership of property do exhibit disparities, depending on biological and social history. Some groups are or have been systematically discriminated against. Also, it is a fact that many kinds of production can take place most efficiently only in units too large for truly perfect competition. And unregulated factories do tend to dump their wastes into the air, water, and land.

Let us review briefly how these market failures might lead to a call for government activity:

▪ *The breakdown of perfect competition.* When monopolies or oligopolies inhibit rivalry or drive firms out of business, government may want to apply antitrust policies or regulation, or even to break up large firms.

▪ *The existence of significant externalities*—too much air pollution or too little investment in science

and engineering. As we will see later in this chapter, government may need to control the emissions of polluters or to support basic science.

▪ *Discrimination in labor markets.* When some groups are discriminated against or excluded from high-paid jobs, government may decide to step in, outlaw discriminatory actions, and break down the barriers between noncompeting groups.

Clearly, there is much on the agenda of possible allocational problems for government to handle.

Income Redistribution

One of the first lessons we learned is that the invisible hand might be marvelously efficient while producing a very unequal or unfair distribution of income. Under laissez-faire, people end up rich or poor depending on their inherited brains or wealth, on their talents and efforts, on the prices of their skills, and sometimes on how lucky they were in finding oil. To some people, the distribution of income arising from unregulated competition looks as arbitrary as the Darwinian distribution of food and plunder among animals in the jungle.

In the poorest societies, there is little excess income to take from the better off and provide to the unfortunate. But as societies become more affluent, they devote more resources to human services. The welfare states of North America and Western Europe now devote a significant share of their incomes to maintaining minimum standards of health, nutrition, and income.

Most advanced economies now rule that children shall not go hungry because of the economic circumstances of their parents; that poor people shall not die young because of insufficient money for needed medical care; that the old shall be able to live out their years with some minimum of income. These government programs are provided in the United States by transfer programs (such as food stamps, Medicaid, and social security) and by redistributive taxes (which raise a greater proportion of taxes from high-income persons and levy little or no taxes on the poor).

This analysis of the four functions of government concludes our survey of the normative view of government's role, of how government ought to behave to improve the economy's functioning.

B. PUBLIC-CHOICE THEORY

The first section of this chapter described the normative role of government in a modern economy. But do governments in fact follow the prescriptions laid down by economists and philosophers? Do governments constantly labor to create the just and efficient society? Do governments use a "visible hand" to ensure that public-policy decisions serve to make the economy operate more smoothly and effectively? Or are there "government failures" that parallel market failures such as monopoly and pollution?

These questions are the domain of **public-choice theory,** which is the branch of economics that studies the way that governments make decisions. Here we ask how governments decide on the level of taxes and public consumption and on the size of transfer payments, and we inquire into inconsistencies in legislative decisions. Public-choice theory asks about the *how*, *what*, and *for whom* of the public sector, just as supply-and-demand theory analyzes choices in the private sector.*

HOW GOVERNMENTS CHOOSE

In the private sector, people express their views by casting what we have metaphorically called "dollar votes" for the goods they desire. In the political sphere, they cast real votes—for representatives and for Presidents. Let's review how people vote and what the consequences are.

The Political Game

The game of politics, like the market, has its rules and its players. These are well known to students of political science, but they are worth reviewing briefly. Political decision making operates within a set of *rules:* these are the basic constitution and voting system (in the United States a powerful President and two legislative houses pass federal laws). The most important rule of the game for our purpose is that decisions are made by elected representatives.

Who are the *players*? One set of players is voters (or consumers) whose needs and wants a democracy is ultimately supposed to serve. The other major players are the elected representatives, or politicians. This group performs a function much like that of firms in a market economy—they are the entrepreneurs who interpret the public's demand for collective goods and find ways of supplying these goods.

What drives politicians? Most political figures are motivated by a combination of pragmatism and ideology—joining the quest for electoral survival with their fundamental beliefs about how the nation should be governed. Some change their positions quickly as the political winds shift. Others feel so deeply about issues that they are willing to risk defeat in defense of their ideals. But the theory of public choice cuts through this thicket of complex motivations by making a simple assumption: *politicians are assumed to behave so as to maximize their chances of election.* They are assumed to be vote maximizers—just as firms are taken to be profit maximizers.

---

*Since the time of Adam Smith, economists have focused most of their energy on understanding the workings of the marketplace. But serious thinkers have also pondered the government's role in society. Joseph Schumpeter pioneered public-choice theory in *Capitalism, Socialism, and Democracy* (1942), and Kenneth Arrow's Nobel Prize–winning study on social choice (analyzed later in this chapter) brought mathematical rigor to this field. But the landmark study of Anthony Downs, *An Economic Theory of Democracy* (1957), first sketched a powerful new theory in which politicians set economic policies in order to be re-elected. Downs showed how parties will tend to move toward the center of the political spectrum and suggested that it is highly irrational for people to vote given the small likelihood of any individual's affecting the outcome.

Further studies of James Buchanan and Gordon Tullock in *The Calculus of Consent* (1959) defended checks and balances and advocated the use of unanimity in political decisions—arguing that unanimous decisions do not coerce anyone and therefore impose no costs. For this and other works, Buchanan received the Nobel Prize in 1986. This conservative brand of economics received careful study by the Reagan administration during the early 1980s and was applied to such areas as farm policy, regulation, and the courts and formed the theoretical basis for a proposed constitutional amendment to balance the budget.

Poised between voters and politicians stand organizations known as *interest groups*. These represent people or businesses who have joined together to lobby for a narrow set of interests or issues. The National Rifle Association defends the right of citizens to bear arms; the Iron and Steel Institute attempts to limit steel imports; the American Medical Association lobbies against government regulation of medicine. In each case, a coalition forms to ensure that the incomes and privileges of its members are protected. Sometimes, interest groups assume a degree of political power far beyond the numerical size of their membership. When this happens, we have a case of nonrepresentative government, and of interest groups who "capture" regulatory agencies or political influence.

There are other players as well, although we will not examine them in our survey of public choice. One important set of participants (such as generals in the Pentagon or farmers in the Agriculture Department) runs executive agencies. Although they exercise great power because of their expertise and long experience, these bureaucrats are ultimately subject to supervision by the political leaders.

In summary, public-choice theory describes how governments make decisions about taxation, expenditure, regulation, and other economic policies. Like the game of markets, the game of politics must match up people's demands for goods with the economy's capability to supply goods. The major difference lies in the fact that the central entrepreneurs of politics— politicians—are oriented to win elections, while the central organizations in markets—business firms— aim to earn profits.

MECHANISMS FOR PUBLIC CHOICE

Government economic policies are not determined in a vacuum or by a computer. Rather, in every nation there is a political system or mechanism for making collective decisions, for public choice. In the balance of this section we ask, How does such a mechanism work in theory and in practice? Moreover, we focus our attention on decision processes, particularly on voting systems, in democratic countries.

Before launching into this analysis, we should re-

mind ourselves what public choice accomplishes: it is the process whereby individual preferences are combined into collective decisions. A democratic society stresses the importance of individual values and tastes in such an aggregation—"one person, one vote" expresses this individualistic underpinning of our political system. A crucial problem arises just because we must aggregate millions of opinions into a single decision. The United States has 250 million views about the defense budget or welfare or abortion or drugs. But in the end, there can be only one federal law, only one defense budget, only one welfare policy, and so forth. A red light means stop for everyone because political choices are indivisible for a nation. Such decisions are coercive compared to private decisions about ice cream or bread or concerts, where your choice to eat ice cream does not bind my decisions. *Unlike private decisions, collective choice contains an essential indivisibility with but one outcome on any particular issue.*

Outcomes of Collective Choice

What is the effect of collective decisions? Figure 32-3 shows the possibilities. For this diagram we imagine a society in which there are two kinds of people, A's and B's. They may be rich and poor, Republicans and Democrats, or farmers and urban dwellers. For the moment, think of each as a unified group with homogeneous interests and tastes.

Consider first a society that shunned any kind of government. Such a world was described by the great seventeenth-century philosopher Thomas Hobbes as one where there was "no place for industry, because the fruit thereof is uncertain; no culture of the earth, no navigation, no arts; continual fear of violent death; and the life of man, solitary, poor, nasty, brutish, and short."[2] Even if some rudimentary laws and constitutions were in place, a pure laissez-faire economy would find itself with relatively low incomes, as shown at point *E* in Figure 32-3.

Next consider the potential for a society which undertook sensible collective actions. It could build highways and encourage railroads. Public-health

---

[2]Thomas Hobbes, *Leviathan* (1651). This quotation has been shortened and rendered into modern English.

COLLECTIVE ACTION

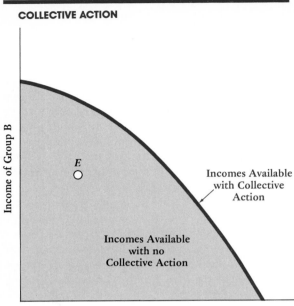

Figure 32-3   The logic of collective action

The graph shows economic performance with and without collective action for a society made up of two kinds of people. Point E marks the outcome of pure laissez-faire, where governments build no roads, vaccinate no children, and "leave things alone."

With collective actions like road-building, support of science and health, regulation of the money supply, and so forth, everybody's incomes can be improved as society moves from E toward the red frontier. Public-choice theory describes how society decides which collective actions it should undertake.

measures could wipe out malaria, smallpox, and plague. Government-supported science could probe space or molecular structure, thereby leading to vast technological improvements. Monetary policies could lead to a sound currency and financial system, thereby allowing people to save and businesses to invest. Police could make the streets and homes safer. Pollution-abatement programs could clean the air and water and produce a healthier and more productive populace. Income-support measures could provide food and medical care for those who are unable to

care for themselves. *Successful public-sector activities push out the frontier of what the economy can produce, as the outer red frontier in Figure 32-3 illustrates.*

Is Public Choice Efficient?

When we think of the many helpful activities undertaken by government, we might ask whether collective choice always enhances efficiency. Few would argue that wiping out plague or launching communications satellites was harmful. But is there a "visible-hand" theorem, whereby the visible hand of government guides the economy toward an efficient and equitable economic allocation of public goods and income?

We will later see that the answer is, No. As Figure 32-4 illustrates, collective decisions can be divided into three general categories: harmful, redistributive, and efficient. A first and probably rare *harmful* case arises when governments take steps that make everyone worse off. If a particular strategy leads to nuclear war, that will surely be an abject failure. Such failures are illustrated by the movement from initial point E to point W in Figure 32-4.

Second, there are simple *redistributive* outcomes, shown by the arrow from E to R. In these cases society may tax one group and subsidize another, or may impose a tariff on a product that helps factors of production in that industry but hurts consumers, or may build an inefficient dam that benefits one group while hurting another.

Finally, collective actions may produce *Pareto improvements,* which represent actions that lead to improvements in everyone's satisfaction; they make everyone better off and no one worse off. A Pareto improvement is shown by the arrow moving northeast in Figure 32-4 from point E to point P. Examples of Pareto improvements would be governments supporting a new scientific advance (like communications satellites) or helping disseminate a public-health measure (like a smallpox or polio vaccine).

This distinction among the three kinds of outcomes is of great importance, for, as we will see, collective action cannot construct foolproof rules that always make everyone better off.

ALTERNATIVE DECISION RULES

Different societies have evolved diverse ways of making collective decisions. Traditional societies were often governed by an informally selected council of elders. Many European countries relied on absolute monarchies until two or three centuries ago. Venice was ruled by an elaborate oligarchy for 500 years. Countries of Western Europe and North America today are governed by their elected representatives, some by a strong executive branch and others by a powerful parliament.

In public-choice theory, we look behind the particular forms of government to the underlying choice process. Do systems that rely on consensus or unanimity produce efficient and consistent decisions? What does ''the will of the majority'' really mean? Are the decisions of collective choice always fair and efficient?

Unanimity

Many social and economic thinkers have stressed the advantages of making decisions by consensus or by unanimity. This approach requires that everybody agree with collective decisions. Figure 32-5(a) illustrates how decisions by consensus proceed. No decision can be made without the accord of each person, so each decision must improve (or not worsen) each person's income (or, more generally, each person's level of satisfaction). It must therefore move society northeast toward the income-possibility frontier in Figure 32-5(a)—a process shown by the arrows. A voting system based on unanimity would guarantee that all decisions be Pareto improvements, never making anyone worse off. In addition, because each voter must agree with any decision, there can never be any coercion of minorities by larger groups.

Unfortunately, a rule of unanimity poses several practical shortcomings. As anyone knows who has ever tried to get a group of people to agree to anything, generating consensus takes enormous amounts of time and energy. One skeptic can hold up any measure, no matter how worthwhile that measure might be.

Even worse, once the last skeptic realized how powerful he was, he could blackmail those who favored the measure. If a $100 million pollution-control

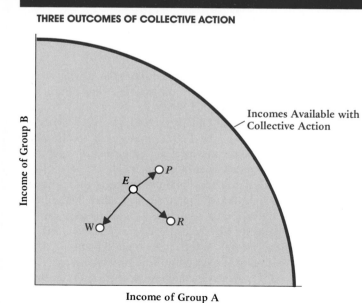

THREE OUTCOMES OF COLLECTIVE ACTION

Income of Group B

Income of Group A

Incomes Available with Collective Action

Figure 32-4   Collective actions can improve or hurt all or simply redistribute incomes

Starting at the laissez-faire point *E*, we can distinguish three kinds of outcomes. Optimistically, we might make everyone better off by moving to point *P*. Or there might be massive government failures (like war) which make everyone worse off as society moves from *E* to *W*. Very often programs are redistributive, taking resources from group B and transferring them to group A, as in the movement from *E* to *R*.

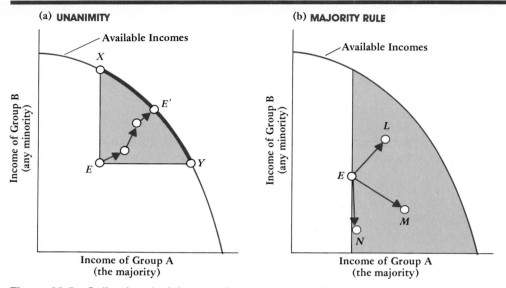

Figure 32-5   Collective decisions under unanimity and majority rule

The left panel illustrates outcomes when decisions require unanimity: no one can be made worse off if each person must agree to each decision. Hence, starting at *E*, all outcomes must lie in the region *EXY*.

Under majority rule, shown on the right, group A can decide issues and would vote for any proposal improving its income or moving rightward into the shaded region. Some decisions may be efficient and fair (as in movement to *L*) or inefficient and unfair (as in movement to *N*).

or road-building program could be vetoed by a single person, this person could hold out for any number of pet projects, delaying the vote and enriching himself or his constituents in the process. Such a problem is occasionally seen in majoritarian voting systems on close votes, but it would occur more frequently and be far more intractable under a system requiring unanimous consent.

In the end, it is likely that the unanimous voting system would be so rife with bargaining and blackmail and delay that virtually nothing would be accomplished. No laws would be passed. The system would be at an impasse or have to creak along with existing arrangements. Instead of moving northeast from point *E*, it could simply stay at point *E* (wherever *E* might happen to be). Thus government by unanimity is likely to preserve the status quo, however bad or good it is.

Majority Rule

Virtually all representative institutions, as well as participatory groups, rely on majority rule for making decisions. Under this system, a law or rule is adopted when more than half the voters approve it. Majority rule is used in the U.S. Congress, in the Supreme Court, in state and local governments, as well as in most corporate boards and clubs.

An idealized description of majority rule is shown on the right side of Figure 32-5. Assume that group A is in the majority. In a pure economic calculation, it will vote for any measure that increases its real income. Thus any of the three points shown—*L*, *M*, or *N*—would win over point *E* by majority vote. Of the three, *M* produces the highest income for group A and would be the ultimate winner in majority voting among the four choices.

The outcomes shown in Figure 32-5*(b)* suggest some important points about majority rule. First, majority rule does not guarantee Pareto improvements. The majority would prefer point *M* to point *E*, but point *M* makes one group of voters (those in group B) worse off. In addition, majority rule may lead to a "tyranny by the majority." Majorities can impose their political will on minorities, through discrimination, income distribution, or even slavery. Such tyranny is not possible under unanimity.

But note that majority decision making does rule out what we have called government failure. In choosing among alternatives, the electorate might well make some people worse off, but, except by mistake, it will not choose an alternative that makes everyone worse off. So majority decisions rule out events represented by the arrow leading to *W* in Figure 32-4.

Avoiding Tyranny by the Majority The possibility of tyranny by the majority has haunted political thinkers for three centuries. Because deep thinkers like James Madison and Alexander Hamilton feared such coercive political activity, they proposed the use of *supermajorities* in many important issues. (Supermajorities require that a measure obtain more than a simple majority, say, two-thirds of the votes, in order to pass.) The U.S. Constitution requires supermajorities for constitutional amendments and for overriding presidential vetoes. These are cases in which, in the interests of protecting minorities, a preference is given to protecting the status quo.

During the last decade, many people have proposed extending rule by supermajority to the federal budget process. Critics argue that the usual budget process allows majorities to pass extravagant spending laws, expanding the scope of government and incurring large budget deficits. We are witnessing, they say, a big-spending majority using majority rule to impose its beliefs upon the minority.

The proposed solution is to require supermajorities for the passage of economic legislation that would lead to budget deficits or to an expansion of government expenditure programs. In the early 1980s, conservatives proposed a constitutional amendment to balance the federal budget: this would require a super-majority of 60 percent, rather than the usual 50 percent, to increase the share of government spending or to run a budget deficit. When the constitutional amendment failed, Congress passed the *Gramm-Rudman* bill, which mandated a gradual reduction of federal budget deficits and a balanced budget in the early 1990s; moreover, the bill established certain procedures that required supermajorities when budget deficits exceeded certain stated targets.[3]

Cyclical Voting and the Voting Paradox

We hear much about the "will of the majority" and "letting the majority have its way." In one of the deepest criticisms of majority rule, Nobel laureate Kenneth Arrow of Stanford demonstrated certain fundamental flaws and inconsistencies that could result from majority decisions. We will illustrate Arrow's results with the help of a simple example of three individuals choosing among three different options.

The situation is illustrated in Table 32-1 on the next page. Each of three individuals has one vote. They must choose among three different levels of defense spending: high, medium, and low. Moreover, the three different people have quite different ideas about the way the country should be defended. Jones is a hawk, but his second choice is a small army rather than a middle-sized one. Smith is a centrist: she likes both guns and butter. Brown is a pacifist, preferring the smallest possible army.

Now line this group up and try to decide the defense issue by majority vote. As Table 32-1 shows, low spending beats medium spending; medium spending beats high spending; high spending beats low spending. We see here the voting paradox:

The *voting paradox* arises when no single program can command a majority against all other programs.

Setting the Agenda There are many important implications of the voting paradox, but one particular one should be mentioned. This is the importance of the *agenda,* or the order of business. Because of the

---

[3]A more extensive discussion of the Gramm-Rudman bill and its implementation is provided in Chapter 17.

VOTER'S PREFERENCE AMONG DIFFERENT PROPOSALS ON DEFENSE SPENDING		
VOTER	**LOW SPENDING**	**MEDIUM SPENDING**	**HIGH SPENDING**
Jones	2	3	1
Smith	3	1	2
Brown	1	2	3

Table 32-1 How cyclical voting or the voting paradox arises

Jones wants a strong army or little defense. Smith is a centrist and prefers a modest defense outlay. Brown is a pacifist.

Under majority voting, each person votes in favor of his or her preferred program. When the programs are voted upon, low spending beats medium spending 2 to 1; medium spending beats high spending 2 to 1; and high spending beats low spending 2 to 1. Like a dog chasing its tail, the majority voting rule here cycles around endlessly. Nor is there any way to resolve the paradox except by arbitrary voting procedures.

need to economize on time, legislatures must have a set of procedures. They cannot allow endless cycling around on issues where opinions are divided.

But the voting paradox shows that the agenda may be crucial to the outcome—that the order of votes may determine which program prevails. Let's return to our example of defense in Table 32-1. Say that the Congress has to decide on a defense policy, but it is divided into three equal camps whose preferences are like those shown in Table 32-1. Enter the Rules Committee. By manipulating the order of votes, the Rules Committee can actually determine the winner. Suppose that the Rules Committee is run by pacifists. It can set the agenda in a way to guarantee its desired outcome. That is, the group starts with a vote between high and medium spending; medium spending wins by 2 votes to 1. Then the winner is pitted against low spending, with low spending the victor. Low spending has won because of the order of the voting.

But suppose the Rules Committee is dominated by the hawkish Committee on the Present Danger. Can you see how it could engineer the high-defense outcome? By starting the low against the medium, and then letting high take on the winner.

This example suggests why chairpersons and rules committees are so important in legislatures: the power to set the agenda is often the power to determine the outcome.

Arrow's Theorem Have political theorists devised a way of eliminating cycling and making good decisions? Certainly unanimity will never solve the problem, for no program in Table 32-1 commands a majority against all other possible programs. Kenneth Arrow investigated the question of whether *any* good voting scheme exists that would avoid cyclical outcomes. His surprising conclusion is that *there exists no majority-rule voting scheme that guarantees efficiency, respects individual preferences, and does not depend on the agenda.* Put differently, no voting scheme has ever been devised—and Arrow proved it is impossible to find one—that can guarantee majority voting will be consistent and will move the society to its most desirable point. In other words, the cyclical voting outcome illustrated in Table 32-1 cannot be ruled out no matter how ingenious are the rules or procedures.

APPLICATIONS OF PUBLIC-CHOICE THEORY

Public-choice theory is fascinating not only for the light it throws on the democratic process. It also helps us understand important aspects of American and other political systems—their strengths as well as their weaknesses.

People today sometimes dwell upon wasteful government activities—pointing to the purchase by the military of a screwdriver for $250 or to a foolish regulation about the height of toilet seats. And who can doubt that governments sometimes make foolish decisions? But we must not overlook the fact that governments have built roads, conquered diseases, safeguarded borders, and provided the countless socially necessary ingredients for an advanced civilization. Recall Hobbes' saying that without government to protect us, life would be nasty, brutish, and short.

But while governments play a central role in modern economies—combating externalities, stabilizing the business cycle, and redistributing income—they are no more perfect than the market. Just as capitalism never attains the perfection of atomistic markets, so do democracies sometimes fail to respond to market failures in the most effective way. There are government failures as well as market failures:

Government failure arises when state actions fail to improve economic efficiency or when the government redistributes income to the wrong people.

What are the important kinds of government failures?

The Bureaucratic Imperative

Few can resist the temptation to increase their own influence or power. Governments are the same. They often do too much for too long. One reason for the tendency of government to overexpand is that there is no profit check (or what businesspeople call "the bottom line") on individual projects. If the government builds too many dams, too many bombers, too many fancy government office buildings—there is no profit-and-loss statement by which the economic worth of these projects can be calculated. The only support such projects need is a legislative majority, and this may be obtained by the small minority's providing campaign financing for a sufficient number of legislators. Once they have come into existence, programs develop a strong constituency from those who work in them or those who benefit from their activities.

Whatever the source, it seems clear that governments often have a great deal of trouble stopping a project once it has started. A classic example is the "breeder reactor." This project involved an advanced nuclear power system to replace the current generation of nuclear reactors when uranium runs out. The government designed the Clinch River Breeder Reactor in the late 1960s when everyone thought nuclear power would grow very rapidly. By the mid-1970s, studies showed that the breeder reactor was going to be economically unviable. By the late 1970s, it was clear that nobody was ordering nuclear power plants any more, and many utilities were canceling plants under construction. Yet the government continued spending hundreds of millions of dollars funding the Clinch River project until 1983.

As one wit said in this regard, governments often behave like the little boy who said, "I know how to spell 'banana,' but I don't know when to stop."

Short Time Horizons Elected political leaders in the United States must face elections frequently—every 2, 4, or 6 years—and often compete in hotly contested districts. Electoral pressures may lead to myopia or short time horizons in political decisions.

The syndrome of short time horizons was illustrated time and again during the 1980s by battles over the federal budget deficit. Almost everyone agreed that the high budget deficit was harmful to saving and investment—the Congress, the President, economic experts, and business spokespersons. Almost everyone agreed that if the budget deficit were not reduced, productivity and prosperity would be imperiled. Yet, again and again, the federal government was unable to take the necessary steps.

What was the source of the failure? The rub came because deficit reduction required painful steps *today* to improve economic performance *in the future*. Taxes would have to be raised or spending cut in the present in order to increase saving, investment, and productivity. But Congress had great difficulty taking the necessary steps. In 1982, 1984, 1986, and 1988, politicians were running for office; they were more concerned about their reelection than about economic problems arising in the distant future. And the political aspirants thought that voters would pay more attention to the taxes raised or spending cuts enacted than to the long-term benefits of deficit reduction. Thus Congress decided to procrastinate—again and again. This defect is, in essence, a case of nonrepresentative voting, for only today's citizens cast a vote.

The tendency to focus only upon the next election may lead governments to introduce and maintain programs with short payoff periods and to steer clear of those with immediate costs and diffuse future benefits. We saw in Chapter 10 that it might lead to a "political business cycle," with a splurge of spending right before elections.

However, a tendency toward short time horizons does not necessarily lead to government that is too big or too small; rather, it may lead to a proconsumption bias in government programs. That is, programs receive favorable treatment when they boost present consumption relative to future consumption, and long-term investments (research, conservation, and protection of the environment) may experience rough sledding in periods of particularly close political elections.

This review of government failures may suggest that public choice in political democracies is always shortsighted, venal, and antisocial. No reading of history could justify such a cynical conclusion. History is also full of political leaders who have taken far-sighted and wise measures—some popular, some unpopular. But public choice reminds us that collective choice in democracies is not guided by an invisible hand that always leads to an optimal or even efficient outcome. Democracies have elected Hitler and Mussolini and Peron, along with Lincoln and Churchill and Kennedy. Just as economists must concern themselves with corrections for market failures, so must public-choice analysts examine ways of avoiding government failures.

C. Public Choice and Externalities

Of all the economic problems requiring government action, some of the most serious arise when a market generates external effects or externalities. It is here that the need for sound decisions tests a nation's mechanisms for public choice and its legislature's ability to avoid short time horizons and interest-group politics. In this final section we explore the nature of externalities, describe why they produce economic inefficiencies, and analyze potential remedies.

Begin with the definition of an externality:

An **externality** or spillover effect occurs when production or consumption inflicts involuntary costs or benefits on others; that is, costs or benefits are imposed on others yet are not paid for by those who impose them or receive them. More precisely, an externality is an effect of one economic agent's behavior on another's well-being, where that effect is not reflected in dollar or market transactions.

Externalities come in many guises. Some are positive (external economies), while others are negative (external diseconomies). Thus when I dump a barrel of acid into a stream, it kills fish and plants. Since I don't pay anyone for this damage, an external diseconomy occurs. When you discover a better way to clean up oil spills, the benefit will spill over to many people who do not pay for it. This is an external economy.

Some externalities are pervasive, while others have only small spillover components. When a carrier of bubonic plague entered a town during the Middle Ages, a quarter of the population could be felled by the Black Death. On the other hand, when you chew an onion at a football stadium on a windy day, the external impacts are hardly noticeable.

Public vs. Private Goods

To illustrate the concept of external effects, we consider the extreme example of a public good, which is a commodity that can be provided to everyone as easily as it can be provided to one person.

The case par excellence of a public good is national defense. Nothing is more vital to a society than its security. But national defense, as an economic good, differs completely from a private good like bread. Ten loaves of bread can be divided up in many ways among individuals, and what I eat cannot be eaten by others. But national defense, once provided, is enjoyed automatically by all persons. It matters not whether you are hawk or dove, pacifist or militarist, old or young, ignorant or learned—you will receive the same amount of national security from the army as does every other resident of the country.

Note therefore the stark contrast: the decision to provide a certain level of a public good like national defense will lead to a number of submarines, cruise missiles, space lasers, and tanks to protect each of us. By contrast, the decision to eat a private good like bread is an individual act. You can eat four slices, or two, or a whole loaf; the decision is purely your own and does not commit me to eat a particular amount of bread.

The example of national defense is a dramatic and extreme case of a public good. But when you think of a smallpox vaccine, a park concert, the damming of a river upstream to prevent flood damage downstream—indeed, when you think of almost any government activity—you will often find elements of public goods involved. In summary:

Public goods are ones whose benefits are indivisibly spread among the entire community, whether or not individuals desire to purchase the public good. **Private goods,** by contrast, are ones that can be divided up and provided separately to different individuals, with no external benefits or costs to others. Efficient provision of public goods often requires government action, while private goods can be efficiently allocated by markets.

In addition to public goods, we often see public "bads," which are public goods that impose costs uniformly across a group. Most public bads, or externalities, are associated with processes of production and are unintended by-products of firms' activities. One critical externality is the "greenhouse effect," which results from the buildup of carbon dioxide and other atmospheric trace gases. Scientific studies indicate that, in the coming decades, these gases will cause the climate to become warmer, oceans to rise, and monsoons to shift. Nobody is producing carbon dioxide in order to change the climate. Rather, this externality results unintentionally from the burning of fossil fuels and from other economic activities.

Other examples of public bads or externalities include: the air and water pollution that results from chemical production, energy production, and use of automobiles; "acid rain," which appears to come from long-distance transportation of sulfur emissions from power plants; radioactive exposure from atmospheric tests of nuclear weapons or from accidents like that at the Soviet plant in Chernobyl; depletion of the ozone layer from buildup of chlorofluorocarbons; and many other examples. Note that in all these cases, those who caused the external effect did not desire the outcome. The externalities were the unintentional but noxious side effects of productive activities.

The economy generates favorable as well as unfavorable externalities. The most important favorable externalities are those associated with the generation of knowledge. When inventors at Bell Telephone Laboratories invented the transistor in 1948, this invention ushered in the electronic age, producing fast computers, electronic telephone switches, stereo equipment, digital watches, and countless other useful products. Did Bell Labs profit from the value of the inventions outside the telephone industry? Very little. Rather, the transistor revolution was an externality whose benefits accrued to consumers around the world.

Nor is the transistor an isolated example. Inventions and discoveries over the ages—from the wheel and fire to the personal computer and superconductivity—inevitably spill over to benefit consumers many times more than they do their inventors.

MARKET INEFFICIENCY WITH EXTERNALITIES

Our discussion of public goods and externalities suggests that public goods will not be efficiently provided by a pure market mechanism. No one can capture and sell the benefits of national defense, so this role is left to the government; the benefits of basic science are too diffuse for profit-oriented firms to find economically attractive, so basic science is supported by government and takes place in universities; firms will not voluntarily restrict emissions of noxious chemicals or abstain from dumping PCBs in landfills, so government must regulate pollution. These are generally held to be legitimate government functions, according to Abraham Lincoln's dictum that government is "to do for the people what needs to be done, but which they cannot, by individual effort, do at all, or do so well, for themselves." Let us explore the implications of Lincoln's view for government policy on externalities.

Analysis of Inefficiency

Why do external diseconomies like pollution lead to economic inefficiency? Take a hypothetical coal-burning steel firm, American Steel, Inc., that generates an external diseconomy by spewing out tons of noxious sulfur dioxide fumes. Some of the sulfur harms the steel company, requiring more frequent repainting and raising the firm's medical bills. But most of the damage is "external" to the firm, settling throughout the region, harming vegetation and buildings, and causing various kinds of respiratory ailments in people.

Being a sound profit-maximizing enterprise, American Steel needs to decide how much pollution it should emit. With no pollution cleanup, its workers and plant will suffer. Cleaning up every little speck, on the other hand, will require heavy expenses for low-sulfur cleaner fuels, recycling systems, scrubbing equipment, and so forth—so much expense, indeed, that American Steel could not hope to compete with other steelmakers.

The managers therefore decide to clean up just to the point where the firm's extra cost of pollution damage (marginal private damage) is equal to the extra cost of cleanup (marginal cost of abatement). The firm's engineers tell management that at the designated pollution rate of 200 tons per period, an extra ton of pollution will cost $10 in damages to the firm; at the same time, cleaning up an additional ton of pollutant will cost $10. The firm has found its private optimal level of pollution: at 200 tons of pollution the marginal private damage to the firm just equals the marginal cost of abatement. Put differently, when American Steel produces steel in a least-cost manner, it will set its pollution limit at 200 tons.

At this point, an environmental specialist decides to undertake an audit of the steel firm. The auditor is interested in costs to society as well as private costs to American Steel. In examining social costs, the auditor finds that the social costs—including health and property damage in neighboring regions—are 4 times the private costs to American Steel. The damage from each extra ton costs American Steel $10, but the rest of society suffers additional damage of $30 per ton. Why doesn't American Steel include the $30 of additional social damages in its cost calculations? The $30 is excluded because these damages are "external" to the firm and cost it nothing.

We now see how pollution and other externalities lead to inefficient economic outcomes. Allowing firms to pollute in a laissez-faire and unregulated way generates social costs greater than the social benefits— the damages from the extra unit of pollution are much greater than the costs of cleaning up that unit.

In a laissez-faire or unregulated environment, firms will determine their pollution levels by equating the marginal private damage from pollution with the marginal cost of abatement. When the pollution spillovers are significant, the private equilibrium will produce inefficiently high levels of pollution and too little cleanup activity.

Socially Efficient Pollution Let's go a step further and ask about the optimal level of pollution. Why should we allow any pollution? Surely, you might think, a well-managed economy should clean up all its pollution. The surprising answer is that the socially efficient level of pollution is not zero. Efficiency requires that the marginal *social* damage from pollution equal the marginal social costs of abatement. This equality occurs when the benefits to health and property of reducing pollution by 1 unit just equal the costs of that reduction, and equality is unlikely to be attained at a "zero-discharge" level of pollution.

How might an efficient level of pollution be determined? Economists recommend an approach known as *cost-benefit analysis,* in which efficient standards are set by balancing the costs of abatement against the benefits of pollution reduction. In the case of American Steel, suppose that engineers and public-health authorities study the cost data for abatement and environmental damage. They determine that incremental costs and benefits are equalized when the amount of pollution is reduced from 200 tons to 100 tons. At the efficient pollution rate, they find that the marginal cost of abatement is $20 per ton, while the marginal damage from one extra ton is also $20.

Why is 100 tons the efficient level of pollution? Because at this emissions rate the net value of production (i.e., the utility of the product less the damages from pollution) is maximized. If American Steel were to emit more than 100 tons of pollution, the incremental damage from pollution would outweigh the savings from lower levels of abatement. On the other hand, if pollution were to be cut below 100 tons, the costs of pollution cleanup would be greater than the gains from cleaner air. Here again, as in many areas, we find the most efficient outcome by equating marginal cost and marginal benefit of an activity.[4]

[4] A geometric approach to understanding American Steel's laissez-faire equilibrium and the optimal pollution level is given in question 10 at the end of this chapter.

Use of cost-benefit analysis will show why the extreme environmentalist position of ''no risk'' or ''zero discharge''—to prohibit any pollution—will generally be wasteful. To reduce pollution to zero will generally impose astronomically high costs, while the marginal benefits of reducing the last few grams of pollution may be quite modest. In some cases, it may even be impossible to continue to produce with zero emissions, so a no-risk philosophy might require closing down the steel industry or banning all vehicular traffic. In most cases, economic efficiency calls for a compromise—a substantial but not complete reduction of emissions—balancing the value of the industry's output against the damage from pollution.

An unregulated market economy will generate levels of pollution (or other externalities) such that the marginal *private* damage of pollution equals the marginal private costs of abatement. The efficient outcome arises when marginal *social* damage equals marginal social abatement costs. Thus in an unregulated economy there will be too little abatement and too much pollution.

Spillovers from Research The case of external economies is similar. Take research on corn farming. A single farmer will reap but a small benefit from improving the state of corn technology; the bulk of any benefits will spill over to others. Therefore, no profit-maximizing farmer will invest much in agricultural research. Nevertheless, the overall economy will benefit greatly from learning about and adopting new miracle seeds or improved crop rotation in corn farming. Adding up all the millions of marginal private benefits leads to a very substantial marginal social benefit of corn research—but individuals will not undertake much of this beneficial research on their own.

Indeed, it was just this externality that led to the Schumpeterian hypothesis. Schumpeter reasoned that, because monopolies could capture almost all the returns to innovation, externalities would be less pernicious for monopolistic than for competitive industries. Because monopolies could appropriate a significant portion of the economic gains from invention, according to Schumpeter, invention and innovation would be relatively rapid in concentrated industries.[5]

[5]See Chapter 25 for a further discussion of the Schumpeterian hypothesis.

POLICIES TO CORRECT EXTERNALITIES

A casual observer of modern society will note the pervasive presence of externalities. Harmful externalities include air and water pollution, unsafe factories and accidental nuclear releases, perils from drunk drivers or gargantuan trucks, strip-mined land or abandoned buildings. In earlier centuries, unsuspecting people could be struck down by plague or smallpox, while today the deadly AIDS virus can infect health-care professionals or unwary partners in drugs or sex. Such externalities are realities that call for government action in modern society.

We benefit from positive externalities as well. Inventors like Edison (light bulb and phonograph), Bell (telephone), Salk (polio vaccine), Farnsworth (television), Carrier (air conditioning), and Carlson (xerography) garnered but a small fraction of the profound benefits of their work. Think also of the radio and TV signals that we receive free of charge or of the public-health policies that have all but eradicated smallpox, polio, typhus, and malaria. For all these externalities, governments have alleviated inefficient, laissez-faire outcomes by taking collective action. What are the weapons that government can use to combat inefficiencies arising from externalities?

Government Policies

Governments today take a number of different steps to combat externalities, using either direct controls or financial incentives to induce firms to decrease harmful externalities or to increase beneficial activities. In this section we focus primarily upon government steps to restrain pollution and other harmful activities.

Direct Controls For almost all pollution, as well as health and safety externalities, governments rely on direct controls. Here, a firm is ordered to reduce the external effect in question.

For example, under the 1970 Clean Air Act, allowable emissions of three major pollutants were reduced by 90 percent. In 1977, utilities were told to reduce sulfur emissions on new plants by 90 percent. In 1984, firms were required to reduce the amount of asbestos in their plants to no more than two fibers per cubic centimeter of air. And so it goes with regulation.

How does the government enforce a pollution regulation? Let us continue our example of American Steel, which might have been told that it can emit no more than 100 tons of particulate matter. The state Department of Environmental Protection would not tell American Steel *how* to meet the standard, as long as the standard is met. If standards are appropriately set, and if the firm duly complies, then the outcome might approach the ideal, efficient pollution level described in the last section.

Unfortunately, pollution-control programs seldom work in such an ideal fashion. Rather, direct controls have been shown to suffer from severe government failures of the kind discussed in section B of this chapter.

What failures arise in government pollution-abatement programs? We described above the necessity for comparing costs and benefits in determining the most efficient level of pollution. In reality, cost-benefit comparisons are often not performed. Indeed, for some regulatory programs, the law prohibits a cost-benefit comparison as a way of setting standards. Rather, the 1970 Clean Air Act has often been interpreted to require that the marginal social damage be essentially zero. Taken literally, this policy would require zero emissions—an absurdly costly approach in most cases, as we sketched in the last section.

Second, enforcement is often haphazard. If the penalities for exceeding the standard are very harsh, the firm does face the right incentives. But for most programs, the penalties for noncompliance are minimal (a few thousand dollars plus legal fees). As a result, the firm has a very strong incentive to ignore or evade the pollution standard. Only fines in the hundreds of millions of dollars could correct this incentive problem.

Finally, standards are inherently a very blunt tool. They are generally the same for large firms and small firms, for steel mills in cities and in rural areas, and for acutely hazardous substances and mildly toxic ones. Such rules do not efficiently allocate pollution reduction among firms so that those whose marginal costs of pollution abatement are lowest do the most abatement. In numerous studies it has been shown that, because of the bluntness of pollution standards,

the nation is paying about twice as much as it would for the same pollution reduction efficiently engineered.

Emissions Taxes In order to avoid some of the pitfalls of direct controls, many economists have suggested a new instrument: pollution or emissions taxes requiring firms to pay a tax on their pollution equal to the amount of external damage. If American Steel were imposing external costs of $30 per ton on the surrounding community, then the appropriate emissions charge would be $30 per ton. In calculating its private costs, American Steel would find that each ton of pollution would cost it $10 of direct costs plus $30 in fees, for a total of $40 per ton of pollution. By equating the total cost (direct plus emissions fee) with the abatement cost, the firm would be led to curb its pollution back to the efficient level of pollution. If the emissions fee were correctly calculated—a big if!—then profit-minded firms would be led as if by a repaired invisible hand to the optimal point where marginal social costs and marginal social benefits of pollution are equal.

Emissions taxes (or externality taxes more generally) have been proposed by economists on numerous occasions as a way of reducing pollution or externalities in a flexible and efficient manner. Legislatures have been loathe to adopt this suggestion, and today only a handful of externality taxes exist, as compared with thousands of regulations.

Private Approaches

Surprisingly, not all solutions involve direct government action. Two private approaches may provide a moderately efficient outcome: private negotiations and liability rules.

Negotiation and the Coase Theorem Let's say that the government decides not to intervene. A startling analysis by Chicago's Ronald Coase suggested that voluntary negotiations among the affected parties would in some circumstances lead to the efficient outcome.[6]

The conditions under which this might occur arise

[6]Ronald Coase, "The Problem of Social Cost," *Journal of Law and Economics* (October 1960).

when there are well-defined property rights and the costs of negotiations are low. Thus, say that I am spilling chemicals upstream from you and doing damage to your fish ponds. Further, say that you can sue me for damage to your fish. In such a case, Coase argued, the two of us would have a powerful incentive to get together and agree on the efficient level of dumping.

Some have tried to take Coase's suggestion even further, arguing that efficient bargains *will* occur. But this conclusion is surely too optimistic. To say that there is room for an efficient, cost-saving bargain does not mean that a deal will always be struck—as the history of war, labor-management disputes, and the theory of games amply demonstrate.[7]

Nevertheless, Coase's analysis does point to certain cases where private bargains may help alleviate externalities—namely where there are few parties and where the gainers and losers from the externalities are clearly identified.

Liability Rules A second approach relies on the legal framework of liability laws or the tort system rather than upon direct government issuance of rules or regulations. Here, the generator of externalities is legally liable for any damages caused to other persons.

In some areas, this doctrine is well established. Thus, in most states, if you are injured because of negligent behavior of the driver of an automobile, you can sue for damages. Or, if a company's workplace is demonstrably unhealthful, a worker can sue the company for compensation (indeed, a number of asbestos-producing companies are in bankruptcy proceedings because of such claims).

Returning to our steel example, how would a perfect liability system contain the externality? If American Steel caused $30 of damages per ton of output, the victims would recover these damages through the courts. Thus the total cost faced by the firm would be $40 per ton ($10 of direct costs plus $30 of legal damages). Faced with such costs, firms would have strong incentives to reduce pollution back toward the efficient level analyzed above.

Unfortunately, liability rules have shortcomings no less than other systems of attacking externalities. The major difficulty of a liability system resides in the high costs of litigating damages.

■　■　■

We have now completed our introductory survey of the theory of government's role in the economy. This review is a sobering reminder of the responsibilities and shortcomings of collective action. On the one hand, responsible and representative governments must defend their borders, stabilize their economies, protect the public health, and regulate pollution. On the other hand, many policies to pursue the public interest suffer from inefficiencies and inconsistencies.

Does this mean we should abandon the visible hand of government for the invisible hand of markets? Economics cannot answer such a deep political question; all it can do is examine the strengths and weaknesses of both collective and market choices, and point to mechanisms (such as pollution taxes or liability rules) where a repaired invisible hand may be more efficient than the extremes of either pure laissez-faire or unbridled bureaucratic rule making.

---

[7]Those who have studied Chapter 25's appendix will recognize that the theory of games can be fruitfully applied to the bargaining situations involved in this kind of an externality. What lessons emerge?

Recall that a two-person game often ends up at inefficient outcomes. The "prisoner's dilemma" game resembles a situation where polluters' private interests lead them to high levels of soot and wastes. This could well be a long-term equilibrium point of the pollution game. Moreover, there is no theorem from game theory proving that an invisible hand will lead two or more bargainers to the Pareto-efficient level of pollution. Coase never proved such a result, nor has anyone else.

SUMMARY _____

A. Government's Role in a Modern Economy

1. The economic role of government has grown vastly. More and more activities in our complex, interdependent society have come under direct regulation and control.
2. A modern welfare state performs four economic functions: *(a)* It sets the economic framework—laws, constitutions, and rules of the economic game. *(b)* It establishes macroeconomic stabilization policy to even out the peaks and troughs of unemployment and to contain inflation. *(c)* It allocates resources to collective goods by taxing, spending, and regulating when market failure becomes important. *(d)* It redistributes resources by social welfare transfers.

B. Public-Choice Theory

3. In the normative theory of the state, government has the four functions discussed in section A. Public-choice theory analyzes how governments actually behave. In a complex and interdependent modern economy, government actions can serve to increase society's real income.
4. Public choice involves the aggregation of individual preferences into a collective choice. Under unanimity, all decisions must be made by consensus. Unanimity has the ideal property that all decisions are Pareto improvements (no one can be hurt), but the costliness of persuading everyone is so great that, in practice, no decisions are likely to be made under unanimity.
5. Thus most committees and legislative bodies use majority rule, which ensures that decisions will improve the welfare of at least half the voters. But majority rule suffers from a problem of "tyranny by the majority," and of the possibility of cyclical voting whereby, in the face of diverse tastes, no single program may command a majority.
6. Just as the invisible hand can break down, so there are government failures. These are cases where, because of the need for less-than-unanimous decisions, inefficient or inequitable outcomes can arise. Important cases are capture of a legislature by well-financed minorities or lobbies, the tendency of governments to finance too large programs for too long, and the short time horizons that plague competitive electoral arrangements.

C. Public Choice and Externalities

7. One major example of market failure that may require collective actions is external effects. These occur when the costs or benefits of an activity spill over to other people, without those other people being paid (or paying) for the costs (or benefits) received.
8. The most extreme example of an externality arises for public goods, like defense, where all consumers in a group share equally in the consumption and cannot be excluded. Less extreme examples like public health, inventions, parks, and dams also show public-good properties. These contrast with private goods, like bread, which can be divided and provided to a single individual.

9. Markets with externalities like pollution exhibit economic inefficiency: they will have laissez-faire or market equilibria in which the private marginal abatement costs and private marginal damages are equalized, rather than the social marginal abatement costs and social marginal damages being equal.

10. There are numerous steps by which governments can internalize or correct the inefficiencies arising from externalities. Alternatives include decentralized solutions (such as negotiations or legal liability rules) and government-imposed approaches (such as pollution emission standards or emissions taxes). Our experience indicates that all approaches show considerable inefficiency.

CONCEPTS FOR REVIEW

four functions of government:
  framework, stabilization, allocation,
  and distribution
market failures
private vs. public goods
public choice by: unanimity, majority
  rule
voting paradox

government failures: capture, myopia,
  bureaucracy
externalities
inefficiency of externalities
social vs. private cost
remedies for externalities: bargaining,
  liability, standards, and taxes

QUESTIONS FOR DISCUSSION

1. Name things government does now that it once didn't do. Can you think of things government used to do that it no longer does? What does this changing pattern of government activity indicate about the changing role of government in steering the economy?

2. Between now and 2000, would you expect the government's share in the national income to change? Why? What factors affect your answer?

3. It is useful to think of a spectrum of goods from purely public to purely private. On a piece of paper, draw a continuum and fill it with examples that are purely private, mostly private, half-and-half, mostly public, purely public. Under what conditions would you allow the market to allocate resources and when would you have the government make the economic decisions?

4. "The radical doctrines of three decades ago are the conservative doctrines of today." Is this ever true? Always true? Evaluate.

5. Evaluate critically the statement on the proper role of government attributed to Abraham Lincoln on page 771. Could believers in big government as well as believers in small government both agree with it?

6. "Local public goods" are ones that mainly benefit the residents of a town or state—such as beaches or schools open only to town residents. Is there any reason to think that towns might act competitively to provide the correct amount of local public goods to their residents? If so, does this suggest an economic theory of "fiscal federalism" whereby local public goods should be locally supplied?

7. Consider each of the following externalities. Decide whether it is serious enough to warrant collective action, and which of the four remedies considered in the chapter you would think to be most efficient.

(a) Steel mills emitting sulfur oxides into the Birmingham air
(b) Drunk drivers running into people or bushes
(c) People smoking in airplanes
(d) Students smoking in their single rooms
(e) Drivers under the influence of alcohol involving 25,000 fatalities per year
(f) Drivers under 21 under the influence of alcohol

8. Can you see why a market allocation of bread proceeds by unanimity? Why is this not possible for national defense? Does this difference suggest why the bread allocation may lead society to the utility-possibility frontier, while the national defense allocation may not?

9. In considering whether you want a pure laissez-faire economy or government regulation, discuss whether there should be government controls over: prostitution, drugs, and alcohol. Should there be a free market for body organs, adopted babies, and surrogate parenting?

10. Advanced problem: Figure 32-6 illustrates the pollution example of American Steel discussed in section C. The downward-sloping black curve shows the marginal cost of reducing pollution at each pollution level, while the solid red line measures the

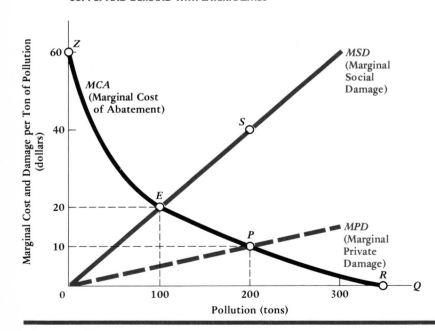

SUPPLY AND DEMAND WITH EXTERNALITIES

Figure 32-6 Inefficiency arising from externalities

marginal social damage exacted by American Steel's pollution. The dashed line, by contrast, shows the marginal private damage done by American Steel to itself.

Explain why point P represents the inefficient laissez-faire and unregulated outcome. Further explain why point E is the efficient outcome.

For extra credit, try to show how each of the four policy approaches (see pp. 773–775) moves the private equilibrium from P to E.

11. W. Averell Harriman, the eminent American diplomat who negotiated the nuclear test-ban treaty, once stated, "The difficulty of negotiating an agreement rises with the square of the number of participants." What is the implication of Harriman's Law for

(a) the feasibility of unanimity as a method of choosing the defense budget?

(b) the workability of the Coase approach as a market solution to externalities like pollution?

(c) the need for governments to pass coercive laws—ones that interfere with some individuals' choices—deciding where nuclear wastes are stored?

(d) Justice Holmes' dictum that "taxes are the price we pay for a civilized society"?

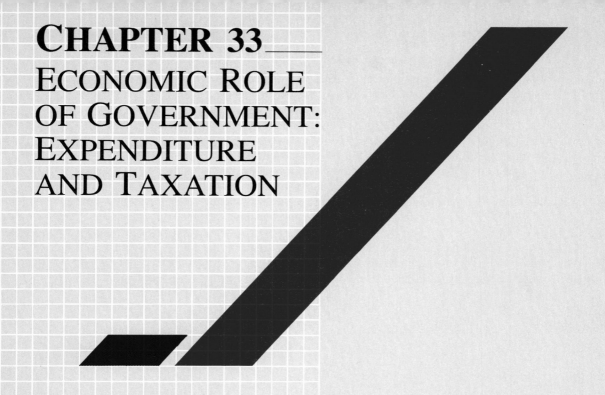

CHAPTER 33___
ECONOMIC ROLE
OF GOVERNMENT:
EXPENDITURE
AND TAXATION

The spirit of a people, its cultural level, its social structure, the deeds its policy may prepare, all this and more is written in its fiscal history. . . . He who knows how to listen to its messenger here discerns the thunder of world history more clearly than anywhere else.

Joseph Schumpeter

THE LAST CHAPTER analyzed the purposes underlying government intervention. We now examine the actual tax and spending behavior of different levels of American government. Section A begins with a brief discussion of the expenditures of government on the federal, state, and local level. We see, as well, some of the major changes in fiscal programs wrought under the Reagan administration. Section B then turns to the principles of taxation. We survey the federal tax system, and then review taxation at the state and local levels.

Finally comes the problem of tax incidence—upon whom does the burden of each tax ultimately fall? How does the tax burden on rich and poor compare with the transfer payments (such as welfare or social security benefits) received by each income group? The answers to these questions will help us to understand the message of fiscal history for different groups in our society.

A. GOVERNMENT EXPENDITURES

FEDERAL, STATE, AND LOCAL FUNCTIONS

Each American faces three levels of government: federal, state, and local. Before the twentieth century, local government was by far the most important of the three. The federal government did little more than pay for national defense, meet pensions and interest payments on past wars, finance a few public works, and pay salaries of government officials. Most of its tax collection came from liquor and tobacco excises and tariffs levied on imports. Life was simple. Local gov-

ernments performed most functions and depended primarily on property taxes for their finance.

Figure 33-1 plots the trends in government spending. You can see that the share of federal spending in GNP tripled during the Great Depression and bulged temporarily during World War II. Since 1940, federal spending has surpassed state and local spending.

Federal Expenditures

The U.S. government is the world's biggest business. It buys more automobiles and steel, meets a bigger

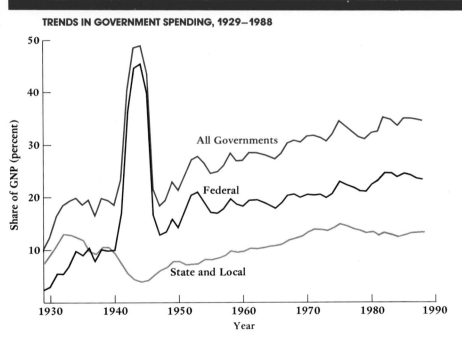

TRENDS IN GOVERNMENT SPENDING, 1929–1988

Figure 33-1   The share of government spending grew in war and peace

Federal spending rose rapidly in the Great Depression and bulged during World War II. In the 1960s and 1970s, government spending on income-support payments showed the steepest trends, while in the 1980s interest payments and defense spending grew most rapidly. Note how little the Reagan administration's policies succeeded in slowing the trend toward larger government spending. (Source: U.S. Department of Commerce.)

FEDERAL EXPENDITURE IN FISCAL YEAR 1989

	BUDGET (billions of dollars)	PERCENTAGE OF TOTAL
1. National defense, veterans, and international affairs	337	31
2. Social security	234	21
3. Interest on public debt	152	14
4. Income security	135	12
5. Health	132	12
6. Transportation, commerce, development	41	4
7. Education, training, employment	37	3
8. Agriculture	22	2
9. Energy, natural resources, environment	19	2
10. General government, justice	19	2
11. Science, space, technology	13	1
12. Miscellaneous and offsetting receipts	−47	−4
Net total	1,094	100

Table 33-1   Federal spending is dominated by defense and income support

Almost one-third of federal spending is to pay for defense and past wars. Almost half today is for rapidly growing "entitlement programs"—income security, social security, and health. Note how small is item 10's traditional cost of government. (Source: Office of Management and Budget, *Budget of the U.S. Government, Fiscal Year 1989.*)

payroll, and handles more money than any organization anywhere. The numbers involved in federal finance are astronomical—in the billions and trillions of dollars. The federal budget for 1989 is projected to be $1094 billion; this enormous number amounts to $4380 for each American or approximately 2.6 months of annual GNP.

Table 33-1 lists the major categories of federal expenditure for fiscal year 1989 (the federal fiscal year 1989 covers October 1, 1988, through September 30, 1989). By far the largest item is national security and international affairs, which includes the cost of equipping and staffing the Department of Defense. The most rapidly expanding item in the last two decades has been "entitlement programs"—those that provide benefits or payments to any persons who meet certain eligibility requirements set down by law. The major entitlements are social security (old-age, survivors, and disability insurance), health programs (in-

cluding Medicare for those over 65 and Medicaid for indigent families), and income security programs (including payments for food, unemployment insurance, and cash payments to the poor).

Another category includes programs for specific sectors of the economy: supporting agriculture, giving grants to local governments for sewage systems, and supporting space exploration. A final category is general government, those traditional functions of government such as paying for Congress, the judiciary, and the President. It is surprising to see that these traditional functions are dwarfed by all the rest.

Looking back at Figure 33-1, you might wonder why government's share in the economy has grown so rapidly in recent years. Virtually the entire growth in federal spending can be accounted for by entitlement programs, which have grown from 20 percent of the budget in 1960 to 45 percent in 1989. Taken together, all other programs have actually shrunk since 1960.

The federal government budget has grown during the last quarter-century because the populace has voted larger and larger transfer payments to itself.

State and Local Expenditures

Turn now to spending by state and local governments. Although outlays at lower levels are but two-thirds of federal amounts, many essential functions are performed by these smaller jurisdictions. Figure 33-2 illustrates the way states and localities spend their money. By far the largest item is education, for most of the nation's children are educated in schools financed primarily by local governments. Only at the college level does the private sector become a significant part of education expenditures. By attempting to equalize the educational resources available to every child, the nation helps to level out the otherwise great disparities in economic opportunity.

Fiscal Federalism

Students of American government are familiar with a division of political responsibilities among the different levels of government. A similar division of labor occurs in economic affairs. Ours is a *fiscal federalism* as well as a political federalism. The federal government is firmly entrenched in affairs that concern the entire nation—paying for defense, space, and foreign affairs. Local governments educate children, police streets, and remove garbage. States build highways and administer welfare programs.

As you examine Table 33-1 and Figure 33-2, you can see how the different kinds of expenditures are parceled out among the three levels of governments. Designing the appropriate system of fiscal federalism requires understanding the degree of spillover or externality in government programs (recall the discussion of externalities in Chapter 3 and in the last chapter). Generally, localities are responsible for "local public goods," activities whose spillovers to other regions are small. Since libraries are used by townspeople and streetlights illuminate city roads, these are appropriately paid for by local residents. Many federal functions, by contrast, spill over to all the nation's citizens (that is, federal activities cover "na-

PURPOSES OF STATE AND LOCAL EXPENDITURES, FISCAL 1985

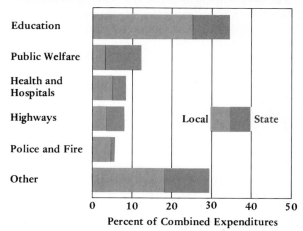

Figure 33-2   State and local governments concentrate on local public goods

Major state and local programs include education, welfare for local residents, financing hospitals, maintaining the streets, and similar tasks. In the division of labor among governments, cities pave their streets and states construct highways between cities, while the federal government pays for 90 percent of interstate highways. Do you see a pattern of fiscal federalism here? (Source: U.S. Bureau of the Census, *Government Finances in 1984–85*.)

tional public goods"). For example, an AIDS vaccine would benefit people from every state, not just those living near the laboratories where it is discovered; similarly, missiles sitting in North Dakota silos defend the entire country, not just the borders of the state where they are housed. Hence an efficient system of fiscal federalism will take into account the nature of the spillovers in government programs.[1]

The boundaries between the fiscal functions change over time. Hamilton, Roosevelt, and Johnson were leaders who broadened the federal role, while Presidents Jefferson, Coolidge, and Reagan attempted to check or reverse the accretion of fiscal powers at the

[1]What about world public goods like the global environment and climate, or global peril to species or rain forests, or the condition of the oceans? Does the lack of a world government suggest that global spillovers or externalities receive inadequate government attention?

federal level. In recent years, the most heated debates in economic policy have concerned the appropriate level for administering government programs. Liberals and conservatives debate about which level of government—federal, state, or local—should finance and administer programs like health care, food stamps, and welfare support for the poor. These are issues of the *balance of fiscal powers*.

B. ECONOMIC ASPECTS OF TAXATION

Taxes are what we pay for a civilized society.
        Justice Oliver Wendell Holmes

Obviously the government needs money to pay for its expenditure programs. It gets this money mainly from taxes, and also, in recent years, from borrowing. But if we look behind the money flows, what the government needs to build a missile or run a school is real economic resources. Government needs aluminum and teachers, or more generally, government has to draw upon the economy's scarce land, labor, and capital.

In choosing the structure of taxation, governments are in reality deciding how the needed resources shall be drawn from the nation's households and businesses and put into collective consumption and investment. So the money raised through taxation is the vehicle by which real resources are transferred from private goods to collective goods.

PRINCIPLES OF TAXATION

In the distant past, taxes were levied by those in power against those out of power. A nobleman in the court of Louis XIV might go scot-free, while a peasant in Normandy was heavily burdened. Such arbitrary distribution of taxes eventually gave way to more thoughtful fiscal principles as economists and political philosophers developed more rational approaches to tax policy.

Benefit vs. Ability-to-Pay Principles

Of the many principles underlying optimal taxation, two can be distinguished:

- That different people should be taxed in proportion to the benefit they receive from government programs. Just as people pay private dollars in proportion to their consumption of private bread, isn't it reasonable that a person's taxes should be related to his or her use of public roads or parks? This is the **benefit principle.**

- That the amount of taxes people pay should relate to their income, wealth, or ability to pay. Stated differently, taxation should be arranged to help accomplish what society regards as the proper and equitable distribution of incomes.[2] This is the **ability-to-pay principle.**

Horizontal and Vertical Equity In addition to these general principles, tax systems attempt to incorporate modern views about fairness or equity. One important principle is that of **horizontal equity,** which states that those who are essentially equal should be taxed equally.

The notion of equal treatment of equals has deep roots in Western culture. If you and I are alike in every way except the color of our eyes, all principles of taxation would hold that we should pay equal

---

[2]Economists following in the utilitarian tradition (see the discussion of utilitarianism in Chapter 19) used to argue that the utilities or satisfactions of different people can be added together to form a total social utility or satisfaction. Thus, if each extra dollar brings less and less extra satisfaction to each of us, and if the rich and poor are alike in their capacity to enjoy consumption, a dollar taxed away from a millionaire and given to a poor person is supposed to add more to total social utility than it subtracts. This suggests that, because those with higher income (or higher ''abilities to pay'') have less extra satisfaction from their last dollars than do poorer people, putting a larger tax share on higher-income people will increase total social satisfaction. See Chapter 19 for a discussion of the law of diminishing marginal utility; the appendix of Chapter 24, and especially Figure 24A-2, provides an illustration of how redistributing income from high-income to low-income individuals can raise the average utility or satisfaction of the population.

taxes. In the case of benefit taxation, if we receive exactly the same services from the highways or parks, the principle of horizontal equity states that we should therefore pay equal taxes. Or if a tax system followed the ability-to-pay approach, horizontal equity would dictate that people who have equal incomes should pay the same taxes.

In the last decade, unequal treatment in the American income-tax system led many to question its fairness. In 1976 President Carter called the tax code a "disgrace to the human race," and in 1986 President Reagan successfully negotiated a massive tax reform bill that tended to equalize taxation of equal incomes.

A more difficult issue, that of **vertical equity,** concerns the treatment of unequals, or the treatment of people in different circumstances. A traditional statement of this principle is: If equals are to be taxed equally, then unequals should be taxed unequally.

Unfortunately, this doctrine provides little guidance for resolving society's tax-policy issues. Imagine that A and B are alike in every respect except that B has 10 times the property and income of A. Does that mean that B should pay the same absolute tax dollars for police protection as A? Or that B should pay the same percentage of income in taxes to defray police expenses? Or if the police need more time to protect the property of well-to-do B, is it not fair for B to pay a larger fraction of income in taxes?

The principles of public finance simply cannot provide the best tax formula. It is one thing to say that the rich have greater ability to pay taxes than the poor or that they receive greater benefits. But general and abstract principles of taxation cannot resolve fundamental political questions of how differently unequals should be treated or how to define equity.

Pragmatic Compromises in Taxation

How have societies resolved these thorny philosophical questions? Governments have generally adopted pragmatic solutions that are based on neither benefit nor ability-to-pay approaches. Political representatives know that taxes are highly unpopular. After all, the cry of "taxation without representation" helped launch the American Revolution. Modern tax systems are an uneasy compromise between lofty principles and political power. As the canny French finance minister Colbert wrote three centuries ago, "Raising taxes is like plucking a goose: you want to get the maximum number of feathers with the minimum amount of hiss."

What practices have emerged? Where various public services at the local and national levels primarily benefit recognizable groups, and where those groups have no special claim for favorable or unfavorable treatment by virtue of their average incomes or other characteristics, modern governments generally rely on taxes of the benefit type.

Thus, local roads are usually paid for by local residents. Water and sewage treatment are often treated like private goods. Taxes collected on gasoline may on the whole be specifically devoted (or "earmarked") for roads.

Progressive and Regressive Taxes On the other hand, considerable reliance has been placed on *graduated income taxes*. A family with $50,000 of income is taxed more than one with $20,000 of income. Not only does the higher-income family pay a larger income tax, but it in fact pays a progressively higher fraction of its income.

This "progressive" tax is in contrast to a strictly "proportional" tax, which makes all taxpayers pay exactly the same proportion of income. A "regressive" tax takes a larger fraction of income in taxes from poor than from rich families.

A tax is called *proportional, progressive,* or *regressive* depending upon whether it takes from high-income people the same fraction of income, a larger fraction of income, or a smaller fraction of income than it takes from low-income people.

The different kinds of taxes are illustrated in Figure 33-3 on the next page. What are some examples? A personal income tax that is graduated to take more and more out of each extra dollar of income is progressive. A comprehensive sales tax will be mildly regressive. But a tax that is strictly proportional to the size of one's estate left at death is progressive since the person with twice the income tends on the average to have and bequeath more than twice the wealth. (It should be noted that the words "progressive" and "regressive" are technical economic terms relating to the proportions that taxes bear to different incomes. Do not interpret them in emotional or political terms.)

RELATION OF TAXES AND INCOME

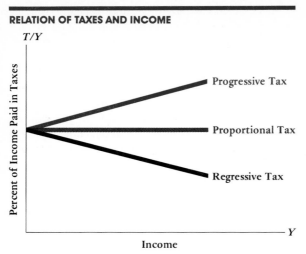

Figure 33-3 Progressive, proportional, and regressive taxes

Taxes are progressive if they take a larger fraction of income as income rises; proportional if taxes are a constant fraction of income; and regressive if they place a larger relative burden on low-income families than on high-income families.

Direct and Indirect Taxes Aside from their degree of progressivity, taxes can also be classified as direct or indirect.

Indirect taxes are usually defined as taxes that are levied on goods and services and thus only ''indirectly'' on individuals. Examples are excises and sales taxes, cigarette and gasoline taxes, tariff duties on imports, and property taxes.

Over the last century, legislatures in all democracies have increasingly relied upon **direct taxes,** which are levied directly upon individuals or firms. Examples of direct taxes are personal income taxes, social security or other payroll taxes, and inheritance and gift taxes. Corporation income taxes are also treated as direct taxes, because people receive the income of corporations. A major reason direct taxes have become increasingly popular is that these taxes can easily be tailored to fit personal circumstances, such as size of family, income, age, and more generally the ability to pay. By contrast, adjusting indirect taxes for personal situations is relatively difficult.

FEDERAL TAXATION

Let us begin our analysis of taxation with a survey of the federal system of taxation in place in the late 1980s. Table 33-2 provides an overview of the major taxes and shows whether they are progressive, proportional, or regressive.

Sales and Excise Taxes

Although no national sales tax has been passed, there are a number of federal excise taxes on specific commodities such as cigarettes, alcohol, and gasoline. Sales and excise taxes are generally regressive, because consumption in general, and purchase of these items in particular, takes a larger fraction of the income of a poor family than of a rich one.

Many economists and political leaders have argued for relying much more heavily on sales or consumption taxes than the United States has up to now. They reason that the country would like to encourage people to work hard and to earn income, and similarly that people should plough back those incomes into investment in plant and equipment rather than spend their earnings on consumption goods. To bring about this change in behavior, they argue, the country should substitute consumption taxes for income taxes. Critics of consumption taxes hesitate to move in that direction because of the regressive nature of sales taxes.

This debate is unlikely to be resolved in the near future. Nonetheless, these issues will be vital as the nation decides how to reduce its government deficits, whether to raise taxes, and what role consumption taxes should play in the coming years.

Social Insurance Taxes

Virtually all industries now come under the Social Security Act. Workers receive retirement benefits that depend upon their earnings history and past social security taxes. The social insurance program also funds a disability program and health insurance for the poor and elderly.

To pay for these benefits, employees and employers are charged a ''payroll tax.'' In 1988, this con-

Federal Tax Receipts, Fiscal Year 1989

	RECEIPTS (billions of dollars)	
Progressive		
Individual income taxes		412
Death and gift taxes		8
Corporation income taxes		118
Proportional		
Payroll taxes		355
Regressive		
Excise taxes		52
Tobacco and alcohol	11	
Customs duties	17	
Highways and airports	18	
Other	6	
Other taxes and receipts		20
Total		**965**

Table 33-2 Income and payroll taxes are the main federal revenue sources

Graduated progressive taxes are still the leading source of federal revenues, but proportional payroll taxes are closing fast. (Source: Office of Management and Budget, *Budget of the U.S. Government, Fiscal Year 1989.*)

sisted of a total of 15 percent of all wage income below a ceiling of about $45,000 a year per person.

The payroll tax has been the fastest growing part of federal revenues, rising from nothing in 1929, to 18 percent of revenues in 1960, to 36 percent in 1988.

As Table 33-2 shows, the payroll tax is intermediate in terms of progressivity; that is, it is close to being a proportional tax since it taxes a fixed fraction of employment earnings, but it has some regressive features in that it exempts property income and does not tax any earnings above $45,000 (for 1988).

Corporation Income Taxes

After a corporation has paid all its expenses and reckoned its annual income, it must pay part of its income to the federal government. The top federal corporation tax rate in 1988 is set at 34 percent of corporate profits. Small corporations pay a slightly lower tax rate on their first $75,000 of profits.

The corporation income tax is probably the most controversial of federal taxes. Many economists oppose this tax, arguing that the corporation is but a legal fiction. By taxing first corporate profits, then the dividends paid by corporations and received by individuals, the government subjects corporations to double taxation.[3] The double taxation means that income from corporations is the most heavily taxed part of the economy, and corporate investment is thereby discouraged.

Some economists advocate abolition of the corporation income tax. They would instead credit corporate-source income to the corporation's owners and tax the income at personal tax rates. Studies indicate that this step would improve the efficiency of the economy by a few billion dollars.

Those who advocate retaining the corporation tax do so on several grounds. They argue that the corporation tax is our most progressive tax, so its abolition would lower the degree of progressivity of the overall tax system (a result they do not favor). Some feel that a wide variety of taxes at low rates is a good idea. Others think that it is impractical to tax individuals on corporate income which has not actually been paid out to individuals. Some worry that the political system would be unwilling to write a more efficient substitute for the corporate tax and would probably increase regressive sales taxes. Some simply lean on the adage, "An old tax is a good tax."

While economists debated the corporation tax, circumstances changed. Businesses attacked the tax, and its revenues fell sharply as tax credits were enacted and depreciation allowances became more generous. The share of federal revenues raised by the corporation tax fell from 33 percent in 1951 to 9.8 percent in 1987. By the mid-1980s, many large corporations paid no taxes, and liberal groups pilloried a tax system under which a working family that earned $15,000 paid more taxes than some multinational companies with $10 billion of sales.

The Tax Reform Act of 1986 placed a hefty new tax burden on corporations. It repealed the investment tax credit and repealed a number of generous tax shelters.

[3]See the discussion of this issue in Chapter 20.

The net effect was to increase federal taxes on companies by about one-quarter for the late 1980s.

Value-Added Taxes

Finally, mention should be made of a tax that has been widely used by the Common Market countries of Europe. The **value-added tax,** or VAT, as it is called for short, collects taxes at each stage of production. Thus, for a loaf of bread, VAT is collected at the farmer's wheat stage of production, also at the miller's flour stage of production, at the baker's dough stage, and finally, at the grocer's delivered-loaf stage.

How, then, does it differ from a so-called turnover tax, widely used in the U.S.S.R and by Common Market countries before VAT? A turnover tax simply taxes every transaction made: wheat, flour, dough, bread. VAT is different because it does not include in the tax on millers' flour that part of its value which came from the wheat bought from the farmer. Instead, VAT taxes millers only on the wage and salary cost of milling, and on the interest, rent, royalty, and profit cost of this milling stage of production. That is, the raw-material costs used from earlier stages are subtracted from the selling price in calculating "value added" and the VAT on the value added. (Table 6-3 in Chapter 6 on national-income accounting explained this.)

It is easily seen, then, that VAT is essentially the same as a national sales tax. (Again, this was seen in Chapter 6; Table 6-3 showed that the sum of values added equals final sales.)

From time to time, Congress becomes infatuated with the idea of a VAT. Why so? In part, the appeal arises because the VAT is a tax on consumption, and many economists think that the United States should change its tax structure toward one based on consumption and away from one based on income.

In addition, some people may support VAT as a tax which has a good public image—it is a politically palatable sales tax, a sales tax that has been presented in a way that the electorate might accept. One pundit called VAT "the Sexy European."

Overall, is VAT a good idea? As with old age, it depends on the alternative. The most objective way of analyzing it would be to call VAT a national sales tax and then to compare it with other taxes.

The Individual Income Tax

The most important and complex tax—affecting everybody in the nation—is the individual income tax. All advanced industrial countries tax the incomes of their residents and citizens, but this tax is particularly important in the United States. Of all taxes, this one is most carefully tailored to the individual's ability to pay.

The individual income tax arrived late in our nation's history, for the Constitution forbade any direct tax that was not apportioned among the states according to population. In 1913, the Sixteenth Amendment to the Constitution provided that "Congress shall have power to lay and collect taxes on income, from whatever source derived, without apportionment among the several States. . . ."

The individual income tax raised much controversy but little revenue until World War II. Then, to raise money for the war effort, tax rates were increased sharply with the top tax rate reaching 94 percent in 1944–1945. After the war, the income tax continued as the most significant federal tax with the tax rate paid by those with highest incomes reduced to 70 percent in 1965, 50 percent in 1982, and 28 percent in 1988.

Periodically, the country rises up and, literally or figuratively, revolts against its tax system. The most recent revolt occurred in the mid-1980s when the perceived inequities in the system led political figures as disparate as liberal Senator Bill Bradley and conservative President Ronald Reagan to join forces in an assault on the tax code. The result was the landmark Tax Reform Act of 1986, which represented the most sweeping change in the tax code in a generation (some of the major features will be discussed below).

How does the federal income tax work? The principle is simple, although the forms are complicated. You start by calculating your income; you then subtract certain expenses, deductions, and exemptions, obtaining taxable income; you then calculate your taxes from a tax table.

The calculation of individual taxes is illustrated for a simple case in Table 33-3. This table shows the taxes faced by a family of four in 1988, after the 1986 Tax Reform Act was fully phased in.

(1) ADJUSTED GROSS INCOME (before exemptions and deductions)	(2) INDIVIDUAL INCOME TAX	(3) AVERAGE TAX RATE, PERCENT (3) = [(2) ÷ (1)] × 100	(4) MARGINAL TAX RATE (= tax on extra dollar)	(5) DISPOSABLE INCOME AFTER TAXES (5) = (1) − (2)
$ 5,000	$ −700	−14.0%	−14%	$ 5,700
10,000	−800	−8.0	14	10,800
20,000	1,080	5.4	15	18,920
50,000	5,148	10.3	28	44,852
100,000	16,348	16.3	33	83,652
150,000	29,563	19.7	33	120,437
200,000	42,763	21.4	28	157,237
1,000,000	221,816	22.2	28	778,184
10,000,000	2,237,816	22.4	28	7,762,184

Table 33-3   Federal income tax for a family of four, 1988

The table shows the average and marginal federal tax rates as well as total taxes and disposable incomes for a representative four-person family in 1988. Because of the earned-income tax credit, low-income workers with children get a tax rebate (this being a small "negative income tax"). Income is taxed first at 15 percent, then at 28 percent, then at 33 percent for high-income families until the *average* tax rate on taxable income reaches 28 percent. For the very highest incomes, the marginal tax rate is again 28 percent. [Source: U.S. Internal Revenue Service. This table assumes that deductions are the greater of the standard deduction ($5,000 for 1988) or 20 percent of income.]

Column (1) shows different levels of "adjusted gross income"—that is, wages, interest, dividends, and other income earned by the household.

Assuming that our household has four people, and takes certain deductions, column (2) shows the tax due. Note that the tax is actually negative for those with wage incomes of $5000 and of $10,000, indicating that the government is transferring income to low-income families. For people with positive taxes, the lowest "marginal tax rate," or extra tax per dollar of extra income, is 15 percent.[4] Taxes then rise rapidly in relation to income. Indeed, when income climbs to $10 million, around 22 percent will go to the government. The current top marginal rate of 28 percent is well below the 70 percent rate of the late 1960s or the 94 percent rate of the 1940s.

Column (3) shows just how progressive the personal income-tax code really is. A $50,000-a-year family is made to bear a relatively heavier burden than a $20,000-a-year family—the former pays 10 percent of income in taxes, while the latter pays but 5 percent. Someone earning $1 million each year is made to bear a still heavier relative burden.

Column (4) records the important marginal tax rate at each level of income. This begins at minus 14 percent for poor families, rises to 15 percent for those just entering the positive tax system, increases to 33 percent, then has a tax rate at the highest incomes of 28 percent.

Column (5) shows the amount of "disposable income left after taxes." Note that it always pays to get more income: even when a star tennis player moves into a higher tax bracket, the move gives her more income to keep. Confirm that the government never takes more than 33 cents out of each extra dollar.

[4]Note our friend "marginal," meaning extra. The notion of marginal tax rates is extremely important in modern economics. Remember the idea that people are affected by the extra costs or benefits that occur—"let bygones be bygones." Under this principle, the major effect of any taxes on incentives to supply capital or labor comes from the marginal tax rate. This notion has formed the intellectual core of modern "supply-side economics."

TOP TAX RATES IN MAJOR COUNTRIES

COUNTRY	TOP MARGINAL TAX RATE*
Japan	75%
France	65
Britain	60
Germany	56
Sweden	44
Denmark	40
Canada	34
United States	28

*The additional amount of taxes per dollar of additional taxable income paid by taxpayers with the highest incomes.

Table 33-4   U.S. has the lowest tax rates and the broadest base, 1988

Under the impact of both tax reformers and supply siders, the U.S. has lowered the tax rate on highest incomes from 92 percent in 1964 to 28 percent in 1988. This was accomplished by including many items of tax preference in taxable income. [Source: OECD, *Personal Income Tax Systems under Changing Economic Conditions* (Paris, OECD, 1986), updated by authors.]

Erosion of the Tax Base The U.S. government collects a larger fraction of its revenues from income taxes than most countries. It is interesting to note that the United States also has the lowest tax rates of any major industrial country. Table 33-4 shows that, after the Reagan economic revolution, the United States now has top individual tax rates far below those of other major industrial countries. How can the United States raise so much in taxes with such low tax rates? This paradox is easily answered: the American tax system includes more items in the definition of "taxable income" than do other countries'. That is to say, the number of exclusions and deductions from taxable income are fewer here than elsewhere.

At the same time, while most people face marginal tax rates of 15 or 28 percent, individual income taxes nonetheless average less than 10 percent of GNP. The difference arises because several items of income are excluded from taxation. Some call these untaxed items "loopholes," while more neutral terms are "tax preference" and "tax expenditure." The nature of tax expenditures is that these sources of income

receive preferential tax treatment. What are some of the untaxed items?

First, there are exemptions of $1950 per person for 1988. In addition, a married couple may take a "standard deduction," or subtraction from income, of $5000 in 1988. (Both these amounts increase each year with inflation.)

Second, some income avoids taxation by going to the "underground economy": cheating by farmers, doctors, or sales agents with fake expense accounts. In recent years the government estimates that 10 percent of taxable income is not reported.

Third, and more important than evasion, is legal tax avoidance. This is possible because Congress legislates many tax preferences that let certain income go lightly taxed or not taxed at all. There are so many preferences that they could fill a book (indeed, they do fill the IRS Code!). Examples include interest on state and local bonds, partial exclusion of social security benefits and payments for pensions, deductibility of most state and local taxes, and special treatment of income in certain industries such as oil and gas. Many tax preferences were trimmed in the 1986 tax act, and Table 33-5 shows the most important remaining ones.

The Flat Tax

Because of the continual erosion of the tax base by expansion of tax preferences, many have suggested a fundamental reform of the personal income-tax system called the "flat tax." This suggestion would include two steps:[5]

▪ Eliminate all loopholes by taxing all income once.

▪ Tax all income above an exemption level at a fixed (or flat) rate of around 20 percent.

At a stroke, this system would eliminate the preference for housing and medical care, while lowering the tax rate on capital income and high wages and sala-

---

[5]One of the earliest proposals for a flat tax was presented in Milton Friedman, *Capitalism and Freedom* (University of Chicago Press, 1963). A careful recent analysis is contained in Robert Hall and Alvin Rabushka, *Low Tax, Flat Tax, Simple Tax* (McGraw-Hill, New York, 1983).

TAX EXPENDITURES, 1989

	BILLIONS
1. Exclusion of pension contributions	$ 53.5
2. Deductibility of mortgage interest on owner-occupied homes	32.2
3. Exclusion of employer contributions for medical expenses	27.7
4. Deductibility of state and local taxes (other than on owner-occupied homes)	17.3
5. Exclusion of social security benefits	13.5
6. Capital gains carryover at death	12.5
Total:	
Top 6 items	**$156.7**
All individual tax expenditures	**$246.7**

Table 33-5 Tax preferences erode the tax base

Analysts have devised the term "tax expenditures" to reflect the fact that Congress can spend money directly by writing a check or indirectly by giving a tax break. The table shows the major tax preferences or tax expenditures. These are calculated by determining the amount of income excluded from the tax base and multiplying these numbers by the applicable tax rate. (Source: Office of Management and Budget, *Budget of the U.S. Government, Fiscal Year 1989.*)

ries. It would put thousands of tax lawyers out of business. The economy would become more efficient as people spent less time worrying about the impact of their actions on taxes and more time worrying about production of aircraft and computers and generation of innovations.

The rationale behind the flat tax was influential in the 1970s and 1980s and helped pave the way to the landmark Tax Reform Act of 1986.

THE REAGAN FISCAL REVOLUTION

From the election of Franklin Roosevelt in 1932 to the defeat of Jimmy Carter in 1980, the United States experienced a steady growth in the scale and scope of government. As we have seen, the federal government assumed countless new tasks, undertook to build dams and regulate power plants, increased its tax take and bolstered income-support programs, enacted social security, and printed food stamps. At the end of the 1970s, conservatives remonstrated that the United States was becoming a planned economy.

President Reagan came into office in 1981 with a different vision of how the economy should be managed. This view held that individual initiative and unfettered markets would produce the best possible economic outcome. President Reagan stated his philosophy succinctly:

> My program [is] a careful combination of reducing incentive-stifling taxes, slowing the growth of federal spending and regulations, and a gradually slowing expansion of the money supply. . . . That environment will be an America in which honest work is no longer discouraged by ever-rising prices and tax rates.

In February 1981 the Reagan administration introduced its "New Economic Policy." Although some shifts occurred, the fundamental tenets were generally followed closely through the next 8 years.

Overall Economic Policy

The Reagan years stressed managing the "supply side" rather than the "demand side" of the economy. In practice, this meant that economic policy should take microeconomic measures to improve productivity and economic efficiency rather than focusing upon macroeconomic steps to stabilize the overall economy.[6] Under the Reagan approach, macroeconomic policies, such as those involving the rate of growth of the money supply or the level of government spending, should be set with long-run expenditure goals in mind and not be "fine-tuned" in reaction to the business cycle. The Reagan economic philosophy advocated a return to the policy of the pre-Depression era, when the federal government took no active responsibility for managing the macroeconomy.

The performance of the economy during the Reagan years, as sketched briefly in Table 33-6, showed little improvement in most of the major indexes of

[6]An analysis of supply-side economics, along with a comparison with the demand-side (or Keynesian) approach, is contained in Chapter 10.

POLICY AREA	ECONOMIC PERFORMANCE	
	EARLY PERIOD (1960–1980)	REAGAN YEARS (1981–1988)
Economic policy and performance		
Growth of money supply (% per year)	5.5	8.6
Unemployment rate (%)	5.6	7.5
Inflation rate (% per year)	5.1	4.7
Productivity growth (% per year)	1.9	1.5
Personal savings rate (% of income)	7.3	5.2
Budget policy		
Spending/GNP (%)	20.2	24.0
Non-defense spending/GNP (%)	13.2	17.8
Taxes/GNP (%)	19.1	19.9
Deficit/GNP (%)	1.1	4.1
Tax policy		
Income taxes/total taxes (%)	60	73
Top tax rate (%, end of period)	50	28

Table 33-6   Economic performance in the Reagan and prior years

During the Reagan years, little improvement occurred in overall economic performance or in the share of GNP devoted to spending or taxation. The burden of the individual income tax grew relative to other taxes, and non-defense programs were trimmed. [Source: *Economic Report of the President 1988* (GPO, Washington) and updated by authors.]

economic policy: unemployment was higher than in the previous two decades; inflation averaged approximately the same rate (although it fell relative to the 1970s); while productivity growth and the personal savings rate deteriorated from the previous two decades. It is clear that "Reaganomics" produced no dramatic changes in American economic performance during the 1980s.

Budget Policy

The Reagan administration advocated a strong military buildup, maintenance of middle-class income-support programs like social security, and a draconian cutback of other civilian programs. The military buildup was based on the Reagan administration's belief that the Soviets had outpaced American military power. The attempt to cut nonmilitary programs stemmed from the President's philosophy that government intervention stifled initiative and innovation.

The Reagan budgetary philosophy was only partially successful. Defense spending grew rapidly during the Reagan period, but the other goals were blunted. Overall, government spending as a share of GNP grew from 20 percent in the 1960s and 1970s to 24 percent in the Reagan years. Moreover, whereas Reagan took office preaching the doctrine of balanced budgets, the 1980s were a period of the highest peacetime budget deficits in half a century. Finally, the attempt to cut civilian spending was thwarted by political forces that successfully protected their own spending programs.

Regulatory Relief

The 15 years prior to the Reagan government represented the heyday of regulatory institution-building. The United States legislated programs to deal with traffic safety, air and water pollution, hazards of the workplace, mine safety and strip mining, the dangers of nuclear power and toxic wastes, and even the safety of lawn mowers and toys. The Reagan administration believed that this regulation was overambitious in intent and overzealous in administration—and that the United States needed "regulatory relief."

The Reagan administration's attack on regulatory

programs was less visible but in many ways more effective than the budget or economic programs. No major regulatory programs were ended, and no major regulatory legislation was repealed. But virtually all regulatory programs were curbed; few new regulations were issued, enforcement was relaxed, and rules were generally interpreted in ways sympathetic to free-market advocates. In contrast to the late 1970s, by the end of the 1980s few voices were heard to argue that excessive regulation was hamstringing American business.

Tax Policy

The Reagan years produced a string of tax changes, with landmark legislation enacted in both 1981 and 1986. The 1981 Economic Recovery and Tax Act (ERTA) produced a major cut in both business and individual taxes. In keeping with the essence of supply-side economics, personal tax rates were cut across the board by 25 percent. The supply siders had contended, and the Reagan administration appeared to accept, that this major cut in tax rates would not markedly reduce tax revenues (this contention is further discussed in the section on the Laffer curve, pages 795–797 below). Evidence to date suggests, however, that the tax cuts led to a roughly proportional drop in tax revenues.

A further step came when President Reagan embraced the flat tax advocated by both tax reformers and supply siders (see pages 790–791 above). The monumental Tax Reform Act (TRA) of 1986 included a number of important new features:[7]

• Marginal tax rates were lowered from a top rate of 50 percent to a top rate of 28 percent for individuals and from 46 percent to 34 percent for corporations.[8]

---

[7]A nontechnical appraisal of the 1986 tax reform is contained in *The Journal of Economic Perspectives* (Summer 1987). This new economic journal, under the aegis of the American Economic Association, was launched in 1987 to present important economic ideas and results to the general audience of economists.

[8]The tax structure under the 1986 TRA has a peculiarity at the top end of the individual income tax. The *marginal* tax rate of wealthy persons (those with taxable incomes from $71,900 to $149,250 for a family of four) rises from 28 percent to 33 percent. This increase has the effect of raising the *average* tax rate to 28 percent. Above the top limit, the marginal tax rate then falls back to 28 percent for incomes above $149,250.

• The overall impact of the TRA was "revenue neutral"—meaning that it neither raised nor lowered total revenues. However, this neutrality was attained by raising taxes on corporations by $25 billion per year and lowering taxes on individuals by the same amount over the 1987–1991 period.

• Numerous tax preferences were trimmed. The most significant changes were that capital gains (income earned from sale of assets like common stocks and houses) are now taxed as ordinary income rather than at preferential rates; sales taxes are no longer deductible from income; interest paid on consumer loans and student debt is no longer deductible. In addition, the investment tax credit, a kind of fiscal "discount" for purchases of investment goods, was repealed.

Critics of the tax bill point to three shortcomings: First, as Table 33-5 shows, many tax preferences remain. Second, some believe that the increase in the burden of the corporation income tax will harm business investment. Finally, those whose primary concern is the federal budget deficit argue that tax reform is a glittery distraction from the premier economic problem of the decade, the bloated deficit.

The overall impact was to trim back many tax preferences, lessening the erosion of the tax base and allowing marginal tax rates to be cut in ways undreamt of a decade ago. Many hope that the new tax system will tilt the balance more toward rewarding honest labor than tax avoidance.

Distributional Impact What is the impact of the 1986 Tax Reform Act upon the distribution of income? At first blush, it might appear that high-income individuals will benefit by the quantum reduction in the marginal tax rates (from 50 percent to 28 percent at the top). In fact, because the tax base is significantly broadened, and in particular because the effective rate of corporation tax was raised significantly, the effect on taxes of the 1986 TRA was mildly progressive. Table 33-7 shows estimates of the percent change in total tax liabilities by income group. It finds that taxes will be lowered for the bottom end of the income distribution and raised for the top tenth. The higher tax in the top tenth results mainly from the higher corporation tax, which is assumed to fall on the owners of capital.

IMPACT OF TAX REFORM

	PERCENT CHANGE IN:	
INCOME GROUP	FEDERAL INDIVIDUAL AND CORPORATE INCOME TAXES	TOTAL FEDERAL TAXES
Top tenth of households	+3	+2
Top 5%	+4	+3
Top 1%	+5	+5
Second tenth	−6	−4
Third	−6	−3
Fourth	−7	−4
Fifth	−8	−4
Sixth	−12	−6
Seventh	−16	−7
Eighth	−24	−10
Ninth	−32	−11
Bottom tenth	−44	−16

Table 33-7   Change in federal taxes as a result of the 1986 Tax Reform Act
The 1986 Tax Reform Act broadened the tax base, increased personal exemptions and deductions, and lowered marginal tax rates. Overall, the impact was to lower the tax burden on the low-income groups and raise taxes on the highest tenth of households. In this calculation, income from corporations is imputed to households according to their ownership of stocks, and the corporation tax is assumed to fall upon the owners of capital. [Source: Joseph A. Pechman, "Tax Reform: Theory and Practice," *The Journal of Economic Perspectives* (Summer 1987), p. 20.]

Overall Assessment

What will be the impact of the Reagan fiscal revolution on the overall economy? The answer will become clear only in the years to come. The evidence to date suggests that the large fiscal deficits have led to major changes in the patterns of saving and investment, significantly lowering private saving in response to higher levels of public dissaving in the form of budget deficits. Many reform proposals—particularly tax and regulatory reform—will need a decade or more before potential benefits can be assessed. Perhaps the most important impact lies in the changing attitudes about government. In the 1980s, for the first time in half a century, a President consistently spoke of the need for self-reliance and of the perils when a free people lean too heavily on the economic intervention of government. Public attitudes indicate that at dec-

ade's end many Americans continue to share President Reagan's vision of minimal government.

TAXES AND EFFICIENCY

The recent tax reforms lead to one of the most important questions about taxation, especially progressive taxation. Is there an adverse effect of high marginal tax rates? Do high tax rates discourage work, saving, and risk taking?

The impact of tax rates on work effort is unclear. We have seen in Chapter 28 that taxation has an ambiguous effect on the total number of hours worked because the labor supply curve may be backward-bending. Some people may, as a result of progressive taxes, prefer more leisure to more work. Other people may work harder in order to make their million. Many doctors, artists, celebrities, and business executives, who enjoy their jobs and the sense of power or accomplishment that they bring, will work as hard for $150,000 as for $200,000.

The effect of high taxes on property income is more clear-cut. Studies have determined that taxing a particular kind of capital or property will cause resources to move to lower-taxed sectors. For example, if corporate capital is double-taxed, some of people's savings will flow to non-corporate sectors like housing. If risky investments are treated unfavorably, then investors will prefer safer havens.

The most important effect may arise not from *levels* of taxation, but from *differences* in tax rates. There are a sufficient number of respectable "tax shelters" open to wealthy people so that they may typically pay much less than the high tax rates shown in Table 33-3. They may invest in tax-exempt bonds, drill for oil and

gas, or put their money in vacation homes. In these sheltered sectors, investors may face low taxes or no taxes at all. Hence high marginal tax rates may have the effect of diverting economic activity to lightly taxed sectors.

The Laffer Curve

From this brief review of the effects of tax rates on economic activity, we can turn to an important movement that sprang up around 1980. The supply-side school argued that the disincentive effects of high marginal tax rates were responsible for many of the nation's ills—low saving, recession, stagnant productivity, and high inflation. Led by Arthur Laffer, along with Jude Wanniski, Norman Ture, and Paul Craig Roberts, this group emphasized the importance of low marginal tax rates for good economic perform-

THE LAFFER CURVE IN THEORY AND REALITY

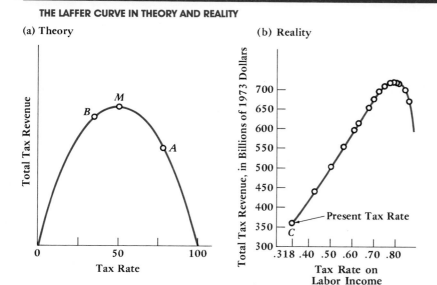

Figure 33-4   Evidence indicates that lowering tax rates would lower revenues

The Laffer curve predicts that tax revenues respond to different tax rates. In the theoretical Laffer curve on the left, a tax rate of 50 percent produces maximal revenues. By reducing taxes from point *A* to point *B*, revenues might rise even as tax rates fall.

Careful empirical studies, such as in **(b)** at right, find a curve that leans sharply to the right, with the U.S. tax system approximately at point *C*. In this realistic case, small movements in tax rates will have roughly proportional effects on revenues. [Source: Don Fullerton, "Relationship between Tax Rates and Government Revenue," *Journal of Public Economics* (October 1982).]

ance. One of the major analytical tools introduced by this group was the *Laffer curve*.

The theoretical Laffer curve is shown on the left side of Figure 33-4 on the previous page. The general shape can be seen in the following way: clearly at a zero tax rate there will be no revenues. Also, when taxes reach 100 percent, no one would be silly enough to work, so again there would be no revenues. The two ends of the curve are thus tacked down.

What lies in between? As tax rates rise from zero, according to this view, total revenues rise. Then, at some point, people begin to work less, save less, and divert their activity to the underground economy. Thus at, say, point M in Figure 33-4(a), the total revenue received by the Treasury is maximized. The curve is sometimes drawn so that the peak of the Laffer curve comes at a 50 percent tax rate, although it is not clear that Laffer or other members of the supply-side school consistently argued that the maximum revenue point comes at a tax rate of 50 percent.

What happens when the tax rate rises above point M in Figure 33-4(a)? The disincentive effect outweighs the revenue effect. So government tax revenues actually begin to decline even though tax rates are raised. If you believe that the economy is to the right of the maximum-revenue point in Figure 33-4(a), then you could recommend a policy of having your cake and eating it too—lower tax rates, increase economic efficiency, and raise revenues.

How did mainstream economists react to this radical new theory? Of course, if the Laffer curve were as depicted in Figure 33-4(a), who would not endorse a cut in tax rates at point A? But the economic evidence did not support the supply-side proposition. Figure 33-4(b) shows a real-world Laffer curve constructed by Virginia's Don Fullerton after examining several econometric studies of the response of work effort to tax rates. The maximum-revenue point appears to be far to the right of the tax rates that the economy has seen in the last few decades. The current tax rates are shown as point C. Fullerton's survey predicts that a cut in taxes would produce an almost-proportional reduction in tax revenues.

The Supply-Side Experiment Supply-side economists in 1980 proposed a bold solution to America's economic ills. They argued, in effect, that the U.S. economy was on the wrong side of the great revenue-divide, say at point A in Figure 33-4(a). They persuaded President Reagan, and he persuaded Congress, to cut personal tax rates by 25 percent by 1983.* Supply siders promoted the cuts as the needed stimulants for America's sick economy and argued that the cuts would produce no side effects such as increasing budget deficits.

What is the evidence to date? History gives little comfort to the supply-side prescription. Personal savings rates declined, rather than rose, after the tax cuts.[9] The Laffer-curve prediction that revenues would rise following the tax cuts has proven false; indeed, federal revenues shrank and the federal budget consequently moved from approximate balance in 1979 to a gaping $200 billion deficit after 1983.

[9]A full discussion of the determinants of saving is provided in Chapter 7, with a graphical history of recent trends displayed in Fig. 7-11.

---

*One of the puzzles about the supply-side revolution is how an obscure idea, which received virtually no support from empirical studies or from mainstream economists, could have achieved such legislative success in a few months. This question is addressed by David Stockman. Stockman was one of the architects of supply-side policies when he served as Director of the Office of Management and Budget during the Reagan administration from 1981 to 1984. This is how Stockman describes President Reagan's conversion to the Laffer curve:

In January 1980, Governor Reagan's campaign managers had sent him to school for a few days to get brushed up on the national issues. There, Jack Kemp, Art Laffer, and Jude Wanniski thoroughly hosed him down with supply-side doctrine.

They told him about the "Laffer curve." It set off a symphony in his ears. He knew instantly that it was true and would never doubt it a moment thereafter.

He had once been on the Laffer curve himself. "I came into the Big Money making pictures during World War II," he would always say. At that time the wartime income surtax hit 90 percent.

"You could only make four pictures and then you were in the top bracket," he would continue. "So we all quit working after four pictures and went off to the country."

High tax rates caused less work. Low tax rates caused more. His experience proved it.

The quotation is from Stockman's *The Triumph of Politics* (Avon, New York, 1987).

Subtle effects may yet appear, and, given the difficulty of performing controlled experiments in economics, no definitive appraisal of the supply-side tax cuts may be possible. But the central prediction of the supply-side economists—that working and saving would increase dramatically as marginal tax rates were cut—has up to now been far off the mark. By conventional scientific standards, the supply-side experiment suggests that the underlying theory should be rejected.

STATE AND LOCAL TAXES

Turn now to public finance other than federal. Although the federal government raises more taxes than other levels of government, these lower levels are important in their own right.

To see the main source of funds that finance state and local expenditures, turn to Figure 33-5.

Property Tax

The property tax accounts for about 30 percent of the total revenues of state and local finance. Figure 33-5 shows that localities are the main recipient of property taxes.

The property tax is levied primarily on real estate—land and buildings. Each locality sets an annual tax rate. Chicago, for example, sets a nominal tax rate of 10.2 percent of "assessed value" (i.e., of the value as determined by the city). If my house has been assessed at $100,000, my tax is $10,200. However, in most places assessed valuations tend to be but a fraction of true market value. In Chicago, assessments are about 16 percent of market value, so the true tax rate is only 1.63 percent of market value.

The property tax became controversial in the 1970s. During the housing boom of the 1970s, housing valuations and taxes skyrocketed. Taxpayers revolted. In Massachusetts, voters passed Proposition $2\frac{1}{2}$, limiting tax payments to $2\frac{1}{2}$ percent of market value. Today, almost half the states have imposed limitations on property or other taxes; these will prevent state and local taxes from rising as rapidly as they did in the 1970s. They have also led several cities and states into severe fiscal crises as these governments ran out of tax funds and were forced to cut services.

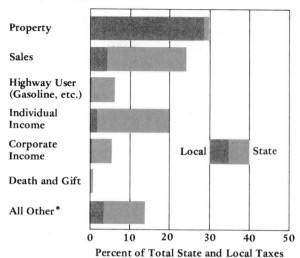

SOURCES OF STATE AND LOCAL TAX REVENUE, FISCAL YEAR 1985

*Does not include federal revenue sharing

Figure 33-5   Property and sales taxes dominate at state and local levels

Note especially the heavy reliance of localities on the property tax. Houses, land, and other fixed real-estate assets are one of the few tax bases that cannot easily flee to the next town to avoid a city's tax. (Source: U.S. Bureau of the Census, *Government Finances in 1984–85*.)

Sales Taxes

States get most of their revenues from general retail sales taxes. Each purchase at the department, drug, or clothing store incurs a percentage tax. (Sometimes food and other necessities are exempt.)

Also, states usually add their own liquor and tobacco excises to the federal excises. Such taxes are often tolerated because most people—including many cigarette smokers and moderate drinkers—feel that there is something vaguely immoral about tobacco and alcohol. They think these "sin taxes" stun two birds with one stone: the state gets revenue, and vice is made more expensive.

Other Taxes

Most states tax the net income of a corporation and collect miscellaneous other fees from business enterprises. Forty-five states imitate the federal government, but on a much smaller scale, by taxing individuals according to the size of their incomes. Even a few cities tax incomes earned by those who live or work there.

There are other miscellaneous revenues. Many states tax bequests. Some states, such as Nevada and New Jersey, tax slot machines and racetrack betting or legitimize gambling by operating lotteries. And most states levy "highway user taxes" on gasoline.

Intergovernmental Grants-in-Aid

A further revenue source for lower levels of government are *grants-in-aid,* which represent financial aid that states and localities receive from higher levels of government.

Many public-finance specialists feel that the federal government is a more efficient tax collector than are states and localities. Below the national level, people can avoid taxes by going to other states or towns. On the other hand, few people emigrate from the United States to avoid taxes. Hence, taxes levied at the national level are less likely to cause distortions than those levied on mobile people or capital at the state and local level.

In the 1960s and 1970s, the federal government stepped up its grants-in-aid to states and localities through general revenue sharing (transfers not tied to particular government programs). By 1980, states and cities received one-fifth of all revenues from Washington. But the federal grants-in-aid were cut sharply during the Reagan years. He viewed these as a kind of public dole, and by 1988 general revenue sharing had been abolished.

CONCLUSION: THE THORNY PROBLEM OF TAX INCIDENCE

In concluding this survey of taxes, let us turn to the issue of tax incidence. Even if the electorate has made up its mind about how it would like the tax burden to be allocated, the following difficult issues remain:

Who ultimately pays a particular tax? Does its burden stay on the person or firm who actually pays the tax? Or is the tax shifted? We should not assume that

the people or firms who send the tax monies to the government will end up paying that tax. Businesses may be able to shift the tax "forward" onto their customers by raising their price as much as the tax, or businesses may shift the tax "backward" onto their suppliers (owners of labor, land, and other factors), who find themselves with lower wages, rents, and other factor prices than they would have enjoyed had there been no tax.

Economists therefore are concerned primarily with the final **incidence** of the tax—the way its burden ultimately is borne and its total effects on work effort, saving, commodity prices, factor prices, resource allocations, and the composition of production and consumption.

Tax-incidence questions include: Does a 5-cent-a-gallon tax on gasoline raise the price at the pump by 5 cents, so that the incidence is on the consumer? Or does the tax lower the price of crude oil so that the incidence is on the oil producers? Or is the incidence somewhere in between? Does it change coal prices? And does the tax kill off oil production, so that it has incidence effects beyond those which show up in money prices and wages and even beyond the burdens that you can allocate among the different citizens?

Parts Four and Five developed some of the important tools that are needed to tackle this thorny problem. In some simple cases, involving only supply of and demand for a single commodity, incidence analysis is straightforward. In other cases, there are effects that cascade through the economy, making analysis extremely complex and sometimes requiring general-equilibrium approaches.

What is the *fiscal* incidence of the government tax and transfer system as a whole? Economists have attempted to answer this question of the overall degree of progressivity or regressivity by allocating all taxes and transfer payments to different groups. Such a study can be only approximate, since no one is sure how the corporation tax or the property tax gets shifted.

The conceptual experiment we want to make is:

- To measure incomes without taxes and transfers
- Then to measure incomes with taxes and transfers
- And finally to measure *incidence* as the difference between these two situations

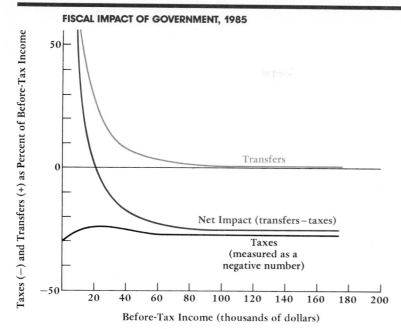

Figure 33-6   Who pays the taxes? Who benefits from transfers? What is government's net fiscal impact?

How has the modern welfare state affected the real income of its citizens? The lower black line shows that federal taxes are regressive at low levels of income, then become progressive after that point. The light red line of federal transfer programs at the top—items such as welfare, social security, and unemployment insurance—is highly progressive, being concentrated in lower-income groups. Therefore, the net impact, or "incidence," of federal taxes and transfers is highly progressive, as is shown by the downward-sloping red line. Because of taxes and transfers, income after government tax and transfer programs is more equally distributed than is income from market sources alone.

[Source: The methodology is described in Joseph Pechman, *Who Bears the Tax Burden* (Brookings Institution, Washington, 1974), Variant 1C. The data shown, based on unpublished tabulations made available by Dr. Pechman, are for 1985.]

Of course, economists are not magicians who can make such controlled experiments, but they take careful measurements and use good judgment to estimate the effects of taxes and spending as best they can.

Incidence of Federal Taxes and Transfers

Figure 33-6 shows the results of a recent study of the incidence of all federal taxes and transfers. The fed-eral tax system is slightly regressive at the low end, and then it becomes roughly progressive at higher incomes.

However, taxes are only half the story. Transfers are a substantial fraction of income for low-income households; that is, the poor receive proportionally much more in government programs than do the middle classes or the upper classes. Therefore, when the transfers and taxes are added together to get net fiscal incidence, we find that government programs as a whole are very progressive.

This pattern of net fiscal impact is similar to that found in most modern welfare states. As one recent survey of the subject concluded:

> The evidence for almost all countries suggests that the tax system overall has almost no effect on income distribution. . . . This results from the progressive impact of income taxes being offset by regressive taxes, notably employers' social security contributions and indirect taxes. . . . When tax, transfer, and expenditure programmes are viewed together, it is apparent that public expenditure programmes, particularly the provision of cash transfers, have been almost totally responsible for the changes in income distribution which governments have brought about. . . .[10]

[10]Peter Saunders, "Evidence on Income Redistribution by Governments," OECD, Economics and Statistics Department, Working Papers, No. 11 (January 1984).

SUMMARY

A. Government Expenditures

1. The American system of public finance is one of fiscal federalism. The federal government concentrates its direct spending on issues of national concern, on national public goods like defense and space exploration. States and localities generally focus on local public goods—those whose benefits are largely confined to local or state boundaries.

2. Government spending and taxation today takes approximately one-third of total GNP. Of this total, 70 percent is spent at the federal level, and the balance is divided between state and local governments. Only a tiny fraction of government outlays is devoted to traditional activities like police and the courts.

B. Economic Aspects of Taxation

3. Notions of "benefits" and "ability to pay" are two principal theories of taxation. Justice implies taxing equals equally, unequals unequally. A tax is progressive, proportional, or regressive as it takes a larger, equal, or smaller fraction of the incomes from rich families than from poor families. Direct and progressive taxes on incomes are in contrast to indirect and regressive sales and excise taxes.

4. More than half of federal revenue comes from progressive personal and corporation income taxes. The rest comes from proportional or regressive taxes on payrolls or consumption goods. Local governments raise most of their revenue from property taxes, while sales taxes are most important for states.

5. The individual income tax is levied on "income from whatever source derived," less certain exemptions and deductions. The 1986 Tax Reform Act completely overhauled the federal income tax, trimming many tax preferences and lowering marginal tax rates substantially. Even with its lower tax rates, the individual income tax is progressive, placing higher average tax burdens on rich than on poor people.

6. The fastest-growing federal tax is the payroll tax, used to finance social security. This is an "earmarked" levy, with funds going to pay public pensions and health and disability benefits. Because there are visible benefits at the end of the stream of payments, the payroll tax has elements of a benefit tax. The corporation tax had almost withered away over the last four decades but was reinvigorated in the 1986 Tax Reform Act.

7. The Reagan fiscal revolution (1981–1988) stood on four pillars: an economic policy that moved away from Keynesian demand management toward concern with promoting free and unfettered private enterprise; a budget policy that bolstered defense, cut civilian programs, and gave little weight to the potential damage done by fiscal deficits; a regulatory program reducing the burden of federal regulations, especially those in health, safety, and the environment; and, most important, lower tax rates and burdens. While many Reagan initiatives fared poorly, the tax programs, especially the supply-side tax cuts of 1981–1983 and the tax reform of 1986, changed the tax structure more drastically than any changes since World War II.

8. Economists are divided on the extent to which taxes hurt incentives to work or save. An extreme view of this debate is provided by the supply siders. According to the theory shown in the Laffer curve, tax rates in the late 1970s were so high that revenues were actually reduced. This extreme view has not received empirical support.

9. The incidence of a tax refers to its ultimate economic burden and to its total effect on prices and other economic magnitudes. Those upon whom a tax is first levied may succeed in shifting part of its burden forward or backward. The tools of Parts Four and Five help in tackling this difficult problem. The progressiveness in benefits of transfer programs offsets the regressiveness of our tax structure at low incomes, so the net fiscal impact of government in today's welfare state is highly progressive.

CONCEPTS FOR REVIEW

benefit and ability-to-pay principles	1986 Tax Reform Act
direct and indirect taxes	incentive effects
progressive, proportional, regressive taxes	Laffer curve in theory and reality
tax incidence and shifting	fiscal federalism and local vs. national public goods
Reagan fiscal revolution: four elements	fiscal incidence

QUESTIONS FOR DISCUSSION

1. Make a list of different federal taxes in order of their progressiveness. If the federal government were to trade in income taxes for consumption or sales taxes, what would be the effect in terms of overall progressiveness of the tax system?

2. "Since people don't change their smoking habits much as a result of taxation, and since the poor smoke, a tax on cigarettes is really no different from a tax on bread." Do you agree? If so, what ought to be done? Is there a way of providing economic incentives not to smoke (drink, gamble, . . .) and not hurt lower-income groups as a whole?

3. Should marijuana and other drugs be made legal and taxed to raise revenue? Should gambling be made legal everywhere, as it is in some states, to provide a cheerful source of tax revenues?

4. "I favor progressively taxing what people spend to consume, not what they earn. My consumption tax would encourage more saving and investment—since we'd then no longer double-tax both saving and the fruits of that saving." Analyze this argument in favor of taxing consumption.

5. Proponents of supply-side economics point to the experience of the 1960s as evidence that the United States was in 1960 on the wrong side of the peak of Mt. Laffer in Figure 33-4(a). They note, "After the Kennedy-Johnson tax cuts of 1964, federal revenues actually rose from $110 billion in 1963 to $133 billion in 1966. Therefore, cutting taxes raises revenues." What fallacies are being committed here? (HINT: *Post hoc, ergo propter hoc.*) What would be a proper analysis?

6. Is it possible that some taxes *promote* economic efficiency? Consider, for example, taxes on sulfur emissions or firms with a poor safety record. Construct a list of taxes that you think would increase rather than decrease efficiency. How many are on the books? Can you think of reasons why Congress passes so few efficiency-promoting taxes?

7. The following table gives the data for a hypothetical tax system:

(1) ADJUSTED GROSS INCOME	(2) DEDUCTIONS AND EXEMPTIONS	(3) TAXABLE INCOME	(4) INDIVIDUAL INCOME TAX
$ 5,000	$ 5,000	$ 0	$ 0
10,000	9,000	1,000	150
20,000	12,000	8,000	1,200
50,000	20,000	30,000	4,500
100,000	30,000	70,000	14,500
500,000	100,000	400,000	97,000

At each income level, calculate the marginal and average tax rates on taxable income. If adjusted gross income is used as an income base, is this system one which is progressive, proportional, or regressive?

8. Using the data from columns (1) and (2) in question 7, construct a hypothetical flat tax with a tax rate of 20 percent on taxable income (for a discussion of the flat tax, see page 790). Calculate the average tax as a percent of adjusted gross income. Is such a flat tax progressive or proportional using adjusted gross income as an income base? Is it more or less progressive than the conventional income tax that is illustrated in question 7?

9. Consider the following data on taxes, wages, and hours of work:

TAX RATE	PRE-TAX WAGE RATE	POST-TAX WAGE RATE	HOURS OF WORK	PRE-TAX EARNINGS	TAX REVENUES
0%	$10/hour	————	2,000	————	————
10	10	————	2,000	————	————
20	10	————	1,950	————	————
30	10	————	1,900	————	————
40	10	————	1,850	————	————
50	10	————	1,800	————	————
60	10	————	1,700	————	————
70	10	————	1,600	————	————
80	10	————	1,300	————	————
90	10	————	600	————	————
100	10	————	0	————	————

Complete the blank items in the table. Draw a Laffer curve on a sheet of graph paper. At what tax rate does the government collect maximal revenue? Explain in words what is happening in the economy as the tax rate increases.

10. Some public goods are local, spilling out to residents of small areas; others are national, benefiting an entire nation; some are global, having an effect upon the entire globe. A private good is one where the spillover is negligible. For the following goods or services, describe the extent of the spillover, indicate the level of government that could design policies most efficiently, and suggest one or two appropriate government actions that could solve the externality:

(a) An AIDS vaccine.

(b) A pollution-abatement program to prevent acid rain from killing off lakes in the northeast that are dying as a result of sulfur emissions from states in the midwest.

(c) Coastal defenses on the south coast of Britain.

(d) Noise from a factory in a residential area.

(e) A glass of orange juice.

(f) Global chlorofluorocarbon emissions that deplete stratospheric ozone and increase the incidence of skin cancer.

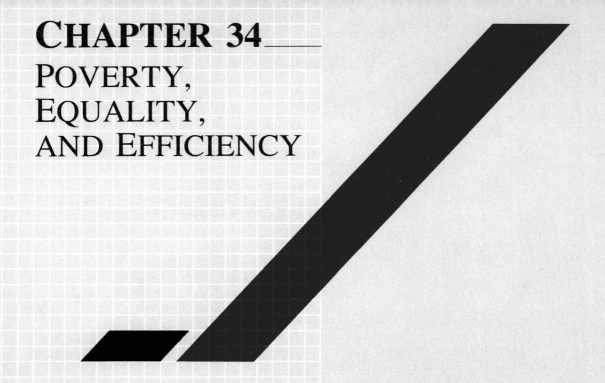

CHAPTER 34
POVERTY, EQUALITY, AND EFFICIENCY

[The conflict] between equality and efficiency [is] our biggest socioeconomic tradeoff, and it plagues us in dozens of dimensions of social policy. We can't have our cake of market efficiency and share it equally.

Arthur Okun (1975)

WE LIVE IN A double-standard economy. Our laws proclaim the rights of man and woman, the principle of one-person one-vote, and equality of opportunity. This is the rhetoric of modern democracy. But the institutions of modern capitalism speak otherwise. On city streets, people are told, "Work or go hungry" and "Economic power goes to those who are white, male, and well connected."

Which face is reality? The answer is both, to some degree. Democratic countries value equality of opportunity and of outcome. They have taken steps to raise all toward the living standards and political power of the more fortunate. But in some areas, the steps are tentative. The modern welfare state has found limits to its affluence. And as nations attempt to equalize incomes among their citizens, they encounter greater and greater effects on incentives and efficiency. Today, people are asking, how much of the social pie is being sacrificed in order to divide it more equally?

In earlier chapters, we have met each of these problems separately. In Chapter 26, we first began to discuss issues of income distribution—its measures as well as sources of inequality. The next chapters focused in on how markets determine incomes, as well as on the possible inefficiencies from taxation.

In this chapter, we return to the problem by examining poverty and its eradication, along with the possible inefficiencies that arise from policies to enhance equality. We begin by analyzing the definition and sources of poverty. The next section examines the tradeoffs between equality and efficiency, asking whether attempts to distribute the nation's income more equally might make it smaller. In the final section we review antipoverty programs in the United States along with proposals for reform.

MEASUREMENT AND TRENDS IN POVERTY

The Bible says, "The poor, ye shall always have with you." And this was the view of the classical economists and most people until very recently; the classical economists preached an economics that was the dismal science of unalterable distribution of income.

The wages of labor, the rent of land, the profit of capital were determined by economic law, and not by political power. If labor unions or reform political parties tried to use the state to modify these facts of life, they would be ineffective in the end. Such well-meaning attempts would beget a smaller national output, which would probably still get distributed in about the same way. Vexation and violence brought about by trying to alter this would merely produce chaos and class warfare. This was the doctrine that the classical economists believed.

In the 1960s, the United States would not accept limited aspirations. We would send a man to the moon, banish unemployment, and export democracy to every corner of the globe. Persuaded by those who held ours was a boundlessly affluent society, President Kennedy, before his 1963 assassination, mapped out a "war on poverty." And the first head of the poverty program prophesied that by 1976, for our bicentennial, poverty could be abolished in the United States.

Before we learn the fate of these lofty dreams, we must carefully examine the definition of poverty, a surprisingly elusive concept.

What Is Poverty?

The word "poverty" means different things to different people. While virtually everybody agrees that poverty occurs when people have inadequate incomes, nonetheless the exact line between the poor and the non-poor is hard to draw. Economists have therefore devised certain techniques which provide the official definition of poverty.

To begin with, analysts adopted from social-service workers budgets that purport to measure the cost of living at the subsistence level. As a check, economists have noted that poor families generally spend one-third of their income on food; hence, from calculations on the cost of a subsistence food budget, they can calculate a minimum-subsistence income by multiplying the minimum-food budget by a factor of 3.

These two methods agree fairly well. They indicate that the subsistence cost of living for an urban family of four is about $12,100 in 1988; this figure represents the "poverty line" or demarcation between those the government labels poor and non-poor. The poverty line also varies by family size and is adjusted over time by the consumer price index to reflect changes in the cost of living.

While an exact figure for measuring poverty is helpful, its use raises numerous conceptual issues. In measuring income, only cash payments are included; therefore, some important in-kind benefits such as food stamps or medical care are omitted. Because of these omissions, the extent of poverty is overestimated. In addition, "poverty" is a relative term. The notion of a subsistence budget includes subjective questions of taste and social convention. Today's minimal food budget of $4000 per year in the United States would please an Indian maharaja and far surpasses the physiological minimum of $360 per year (see footnote 1 in Chapter 2). Minimal housing standards today include plumbing that would have been out of reach of the most affluent citizen of the seventeenth century.

We should keep these conceptual issues in mind as we listen to debates about changes in the poverty population, the hardships visited upon the poor, and issues of income redistribution.

POVERTY IN MAJOR GROUPS

POPULATION GROUP	PERCENT OF GROUP IN POVERTY
White	11.0
Black	31.1
Hispanic	27.3
Black children under 15	44.0
Elderly (i.e., 65 and over)	12.4
College education (≥1 yr)	5.0
Families headed by women	38.3
Average	**13.6**

Table 34-1   Incidence of poverty in different groups, 1986

What is the percent of each group whose cash incomes fell below the 1986 poverty line of $11,203? Whites, college-educated persons, and, surprisingly, the elderly have lower-than-average poverty rates. Blacks, Hispanics, and female-headed households have much higher poverty rates than average. (Source: U.S. Bureau of the Census, *Money Income and Poverty Status of Families and Persons in the United States,* 1986.)

Who Are the Poor?

Poverty does not occur randomly across the population; some groups are more poverty-prone than others. Table 34-1 shows the incidence of poverty in different groups for 1986. While 13.6 percent of the total population was counted as falling below the 1986 poverty line of $11,203, the rate among black families was almost 3 times that of whites. Perhaps the most ominous trend is that among families headed by women—a rapidly growing group—38 percent fell below the poverty line.

No discussion of poverty would give an accurate picture without an analysis of the position of minorities. Blacks, Hispanics, and American Indians find almost one-third of their members with below-standard incomes. What are the characteristics of minority groups like black families?

Table 34-2 shows at a glance the relative economic position of the white and black populations. Thirty-one percent of the black population has less than a minimum-subsistence income. The U.S. population

is only 12 percent black, but the poor are 28 percent black.

Many of the poor are untrained, stuck in economically stagnant rural areas, or isolated in city ghettos. Yet many are also active job seekers in urban labor markets.

Why is it that so many female-headed or black families are poor? Experienced observers insist, as we saw in Chapter 28, that blatant racial or gender discrimination that pays men or whites higher rates for the same kind and volume of work is becoming rare.

How can we reconcile this sanguine view of labor markets with the economic inequalities that clearly prevail among the sexes and races—as shown in Tables 34-1 and 34-2? Two answers stand out: First, poorer groups often have less education and training and therefore do not qualify for high-paying jobs. A second answer to the paradox lies, as we saw in our analysis of discrimination in Chapter 28, in the phenomenon of noncompeting groups. Discrimination today generally works not by blatantly excluding blacks and minorities from schools or jobs but by the more subtle means of disqualifying them, by reason of lack of suitable education and training, from the best positions in the professions or in executive and managerial areas.

Sources of Poverty

Why do so many people remain poor while others enjoy fabulous wealth? Let's review some of the major sources of income inequality that were uncovered in Chapter 26.

Differences in Property Wealth   The greatest disparities in income arise from differences in wealth—from the fact that the poor have virtually no assets while the wealthiest have net worths in the millions. After John D. Rockefeller gained a fortune by shrewd combinations of oil and steel firms, his heirs moved to the top of the pyramid of wealth, status, and power. The history of such great fortunes—associated with names like Mellon or Ford or Getty or MacArthur, read on the walls of museums or college buildings or foundations—shows that differences in wages and personal characteristics are dwarfed by differences in wealth and property income.

WORKER CHARACTERISTICS	WHITE	BLACK
Income		
Median income of families	$30,809	$17,604
Percent of persons in poverty	11.0	31.1
Percent of families with incomes of		
$25,000 or more	58.5	33.1
Education		
Percent of persons 25–29 years old who have		
completed high school	86.9	79.0
Percent of persons 25–34 years old who are		
college graduates	25.9	13.1
Unemployment rates (percent)		
Adult men	5.2	12.9
Adult women	4.9	11.4
Teenagers	15.3	42.4
Occupation		
Percent of labor force who are		
scientists or engineers	2.01	0.44
Percent of labor force who		
are doctors	0.47	0.15

Table 34-2   Discrimination and inequality of opportunity, 1985 or 1986

Because of racial discrimination and less education, blacks still find fewer good jobs. The incidence of unemployment compounds the inequality. Black Americans tend to be particularly underrepresented in managerial and professional positions. (Source: U.S. Bureau of the Census; U.S. Bureau of Labor Statistics.)

The Rockefellers and the Gettys are but the smallest splinter on the top of the pyramid of wealth. At the bottom lie people who come into this world with little more than a gasp for air and leave their children with but a few precious memories. The poor own few material goods and therefore earn no income on their nonexistent wealth.

Differences in Personal Ability Some of the income differences among people arise from different skills and abilities. With the emphasis on test scores, people sometimes think that intelligence quotient (IQ) plays an important role in how much people earn. Measured abilities are probably overemphasized; traits like energy, luck, willingness to run risks, and ambition can be just as important. As Mark Twain might have said, "You don't have to be smart to make money. But you *do* have to know how to make money."

What are the roots of economically advantageous abilities? Some are inherited, but even within families there are generally major differences in physical and mental abilities. Indeed, social scientists today think that the importance of inheritance is often exaggerated. Our traits are determined as much by our environment as by our parents' genes. Children of the affluent probably don't start ahead of the poor, but they are helped by their environment at every stage. As the Bible tells us, "To those who have shall be given." A child of poverty often experiences crowding, poor nutrition, run-down schools, and overworked teachers. Some believe that the scales are tipped against many inner-city children before they are 10 years old.

Differences in Education and Training In addition to early influences, lack of education has been one of

HOW FARED THE POOR?

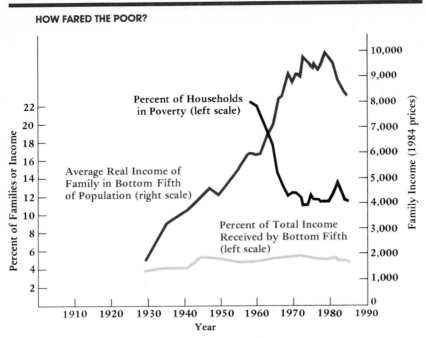

Figure 34-1 Trends in poverty and inequality

This shows three important indicators of the trends in poverty.

The upward-sloping heavy red line shows the average family income (in constant 1988 prices) of a family in the bottom fifth of the population. Note how sharply it has risen since 1929, and how incomes of the poor have fallen in the 1980s.

However, this rise in the absolute incomes of the poor has been mainly due to a rise in average income. The lighter red line shows that the share of the bottom fifth of the population has changed little since the late 1940s.

The black line shows the fraction of the population that is below the official poverty line. It shrank sharply during the 1960s, but has actually risen in the last few years. (Source: U.S. Bureau of the Census.)

the greatest barriers to equality over the ages. Before the twentieth century, there was a vast gulf between the educated upper classes and the illiterate masses. Many groups and classes were excluded from important educational institutions. Until 1954, blacks were segregated into separate school systems in the south of the United States. The poor simply could not afford the time or the funds for a college education, and few could succeed in working their way through medical or law school. Women were excluded from many of the best colleges and universities. Some schools barred women from entry into fields like medicine or

engineering. In short, college was until recently the province of the privileged.

Such class differences persist even today, for few poor families can afford to send their children to business school or medical school—and these children are thus excluded from a whole set of high-paying professions.

Trends in Inequality and Poverty

Many social and political changes have shaken our society over the last century. How have these affected poverty and inequality? The country has experienced increased levels of educational attainment, the drive for racial and sexual equality, government transfer programs, and progressive taxation. How have these affected the share of the population living in poverty?

Figure 34-1 shows the trends in poverty as measured by three important indicators. In *absolute* terms, the bottom fifth of the population has fared well over this century: the real income of the bottom fifth of the population has grown sharply since the 1920s. The poor have shared the growing prosperity with the middle class and the affluent. Indeed, as the light red line shows, the share of the national pie taken by the poorest fifth has increased slightly since the numbers were first collected.

What about poverty as officially measured? The black line in Figure 34-1 shows that the percent of the population in poverty dropped sharply from the late 1950s to the early 1970s. Since 1980, however, rising unemployment, declining generosity of transfer programs, and the increasing number of female-headed households have reversed the earlier trend, producing a sharp increase in the poor population.[1]

Recall that people predicted that poverty could be abolished by the mid-1970s. In fact, the millennium did not arrive in 1976. Let's turn to see why many people retreated from the heady ideas of the 1960s and instead began to trim back the antipoverty programs in the 1980s.

THE COSTS OF EQUALITY

Although the poor earn but a small fraction of national income, they have made great strides in absolute living standards. Real wages have risen steadily over the last century; manufacturing workers today

earn real wages 10 times what their great-grandfathers got. Few socialists or communists today doubt that capitalism has been a mighty engine for increasing the real wages of poor as well as rich. These facts lead apologists for today's order to say:

> Our system is the best hope for poor people; look at the national doughnut and see how it has grown.

But these cheerful tales will not still the critics of capitalism. They reply:

> Don't talk to me about growing doughnuts; look at the gaping hole that still remains.

Good is not good enough, they say. Why not the best? Why should we permit children to go hungry or homeless in this most affluent of societies?

Political philosophers over the ages have debated the proper extent of equality, wondering how much inequality society should permit. A democratic society holds central the principle of equality of *political rights*. The United States guarantees such things as the right to vote, trial by jury, free speech and practice of religion, and so forth. These rights have been universally recognized only late in human societies, but most people accept the desirability of these fundamental political birthrights.

A more radical view of a political democracy argues that people should also have equal *economic opportunity*. In this view, all people should play the economic game by the same rules on the same field. All would have equal access to the best schools and training and jobs. Discrimination on the basis of race or gender or religion would have long since disappeared. Rich parents could not buy admission to top colleges or jobs in the family firm for their fortunate offspring. This world of equal opportunity was pursued by liberals of the 1960s and 1970s, but inequalities of opportunity have proven very stubborn, and even America of the 1980s falls far short of this ideal.

A third and most far-reaching ideal is equality of *economic outcome*. In this radical utopia, people would have the same consumption whether they are smart or dull, eager or lazy, lucky or ill-fated. Wages would be the same for doctor and nurse, lawyer and

---

[1]Official statistics overstate the extent of poverty because they omit noncash benefits. Including noncash benefits poses measurement problems because it is difficult to estimate the value of noncash benefits to recipients. Should they be valued (A) at the market value of the goods even though the household would not have bought them or (B) at the beneficiary's stated valuation? The Census Bureau used a number of techniques and found that the standard definition of poverty overestimates the number of poor people. In 1985, for example, the official poverty rate was 14 percent of the population, while the poverty rate including noncash benefits of food and housing was calculated to be 12.5 percent using technique A and 12.8 percent using technique B.

secretary. People could live in large houses and drive fancy cars even if they were lazy workers or refused to save from their incomes. While this utopian dream was pursued by idealists of the nineteenth century, even the most radical socialist or communist today recognizes that some differences in economic outcome are necessary if the economy is to function efficiently. Without some differential reward for different kinds of work, how can we ensure that different jobs get done, that people will do the unpleasant as well as the pleasant work, that labor will flow into new occupations, and that people will work at night as well as day and on offshore oil derricks as well as in pleasant cities? Insisting on equality of outcomes would severely hamper the functioning of the economy.

Equality vs. Efficiency

This discussion suggests that steps to reduce the extent of inequality may harm the efficiency of the economy. In taking steps to redistribute income from the rich to the poor, we may reduce the amount of national income available to distribute. On the other hand, if equality is an ethical good, it is one worth incurring some cost for. The question of how much we are willing to pay in reduced efficiency for greater equity was addressed by Arthur Okun in his "leaky bucket" experiment:

> If we value less inequality, we'll approve when a dollar is taken in a bucket from the very rich and given to the very poor.[2]

But suppose the bucket of redistributive taxation has a leak in it. Suppose only a fraction—maybe two-thirds—of each dollar the rich lose actually reaches the poor. Then redistribution in the name of equity has harmed another economic goal, efficiency.

Okun has thus raised a fundamental dilemma. While there are many public programs (such as child nutrition or free public education) that may both increase equality and increase total output, in other cases a conflict between equity and efficiency arises.

[2]Arthur M. Okun, *Equality and Efficiency: The Big Tradeoff* (Brookings Institution, Washington, D.C., 1975).

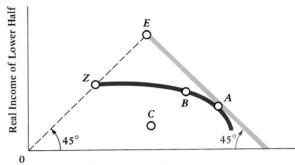

REDISTRIBUTION AT COST OF INEFFICIENCY

Figure 34-2   Redistributing income may harm economic efficiency

Point *A* marks the most efficient outcome, with maximal GNP. If society could redistribute with no loss of efficiency, the economy would move to point *E*. Because redistributive programs generally create distortions and efficiency losses, the path of redistribution might move along the heavy red line *ABZ*. Society must decide how much efficiency to sacrifice to gain greater equality. Why would everyone want to avoid inefficient redistributional programs that take the economy to point *C*?

Redistributional measures like the progressive income tax analyzed in Chapter 33 will probably reduce real output somewhat by reducing incentives to work and save. In the end, the optimal amount of redistribution will be affected by the extent to which redistribution changes the size of the total national output. As a country considers its income-distribution policies, therefore, it will want to weigh the increased fairness of redistribution against the reduction in national income that occurs because of redistribution.

Economic Costs of Redistribution Okun's analysis suggests that policies to redistribute income from one group to another are likely to reduce the total output of an economy. We can illustrate how attempts to achieve greater equality may retard efficiency using the "income-possibility curve" of Figure 34-2. This graph shows the incomes available to different groups when government uses tax and transfer programs to redistribute income.

We begin by dividing the population into two

halves; the real income of each group is measured on the axes of Figure 34-2. Start by examining point *A,* which is the pre-redistribution point. At point *A,* no taxes are levied and no transfers are given, so people simply live with their market incomes. If the economy is workably competitive, point *A* will contain no economic distortions, so the outcome is efficient and national income is maximized.

What is the problem? At point *A,* the upper-income group receives substantially more income than the lower half. The Congress might object to the extent of inequality and take steps to move the distribution toward the point of equal incomes at *E.* If such steps could be taken without reducing GNP, the economy would move along the light red line from *A* to *E.* The slope of the *AE* line is −45°, reflecting the assumption about efficiency that every dollar taken from the upper half increases the income of the lower half by exactly $1. Along the 45° line, total national income is constant, indicating that redistributional programs have no impact upon the total size of GNP.

Generally, however, redistributional programs will affect the efficiency of the economy. If a country redistributes income by imposing high tax rates on the wealthiest people, their saving and work effort may be reduced or misdirected, thereby lowering total national output. They may spend more money on tax lawyers, send funds to Swiss bank accounts, decide to save less for retirement, or put less money into the risky ventures that speed technological change. Similarly, if a guaranteed floor beneath the incomes of the poor is high enough, they may look less hard for jobs, or they may stay on welfare programs longer. All these reactions to redistributive programs reduce the total size of real national income.

Put differently, when high tax rates and generous transfer programs reduce saving and work effort, this results in a lower total national income. For every $100 of taxation on the rich, the income of the poor might increase by only $80 or $60 or $40, with the rest dissipated in wasted effort or administrative costs. In this case, the bucket of redistribution has developed a leak, so that only a fraction of the resources taken from the rich are actually delivered to the poor. We can depict the case of costly redistribution by the heavy *ABZ* curve in Figure 34-2. Here, the hypothetical frontier of real incomes bends away from

the 45° line because taxes and transfers cause inefficiencies.

Indeed, experience has shown that in some cases the distortions due to interference can become so great that the attempt to help one social class at the expense of another can end in hurting them both. Or, in the opposite case, an action that looks like it is aimed to benefit the rich finally ends by benefiting all.

A recent example will illustrate why equity and efficiency are not always at war. In 1981, President Reagan completed the decontrol of oil prices. Some complained that the decontrol was a giveaway to the rich. Yet oil and gasoline prices fell after decontrol, and many believe that the greater efficiency allowed by a freer oil market was responsible. The movement was as if from point *C* to point *B* in Figure 34-2. Even though it was attacked as a pro-oil-company action, this step may have improved the fortunes of virtually all Americans.

How Big Are the Leaks?

Okun characterized our redistributive system of taxes and transfers as a leaky bucket. But how big in fact are the leaks? Is the economy closer to Figure 34-2's point *A,* where the leaks are negligible? Or to *B,* where they are substantial? Or to Z, where the redistributive bucket is in fact a sieve? To answer this, we must examine the major inefficiencies induced by high tax rates and by generous income-support programs: administrative costs, damage to work and savings incentives, and socioeconomic costs.

Administrative Costs The government must hire tax collectors to gain revenue and social security accountants to disperse it. These are clear inefficiencies or regrettable necessities, but they are small: the Internal Revenue Service spends only half a penny on administrative costs for each dollar of collected revenues.

Damage to Work Effort As the taxman's bite is larger and larger, might I not find myself discouraged and end up working less? (Recall last chapter's Laffer curve, which convinced some that tax rates were so high that total revenues are actually lower than they would be at more modest tax rates.)

Whatever the rhetoric, the empirical evidence suggests that the actual damage of taxes on work effort is very limited. Chapter 28 found that the labor supply curve may actually be backward-bending, indicating that a tax on wages would increase rather than decrease work effort. Of the many studies of this subject, few find the effect of taxes on work effort to be very substantial. More important, perhaps, are the impacts of welfare and transfer systems on poor people, a controversial topic to which we will shortly return.

A Drain on Saving? Perhaps the most important potential leakage from the revenue bucket is in the savings component. Many analysts believe that high tax rates discourage saving and investment, and this belief has triggered the major reduction in taxes on property income over the last decade.

This claim was assessed by Okun long before the rise of supply-side economics:

> If progressive taxation had had a massive and dominant effect on saving and investment, the evidence would be loud and clear in the aggregate data. In 1929, when all federal tax rates were low and barely progressive, the nation saved and invested 16 percent of GNP; in 1973, with all the allegedly onerous "soak the rich" taxes, it saved and invested 16 percent of GNP.[3]

And, it should be added, after the major "supply-side" tax cuts of the early 1980s, the national savings rate fell to the lowest levels since the Great Depression.

Whatever are recent trends, the potential for an adverse effect on saving is present. Economists will be looking for it in coming years.

Social Costs or Benefits Some claim that the leaks cannot be found in the cost statistics of the economist; instead, the costs of equality are seen in attitudes rather than in dollars. Is the business ethic downplayed? Are students so turned off by the prospect of high taxes that they turn on to drugs and idleness? Is the welfare system leading to a permanent underclass, a society of people who are trapped in a culture of dependency?

[3]Okun, *Equality and Efficiency*, p. 98.

Studies of such questions are few. But, some argue, the opposite case looks just as strong. Doesn't the drive for equality allow many more talents to compete in the mainstream? Don't many low-income programs improve health, education, and the long-run productivity of poor groups and of the nation as a whole? Aren't invention, the arts, and politics likely to be more vital when 80 percent of the population is not excluded by discrimination?

Many analysts would go further, criticizing the notion that policies to improve the lot of the poor necessarily invoke a dilemma of efficiency against equality, arguing as follows. The sources of poverty are rooted in disadvantaged backgrounds, malnourishment in the early years, broken families, illiteracy at home, poor education, and lack of job training. Poverty begets poverty. What the nation needs, then, are programs that break through the vicious cycle of malnutrition, poor education, low productivity, low incomes, leading to yet another generation of poverty. Programs providing health care and adequate food for poor families [such as the federal Women, Infants, and Children (WIC) Program] will *increase* productivity and efficiency rather than decrease output. By breaking the vicious cycle of poor education, high unemployment, and low incomes today, we will be raising the skills and human capital of poor people thus raising their efficiencies tomorrow. In this view, then, programs to break the cycle of poverty are investments in humans; like all investments, they require resources set aside today to increase productivity tomorrow. It would hence be a tragic error, in this approach, to view programs to assist the poor as a drain on the nation's productive resources.

Adding Up the Leaks

We can try to add up all the leaks from the bucket of redistribution. How big are they? Okun argued that the leaks are small, particularly when funds for redistributive programs are drawn from the tap of a broad-based income tax. As we will see in the next section, other people disagree, pointing to the dizzying array of tax loopholes and transfer programs as confusing and destructive of economic efficiency.

What is the truth? In fact, while economists have firm opinions on the cost of redistribution, the truth has proved elusive. A final estimate of the cost of equality awaits the findings of much painstaking research by future generations of social scientists.

ANTIPOVERTY POLICIES: PROGRAMS AND CRITICISMS

We have taken the measure of poverty and have faced the social dilemma involved in trading off efficiency for equality. What weapons can a nation deploy to reduce the social and economic hardships of low incomes? Have these programs produced counterproductive responses in the low-income population? What reforms could ameliorate the problems of today's welfare system? We address these issues in this final section.

The Rise of the Welfare State

We noted at the beginning of this chapter that the early classical economists believed the distribution of income was unalterable. They argued that attempts to alleviate poverty by government interventions in the economy were foolish endeavors that would simply end up reducing total national income.

By the end of the nineteenth century, however, political leaders in Western Europe took steps that marked a historic turning point: the beginning of the welfare state. Bismarck in Germany, Gladstone and Disraeli in Britain, followed by Franklin Roosevelt in the United States introduced a new concept of government responsibility for the welfare of the populace. More specifically, the *welfare state* is a society in which the government modifies market forces to protect individuals against specified contingencies and to guarantee people a minimum standard of living irrespective of their market incomes.

Important provisions in the welfare state include public pensions, accident and sickness insurance, unemployment insurance, health insurance, food and housing programs, family allowances, and income supplements for certain groups of people. These policies were introduced gradually from 1880 through the modern era, although some programs have not been universally provided (e.g., unlike many countries, the United States does not offer universal national health insurance).

Voting-Class Interests What forces led to the creation of the welfare state? In retrospect, there is no mystery about the spread of this social movement over the last century. With the rise of mass democracies and universal male suffrage, the poor began to outnumber the rich at the ballot box. Chapter 32's public-choice theory would predict that the low-income groups, the elderly, and labor unions would press for legislation to redistribute income away from the few rich to the poor, old, or laboring classes. Today, there is wide support for the programs of the welfare state, and even the conservative governments of the 1980s were unable to roll back the generosity of public pensions and similar programs. These are taken for granted as economic birthrights in all modern industrial democracies.

Income-Support and Welfare Programs

What are the major income-support or welfare programs of today? They are the following.

Food Stamps After the people rediscovered hunger in this most affluent of societies in the 1960s, the United States instituted the food-stamp program. Under this program, low-income families receive stamps or coupons that permit them to purchase food at a small fraction of its market cost.

Welfare Assistance In every locality there exists some apparatus for help to the destitute. These programs offer "in-kind" aid (that is, direct aid in food, clothing, or housing) as well as straight income transfers.

The most visible and controversial form of welfare assistance is AFDC (Aid to Families with Dependent Children). This income support goes to poor parents with small children. Governments also provide income support for the aged, blind, and disabled who demonstrate a need for aid.

Because the minimum standards for income support provided by the modern welfare state rose rapidly, the costs of welfare programs rose almost tenfold from 1960 to 1975. But in the late 1970s, taxpayers became uneasy about supporting a growing group of indigents. Public opinion began to swing

FEDERAL PROGRAMS FOR THE POOR, 1989

PROGRAM	AMOUNT (billions)	PERCENT OF TOTAL FEDERAL SPENDING
All income-support programs	**$435.3**	**39.8**
General programs	334.2	30.5
Social security	233.8	
Medicare	84.0	
Unemployment insurance	16.4	
Programs for the poor	101.1	9.2
Aid to aged, blind, disabled	12.5	
Aid to families with dependent children	10.8	
Medicaid	32.7	
Food stamps and child nutrition	20.8	
Housing	14.9	
Other	9.4	

Table 34-3   Most federal income-support dollars go for general programs like social security

Federal programs for income support are largely concentrated on the population as a whole, rather than on the poor. Only $23 billion is spent on programs that increase poor families' incomes. Note as well the high cost of health programs for both the poor and the non-poor. (Source: Office of Management and Budget, *Budget of the United States Government, 1989*.)

against welfare programs, and their fiscal support was cut sharply after 1978.

Medicaid One of the most rapidly growing programs is medical care for low-income families. This program is unusual in that its benefits are generally not reduced as income rises: a family either qualifies or does not.

Other Programs There are numerous other income-support programs, some of which are more or less targeted at poor families. Housing programs, social security, and disability benefits tend to bolster the incomes of the poor more than the population as a whole—even though they are not always specifically designed for low-income families.

Overall Totals How much do all federal programs add up to in terms of budget expenditures? Table 34-3 shows the level of federal spending for income-support programs for both the general population and poor households. All federal poverty programs today amount to 9 percent of the total federal budget.

Even though the federal programs to assist the poor form a relatively modest part of the budget, they have dulled the sharp edge of poverty. They have provided a financial safety net that has all but eradicated the grinding poverty of earlier periods (for an estimate of the way government transfer programs raise the incomes of the worst-off families, look back to Figure 33-6).

Two Views of Poverty

Debates about policies to cure the poverty problem are sometimes rooted in divergent views of the roots of poverty. Proponents of strong government action see poverty as the result of social and economic conditions over which the poor have little control. They stress malnutrition, poor schools, broken families, lack of job opportunities, and a host of similar factors as central determinants of the fate of the poor. Someone holding this view would quite naturally tend to think that government bears a responsibility to alleviate poverty—either by providing income to the poor or by curing the conditions that produce poverty.

A second view holds that poverty grows out of maladaptive individual behavior—behavior which is the responsibility of individuals and is properly cured by the poor themselves. In earlier centuries, this view held that the poor were shiftless, lazy, or drunk, as in the case of a charity worker who wrote almost a century ago that "want of employment . . . is, as often as not, [caused by] drink." Today, people often point to the government as culprit, arguing that the patchwork quilt of welfare programs leads people to be dependent upon government programs rather than upon their own ingenuity. Such views often lead critics to advocate cutting back on welfare programs so that people will develop their own resources.

This debate was succinctly summarized by the eminent social scientist William Wilson:

> Liberals have traditionally emphasized how the plight of disadvantaged groups can be related to the problems of the broader society, including problems of discrimination and social class subordination. . . . Conservatives, in contrast, have traditionally stressed the importance of different group values and competitive resources in accounting for the experiences of the disadvantaged.[4]

Few analysts of the problems of poverty and the welfare system fall into either of these two extreme categories. Nonetheless, much of today's debate about welfare can be better understood once these two views and their implications are factored into the political equation.

Are We Losing Ground?

The American welfare system has been a social battleground for half a century. The debate heated up with the publication of Charles Murray's 1984 study, *Losing Ground*.[5] Murray starts with the paradoxical observation that, even though federal antipoverty programs expanded greatly in the 1960s, the number of poor people has risen sharply. He traces the cause of this trend to the increasing tendency during the 1960s to view poor people as victims of circumstance rather than as personally responsible for their economic distress. The result was to change the rules of the game, extending notions of equality beyond earlier notions of equality of opportunity to equality of outcome. As a result, dependency on government programs rose and the number of poor people *increased* over time. Let's examine his analysis in detail.

Incentive Problems of the Poor   Murray pointed out, as have many other analysts in the past, that the current welfare system severely reduces the incentives of low-income adults to seek work. He noted that the "effect of the new rules was to make it profitable for the poor to behave in the short term in ways that were destructive in the long run."[6]

It might be surprising, after all the publicity aired about how people pay such high taxes, to hear that the worst incentive problems are faced by low-income families. Poor people face high marginal "tax" rates (or, more accurately, "benefit-reduction rates") because welfare benefits get sharply reduced as earnings rise. If a person on welfare gets a job, the government will trim back food stamps, cash welfare payments, and rent subsidies. If the wage earner is unlucky enough to land a good job, the family may even lose its public medical benefits.

The following calculation for a family of three (mother and two children) will illustrate the problem. We choose the example of Pennsylvania because the AFDC benefits in that state are close to the national average. In 1987, if the mother did not have a job, the family would receive AFDC benefits of $4584 and food stamps worth $1549, for a total disposable income of $6133. Suppose the parent takes a full-time job earning $8000 a year. She would lose all the AFDC benefits, but would retain $1306 worth of food stamps. After child-care and work-related expenses of $2400, disposable income would equal $6906. The net gain from taking this $8000 job would be a gain in

[4]William Julius Wilson. "Cycles of Deprivation and the Underclass Debate." *Social Service Review,* vol. 59, December 1985, pp. 541–559.

[5]Charles Murray, *Losing Ground: American Social Policy, 1950–1980* (Basic Books, New York, 1984).

[6]Murray, *Losing Ground,* p. 9.

disposable income of $773 a year; the increase in disposable income is only 9.7 percent of the increase in earnings. In this example we can see why people sometimes say that the "tax rate" on low-income people is often around 90 percent. [This example is actually not the worst case. The family may also lose medical benefits (Medicaid) worth $1537, indicating that the family may actually have a *lower* living standard after the parent takes a full-time job.]

We can usefully consider benefit reductions as a kind of "tax." In these terms, the tax rates on the working poor can easily reach 90 percent—far above the rate faced by the richest Americans and surely a major disincentive to the avid pursuit of work.

One of the harshest criticisms of the current welfare system is that it provides incentives for family dissolution—and that this is occurring at a time when intact families are already an endangered species. Most states refuse to provide welfare support to a family in which both parents are present, reasoning that the second parent can be expected to support the children. In such cases, the parent (usually the father) of a family on welfare may find that his family's income rises sharply if he leaves home and disappears. Only then can his wife and children continue to get welfare support.

In this age of concern about the dulling effect of high taxes, it is ironic that our current welfare system of cash aid, food stamps, and other benefits contains major disincentives for the poor. A person on welfare can lose 80 or 90 or even 100 percent of any earnings because benefits are reduced as earnings increase.

While the perverse incentives faced by the poor have been lamented by liberals and conservatives for decades, Murray pursues the argument a step further by arguing that the programs have torn the social fabric of poor families. Not only did the programs demonstrably fail to cure poverty, but they also created dependency by discouraging work, reduced the labor-force participation of poor groups, helped break up families, and promoted out-of-wedlock births and single-parent families. In short, instead of curing poverty, the welfare system was creating a population sinking slowly and inescapably into the quicksand of dependency on federal welfare programs.

Murray then goes on to consider changes:

The proposed program . . . consists of scrapping the entire federal welfare and income-support structure for working persons, including AFDC [Aid to Families with Dependent Children], Medicaid, Food Stamps, Unemployment Insurance, Workers' Compensation, subsidized housing, disability insurance, and the rest. It would leave the working-aged person with no recourse whatsoever except the job market, family members, friends, and public or private locally funded services.[7]

Murray's analysis proved extremely influential in shaping the Reagan administration's policies on income-support programs. While not proposing to repeal any major income-support programs, during most of his term President Reagan labored to curb their benefits in a war of attrition on antipoverty programs. The extent of success can be seen in the fact that from 1981 to 1988, the share of the federal budget spent on low-income support programs rose from 8.9 to 9.2 percent of total federal spending.

Alternative Approaches Murray's analysis was severely attacked by other social scientists. While the basic facts were accepted, Murray's interpretation, critics charged, fell prey to the post hoc fallacy.[8] Critics made the following points:

- The increase in poverty appeared to be attributable more to slow economic growth and high unemployment than to changes in federal programs.

- Other factors than welfare programs appear to lie behind the major decline in the fraction of black and other poor youths with jobs—high overall unemployment, changing schooling patterns, regional migration, and a smaller army being the most important.

- Murray points to declining SAT (Scholastic Aptitude Test) scores as an indication of the increasing gap between black and white students. Careful study of the data indicates that black students have improved their relative performance between 1965 and 1980.

---

[7]Murray, *Losing Ground*, pp. 227–228.

[8]A succinct and readable summary of criticisms is contained in University of Wisconsin-Madison, Institute of Research on Poverty, *Focus*, vol. 8, no. 3, Fall–Winter 1985.

■ On the most controversial issue of whether the welfare system promotes family breakup and whether young women are encouraged to have children to get on the welfare rolls, careful studies by researchers such as Harvard's David Ellwood and Mary Jo Bane find some evidence that the welfare system promotes single-parent families. But they, along with virtually all others who have studied the problem, find no evidence that generous welfare payments encourage out-of-wedlock births or a higher birth rate among those likely to be on welfare. Ellwood and Bane conclude that ''welfare simply does not appear to be the underlying cause of the dramatic changes in family structure of the past few decades.''

■ A study at the University of Michigan, following a large number of families for 18 years, uncovered some startling facts concerning the behavior of ''poverty families.'' Contrary to stereotype, they found that poverty typically lasts at most a few years, that most welfare recipients work while on welfare, and that welfare dependency is not transmitted from generation to generation. (See Question 6 at the end of this chapter for an analysis of the integrational transmission of poverty.)

The Negative Income Tax

Contemplating the enormous potential effects on the efficiency of the economy as well as on the social structure of the country, economists of varied political persuasions have concluded that the welfare system needs a fundamental reform. Conservatives like Milton Friedman of Chicago and liberals like James Tobin of Yale agree that it will be both cheaper and more humane to replace or supplement the incoherent set of income-support programs with a single unified program of cash assistance.

This reform, analyzed and supported by many economists, is sometimes called the **negative income tax.** Other plans with different (and more appealing) names have been put forth over the years. Most of them share the goal of creating a uniform, national income-support program that maintains sufficient economic incentives for poor people to work. We will analyze a typical plan below, labeling it a ''negative income tax.''

How It Works The basic notion is simple. When I make $20,000 a year, I pay positive income taxes (as seen back in Table 33-3). When I earn an extra thousand dollars, I pay extra taxes of $150, leaving me $850 of additional disposable income. Thus the incentive to earn more is preserved.

Next consider a poor family earning, say, $8000 in 1988. The Congress might decide that such a family deserves an income above $8000, especially if it has earned its $8000 by work and if the family has small children to support. The government wants to provide further income support. Put differently, the family should not pay taxes on its income but receive a *negative* income tax.

A major problem arises: How can the government provide income support without hurting the family's incentives to work? The negative income tax might aim to raise the incomes of the poor and still maintain incentives to work hard. The way to do this, argue proponents of the negative income tax, is to provide a basic allowance and then allow the family to keep a significant portion of any earnings. By this reasoning, just as people with high incomes can keep most of their earnings if they earn more money, similarly a poor family could keep much of its additional earnings if a family member gets a job.

Possible Formula How might a negative income tax work in practice? The idea is to provide each household with a basic allowance, say $4500 for a family of four. The family would then keep a fraction of any additional earnings (perhaps 40 percent) and the basic allowance would be reduced by the complementary fraction (in this example, by 60 percent). This kind of scheme was proposed by Presidents Nixon and Carter in the 1970s.

Table 34-4 shows a hypothetical negative income tax with a basic allowance of $4500 and a ''tax rate'' or benefit-reduction rate of 50 percent. This example shows the government can simultaneously support the poorest families and maintain an incentive for families to seek gainful employment. Compare this approach with that of the current welfare system, examined in the last section, to see how the current system destroys incentives while the negative income tax enhances incentives.

POSSIBLE FORMULA FOR NEGATIVE INCOME TAX

MARKET EARNINGS	ALGEBRAIC TAX (+ if tax; − if benefits received)	AFTER-TAX INCOME
$ 0	−$4,500	$4,500
4,000	− 2,500	6,500
7,000	− 1,000	8,000
8,000	− 500	8,500
9,000	0	9,000
10,000	+ 500	9,500

Table 34-4   Negative income tax sets minimum-income standards, preserving incentives and efficiency

Above an exemption level, people naturally expect to pay positive taxes that rise with their incomes. Under a negative income tax plan, the principle is extended below the poverty line by allowing the poor to receive income support—in essence, to receive negative taxes.

The plan in the table starts with a "basic allowance" of $4500 and then reduces benefits (or "taxes income") at the rate of 50 percent of any earnings. Under this plan, incentives to work are maintained, as can be seen in the last column: after-tax income rises significantly when the family increases its market income.

In the design of a negative income tax, crucial economic and social questions arise: Should the program include single persons along with families? Should supported persons be required to work (in a system known as "workfare")? How should college students be treated? And, most important, should the support levels be minimal so that welfare provides an inadequate living standard, thereby interfering minimally with work incentives and keeping the welfare rolls small (the approach traditionally favored by conservative groups)? Or should the negative income tax be generous, supplementing incomes at or above the poverty line, risking major disincentive effects and swelling the welfare rolls?

Pros and Cons The negative income tax has been actively debated in the economic and political arena for four decades, yet it has never been enacted. What are the terms of the debate?

Advocates point to numerous advantages over the current complex system of benefits. A negative income tax would help set a national minimum standard of living for the poor; it would be much less demeaning than the current system; it could be simply administered by the Internal Revenue Service or another agency; and it could help reduce incentives for people to migrate to high-benefit states. Most important, it could replace the current system, with its virtually prohibitive work disincentives, with one that provides incentives for the poor to provide for themselves.

Opponents of the system raise a number of questions. Wouldn't it end up costing the government a great deal more money? Shouldn't we leave provision of aid to the poor to the states, who have to live with the results? Do we really want to make it easier and more dignified for people to be on the dole? Shouldn't people be required to work if they are to get welfare? Isn't it better to have government aid in kind, with provision for food, shelter, and medical care, rather than give cash to those who may have not succeeded in managing their finances in the past? And most important, won't more generous cash assistance reinforce the cycle of dependency, hurt the incentive to work, and be a drain on the economy? Opponents feel that the answers to these questions support restricting rather than expanding the welfare system.

Experimental Evidence It is often difficult to test economic theories or policies in the laboratory of real-world human experience. But in the case of the negative income tax, economists helped undertake an impressive set of real-world experiments to measure the effects of a negative income tax on people's behavior.

The "negative income tax experiments" involved several thousand families in New Jersey, Indiana, Seattle, and Denver. The experiments divided a randomly selected group of families into "control" groups that would receive no special treatment and "experimental" groups that would live under a negative income tax plan for a few years. The central question was how people would react to income supplements such as those sketched in Table 34-4.

These information experiments showed that families in the more generous plans (say, obtaining 100 percent of the poverty line as the basic allowance) reduced their hours of work markedly—by as much as 15 percent. When extrapolated to the entire population, this work reduction—the leak in Okun's redistributive bucket—would reduce GNP by 15 to 30 percent of the measured budget cost of the program. On the other hand, experiments with smaller benefit levels produced much smaller reductions in work effort of the affected people.

Recent Reforms Are these costs large or small? Those who care more about the poor than about economic efficiency find much justice in a generous negative income tax program. By contrast, those primarily concerned with efficiency and who hold the poor responsible for their own economic condition argue for curbing existing welfare programs.

How has the electorate responded to the tug-of-war between efficiency and redistribution? In fact, beginning about 1975, cash assistance to low-income families has been steadily reduced. A clear message about the responsibility of people to provide for themselves came in the 1988 Welfare Reform Act, which will require many welfare recipients to work or to enter training programs. Faced with the alternative approaches to poverty, America has moved away from the carrots of government assistance and toward the sticks of market necessity.

SUMMARY

1. In the last century economists believed that inequality was a universal constant, unchangeable by public policy. This view does not stand up to scrutiny. Poverty has made a glacial retreat over the last few decades; absolute incomes of the bottom part of the income distribution have risen sharply.

2. Poverty is essentially a relative notion. In the United States, poverty was defined in terms of the adequacy of spending on food in the early 1960s. By this standard of measured income, little progress has been made in the last decade.

3. Poverty has many roots. The important ones are: *(a)* discrimination against minorities, *(b)* little property wealth, *(c)* a less advantageous home background, and *(d)* impediments to education, job opportunities, or training.

4. Political philosophers point to three types of equality: *(a)* equality of political rights, such as the right to vote; *(b)* equality of opportunity, providing equal access to jobs, education, and other social systems; and *(c)* equality of outcome, whereby people are guaranteed equal incomes or consumptions. Whereas the first two types of equality are today widely accepted in most advanced democracies like the United States, equality of outcome is extremely controversial and unacceptable to many.

5. Equality has costs as well as benefits; the costs show up as drains from Okun's "leaky bucket." That is, attempts to reduce income inequality by progressive taxation or welfare payments may harm economic incentives to work or save and may thereby reduce the size of national output. Potential leakages are administrative costs and reduced hours of work or savings rates, along with intangible socioeconomic impacts.

Murray argued that the leakages are so high that in the long run the poor are actually losing ground under the current welfare system, although other analysts question Murray's results.

6. Major programs to alleviate poverty are: welfare payments, food stamps, Medicaid, and a group of smaller or less targeted programs. As a whole, these programs are criticized because they impose high benefit-reduction rates (or marginal "tax" rates) on low-income families when families begin to earn wages or other income.

7. Prominent among proposals to reform the income-support system for the poor stands the negative income tax. This would replace the dizzying array of existing programs with a unified, cash income supplement. The supplement would be reduced (that is, income would be "taxed") at a moderate rate (say one-third or one-half), so that low-income families would have a significant incentive to seek market employment. Because of debates about the effects of such an income-supplement plan on the work ethic, on family structure, and on the federal budget, no such plan has yet been politically acceptable.

CONCEPTS FOR REVIEW

poverty
welfare state
equality: political, of opportunity, of
  outcome
Okun's "leaky bucket"
income-possibility curve: ideal and
  realistic cases
two views of poverty
Murray's theory of losing ground

causes of inefficiency in redistribution:
  administration, work, saving, social
  impacts
income-support programs: welfare, food
  stamps, Medicaid
negative income tax: basic allowance,
  tax rate
benefit-reduction rate (marginal tax
  rate)

QUESTIONS FOR DISCUSSION

1. From 1945 to 1988, measured inequality of incomes in the United States didn't change much. Is this an indictment of American capitalism, in your view? Or is it a symptom of the difficulty of constructing programs to lower income inequalities?

2. Discuss the three different kinds of equality. Why might equality of opportunity not lead to equality of outcome? Should persons of different abilities be given the same access to jobs and education? What might be done to ensure equality of outcome? How might such steps lead to economic inefficiencies?

3. Analyze Murray's viewpoint on the theory of losing ground and that of his critics. Which view coincides with your personal experience or reading of history? Where would your views lead you on the issue of the pros and cons of the negative income tax?

4. Many people continue to argue about what form assistance for the poor should take. One school says, "Give people money and let them buy health services and the foods they need." The other school says, "If you give money for milk to the poor, they will spend it on beer. Your dollar goes further in alleviating malnourishment and disease if you provide the services in kind. The dollar that you earn may be yours to spend, but society's income-support dollar is a dollar that society has the right paternalistically to channel directly to its targets.''

The argument of the first might rest on demand theory: let each household decide how to maximize its utility on a limited budget. Chapter 19 shows why this argument might be right. But what if the parents' utility includes mainly beer and lottery tickets and no milk or clothing for the children? Might you agree with the second view? From your own personal experience and reading, which of these two views do you think is more accurate? Explain your reasoning.

5. One of the central dilemmas in designing a negative income tax is the necessity to raise benefit-reduction (or tax) rates when basic allowances increase. If you examine Table 34-4, consider different constant-tax-rate programs that have a breakeven point (or zero-tax point) at $9000. What is the benefit-reduction rate when the basic allowance is $2700? $7200? $9000?

Does the rise of the tax rate as the basic allowance increases suggest that there will be increasing inefficiency as equality is pursued more vigorously—that Okun's bucket will become leakier as antipoverty programs become more egalitarian? Does this suggest why Figure 34-2 curves inward as more income is transferred from rich to poor?

6. Advanced problem (using probability theory): Critics of the welfare system argue that poverty programs have created ''a spider web of dependency,'' fostering a culture in which the ''breakdown of the family . . . has reached crisis proportions'' (President Ronald Reagan, ''State of the Union,'' 1986). Using the theory of transition probabilities, we can calculate the extent to which welfare dependency may be transmitted from one generation to another.

Say that society is divided into two classes, a class on welfare or AFDC (the Ws) and a class not on welfare (the Ns). Studies of family patterns show the following intergenerational patterns of welfare dependency, focusing on females:

WELFARE DEPENDENCE OF PARENTS:	WELFARE DEPENDENCE OF DAUGHTERS	
	NO	YES
No	0.90	0.10
Yes	0.60	0.40

Source: G. J. Duncan, "Welfare Dependence Within and Across Generations," *Science* (January 29, 1987).

This table shows that only 10 percent of daughters of non-welfare parents are observed on welfare when they are young adults, whereas 40 percent of daughters of parents on welfare were found on welfare as young adults. That is, of 100 daughters of W parents, 40 are found on welfare as young adults and 60 are not on welfare. Of 100 daughters of N parents, only 10 daughters are on welfare as young adults.

Assuming that a population of 100 (million) is initially equally divided between Ns and Ws, calculate the experience of the daughters of the Ns and Ws for a few generations. (HINT: Apply the transition probabilities in the table to each group to get the new number of Ns and Ws for each generation.) Can you estimate the ultimate (or equilibrium) number of Ns and Ws?

Say that the social structure was in equilibrium and a welfare reform proposal like a negative income tax changed the second row to (0.80, 0.20). Trace out the new pattern of Ns and Ws. How would this reform change the equilibrium number of welfare families? If the average time between generations is 20 years, how many years would it take for the social structure to get 99 percent of the way from its AFDC equilibrium to its negative-income-tax equilibrium? Does the length of time to equilibrate suggest why social movements like civil rights or women's liberation take so long to bear fruit?

CHAPTER 35

THE WINDS OF CHANGE: ALTERNATIVE ECONOMIC SYSTEMS

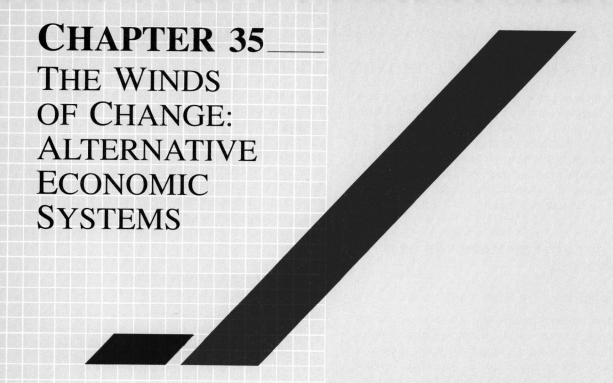

Come writers and critics
Who prophesize with your pen
And keep your eyes wide
The chance won't come again
And don't speak too soon
For the wheel's still in spin . . .
For the times they are a-changin'.

Bob Dylan

THIS BOOK FOCUSES most of its attention upon the workings of mixed capitalist economies like the United States. This attention is warranted given the economic role of the advanced democracies—accounting for 60 percent of world income and serving as models for an increasing number of middle-income countries.

But we cannot ignore a world filled with competing economic ideologies and alternative economic systems. Marxism claims the allegiance of nearly 2 billion people, while socialism has been championed by many of the great Western thinkers. Above all, we must remember that neither economies nor economic theories remain untouched by time: economics evolves incessantly in a Darwinian struggle of ideas, technologies, and armies.

We turn in this chapter, therefore, to look backward in time and outward in space—backward to see how economic theories have evolved over time, and outward to see how other economies are organized and how they perform. Such travel in foreign lands will help us better understand our own.

A. EVOLUTION OF ECONOMIC THOUGHT

We begin with an excursion into the history of economic thought. This trip will deepen our understanding of the roots of the language of modern economics just as studying Latin enriches our understanding of modern languages. Once you know how today's economic theories grew out of the past, you will be better prepared for the modifications those theories will surely undergo in the future.[1]

THE GROWTH OF MAINSTREAM ECONOMICS

Early Roots

Economic thinking began with Aristotle and continued through the teachings of the medieval Scholastics. These early stirrings dealt largely with normative doctrines such as the idea of a ''just price,'' which purported to tell the genuine value of a commodity. The Scholastics rejected interest on loans as unjust ''usury,'' and prohibitions of usury survive today as interest-rate ceilings in many states and countries.

Perhaps the first systematic thinkers were the *mercantilists* of the seventeenth and eighteenth centuries. This group of pamphleteers devised policies to buttress the military and economic powers of emerging nation-states. Especially powerful in England and France, they espoused the accumulation of gold and silver and promoted protectionist steps like Britain's Navigation Acts that eventually kindled the American Revolution.

Mercantilist practices spawned numerous ideas. David Hume (1711–1776) propounded his brilliant gold-flow mechanism (see Chapter 40) to demonstrate how the mercantilists' gold inflow would eventually end up raising prices rather than output. The group known as the *Physiocrats* (or *''philosophes''*) reacted powerfully to the excesses of French mercantilism under Colbert, Louis XIV's finance minister. This group pronounced agriculture the only source of economic surplus and attempted to remove trade restrictions from corn and other sectors. A remarkable depiction of the economy as a circular flow, still used in today's texts (see page 42), was made by Quesnay, Louis XIV's court physician. His scheme stressed that the different elements of the economy are as integrally tied together as are the blood vessels of the body.

Classical Economics: Smith, the Prophet of Laissez-Faire

The family tree of economics, shown on the back endpaper, traces the lineage of modern economics. The early influences converge in the publication in 1776 of *The Wealth of Nations* by Adam Smith (1723–1790), which we can mark as the birthdate of modern economics.

After beginning his career as a moral philosopher, Smith turned to the study of political economy, which culminated in his classic work. Smith's contributions were legion. He discussed the foundation of prices and the distribution of income, analyzed various theories of wages, and performed one of the earliest empirical studies of inflation.

But of all his contributions to economic analysis, the boldest was his recognition that the market mechanism is a self-regulating natural order and that the price system organizes the behavior of people and does so in an automatic fashion without central direction. To mercantilists who were eager to interfere with markets, Smith's message in effect said:

> You think that you are improving the economy with your well-meaning laws and regulations. You are not. In a laissez-faire system, the oil of self-interest will keep the economic gears turning in a miraculous fashion. No planners are necessary; no government need issue edicts to control prices or mandate production. The market will solve all our problems.

Adam Smith was a worldly student of history, politics, and economics. He drew upon his vast store-

---

[1]Good introductions to the history of economics are Robert L. Heilbroner, *The Worldly Philosophers*, 5th ed. (Simon and Schuster, Inc., New York, 1980), or Mark Blaug, *Economic Theory in Retrospect*, 3d ed. (Cambridge University Press, London, 1978). The standard advanced reference is the posthumous classic, Joseph A. Schumpeter, *History of Economic Analysis* (Oxford University Press, New York, 1957).

house of knowledge, not on purely deductive reasoning, when he wrote his famous words about the invisible hand:

> Every individual . . . neither intends to promote the general interest, nor knows how much he is promoting it. He intends only his own security, his own gain. And he is in this led by an invisible hand to promote an end which was no part of his intention. By pursuing his own interest he frequently promotes that of society more effectually than when he really intends to promote it.

Smith was unable to prove the essence of his invisible-hand doctrine. Indeed, until the 1940s no one knew how to prove, or even to state properly, the kernel of truth in this proposition about perfectly competitive markets.

Smith's approach, instead, was to prove by example. He enumerated countless cases of government follies. He mined ancient and contemporary history for illustrations of how well-meaning government interferences in economic affairs had had harmful effects upon nations.

His book is a masterpiece. It is a practical handbook that might be entitled, *How to Make the GNP Grow*. And at the same time, it lays the foundations for modern general-equilibrium analysis of supply and demand.

Spirit of the Bourgeois Age But, of course, its many excellences are not enough to explain why *The Wealth of Nations* had so dramatic an impact on the century to follow. Just as important was the fact that the rising business classes needed a spokesperson for their interests. Smith provided them with the laissez-faire ideology that served their purposes, offering intellectual support for free enterprise with minimal government interference.

This does not imply that Smith was a flunky for the business classes. Actually, he had a healthy distrust of business owners. He wrote, for example, "People of the same trade seldom meet together, even for merriment and diversion, but the conversation ends in a conspiracy against the public, or in some contrivance to raise prices."

Smith was definitely on the side of the common people. But his advocacy of laissez-faire was derived from his conviction that the road to economic inefficiency is paved with good intentions. To replace monopolistic businesses with government regulation of the economy would, he thought, probably make a bad situation worse rather than better.

Smith's eclectic and pragmatic views ushered in the Industrial Revolution and the golden age of capitalism.

Classical Economics: Malthus and Ricardo

In the half-century after *The Wealth of Nations* appeared, the law of diminishing returns was discovered. Ironically, just as the Industrial Revolution in the West was offsetting the dire workings of that dismal law, The Reverend T. R. Malthus (1766–1834) enunciated the *iron law of wages,* holding that population growth will inevitably drive workers' wages down to the bare margin of subsistence.

The central figure of the age, however, was David Ricardo (1772–1823), from whose thinking both neoclassical and modern economics derive. Ricardo never went to college. Born to an affluent family, he was cut off by his father with £800 for having married outside his Jewish faith. Within 12 years, he retired from being a stockbroker with a nest egg in the millions.

Once established and affluent, he chanced to read Adam Smith. Fascinated, Ricardo believed that there were basic errors in Smith's analysis and also gaps in his macroeconomic writings. Had it not been for the insistent advice of James Mill, father of John Stuart Mill, Ricardo would have remained no more than a pamphlet writer and member of Parliament. But the elder Mill browbeat Ricardo into writing his *Principles of Political Economy and Taxation* (1817), and Ricardo's fame was secure.

One of Ricardo's contributions lay in a thorough analysis of the nature of economic rent—a theory that survives almost intact today in the form seen in Chapter 27. He presented a careful analysis of the labor theory of value (of which more is to come in our analysis of Marxian theories). His analysis of the burden of the public debt is an apt warning for the 1980s. But his major accomplishment was to analyze the laws of income distribution in a capitalist economy.

Stagnant Wage Predictions and Class Oppositions For a full half-century, from 1820 to 1870, Ricardo kept economists and statesmen hypnotized. Yet, like Malthus, he bet on the wrong horse of diminishing returns just when the technological advances of the Industrial Revolution were outpacing that law.

Ricardo's vision was that rents would rise and land would form the bottleneck to economic growth. In the century to come, in fact, landowners would wither away in importance, and capitalists would replace them as captains of the economic order.

For Ricardo, the law of distribution was the most important part of economic theory. He studied the distribution of the national product among the major classes of society: wages for workers, profits for capitalists, and rents for landowners. With a total social product limited by diminishing returns, Ricardo emphasized that what was gained by one social class had to be taken away from another one. Ricardo presented an autumnal view of capitalism—of an economy on its way to an inevitable rendezvous with pervasive poverty—that attracted both intellectuals and the general public, both capitalists and socialists, over the next century.

No wonder the capitalists liked Ricardo. They could find quotations in his work to prove that trade unions and reforms can do little for the masses.

No wonder the socialists liked Ricardo. They found in him a proof that capitalism would have to be destroyed if workers were to win their rightful share of national output.

Decadence in Classical Economics Historians of science observe that the progress of science is discontinuous. New schools of thought rise, spread their influence, and convince skeptics.

But schools, like people, are subject to hardening of the arteries. Students learn the embalmed truth from their teachers and sacred textbooks. The imperfections in the orthodox doctrines are ignored or glossed over as unimportant.

Decadence and senility set in. Thus, John Stuart Mill, an outstanding economist of the mid-nineteenth century, could write in his classic, *Principles of Political Economy:* ''Happily, there is nothing in the laws of Value which remains for the present and any future writer to clear up. . . .''

Classical economics had grown stale. The time had come for new blood.

The Great Schism A century ago the family tree of economics branched. One branch grew from Karl Marx's *Capital* (1867, 1885, 1894) and his earlier writings. This line, important for understanding the economic organization of communist countries, will be analyzed in section B of this chapter. The other branch continued the tradition of Smith and Ricardo, through the neoclassical thinkers and Keynesian economics to the present-day era of modern mainstream economics.

Neoclassical Economics

Classical writers emphasized costs to the neglect of demand. It was as if they were working with horizontal supply curves and ignored the role of demand curves. Around 1870, three scholars independently laid the foundation for modern economics by devising an analysis that could synthesize both demand elements and cost elements. They were W. Stanley Jevons (1835–1882) in England, Carl Menger (1840–1921) in Austria, and Léon Walras (1834–1910) in Switzerland.

The key element in the neoclassical revolution was to understand how consumer preferences (called ''utility'') enter into the demand for commodities. The neoclassical economists showed that demand depends upon marginal utility and thereby provided the missing link in a complete theory of the market mechanism. (A modern version of the neoclassical theory of utility forms the basis of the theory of demand derived in Chapter 19.)

Finally, particularly in the deep mathematical analysis of Léon Walras, the analysis of general competitive equilibrium was achieved. Walras discovered how to analyze the economy as a whole—as a simultaneous general equilibrium of all the labor, land, and product markets. The late Joseph Schumpeter (1883–1950) used to say that of all great economists, surely Walras was the greatest—for it was he who discovered general equilibrium.

Welfare Economics and Policy Concerns

Economists have always been concerned with applying their theories to public policy. Ever since Adam Smith began to analyze the harmful effects of government regulation of the market, economists have devised technical tools—such as consumer surplus and Pareto efficiency—that could measure the losses that arise from misplaced government interferences with a competitive equilibrium. But don't think neoclassical economists were devotees of laissez-faire. A few were, but most were not. Since the Industrial Revolution, the great economists on the whole have been critical of capitalism's inequality. Around the time of World War I, Cambridge economist A. C. Pigou emphasized the case against laissez-faire and in favor of government action: he argued that government is necessary to mitigate inequality, offset monopoly distortions, and correct for externalities.

Even as economics became more "scientific," it never lost its interest in policy. Most of the great economists tell us in their autobiographies that they became economists to help improve the world. Many were radical believers in the need for drastic changes in the established regimes. But, however much the great economists wanted to bring about a more just economic order, they insisted that plans for alternative economic systems be practical.

A fascinating biography of a radical is that of the great Scandinavian economist Knut Wicksell (1851–1926). Wicksell was a counterculture bohemian who believed in birth control—heresy in the 1870s. When the Czar's army stood on the Swedish borders, Wicksell disregarded the prevalent nationalism of the day and advised his fellow citizens to dismantle their army.

Though he never hesitated to speak out on behalf of unpopular causes, in economic issues Wicksell was a hard-headed realist who criticized utopian socialist ideas. His practical reform proposals anticipated the modern Swedish welfare state, with its income redistribution and transfer benefits.

Today as well, the giants of modern economics keep one eye upon the policy implications of their theoretical studies. Economists of the late twentieth century study government deficits, the money supply, energy markets, and poverty not only because they are fascinated by economic behavior. They also search endlessly for better ways that the government can help (or stop hindering) economic progress.

The Keynesian Revolution

In the years after World War I, economics made great strides in describing and analyzing the economic world of developed and developing regions. One enormous hole, however, still remained. Economists had gone far in describing the business cycle. But neoclassical economics lacked a well-developed macroeconomics to match its microeconomics.

Finally, with the Great Depression came the breakthrough in the *General Theory of Employment, Interest, and Money* (Macmillan, London, 1936) by John Maynard Keynes. Economics would never be the same.

Keynes' breakthrough mortally wounded belief in Say's Law (that held overproduction to be impossible). The neoclassical theories of money and the price level earlier developed by Alfred Marshall (1842–1924) and Yale's Irving Fisher (1867–1947) were given a more fruitful restatement in terms of the Keynesian concepts. And the insights and challenges of the Keynesian revolution have inspired a new generation of theorists to try to understand why wages and prices tend to be sticky, why nominal variables like money have real impacts, and how government fiscal and monetary policies can affect the macroeconomy.

Mainstream Economics

As we move on from Keynesian thought, we encounter the primary subject of this book, the modern mainstream economics that prevails in the mixed capitalist economies of North America, Western Europe, and Japan. The better understanding of both microeconomics and macroeconomics has led to a markedly better working of the mixed economy. The era since World War II has witnessed a growth in world output and living standards unmatched in recorded history.

But we should not glorify past achievements. The

advanced industrial economies have not attained economic nirvana. They cannot attain stable prices and full employment; poverty is on the rise; the international banking system is threatened by staggering debts of developing countries; American farmers are in bankruptcy courts in droves; tens of thousands of toxic waste sites plague our landscape; unemployment in Europe is at its highest levels since the Great Depression.

This sobering reminder of the ailments of a mixed economy should make us sensitive to the *critiques* of mainstream economics that have prevailed in the past and will undoubtedly continue to flourish in the future.

MODERN CRITIQUES

Modern economics is not without its critics. They range from dissenters who question small points here or there to those who reject the entire logical structure. We concentrate here on the major non-Marxist critics, reserving Marxist thought for section B of this chapter.

Chicago School

Starting at the right end of the political spectrum, we encounter first a group of **libertarians**—those who emphasize the central importance of personal freedom in economic and political affairs. These modern-day apostles of laissez-faire and the minimal state include primarily economists associated with the University of Chicago: Frank Knight, Henry Simons, and Milton Friedman, along with Austrian-born economist Friedrich Hayek.

The libertarians remind us of the accomplishments of the market mechanism and warn us of the penalties falling upon any society that ignores the market's guiding hand. In reading their works, we recall how governmental attempts to solve problems can create other difficulties. The libertarians point out that rent controls often lead to housing shortages; that labor unions raise wages and cause unemployment in unionized industries; and that putting price controls on gasoline leads to long lines at gasoline stations.

People of all political persuasions should study Friedman's *Capitalism and Freedom*.[2] It is a rigorous and persuasive elucidation of an important point of view which held sway among conservative thinkers in the 1980s. You might ask yourself whether you are for or against: Social security? Flood relief? Government inspection and regulation of food and drugs? Minimum wages? Mandatory installation of seat belts in cars? Compulsory and free public schooling? Prohibition of open sale of heroin? Compulsory licensing of doctors? Establishment of national parks like Yellowstone or Grand Canyon?

If you read Professor Friedman's work, or collections of his *Newsweek* columns, you will see that he argues cogently against each one of these programs. He opposes them both because he sees them as interferences with personal freedom and because he thinks they fail to achieve their goals. Although you may, on reflection, agree with few or many of the positions advocated, as a thoughtful citizen you must grapple with the issues that Friedman addresses.

Rational-Expectations Macroeconomics Related to the libertarians are a group of free-market macroeconomists, called the **rational-expectations school,** founded in the early 1970s by Robert Lucas at the University of Chicago and Stanford's Thomas Sargent. This school shares the libertarians' skepticism about government policies, arguing that systematic macroeconomic policies to combat unemployment will only end up causing inflation. Better a passive monetary and fiscal policy, they say, than one futilely trying to straighten out every twist and turning point of the business cycle.

The rational-expectations argument fell on deaf ears among older mainstream economists who fought to inject Keynesian thinking into national policymaking. But younger macroeconomists often take inspiration from the techniques of this new approach. And the Reagan administration flirted with both libertarian and rational-expectations views, arguing in the 1982 *Economic Report of the President* that limiting the role of both macroeconomic and microeconomic poli-

---

[2]The University of Chicago Press, Chicago, 1962, hardcover and paperback. See also M. Friedman, *An Economist's Protest* (Thomas Horton & Co., Glen Ridge, N.J., 1972), a collection of his *Newsweek* columns.

cies would in the end expand personal freedom and economic growth. Let us hear this viewpoint:

> Political freedom and economic freedom are closely related. Any comparison among contemporary nations or examination of the historical record demonstrates two important relationships between the nature of the political system and the nature of the economic system: [1] All nations which have broad-based representative government and civil liberties have most of their economic activity organized by the market. [2] Economic conditions in market economies are generally superior to those in nations . . . in which the government has the dominant economic role. . . .
>
> A major objective of this Administration's economic program is to reduce the Federal Government's role in economic decision making while strengthening the economic role of individuals, private organizations, and State and local governments.[3]

Dissenters from the Left

During most of the two centuries since the Industrial Revolution, the most vocal critics of capitalism have fired their salvos from the left. Socialists like Marx and Engels, communists like Lenin, anarchists like Proudhon, neo-Marxists of the 1950s like Baran and Sweezy—all these critics argued that capitalism is fatally flawed and must be replaced by a more efficient and equitable economic system. Who today takes up the revolutionary banner, calling for dismantlement of Western-style capitalism?

Indeed, the voices for radical restructuring today are few. One economist who has voiced his criticisms over the last three decades is Harvard's John Kenneth Galbraith. Writing in *American Capitalism, The Affluent Society,* and *The New Industrial State,* Galbraith has challenged prevailing views about consumers and firms. Among his major points were:

▪ Today's economy is directed by large bureaucracies, not by perfectly competitive markets. The technostructure (the educated elites who run firms, governments, and universities) ultimately makes the decisions that guide countries of both East and West.

[3]*Economic Report of the President, 1982* (Government Printing Office, Washington), pp. 27–28.

The idea that small firms are responsible for much of production, or that small inventors bring forth the major inventions, is a convenient myth designed to perpetuate belief in the market system.

▪ Consumers are not masters of their own minds. Advertising shapes our preferences. The outcomes of markets are determined as much by Madison Avenue as by genuine needs.

▪ Ours is a society in which the public sector starves while the private sector lives high on the hog. Public goods like parks are neglected; roads crumble; bridges collapse.

Galbraith's views about the paradoxes of an affluent society were heeded by political figures and economists alike during the 1950s and 1960s.

The Japanese Mystique America was the birthplace of the "factory system," mass production, the assembly line, and giant factories stretching over acres of land. While Adam Smith expounded the theoretical virtues of division of labor, American entrepreneurs developed its practice to the nth degree in large automobile plants employing 15,000 workers. After Henry Ford introduced mass production of the Model T Ford, workers came to be viewed as little more than highly versatile, all-purpose machines.

As long as the United States remained king of the economic mountain, the defects of the factory system seemed a small price to pay for its marvelous contribution to productivity and living standards. Would we not rather work all day in a factory and be able to buy cars and radios and home appliances than stay on the farm and spend all day washing our clothes in a tub?

During the 1970s and 1980s, America began to fall behind Japan and other countries of the Pacific Rim in the economic race. One industry after another was conquered by Japan or Korea or Singapore. Steel, shipbuilding, radios, television, cameras, automobiles—all these industries fell under the domination of innovative firms from East Asian countries. While advanced industrial countries struggled with inflation or unemployment, while Latin American countries staggered under heavy debt burdens, while socialist countries of Eastern Europe attempted to modernize their obsolete manufacturing industries, the countries of the Pacific Rim moved steadily and rapidly ahead. A striking example of success was the city-state of Singapore. So rapidly had this country of 3 million advanced that, by the end of the 1980s, it exported 20 percent more machinery to the West than did all the socialist countries of Eastern Europe.

As traditional capitalist countries began to falter, many economists asked whether the old factory system of giant bureaucratic corporations operating huge factories had outlived its usefulness. Taking inspiration from Japanese-style management, these economists argued that "Small is beautiful" and pointed to supposedly contented Japanese workers and to Japan's astounding productivity growth since World War II. MIT's Lester Thurow, Harvard's Robert Reich, and others argued for redesigning the workplace on cooperative rather than competitive lines. These scholars argued in effect:

> People work for satisfaction as well as for money; men and women prize jobs which allow them to express their creativity and need for community. Workers must feel themselves part of the management team—sharing information and ideas, designing their jobs, helping to improve the quality of work and of the final output.[4]

Although this group of economists has spawned numerous suggestions, one common theme has been to introduce profit sharing into compensation. MIT's Martin Weitzman has analyzed a compensation system that shares revenues or profits with workers, a system modeled on the Japanese bonus system. He reasons that if workers are paid a share of profits or revenues rather than a straight hourly wage, the marginal cost of labor will decline relative to a straight wage system. Firms will choose to retain their workers during recessions, and the overall unemployment rate will decline.

Another strand running through this critique is that American management has lost touch with production. Trained in financial wizardry at the top business schools, today's MBAs feel more at home reading a balance sheet than managing a production line. They pay more attention to this quarter's bottom line than to the long-term viability of radical new products. They look to getting rich fast with takeovers or arbitrage rather than getting rich slowly through the tedious process of constant innovation and better new products. Some say that the modern company is suffering from "corpocracy"—corporate bureaucracy which makes management sluggish, risk-averse, and poorly adapted to the dynamic world of international competition.

How do traditional economists respond to the analyses of these dissenters from the left? Some argue that the dissenters commit the *post hoc* fallacy, associating Japanese success with the bonus system or with a particular form of corporate organization without any proof that these elements are responsible for Japanese success.

Others charge that their writings lack originality. Those who criticize large corporations today echo the Galbraithian logic; much of Galbraith's argument in *The Affluent Society* can be found in works of earlier writers and is derivative even in title from *The Acquisitive Society* (1920) by the English economic historian R. H. Tawney (1880–1962). But criticisms of lack of originality miss the point. Great advances in technology often arise from the innovator rather than the inventor. And, in the history of ideas, the thinker who creates a new synthesis and speaks in a telling fashion to a new age is the one who plays the pivotal role in history.

Radical Economics

Finally, we move to the truly radical end of the spectrum, to thinkers who would entirely reshape today's mixed capitalist regime.

The Rise of the New Left Two decades ago, in the swirl of civil rights activism and revulsion against the Vietnam war, a school called the *new left* and a group called the Union of Radical Political Economics began to organize their ideas.

To give the flavor of this critique, here are the words of one of its most prominent members, John G. Gurley of Stanford, a former mainstream monetary economist who became an eloquent advocate of radical economics:

---

[4]Among the important recent studies, see Lester Thurow, *The Zero-Sum Solution* (Simon and Schuster, New York, 1985), Robert Reich, *The New American Frontier* (New York Times Publishers, New York, 1983), and Martin Weitzman, *The Share Economy* (Harvard University Press, Cambridge, Mass., 1986).

[This is a] time when the assumptions and methods of economics are being challenged. . . . Some of the attacks have reflected dissatisfaction with the many trivial problems that economists seem to spend so much of their time on. Still others have questioned the economic goals so widely accepted by economists, especially that of ever-increasing GNP, and a few have examined this issue within the wider framework of ecological systems.

Many of the attacks on present-day economics have taken the form of radical analyses of U.S. imperialism— of how the United States profits from its leading role in the hierarchical structure of rich and poor countries that make up the international capitalist system. Other radical analyses have examined how certain groups in the United States itself profit from the maintenance of a hierarchical class structure which produces both wealth and poverty, both privilege and oppression. These analyses, which generally conclude that capitalism is largely responsible for such social and economic disparities, accordingly deny that capitalist society is able (i.e., willing) to solve these problems.[5]

The Radical Critique Today

After an early wave of enthusiasm, the new left went underground. It hibernated during the turbulent 1970s as market economies were beset with inflationary storms arising from supply shocks. As a conservative front spread over the Western democracies—the Reagan presidency in the United States, the Thatcher government in Britain, conservative movements in Western Europe—radical movements were quiescent. But a few scholars kept the faith, particularly a group at the University of Massachusetts in Amherst. What were the major themes in their criticisms?[6]

▪ *Rejection of modern macroeconomics.* Modern mainstream macroeconomics says that there is a natural rate of unemployment—today around 6 percent— below which the economy cannot go without running the straits of inflation. Radicals reject the premise that prices and wages should be free to inflate freely. They

would impose wage-and-price controls as a way of containing inflation, thereby allowing lower levels of unemployment.

With the resources freed up by wage-and-price controls, the new radicals would pour funds into public capital—railroads, pollution control, education, and training.

▪ *Countering imperialism.* One radical note heard in Gurley's trumpet call quoted above has resonated on college campuses: the need to fight American imperialism in South Africa. Harking back to the doctrines of Hobson and Lenin, radicals denounce American companies and accuse them of profiting from the racist policies of apartheid in South Africa. A rising storm of marches, protests, sit-ins, and shanties built in protest has forced many colleges and universities to sell their shares of companies operating in South Africa. Radicals see this movement as the first step in cleansing capitalism of its imperialist stain.

▪ *Greater equity.* The new left shares with the old left a revulsion against the great inequalities generated by markets. The radicals would counterattack the movement against progressive taxation, hoping to tax wealthy groups heavily and redistribute the funds to the poor. They recognize, however, that the most effective redistributional programs are provided by spending (on welfare, food stamps, or housing programs) rather than by redistributive taxation.

▪ *Rejection of markets.* Modern economics views markets as good judges of people's tastes and of the social costs of production. Today's radical economists dissent. Like Galbraith, they feel that our tastes are manipulated by advertising to favor trivial consumption. How can a nation spend billions of dollars playing video games, buying lethal cigarettes, or purchasing brand-name drugs instead of identical but cheaper generic products—all at a time when millions go without food, shelter, and adequate medical care? How can the nation permit firms to continue to foul our environment with sulfurous fumes and toxic wastes? Radicals call for democratic planning to replace the distorted judgments of markets.

▪ *Democratic planning.* Many radicals call for deliberate policies to reverse the decline of our basic manufacturing industries. Some call for a planning mechanism to channel funds into growth industries

---

[5]This quotation is taken from ''The State of Economics,'' *The American Economic Review,* vol. LXI (May 1971, Papers and Proceedings).

[6]See particularly Samuel Bowles, David Gordon, and Thomas Weisskopf, *Beyond the Waste Land* (Anchor Press, Garden City, N.Y., 1983).

while easing declining industries into their graves. But while the radical economists are more sympathetic to democratic or participatory planning than libertarians, they are suspicious of government bureaucracy, and they definitely reject Soviet communism as repressive and destructive of individual liberty.

Appraisal What is the verdict on the theories of the new left? One of the most thoughtful surveys comes from a Swedish economist, Assar Lindbeck.[7] This twentieth-century de Tocqueville studied radical economics while visiting the United States.

Lindbeck points out that the new left mistrusts both the market and state bureaucracy. But that is one dislike too many, for these two systems are the only mechanisms known to society by which a complex modern economy can allocate its resources. How can we plan without a government planning agency? How can we allow markets to distribute corn and labor without allowing corn prices and wages to reflect supply and demand? No answers to this fundamental challenge have come forth.

What has happened to the views expressed by the new left? While we cannot yet judge their ultimate contribution, they have up to now had little impact on mainstream economics. Whatever may be the merits of their arguments, the economists of the new left have been unable to convince their professional colleagues that radical approaches are fruitful ways of attacking today's unsolved economic problems.

B. MARXISM AND ALTERNATIVE ECONOMIC SYSTEMS

Crises of Capitalism

Since the Industrial Revolution, capitalism has been plagued by crises, inequality, and depressions. In the midst of each peril, prophets would pronounce capitalism as dying or worse. Others foretold a mechanical timetable of inevitable progression—savagery to feudalism, feudalism to capitalism, capitalism to socialism, socialism to communism—but these timetables generally proved wrong. After World War I, new democratic governments sprouted all over Europe, and an impartial observer in 1925 might have pronounced the future of capitalism secure. Yet, a decade later, country after country succumbed to dictatorship. Totalitarian fascism covered the map of Europe, displacing the market economies of an earlier era and raising questions about the future of capitalism and democracy.

After World War II, the critics of capitalism were once again confounded. The mixed economies of the West and Japan formed a common pattern of rapid growth and expanding international trade. The insights of the Keynesian revolution propelled market economies to the most rapid and sustained period of expansion ever seen.

Soon, however, Western capitalism fell victim to its own success. Rapid income growth allowed the welfare states in North America and Western Europe to raise income-support and social security programs to unimagined levels. When the oil crisis of the 1970s hit the market economies, they had developed a brittleness. Inflation soared. Unemployment rose. Government deficits began to climb. The external debt burdens of many middle-income countries, especially in Latin America, dragged down their economic growth. The international financial system tottered on the edge of massive defaults in the early 1980s. Once again, critics from left and right set forth grand schemes to revive the sick economies of the West.

As economists and philosophers waged the age-old debate about market mechanism versus government direction, yet another unanticipated shift among nations emerged in the 1980s. While Europe stagnated and North America drowned in deficits, the insular and peninsular countries of the Pacific Rim showed remarkable agility and strength. Japan weathered oil shocks, world recession, and unprecedented turbulence in foreign markets. South Korea, Taiwan, Hong Kong, and Singapore also grew rapidly in the face of

---

[7]*The Political Economy of the New Left—An Outsider's View* (Harper & Row, New York, 1971).

a wide variety of economic vicissitudes. These countries were mixed economies par excellence, relying on markets to innovate, imitate, produce, and sell their products, while the government provided fiscal and monetary guidance and steered the economy in desired directions. In response to the success of the Pacific Rim countries, economists from both capitalist and socialist countries studied the Japanese model, hoping to find the magic formula for future economic success. (Recall the discussion of the ideas of Weitzman, Thurow, and Reich earlier in this chapter.)

A Bouquet of Isms

Philosophers have always had visions of a more perfect society: Plato's Republic, Sir Thomas More's Utopia, and Marx's dictatorship of the proletariat were among the most influential. Visionaries often start by decrying society's concrete ills and then contrast them with the ideal features of a vaguely defined utopia. But beyond agreeing that the present order has faults, different schools of reform often have little in common.

At one extreme are anarchists, who believe in the elimination of all government. At the other extreme are advocates of absolute communism, with the government operating a totalitarian, collectivized economic order and with all decisions about production, consumption, and distribution made by the state.

In between the extremes of anarchism and communism lie the major categories of economic systems that we study in this book:

1. *The market economy.* In pure form, this system is found in laissez-faire capitalism. Although pure laissez-faire never existed, it was closely approached in nineteenth-century Britain. Because most of this book is devoted to describing the functioning of the market economy and the mixed economy that evolved from it, we need not dwell further on this economic system.

2. *Marxism.* Although Karl Marx was primarily a critic of capitalism, he believed that capitalism would be succeeded by socialism, which in turn would give way to communism. His powerful arguments have influenced economic planners in Europe, in the So-

viet Union, in China, and in many developing countries.

3. *Socialism.* One offshoot from the Marxist tree was socialist thinking, which encompasses a wide variety of different approaches. In the nineteenth century, socialists were often revolutionaries who tried to topple governments through violent means; when they succeeded, they often substituted government ownership of factories and land for private ownership. Twentieth-century socialism is widespread, particularly in Western Europe, where democratic socialist governments expanded the welfare state, nationalized industries, and planned the economy.

4. *Soviet communism.* The most thoroughgoing practical alternative to the market economy has taken place in the Soviet Union since 1917, with some features of the Soviet system adopted by Eastern Europe and in China. Under Soviet communism, the state owns all the land and most of the capital, sets wages and most prices, and directs the microeconomic operation of the economy.

The rest of this chapter is devoted to explaining the economic ideas behind the last three of these economic systems.

The Central Dilemma: Market vs. Command

In surveying alternative economic systems, a student might become discouraged about the thousand and one different "isms" that dot the political landscape. And indeed, there is great variety in the way countries organize their economies. But one central theme dominates the entire discussion about different approaches to economic organization and economic reform movements: Should the economy rely primarily upon the private market or upon government commands to answer the questions of *how, what,* and *for whom*? Before we turn to a detailed discussion of the roles of market and command, we first pose this central question in a concise manner.

First, recall that we are discussing the organization of an economic system. What is an *economic system*? It consists of a network of relations and organizations that: sets the laws and regulations that govern economic activity; determines the property rights and ownership of factors of production; distributes the decision-making power over production and consumption; determines the incentives motivating the different decision makers; and in the end determines *what* gets produced, *how* it gets produced, and *for whom* the output is produced.

One important system for determining these questions is the *market*. Under the market system, people act voluntarily and primarily for financial gain or personal satisfaction. Firms buy factors and produce outputs, selecting inputs and outputs in order to maximize their profits. Consumers supply factors and buy consumer goods to maximize their satisfactions. Agreements on production and consumption are made voluntarily and with the use of money, at prices determined in free markets, and on the basis of arrangements between buyers and sellers. Although individuals differ greatly in terms of economic power, the relations between individuals and firms are horizontal in nature, essentially voluntary, and non-hierarchical.

The other major system of organization is a *command economy,* where direction is given by government bureaucracy. In this approach, people are linked by a vertical relationship, and control is exercised by a multilevel hierarchy. A plan for the economy is established at the top level of government, and this plan is subdivided and transmitted down the bureaucratic ladder, with the lower levels executing the plan with increasing attention to detail. Individuals are motivated by coercion and legal sanctions; organizations compel individuals to accept orders from above. Transactions and commands may or may not use money; trades may or may not take place at established prices. The planning bureaucracy determines *what* goods are produced, *how* they are produced, and *who* gets the fruits of productive activity.

The tension between markets and command runs through all discussions about comparative economic systems.

MARXISM

Biography of Karl Marx

Karl Marx (1818–1883) was educated at Bonn and Berlin—starting in law, until the charms of philoso-phy drew him away from a legal career. Along with many German intellectuals, Marx was mesmerized by the philosophical teachings of G. W. F. Hegel. But while Hegel emphasized the supremacy of spirit, Marx stressed the primacy of matter over mind. He identified technological breakthroughs and the accompanying changes in social and economic relations—particularly the accumulation of capital—as the motive forces of history. He thought that these forces, which he called economic determinism, would lead to the inevitable triumph of communism.

When a professional career was closed to Marx because of his truculent and quarrelsome personality and his radical ideas, he turned to journalism. Each radical paper he edited was plagued by financial troubles or the Prussian censor.

Exile followed, and Marx ultimately settled in London, where he led an uneventful life of study, much of it spent in the library of the British Museum. He pursued his vision of economic determinism through thick and thin. However, he would have experienced even more of the thin but for the friendship of Friedrich Engels, his lifelong collaborator and financial angel.

These biographical details can barely hint at the power of Marx's ideas, of which the British intellectual historian Isaiah Berlin wrote, ''No thinker in the nineteenth century has had so direct, deliberate, and powerful an influence on mankind as Karl Marx.''

Marx's Theories Unlike most of the early theories we have reviewed, those of Marx are alive and vitally important today. One can hardly understand the developments in the Soviet Union and Eastern Europe today without an appreciation of Marx's influence. What are the major features on the enormous canvas painted by this intellectual master? We will review here his labor theory of value, his theory of surplus value, and his vision of the laws of motion of a capitalist society.

Marx's economics begins with the *labor theory of value*. Marx assumed that what gives value to a commodity is the total amount of labor power used to produce it—both the direct labor and the indirect labor embodied in buildings or machinery used up in the productive process. Marx realized that market prices under competitive capitalism would not necessarily equal labor values. Why not? Because capitalists receive an excess in revenues over labor costs—a surplus value.

By *surplus value* Marx meant the difference between revenues and total labor costs (total labor costs include direct costs of hired labor and indirect costs of labor used to produce capital goods and therefore "embodied" in capital). How does the difference arise? It arises because workers are forced to sell their labor to capitalists, and because capitalists pay workers for only part of the value of their output. In the simple case where no machinery is used up, the rate of surplus value (or *rate of exploitation*) is simply the ratio of profits to wages.

Someone who had mastered the concepts of modern economics might ask, What is gained by viewing a capitalist economy through Marxist lenses? A careful study shows that Marx's theory of prices differed little from that of Ricardo a half-century earlier. Rather, the essence of Marx's vision was to attempt to expose the nature of profit. Marx hoped to show that profits—that part of output that is produced by workers but received by capitalists—amount to "unearned income."

Using his labor theory of value, Marx described the transition to a socialist society in which "the expropriators are expropriated"; that is, where workers wrench back the surplus value for themselves.

Prophecies If Marx's thinking had progressed no further than his labor theory of value and the concept of exploitation, he would have remained but a minor figure. But he pressed on. Drawing upon these concepts, he claimed to have deduced scientifically the inevitable transition from capitalism to socialism. What did he foresee?

In Marx's world, capitalists are driven to accumulate, for the pursuit of wealth becomes an end in itself and not a means for later consumption. As capital accumulates, the rate of profit falls. Under pressure to squeeze out ever more surplus value, the working class becomes increasingly "immiserized"—by which Marx meant that working conditions would deteriorate and workers would grow progressively alienated from their jobs. A growing "reserve army of the unemployed" would prevent wages from rising above the subsistence level.

As profits decline and investment opportunities at home become exhausted, the ruling capitalist classes resort to *imperialism*. Capital tends to seek higher rates of profit abroad. And, according to this theory (particularly as later expanded by Lenin), the flag follows trade; that is, the foreign policies of imperialist nations are directed toward securing colonies and then mercilessly milking surplus value from them.

But the capitalist system cannot continue this unbalanced growth forever. Marx foresaw ever-growing inequality under capitalism, along with a gradual emergence of class consciousness on the part of the downtrodden proletariat. The requirement for larger and larger firms would culminate in the demise of competition and the formation of monopoly capitalism. Business cycles would become ever more violent as the masses suffered from lack of purchasing power resulting in underconsumption.

Finally, a cataclysmic depression would sound the death knell of capitalism. Like an overripe fruit ready to fall off the tree, capitalism would have grown into a fat monopoly that could be plucked by the workers in a sudden and violent revolution.

These were the prophecies that inspired generations of radicals, of the old and new left. As these positions hardened, later-day Marxists would argue about whether immiseration of the workers referred to real wages or labor's share, about whether peaceful evolution could be a substitute for violent revolution, and about whether socialism was the first or the last stage on the road to communism.

As the decades passed, it became clear that Marx's drama was not being played according to his script. Workers were enjoying ever-growing real wages and shorter hours, and labor's share of national income was slowly growing. Workers were gaining political power through ballots not bullets. The rate of profit showed no tendency to decline for innovations constantly replenished the stock of domestic investment opportunities.

In the area of business cycles, Marx's predictions seemed to be validated by deep depressions in the 1890s and 1930s. But how could Marx foretell that Keynes' *General Theory* in 1936 would point the way to successful macroeconomic management, a shrinking reserve army of the unemployed, and a level of economic stability never seen before?

History has not been kind to the Marxist prophesies over the century since *Capital*. But, as we have repeatedly seen, history rarely follows any script written by mere mortals.

The *economic interpretation of history* is one of Marx's lasting contributions to Western thought. Marx argued that economic interests lie behind and determine our values. Why do business executives vote in favor of conservative candidates, while labor leaders support candidates who advocate raising the minimum wage or increasing unemployment benefits? The reason, Marx holds, is not that people's opinions are shaped by reasoned discourse and impartial analysis. Rather, people's beliefs and ideologies reflect the material interests of their social and economic class.

Some reflection will suggest that this approach is hardly foreign to mainstream economics. In proposing his economic theory of history, Marx has generalized Adam Smith's analysis of self-interest away from the dollar voting of the marketplace to the ballot voting of elections and the bullet voting of the barricades. When the economic theory of history is today formalized in terms of utility and voting decision rules, we recognize the embryo of modern public-choice theories.

Our brief review of Marxian economics can only touch upon the sweeping analysis of this great and controversial figure. In the end, Marx's greatest contribution was to show how the economy is constantly undergoing technological change and social evolution. Each social system contains the elements of its own destruction. Hence, once we understand Marx's approach to history, we can no longer believe, as did the complacent historians of nineteenth-century Britain, that laissez-faire British capitalism was the culmination of human civilization. Nor can we fall into the fallacy that the triumph of the proletariat will inevitably bring an end to the class struggle,[8] or even that the pinnacle of economic achievement has been reached in the mixed economy of twentieth-century America.

"All these will pass away." This is Karl Marx's ultimate thesis.

SOCIALISM

As a doctrine, socialism developed from the ideas of Marx and other radical thinkers of the nineteenth century. Socialism is a middle ground between laissez-faire capitalism and the Soviet communism to which we next turn. A few common elements characterize most socialist philosophies:

- *Government ownership of productive resources.* Socialists believe that the role of private property should be reduced. Key industries such as railroads, coal, and steel should be nationalized (that is, owned and operated by the state).

Although government ownership of industry was the traditional goal and definition of socialism, enthusiasm for nationalization has ebbed in West Germany, the United Kingdom, and Sweden. The major exception to the disenchantment with government ownership was Mitterrand's France, where dozens of firms and banks were nationalized in 1981.

- *Planning.* Socialists are suspicious of the free play of profit motives relied upon in a market economy. They insist that a planning mechanism be introduced to coordinate different sectors. In recent years, planners have emphasized subsidies to promote the rapid development of "high-technology" industries, such as computers and biotechnology; these plans are sometimes called "industrial policies."

In many European countries, capitalist management is diluted by "codetermination"—a process wherein representatives of workers and the public sit as company directors.

- *Redistribution of income.* Inherited wealth and the highest incomes are to be reduced by the militant use of government taxing powers. (In some countries, marginal tax rates have reached 98 percent.) Social security benefits, free medical care, and cradle-to-grave welfare services collectively provided out of progressive-tax sources increase the well-being of the less privileged classes and guarantee minimum standards of living.

---

[8]Only a supersophisticated Marxist could have coined the wry joke recently heard in Eastern Europe: "Under capitalism, it's a case of man exploiting man. Under socialism, it's the other way around."

■ *Peaceful and democratic evolution.* Socialism, as distinct from communism, often advocates the peaceful and gradual extension of government ownership—evolution by ballot rather than revolution by bullet.

Convergence with Capitalism If many of the features of modern socialism sound familiar to Americans, that is no accident. The practices in socialist countries—in Scandinavia, France, and pre-Thatcher Britain—sound more and more like what the United States itself became in the five decades from F. D. Roosevelt to Carter. Even the attempts to shrink the federal role during the Reagan years have left most of the earlier welfare programs intact.

With pardonable exaggeration, John Kenneth Galbraith and the Dutch economist Jan Tinbergen point to a political convergence, all around the world, to a single approach to economic organization: the new world is neither capitalist nor socialist, but dominated by the mixed economies.

SOVIET COMMUNISM

Debate about economic philosophies generally takes place in learned journals and university lecture halls. With Marxism, however, arguments about economic systems spilled over onto the battlefields of Europe and Asia. Marx thought that capitalism would yield to socialism, and that, after a transitional phase, socialism would yield to communism. In reality, the great experiment came when the Bolsheviks seized power in economically backward Russia during a period that the American writer John Reed called "ten days that shook the world." Since the revolution in 1917, the Soviet Union has grown into a mighty military and economic power.

We turn now to a detailed study of the workings of the Soviet economy. This subject is of great importance not only because the Soviet Union is locked in a political struggle with the United States. In addition, the Soviet economy is proof that, contrary to what many skeptics had earlier believed, a socialist command economy can function and even thrive. That is, a society in which the major economic decisions are made administratively, without profits as a central

motive force for production, can grow rapidly over long periods of time.

In this section we will review the major issues of the Soviet economy: What are the high points of Soviet economic history? How is the economy organized? Who makes decisions and what motivates managers? And how successful has the Soviet economy been in achieving its goals of rapid industrialization?

Soviet History

Czarist Russia grew rapidly from 1880 to 1914 but was considerably less developed than industrialized countries like the United States or Britain. World War I brought great hardship to Russia and allowed Lenin and Trotsky—promising power to the workers and land to the peasants—to seize power in a rapid coup. Immediately upon taking power, the Soviet leaders were in a quandary. They had no economic blueprint to guide them. Marx had written extensively about the faults of capitalism, but he had speculated little about the design of the promised land.

From 1917 to 1933, the U.S.S.R. experimented with different socialist models before settling on the centralized version that prevails today.[9] It first tried "war communism," a thoroughly centralized command economy which even toyed with the abolition of money. When that failed, the Soviet leaders instituted the "New Economic Policy," which privatized small-scale trade and decentralized some industries. But dissatisfaction with the pace of industrialization led Stalin and his colleagues to undertake a radical new venture around 1928—collectivization of agriculture and forced-draft industrialization.

The collectivization of Soviet agriculture in 1929–1935 presented one of the great dramas of modern history. While the events are clouded by lack of objective records, it appears that the main reasons for the "great turn" were: first, that Stalin and others wanted to eliminate the more affluent peasants (the "kulaks"), who had formed a core of opposition to Soviet policy. Second, there was a sharp turning

---

[9]A highly readable history of developments in Soviet economic history is contained in Alec Nove, *An Economic History of the U.S.S.R.* (Penguin, Baltimore, revised 1982).

against reliance on markets. Third, grain deliveries to the state—a kind of tax on the farmers—had dropped sharply. In the end, Stalin hoped that he could raise more resources—levy more grain—from the peasants if they were forced into collective farms than if they operated under free enterprise.

The result was that, from 1929 to 1935, 94 percent of Soviet peasants were forced to join collective farms. In the process, many wealthy peasants were deported, and conditions deteriorated so much that millions perished.

The other part of the Soviet "great leap forward" came through the introduction of economic planning for rapid industrialization. In the late 1920s, the communist party spoke of the need to surpass the capitalist countries through planning for rapid growth of heavy industry.

In response, the Soviets created the first 5-year plan, covering 1928–1933. It called for increasing investment by 150 percent over 5 years. Already the emphasis of Soviet planning was established: heavy industry was to be favored over light industry, and consumer goods were to be the residual sector after all the other priorities had been met. Another feature of the first plan was its emphasis on "giantism"—enormous long-term projects, such as the great Dnieper dam, absorbing massive amounts of capital.

Soviet economic history since the 1930s has been a continual drama: preparation for and ultimate victory over the German invaders in World War II; continued use of "high-pressure planning" accompanied by rapid growth of industry; heavy investment in defense, which today takes around 15 percent of GNP; increasingly stern pressures for intellectual conformity along with repression of deviant ideas in the Stalinist period; some relaxation during the Khrushchev and Brezhnev periods; and attempts to reinvigorate the Soviet economy under young new leadership during the Gorbachev era.

The Soviet Economy Today

Having seen how Marxian economics sprouted in the nineteenth century, developed into a full-grown ideology, and flourished in underdeveloped Russia—we now turn to examine the Soviet economy today. This study of how the world's largest command economy

works in practice forms an invaluable supplement to our understanding of economic processes.[10]

Here, as for a market economy, we want to understand how the three basic economic problems get decided: *What* shall be produced? *How* shall it be produced? And *for whom* shall the goods be made? In broad outline, the picture is this.

The state owns almost all means of production—factories, equipment, and land. The major decisions about production and inputs are made by command from above, in accordance with the plan or the planners' wishes. In areas where the economy interacts with households—for consumer goods and in labor markets—prices are set by planners so that consumer demand more or less clears the markets. But the key difference from a market economy is that the direction of economic activity is set by the state, not by consumers.

What In a command economy like the Soviet Union, the broad categories of output are determined by political decisions. Military spending has always been accorded a large fraction of output and scientific resources, while the other major priority has been investment, with a share of GNP ranging between 30 and 40 percent (as compared with 15 percent for the United States). Consumption claims the residual output after the quotas of higher-priority sectors have been filled.

By contrast with those of a mixed capitalist system, prices and incomes in the Soviet economy have little say in the allocation of GNP among the different sectors. Rather, planners start by deciding on the division of the pie between sectors; then they use incomes and prices to help attain their planning goals.

We can illustrate the operation of Soviet planning using consumer goods as an example. Consumers' incomes are determined by wages, which in turn are set at levels needed to persuade workers to move into the priority sectors; Soviet planners rejected the notion of equal wages for all as naive "equality monger-

---

[10]An objective study of the Soviet economic system is provided by Paul R. Gregory and Robert C. Stuart, *Soviet Economic Structure and Performance,* 2d ed. (Harper & Row, New York, 1981). A recent appraisal of the Soviet economy and prospects for reform is contained in Marshall I. Goldman, *Gorbachev's Challenge* (Norton, New York, 1987).

ing.'' But does this mean that consumption decisions are left to the marketplace? Not at all. Rather, planners first decide on the levels and distribution of consumer goods (so much total consumption, so many automobiles, so many radios, and so forth); then consumer prices are set so that demand and supply more or less balance.

More precisely, Soviet planners set *turnover taxes* in order to reduce the demand for consumer goods. This process is illustrated in Figure 35-1, where the different components of the retail price are shown. The key point to see is that the excess demand for goods can be reduced by levying a steep tax on retail purchases. For many commodities, however, prices are set incorrectly. When prices are set too low (as is the case in Figure 35-1), there is excess demand and consumers are forced to wait in long lines; in effect, lines rather than prices are rationing out goods. In other cases, prices are set too high and goods languish on the shelves of department stores.

The role of *prices* in the Soviet economy clearly differs greatly from that in a market economy. What are the principles of price determination? With few exceptions, prices are determined by planners, not by enterprises. We have already seen that retail prices (including taxes) are set to clear markets. Wholesale prices—those used by firms—by contrast serve as accounting prices. They are set on the basis of average costs of production (including a small markup) for the industry as a whole. Western observers stress that industrial prices (such as those on goods like steel) serve virtually no allocational role.

One other feature of Soviet pricing should be noted: Prices are virtually unchanged for long periods of time, being ''reformed''only once or twice a decade. The stickiness of Soviet prices, together with their basis in average costs rather than in marginal costs, makes them often very unreliable indicators of true economic costs.

A Western economist might ask, ''How can you run an economy where you don't know what goods are really worth?'' To this an orthodox Soviet economist might reply, ''The whole purpose of planning is to *avoid* the mistakes of the market. We prefer to have goods that society really needs (as determined by the communist party), rather than to devote our economy to the follies of the market, producing endless quanti-

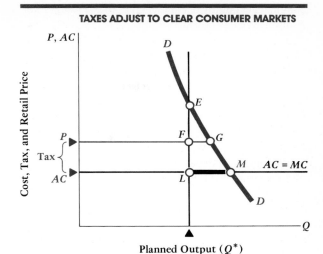

TAXES ADJUST TO CLEAR CONSUMER MARKETS

Figure 35-1   In Soviet consumer markets, taxes are levied to reduce consumer demand

Soviet planners recognize that setting prices at average cost will cause drastic shortages: price at *AC* will cause shortage equal to quantity demanded *M* minus planned quantity *Q**, leading to shortage amount *LM*.

By setting turnover tax *LF*, raising retail price to *P*, planners can curb shortages or gluts. Prices are generally held fixed for several years, so wasteful mismatches of supply and demand (such as *FG*) are endemic to the Soviet economy.

ties of polluting automobiles, computer games, and designer jeans. If we wanted consumers to be sovereign, we could use the market. But we don't.''

One of the major complaints about the Soviet economy has been the shoddy quality of the goods it produces. The nuclear disaster at Chernobyl demonstrated to the world problems of Soviet quality control. Less publicized examples are that 70 percent of the television sets made by one association were rejected each year for poor quality and that 20 percent of the Soviet food harvest rots because of poor handling. In recent years, Soviet leaders have launched campaigns to improve worker morale and to raise the sense of pride in the quality of goods.

How How does the Soviet economy decide upon the techniques of production? On what basis does this command economy decide whether to use steel or aluminum, nuclear power or coal, labor or machinery? These questions can be subdivided into the question of who makes the decisions and what criteria are used.

In large part, the decisions about *how* goods are to be produced are made by the planning authorities. Planners first decide on the quantities of final outputs (the *what*). They then use a technique called *material balances* to work backward from outputs to the required inputs and the flows among different firms. Investment decisions are specified in great detail by the planners, while firms have considerable flexibility in deciding upon their mix of labor inputs.

What motivates managers to fulfill the plans? Clearly no planning system could specify all the activities of all the firms—this would require billions and billions of commands every year. Many details must be left to the managers of individual factories. The key problem then devolves to *inadequate managerial incentives,* which have been a recurrent problem of the Soviet economy.

In contrast to a market economy, the primary goal of Soviet firms is to fulfill the plan rather than to earn profits. Soviet managers face a number of targets by which they are judged. The major target is output (or more precisely, ''realized output'' or sales); subsidiary targets include labor productivity, the product mix, and, in recent years, profits.

Soviet managers are then judged on how well their enterprise fulfills the plan: they get large bonuses if they meet the plan, while they may be dismissed if they fall short of the plan.

While much of the Soviet system may sound unfamiliar, some aspects resemble features of the American economy. Successful bureaucrats in the U.S.S.R. are ''organization people''—they are obedient but resourceful, obsequious to those above and arrogant to those below. Ability counts, ability not only to master a technical engineering problem, but also to get along with people. Some complain here of the businessperson's three-martini lunch; similarly, the Soviet press often contains reports of padding of expense accounts or business junkets to a Black Sea resort.

The managerial incentive system has given rise to significant distortions in the Soviet economy. Be-

cause such high priority is given to meeting the output or sales target, managers often hoard inputs like steel that might cause bottlenecks if they became scarce because of shortages or transport delays. Moreover, because output targets do not contain quality dimensions, there is an incentive to produce low-quality goods. Thus, if the target is 10,000 shirts, the firm might use rough cloth and sew a crooked seam. Stories are told of transportation enterprises that move carloads of water back and forth in order to fulfill their output target of logging so many physical ton-miles.

But it would be misleading to dwell on the shortcomings. Every economy has its contradictions and difficulties with incentives—witness the paradoxes raised by the separation of ownership from control in America, discussed in Chapters 20 and 25.

What counts is results, and there can be no doubt that the Soviet planning system has been a powerful engine for economic growth.

For Whom We have already discussed the question of who is served by the Soviet economy. The entire system is designed to attain the goals of the planners and the ultimate political leaders of the communist party. The priority has, since 1930, been national security and rapid economic growth. In recent years, however, the consumer has been given greater priority. A much larger share of investment now goes to agriculture and light industry than in the time of Stalin. But the system is still very far from being driven by consumer preferences.

Because of the high priority of investment and defense, consumption's share of GNP is only 53 percent (as opposed to 66 percent in the United States). Consumption is not equally distributed, however. Wage rates are determined centrally to clear labor markets. In the early stages of industrialization, Soviet planners set large differentials between skilled and unskilled workers to reflect the scarcity of skilled labor. In the 1930s, the differential was as high as 8 to 1, whereas today, because of the increased number of educated workers, wage differentials have declined to 2 to 1.

In the *Communist Manifesto,* Marx wrote, ''To each according to his needs.'' Soviet leaders have decided that such a utopian society is many years away, and that material incentives for workers must continue to play a key role in deciding the distribution of consumer goods.

Comparative Economic Performance

Since 1945 the United States and the Soviet Union have engaged in a superpower competition for public opinion, for military superiority, and for economic dominance. Premier Nikita Khrushchev boastfully predicted that the U.S.S.R. would bury the United States economically. Moreover, in that era—when the American economy stagnated while Soviets thrust the first missile into space—many objective analysts believed that the Soviets might well outstrip their capitalist rivals.

How does the economic performance of the world's largest command economy compare with that of the mixed economies? In answering this question, we examine the key indicators of economic growth, equality of income, and absence of inflation and unemployment.

Economic Growth The central objective of Soviet leaders since the late 1920s has been rapid industrialization. It is hence appropriate to compare growth in GNP of the U.S.S.R with that of other countries. As Table 35-1 shows, Soviet economic growth since the 1920s has indeed been impressive. Measured Soviet real GNP has grown more rapidly over the long run than have most of the major market economies. While the growth experience has been impressive, some historians note that the growth has been achieved by brute force, by emphasizing rapid growth of many commodities that have not necessarily been highly valued by consumers. Quantity, not quality, has been the goal.

What have been the sources of economic growth? Studies indicate that the pace of growth in the Soviet Union has been rapid because of extensive growth—very large increases in inputs of capital and labor. The rate of productivity growth (that is, the rate of growth of output per unit of input) has in recent years been markedly lower than that of major market economies.

But recent years have not seen a continuation of the earlier trend of more rapid growth under communism than in market economies. By some analysts' reckon-

THE U.S.S.R. HAS GROWN RAPIDLY UNDER PLANNING

COUNTRY AND PERIOD	AVERAGE GROWTH RATE OF GNP (percent per year)
Soviet Union	
1885–1913	3.3
1928–1987	4.2
United States	
1834–1929	4.0
1929–1987	3.0
United Kingdom	
1855–1987	2.1
Germany	
1850–1987	2.8
Japan	
1874–1987	4.5

Table 35-1 Long-term growth of GNP in the Soviet Union and other major countries

The planned Soviet economy since 1928 has grown more rapidly than the economy of Czarist Russia and has outpaced most major market economies. Only Japan and the United States in its rapid-growth phase equalled Soviet economic growth. (Source: Gur Ofer, "Soviet Economic Growth: 1928–1985," *Journal of Economic Literature*, Dec. 1987 and CIA, *Impact of Gorbachev's Policies*, July 1988, SOV 88-10049.)

ing, indeed, the U.S. growth has outstripped Soviet growth in the last decade; in the last 5-year period, Soviet GNP has grown at only 2.1 percent per year. What caused the slowdown? Factors include: a lack of major innovations, a string of disastrous harvests, increasing burdens of military spending, escalating costs of producing energy in the far east and north of the U.S.S.R., and the strain of using a cumbersome planning apparatus to deal with the demands of an economy with a growing need for technological sophistication.

Where does the Soviet economy stand today? Overall, Soviet GNP was about 57 percent of American GNP in 1987. On a per capita basis, however, Soviet output was only 49 percent of that of the United States. There remains a large gap between the most advanced capitalist countries and the Soviet Union, and that gap is not closing.

Income Distribution One of the major complaints levied by Marx and many socialists and radicals has been that capitalism permits surplus value or un-earned profits to flow to capitalists, making capitalism a very unequal, class-ridden society. By contrast, a socialist society would share the return to capital among the workers, thereby allowing much greater equality than a market economy.

In practice, communist planners have allowed sizable but declining wage differentials. And the privileges of the capitalist class have been replaced by generous benefits for the ruling party elites. Recent estimates of income distribution indicate that, except for the absence of a super-rich class, the income distribution in the Soviet Union and Eastern Europe shows a striking similarity to that in Western countries.

Inflation and Unemployment Finally, what of the scourges of capitalism, unemployment and inflation? The answer appears to be that there is effectively none of either in the U.S.S.R. Labor is generally in short supply, because of the ambitious economic plans. Further, controlled prices tend to be quite stable, so measured inflation is absent. Whatever the flaws of Soviet communism, the problems of open inflation and unemployment are not among them.

■　■　■

How do these diverse elements of performance add up? Such an evaluation is beyond mere economic science. The Soviet model has surely demonstrated that a command economy is capable of mobilizing resources for rapid growth and awesome military power. But it has done so in an atmosphere of great human sacrifice—even loss of life—and political repression. Is such a frightful human toll worth the economic gains? This is one of the most profound dilemmas of human society.

Economic Reforms

Although the socialist economies of the Soviet Union and Eastern Europe grew rapidly for many years, they began to stagnate in the 1970s and 1980s. The promise of the Soviet model lost its allure for other coun-tries as growth slowed and as high-technology industries of the United States, Western Europe, and the Pacific Rim left the Soviet-style economies far behind. The technological backwardness of Soviet planning is symbolized by the fact that the planning apparatus, which compiles thousands of material balances and sets most prices, performs most calculations manually, sometimes even on abacuses!

On many occasions in Soviet history, leaders have attempted to reform Soviet communism. Some of the most thorough reforms have taken place in China and Hungary, but the most visible set of reforms were the reforms launched under Soviet General Secretary Mikhail Gorbachev. We first sketch the nature and content of the reforms and then comment on the outlook for their success.

More or Less Centralization? The key debate has been between those who want better centralized planning and those who want to decentralize decisions and give leading roles to prices and profits.

The proponents of *better centralization* stress that planning directives can be improved by use of the new tools of mathematical economics. They would introduce input-output techniques (such as those developed by Russian-born former Harvard economist Wassily Leontief, described in Chapter 36's appendix). Some (Nobel-laureate Kantorovich and academician Novozhilov) would apply linear programming techniques to estimate the appropriate scarcity prices to use in plans. Thus proponents of centralization would retain the key elements of the command economy, but improve the precision of its commands.

At the other pole are those who press for greater *decentralization* of decision making. This group stresses that a modern economy is too complex to be operated with as high a degree of centralization as prevails in the Soviet Union. They note that use of highly aggregated output quotas leads to distortions; distortions are exacerbated by use of prices that are poor indicators of true economic scarcity.

In recent years, the decentralizers have become dominant. The key insight, first put forth by Soviet economist Evsei Liberman in 1956, was that production must be subordinated to profit as an incentive for managers. By targeting profits, Soviet managers would be forced to pay greater attention to costs, quality, and innovation, as must a manager in a market economy. Managers would no longer be rewarded for producing large quantities of unsold and defective goods.

The Gorbachev Reforms

General Secretary Gorbachev faced a crisis in the Soviet economy upon assuming leadership in 1985. Growth in the Soviet economy had slowed sharply, defense continued to drain a substantial fraction of the output and technological capability, and leadership and worker morale seemed at a low ebb. Gorbachev argued that the traditional Soviet system was too centralized and clumsy for effective management of an increasingly sophisticated economy. The economy, in the view of many Soviet economists, needed fundamental reform.[*]

Gorbachev's first efforts were aimed at improving morale and renewing the leadership of his country. He instituted a policy of *glasnost* (openness) to promote candor and reduce ideological rigidity, increased tolerance toward minorities, and replaced many of the aged "revolutionaries" with younger comrades.

The boldest restructuring, called *perestroika,* calls for a major reform of the management of Soviet industry. In June 1987 and July 1988, the Soviet government approved a "New Economic Mechanism" to change the relation between the state and enterprises over the period to 1991. These are the major contours of the Gorbachev reforms:

- The degree of control of the planning apparatus over the economy is to be reduced and the autonomy of enterprises will be enhanced. Fewer industries will receive quantitative planning targets (e.g., tons of steel or number of radios). Enterprises will determine a larger number of prices, although the prices will continue to be scrutinized by the state.

- Enterprises will become largely self-financing. That is, they will be able to retain much of their profits for bonuses and investment. The reform even contemplates the discipline of bankruptcy when an enterprise has persistent losses. The role of the profit motive is clearly increased.

- Firms will now be able to compete in international trade rather than having to make all sales and purchases through the Ministry of Foreign Trade. It is proposed that firms will be able to retain some of their

[*]In 1987, an obscure Soviet economist, N. P. Shmelev, was catapulted into prominence with a trenchant critique of Soviet planning in a Soviet periodical, *Novi Mir*. Excerpts from this eloquent tract illustrate some of the themes of the reform economists and demonstrate the extent to which open criticism was tolerated during the early Gorbachev years. Shmelev wrote, "Our economy has been ruled for too long by decree instead of by the ruble. Today's administrative system of management is unable to concern itself with improving output quality or increasing production efficiency." He complains that planners spend their time "watching with the utmost vigilance to ensure that shoemakers stitch shoes and pastry-cooks bake pies. . . . Everything is swamped in a foul bureaucratic morass of departments. Great authority, intelligence, and strength are needed for the day-to-day struggle against the bureaucracy."

Critics of the Soviet economy have pointed out that state enterprises act as monopolists and therefore have an iron grip on markets. Shmelev castigates the monopolistic tendencies in a manner reminiscent of critics of American big business, arguing for greater competition and for breaking the dominance of the producer over the consumer: "Choice, competition—that is an objective condition without which no economic system can be viable or at least sufficiently efficient. Any monopoly inevitably leads to stagnation, and absolute monopoly to absolute stagnation."

Soviet communism has proclaimed the right of every worker to a job and contrasts the absence of unemployment in the Soviet Union with the high unemployment prevalent in many capitalist countries.

Shmelev says the unspeakable by suggesting that the threat of unemployment will be necessary to discipline workers: "Let us not close our eyes to the economic harm done by our parasitical confidence in guaranteed work. Today it is, I believe, clear to everyone that we owe disorderliness, drunkenness, and shoddy work largely to excessively full employment. A real danger of losing your job and going onto a temporary allowance or being obliged to work wherever you are sent is a very good cure for laziness, drunkenness, and irresponsibility."

Western economists wait eagerly to see whether such open critiques have an impact on the course of Soviet reform.

earnings of foreign currencies. In addition, the reformers have suggested that they may make the ruble convertible into foreign currencies and that the Soviet Union may join major international economic institutions like the International Monetary Fund (IMF) and the General Agreement on Tariffs and Trade (GATT).[11]

▪ The stated purpose of the reforms is to make the Soviet economy more productive and to increase the volume and quality of consumer goods. The objective was stated by Secretary Gorbachev in 1986:

> We would welcome any opportunity to switch resources and forces from defense into civilian sectors, into increasing people's prosperity.

Outlook for Reform The Gorbachev reforms are in their infancy, and no assessment will be possible for many years. A sober assessment of the chances for success finds many pitfalls along the road to achieving the goals. First, things may get worse before they get better. The Soviet economy is a delicately balanced web of interests and classes. A thoroughgoing reform may disrupt the normal channels of commerce and actually slow economic growth for a time. In addition, there will be strong resistance from the entrenched bureaucracy that wishes to maintain its economic power. Past reform efforts have always been laid low by central planners.

Second, the Soviet leaders are moving into uncharted waters. There are no clear precedents for a mixed socialist economy. Many questions arise for the future performance of a system with elements of both plan and market: Will profit incentives steer the economy in the wrong direction? Will enterprises fire workers and jack up prices, producing the scourges of inflation and unemployment in a socialist economy? Will decentralization of foreign trade to enterprises lead to a wave of imports? Will workers revolt against the new material incentives?

Or, most likely of all, will the reform movement simply be strangled by the opposition of those who currently enjoy privilege and high status under the old regime of centralized planning?

A recent study of the Gorbachev reforms concludes with the following words:

> All this is not to argue that there will be no reform. Some improvements will occur, probably in foreign trade, joint ventures, agriculture, and the service sector. . . . It is also likely that enterprise managers will end up with more power and more financial autonomy, but not as much as they need to free themselves from the petty tutelage of central officials. In other words, there will be improvements and improved productivity, but not the breakthroughs Gorbachev seems eager to achieve.
>
> Gorbachev confronts an unpleasant dilemma. Without a radical economic and political upheaval, the Soviet Union will probably be unable to sustain its economic power. . . . Essential to such an upheaval, however, is a decision to slash Soviet military expenditures and divert more resources to decentralized consumption and innovation, but this in turn will force, at the very least, a temporary reduction of military might and prestige. . . . Moreover, there is always the chance that, in the process of doing all this, Gorbachev will fail in bringing about economic reform but succeed in relegating the Soviet Union to a lesser military and political position.[12]

With this overview of the Soviet economic reform movement, we conclude our analysis of alternative economic systems. And, indeed, the circle is closed, for we see that the underlying motive for reform stems from the need to confront economic scarcity and to face the age-old dilemma of guns versus butter. No lesson could better illustrate the central tenet of economics—that scarcity and the limitation of economic goods is pervasive no matter what the form of economic organization.

---

[11]The mission and function of these international organizations are discussed in Chapter 40.

[12]Marshall I. Goldman, *Gorbachev's Challenge* (Norton, New York, 1987), pp. 260–262.

SUMMARY

A. Evolution of Economic Thought

1. Growing from roots in nationalist and protectionist mercantilism, political economy as a discipline began with the classical economists: Adam Smith, whose invisible-hand doctrine proclaimed a beneficial natural order in the price system and who severely criticized government interference in the marketplace, and Malthus and Ricardo, the gloomy prophets of diminishing returns and of the struggle over distribution of limited social income among the wage workers, landowners, and profit-seeking capitalists.

2. Flagging classicism gave way a century ago to neoclassical economics, which provided a synthesis of utility and costs, marginalism extended beyond Ricardian rent analysis to all factors of production, and modern welfare economics studying government policies for changing the income distribution or for correcting microeconomic inefficiencies.

3. The Keynesian revolution added to the microeconomics of neoclassical economics an overdue macroeconomics that eventually synthesized fiscal and monetary analysis.

4. Important counterweights to modern mainstream economics have come from both left and right. Conservative libertarian critics stress that planning and government intervention imperil personal freedoms along with economic efficiency, while rational-expectations macroeconomists argue that systematic policies cannot cure business cycles. Galbraithian iconoclasm questions whether consumer tastes are shaped by advertising, while other economists fret over corpocracy that weakens innovativeness in large businesses. Radical economists denounce inequality, pollution, and imperialism.

B. Marxism and Alternative Economic Systems

5. In reaction to the periodic crises and depressions of capitalism, critics have spawned "isms" of the Marxist, socialist, and communist varieties.

6. The Marxian offshoot from Ricardian classicism has played a pivotal role in intellectual and political history. Scientific socialism purports to predict the laws of motion of capitalism: exploitation and pauperization, class struggle and class-conditioned ideology, imperialism, cyclical crises, and ultimate proletarian victory.

7. Socialism is a middle ground between capitalism and communism, stressing government ownership of the means of production, planning by the state, income redistribution, and peaceful transition to a new world.

8. Historically, Marxism took its firmest roots in semifeudal Russia. A study of the *what, how,* and *for whom* of the command economy in the Soviet system shows a much greater central planning of broad elements of resource allocation (particularly the emphasis on defense, a high rate of investment, and rapid industrialization). The Soviet economy has grown very rapidly since the 1920s. But recent stagnation leaves a large gap between the standards of living of the U.S.S.R. and advanced capitalist countries, and the slow growth has provoked significant reform proposals during the Gorbachev years.

CONCEPTS FOR REVIEW

mercantilism
Adam Smith's attack on government, espousal of the invisible hand
Ricardian diminishing returns, class conflicts
neoclassical economics
Chicago School libertarianism
Japanese mystique

new left and radical economics
Marxist laws of economic evolution
socialism, communism, Marxism
centralized planning, Soviet style
what, how, for whom in the Soviet Union
two poles of communist reform
Gorbachev reforms

QUESTIONS FOR DISCUSSION

1. Make a list of the key alternative economic systems, describing each and its history.

2. Analyze the way that *what, how,* and *for whom* are solved in the Soviet command economy, and compare your analysis with the solution of the three central questions in a market economy.

3. Which parts of a modern American economics textbook would be well—or badly—received by socialist or Soviet thinkers?

4. Libertarian economists argue that the government should not regulate the quality of drugs, require seat belts, or have speed limits on highways. Devise the kind of argument a libertarian might use to support such views. Construct some opposing arguments.

5. Review the list of reservations that libertarians lodge against government interferences in the modern mixed economy (page 828). In your view, which of these interferences expand and which reduce economic freedoms? On which would you agree with Friedman's opposition?

6. Consider the Soviet and American economic models. What are the strong or weak points of each in the following tasks:

  (a) Setting a high ratio of investment to GNP
  (b) Matching shoe sizes or colors with consumer tastes
  (c) Controlling inflation and unemployment
  (d) Inventing new products or processes

7. Prices and profits play a central role in the allocation of resources in a market economy; explain briefly. Then contrast their role in a Soviet-style command economy.

8. Advanced problem: The basic technique of Soviet planning is material balances. Under this technique, the total demand of each commodity is (in principle) adjusted to equal the total supply. More precisely, demands are set so that the sum of all demands for intermediate goods (e.g., corn for seed) plus final demands (e.g., corn for muffins) is equal to the supplies (e.g., production, imports, and decline in inventories of corn).

Recalling the principles of an efficient allocation of resources (particularly that in Chapters 23 and 31), evaluate whether a material balance plan is assured to achieve allocative efficiency. [HINTS: Draw a marginal-cost-based supply curve and a marginal-utility-based demand diagram. Choose an arbitrary level of output, and assume this is sold at the price where output is equal to quantity demanded (i.e., the price is determined by the intersection of the planner's quantity with the demand curve). Does $MC = MU$? Can you see anything in the material-balancing technique that satisfies the fundamental conditions for allocative efficiency?] Does your analysis suggest why Soviet economists are critical of the current system and propose introducing reforms such as decentralization or better planning techniques?

PART SEVEN

ECONOMIC GROWTH
AND INTERNATIONAL
TRADE

CHAPTER 36

ECONOMIC GROWTH: THEORY AND EVIDENCE

The Industrial Revolution was not an episode with a beginning and an end. . . . It is still going on.

E. J. Hobsbawm,
The Age of Revolution (1962)

MOST ANALYSES and popular discussions of economic issues focus upon short-run concerns like the latest data on inflation or unemployment, the latest twist or turn in Federal Reserve policy, and the travails of the computer or auto industry.

But such concerns are only ripples in the longer wave of economic growth. Year in and year out, advanced economies like the United States accumulate larger quantities of sophisticated capital equipment, push out the frontiers of technological knowledge with new process and product innovations, and increase their potential per capita GNP. If we look at individual industries, we see an incessant change and evolution: industries producing horseshoes or steam engines decline and disappear; steel and textiles fight for their livelihood against lower-cost foreign producers; aircraft and microcomputers become the new buttress of America's industrial system—for a while.

Here in Part Seven, we turn to these long-run questions of economic growth and international trade. We begin in this chapter by examining the history and quantitative record of American economic growth, along with the economic theories that explain this trend.

Chapter 37 also looks at growth and trade, focusing

851

primarily on problems of economic development of poorer countries. We see what barriers keep poor nations poor and what steps they can take to improve their economic fortunes.

The last three chapters then examine issues of international trade and finance. Chapter 38 begins with the theory of comparative advantage, which offers some of the most profound insights in all of economic analysis. This theory shows why it pays for a country to trade even though foreigners are more efficient (or inefficient) in the production of every commodity.

Chapter 39 then applies comparative advantage to analyze the question of protectionism: Should a na-

tion protect its industries from imports of more efficient foreign nations? What are the dubious and what the valid reasons for imposing barriers to international trade?

In the final chapter, we address issues of international finance. We shall see how the gold and dollar standards collapsed, to be replaced by today's system of market-determined exchange rates. We shall also see how the U.S. trade deficit of the late 1980s threatens today's trade and payments systems.

With these final topics, we will have completed our survey of modern economics.

A. THE THEORY OF ECONOMIC GROWTH

Nations have long regarded their economic growth as a central economic and political objective. In the United States, presidents have campaigned on platforms proclaiming the need to ''get the country moving again.'' Other countries, like the Soviet Union, have made untold sacrifices to speed their industrialization. But what exactly is economic growth?

Formally, **economic growth** represents the expansion of a country's potential GNP. In terms of Chapter 2's production-possibility frontier *(PPF)*, we can visualize economic growth as the outward shift of the *PPF*.

In studying the process of economic growth, however, we should also understand what growth means for ordinary people. To see what economic growth has brought to America, let's go back a century to 1888 and look at a family's daily existence. Most people worked on farms, and a day's work lasted for 10 to 12 hours for 6 or 7 days a week. The average worker would earn about $1 per hour in terms of today's prices. But what goods and services could be bought with such meager earnings? The average home had no electricity, no telephone, no radio or television or stereo, no running water, no toilets, and no central heating. Local transportation was by foot or by horse on unpaved pathways, and the lucky few who could travel to neighboring cities went by rail. Public health was rudimentary, and few safe and effective drugs were available to combat the many dreaded illnesses of the time.

To understand economic growth, compare the everyday life of the present-day American with the last paragraph. The enormous difference in the standards of private consumption and public services is a dramatic illustration of the effect of economic growth.

In the first part of this chapter, we inquire into the economic processes that lead to growth. *Theories of economic growth* study the factors that lead to economic growth over time and analyze the forces that allow some nations to grow rapidly, some slowly, and others not at all.

We also inquire into the causes of the economic growth of nations. Are there stages of history? What is the economic process by which living standards rise and capital is accumulated? Can we discern patterns of economic growth in industrial countries? And has the period since the early 1970s witnessed a change in the patterns of economic growth?

We want to know, as well, the sources of economic growth. Did our living standards rise because of more capital or because of technological progress? And what can a nation do to improve its economic performance? All these questions are central issues addressed by growth theory and policy in this chapter.

STAGES OF HISTORY

Voltaire wrote that history is but a fable agreed upon. Until recently, many writers regarded economic history as a series of stages, one unfolding predictably after another. One catalog of the possible stages was described more than a century ago by Friedrich List, in his 1841 *National System of Political Economy.* According to List, Karl Marx, and others, European society has evolved toward higher forms of economic organization. First came primitive cultures, with marauding hunters and self-sufficient tribal families cultivating crops. Gradually, as elbow room became scarce, the primitive economy evolved into feudalism. In the Middle Ages, a settled chain of command and exploitation—based largely on ownership of land—governed all economic and social life from king down to serf.

When the Renaissance and Reformation led to the Industrial Revolution, the curtain came down on feudalism, and civilization was ushered onto the stage of bourgeois, middle-class capitalism. Peasants were driven from the countryside and forced into the cities as a working class (or ''proletariat''). Rivers were dammed to harness water power, and the invention of the steam engine enabled the energy of wood and coal to replace the energy of beast and man.

Some, such as British historians of the Victorian age, believed that an almost-perfect economic state had been reached under laissez-faire capitalism. The only remaining step toward perfection would be to dismantle tariffs and the few other government interferences in the marketplace. The state would wither away.

Others, particularly socialist writers like Marx, believed that one more act was to follow in the drama of economic development. Capitalism was to be but a passing phase, succeeded in its turn by socialism or communism, just as capitalism had succeeded dying feudalism. In 1849, Marx and Engels wrote in *The Communist Manifesto:*

> The modern bourgeois society has sprouted from the ruins of feudal society. . . . The modern laborer . . . becomes a pauper. . . . What the bourgeoisie therefore produces . . . are its own grave diggers. Its fall and the victory of the proletariat are equally inevitable.

Fact and Fiction

Events rarely agree with the fables written by historians or economists. Victorian capitalism yielded to the welfare state. Moreover, the revolutions that Marx and Engels predicted for France and Germany failed to materialize. And real wages, instead of falling or remaining constant in the century since Marx's 1867 *Capital,* have instead risen dramatically under industrial capitalism.

Another frequent prophesy was that capitalism would be racked by ever-deepening depressions. And indeed, the Great Depression of the 1930s was one of the worst the capitalist system has ever known. But who could foresee that Keynes would develop the macroeconomic theories that allow today's market economies to use fiscal and monetary policies to moderate business cycles and combat chronic slumps? Few economists today predict that capitalism will collapse under the weight of one final great depression.

What has been the major surprise in economic development of the last half of the twentieth century? The single most surprising development of our age has been the unpredicted vigor of market economies. Miracles of sustained growth in production and living standards have taken place in Japan, Germany, Italy, France, Scandinavia, and North America.

Social prophets of the 1940s and 1950s, such as Schumpeter and Toynbee, thought of the mixed economy as ''capitalism in an oxygen tent.'' But the growth experience of the third quarter of the twentieth century revealed that a market economy could perform favorably in comparison with past epochs of capitalism or present developments under communism. Sages of an earlier age would be astounded to find that virtually all the major economies have rediscovered the central role of market forces as a way of guiding resource allocation.

Then the 1970s ushered in the ''age of stagflation,'' in which rising inflation and unemployment were to appear simultaneously as the growth in living standards slowed sharply. This development was on no scholar's timetable—not seen in the crystal ball of Spengler, Toynbee, Marx, Schumpeter, or Galbraith. We live in a world no prophet ever predicted!

The twists and turns of economic history serve as fair warning: Not even the most brilliant social scientist can predict the future outcome of complex economic, social, and political factors.

ECONOMIC THEORIES

Let us turn now to various economic theories that can help us to understand history. From the earliest days of political economy, economists have applied their tools to help explain the evolution of output and wages, and the process of long-term economic growth generally.

The "Magnificent Dynamics" of Smith and Malthus

In *The Wealth of Nations* (1776), Adam Smith wrote a handbook of economic development. He began with a hypothetical golden age—"that original state of things, which precedes both the appropriation of land and the accumulation of [capital] stock"—when labor alone counted, when land was freely available to all, and before there was any capital to speak of.

What determines pricing and distribution in this simple and timeless dawn? Prices and outputs depend here on labor alone. Every commodity trades at prices proportional to the amount of work required to produce it. If beavers take twice the time to find and trap as deer, then beavers will cost twice as much as deer. An economy in which prices are determined by the amount of labor that goes into the production of each commodity is governed by the **labor theory of value.**

The determination of price by average labor cost alone would apply no matter how many goods there were. Supply and demand are operating in this golden age, but the situation is so simple that we do not need elaborate *DD* and *SS* curves. The long-run *SS* curves for the different goods are simple horizontal lines at the stated labor costs; average labor costs therefore determine prices.

Now consider the dynamics of such an economy. Life is pleasant in the golden age. Babies are born, and the population doubles every 25 years. Since land is plentiful, people spill over onto more acres. National output exactly doubles as population doubles. Price ratios of deer and beaver remain exactly as before.

What about real wages? Wages still get all the national income, there being as yet no subtractions for land rent or interest on capital. Because output expands in step with population and land is not a drag on

output, diminishing returns do not set in. The real wage per worker is therefore constant over time.

That would be the end of the story until, say, some clever inventor found a new way of doing in 1 hour what used to take 2 hours. This would raise the national product per capita. A balanced improvement in the productivity of labor would leave the price ratio of beaver to deer unchanged, but it would double the real wage rate. In this world of the labor theory of value, inventions can only raise wages and speed the pace of balanced economic growth.[1]

Scarce Land and Diminishing Returns Once all land becomes fully populated, the golden age in which only labor counts would come to an end. As we saw in Chapter 2, once the frontier of virgin land disappears, balanced growth of land and labor inputs along with their outputs is no longer possible. New laborers begin to crowd onto existing arable soils. For the first time, private property in land springs up. Now land is scarce, and a rent is charged to ration it.

Growth does take place in this classical world of Adam Smith and Thomas Malthus. Population still grows, and so does national product. But output now must grow more slowly than does population. Why? Because, with new laborers added to fixed land, each worker now has less land to work with. Naturally, therefore, the law of diminishing returns comes into operation. The increasing labor-land ratio leads to a declining marginal product of labor and hence to declining real wage rates. The classical economists believed that a conflict of interests arises between classes. More babies mean lower per capita incomes and wage rates; lower wage rates mean higher rent rates per acre of land. Landlords gain at the expense of labor. This gloomy picture led Thomas Carlyle to criticize economics as "the dismal science."

Paradise Lost and Regained How bad can things get? The dour Reverend T. R. Malthus thought that population pressures would drive the economy to a point where workers were at the minimum level of subsistence. We will return to Malthus in the next

---

[1] Question 6 at the end of this chapter will apply the production-possibility frontier to Smith's beaver-deer economy.

chapter's analysis of population trends, but we can outline his theory briefly here.

Malthus reasoned that whenever wages were above the subsistence level, population would expand, while below-subsistence wages would lead to high mortality and population decline. Only at subsistence wages could there be lasting equilibrium. Humans are destined to a life that is brutish, nasty, and short.

What did Malthus forget, or at least underestimate? He overlooked the future contribution of invention and technology. He failed to realize how technological innovation could intervene—not to repeal the law of diminishing returns but to more than offset it. He stood at the brink of a new era and failed to anticipate that the succeeding two centuries would show the greatest scientific and economic gains in history—a chastening fact, and one to keep in mind while listening to modern Malthusians sing out their baleful dirge.

Economic Growth with Capital Accumulation

We have seen how the classical economists stressed the role of scarce land in economic growth. But history records how entrepreneurs and capital—not landowners and land—have called the tune since the early nineteenth century. Land did not become increasingly scarce. Instead, inventions and new machines led to the introduction of power-driven machinery, factories that gathered teams of workers into giant firms, railroads and steamships that joined together the far points of the world, and iron and steel that built stronger machines and faster locomotives. As capitalist economies entered the twentieth century, important new industries grew up around the telephone, the automobile, and electric power. Capital accumulation and new technologies became the dominant force affecting economic development.

To understand how capital accumulation and technological change affect the economy, we consider the basic **neoclassical growth model** to explain economic growth. This approach was pioneered by MIT's Robert Solow, who was awarded the 1987 Nobel Prize for this and other contributions to economic growth theory.* The neoclassical growth model serves as the basic tool for understanding the growth process in advanced countries and has been applied, using "growth accounting," to empirical studies of the sources of economic growth.

Basic Assumptions The neoclassical growth model describes an economy in which a single homogeneous output is produced by two types of inputs, capital and labor. In contrast to the Malthusian analysis, labor growth is determined by forces outside the economy and is unaffected by economic variables.

The major new ingredients in the neoclassical growth model are capital and technological change. For the moment, we assume that technology is unchanged and focus on the role of capital in the growth process. What do we mean by capital? Capital goods consist of the great variety of durable tangible goods that are used to make other goods. They include struc-

---

*Robert M. Solow was born in Brooklyn, was educated at Harvard, and then moved to MIT in 1950. In the next few years he developed the neoclassical growth model and applied it in a number of studies using the growth-accounting framework discussed in the second half of this chapter. According to the committee that awards the Nobel Prize, "The increased interest of government to expand education and research and development was inspired by these studies. Every long-term report . . . for any country has used a Solow-type analysis."

Solow is known for his enthusiasm for economics as well as for his humor. He worries that many economists' penchant for publicity leads them to overestimate their knowledge. He criticized economists for "an apparently irresistible urge to push their science further than it will go, to answer questions more delicate than our limited understanding of a complicated question will allow. Nobody likes to say 'I don't know.'"

Many believe that Solow is one of the few living economists who can write well. At the same time, Solow worries that economics is terrifically difficult to explain to the public. At his news conference after winning the Nobel Prize, Solow quipped, "The attention span of the people you write for is shorter than the length of one true sentence." Nonetheless, Solow continues to labor for his brand of economics, and the world increasingly listens to the apostle of economic growth at MIT.

tures like factories and houses, equipment like computers and machine tools, and inventories of finished goods and goods-in-process.

It is convenient for our purposes to simplify by assuming that there is a single versatile kind of capital good (call it K). We then measure the aggregate stock of capital as the total number of capital goods. In our real-world calculations, we approximate the universal capital good as the total dollar value of capital goods (i.e., the constant-dollar value of equipment, structures, and inventories). Under perfect competition and without risk or inflation, the rate of return on capital is also equal to the real interest rate on bonds and other financial assets.

Turning now to the economic-growth process, economists stress the importance of **capital deepening,** which occurs when the quantity of capital per worker increases over time. Important examples of capital deepening include the increase in farm machinery and irrigation systems on the farm, of railroads and highways in transportation, and of computers and communications systems in banking. In each of these industries, societies have invested heavily in capital goods, increasing the amount of capital per worker. As a result, the output per worker has increased enormously in farming, transportation, and banking.

What happens to the return on capital in the process of capital deepening? For a given state of technology, a rapid rate of investment in plant and equipment tends to depress the return on capital (the real interest rate). This occurs because the most worthwhile investment projects get constructed first, after which the investments become less and less valuable. Once a full railroad network or telephone system was constructed, new investments would branch into more sparsely populated regions or duplicate existing lines. The rates of return on these late investments would tend to be depressed relative to high returns on the first lines between densely populated regions.

In addition, the wage rate paid to workers will tend to rise as capital deepening takes place. Why so? Each worker has more capital to work with and his or her marginal product therefore rises. As a result, the competitive wage rate rises along with the marginal product of labor. We will see the wage rate rise for farm labor, transport workers, or bank tellers as in-

creases in capital per worker raise marginal products in those sectors.

We can summarize the impact of capital deepening in the neoclassical growth model as follows:

Capital deepening occurs when the supply of capital grows more rapidly than the labor force. In the absence of technological change, capital deepening will produce a growth of output per worker, of the marginal product of labor, and of wages; it also will lead to diminishing returns on capital and a consequent decline in the real interest rate.

Geometrical Analysis of the Neoclassical Model

We can analyze the effects of capital accumulation using Figure 36-1. The left-hand panel shows the relationship between the capital-per-worker ratio on the horizontal axis and the rate of return on capital, or the real interest rate, on the vertical axis. This DD curve is downward-sloping to reflect the fact that, for a given amount of labor, capital accumulation forces its marginal product to decline. This diminishing marginal productivity of capital is just the principle of diminishing returns applied to capital rather than to labor.

Figure 36-1(b) displays a new graph, called the *factor-price frontier*. This frontier shows the relationship between the competitively determined wage rate and the competitive real interest rate. As capital deepens, the economy moves down and to the right on the factor-price frontier; that is, the real interest rate falls and the wage rate must simultaneously rise. Conversely, if a great war were to destroy much of a nation's capital, the capital-labor ratio would fall, the real interest rate would rise, and the wage rate would fall—this would represent a movement up and to the left along the factor-price frontier.

Let's use Figure 36-1 to analyze the course of the economy when capital accumulation takes place. Say the economy is initially at point A with relatively little capital per worker.

In the absence of technological change, capital accumulation takes us down the red DD curve from A to B. Indeed, at some point the real interest rate might decline so far that people feel that it no longer pays them to save anything for enhanced future consump-

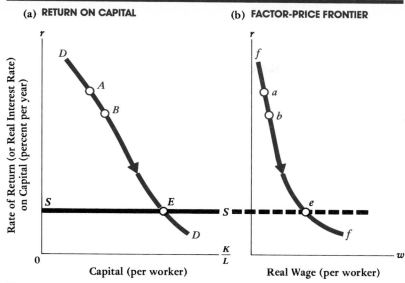

Figure 36-1   Capital accumulation raises output and wages, but depresses the return (or interest rate) on capital

(a) Adding more capital goods to a fixed amount of labor will (in the absence of technological change) lead to diminishing returns on capital. Thus the real interest rate falls as capital increases, as is shown by the arrow on the DD curve. Capital accumulation drives the real interest rate (or the rate of return on capital) down from A to B to E. Eventually, the interest rate may reach a point (on SS) where no further capital accumulation takes place.

(b) We can see the behavior of wages in the factor-price frontier. Capital accumulation drives up wages at the same time that the rate of return on capital (or profit rate) is beaten down.

tion. The SS line in Figure 36-1 shows the level of interest rates at which the economy's net saving is zero. At point E, the diminished desire for saving snuffs out further capital accumulation.

The same process is also shown by the factor-price frontier ff in Figure 36-1(b). In that graph, economic growth begins at an initial low-wage, high-interest equilibrium at point a. Then capital deepening moves the economy to point b with a higher wage rate and a lower real interest rate. Finally, as capital deepening ceases, the economy comes into equilibrium at point e with a still higher capital-output and capital-labor ratio.

Note that our earlier summary of the impact of capital deepening is verified by the analysis in Figure 36-1.

Long-Run Steady State What is the long-run equilibrium in the neoclassical growth model without technological change? It is one in which capital deepening ceases, real wages begin to stagnate, and real interest rates stop falling. The stagnation may come at a high level of income and output if a great deal of capital has been accumulated. This vision of a "steady state," while not one of constant improvement in incomes and output, is nevertheless more optimistic than the dismal view of Malthus and Ricardo.

Technological Change and Continued Growth

A glance at economic history will reveal that the stagnationist's view of constant wages and profits was

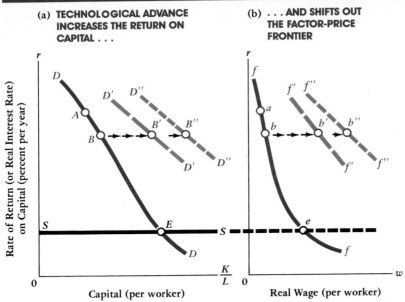

Figure 36-2   Technological advance shifts out curves, raising output and wages

Inventions and technological advance increase capital's productivity and the output that can be paid to factors of production. Hence, the productivity of capital marches out from *DD* to *D'D'* to *D"D"*, and the factor-price frontier moves from *ff* to *f'f'* to *f"f"*. These rightward shifts allow higher wages and productivity over time (as seen by shifts from *B* to *B'* to *B"* and from *b* to *b'* to *b"*).

Historically, the pace of technological change has been just fast enough to offset diminishing returns on capital—keeping interest and profit rates almost unchanged, while real wages grew steadily.

also not in history's script. Rather, a never-ending stream of inventions and technological change led to a vast improvement in the production possibilities of Europe, North America, and Japan. What is meant by **technological change**? This denotes changes in the processes of production or introduction of new products such that more or improved output can be obtained from the same bundle of inputs. Among process inventions that have greatly increased productivity were the Hall process for producing aluminum, the Bessemer process for producing steel, and automatic looms that replaced earlier handlooms. The most dramatic technological changes include product inventions such as the telephone, the airplane, and the computer.

How can we represent technological change in our neoclassical growth model? Technological change means that more output can be produced with the same inputs of capital and labor. Technological change shifts out the *PPF*. In terms of our growth diagram, technological change shifts outward and upward the marginal product curve on the left of Figure 36-1, and it shifts out the factor-price frontier on the right side of Figure 36-1.

Figure 36-2 presents an important interpretation of economic growth. These graphs show that—instead of moving to a steady state with constant output, wage rates, and interest rates—inventions increased the amount of output that each unit of input could produce. As a result of technological progress, capital per worker, output per worker, and wages per worker grow over time, yet the real interest rate does not decline. If no invention had occurred, perhaps Marx would have been proven correct in his prophecy of the falling rate of profit. But invention increases the productivity of capital and repeals the law of the falling rate of profit. In the race between diminishing returns and advancing technology, technology has won by several lengths.

Bias of Invention Not all inventions are even-handed. Some favor capital, others labor. Machines and tractors reduce the need for labor and increase the demand for capital—they are thus called "labor-saving inventions." Such inventions are ones that increase profits relative to wages. An invention that reduces the capital requirement more than the labor requirement (such as introducing multiple-shift workdays) is "capital-saving," and raises wages relative to profits. In between are "neutral inventions,"

which have no major effect on the relative demands of or returns to different factors. Since the Industrial Revolution, inventions appear to have been labor-saving on balance.*

■   ■   ■

We have now completed our survey of the important theoretical approaches to economic growth. In advanced market economies, economic growth is largely determined by the growth of inputs (particularly labor and capital) and by technological change. But what are the relative contributions of labor, capital, and technology? To answer this question, we turn to an analysis of the quantitative aspects of growth and of the important approach known as growth accounting.

B. THE TRENDS AND SOURCES OF ECONOMIC GROWTH

Theories can take us only so far. It is time to examine the underlying trends of economic growth—of output, productivity, wages, and other important magnitudes. In addition, we will examine the forces lying behind these trends.

THE STYLIZED FACTS OF ECONOMIC GROWTH

Thanks to the painstaking gathering of data and construction and analysis of national accounts by Simon Kuznets, John Kendrick, Edward Denison, and many

others, we can discern several patterns of economic development in the United States and other advanced nations.

The graphs of Figure 36-3 depict the key trends of economic development for the United States in this century. Similar findings apply abroad.

Figure 36-3(a) shows the trends in real GNP, the capital stock, and population. Population and employment have more than tripled since 1900. At the same time, the stock of physical capital has risen more than eightfold. Thus the amount of capital per worker (the K/L ratio) has increased by a factor of

---

*The impact of inventions has concerned economists since the Industrial Revolution. The tools of this chapter will allow us to analyze patterns of invention and growth in a competitive economy. Here are two examples:

■ Marx predicted that in the course of capitalism the rate of return on capital would fall and the working class would be impoverished. Using the factor-price frontier, however, you can see that there

is one too many dire prediction here. If the rate of profit falls, then the real wage rate must rise. And because inventions must shift out the factor-price frontier, it would be surprising if one of the factor prices declined sharply.

■ Some today argue that robots and machines will make humans economically obsolete. Human labor will, under this gloomy view, follow the horse's role in history—from being a central economic factor to being a mere luxury.

To analyze this view, recall that robots are a different kind of capital good. The robotization of the economy suggests, then, that inventions will be highly labor-saving, and that as a result the real interest rate will rise so much that wages will decline drastically. Hence the key variable to watch in the robotization of America, then, is movements in the rate of return on capital.

PATTERNS OF ECONOMIC GROWTH

(a) Output, Labor, Capital

(b) Capital-Output Ratio

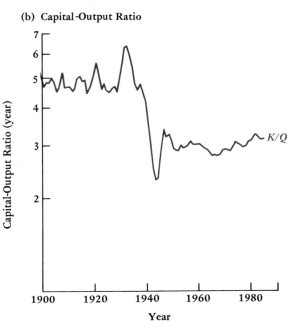

(c) Real Wages and Output per Worker

(d) Real Interest Rate

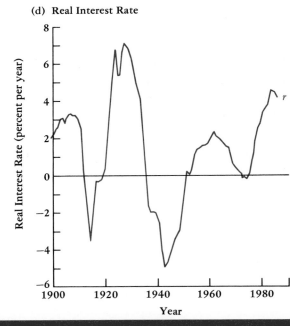

almost three. Clearly, a great deal of capital deepening has occurred.

What about the growth in output? Has output grown less than in proportion to capital, as would occur in a model that ignored technological change? No. The fact that the output curve in Figure 36-3(a) is not in between the two factor curves, but actually lies above the capital curve, shows that technological progress must have increased the productivity of capital and labor.

Indeed, the capital-output ratio—shown in Figure 36-3(b)—has fallen over time, rather than rising as would be expected in the capital-accumulation model without technological progress.

Rising Wages and Trendless Profit Most people judge capitalism by the movements in real wages (i.e., money wages corrected for movements in the price level). Real wages have indeed risen steadily, as seen in Figure 36-3(c). This is in accordance with what one would expect from the growth in the capital-labor ratio and from favorable technological trends.

The real interest rate (i.e., the money interest rate minus the rate of inflation) is shown in Figure 36-3(d). These data—or data on the rate of return or profits earned by corporations—do not show the decline that would be predicted from simple deepening of capital and diminishing returns. Interest rates and profit rates fluctuate greatly in business cycles and wars but display no strong trend upward or downward for the whole period. Either by coincidence, or because of an economic mechanism inducing this pattern, technological change has just about offset diminishing returns.

Output per worker-hour is the solid black curve in Figure 36-3(c). As could be expected from the deepening of capital and from technological advance, Q/L has risen steadily.

When wages rise at the same rate as output per worker, this does not mean that labor has captured all the fruits of productivity advance. It means, rather, that labor has kept about the same share of total product, with capital also earning about the same relative share throughout the period. Actually, a close look at Figure 36-3(c) shows that real wages have grown slightly faster than has output per worker-hour over the last nine decades. This trend implies a slow upward creep in the share of labor in GNP, with capital's share declining gently.

Seven Basic Trends of Economic Development

These basic facts of economic history in the advanced nations can be summarized approximately by the following trends:

Trend 1. Population and the labor force have grown, but at a much more modest rate than the capital stock, resulting in capital deepening.

Trend 2. There has been a strong upward trend in real wage rates.

Trend 3. The share of wages and salaries relative to the total return on property has edged up very slightly over the long run.

Trend 4. Instead of observing a fall in the rate of return on capital or the real rate of interest, we observe major oscillations of profits during business cycles with no strong upward or downward trend in this century.

Trend 5. Instead of observing a steady rise in the capital-output ratio as the deepening of capital in-

Figure 36-3 Economic growth has displayed striking long-run regularities

(a) Capital stock has grown faster than population and labor supply. Nonetheless, total output has grown even more rapidly than capital.
(b) Capital-output ratio declined sharply during first half of the twentieth century, but has remained steady over the last three decades.
(c) Real wages have grown steadily, if anything somewhat faster than average product per person-hour. Note the slowdown of growth in output, real wages, and productivity since 1973. Has the Industrial Revolution come to an end?
(d) Without invention and technological change, deepening of capital relative to labor would depress real interest rate and raise the capital-output ratio. In fact, real interest rate has been trendless over the last nine decades, suggesting that technological change has just about offset diminishing returns to capital accumulation. Hence, static curves of Fig. 36-1 must have been shifting rightward as in Fig. 36-2. (Source: U.S. Departments of Commerce and Labor, Federal Reserve Board, Bureau of the Census, and historical studies by John Kendrick.)

vokes the law of diminishing returns, the capital-output ratio has actually declined since 1900, although little change has occurred since 1950.

Trend 6. For most of the twentieth century, the national savings rate in the United States (equal to private national saving divided by GNP) has been stable. The ratio of gross investment to GNP has also been nearly constant over this period. Since 1980, however, the large federal government deficit has led to a sharp decline of the national savings rate.

Trend 7. After removing effects of the business cycle, national product has grown at a stable rate of 3 to 4 percent per year. Moreover, this growth rate has been so much higher than a weighted average of capital, labor, and resource inputs that technological innovation must have played a key role in economic growth.

One further point about the curves of Figure 36-3 and our seven trends should be recognized. The persistence of the trends might suggest that they have taken on a certain invulnerability or inevitability—that we can forever expect our economy to generate rapid growth in output per worker, real wages, and real output.

That view should be resisted, for it misreads the lessons of history and economic theory. While trends have been persistent, a closer examination shows major waves or deviations during periods of a decade or more. Moreover, there is no theoretical reason why technological innovation should remain high, forever raising living standards and offsetting diminishing returns. The most recent deviant period, since 1973, has witnessed a marked slowdown in growth of output, real wages, and output per worker. While it is impossible to say how long this period of diminished macroeconomic performance will persist, we must emphasize that there is no *logical* reason why the future cannot be sharply divergent from the first three-quarters of the twentieth century.

Analyzing the Economic Growth of the Mixed Economy

While these seven trends are not like the unrepealable laws of chemistry, they do portray fundamental his-

torical facts about economic growth. How do they fit into our economic theories?

Trends 2 and 1—higher wage rates when capital deepens—fit nicely together with classical and neoclassical theories of production and distribution. Trend 3—that the wage share has grown only very slowly—is an interesting coincidence that is consistent with a wide variety of production functions relating Q to L and K.

Trends 4 and 5, however, warn us that neoclassical theory cannot hold in static form. A steady profit rate and a declining, or steady, capital-output ratio cannot hold when the K/L ratio is rising in a world with unchanging technology; taken together, they contradict the basic law of diminishing returns under deepening of capital.

We must therefore recognize the key role of technological progress in explaining the seven trends of modern economic growth. Indeed, given the ample evidence of the contribution of science, technology, and engineering to the economy, it would be difficult to ignore advancing technology.

The trends confirm, then, the hypothesis of technological progress shown in Figure 36-2. In those diagrams, technological change is shown by a rightward shift in the marginal-product-of-capital curve [DD in Figure 36-2(a)] and in the factor-price frontier [ff in Figure 36-2(b)]. Advancing technology might then lead to the rightward move in Figure 36-2(a) from B on DD to B' on $D'D'$ to B'' on $D''D''$, with a similar rightward movement in the right-hand panel.

Note that this movement will be consistent with trends 1 to 7. The tendency toward diminishing returns has just been offset by technological change, with the real interest rate changing little and the wage rate rising somewhat more rapidly than output per head.

THE SOURCES OF ECONOMIC GROWTH

Economists have not rested contentedly with trends and theories. Under the leadership of Robert Solow, John Kendrick, and Edward Denison, economic archaeologists have begun to ferret out the sources of economic growth. By combining the theories such as those in Figure 36-2 with the seven trends, we now have a much better understanding of why nations grow.

The Growth-Accounting Approach[2]

Detailed studies of economic growth rely on what is called **growth accounting.** This technique is not a balance sheet or national product account of the kind we met in Chapters 6 and 20. Rather, it is a way of exhaustively accounting for the ingredients that lead to the observed growth trends.

In our simple model shown in Figure 36-2, growth in output or Q can be decomposed into three separate sources: growth in labor or L, growth in capital or K, and technological innovation itself. Momentarily ignoring technological change, an assumption of constant returns to scale means that a 1 percent growth in L together with a 1 percent growth in K will lead to a 1 percent growth in output.

Suppose L grows at 1 percent and K at 5 percent. It is tempting, but wrong, to guess that Q will then grow at 3 percent, the simple average of 1 and 5. Why wrong? Because the two factors do not necessarily contribute equally to output. Rather, the fact that in recent years three-fourths of GNP goes to labor while only one-fourth goes to capital suggests that labor growth will contribute more to output than will capital growth.

If labor's growth rate gets 3 times the weight of K's, then we can calculate the answer as follows: Q will grow at 2 percent per year ($= \frac{3}{4}$ of 1% $+ \frac{1}{4}$ of 5%). To growth of inputs, we also add technological change and thereby obtain all the sources of growth.

Hence, output growth per year follows the *fundamental equation of growth accounting:*

$$\% \ Q \ \text{growth} = \tfrac{3}{4}(\% \ L \ \text{growth}) + \tfrac{1}{4}(\% \ K \ \text{growth}) + \text{T. C.}$$

where T. C. represents technological change (or total factor productivity) that raises productivity, and where $\frac{3}{4}$ and $\frac{1}{4}$ are the relative contributions of each input to economic growth, given by their relative shares of national income (of course, these fractions would be replaced by new fractions if the relative shares of the factors were to change).

If we seek to explain per capita growth, matters are simpler, since this enables us to get rid of L as a separate growth source. Now, using the fact that capital gets one-fourth share of output, we have

$$\% \frac{Q}{L} \text{growth} = \tfrac{1}{4}\left(\% \frac{K}{L} \text{growth} \right) + \text{T. C.}$$

This relation shows clearly how capital deepening would affect per capita output if technological advance were zero. Output per capita would grow only one-fourth as fast as capital per capita, reflecting diminishing returns.

One final point remains: We can measure Q growth, K growth, L growth, as well as the shares of K and L. But how can we measure T. C. (technological change)? We cannot. Rather, we must *infer* T. C. as the residual or leftover after the other components of output and inputs are calculated. Thus if we examine the equation above, T. C. is calculated by subtraction as

$$\text{T. C.} = \% \ Q \ \text{growth} - \tfrac{3}{4}(\% \ L \ \text{growth})$$
$$- \tfrac{1}{4}(\% \ K \ \text{growth})$$

We can now ask critically important questions about economic growth: What part of per capita output growth is due to capital deepening and what part is due to technological advance? Does society progress chiefly by dint of thrift and the forgoing of current consumption? Or is our rising living standard the reward for the ingenuity of inventors and the daring of innovator-entrepreneurs?

Numerical Example For a first answer, substitute representative numbers for the period 1900–1986 into our equation above for the growth of Q/L, or per capita output. Since 1900, L has grown 1.5 percent per year, K has grown 2.5 percent per year, while Q has grown 3.1 percent per year. Thus, by arithmetic, we find that

$$\% \frac{Q}{L} \text{growth} = \tfrac{1}{4}\left(\% \frac{K}{L} \text{growth} \right) + \text{T. C.}$$

becomes

$$2.1 = \tfrac{1}{4}(1) + \text{T. C.} = 0.25 + 1.85$$

---

[2]This section contains advanced materials, so short courses may skip right to "Detailed Studies" in the next section.

Thus of the 2.1 percent-per-year increase in output per worker, about 0.25 percentage point is due to capital deepening, while an astounding 1.85 percent per year stems from T. C. In careful studies of economic growth, such as those described in the next sections, T. C. is usually called "total factor productivity," which includes advances in knowledge, economies of scale, and a host of other factors.

Detailed Studies

More thorough studies refine the simple calculation but show quite similar conclusions. Table 36-1 presents the results of studies by Edward Denison and the Department of Labor analyzing the sources of growth over the 1948–1986 period. Over this period, GNP grew at an average rate of 3.2 percent per year. Input growth (of capital, labor, and land) contributed 1.8 percentage points per year, while **total factor productivity**—the growth of output less the growth of the weighted sum of all inputs—average 1.4 percent annually.

Somewhat more than one-half of the growth in output in the United States can be accounted for by the growth in labor and capital. The remaining growth is a residual that can be attributed to education, innovation, economies of scale, scientific advances, and other factors.

Growth accounting yields many dividends in understanding economic growth. For example, many people have wondered why countries like Japan or the Soviet Union have grown so much more rapidly than the United States during most of the postwar period.

Using growth accounting, scholars have uncovered some surprising answers to this puzzle. Over most of the postwar period Japan's GNP grew at an amazing 10 percent per year. Empirical analysis indicates that this was partly due to very rapid growth in inputs. In addition, Japan had extremely rapid technological change over this period compared to other industrial countries.

Analyses of Soviet growth show a different pattern, as the last chapter's discussion foreshadowed. The U.S.S.R. grew at a pace of almost 5 percent annually

CONTRIBUTION OF DIFFERENT ELEMENTS TO GROWTH IN REAL GNP, UNITED STATES, 1948–1986

	IN PERCENT PER YEAR	AS PERCENT OF TOTAL
Real GNP Growth	**3.2**	**100**
Contribution of Inputs	**1.8**	**56**
Capital	0.9	28
Labor	0.9	28
Land	0.0	0
Total Factor Productivity Growth	**1.4**	**44**
Education	0.4	13
Advances in knowledge and other	1.0	31

Table 36-1   Education and advances in knowledge outweigh capital in contributing to economic growth

Studies using the techniques of growth accounting break down the growth of GNP in the private business sector into its contributing factors. These studies find that capital growth is only a modest contributor, accounting for about one-fourth of total GNP growth. Education, technological change, and other sources make up almost one-half of total GNP growth and six-tenths of the growth of output per worker. [Source: Edward F. Denison, *Trends in American Economic Growth, 1929–1982* (Brookings, Washington, D.C., 1985), U.S. Department of Labor, "Multifactor Productivity Measures, 1986," October, 1987, and updated by authors.]

LABOR PRODUCTIVITY GROWTH BY BUSINESS SECTOR
(average annual percent change)

| | | | NONFARM | |
| | TOTAL | | MANUFACTURING | NONMANUFACTURING |
PERIOD	BUSINESS	FARM		
1948–1973	2.9	6.5	2.8	1.9
1973–1981	0.6	4.6	1.3	−0.1
1981–1986	1.7	3.3	4.5	0.4

Table 36-2 Labor productivity growth by sector, 1948–1986

Labor productivity in the total business sector slowed sharply after 1973 with the most dramatic decline occurring in nonmanufacturing areas like services. Manufacturing productivity growth regained ground in the 1980s. (Source: Council of Economic Advisers, *Economic Report of the President, 1987;* U.S. Department of Agriculture; U.S. Department of Labor, Bureau of Labor Statistics.)

since its big push forward around 1930. It appears, however, that the high growth rate came primarily from forced-draft increases in capital and labor inputs. The estimated pace of growth in total factor productivity for the U.S.S.R. over the last half-century has been slower than that in the United States.

The Productivity Slowdown

We noted earlier that the rapid growth in output and productivity slowed abruptly around 1973. This break is seen in Figure 36-3*(c),* in which the *Q/L* curve (representing labor productivity) begins to flatten out in the early 1970s. What were the causes of the abrupt slowdown in productivity growth?

The basic facts are shown in Table 36-2, which provides data on the growth of productivity in the U.S. economy both for the entire business sector and for different subsectors. This table indicates that the growth in labor productivity (measured by GNP originating in a sector divided by the number of hours worked in that sector) slowed in all sectors in the 1970s with productivity growth in the nonmanufacturing areas declining most sharply. Among the areas showing the sharpest deterioration in productivity are mining, construction, and services. Similar patterns, with a slowdown of productivity growth in the aggregate and in most sectors after 1973, are found in all major industrial countries.

What lay behind the unexpected decline in productivity growth? This is still a major puzzle for economists. Most studies point to a number of unfavorable factors converging on the American economy at about the same time, and tending to reduce productivity growth. Some examples are the following:

- In the late 1960s and early 1970s, environmental regulations required firms to spend money on plant and operations to improve their impacts on health and safety, yet these improvements did not show up as measured output increases. One of the most dramatic cases was in underground mining, in which productivity declined sharply.

- The increase in energy prices in the early 1970s led firms to substitute capital and labor for energy. As a result, the productivity of labor and capital declined relative to earlier growth rates.

- The 1970s witnessed an infusion of inexperienced, low-wage workers into many nonmanufacturing sectors, particularly into service industries like fast-food outlets. This infusion increased the share of employment in the low-productivity sectors and thereby lowered overall productivity growth.

Other factors mentioned in studies of the productivity slowdown are a lower level of expenditure on civilian research and development, lower levels of investment in plant and equipment, and higher

A MENU FOR GROWTH

GROWTH-ENCOURAGING STEPS	ESTIMATED POTENTIAL FOR INCREASING REAL ECONOMIC GROWTH, 1990–2000
1. Increase net national investment and savings rate by one-third (i.e., from 6 to 8% of GNP)	0.16% per year
2. Increase civilian research and development by one-fifth (i.e., from 2 to 2.4% of GNP)	0.18
3. Lower the natural rate of unemployment by 1% of the labor force	0.20
4. Eliminate all strikes	0.01
5. Reach an arms-control agreement that allows government to reduce strategic programs and increase government investment	0.10
Total	**0.65% per year**

Table 36-3   How can the United States grow faster?
This menu of growth shows the kinds of steps that might be taken to speed the growth of potential output and labor productivity. It should be emphasized that *each* of these steps would be extremely difficult to accomplish, but they are on the whole within the realm of the feasible. [Source: Edward Denison, *Sources of Growth in the United States* (Committee for Economic Development, New York, 1961); calculations by authors.]

inflation. However, when all the careful studies have been completed, all these factors can explain only a fraction of the slowdown. The productivity slowdown of the 1970s and 1980s continues to be an unsolved economic mystery.

Speeding Economic Growth

In response to the lagging productivity growth, many have called for policies to restore the earlier rapid productivity improvement. What kinds of steps are possible to speed growth? A study by Edward Denison investigated this subject in detail, and the results appear in Table 36-3.

These figures show that raising the growth rate of potential output or of productivity per worker is possible but difficult. The most obvious way to grow more rapidly is to increase the national savings and invest-

ment rate; this could be accomplished by changing the mix of fiscal and monetary policy toward one more favorable to capital accumulation (say, by lowering real interest rates and incurring a smaller budget deficit). A very ambitious program might succeed in raising national net investment by 2 percent of GNP. This would lead to an increase of slightly less than two-tenths of a percentage point in the annual growth rate of potential GNP and of labor productivity over the following decade.

One cannot help but be impressed by the smallness of the numbers shown in Table 36-3. Increasing productivity growth is not impossible, but no easy paths have yet been found.

Epilogue

This review of growth accounting and the way that

the United States might revitalize its economic growth brings us to the end of our discussion of economic growth in advanced countries. We have seen how technological progress has allowed the advanced industrial economies to escape from snares foreseen by Malthus and Marx. History—while full of twists and turns—shows a remarkable pattern of growth in wages and living standards in capitalist countries.

But the laws of motion for the advanced countries have not held true for all countries of the developing world. These poorer countries find themselves trapped in a cycle of poverty. The next chapter shows that Malthus has been a prophet outside his own land.

SUMMARY

A. The Theory of Economic Growth

1. Many writers have tried to read into economic history a linear progression through inevitable stages, such as primitive economy, feudalism, capitalism, and some form of communism. History has not agreeably stuck to such timetables. In particular, the advanced market economies have grown more rapidly over the last four decades than social prophets foresaw.

2. The classical models of Smith and Malthus describe economic development in terms of fixed land and growing population.

In the absence of technological change, increasing population ultimately exhausts the supply of free land. The resulting increase in population density triggers the law of diminishing returns: fixity of land keeps output from growing proportionally to increased labor. With less and less land to work, each new worker adds less and less extra product; the decline in labor's marginal product means a decline in the competitively earned real wage. As each acre of land gets more and more labor to work with, its marginal product and competitively earned rent go up. The Malthusian equilibrium comes when the wage has fallen to the subsistence level, below which the supply of labor will not reproduce itself. However, in reality, technological change has kept economic development progressing in industrial countries by continually shifting the productivity curve of labor upward.

3. Growth theories incorporating capital accumulation form the core of modern analysis. This approach examines a world where labor grows for non-economic reasons while capital is accumulated in response to profit rates. In the beginning, there is a gradual increase of the amount of capital per worker, or "capital deepening." In the absence of technological change and innovation, an increase in capital per worker would not be matched by a proportional increase in output per worker because of diminishing returns. Hence, capital deepening would lower the rate of return on capital (equal to the real interest rate under risk-free competition).

4. The fundamental factor-price frontier depicts how wages must rise when the return on capital or real interest rate falls. In a world with capital deepening, the downward trend in the real interest rate leads to a rise in real wages along the factor-price frontier.

5. Technological change, increasing the output produced for a given bundle of inputs, pushes outward and rightward both the capital-productivity curve and the factor-price frontier, allowing output to rise even more rapidly than capital and labor inputs.

B. The Trends and Sources of Economic Growth

6. Numerous trends of economic growth are seen in data for this century. Among the most important are that real wages and output per hour have risen steadily (at least until the early 1970s); that the real interest rate has moved trendlessly; and that the capital-output ratio has declined.

7. Some of the major trends are consistent with the simple model of capital accumulation. In general, however, we must augment the simple model by introducing technological advance if all trends are to be explained. Thus, a trendless interest and profit rate cannot be consistent with capital deepening unless there is technological advance shifting out production functions; nor can the capital-output ratio fall in the simple model without this advance. We thus recognize what common sense tells us—that technological advance increases the productivity of inputs and shifts out both the productivity-of-capital curve and factor-price frontiers.

8. The last trend—relatively stable growth in potential output over the last nine decades—raises the important question of the sources of economic growth. Using quantitative techniques, growth accountants have determined that "residual" sources—such as innovation and education—outweigh capital deepening in their impact on GNP growth or labor productivity. This technique also shows the great difficulty a country has in attempting to add even a few tenths of a percentage point to its underlying potential GNP growth rate.

CONCEPTS FOR REVIEW

Smith's golden age
Malthus' limited land
neoclassical growth model
real interest rate and rate of return on
  capital
K/L rise as capital deepens
capital-output ratio, K/Q
factor-price frontier

marginal product
seven trends of economic growth
growth accounting
% Q growth = $\frac{3}{4}$(% L growth) + $\cdots$
% Q/L growth = $\frac{1}{4}$(% K/L growth)
  + T. C.
Q growth from more K, from
  inventions

QUESTIONS FOR DISCUSSION

1. Describe some of the major prophesies about economic growth. Why did each prove wrong? From *Business Week, Fortune,* or the *Economist,* collect some predictions about the future of the American economy. List some of the ways they might be inaccurate.

2. "If the government subsidizes science and invention and controls stagflation and cycles, we can expect growth that would astound the classical economists." Evaluate critically.

3. "Without population growth or technological change, persistent capital accumulation would ultimately destroy the capitalist class.'' Explain why such a scenario might lead to a zero interest rate and to a disappearance of profits.

4. Since labor's share shows a slight uptrend and the capital-output ratio a slight downtrend, since the interest rate fluctuates considerably, since the ratio of private net investment to private GNP is volatile—in view of these facts, would you be much surprised if the basic trends on pp. 861–862 were to fluctuate sharply in the future?

5. Recall the growth-accounting formula on page 863. Calculate the rate of growth of output if labor grows at 1 percent per year, capital grows at 4 percent per year, and technological change is $1\frac{1}{2}$ percent per year.

How would your answer change if:

(a) Labor growth slowed to 0 percent per year?

(b) Capital growth increased to 5 percent per year?

(c) Labor and capital had equal shares in GNP?

Also, calculate for each of these questions the rate of growth of output per worker.

6. Using the graphical *PPF* of Chapter 2, analyze Adam Smith's beaver-deer economy as follows.

Assume that catching a deer takes 2 hours, while trapping a beaver requires 4 hours. For a society with 100 hours of labor, first draw the *PPF* as a straight line—going from the intercept on the vertical axis of the 50 deer producible with that much labor, to the intercept on the horizontal axis of 25 beavers. The absolute slope of this *PPF* gives the 2-to-1 price ratio prevailing at any point where both goods were being produced and consumed. (The marginal-utility and indifference-curve analysis of Chapter 19 is still needed to tell where society ends up on the *PPF*.)

What would happen to the *PPF* if the amount of labor doubled with exactly the same technology? Also, show the effect of a doubling of labor productivity in both industries.

7. Political candidates have proposed the following policies to speed economic growth for the 1990s. For each, explain qualitatively the impact upon the growth of potential output and of per capita potential output. If possible, give a quantitative estimate of the increase in the growth of potential output and per capita potential output over the next decade:

(a) Cut the federal budget deficit by 2 percent of GNP, increasing the ratio of investment to GNP by the same amount.

(b) Increase the federal subsidy to research and development (R&D) by $\frac{1}{4}$ percent of GNP, assuming that this subsidy will increase private R&D by the same amount and that R&D has a social rate of return that is 3 times that of private investment.

(c) Increase defense spending by 1 percent of GNP, with multiplier effects leading to at least twice as large an impact upon aggregate demand.

(d) Increase the labor-force participation rate of females so that total labor inputs increase by 1 percent.

(e) Increase investments in ''human capital'' (or education and on-the-job training) by 1 percent of GNP.

8. A brooding pessimist might argue that 1973 marked a watershed—the end of the great expansion that began with the Industrial Revolution. Assume that all the features of the earlier era were still present today *except* that technological change and innovation were to cease. What would the new seven trends look like for coming decades?

What would happen to the important real wage? What steps could be taken to counter-act the new trends and to put the economy back on the earlier path?

9. Advanced problem: Many fear that robots will do to humans what tractors and cars did to horses—the horse population declined precipitously early in this century after technological change made horses obsolete.

If we treated robots as a particularly productive kind of K, what would their intro-duction do to the DD and ff curves in Figure 36-1? Can total output go down with a fixed labor force? Under what conditions would the real wage decline? Can you see why the horse analogy might not apply?

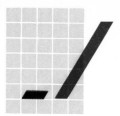

APPENDIX: 36
Modern Economic-Growth Theories

Economics, not being a settled subject, is itself still undergoing development. While the broad facts of historical development discussed in the chapter are not in dispute, different interpretations of them are given by different authors. Some further ideas associated with the names of Joseph A. Schumpeter, W. W. Leontief, and other economists are sketched briefly in this appendix.

SCHUMPETERIAN INNOVATION

Joseph Schumpeter (1883–1950) of Vienna and Harvard was author of two economic classics: *The Theory of Economic Development* (English ed., Harvard University Press, Cambridge, Mass., 1934) and his posthumous *History of Economic Analysis* (Oxford University Press, New York, 1954).

Schumpeter emphasized the role of the innovator—i.e., the inventor, the developer, the promoter, the person who initiates and recognizes technological improvements and who succeeds in getting them introduced. Schumpeter regarded the innovators as the dynamic actors of capitalism, who rule profitably for a day, only to have their profits nibbled away by imitating competitors.

Figure 36-1(*a*) represents well Schumpeter's notion of what would happen if all innovations ceased. Competition and capital accumulation would quite quickly push society down the curve of diminishing returns *DD*. Indeed, Schumpeter thought that the long-run *SS* horizontal line at which the supply of new saving will disappear would be at a zero rate of interest and profit, being properly drawn in Figure 36-1(*a*) on the horizontal axis itself.

But now Schumpeter plays his trump card. Innovation is periodically shifting the *DD* curve upward and outward. Profits and interest are like a violin string plucked by innovation; without innovation profits die down to nothing, but then along comes a new innovation to pluck them back into dynamic motion again. Thus profits arise because of constant birth of new products and new markets.

The profits due to innovation, we have seen, will be competed away by imitators with labor and consumers soon benefiting from price reductions. The innovation-induced rise in interest rates will soon coax out saving and capital formation until the accumulation of the augmented capital stock leads to diminishing returns, a "profit squeeze," and minimal interest. But then along comes a new burst of innovations—e.g., railroads, electricity, computers, superconductors—to pluck the system back into dynamic motion, and we are off on a new repetition of the process.[1]

---

[1] As can be seen by readers of his stimulating *Capitalism, Socialism and Democracy* (Harper & Row, New York, 1942), Schumpeter was more than an economist. Believing the economic system to be itself essentially stable, Schumpeter advanced sociological and political reasons for his predicted decay of capitalism. He held that the very efficiency of capitalism will be its ruin, as intellectuals and the masses come to despise the market ideology and contrive to introduce hampering government interferences in the name of welfare. Unlike Marx, who thought capitalism would die of its own cancers, Schumpeter thought it would eventually commit suicide as children of the capitalist class became disaffected and introduced socialism. His forecast had an eerie ring of truth as radical students invaded their colleges and burned their parents' bank buildings in the 1960s and 1970s.

NEOCLASSICAL GROWTH MODEL

The birth of modern growth theory can be traced to an important contribution to the concept of balanced (or "exponential") growth developed by Sir Roy Harrod in England and Professor E. Domar in the United States.[2] This theory attempts to use a rigorous economic approach, known as *neoclassical growth theory*, to explain the major trends of modern economic history sketched in the main body of this chapter.

Suppose hours of labor L grow steadily at about 1 percent per year. And for extreme simplicity, assume that technological change is "labor-augmenting"—in effect making each person's efficiency as a worker grow at another 2 percent per year. Either because of more scientific methods of production or better education, it is as if 100 workers can this year do what it took 102 to do last year. This process of improved efficiency is repeated indefinitely. While *actual L* in its human-hour units is growing at but 1 percent per year, the number of *efficiency units of labor L^** is growing at 3 percent per year because of the annual 2 percent efficiency improvement. This leads to the concept of the natural rate of growth.

The **natural rate of growth** in a neoclassical model is the percentage growth per year of its labor supply expressed in "efficiency units" (which means natural labor units as augmented by the increase in technological efficiency of each person-hour); as a condition of balanced growth, output and capital must also be growing at this same natural rate.

With GNP (or Q) and with L^* growing steadily at this natural rate of 3 percent per year, the stock of capital K must also grow at the same natural rate of 3 percent per year if it is to keep in balance. How much net investment is required each year to keep K growing at this natural rate of 3 percent? In other words, how much must people be steadily saving and investing out of their annual potential output to keep growth of output and capital just balanced?

The needed saving-income, or saving-GNP, ratio depends on the numerical value of the capital-output ratio K/Q times the natural growth rate.

We are now in a position to write down the arithmetic formula relating three historical things: the natural rate of growth of 0.03 per year, or in the general case g per year; the historical capital-output ratio of, say, $3\frac{1}{3}$, or in the general case K/Q; the required saving-GNP ratio of 0.10, or in the general case s. We get the *balanced-growth equation:*[3]

$$0.10 = 0.03 \times 3\tfrac{1}{3} \qquad \text{or more generally} \qquad s = g \times \frac{K}{Q}$$

---

[2] R. F. Harrod, *Towards a Dynamic Economics* (Macmillan, London, 1948); E. D. Domar, *Essays in the Theory of Economic Growth* (Oxford University Press, New York, 1957). The same discussion of interacting accelerator-multiplier models in Chapter 10 is here applied to the trend of economic development rather than to the business-cycle deviations from that trend.

[3] Thus, suppose Q is $3000 billion per year and that the capital stock is about $3\frac{1}{3}$ times as great, being $10,000 billion. Then, to add 3 percent to K this year we must have net investment of $300 billion (equals $0.03 \times \$10,000$ billion), which means that people must be saving and investing exactly 10 percent (equals $3\% \times 3\frac{1}{3}$) of their incomes. [Check your understanding by showing that a 4 percent natural growth rate would in this case require a $13\frac{1}{3}$ percent (equals $4\% \times 3\frac{1}{3}$) saving ratio out of income, and that a 3 percent natural growth rate with a K/Q ratio of only 2 would require only a 6 percent saving-income ratio.]

This relationship determines the amount of voluntary saving and investment that is needed in the long-run equilibrium of the neoclassical growth model.[4]

Explaining the Trends

Can this simplified neoclassical growth model account for all seven of the basic trends listed earlier? Let us check off the trends.

The model certainly gives a deepening of capital relative to hours of actual L, since K grows at 3 percent and L only at 1 percent. [However, in this simplified model, an observer who concentrates only on L^*, labor in efficiency units, will see a constant (K/L^*).]

Trend 2 is verified also. The wage rate rises at 2 percent per year. Why? Because actual persons $(L$, not $L^*)$ collect the marginal product of their increased efficiency.

A slightly modified version of trend 3 is verified and is no longer a coincidence. Because technological change is labor-augmenting, making each person take on "the strength of ten," the balanced growth in K and L^* means we are dividing shares between the factors in precisely the same way as before. We thus have constant shares of labor and capital, not an upward creep of labor's share.

Trend 4's constancy of the real interest rate is now precisely verified, being neither an approximation nor a coincidence. Each unit of K, being matched exactly by the same amount of L^* as before, experiences no diminishing returns and has imputed to it the same competitive real interest rate.

Trend 5 is also verified in slightly modified form, since the natural rate of balanced growth assumes from the beginning an unchanged K/Q ratio.

Trend 6's constancy of the saving-income ratio is verified from the balanced-growth equation for the case of the natural rate of balanced growth at the same compound interest rate per year: $s = $ constant $g \times$ constant K/Q.

And the centrally important trend 7 is also verified, for output is growing steadily and rapidly at 3 percent each year.

INPUT-OUTPUT TABLES

Often, the analysis of economic growth must go beyond the highly simplified, aggregate analysis of the neoclassical model. Countries on the road to economic development need to plan the output growth of individual sectors; advanced countries may want to trace the implications of changes in defense spending upon the steel, oil, and electronics industries. An important tool for those addressing these issues is **input-output analysis,** which shows the flow of products among the many industries of an economy.

Input-output analysis was developed by the Russian-born Harvard economist, Wassily Leontief, and is a modern-day realization of the eighteenth-century dream of the physiocratic economist, François Quesnay, who first envisaged the *Tableau*

---

[4]This is really the $I = S$ schedule equality of Part Two. In the case of the natural growth rate, $g = I/K$ or $I = gK$; hence, $I/Q = S/Q = s = g(K/Q)$, which gives the balanced-growth equation.

WARTIME INTERINDUSTRY FLOWS *(billions of dollars)*

	AGRICUL- TURE	MANUFAC- TURING	HOUSEHOLD FINAL CONSUMPTIONS	GROSS OUTPUT
Agriculture		1,000	500	1,500
Manufacturing	500		1,500	2,000
Household labor and other factors	1,000	1,000	___	
Gross inputs	1,500	2,000		3,500

Table 36A-1   The input-output table dissects the economy's structure
Each industry appears twice, in a row and column: its row lists the allocation of its total gross output as inputs for other industries and for final consumption; also, its column shows inputs needed to produce it.

The black totals show gross outputs, inclusive of amounts needed as intermediate inputs. To compute GNP without double counting, we add only the factor payments (or the "value added") of the red-shaded row, or alternatively, only the final-consumption flows of the red-shaded column. (Fill in the proper GNP in the indicated blank, and check it two ways.)

Économique, or circular flow of economic life. Dozens of nations—such as France, Norway, Egypt, the United States, the United Kingdom, the Soviet Union, and India— have computed input-output tables as an amplification of their national income data and as a possible aid in development planning.[5]

We can illustrate input-output analysis showing first a wartime situation and then the transformation into a peacetime economy. This example indicates in a highly simplified way the kind of calculations that a centrally planned economy might make as it estimated the changes required for a massive shift in resource allocation.

For this example, Table 36A-1 shows a wartime flow of product with only manufacturing (e.g., guns) and agriculture (e.g., butter) as sample industries. A realistic input-output table would have hundreds of industries. Here is its general idea. Each industry is listed twice: in a row as an output, and in a column as a needed input. In addition, the final consumption of households is treated as an extra column and their labor (or other primary factors of production) as an extra row. These household figures are the numbers that enter into national income or net national product and are in the colored parts

[5] For additional discussion of theory and applications see Wassily Leontief, *The Structure of the American Economy, 1919–1929* (Harvard University Press, Cambridge, Mass., 1941; 2d ed.: *1919–1939*, Oxford University Press, New York, 1951); or Wassily Leontief, *Input-Output Economics* (Oxford University Press, New York, 1966). As part of the price that Leontief has to pay to make Walras' general equilibrium empirically measurable, he is forced to make the technical assumption that all factor proportions—to each other and to total output—are technologically fixed or constant.

Modern techniques, such as those of Harvard's Dale Jorgenson, allow flexible input-output coefficients in a more complex "trans-logarithmic" production function.

of the table. Actual input-output tables also include government, foreign trade, investment, and other sectors.

The gross value of agricultural output is shown by the black $1500 (billion) twice: at its row's right as the sum of all the places where farm output went—$1000 as input to manufacturing plus $500 directly consumed by households as food—and at its column's bottom as the sum of the $500 cost it paid for manufacturing inputs (chemical fertilizers, etc.) and the $1000 cost it paid for labor inputs.

Give a similar interpretation of the $2000 gross total for manufacturing.

The table also shows our old friend GNP (which will also be NNP if our example is simple enough to ignore depreciation). With no government or investment in the picture, GNP equals the sum of the third column's red final products, or alternatively GNP equals the sum of all factor costs or values added shown in the third row's red wages.

GNP definitely does not include the intermediate purchases of one sector from another; the gross black total of $3500 definitely involves double counting. Verify that GNP = $2000.

This input-output table is more than a record of past history. How do planners hope to use it? They employ it to forecast the effects of changing consumption requirements.

Thus suppose Table 36A-1 refers to a wartime situation where manufacturing employment and output have been swollen by military needs. Now suppose "peace breaks out." What will have to be planned for the new deployment of labor and other inputs if full employment is still to be maintained? Suppose we now want to double agriculture's final consumption, from the old red $500 to new $1000, exactly compensating by cutting the military manufacturing sector back from $1500 to $1000. Assuming fixed input-output coefficients, the analyst can solve linear equations for the new peacetime state and show that it must then be in the configuration given in Table 36A-2. Ten percent of the workers, calculation shows, must be shifted from war work

PEACETIME INPUT-OUTPUT FLOWS (all numbers in billions)

	AGRICUL-TURE	MANUFAC-TURING	HOUSEHOLD FINAL CONSUMPTIONS	GROSS TOTALS
Agriculture		800	1,000	1,800
Manufacturing	600		1,000	1,600
Household labor and other factors	1,200	800	2,000	
Gross totals	1,800	1,600		3,400

Table 36A-2 Input-output table helps nations plan

End of war causes a shift from guns to butter: agricultural final consumption goes up by $500 billion; manufacturing final consumption goes down by the same amount. Using fixed input-output coefficients from Table 36A-1, we can calculate the needed changes in gross outputs, labor, and intermediate inputs. The same table helps in development planning.

to peace work. Similarly, the input-output table can help developing economies plan for major shifts in the structure of their economies.

SUMMARY TO APPENDIX

1. Schumpeter's stress on innovation, followed by competitive erosion of profit, highlights an important part of the growth process.

2. The neoclassical growth model uses the concept of the "natural rate of growth" g, which is determined by population growth and technological change. If K and Q are to grow at this balanced rate, the required fraction of income that has to be voluntarily saved is given by the *balanced-growth equation, $s = g(K/Q)$*.

3. By working carefully through the neoclassical growth model, we see how it can be made consistent with the seven major trends of growth in a modern economy. The major insight is to allow for continual improvement in the "quality" of labor; that is, one person a decade ago becomes 10 or 20 percent more efficient today. By incorporating this assumption of labor-augmenting technological change, we see that many of the trends of growth are produced over the long run.

4. Input-output tables give a useful picture of the relationships lying behind aggregate GNP data. By positing fixed input-output coefficients, a planner can use this technique to program a shift from a war pattern of consumption to a peace pattern or to achieve any other developmental target goal.

CONCEPTS FOR REVIEW

innovation and competition
capital deepening, varying K/Q
natural growth rate
$s = g(K/Q)$

labor-augmenting technological change;
  seven trends explained
input-output table

QUESTIONS FOR DISCUSSION

1. Explain the basic idea of the two-way input-output table.

2. Return to the input-output system given in Table 36A-1. Instead of peace breaking out, assume that the war becomes even hotter. Manufacturing guns must rise to 1750 while only 250 can be spared for agricultural butter. Work out the full input-output tableau for this new situation. (The key assumption you need is that for every $3 of agriculture you need a fixed $2 of labor and $1 of manufacturing, while for every $2 of manufacturing, equal $1 inputs of labor and agriculture are needed.)

3. Assume that the capital-output ratio is 3 and the savings rate is 9 percent of GNP. What is the natural growth rate of the economy in the neoclassical growth model?

4. What might Schumpeter have meant by the following statement: "Capitalism creates a critical frame of mind which, after having destroyed the moral authority of so many other institutions, in the end turns against its own" (*Capitalism, Socialism and Democracy*, p. 143)?

CHAPTER 37

THE ECONOMICS OF DEVELOPING COUNTRIES

I believe in materialism.
I believe in all the proceeds of a healthy materialism—
good cooking, dry houses, dry feet, sewers, drain
pipes, hot water, baths, electric lights, automobiles,
good roads, bright streets, long vacations away from
the village pump, new ideas, fast horses, swift
conversation, theatres, operas, orchestras, bands—I
believe in them all for everybody. The man who dies
without knowing these things may be as exquisite as a
saint, and as rich as a poet; but it is in spite of, not
because of, his deprivation.

Francis Hackett

ALL THE ECONOMIC PRINCIPLES we have learned can now be brought to bear on one of today's most challenging issues—the problem of poor societies striving for economic development. Of the 5 billion people on the globe, perhaps 1 billion live in a state of absolute poverty—barely able to eke out enough food to survive from day to day. At the same time that poor countries are struggling to rise out of abject poverty, the rapid growth of population has reduced the benefits of improved agricultural technologies and of increased food production.

This great disparity in incomes leads people to ask: What causes the great difference in the wealth of nations? Can the world peacefully survive with poverty in the midst of plenty, with agricultural surpluses in America alongside starvation in Africa? What steps can poorer nations take to improve their living standards?

This chapter explores some of the obstinate problems facing less developed countries. After section A describes what we mean by a developing country, section B explores the causes and consequences of population growth. Section C then examines the nature of, sources of, and solutions to global poverty.

877

A. DEVELOPING COUNTRIES

Before turning to an analysis of population and development theory, let's ask what is meant by a developing country, or a less developed country (LDC).

Definitions

A **developing country** is one with real per capita income that is low relative to that in advanced countries like the United States, Japan, and those in Western Europe.

This standard definition conceals much of the human side of development. Developing countries have populations with poor health, low levels of literacy, inadequate dwellings, and meager diets.

Table 37-1 is a key source of data for understanding the major players in the world economy, as well as indicators of underdevelopment. Countries are grouped into the categories of low-income, middle-income, and high-income market economies. In addition, there are two nonconforming groups—the high-

COUNTRY GROUP	POPULATION		GNP 1985 ($ billions)	PER CAPITA GNP 1985 ($)	ADULT LITERACY 1980 (%)	LIFE EXPEC-TANCY AT BIRTH (years)	AGRICUL-TURAL EMPLOY-MENT 1980 (% of labor force)
	LEVEL 1985 (millions)	GROWTH 1965–1985 (% per year)					
Low-income economies (e.g., China, India)	2,439	2.2	659	270	52	60	72
Middle-income economies (e.g., Brazil, Philippines, South Korea)	1,242	2.4	1,602	1,290	65	62	43
High-income oil exporters (e.g., Saudi Arabia, Libya)	18	5.0	180	9,800	32	63	35
European centrally planned economies (e.g., U.S.S.R., East Germany)	363	1.0	2,430	7,630	99	69	22
High-income market economies (e.g., U.S.A., West Germany, Japan)	737	0.8	8,708	11,810	99	76	7

Table 37-1   Important indicators for different groups of countries

Countries are grouped by the World Bank into five major categories. In each, two or three important countries are listed. Note how well the indicators are correlated across most of the groups, with low-income economies having low per capita incomes, low literacy and life expectancy, and a very large fraction of the labor force in agriculture. (Source: World Bank, *World Development Report, 1987.*)

income oil exporters (like Saudi Arabia) and the communist countries of Eastern Europe.

A number of interesting features emerge from the table. Clearly, low-income countries are much poorer than advanced countries like the United States. Their calculated per capita incomes are about one-fortieth of those in high-income countries. (This comparison is distorted by use of official exchange rates to compare living standards. A newer technique, looking at "purchasing-power parity," or what incomes will buy, suggests that incomes in poorer countries are probably understated by a factor of 3—but a large gap still remains.)

In addition, many of the social and health indicators show the effects of poverty in low-income nations. Life expectancy is low, and educational attainment and literacy are modest, reflecting low levels of investment in human capital. And most people live and work on farms, whereas few do in wealthier countries.

Table 37-1 also shows that there is a great diversity among developing countries. Some remain at the ragged edge of starvation—these are the very poorest countries like Chad, Bangladesh, or Ethiopia. Others have found that combination of ingredients that can propel them into the category of middle-income countries. The more successful—countries like South Korea, Taiwan, and Singapore—are called the "newly industrializing countries," or "NICs." The NICs have been enormously successful in raising their living standards and in penetrating the traditional markets of advanced industrial countries. Yesterday's successful developing countries, which are today's NICs, will probably be tomorrow's advanced countries.

Life in Low-Income Countries

To bring out the contrasts between advanced and developing economies, imagine that you are a typical 21-year-old in one of the low-income countries, such as Haiti, India, or Bangladesh.

You are poor: even after making generous allowance for the goods that you produce and consume, your annual income averages barely $270 as compared to $14,000 for your counterpart in North America; perhaps you can find cold comfort in the thought that only 1 person in 4 in the world averages more than $3000 in annual income.

For each of you who can read, there is one like you who is illiterate. Your life expectancy is four-fifths that of the average person in an advanced country; already one or two of your brothers or sisters have died before reaching adulthood.

Most people in your country work on farms. Few can be spared from food production to work in factories. You work with but one-sixtieth the horsepower of a prosperous North American worker. You know little about science, but much about your village traditions.

As a citizen in one of the 37 countries in the poorest parts of Africa and Asia, you and your fellows together constitute 50 percent of the world population. But you must divide among you only 5 percent of world income. You are often hungry, and the food you eat is mainly roughage or rice. While you may get some primary schooling, you are unlikely to go on to high school, and only the wealthiest go to a university. You work long hours in the fields without the benefit of machinery. At night you sleep on a mat. You have little household furniture, perhaps a table and a radio. Your only mode of transportation is an old pair of boots.

Such is the way of life in the poorest countries. But we must be careful not to think that all developing countries fit into the same mold. There is enormous diversity among countries. While the description given above may apply to peasants in Bangladesh or Ethiopia, it would be increasingly outdated for citizens of many newly industrializing countries like South Korea or Taiwan.

B. POPULATION AND ECONOMIC CONDITIONS

Some nations are endowed with few people, enjoying a vast continent teeming with minerals and fertile land; others see their people crowded into small plots, leaving no tillable corner untouched. The theory of population can help to explain such disparities among countries.

THE LEGACY OF MALTHUS

One of the earliest writers to analyze the relation between population and the economy was Thomas Malthus. He first developed his views while arguing at breakfast against his father's perfectionist view that the human race was getting ever better. Finally the son became so agitated that he wrote a book. Malthus' *Essay on the Principle of Population* (1798) was an instantaneous best-seller and since then has influenced the thinking of people all over the world about population and economic growth.

Malthus first took the observation of Benjamin Franklin that, in the American colonies where resources were abundant, population tended to double every 25 years or so. Malthus postulated a universal tendency for population—unless checked by limited food supply—to grow exponentially, or by a geometric progression.[1] Eventually, a population which doubles every generation—1, 2, 4, 8, 16, 32, 64, 128, 256, 512, 1024, . . . —becomes so large that there is not enough space in the world for all the people to stand.

All this left members of the "perfectionist school" unimpressed. So at this point Malthus unleashed the devil of diminishing returns. He argued that because land is fixed while labor inputs keep growing, food could grow only by an arithmetic progression and not by a geometric progression. (Compare 1, 2, 3, 4, . . . , with 1, 2, 4, 8, ...) Malthus concluded:

As population doubles and redoubles, it is exactly as if the globe were halving and halving again in size—until finally it has shrunk so much that the supply of food falls below the level necessary for life.

When the law of diminishing returns is applied to a fixed supply of land, food production tends not to keep up with a population's geometric-progression rate of growth.

---

[1]Exponential (or geometric) growth occurs when a variable increases at a constant proportional rate from period to period. Thus, if a population of 200 is growing at 3 percent per year, it would equal 200 in year 0, $200 \times (1.03)$ in year 1, . . . , $200 \times (1.03)^{10}$ in year 10, and so on. Money earning compound interest grows geometrically. For example, at 6 percent compound interest, money doubles in value every 12 years. It has been estimated that the \$24 received by the Indians for Manhattan Island would, if deposited at compound interest, be worth as much today as all property on the island.

Now, Malthus did not say that population would increase at these rates. This was only its tendency if unchecked. He wrote at length to show that, in all places and at all times, checks do operate to hold population down. And in his later, little-read editions, Malthus retreated from his gloomy doctrine, holding out hope that population growth could be slowed by birth prevention, rather than by pestilence, famine, and war.

This important application of diminishing returns illustrates the profound effects a simple theory can have. Malthus' ideas had wide repercussions. His book was used to support a stern revision of the English poor laws. Under the influence of Malthus' writings, poverty was considered a result of laziness, to be made as uncomfortable as possible. His opinions also bolstered the argument that trade unions could not improve the welfare of workers—since any increase in their wages would allegedly only cause workers to reproduce until all were reduced to a bare subsistence.

Flawed Prophecies of Malthus Despite his careful statistical studies, it is thought today that Malthus' views were oversimplified. In his discussion of diminishing returns, Malthus never fully anticipated the technological miracles of the Industrial Revolution.

In the century following Malthus, technological advance shifted out the production-possibility frontiers of countries in Europe and North America, as we saw in Chapter 36. This rapid technological change allowed output to far outstrip population, resulting in a rapid rise in real wages.

Nor did Malthus anticipate that after 1870 population growth in most Western nations would begin to decline just as living standards and real wages grew most rapidly.

Nevertheless, the germs of truth in his doctrines are still important for understanding the population behavior of India, Ethiopia, China, and other parts of the globe where the balance of numbers and food supply is a vital consideration.

The New Malthusians

Economics often sees older ideas reappearing in new garb, transformed by recent events or scientific devel-

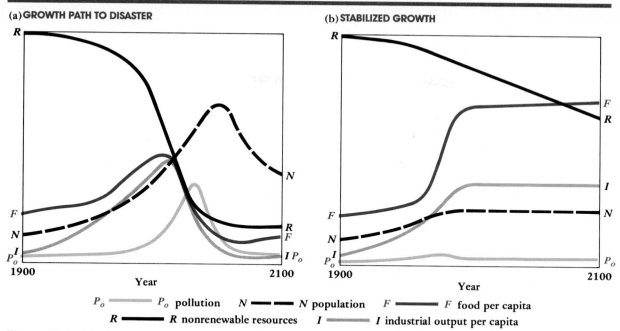

(a) GROWTH PATH TO DISASTER

(b) STABILIZED GROWTH

P_o ▬▬▬ P_o pollution N ▬ ▬ ▬ N population F ▬▬▬ F food per capita

R ▬▬▬ R nonrenewable resources I ▬▬▬ I industrial output per capita

Figure 37-1   Limits-to-growth school projected economic disaster could be prevented by limiting resource use

Rapid population growth (*NN* in black) leads inexorably to black *RR* curve of declining resources, and to worsening pollution (*P_oP_o* in light red). Doomsday prediction in **(a)**: imminent decline in available food per capita (*FF* in red) and decline in industrial output (*II* in gray).

   Economic decline is averted on right by stopping both economic growth and population growth immediately. The Club of Rome recommends recycling resources and shifting to services that don't use up resources. If billions of people in poor countries are to share equitably in stabilized world output, the U.S. standard of living must halve and halve again. (Source: Donella Meadows et al., *The Limits to Growth*, 1972.)

opments. In recent decades, many observers of the global environment have become alarmed by potential resource depletion and environmental degradation. The prices of many natural resources soared in the 1970s and 1980s. In addition, scientists pointed to rising levels of carbon dioxide and other atmospheric trace gases, to depletion of stratospheric ozone, to acid rain, and to dying forests. Are these the early-warning signs of the end of the industrial era and the beginning of an inevitable economic decline?

   One of the most dramatic and controversial attempts to answer these concerns was made by a group of European intellectuals known as the Club of Rome. In Jay Forrester's *World Dynamics* (1971) and the

best-seller by Dennis Meadows and co-authors, *The Limits to Growth* (1972), a computerized model of the world economy was constructed. The model assumed that population behaved in a Malthusian manner, that natural resources were essential but limited, and that technological advance was absent. Based on these assumptions, the Club of Rome models made a series of predictions about the global future. Two of their simulations are shown in Figure 37-1.

Steady-State Economics   Figure 37-1(*a*) shows the group's forecast of rising pollution, exhaustion of natural resources, and inevitable fall in future per capita real incomes. This forecast exactly parallels Malthus' early view that a decline toward subsistence could not be avoided.

Then, in Figure 37-1(b), we see, as in later editions of Malthus, how humanity can forestall its fate if it undertakes drastic measures: abolishing all population growth immediately, reducing output, and concentrating on food, services, and recycling resources.

Here we have warmed-over Malthus. But now the simple geometric and arithmetic progressions have been dressed up in computer models in which biological exponential growth collides with limited resources and stagnant technology.

Appraisal The neo-Malthusians posed a dilemma that distressed many readers. Most economists, in contrast, remembered the analysis and prophesies of Malthus and were skeptical. After a careful analysis of their structure, the models were sometimes labelled ''PIPO''—or ''pessimism in, pessimism out.'' This phrase conveys the idea that the doomsday nature of the conclusions arises from the pessimistic nature of the assumptions. Critics argued that these models ignored the role of prices as signals of scarcity, rejected the possibility of technological change outpacing resource scarcity, and assumed that population would grow rapidly if affluence were to prevail. It was, in one economist's words, ''the computer that cried wolf.''

But perhaps, for some countries, the wolf is there. In some areas, population *is* outrunning food supplies. While the doomsday models may be largely irrelevant for advanced countries, some enduring truth remains for poor regions. Let's examine what modern population theory says concerning the relationship between population and economic growth.

MODERN VIEWS ON POPULATION

Malthus and others thought that if the negative checks of pestilence, war, and famine subsided, population would shoot up. The history of developed countries followed a different route. Populations have stabilized in most advanced countries. These countries have made the transition from high birth and death rates in preindustrial times to low birth and death rates today. Before we can fully understand this important shift, we must master some of the concepts of modern **demography,** the study of the behavior of population.[2]

Birth and Death Rates

Basic to understanding population are the concepts of *crude birth and death rates*. These are simply the number of births or deaths per year per 1000 people. If we subtract the death rate from the birth rate, we get the rate of population growth.[3] Birth, death, and population growth rates for representative countries are shown in Table 37-2.

The Demographic Transition

We are now in a position to understand the demographic transition that occurs during the course of economic development. An idealized picture of the stages is shown in Figure 37-2. Here, population growth proceeds through four stages:

1. Preindustrial society, in which high birth and death rates lead to low population growth.

2. Early development, in which advances in medical technology lead to a decline in death rates with little effect on the birth rate. Thus population spurts upward.

3. Later development, in which lower infant mortality, urbanization, and education lead many couples to desire smaller families, cutting back the birth rate. Population growth may be rapid, but it is slowing.

4. Maturity, in which couples practice birth control successfully and both spouses tend to work outside the home. The desired (and actual) number of children per family drops to around 2, so net population growth is close to zero.

---

[2]An informative summary of the relationship between population and the overall economy is contained in Gary Becker's presidential address to the American Economic Association, ''Family Economics and Macro Behavior,'' *American Economic Review* (March 1988), pp. 1–13.

[3]When applied to a specific country, this calculation assumes no migration. If there is net immigration (or emigration), then this figure would have to be added to (or subtracted from) births minus deaths to get net increase in population.

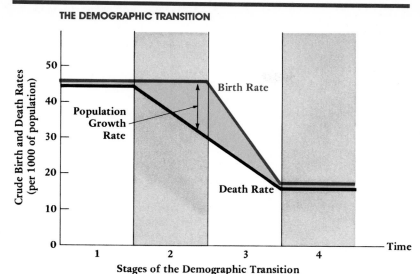

THE DEMOGRAPHIC TRANSITION

Figure 37-2   The stages of the demographic transition

This figure shows how countries have often made the transition from slow population growth with high birth and death rates to slow population growth with low birth and death rates.

Stage 1: Traditional society with little growth.

Stage 2: With the introduction of modern medical techniques, deaths fall but births stay high. Thus population growth rises.

Stage 3: The birth rate begins to recede as couples desire fewer children. Thus population growth diminishes.

Stage 4: In a mature society, couples have around 2 children, so population stabilizes.

We see, then, that the pessimistic population forecasts of Malthus and the neo-Malthusians appear correct in stages 1 and 2. But affluence in stages 3 and 4 leads to declining population growth. It is just this transition to low population growth that is the greatest hope for the economic development of many poor countries.

Population Explosion

The demographic transition to low population growth holds out hope that many poor countries will not get forever caught in a Malthusian trap. But the transition evidently has not been completed yet, as is shown by Table 37-2. Historical trends and projections for the future are shown in Table 37-3. Faced with the prospect of continued rapid population growth, many observers fear the globe will have to display signs saying, "Standing Room Only."

Controlling Population Growth In the face of the Malthusian specter, countries have begun to take an active role in curbing growth of population, even when such actions run against prevailing religious norms. Many countries have introduced educational campaigns, subsidized birth control, or, in extreme cases, mandatory sterilization. China has been particularly vigorous in curbing population growth among its more than 1 billion inhabitants.

Slowly, we begin to see the results of economic development and birth control. The birth rate in poor countries has declined from 43 per 1000 in 1965 to 29

SOURCES OF POPULATION GROWTH, 1985 *(rates per 1,000 of population per year)*

	BIRTH RATE	DEATH RATE	NATURAL GROWTH RATE
Low-income countries			
Zambia	49	15	34
Malawi	54	22	32
India	33	12	21
Middle-income countries			
Venezuela	31	5	26
Brazil	29	8	21
Thailand	26	8	18
High-income countries			
United States	16	9	7
France	14	10	4
United Kingdom	13	12	1
West Germany	10	11	−1

Table 37-2   Birth, death, and population growth rates, 1985

Data for three groups of countries illustrate how patterns of population growth change with levels of development. Poor countries have high birth and death rates. When health conditions improve in the course of economic growth, countries experience a fall in death rates with little change in birth rates. Consequently their population growth sometimes exceeds that of poorer countries. In the richest countries, birth rates fall as well, and population stabilizes. (Source: World Bank, *World Development Report, 1987.*)

per 1000 in 1985. Although these countries are probably still in stage 2 of the demographic transition (see Figure 37-2), their population growth rates have stabilized over the last two decades. The struggle against poverty induced by excessive population growth is still underway on two-thirds of the globe.

POPULATION OF THE WORLD *(in millions)*

	1800	1940	1986	2000 (PROJECTED)
Europe (including all of U.S.S.R.)	188	575	773	827
North, South, and Central America	29	274	686	844
Asia, Africa, and Oceania	702	1,446	3,485	4,451
World	**919**	**2,295**	**4,944**	**6,122**

Table 37-3   World population has more than quintupled since 1800

Even with birth rates falling generally, the population of the less developed world will grow relative to the developed world. [Source: *Statistical Abstract, 1987* (U.N.).]

C. THE PROCESS OF ECONOMIC DEVELOPMENT

Having seen what it means to be a developing country, we now turn to an analysis of the nature of the development process.

THE FOUR ELEMENTS IN DEVELOPMENT

In the last chapter, which examined economic growth, we explored how a nation expands its productive potential over time. The ingredients for growth in less developed countries are no different; the engine of economic progress must ride on the same four wheels, no matter how rich or poor the country. The four central factors are:

- Human resources (labor supply, education, discipline, motivation)
- Natural resources (land, minerals, fuels, climate)
- Capital formation (machines, factories, roads)
- Technology (science, engineering, management, entrepreneurship)

Let's see how each of the four wheels contributes to growth, as well as how public policy can steer the growth process in desirable directions.

Human Resources

We have already dealt at length with the problems of population growth in developing countries. Countries must also be concerned with the quality of their human resources. When planners draw up blueprints for hastening economic development, they emphasize the following specific programs:

- Control disease and improve health and nutrition—both to make people happier and to make them more productive workers. Accordingly, do not look on health-care clinics and sewerage projects as luxuries but rather as vitally useful social capital.
- Improve education, reduce illiteracy, and train workers. Educated people become more productive

workers when they can use capital more effectively, adopt new technologies, and learn from their mistakes. For advanced learning in science, engineering, medicine, and management, countries will benefit by sending their best minds abroad to bring back the newest advances. But beware of the *brain drain*, in which the most able people get drawn off to high-wage countries in Europe and North America.

Many economists believe that the quality of labor inputs is the single most important barrier to economic development. Virtually every other ingredient in production—capital goods, raw materials, and technology—can be bought or borrowed from advanced countries. But the application of high-productivity techniques of production to local conditions almost always requires management, production workers, and engineering know-how found only in a literate and highly skilled work force. Modern technologies are often embodied in capital goods, as can be seen in telecommunications devices, computers, nuclear power stations, and fighter aircraft; but these capital goods require complementary trained labor for effective use and maintenance. The crucial role of skilled labor has been shown again and again when sophisticated mining, defense, or manufacturing machinery fell into disrepair and disuse because the labor force of developing countries had not acquired the necessary maintenance skills.

Natural Resources

Some poor countries of Africa and Asia have been poorly endowed by nature, and such land and minerals as they do possess must be divided among dense populations. The romantic notion that there remain in these countries areas of overlooked valuable resources has largely been exploded by geographers.

Perhaps the most important natural resource of developing countries is arable land. As Table 37-1 shows, much of the labor force is employed in farming. Hence the productive use of land—with appropriate conservation, fertilizers, and tillage—will go far in increasing a poor nation's output. Moreover, landownership patterns are a key to providing farmers strong incentives to invest in capital and technologies that will increase their land's yield. If farmers own the land, they will be willing to make improvements, invest in irrigation systems, and undertake appropriate conservation practices.

Capital Formation

While the hands of people are much the same the world around, workers in advanced countries have their hands on a great deal more capital—and are therefore much more productive.

Accumulating capital, as we have seen, requires a sacrifice of current consumption over many decades. But there's the rub: the poorest countries are already near a subsistence standard of living. At such income levels, reducing current consumption imposes great economic hardship.

In advanced economies, 10 to 20 percent of income may go into capital formation. By contrast, the poorest agrarian countries are often able to save only 5 percent of national income. Moreover, much of the low level of saving goes to provide the growing population with housing and simple tools. Little is left over for development.

But let's say a country has succeeded in hiking up its rate of saving. Even so, it takes many decades to accumulate the railroads, electricity-generating plants, equipment, factories, and other capital goods that underpin a productive economic structure.

In many developing countries, the single most pressing problem is too little saving. Particularly in the poorest regions, urgent current consumption competes with investment for scarce resources. The result is often too little investment in the productive capital so necessary for rapid economic progress.

It must be emphasized that undersaving is not a universal syndrome. Many of the more successful middle-income countries—South Korea, Taiwan, Hong Kong, and Singapore—have succeeded in raising the share of their output devoted to investment to 20 or 30 percent. These are the countries that provide models to emulate.

Social Overhead Capital and Externalities When we think of capital, we must not concentrate only on trucks and steel mills. Many large social investments must precede industrialization, or even efficient marketing of farm products.

To develop, a private economy must have **social overhead capital.** These are the large-scale projects that precede trade and commerce—roads, railroads, irrigation projects and dams, public-health spraying against malarial mosquitoes, etc. All these involve large investments that tend to be indivisible with increasing returns to scale. No small farm or family can profitably undertake to build a railroad system; no pioneering private enterprise can hope to make a profit from a telephone or irrigation system before the markets have been developed. These large-scale investment projects spread their benefits widely across the economy.

Often these projects involve external economies, or spillovers that private firms cannot capture. For example, a regional agricultural adviser can help all farmers in an area; a public-health program inoculating people against typhoid or diphtheria protects the population beyond those inoculated; a dam produces widespread benefits. In each of these cases it would be impossible for an enterprising firm to capture the social benefits because the firm cannot collect fees from the thousands or even millions of beneficiaries. Because of the large indivisibilities and external effects, the government must step in, provide the necessary funds and initiative, and ensure that these social overhead investments are undertaken.

Foreign Borrowing and the Debt Crisis

If there are so many obstacles to finding domestic saving for capital formation, why not rely more heavily on foreign sources? Does not economic theory tell us that a rich country, which has depleted its own high-yield investment projects, can benefit both itself and the recipient by investing in high-yield projects abroad?

Actually, prior to 1914, economic development did proceed in this fashion. Britain in its heyday saved about 15 percent of its GNP and invested fully half this amount abroad. And during most of the period after World War II, the United States and other advanced countries lent large sums to developing countries. The figures on foreign investment in low- and middle-income countries show an impressive record of capital transfer: foreign loans averaged $112 billion annually in the period 1980–1982. Investors in wealthy countries sent their funds abroad in search of higher returns than were available at home; poor countries, hungry for funds to finance investment projects or even consumption, welcomed this flow of foreign capital. These loans were particularly useful during the 1970s, when rapidly rising oil prices imposed severe hardships on many oil-importing, developing countries.

By the end of the 1970s, however, the extent of foreign borrowing by developing countries had become unsustainably large. Total outstanding debt grew almost 20 percent per year and increased by almost $500 billion from 1973 to 1982. By 1982, 63 percent of the debt of major developing countries was owed to banks, and this debt was generally of very short maturity. Some of these loans were put to good use in investments in oil drilling, textile factories, and coal-mining equipment, but part simply raised consumption levels.

As long as the exports of these countries grew at the same rate, all was well. But with the rise in international interest rates and the slowdown in the world economy after 1980, many countries found that their borrow-and-invest strategy had led them to the brink of financial crisis. Some countries (such as Bolivia and Peru) needed all their export earnings simply to pay the interest on their foreign debt. Others found themselves unable to meet debt-repayment schedules; almost all indebted developing countries were staggering under heavy debt-service burdens (i.e., the need to repay the interest and principal on their loans). As a result, country after country, particularly the large Latin American ones, failed to make interest payments and had their debts ''rescheduled'' (i.e., the repayment was postponed). In 1987, some countries unilaterally suspended payments of interest and principal while continuing to promise future payments.

By the late 1980s, the debt crisis simmered quietly on the back burner, neither solved nor causing immediate turmoil on the world's financial markets. What does economic history suggest will be the future course of events in the area of foreign debt? If no severe shocks hit the world economy, indebted countries can probably move back toward lower levels of foreign debt. If, however, a severe shock to output, interest rates, or confidence occurs, then the international financial system may find itself unable to continue financing trade and growth in both advanced and poorer countries. The exact shape and course of such a crisis in the international financial system cannot be foreseen.

Technological Change and Innovations

In addition to the fundamental factors of population, natural resources, and capital formation, there is the vitally important fourth factor of technology. Here developing countries have one potential advantage: they can hope to benefit by relying on the technological skills of more advanced nations.

Imitating Technology Poor countries do not need to find modern Newtons to discover the law of gravity; they can read about it in any physics book. They don't have to go through the slow, meandering climb of the Industrial Revolution; in a machinery catalogue they can find tractors, computers, and power looms undreamed of by the great inventors of the past.

Japan and the United States clearly illustrate this in their historical developments. Japan joined the industrial race late and only at the end of the nineteenth century sent students abroad to learn Western technology. The Japanese government took an active role in stimulating the pace of development and in building railroads and utilities. Relying on the adaptation of foreign technologies, Japan moved into its position today as the world's second-largest industrial economy.

The case of the United States itself provides a hopeful example to the rest of the world. Until the 1930s, America did not reach the front rank in the field of pure science. Yet for a century its applied technology was outstanding. Examine one by one the key inventions involved in the automobile. Where did they originate? Mostly abroad. Nevertheless, Henry Ford and General Motors applied foreign inventions and outproduced the rest of the world. The examples of the United States and Japan show how countries can thrive by adapting foreign science and technology to local market conditions.

Entrepreneurship and Innovation From the histories of Japan and the United States, it might appear that adaptation of foreign technology is an easy recipe for development. You might say: "Just go abroad; copy more efficient methods; put them into effect at home; then sit back and wait for the extra output to roll in."

Of course, it does not work quite this way. A few technical experts armed with a roll of blueprints cannot solve all a poor country's problems. There are thousands of cultural and economic barriers to progress.[4]

Experience shows that to make advanced technologies work requires entrepreneurs to take those ideas and employ them. It is no cut-and-dried task to adapt advanced foreign technology to an underdeveloped country's own use. Remember, the advanced technology was itself developed to meet the special conditions of the advanced countries—conditions like high wages, plentiful capital relative to labor, and ample skilled engineers. These conditions do not prevail in poorer countries.

One of the key tasks of economic development is the fostering of an entrepreneurial spirit. A country cannot thrive without a group of owners or managers willing to undertake risks, open new plants, adopt new technologies, confront labor strife, and import new ways of doing business. Government can help entrepreneurship by setting up extension services for farmers, educating and training the work force, establishing management schools, and making sure that government itself maintains a healthy respect for the role of private initiative.

Vicious Cycle

We have emphasized that poor countries face great obstacles in combining the four elements of progress—labor, capital, resources, and entrepreneurship. In addition, countries find that the difficulties reinforce each other in a *vicious cycle of poverty*.

---

[4]A recent example illustrates how custom can frustrate a nation's attempt to adopt modern technology. A country attempting to introduce personal computers started to teach managers to use them in their day-to-day operations. Many of the men refused to use the new technology, which required typing at a keyboard, saying that "typing is women's work and is demeaning to men."

Figure 37-3 illustrates how one hurdle raises yet other hurdles. Low incomes lead to low saving; low saving retards the growth of capital; inadequate capital prevents introduction of machinery and rapid growth in productivity; low productivity leads to low incomes. Other elements in poverty are self-reinforcing. Poverty is accompanied by low levels of skill and literacy; these in turn prevent the adaptation of new and improved technologies.

Because overcoming the barriers of poverty often requires a concerted effort on many fronts, some development economists recommend a "big push" forward to break the vicious cycle. If a country is fortunate, simultaneous steps to invest more, develop skills, and curb population growth can break the vicious cycle of poverty and create a virtuous cycle of rapid economic development.

STRATEGIES OF ECONOMIC DEVELOPMENT

We see how countries must combine labor, resources, capital, and technology in order to grow rapidly. But to say this provides no answers—saying that successful countries must grow is like saying that an Olympic sprinter must run like the wind. The deeper questions are: Why do some countries succeed in running faster than others? How do poor countries ever get started down the road of economic development?

Comprehensive Theories

Historians and social scientists have long been fascinated by the differences in the pace of economic growth among nations. Some early theories stressed climate, noting that all advanced countries lie in the earth's temperate zone. Others have pointed to the importance of custom, culture, or religion as key factors. Max Weber emphasized the "Protestant ethic" as a driving force behind capitalism, motivating many to seek personal gain and call it "God's gold." More recently, Mancur Olson has argued that nations begin to decline when their decision structure becomes brittle and when interest groups or oligarchies prevent social and economic change.

No doubt each of these theories has some validity

THE VICIOUS CYCLE OF UNDERDEVELOPMENT

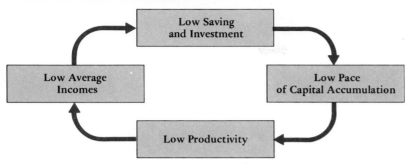

Figure 37-3   Many obstacles to development are reinforcing

Obstacles to development are closely related, as shown in this example of the vicious cycle of poverty. Low levels of income prevent saving, retard capital growth, hinder productivity growth, and keep income low. Successful development may require taking steps to break the chain at many points.

for a particular time and place. But they do not hold up as universal explanations of economic development. Weber's theory leaves unexplained why the cradle of civilization appeared in the Near East and Greece while European tribes who were later to dominate the world lived in caves, worshipped trolls, and wore bearskins. Where is the Protestant ethic in a sleek Japanese factory in which workers gather to pay homage to Buddha? How can we explain that a country like Japan, with a rigid social structure and powerful lobbies in many sectors, has become the world's most productive economy?

To understand the diversity of economic experience, we must turn to broader explanations.

Recent Approaches to Development

For decades economists have been intensely interested in economic development. The following account represents a montage of important ideas developed in recent years. Each theory attempts to describe how countries break out of the vicious cycle of poverty and begin to mobilize the four forces behind growth—the labor, resources, capital, and technology just discussed.

The Takeoff Human history is long, and the era of economic development has been both recent and brief. During most of history, life was nasty, brutish, and short. But, in a few places over a brief period, superior production techniques were introduced. Great inequality of income allowed a few to funnel saving into capital formation. Economic development could take place.

So dramatic was the discontinuity between earlier periods and the Industrial Revolution that scholars like W. W. Rostow developed a theory stressing stages of economic growth. One of Rostow's stages is called the *takeoff,* the analogy being with an airplane, which can fly only after attaining a critical speed.

Different countries had their takeoffs in different periods: England at the beginning of the eighteenth century, the United States around 1850, Japan in 1910, and Mexico after 1940.

The takeoff is impelled by ''leading sectors,'' such as a rapidly growing export market or an industry displaying large economies of scale. Once these leading sectors begin to grow rapidly, a process of *self-sustaining growth* (the takeoff) occurs. Growth leads to profits; profits are reinvested; capital and productivity and per capita incomes spurt ahead. The virtuous cycle of economic development is under way.

The Backwardness Hypothesis A second view emphasizes the international context of development. We saw above that poorer countries have important

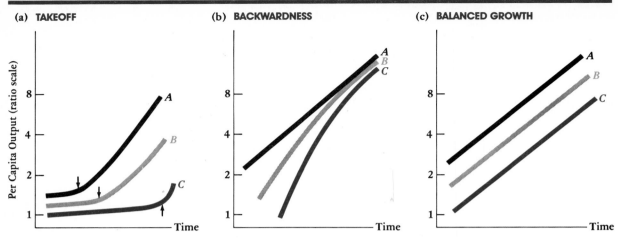

Figure 37-4   Three views of the development process for countries A, B, and C

Three modern theories of economic development can be seen in diagrammatic form. Consider advanced country A, middle-income country B, and low-income country C. Note that output is shown on a ratio scale. This means that the *slope* of each line represents the *growth* rate of output. Thus a constant slope, as in part **(c)**, indicates a constant annual growth rate for output; while an increasing slope in part **(a)** indicates an increasing growth rate. What is occurring in part **(b)**?

In part **(a)**, leading sectors such as exports promote a takeoff (shown by arrows) into rapid self-sustaining growth. In part **(b)**, backward countries rely on and adopt technologies invented by richer countries. They thus grow rapidly and gradually catch up with advanced countries. In the final scheme **(c)**, countries run at the same speed, but some countries began the growth process earlier than others. The relative gap between countries is roughly constant. [Adapted from Bruce Herrick and Charles P. Kindleberger, *Economic Development* (McGraw-Hill, New York, 1983).]

advantages that the first pioneers along the path of industrialization did not. Today's developing nations can draw upon the capital, skills, and technology of more advanced countries. This hypothesis, advanced by Alexander Gerschenkron of Harvard, suggests that *relative backwardness* itself may aid development. Countries can buy modern textile machinery, efficient pumps, miracle seeds, chemical fertilizers, and medical supplies. Because they can lean on the technologies of advanced countries, today's developing countries can grow more rapidly than did Britain or Western Europe in the period 1780–1850.

Balanced Growth Theories like the takeoff or backwardness hypotheses have been successful at catching the attention of scholars and experts. But we must step back and assess history to see whether they fit the facts. Along with the earlier two theories, some writers suggest that growth is a *balanced* process with countries progressing steadily ahead. Economic de-

velopment might more resemble the tortoise, making continual progress, than the hare, who runs in spurts and then rests when exhausted.

The three alternatives can be seen graphically in Figure 37-4. Here we see how the takeoff, the backwardness hypothesis, and the balanced-growth views would appear over time for three countries—advanced A, middle-income B, and low-income C.

Which of these three views appears most closely to explain history? One of the most careful studies is that of Nobel laureate Simon Kuznets.[5] He examined the history of 13 advanced countries over long time periods going back as far as 1800. His conclusion was that the balanced-growth model is most consistent with these countries' histories—with no significant rise or fall in economic growth as development progressed.

Note one further important difference between the

[5]Simon Kuznets, *Economic Growth of Nations* (Harvard University Press, Cambridge, Mass., 1971).

three theories. The takeoff theory suggests that there will be increasing divergence among countries (some flying rapidly, while others are unable to leave the ground). The backwardness hypothesis suggests convergence, while the Kuznets view suggests roughly constant differentials. Empirical evidence shown in Table 37-4 indicates that there has been little change in the relative gap between advanced and developing countries in the last quarter-century (although the performance of individual countries has varied greatly from the average)—a pattern of growth rates most consistent with the balanced-growth view.

A Rich Mosaic The three views just sketched can do no more than begin to describe the ideas put forth in recent years to analyze the process of economic development. Nor are some theories right while others

are wrong. Rather, the developing world is a highly diverse group of nations, with different backgrounds, cultures, economic resources, and political systems. Development economists are today shying away from comprehensive theories that purport to be universal explanations of human history. Rather, each country tends to be viewed as an individual with special resources and needs, requiring prescriptions that fit the particular case.

Issues in Economic Development

To say that countries must encourage rapid growth in capital and technology does not answer *how* these key ingredients are to be deployed. Among the vast array of issues that arise in development planning, we focus here on three recurrent themes: the balance between industry and agriculture, the role of outward orientation, and the risks of overspecialization.

Industrialization vs. Agriculture In most countries, incomes in urban areas are almost double those in rural agriculture. And in affluent nations, large parts of total resources are devoted to manufacture. Hence, many nations jump to the conclusion that industrialization is the cause rather than the effect of affluence.

We must be wary of such inferences, which often fall into the *post hoc* fallacy. You sometimes hear, "Rich people drive expensive cars, but driving an expensive car will not make you rich." Similarly, there is no economic justification for every poor country to insist upon having its own national airline and large steel mill. These are often ornamental luxuries rather than the necessities of economic growth.

The lesson of decades of attempts to accelerate industrialization at the expense of agriculture has led many analysts to rethink the role of farming. Industrialization tends to be capital-intensive, pulls workers into crowded cities, and often produces high levels of unemployment. Raising productivity on farms may require less capital, while providing productive employment for surplus labor.

Indeed, if Bangladesh could increase the productivity of its farming by 20 percent, that would do more to release resources for the production of comforts than would primary reliance on promoting industry.

RECENT GROWTH TRENDS

COUNTRY GROUP	RATE OF GROWTH OF REAL GNP (% per year)	
	1965–1980	1980–1985
Low-income		
China and India	5.3	8.3
Other low-income	3.2	2.8
Middle-income		
Lower-middle	6.3	1.6
Upper-middle	6.6	1.7
High-income oil exporters	7.5	−2.2
Industrial market economies	3.7	2.3

Table 37-4 Poorer countries are slowly closing the income gap

Data on the growth in total output show that poor countries were unable to close the gap between themselves and the industrial market economies during the 1960s, although middle-income or newly industrializing countries grew rapidly. Stagnation in high-income market economies during the 1970s allowed the relative output gaps to close by 10 to 25 percent. (Source: World Bank, *World Development Report, 1987*.)

Inward vs. Outward Orientation Since all countries engage in international trade, a key question soon emerges in a development strategy: Should countries attempt to be self-sufficient, replacing most imports with domestic production (sometimes called a strategy of *import substitution*)? Or should a country strive to pay for its needed imports by improving efficiency and competitiveness, developing foreign markets, and giving incentives for exports (a strategy of *outward orientation*)?

Policies of import substitution have often been popular in Latin America. The policy most frequently used toward this end has been to build high tariff walls around manufacturing industries so that local firms can produce and sell goods that would otherwise be imported. For example, Brazil and Mexico have placed high tariffs on automobiles so that firms in those countries would assemble autos at home rather than importing much less expensive cars from North America or Japan.

Critics observe that such subsidized import substitution generally limits competition, dampens innovation and productivity growth, and keeps the country's real income low. The consumers and the entire economy might be better off if the emphasis on import substitution were replaced by the quite different emphasis on outward orientation. Outward expansion sets up a system of incentives that stimulates exports rather than restricting imports. Important features of this approach are maintaining a competitive foreign exchange rate, choosing foreign-trade policies that encourage firms to produce for export, and minimizing unnecessary government regulation of businesses, especially of small firms.

The success of outward-expansion policies is best illustrated by the East Asian NICs. A generation ago, countries like Taiwan, South Korea, and Singapore had per capita incomes one-quarter to one-third of those in the wealthiest Latin American countries. Yet, by saving large fractions of their national incomes and channeling these to high-return export industries, the East Asian NICs overtook every Latin American country by the late 1980s. The secret to success was not a complete laissez-faire policy, for the governments in fact engaged in some planning and interventions. Rather, the outward orientation allowed the

countries to reap economies of scale and the benefits of international specialization to increase employment, effectively use domestic resources, enjoy rapid productivity growth, and provide enormous gains in their citizens' living standards.

A recent study of the economic prospects of Latin America concludes with the following assessment of the effects of outward expansion:

> Outward orientation is the keystone of the strategies of virtually all the "success stories" [of economic development]—in East and southeast Asia, in Latin America in certain periods, in Turkey, and elsewhere. Even where success has been limited, as in Africa, relatively outward-oriented countries have done much better than inward-oriented.[6]

But will the advanced countries allow their own declining manufacturing industries to be outcompeted by exports from countries pursuing outward expansion? Or will they succumb to the temptation to shut out such imports by their own protective tariffs and quotas? These are real issues debated in the name of "protection" and "industrial policies" during the 1980s—policies that we will discuss in the next two chapters.

The Dangers of Overspecialization We have repeatedly emphasized the economic gains from specialization, whether within a nation or among nations, because division of labor allows a vast increase in the quantity and variety of producible goods and services. But cannot a nation become dangerously overspecialized? Imagine the fate of a nation with big cost advantages that specialized completely in horseshoe manufacture in 1900, in production of vacuum tubes in 1945, or in nuclear reactor sales in 1975?

Countries should be concerned about their degree

---

[6] Bela Belassa et al., *Toward Renewed Economic Growth in Latin America* (Institute for International Economics, Washington, D.C., 1986), p. 24. This study points out that microeconomic government regulations may be as important as macroeconomic policies, with the following example: "The state as regulator has stifled much entrepreneurial initiative throughout [Latin America]. In several countries, numerous licenses are needed even to begin exporting—hardly an auspicious framework within which to promote outward expansion. In Peru, it recently took 289 days to register a new corporation—compared with four hours in Miami" (p. 30).

	EXPORTS OF THE MOST IMPORTANT PRODUCT		
COUNTRY	AS % TOTAL EXPORTS	AS % GNP	COMMODITY
Iran	98.0	34.6	Oil
Nigeria	97.3	16.0	Oil
Saudi Arabia	93.0	34.6	Oil
Zambia	83.8	21.7	Copper
Venezuela	82.6	21.7	Oil
Colombia	53.2	6.4	Coffee
South Africa	42.1	13.6	Gold
Tanzania	38.5	2.9	Coffee
Jamaica	38.0	11.4	Alumina
Sweden	9.7	3.0	Paper
United States	2.5	0.1	Corn

Table 37-5   Degree of specialization in exports, 1984

Many countries, particularly oil exporters, are dangerously specialized in a single commodity. By putting all their eggs in one basket, such countries ride the roller coaster of primary commodity prices. Advanced countries like the United States tend to be much more diversified and therefore suffer little from price swings in individual sectors. (Source: International Monetary Fund and U.S. Department of Commerce.)

of diversification. If Venezuela exports mainly oil, or Colombia mainly coffee, then price fluctuations in these markets will have large impacts on their foreign-trade balances and real incomes. Table 37-5 shows the degree to which some economies engage in "monoculture"—that is, have most of their exports concentrated in a single product. The oil-exporting countries are the most vulnerable to the dangers of overspecialization, followed by producers of other primary commodities.

When a country is overspecialized, prudent planning suggests that special efforts should be taken to diversify into different areas (particularly areas where the price swings are independent of, or even inverse to, those in their current area of specialization).[7] If coffee demand and supply are volatile, and if sound investment opportunities can be found in coal mining or cut flowers, a country like Colombia may be well advised to discourage the market's tendency to specialize in coffee production.

Don't put all your beans in one bag is a good rule for countries as well as people.

[7]Recall our discussion of portfolio theory in Chapter 11's analysis of optimal investment strategies.

SUMMARY

A. Developing Countries

1. Most of the world consists of developing countries: countries with low per capita incomes relative to the most advanced economies. Such countries often exhibit rapid population growth, low literacy, and a high proportion of their populations living and working on farms. Within the group of developing countries, some are middle-income newly industrializing countries, or NICs. This group has been successful in breaking the vicious cycle of underdevelopment.

B. Population and Economic Conditions

2. Malthus' theory of population rests on the law of diminishing returns. He thought that population, if unchecked, would tend to grow at a geometric (or exponential) rate, doubling every generation or so. But each member of the growing population would have less land and natural resources to work with. Therefore, because of diminishing returns, income could at best grow at an arithmetic rate; output per person would tend to fall so low as to lead to a stable population at a subsistence level of near-starvation.

3. In the 1970s, the Club of Rome school presented computer models of the global economy. This neo-Malthusian view foresaw the likelihood of impending collapse in living standards as population and production pushed against limited land and environmental capacity.

4. Malthus and his followers over the last century and a half have been criticized on several grounds: for ignoring the possibility of technological advance and for overlooking the significance of birth control as a force in lowering population growth.

5. The most important development in population theory has been to understand the demographic transition. This is the four-stage process by which a traditional society moves from stable population with high birth and death rates to stable population with low birth and death rates. In the interval, countries generally find that their death rates fall before their birth rates, so that a population explosion may occur. Many poorer and middle-income countries are still in the middle of their demographic transition.

C. The Process of Economic Development

6. The key to development lies in four fundamental factors: human resources, natural resources, capital formation (domestic or imported), and technology. Population causes problems of explosive growth as death rates fall before birth rates fall; the Malthusian prediction of diminishing returns stalks less developed countries. On the constructive agenda, improving the population's health, education, and technical training has high priority.

7. Rates of productive capital formation in poor countries are low because incomes are so low that little can be saved for the future. The financing of growth in poorer countries has always been an unstable link in the productive mechanism. The most recent crisis arose when many middle-income countries borrowed heavily in the 1970s to finance ambitious development programs. The economic slowdown of the early 1980s left them with swollen debts, unable to export enough to cover their expenses. The continuing problem of high debt burdens looms over financial markets, threatening to disrupt trade and finance in the 1990s.

8. Technological change is often associated with investment and new machinery. It offers much hope to the developing nations inasmuch as they can adapt the more productive technologies of advanced nations. This requires entrepreneurship. One task of development is to spur internal growth of the scarce entrepreneurial spirit.

9. Numerous theories of economic development help explain why the four fundamental factors are present or absent at a particular time. Geography and climate, custom, religion and business attitudes, class conflicts and colonialism—each affects economic development. But none does so in a simple and invariable way.

More impressive are the takeoff hypothesis (whereby increasing returns and social overhead capital combine to allow a rapid growth in a short period); the backwardness view (in which less advanced countries can converge quickly toward the more advanced by borrowing their technology and technologists); and the balanced-growth thesis (in which countries tend to grow at pretty much the same rate whether advanced or backward).

CONCEPTS FOR REVIEW

developing country, LDC
indicators of development
four elements in development:
    human resources
    natural resources
    capital
    technology and innovation
Malthusian population theory

neo-Malthusians
demographic transition (stages 1, 2, 3, 4)
social overhead capital, externalities
takeoff, backwardness, balanced-growth hypotheses
overspecialization in exports

QUESTIONS FOR DISCUSSION

1. Examine each of the countries in Table 37-2. Can you say where each is in its demographic transition?

2. Generally, many economists believe that the state should not interfere in a market where there are no important externalities—this being the ''liberal'' or laissez-faire tradition. Are there externalities in population growth that would lead to positive or negative spillovers? Consider such items as education, national defense, roads, beaches, and the distribution of geniuses like Mozart or Einstein.

3. How many children were there in your great-grandparents' family? In your parents' family? How many do you expect to be in your own family? What factors led to these decisions?

4. A *geometric progression* is a sequence of terms $(g_1, g_2, \ldots, g_t, g_{t+1}, \ldots)$ in which each term is the same multiple of its predecessor, $g_2/g_1 = g_3/g_2 = \cdots = g_{t+1}/g_t = \beta$. If $\beta = 1 + i > 1$, the terms grow exponentially like compound interest. An *arithmetic progression* is a sequence $(a_1, a_2, a_3, \ldots, a_t, a_{t+1}, \ldots)$ in which the difference between each term and its predecessor is the same constant: $a_2 - a_1 = a_3 - a_2 = \cdots = a_{t+1} - a_t = \alpha$. Give examples of each. Satisfy yourself that any geometric progression with $\beta > 1$ must eventually surpass any arithmetic progression.

5. Recall that Malthus asserted that unchecked population would grow geometrically, while food supply—constrained by diminishing returns—would grow only arithmetically. Use a numerical example to show why per capita food production must decline if population is unchecked while diminishing returns lead food production to grow more slowly than labor inputs.

6. Would you expect everyone to agree with the praise of material well-being expressed in the chapter's opening quotation?

7. Delineate each of the four important factors driving economic development. With respect to these, how was it that the high-income oil-exporting countries became rich? What hope is there for a country like Bangladesh that has very low per capita resources of capital, land, and technology?

8. Some fear the ''vicious cycle of underdevelopment.'' Rapid population growth eats into whatever improvements in technology occur. With a low per capita income, the country cannot save and invest but must engage in subsistence farming. With most of the population on the farm, there is little hope for education, decline in fertility, or industrialization. If you were to advise such a country, how would you break through the vicious cycle?

9. Compare the situations faced by a developing country today and by a country at an equivalent level of per capita income 200 years ago. Considering each of the four wheels of economic development, explain the advantages and disadvantages that to-day's developing country might experience.

10. Advanced problem for those who have also studied Chapter 36: We can extend our growth-accounting equation to include three factors and write the following equation:

$$g_Q = s_L \, g_L + s_K \, g_K + s_R \, g_R + \text{T. C.}$$

where g_Q = the growth rate of output, g_i = the growth rate of inputs (i = inputs to production = L for labor, K for capital, and R for land and other natural resources), and s_i = the contribution of each input to output growth as measured by its share of national income ($0 \leq s_i \leq 1$ and $s_L + s_K + s_R = 1$). T. C. measures technological change.

(a) In the poorest developing countries, the share of capital is close to zero, most resources are agricultural land (which is constant), and there is little technological change. Can you see why per capita output is likely to be stagnant or even to decline (i.e., $g_Q < g_L$)? Explain the Malthusian hypothesis in terms of this model.

(b) In advanced industrial economies, the share of land and resources drops to virtually zero. Why does the generalized growth-accounting equation then become identical to that given in Chapter 36? Can you explain why the Malthusian hypothesis would fail in terms of this equation?

(c) According to the neo-Malthusians, T. C. is close to zero, the available supply of natural resources is declining, and the share of resources is large and rising. Does this explain why the future of industrial societies might be bleak? What assumptions of the neo-Malthusians might you question?

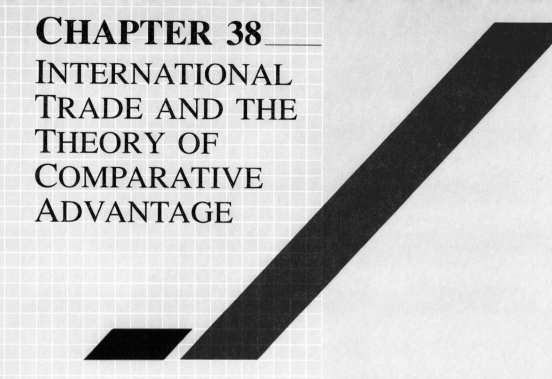

CHAPTER 38____
INTERNATIONAL TRADE AND THE THEORY OF COMPARATIVE ADVANTAGE

The benefit of international trade—a more efficient employment of the productive forces of the world.

John Stuart Mill

WE HAVE SEEN again and again how specialization increases productivity and living standards. We will now apply this principle to the field of *international trade and finance,* the process by which nations export and import goods, services, and financial capital. International trade and finance is related to some of the most controversial questions of today: Why does the United States import shoes and textiles and export food and computers? Why is American agriculture so different from Dutch farming? Why do Japan and Germany generally have large trade surpluses while Mexico and the Philippines usually run trade deficits? And how did it come to pass that the United States, which a few years ago was the world's largest creditor nation, has now become the largest debtor nation of all?

The answers to these questions are provided by a careful study of international trade and finance.

International vs. Domestic Trade

International trade is vital for one basic reason: it expands a nation's consumption possibilities. Trade allows a nation to consume more of all goods than would be possible if its borders were closed to the products of other countries.

For example, Japan sells us cameras; we sell Australians computers; Australians complete the circle by selling the Japanese coal. By specializing in its areas of greatest relative productivity, each nation ends up consuming more than it could produce alone. As a result of nations being increasingly open to trade, the world economy can move toward its production-possibility curve; trade restrictions force the world to be inside its *PPF*. This point is the simple yet elusive essence of foreign trade.

Our task in the remaining chapters centers on this essential point about trade. We start by examining the mechanics of trade, the central principle of comparative advantage, and the pros and cons of tariffs and quotas. We then see how different kinds of money (or foreign exchange) get traded to determine foreign exchange rates. And finally, we observe how the international financial system weathered a severe crisis in the 1970s, which led to a new floating exchange-rate system, only to find that severe trade imbalances emerged as a result of exchange-rate misalignments in the 1980s.

The analysis of international trade differs from the analysis of self-sufficient economies in two respects. First, it involves trade among different nations: formidable political problems sometimes arise concerning whether foreigners will be discriminated against or treated equally—this is the problem of protectionism, which will occupy us in Chapter 39.

The other new feature introduced by international trade is that different nations use different currencies. I want to pay for a Japanese car in dollars, while Toyota wants to be paid in Japanese yen. As we will see in Chapter 40, the international financial system must provide for a smooth flow of dollars, yen, and other currencies—or else risk a breakdown in trade such as was experienced in the 1930s.

Economic protectionism and a diversity of national currencies are at the heart of international economic issues today.

A. ECONOMIC BASIS FOR INTERNATIONAL TRADE

Trends in Foreign Trade

We begin by examining the patterns of international trade for the United States and for the entire trading system. Figure 38-1 is a "trade map," showing how the world would look if each country's geographical size were proportional to its share of world trade. Notice how large the United States, Western Europe, and Japan loom, while the U.S.S.R. and China appear as but tiny principalities.

An important factor is the degree of openness of an economy. An economy is *open* to the extent that it exchanges goods, services, or factors of production with the rest of the world. A useful way to measure openness is the ratio of a country's exports or imports to its GNP. What are the dimensions of trade for the United States? Figure 38-2, showing the degree of openness of the U.S. economy from 1929 to 1988, reveals that the United States has been one of the least open (or most self-sufficient) economies in the world. Many nations, particularly in Western Europe and East Asia, export and import up to 50 percent of their GNP.

The degree of openness is much higher in many U.S. industries—such as steel, textiles, and shoes—than it is for the U.S. economy as a whole. Table 38-1 shows the commodity composition of U.S. foreign trade for 1986. Two important features stand out from these data. First, we see that the United States exports surprisingly large amounts of primary commodities (such as food) and imports large quantities of sophisticated, capital-intensive manufactured goods (like automobiles or telecommunications equipment). Second, we find a great deal of two-way, or intra-industry, trade. That is, even within a particular industry (like textiles or steel), the United States both exports and imports at the same time.

What economic principles lie behind the patterns of international trade? Let us review the major reasons why nations trade with other countries rather than produce all their own goods and services.

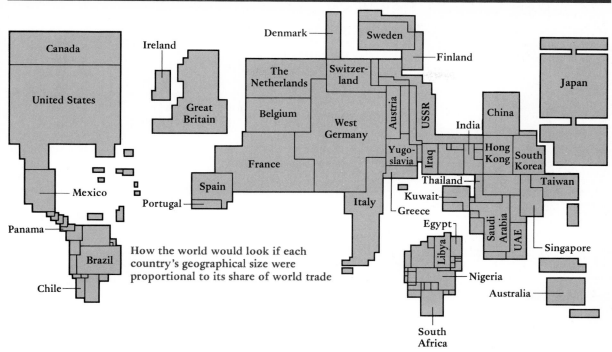

Figure 38-1 Countries of the world scaled to their international trade

In this map, the area of each country is drawn proportional to its share of total world trade in 1985. Compare the size of the advanced industrial countries with that of Africa and Asia. [Adapted from Michael Kidron and Ronald Segal, *The New State of the World Atlas* (Simon and Schuster, New York, 1987).]

THE SOURCES OF INTERNATIONAL TRADE

Nations find it beneficial to participate in international trade for many reasons: because of diversity in the conditions of production among regions, because of decreasing costs of production, and because of differences in tastes. Let us review each of these briefly before analyzing the ultimate reason for trade—comparative advantage.

Diversity in Conditions of Production

In many cases, two countries or regions will have extremely diverse conditions of production. We might consider the economies of North and South America, or of the tropics and the temperate zone. Each region has certain endowments of natural resources, land, labor, capital, and technology, and as a result the producible goods and services may differ greatly among regions.

Trade may therefore take place because of the diversity in productive possibilities among countries. As examples, look at foods and recreational activities. Countries with tropical climates will naturally specialize in sunbathing, surfing, snorkeling, coffee, and citrus fruits; these goods and services will be traded for other commodities. Countries with frostier climates are advantageous for producing goods and services like maple syrup, salmon, skiing, and reindeer meat.

Decreasing Costs

A second reason for trade arises when there are increasing returns to scale, or decreasing costs of large-

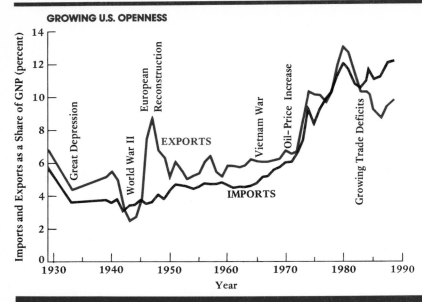

Figure 38-2 The United States has become more exposed to the winds of international competition

Like all major industrial countries, the United States has opened its borders to greater amounts of foreign trade over the last half-century. The greatest growth of the dollar value of imports came with higher oil prices and with the rise in the dollar's foreign exchange rate. In the late 1980s, imports far outdistanced exports, causing the United States to become the world's largest debtor nation. (Source: U.S. Department of Commerce.)

U.S. TRADE, 1986

COMMODITY CLASSIFICATION	SHARE OF EACH COMMODITY AS % OF TOTAL	
	EXPORTS	IMPORTS
Primary commodities:		
Oil, coal, and other fuels	4	10
Food	10	7
Other	9	3
Manufactures:		
Motor vehicles	9	18
Computers and machinery	37	26
Other	26	32
Other	5	4
Total	100	100

Table 38-1 The United States exports surprising amounts of primary goods, imports much manufactures

The composition of United States total merchandise exports and imports for recent years shows a number of surprises. The United States exports a large volume of primary commodities, especially food and coal, largely because of its ample resource base. At the same time, the United States imports many manufactures, like cars and cameras, even though manufacturing is highly capital-intensive. (Source: U.S. Bureau of the Census.)

scale production. Recall from earlier chapters that many manufacturing processes enjoy economies of scale; that is, they tend to have lower average costs of production as the volume of output expands. And what better way to expand production than to sell output in the vast global marketplace?

How might the scenario run? Suppose that a particular country gets a head start in a given sector. It might be Britain in textiles in the early 1800s, the United States in telecommunications in the late 1800s, or Japan in consumer electronics in the 1980s. Once the country begins to produce and export the product, the economies of scale give it a significant cost and technological advantage over other countries, so it can outcompete its foreign rivals. In the extreme, countries would all specialize in different products: all the economies of mass production would be realized as each country produced and exported the goods in which it had a head start and imported those goods for which foreigners were further down the cost curves.

The example of decreasing cost helps explain the important phenomenon of extensive intra-industry trade shown in Table 38-1 above. Why is it that the United States both imports and exports automobiles? The reason is that the United States has exploited the economies of scale in large-car production and is specialized there, while Japan enjoys a cost advantage in small cars and tends to specialize and export in that part of the market. Similar patterns of specialization are seen in computers, steelmaking, textiles, and many other manufactured products.

Differences in Tastes

Yet a third cause of trade lies in preferences. Even if the conditions of production were identical in all regions, countries might engage in trade if their tastes for goods were different.

For example, suppose that Norway and Sweden produce fish from the sea and meat from the land in about the same amounts, but the Swedes have a great fondness for meat while the Norwegians are partial to fish. In this case, a mutually beneficial export of meat from Norway and fish from Sweden would take place. Both countries would gain from this trade; the sum of human happiness is increased, just as when Jack Sprat trades fat meat for his wife's lean.

THE PRINCIPLE OF COMPARATIVE ADVANTAGE

Uncommon Sense

The three reasons for trade listed above provide the common-sense reasons for international trade. But there is a deeper principle underlying *all* trade—in a family, within a nation, and among nations—that goes beyond common sense. The theory, called the principle of **comparative advantage,** holds that a country will trade with other regions even if it is absolutely more efficient or more inefficient in the production of every good.

Say that the United States has higher output per worker (or per unit of input) than the rest of the world in computers and steel. But suppose the United States is relatively more efficient in computers than it is in steel—for example, U.S. productivity might be 50 percent higher than other countries in computers and 10 percent higher in steel. In this case, it would benefit the United States to export that good in which it is relatively more efficient (computers) and import that good in which it is relatively less efficient (steel).

Or consider a poor country like India. How could impoverished India, whose productivity per worker is but a fraction of that of advanced countries, hope to export any of its textiles or wheat? Surprisingly, according to the doctrine of comparative advantage, India can and will trade with countries that are absolutely more efficient. How so? By exporting the goods in which it is relatively more efficient (like wheat and textiles) and importing the goods in which it is relatively less efficient (like turbines and super-computers).

The principle of comparative advantage holds that each country will specialize in the production and export of those goods that it can produce at relatively low cost (in which it is relatively more efficient than other countries); conversely, each country will import those goods which it produces at relatively high cost (in which it is relatively less efficient than other countries).

This simple principle provides the unshakable basis for international trade. It is the task of the balance of this section to explain the logic of the principle of comparative advantage.

The Logic of Comparative Advantage

The rapid growth in the volume of international trade leads us to ask why countries specialize in the particular commodities that they do. All countries can produce wheat, textiles, steel, and aircraft, yet the United States tends to specialize in the production and export of wheat and aircraft while importing a substantial fraction of its textiles and steel. What economic forces lie behind this international division of labor? Moreover, what are the economic gains and losses that flow from opening a nation's borders to international trade? Would countries be better off if they put tariffs and quotas on their imports, or even if they completely closed their borders to all trade?

The key to answering these questions lies in the principle of comparative advantage. We begin with a simple example of specialization among people and then move to the more general case of specialization and comparative advantage among nations.

Lawyers and Secretaries A traditional way to explain comparative advantage is the case of the best lawyer in town who is also the best typist in town. How should the lawyer spend her time? Should she write and type her own legal briefs? Or should she specialize in law and leave the typing to her secretary? Clearly, the lawyer should concentrate on legal activities, where her *relative* or *comparative* skills are most effectively used, even though she has *absolutely* greater skills in both typing and legal work.

Or look at it from the secretary's point of view. He is a fine typist, but to undertake legal research and write a brief would be laborious at best and impossible at worst. He is *absolutely* less efficient than the lawyer in both legal research and in typing, but he is *relatively* or *comparatively* more efficient in typing.

The upshot of this analysis is that the most efficient outcome is for the lawyer to specialize in legal work and the secretary to concentrate on typing. The keys to this conclusion are the terms "absolute" and "relative." The most efficient and productive pattern of specialization is that people or nations should concentrate on activities in which they are relatively or comparatively more efficient than others; this efficient pattern of specialization may imply that people or nations specialize in areas in which they are absolutely less efficient than others. And even though individual people or countries may be absolutely less or more efficient than all other people and countries, each and every person or country will have a definite comparative advantage in some goods and a definite comparative disadvantage in other goods.

Ricardo's Analysis of Comparative Advantage

Let us illustrate the fundamental principles of international trade by considering America and Europe of a century ago. In America, land and natural resources were then very plentiful relative to labor and capital. But in Europe, people and capital were plentiful relative to land.

What will be the patterns of trade in this case? If labor (or resources more generally) is absolutely more productive in America than in Europe, does this mean that America will import nothing? And is it economically wise for Europe to impose a protective tariff to prevent imports from entering its markets?

These questions were first answered by the English economist David Ricardo in 1817. Ricardo supplied a beautiful proof that international specialization benefits a nation, calling the result the law of comparative advantage.

For simplicity, Ricardo worked with only two countries and only two goods, and he chose to measure all costs in terms of labor-hours. We shall follow his lead here, analyzing food and clothing for Europe and America.[1]

Table 38-2 portrays the principle of comparative advantage. In America a unit of food costs 1 hour of labor and a unit of clothing costs 2 hours of labor. In Europe the cost is 3 hours of labor for food and 4 hours of labor for clothing. We see that America has *absolute advantage* in both goods, for it can produce them with greater absolute efficiency than can Eu-

---

[1]The analysis of comparative advantage with many countries and many commodities is presented later in this chapter.

AMERICAN AND EUROPEAN LABOR REQUIREMENTS FOR PRODUCTION

PRODUCT	NECESSARY LABOR	
	IN AMERICA	IN EUROPE
1 unit of food	1 labor-hr.	3 labor-hr.
1 unit of clothing	2 labor-hr.	4 labor-hr.

Table 38-2   Comparative advantage depends only on relative costs

In a hypothetical example, America has lower labor costs in both food and clothing. American labor productivity is between 2 and 3 times Europe's (twice in clothing, thrice in food). Yet it benefits both regions to trade with each other.

rope. However, America has *comparative advantage* in food, while Europe has comparative advantage in clothing, because food is relatively inexpensive in America while clothing is relatively less expensive in Europe.

From these facts, Ricardo proved that both countries will benefit if they specialize in their areas of comparative advantage—that is, if America specializes in the production of food while Europe specializes in the production of clothing. In this situation, America will export food to pay for European clothing while Europe exports clothing to pay for American food.

To analyze the effects of trade and the benefits of specializing in areas of comparative advantage, we must measure carefully the amounts of food and clothing that will be produced and consumed in each country *(a)* if there is no international trade and *(b)* if there is free trade with each country specializing in its area of comparative advantage.

Before Trade Start by examining what occurs in the absence of any international trade, say because all trade is illegal or because of a prohibitive tariff. Table 38-2 shows the real wage of the American worker for an hour's work as 1 unit of food or $\frac{1}{2}$ unit of clothing. The European worker is less well off in a no-trade position, getting only $\frac{1}{3}$ unit of food or $\frac{1}{4}$ unit of clothing per hour of work.

Clearly, if competition prevails in each isolated region, the prices of food and clothing will be different in the two places because of the difference in production costs. In America, clothing will be 2 times as expensive as food because it takes twice as much labor to produce a unit of clothing as a unit of food. In Europe, clothing will be only $\frac{4}{3}$ as expensive as food.

After Trade Now allow free trade and repeal all tariffs, and, for simplicity, assume that there are no transportation costs. In this case, goods will flow from low-price regions to high-price regions. Indeed, with no transportation costs, the prices of clothing and food in the two regions must be equalized, just as the water in two connecting pipes must come to a common level once you remove the barrier between them.

What is the flow of goods when trade is opened up? When people inspect the prices of goods in different regions, they will find that clothing is relatively more expensive in America and food is relatively more expensive in Europe. Firms will then buy where goods are cheap and sell where they are expensive. Given these relative prices, this means that food will soon be shipped from America to Europe and clothing from Europe to America.

As European clothing penetrates the American market, American clothiers will find prices falling and profits shrinking, and they will begin to shut down their factories. The opposite will occur in Europe. European farmers will find that the prices of foodstuffs begin to fall when American products hit the European markets; they will suffer losses, some will go bankrupt, and resources will be withdrawn from farming.

After all the adjustments to international trade have taken place, what will we find? We will see that the prices of clothing and food are equalized in Europe and America. At what level will prices equalize? We cannot know the exact level of prices without further information, but we do know that the relative prices of food and clothing must lie somewhere in between the European price ratio (which is $\frac{3}{4}$ for the ratio of food to clothing prices) and the American price ratio (which is $\frac{1}{2}$). Let us say that the final price ratio is $\frac{2}{3}$ (the exact reasoning will be explained in the next section), so that 2 units of clothing trade for 3 units of food. For simplicity, say we measure prices in American dollars; we have then found that under free trade the price of food is $2 per unit while the price of clothing is $3 per unit.

Moreover, the regions have shifted their productive activities; America has withdrawn resources from clothing and invested in food while Europe has contracted its farm sector and expanded its clothing manufacture. In short, under free trade, countries shift their production toward their areas of comparative advantage.

The Economic Gains from Trade

What are the economic effects of opening up the two regions to international trade? America as a whole benefits from the fact that imported clothing costs less than clothing produced at home. Likewise, Europe benefits from specializing in clothing and getting food more cheaply by importing than it can by domestic production.

We can most easily reckon the gains from trade by calculating the effect of trade upon the real wages of workers. Real wages are measured by the amount of goods and services that a worker can buy with an hour's pay. By examining Table 38-2, we can see that the real wages after trade will be greater than the real wages before trade for workers in both Europe *and* America. For simplicity, assume that each worker buys 1 unit of clothing and 1 unit of food. Before trade, this bundle of consumer goods costs an American worker 3 hours of work and a European worker 7 hours of work.

After trade has opened up, recall that the price of clothing is $3 per unit while the price of food is $2 per unit. An American worker must still work 1 hour to buy a unit of food; but at the price ratio of 2 to 3, the American worker need work only $1\frac{1}{2}$ hours to produce enough to buy 1 unit of European clothing. Therefore the bundle of goods costs the American worker $2\frac{1}{2}$ hours of work when trade is allowed—this represents an increase of $16\frac{2}{3}$ percent in the real wage of the American worker.

For European workers, a unit of clothing will still cost 4 hours of labor in a free-trade situation, for clothing is domestically produced. To obtain a unit of

food, however, the European worker need only produce $\frac{2}{3}$ of a unit of clothing (which requires $\frac{2}{3} \times 4$ hours of labor) and then trade that $\frac{2}{3}$ unit for 1 unit of American food. The total European labor needed to obtain the bundle of consumption is then $4 + 2\frac{2}{3} = 6\frac{2}{3}$, which represents an increase in real wages of about 5 percent over the no-trade situation.

In summary, when trade has opened up, and when each country concentrates on its area of comparative advantage, everyone is better off. Workers in each region can obtain a larger quantity of consumer goods for the same amount of work when people specialize in the areas of comparative advantage and trade their own production for goods in which they have a relative disadvantage. When borders are opened to international trade, the national income of each and every trading country rises.

Effects of Tariffs and Quotas

We have analyzed the cases of free trade and no trade. What are the impacts of **tariffs** (which are taxes levied on imports) and **quotas** (which are quantitative restrictions on imports)?

One effect of restrictions on foreign trade is easily seen from our discussion up to this point. We know that foreign trade benefits a nation relative to a no-trade situation. It follows therefore that a prohibitive tariff or quota (that is, one that is stringent enough to shut off all foreign trade) will unambiguously hurt a country.

More generally, we will see below that economic protectionism (meaning that a country restricts imports to ''protect'' domestic industries) will lower incomes. This, then, is the second major finding of the economics of international trade:

An ill-designed tariff or quota, far from helping consumers in a country, will instead reduce their real incomes by making imports expensive and by making the whole world less productive. Countries lose from protectionism because reduced international trade eliminates the efficiency inherent in specialization and division of labor.

These two color-highlighted principles are the foundation of the economic analysis of international trade.

EXTENSIONS TO MANY COMMODITIES AND COUNTRIES

The world of international trade consists of more than two countries and two commodities. What happens when more realistic situations are involved? As we will see, the conclusions are essentially unchanged.

Many Commodities

First note that up to now we've simplified the analysis by considering only two commodities, food and clothing. In reality, exchange involves thousands of goods, but the advantages of trade are not diluted when the number of goods is multiplied.

When two countries produce many commodities at constant costs, they can be arranged in order according to their comparative advantage or cost. For example, the commodities might be wheat, aircraft, computers, automobiles, wine, and shoes—all arranged in the comparative-advantage sequence shown in Figure 38-3. This means that of all commodities, wheat costs are lowest in America relative to Europe. Europe has its greatest comparative advantage in shoes, while its advantage in wine is not quite so great. And so forth.

From the beginning we can be virtually sure of one thing. The introduction of trade will cause America to produce and export wheat, and assuredly Europe will produce and export shoes. But where will the dividing line fall? Between automobiles and computers? Or will America produce automobiles and Europe confine itself to wine and shoes? Or will the dividing line fall on one of the commodities rather than between them—so that, say, automobiles might be produced in both places?

You will not be surprised to find that the answer depends upon the comparative strength of international demands for the different goods. We can think of the commodities as beads arranged on a string according to their comparative advantage; the strength of supply and demand will determine where the dividing line between American and European production will fall. An increased demand for aircraft and wheat, for example, would tend to turn the prices in the direction of America and make us so prosperous that it no longer benefits us to continue to produce our own wine.

Many Countries

So much for the complications introduced by many commodities. What about the case of many countries? Introducing many countries need not change our analysis. As far as a single country is concerned, all the other nations with whom it trades can be lumped together into one group as "the rest of the world." The advantages of trade have no special relationship to national boundaries. The principles already developed apply between groups of countries and, indeed, between regions within the same country. In fact, they are just as applicable to trade between our northern and southern states as to trade between the United States and Canada.

Triangular and Multilateral Trade

With many countries brought into the picture, America will find it beneficial to engage in *triangular* or *multilateral trade*. Each country trades with a multitude of other countries, and generally *bilateral* (or two-country) trade is unbalanced.

A simple example of this comes in the triangular trade flows illustrated in Figure 38-4, in which the

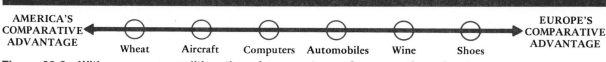

AMERICA'S COMPARATIVE ADVANTAGE ←— ○ Wheat   ○ Aircraft   ○ Computers   ○ Automobiles   ○ Wine   ○ Shoes —→ EUROPE'S COMPARATIVE ADVANTAGE

Figure 38-3   With many commodities, there is a spectrum of comparative advantages

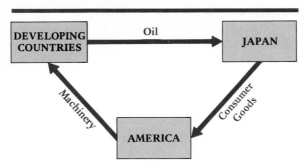

Figure 38-4 Triangular trade benefits all

Advantages of multilateral trade would be much reduced if bilateral balancing were required.

arrows show the direction of exports. America buys consumer goods from Japan, Japan buys oil and primary commodities from developing countries, and developing countries buy machinery and computers from America. In reality, trade patterns are even more complex than this triangular example.

The multilateral nature of trade should give caution to those who argue for bilateral balance between particular countries, as was the case in recent proposals in the United States. What would happen if all nations signed bilateral trade agreements that balanced trade between each pair of countries? Trade would be sharply curbed; imports would balance exports, but at the level of whichever was the smaller. The gains from trade would be severely reduced.

This completes our introductory analysis of the economic reasons for international trade. In the next section we provide a more systematic study of the economics of trade using production-possibility frontiers.

GRAPHICAL ANALYSIS OF COMPARATIVE ADVANTAGE[2]

Having presented the essence of comparative advantage, we now further develop the analysis with the help of the production-possibility frontier (PPF). We continue the numerical example based upon labor

[2]This section's advanced material on comparative advantage may be omitted in short courses.

costs, but the theory is equally valid in a competitive world with many different inputs. With the help of this analysis, we can see vividly how trade increases a nation's consumption possibilities.

America without Trade

Chapter 2 introduced the PPF, which indicates the combinations of commodities that can be produced with a society's given resources and technology. Using the simple production data shown in Table 38-2, and assuming that both Europe and America have 600 units of labor, we can easily derive each region's PPF. The table attached to Figure 38-5 shows the possible levels of food and clothing that America can produce with its inputs and technology. Figure 38-5 plots the production possibilities; the red line DA shows America's PPF. The PPF has a slope of $-\frac{1}{2}$, for this represents the terms on which food and clothing can be substituted in production; in competitive markets, the price ratio of food to clothing will also be one-half.

So far we have only been discussing production. However, if America is isolated from all international trade, then what it can produce is also what it can consume. Given the incomes and demands in the marketplace, point B in Figure 38-5 marks America's production and consumption in the absence of trade. Without trade, America produces and consumes 400 units of food and 100 units of clothing.

We can do exactly the same thing for Europe as we did for America. The only difference is that Europe's PPF will look different from America's because Europe's efficiencies in producing food and clothing are different. Europe's price ratio is $\frac{3}{4}$, reflecting Europe's relative productivity in food and clothing. (Question 3 at the end of this chapter asks you to construct Figure 38-5 and its accompanying table for Europe.)

Opening Up to Trade

Now admit the possibility of trade between the two regions. Food can be exchanged for clothing at some price ratio, or at some **terms of trade,** which denote the ratio of export prices to import prices. To indicate the trading possibilities, we put the two PPFs to-

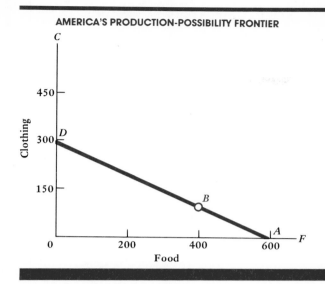

AMERICA'S PRODUCTION-POSSIBILITY FRONTIER

AMERICA'S PRODUCTION-POSSIBILITY SCHEDULE *(1 to 2 constant-cost ratio)*

POSSIBILITIES	FOOD (units)	CLOTHING (units)
A	600	0
B	400	100
C	200	200
D	0	300

Figure 38-5   Table and graph give American production data

The constant-cost line *DA* represents America's domestic production-possibility frontier. America will produce and consume at *B* in the absence of trade.

gether in Figure 38-6, p. 908. America's red *PPF* shows its domestic production possibilities, while Europe's black *PPF* shows the terms on which it can domestically substitute food and clothing. Note that Europe's *PPF* is drawn closer to the origin than America's. Why? Because Europe has lower productivities in both industries; it has an absolute disadvantage in the production of both food and clothing.

However, Europe need not be discouraged by its absolute disadvantage, for it is the difference in *relative* productivities or *comparative* advantage that makes trade beneficial. The gains from trade are illustrated by the outer lines in Figure 38-6. If America could trade at Europe's relative prices, it could produce 600 units of food and move northwest along the outer black line in Figure 38-6(*a*)—where the black line represents the price ratio or terms of trade that are generated by Europe's *PPF*. Similarly, if Europe could trade with America and not affect America's relative prices, then Europe could specialize in clothing and move southeast along the red line in Figure 38-6(*b*)—where the red line is America's pre-trade price ratio.[3]

[3]This discussion shows why little countries have the most to gain from international trade: they affect world prices the least and therefore can trade at world prices very different from domestic prices. Why might large countries gain least from international trade?

Equilibrium Price Ratio Once trade opens up, some set of prices must reign in the world marketplace. What will be the final prices at which the regions trade food and clothing? To dramatize this question, let us suppose that an auctioneer stands in mid-ocean and attempts to find the prices that balance supply and demand. That is, he wants to find the food and clothing prices at which the offers of food and clothing are exactly equal. He does this by calling out prices and adjusting them when imbalances occur. When he arrives at the equilibrium price level, he raps his gavel and shouts, "Going, going, gone!"

What will be the final prices? Although we can determine what the price range will be, without further information we cannot specify the exact price ratio. We can say at the outset, however, that the prices must lie somewhere between the prices of the two regions. That is, we know that the relative price of food and clothing must lie somewhere in the region $[\frac{1}{2}, \frac{3}{4}]$.

The final price ratio will depend upon the relative demands for food and clothing. If food is very much in demand, then the food price would be relatively high. If food demand were so high that Europe produced food, then the price ratio would be at Europe's relative prices of $\frac{3}{4}$. On the other hand, if clothing demand were relatively high, then the relative price of

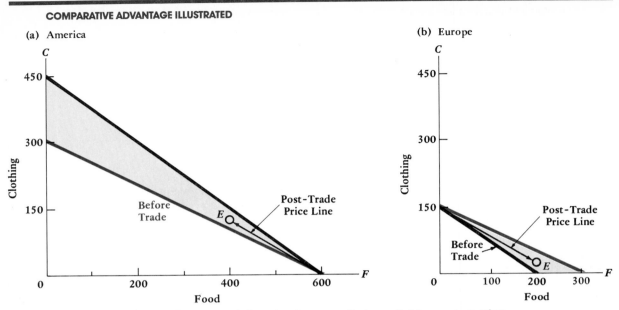

Figure 38-6 By trade, both Europe and America improve their available consumption

If no trade is allowed, each country must be satisfied with its own production. It is therefore limited to its production-possibility curve, shown for each country as the line marked "Before Trade." After borders are opened and competition equalizes relative prices of the two goods, the relative price line will be given by the arrow. It lies somewhere between the red price line (America's prices before trade) and the black price line (Europe's prices before trade).

If each region is faced with prices given by the arrows, can you see why its consumption possibilities must improve?

clothing would rise; if clothing demand were so strong that America produced clothing, then the terms of trade would be according to America's price ratio of $\frac{1}{2}$. If countries specialize completely in the area of their comparative advantage, with Europe producing only clothing and America producing only food, then the price ratio will lie somewhere between $\frac{1}{2}$ and $\frac{3}{4}$. The exact ratio will depend on the strength of demand.[4]

For our example, we assume that the levels of demand are such that the final price ratio is $\frac{2}{3}$, with 3 units of food selling for 2 units of clothing. With this price ratio, each country can then specialize—America in food and Europe in clothing—and export

some of its production to pay for imports at the world price ratio of $\frac{2}{3}$.

Figure 38-6 illustrates how trade will take place. Each country will face a *consumption-possibility curve* according to which it can produce, trade, and consume. This consumption-possibility curve begins at a country's best point of specialization and then runs out at the world price ratio of $\frac{2}{3}$. Figure 38-6(a) shows America's consumption possibilities as a thin black arrow with slope of minus $\frac{2}{3}$ coming out of its best production point at 600 units of food and no clothing. Similarly, Europe's post-trade consumption possibilities are shown in Figure 38-6(b) by the black arrow running southeast from its point of best specialization with a slope of minus $\frac{2}{3}$.

The final outcome is shown by the points E in Figure 38-6. At this free-trade equilibrium, Europe spe-

---

[4]Question 14 at the end of this chapter shows how relative supplies and demands interact to determine the final price ratio.

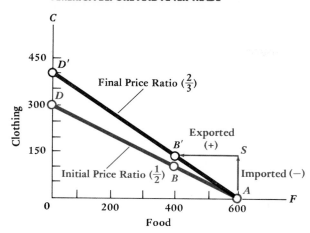

Figure 38-7   Free trade expands consumption options of America

The red line *DA* represents America's domestic production-possibility curve; the black line *D'A*, its new consumption-possibility curve when it is able to trade freely at the price ratio 2/3 and in consequence has decided to specialize completely in the production of food (at *A*). The red arrows from *S* to *B'* and *A* to *S* show the amounts exported (+) and imported (−) by America. As a result of free trade, America ends up at *B'* with more of both goods available than before trade at *B*.

cializes in producing clothing and America specializes in producing food. Europe exports $133\frac{1}{3}$ units of clothing for 200 units of America's food. Both regions are able to consume more than they would produce alone; both regions have benefited from international trade.

Figure 38-7 illustrates the benefits of trade for America. The red inner line shows the *PPF,* while the black outer line shows the consumption possibilities at world prices of $\frac{2}{3}$. The red arrows show the amounts exported and imported. America ends up at the point *B'*. By trading it can now move onto the black line *D'A* just as if a fruitful invention had been made and pushed out its *PPF*.

The lessons of this analysis are summarized in Figure 38-8. This figure shows the *world* production-possibility frontier. How is the world *PPF* obtained? This represents the maximum output that can be ob-

tained from the world's resources when goods are produced in the most efficient manner, that is, with the most efficient division of labor and regional specialization.

The world *PPF* is built up from the two national *PPF*s (see Fig. 38-6) by determining the maximum level of world output that can be obtained from the individual country *PPF*s. For example, the maximum quantity of food that can be produced (with no clothing production) is seen in Figure 38-6 to be 600 units in America and 200 units in Europe, for a world maximum of 800 units. This same point (800 food, 0 clothing) is then plotted in the world *PPF* in Figure 38-8. Additionally, we can plot the point (0 food, 450 clothing) in the world *PPF* by inspection of the national *PPF*s. All the individual points in between can be constructed by a careful calculation of the maximum world outputs that can be produced if the two regions are efficiently specializing in the two goods.

Before opening up borders to trade, the world is at

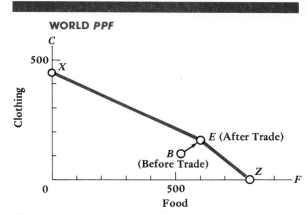

Figure 38-8   Free trade allows world to move to its production-possibility frontier

We here show the effect of free trade from the viewpoint of the world as a whole.

Before trade is allowed, each region is on its own national *PPF.* Without trade, regions are producing goods in which they are relatively inefficient, so the world is *inside* the world *PPF,* shown as the red line *XEZ.*

Free trade allows each region to specialize in the goods in which it has comparative advantage. As a result of the specialization, the world as a whole moves out to point *E,* which is on the world *PPF.*

point *B*. This is an inefficient point—inside the world *PPF*—because regions have different levels of *relative* efficiency in different goods.

After opening the borders to trade, the world moves out to point *E*, the free-trade equilibrium. At *E*, countries are specializing in areas of comparative advantage. With free trade in competitive markets, the world is on the outer limit of its production-possibility frontier.

Qualifications and Conclusions

We have now completed our analysis of the elegant theory of comparative advantage. Its conclusions apply for any number of countries and commodities; advanced books show how it can be generalized to handle many inputs instead of labor alone and that it applies when there are changing factor proportions and diminishing returns.

But having understood this theory, we must also recognize its limitations. The major defect lies in its classical assumptions, for it assumes a smoothly working macroeconomic setting, with rapidly adjusting prices and wages and no involuntary unemployment. Would the theory still hold if autoworkers, laid off when the share of Japanese cars sold in the American market rises rapidly, cannot easily find new jobs? What if an overvalued foreign exchange rate on the dollar leads to a loss of 2 million manufacturing jobs that are not transferred to other sectors? In such cases, trade might well push a nation *inside* its *PPF* as un-

employment rose and GNP fell, and the gains from trade along with the theory of comparative advantage would fail.

Given this reservation, there can be little wonder that the theory of comparative advantage sells at a big discount during periods of major macroeconomic dislocations. During the Great Depression of the 1930s, as unemployment soared and real outputs fell, all nations built high tariff walls at their borders and the volume of foreign trade shrank sharply. Comparative advantage gained prestige in the 1950s and 1960s, as economies prospered and lower trade barriers promoted economic integration among the world's industrial nations. But the theory was again eclipsed in the 1980s as a high dollar exchange rate and protectionism in many indebted countries, along with mounting trade deficits and stagnant manufacturing, crippled the U.S. economy. These epochs of history are an apt reminder that the classical theory of comparative advantage retains its social relevance only when exchange rates, prices, and wages are at appropriate levels and when macroeconomic policies banish major business cycles or trade dislocations from the economic scene.

Oversimplified as it is, the theory of comparative advantage provides a most important glimpse of truth. Economics has uncovered few deeper principles. A nation that neglects comparative advantage may pay a heavy price in terms of living standards and economic growth.

B. THE BALANCE OF INTERNATIONAL PAYMENTS

BALANCE-OF-PAYMENTS ACCOUNTS

Almost daily we can read about the U.S. trade balance, the growing indebtedness of the United States, or the need for balance-of-payments adjustments in Latin American countries. In order to master the elements of international trade, a general understanding of the nature of balance-of-payments accounting is essential.

Up to now we have treated international trade as if

nations simply barter goods—oil for aircraft or bananas for computers. In fact, international exchange, like domestic exchange, takes place through the medium of money, and the monetary flows into and out of a country are measured in a nation's balance of payments.

What exactly do we mean by a country's **balance of international payments**? These are the accounting statements that measure all the economic flows coming into and going out of a country—they form an overall measure of the flows of goods, services, and capital between a country and the rest of the world.

For the United States, the U.S. Department of Commerce keeps records, makes official estimates of all international transactions, and publishes the U.S. balance-of-payments statistics. These include data on merchandise exports and imports, money lent or borrowed abroad, tourist expenditures, interest and dividends paid or received, and so forth.

The balance of international payments is listed in four sections:

I.   Current account
     Private:
          Merchandise (or "trade balance")
          Invisible or service items (travel, transportation, income on investments, and other)
     Governmental exports and grants

II. Capital account
     Private
     Government

III. Statistical discrepancy

IV. Official settlements

We will now explain each of these major components of the balance of payments.

Debits and Credits

Like other accounts, balance-of-payments accounts record pluses and minuses. Here a plus item is called a *credit*, while a negative is called a *debit*.

In general, exports are **credits** and imports are **debits.** A good rule to use in deciding how any item should be treated is to ask whether it earns foreign currencies for the country. *Foreign currencies* are other countries' monies. For the United States, foreign currencies include German marks, Mexican pesos, and Japanese yen.

Remember the following rule:

Is an item like one of our exports providing us with more foreign currencies? Such an export-type item is called a "credit item." Or is the item like one of our imports, causing us to use up our stock of foreign currencies? Such an import-type item is called a "debit item."

How is the U.S. import of a Toyota recorded? It is clearly a debit, for it depletes our stock of Japanese yen. Or, how shall we treat interest and dividend income on investments received by Americans from abroad? Clearly, they are credit items like exports because they provide us with foreign currencies. Similarly, when we pay interest and dividends to foreigners this is a debit item—like imports, such items use up our foreign currencies.

Details of the Balance of Payments

Balance on Current Account   The totality of items under section I is usually referred to as the *balance on current account*. This important magnitude summarizes the difference between our total exports of goods and services and our total imports of them. It is almost identical to the "net exports" discussed in Chapter 6's national accounts.

Centuries ago, writers concentrated on the *trade balance,* which consists of merchandise imports or exports. The composition of merchandise imports and exports was shown in Table 38-1 at the beginning of this chapter; it consists mainly of primary commodities (like food and fuels) and manufactured goods. In an earlier era, the mercantilists strove for a trade surplus (where exports exceed imports), calling this a "favorable balance of trade." They hoped to avoid an "unfavorable trade balance," by which they meant a trade deficit (where imports exceed exports). This choice of terms has carried over to today as many nations seek trade surpluses; economics teaches, however, that trade deficits are sometimes economically advantageous for countries that need an infusion of foreign capital.

In addition to the trade balance, we must not forget the increasing role played by *services* or "invisibles." These consist of such items as shipping, financial services, and foreign travel. The service component was an important positive or credit item for the United States from World War II until the 1980s, although the U.S. international debt position has eroded this surplus item in the late 1980s.

U.S. BALANCE OF PAYMENTS, 1987 *(in billions of dollars)*

SECTION	(a) ITEMS	(b) CREDITS (+)	(c) DEBITS (−)	(d) NET CREDITS (+) OR DEBITS (−)
I.	**Current account**			
	1. Merchandise trade balance	$250	−$410	−$160
	2. Services, transfers, other			6
	3. **Balance on current account**			−154
II.	**Capital account**			
	[lending (−) or borrowing (+)]			
	4. Capital flows	211	−85	
	5. **Balance on capital account**			126
III.	**Statistical discrepancy**			19
	6. **Total needing to be offset**			−9
	(line 3 + line 5 + statistical discrepancy)			
IV.	**Official settlements**			
	7. **Official settlements balance**			9
	(net change in U.S. official assets)			
	8. **Formal overall net total**			0

Table 38-3   By definition, current account plus capital account plus statistical discrepancy must be offset by official government settlements
(Source: Adapted from U.S. Department of Commerce.)

Table 38-3 presents helpful official data on the balance of international payments of the United States for 1987. Note its four main divisions: current and capital accounts, statistical discrepancy, and official settlement items. Each row is numbered to make reference easy. Then, after each item has been listed by name in column (a), we list in column (b) the credits. In column (c), we list the debits. In column (d) are the net credits or debits; it shows a credit if the item added to our stock of foreign currencies or a debit if, on balance, it subtracted from our foreign currency supply.

Thus, in 1987 our merchandise exports gave us credits of $250 billion. But our merchandise imports gave us debits of $410 billion. The *net* difference between credits and debits was a debit of $160 billion. This "trade deficit" is listed in column (d), on the first row. (Be sure you know why the algebraic sign is shown as − rather than as +.)

Table 38-3 shows that services or invisible items plus transfers were slightly in surplus. Our current account deficit was thus $154 billion for 1987.

Capital Account We have now completed analysis of the current account. But how did the United States "finance" its $154 billion current account deficit in 1987? The United States must have either borrowed or run down its assets. For it is definitional that what you buy you must either pay for or owe for. And this fact of double-entry bookkeeping means that the balance of international payments as a whole must by definition show a final zero balance.

So turn now to capital movements: these are loans private citizens or governments make to or receive from foreign private citizens or governments. Such capital movements occur, for example, when a Japanese pension fund buys U.S. government securities or when an American buys stock in a British firm.

It is easy to decide which are credit and which are debit items in the capital account if you use the following rule: Always think of the United States as exporting and importing stocks, bonds, or other securities—or, for short, exporting and importing IOUs in return for foreign currencies. Then you can treat these exports and imports like any other exports and imports. When we borrow abroad to finance a current account deficit, we are sending IOUs (like Treasury bills) abroad and gaining foreign currencies. Is this a credit or a debit? Clearly this transaction gives rise to a credit.

Similarly, if our banks lend abroad to finance a steel mill in Brazil, this means the U.S. banks are importing IOUs from Brazilians and losing foreign currencies; this is clearly a debit item.

Line 5 shows that in 1987 the United States was a net *borrower:* we were doing more borrowing abroad than foreigners were doing here. We were the net exporters of IOUs in the amount of $126 billion.

Part III shows that there was a modest statistical discrepancy (the net sum of all unrecorded transactions) accounting for $19 billion.

Adding all current and capital account items to the statistical discrepancy, we find a net deficit of $9 billion.

Official Settlements When the United States was on the gold standard and the government followed a virtual hands-off or laissez-faire policy, any net deficit on line 6 had to be settled by the nation's exporting gold. Now that countries are no longer on the gold standard, they must provide the funds (in domestic or foreign currencies) to balance their books. These balancing flows provided by governments are called "official settlements." The most common way of providing official settlements today is for countries to buy or sell U.S. government securities. In 1987, you can see in line 7 that there was a small subtraction ($9 billion) from U.S. official assets. In other years, official settlements have run in the tens of billions of dollars.

This summarizes the essentials of balance-of-payments accounting. We turn next to a broad survey of how nations' balance-of-payments positions develop over time.

STAGES OF THE BALANCE OF PAYMENTS

A review of the economic history of advanced industrial countries finds that they go through four stages in their balance of payments as they grow from a young debtor to a mature creditor. This sequence is found, with variations depending upon their particular histories, in the advanced countries of North America, Europe, and Southeast Asia. We can illustrate the stages by recounting briefly the history of the balance of payments of the United States.

■ *Young and growing debtor nation.* From the Revolutionary War until after the Civil War, we imported on current account more than we exported. Europe lent us the difference in order to build up our capital stock. We were a typical young and growing debtor nation.

■ *Mature debtor nation.* From about 1873 to 1914, the U.S. balance of trade moved into surplus. But growth of the dividends and interest that we had to pay abroad on our past borrowing kept our current account more or less in balance. Capital movements were also nearly in balance as our lending just offset our borrowing.

■ *New creditor nation.* During World War I, we expanded our exports tremendously. American citizens and our government lent money to allies England and France for war equipment and postwar relief needs. We emerged from the war a creditor nation.

■ *Mature creditor nation.* In the fourth stage, earnings on foreign capital and investments provided a large surplus on invisibles (running as high as $40 billion per year in the early 1980s); often this was matched by a deficit on visibles or merchandise trade.

This pattern was followed by the United States through the early 1980s. Countries like Japan and West Germany today play the role of mature creditor nations as they enjoy large current account surpluses which they in turn invest abroad.

The United States, surprisingly, has moved out of the mature creditor nation stage, as is shown in the balance-of-payments data in Table 38-3. We have now once again become a debtor nation, borrowing large amounts from stage-four countries. The difference between this new situation and stage one is that the borrowings are now for consumption rather than for investment.

Some economists wonder whether the United States has entered a fifth stage, that of *senile debtor nation*. They note that the macroeconomic policy mix of tight money and high government deficits of the 1980s has driven the national savings rate (equal to total private saving, foreign and domestic, divided by NNP) from 8 percent to 2 percent over the last decade. The United States is now unable to generate a volume of saving sufficient to provide its capital requirements and must turn to thriftier people abroad to do our saving for us. The counterpart of American dissaving is that foreigners, particularly Japanese investors, are purchasing substantial American assets for their portfolios.

Is this new stage of the U.S. balance of payments a transient period, or does it mark the beginning of a long period of "structural" trade deficits that will last for decades to come? No one can answer this question with certainty. As long as foreign countries continue to desire to accumulate American investments, the pattern of large capital inflows and current account deficits can continue. But eventually, foreign portfolios are likely to become saturated with U.S. investments. At that point, if macroeconomic policies and savings patterns in the United States have not changed, changes in trade flows and exchange rates will put an end to the rapid buildup of foreign indebtedness.

■   ■   ■

We have now reviewed the principles underpinning the trade of nations and have seen how this trade is recorded in the balance of payments. But we might ask, Do the actual trading flows and practices of nations recorded in balance-of-payments accounts actually reflect nations' attempts to exploit their comparative advantages? Or are trade policies a product of superstition and political compromises between warring political factions? Why do countries so often interfere with free trade? Is there a sound intellectual basis for protectionism? It is to these questions that we turn in the next chapter.

SUMMARY

A. Economic Basis for International Trade

1. As soon as diversities in productivities arise within a country, specialization and exchange become beneficial. The same holds for nations. International exchange allows an efficient degree of specialization and division of labor—one that is more efficient than having to rely solely on domestic production.

2. Diversity is the fundamental reason that nations engage in international trade. Within this general principle, we see that trade occurs: because of differences in the conditions of production, such as when countries in the tropics produce coffee and bananas while temperate countries produce wheat and salmon; because of decreasing costs (or economies of scale)—particularly in manufacturing industries—whereby countries that get a head start in a particular industry make further gains in productivity to stay ahead of others; and because of diversity in tastes.

3. The most profound reason for international trade is the Ricardian principle of comparative advantage. This principle holds that trade between two regions is advantageous even if one country is absolutely more or less productive than the other in all commodities. As long as there are differences in *relative* or *comparative* efficiencies among countries, every country must enjoy a comparative advantage or a comparative disadvantage in some goods. Powerful benefits will arise when countries specialize in production in their areas of comparative advantage, exporting those goods and trading them for goods in which other nations have a comparative advantage.

4. The law of comparative advantage predicts more than just the geographical pattern of specialization and direction of trade. It also demonstrates that both countries are made better off and that the real wages (or, more generally, returns to the factors of production taken as a whole) are improved by trade and the resulting enlarged totals of world production. Quotas and prohibitive tariffs that are designed to ''protect'' workers or industries will often hurt real wages and total factor returns—not help them.

5. When there are many goods or many countries, the same principles of comparative advantage apply. With many commodities, we can arrange products along a continuum of comparative advantage, from relatively more efficient to relatively less efficient. We know that a country will produce and export the commodity in which it has greatest comparative advantage and import that one in which it has greatest comparative disadvantage. With many countries, trade may be ''triangular,'' with countries having large bilateral (or two-sided) surpluses or deficits with other individual countries. Triangular trade may allow many imbalances in bilateral trade, but this reflects the fact that a nation's accounts must balance only multilaterally—between a nation and the rest of the world. Imposing bilateral balance would hamper economic efficiency.

B. The Balance of International Payments

6. The balance of international payments is the set of accounts that measures all the economic flows into and out of a nation. It includes exports and imports of goods, services, and financial capital. Exports are credit items, while imports are debits. More generally, a country's credit items are transactions that make foreign currencies available to it; debit items are ones that reduce its holdings of foreign currencies.

7. The major components of the balance of payments are:

I. Current account (including the merchandise or trade balance along with services and government transfers)

II. Capital account (private and government purchases and sales of assets like stocks, bonds, and real estate)

III. Statistical discrepancy

IV. Changes in official reserve assets

The rule of balance-of-payments accounting is that the sum of all items must equal zero: $I + II + III + IV = 0$.

8. Historically, countries tend to go through stages of the balance of payments: from the young debtor borrowing for economic development, through mature debtor and young creditor, to mature creditor nation living off earnings from past investments. In the 1980s, the United States moved to yet a different stage where disappearing domestic saving has again led it to borrow heavily abroad and become a debtor nation.

CONCEPTS FOR REVIEW

open economy
sources of trade: cost differences,
  decreasing costs, differences in tastes,
  comparative advantage
absolute and comparative advantage
  (disadvantage)
principle of comparative advantage
economic gains from trade
effects of tariffs and quotas
spectrum of comparative advantage
triangular and multilateral trade

terms of trade
consumption vs. production possibilities
  with trade
world vs. national *PPF*s
balance of payments (current account,
  capital account, official settlements)
balance of payments must total zero:
  $I + II + III + IV = 0$
debits and credits
stages of balance of payments

QUESTIONS FOR DISCUSSION

1. "Buying a good abroad cheaper than we can produce it at home is to our advantage." Is this consistent with comparative advantage?

2. For each of the following, state whether or not it is correct and explain carefully your reasoning. If the quotation is incorrect, provide the correct statement.

(a) "We Mexicans can never compete profitably with the Northern colossus. Her factories are too efficient, she has too many computers and machine tools, and her engineering skills are too advanced. We need tariffs, or we can export nothing!"

(b) "Because of international trade, a nation can consume outside its production-possibility curve."

(c) "If American workers are subjected to the unbridled competition of cheap foreign labor, our real wages must necessarily fall drastically."

(d) "The current account for a country need not balance bilaterally (or with each country), but it must balance multilaterally (or with all countries)."

(e) "The principle of comparative advantage applies equally well to families, cities, and states as it does to nations and continents."

3. Construct Figure 38-5 and its accompanying table for Europe assuming that Europe has 600 units of labor and that labor productivities are given in Table 38-2.

4. What if the data in Table 38-2 changed from (1, 2; 3, 4) to (1, 2; 2, 4)? Show that all trade is killed off. Use this to explain the adage, *"Vive la différence!"* (freely translated as, "Let diversity thrive!").

5. *Follow-up to question 4:* Suppose that the two countries in Table 38-2 are Korea and America. What are the gains from trade between the two countries? Now suppose that Korea adopts American technology, grows rapidly, and has an identical technology to the American column of Table 38-2. What will happen to international trade? What will happen to Korean living standards and real wages? What will happen to American living standards? Is there a lesson here for the impact of converging economies on trade and welfare?

6. Why do the largest gains to trade flow to small countries whose pre-trade prices are very different from prevailing world prices?

7. Why might a newly discovered continent have a comparative advantage in the production of food and raw materials?

8. Draw up a list of items that belong on the credit side of the balance of international payments and another list of items that belong on the debit side. What is meant by a trade surplus? By the balance on current account? Why the term "invisible items"?

9. Construct hypothetical balance-of-payments accounts for a young debtor country, a mature debtor country, a new creditor country, and a mature creditor country.

10. A Mideast nation suddenly discovers huge oil resources. Show how its balance of trade and current account suddenly turn to surplus. Show how it acquires assets in New York as a capital account offset. Later, when it uses the assets for internal development, show how its current and capital items reverse their roles.

11. A nation records the following data for 1991: Exports of automobiles ($100) and corn ($150); imports of oil ($150) and steel ($75); tourist expenditures abroad ($25); lending to foreign countries ($50); borrowing from foreign countries ($40); official settlements ($30 accumulation by domestic central bank). Calculate the statistical discrepancy and create a balance-of-payments table like Table 38-3.

12. A U.S. senator recently wrote the following:

> Trade is supposed to raise the incomes of all nations involved—or at least that is what Adam Smith and David Ricardo taught us. If our economic decline has been caused by the economic growth of our competitors, then these philosophers—and the entire discipline of economics they founded—have been taking us on a 200-year ride.

Explain why the first sentence is correct. Also explain why the second sentence does not follow from the first. Can you give an example of how economic growth of country J could lower the standard of living in country A? [HINT: The answer to question 5 will help uncover the fallacy in the quotation.]

13. For the period 1980–1982, the current account balances of the United States and Japan were each around zero (with imports approximately equalling exports). Yet during this period, the United States had a $15 billion bilateral trade deficit with Japan. Can you see how such a pattern might reflect comparative advantages of the two countries?

Many are calling for "reciprocity legislation," in which *bilateral* United States–Japanese trade would be balanced. What would the effect of this be on the efficiency of the *multilateral* trading system?

14. Advanced problem: To determine the final price ratio for our analysis of trade between Europe and America, we can use John Stuart Mill's "reciprocal demand curves," shown in Figure 38-9. In this diagram, we measure the supply and demand for clothing imports and exports. The $D_a D_a$ demand curve measures America's demand for clothing, while the $S_e S_e$ supply curve measures Europe's supply of clothing. These are not ordinary demand curves, however, for clothing is traded for food, not for money. Therefore, the price ratio here is the price of clothing in terms of food rather than in terms of dollars, and the price ratio, P_C/P_F, is measured on the vertical price axis.

RECIPROCAL DEMANDS

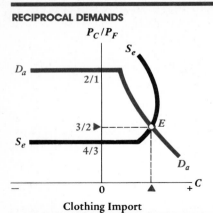

Clothing Import   Figure 38-9   Price determination in international trade

This diagram then finds the equilibrium price ratio as the intersection of supply and demand. Explain the diagram. Then show what would happen if America's demand for clothing were extremely weak. What would happen if America's clothing demand were very large? Explain the proposition in the chapter that the price ratio must lie in the range $[\frac{1}{2}, \frac{3}{4}]$.

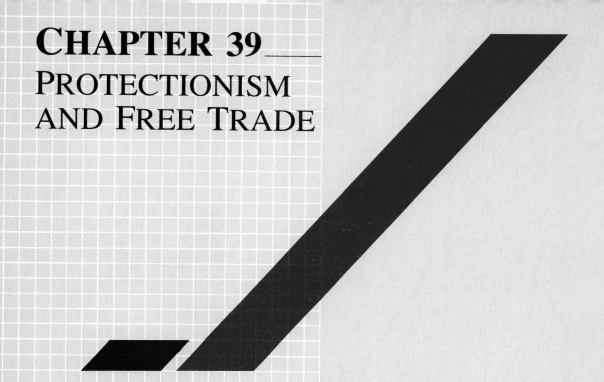

CHAPTER 39
PROTECTIONISM AND FREE TRADE

To the Chamber of Deputies: *We are subjected to the intolerable competition of a foreign rival, who enjoys such superior facilities for the production of light that he can* inundate *our* national market *at reduced price. This rival is no other than the sun. Our petition is to pass a law shutting up all windows, openings and fissures through which the light of the sun is used to penetrate our dwellings, to the prejudice of the profitable manufacture we have been enabled to bestow on the country.*
Signed: *Candle Makers.*

F. Bastiat

THE THEORY OF COMPARATIVE ADVANTAGE shows how countries can benefit from specialization and international division of labor. Nonetheless, during the 1980s, legislatures were besieged by groups lobbying for "protective" measures—barriers to imports in the form of tariffs or quotas. In the United States, the Congress and the President struggled over the passage of bills to protect domestic industries from inexpensive imports from other industrial countries.

Is a protectionist stance sound economic policy? Economists generally agree that it is not, for they have learned that trade promotes a mutually beneficial division of labor among nations and that free and open trade allows each nation to expand its production and consumption possibilities, raising the world's living standard.

But many people today disagree with the economists' argument. Just as Alexander Hamilton wanted to build tariff walls around our manufacturing industries in 1789, so today people argue that we need to protect our industries against foreign competition.

In this chapter we begin by showing how tariffs affect prices and outputs in an industry. We then evaluate the arguments for and against economic protectionism.

FREE TRADE IN CLOTHING

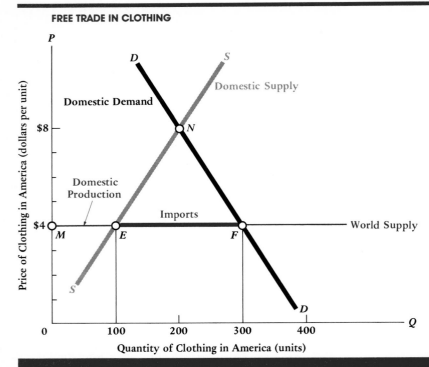

Figure 39-1   American production, imports, and consumption with free trade

We see here the free-trade equilibrium in the market for clothing. America has a comparative disadvantage in clothing. Therefore, at the no-trade equilibrium at *N*, America's price would be $8, while the world price is $4.

Assuming that American demand does not affect the world price of $4 per unit, the free-trade equilibrium comes when America produces *ME* (100 units) and imports the difference between demand and domestic supply shown as *EF* (or 200 units).

SUPPLY-AND-DEMAND ANALYSIS OF TRADE AND TARIFFS

The last chapter analyzed the theory of comparative advantage, using as a specific example a situation in which Europe had a comparative advantage in clothing while America's comparative advantage lay in food production. In what follows we will see how supply-and-demand analysis can illuminate the determination of prices and quantities in foreign trade; we will then analyze the impact of tariffs.

Supply-and-Demand Analysis of a Single Traded Good

Consider only the clothing market in America. Assume for simplicity that America cannot affect the world price of clothing; this assumption will allow us to analyze supply and demand very easily. (The more realistic case where a country can affect world prices will be considered later in this chapter.)

Figure 39-1 shows the supply and demand curves for clothing in America. The demand curve of American consumers is drawn as *DD* and the domestic supply curve of American firms as *SS*. We assume that the price of clothing is determined in the world market (assumed to be much larger than the American market) and is equal to $4 per unit.

Later on, we must recognize that transactions in international trade take place in a variety of different currencies (U.S. dollars, Japanese yen, British pounds, and so forth). But for now we can simplify by translating each of those foreign currencies into dollars. For example, French suppliers would normally want to be paid in francs. But we can turn the French supply schedule into a dollar supply curve by using the current exchange rate. (Thus, if clothing sold for 24 francs a unit, and if the French franc sold for 6 francs to the dollar, we would simply use a scale of $4 per unit for French clothing.)

No-Trade Equilibrium   For the moment, let's suppose that transportation costs or tariffs for clothing were prohibitive (say, $100 per unit of clothing).

Where would the no-trade equilibrium lie? In this case, the American market for clothing would be at the intersection of domestic supply and demand, shown at point *N* in Figure 39-1. At this no-trade point, prices would be relatively high at $8 per unit, and domestic producers would be meeting all the demand.

Free Trade Next open up trade in clothing. For simplicity, assume that there are no transport costs, tariffs, or quotas. Then the price in America must be equal to the world price. Why? Because if the American price were above the European price, sharp-eyed entrepreneurs would buy where clothing was cheap (Europe) and sell where clothing was expensive (America)—Europe would export clothing to America. Once trade flows fully adapted to supplies and demands, the price in America would equal the world price level (adjusted for transportation costs and for tariffs or other trade barriers).

Figure 39-1 illustrates the impact of international trade upon prices, quantities, and trade flows for this clothing example. The horizontal red line at $4 represents the supply curve for imports; it is horizontal, or perfectly price elastic, because American demand is assumed to be too small to affect the world price of clothing.

Once trade opens up, a flood of imports comes into America, lowering the price of clothing to the world price of $4 per unit. At that level, domestic producers will supply the amount *ME*, or 100 units. But at that low price consumers will want to buy 300 units. The difference, shown by the heavy red line *EF*, is the amount of imports.

Who decided that we would import just this amount of clothing, and that domestic producers would supply only 100 units? A planning agency? A cartel of clothing firms? Labor unions? No, the amount of trade was determined by supply and demand.

Moreover, we can say that the level of prices in the no-trade equilibrium determined the direction of the trade flows. America's no-trade prices were higher than Europe's, so goods flowed into America. Remember this paradoxical rule: *Under free trade, goods flow uphill from low-price regions to high-price regions.* Clothing flows uphill from the low-priced European market to the higher-priced

American market when markets are opened to free trade.

Before we move on to analyze the impact of tariffs upon trade, pause first to consider the relationship of the supply and demand curves just analyzed to the theory of comparative advantage in the last chapter. The supply and demand curves are highly useful for understanding the forces operating upon a single industry, but they are incomplete. Why do the schedules determine a higher no-trade equilibrium clothing price in America than in Europe? Why does trade in clothing flow from Europe to America? To answer these questions we have to analyze the supplies and demands for all industries, as we did in last chapter's general-equilibrium analysis of an economy's comparative advantage along Ricardian lines. The same principles of comparative advantage explain why Europe would export clothing and import food.[1]

Tariffs and Quotas

For centuries, one of the major tools that governments have used to raise revenues and to influence the development of individual industries is the imposition of tariffs and quotas. From the eighteenth century—when the British Parliament attempted to impose tariffs on tea, sugar, and other commodities on its American colonies—until today, tariff policy has proved fertile soil for revolution and political struggle.

We can understand the economic impacts of tariffs and quotas using our supply-and-demand analysis. To begin with, note that a **tariff** is a tax levied on imports. Table 39-1 shows some representative tariff rates in the mid-1980s for the United States and Japan. To take an example, the United States today has a 2.5 percent tariff on automobiles. If a foreign car costs $10,000, then the domestic price including the tariff would be $10,250. A **quota** is a limit on the quantity of imports. The United States has quotas on products like cheese, textiles, and beef.

Prohibitive Tariff The easiest case to analyze is a "prohibitive tariff"—one that is so high as to com-

[1] Economists explain that these supply and demand curves depict only "partial equilibrium." They must be anchored in "general-equilibrium" analysis, of which Chapter 38's Ricardian theory of comparative advantage is a special case.

COMMODITY CLASS	AVERAGE TARIFF RATE, 1987	
	UNITED STATES	JAPAN
Agricultural products	1.8	18.4
Food products	4.7	25.4
Wearing apparel	22.7	13.8
Printing and publishing	0.7	0.1
Iron and steel	3.6	2.8
Transport equipment	2.5	1.5
Average, industrial products	4.4	2.8

Table 39-1   Average tariff rates for United States and Japan

The average tariff rates for industrial countries like the United States and Japan are relatively low today. High tariffs or import quotas are generally found in politically sensitive sectors like agriculture in Japan and clothing in the United States. [Source: Congressional Budget Office, *The GATT Negotiations and U.S. Trade Policy* (U.S. Government Printing Office, Washington, June 1987).]

pletely discourage any imports. Looking back at Figure 39-1, what will happen if the tariff on clothing is more than $4 per unit (that is, more than the difference between America's no-trade price of $8 and the world price of $4)? This tariff would be so high as to be *prohibitive,* shutting off all clothing trade.

Why? Because any importer who buys clothing at the world price of $4 can sell it in America for at most the no-trade price of $8. But the tariff the importer has to pay would come to more than the difference between U.S. and world price. Prohibitive tariffs thus kill off all trade.

Nonprohibitive Tariff More moderate tariffs (less than $4 per unit of clothing) would injure but not kill off trade. Figure 39-2 shows the equilibrium in the clothing market with a $2 tariff. Again assuming no transportation costs, a $2 tariff means that foreign clothing will sell in America for $6 per unit (equal to the $4 world price plus the $2 tariff).

The equilibrium result of a $2 tariff is to lower domestic consumption (or quantity demanded) from 300 units in the free-trade equilibrium to 250 units after the tariff is imposed, to raise the amount of domestic production by 50 units, and to lower the quantity of imports by 100 units. This example summarizes the economic impact of tariffs:

A tariff will tend to raise price, lower the amounts consumed and imported, and raise domestic production.

Quotas Quotas have the same qualitative effect as tariffs. A prohibitive quota (prohibiting all imports) would achieve the same result as a prohibitive tariff. The price and quantity would move back to the no-trade equilibrium at *N* in Figure 39-2. A less stringent quota might limit imports to 100 clothing units; this quota would equal the heavy red line *HJ* in Figure 39-2. A quota of 100 units would lead to the same equilibrium price and output as did the $2 tariff.

There is thus no essential difference between tariffs and quotas. Some subtle differences arise, however. A tariff at least gives revenue to the government, perhaps allowing other taxes to be reduced and thereby offsetting some of the harm done to customers in the importing country. A quota, on the other hand, puts the profit from the resulting price difference into the pocket of the importers lucky enough to get a permit or license to import. They can afford to wine and dine the officials who give out import licenses and may even engage in bribery.

For these reasons, in choosing between tariffs and quotas, economists generally regard tariffs as the lesser evil. However, they advise that, if governments are determined to interfere with comparative advantage by imposing quotas, the government should auction off the scarce import-quota licenses. An auction will ensure that the government rather than the importer or the exporter gets the revenue from the scarce right to import; and in addition, the bureaucracy will not be tempted to allocate quota rights by bribery, friendship, or nepotism.

Transportation Costs What of transportation costs? The cost of moving bulky and perishable goods has the same effect as tariffs, reducing the extent of beneficial regional specialization. For example, if it costs $2 per unit to transport clothing from Europe to the United States, the supply-and-demand equilibrium

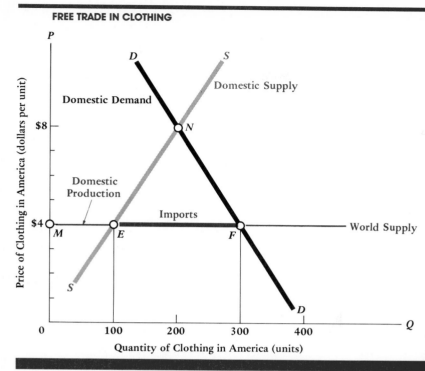

FREE TRADE IN CLOTHING

P

Price of Clothing in America (dollars per unit)

D

Domestic Demand

S

Domestic Supply

$8 — *N*

Domestic
Production

$4 — *M*   *E*   Imports   *F*   World Supply

S

D

0   100   200   300   400   *Q*

Quantity of Clothing in America (units)

Figure 39-2   A tariff lowers imports and consumption, raises domestic production and price

Starting from the free-trade equilibrium in Fig. 39-1, America now puts a $2 tariff on clothing imports. The price of European clothing imports rises to $6 (including the tariff).

The market price rises from $4 to $6, so the total amount demanded falls. Imports shrink from 200 units to 100 units, while domestic production rises from 100 to 150 units.

would look just like Figure 39-2, with the American price $2 above the European price.

But there is one difference: transport costs are imposed by nature—by distances, mountains, and rivers. Restrictive tariffs are squarely the responsibility of nations. Indeed, one economist called tariffs ''negative railroads.'' This idea illustrates dramatically that a tariff has the same economic impact as throwing sand in the engines of vessels that transport goods to our shores from other lands.

The Economic Costs of Tariffs

In the last chapter, we saw that all countries would benefit by opening up their borders to international trade. We can also use our supply-and-demand apparatus to analyze the economic costs of tariffs.

What happens when America puts a tariff on clothing, such as the $2 tariff shown in Figure 39-2? We have seen that there are three effects: *(a)* The domestic producers, operating under a price umbrella provided by the tariff, can now expand production;

(b) consumers are faced with higher prices and therefore reduce their consumption; and *(c)* the government gains tariff revenue. What is the net economic impact of the tariff?

Tariffs create economic inefficiency. More precisely, when tariffs are imposed, the economic loss to consumers exceeds the revenue gained by the government plus the extra profits earned by producers.

Diagrammatic Analysis[2]

The economic analysis of a tariff's impact is shown in Figure 39-3. This shows the same curves as those in Figure 39-2, but three new areas are highlighted. Let's investigate each:

A. A tariff raises the price in domestic markets from $4 to $6. Firms are thereby induced to produce

[2]The section on diagrammatic analysis is somewhat technical and can be skipped in short courses or in those courses which have not covered Part Four.

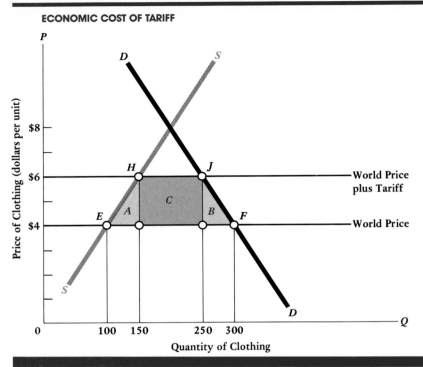

ECONOMIC COST OF TARIFF

Figure 39-3 Imposing a tariff raises revenues and leads to inefficiency

This diagram shows the same situation as that in Fig. 39-2. We have shown the impact of the tariff as three effects. Region *A* is the cost of the inefficiency in production induced by a higher domestic price. Triangle *B* is the loss in consumer surplus from the inefficiently high price. Region *C* is the tariff revenue gained by the government—a transfer from consumers to the government but not an efficiency loss.

more—i.e., to bring on line factories whose marginal costs for producing are between $4 and $6 per unit. Bringing on these high-marginal-cost plants is inefficient, for the clothing produced by those factories could be bought from abroad at $4.

We can easily measure the amount of this waste as the area *A* in Figure 39-3. This area is the sum of the marginal costs of domestic producers (represented by the domestic supply curve) minus the marginal costs of foreign producers ($4). The total loss in *A* is $50 (which, by geometry, is equal to $\frac{1}{2}$ times the tariff times the induced domestic production).

B. In addition, there is a loss of consumer surplus from the too-high price. Recall that the demand curve represents consumers' marginal utilities, or the value of the different units of clothing. The resource cost of each unit of clothing is the world price, $4. Hence, the triangle *B* measures the loss in consumer satisfaction from having to cut back on consumption. It is also equal to $50 (which is calculated as equal to one-half the price difference times the consumption reduction).

C. Area *C* is simply the tariff revenue, equal to the amount of the tariff times the units of imports. Revenues in Figure 39-3 are $200. Note that, unlike triangles *A* and *B*, revenue rectangle *C* need not be an efficiency cost or a deadweight loss. The government revenues raised by tariffs can be employed to finance useful government programs or can be returned to consumers for their own purposes.

Figure 39-3 illustrates one feature that is important in understanding the politics and history of tariffs. When a tariff is imposed, part of the impact is upon economic efficiency but the largest effect is often redistributive. In the example shown in Figure 39-3, areas *A* and *B* represent efficiency losses from inefficiently high domestic production and inefficiently low consumption, respectively. Under the simplifying assumptions used above, the efficiency losses are equal to the two little triangles and sum up to $100. The redistribution involved and shown as area *C* is much larger, however, equalling $200 raised in tariff revenues levied upon consumers of the commodity. Consumers will be unhappy about the higher product cost, and producers may attempt to capture the potential revenues by shifting from tariffs to quotas. We can see why battles over import restrictions generally center more on the redistributive gains and losses than on the impacts upon economic efficiency.

In summary:

Imposing a tariff has three effects. It encourages inefficient domestic production; it induces consumers to reduce their purchases of the tariffed good below efficient levels; and it raises revenues for the government. Only the first two of these necessarily impose efficiency costs on the economy.

An Example of Tariffs on Textiles

Let's put some flesh on these analytical bones by discussing the impacts of a particular tariff, such as a tariff on clothing. Today, tariffs on imported textiles and apparel are among the highest tariffs levied by the United States (see Table 39-1). How do consumers and producers feel the impact of these high tariffs?

To begin with, domestic clothing prices are raised. It costs more to buy a suit or dress than it would under free trade. Because of the higher prices, many factories—ones that would otherwise be bankrupt in the face of a declining comparative advantage in textiles—remain open. They are only marginally profitable, but they somehow manage to eke out enough sales to continue domestic production. A few more workers are employed in textiles than would otherwise be the case although, because of pressure from foreign competition, real wages remain among the lowest of any manufacturing industry.

From a national point of view, we are wasting resources in textiles. These workers, materials, and capital would be more productively used in other sectors—perhaps in producing computers or corn or aircraft. The nation's productive potential is lower because we keep factors of production in an industry like textiles where we have lost our comparative advantage.

Consumers are of course paying for this protection of the textile industry. They face higher prices. They get less satisfaction from their incomes than they would if they could buy textiles at Hong Kong or Singapore prices, that is, at prices that exclude the high tariffs. Consumers are induced to cut back on their clothing purchases, channeling funds into food or transportation or recreation, whose relative prices are lowered by the tariff.

In addition, the government gets a few million dollars of revenues from tariffs on textiles. These revenues can be used to buy useful public goods or to reduce other taxes, so (unlike the consumer loss or the productive inefficiency) this is not a real social burden.

■   ■   ■

Now that we have completed our analysis of the way that tariffs affect the price and quantity of a good, we turn to an analysis of the arguments for and against protecting a nation's industries against foreign trade.

THE ECONOMICS OF PROTECTIONISM

The arguments for tariff or quota protection against the competition of foreign imports take many different forms. Here are the main categories:

■ Certain non-economic arguments that suggest it is desirable to sacrifice economic welfare in order to subsidize other national objectives

■ Arguments that are economically false: some that are clearly defective and some whose falsity can be detected only by subtle and sophisticated economic reasoning

■ A few analyses that are invalid in a perfectly competitive full-employment world, but that contain kernels of truth for a nation large enough to affect its import or export prices, as well as for a nation suffering from unemployment

Many of these arguments are a century old; others have been promoted by the "new wave" theorists of protection. The best way to evaluate the arguments is by a careful economic analysis.

Non-Economic Goals

Let us begin with the first category, for they are most easily considered. If you ever are on a debating team given the assignment to defend free trade, you will strengthen your case at the beginning by conceding that economic welfare is not the only goal of life. A nation surely should not sacrifice its liberty and national security for a few dollars of extra real income gained in trade.

Consider the example of oil. If oil is considered necessary for national defense, the economist should not assert that it is wrong to protect the oil industry. The case for protection is strengthened if foreign oil is controlled by a hostile power or by a cartel that may, on some future occasion, cut off supplies for political reasons. An advocate of protection might conclude that the nation should severely limit imports of oil into the United States.

A close look, however, will reveal faults in this argument. Suppose the nation consumes 15 million barrels of oil a day, of which essential military and civilian needs are 5 million barrels a day. Moreover, our productive capacity is 9 million barrels a day. An appropriate policy would seem to be to ensure that the nation always has access to 5 million barrels a day of oil resources. Clearly, then, there is no need to restrict oil imports to guarantee the essential oil needs of the nation.

In some cases, a nation might not produce enough of a product for its essential military needs. This might be true for cobalt or copper. The domestic copper industry might come before Congress and lobby for a high tariff on copper, arguing that only by this means can the nation guarantee an adequate supply in wartime. A careful analysis of this contention often reveals that there are more efficient ways of ensuring the needed amount of strategic materials than by raising tariffs—a particularly useful policy being the storage of such materials in a strategic stockpile. The United States today does in fact have large stocks of major materials as a way of providing adequate supplies if imports are curbed.

The National Way of Life Proponents of protection can muster yet other arguments to their defense. Sometimes it is argued that the nation's scientific resources (in aircraft, microelectronics, or computers) will wither away if they are not kept hard at work protected from foreign competition. In addition, tariffs are sometimes seen as part of a social strategy—to preserve the farm, the culture of New England or New York, or the centuries-old tradition of Swiss watchmaking.

A thoughtful analyst cannot dismiss such objectives out of hand. But most economists prefer the use of subsidies rather than tariffs as a way of attaining non-economic goals. A subsidy makes direct payments to a person or a firm for the desired service; for example, if Switzerland desires to maintain its watch industry, it may provide low-interest (or subsidized) loans to watch manufacturers. Subsidies are held superior because they are more visible and can be debated openly; they do not raise all prices, but only those of the subsidized goods or workers; and they are subject to periodic review by legislatures.

There are many non-economic goals in a humane society. But to attain them by economic protectionism is usually an inefficient and costly route to follow.

Grounds for Tariffs Not Based on Sound Economics

Mercantilism To Abraham Lincoln has been attributed the remark, "I don't know much about the tariff. I do know that when I buy a coat from England, I have the coat and England has the money. But when I buy a coat in America, I have the coat and America has the money."

This reasoning represents an age-old fallacy typical of the so-called mercantilistic writers of the seventeenth and eighteenth centuries. They considered a country fortunate which sold more goods than it bought because such a "favorable" balance of trade meant that gold would flow into the country to pay for its export surplus.

The mercantilist argument confuses the means and the ends of economic activity. Accumulating gold or other monies will not improve a country's living standard. Money is worthwhile not for its own sake, but for what it will buy from other countries. Most economists today therefore reject the idea that raising tariffs to run a trade surplus will improve a country's economic welfare.

Tariffs for Special-Interest Groups The single most important source of pressure for protective tariffs comes from powerful special-interest groups. Both business and labor know very well that a tariff on their products will help *them,* whatever its effect on total production and consumption. This barrier to free trade was understood by Adam Smith, who wrote:

> To expect . . . freedom of trade . . . is as absurd as to expect . . . Utopia. Not only the prejudices of the public, but what is much more unconquerable, the private interests of many individuals, irresistibly oppose it.

A century ago, outright bribery was used to get the votes necessary to pass tariff legislation. Today, powerful political action committees (PACs)—financed by industries or labor and in turn making millions of dollars of campaign contributions to members of Congress—drum up support for tariffs or quotas on textiles, autos, steel, sugar, and other goods.

Why do the proponents of protectionism continue to wield such a disproportionate influence in Congress when free trade is so beneficial to the nation as a whole? The answer lies in the dynamics of interest-group politics in our democratic system (a topic analyzed in Chapter 32's discussion of public choice). Free trade helps everybody a little, while protection helps a few people a great deal. If political votes were cast in proportion to total economic benefit, every nation would legislate most tariffs out of existence.

But all dollars of economic interests do not always get proportional representation. It is much harder to organize the masses of consumers and producers to agitate for the benefits of free trade than it is to organize a few companies or labor unions to beat the drums against "cheap foreign labor" or "unfair Japanese competition." Usually, those few firms, farmers, or labor unions who seek protection are the best represented and the most active in the political arena. Their trade groups have many millions of dollars to spend lobbying and supporting friendly legislators while the consumers who lose from protection have but a few poorly funded groups to counter protectionist arguments. In every country, the tireless enemies of free trade are the special interests of protected firms and workers.

Competition from Cheap Foreign Labor Another argument for protection, gauged to appeal to workers, has been the most popular of all in American history. This argument holds, "How can American workers possibly compete with goods produced by cheap foreign labor—whether by Koreans making circuit boards and earning only $2 an hour or by Brazilians earning $1 an hour making carbon steel? We need tariffs on foreign goods so that we can compete effectively."

The flaw in the argument is that it ignores the basic principle of comparative advantage. The reason American workers have higher wages is that they are on average more productive. If our equilibrium wage is 10 times that in East Asia, it is because we are on average roughly 10 times more productive in the manufacture of tradable goods.

To put this differently, the principle of comparative advantage shows that it will be beneficial for country A to trade with country B even if country B can produce every good more efficiently than can country A. Trade flows according to comparative advantage, not absolute advantage. If America has higher relative costs than East Asia in basic steel, textiles, shoes, and circuit boards, then America will benefit by importing those goods. Instead of protecting unproductive industries, America should concentrate on areas where its labor is relatively more productive—on sectors like farming, aircraft, petrochemicals, and customized integrated circuits.

Having shown that the nation gains from importing the goods produced by "cheap foreign labor" when those goods are relatively cheap to produce abroad, we should not ignore the costs that this strategy may temporarily impose on the affected workers and firms. If plants in a particular locality are unexpectedly shut down because production moves overseas, the local labor market may be inundated with job seekers. Older workers with outdated job skills may

have trouble finding attractive jobs and suffer a decline in their real incomes. The difficulties of displaced workers will be greater when the overall economy is depressed or when the local labor markets
have high unemployment. Over the long run, labor
markets will reallocate workers from declining to
advancing industries, but the transition may be painful for many people.

In summary, the economic answer to the "cheap
foreign labor" argument rests on the comparative-
advantage analysis. This shows a country will benefit
from trade even though its wages are far above those
of its trading partners. High wages come from high
efficiency, not from tariff protection.

Tariffs for Retaliation While many people would
agree that a world of free trade would be the best of
all possible worlds, they note that this is not the world
we live in. They reason, "As long as other countries
impose import restrictions or otherwise discriminate
against our products, we have no choice but to play
the same game in self-defense. We'll go along with
free trade only as long as it is fair trade. But we must
play on a level playing field."

While this argument seems sensible, it is not well
grounded in economic analysis or history. As we have
seen, when another country increases its tariffs, this is
akin to increasing its transportation costs. But if
France decided to let its roads go to ruin, should we
therefore chop holes in ours? If a country decided to
lay mines in its harbors, should we mine ours? Few
would think so. Similarly, if other countries injure
their economies' vitality by imposing tariffs on their
imports, it would not be economically beneficial to
add injury to injury by adding tariffs on ours.

The only possible sense in the argument that we
should retaliate when a foreign country raises tariffs is
that our threat of retaliation may deter the country
from raising tariffs in the first place. This rationale
was explicitly given by the U.S. government in a
1982 analysis of protection (in the *Economic Report
of the President*):

> Intervention in international trade . . . , even though
> costly to the U.S. economy in the short run, may, how-
> ever, be justified if it serves the strategic purpose of in-

creasing the cost of interventionist policies by foreign
governments. Thus, there is a potential role for carefully
targeted measures . . . aimed at convincing other countries to reduce their trade distortions.

But this argument should be used with great caution. Just as building missiles leads to an arms race as
often as to arms control, protectionist bluffs may end
up hurting the bluffer as well as the opponent. Historical studies show that retaliatory tariffs usually lead
other nations to raise their tariffs still higher and are
rarely an effective bargaining chip for multilateral tariff reduction.

Import Relief Today, relatively little direct tariff
business is conducted on the floor of Congress. Congress realized that tariff politics was too hot to handle
and delegated most authority to the President. Most
trade barriers are erected as a result of a complaint
filed by an industry that feels itself to be adversely
affected by foreign competition. In most circumstances, the complaint is analyzed by the International
Trade Commission, which makes recommendations
for final action by the President. Among the important kinds of actions are the following:

- *The escape clause* allows temporary import relief
(tariffs, quotas, or export quotas negotiated with other
countries) when an industry has been "injured" by
imports. Injury occurs when the output, employment,
and profits in a domestic industry have fallen while
imports have risen. We have seen such "escape
clause" relief provided for televisions, shoes, steel,
CB radios, and even nuts and bolts.

- *Antidumping tariffs* are levied when foreign countries sell in the United States at prices below their
average costs or at prices that are lower than in the
home market. Such duties have been levied on steel
imports and semiconductor chips.

- *Retaliation for unfair trade practices* is imposed
when other countries discriminate against, or unjusti-
fiably restrict, U.S. commerce. Since 1985, for example, the United States has initiated actions against
Japan for restricting sales of American cigarettes,
against Korea for restrictions on insurance, against
Taiwan for restrictions on alcoholic beverages, and

against Brazil for restrictions in the computer industry.

What is the justification for such retaliatory measures or for protecting an industry threatened by imports? While import relief may sound reasonable, it actually runs completely counter to the economic theory of comparative advantage. A nation gains from trade by specializing, i.e., by giving up certain activities and moving resources into other industries which enjoy a comparative advantage. Suppose an industry (say, steel) formerly had a comparative advantage but has lost it—because other industries have had greater technological improvements, because the domestic factors it uses have become more expensive when they have become more valuable elsewhere, or for any other reason. The theory of comparative advantage says that this industry *ought* to be injured by imports. Indeed, it ought to be killed off by the competition of more productive industries.

This sounds ruthless indeed. No industry willingly dies. No region gladly undergoes conversion to new industries. Often the shift from old to new industries involves considerable unemployment and hardship. The weak industry and region feel they are being singled out to carry the burden of progress.

A compromise that recognizes the costs of adjusting to economic dislocations is to introduce tariff reductions gradually, so that unemployed workers will have time to move to regions with growing job opportunities. Also, as has occurred since the 1962 Trade Act and was strengthened in the 1988 Trade Act "trade adjustment assistance," or federal aid to displaced factors of production is given. Such assistance may help shift factors from declining to growing industries, share the burden among the strong and the weak, and lessen effective opposition to a free and open trading system.

Many economists and political leaders feel that adjustment assistance is the most efficient and humane way to respond to the inevitable dislocations wrought by changing patterns of comparative advantage. As Victoria Curzon Price noted, "Trade liberalization coupled with adjustment assistance is a typical example of the . . . capacity for moving forwards while looking backwards."

Arguments for Protection under Dynamic Conditions

Finally, we can consider three arguments for protection that may have true economic merit:

- Tariffs may move the terms of trade in favor of a country.
- Temporary tariff protection for an "infant industry" with growth potential may be efficient in the long run.
- A tariff may under certain conditions help reduce unemployment.

Let's examine each of these arguments.

The Terms-of-Trade or "Optimal-Tariff" Argument

One valid argument for a country's imposing tariffs on its trade is that it will "shift the terms of trade in its favor and against foreign countries." Recall that *terms of trade* represent the ratio of export prices to import prices. To shift the terms of trade against foreigners means that levying tariffs on imports will reduce the world price of imports while increasing the prices of our exports. By shifting the terms of trade in our favor, we can export less of our wheat and aircraft in order to pay for imports of oil and cars. The set of tariffs that maximizes our domestic real incomes is called the *optimal tariff*.

The terms-of-trade argument, which goes back 150 years to the free-trade proponent John Stuart Mill and has been recently dusted off by "new wave" theorists, is the only one that would be valid under conditions of full employment and perfect competition. We can understand it in a simple case by considering an optimal tariff on oil. Mill would note that the optimal tariff on oil will raise the price here above the foreign price. But with our demand now curtailed, and because we are a significant part of the world demand for oil, the world market price of oil will be bid down. So part of the tariff really falls on the foreigner.[3] (We

---

[3] The analysis is exactly like that of domestic monopolists who raise P above MC, stopping where $MR = MC$. This approach has been presented as an argument for a large tariff on imported oil. Proponents of an oil tariff argue that a higher domestic price will depress the demand for OPEC's oil and thereby lower the price of imports (see question 10 at the end of this chapter).

can see that a very small country could not use this argument since a tiny country cannot affect world prices.)

Have we not therefore found a theoretically secure argument for tariffs? The answer would be yes if we could forget that this is a "beggar-thy-neighbor" policy and ignore the reactions of other countries. But other countries are likely to react. After all, if the United States were to impose an optimal tariff of 30 percent on its imports, why should the European Community and Japan and Brazil not put 30 or 40 percent tariffs on their imports? In the end, as every country calculated and imposed its own domestic optimal tariff, the overall level of tariffs might climb to 30 or 50 percent.

But such a situation would surely not in the end represent an improvement of either world or individual economic welfare. When *all* countries impose optimal tariffs, it is likely that *everyone's* economic welfare will decline as the impediments to free trade become great. All would benefit if countries were to gather and negotiate an abolition of trade barriers.

Tariffs for "Infant Industries"

In his famous *Report on Manufactures* (1791), Alexander Hamilton proposed to encourage the growth of manufacturing by protecting youthful industries from foreign competition. According to this doctrine, which received the cautious support of free-trade economists like John Stuart Mill and Alfred Marshall, there are lines of production in which a country could have a comparative advantage if only they could get started.

But such "infant industries" would not be able to weather the initial period of start-up and experimentation if they were forced to face unprotected the gales of international competition. On the other hand, if given some temporary shelter, they might develop economies of mass production, a pool of skilled labor, inventions well adapted to the local economy, and the technological efficiency typical of many mature industries. Hence, although protection will at first raise prices to the consumer, the industry will be so efficient once it has grown up that cost and price will actually have fallen. If the benefit to consumers at that later date would be more than enough to make up for the higher prices during the period of protection, a tariff is justified.

This argument must be carefully weighed. Historical studies have turned up some genuine cases of infant industries that grew up to stand on their own feet. And studies of successful newly industrialized countries (such as Singapore and Korea) find that they have often protected their manufacturing industries from imports during the early stages of industrialization. But the history of tariffs reveals even more contrary cases of perpetual infants unable to shed their diapers after many years of protection from international trade.

Tariffs and Unemployment

Historically, a powerful motive for protection has been the desire to increase employment during a period of recession or stagnation. How might protection create jobs? A tariff will raise the price of imports and therefore divert demand toward domestic production; Figure 39-2 demonstrates this impact. As domestic demand increases, firms will hire more workers, and unemployment will fall.[4] This too is a "beggar-thy-neighbor" policy, for it raises domestic demand at the expense of output and employment in other countries.

However, while economic protection may raise employment, it does not constitute an effective program to pursue high employment, efficiency, and stable prices. Macroeconomic analysis shows that there are other ways of reducing unemployment than by imposing import protection (these topics were covered in Parts Two and Three). By the appropriate use of monetary and fiscal policy, a country can increase output and lower unemployment. More importantly, the use of general macroeconomic policies will allow workers displaced from low-productivity jobs in industries losing their comparative advantage to move to high-productivity jobs in industries enjoying a comparative advantage.

This lesson was amply demonstrated during the 1980s. From 1982 to 1987, the United States created

---

[4] Those who have studied the chapters on macroeconomics in Parts Two and Three can understand the mechanism by which tariffs increase employment as follows: Recall that higher investment or government spending increases aggregate demand, output, and employment. By similar reasoning, greater protection or higher tariffs lower imports, increase net exports (equal to exports minus imports), and thereby increase aggregate demand. The higher net exports will have a multiplier effect much like that of investment or government spending on goods and services.

15 million net new jobs while maintaining open markets and low tariffs and sharply increasing its trade deficit; by contrast, the European Community created virtually no new jobs while moving toward a position of trade surpluses.

Another way of analyzing the impact of trade barriers upon employment is to measure the "cost of a job created by import restraints." Numerous economic studies have analyzed the economic cost imposed when tariffs or quotas are put upon an industry. As an example, consider the voluntary import quotas on Japanese cars during the 1980s. According to government studies, these quotas increased employment in the automobile industry by around 30,000 workers during 1983 and 1984. For the 7 million cars bought annually during that period, it is estimated that consumers paid an average of $500 per car more than they would have without the quotas. The consumer cost per job then averaged about $3.5 billion/30,000 = slightly over $100,000 per job.[5] Calculations such as these show how inefficient tariffs are as a technique for increasing employment.

In summary, tariffs and import protection are an inefficient way to create jobs or to lower unemployment. A more effective way to increase productive employment is through domestic monetary and fiscal policy.

Other Barriers to Trade

While this chapter has usually spoken of tariffs, almost everything it has said would apply equally well to any other impediments to trade. Quotas have much the same effects as tariffs, for they prevent the comparative advantages of different countries from being determined in the marketplace. In recent years, countries have negotiated quotas with other countries. The United States, for example, forced Japan to put "voluntary" export quotas on automobiles and negotiated similar export quotas on televisions, shoes, and steel.

Finally, we should mention the so-called non-tariff barriers (or NTBs). These consist of informal restrictions or regulations that make it difficult for countries to sell in foreign markets. The growth of NTBs was

one of the major problems faced by trade negotiators in the 1980s.

MULTILATERAL TRADE NEGOTIATIONS

This completes our discussion of the political economy of tariffs. Given the tug of war between the economic benefits of free trade and the political appeal of protection, which force has prevailed? The history of tariffs, shown in Figure 39-4, has been a bumpy one. For most of the life of the American republic, we have been a high-tariff nation. The pinnacle came after the infamous Smoot-Hawley tariff of 1930. This was opposed by virtually every American economist, yet it sailed through Congress.

The trade barriers erected during the Depression helped raise prices and exacerbated that period's economic distress. The 1930s witnessed trade wars in which countries attempted to raise employment and output by raising trade barriers at the expense of their neighbors. Nations soon learned that at the end of the tariff game, all were losers.

Negotiating Free Trade

As nations gathered at the end of World War II, they designed a number of institutions that could promote peace and economic prosperity by encouraging cooperative policies. One of the most successful of these was the General Agreement on Tariffs and Trade (GATT), whose charter speaks of raising living standards through "substantial reduction of tariffs and other barriers to trade and the elimination of discriminatory treatment in international commerce." The GATT currently has 92 member countries; these account for 85 percent of international trade.

Among the principles underlying the GATT are: (1) countries should work to lower trade barriers; (2) all trade barriers should be applied on a nondiscriminatory basis (i.e., all nations should enjoy the "most-favored-nation" status); (3) when a country increases its tariffs above agreed-upon levels, it must compensate its trading partners for their economic injury; and (4) trade conflicts should be settled by consultations and arbitration.

---

[5] These figures are drawn from Congressional Budget Office, *Has Trade Protection Revitalized Domestic Industries?* (U.S. Government Printing Office, Washington, 1986), Chap. V.

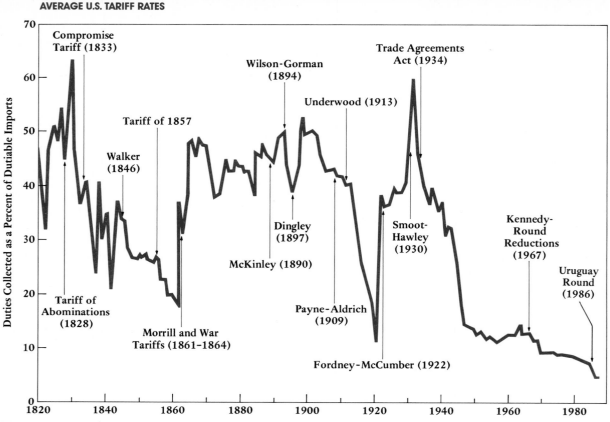

AVERAGE U.S. TARIFF RATES

Figure 39-4 America was historically a high-tariff nation

Duties were high for most of our nation's history, but have come down in a series of trade negotiations since the 1930s. The newest threat comes from non-tariff barriers, particularly negotiated quotas. Workers and firms in industries such as textiles, shoes, steel, and autos want competing imports kept out in order to maintain their wages and profits. The overall effect of high tariffs is to depress a nation's real wages as it loses the efficiencies of specialization and regional division of labor.

The history of trade negotiations has proved one of the major successes in international economic cooperation. Every few years, all major industrial countries gather under the auspices of the GATT to identify major trade barriers and negotiate their removal. The current negotiations are called the "Uruguay Round." In addition to the traditional goal of reducing tariff and quota barriers, the new round has undertaken the ambitious goals of reducing trade barriers in services or invisibles. Some of the targets are opening up financial markets (such as banking and insurance), protecting intellectual property rights (through patents, copyrights, and trade secrets), and removing barriers to investment (such as limits on foreign ownership of firms and currency restrictions).

Recent Steps At the end of the 1980s, governments took a number of steps to promote free trade or to broaden markets. Among the most important were the following:

■ In 1987, the United States and Canada negotiated a set of principles for free trade between the two countries. This agreement was particularly significant because Canada is the United States' largest trading partner, with total trade flows between the two of $130 billion in 1987. Trade barriers have remained high between the two nations: Canada has among the highest tariff rates of any major industrial country, and Canada curtails foreign investment on nationalist grounds. Canada in turn seeks abolition of U.S. tariffs and non-tariff barriers along with better access to U.S. government procurement. Economists have estimated that a free-trade agreement would raise Canadian real incomes by 5 percent and those of the United States by 1 percent. As of the end of 1988, the two governments had not yet ratified the free-trade pact.

■ "Europe 1992" is another movement toward regional free trade. This plan for the 12 nations of the European Community, designed to be completed by 1992, will reduce all internal tariff and regulatory barriers to trade, will harmonize taxes and subsidies, and will allow companies operating in Europe to manage their production and trade with much the same freedom as do companies in the United States.

■ In late 1988, the United States completed and enacted landmark trade legislation. The 1988 Trade Acts, drafted in response to the enormous trade deficits of the mid-1980s, attempted to require "fair" trade as well as free trade. Table 39-2 summarizes the high points of the 1988 trade legislation.

Appraisal How successful have nations and the GATT been in achieving the goals of reducing trade barriers? Figure 39-4 shows dramatically how, as a result of the many rounds of successful tariff negotiations, the United States has ceased to be a high-tariff

HIGHLIGHTS OF 1988 TRADE ACTS

■ Require 60-day notice for major plant shutdowns and layoffs.

■ Grant negotiating authority to cut tariffs up to 50 percent in the Uruguay Round and authorize other tariff negotiations.

■ The government is required to investigate, and is authorized to retaliate against, countries that maintain numerous and pervasive "unfair trade barriers."

■ President has authority to block foreign takeovers of domestic companies if takeover is a threat to national security.

■ Repeal Windfall Profits Tax and weaken foreign anti-bribery laws.

■ Expand trade adjustment assistance to aid workers displaced by plant closings or modernizations.

Table 39-2 1988 Trade Acts authorize trade negotiations while protecting against foreign trade barriers

nation. Indeed, the average tariff rate in the United States has fallen to less than one-tenth of the level reached under the Smoot-Hawley tariff, and similar reductions have been achieved in other nations. But the political proponents of protection remain powerful. Many feel that the industrial world is always perilously near the point where a spark of protection and retaliation like that of the 1930s might ignite a major trade war between nations. Up to now, however, the forces of conciliation have prevailed.

SUMMARY

1. Completely free trade equalizes prices at home with those in world markets. Under trade, goods flow uphill from low-price to high-price markets.

2. A tariff raises the domestic prices of imported goods, leading to a decline in con-

sumption and imports along with an increase in domestic production. Quotas have very similar effects and may, in addition, cost the government revenues.

3. A tariff causes economic waste. The economy suffers losses from decreased home consumption and from wastage of resources on goods lacking comparative advantage. The losses generally exceed government revenues from the tariff.

4. Most arguments for tariffs are simply rationalizations for special benefits to particular pressure groups and cannot withstand analysis. Only three arguments can stand up to careful analysis: *(a)* The terms of trade or "optimal tariff" can in principle raise a country's consumption at the expense of its trading partners. *(b)* Under dynamic conditions, tariffs might push an economy toward fuller employment, but monetary or fiscal policies could attain the same employment goal with fewer inefficiencies. *(c)* The only exception of any practical importance in a full-employment economy is provided by the case of infant industries that need temporary protection in order to realize their true long-run comparative advantages.

CONCEPTS FOR REVIEW

price equilibrium with and without trade
tariff, quota
effects of tariffs on price, imports,
  domestic production
mercantilist, cheap foreign labor,
  retaliatory arguments

terms-of-trade shifts and the optimal
  tariff
unemployment and tariffs
infant-industry tariff
GATT and trade negotiations

QUESTIONS FOR DISCUSSION

1. What do you think are the single most favorable arguments for and against protection?

2. What arguments have been made for import protection of the computer or automobile industries? Weigh the pros and cons. Present your point of view carefully.

3. Comment critically on the infant-industry argument for tariffs. What is its relation to comparative advantage? What are today's infant industries?

4. The 1988 Trade Act allows for tariff protection for industries "injured" by imports. Construct the best possible defense for this provision; attack it with the most important opposing arguments.

5. Since the 1930s, industrial nations have negotiated a series of agreements in which they lowered their tariff barriers. Explain how a mutual reduction of tariffs helps countries in *four* ways. (HINT: Each side's tariff reductions helps both itself and its trading partners.)

6. The "new wave" of protectionism put forth during the 1980s made the following arguments for protecting domestic industries against foreign competition:

(a) "In some situations, a country could improve its standard of living by imposing protection if no one else retaliated."

(b) "If the marketplace is not working well, and there is excessive unemployment, tariffs might lower the unemployment rate."

(c) "A country might be willing to accept a small drop in its living standard to preserve certain industries that it deems necessary for national security, such as shipping or steel, by protecting them from foreign competition."

(d) "Wages in Korea are but one-tenth of those in the United States. Unless we limit the imports of Korean manufactures, we face a future in which our trade deficit continues to deteriorate under the onslaught of competition from low-wage East Asian workers."

In each case, relate the argument to one of the traditional defenses of protectionism. State the conditions under which it is valid and decide whether you agree with it.

7. (For those who have studied Chapter 25's appendix on game theory.) Examine the payoff matrix in Figure 39-5 and explain how these data illustrate the optimal-tariff or terms-of-trade argument for tariffs. Describe how nations acting noncooperatively might well end up in an equilibrium with high tariff barriers. Further explain how a negotiated reduction of tariffs will benefit *all* countries.

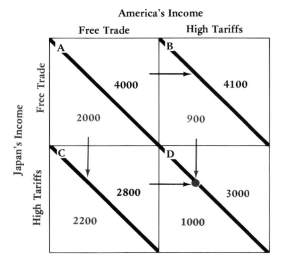

Figure 39-5   Payoff matrix for international trade

8. Why might the political system lead to high tariffs even though these reduce overall national income? Using this analysis, explain why the United States imposes high duties on textiles and sugar but not on bananas or coffee?

9. The United States has quotas on steel, shipping, automobiles, textiles, and many other products. Economists estimate that by auctioning off the quota rights, the Treasury would gain at least $10 billion annually. Use Figure 39-3 to analyze the economics of quotas as follows: Assume that the government imposes a quota of 100 on imports, allocating the quotas to importing countries on the basis of last year's imports. What would be the equilibrium price and quantity of clothing? What would be the efficiency losses from quotas? Who would get revenue rectangle C? What would be the effect of auctioning off the quota rights?

10. Consider a situation in which the industrial countries import all their oil from oil-exporting OPEC countries and where OPEC countries are competitive suppliers with a completely inelastic supply curve. What would be the effect on oil imports, OPEC oil prices, and industrial-country oil prices if all oil-consuming countries placed a $10-per-barrel import tariff on oil? Which tariff argument might be used to support such a tariff on oil imports?

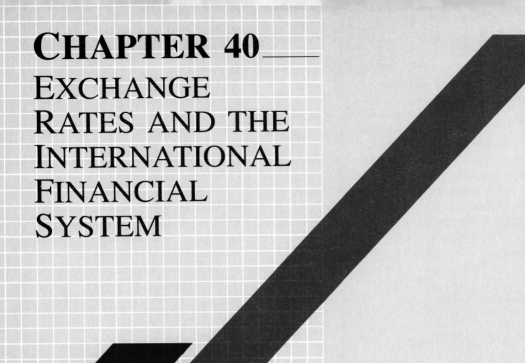

CHAPTER 40

EXCHANGE RATES AND THE INTERNATIONAL FINANCIAL SYSTEM

*Before I built a wall I'd ask to know
What I was walling in or walling out . . .*

Robert Frost

DURING THE 1970s AND 1980s, Americans woke up to discover their economic interdependence with the rest of the world. Time and again, people saw how world events could affect financial or goods markets in the United States. Bad harvests in the Soviet Union drove up food prices in American grocery stores. Technological advances in the Japanese automobile industry threw people out of work in Detroit. The overthrow of the Shah of Iran drove oil prices from $14 to $32 per barrel, produced a great inflation, and thereby contributed to the deepest recession since the 1930s. A mounting trade deficit at home plus rising interest rates abroad triggered a stock market panic that wiped out over $500 billion in American wealth in one day.

Economically, no nation is an island unto itself. When the bell tolls for one nation, it tolls for all.

What are the economic mechanisms that increasingly link nations together? We saw in the last two chapters the way international trade allows nations to specialize in areas of comparative advantage, exporting goods in which they have relative efficiency and importing those in which they are relatively inefficient. But how does international exchange take place? Not by bartering American computers for Japanese cars, but through the medium of money—by buying or selling commodities for dollars or yen or pounds or francs or other currencies. A full understanding of the mechanism of international trade requires a mastery of the principles of international finance.

This concluding chapter surveys the essentials of exchange rates and of the international financial system. The first section examines exchange rates between different currencies and explains different exchange-rate systems. The second part analyzes how the fixed exchange-rate system (known as the Bretton Woods system) fueled the great postwar expansion but then broke down in the 1970s. It also examines how nations today are struggling to rebuild a workable international financial system.

The history of international finance has been marked by alternating periods of smooth functioning, breakdown, and reconstruction. The late 1980s was a period in which many economists and policymakers felt a strong dissatisfaction with the current international financial system; they searched actively for a more stable system. But, however severe the shortcomings of today's or any era's system, we must recognize the essential role of exchange rates in lubricating the wheels of international trade. Some have said of our current international financial system what is said of democracy: Although it is a highly imperfect system, we know of nothing better.

A. The Determination of Foreign Exchange Rates

FOREIGN EXCHANGE RATES

We are all familiar with domestic trade. When I buy Florida oranges or California shirts, I naturally want to pay in dollars. Luckily, the orange grower and the shirt manufacturer are willing to accept U.S. dollars for their expenses. Trade can be carried on in dollars. Economic transactions within a country are relatively simple.

If I want to buy a British bicycle, however, matters become more complicated. I must ultimately pay in British money, or "British pounds," rather than in dollars. Similarly, if the British want to buy U.S. merchandise, they must obtain U.S. dollars. And the requirement to obtain foreign currencies holds for other countries as well.

We see, then, that international trade introduces a new element: the **foreign exchange rate,** which denotes the price of a foreign country's currency in terms of our own.

Here are some examples: The U.S. dollar price of a British pound was recently $1.80; for a British resident wanting to buy U.S. goods, the price of a dollar was £1/$1.80 = £0.56. There is also a foreign exchange rate between U.S. dollars and the currency of each and every country. In mid-1988, the foreign exchange rate was 60 cents for a German mark, 18 cents for a French franc, 80 cents for a Canadian dollar, and 0.8 cent for a Japanese yen. For foreigners desiring to buy dollars, the reciprocal prices were 1.67 German marks, 5.56 French francs, 1.25 Canadian dollars, or 125 Japanese yen for each U.S. dollar.

Given the foreign exchange rate, it is now possible for me to buy my English bicycle. Suppose its quoted price is £100 (i.e., 100 British pounds). All I have to do is look in the newspaper for the foreign exchange rate for pounds. If this is $1.80 per pound, I simply go to a bank with $180 and ask that the money be used to pay the English bicycle exporter. Pay with what? The bank pays with pounds, of course, the kind of money the exporter needs.

You should be able to show what British importers of American grain have to do if they want to buy, say, a $36,000 shipment from an American exporter. Here pounds must be converted into dollars. You will see that, when the foreign exchange rate is $1.80 per pound, the grain shipment costs them £20,000.

Businesses and tourists do not have to know anything more than this for their import or export transactions. But the true economics of foreign exchange rates cannot be grasped until we find out why the foreign exchange rate is at a given level.

What economic principles determine foreign exchange rates? And what forces underlie their movements?

THE FOREIGN EXCHANGE MARKET

To understand the determination of the foreign exchange rate, we need to analyze the workings of the foreign exchange market. The **foreign exchange market** is the market in which currencies of different countries are traded; it is here that the foreign exchange rate is determined. Foreign exchange is traded at the retail level in many banks and firms specializing in that business. Organized markets in New York, Tokyo, London, and Zurich trade hundreds of billions of dollars worth of currencies each day.

We can use our familiar supply and demand curves to illustrate how markets determine the price of foreign currencies. Figure 40-1 shows the supply and demand for British pounds in a simplified example in which we consider only the bilateral trade between Britain and the United States. The demand for British pounds comes from people who need pounds to purchase British goods, services, or financial instruments; the supply of pounds arises from people who are supplying goods, services, or investments to the British. The price of foreign exchange—the foreign exchange rate—settles at that price where supply and demand are in balance.

To understand this relationship in greater depth, let us begin on the demand side. The demand for British pounds originates when Americans need pounds to buy British bicycles and other commodities, to vacation in Wales, to hire British insurance services, and for similar items in the British current account (recall Chapter 38's discussion of the balance of payments). In addition, foreign exchange is required if American firms want to buy land in London or to purchase shares in British companies. In short, we demand foreign currencies when we purchase foreign goods, services, and assets. The demand curve shown in Figure 40-1 is represented by the downward-sloping *DD* curve, with the vertical axis representing the price of the British pound. The demand curve slopes downward to indicate that as the price of the British pound

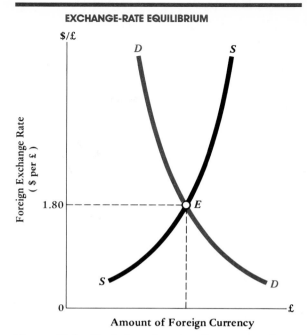

EXCHANGE-RATE EQUILIBRIUM

Figure 40-1   Market exchange rate comes when supply and demand for goods, services, and capital flows are in balance

Behind *DD* is the desire to import British goods, buy British securities, visit the Bard's grave, and so forth. Behind the supply of pounds to be traded for dollars *SS* is the desire for U.S. export goods, services, and capital. If the rate were above *E*, there would be an excess of foreign currency; market forces would push the exchange rate back down to *E*, where the supply and demand for foreign currency are just in balance.

falls, foreigners tend to want to buy more British goods. For example, if the pound were to fall from $1.80/£ to $1.20/£, other things being equal, Americans would want to buy more British bicycles and spend more time visiting Britain.

What lies behind foreigners' supply of their currency (represented in Figure 40-1 by the *SS* supply curve of British pounds)? The British supply their currency when they import goods, services, and assets. For example, when a British student buys an American book or takes a trip to the United States, she supplies the British pounds necessary for the ex-

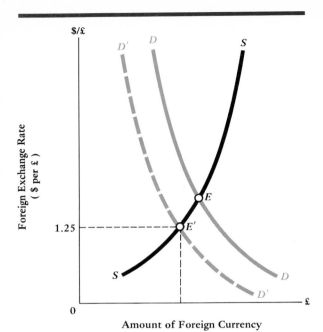

Figure 40-2   A decrease in American imports leads to a higher dollar exchange rate

Suppose Americans travel less to Britain or decide to withdraw troops from Europe. This will lower the imports from Britain and decrease the demand for British pounds, shifting the *DD* curve to the left to *D'D'*. As a result, the exchange rate of the pound falls to $1.25 per £1 (similarly, the exchange rate of the dollar rises to £0.80/$). At the new exchange rate at *E'*, British exports are stimulated and American imports curbed until the supply and demand for British pounds are once more in balance. (What would be the impact of a decision by the British government never to buy American military equipment?)

pense. Or when the British government purchases an American supercomputer for weather forecasting, this adds to the supply of British pounds. Hence, the British supply pounds to pay for their purchases of foreign goods, services, and financial assets. The *SS* curve in Figure 40-1 slopes upward to indicate that as the pound's value rises (and the dollar therefore becomes less expensive) British residents will want to buy more foreign goods, services, and investments and will therefore supply more of their currency to the foreign exchange market.

The supply and demand for British pounds interact in the foreign exchange market. Market forces move

the foreign exchange rate up or down to balance the inflows and outflows of pounds; the price will settle at the equilibrium foreign exchange rate at which the pounds willingly bought just equal the pounds willingly sold.

The balance of supply and demand for foreign exchange determines the foreign exchange rate of a currency. At the market exchange rate of $1.80 per £1, shown at point *E* in Figure 40-1, the exchange rate is in equilibrium, having no tendency to rise or to fall.

We saw above that the exchange rate is a reciprocal relationship. Just as we sell a British pound for $1.80, we buy a dollar for £0.56. We could also have drawn the reciprocal demand-and-supply relationship by analyzing the demand and supply of U.S. dollars. In our simplified bilateral trading world, the British supply of pounds would translate into a demand for dollars, while the American demand for pounds would have represented a supply of dollars. We could then have drawn the supply and demand for the dollar foreign exchange, and the equilibrium would have come at £0.56/$ rather than $1.80/£.

Moreover, this supply and demand for foreign exchange exists for every currency. And in a world of many nations, it is the many-sided exchange and trade, with demands and supplies coming from all quarters, that determines the entire array of foreign exchange rates.

Effects of Changes in Trade   What would happen if there were changes in the volume of international trade? For example, what would be the result if the United States withdrew its troops from Europe or decided to curb imports from Britain, or if we traveled less abroad because domestic airfares were lower?

In each case, America's demand for foreign currencies would decrease. The result is shown in Figure 40-2 for the case where the shift affects Britain. The decline in purchases of goods, services, and investments decreases the demand for foreign currencies. This change is represented by a leftward shift in the demand curve. The result will be a lower price of foreign currencies, that is, a lower exchange rate on the pound and a higher exchange rate for the dollar. How much will exchange rates change? Just enough so that American exports and capital flows are increased, and British imports and capital flows decreased, until supply and demand are again in balance. In the example shown in Figure 40-2, the pound has declined from $1.80 to $1.25 per £1.

Terminology for Exchange-Rate Changes

Foreign exchange markets have a special vocabulary. A doubling of the pound is a halving of the dollar. By definition, a fall in the price of one currency in terms of one or all others is called a "depreciation." A rise in the price of a currency in terms of another currency is called an "appreciation." In our example above, when the price of the pound went from $1.80 to $1.25, the pound depreciated and the dollar underwent an appreciation.

The term "devaluation" is often confused with the term "depreciation." Devaluation is confined to situations in which a country has officially pegged its exchange rate to another currency or to gold and in which the pegged rate or parity is changed by raising the price of the other currency or gold.

For example, when the United States in 1971 changed the official price of gold from $35 to $38 per ounce, we say the dollar was devalued. But when the dollar fell from 150 yen/$ to 120 yen/$, we say that the dollar depreciated.

When a country's foreign exchange rate has declined relative to that of another country, we say that the domestic currency has **depreciated** while the foreign currency has **appreciated.**

When a country's official foreign exchange rate (relative to gold or other currencies) is lowered, we say that the currency has undergone a **devaluation,** while an increase in the official foreign exchange rate is called a **revaluation.**

THREE MAJOR EXCHANGE-RATE SYSTEMS

Having reviewed the principles underlying the market determination of exchange rates, we can now turn to an analysis of the **exchange-rate system,** which denotes the set of rules, arrangements, and institutions under which payments are made and received for transactions reaching across national boundaries.

At the outset, we must ask why there is an exchange-rate system to regulate exchange rates, when there is no "lettuce system" to regulate lettuce prices or even a "machinery system" to affect the machinery market. The reason is that all governments feel that the foreign exchange rate is too important to be left to the unregulated market. Foreign exchange rates affect output, inflation, foreign trade, and many other central economic goals, so it is natural that governments will choose to try to affect exchange markets in ways they think favorable for their political and economic health.

The importance of the international monetary system was well stated by international economist Robert Solomon:

> Like the traffic lights in a city, the international monetary system is taken for granted until it begins to malfunction and to disrupt people's lives. . . . A well-functioning monetary system will facilitate international trade and investment and smooth adaptation to change. A monetary system that functions poorly may not only discourage the development of trade and investment among nations but subject their economies to disruptive shocks when necessary adjustments to change are prevented or delayed.[1]

In understanding the functioning of the exchange-rate system, three important cases should be studied:

- The gold standard

- The case of "pure" floating exchange rates, in which prices fluctuate incessantly according to supply and demand (much as the price of soybeans fluctuates in response to market conditions)

- Today's system of "managed floating" exchange rates, which involves some currencies whose values float (or fluctuate) freely in the market; some currencies whose values are determined by a combination of government intervention and the market; along with others that are pegged or fixed to one currency (such as the dollar) or a group of currencies

---

[1] Robert Solomon, *The International Monetary System, 1945–1976: An Insider's View* (Harper & Row, New York, 1977), pp. 1, 7.

THE CLASSICAL GOLD STANDARD

Historically, one of the most important exchange-rate systems was the gold standard. This system, which provided for fixed exchange rates among participating countries, held sway in its purest form during the period 1880–1913. As we will describe, most countries defined their currencies in terms of a fixed amount of gold, thereby establishing fixed exchange rates among the countries on the gold standard.

The functioning of the gold standard can be seen easily by a simplified example. Suppose people everywhere insisted on being paid in bits of pure gold metal. Weight alone would count, so long as there was a guarantee of purity. Then buying a bicycle in Britain would merely require payment in gold at a price expressed in ounces of gold. By definition there would be no foreign-exchange-rate problem. Gold would be the common world currency.

The gold standard evolved into essentially this system. It became customary for each country to issue gold coins carrying the seal of the state to guarantee purity and weight. Once gold coins became the medium of exchange—money—foreign trade was no different from domestic trade; everything could be paid for in gold. The only difference would arise if people chose different *units* for their coins. Thus, Queen Victoria chose to make her coins about $\frac{1}{4}$ ounce of gold (the pound) and President McKinley chose to make his unit $\frac{1}{20}$ ounce of gold (the dollar). In that case, the British pound, being 5 times as heavy as the dollar, would naturally have an exchange rate of $5 to £1.

That is essentially how the pre-1914 gold standard worked. Of course, countries tended to use their own coins. But anyone was free to melt down coins and sell them at the going price of gold. So, except for the costs of melting down, shipping across the oceans, and recoining, all countries on the gold standard had exchange rates that were fixed; the exchange rates (also called "par values" or "parities") between the different currencies were determined by the gold content of their monetary units.

Only minor qualifications need be brought to the gold-standard example analyzed above. Gold being quite inconvenient to carry around for spending purposes, governments inevitably issued paper certificates that were pledged to be redeemable in gold metal. People had the right to turn in gold for certificates and certificates for gold, and they often exercised that right. Also, in those days ocean transport was slow and costly, so exchange rates fluctuated in a narrow band between "gold points."*

Hume's Gold-Flow Equilibrating Mechanism

Now that we have seen the mechanics of foreign exchange, we ask a deeper question: Under the gold standard, what kept America from buying more British goods and services and lending more capital to Britain than Britain did from us? Put differently, what kept us from demanding more British pounds than Britain wanted to supply? We would have had to ship gold to Britain to pay for our trade deficit. Wouldn't we eventually lose all our gold?

Mercantilists fretted that there would be a drain of a country's gold and argued that this drain should be halted by the government's placing tariffs and quotas on imports, subsidies on exports, and numerous other interferences.

Mercantilism came under attack from Adam Smith.

---

* Thus, if it costs 2 cents to ship $\frac{1}{4}$ ounce of gold either way across the Atlantic Ocean (inclusive of insurance and interest costs), could the exchange rate depart a little from $5? Yes. In New York, the quoted price of a pound could rise to as much as $5.02 before it would pay an arbitrager to get gold bars and ship them to London to be exchanged for pounds; a price higher than $5.02 could not prevail because enough gold would be flowing to keep the price no higher than the upper "gold point." It should be evident that the pound could fall only to $4.98. When the exchange rate got down to this lower gold point, it would be cheaper for gold to be shipped from Europe to America.

All this actually happened (except that $5 is substituted here for the correct pre-1914 parity of $4.87 to simplify the arithmetic, and the shipping costs are only approximate). Before 1914, the foreign exchange rate of the pound and dollar stayed essentially stable, varying but a trifle from these weight-determined mint parities until the gold points were touched and gold flowed in the indicated direction.

But the clearest refutation of mercantile reasoning flowed from the pen of David Hume, the great British philosopher, in 1752. His argument is as important today as then for understanding how trade flows get balanced.

Hume first pointed out that all countries could not be simultaneously losing gold. Where would it go, into the sea? And even if a single nation were to lose a good deal of its gold, that would be no tragedy if prices were to adjust as well. Suppose Britain lost half of its gold. If at the same time all prices and incomes in Britain were exactly halved, then no one in the country would be any better or worse off. Even though people have only half as much gold, that smaller quantity will buy the same quantity of goods and services. The *real* value of monetary gold (that is, the quantity of real commodities that the gold will buy) has remained unchanged. So, Hume argued, losing half or nine-tenths of a nation's gold is of no concern if the nation merely ends up with a balanced reduction of all prices and costs.

The second part of Hume's reasoning showed that there is an automatic mechanism that tends to keep international payments in balance under the gold standard. This explanation rested in part upon the quantity theory of prices outlined in Chapter 16. Before turning to Hume's explanation, it is well to recall the quantity theory.

Gold and the Quantity Theory Hume was, in fact, one of the earliest proponents of the quantity theory of prices. Under this doctrine, the overall price level in an economy is proportional to the supply of money. Under the gold standard, gold formed an important part of the money supply—either directly, in the form of gold coins, or indirectly, when governments used gold as backing for paper money.

What would be the impact of a country losing gold? First, the country's money supply would decline either because gold coins would be exported or because some of the gold backing for the currency would leave the country. Putting both these consequences together, we would find that a loss of gold leads to a reduction in the money supply. The next step, according to the quantity theory, is that prices and costs change proportionally to the change in the money supply. If Britain loses 10 percent of its gold to pay for a trade deficit, the quantity theory predicts that Britain's prices, costs, and incomes would fall 10 percent. If gold discoveries in California lead to a sharp increase in gold supplies, we would expect to see a proportional increase in the price level in the United States.

The Four-Pronged Mechanism We now can explain Hume's brilliant theory of how international payments equilibrium arises. It runs as follows: Suppose that America runs a large trade deficit and begins to lose gold. According to the quantity theory of prices, this loss of gold reduces America's money supply and thence drives down America's prices and costs.

As a result, (1) America decreases its imports of British and other foreign goods that have become relatively expensive; moreover, (2) because America's domestically produced goods are now relatively inexpensive on world markets, America's exports increase.

The opposite effect occurs in Britain and other foreign countries. When Britain's exports grow rapidly, it receives gold in return. Britain's money supply increases, driving up British prices and costs according to the quantity theory.

Two more prongs of the Hume mechanism now come into play: (3) British and other foreign exports have become more expensive, so the volume of goods exported to America declines; and (4) British citizens, faced with a higher domestic price level, now import more of America's low-priced goods.

The result of Hume's four-pronged gold-flow mechanism is to improve the balance of payments of the country losing gold and to worsen that of the country gaining the gold. In the end, an equilibrium of international trade and finance is reestablished at new relative prices that keep trade and international lending in balance with no net gold flow. This equilibrium is a stable one and requires no tariffs or other government intervention.

FLEXIBLE EXCHANGE RATES

Having seen how a gold standard works, we turn next to the case of flexible exchange rates. A system of

flexible exchange rates is one in which the foreign exchange rate is predominantly determined by the market forces of supply and demand. That is, in a flexible exchange-rate system, the relative prices of currencies are determined by buying and selling among people, firms, and governments.

We saw that under the gold standard the dollar and the pound were tied in a $5-to-£1 relationship. But what would have happened in 1913 if the United States decided not to define its dollar in terms of a fixed weight of gold? Would the dollar have sold for $4 per £1? Or $6 per £1? The world has learned during the period after 1973 that flexible exchange rates tend to fluctuate widely, as we will see later in this chapter.

Within the class of flexible exchange-rate systems, we can distinguish the two important subcases of a *free-floating* system and a *managed-floating* system depending on the degree of government intervention. The government **intervenes,** or engages in exchange-rate intervention, when it buys or sells its own or foreign currencies to affect exchange rates. For example, the Japanese government on a given day might buy $1 billion worth of Japanese yen with U.S. dollars. This would cause a rise in value, or appreciation, of the yen. Governments generally tend to intervene heavily when they believe their country's foreign exchange rate is higher or lower than is desirable.

A **freely floating** exchange rate is one determined purely by supply and demand without any government intervention. When the government intervenes in exchange markets to affect its exchange rate, this system is called **managed floating.**

The first case we examine is of freely floating exchange rates.

Freely Floating Exchange Rates

In a system of freely floating exchange rates, the prices will be determined by the forces of supply and demand, as was illustrated at the beginning of this chapter. Say that at an exchange rate of $1.50 per £1, Americans are importing many British goods, while the British import few American goods. This means that Americans will be demanding a large quantity of

British pounds to buy British goods, while the British will be supplying few British pounds.

What will be the outcome? Our excess demand for British pounds will bid up the price of pounds (or, in other words, will bid down the price of the dollar).

How far will exchange rates move? Just far enough that—at the new higher price of, say, $2 for the British pound—the foreign exchange market is in equilibrium. The price of the pound must move up until the diminished quantity of British pounds demanded is equal to the increased supply of British pounds.

Two main steps are involved: (1) With the pound more expensive, it will cost more to import British goods, services, and investments, causing our demand for imports to fall off in the usual fashion. (2) With the dollar now cheaper, our goods will cost less to foreigners. They will want to purchase more of our export goods. (If we look at these two effects from both their viewpoint and our own, we have something much like the four-pronged mechanism of Hume.)

Managed Floating Exchange Rates

In the freely floating exchange-rate system just described, the government was passive. It allowed the foreign exchange market to determine the value of the dollar (just as it allows markets to determine the value of oats, GM stock, or copper).

Few countries, in reality, allow their currencies to float freely. Rather, they intervene—buying and selling currencies—to prevent wide swings in exchange rates, or even to maintain a *parity* (an announced target exchange rate with other countries).

A particularly important example of a managed exchange-rate system, known as *pegged exchange rates,* prevailed during the period from World War II until 1971. Called the "Bretton Woods system," it allowed countries to set fixed parities or pegged exchange rates with each other; the rates might be $2.40 per British pound, 4 German marks per $1, and so forth. Countries then took steps to defend the set of exchange rates. From time to time, when exchange rates deviated too far from the official rates, countries would adjust the official parities. The essence of the Bretton Woods system, then, was that the exchange rates were fixed but adjustable—that is, fixed in the short run but adjustable in the long run.

Today, we see a variety of different exchange-rate systems coexisting. The European countries have joined together in a system similar to the Bretton Woods system. But each of the three major currency areas—the U.S. dollar, the Japanese yen, and the European currencies—have floated more or less freely against the others over the period since 1973. Many countries in Latin America peg their exchange

rates to the U.S. dollar. In addition, almost all countries tend to intervene whenever markets become "disorderly" or when exchange rates seem far out of line with what is thought appropriate given price levels, trade flows, and historical levels of exchange rates. This system—with a mixture of different components—is called *managed floating*. We return to a full discussion of this system in a later section of this chapter.

B. EVOLUTION OF THE INTERNATIONAL MONETARY SYSTEM

Now that we have surveyed the highlights of exchange rates and of the international monetary system, we will analyze the history of international economic institutions along with current problems of international finance.

In the balance of this chapter, we will describe how the industrial countries organized trade and finance after the economic and physical devastation of the Great Depression and World War II. This era marked the establishment of the General Agreement on Tariffs and Trade (the GATT) as well as the design of the Bretton Woods system. The Bretton Woods system survived until the early 1970s, after which it was replaced by a host of different systems in today's international economy.

Finally, we will review the major issues of international finance facing major countries today. Should the United States and other countries continue to allow their currencies to float flexibly? Or should we return to some kind of fixed exchange-rate system? Should gold be returned to its former place as the kingpin of the international currency system, or should some form of international money be devised? This last section discusses these central issues for the 1990s.

BUILDING INTERNATIONAL INSTITUTIONS AFTER WORLD WAR II

In the winter of 1946, Europe and Japan were buried under mountains of rubble. America alone emerged

with her economy intact, able to meet the urgent need to rebuild the countries of allies and foes alike. In contrast to the bitter recriminations that followed World War I—with hyperinflations, revolutions, and the Great Depression—the international political system after World War II responded to the needs by constructing durable institutions within which the international economy could recover quickly. The four major economic institutions of the 1940s—the GATT (described in Chapter 39), the Bretton Woods exchange-rate system, the International Monetary Fund, and the World Bank—stand as monuments to wise and farsighted statecraft.

The Bretton Woods System

The economic and social turmoil of the 1930s deeply impressed economic thinkers of the 1940s. They were determined to avoid the economic chaos and competitive devaluations of the Great Depression.

In order to map out a new international economic order, the United States, Britain, and their major allies gathered in Bretton Woods, New Hampshire, in 1944. Under the intellectual leadership of J. M. Keynes and the American diplomat H. D. White, this landmark conference hammered out an agreement that led to formation of the International Monetary Fund (IMF), the World Bank, and the Bretton Woods exchange-rate system. For the first time in history, nations agreed upon a system for regulating the international financial system. Even though some of the rules have changed since 1944, the basic institutions designed there play even more vital roles today than many imagined at the time.

The conference designed a framework for managing exchange rates that is known as the *Bretton Woods system*. Those who attended the Bretton Woods conference remembered well the failings of the earlier gold standard. Among the severest critic of the gold standard was Lord Keynes, who wrote at the beginning of his career:

> If . . . gold is at last deposed from its despotic control over us and reduced to the position of a constitutional monarch, a new chapter of history will be opened. Man will have made another step forward in the attainment of self government.[2]

Under the Bretton Woods system, gold was established as a dual monarch along with the dollar. Instead of using gold as the only international money, each currency had an established parity that was set in terms of both the U.S. dollar and gold. As the key or reserve currency, the parity of the dollar was pegged in terms of gold, initially at $35 per ounce of gold. Other currencies were defined in terms of both gold and the dollar. For example, the parity of the British pound was set at £12.5 per ounce of gold. Given the gold price of the dollar, this implied an official exchange rate between the dollar and the pound of $35/£12.5 = $2.80 per £1, which was thereby set as the official parity on the pound. Under the Bretton Woods system, therefore, because each currency's parity was set in terms of gold and the dollar, a set of exchange rates *among* currencies was fixed by international agreement.

The Bretton Woods system succeeded in keeping exchange rates fixed for most of the period from 1945 until 1971. However, whenever one currency got too far out of line with its appropriate or ''fundamental'' value, the parity could be adjusted. The German mark was adjusted upward, or revalued, on several occasions, while the British pound was devalued from $2.80 per £1 to $2.40 per £1 in 1967.

The ability to adjust exchange rates when fundamental disequilibrium arose was the central distinc-

---

[2] *Economic Journal,* December 1914.

tion between the Bretton Woods system and the gold standard, making the former a *fixed but adjustable* exchange-rate system. The changes in exchange rates would ideally be worked out among countries in a cooperative way. By having a fixed but adjustable system, the designers of Bretton Woods hoped to have the best of two worlds: (1) the *stability* of the gold standard, a world in which exchange rates would be predictable from one month to the next, thereby encouraging trade and capital flows, along with (2) the *adaptability* of flexible exchange rates, under which persistent relative price differences among countries could be adjusted to by exchange-rate changes rather than by the painful deflation and unemployment necessary under the gold standard.

The International Monetary Fund (IMF)

Another major contribution of the Bretton Woods conference was the establishment of the International Monetary Fund (or IMF), which today continues to administer the international monetary system and to operate as a central bank for central banks. Member countries subscribe by lending their currencies to the IMF; the IMF then relends these funds to help countries in balance-of-payments difficulties. In recent years, the IMF has played a useful role in helping middle-income countries with balance-of-payments deficits and in organizing a cooperative response to the international debt crisis.

How would an IMF mission operate today? Let us say that Mexico has a balance-of-payments deficit. It is having trouble paying interest and principal on its $110 billion of government-guaranteed foreign loans. American and Japanese banks are unwilling to provide any funds. (See the analysis of the international debt problem in Chapter 37.)

At this point the IMF might send a team of specialists to pore over the country's books; it would come up with an austerity plan for Mexico, generally involving slowing GNP growth and cutting imports. When Mexico and the IMF agree on the plan, the IMF will lend Mexico $1 or $2 or $8 billion to ''bridge'' the country over until its balance of payments improves. In addition, there is likely to be a ''debt rescheduling,'' wherein banks lend more funds and stretch out existing loans.

If the IMF program is successful, the country's balance of payments soon will regain health, and the country will resume economic growth.

The World Bank

The Bretton Woods conference also established the World Bank. The Bank is capitalized by lending nations who subscribe in proportion to their economic importance. The Bank can use its capital to make international loans to countries whose projects seem economically sound but who cannot get private loans at low interest rates.

As a result of such long-term loans, goods and services flow from the advanced nations to developing countries. In recent years, the World Bank has made new loans averaging $8 billion per year.

While the loans are being spent, the advanced world is forgoing domestic spending. When the loans are being ''serviced'' or repaid, the advanced nations can enjoy somewhat higher imports of useful goods. Production in the borrowing lands will have risen by more than enough to pay interest on the loans; wages and living standards generally will be higher, not lower, because of what foreign capital has added to the GNP of the borrowing country.

Demise of the Bretton Woods System

During the first three decades after World War II, the world was on a dollar standard. The U.S. dollar was the key currency; most international trade and finance were carried out in dollars and payments were most often made in dollars. Exchange-rate parities were set in dollar terms, and private and government reserves were kept in dollar balances.

The world economy thrived during this period. The industrial nations began to lower trade barriers and to make all their currencies freely convertible. The economies of Europe and East Asia recovered from war damage and grew at spectacular rates. But recovery contained the seeds of its own destruction. Dollars began to pile up abroad as Germany and Japan developed trade surpluses while U.S. deficits were fueled

by heavy spending for military programs abroad (including the Vietnam war) and growing overseas investment by American firms. By the 1960s, the United States began to incur balance-of-payments deficits, and dollar holdings abroad grew from next to nothing in 1945 to $50 billion in the early 1970s.

By 1971, the international economy was experiencing severe strains. The amount of liquid dollar balances grew so large that governments had difficulty defending the official parities. People began to lose confidence in the ''almighty dollar.'' And the lowered barriers to capital flows meant that billions of dollars could cross the Atlantic in minutes. Many economists believe that by 1971 the world had crossed an irreversible threshold and that countries could no longer maintain fixed exchange rates in the face of enormous pools of mobile financial capital.

In August 1971, President Nixon formally severed the link between the dollar and gold, bringing the Bretton Woods era to an end. No longer would the United States automatically convert dollars into other assets; no longer would the Treasury trade dollars for gold at $35 per ounce; no longer would the United States set an official parity of the dollar relative to gold or other currencies and then defend those exchange rates at all costs. As the United States abandoned the Bretton Woods system, the world moved into the modern era of managed flexible exchange rates.

Today's System of Managed Floating Exchange Rates

When an old system breaks down, it does not mean a perfected new system is at hand to be adopted. Conference after conference was held in the 1970s by the leading IMF member countries trying to agree on a new system to replace Bretton Woods. But countries could not agree on a new system. So without anyone having planned it that way, the world has moved on to a managed floating exchange-rate system. How does this system work? The following describes how exchange rates have been determined since the breakdown of the Bretton Woods system:

- A very few countries allow their currencies to

float freely, as the United States did during the mid-1970s and during the first years of the Reagan administration. In this approach, a country abstains from virtually all exchange-market intervention, allowing markets to determine its currency's value.

▪ Most major countries have *managed but flexible* exchange rates—this group including today the United States, Japan, and the United Kingdom. Under this system, a country will buy or sell its currency to reduce the day-to-day volatility of currency fluctuations. In addition, a country will sometimes engage in systematic intervention to move its currency toward what it believes to be a more appropriate level. Such a strategy prevailed for Britain, Canada, Japan, and the United States during most of the period from 1973 to 1988.

▪ Some countries pursue *flexible rates with target zones,* whereby they individually or collectively set broad zones within which currencies can fluctuate, intervening to keep exchange rates within these zones.

▪ Many countries, particularly small ones, *peg* their currencies to a major currency or to a "basket" of currencies. This approach or the next one is followed by virtually all small countries. Sometimes, the peg is allowed to glide smoothly upward or downward in a system known as a *gliding* or *crawling peg* (see question 8 at the end of this chapter).

▪ Finally, some countries gather in a *currency block* in order to stabilize exchange rates among themselves while allowing their currencies to move flexibly relative to the rest of the world. The most important of these blocks is the European Monetary System (discussed below).

We return to a discussion of recent proposals for international monetary reform toward the end of this chapter.

CURRENT INTERNATIONAL ECONOMIC PROBLEMS

Such is the shape of today's international financial system. We turn now to analyze some of the major issues on the international scene. These are the role of gold, the problem of the U.S. current-account deficit, and an evaluation of the managed floating exchange-rate system.

What Role for Gold?

After 1971, nations dropped the pretense that their currencies were freely convertible into gold. Yet many people continue to lobby for the use of gold in the international monetary system. What are the current proposals?

Currently, gold is held both in the free market and by governments. Free-market gold is owned by many people who either believe that a great inflation will drive gold's price sky-high or who distrust paper currencies. Most gold today is held by national treasuries or by the IMF. Official gold holdings are part of a nation's international reserves—along with dollars, German marks, and other reserve currencies. Hard-pressed nations can sell off or pledge their gold when they encounter balance-of-payments difficulties.

Two decades ago, specialists in international finance hoped to replace gold with "paper gold." They reasoned that just as national trade moved from gold to managed paper currencies, so should international trade move to a paper reserve asset that would be managed by the IMF. The result was the creation of the *special drawing right* (or SDR), which became an international money. What exactly is this SDR?

In the first place, the SDR is a new unit of account, a basket of five major currencies of the world (the U.S. dollar, the German mark, the French franc, the British pound, and the Japanese yen). Each is given a weight depending upon its importance. A basket of currencies is more diversified than is any one currency; that is why some private transactions are also beginning to be expressed in SDR units.

Second, the SDR is also used as an international reserve asset. SDRs can be used in a very limited way to buy key currencies from the IMF and to perform other minor functions.

A decade ago, some enthusiasts believed that the SDR would displace gold as the new international money, becoming the major reserve asset held by governments. This hope has been largely dashed. The SDR lacked the single requirement for being money.

It was not accepted because it was not accepted. Why was the SDR not accepted? Fundamentally because it did not have any intrinsic value (like that of gold), nor was it backed by a powerful government (as is the dollar). Without value as a commodity money or backing as fiat money, SDRs simply never became common coin.

A Return to Gold? In the early 1980s, many people—prominently led by supply-side economists like Arthur Laffer and Columbia's Robert Mundell—called for a return to the gold standard. Others urged a more broadly based commodity standard as the link between money and the real world.

These clarion calls for a return to the golden age are based on the observation that the general price level has no anchor. Prices can be stable, rising 10 percent a year, or galloping at 100 percent a year. Nothing stands between a stable currency and ruinous hyperinflation but the weak flesh of political resolve. By anchoring the price level to gold or commodities, it is argued, we can once and for all banish the specter of inflation from our lands.

Critics of the gold standard disagree. They concede that gold provides an anchor—but an anchored ship is often more dangerous than one under way. Critics of gold would rather trust the fate of inflation and the price level to the fiscal and monetary policies of human governments than to the vagaries of South African mine production, Russian gold sales, or the highly inelastic supply and demand curves for gold. They add that during the period of the gold standard, from 1870 to 1914, inflation and output were more volatile than over the last four decades of the dollar standard. The cruel dilemmas of macroeconomics—the large social cost of disinflation or of unemployment—would not magically disappear with the wave of a golden wand.

What is the likely role for gold in the coming years? Those who regard gold as a barbaric relic of an earlier age have not succeeded in barring gold from discussions about international finance. Those who hanker to launch a gold standard to do battle against inflationary government policies have found the winds of professional and political opinion blowing against them. From time to time—as when the United States establishes a gold commission in the early 1980s or when a Treasury secretary floats a proposal to include gold as an indicator of inflationary trends in the late 1980s—hopes are rekindled in the hearts of gold bugs. But, funeral by funeral, the advocates of a revived gold standard lose their influence.

The Volatile Dollar

We have seen how strains in the Bretton Woods system led to its breakdown in the early 1970s. During the years that followed, industrial countries attempted to find a system that secured the twin advantages of the earlier system—stability of exchange rates in the short run with adaptability of exchange rates over the long run. Figure 40-3 shows the average exchange value of the dollar against major currencies over this period. Note how stable the dollar's exchange rate was until the Bretton Woods system broke down in 1971; also examine the steady depreciation of the dollar from 1971 to 1980.

The decade of the 1980s witnessed a dramatic cycle of dollar rise and decline, or appreciation and depreciation. The rise of the dollar began in 1980 after a tight U.S. monetary policy drove interest rates up sharply. Real interest rates averaged around zero during the period from 1954 to 1978 but rose to an average of 4 percent per year in the 1980–1984 period.

High interest rates, a conservative administration in the United States, and a cut in U.S. tax rates attracted mobile funds from other currencies into U.S. dollars. These events coincided with economic difficulties in continental Europe along with political unrest and a debt crisis in many Latin American countries. Foreigners asked in effect, "Why risk your nest egg in socialist France or in strife-torn Brazil when you can obtain a high real return on your funds in the safe dollar?"

Figure 40-3 shows the result: from 1979 to early 1985, the exchange rate on the dollar rose 80 percent. Indeed, the dollar rose to levels far above those attained just before the Bretton Woods system collapsed because of an "overvalued dollar" in 1971. Many economists and policymakers became convinced that the dollar was overvalued in 1985, and a swift decline soon followed. Over the next 3 years, the dollar lost almost all the value that it had gained in the early 1980s.

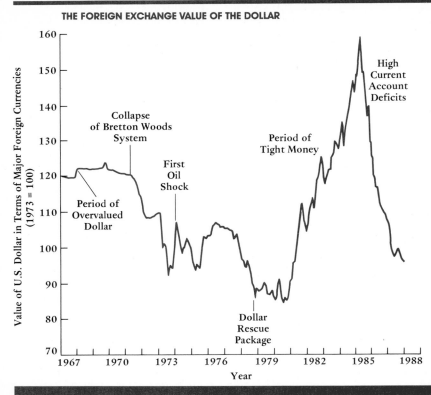

THE FOREIGN EXCHANGE VALUE OF THE DOLLAR

Value of U.S. Dollar in Terms of Major Foreign Currencies (1973 = 100)

- Period of Overvalued Dollar
- Collapse of Bretton Woods System
- First Oil Shock
- Period of Tight Money
- High Current Account Deficits
- Dollar Rescue Package

Figure 40-3 The dollar has shown extreme instability under flexible exchange rates

Before the collapse of the Bretton Woods system, the dollar's value was stable in exchange markets. After 1971, the dollar first drifted down, next rose sharply during the high-interest-rate era of the early 1980s, then collapsed as U.S. interest rates fell and the U.S. trade deficit mounted. The instability shown here has led many to question the usefulness of flexible exchange rates. (Source: Federal Reserve System.)

Impacts of the Overvalued Dollar What were the impacts of U.S. financial policies and the overvaluation of the dollar in the 1980s? The consequences were profound not only for the United States but for virtually the entire world economy.

The first results came from the impact of the high interest rates slowing economic growth in the United States and abroad. We have learned in Chapters 5 through 17 that high interest rates tend to reduce business and residential investment, thereby reducing aggregate spending, slowing economic activity, and raising unemployment. The United States experienced an economic slowdown beginning in 1980, with the trough of the recession coming in 1982.

In addition, the high U.S. interest rates pulled up the interest rates of other major countries. These high interest rates slowed investment in other industrial economies, triggering a sharp slowdown in overall economic activity in the industrial world starting in 1981, a slowdown from which the European econo-

mies had not fully recovered by the late 1980s. In addition, high interest rates led to increased debt-service burdens in poor and middle-income countries (especially the Latin American economies).

The next reaction came in exchange markets. As we saw, the high dollar interest rates pulled up the exchange rate on the dollar. As the dollar rose, this tended to increase American export prices abroad and reduce the prices of goods imported into the United States. As a result, America's exports declined while its imports mounted sharply. The data on imports and exports illustrate the impacts: from 1980 to 1985, the prices of imported goods and services fell by 1 percent, while the prices of our exports in foreign currencies rose over 60 percent. In response, the volume of imports rose 42 percent while export volumes fell 5 percent.

The impact on the overall economy is measured by the changes in *real net exports,* which measure the trade balance in volume terms; more precisely, real net exports are the volume of exports minus the volume of imports, where both are measured in constant dollars. Figure 40-4 shows the dramatic impact of the rising exchange rate of the dollar upon real net exports. From the peak in 1980 to the trough in 1986, real net exports declined by $195 billion, a decline representing 5.2 percent of 1986 GNP (all these figures are in 1982 prices).

What was the impact of the decline in real net exports upon the American economy? As we learned in the macroeconomic chapters, a decline in real net exports has a contractionary multiplier impact upon domestic output and employment. When foreigners spend less here and Americans spend more abroad, the demand for American goods and services declines, our real GNP falls, and unemployment tends to rise. Economic studies indicate that the fall in real net exports was a major contributor to the deep recession in the early 1980s and tended to retard the growth of real GNP during the entire 1980s.

Deindustrialization of America The overvalued dollar produced severe economic hardships in many U.S. sectors exposed to international trade. Industries like automobiles, steel, textiles, and agriculture found the demand for their products withering as their prices rose relative to the prices of foreign competitors. Unemployment in the manufacturing heartland rose sharply as factories were closed and the midwest became known as the "rust belt."

The political response to the soaring trade deficit took many forms. Economists tended to emphasize macroeconomic forces such as the overvalued dollar, tight monetary policy, and a growing fiscal deficit. They called for fiscal austerity, which would force down the dollar's exchange rate and stem the rising trade deficit.

Many non-economists interpreted America's trade problems as indicative of "America in decline." They sometimes called for economic protection against stronger trading partners like Japan, Korea,

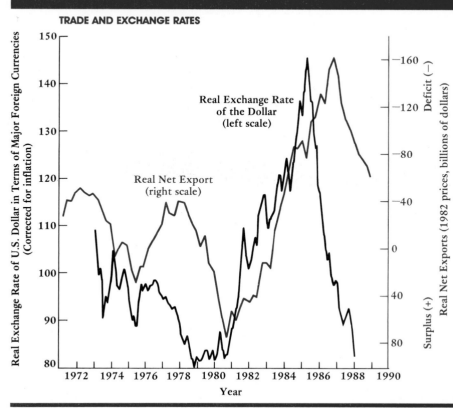

TRADE AND EXCHANGE RATES

Figure 40-4   Real net exports react to exchange rate changes, but with a time lag

The rising real exchange rate of the dollar during the early 1980s increased U.S. export prices and reduced prices of imported goods into the United States. As a result, real net exports (that is, exports minus imports, both measured in constant 1982 prices) fell sharply. After the dollar began to fall in 1985, real net exports began to react only after a considerable time lag. (Source: Real exchange rate is trade-weighted exchange rate corrected for differences in national price levels, from Federal Reserve Board; real net exports from U.S. Department of Commerce.)

and Western Europe. Others argued for "industrial policies," fiscal aid to beleaguered industries to help stem the "deindustrialization of America."

The Dollar's Decline In early 1985, the dollar peaked and began a sharp decline. The reversal was caused in part by governments who used intervention to sell dollars and buy other currencies, in part by speculators who believed that the dollar was overvalued, and in part by lower relative dollar interest rates. As can be seen in Figure 40-4, the dollar declined steadily for the next 3 years, and by mid-1988 it had lost all the ground gained between 1980 and 1985.

The recovery in U.S. net exports was surprisingly slow, and the current and trade accounts remained deeply in deficit at the end of 1988. What was the reason for the slow improvement after the dollar's decline? Trade flows react to exchange-rate changes with a substantial lag because both prices and volumes change slowly in response to exchange-rate movements. Prices react slowly because importers into the United States tend to keep their dollar prices stable and squeeze their profit margins rather than lower their market shares. When importers ultimately raise their prices, people substitute domestic for imported goods only after they have evaluated and selected new products: brand loyalties become entrenched, so that Toyotas and Canons may retain a substantial market share many years after these products have migrated to the high end of the price range. All these forces imply that the full reaction to the exchange-rate depreciation of 1985–1988 may not be felt until the early 1990s. As a result, the United States may continue to experience deficits in its trade and current accounts and in its real net exports for a substantial period of time.

The Lessons of Interdependence The turbulent 1980s marked the era in which the United States fully realized its economic interdependence with the rest of the world. It saw its domestic monetary and fiscal policies spill over to affect exchange rates and trade flows; the country even found its unemployment rate buffeted by the ups and downs of foreign trade. From our vantage point, the central lesson of the 1980s is clear: In a world where economies are increasingly linked by trade and capital flows, interdependence is

unavoidable. No walls can prevent domestic actions from spilling over territorial boundaries. National strengths can be leveraged in a global marketplace, while national weaknesses fall prey to intense foreign competitors. Isolationism is today no more feasible in economic affairs than it is in political or military affairs.

Assessment of Flexible Exchange Rates

The year 1989 marks almost two decades of experience with flexible exchange rates. How well have they functioned? Figure 40-5 tells the story of how different currencies have evolved over the 1970s and 1980s. Note how much greater are the fluctuations after the flexible-rate regime began in 1973.

Many economists and policymakers, having lived through the violent ups and downs of the last two decades, have concluded something like the following:

> We had high hopes that flexible exchange rates would allow our economies to adjust to changes in national economic conditions without unacceptable business cycles or currency fluctuations. But currencies left to free markets wander around like a bunch of drunken sailors. We must put some kind of controls on these wayward exchange rates by moving back toward the fixed or stable exchange rates of the Bretton Woods period.

A careful examination of the historical record will find that flexible exchange rates have indeed performed less well than their advocates had hoped. Exchange rates have been extremely unstable, with key currencies like the dollar appreciating by almost four-fifths in the early 1980s only to lose an equal amount within a few years. The sharp currency movements have, moreover, had unwelcome macroeconomic effects, with the dollar's rise causing a severe external deficit in the United States and turning it into the world's largest debtor. Critics of flexible exchange rates argue that the exchange rate is too important a price to be left to the free market and that it must be brought under the control of governments and central banks.

The EMS Many countries have moved to curb exchange-market fluctuations. One early step was the

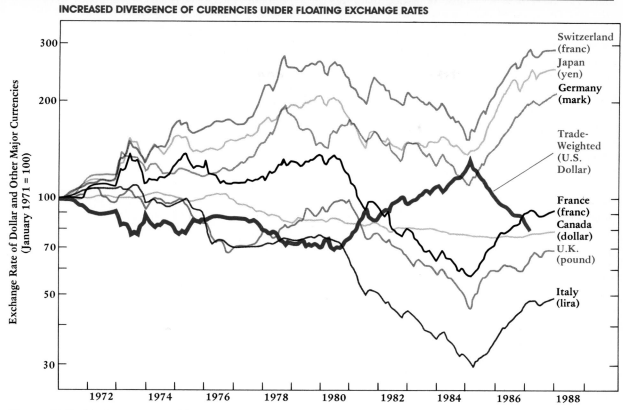

INCREASED DIVERGENCE OF CURRENCIES UNDER FLOATING EXCHANGE RATES

Figure 40-5   Exchange rates float against the dollar—some managed, some free

Before the 1971 demise of Bretton Woods, all parities were pegged to each other. Since then, they have floated up or down with supply and demand. Note how the dollar appreciated from 1980 to 1985 and then depreciated in the late 1980s. Many economists and policymakers view this volatility with alarm and advocate a return to fixed or more stable exchange rates. (Source: International Monetary Fund.)

creation in 1978 of a currency block known as the European Monetary System (or EMS). This system comprises a group of West European countries, notably Germany, France, and Italy, which have re-created a system, similar to the earlier Bretton Woods regime, in which countries intervene to keep their relative exchange rates within narrow limits.

This arrangement is often called the "snake," getting its name because the exchange rates of the group slither up and down relative to the dollar or the yen. But each currency relative to all others in the EMS must remain within the narrow band that constitutes the snake's diameter.

This has some of the advantages of both worlds: the French and the Germans can conveniently transact with each other on quite predictable currency terms. At the same time, any fundamental change in world affairs, such as the major shift in American monetary policy in 1979 or the stock market crash of October 1987, can be absorbed by having the EMS exchange rates float flexibly upward or downward.

The European Monetary System has been moderately successful in reducing short-run exchange-rate fluctuations among European countries. But this has not prevented periodic crises—particularly as French economic difficulties under President Mitterrand's Keynesian socialism drove down the value of the French franc and led it to break through the skin of the snake on numerous occasions, or as German surpluses periodically caused a revaluation of the mark.

Target Zones   Another set of proposals for stabilizing exchange rates would have governments take forceful policy steps to keep exchange rates within certain *target zones*. At the informal end of the spectrum were practices in the mid-1980s, such as the Louvre accord of 1987. Under this arrangement, the largest countries attempted to stabilize their currencies within agreed "reference ranges." The ranges were set by private negotiations among governments and were not announced as formal targets. When the United States became dissatisfied with other governments' policies in October 1987, it abandoned the reference ranges and allowed the dollar to fall sharply.

More wide-ranging proposals by economists would go further toward a regime of fixed exchange rates. One ambitious proposal by John Williamson and Marcus Miller would have governments formally agree on goals for macroeconomic variables (such as nominal GNP) along with target zones for real (or price-adjusted) exchange rates. If national or world conditions deviated from targets, countries would take fiscal- or monetary-policy measures to correct the imbalances. This ambitious program, along with other proposals to replace the flexible exchange-rate non-system, will be debated in the years to come.

Floating Rates and Discipline   We saw that under fixed exchange rates, such as the gold standard, a country would be under very tight discipline. If domestic prices began to rise and a balance-of-payments deficit occurred, gold would leave the country, leading to monetary contraction and recession or worse. A similar (albeit somewhat less powerful) chain of events would occur under the Bretton Woods system.

Under a floating-rate system, these earlier constraints are removed. Countries are now free to determine their own domestic price levels: they can be high-inflation countries or low-inflation countries—through their domestic macroeconomic policies—without automatically triggering a balance-of-payments crisis. But removing the old constraints leads to new ones. Freedom to choose price levels does not mean that a nation can have any *real* wage rate it chooses. Let's see why not.

Suppose the United States raises money wage rates 50 percent overnight. Our costs are now high. Our exports can no longer compete. The dollar floats down to correct the imbalance. That makes imports (raw materials, etc.) more expensive, which raises U.S. prices. In the end, our prices are likely to rise about as much as money wage rates rose.

The moral here is that floating exchange rates do indeed remove the discipline of the gold or dollar standard on the *nominal* price and wage levels. But nothing can remove the irreducible constraint of a system's real productivity level. Flexible exchange rates remove one set of constraints (the straightjacket of gold) and impose another (the harsh verdict of markets about a currency's true value).

America in Decline?

At the end of the 1980s, many observers worried that the United States was traveling rapidly down the road to economic and political decline. They pointed to a variety of symptoms: a declining national savings rate, a persistent federal budget deficit, slow productivity growth, and a large external deficit, which was turning the United States into the world's largest debtor nation. At the same time, the country appeared to lack the political will to take forceful steps to reverse these trends.

Against this backdrop, Yale historian Paul Kennedy published a massive study of economic change and political conflict, *The Rise and Fall of the Great Powers.*[3] Kennedy argued that, because of underlying long-term economic trends, the United States was likely to suffer a significant decline in political and military power in the decades to come.

Having reviewed five centuries of economic, political, and military history, Professor Kennedy puts forth the following theses:

1. "The historical record suggests that there is a very clear connection in the long run between an individual Great Power's economic rise and fall and its growth and decline as an important military power (or world

[3] Paul Kennedy, *The Rise and Fall of the Great Powers: Economic Change and Military Conflict from 1500 to 2000* (Random House, New York, 1987). See especially the introduction, chapter 1, and chapter 8.

empire). . . . Both wealth and power are always relative. . . .'' He buttressed his argument by a thorough historical study of Spain, France, the British Empire, the Soviet Union, and the United States.

2. ''The relative strengths of the leading nations in world affairs never remain constant, principally because of the uneven rate of growth among different societies and of the technological and organizational breakthroughs which bring a greater advantage to one society than to another.'' Economic and technological developments from the development of steam power to the introduction of nuclear weapons illustrate the way technology changes the economic and political fortunes of nations differently and unpredictably.

Kennedy then applied these lessons of history to world economic and political affairs today. He noted that the United States' share of world GNP and manufacturing has declined significantly since its zenith in 1945; that many critical industries and skills have declined, to be replaced by those of foreign countries; that the political consensus has become less favorable to economic growth; and that high defense spending and research and development (R&D) has sapped the nation's civilian economy. At the same time, other regions—particularly Japan, China, and the European Community—are growing rapidly, producing an increasing share of world GNP and manufacturing, and possessing the potential of becoming Great Powers. From these and other facts, Kennedy concluded:

> The only answer to the question . . . of whether the United States can preserve its existing [military and political] position is ''no''—for it simply has not been given to any one society to remain permanently ahead of all the others, because that would imply a freezing of the differentiated patterns of growth rates, technological advance, and military developments which has existed since time immemorial. . . . One is tempted to paraphrase Shaw's deadly serious quip and say, ''Rome fell; Babylon fell; Scarsdale's turn will come.''[4]

Kennedy's thesis provoked a storm of debate and criticism. Some argued that the lessons of Europe do not apply to a continental power like the United States; others contend that America has the means if not necessarily the will to regain its earlier economic preeminence; yet another group believes that, as the exchange rate of the dollar falls, American industry will reconquer sectors lost to foreigners.

Only the future will reveal the correct forecast. But as the debate continues in the years to come, Kennedy's bold hypothesis serves as a stern reminder of the continuing importance of productive efficiency and economic growth. At a deeper level, we recognize in his words the age-old dilemma of choice—guns vs. butter vs. machines. Should the nation spend vast amounts on armaments to protect its vital interests abroad, but run the risk of economic decline that will weaken it in the future? Or should the country enjoy the fruits of its past investments with high consumption today and let the future take care of itself? Or should the nation devote more resources to investment in machines and education and research, thereby ensuring a higher level of production of guns and butter and machines in the future?

There are no right answers to such profound questions about the ultimate economic goals of society. Rather, these final reflections on the economic dilemmas facing America take us full circle to the first question asked in the book: Why study economics? Even though industrial countries are many times wealthier than they were in the age of Adam Smith, the vitality of economics knows no diminishing returns. The catalogue of unsolved economic questions remains long while the list of secure answers is short. Much useful work remains for those who would pursue the purest economic theory or apply economic analysis to the thorniest political problems. As you contemplate further study of our exciting science, take heart from the words of this century's greatest economist:

> For the next twenty-five years, economists will be the most important group of scientists in the world. And it is to be hoped—if they are successful—that after that they will never be important again.[5]

---

[4]The quotes above are from Kennedy, ibid., pp. xxii, xv, and 533.

[5]John Maynard Keynes, ''The Dilemma of Modern Socialism,'' *Political Quarterly,* 1932.

SUMMARY

A. The Determination of Foreign Exchange Rates

1. International trade involves use of different national currencies, which are linked by relative prices called foreign exchange rates. When Americans import British goods, they ultimately need to pay in British pounds. In the foreign exchange market, British pounds might trade for $1.80 per £1 (or reciprocally, $1 would trade for £0.56).

2. In the foreign exchange market involving only two countries, the demand for British pounds comes from Americans who want to purchase goods, services, and investments; the supply of British pounds comes from Britons who want to import commodities or financial assets from America. The interaction of these supplies and demands determines the foreign exchange rate. More generally, foreign exchange rates are determined by the complex interplay of many countries buying and selling among themselves. When trade or capital flows change, this shifts supply and demand and changes the equilibrium exchange rate.

3. When the market price of a currency falls, this is a depreciation; a rise in a currency's value is called an appreciation. In a system where governments announce official foreign exchange rates, a decrease in the official exchange rate is called a devaluation while an increase is a revaluation.

4. A well-functioning international economy requires a smoothly operating exchange-rate system, which denotes the rules and institutions which govern transactions among nations. Three important exchange-rate systems are: *(a)* the gold standard, in which countries define their currencies in terms of a given weight of gold and then buy and sell gold to balance their international payments; *(b)* a pure floating exchange-rate system, in which a country's foreign exchange rate is entirely determined by market forces of supply and demand; and *(c)* a managed floating exchange-rate system, in which government interventions and market forces interact to determine the level of exchange rates.

5. Classical economists like David Hume explained adjustments to trade imbalances by the gold-flow mechanism. Under this process, gold movements would change the money supply and the price level. For example, a trade deficit would lead to a gold outflow which would *(a)* raise exports and *(b)* curb imports of the gold-losing country while *(c)* reducing exports and *(d)* raising imports of the gold-gaining country.

B. Evolution of the International Monetary System

6. After World War II, countries invented a group of international economic institutions that would help organize international trade and finance. These included the International Monetary Fund (IMF) to oversee exchange-rate systems and help countries with their balance of payments; the World Bank, which lends money to low-income countries; and the Bretton Woods exchange-rate system. The Bretton Woods system allowed countries to "peg" their currencies to the dollar and to gold, providing fixed but adjustable exchange rates. When official parities deviated too far from fundamentals, countries could adjust parities and achieve a new equilibrium without incurring the hardships of inflation or recession.

7. When the Bretton Woods system broke down in 1971, it was replaced by today's system of generally flexible exchange rates. Some large countries allow their currencies to float independently; most small countries peg their currencies to the dollar or to other currencies; and most European countries adhere to the European Monetary System (EMS), which resembles closely the Bretton Woods system. Governments often intervene when their currencies get too far out of line with fundamentals or when exchange markets become disorderly.

8. Gold no longer has the key official role that it did under the automatic gold standard. Today, gold's price is determined on competitive markets, much as is that of wheat or GM stock. Monetary reformers hoped that special drawing rights (SDRs or "paper gold") would replace gold as an international money, but instead the dollar has replaced gold as the standard of value and intervention currency. The hope for a return to gold lingers in the hearts of gold bugs and supply siders, but few central bankers believe that such a reform is either realistic or desirable.

9. The most dramatic development of the last few years has been the rise and fall of the dollar. After a decade in which it drifted downward, the dollar surged in 1980. The appreciation led to a sharp fall in real net exports, exacerbating the 1980–1982 recession. The fall in the dollar after 1985 has been slow to cure the enormous trade deficit of the United States.

10. Floating exchange rates appear to remove the automatic discipline of the earlier gold or dollar standards—allowing countries to pursue their own inflationary or noninflationary policies. But in fact a new discipline emerges—that of markets which move exchange rates in response to divergent relative price levels or interest rates, or even to people's expectations about prices or interest rates.

CONCEPTS FOR REVIEW

foreign exchange rate
supply of and demand for foreign
  currencies
currency: appreciation and depreciation;
  revaluation and devaluation
exchange-rate systems: gold standard,
  freely floating, managed floating
Hume's four-pronged gold-flow
  mechanism

fixed exchange rates; pegged parities
intervention
World Bank and IMF
SDR
Bretton Woods conference
Bretton Woods system and its
  breakdown, EMS

QUESTIONS FOR DISCUSSION

1. Define the following and explain the significance of each: foreign exchange rate, gold standard, Bretton Woods system, and freely floating exchange rate.

2. The following table shows some foreign exchange rates (in dollars per unit of foreign currency) as of October 7, 1988:

CURRENCY	PRICE ($ per unit of foreign currency)	PRICE (foreign currency per $1)
Britain (pound)	1.699	
France (franc)	0.1577	
Japan (yen)	0.00750	
South Korea (won)	0.00140	
West Germany (mark)	0.5370	

Fill in the last column of the table with the reciprocal price of the dollar in terms of foreign currencies, being especially careful to note the relevant units.

3. International reserves are a kind of international money: they are used by nations or central banks to settle accounts among countries. Explain how gold, the dollar, and SDRs could serve as reserves under different exchange-rate systems.

4. Figure 40-1 shows the demand and supply for British pounds in an example where Britain and the United States trade only with each other. Describe the reciprocal supply and demand schedules for U.S. dollars. Explain why the supply of pounds is equivalent to the demand for dollars. Also explain the schedule that corresponds to the demand for pounds. Find the equilibrium price of dollars in this new diagram and relate it to the equilibrium in Figure 40-1.

5. James Tobin has written, "A great teacher of mine, Joseph Schumpeter, used to find puzzling irony in the fact that liberal devotees of the free market were unwilling to let the market determine the prices of foreign currencies . . . " [*National Economic Policy* (Yale University Press, New Haven, Conn., 1966), p. 161]. What are some reasons why economists might allow the foreign exchange market to be an exception to a general inclination toward free markets?

6. Show an initial equilibrium in the foreign exchange market for Japanese yen (similar to that for pounds in Figure 40-1). Let the initial equilibrium be 150 yen to the dollar and consider the impact on the market equilibrium of the following:

    (a) The Japanese government decides to sell very large quantities of yen at 160 yen to the dollar.

    (b) Higher interest rates in New York lower the demand for yen.

    (c) The demand for Toyotas and Hondas by Americans increases sharply.

    (d) Japan pays the United States in dollars for American forces in the Far East.

7. In the Louvre accord in 1987, major countries agreed to keep their currencies within "reference zones." Say that the United States and Germany agree to keep the German mark in the range of 1.60 to 1.80 marks to the dollar. Show with the help of a supply-and-demand diagram how the governments could implement this policy.

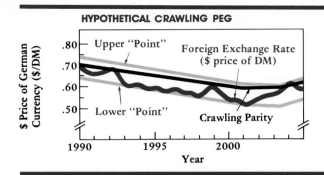

HYPOTHETICAL CRAWLING PEG

Figure 40-6   Crawling peg allows orderly adjustment of exchange rates

8. Figure 40-6 shows a proposal for a ''gliding peg'' or ''crawling peg'' for the exchange rate between the dollar and the German deutsche mark (DM). Such a system lets an exchange rate change a few percent per year. What are its pros and cons relative to fixed exchange rates or freely floating rates?

9. Show in a supply-and-demand diagram how government intervention would change a nation's exchange rate. What would be the effect on the dollar if the United States sold dollars for foreign currencies? Why would intervention be ineffective if, as some believe, the supply of dollars is virtually perfectly elastic?

10. Suppose a country discovers oil, but it takes a decade actually to exploit the new find. What would happen to the country's trade balance after oil begins to flow onto world markets? What might happen to the nation's freely floating currency today once people realize that the trade balance will soon turn favorable? Why would the trade balance thus turn *unfavorable* in the period before the oil is actually recovered?

11. The 1988 *Economic Report of the President* states:

> Dollar appreciation, not slow productivity growth or spiraling wage costs, was the primary cause of the decline in the international competitiveness [i.e., the large trade deficit] of U.S. manufacturing in the first half of the 1980s.

Explain how each of the three factors listed might produce a trade deficit. If domestic prices are determined by a markup relationship in which price is proportional to the wage rate divided by productivity (output per worker), what would the quotation imply about differential rates of inflation in the United States and abroad? Refer to a source book with international data on exchange rates and prices (such as the *Economic Report*) to verify the statement.

12. Consider the following three exchange-rate systems: classical gold standard, freely floating exchange rates, and Bretton Woods system. Compare and contrast the three systems with respect to the following characteristics:

(a) Roles of government vs. market in determining exchange rates

(b) Degree of exchange-rate volatility

(c) Method of adjustment of relative prices across countries

(d) Need for international cooperation and consultation in determining exchange rates

(e) Potential for establishment and maintenance of severe exchange-rate misalignment

13. The 1984 *Economic Report of the President* states:

> In the long run, the exchange rate tends to follow the differential trend in the domestic and foreign price level. If one country's price level gets too far out of line with prices in other countries, there will eventually be a fall in demand for its goods, which will lead to a real depreciation of its currency.

The first sentence espouses the "purchasing-power parity" or "PPP" theory of exchange rates. The PPP theory, which was proposed by David Ricardo in 1817 and by Sweden's Gustav Cassel around 1916, holds that floating exchange rates will move in proportion to relative prices in different countries; that is, if prices in the United States are rising 7 percent annually while those in Germany are rising 3 percent annually, the PPP theory holds that the U.S. dollar will tend to depreciate about 4 percent annually relative to the German mark. Explain the reasoning behind the PPP theory of exchange rates. In addition, using a supply-and-demand diagram like that of Figure 40-1, explain the sequence of events, described in the second sentence of the quotation, whereby a country whose price level is relatively high will find that its exchange rate depreciates.

EPILOGUE

WE HAVE COME a long way in our studies. We have encountered the major problems of the day in both microeconomics and macroeconomics. Economies here and abroad are strained by stubborn unemployment, poverty in the midst of plenty, the heavy debt burdens of middle-income countries and middle-income families, rising pollution levels, government fiscal imbalances, and volatile financial markets.

Our economic investigation has presented many solutions to these entrenched problems. We have learned that the first step toward fruitful application is finding the correct analysis. When unemployment or inflation imperils our prosperity, we must sort through the competing claims of monetarist, Keynesian, supply-side, and rational-expectations doctrines to find the most applicable solution. If global pollution threatens to change our climate, we must explore different approaches to correcting externalities. In finding the right answer, there is no substitute for economic analysis, statistical studies, and a careful review of the historical record.

An economics textbook today is inevitably weighed down by gloomy thoughts about the problems aplenty facing modern societies. Indeed, economists have long been known for their dire predictions.

Remember that at the beginning of the nineteenth century Reverend Malthus condemned the human race to perpetual poverty as unbridled population growth dragged down living standards. It was then that Thomas Carlyle baptized economics "the dismal science." Is it possible that, by constantly reminding people about constraints and production-possibility frontiers, economists have subtly persuaded themselves that there are stringent limits to growth and happiness?

The statistics of economic history reveal that Malthus and Carlyle were dead wrong. Shortly after they issued their baleful predictions, Europe and North America entered an unprecedented century and a half of tremendous growth in real wages, life expectancies, and living standards.

We remind ourselves of the Malthusian errors as an antidote to the pervasive gloom that infects many economic circles today. In the late 1980s, the United States was burdened by large fiscal and external deficits, rising inflation, and the threat of a serious recession. After the stock-market meltdown of October 1987, many drew the parallel between the supply-side euphoria of the 1980s and the speculative atmosphere of the roaring 1920s. Some forecast that the 1990s would be a rerun of the 1930s, with a trade war, deflation, a Great Depression, and social unrest in the industrial world.

In the midst of these fretful thoughts, we recall a famous prophesy made by John Maynard Keynes in 1930. In a crumbling world economy, Keynes was able to look beyond the looming Great Depression and offer a startling vision of the economic future of the human race:

> [S]uppose that a hundred years hence we are all of us . . . eight times better off . . . than we are today. . . . Assuming no important wars and no important increase in population, the *economic problem* may be solved. . . . This means that the economic problem is not—if we look into the future—*the permanent problem of the human race.*

Why, you may ask, is this so startling? It is startling because—if instead of looking into the future, we look into the past—we find that the economic problem, the struggle for subsistence, always has been hitherto the primary, most pressing problem of the human race—not only of the human race, but of the whole of the biological kingdom from the beginnings of life in its most primitive forms.

> Thus we have been expressly evolved by nature—with all our impulses and deepest instincts—for the purpose of solving the economic problem. If the economic problem is solved, mankind will be deprived of its traditional purpose. . . . I think with dread of the readjustment of the habits and instincts of the ordinary man, bred into him for countless generations, which he may be asked to discard within a few decades.

> To use the language of today—must we not expect a general "nervous breakdown"? . . . Thus for the first time since his creation man will be faced with his real, his permanent problem—how to use his freedom from pressing economic cares, how to occupy the leisure, which science and compound interest will have won for him, to live wisely and agreeably and well. . . .

> There are changes in other spheres too which we must expect to come. When the accumulation of wealth is no longer of high social importance, there will be great changes in the code of morals. We shall be able to rid ourselves of many of the pseudo-moral principles which have hag-ridden us for two hundred years, by which we have exalted some of the most distasteful human qualities into the position of the highest virtues. . . . The love of money as a possession—as distinguished from the love of money as a means to the enjoyments and realities of life—will be recognized for what it is, a somewhat disgusting morbidity, one of those semi-criminal, semi-pathological propensities which one hands over with a shudder to the specialists in mental disease.

> But beware! the time for all this is not yet. For at least another hundred years we must pretend to ourselves and to every one that fair is foul and foul is fair; for foul is useful and fair is not. Avarice and usury and precaution must be our gods for a little longer still.[1]

We close with Keynes' vision to remind ourselves that the future is longer than the present. Today's dilemmas will soon be part of history. New and unforeseen problems will emerge. The age-old struggle between scientific advance and the law of diminishing returns will continue. But if history is a guide to the

---

[1] J. M. Keynes, "Economic Possibilities for Our Grandchildren," reprinted in his *Essays in Persuasion* (Macmillan, London, 1933).

future, we can expect that our economic fortunes will continue to improve in the coming decades.

If economic progress does indeed continue, then Keynes' reflections may pose the crucial question for affluent societies: *affluence for what*? How shall we use the resources and time that technological progress liberates from drudgery? For arms? For grain and tractors for poor lands? For classrooms and test tubes? For poetry and ballet? For baseball and tennis? For yachts and furs?

The deepest economic question facing advanced economies is not *how, what,* or *for whom*—but *for what*? One answer was given by the first Keynesian President, John F. Kennedy, who shared his vision of the just society a quarter-century ago: "Now the trumpet summons us again—not as a call to bear arms [but in] a struggle against the common enemies of man: tyranny, poverty, disease, and war itself."

Ultimately, this might serve as the trumpet call for our science as well. The heart has reasons that reason will never know. Economics, poised between an art and a science, can combat the common enemies of humanity by combining reasons drawn from history with purposes drawn from the heart.

GLOSSARY OF TERMS[1]

Ability-to-pay principle (of taxation) The principle that one's tax burden should increase with one's relative income or wealth. This principle does not specify *how much* more those who are better off should pay.

Absolute advantage (in international trade) The ability of country A to produce a commodity more efficiently (i.e., with greater output per unit input) than country B. Possession of such an absolute advantage does not necessarily mean that A can export this commodity

[1]Words in bold type within definitions appear as separate entries in the glossary. For a more detailed discussion of particular terms, the text will provide a useful starting point. More complete discussions are contained in Douglas Greenwald, ed., *Encyclopedia of Economics* (McGraw-Hill, New York, 1983); David W. Pearce, *The Dictionary of Modern Economics,* rev. ed. (The MIT Press, Cambridge, Mass., 1983); *International Encyclopedia of the Social Sciences* (Collier and Macmillan, New York, 1968); and John Eatwell, Murray Milgate, and Peter Newman, *The New Palgrave: A Dictionary of Economics* (Macmillan, London, 1987), four volumes.

to B successfully. Country B may still have the **comparative advantage.**

Accelerator principle A theory of investment spending which holds that the level of investment is governed by the rate of increase in real GNP. That is, there will be positive (or high) net investment when GNP is rising, and there will be zero (or low) net investment when GNP is just holding steady (even if GNP is already very high).

Actual, cyclical, and structural budget The **actual budget** deficit or surplus is the amount recorded in a given year. This is composed of the **structural budget,** which calculates what government revenues, expenditures, and deficits would be if the economy were operating at potential output; and the **cyclical budget,** which measures the effect of the business cycle on the budget.

Adaptive expectations See **expectations.**

Adjustable peg An exchange-rate system in which countries maintain a fixed or "pegged" exchange rate with re-

spect to other currencies. This exchange rate is subject to periodic adjustment, however, when it becomes too far out of line with fundamental forces. This system was used for major currencies during the Bretton Woods period, from 1944 to 1971.

Administered prices (or inflexible prices) A term originated by Gardner C. Means to describe prices that are not "flexible" (refer to **price flexibility**). Administered prices are typically set by imperfectly competitive firms and may stay at the same level for a period of weeks or months.

Aggregate demand Total planned or desired spending in the economy as a whole during a given period. It is determined by the aggregate price level and influenced by domestic investment, net exports, government spending, and the money supply.

Aggregate demand *(AD)* curve The curve showing the relationship between the quantity of goods and services that people are willing to buy and the aggregate price level. As in any demand curve, important variables lie behind the aggregate demand curve, e.g., government spending, exports, and the money supply.

Aggregate supply The total value of goods and services that firms would willingly produce in a given time period. Aggregate supply is a function of the available inputs, technology, and the price level.

Aggregate supply *(AS)* **curve** Curve showing the relationship between the real output that firms would willingly supply and the aggregate price level. The *AS* curve tends to be vertical at potential output in the very long run but may be relatively flat in the short run because of inflexible wages and prices (such as labor contracts) built into the economy.

Allocative efficiency An economic outcome in which no reorganization or trade could occur that would raise the utility or satisfaction of one individual without lowering the utility or satisfaction of another individual. This is sometimes stated as "you cannot make anyone better off without making someone else worse off." Such an outcome is thus on the utility-possibility frontier. Under certain limited conditions, perfect competition leads to allocative efficiency. Also called **Pareto efficiency.**

Antitrust legislation Laws prohibiting monopolization, restraints of trade, and collusion among firms to raise prices or inhibit competition.

Appreciation (of a currency) See **depreciation** (of a currency).

Arbitrage The act of buying a currency or a commodity in one market and simultaneously selling it for a profit in another market. Arbitrage is an important force in eliminating price discrepancies, thereby making markets function more efficiently.

Asset A physical property or intangible right that has economic value. Important examples are plant, equipment, land, patents, copyrights, and financial instruments such as money or bonds.

Asset demand for money See **demand for money.**

Asset, intangible Asset that is not physical or financial in nature, such as the extra value placed on a firm because

it is a going concern with a recognized name (its **goodwill**).

Automatic (or **built-in**) **stabilizer** The property of a government tax and spending system that cushions income changes in the private sector. Examples include unemployment insurance and progressive income taxes.

Average cost Refer to **cost, average.**

Average cost curve, long-run (LRAC, or **LAC)** The graph of the minimum average cost of producing a commodity for each level of output, assuming that technology and input prices are given but that the producer is free to choose the optimal size of plants.

Average cost curve, short-run (SRAC) The graph of minimum average cost of producing a commodity, for each level of output, using the given state of technology, input prices, and existing plant.

Average product Total product or output divided by the quantity of one of the inputs. Hence, the average product of labor is defined as total product divided by the amount of labor input, and similarly for other inputs.

Average propensity to consume See **marginal propensity to consume.**

Average revenue Total revenue divided by total number of units sold—i.e., revenue per unit. Average revenue is generally equal to price.

Average variable cost Refer to **cost, average variable.**

Balance of international payments A statement showing all a nation's transactions with the rest of the world for a given period. It includes purchases and sales of goods and services, gifts, government transactions, and capital movements.

Balance of trade The part of a nation's balance of payments that deals with merchandise (or visible) imports or exports. When "invisibles," or services, are included, the total accounting for imports and exports of goods and services is called the **balance on current account.**

Balance on current account See **balance of trade.**

Balance sheet A statement of a firm's

financial position as of a given date, listing **assets** in one column, **liabilities** plus **net worth** in the other. Each item is listed at its actual or estimated money value. Totals of the two columns must balance because net worth is defined as assets minus liabilities.

Balanced budget See **budget, balanced.**

Bank, commercial A financial intermediary whose prime distinguishing feature until recently was that it accepts checking deposits. Also it holds savings or time deposits and money market deposit accounts; sells traveler's checks and performs other financial services; and lends to individuals and firms. Since 1980, savings banks and other depository institutions have been allowed to accept checking accounts and are thus becoming more like commercial banks.

Bank money Money created by banks, particularly the checking accounts (part of M_1) that are generated by a multiple expansion of bank reserves.

Bank reserves Refer to **reserves, bank.**

Barriers to competition Factors that reduce the amount of competition or the number of producers in an industry, allowing greater economic concentration to occur. Important examples are legal barriers, regulation, and product differentiation.

Barter The direct exchange of one good for another without using anything as money or as a medium of exchange.

Benefit principle (of taxation) The principle that people should be taxed in proportion to the benefits they receive from government programs.

Bond An interest-bearing certificate issued by a government or corporation, promising to repay a sum of money (the principal) plus interest at specified dates in the future.

Breakeven point For an individual, family, or community (in macroeconomics), that level of income at which 100 percent is spent on consumption (i.e., the point where there is neither saving nor dissaving). Positive saving begins at higher income levels.

Breakeven price (or **level,** or **point)**

For a business firm, that level of price at which the firm "breaks even," covering all costs but earning no profit.

Budget, balanced A budget in which total expenditures just equal total receipts (excluding any receipts from borrowing).

Budget constraint See **budget line.**

Budget deficit For a government, the excess of total expenditures over total receipts, with borrowing not included among receipts. This difference (the deficit) is ordinarily financed by borrowing.

Budget, government A statement showing, for the government in question, its planned expenditures and revenues for some period (typically 1 year).

Budget line A line indicating the combination of commodities that a consumer can buy with a given income at a given set of prices. If the graph shows food and clothing, then each point on the line represents a combination of food and clothing that can be bought for a certain income level and with a given set of prices for the two goods. Also sometimes called the **budget constraint.**

Budget surplus Excess of government revenues over government spending; opposite of **budget deficit.**

Built-in stabilizer See **automatic stabilizer.**

Business cycles Fluctuations in overall economic activity, characterized by the simultaneous expansion or contraction of output in most sectors. In modern parlance, business cycles are said to occur when actual GNP rises relative to potential GNP (an expansion) or falls relative to potential GNP (a contraction or recession).

$C + I, C + I + G,$ or $C + I + G + X$ **schedule** A schedule showing the planned or desired levels of aggregate demand for each level of GNP, or the graph on which this schedule is depicted. The schedule includes consumption (C), investment (I), government spending on goods and services (G), and net exports (X).

Capital (capital goods, capital equipment) (1) In classical and neoclassical economic theory, one of the triad of productive inputs (land, labor, capital). Capital consists of durable produced goods that are in turn used in production. The major components of capital are equipment, structures, and inventory. When signifying capital goods, the reference is also made to real capital. (2) In accounting and finance, "capital" means the total amount of money subscribed by the shareholder-owners of a corporation, in return for which they receive shares of the company's stock.

Capital consumption allowance See **depreciation.**

Capital deepening In economic growth theory, a rise in the capital-labor ratio. Contrast with **capital widening.**

Capital gains The rise in value of a capital asset, such as land or common stocks, the gain being the difference between the sales price and the purchase price of the asset.

Capital markets Markets in which financial resources (money, bonds, stocks) are traded. These, along with **financial intermediaries,** are institutions through which savings in the economy are transferred to investors.

Capital-output ratio In economic-growth theory, the ratio of the total capital stock to annual GNP.

Capital widening A rate of growth in real capital stock just equal to the growth of the labor force (or of population), so that the ratio between total capital and total labor remains unchanged (contrast with **capital deepening**).

Capitalism Traditionally defined as an economic system in which most property (land and capital) is privately owned. In such an economy, private markets, with little government intervention, are the prime instruments used to allocate resources and generate incomes.

Cartel An association of producers in a given industry whose purpose is to restrict or bar competition in the industry. They do this by colluding on the prices, by dividing markets, or by engaging in other anticompetitive practices. Cartels are illegal under U.S. antitrust laws.

Central bank A government-established agency (in the United States, the Federal Reserve System) responsible for controlling the nation's money supply and credit conditions and for supervising the financial system, especially commercial banks.

Change in demand vs. change in quantity demanded A change in the quantity buyers want to purchase, prompted by any reason other than a change in price (e.g., increase in income, change in tastes, etc.), is a "change in demand." (In graphical terms, it is a shift of the demand curve.) If, in contrast, the decision to buy more or less is prompted by a change in the good's price, then it is a "change in quantity demanded." (In graphical terms, a change in quantity demanded is a movement along an unchanging demand curve.)

Change in supply vs. change in quantity supplied This distinction is the same for supply as for demand, so see **change in demand vs. change in quantity demanded.**

Checking accounts (or **bank money**) A deposit in a commercial bank or other financial intermediary upon which checks can be written and which is therefore transactions money (or M_1). The major kinds of checking accounts are demand deposits (which can be withdrawn without notice and do not bear interest) and **NOW accounts** (which are indistinguishable from traditional demand deposits except that they earn interest). Checking accounts form the bulk of M_1.

Chicago School of Economics A group of economists (among whom Henry Simons, F. A. von Hayek, Milton Friedman, and George Stigler have been the most prominent) who believe that competitive markets free of government intervention will lead to the most efficient operation of the economy.

Classical economics The predominant school of economic thought prior to the appearance of Keynes' work, founded by Adam Smith in 1776. Other major figures who followed him include David Ricardo, Thomas Malthus, and John Stuart Mill. By and large, this school believed that economic laws (particularly individual self-interest and competition) determine prices and factor rewards and that the price system is the best possible device for resource allocation. Their macroeconomic theory rests on **Say's Law of Markets.**

Clearing market A market in which prices are sufficiently flexible to equilibrate supply and demand very quickly. In markets that clear, there is no rationing, unemployed resources, or excess demand or supply. In practice, this is thought to apply to many commodity and financial markets but not to labor or many product markets.

Closed economy See **open economy.**

Coase theorem A view (not actually a theorem) put forth by Ronald Coase that externalities or economic inefficiencies will be corrected by bargaining between the affected parties.

COLA (cost-of-living adjustment) See **escalator clause.**

Collective bargaining The process of negotiations between a group of workers (usually a union) and their employer. Such bargaining leads to an agreement about wages, fringe benefits, and working conditions.

Collusion Agreement between different firms to cooperate by raising prices, dividing markets, or otherwise restraining competition.

Collusive oligopoly A market structure in which a small number of firms (i.e., a few oligopolists) collude and jointly make their decisions. When they succeed in maximizing their joint profits, the price and quantity in the market closely resemble those prevailing under monopoly.

Command economy A mode of economic organization in which the key economic functions—*what, how,* and *for whom*—are principally made by government directive. Also called a "centrally planned economy."

Commodity money Money with **intrinsic value**; also, the use of some commodity (cattle, beads, etc.) as money. As monetary transactions become more widespread, the use of commodity money becomes increasingly

awkward. Hence the gradual transition to **fiat money** (paper money).

Common stock The financial instrument representing ownership and, generally, voting rights in a corporation. A certain share of a company's stock gives the owner title to that fraction of the votes, net earnings, and assets of the corporation.

Communism At the same time (1) an ideology, (2) a set of political parties, and (3) an economic system. A communist economic system is one in which private ownership of the means of production, particularly industrial capital, is prohibited (for such ownership of capital goods is believed to result in exploitation of workers). In addition, communism holds that income should be distributed equally, or, more ideally, according to "need." In today's communist countries (the Soviet Union, China, and Eastern Europe) most capital and land are owned by the state. These countries are also characterized by extensive central planning, with the state setting many prices, output levels, and other important economic variables.

Comparative advantage (in international trade) The law of comparative advantage says that a nation should specialize in producing and exporting those commodities which it can produce at *relatively* lower costs, and that it should import those goods in which it is a *relatively* high-cost producer. Thus it is a comparative advantage, not an **absolute advantage,** that should dictate trade patterns.

Compensating differentials Differences in wage rates among jobs that serve to offset or compensate for the nonmonetary differences of the jobs. For example, unpleasant jobs that require isolation for many months in the Arctic usually pay wages much higher than those for similar jobs nearer to civilization.

Competition, imperfect Refers to markets in which perfect competition does not hold because at least one seller is large enough to affect the market price and therefore faces a downward-sloping demand curve. Imperfect competition refers to any kind of imperfection—

pure **monopoly**, **oligopoly**, or **monopolistic competition.**

Competition, perfect A market situation in which (1) the number of sellers and buyers is very large and (2) the products offered by sellers are homogeneous (or indistinguishable). Under such conditions, no firm can affect the market price, and each firm faces a horizontal (or perfectly elastic) demand curve.

Competitive equilibrium The balancing of supply and demand in a market or economy characterized by **perfect competition.** Because perfectly competitive sellers and buyers have no power to influence the market, price will move to the point at which price equals both marginal cost and marginal utility.

Competitive market See **competition, perfect.**

Complements Two goods which "go together" in the eyes of consumers (e.g., left shoes and right shoes). Goods are **substitutes** when they compete with each other (as do gloves and mittens).

Compound interest Interest computed on the sum of all past interest earned as well as on the principal. For example, suppose $100 (the principal) is deposited in an account earning 10 percent interest compounded annually. At the end of year 1, interest of $10 is earned. At the end of year 2, the interest payment is $11, $10 on the original principal and $1 on the interest—and so on in future years.

Concentration ratio The percentage of an industry's total output accounted for by the largest firms, typically the largest four or eight firms.

Conglomerate A large corporation producing and selling a variety of unrelated goods (e.g., some cigarette companies have expanded into such unrelated areas as liquor, car rental, and movie production).

Conglomerate merger See **merger.**

Constant returns to scale See **returns to scale.**

Consumer price index (CPI) The most widely used index of the cost of living. It is a **price index** of the cost of a fixed basket of consumer goods in which the weight assigned to each commodity is the share of expenditures on that commodity by urban consumers in 1982–1984.

Consumer sovereignty The outcome of a pure market or price system in which consumers are the ultimate dictators of the kind and quantity of commodities to be produced. Consumers are said to exercise this power by bidding up the prices of those goods they want most; and suppliers, following the lure of higher prices and profits, produce more of those goods. Consumer sovereignty is limited when consumers lack complete information or when tastes are manipulated by producer advertising.

Consumer surplus The difference between the amount that a consumer would be willing to pay for a commodity and the amount he or she actually pays. This difference arises because the marginal utility (in dollar terms) of the first unit bought exceeds the price. Only for the last unit is marginal utility equal to price. Thus the monetary equivalent of the total utility of the commodity consumed may be well above the amount spent. Under quite rigorous assumptions, the money value of consumer surplus can be measured (using a demand-curve diagram) as the area under the demand curve but above the price line.

Consumption In macroeconomics, the total spending, by individuals or a nation, on consumer goods during a given period. Strictly speaking, consumption should apply only to those goods totally used, enjoyed, or "eaten up" within that period. In practice, consumption expenditures include all consumer goods bought, many of which last well beyond the period in question—e.g., furniture, clothing, and automobiles.

Consumption function A schedule relating total consumption to the level of income. The measure of income used might be disposable income (*DI)* or in the case of the national consumption function, GNP. Total wealth and other variables are also frequently assumed to influence consumption.

Consumption-possibility line Refer to **budget line.**

Corporate income tax A tax levied on the annual net income of a corporation.

Corporation The predominant form of business organization in modern capitalist economies. A corporation is a firm owned by individuals or other corporations and has the same rights to buy, sell, and make contracts as a person would have. It is legally separate from those who own it, so its owners have "limited liability." At worst, they can lose their investment in the corporation; beyond that, they are not responsible for its liabilities.

Correlation The degree to which two variables are systematically associated with each other.

Cost, average Total cost (refer to **cost, total**) divided by quantity of goods produced. Short-run and long-run average costs are associated respectively with short-run and long-run total costs.

Cost, average variable Total variable cost (refer to **cost, variable**) divided by quantity of output produced.

Cost, fixed The cost a firm would incur even if its output for the period in question were zero. Total fixed cost is made up of such individual fixed costs as interest payments, mortgage payments, and directors' fees.

Cost, marginal The increase in total cost required to produce 1 extra unit of output (or the reduction in total cost from producing 1 unit fewer). Short-run and long-run marginal costs are associated with short-run and long-run total costs, respectively.

Cost, minimum The lowest attainable cost per unit (whether average, variable, or marginal). Every point on an average cost curve is a minimum in the sense that it is the best the firm can do with respect to cost for the output which that point represents. Minimum average cost is the lowest point, or points, on that curve.

Cost-push inflation Inflation originating on the supply side of markets, such as from a sharp increase in wages or oil prices (i.e., for reasons other than excess demand for goods, which leads to

demand-pull inflation). In the aggregate supply-and-demand framework, cost-push is illustrated as an upward shift of the *AS* curve.

Cost, total The minimum attainable total cost, given a particular level of technology and set of input prices. Short-run total cost takes existing plant and other fixed costs as given. Long-run total cost is the cost that would be incurred (again, given the level of technology and input prices) if the firm had complete flexibility with respect to all inputs and decisions.

Cost, variable Total cost incurred minus fixed cost. That is, the costs that vary with the level of output, such as raw materials, labor, and fuel costs.

Craft union A union with membership restricted to those having the same skill or craft (e.g., carpenters, machinists, electricians).

Crawling (or **sliding) peg** A technique for managing a nation's exchange rate that allows the exchange rate (or the bands around the rate) to "crawl" up or down by a small amount each day or week (say, 0.25 percent per week).

Credit The use of someone else's funds in exchange for a promise to pay (usually with interest) at a later date. The major examples are short-term loans from a bank, credit extended by suppliers, or commercial paper.

Cross elasticity of demand A measure of the influence of a change in one good's price on the demand for another good. More precisely, the cross elasticity of demand equals the percentage change in quantity demanded of good A when the price of good B changes by 1 percent, assuming other variables are held constant.

Crowding out Proposition that government spending or deficits or government debt reduces the amount of business investment. Although the term is often used loosely, there are two general conditions in which genuine crowding out may occur. First, government spending may crowd out investment because of resource limitations (if the economy is at full employment); second, deficits may raise interest rates and choke off interest-sensitive investment.

Currency Coins and paper money.

Currency appreciation (or depreciation) See **depreciation** (of a currency).

Current account See **balance of trade.**

Cyclical budget See **actual, cyclical, and structural budget.**

Cyclical unemployment See **frictional unemployment.**

Deadweight loss Loss of consumer surplus or producer surplus due to departures of output from its most efficient level. Thus when a monopolist raises its price, the loss in consumer satisfaction is more than the gain in the monopolist's revenue—the difference being the deadweight loss to society due to monopoly.

Debit An accounting term signifying an increase in assets or decrease in liabilities. In balance-of-payments accounting, a debit is an import (or equivalent) item.

Decreasing returns to scale See **returns to scale.**

Deficit spending Government expenditures on goods and services and transfer payments in excess of its receipts from taxation and other revenue sources. The difference must be financed by borrowing from the public.

Deflating (of economic data) The process of converting "nominal" or current-dollar variables into "real" terms. This is accomplished by dividing current-dollar variables by a general price index.

Deflation A fall in the general level of prices. Also sometimes used, incorrectly, to mean a fall in GNP or an increase in unemployment.

Demand curve A schedule or curve showing the quantity of a good that buyers would purchase at each price, other things equal. Normally a demand curve has price on the vertical or Y axis and quantity demanded on the horizontal or X axis. Also see **change in demand vs. change in quantity demanded.**

Demand for money A summary term used by economists to explain why individuals and businesses hold money.

The major motivations for holding money rather than other assets are (1) **transactions demand,** signifying that people need money to purchase things, and (2) **asset demand,** relating to the desire to hold a very liquid, risk-free asset. Note that the demand for money is a demand for a stock, not a flow.

Demand-pull inflation Price inflation caused by an excess demand for goods in general, caused, for example, by a major increase in aggregate demand. Often contrasted with **cost-push inflation.**

Demography The study of the behavior of a population.

Depreciation (of an asset) A decline in the value of an asset. In both business and national accounts, depreciation is the dollar estimate of the extent to which capital has been "used up" or worn out over the period in question. Also termed **capital consumption allowance** in national income accounting.

Depreciation (of a currency) A nation's currency is said to depreciate when it declines relative to other currencies. For example, if the foreign exchange rate of the dollar falls from 6 to 4 French francs per U.S. dollar, the dollar's value has fallen, and the dollar has undergone a depreciation. The opposite of a depreciation is an **appreciation,** which occurs when the foreign exchange rate of a currency rises. In flexible exchange-rate systems, currencies depreciate and appreciate largely as a result of the market forces of supply and demand.

Depression A prolonged period characterized by high unemployment, low output and investment, depressed business confidence, falling prices, and widespread business failures. A milder form of business downturn is a **recession,** which has many of the features of a depression to a lesser extent; the precise definition of a recession today is a period in which real GNP declines for at least two consecutive calendar quarters.

Derived demand The demand for a factor of production that results from (is "derived" from) the demand for the final good to which it contributes. Thus

the demand for tires is derived from the demand for automobile transportation.

Devaluation A decrease in the official price of a nation's currency, as expressed in the currencies of other nations or in terms of gold. Thus when the official price of the dollar was lowered with respect to gold in 1971, we say that the dollar was devalued. The opposite of devaluation, occurring when a nation raises its official foreign exchange rate relative to gold or other currencies, is called **revaluation.**

Developing countries See **less developed country.**

Diminishing marginal utility, law of The law which says that, as more and more of any one commodity is consumed, its marginal utility declines.

Diminishing returns, law of The law of production stating that the incremental output from successive increases of one input will eventually diminish when other inputs are held constant. Technically, the law is equivalent to saying that the marginal product of the varying input declines after a point.

Direct taxes Those levied directly on individuals or firms, such as taxes on income, labor earnings, and profits. Direct taxes contrast with **indirect taxes,** which are those levied on particular commodities and thus only indirectly on people, and include sales taxes and taxes on property, alcohol, imports, and gasoline.

Discount rate (1) The interest rate charged by a Federal Reserve Bank (the central bank) on any loan that it makes to a commercial bank. (2) The rate used to calculate the present value of some asset.

Discounting (of future income) The process of converting future income into an equivalent present value. This process takes a future dollar amount and reduces it by a discount factor that reflects the appropriate interest rate. For example, if someone promises you $121 in 2 years, and the appropriate interest rate or discount rate is 10 percent per year, then we can calculate the present value by discounting the $121 by a discount factor of $(1.10)^2$. The rate at which future incomes are discounted is called the **discount rate.**

Discrimination Differences in earnings that arise because of personal characteristics that are unrelated to job performance, especially those related to gender, race, or religion.

Disequilibrium An economy not in the state of **equilibrium.** This may arise when shocks (to income or prices) have shifted demand or supply schedules but the market price (or quantity) has not yet adjusted fully. In macroeconomics, unemployment is often thought to stem from market disequilibria.

Disinflation The process of reducing a high inflation rate. Thus, the deep recession of 1980–1983 led to a sharp disinflation over that period.

Disposable income *(DI)* Roughly, take-home pay, or that part of the total national income that is available to households for consumption or saving. More precisely, it is equal to GNP *less* all taxes, business saving, and depreciation *plus* government and other transfer payments and government interest payments.

Dissaving Negative saving; spending more on consumption goods during a period than the disposable income available for that period (the difference being financed by borrowing or drawing on past savings).

Distribution In economics, the manner in which total output is distributed among individuals or factors (e.g., the distribution of income between labor and capital). National-income theory recognizes five categories of income (hence, implicitly, five groups of recipients): (1) wages and salaries; (2) interest payments; (3) rental income; (4) corporation profits; and (5) earnings from unincorporated business.

Division of labor A method of organizing production whereby each worker specializes in one small stage of production. Specialization of labor yields higher total output because labor can become more skilled at a particular task and because specialized machinery can be introduced to perform more carefully defined subtasks.

Downward-sloping demand, law of The rule that says that when the price of some good or service falls, consumers will purchase more of that good when other things are held equal.

Duopoly A market structure in which there are only two sellers. Compare with **oligopoly.**

Durable goods Equipment or machines that are normally expected to last longer than 3 years, e.g., computers, trucks, and automobiles.

Easy-money policy The policy of a central bank to increase the money supply to reduce interest rates. The purpose of such a policy is to increase investment, thereby raising GNP. Contrast with **tight-money policy.**

Econometrics The branch of economics that uses the methods of statistics to measure and estimate quantitative economic relationships.

Economic good A good that is scarce relative to the total demand for it. It must therefore be rationed, usually by charging a positive price.

Economic growth Increase in the total output of a nation over time. Economic growth is usually measured as the annual rate of increase in a nation's real GNP (or real potential GNP).

Economic regulation See **regulation.**

Economies of scale Increases in productivity, or decreases in average cost of production, that arise from increasing the size or scale of plant. For example, a firm operating with large volumes can often get quantity discounts on large purchases or can subdivide tasks to attain greater efficiency.

Economies of scope Economies of producing multiple goods or services. Thus economies of scope exist if it is cheaper to produce both good X and good Y together rather than separately. For example, an airline selling trips from New York to Chicago and back can produce air transportation more cheaply than one selling only one-way routes.

Efficiency The use of economic resources that produces the maximum level of satisfaction possible with the given inputs and technology. A shorthand expression for **allocative efficiency.**

Efficient-market theory See **random-walk theory** (of stock market prices).

Elastic demand (with respect to price) The situation in which price elasticity of demand exceeds 1 in absolute value. This signifies that the percentage change in quantity demanded is greater than the percentage change in price. In addition, elastic demand implies that total revenue (price times quantity) rises when price falls because the increase in quantity demanded is so large. Contrast with **inelastic demand.**

Elasticity A term widely used in economics to denote the responsiveness of one variable to changes in another. Thus the elasticity of X with respect to Y means the percentage change in X for every 1 percent change in Y. For especially important examples, see **price elasticity of demand** and **price elasticity of supply.**

Employed According to official U.S. definitions, persons are employed if they perform any paid work, or if they hold jobs but are absent because of illness, strike, or vacations. Also see **unemployment.**

Entrepreneur In general terms, the person who organizes production. The person who performs this function hires inputs, manages day-to-day operations, and bears risk. An important role of the entrepreneur is to take risks by engaging in **innovation.**

Equilibrium The state in which an economic entity is at rest or in which the forces operating on the entity are in balance so that there is no tendency for change.

Equilibrium, competitive See **competitive equilibrium.**

Equilibrium (for a business firm) That position or level of output in which the firm is maximizing its profit, subject to any constraints it may face, and therefore has no incentive to change its output or price level. In the standard theory of the firm, this means that the firm has chosen an output at which marginal revenue is just equal to marginal cost.

Equilibrium (for the individual consumer) That position in which the consumer is maximizing utility, i.e., has chosen the bundle of goods which, given income and prices, best satisfies the consumer's wants.

Equilibrium, general See **general equilibrium.**

Equilibrium, macroeconomic A GNP level at which intended aggregate demand equals intended aggregate supply. At the equilibrium, desired consumption (C), government expenditures (G), investment (I), and net exports (X) just equal the quantity that businesses wish to sell at the going price level.

Equity capital Funds supplied by the owner of a business. Such an investment yields a share in the ownership along with the corresponding risk of loss and the chance of profit.

Escalator clause Provisions in a contract that tie payments to a price index. When the escalation is complete (i.e., when a 10 percent increase in the price index results in a 10 percent increase in the contract price) the obligation is converted from a nominal to a real one. The most important escalators are cost-of-living adjustments (**COLAs**) in wage contracts, which raise wage rates when the consumer price index increases.

Exchange rate See **foreign exchange rate.**

Exchange rate system The set of rules, arrangements, and institutions under which payments are made among nations. Historically, the most important exchange rate systems have been the gold exchange standard, the Bretton Woods system, and today's flexible exchange rate system.

Excise tax vs. sales tax An excise tax is one levied on the purchase of a specific commodity or group of commodities (e.g., on alcohol or tobacco). A **sales tax** is one levied on all commodities with only a few specific exclusions (e.g., on all purchases except food).

Exclusion principle A criterion by which public goods are distinguished from private goods. When a producer sells a commodity to person A—and can easily exclude B, C, D, . . . from enjoying the benefits of the commodity—the exclusion principle holds and the good is a private good. If, as in public health or national defense, people cannot easily be excluded from enjoying the benefits of the good's pro-

duction, then the good has public-good characteristics.

Expectations Views or beliefs about uncertain variables (such as future interest rates, prices, or tax rates). Expectations are said to be **rational** if they are not systematically wrong and use all available information. Expectations are said to be **adaptive** if people assume the future will be pretty much like the past but change or adapt their expectations if they have made forecast errors in the past.

Exports Goods or services that are produced in the home country and sold to another country. These include merchandise trade (like cars) and services (like transportation or interest on loans and investments). **Imports** are simply flows in the opposite direction—into the home country from another country.

External diseconomies A firm's actions that impose uncompensated costs on other parties. Steel factories that emit smoke and sulfurous fumes harm local property and public health, yet the injured parties are not paid for the damages. The pollution is an external diseconomy.

External economies Economies that occur if a firm's operations yield positive benefits to others without those others paying. A firm that hires a security guard scares thieves from the neighborhood, thus providing external security services. Together with external diseconomies, these are often referred to as **externalities.**

External vs. induced change External change is any change in a variable that is caused by circumstances outside the system. It is contrasted with induced change, which is caused by the internal workings of the economic system. Changes in the weather are external; changes in consumption are often induced by changes in income.

Externalities An activity that affects others for better or worse, without those others paying or being compensated for the activity. Externalities exist when private costs or benefits do not equal social costs or benefits. The two major species are **external economies** and **external diseconomies.**

Factors of production Productive inputs: the machinery, equipment, tools, labor services, land, and raw materials needed to produce goods and services. Also called **inputs.**

Fallacy of composition Fallacy of assuming that what holds for individuals also holds for the group.

Federal Reserve notes Paper money, issued by the **Federal Reserve System,** which today comprises almost all the paper money in the United States.

Federal Reserve System The **central bank** of the United States.

Fiat money Money, like today's paper currency, without **intrinsic value** but decreed (by fiat) to be legal tender by the government. Fiat money is accepted only as long as people have confidence that it will be accepted.

Final good A good that is produced for final use and not for resale or further manufacture. Compare with **intermediate goods.**

Financial intermediary An institution that receives funds from savers and lends them to borrowers. These include depository institutions (such as commercial or savings banks) and non-depository institutions (such as money market mutual funds, brokerage houses, insurance companies, or pension funds).

Firm (business firm) The basic, private producing unit in a capitalist or mixed economy. It hires labor and buys other inputs in order to make and sell commodities.

Fiscal-monetary mix Refers to the combination of fiscal and monetary policies used to influence macroeconomic activity. A tight monetary–loose fiscal policy will tend to encourage consumption and retard investment, while an easy monetary–tight fiscal policy will have the opposite effect.

Fiscal policy A government's program with respect to (1) the purchase of goods and services and spending on transfer payments, and (2) the amount and type of taxes. Fiscal policy and monetary policy are the major tools used by governments to regulate the macroeconomy.

Fixed cost Refer to **cost, fixed.**

Fixed exchange rate See **foreign exchange rate.**

Flexible exchange rates A system of foreign exchange rates among countries wherein the exchange rates are predominantly determined by private market forces (i.e., by supply and demand) without government's setting and maintaining a particular pattern of exchange rates. Also sometimes called **floating exchange rate.** When the government refrains from any intervention in exchange markets, the system is called a pure floating exchange-rate system.

Floating exchange rates See **flexible exchange rates.**

Flow vs. stock A flow variable is one that has a time dimension or that flows over time (like a stream). A stock variable is one that measures a quantity at a point of time (like the water in a lake). Income represents dollars per year and is thus a flow. Wealth as of December 1990 is a stock. Similarly, investment is a flow, while the total inventory of computers is a stock.

Foreign exchange Currency or other financial instruments that allow one country to settle amounts owed to other countries.

Foreign exchange rate The rate, or price, at which one country's currency is exchanged for the currency of another country. For example, if one British pound costs $1.80, then the exchange rate for the pound is $1.80. A country has a **fixed exchange** rate if it "pegs" its currency at a given exchange rate and then stands ready to defend that rate. An exchange rate which is not fixed is said to "float." See also **flexible exchange rates.**

Fractional-reserve banking A regulation in modern banking systems whereby financial institutions are legally required to keep a specified fraction of their deposits in the form of deposits with the central bank (or in vault cash). In the United States today, large banks must keep 12 percent of checking deposits in reserves.

Free enterprise system Usually has the same meaning as **capitalism.**

Free goods Those goods that are not **economic goods.** Like air or seawater, they exist in such large quantities that they need not be rationed out among those wishing to use them. Thus, their market price is zero.

Free trade A policy whereby the government does not intervene in trading between nations—by tariffs, quotas, or other means.

Frictional unemployment Temporary unemployment caused by incessant changes in the economy. It takes time, for example, for new workers to search among different job possibilities; even experienced workers often spend a minimum period of unemployed time moving from one job to another. Frictional is thus distinct from **cyclical unemployment,** which results from a low level of aggregate demand in the context of sticky wages and prices.

Full employment A term that is used in many senses. Historically, it was taken to be that level of employment at which no (or minimal) involuntary unemployment exists. Today, economists rely upon the concept of the **natural rate of unemployment** to indicate the highest sustainable level of employment over the long run.

Galloping inflation See **inflation.**

Game theory Theory seeking to draw a parallel between the behavior of participants in games of chance and strategy (such as poker and chess) and behavior of firms or people in small groups, particularly in oligopolies.

General equilibrium An equilibrium state for the economy as a whole in which prices of all goods and services are such that all markets are simultaneously in equilibrium. Since at these prices producers want to supply exactly the amount of goods that consumers want to buy, there are no pressures encouraging any agent in the economy to change behavior. By contrast, a **partial equilibrium** is an equilibrium condition in only one market.

GNP See **gross national product.**

GNP deflator The "price" of GNP, that is, the price index that measures the average price of the components in GNP relative to a base year.

GNP gap The difference or gap between potential GNP and actual GNP; in Keynesian macroeconomics, taken to measure the macroeconomic loss due to inadequate aggregate demand.

Gold standard A system under which a nation (1) declares its currency unit to be equivalent to some fixed weight of gold, (2) holds gold reserves and will buy or sell gold freely at the price so proclaimed, and (3) puts no restriction on the export or import of gold. With two or more countries on the gold standard, this sets a "gold parity price," or exchange rate, between their currencies. If the "gold content" of the pound is 5 times that of the dollar, then the pound will sell for $5 in the foreign exchange market. Great Britain in the latter half of the nineteenth century was the classic example of the operation of the gold standard. Today, no nation is fully on (or even close to) the gold standard.

Goodwill Refer to **asset, intangible.**

Government debt The total of government obligations in the form of bonds and shorter-term borrowings. Government debt held by the public excludes bonds held by quasi-governmental agencies such as the Federal Reserve System.

Graduated income tax See **income tax, personal.**

Gresham's Law A law first attributed to Sir Thomas Gresham, adviser to Queen Elizabeth I of England, who stated in 1558 that "bad money drives out good"—i.e., that if the public is suspicious of one component of the money supply, it will hoard the "good money" and try to pass off the "bad money" to someone else.

Gross national product, nominal (or **nominal GNP**) The value, at current market prices, of all final goods and services produced within some period by a nation (without any deduction for depreciation of capital goods).

Gross national product, real (or **real GNP**) Nominal GNP corrected for inflation, i.e., real   GNP = nominal

GNP/GNP deflator. An increase in real GNP indicates the increase in the physical volume of output for that period and excludes any price increases.

Growth accounting A technique for estimating the contribution of different factors to economic growth. Using marginal-productivity theory, growth accounting decomposes the growth of output into the growth in labor, land, capital, education, technical knowledge, and other miscellaneous sources.

Hedging A technique for avoiding a risk by making a counteracting transaction. For example, if a farmer produces wheat that will be harvested in the fall, the risk of price fluctuations can be offset, or hedged, by selling in the spring or summer the quantity of wheat that will be produced.

Herfindahl index (of market power) A measure of concentration for an industry, calculated as the sum of squared market shares of the individual firms.

High-powered money Same as **monetary base.**

Horizontal integration Refer to **integration, vertical vs. horizontal.**

Horizontal merger See **merger.**

Horizontal vs. vertical equity Horizontal equity refers to the fairness or equity in treatment of persons in similar situations; the principle of horizontal equity states that those who are essentially equal should receive equal treatment. Vertical equity refers to the equitable treatment of those who are in different circumstances; there are no universally accepted practical applications of vertical equity, although some hold that vertical equity requires progessssive taxation.

Human capital The stock of technical knowledge and skill embodied in a nation's work force, resulting from formal education and on-the-job training.

Hyperinflation See **inflation.**

Imperfect competition Refer to **competition, imperfect.**

Imperfect competitor Any firm that buys or sells a good in large enough quantities to be able to affect the price of that good.

Implicit-cost elements Costs that do not show up as explicit money costs but nevertheless should be counted as such. For example, if you run your own business, then in reckoning your profit you should include as one of your implicit costs the wage or salary you could have earned if you had worked elsewhere. Sometimes called **opportunity cost** although opportunity cost has a broader meaning.

Imports See **exports.**

Incidence The ultimate economic burden of a tax (as opposed to the legal requirement for payment). Thus a sales tax may be paid by a retailer, but it is likely that the incidence falls upon the consumer. The exact incidence of a tax depends on the price elasticities of supply and demand.

Income The flow of wages, interest payments, dividends, and other receipts accruing to an individual or nation.

Income effect (of a price change) Change in the quantity demanded of a commodity because the change in its price has the effect of raising or lowering a consumer's real income. Thus it supplements the **substitution effect** of a price change.

Income elasticity of demand The demand for any given good is influenced not only by the good's price but by buyers' incomes. Income elasticity measures this responsiveness. Its precise definition is: percentage change in quantity demanded divided by percentage change in income. Compare with **price elasticity of demand.**

Income statement A company's statement for a specified time period (usually a year), showing sales or revenue earned during that period, all costs properly charged against the goods sold, and the profit (net income) remaining after deduction of such costs. Also called a **profit-and-loss statement.**

Income tax, negative Refer to **negative income tax.**

Income tax, personal Tax levied on the income received by individuals, either in the form of wages and salaries ("earned" income), or income from property, such as rents, dividends, or interest ("unearned" income). In the United States, personal income tax is **graduated,** meaning that people with higher incomes pay taxes at a higher average rate than people with lower incomes.

Income velocity of money Refer to **velocity of money.**

Incomes policy A government policy that attempts directly to restrict wage and price change in an effort to slow inflation. Such policies range from voluntary wage-price guidelines to outright legal control over wages, salaries, and prices.

Increasing relative costs, law of The law of scarcity for an economy with full employment states that if a society wants more of good A, it must sacrifice some output of another good, B. The law of increasing relative costs says that if a society wants more and more of good A, the quantity of B that must be sacrificed, for each extra unit of A, will increase as the production of A increases. In terms of a **production-possibility frontier,** this law is illustrated by a curve that is bowed outward (like a dome).

Increasing returns to scale See **returns to scale.**

Independent goods Goods whose demands are relatively independent. More precisely, goods A and B are independent when a change in the price of good A has no effect on the quantity demanded of good B, when factors other than A's price are held equal.

Indexing (or **indexation**) A mechanism whereby prices or payments are adjusted to reflect movements in a price index. Labor contracts are the most important example (see **escalator clause**).

Indifference curve A curve drawn on a graph whose two axes measure amounts of different goods consumed. Each point on one curve (indicating different combinations of the two goods) yields exactly the same level of satisfaction for a given consumer. That is, the consumer is indifferent between any two points on an indifference curve.

Indifference map A graph showing a family of indifference curves for a consumer. In general, curves that lie farther northeast from the graph's origin represent higher levels of satisfaction.

Indirect taxes See **direct taxes.**

Induced change See **external vs. induced change.**

Industry Group of firms producing similar or identical products.

Inelastic demand (with respect to price) The situation in which price elasticity of demand is below 1 in absolute value. This signifies that when price changes by 1 percent, the quantity demanded changes by less than 1 percent. Alternatively, when price declines, total revenue declines, and when price is increased, total revenue goes up. Perfectly inelastic demand means that there is no change at all in quantity demanded when price goes up or goes down. Contrast with **elastic demand** and **unit-elastic demand.**

Infant industry In foreign-trade theory, an industry that has not had sufficient time to develop the experience or expertise, or that has not developed sufficiently to exploit the economies of scale needed to compete successfully with more mature industries producing the same commodity in other countries. Infant industries are often thought to need tariffs or quotas to protect them while they develop.

Inferior good A good whose consumption goes down as income rises.

Inflation The inflation rate is the percentage annual increase in a general price level, commonly measured by the consumer price index (CPI) or some comparable price index. **Hyperinflation** is inflation so severe—1000, 1 million, or even 1 billion percent a year—that people try to get rid of their currency before prices rise further and render the money worthless. **Galloping inflation** is a rate of 50 or 100 or 200 percent annually. **Moderate inflation** is a price-level rise that does not distort relative prices or incomes severely.

Innovation A term particularly associated with Joseph Schumpeter, who meant by it (1) the bringing to market of a new and significantly different product, (2) the introduction of a new production technique, or (3) the opening up of a new market. Contrast with **invention.**

Input See **factors of production.**

Input-output table A table showing the flows of goods among industries.

Integration, vertical vs. horizontal The production process is one of stages—e.g., iron ore into steel ingots, steel ingots into rolled steel sheets, rolled steel sheets into an automobile body. Vertical integration is the combination in a single firm of two or more different stages of this process (e.g., iron ore with steel ingots). Horizontal integration is the combination in a single firm of different units that operate at the same stage of production.

Interest The return paid to those who lend money.

Interest rate The price paid for borrowing money for a period of time, usually expressed as a percentage of the principal per year. Thus, if the interest rate is 10 percent per year, then $100 would be paid for a loan of $1000 for 1 year.

Intermediate goods Goods that have undergone some manufacturing or processing but have not yet reached the stage of becoming final products. For example, steel and cotton yarn are intermediate goods.

Intervention An activity in which a government buys or sells its currency in the foreign exchange market in order to affect its currency's exchange rate. For example, the U.S. government would buy U.S. dollars when it wants the exchange rate on the dollar to rise, or appreciate.

Intrinsic value (of money) The commodity value of a piece of money (e.g., the market value of the weight of copper in a copper coin).

Invention The creation of a new product or discovery of a new production technique; to be distinguished from **innovation.**

Investment (1) Economic activity that forgoes consumption today with an eye to increasing output in the future. The major forms of investment are in tangible capital (structures, equipment, and inventories) and in intangible investments (education or "human capital," research and development, and health). Net investment is the value of total investment after an allowance has been made for depreciation. Gross investment is investment without allowance for depreciation. (2) In finance terms, investment has an altogether different meaning: the purchase of a security, such as a stock or a bond.

Investment demand The schedule showing how the level of investment responds to the cost of borrowing (or more specifically, to the real interest rate). Behind this relationship lies an assumption that firms select only profitable investment projects, and that as the cost of borrowing rises, fewer projects can earn a profit.

Investment schedule or **function** See **investment demand.**

Invisible hand A concept introduced by Adam Smith in 1776 to describe the paradox of a laissez-faire market economy. The invisible-hand doctrine holds that, with each participant pursuing his or her own private interest, a market system nevertheless works to the benefit of all as though a benevolent invisible hand were directing the whole process.

Iron law of wages In the economic theories of Malthus and Marx, the theory that there is an inevitable tendency in capitalism for wages to be driven down to a subsistence level.

Keynesian economics The body of thought developed by John Maynard Keynes culminating in his *General Theory*. The central theme was that (primarily because of sticky wages) a capitalist system does not automatically tend toward a full-employment equilibrium. According to Keynes, the resulting "underemployment equilibrium" could be cured by fiscal or monetary policies to raise aggregate demand.

Labor force In official U.S. statistics, the population 16 years of age and older who are either working or looking for work.

Labor-force participation rate Ratio of those in the labor force to the entire population 16 years or older.

Labor supply The number of workers (or, more generally, the number of labor-hours) available to an economy. The principal determinants of labor supply are population, real wages, and social traditions.

Labor theory of value The view, often associated with Karl Marx, but developed earlier, that every commodity should be valued solely according to the quantity of labor required for its production.

Laissez-faire ("Leave us alone") The view that government should not interfere in economic activity. As expressed by classical economists like Adam Smith, this view held that the role of government should be limited to (1) maintenance of law and order, (2) national defense, and (3) provision of certain public goods that private business would not undertake (e.g., public health and sanitation).

Land In classical and neoclassical economics, one of the three basic factors of production (along with labor and capital). More generally, land is taken to include land used for agricultural or industrial purposes as well as natural resources taken from above or below the soil.

Least-cost production rule The rule that the cost of producing a specific level of output is at its minimum when the ratio of the marginal revenue product of each input to the price of that input is the same for all inputs.

Legal tender Money that by law must be accepted as payment for debts. All U.S. coins and currency are legal tender, but checks are not.

Less developed country (LDC) A country with a per capita income far below that of a "developed" nation (the latter usually includes most nations of North America or Europe).

Liabilities In accounting, debts owed to other firms or persons.

Libertarianism (also sometimes called "liberalism") An economic philosophy that emphasizes the importance of personal freedom in economic and political affairs. Libertarian writers, including Adam Smith in an earlier age and Milton Friedman and James Buchanan today, hold that people should be able to follow their own interests and desires; government activities should be limited to guaranteeing contracts and to provision of police and national defense, thereby allowing maximum personal freedom.

Limited liability The restriction of an owner's loss in a business to the amount of capital that the owner has contributed to the company. This limitation allows people to invest in a corporation without fear of losing all their personal assets should the corporation become unprofitable. Limited liability was an important factor in the rise of large corporations. By contrast, owners in partnerships and individual proprietorships generally have **unlimited liability** for the debts of those firms.

Long run A term used to denote a period over which full adjustment to changes can take place. In microeconomics, it denotes the time over which firms can enter or leave an industry and the capital stock can be changed. In macroeconomics, it is often used to mean the period over which all prices, wage contracts, tax rates, and expectations can fully adjust.

Lorenz curve A graph showing cumulative percentage of population on the horizontal axis and cumulative percentage of income received on the vertical axis. It is used to show the degree of equality or inequality in income distribution. The greater the departure of the Lorenz curve from the 45° line, the more unequal the distribution of income.

Lump-of-labor hypothesis The belief that there is only a fixed amount of work to be done so that, if you work faster or if new and better machines are introduced, the only result can be to raise unemployment.

M_1, M_2 Refer to **money supply.**

Macroeconomics Analysis dealing with the behavior of the economy as a whole with respect to output, income, the price level, and unemployment. To be contrasted with **microeconomics,** which deals with the study of individual firms, people, or markets.

Malthusian theory of population growth The belief, first expressed by Thomas Malthus, that the "natural" tendency of population is to increase at a geometric rate (1, 2, 4, 8, . . .) whereas food supply tends to increase at an arithmetic rate (1, 2, 3, 4, . . .). Per capita food production would thus decline over time, thereby putting a check on population.

Managed float The most prevalent exchange-rate system today. In this system, a country occasionally intervenes to stabilize its currency.

Marginal cost Refer to **cost, marginal.**

Marginal product (MP) (sometimes **marginal physical product**) The extra output resulting from 1 extra unit of a specified input when all other inputs are held constant.

Marginal product theory of distribution A theory of the distribution of income proposed by John B. Clark, according to which each productive input is paid according to its **marginal product.**

Marginal propensity to consume (MPC) That fraction of an additional dollar of disposable income which a family or community would spend on additional consumption (the remainder being saved). Not the same thing as the **average propensity to consume,** which is the ratio of total consumption to total disposable income.

Marginal propensity to import (MPm) In macroeconomics, the increase in the dollar value of imports resulting from each dollar increase in the value of GNP.

Marginal propensity to save (MPS) That fraction of an additional dollar of disposable income that a family or community would save (rather than consume). Note that, by definition: $MPC + MPS = 1$.

Marginal revenue (MR) The additional revenue a firm would obtain if it sold 1 extra unit of output. In perfect competition, MR equals price. Under imperfect competition, MR is less than price because, in order to sell the extra unit, the price must be reduced on all prior units sold.

Marginal revenue product *(MRP)* (of an input) Equals marginal revenue multiplied by marginal product. It is the extra revenue that would be brought in if a firm were to buy 1 extra unit of an input, put it to work, and sell the extra product it produced.

Marginal tax rate For an income tax, the percentage of the last dollar of income paid in taxes. If a tax system is progressive, the marginal tax rate is higher than the average tax rate.

Marginal utility *(MU)* The additional or extra satisfaction yielded from consuming 1 additional unit of a commodity, with amounts of all other goods consumed held constant.

Market An arrangement whereby buyers and sellers interact to determine the prices and quantities of a commodity. Some markets (such as the stock market or a flea market) take place in physical locations; other markets are conducted over the telephone or are organized by computers.

Market economy An economy in which the *what, how,* and *for whom* questions concerning resource allocation are primarily determined by supply and demand in markets. In this form of economic organization, firms, motivated by the desire to maximize profits, buy inputs and produce and sell outputs. Households, armed with their factor incomes, go to markets and determine the demand for commodities. The interaction of firms' supply and households' demands then determines the prices and quantities of goods.

Market equilibrium Same as **competitive equilibrium.**

Market failure An imperfection in a price system that prevents an efficient allocation of resources. Important examples are **externalities** and **imperfect competition.**

Market power The degree of control that a firm or group of firms has over the price and production decisions in an industry. In a monopoly, the firm has a high degree of market power while firms in perfectly competitive industries have no market power. Concentration ratios are the most widely used measures of market power.

Market share Fraction of an industry's output accounted for by an individual firm or group of firms.

Market socialism A socialist economy in which most microeconomic questions are left to the market mechanism. The state would own most capital and land and would direct investment, but the techniques of production, pricing, and the exact composition of the output would be left to supply and demand.

Markup pricing The pricing method used by many firms in situations of imperfect competition; under this method they estimate average cost and then add some fixed percentage to that cost in order to reach the price they charge.

Marxism The set of social, political, and economic doctrines developed by Karl Marx in the nineteenth century. As an economic theory, Marxism predicted that capitalism would collapse as a result of its own internal contradictions, especially its tendency to exploit the working classes. The conviction that workers would inevitably be oppressed under capitalism was based on the iron law of wages, which holds that wages would decline to subsistence levels.

Mean In statistics, the same thing as "average." Thus for the numbers 1, 3, 6, 10, 20, the mean is 8.

Median In statistics, the figure exactly in the middle of a series of numbers ordered or ranked from lowest to highest (e.g., incomes or examination grades). Thus for the numbers 1, 3, 6, 10, 20, the median is 6.

Mercantilism A political doctrine perhaps best known as the object of Adam Smith's attack in *The Wealth of Nations*. Mercantilists emphasized the importance of balance of payments surpluses as a device to accumulate gold. They therefore advocated authoritarian control of economic policies, believing that laissez-faire policies might lead to a loss of gold.

Merger The acquisition of one corporation by another, which usually occurs when one firm buys the stock of another. Important examples are: (1) **vertical mergers,** which occur when the two firms are at different stages of a production process (e.g., iron ore and steel), (2) **horizontal mergers,** which occur when the two firms produce in the same market (e.g., two automobile manufacturers), and (3) **conglomerate mergers,** which occur when the two firms operate in unrelated markets (e.g., golf balls and oil refining).

Microeconomics Analysis dealing with the behavior of individual elements in an economy—such as the determination of the price of a single product or the behavior of a single consumer or business firm. To be contrasted with **macroeconomics,** which studies economic aggregates (total national product, total employment, inflation, money supply, etc.).

Minimum cost Refer to **cost, minimum.**

Mixed economy The dominant form of economic organization in non-communist countries. Mixed economies rely primarily on the price system for their economic organization but use a variety of government interventions to cope with macroeconomic instability and market failures.

Model A formal framework for representing the basic features of a complex system by a few central relationships. Models take the form of graphs, mathematical equations, and computer programs.

Moderate inflation See **inflation.**

Momentary run That period of time that is so short that production is fixed.

Monetarism A school of thought holding that changes in the money supply are the major cause of macroeconomic fluctuations. For the short run, this view holds that changes in the money supply are the primary determinant of changes in both real output and the price level. For the longer run, real output tends toward potential GNP, while prices tend to move proportionally to the money supply. Monetarists often conclude that the best macroeconomic policy is one with a stable growth in the money supply of 3 to 5 percent per year.

Monetary base The net monetary liabilities of the government held by the public. In the United States, the monetary base is equal to currency and bank reserves. Sometimes called **high-powered money.**

Monetary policy The objectives of the central bank in exercising its control over money, interest rates, and credit conditions. The instruments of monetary policy are primarily open-market operations, reserve requirements, and the discount rate. (Refer also to **easy-money policy, tight-money policy.**)

Money Anything that serves as a medium of exchange, i.e., is widely accepted as a means of payment. (For the items constituting money in a developed economy, refer to **money supply.**)

Money demand schedule The relationship between holdings of money and interest rates. As interest rates rise, bonds and other securities become more attractive, lowering the demand for money. See **demand for money.**

Money funds Shorthand expression for very liquid short-term financial instruments whose interest rates are not regulated. The major examples are money market mutual funds and commercial bank money market deposit accounts.

Money market A term denoting the set of institutions that handle the purchase or sale of short-term credit instruments like Treasury bills and commercial paper. Unlike a stock market, the money market is not located in a place—it is rather a network of brokers, buyers, and sellers.

Money supply The narrowly defined money supply (M_1) consists of coins, paper currency, plus all demand or checking deposits; this is narrow, or transactions, money. The broadly defined supply (M_2) includes all items in M_1 plus certain liquid assets or near monies—savings deposits, money market funds, and the like.

Money-supply multiplier The ratio of the increase in the money supply (or of deposits) to the increase in bank reserves. Generally, the money-supply multiplier is equal to the inverse of the required reserve ratio. For example, if the required reserve ratio is 0.125, then the money-supply multiplier is 8.

Money, velocity of See **velocity of money.**

Monopolistic competition A market structure in which there are many sellers who are supplying goods that are close, but not perfect, substitutes. In such a market, each firm can exercise some effect on its product's price.

Monopoly A market structure in which a commodity is supplied by a single firm. Also see **natural monopoly.**

Monopsony The mirror image of monopoly: a market in which there is a single buyer. A "buyer's monopoly."

Multiplier A term in macroeconomics denoting the change in an induced variable (GNP, money supply, imports) per unit of change in an external variable (government spending, income, exports, or bank reserves). The investment multiplier refers to the increase in GNP that would result from a $1 increase in investment. In the simple multiplier model, the investment (or government expenditure) multiplier exceeds 1 because the original spending increase sets off a series of further "induced" spending increases.

Multiplier model In macroeconomics, a theory developed by J. M. Keynes that emphasizes the importance of changes in autonomous expenditures (especially investment, government spending, and net exports) in determining changes in output and employment. Also see **multiplier.**

National debt Same as **government debt.**

National income and product accounting A set of accounts that measures the spending, income, and output of the entire nation for a quarter or a year.

Natural monopoly A firm or industry whose average cost per unit of production falls sharply over the entire range of its output, as for example in local electricity distribution. Thus a single firm, a monopoly, can supply the industry output more efficiently than can multiple firms.

Natural rate of growth The rate of growth of the labor force, plus the rate of growth of labor productivity. Thus, if the labor force is growing at 1 percent per year, and output per labor-hour is growing at 2 percent per year, the natu-ral rate of growth of the economy is 3 percent per year.

Natural rate of unemployment The unemployment rate at which pressures on wages are in balance, so they neither increase nor decrease the rate of inflation. Equivalently, the unemployment rate at which the long-run Phillips curve is vertical.

"Near-money" Financial assets that are risk-free and so readily convertible into money that they are close to actually being money. Examples are money funds and Treasury bills.

Negative income tax A plan for replacing the current complex set of income-support programs (welfare, food stamps, etc.) with a unified program. Under such a plan, poor families would receive an income-support payment (or "negative" tax) whose size would depend on their income.

Neoclassical growth model A theory or model for explaining long-term trends in economic growth of industrial economies. This model emphasizes the importance of capital deepening (i.e., a growing capital–labor ratio) and technological change in explaining the growth of potential real GNP.

Net economic welfare (NEW) A measure of national output that corrects several limitations of the GNP measure.

Net exports In the national product accounts, exports of goods and services minus imports of goods and services.

Net investment Gross investment minus depreciation of capital goods.

Net national product (NNP) GNP less an allowance for depreciation of capital goods.

Net worth In accounting, total assets minus total liabilities.

NNP See **net national product.**

Nominal GNP See **gross national product, nominal.**

Nominal (or money) interest rate The **interest rate** paid on different assets. This represents a dollar return per year per dollar invested. Compare with the **real interest rate,** which represents the return per year in goods per unit of goods invested.

Normative vs. positive economics Normative economics considers "what ought to be"—value judgments, or goals, of public policy. Positive economics, by contrast, is the analysis of facts and data, "the way things are."

NOW (negotiable order of withdrawal) account An interest-bearing checking account. See also **checking accounts.**

Okun's Law Empirical relationship, uncovered by Arthur Okun, between cyclical movements in GNP and unemployment. The law states that when actual GNP declines 2 percent relative to potential GNP, the unemployment rate increases by about 1 percentage point. (Earlier estimates placed the ratio at 3 to 1.)

Oligopoly A situation of imperfect competition in which an industry is dominated by a small number of suppliers.

Open economy An economy that engages in trade (i.e., imports and exports) of goods and capital with other countries. A **closed economy** is one that has no imports or exports.

Open-economy multiplier In an open economy (i.e., one open to international trade), income leaks into imports as well as into saving. Therefore, the open-economy multiplier for investment or government expenditure is given by

$$\frac{\text{Open-economy}}{\text{multiplier}} = \frac{1}{MPS + MPm}$$

where MPS = marginal propensity to save and MPm = marginal propensity to import.

Open-market operations The activity of a central bank in buying or selling government bonds to influence bank reserves, the money supply, and interest rates. If securities are bought, the money paid out by the central bank increases commercial bank reserves, and the money supply increases. If securities are sold, the money supply contracts.

Opportunity cost The value of the next best use (or opportunity) for an economic good, or the value of the sacrificed alternative. Thus, say that the inputs used to mine a ton of coal *could* have been used to grow 10 bushels of wheat. The opportunity cost of a ton of coal is thus the 10 bushels of wheat that *could* have been produced but were not. Opportunity cost is particularly useful for valuing non-marketed goods such as environmental health or safety.

Option A contract allowing a party to buy or sell a commodity or a security at a given price during a specified period of time. Options today are widely traded for common stocks, bonds, foreign exchange, and many raw materials.

Other things equal A phrase that signifies that a factor under consideration is changed while all other factors are held equal or constant. For example, a demand curve states that the quantity demanded will decline as the price rises, as long as other things (such as incomes) are held equal.

Output See **total product.**

Paradox of thrift The paradox, first noted by J. M. Keynes, that a community's decision to save more (to be more thrifty) may result in its actually saving less. To save more is to spend less on consumer goods; to spend less on consumer goods may reduce aggregate demand and GNP; this may lead to lower induced investment, lower incomes, and ultimately, reduced saving.

Paradox of value The paradox that many necessities of life (e.g., water) have a low "market" value, while many luxuries (e.g., diamonds) that have little "use" value have a high market price. It is explained by the fact that a price does not reflect the total utility of a commodity but its marginal utility.

Pareto efficiency (or **Pareto optimality**) See **allocative efficiency.**

Partial-equilibrium analysis Analysis that concentrates upon the effect of changes in an individual market, holding "other things equal" (for example, disregarding changes in income). Partial-equilibrium analysis might be used to assess the effect of a gasoline-price rise on demand for gasoline. But if the price rise causes GNP to decline, this will "feed back" into the gasoline market; partial-equilibrium analysis does not consider this feedback effect.

Partnership An association of two or more persons to conduct a business which is not in corporate form and does not enjoy limited liability.

Patent An exclusive right granted to an inventor to control the use of an invention lasting, in the United States, over a period of 17 years. They create temporary monopolies as a device for rewarding inventive activity and are the principal tool for promoting invention among individuals or small firms.

Perfect competition Refer to **competition, perfect.**

Phillips curve A graph first devised by A. W. Phillips, showing the tradeoff between unemployment and inflation. The view that first evolved from Phillips' work was that the lower the rate of unemployment, the higher the rate of inflation. In modern mainstream macroeconomics, the downward-sloping "tradeoff" Phillips curve is generally held to be valid only in the short run; in the long run, the Phillips curve is usually thought to be vertical at the natural rate of unemployment.

Portfolio theory An economic theory that describes how rational investors allocate their wealth among different financial assets—that is, how they put their wealth into a "portfolio." For example, a family might have a portfolio of $50 in cash, $400 in a checking account, and $2500 in a money market mutual fund.

Positive economics Refer to **normative vs. positive economics.**

***Post hoc, ergo propter hoc* fallacy** ("After this, therefore because of this") This fallacy arises when it is assumed that because event A precedes event B, it follows that A *causes* B.

Potential GNP The maximum level of GNP that can be sustained with a given state of technology and population size without accelerating inflation; sometimes called "high-employment output." Today, generally taken to be equivalent to the level of output corresponding to the natural rate of unemployment.

Potential output Same as **potential GNP.**

Poverty Today, the U.S. government defines the "poverty line" to be the minimum adequate standard of living.

PPF See **production possibility frontier.**

Present value (of an asset) Today's value for an asset that yields a stream of income over time. Valuation of such time streams of returns requires calculating the present worth of each component of the income, which is done by applying a discount rate (or interest rate) to future incomes.

Price elasticity of demand A measure of the degree to which quantity demanded by buyers responds to a price change. The elasticity coefficient, or quantitative measure of elasticity, is: percentage change in quantity bought divided by percentage change in price. In figuring percentages, use the averages of old and new quantities in the numerator and of old and new prices in the denominator; disregard the minus sign. (Refer also to **elastic demand, inelastic demand, unit-elastic demand.**)

Price elasticity of supply Conceptually similar to **price elasticity of demand,** except that it measures the supply responsiveness to a price change. More precisely, the price elasticity of supply measures the percentage change in quantity supplied divided by the percentage change in price. Supply elasticities are most useful in perfect competition, where the suppliers are "price-takers" (i.e., have no individual influence in the setting of market price).

Price flexibility Price behavior in "auction" markets (e.g., for many raw commodities or the stock market), in which prices immediately respond to changes in demand or in supply. (In contrast, refer to **administered prices.**)

Price index An index number that shows how the average price of a bundle of goods has changed over a period of time. In computing the average, the prices of the different goods are generally weighted by their economic importance (e.g., by each good's share of total consumer expenditures in the **consumer price index**).

Private good See **public good.**

Producer price index The **price index** of goods sold at the wholesale level (such as steel, wheat, oil).

Product, average See **average product.**

Product differentiation The existence of characteristics that make similar goods less than perfect substitutes. Thus locational differences make the gasoline sold at separate points imperfect substitutes. Firms enjoying product differentiation face a downward-sloping demand curve instead of the horizontal demand curve of the perfect competitor.

Product, marginal See **marginal product.**

Production function A relation (or mathematical function) specifying the amount of output that can be achieved with given inputs. Applies to a firm or, as an "aggregate production function," to the economy as a whole.

Production-possibility frontier (*PPF*) A graph showing the menu of goods that can be produced by an economy. In a frequently cited simple case, the choice is reduced to two goods, guns and butter. Points outside the *PPF* (to the northeast of it) are unattainable. Points inside it would be inefficient since resources are not being fully employed, resources are not being used properly, or outdated production techniques are being utilized.

Productivity A term referring to the ratio of output to inputs (total output divided by labor inputs is "labor productivity"). Productivity increases if the same quantity of inputs produces more output. Labor productivity increases because of improved technology, improvements in labor skills, or capital deepening.

Productivity growth The rate of increase in **productivity** from one period to another. For example, if an index of labor productivity is 100 in 1987 and 103 in 1988, the rate of productivity growth is 3 percent per year for 1988 over 1987.

Productivity of capital, net Refer to **rate of return.**

Profit (1) In accounting terms, total revenue minus costs properly chargeable against the goods sold (refer to income statement). (2) In economic theory, the difference between sales revenue and the full opportunity cost of resources involved in producing the goods.

Profit-and-loss statement Refer to **income statement.**

Progressive, proportional, and **regressive taxes** A progressive tax weighs more heavily upon the rich; a regressive tax does the opposite. More precisely, a tax is progressive if the average tax rate (i.e., taxes divided by income) is higher for those with higher incomes and regressive if the average tax rate declines with higher incomes. A graduated income tax would be progressive; a sales tax on food would be regressive. A proportional tax is one in which the average tax burden is equal at all levels of income.

Proportional tax Refer to **progressive, proportional,** and **regressive taxes.**

Proprietors' income In national-income accounting, the net income earned by the owners of unincorporated firms (individual proprietorships and partnerships).

Proprietorship, individual A business firm owned and operated by one person.

Protectionism Any policy adopted by a nation to protect domestic industries against competition from imports (most commonly, by a tariff or quota imposed on such imports).

Public choice Branch of economics and political science dealing with the way that governments make economic choices: the *what, how,* and *for whom* of the public sector. The theory differs from the theory of markets in emphasizing the role of vote maximizing played by politicians, which contrasts to profit maximizing by firms.

Public debt See **government debt.**

Public good A commodity whose benefits may be provided to all people (in a nation or town) at no more cost than that required to provide it for one person. The benefits of the good are indivisible, and people cannot be excluded from using it. For example, a public-health measure that eradicates smallpox protects all, not just those paying for the vaccinations. To be contrasted with **private goods,** such as bread, which, if consumed by one person, cannot be consumed by another person.

Quantity demanded See **change in demand vs. change in quantity demanded.**

Quantity equation of exchange A tautology, $MV \equiv PQ$, where M is the money supply, V is the income velocity of money, and PQ ("price times quantity") is the money value of total output (nominal GNP). The equation must always hold exactly since V is defined as PQ/M.

Quantity supplied See **change in supply vs. change in quantity supplied.**

Quantity theory of prices A theory of the determination of output and the overall price level holding that prices (P) move proportionately with the money supply (M). This theory begins with the quantity equation, $MV \equiv PQ$. It then assumes that velocity (V) is a constant or smoothly growing trend, while output (Q) is always at full employment. Under these assumptions, a k percent increase in M will produce a k percent increase in P.

Although few macroeconomists hold to the strict and literal version of the quantity theory of prices, it does have some validity in periods when the money supply changes greatly. A more cautious approach put forth by monetarists holds that the money supply is the most important determinant of changes in nominal GNP (see **monetarism**).

Quota A form of protectionism in which the total quantity of imports of a particular commodity (e.g., sugar or cars) during a given period is limited.

Random-walk theory (of stock market prices) Increasingly called the **efficient-market hypothesis.** A view that holds that all currently available information is already incorporated into the price of

common stocks (or other assets). Consequently, the stock market offers no bargains that can be found by looking at old or "stale" information or at easily available information (like recent price movements). Stock prices do change, however—on the basis of *new* information. If we assume that the chances of good news and of bad are 50:50, then stock prices will follow a "random walk," i.e., are equally likely to move up or down.

Rate of return (or **return**) **on capital** The yield on an investment or on a capital good. Thus, an investment costing \$100 and yielding \$12 annually has a rate of return of 12 percent per year.

Rational expectations (1) For the narrow definition, see **expectations.** (2) More generally, part of a view of the economy held by proponents of **rational-expectations macroeconomics.**

Rational-expectations macroeconomics (sometimes new classical macroeconomics) A school, led by Robert Lucas and Thomas Sargent, holding that markets clear quickly and that expectations are rational. Under these and other conditions it can be shown that predictable macroeconomic policies have no effect on real output or unemployment.

Real GNP GNP adjusted for price change. Real GNP equals nominal GNP divided by the GNP deflator. See **gross national product, real.**

Real interest rate The interest rate measured in terms of goods rather than money. It is thus equal to the money (or nominal) interest rate less the rate of inflation.

Real wages The purchasing power of a worker's wages in terms of goods and services. Measured by the ratio of the money wage rate to the consumer price index.

Recession Downturn in real GNP for two or more successive quarters (see **depression**).

Regressive tax Refer to **progressive, proportional,** and **regressive taxes.**

Regulation Government laws or rules designed to change the behavior of firms. The major kinds are **economic**

regulation (which affects the prices, entry, or service of a single industry, such as airlines) and **social regulation** (which attempts to correct externalities that prevail across a number of industries, such as air or water pollution).

Rent, economic This term was applied by nineteenth-century British economists to income obtained from ownership of land. The total supply of land available in a nation or in the world is (with minor qualifications) fixed, and the return paid to the landowner is rent. The term is often extended to the return paid to any factor in fixed supply—i.e., to any input having a perfectly inelastic or vertical supply curve.

Required reserves See **reserves, bank.**

Reserve army of the unemployed A term used in Marxian economics. In Marx's argument, there are always unemployed laborers seeking work. Employers can point to, and if necessary draw upon, this army to enforce the **iron law of wages**—i.e., to hold wages down to the level where workers can just manage to survive.

Reserves, bank That portion of deposits that a bank sets aside in the form of vault cash or non-interest-earning deposits with Federal Reserve Banks. In the United States, banks are required to hold 12 percent of checking deposits (or transactions accounts) in the form of reserves.

Reserves, international Every nation holds at least some reserves, in such forms as gold, currencies of other nations, and special drawing rights. International reserves serve as "international money," to be used when a country encounters foreign liquidity or balance-of-payments difficulties. If a nation were prepared to allow its exchange rate to float freely, it would need no reserves.

Resource allocation The manner in which an economy distributes its resources (its factors of production) among the potential uses so as to produce a particular set of final goods.

Retained earnings The part of a corporation's profit (net income) not paid out as dividends to shareholders but instead retained by the corporation, normally to expand its operations. The same as **undistributed profit.**

Returns to scale The rate at which output increases as all inputs are increased together. For example, if all the inputs double and output is exactly doubled, that process is said to exhibit **constant returns to scale.** If, however, output grows by less than 100 percent when all inputs are doubled, the process shows **decreasing returns to scale**; if output more than doubles, the process demonstrates **increasing returns to scale.**

Revaluation An increase in the official foreign exchange rate of a currency. (See **devaluation.**)

Revenue, average Refer to **average revenue.**

Revenue, marginal Refer to **marginal revenue.**

Revenue, total Price times quantity, or total sales.

Sales tax See **excise tax vs. sales tax.**

Saving The difference between disposable income and consumption expenditures.

Savings function The schedule showing the amount of saving that households or a nation will undertake at each level of income.

Say's Law of Markets The theory that "supply creates its own demand." J. B. Say argued in 1803 that, because total purchasing power is exactly equal to total incomes and outputs, excess demand or supply is impossible. Keynes attacked Say's Law, pointing out that an extra dollar of income need not be entirely spent (i.e., the marginal propensity to consume is not necessarily unity).

Scarcity, law of The principle that most things that people want are available only in limited supply (the exception being **free goods**). Thus goods are generally scarce and must somehow be rationed, whether by price or some other means.

Securities A term used to designate a wide variety of financial assets, such as stocks, bonds, options, and notes; more precisely, the document used to establish ownership of these assets.

Separation of ownership and control A characteristic of most large corporations in the United States today: they are owned by their shareholders but operated and controlled by their professional managers. In such situations, the actual control exercised by shareholders is negligible.

Short run Period in which all factors cannot adjust fully. In microeconomics, the capital stock and other "fixed" inputs cannot be adjusted and entry is not free in the short run. In macroeconomics, prices, wage contracts, tax rates, and expectations may not fully adjust in the short run.

Shutdown price (or **point,** or **rule)** In the theory of the firm, the shutdown point comes at that point where the market price is just sufficient to cover average variable cost and no more. Hence, the firm's losses per period just equal its fixed costs; it might as well shut down.

Single-tax movement A nineteenth-century movement, originated by Henry George, holding that continued poverty in the midst of steady economic progress was attributable to the scarcity of land and the large rents flowing to landowners. The "single tax" was to be a tax on economic rent earned from landownership.

Slope In a graph, the change in the variable on the vertical axis per unit of change in the variable on the horizontal axis. Upward-sloping lines have positive slopes, downward-sloping curves (like demand curves) have negative slopes, and horizontal lines have slopes of zero.

Social overhead capital (sometimes called infrastructure) The essential investments on which economic development depends, particularly for transportation, power, and communications. Because of the high capital cost and indivisibilities involved, social overhead capital generally depends on government planning and economic support, especially in less developed countries.

Social regulation See **regulation.**

Socialism A political theory that holds that all (or almost all) the means of production, other than labor, should be owned by the community. This allows the return on capital to be shared more equally than under capitalism.

Speculator Someone engaged in speculation, i.e., who buys (or sells) a commodity or financial asset with the aim of profiting from later selling (or buying) the item at a higher (or lower) price.

Spillovers Same as **externalities.**

Stagflation A term, coined in the early 1970s, describing the coexistence of high unemployment, or *stag*nation, with persistent in*flation*. Its explanation lies primarily in the inertial nature of the inflationary process.

Stock, common Refer to **common stock.**

Stock market An organized marketplace in which common stocks are traded. In the United States, the largest stock market is the New York Stock Exchange, on which are traded the largest American companies.

Stock vs. flow See **flow vs. stock.**

Structural budget See **actual, cyclical, and structural budget.**

Structural unemployment Unemployment resulting from the fact that the regional or occupational pattern of job vacancies does not match the pattern of worker availability. There may be jobs available, but unemployed workers may not have the required skill; or the jobs may be in different regions from where the unemployed workers live.

Subsidy A payment by a government to a firm or household that provides or consumes a commodity. For example, governments often subsidize food by paying for part of the food expenditures of low-income households.

Substitutes See **complements.**

Substitution effect (of a price change) The tendency of consumers is to consume more of a good when its relative price falls (to "substitute" in favor of that good), and to consume less of the good when its relative price increases (to "substitute" away from that good). This substitution effect of a price change leads to a downward-sloping demand curve. Compare with **income effect.**

Supply and demand, law of The "law" that stipulates that (under perfect competition) market price will move to the level at which the quantity purchasers wish to buy just equals the quantity that sellers wish to sell.

Supply curve A schedule showing the quantity of a good that suppliers in a given market would be prepared to sell at each price, holding other things equal.

Supply shock In macroeconomics, a sudden change in production costs or productivity that has a large and unexpected impact upon aggregate supply. As a result of a supply shock, real GNP and the price level change unexpectedly. For example, when oil prices rose sharply in 1978–1979, inflation increased sharply and real output fell.

Supply-side economics A view emphasizing policy measures to affect aggregate supply or potential output. This approach holds that high marginal tax rates on labor and capital incomes reduce work effort and saving; a cut in marginal tax rates will thereby increase factor supplies and total output. An extreme view, put forth by Arthur Laffer, is that a cut in taxes may actually raise total tax revenues.

Surplus value A term used in Marxian economics to refer to the excess of a price over the value of the total direct and indirect labor that went into the manufacture of the good. See also **labor theory of value.**

Tariff A levy or tax imposed upon each unit of a commodity imported into a country.

Tax incidence See **incidence.**

Technological change The introduction of a new production method, yielding product improvements or cost reduction and thereby raising productivity. It results in an outward shift in the production-possibility curve.

Technological progress Same as **technological change.**

Terms of trade A phrase usually employed with respect to international trade, referring to the "real" terms at which a nation sells its export products and buys its import products. It equals the ratio of an index of export prices to an index of import prices.

Tight-money policy A central bank policy of restraining or reducing the money supply and of raising interest rates. This policy has the effect of slowing the growth of real GNP, reducing the rate of inflation, or raising the nation's foreign exchange rate. Contrast with **easy-money policy.**

Time deposit Funds, held in a bank, that have a minimum "time of withdrawal." Included in broad money (M_2) but not in M_1 because they are not accepted as a means of payment.

Token money Money with little or no intrinsic value.

Total cost Refer to **cost, total.**

Total factor productivity An index of productivity that measures total output per unit of total input. The numerator of the index is total output (say GNP), while the denominator is a weighted average of inputs of capital, labor, and resources. The growth of total factor productivity is often taken as an index of the rate of technological progress.

Total product (or **output**) The total amount of a commodity produced measured in physical units such as bushels of wheat, tons of steel, or number of haircuts.

Total revenue Refer to **revenue, total.**

Trade barrier Any of a number of protectionist devices by which governments discourage imports. Tariffs and quotas are the most visible barriers, but in recent years non-tariff barriers (or NTBs), such as burdensome regulatory proceedings, have replaced more traditional measures.

Transactions demand for money See **demand for money.**

Transfer payments, government A payment made by a government to an individual, for which that individual performs no current service in return. Examples are social security payments

and unemployment insurance. Transfer payments are usually intended to change the distribution of income by aiding particular groups (e.g., the poor, the blind, or the aged).

Treasury bills (T-bills) Short-term bonds or securities issued by the federal government.

Underground economy Unreported economic activity. The underground economy includes otherwise legal activities not reported to the taxing authorities (such as garage sales or services "bartered" among friends) and illegal activities (such as the drug trade, gambling, and prostitution).

Undistributed profit Same as **retained earnings.**

Unemployment (1) In economic terms, involuntary unemployment occurs if there are qualified workers who would be willing to work at prevailing wages but cannot find jobs. (2) In the official (U.S. Bureau of Labor Statistics) definition, a worker is unemployed if he or she (*a*) is not working and (*b*) either is waiting for recall from layoff or has actively looked for work in the last 4 weeks.

Unemployment, frictional See **frictional unemployment.**

Unemployment, structural See **structural unemployment.**

Unit-elastic demand (with respect to price) The situation between **elastic demand** and **inelastic demand,** in which price elasticity is just equal to 1 in absolute value. This means that when price changes by 1 percent, quantity demanded changes by 1 percent (in the opposite direction). In addition, when price changes, total revenue ($P \times Q$) is unchanged. See also **price elasticity of demand.**

Unlimited liability See **limited liability.**

Usury The charging of an interest rate above a legal maximum on borrowed money.

Utility-possibility frontier Analogous to the **production-possibility frontier.** A graph showing the utility or satisfaction of two consumers (or groups), one on each axis. It is downward-sloping to indicate that redistributing income from A to B will lower the utility of A and raise that of B. Points on the utility-possibility frontier display **allocative (or Pareto) efficiency.** For the allocation implied by these points, it is impossible to devise feasible outcomes that would make one party better off without making someone else worse off.

Utility, total The total satisfaction derived from the consumption of commodities. To be contrasted with **marginal utility,** which is the additional utility arising from consumption of an additional unit of the commodity.

Value added The difference between the value of goods produced and the cost of materials and supplies used in producing them. In a $1.00 loaf of bread embodying $0.60 worth of wheat and other materials, the value added is $0.40. Value added consists of the wages, interest, and profit components added to the output by a firm or industry.

Value-added tax (or **VAT**) A tax levied upon a firm as a percentage of its value added.

Value, paradox of See **paradox of value.**

Variable A magnitude of interest that can be defined and measured. Important variables in economics include prices, quantities, interest rates, exchange rates, dollars of wealth, and so forth.

Variable cost Refer to **cost, variable.**

Velocity of money Money, in serving its function as medium of exchange, moves from buyer to seller to new buyer and so on. Its "velocity" refers to the "speed" of this movement. The **income velocity of money** is defined, more precisely, as nominal GNP divided by the (average) total money supply for the period in question, or $V \equiv P \times Q/M \equiv GNP/M$.

Vertical equity See **horizontal vs. vertical equity.**

Vertical integration Refer to **integration, vertical vs. horizontal.**

Vertical merger See **merger.**

Wealth The net value of tangible and financial items owned by a nation or person. It equals all assets less all liabilities.

Welfare economics The normative analysis of economic systems, i.e., the study of what is "wrong" or "right" about the economy's functioning.

What, how, and for whom The three fundamental problems of economic organization. *What* is the problem of how much of each possible good and service will be produced with the society's limited stock of resources or inputs. *How* is the choice of the particular technique by which each good of the *what* shall be produced. *For whom* refers to the distribution of consumption goods among the members of that society.

Yield Same as the **interest rate** or **rate of return** on an asset.

INDEX

Page references in **boldface** indicate Glossary terms.

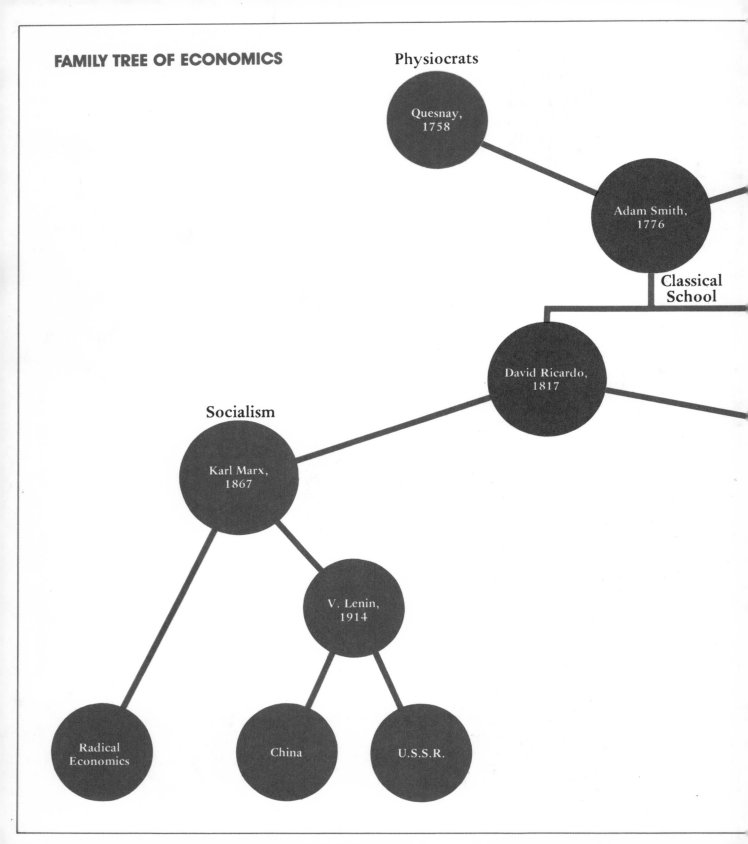

FAMILY TREE OF ECONOMICS

Physiocrats

Quesnay, 1758

Adam Smith, 1776

Classical School

David Ricardo, 1817

Socialism

Karl Marx, 1867

V. Lenin, 1914

Radical Economics

China

U.S.S.R.